The Oxford Handbook of Evolutionary Family Psychology

OXFORD LIBRARY OF PSYCHOLOGY

EDITOR-IN-CHIEF

Peter E. Nathan

AREA EDITORS:

Clinical Psychology
David H. Barlow

Cognitive Neuroscience
Kevin N. Ochsner and Stephen M. Kosslyn

Cognitive Psychology
Daniel Reisberg

Counseling Psychology
Elizabeth M. Altmaier and Jo-Ida C. Hansen

Developmental Psychology
Philip David Zelazo

Health Psychology
Howard S. Friedman

History of Psychology
David B. Baker

Industrial/Organizational Psychology
Steve W. J. Kozlowski

Methods and Measurement
Todd D. Little

Neuropsychology
Kenneth M. Adams

Personality and Social Psychology
Kay Deaux and Mark Snyder

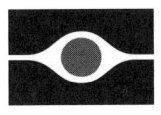 OXFORD LIBRARY OF PSYCHOLOGY

Editor-in-Chief PETER E. NATHAN

The Oxford Handbook of Evolutionary Family Psychology

Edited by
Catherine A. Salmon
Todd K. Shackelford

OXFORD
UNIVERSITY PRESS

OXFORD
UNIVERSITY PRESS

Published in the United States of America by Oxford University Press, Inc.,
198 Madison Avenue, New York, NY, 10016
United States of America

Oxford University Press, Inc., publishes works that further Oxford University's
objective of excellence in research, scholarship, and education

Oxford is a registered trade mark of Oxford University Press
in the UK and in certain other countries

© Oxford University Press, Inc. 2011

All rights reserved. No part of this publication may be reproduced, stored in a retrieval system,
or transmitted, in any form or by any means, without the prior permission in writing of
Oxford University Press, Inc., or as expressly permitted by law, by licence, or under terms agreed
with the appropriate reproduction rights organization. Inquiries concerning reproduction outside
the scope of the above should be sent to the Rights Department, Oxford University Press, Inc.,
at the address above

You must not circulate this work in any other form and you must impose this same condition
on any acquirer

_____

Library of Congress Cataloging-in-Publication Data
The Oxford handbook of evolutionary family psychology / edited by
Catherine Salmon and Todd K. Shackelford.
   p. cm. — (Oxford library of psychology)
  Includes bibliographical references and index.
  ISBN 978-0-19-539669-0 (hardcover : alk. paper) 1. Families. 2. Families—Psychological
aspects. I. Salmon, Catherine. II. Shackelford, Todd K. (Todd Kennedy), 1971–
III. Title: Handbook of evolutionary family psychology.
  HQ734.O94 2011
  306.85—dc22   2010044161
_____

978-0-19-539669-0
1 3 5 7 9 10 8 6 4 2

Typeset in Adobe Garamond
Printed on acid-free paper
Printed in the United States of America

To Margo Wilson, for inspiring our interest in the study of human and animal families

SHORT CONTENTS

Oxford Library of Psychology   ix

About the Editors   xi

Contributors   xiii

Table of Contents   xv

Chapters   1—398

Index   399

OXFORD LIBRARY OF PSYCHOLOGY

The *Oxford Library of Psychology*, a landmark series of handbooks, is published by Oxford University Press, one of the world's oldest and most highly respected publishers, with a tradition of publishing significant books in psychology. The ambitious goal of the *Oxford Library of Psychology* is nothing less than to span a vibrant, wide-ranging field and, in so doing, to fill a clear market need.

Encompassing a comprehensive set of handbooks, organized hierarchically, the *Library* incorporates volumes at different levels, each designed to meet a distinct need. At one level are a set of handbooks designed broadly to survey the major subfields of psychology; at another are numerous handbooks that cover important current focal research and scholarly areas of psychology in depth and detail. Planned as a reflection of the dynamism of psychology, the *Library* will grow and expand as psychology itself develops, thereby highlighting significant new research that will impact on the field. Adding to its accessibility and ease of use, the *Library* will be published in print and, later on, electronically.

The *Library* surveys psychology's principal subfields with a set of handbooks that capture the current status and future prospects of those major subdisciplines. This initial set includes handbooks of social and personality psychology, clinical psychology, counseling psychology, school psychology, educational psychology, industrial and organizational psychology, cognitive psychology, cognitive neuroscience, methods and measurements, history, neuropsychology, personality assessment, developmental psychology, and more. Each handbook undertakes to review one of psychology's major subdisciplines with breadth, comprehensiveness, and exemplary scholarship. In addition to these broadly conceived volumes, the *Library* also includes a large number of handbooks designed to explore in depth more specialized areas of scholarship and research, such as stress, health and coping, anxiety and related disorders, cognitive development, or child and adolescent assessment. In contrast to the broad coverage of the subfield handbooks, each of these latter volumes focuses on an especially productive, more highly focused line of scholarship and research. Whether at the broadest or most specific level, however, all of the *Library* handbooks offer synthetic coverage that reviews and evaluates the relevant past and present research and anticipates research in the future. Each handbook in the *Library* includes introductory and concluding chapters written by its editor to provide a roadmap to the handbook's table of contents and to offer informed anticipations of significant future developments in that field.

An undertaking of this scope calls for handbook editors and chapter authors who are established scholars in the areas about which they write. Many of the nation's and world's most productive and best-respected psychologists have agreed to edit *Library* handbooks or write authoritative chapters in their areas of expertise.

For whom has the *Oxford Library of Psychology* been written? Because of its breadth, depth, and accessibility, the *Library* serves a diverse audience, including graduate students in psychology and their faculty mentors, scholars, researchers, and practitioners in psychology and related fields. Each will find in the *Library* the information they seek on the subfield or focal area of psychology in which they work or are interested.

Befitting its commitment to accessibility, each handbook includes a comprehensive index, as well as extensive references to help guide research. And because the *Library* was designed from its inception as an online as well as a print resource, its structure and contents will be readily and rationally searchable online. Further, once the *Library* is released online, the handbooks will be regularly and thoroughly updated.

In summary, the *Oxford Library of Psychology* will grow organically to provide a thoroughly informed perspective on the field of psychology, one that reflects both psychology's dynamism and its increasing interdisciplinarity. Once published electronically, the *Library* is also destined to become a uniquely valuable interactive tool, with extended search and browsing capabilities. As you begin to consult this handbook, we sincerely hope you will share our enthusiasm for the more than 500-year tradition of Oxford University Press for excellence, innovation, and quality, as exemplified by the *Oxford Library of Psychology*.

Peter F. Nathan
Editor-in-Chief
Oxford Library of Psychology

ABOUT THE EDITORS

Catherine A. Salmon
Catherine A. Salmon, Ph.D., is Associate Professor of Psychology at the University of Redlands. Her research interests are in the areas of kinship and birth order, sexuality, and eating disorders. She is the co-author of *Warrior Lovers: Erotic Fiction, Evolution and Female Sexuality*, and co-editor of *Evolutionary Psychology, Public Policy, and Personnel Decisions* and *Family Relationships: An Evolutionary Perspective*.

Todd K. Shackelford
Todd K. Shackelford received his Ph.D. in Evolutionary Psychology in 1997 from the University of Texas at Austin, his M.A. in psychology from the University of Michigan in 1995, and his B.A. in psychology from the University of New Mexico in 1993. In 2010, Shackelford joined Oakland University as Professor and Chair of the Department of Psychology. Shackelford was previously Professor of Psychology at Florida Atlantic University, where he was Founder and Chair of the Evolutionary Psychology Ph.D. program and Director of the Evolutionary Psychology Lab. Shackelford has published over 200 peer-reviewed articles and chapters in edited volumes and has co-edited six volumes.

CONTRIBUTORS

Joshua M. Ackerman
Sloan School of Management
Massachusetts Institute of Technology
Cambridge, MA

Kermyt G. Anderson
Department of Anthropology
University of Oklahoma
Norman, OK

John Archer
School of Psychology
University of Central Lancashire
Preston, UK

Drew H. Bailey
Department of Psychological Sciences
University of Missouri
Columbia, MO

Jay Belsky
Institute for the Study of Children,
Families and Social Issues
Birkbeck University of London
London, UK

Carol M. Berman
Department of Anthropology
Graduate Program in Evolution,
Ecology and Behavior
University at Buffalo
Buffalo, NY

David F. Bjorklund
Department of Psychology
Florida Atlantic University
Boca Raton, FL

Bernard Chapais
Department of Anthropology
University of Montreal
Montreal, Quebec, Canada

Lisa M. DeBruine
School of Psychology
University of Aberdeen
Aberdeen, United Kingdom

Marco Del Giudice
Center for Cognitive Science
Department of Psychology
University of Turin
Turin, Italy

Emily H. DuVal
Department of Biological Science
Florida State University
Tallahassee, FL

Harald A. Euler
Department of Psychology
University of Kassel
Kassel, Germany

Mark V. Flinn
Departments of Anthropology and
Psychological Sciences
University of Missouri
Columbia, MO

David C. Geary
Department of Psychological Sciences
University of Missouri
Columbia, MO

Aaron T. Goetz
Department of Psychology
California State University, Fullerton
Fullerton, CA

Gregory Gorelik
Department of Psychology
Florida Atlantic University
Davie, FL

Peter Hepper
School of Psychology
Queen's University of Belfast
Belfast, United Kingdom

Ashley D. Hoben
Department of Social Psychology
University of Groningen
Groningen, The Netherlands

Benedict C. Jones
School of Psychology
University of Aberdeen
Aberdeen, United Kingdom

Alan H. Krakauer
Department of Evolution and Ecology
University of California, Davis
Davis, CA

Daniel Brian Krupp
Department of Psychology, Neuroscience & Behaviour
McMaster University
Hamilton, Ontario, Canada

James Malcolm
Department of Biology
University of Redlands
Redlands, CA

Douglas W. Mock
Department of Zoology
University of Oklahoma
Norman, OK

Jonathan Oxford
Department of Psychological Sciences
University of Missouri
Columbia, MO

Justin H. Park
Department of Experimental Psychology
University of Bristol
Bristol, United Kingdom

Elizabeth S. Paul
School of Veterinary Science
University of Bristol
Bristol, United Kingdom

Virginia Periss
Department of Psychology
Florida Atlantic University
Boca Raton, FL

Thomas V. Pollet
Department of Social Psychology
University of Groningen
Groningen, The Netherlands

Hector N. Qirko
Department of Sociology and Anthropology
College of Charleston
Charleston, SC

Gorge A. Romero
Department of Psychology
California State University, Fullerton
Fullerton, CA

Catherine A. Salmon
Department of Psychology
Redlands University
Redlands, CA

James A. Serpell
School of Veterinary Medicine
University of Pennsylvania
Philadelphia, PA

Todd K. Shackelford
Department of Psychology
Oakland University
Rochester, MI

Anthony A. Volk
Department of Child and Youth Studies
Brock University
St. Catharines, Ontario, Canada

TABLE OF CONTENTS

Part One • Introduction
1. Toward an Evolutionary Psychology of the Family   3
   Catherine A. Salmon and Todd K. Shackelford
2. Evolutionary Anthropology of the Human Family   12
   Mark V. Flinn
3. The Evolutionary History of Pair-bonding and Parental Collaboration   33
   Bernard Chapais
4. The Evolution of Relationships in Nonhuman Families   51
   Douglas W. Mock

Part Two • Human Families
5. Parent–Child Relationships   65
   Marco Del Giudice and Jay Belsky
6. Parent–Offspring Conflict   83
   Catherine A. Salmon and James Malcolm
7. Stepparenting, Divorce, and Investment in Children   97
   Kermyt G. Anderson
8. Adoption: Forms, Functions, and Preferences   113
   Anthony A. Volk
9. An Evolutionary Perspective on Siblings: Rivals and Resources   128
   Thomas V. Pollet and Ashley D. Hoben
10. Trials and Tribulations of Childhood: An Evolutionary Perspective   149
    Virginia Periss and David F. Bjorklund
11. Family Violence: How Paternity Uncertainty Raises the Stakes   169
    Aaron T. Goetz and Gorge A. Romero
12. Grandparents and Extended Kin   181
    Harald A. Euler

Part Three • Animal Families
13. Kin Recognition   211
    Peter Hepper
14. Kin Selection and Cooperative Courtship in Birds   230
    Alan H. Krakauer and Emily H. DuVal
15. Primate Kin Preferences: Explaining Diversity   248
    Carol M. Berman

Part Four • Fictive Families

16. Pet Keeping: A Case Study in Maladaptive Behavior   281
    John Archer
17. Pets in the Family: An Evolutionary Perspective   297
    James A. Serpell and Elizabeth S. Paul
18. Fictive Kinship and Induced Altruism   310
    Hector N. Qirko
19. Passion and Compassion: Psychology of Kin Relations Within and Beyond the Family   329
    Justin H. Park and Joshua M. Ackerman
20. Cooperation and Conflict in the Light of Kin Recognition Systems   345
    Daniel Brian Krupp, Lisa M. DeBruine, and Benedict C. Jones

Part Five • Conclusions and Future Directions

21. Reflections on the Human Family   365
    David C. Geary, Drew H. Bailey, and Jonathan Oxford
22. Between Conflict and Cooperation: New Horizons in the Evolutionary Science of the Human Family   386
    Gregory Gorelik, Todd K. Shackelford, and Catherine A. Salmon

Index   399

PART 1

Introduction

CHAPTER 1

Toward an Evolutionary Psychology of the Family

Catherine A. Salmon *and* Todd K. Shackelford

Abstract

Kinship has been central to evolutionary biological analyses of social behavior since Hamilton (1964) extended the concept of Darwinian fitness to include an individual's actions that benefit not only direct descendents but also collateral kin. No longer were organisms simply reproductive strategists, they also were nepotistic strategists. This concept revolutionized how biologists understand social interaction and influence. This chapter provides an overview of some of the ways evolutionary psychologists see humans as nepotistic strategists, introducing concepts that will be important to understanding the chapters on animal and human kinship to follow.

Keywords: Adaptation, inclusive fitness, kin selection

Introduction

What do you think of when you think about family? Parents, children, spouses, or siblings? How about grandparents or cousins? A beloved pet? For most people, relationships with those we think of as our family members are an essential part of our lives. As children, we were dependent on our families for our food and shelter. Our families protected us, loved us, and taught us about the world we were growing up in. Then, as young adults, many of us moved away from our family circles, often to form families of our own. Sometimes this happened close by; at other times, we might move miles away, sometimes even to other continents! But many of us retain strong ties to our natal kin. Relationships with family can be important to our emotional health and can play a significant role in our social success. Family can be a source of great joy as well as great anguish. Our siblings, for example, can be our strongest allies and our most persistent opponents. We need our families, and yet sometimes we have a great difficulty understanding them. Hundreds of books have been published with the goals of helping us understand and improve our family relationships. Many focus on parent–child relations or sibling rivalry and how best to get along.

The current volume focuses on the whys, the reasons behind people's behavior and how a greater understanding of "whys" can help us in our own lives, to better understand our own behavior and that of our family members. It also brings something to the table that is often ignored in the study of families. Humans are not the only species to have families. Many other social species live in groups and have relationships with their parents, offspring, and siblings. Sometimes these relationships are short-lived, but sometimes they can last a long time and often appear to be characterized by strong bonds. Anyone who has read (or seen footage of) Jane Goodall's descriptions of the relationships between chimpanzee mother Flo and her offspring, especially Flint, the son she nursed until her own death, cannot help but see a bond that many human mothers and children feel.

[N]othing did any good, and about three weeks after Flo died, Flint died too. It seems that because Flo had been too old to force the spoiled Flint to become independent, he simply couldn't face life without her. (Goodall, 1996, p. 96).

Goodall also noted that Flint's older sister Fifi tried to help him but eventually had to give up as she had her own infant son to care for. Although we are interested in animal families for their own sakes and hope our readers are too, we also hope that readers will recognize the deeper understanding of human families that can be found through an understanding of similar phenomena in other species.

Throughout this volume, you will see reference to the evolved motivations that underlie behavior. In making claims about the evolved nature of motivations and behavioral mechanisms, we are not judging whether a behavior itself is good or bad or right or wrong in any moral sense. Human and other animal behaviors exist, and evolutionary scientists are interested in understanding why certain behaviors evolved and why they appear in certain contexts. Providing evidence that a behavior is generated by evolved mechanisms—infanticide by mothers, for example, which occurs in humans as well as many other species—says nothing about the moral nature of such an act. Rather, this investigative strategy represents an exploration of the circumstances that would cause such a behavior to have increased the reproductive success of, in this case, ancestral mothers of the species. It is a consideration of what sorts of selection pressures might have caused the evolution of the mechanisms that produce the behavior. In fact, reference to what "is" to justify what "ought to be" is referred to as the *naturalistic fallacy*. Interestingly, the naturalistic fallacy seems to come into play for humans much more frequently than for nonhumans. Few people seem to worry if an evolutionary argument is offered for why a pig or a rabbit kills one of its babies. It's not as if we're condoning the pig's behavior. But if one tries to explain the evolutionary logic of human behaviors judged to be immoral or unseemly, the suspicion is that you're thereby giving it a stamp of approval. But empirical data and the moral realm are logically distinct. No matter how desirable some behavior may be, that does not mean that wishing makes it so, just as the existence of a behavior does not necessarily make it desirable. A better understanding of the evolutionary forces that shaped a behavior and the cues to which the underlying mechanisms are sensitive may allow us to better point behavior in the direction society views as more moral or desirable (an excellent discussion of the naturalistic fallacy and evolutionary moral psychology can be found in Holcomb, 2004).

What Is an Evolutionary Perspective on the Family?

In many ways, early 20th-century thinking about human behavior embraced Charles Darwin, or at least his functional approach to the study of life. To modern biologists and animal behaviorists, an evolutionary approach is second nature. An adaptationist approach to animal families raises no eyebrows. But the last 75 years or so has seen an almost pathological avoidance of biology when it comes to the study of human behavior. In psychology, neobehaviorism, humanism, cognitive theory, modern psychoanalysis, and an assortment of postmodernist explanations have come to dictate the way many academics think about human behavior. We believe it's time for a rather different approach. We need to remember that people are just another type of animal, subject to the forces of natural selection just as all other species are. It's time to revisit the importance of our ancestral history and the selection pressures that built, not only the organs of our body, but also those of our mind. To explain this approach, we first provide a brief review of the process of natural selection, the special role of kinship in evolutionary analyses, and how adaptations can function as decision-makers, highlighting this with regard to kin relationships.

Natural Selection

When we refer to an adaptation, we are talking about an anatomical structure, physiological process, or behavior that made ancestral individuals' more likely to survive and reproduce in competition with other members of their species. Adaptations are shaped, or evolve, through natural selection. The process of natural selection is simply the differential production or survival of offspring by genetically different members of the population (Williams, 1966). If an individual (whether animal or human) is better able to survive and reproduce, he or she is more likely to leave offspring that share his or her traits. Darwin's (1859) logic can be seen in the following:

Assumption 1: Species are capable of overproducing offspring.
Assumption 2: The size of populations of individuals tends to remain relatively stable over time.

Inference 1: A struggle for existence among individuals ensues.

Assumption 4: Individuals differ on traits (adaptations) that enable them to survive and reproduce.

Assumption 5: At least some of the variance in these traits is genetically heritable.

Inference 2: There is differential production or survival of offspring by genetically different members of the population, which is by definition natural selection.

Inference 3: Through many generations, evolution of traits that are more adaptive than others will occur through natural selection.

(*Crawford & Salmon*, 2004)

In other words, some feature of the environment poses a problem for an organism. Genetically based variants contribute to reproduction and survival with regard to that environmental condition. Individuals with those variants will be more successful, passing on their "good genes" and the resulting behavioral repertoire to their offspring.

Although the logic of natural selection is at the heart of all evolutionary explanations of behavior, there are several concepts that Darwin did not develop fully in his own work that have been more thoroughly elucidated in recent years. Kinship theory is arguably the most relevant for this volume on the family.

Kinship Theory

Altruism has long been a topic of interest in the study of both human and animal behavior. To many early evolutionary thinkers, it was a puzzle. Why would individuals be willing to sacrifice anything for another individual? The logic of natural selection would seem to suggest that altruism should not exist, and yet it is found throughout the natural world. Hamilton (1964) demonstrated that altruistic behavior (behavior performed at a cost to oneself for the benefit of another) could evolve if the individuals involved were genetically related. Even though the direct reproductive fitness of the donor is reduced, if his actions aid his own genetic kin, then he receives an indirect fitness benefit. Typically, this idea is expressed by the equation:

$$Br_1 > Cr_2$$

Where B is the benefit to the recipient, r_1 is the genetic correlation between the donor and the recipient's offspring, C is the cost to the donor, and r_2 is the genetic correlation between the donor and its own offspring (Crawford & Salmon, 2004).

In the equation, r represents the probability that the two individuals each have an allele that is a copy of an allele in a common ancestor. Such an allele is called *identical by common descent*, and the probability of such an event is the genetic correlation or coefficient of relatedness between individuals. Br_1 is the indirect benefit to the donor through the recipient's additional offspring, and Cr_2 is the direct cost to the helper because of its decreased offspring. Both sides of the equation refer to changes in the donor's fitness as a result of his or her altruistic actions. This was a new way of thinking about fitness. No longer were organisms simply reproductive strategists (with fitness being measured in own offspring); now, they were also nepotistic strategists (with fitness being measured in one's own reproductive success plus the reproductive success of kin). If an individual's genes are just as likely to be present in a sister as in a daughter, one would expect the evolution of sororal investment in the same way as one expects maternal investment. Kinship theory and Hamilton's understanding of it illuminated our understanding of social interaction and influence, paving the way for future insights into kinship dynamics.

For example, consider conflicts that occur within the family (animal or human). Hamilton (1964) pointed out that kin are valuable in the genetic sense (among others senses) and that what contributes to an individual's inclusive fitness also may contribute to the inclusive fitness of the individual's relatives. The more closely related are two individuals, the greater their shared genetic interests. But, it is important to remember that although there is genetic commonality, there also are genetic differences, and these can lead to conflicts of interest. These conflicts are often apparent when individuals are competing for the same scarce resources, such as mates, food, or social status. Trivers' (1974) analysis of within-family conflict made use of Hamilton's approach. Because the probability of an individual replicating its alleles through its own offspring is 0.5 (the degree of relatedness between parent and offspring), and through its full sibling's offspring (a niece or nephew) is only 0.25, natural selection will favor individuals that seek a greater share of their parent's resources. In other words, we expect a certain degree of sibling competition. In some species, this competition results in the elimination of a sibling competitor. In others, it just means a lot of headaches for the parents. From a parental perspective, they are equally related to all their children and grandchildren, so parents have typically been under selective pressure to resist a particular offspring's demands, especially when offspring are trying to extract more than their fair share of resources.

Consider the case of weaning conflict in a species that produces one offspring at a time. When an offspring is very young, parental fitness typically benefits most from investing highly in this current offspring. It's in the offspring's best interests to extract as many resources as possible, up to a certain point, even at the expense of future siblings the mother could be having. At some point, the value to the offspring (who may be reaching a state of greater independence, able to obtain food on its own, etc.) of monopolizing such resources is outweighed by the costs in terms of its own inclusive fitness. Typically, the mother reaches her own point of diminishing returns before the offspring does (after all, she is equally related to each of her offspring, whereas her current offspring is more closely related to itself than to future siblings). The period between when the mother's fitness is best served by decreasing investment in the current offspring and investing in future offspring (in reproducing again) and when the current offspring's fitness is also best served by the mother investing elsewhere is known in mammalian species as *weaning conflict* (see Trivers, 1974). The mother's fitness returns are decreasing, but the offspring isn't quite ready to give up any investment. Conflict is most intense at such a stage. During this period, the mother's fitness is increased more by investing in additional offspring, whereas a particular offspring's fitness is increased more by continued maternal investment. The conflict ends as the fitness benefits of weaning shift to both mother and offspring (Drake, Fraser, & Weary, 2008; Humphrey, in press; Rehling & Trillmich, 2007).

Harvard professor David Haig (1993; and see Haig, 2002, for review) has investigated parent–offspring conflict at a further level of analysis by considering that there are three sets of genes, each set of which may have different interests. They include genes in the mother, maternally derived genes in the current offspring, and paternally derived genes in the current offspring. With maternal genes having an equal stake in each offspring, they will be selected to transfer resources to offspring as a function of the offspring's likelihood of reproducing. Genes in the current offspring have a greater interest in the current offspring than in future siblings and will be selected to maximize transfer of resources to the current offspring. Some genes can be imprinted with information about their paternal origin. This can create additional conflict if the mother has offspring from different fathers because paternally active genes in the current offspring have no stake in the offspring sired by other males. Haig's work addresses the influence of these conflicts on the evolution of the female reproductive system and how serious health problems for mothers, such as gestational diabetes and preeclampsia, can arise.

Adaptations as Decision-makers

Adaptations can be anatomical, physiological, or behavioral. The beaks of Darwin's finches, often used to characterize the different species of finches living on the Galapagos, provide a classic example of an adaptation that is anatomical in nature (for review, see Grant & Grant, 2007). The dietary options available influenced the survival of birds of varying beak types and sizes, so that today we see finch beaks that are well suited to cracking large seeds in some areas, whereas finches in other environments have beaks that take advantage of other food sources, such as insects. But adaptations can also be understood in terms of processes that carry out the cost–benefit analyses that an ancestral organism required to survive environmental challenges. For example, the fever adaptation can be described as a set of decision processes for dealing with certain types of invading organisms. If you are being invaded by bacteria M, raise your body temperature by X degrees. The increase in body temperature may be enough to destroy the invader, which is beneficial to the individual (which is why when fever is prevented by drugs, resistance to infection is lower). But the adaptation is not cost-free. It takes a nontrivial amount of energy to raise body temperature. Perhaps more importantly, and especially in young children, the rise in body temperature can damage other systems if it is excessively high and prolonged in duration (Williams & Nesse, 1991).

From a decision-maker perspective, adaptations can be seen as decision rules or mental mechanisms designed by natural selection for producing the different behaviors required for ancestral survival, growth, and reproduction. Buss (1999) has suggested the term "evolved psychological mechanisms" for the specialized information-processing mechanisms that organize experiences into adaptively meaningful schemas. These mechanisms focus attention, organize perception and memory, and recruit specialized procedural knowledge that leads to domain appropriate inferences, judgments, and choices when activated by a relevant problem.

Kinship and Human Psychology

Anthropologists have long recognized the importance of kinship to the study of human social behavior, as illustrated by several chapters in this book by anthropologists and the evidence for runaway social selection elegantly presented in Flinn's chapter on an evolutionary anthropology of the family. One might have assumed the same of psychologists. And, it is true that attention to the family has been paid in areas such as developmental psychology and counseling psychology. However, it has been largely ignored in many other areas of psychology, including those areas in which its importance might have seemed obvious, such as social psychology (see Daly, Salmon, & Wilson [1997] for a discussion of the absence of the family in much of social psychology; see Burnstein, Crandall, and Kitayama [1994] and Michalski and Shackelford [2005] for examples of evolutionarily informed social psychological research that takes kinship into account).

Although some areas of psychology do attend to the importance of understanding familial relationships and the roles they play in our lives, the majority have failed to recognize the relevance of the qualitatively distinct types of close relationships found within the family domain. A proper, evolutionarily informed approach to a psychology of the family is by necessity a relationship-specific approach (Wilson & Daly, 1997). Humans, along with other species, have evolved specialized mechanisms for processing information and motivating behavior relevant to the specific demands of being a mate, father, mother, sibling, child, or grandparent. This type of evolutionary perspective on the nature of distinct family relationships provides an insight into our behavior that cannot be found elsewhere. Kinship is not one relationship. It is many different relationships. The challenges that face mothers are different from those that face fathers or siblings.

Relationship-specific Adaptations
Motherhood

There is no more essential mammalian relationship than that between mother and offspring. It should not be surprising, therefore, that it may be the relationship with the most specialized anatomical, physiological, and psychological mechanisms (Hrdy, 2000). The demands of motherhood go beyond conception, gestation, and nursing. Not all offspring are created equal. They are not all equally capable of transforming parental care and investment into the long-term success of parental genes. The result has been strong selection for the strategic allocation of maternal effort. The evolved motivational mechanisms that direct maternal investment decisions are sensitive to a number of offspring attributes, to the material and social situation, and the situation/condition of the mother herself (see Daly & Wilson, 1995, for a review).

However, mothers are not the only interested party. Offspring themselves have a role to play in shaping resource allocation. Parent–offspring conflict (Trivers, 1974) is a feature of sexually reproducing species because of the resultant genetic asymmetries in family relationships. A mother is equally related genetically to any two of her offspring, but each offspring is more closely related to itself than to a sibling (except in the case of identical twins). As a result, mother and offspring do not see eye to eye on the relative fitness value of other offspring or on the allocation of maternal resources. This conflict over maternal resources provides an explanation for some puzzling aspects of mother–offspring interaction, such as weaning conflict (Trivers, 1974) and the dangerously high levels of substances of fetal origin that sometimes accumulate in the blood of pregnant women, including placental lactogen, which up-regulates the fetus's access to maternal glucose stores, resulting in gestational diabetes (Haig, 1993, 2002). Such areas of conflict between parent and offspring are explored further in Chapter 6 by Salmon and Malcolm, as are parent–child relationships more generally in Chapter 5 by Del Giudice and Belsky.

Fatherhood

Significant similarities exist between paternal solicitude and maternal solicitude, but there also are several substantial differences. Parents have been selected to assess offspring quality and need, and for both fathers and mothers, mechanisms motivating solicitude evolved to generate solicitude in relation to cues of the expected impact of any parental investment on the offspring's future success. Both father and mother have been selected to discriminate with respect to cues that the offspring is their genetic child. But it is true that for mammalian mothers the evidence is clear. If you gave birth to it, the baby is yours. For men, due to internal fertilization and relatively concealed ovulation, paternity is never certain (or wouldn't have been in our ancestral past). Putative fathers must depend on sources of information about the mother's likely fidelity, or the child's resemblance to his relatives or to himself. From this, one might predict that paternal affection will be influenced by paternal perceptions of resemblance. And, in fact, people do pay more attention to paternal resemblance than to maternal resemblance, with mothers and their relatives actively promoting perceptions of paternal resemblance (Daly & Wilson, 1982; Regalski & Gaulin, 1993). Issues of paternal investment are discussed by Anderson (Chapter 7), and issues of investment by mothers and fathers in unrelated offspring are addressed by Volk (Chapter 8).

Sibship

An evolutionary perspective also can generate insight into our understanding of sibling relations (Mock & Parker, 1997. Hamilton's (1964) analysis of the evolution of sociality and altruism in haplodiploid insects had at its core the shared genetic interests of sisters in such species. But although siblings, our close genetic kin, can be major allies, they also can be our fiercest competitors, especially for parental resources (Salmon, 1998; Sulloway, 1996). The result is sibling relationships that are often somewhat ambivalent across the lifespan. Thomas Pollet and Ashley Hoben (Chapter 9) illuminates the cooperative and rivalrous nature of sibling relationships.

Grandparenthood

Do we have adaptations designed specifically to deal with the problems faced by grandparental relationships? Or, do these relationships merely co-opt adaptations for parenting? Postmenopausal women make significant contributions to the welfare of their grandchildren in many cultures (Lancaster & King, 1985; Sears, Mace, & McGregor, 2000). Thus, it is reasonable to suspect that mental processes specific to the allocation of grandparental investment may have been the targets of natural selection (Hawkes, O'Connell, Blurton Jones, Alvarez, & Charnov, 1998; Smith, 1988).

Euler and Weitzel (1996) noted that paternity certainty could influence grandparental investment (in addition to its impact on paternal investment). To test their hypotheses, they asked adults to rate the degree of grandparental solicitude they experienced from each of their four grandparents. The results were striking, indicating a strong link between relatedness/paternity certainty and solicitude. Maternal grandmothers were rated the highest on solicitude, followed by maternal grandfathers, paternal grandmothers, and finally paternal grandfathers. From a theoretical perspective, a maternal grandmother has the greatest certainty of her grandchild's relatedness to her. A paternal grandfather faces a different dynamic. He endures two relationship links that can be broken by nonpaternity: the grandchild might not be his son's child, and his son might not be his own biological child (see also Michalski & Shackelford, 2005). Euler (Chapter 12) addresses the nature of grandparental and extended kin relationships.

Mateship

Although mates are rarely close genetic relatives, their relationship is usually considered a family one, with both parties having a shared interest in their joint offspring. The longer the duration of the union, the more likely that they share a similar perspective on the optimal allocation of resources. What is best for one is usually best for the other. But such a harmony of interests can be shattered by extrapair relations. Studies of marital conflict and violence make this point clear. Suspected or actual infidelity is a powerful source of severe conflict and spousal violence (Daly & Wilson, 1988; Wilson & Daly, 1993; for recent reviews, see Goetz & Shackelford, 2009, and Kaighobadi, Shackelford, & Goetz, 2009). Step-relationships bring another factor into the mix. In this case, there is a child who is a potential vehicle of fitness for one partner but not the other. Both parties are aware of the asymmetry in relatedness (as contrasted to instances of female infidelity and subsequent cuckoldry) at the start of or at least very early in their relationship. Nevertheless, stepchildren are at an elevated risk of neglect, abuse, and homicide (Daly & Wilson, 1988, 1995), a reminder that the motivational mechanisms of parental feeling are designed to preferentially direct affection and investment toward one's genetic offspring. Kermyt Anderson (Chapter 7) discusses stepparenting, divorce, and parental investment.

Daly and Wilson (1984) also have suggested that motivational differences produce different methods when it comes to how stepparents or genetic parents kill. Daly and Wilson found, in both Canadian and British national-level databases, that stepfathers were more likely than genetic fathers to commit filicide by beating and bludgeoning, a window into stepparental feelings of bitterness and resentment not seen in genetic fathers. Genetic fathers were more likely than stepfathers to commit filicide by shooting or asphyxiation, which often produce a relatively quick and painless death. Weekes-Shackelford and Shackelford (2004) replicated and extended these findings using a U.S. national-level database of over 400,000 homicides. They also identified similar differences in the methods by which stepmothers and genetic mothers committed filicide. Aaron Goetz and Gorge Romero (Chapter 11) discuss the nature and scope of family violence, with particular attention to the role played by paternity uncertainty.

Kinship and Animal Psychology

When most people think about family, they think about their own relationships, their parents, siblings, and children, maybe cousins, aunts and uncles, and grandparents, too. But we are not the only species that has families and for which kinship plays a significant role. Much of our understanding of human families and the mechanisms that influence family relationships was facilitated by the study of animal behavior and how animals invest in their own offspring (and sometimes in siblings or in the offspring of others). From work on the breeding success of birds, to the strategic allocation of reproductive effort to parenting or mating, to sibling competition and helpers at the nest, animal families not only are interesting in and of themselves, but also are important for the light they shed on human family relationships.

Animal Parenting

Consider the killdeer, a familiar bird in the grasslands of America. It is perhaps best known for its predator distraction display used to protect its chicks. If a predator gets close to its nest, it will attempt to lure the predator away with a display of vulnerability, behaving as though its wing is broken. The energy cost may be low but there is a risk (part of the bird's investment) that the predator will make the parent into a killdeer lunch (Brunton, 1990). How easy it is to appreciate such parental protection, seeing the connection between that and the protective behavior of human parents, as well as that of many other animals.

Although many species of animal, particularly some aquatic ones, make no parental investment after spawning, many do invest in their offspring. Among mammals, it is typically the female who invests the most through provisioning and protection, although it is true that some males contribute significantly as well. Several chapters in the current volume address issues related to animal parenting, including Chapter 15 by Berman; and in Chapter 6, Salmon and Malcolm consider parent–offspring conflict over investment in both animals and humans.

Because animals sometimes behave nepotistically, engaging, for example, in cooperative grooming in Japanese macaques (Glick, Eaton, Johnson, & Worlein, 1986) and in alarm-calling in Belding's ground squirrels (Sherman, 1977; alarm-calling is done typically by females living near female kin), recognizing relatives has been a hot topic in animal family research. Do animals recognize each other as kin by frequency of contact? Phenotypic resemblance? Smell? The research in this area is brought to light in Chapter 13, by Hepper.

And, like humans, not all family relationships are bright and rosy. Books on how to deal with sibling rivalry between one's children abound, and in some animal species such sibling conflict is taken to Cain and Abel–like heights, with siblicide occurring in many species of birds. Siblicide in these cases has been interpreted as an adaptive strategy that benefits the surviving offspring and the parents, as grisly as this may seem (Mock, Drummond, & Stinson, 1990; Mock & Parker 1997).

Fictive Kinship

When we refer to fictive kinship, we are focusing on relationships that appear to be modeled on those of genetic kinship. Godparents or blood-brothers are examples many readers will be familiar with. The focus is on relationships that are kin-like but that are not defined by actual genetic relatedness. In many cases, these relationships may replace missing kin relationships and co-opt the adaptations designed to manage those of genetic kinship. How many people have heard others refer to their pets as their babies? Many people treat their pets like children, buying them toys and treats, showering them with affection and investment. The special bond between people and their pets is addressed by Archer (Chapter 16) and Serpell and Paul (Chapter 17).

Friendship is often treated as a special form of kinship. Close girlfriends may refer to each other as sister, and birthday cards for female friends contain phrases such as "You're like a sister to me." Park and Ackerman (Chapter 19) reflect on the connections between kinship and friendship. Others have pointed out that cues of kinship influence the way we interact with others. Cues of kinship can make us more likely to cooperate with others (as discussed by Krupp, DeBruine, and Jones, Chapter 20), and appeals to the shared interests of kinship ("My brothers and sisters . . . ," "For he who sheds his blood with me today shall be my brother.") have been used over and over again in political and rhetorical speech (Salmon, 1998; Johnson, 1987). In this volume, Hector Qirko touches on how the power of fictive kinship plays a role in our lives today.

Conclusion

This volume is intended to illustrate the many ways in which an evolutionary perspective on the family can contribute to our understanding of behavior, not only of our own family relationships but also of how our evolved psychological mechanisms influence how we react to friends, allies, and our pets. We also hope that it provides insight into the kinship psychology of animals and how similar (and at times different) they are in comparison to our own kinship psychology. Much of the pleasure and pain of family life has been with us over the course of human evolutionary history. Our modern behavior is the product of our evolutionary response to the pressures of living as a social species, just as the behavior of other social animals is a product of such pressures. The next three chapters in this opening section of the volume, by Mark Flinn, Bernard Chapais, and Doug Mock, elaborate on the benefits of bringing an evolutionary perspective to the study of human and animal families. In our final chapter, we return to a consideration of the future of evolutionary approaches to the study of family relationships.

References

Brunton, D.H. (1990). The effects of nesting stage, sex, and type of predator on parental defense by killdeer (*Charadrius vociferous*): Testing models of avian parental defense. *Behavioral Ecology and Sociobiology, 26*, 181–190.

Burnstein, E., Crandall, C., and Kitayama, S. (1994). Some neo-Darwinian decision rules for altruism: Weighing cues for inclusive fitness as a function of the biological importance of the decision. *Journal of Personality and Social Psychology, 67*, 773–789.

Buss, D.M. (1999). *Evolutionary psychology: The new science of the mind* (1st ed.). New York: Allyn & Bacon.

Crawford, C.B., and Salmon, C. (2004). The essence of evolutionary psychology. In C. Crawford and C. Salmon (Eds.), *Evolutionary psychology, public policy and personal decisions* (pp. 23–49). Mahwah, NJ: Erlbaum.

Daly, M., and Wilson, M. (1982). Whom are newborn babies said to resemble? *Ethology and Sociobiology, 3*, 69–78.

Daly, M., and Wilson, M. (1984). A sociobiological analysis of human infanticide. In G. Hausfater and S.B. Hrdy (Eds.), *Infanticide: Comparative and evolutionary perspectives* (pp. 487–502). New York: Aldine.

Daly, M., and Wilson, M. (1988). The Darwinian psychology of discriminative parental solicitude. *Nebraska Symposium on Motivation, 35*, 91–144.

Daly, M., and Wilson, M. (1995). Discriminative parental solicitude and the relevance of evolutionary models to the analysis of motivational systems. In M. Gazzaniga (Ed.), *The cognitive neurosciences* (pp. 1269–1286). Cambridge, MA: MIT Press.

Daly, M., Salmon, C., and Wilson, M. (1997). Kinship: The conceptual hole in psychological studies of social cognition and close relationships. In J.A. Simpson and D.T. Kenrick (Eds.), *Evolutionary social psychology* (pp. 265–296). Mahwah, NJ: Erlbaum.

Darwin, C. (1859). *On the origin of species by means of natural selection or the preservation of favored races in the struggle for life*. London: John Murray.

Drake, A., Fraser, D., and Weary, D.M. (2008). Parent-offspring resource allocation in domestic pigs. *Behavioral Ecology and Sociobiology, 62*, 309–319.

Euler, H., and Weitzel, B. (1996). Discriminative grandparental solicitude as reproductive strategy. *Human Nature, 7*, 39–59.

Glick, B.B., Eaton, G.G., Johnson, D.F., and Worlein, J.M. (1986). Development of partner preferences in Japanese macaques (*Macaca fuscata*): Effects of gender and kinship during the second year of life. *International Journal of Primatology, 7*, 467–479.

Goodall, J. (1996). *My life with the chimpanzees*. New York: Alladin.

Goetz, A. T., and Shackelford, T. K. (2009). Sexual conflict in humans: Evolutionary consequences of asymmetric parental investment and paternity uncertainty. *Animal Biology, 59*, 449–456.

Grant, P. R., and Grant, R. (2007). How and why species multiply: The radiation of Darwin's finches (Princeton Series in Evolutionary Biology). Princeton, NJ: Princeton University Press.

Haig, D. (1993). Genetic conflicts in human pregnancy. *Quarterly Review of Biology, 68*, 495–532.

Haig, D. (2002). *Genomic imprinting and kinship*. New Brunswick, NJ: Rutgers University Press.

Hamilton, W.D. (1964). The genetical evolution of social behaviour. I and II. *Journal of Theoretical Biology, 7*, 1–52.

Hawkes, K., O'Connell, J.F., Blurton Jones, N.G., Alvarez, H., and Charnov, E.L. (1998). Grandmothering, menopause, and the evolution of human life histories. *Proceedings of the National Academy of Sciences of the United States, 95*, 1336–1339.

Holcomb, H. (2004). Darwin and evolutionary moral psychology. In C. Crawford and C. Salmon (Eds.), *Evolutionary psychology, public policy and personal decisions* (pp. 73–95). Mahwah, NJ: Erlbaum.

Hrdy, S.B. (2000). *Mother nature: Maternal instincts and how they shape the human species*. New York: Ballantine.

Humphrey, L.T. (in press). Weaning behavior in human evolution. *Seminars in Cell and Developmental Biology*.

Johnson, G.R. (1987). In the name of the fatherland: An analysis of kin term usage in patriotic speech and literature. *International Political Science Review, 8*, 165–174.

Kaighobadi, F., Shackelford, T. K., and Goetz, A. T. (2009). From mate retention to murder: Evolutionary psychological perspectives on men's partner-directed violence. *Review of General Psychology, 13*, 327–334.

Lancaster, J.B., and King, B.J. (1985). An evolutionary perspective on menopause. In J.K. Brown and V. Kern (Eds.), *In her prime: A new view of middle aged women* (pp. 13–20). Boston: Bergin and Garvey.

Michalski, R. L., and Shackelford, T. K. (2005). Grandparental investment as a function of relational uncertainty and emotional closeness with parents. *Human Nature, 16*, 292–304.

Mock, D.W., Drummond, H., and Stinson, C.H. (1990). Avian siblicide. *American Scientist, 78*, 438–449.

Mock, D.W., and Parker, G.A. (1997). *The evolution of sibling rivalry*. New York: Oxford University Press.

Regalski, J.M., and Gaulin, S.J.C. (1993). Whom are Mexican infants said to resemble? Monitoring and fostering paternal confidence in the Yucatan. *Ethology and Sociobiology, 14*, 97–113.

Rehling, A., and Trillmich, F. (2007). Weaning in the guinea pig (*Cavia aperea f. porcellus*): Who decides and by what measure? *Behavioral Ecology and Sociobiology, 62*, 149–157.

Salmon, C. (1998). The evocative nature of kin terminology in political speech. *Politics and the Life Sciences, 17*, 51–57.

Salmon, C. (2003). Birth order and relationships: Family, friends, and sexual partners. *Human Nature, 14*, 73–88.

Sears, R., Mace, R., and McGregor, I.A. (2000). Maternal grandmothers improve nutritional status and survival of children in rural Gambia. *Proceedings of the Royal Society of London. Series B. Biological Sciences, 267*, 1641–1647.

Sherman, P.W. (1977). Nepotism and the evolution of alarm calls. *Science*, 197, 1246–1253.

Smith, M.S. (1988). Research in developmental sociobiology: Parenting and family behavior. In K. MacDonald (Ed.), *Sociobiological perspectives on human development* (pp. 271–292). New York: Springer.

Sulloway, F.J. (1996). *Born to rebel: Birth order, family dynamics, and creative lives*. New York: Pantheon.

Trivers, R.L. (1974). Parent-offspring conflict. *American Zoologist, 14*, 249–264.

Weekes-Shackelford, V.A., and Shackelford, T.K. (2004). Methods of filicide: Stepparents and genetic parents kill differently. *Violence and Victims, 19*, 75–81.

Williams, G.C. (1966). *Adaptation and natural selection: A critique of some current evolutionary thought*. Princeton, NJ: Princeton University Press.

Williams, G.C., and Nesse, R. (1991). The dawn of Darwinian medicine. *Quarterly Review of Biology, 66*, 1–22.

Wilson, M., and Daly, M. (1993). An evolutionary psychological perspective on male sexual proprietariness and violence against wives. *Violence and Victims, 8*, 271–294.

Wilson, M., and Daly, M. (1997). Relationship-specific social psychological adaptations. In G. R. Bock & G. Cardew (Eds.), *CIBA Foundation symposium on characterizing psychological adaptations* (pp. 253–263). Chichester, UK: John Wiley & Sons.

CHAPTER 2

Evolutionary Anthropology of the Human Family

Mark V. Flinn

Abstract

The family is a key human evolutionary adaptation. The extent and duration of offspring care is extraordinary—and unique in the huge informational transfer via language. Kin relationships are bilateral, complex, variable, multigenerational, and intergroup. Mating relationships are also variable, and influenced by kin in traditional cultures. These aspects of our sociality are biologically embedded in neurological and physiological mechanisms. Analysis of mechanisms such as affiliative and stress hormonal axes can provide clues into the evolution of the emotional and cognitive systems that underpin human family psychology.

Keywords: Child development, family, kinship, hormones, runaway social selection, human evolution

Humans are the species that raises children.
—M. Konner (p. 427), 1991

The human family seems to follow a typical mammalian pattern: intense maternal care, including breastfeeding of an altricial (helpless) offspring, with some support from an assortment of other relatives—fathers, siblings, aunts, and the like. Beyond the shared mammal/primate commonality, however, humans exhibit a suite of highly unusual traits. We are the only species characterized by the combination of stable breeding bonds, extensive paternal effort in a multimale group, lengthy childhood, extended bilateral kin recognition, grandparenting, and controlled exchange of mates among kin groups (Alexander, 1979, 1990b; Chapais, 2008; Daly & Wilson, 1983). These characteristics are important for the theoretical and pragmatic understanding of family relationships and the supporting cognitive, emotional, and physiological mechanisms; they also provide critical insights into the puzzle of human evolution.

In this chapter, I first review a general model for the evolution of human mating, parenting, and kinship patterns based on a process of runaway social selection (Alexander, 2005; Flinn & Alexander, 2007; Flinn et al., 2005, 2007). I then briefly evaluate the fossil evidence and physiological mechanisms that underpin these central aspects of our sociality. My objectives include providing important information and ideas from biological and cultural anthropology that contribute to understanding the evolutionary psychology of the human family.

Brain, Childhood, and Family
Evolution of Mind in the Family Crèche

Information processing (intelligence) and social communication (language) are core human adaptations. By all measures, the human brain that enables these abilities is an astonishing organ. Its cortex comprises about 30 billion neurons of 200 different types, each of which are interlinked by about a thousand synapses, resulting in more than 10^{15} connections working at rates of up to 10^{10} interactions per second (Edelman, 2006; Koch, 1999; Williams & Herrup, 1988). Quantifying the transduction of these biophysical actions into specific mental activities (i.e., thoughts and emotional feelings) is difficult, but it is likely that humans have more information processing capacity than any other species (Roth & Dicke, 2005).

The human brain evolved at a rapid pace: Hominin cranial capacity tripled (from an average of about 450 to 1350 cc) in less than two million years (Lee & Wolpoff, 2003)—roughly 100,000 neurons and supportive cells per generation. Structural changes, such as increased convolutions, thickly myelinated cortical neurons, lateral asymmetries, increased von Economo neurons, expansion of the neocortex, and enhanced integration of the cerebellum also were significant (Allman, 1999; Amodio & Frith, 2006; Schoenemann, 2006; Sherwood et al., 2006; Spoctor et al., 2010). In comparison with most other parts of the human genome, selection on genes involved with brain development was especially intense (Gilbert et al., 2005).

The human brain has high metabolic costs: About 50% of an infant's, and 20% of an adult's, energetic resources are used to support neurological activity (Aiello & Wheeler, 1995; Elia, 1992; Holliday, 1986; Leonard et al., 2007). Thoughts are not free; the high levels of glucose and other energetic nutrients required to fuel human cognition involve significant trade-offs. Although the increase in energetic resources allocated to the brain was accompanied by a corresponding decrease in digestive tissue, this does not explain what the selective pressures for enhanced information processing were, nor why the resources were not reallocated to direct reproductive function (Aiello & Wheeler, 1995). The obstetric difficulties associated with birthing a large-headed infant generate additional problems (Rosenberg & Trevathan, 2002). The selective advantages of increased intelligence must have been high to overcome these costs.

The human brain, in short, is a big evolutionary puzzle. It is developmentally and metabolically expensive. It evolved rapidly and consistently. And it enables unusual human cognitive abilities, such as language, empathy, foresight, consciousness, mental time travel, creativity, and theory of mind (ToM). The advantages of a larger brain may include enhanced information processing capacities to contend with ecological pressures that involve sexually dimorphic activities, such as hunting and complex foraging (Kaplan & Robson, 2002). There is little evidence, however, of sufficient domain-specific enlargement of those parts of the brain associated with selective pressures from the physical environment, including subsistence activities (Adolphs, 2003; Geary & Huffman, 2002). Indeed, human cognition has little to distinguish itself in the way of specialized ecological talents. Our remarkable aptitudes for tool use and other technical behaviors depend primarily on more general aptitudes for social learning and fluid intelligence (Geary, 2005). A large brain may have been sexually selected because intelligence was an attractive trait for mate choice (Miller, 2000). However, there is little sexual dimorphism in encephalization quotient or intelligence psychometrics (Jensen, 1998), nor is there a clear reason why brains would have been a target for sexual selection driven by mate choice uniquely and consistently among hominins.

The human brain did not evolve as an isolated trait. Concomitant changes in other traits provide clues to what selective pressures were important during hominin evolution. Changes in life history patterns accompanied the evident increases in information processing and communication during the Pleistocene (Dean et al., 2001). Gestation (pregnancy) was lengthened, but the resultant infant was even more altricial (Rosenberg, 2004). Human infants must be carried, fed, and protected for a long period in comparison with those of other primates. And yet, humans have shorter interbirth intervals than other hominoids (Walker et al, 2008). Human childhood and adolescence are also exceptionally lengthy (Bogin, 1999; Del Giudice, 2009; Leigh, 2004; Smith, 1994). This extension of the juvenile period appears costly in evolutionary terms. The delay of reproduction until at least 15 years of age involves prolonged exposure to extrinsic causes of mortality and longer generation intervals. Parental and other kin investment continues for an unusually long time, often well into adulthood and perhaps even after the death of the parents. Like the big brain, human life history is an evolutionary puzzle (Hill & Kaplan, 1999; Mace, 2000; Marlowe, 2010; Muehlenbein & Flinn, 2011).

Of course, the child must accumulate energetic resources necessary for physical somatic growth. Whether the lengthening of the human juvenile period was an unavoidable response to an increasing shortage of calories, however, is uncertain. Other hominoids (chimpanzees, gorillas, orangutans) grow at similar overall rates, but mature earlier (Leigh, 2004). Increased body fat is associated with earlier puberty for girls, although psychological and genetic factors are also important (Walvoord, 2010), and the relation is not significant for boys (Lee et al., 2010). Moreover, low birth weight is associated with earlier puberty in some conditions (Karaolis-Danckert et al., 2009). The peculiarities of the human growth curve are also difficult to explain from a simple model of food scarcity—the general timing of growth spurts does not appear linked to a pattern of caloric surpluses. Hence, although it is clear that human female growth and reproductive maturation are sensitive to fat accumulation (Ellison, 2001; Sloboda et al., 2007), the lengthening of the juvenile period during human evolution seems likely to have involved more than simple energetic constraints on growth.

The life history stage of human childhood appears to be an adaptation, at least in part, for the function of enabling cognitive development, including complex social skills and emotional regulation (Alexander, 1987, 1990a; Bogin, 1999; Bjorklund & Pellegrini, 2002; Del Giudice et al., 2009; Flinn, 2004; Konner, 2010). The human child is an extraordinarily social creature, motivated by and highly sensitive to interpersonal relationships (Gopnik et al., 1999). Learning, practice, and experience are imperative for social success. The information processing capacity used for human social interactions is considerable, and perhaps significantly greater than that involved with foraging, locomotion, tool-making, and other subsistence skills (Rilling et al., 2002; Roth & Dicke, 2005; Schoenemann, 2006).

The child needs to master complex dynamic social tasks, such as developing appropriate cognitive and emotional responses during interactions with peers and adults in the local community (Bugental, 2000). The learning environments that facilitate and channel these aspects of human mental phenotypic plasticity appear to take on a special importance (Posner, 2005). Much of the data required for the social behavior necessary to be successful as a human cannot be "preprogrammed" into specific, detailed, fixed responses. Social cleverness in a fast-paced, cumulative cultural environment must contend with dynamic, constantly shifting strategies of friends and enemies, and hence needs information from experiential social learning and creative scenario building (Flinn, 1997; 2006a; Flinn & Alexander, 2007; del Giudice, 2009).

To summarize my argument to this point, human childhood may be viewed as a life history stage that is necessary for acquiring the information and practice to build and refine the mental algorithms critical for negotiating the social relationships that are key to success in our species (Flinn, Muehlenbein, & Ponzi, 2009; Geary & Flinn, 2001). Mastering the social environment presents special challenges for the human child. Social competence is difficult because the targets (other children and adults) are constantly changing and similarly equipped with ToM and other cognitive abilities. Selection for flexible cognitive problem solving would also enhance complementary development of more sophisticated ecological skills, such as hunting and complex extractive foraging (Kaplan et al., 2000).

Human social relationships are especially complex because they involve extensive coalitions. We are extraordinarily cooperative, most exceptionally and importantly in regard to competition with other groups (Alexander, 1979, 2006; Bowles, 2009). Humans are unique in being the only species that engages in group-against-group play (Alexander, 1990b), including team sports. This trait is cross-culturally universal, emerges early in child development, and often is the object of tremendous collective effort.

The family environment is a primary source and mediator of the ontogeny of information processing abilities, including social competencies and group cooperation. Human biology has been profoundly affected by our evolutionary history as unusually social creatures, immersed in networks of family, kin, and dynamic, intercommunity coalitions.

The Human Family

All human societies recognize kinship as a key organizational principle (Brown, 1991). All languages have kinship terminologies and concomitant expectations of obligations and reciprocity (Fortes, 1969; Murdock, 1949). Human kinship systems appear unique in the universal recognition of both bilateral (maternal and paternal) and multigenerational structure, with a general trend for coresidence of male kin, but a dozen or more major variants (Flinn & Low, 1986; Murdock, 1949). These aspects of human kinship link families into broader cooperative systems and provide additional opportunities for alloparental care during the long social childhood. Three species-distinctive characteristics stand out as unusually important in this regard: (a) fathering, that is, extensive and specific investment by males; (b) grandparenting; and (c) networks of kinship that extend among communities and involve affinal (ties by marriage) and consanguineal (ties by blood) relationships (see Fig. 2.1A,B).

Fathers

Mammals that live in groups with multiple males, such as chimpanzees (*Pan troglodytes*), usually have little or no paternal care, because the nonexclusivity of mating relationships obscures paternity (Alexander, 1974; Clutton-Brock, 1991). In contrast, it is common

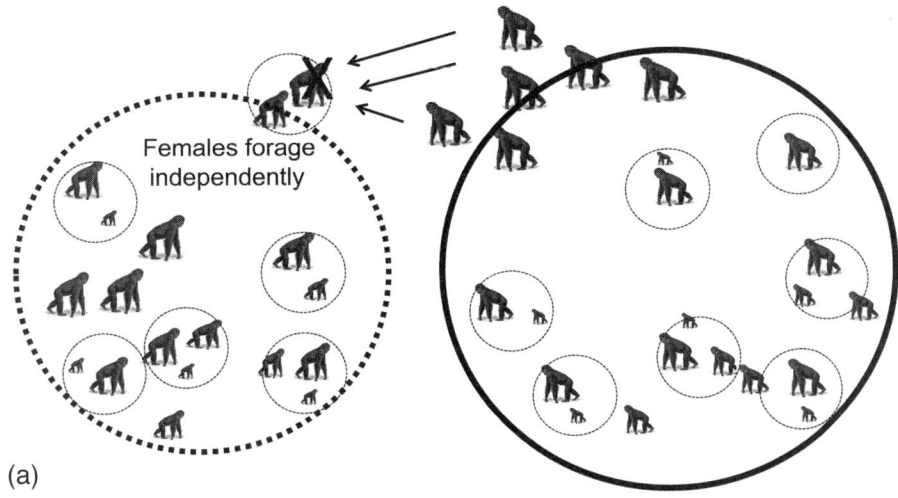

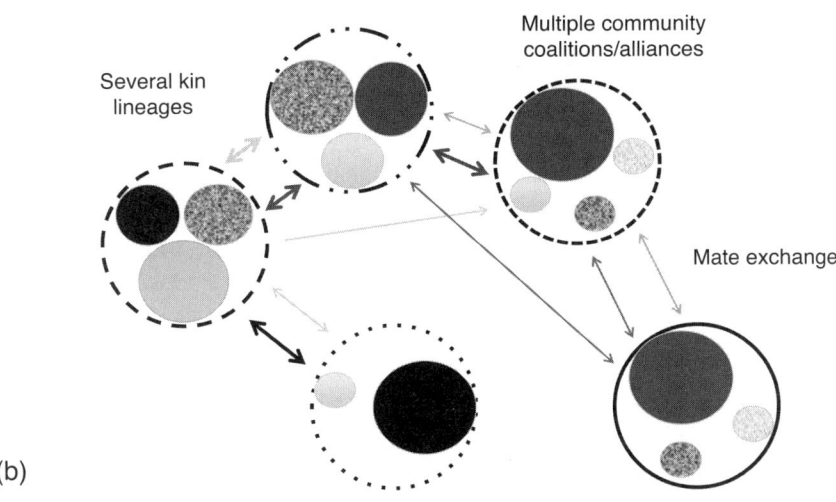

Fig. 2.1 (**A**) Chimpanzee community and intergroup relations. (**B**) Human community and intergroup relations. Chimpanzee (**A**) and human (**B**) social organization and intergroup relations. Lethal intergroup coalitionary aggression occurs in both chimpanzees (male with X in **A**) and humans. Only humans have: (1) functional kin ties that extend among communities (represented by distribution of small colored circles among large colored circles in **B**), (2) mating/marriage exchanges among kin groups, including cousins, in different communities (represented by colored arrows in B), and multiple-community coalitions

for human fathers to provide protection, information, food, and social status for their children (Gray & Anderson, 2010). Paternal care in humans appears to be facilitated by relatively stable pair-bonds, which not only involves cooperation between mates that often endures over the lifespan, but which requires an unusual type of cooperation among coresiding males—respect for each other's mating relationships.

The relatively exclusive mating relationships that are characteristic of most human societies (Flinn & Low, 1986) generate natural factions within the group. Mating relationships also can create alliances in human groups, linking two families or clans together (e.g., Chagnon, 1966). By way of comparison, in chimpanzee communities, it is difficult for even the most dominant male to monopolize an estrous female; usually, most of the males in a community mate with most of the females (Goodall, 1986; Mitani et al., 2010). Chimpanzee males in effect "share" a common interest in the community's females and their offspring. Human groups, in contrast, are composed of family units, each with distinct reproductive interests. Human males do not typically share mating access to all the group's females; consequently, there are usually reliable cues identifying which children are their genetic offspring, and which are those of other males (for exceptions see Beckerman & Valentine, 2002; Walker, Flinn, & Hill, 2010). Because humans live in multimale groups, yet often maintain stable and exclusive mating relationships, the potential for fission along family lines is high. Still, human groups overcome this inherent conflict between family units to form large, stable coalitions.

This unusual tolerance among coresidential males and their families stands in contrast to the norm of polygamous mate competition in group-living nonhuman primates. Selection pressures favoring such tolerance are uncertain, but likely involve the importance of both male parental investment (Alexander, 1990b; Geary & Bjorklund, 2000; Marlowe, 2003) and male coalitions for intraspecific conflict (Alexander, 1990b; Bernhard, Fischbacher, & Fehr, 2006; Flinn et al., 2005; Gavrilets & Vose, 2006; Wrangham, 1999).

The advantages of intensive parenting, including paternal protection and other care, require a most unusual pattern of mating relationships: moderately exclusive pair-bonding in multiple-male groups. No other primate (or mammal) that lives in large, cooperative multiple–reproductive-male groups has such extensive male parental care targeted at specific offspring. Competition for females in multiple-male groups usually results in low confidence of paternity (e.g., bonobos and chimpanzees). Males forming exclusive "pair-bonds" in multiple-male groups would provide cues of nonpaternity to other males, and hence place their offspring in great danger of infanticide (Hrdy, 1999). Paternal care is most likely to be favored by natural selection in conditions in which males can identify their offspring with sufficient probability to offset the costs of investment, although reciprocity with mates is also likely to be involved (Geary & Flinn, 2001; Smuts & Smuts, 1993). Humans exhibit a unique "nested family" social structure, involving complex reciprocity among males and females to restrict direct competition for mates among group members.

It is difficult to imagine how this system could be maintained in the absence of another unusual human trait: concealed or "cryptic" ovulation (Alexander & Noonan, 1979). Human groups tend to be male philopatric (males tending to remain in their natal groups), resulting in extensive male kin alliances, useful for competing against other groups of male kin (LeBlanc, 2003; Wrangham & Peterson, 1996). Females also have complex alliances, but usually are not involved directly in the overt physical aggression characteristic of intergroup relations (Campbell, 2002; Geary & Flinn, 2002). Relationships among human brothers and sisters are life-long, even when residence is in different communities, in contrast with the absence of significant ties or apparent kin recognition after emigration in other hominoids. Parents, grandparents, and other kin may be especially important for the child's mental development of social and cultural maps because they can be relied upon as landmarks who provide relatively honest information. From this perspective, the evolutionary significance of the human family in regard to child development is viewed more as a nest from which social skills may be acquired than simply as an economic unit centered on the sexual division of labor (Flinn & Ward, 2005).

In summary, the care-providing roles of fathers are unusually important in humans, particularly in regard to protection and social power, but are flexible components of the human family, and are linked with the roles of other relatives, including grandparents. In addition to the effects of direct parental care, paternity provides the basis for critical bilateral kinship links that extend across communities and generations. The neuroendocrine mechanisms that underpin human paternal and grandparental psychology are not well studied, but likely involve the common mammalian affiliative hormones oxytocin (OT) and arginine vasopressin (AVP), with additional influence from prolactin (PRL) and the hypothalamic-pituitary-gonadal and hypothalamic-pituitary-adrenal systems (Gray & Campbell, 2009).

Grandparents

Grandparents and grandoffspring share 25% of their genes identical by descent, a significant opportunity for kin selection (Fig. 2.2). Few species, however, live in groups with multiple overlapping generations of kin. Fewer still have significant social relationships among individuals two or more generations apart. Humans appear rather exceptional in this regard. Grandparenting is cross-culturally ubiquitous and pervasive (Murdock, 1967; Sear et al., 2000;

Fig. 2.2 Three generation extended family in a rural community on the island of Dominica. Child well-being is strongly affected by care from grandparents and other relatives (Flinn & Leone, 2006).

Voland et al., 2005). Our life histories allow for significant generational overlaps, including an apparent extended postreproductive stage facilitated by the unique human physiological adaptation of menopause (Alexander, 1974, 1987; Hawkes, 2003).

The significance of emotional bonding between grandparents and grandchildren is beyond doubt. The evolved functions are uncertain, but likely involve the exceptional importance of long-term, extensive, and intensive investment for the human child. The emotional and cognitive processes that guide grand-relationships must have evolved because they enhanced survival and the eventual reproductive success of grandchildren. Leaving children with grandparents and other alloparental care providers allows parents to pursue productive activities that would otherwise be risky or difficult when encumbered with child care. In addition to the physical basics of food, protection, and hygienic care, psychological development of the human child is strongly influenced by the dynamics of the social environment (Dunn, 2004; Hetherington, 2003a, 2003b; Konner, 1991, 2010). Grandparents may have knowledge and experience that are important and useful for helping grandchildren and other relatives survive (Sear et al., 2000; Sear & Mace, 2008) and succeed in social competition (Coe, 2003; Voland, Chasiotis, & Schiefenhövel, 2005). Humans are unusual in the critical role of kin in alloparental care and group coalitions (Hrdy, 2009).

Extended Kinship and Control of Mating Relationships

> The direct application of theory from evolutionary biology to human marriage behavior and mating strategies is . . . not possible until the theory is modified to take into consideration the interdependency of individuals . . . and how their interdependency—coalition alliances—structures human mating behavior. (Chagnon, 1979, p. 88)

Human communities are composed of families embedded in complex kin networks (Fig. 2.3). The importance of kinship in traditional societies is paramount; social power is primarily contingent upon support from relatives. Complex kinship alliances are arguably the most distinguishing social behavioral characteristic of humans in preindustrial cultures, and yet it is rarely discussed in evolutionary psychology or evolutionary economics. Reciprocity in all its various guises (for review see Alexander, 2006, 2010) is inextricably bound up with kinship in traditional societies, perhaps most importantly in regard to the control of mating within the institution of marriage. The vast majority of nonindustrial cultures in the *Ethnographic Atlas* (Murdock, 1967) have rules and preferences specifying what categories of relatives are appropriate for mating/marriage; these rules and preferences involve issues of resultant kin ties, in addition to inbreeding avoidance (Fig. 2.4; for ethnographic examples see Chagnon, 1966; Gough, 1959). It is worth emphasizing that humans are unique in the regulation of mating relationships by kin groups. The reason for controlling who mates with whom is that humans are unique in the great importance of kinship ties for alliances among groups (Fortes, 1969; Levi-Straus, 1949/1969). Mates are usually obtained via strategic negotiation between kin groups. No other species exhibits systematic preferences and prohibitions for mating relationships between specific types of cousins.

If human ancestors had intergroup relations similar to that of chimpanzees (Fig. 2.1a; see Mitani et al, 2010; Wrangham, 1999; Wrangham & Peterson, 1996), it would have been difficult to make even the first steps toward cooperative alliances among males (and females) in different communities. An adult male attempting to establish a relationship with another group likely would be killed as he entered their range. Somehow, our ancestors overcame such obstacles to taking the first steps toward the core human adaptation of intercommunity alliances. It is possible that our ancestors did not have hostile intergroup relations; this seems unlikely, however, on both empirical (LeBlanc, 2003) and theoretical (Alexander, 1990b) grounds. Surely, the most potent factor driving the evolution of the psychological, social, and cultural mechanisms enabling the formation of increasingly large and complex coalitions was competition with other such coalitions (Alexander, 1990b; 2010; Flinn et al., 2005; Gavrilets & Vose, 2006).

Recognition of kinship among individuals residing in different communities is key to intergroup cooperation. Humans are different from other hominoids in the coevolutionary development of (a) stable and moderately exclusive breeding bonds, (b) bilateral kin recognition and relationships, and (c) reciprocity and kin links among coresident families (Alexander, 1990b; Chapais, 2008; Flinn et al., 2007). In short, the family was a critical building block for the evolution of more complex communities, such as the patrilocal band (Steward, 1955), with flexible residence choice with kin in multiple communities and apparent intentional cultivation of ties with relatives in multiple locations.

Hard evidence for the evolutionary trajectory of human family, kinship, and intergroup relations is scarce and indirect; fossils, neurobiology, and physiology, however, provide some important clues.

Paleontological Evidence

Fossils and artifacts can provide useful insights into behavior. Functional analyses of fossilized bone can

Fig. 2.3 Maori male tattooed/engraved with symbols that display genealogy of mother's kin on left side of face, father's kin on right side. Kinship largely determined an individual's status, position, rights, and obligations for Maori (and other traditional cultures)

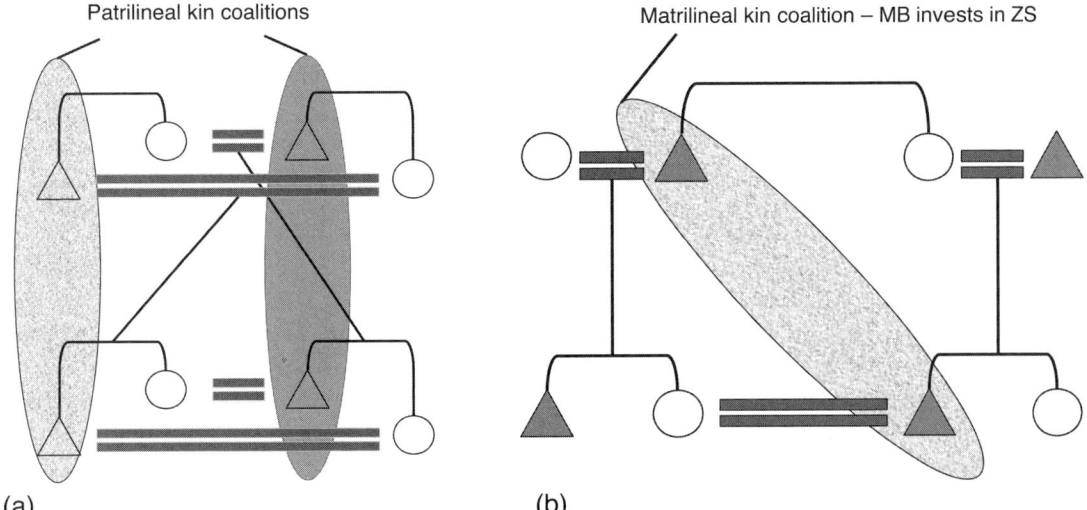

Fig. 2.4 (**A**) Bilateral cross cousin marriage system. (**B**) Matrilateral cross cousin marriage system. Bilateral and matrilateral marriage systems. Males are represented by triangles, females by circles. Mating/marriage relationships are indicated by gray double bars; descent and siblings by black lines. Bilateral cross cousin systems (**A**) involve exchange of mates between patrilateral kin coalitions. Matrilateral cross-cousin systems (**B**) involve enhancement of investment in maternal nephews (i.e., sister's son–ZS) and daughters by males (i.e., mother's brother–MB). The majority of traditional societies in the *Ethnographic Atlas* (Murdock, 1967) have one of these types of cousin marriage systems. Note that rules often apply to second and more distant cousins in bilateral systems

be used to infer behavior such as bipedal locomotion, precision hand grip, use of projectile weapons, diet, and sexual dimorphisms. The temporal sequences of changes in morphological characters indicate the directions of natural selection and can be used to test causal relations. For example, paleontological evidence indicates that bipedal locomotion, canine reduction, meat eating, and tool use predate significant changes in cranial capacity by at least two million years, casting doubt on these factors as critical selective pressures favoring increased human intelligence. Of greater interest to us here in regard to understanding the human family is evidence for parental behavior and patterns of child development.

A prolonged childhood in the latter part of human evolution can be seen in delayed dental maturation rates occurring after the early evolution of *Homo*. The teeth of early *Homo erectus* 1.6 million years developed at similar relatively rapid rates as those of apes and australopithecines (Dean, Leakey, Reid, Shrenk, Schwartz, Stringer, & Walker, 2001; Smith, 1993). However, they are modern in pattern by 800,000 years ago (Bermudez de Castro, Rosas, Carbonell, Nicolas, Rodriguez, & Arsuaga, 1999; cf. Smith et al, 2010), and in rate by 150,000 years ago (Dean, Leakey, Reid, Shrenk, Schwartz, Stringer, & Walker, 2001; Guatelli-Steinberg, Reid, Bishop, & Larsen, 2005). By the appearance of *Homo sapiens* at least, rates of juvenile development appear to have slowed to modern human levels.

During this time period of 1.6 MYA to 0.1 MYA, brain size increased roughly 50%, from 700–900 cc to 1200–1600 cc. At this same time, female body size increased markedly from about 1–1.3 m (3–4 ft) in stature to 1.3–1.5 m (4–5 ft), with a corresponding estimated 50% increase in body mass (McHenry 1992a, 1992b; Ruff, Trinkaus, Walker, & Larsen, 1993). These brain size increases were associated with a change in pelvic structure permitting the birth of larger-brained infants (Ruff, 2002). It may be that this change in body size and pelvic structure permitted the initial brain size increase without altering selection on timing of birth and rate of brain growth. Subsequent brain size increase, however, necessitated more altricial infants, with a greater percentage of brain growth occurring postnatally (Portman, 1941; see also Gunz et al, 2010; Neubauer et al, 2010). This, and the slowing rates of development during this period, may reflect intensified selection for a long period of dependency and learning throughout the evolution of *Homo erectus*, appearing in roughly modern human form by the appearance of *Homo sapiens*.

With the origins of *Homo*, female body size increased dramatically, and although males increased in size, the change was not as pronounced, resulting in a decrease in sexual dimorphism

(McHenry 1992a, 1992b; Ruff, Trinkaus, Walker, & Larsen, 1993). Selection for larger females may have involved increasing fecundity and the ability to produce larger, higher-quality infants, perhaps facilitated by an increasing ability to extract higher-quality resources from the environment (Ungar, Grine, Teaford, & El Zaatari, 2006). A lack of concomitant selection for a similar magnitude of increasing male size may reflect changing male reproductive strategies. Although its magnitude is the subject of current debate, most indications are that *Australopithecus* species were more dimorphic in body mass than were later hominins (Cunningham, Cole, Jungers, Ward, & Wescott, 2005; Plavcan, Lockwood, Kimbel, Lague, & Harmon, 2005; but see Reno, Meindl, McCollum, & Lovejoy, 2005). This change in dimorphism likely reflects changing patterns of social behavior (e.g., Plavcan & Van Schaik, 1997a, 1997b). High levels of sexual dimorphism are associated with extensive and intense mate competition in extant primates (Plavcan, 2000). Reduced dimorphism in hominoids is associated with stable male–female mating relationships (hylobatids, humans) (Plavcan, 2000; Plavcan & Van Shaik, 1997b) and also with male–male coalitions (chimpanzees, humans) (Pawlowski, Lowen, & Dunbar, 1998; Plavcan & Van Shaik, 1997a, 1997b). Both of these systems offer less relative advantage for large male size than do other hominoid social systems. It is reasonable to hypothesize that either, and perhaps both, of these social changes were taking place early in the evolution of *Homo*. An increase in infant altriciality necessitates greater social support for females, and almost certainly paternal and alloparental care. Fairly exclusive mating relationships and cooperative kin networks would have enabled both of these changes.

Neurological and Physiological Mechanisms

Neuroendocrine systems may be viewed as complex sets of mechanisms designed by natural selection to communicate information among cells and tissues. Steroid and peptide hormones, associated neurotransmitters, and other chemical messengers guide the behaviors of mammals in many important ways (Ellison & Gray, 2009; Lee et al., 2009; Panksepp, 2009). For example, analysis of patterns of hormone levels in naturalistic contexts can provide important insights into the evolutionary functions of the neuroendocrine mechanisms that guide human behaviors. Here, I focus on the neuroendocrine mechanisms that facilitate human family relationships.

Hormonal Basis for Attachment and Family Love

Some of the most precious human feelings are stimulated by close social relationships: a mother holding her newborn infant; brothers reunited after a long absence; lovers entangled in each other's arms (Fig. 2.5). Natural selection has designed our neurobiological mechanisms, in concert with our endocrine systems, to generate potent sensations during our interactions with these most evolutionarily significant individuals. We share with our primate relatives the same basic hormones and neurotransmitters that underlie these mental gifts. But our unique evolutionary history has modified us to

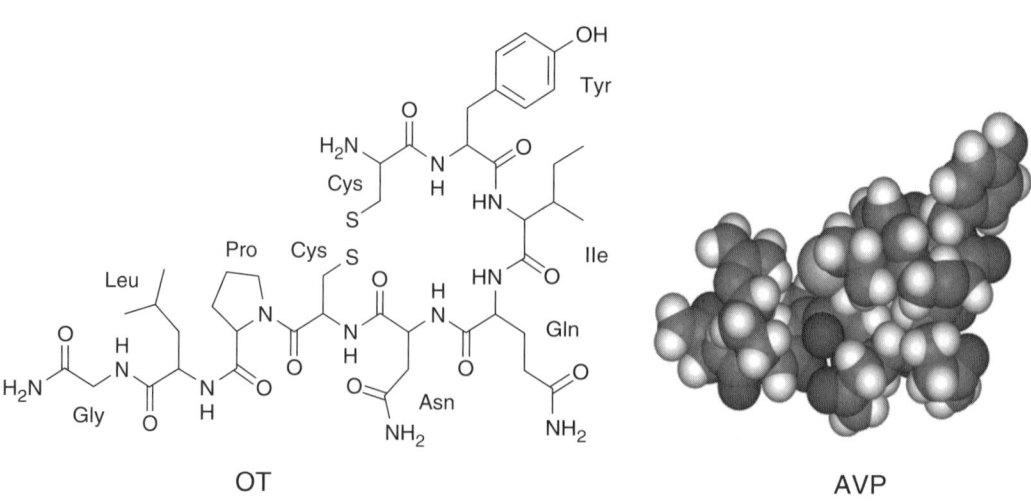

Fig. 2.5 The closely related affiliative neuropeptides, oxytocin (OT) and arginine vasopressin (AVP)

respond to different circumstances and situations; we are rewarded and punished for somewhat different stimuli than were our phylogenetic cousins. Chimpanzees and humans share the delight—the sensational reward—when biting into a ripe, juicy mango. But the endocrine, neurological, and associated emotional responses of a human father to the birth of his child (e.g., Gray et al., 2002, 2006; Storey et al., 2000) are likely to be quite different from those of a chimpanzee male. Happiness for a human (Buss, 2000) has many unique designs, such as romantic love (Fisher et al., 2006), that involve modifications of the neurological receptors and processors of shared endogenous messengers from our phylogenetic heritage.

Attachments or bonding are central in the lives of the social mammals. Basic to survival and reproduction, these interdependent relationships are the fabric of the social networks that permit individuals to maintain cooperative relationships over time. Although attachments can provide security and relief from stress, close relationships also exert pressures on individuals, to which they continuously respond. It should not be surprising, therefore, that the neuroendocrine mechanisms underlying attachment and stress are intimately related to one another. And although more is known about the stress response systems than the affiliative systems, we are beginning to get some important insights into the neuroendocrine mechanisms that underpin human relationships (Alexander et al, 2009; Lee et al., 2009; Panksepp, 2004).

The mother–offspring relationship is at the core of mammalian life, and it appears that some of the biochemistry at play in the regulation of this intimate bond was also selected to serve in primary mechanisms regulating bonds between mates, paternal care, the family group, and even larger social networks (Fisher et al., 2006; Hrdy, 1999; Wynne-Edwards, 2001). Although a number of hormones and neurotransmitters are involved in attachment and other components of relationships, the two peptide hormones, OT and AVP, appear to be primary (Carter, 2002; Curtis & Wang, 2003; Heinrichs & Domes, 2008; Heinrichs, Dawans, & Domes, 2009; Lee et al., 2009; Seltzer, Ziegler, & Pollak, 2010; Young & Insel, 2002), with dopamine, prolactin, cortisol, and other hormones and neurotransmitters having mediating effects.

The hypothalamus is the major brain site where OT and AVP (closely related chains of nine amino acids) are produced. From there, they are released into the central nervous system (CNS), as well as transported to the pituitary where they are stored until secreted into the bloodstream. OT and AVP act on a wide range of neurological systems, and their influence varies among mammalian species and stage of development. The neurological effects of OT and AVP appear to be key mechanisms (e.g., Bartels & Zeki, 2004) involved in the evolution of human family behaviors. The effects of OT and AVP in humans are likely to be especially context dependent, because of the variable and complex nature of family relationships.

Along with OT and AVP, prolactin, estrogen, testosterone, and progesterone are involved in parental care among mammals (Insel & Young, 2001). The roles of these hormones vary across species and between males and females. The effects of these hormones are influenced by experience and context. Among rats, for example, estrogen and progesterone appear to prime the brain during pregnancy for parental behavior. Estrogen has been found to activate the expression of genes that increase the receptor density for OT and prolactin, thus increasing their influence postnatally (Young & Insel, 2002).

Oxytocin is most well known for its role in regulating birth and lactation, but along with AVP, it has also been found to play a central role in maternal care and attachment (Fleming et al., 1999; Young, 2009). Just prior to birth, an increase in OT occurs, which is seen as priming maternal care. An injection of OT in virgin rats has been found to induce maternal care, whereas an OT antagonist administered to pregnant rats interferes with the development of maternal care (Carter, 2002).

Among mammals, hormonal activation initially stimulates maternal behavior among new mothers. Once she has begun to care for her offspring, however, hormones are not required for maternal behavior to continue. Olfactory and somatosensory stimulation from interactions between offspring and mother are, however, usually required for parental care to continue (e.g., Fleming et al., 1999). The stimulation from suckling raises OT levels in rodents and breastfeeding women, which then results in not only milk letdown but also in a decrease in limbic hypothalamic-anterior pituitary-adrenal cortex system (HPA) activity and a shift in the autonomic nervous system (ANS) from a sympathetic tone to a parasympathetic tone. This results in a calmness seen as conducive to remaining in contact with the infant. It also results in a shift from external-directed energy toward the internal activity of nutrient storage and growth (Uvnas-Moberg, 1998).

Experience also affects the neuroendocrine systems involved in the expression of maternal care. The HPA system of offspring during development is influenced by variation in maternal care, which then influences their maternal behavior as adults. Such changes involve the production of, and receptor density for, stress hormones and OT (Champagne & Meaney, 2001; Fleming et al., 1999; Todeschin et al., 2009).

HPA-modulated hormones and maternal behavior are related in humans during the postpartum period (Fleming et al., 1997). During this time, cortisol appears to have an arousal effect, focusing attention on infant bonding. Mothers with higher cortisol levels were found to be more affectionate, more attracted to their infant's odor, and better at recognizing their infant's cry during the postpartum period.

Functional magnetic resonance imaging (fMRI) studies of brain activity involved in maternal attachment in humans indicate that the activated regions are part of the reward system and contain a high density of receptors for OT and AVP (Bartels & Zeki, 2004; Fisher et al., 2006). These studies also demonstrate that the neural regions involved in attachment activated in humans are similar to those activated in nonhuman animals. Among humans, however, neural regions associated with social judgment and assessment of the intentions and emotions of others exhibited some deactivation during attachment activities, suggesting possible links between psychological mechanisms for attachment and management of social relationships. Falling in love with a mate and affective bonds with offspring may involve temporary deactivation of psychological mechanisms for maintaining an individual's social "guard" in the complex reciprocity of human social networks. Dopamine levels are likely to be important for both types of relationship but may involve some distinct neural sites. It will be interesting to see what fMRI studies of attachment in human males indicate because that is where the most substantial differences from other mammals would be expected. Similarly, fMRI studies of attachment to mothers, fathers, and alloparental care providers in human children may provide important insights into the other side of parent–offspring bonding.

Paternal care is not common among mammals (Clutton-Brock, 1991). For evolutionary reasons noted earlier, it is found among some rodent and primate species, including humans. The extent and types of paternal care vary among species. The hormonal influence in parental care among males appears to differ somewhat from that found among females. Vasopressin (AVP) appears to function as a complement to OT (Young & Insel, 2002). Along with prolactin and OT, AVP prepares the male to be receptive to and care for infants (Bales et al., 2004).

Paternal care is more common in monogamous than polygamous mammals and is often related to hormonal and behavioral stimuli from the female. In the monogamous California mouse, disruption of the pair-bond does not affect maternal care but does diminish paternal care (Gubernick, 1988). In some other species with biparental care, however, paternal care is not as dependent on the presence of the female (Young & Insel, 2002). Experience also plays a role in influencing hormonal activation and paternal behavior. Among tamarins, experienced fathers have higher levels of prolactin than do first-time fathers (Ziegler & Snowdon, 1997).

Androgens, including testosterone, also appear to be involved in the regulation of paternal behavior. For example, human fathers tend to have lower testosterone levels when they are involved in childcare activities (Berg & Wynne-Edwards, 2001; Fleming et al., 2002; Gray & Campbell, 2009; Kuzawa et al., 2009), although the relation of these levels with the key paternal role of offspring protection is uncertain. Human males stand out as very different from our closest relatives, the chimpanzees, in the areas of paternal attachment and investment in offspring. Investigation of the neuroendocrine mechanisms that underpin male parental behavior may provide important insights into these critical evolutionary changes.

Like male parental care, bonding between mates is also uncommon among mammals but has been selected for when it has reproductive advantages for both parents (Clutton-Brock, 1991; Carter, 2002; Young et al., 2002). Monogamy is found across many mammalian taxa, but most of the current knowledge related to the neuroendocrine basis of this phenomenon has been obtained from the comparative study of two closely related rodent species. The prairie vole (*Microtus ochrogaster*) mating pair nest together and provide prolonged biparental care, whereas their close relatives, the meadow vole (*Microtus pennsylvanicus*), do not exhibit these behaviors (Young et al., 2002). As with other social behaviors in rodents, OT and AVP have been found to be central in the differences that these related species exhibit with respect to pair-bonding. Pair-bonding occurs for the prairie vole following mating. Vagino-cervical stimulation results in a release of

OT and the development of a partner preference for the female (Carter, 2002). For the male, it is an increase in AVP following mating and not just OT that results in partner preference. Injections of exogenous OT in the female and AVP in the male prairie vole result in mate preference even without mating. This does not occur with meadow voles (Young et al., 2002).

The receptor density for OT and AVP in specific brain regions might provide the basis for mechanisms underlying other social behaviors. Other neurotransmitters, hormones, and social cues also are likely to be involved, but slight changes in gene expression for receptor density, such as those found between the meadow and prairie voles in the ventral palladium (located near the nucleus accumbens, an important component of the brain's reward system), might demonstrate how such mechanisms could be modified by selection (Lim et al., 2004). The dopamine D_2 receptors in the nucleus accumbens appear to link the affiliative OT and AVP pair-bonding mechanisms with positive, rewarding mental states (Aragona et al., 2003, 2006; Curtis & Wang, 2003). The combination results in the powerful addiction that parents have for their offspring.

Given the adaptive value of extensive biparental care and prolonged attachment found in the mating pair and larger family network, it is not surprising that similar neurohormonal mechanisms active in the maternal–offspring bond would also be selected to underlie these other attachments. Although some variation exists among species and between males and females, the same general neurohormonal systems active in pair-bonding in other species are found in the human (Lee et al., 2009; Panksepp, 2004; Wynne-Edwards, 2003). Androgen response to pair-bonding appears complex (e.g. van der Meij et al., 2008), but similar to parent–offspring attachment in that pair-bonded males tend to have lower testosterone levels in nonchallenging conditions (Alvergne et al., 2009; Gray & Campbell, 2009). Moreover, males actively involved in caretaking behavior appear to have temporarily diminished testosterone levels (Gray et al., 2007).

Hormonal mechanisms for another key human adaptation—bonding among adult males to form coalitions or a "band of brothers"—is less well studied. Social effects, such as victories against outsiders, produce elevations in testosterone, but defeating friends does not (Flinn et al., 2009; Fuxjager et al., 2009; Gleason et al., 2009; Wagner, Flinn, & England, 2002). Human males, moreover, may differentially respond to females contingent on whether the females are in a stable breeding bond with a close friend; males have lower testosterone after interacting with the wives of their relatives and friends (Flinn, preliminary data). Involvement of the affiliative neuropeptides (OT and AVP) in relationships among adult males is unknown.

The challenge before human evolutionary biologists and psychologists is to understand how these general neuroendocrine systems have been modified and linked with other special human cognitive systems (e.g., Allman et al., 2001; Blakemore et al., 2004; Ulrich-Lai & Herman, 2009) to produce the unique suite of human family behaviors. Analysis of hormonal responses to social stimuli may provide important insights into the selective pressures that guided the evolution of these key aspects of the human mind.

Stress Hormones: Response to Dynamic Social Environment

The evolutionary scenario proposed in previous sections posits that social environment, with the family as cornerstone, is of paramount importance in a child's world. Throughout human evolutionary history, parents and close relatives provided calories, protection, and information necessary for survival, growth, health, social success, and eventual reproduction. The human mind, therefore, is likely to have evolved special sensitivity to interactions with family care providers, particularly during infancy and early childhood (Bowlby, 1969; Daly & Wilson, 1995; Belsky, 1997, 2005; Geary & Flinn, 2001). The human mind also is likely to have evolved neurological mechanisms that facilitate keeping pace in the rapid and dynamic social arms race.

The family and other kin provide important cognitive "landmarks" for the development of a child's understanding of the social environment.

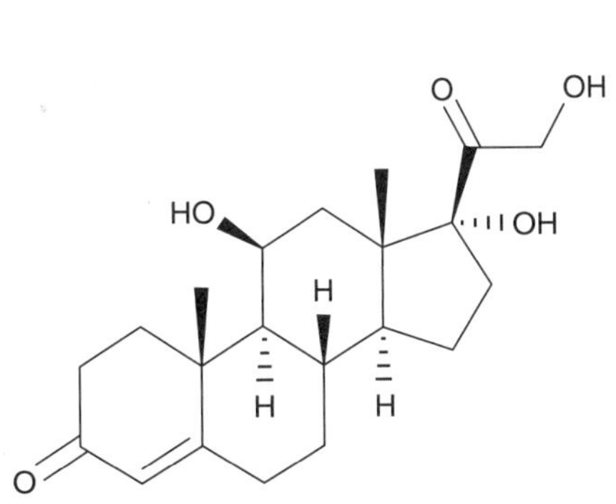

Fig. 2.6 The key human glucocorticoid stress hormone, cortisol

The reproductive interests of a child overlap with those of its parents more than with any other individuals. Information (including advice, training, and incidental observation) provided by parents is important for situating oneself in the social milieu and developing a mental model of its operations. A child's family environment may be an especially important source and mediator of stress, with consequent effects on health.

Psychosocial stressors are associated with increased risk of infectious disease (Cohen et al., 2003) and a variety of other illnesses (Ader et al., 2001). Physiological stress responses regulate the allocation of energetic and other somatic resources to different bodily functions via a complex assortment of neuroendocrine mechanisms. Changing, unpredictable environments require adjustment of priorities. Digestion, growth, immunity, and sex are irrelevant while being chased by a predator (Sapolsky, 1994). Stress hormones (Fig 2.6) help shunt blood, glucose, and so on to tissues necessary for the task at hand. Chronic and traumatic stress can diminish health, evidently because resources are diverted away from important health functions. These costs can be referred to as *allostatic load* (McEwen, 2005; Juster et al., 2010). Such diversions of resources may have special significance during infancy and childhood because of the additional demands of physical and mental growth and development and possible long-term ontogenetic consequences (e.g., see Chisholm et al., 2005; Nepomnaschy & Flinn, 2008; Roozendaal et al., 2009; van der Vegt et al., 2009; Wiedenmayer, 2009).

Investigation of physiological stress responses in the human family environment has been hampered by the lack of noninvasive techniques for measuring stress hormones. Frequent collection of plasma samples to assess temporal changes in endocrine function is not feasible in nonclinical settings. The development of saliva immunoassay techniques, however, presents new opportunities for stress research. Saliva is relatively easy to collect and store, especially under adverse field conditions faced by anthropologists (Ellison, 1988). In this section, I review results from a longitudinal, 22-year study of child stress and health in a rural community on the island of Dominica (for reviews see Flinn, 1999, 2006b; Flinn & England, 1995, 1997, 2003). The research design uses concomitant monitoring of a child's daily activities, stress hormones, and psychological conditions to investigate the effects of naturally occurring psychosocial events in the family environment.

Associations between average cortisol levels of children and household composition indicate that children living with nonrelatives, stepfathers, and half-siblings (stepfather has children by the stepchild's mother), or single parents without kin support had higher average levels of cortisol than did children living with both parents, single mothers with kin support, or grandparents (see gray bars in Figure 2.7). Note, however, that these differences in

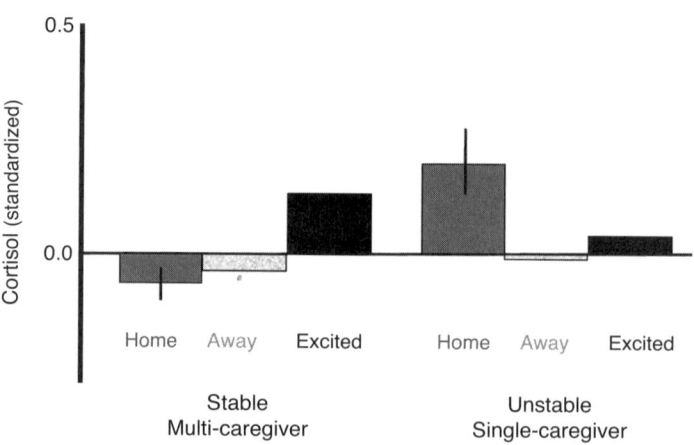

Fig. 2.7 Cortisol and family environment. Children from stable families with multiple care providers (mothers, fathers, aunts, grandparents) have lower cortisol levels when in their home environments (*gray bars*) compared with children from unstable families with few care providers (single mothers, stepfamilies). This relation is reversed, however, during exciting periods such as holidays and sporting events (*black bars*), when children from stable multiple care providers have higher cortisol levels than do children from unstable families. Compiled from data in Flinn & England (1997).

cortisol levels are diminished when comparisons are made during nonstressed conditions. Moreover, the pattern is reversed during the excitement of holidays and other apparently hedonic emotional circumstances. Hence cortisol appears to be elevated during positive as well as negative social challenges.

Several caveats need emphasis. First, not all children in difficult family environments have elevated cortisol levels. Second, household composition is not a uniform indicator of family environment. Some single-mother households, for example, appear more stable, affectionate, and supportive than some two-parent households. Third, children appear differentially sensitive to different aspects of their caretaking environments, reflecting temperamental and other individual differences.

These caveats, however, do not invalidate the general association between household composition and childhood stress. Several possible reasons may underlie this result. Children in difficult caretaking environments may experience chronic stress resulting in moderate-high levels of cortisol (i.e., a child has cortisol levels that are above average day after day). They may experience more acute stressors that substantially raise cortisol for short periods of time. They may experience more frequent stressful events (e.g., parental chastisement or marital quarrelling—see Flinn, 1988; Daly & Wilson, 1988) that temporarily raise cortisol. There may be a lack of reconciliation between parent and child. And, they may have inadequate coping abilities, perhaps resulting from difficult experiences in early development. These early experiences may have long-term effects (e.g., McGowan et al, 2009).

The events in children's lives that are associated with elevated cortisol are not always traumatic or even "negative." Activities such as eating meals, hard physical work, routine competitive play (e.g., cricket, basketball, and "king of the mountain" on ocean rocks), return of a family member who was temporarily absent (e.g., father returning from a job in town for the weekend), and holiday excitement were associated with temporary, moderate increases (about 10%–100%) in cortisol among healthy children. Some of these moderate stressors usually had rapid attenuation (less than 1 hour) of cortisol levels (some stressors had characteristic temporal "signatures" of cortisol level and duration).

High-stress events (cortisol increases from 100% to 2,000%), however, most commonly involved trauma from family conflict or change (Flinn et al., 1996; Flinn & England, 2003). Punishment, quarreling, and residence change substantially increased cortisol levels, whereas calm, affectionate contact was associated with diminished (-10% to -50%) cortisol levels. Of all cortisol values that were more than 2 standard deviations (SD) above mean levels (i.e., indicative of substantial stress), 19.2% were temporally associated with traumatic family events (residence change of child or parent/caretaker, punishment, "shame," serious quarreling, and/or fighting) within a 24-hour period. In addition, 42.1% of traumatic family events were temporally associated with substantially elevated cortisol (i.e., at least one of the saliva samples collected within 24 hours was >2 SD above mean levels). Chronic elevations of cortisol levels sometimes occurred among children in difficult family environments, but this was difficult to assess quantitatively (Flinn, 2009).

Considerable variability was noted among children in cortisol response to family disturbances. Not all individuals had detectable changes in cortisol levels associated with family trauma. Some children had significantly elevated cortisol levels during some episodes of family trauma but not during others. Cortisol response is not a simple or uniform phenomenon. Numerous factors, including preceding events, habituation, specific individual histories, context, and temperament might affect how children respond to particular situations.

Nonetheless, traumatic family events were associated with elevated cortisol levels for all ages of children more than any other factor that we examined. These results suggest that family interactions were a critical psychosocial stressor in most children's lives, although the sample collection during periods of intense family interaction (early morning and late afternoon) may have exaggerated this association.

Although elevated cortisol levels are associated with traumatic events such as family conflict, long-term stress may result in diminished cortisol response. In some cases, chronically stressed children had blunted response to physical activities that normally evoked cortisol elevation. Comparison of cortisol levels during nonstressful periods (no reported or observed crying, punishment, anxiety, residence change, family conflict, or health problem during 24-hour period before saliva collection) indicates a striking reduction and, in some cases, reversal of the family environment-stress association. Chronically stressed children sometimes had subnormal cortisol levels when they were not in stressful situations. For example, cortisol levels immediately after school (walking home from school) and during noncompetitive play were lower among some chronically stressed children. Some chronically stressed children appeared socially "tough" or withdrawn and exhibited little or no arousal to the novelty of the first few days of the saliva collection procedure.

Relations between family environment and cortisol stress response appear to result from a combination of factors including frequency of traumatic events; frequency of positive affectionate interactions; frequency of negative interactions, such as irrational punishment; frequency of residence change; security of attachment; development of coping abilities; and availability or intensity of caretaking attention. Maternal care is probably the most important correlate of household composition that affects childhood stress. Mothers in socially secure households (i.e., permanent amiable coresidence with mate and/or other kin) appeared more able and more motivated to provide physical, social, and psychological care for their children. Mothers without mates or kin support were likely to exert effort in attracting potential mates and may have viewed dependent children as impediments to this. Hence, the coresidence of a father may provide not only direct benefits from paternal care but also may affect maternal care (Belsky et al., 1991; Hill & Hurtado, 1996). Young mothers without mate support usually relied extensively on their parents or other kin for help with child care.

Children born and raised in household environments in which mothers have little or no mate or kin support were at greatest risk for abnormal cortisol profiles and associated health problems. Because socioeconomic conditions influence family environment, they have consequences for child health that extend beyond direct material effects (e.g., see Hosseini et al., 2009; Joëls & Baram, 2009). And because health in turn may affect an individual's social and economic opportunities, a cycle of poor health and poverty may be perpetuated generation after generation (Shonkoff et al., 2009).

Conclusion

Human childhood is a life history stage that appears necessary and useful for acquiring the information and practice to build and refine the mental algorithms critical for negotiating the social coalitions that are key to success in our species (del Giudice et al., 2009). Mastering the social environment presents special challenges for the human child. Social competence is difficult because the target is constantly changing and is similarly equipped with ToM and other cognitive abilities. Here, we suggest that family environment, including care from fathers and grandparents, is a primary source and mediator of the ontogeny of social competencies.

Social competence is developmentally expensive in time, instruction, and parental care. Costs are not equally justified for all expected adult environments. The human family may help children adjust development in response to environmental exigencies for appropriate trades-offs in life history strategies. An evolutionary developmental perspective of the family can be useful in these efforts to understand this critical aspect of a child's world by integrating knowledge of physiological causes with the logic of adaptive design by natural selection. Human biology has been profoundly affected by our evolutionary history as unusually social creatures, including, perhaps, a special reliance upon cooperative fathers, grandparents, and kin residing in other groups. Indeed, the mind of the human child may have design features that enable its development as a group project, guided by the multitudinous informational contributions of its ancestors and codescendants.

Understanding the coevolution of the core human adaptations of stable breeding bonds, biparental care, altricial infancy, prolonged childhood, complex social intelligence, extended kinship networks, and intergroup alliances, presents difficult challenges for evolutionary psychology. The inclusion of ideas and methods from anthropology and the life sciences may prove helpful, and hopefully make the task merrier.

References

Ader, R., Felten, D. L., & Cohen, N. (2001). *Psychoneuroimmunology* (3rd ed.). San Diego: Academic Press.

Adolphs, R. (2003). Cognitive neuroscience of human social behavior. *Nature Reviews, Neuroscience 4*(3), 165–178.

Aiello, L.C., & Wheeler, P. (1995). The expensive-tissue hypothesis: The brain and the digestive system in human and primate evolution. *Current Anthropology, 36*, 199–221.

Alexander, G.M., Wilcox, T., & Farmer, M.E. (2009). Hormone-behavior associations in early infancy. *Hormones and Behavior, 56*(5), 498–502.

Alexander, R.D. (1974). The evolution of social behavior. *Annual Review of Ecology and Systematics, 5*, 325–383.

Alexander, R.D. (1979). *Darwinism and human affairs*. Seattle: University of Washington Press.

Alexander, R.D. (1987). *The biology of moral systems*. Hawthorne, NY: Aldine Press.

Alexander, R.D. (1990a). Epigenetic rules and Darwinian algorithms: The adaptive study of learning and development. *Ethology and Sociobiology, 11*, 1–63.

Alexander, R.D. (1990b). *How humans evolved: Reflections on the uniquely unique species.* Museum of Zoology (Special Publication No. 1). Ann Arbor: The University of Michigan.

Alexander, R.D. (2005). Evolutionary selection and the nature of humanity. In V. Hosle & C. Illies (Eds.), *Darwinism and philosophy* (Chapter 15). South Bend, IN: University of Notre Dame Press.

Alexander, R.D. (2006). The challenge of human social behavior. *Evolutionary Psychology, 4,* 1–32.

Alexander, R.D. (2010). Darwin's challenges and the future of human society. In F. Wayman, P. Williamson, & B. Bueno de Mesquita (Eds.). Prediction: Breakthroughs in science, markets, and politics. Ann Arbor, Michigan: University of Michigan Press.

Allman, J. (1999). *Evolving brains.* New York: Scientific American Library.

Allman, J.M., Hakeem, A., Erwin, J.M., Nimchinsky, E., & Hof, P. (2001). The anterior cingulate cortex: the evolution of an interface between emotion and cognition. *Annals of the New York Academy of Sciences, 935,* 107–117.

Alvergne, A., Faurie, C., & Raymond, M. (2009). Variation in testosterone levels and male reproductive effort: Insight from a polygynous human population. *Hormones and Behavior, 56*(5), 491–497.

Amodio, D.M., & Frith, C.D. (2006). Meeting of minds: The medial frontal cortex and social cognition. *Nature Reviews Neuroscience, 7*(4), 268–277.

Aragona, B.J., Liu, Y., Curtis, J.T., Stephan, F.K., & Wang, Z. (2003). A critical role for nucleus accumbens dopamine in partner-preference formation in male prairie voles. *Journal of Neuroscience* 23, 3483–3490.

Aragona, B.J., Liu, Y., Yu, Y.J., Curtis, J.T., Detwiler, J.M., Insel, T. R., et al. (2006). Nucleus accumbens dopamine differentially mediates the formation and maintenance of monogamous pair bonds. *Nature Neuroscience, 9,* 133–139.

Bales, K.L., Kim, A.J., Lewis-Reese, A.D., & Carter, C.S. (2004). Both oxytocin and vasopressin may influence alloparental behavior in male prairie voles. *Hormones and Behavior, 45*(5), 354–361.

Bartels, A., & Zeki, S. (2004). The neural correlates of maternal and romantic love. *NeuroImage 21,* 1155–1166.

Beckerman, S., & Valentine, P. (Eds.). (2002). *Cultures of multiple fathers: The theory and practice of partible paternity in South America.* Gainesville: University of Florida Press.

Belsky, J. (1997). Attachment, mating, and parenting: An evolutionary interpretation. *Human Nature, 8,* 361–381.

Belsky, J. (2005). Differential susceptibility to rearing influence: An evolutionary hypothesis and some evidence. In B.J. Ellis & D.F. Bjorklund (Eds.), *Origins of the social mind: Evolutionary psychology and child development* (pp. 139–163). New York: Guilford Press.

Belsky, J., Steinberg, L., & Draper, P. (1991). Childhood experience, interpersonal development, and reproductive strategy: An evolutionary theory of socialization. *Child Development, 62,* 647–670.

Berg, S.J., & Wynne-Edwards, K.E. (2001). Changes in testosterone, cortisol, and estradiol levels in men becoming fathers. *Mayo Clinic Proceedings, 76,* 582–592.

Bermudez de Castro, J.M., Rosas, A., Carbonell, E., Nicolas, M.E., Rodriguez, J., & Arsuaga, J.L. (1999). A modern human pattern of dental development in lower Pleistocene hominids from Atapuerca-TD6 (Spain). *Proceedings of the National Academy of Sciences, 96*(7), 4210–4213.

Bernhard, H., Fischbacher, U., & Fehr, E. (2006). Parochial altruism in humans. *Nature, 442*(7105), 912–915.

Bjorklund, D.F., & Pellegrini, A.D. (2002). *The origins of human nature: Evolutionary developmental psychology.* Washington, DC: APA Press.

Bogin, B. (1999). *Patterns of human growth* (2nd edition). Cambridge: Cambridge University Press.

Bowlby, J., (1969). *Attachment.* New York: Basic Books.

Bowles, S. (2009). Did warfare among ancestral hunter-gatherers affect the evolution of human social behaviors? *Science, 324* (5932), 1293–1298.

Brown, D.E. (1991). *Human universals.* Philadelphia: Temple University Press.

Buchan, J.C., Alberts, S.C., Silk, J.B., & Altmann, J. (2003). True paternal care in a multi-male primate society. *Nature, 425*(6954), 179–181.

Bugental, D.B. (2000). Acquisition of the algorithms of social life: A domain-based approach. *Psychological Bulletin, 26,* 187–209.

Buss, D.M. (2000). The evolution of happiness. *American Psychology, 55,* 15–23.

Cameron, N.M., Champagne, F.A., Parent, C., Fish, E.W., Ozaki-Kuroda, K., & Meaney, M.J. (2005). The programming of individual differences in defensive responses and reproductive strategies in the rat through variations in maternal care. *Neuroscience and Biobehavioral Reviews, 29,* 843–865.

Campbell, A. (2002). *A mind of her own: The evolutionary psychology of women.* London: Oxford University Press.

Carter, C.S. (2002). Neuroendocrine perspectives on social attachment and love. In J.T. Cacioppo, G.G. Berntson, R. Adolphs, C.S. Carter, R.J. Davidson, M.K. McClintock, et al. (Eds.), *Foundations in social neuroscience* (pp. 853–890). Cambridge, MA: MIT Press.

Chagnon, N.A. (1966). *Yanomamo.* New York: Holt, Rinehart & Winston.

Chagnon, N.A. (1979). Mate competition, favoring close kin, and village fissioning among the Yanomamo Indians. In N.A. Chagnon & W.G. Irons (Eds.), Evolutionary biology and human social behavior: An anthropological perspective (pp. 86–132). North Scituate, MA: Duxbury press.

Champagne, F.A., & Curley, J.P. (2008). Epigenetic mechanisms mediating the long-term effects of maternal care on development. *Neuroscience and Biobehavioral Reviews, 33,* 593–600.

Champagne, F.A., & Meaney, M. J. (2001). Like mother, like daughter: Evidence for non-genomic transmission of parental behavior and stress responsivity. *Progress in Brain Research, 133,* 287–302.

Chapais, B. (2008). *Primeval kinship: How pair-bonding gave birth to human society.* Cambridge, MA: Harvard University Press.

Chiappe, D., & MacDonald, K. (2005). The evolution of domain-general mechanisms in intelligence and learning. *Journal of General Psychology, 132*(1), 5–40.

Chisholm, J.S., Quinlivan, J.A., Petersen, R.W., & Coall, D.A. (2005). Early stress predicts age at menarche and first birth, adult attachment, and expected lifespan. *Human Nature, 16*(3), 233–265.

Cirulli, F., Francia, N., Berry, A., Aloe, L., Alleva, E., & Suomi, S.J. (2009). Early life stress as a risk factor for mental health: Role of neurotrophins from rodents to non-human primates. *Neuroscience and Biobehavioral Reviews, 33*(4), 493–497.

Clutton-Brock, T.H. (1991). *The evolution of parental care*. Princeton, NJ: Princeton University Press.

Coe, K. (2003). *The ancestress hypothesis: Visual art as adaptation*. New Brunswick: Rutgers University Press.

Cohen, S., Doyle, W. J., Turner, R. B., Alper, C. M., & Skoner, D. P. (2003). Emotional style and susceptibility to the common cold. *Psychosomatic Medicine*, 65(4), 652–657.

Cunningham, D.L., Cole, T. III, Jungers, W.L., Ward, C.V., & Wescott, D. (2005). Patterns of postcranial and body mass dimorphism in hominoids. *American Journal of Physical Anthropology Supplement*, 40, 90.

Curtis, T.J., & Wang, Z. (2003). The neurochemistry of pair bonding. *Current Directions in Psychological Science*, 12(2), 49–53.

Daly M., & Wilson, M. (1983). *Sex, evolution, and behavior*. Boston: Duxbury Press.

Daly, M., & Wilson, M. (1995). Discriminative parental solicitude and the relevance of evolutionary models to the analysis of motivational systems. In: Gazzaniga, M.S. (Ed.), *The cognitive neurosciences* (pp. 1269–1286). Cambridge, MA: MIT Press.

Daly, M., & Wilson, M. (1988). Evolutionary social psychology and family homicide. *Science*, 242, 519–524.

Darwin, C.R. (1871). *The descent of man and selection in relation to sex*. London: John Murray.

Dean, C., Leakey, M.G., Reid, D., Schrenk, F., Schwartz, G.T., Stringer, C., & Walker, A. (2001). Growth processes in teeth distinguish modern humans from *Homo erectus* and earlier hominins. *Nature*, 414, 628–631.

Deater-Deckard, K., Atzaba-Poria, N., & Pike, A. (2004). Mother- and father-child mutuality in Anglo and Indian British families: A link with lower externalizing behaviors. *Journal of Abnormal Child Psychology*, 32(6), 609–620.

de Jong, T.R., Chauke, M., Harris, B.N., & Saltzman, W. (2009). From here to paternity: Neural correlates of the onset of paternal behavior in California mice (*Peromyscus californicus*). *Hormones and Behavior*, 56, 220–231.

Del Giudice, M., 2009. Sex, attachment, and the development of reproductive strategies. *Behavior and Brain Science*, 32, 1–21.

Del Giudice, M., Angeleri, R., & Manera, V., 2009. The juvenile transition: A developmental switch point in human life history. *Developmental Reviews*, 29, 1–31.

Dunn, J. (2004). Understanding children's family worlds: Family transitions and children's outcome. *Merrill-Palmer Quarterly*, 50(3), 224–235.

Edelman, G.M. (2006). *Second nature: Brain science and human knowledge*. New Haven, CT: Yale University Press.

Elia, M. (1992). Organ and tissue contribution to metabolic rate. In J.M. Kinner & H.N. Tucker (Eds.). *Energy metabolism: Tissue determinants and cellular corollaries* (pp. 61–79). New York: Raven Press.

Ellison, P., (1988). Human salivary steroids: methodological considerations and applications in physical anthropology. *Yearbook of Physical Anthropology*, 31, 115–142.

Ellison, P.T. (2001). *On fertile ground, a natural history of human reproduction*. Cambridge, MA: Harvard University Press.

Ellison, P.T., & Gray, P.B. (Eds.) (2009). *Endocrinology of Social Relationships*. Cambridge, MA: Harvard University Press.

Entringer, S., Kumsta, R., Hellhammer, D.H., Wadhwa, P.D., & Wüst, S. (2009). Prenatal exposure to maternal psychosocial stress and HPA axis regulation in young adults. *Hormones and Behavior*, 55, 292–298.

Fisher, H., Aron, A., & Brown, L.L. (2006). Romantic love: A mammalian system for mate choice. *Philosophical Transactions of the Royal Society B –Biological Sciences*, 361, 2173–2186.

Fleming, A.S., Corter, C., Stallings, J., & Steiner, M. (2002). Testosterone and prolactin are associated with emotional responses to infant cries in new fathers. *Hormones and Behavior*, 42, 399–413.

Fleming, A.S., O'Day, D.H., & Kraemer, G.W. (1999). Neurobiology of mother-infant interactions: Experience and central nervous system plasticity across development and generations. *Neuroscience and Biobehavioral Reviews*, 23, 673–685.

Fleming, A.S., Steiner, M., & Corter, C. (1997). Cortisol, hedonics, and maternal responsiveness in human mothers. *Hormones and behavior*, 32(2), 85–98.

Flinn, M. V. (1981). Uterine and agnatic kinship variability. In R. D. Alexander & D. W. Tinkle (Eds.), *Natural selection and social behavior: Recent research and new theory* (pp. 439–475). New York: Blackwell Press.

Flinn, M.V. (1988). Step and genetic parent/offspring relationships in a Caribbean village. *Ethology and Sociobiology*, 9(6), 335–369.

Flinn, M.V., (1997). Culture and the evolution of social learning. *Evolution and Human Behavior*, 18(1), 23–67.

Flinn, M.V. (2004). Culture and developmental plasticity: Evolution of the social brain. In K. MacDonald & R.L. Burgess (Eds.), *Evolutionary perspectives on child development* (pp. 73–98). Thousand Oaks, CA: Sage.

Flinn, M.V. (2006a). Cross-cultural universals and variations: The evolutionary paradox of informational novelty. *Psychological Inquiry*, 17, 118–123.

Flinn, M.V. (2006b). Evolution and ontogeny of stress response to social challenge in the human child. *Developmental Review*, 26, 138–174.

Flinn, M.V., & Alexander, R.D. (2007). Runaway social selection. In S.W. Gangestad & J.A. Simpson (Eds.), *The evolution of mind* (pp. 249–255). New York: Guilford Press.

Flinn, M.V., & Coe, K.C. (2007). The linked red queens of human cognition, coalitions, and culture. In S.W. Gangestad & J.A. Simpson (Eds.), *The evolution of mind* (pp. 339–347). New York: Guilford Press.

Flinn, M.V., & England, B.G. (1995). Childhood stress and family environment. *Current Anthropology* 36(5), 854–866.

Flinn, M.V., & England, B.G. 1997. Social economics of childhood glucocorticoid stress response and health. *American Journal of Physical Anthropology* 102(1), 33–53

Flinn, M. V., & England, B. G., 2003. Childhood stress: endocrine and immune responses to psychosocial events. In J.M. Wilce, (Ed.), *Social & Cultural Lives of Immune Systems* (pp. 107–147). London: Routledge Press.

Flinn, M.V., Geary, D.C., & Ward, C.V. (2005). Ecological dominance, social competition, and coalitionary arms races: Why humans evolved extraordinary intelligence. *Evolution and Human Behavior*, 26(1), 10–46.

Flinn, M.V., & Leone, D.V. (2006). Early trauma and the ontogeny of glucocorticoid stress response: Grandmother as a secure base. *Journal of Developmental Processes*, 1(1), 31–68.

Flinn, M.V., & Leone, D.V. (2009). Alloparental care and the ontogeny of glucocorticoid stress response among stepchildren. In G. Bentley & R. Mace (Eds.), *Substitute parents* (pp. 212–231). Biosocial Society Symposium Series. Oxford: Berghahn Books.

Flinn, M.V., & Low, B.S. (1986). Resource distribution, social competition, and mating patterns in human societies. In D. Rubenstein & R. Wrangham (Eds.), *Ecological aspects of social evolution* (pp. 217–243). Princeton NJ: Princeton University Press.

Flinn, M.V., Muehlenbein, M.P., & Ponzi, D., 2009. Evolution of neuroendocrine mechanisms linking attachment and life history: Social endocrinology of the human child. *Behavioral and Brain Sciences, 32*(1), 27–28.

Flinn, M.V., Quinlan, R.J., Turner, M.T., Decker, S.D., & England, B.G. (1996). Male-female differences in effects of parental absence on glucocorticoid stress response. *Human Nature, 7*(2), 125–162.

Flinn, M.V., Quinlan, R.J., Ward, C.V., & Coe, M.K., 2007. Evolution of the human family: Cooperative males, long social childhoods, smart mothers, and extended kin networks. In Salmon, C., & Shackelford, T. (Eds.), *Family relationships* (Chapter 2, pp. 16–38). Oxford: Oxford University Press.

Flinn, M.V., & Ward, C.V. (2005). Evolution of the social child. In B. Ellis & D. Bjorklund (Eds.), *Origins of the social mind: Evolutionary psychology and child development* (Chapter 2, pp. 19–44). London: Guilford Press.

Flinn, M.V., Ward, C.V., & Noone, R. (2005). Hormones and the human family. In D. Buss (Ed.), *Handbook of evolutionary psychology* (Chapter 19, pp. 552–580). New York: Wiley.

Fortes, M. (1969). *Kinship and the social order.* Chicago: Aldine.

Fuxjager, M.J., Mast, G., Becker, E.A., & Marler, C.A. (2009). The "home advantage" is necessary for a full winner effect and changes in post-encounter testosterone. *Hormones and Behavior, 56,* 214–219.

Gavrilets, S., & Vose, A. (2006). The dynamics of Machiavellian intelligence. *Proceedings of the National Academy of Sciences, 103*(45), 16823–16828.

Geary, D.C. (2005). *The origin of mind: Evolution of brain, cognition, and general intelligence.* Washington, DC: American Psychological Association.

Geary, D.C., & Bjorklund, D.F. (2000). Evolutionary developmental psychology. *Child Development, 71*(1), 57–65.

Geary, D.C., & Flinn, M.V. (2001). Evolution of human parental behavior and the human family. *Parenting: Science and Practice, 1,* 5–61.

Geary, D.C., & Flinn, M.V. (2002). Sex differences in behavioral and hormonal response to social threat. *Psychological Review, 109*(4), 745–750.

Geary, D.C., & Huffman, K.J. (2002). Brain and cognitive evolution: Forms of modularity and functions of mind. *Psychological Bulletin, 128*(5), 667–698.

Gilbert, S.L., Dobyns, W.B., & Lahn, B.T. (2005). Genetic links between brain development and brain evolution. *Nature Reviews Genetics, 6*(7), 581–590.

Gleason, E.D., Fuxjager, M.J., Oyegbile, T.O., & Marler, C.A. (2009). Testosterone release and social context: When it occurs and why. *Frontiers in Neuroendocrinology, 30*(4), 460–469.

Goodall, J. (1986). *The chimpanzees of Gombe: Patterns of behavior.* Cambridge, MA: Belknap Press of Harvard University Press.

Gopnik, A., Meltzoff, A.N., & Kuhl, P.K. (1999). *The scientist in the crib: Minds, brains, and how children learn.* New York: William Morrow & Co.

Gough, E.K. (1959). The Nayars and the definition of marriage. *Journal of the Royal Anthropological Institute, 89,* 23–34.

Gray, P.B., & Anderson, K.G. (2010). *Fatherhood: Evolution and human paternal behavior.* Cambridge, MA: Harvard University Press.

Gray, P.B., & Campbell, B.C. (2009). Human male testosterone, pair bonding and fatherhood. In P.T. Ellison & P.B. Gray (Eds.), *Endocrinology of social relationships.* Cambridge: Harvard University Press.

Gray, P.B., Kahlenberg, S., Barrett, E., Lipson, S., & Ellison, P.T. (2002). Marriage and fatherhood are associated with lower testosterone in males. *Evolution and Human Behavior, 23,* 193–201.

Gray, P.B., Parkin, J.C., & Samms-Vaughan, M.E. (2007). Hormonal correlates of human paternal interactions: A hospital-based investigation in urban Jamaica. *Hormones and Behavior, 52,* 499–507.

Gray, P.B., Yang, C.J., & Pope, H.G. Jr. 2006. Fathers have lower salivary testosterone levels than unmarried men and married non-fathers in Beijing, China. *Proceedings of the Royal Society of London B: Biological Sciences, 273,* 333–339.

Guatelli-Steinberg, D., Reid, D.J., Bishop, T.A., & Larsen, C.S. (2005). Anterior tooth growth periods in Neanderthals were comparable to those of modern humans. *Proceedings of the National Academy of Sciences, 102*(40), 14197–14202.

Gubernick, D.J. (1988). Reproduction in the California mouse, *Peromyscus californicus. Journal of the Mammal, 69,* 857–860.

Gunz, P., Neubauer, S., Maureille, B., & Hublin, J.-J. (2010). Brain development after birth differs between Neanderthals and modern humans. *Current Biology, 20*(21), R921–R922.

Hawkes, K. (2003). Grandmothers and the evolution of human longevity. *American Journal of Human Biology, 15,* 380–400.

Heinrichs, M., Dawans, B.V., & Domes, G. (2009). Oxytocin, vasopressin, and human social behavior. *Frontiers in Neuroendocrinology, 30*(4), 548–557.

Heinrichs, M., & Domes, G. (2008). Neuropeptides and social behaviour: Effects of oxytocin and vasopressin in humans. *Progress in Brain Research, 170,* 337–350.

Hetherington, E.M. (2003a). Intimate pathways: Changing patterns in close personal relationships across time. *Family Relations: Interdisciplinary Journal of Applied Family Studies, 52*(4), 318–331.

Hetherington, E.M. (2003b). Social support and the adjustment of children in divorced and remarried families. *Childhood: A Global Journal of Child Research, 10*(2), 217–236. San Diego: Sage Publications, USA.

Hill, K., & Hurtado, A. (1996). *Ache life history: The ecology and demography of a foraging people.* Hawthorne, NY: Aldine de Gruyter.

Hill, K., & Kaplan, H. (1999). Life history traits in humans: theory and empirical studies. *Annual Review of Anthropology, 28,* 397–430.

Holliday, M.A. (1986). Body composition and energy needs during growth. In F. Falkner & J. M. Tanner (Eds.), *Human growth: A comprehensive treatise.* New York: Plenum Press.

Hosseini, S.M., Biglan, M.W., Larkby, C., Brooks, M.M., Gorin, M.B., & Day, N.L. (2009). Trait anxiety in pregnant women predicts offspring birth outcomes. *Paediatric and Perinatal Epidemiology, 23,* 557–566.

Hrdy, S.B. (1999). *Mother nature: A history of mothers, infants, and natural selection.* New York: Pantheon.

Hrdy, S.B. (2009). *Mothers and others: The evolutionary origins of mutual understanding.* Cambridge: Harvard University Press.

Insel, T.R., & Young, L.J. (2001). The neurobiology of attachment. *Nature Reviews Neuroscience 2*, 129–136.

Jensen, A.R. (1998). *The g factor: The science of mental ability.* New York: Praeger.

Joëls, M., & Baram, T.Z. 2009. The neuro-symphony of stress. *Nature Reviews Neuroscience*, 10, 459–466.

Juster, R-P., McEwen, B.S., & Lupien, S.J. (2010). Allostatic load biomarkers of chronic stress and impact on health and cognition. *Neuroscience & Biobehavioral Reviews, 35*(1), 2–16.

Kaplan, H., Hill, K., Lancaster, J., & Hurtado, A.M. (2000). A theory of human life history evolution: Diet, intelligence and longevity. *Evolutionary Anthropology, 9*, 156–183.

Kaplan, H.S., & Robson, A.J. (2002). The emergence of humans: The coevolution of intelligence and longevity with intergenerational transfers. *Proceedings of the National Academy of Sciences, 99*(15), 10221–10226.

Karaolis-Danckert N., Buyken, A.E., Sonntag, A., & Kroke, A. (2009). Birth and early life influences on the timing of puberty onset: Results from the DONALD (DOrtmund Nutritional and Anthropometric Longitudinally Designed) Study. *American Journal of Clinical Nutrition, 90*(6), 1559–1565.

Koch, C. (1999). *Biophysics of computation. Information processing in single neurons.* New York: Oxford University Press.

Konner, M. (1991). *Childhood.* Boston: Little, Brown.

Konner, M. (2010). *The evolution of childhood: Relationships, emotion, mind.* Cambridge, MA: Harvard University Press.

Kuzawa, C.W., Gettler, L.T., Muller, M.N., McDade, T.W., & Feranil, A.B. (2009). Fatherhood, pairbonding and testosterone in the Philippines. *Hormones and Behavior, 56*(4), 429–435.

Leblanc, S.A. (2003). *Constant battles: The myth of the peaceful, noble savage.* New York: St. Martin's Press.

Lee, H-J., Macbeth, A.H., Pagani, J., & Young 3rd, W.S. (2009). Oxytocin: The great facilitator of life. *Progress in Neurobiology, 88*(2), 127–151.

Lee, J.M., Kaciroti, N., Appugliese, D., Corwyn, R.F., Bradley, R.H., & Lumeng, J.C. (2010). Body mass index and timing of pubertal initiation in boys. *Archives of Pediatrics and Adolescent Medicine, 164*(2), 116–123.

Lee, S.H., & Wolpoff, M.H. (2003). The pattern of evolution in Pleistocene human brain size. *Paleobiology, 29*, 186–196.

Leigh, S.R. (2004). Brain growth, cognition, and life history in primate and human evolution. *American Journal of Primatology, 62*, 139–164.

Leonard, W.R., Snodgrass, J.J., & Robertson, M.L. (2007). Effects of brain evolution on human nutrition and metabolism. *Annual Review of Nutrition, 27*, 311–327.

Levi-Strauss, C. (1949/1969). *Les Structures élémentaires de la parenté* (The elementary structures of kinship). R. Needham (Ed.), J. H. Bell, J. R. von Sturmer, & Rodney Needham (Trans.), 1969. Boston: Beacon Press.

Lim, M.M., Murphy, A.Z., & Young, L.J. (2004). Ventral striatopallidal oxytocin and vasopressin V1a receptors in the monogamous prairie vole (*Microtus ochrogaster*). *Journal of Comparative Neurology, 468*, 555–570.

Mace, R. (2000). Evolutionary ecology of human life history. *Animal Behaviour, 59*, 1–10.

Marlowe, F.W. (2003). A critical period for provisioning by Hadza men: Implications for pair bonding. *Evolution and Human Behavior, 24*(3), 217–229.

Marlowe, F.W. (2010). *The Hadza: Hunter-gatherers of Tanzania.* Berkeley: University of California Press.

McHenry, H.M. (1992a). Body size and proportions in early hominids. *American Journal of Physical Anthropology, 87*, 407–431.

McHenry, H.M. (1992b). How big were early hominids? *Evolutionary Anthropology, 1*(1), 15–20.

McGowan, P.O., Sasaki, A., D'Alessio, A.C., Dymov, S., Labonté, B., Szyf, M., Turecki, G., & Meaney, M.J. (2009). Epigenetic regulation of the glucocorticoid receptor in human brain associates with childhood abuse. *Nature Neuroscience, 12*(3) 342–348.

Miller, G.E. (2000). *The mating mind: How sexual choice shaped the evolution of human nature.* New York: Doubleday.

Mitani, J.C., Watts, D.P., & Amsler, S.J. (2010). Lethal intergroup aggression leads to territorial expansion in wild chimpanzees. *Current Biology, 20*(12), R507–R508.

Muehlenbein, M.P., & Flinn, M.V. (2011). Patterns and processes of human life history evolution. In T. Flatt and A. Heyland (Eds.), *Mechanisms of life history evolution* (Chapter 12). Oxford: Oxford University Press.

Murdock, G.P. (1949). *Social structure.* New York: Macmillan.

Murdock, G.P. (1967). *Ethnographic atlas.* Pittsburgh: University of Pittsburgh Press.

Nepomnaschy, P., & Flinn, M.V. (2008). Early life influences on the ontogeny of neuroendocrine stress response in the human child. In P. Ellison & P. Gray (Eds.), *The endocrinology of social relationships* (Chapter 16), pp. 364–382. Cambridge, MA: Harvard University Press.

Neubauer, S., Gunz, P., & Hublin, J.J. (2010). Endocranial shape changes during growth in chimpanzees and humans: A morphometric analysis of unique and shared aspects. *Journal of Human Evolution, 59*(5), 555–566.

Panksepp, J. (2004). *Affective neuroscience: The foundations of human and animal emotions.* New York: Oxford University Press.

Panksepp, J. (2009). Carving "natural" emotions: "Kindly" from bottom-up but not top-down. *Journal of Theoretical and Philosophical Psychology, 28*(2), 395–422.

Pawlowski, B., Lowen, C.B., & Dunbar, R.I.M. (1998). Neocortex size, social skills and mating success in primates. *Behaviour, 135*, 357–368.

Plavcan, J.M. (2000). Inferring social behavior from sexual dimorphism in the fossil record. *Journal of Human Evolution, 39*, 327–344.

Plavcan, J.M., Lockwood, C.A., Kimbel, W.H., Lague, M.R., & Harmon, E.H. (2005). Sexual dimorphism in *Australopithecus afarensis* revisited: How strong is the case for a human-like pattern of dimorphism? *Journal of Human Evolution, 48*, 313–320.

Plavcan, J.M., & Van Schaik, C.P. (1997a). Intrasexual competition and body weight dimorphism in anthropoid primates. *American Journal of Physical Anthropology, 103*, 37–68.

Plavcan, J.M., & Van Schaik, C.P. (1997b). Interpreting hominid behavior on the basis of sexual dimorphism. *Journal of Human Evolution, 32*(4), 345–374.

Portman, A. (1941). Die Tragzeiten der Primaten und die Dauer der Schwangerschaft beim Menschen: Ein Problem der vergleichenden Biologie. *Revue Suisse de Zoologie, 48*, 511–518.

Posner, M. I. (2005). Genes and experience shape brain networks of conscious control. *Progress in Brain Research, 150*, 173–183.

Reno, P.L., Meindl, R.S., McCollom, M.A., & Lovejoy, C.O. (2005). The case is unchanged and remains robust: *Australopithecus afarensis* exhibits only moderate skeletal dimorphism.

A reply to Plavcan et al. (2005). *Journal of Human Evolution*, 49, 279–288.

Rilling, J., Gutman, D., Zeh, T., Pagnoni, G., Berns, G., & Kilts, C. (2002). A neural basis for social cooperation. *Neuron*, 35(2), 395–405.

Roozendaal, B., McEwen, B.S., & Sumantra Chattarji, S. (2009). Stress, memory and the amygdala. *Nature Reviews Neuroscience*, 10(6), 423–433.

Rosenberg, K. (2004). Living longer: Information revolution, population expansion, and modern human origins. *Proceedings of the National Academy of Sciences*, 101(30), 10847–10848.

Rosenberg, K., & Trevathan, W. (2002). Birth, obstetrics and human evolution. *BJOG: An International Journal of Obstetrics & Gynecology*, 109(11), 1199–1206.

Roth, G., & Dicke, U. (2005). Evolution of the brain and intelligence. *Trends in Cognitive Sciences*, 9(5), 250–257.

Ruff, C.B. (2002). Variation in human body size and shape. *Annual Review of Anthropology*, 31, 211–232.

Ruff, C.B., Trinkaus, E., Walker, A., & Larson, C.S. (1993). Postcranial robusticity in Homo. I: Temporal trends and mechanical interpretation. *American Journal of Physical Anthropology*, 91, 21–53.

Sapolsky, R.M. (1994). *Why zebras don't get ulcers*. New York: W.H. Freeman and Co.

Schoenemann, P.T. (2006). Evolution of the size and functional areas of the human brain. *Annual Review of Anthropology*, 35, 379–406.

Sear, R., Mace, R., McGregor, I. A. (2000). Maternal grandmothers improve the nutritional status and survival of children in rural Gambia. *Proceedings of the Royal Society London B*, 267, 1641–1647.

Sear, R., & Mace, R. (2008). Who keeps children alive? A review of the effects of kin on child survival. *Evolution and Human Behavior*, 29(1), 1–18.

Seltzer, L.J., Ziegler, T.E., & Pollak, S.D. (2010). Social vocalizations can release oxytocin in humans. *Proceedings of the Royal Society London B*, 277, 2661–2666.

Sherwood, C.C., Stimpson, C.D. Raghanti, M.A., Wildman, D.E., Uddin, M., Grossman, L.I., et al. (2006). Evolution of increased glia–neuron ratios in the human frontal cortex. *Proceedings of the National Academy of Sciences*, 103 (37), 13606–13611.

Shonkoff, J.P., Boyce, W.T., & McEwen, B.S. (2009). Neuroscience, molecular biology, and the childhood roots of health disparities: Building a new framework for health promotion and disease prevention. *Journal of the American Medical Association*, 301(21), 2252–2259.

Sloboda, D.M., Hart, R., Doherty, D.A., Pennell, C.E., & Hickey, M. (2007). Age at menarche: Influences of prenatal and postnatal growth. *Journal of Clinical Endocrinology and Metabolism*, 92, 46–50.

Smith, B.H. (1993). The physiological age of KNM-WT 15000. In A. Walker and R. Leakey (Eds.), *The Nariokotome Homo erectus skeleton*. Cambridge, MA: Harvard University Press.

Smith, B.H. (1994). Patterns of dental development in homo, Australopithecus, pan, and gorilla. *American Journal of Physical Anthropology*, 94(3), 307–325.

Smith, T.M., Tafforeau, P., Reid, D.J., Pouech, J., Lazzari, V., Zermeno, J.P., Guatelli-Steinberg, D., Olejniczak, A.J., Hoffman, A., Radovcic, J., Masrour, M., Toussaint, M., Stringer, C., Hublin, J-J. (2010). Dental evidence for ontogenetic differences between modern humans and Neanderthals. *Proceedings of the National Academy of Sciences USA*, doi:10.1073/pnas.1010906107.

Smuts, B.B., & Smuts, R.W. (1993). Male aggression and sexual coercion of females in nonhuman primates and other mammals: Evidence and theoretical implications. *Advances in the Study of Behavior*, 22, 1–63.

Spocter, M.A., Hopkins, W.D., Garrison, A.R., Bauernfeind, A.L., Stimpson, C.D., Hof, P.R., & Sherwood, C.C. (2010). Wernicke's area homologue in chimpanzees (*Pan troglodytes*) and its relation to the appearance of modern human language. *Proceedings of the Royal Society London B*, 277, 2165–2174.

Steward, J.S. (1955). *Theory of culture change*. Urbana, IL: University of Illinois press.

Storey, A.E., Walsh, C.J., Quinton, R.L., & Wynne-Edwards, K.E. (2000). Hormonal correlates of paternal responsiveness in new and expectant fathers. *Evolution and Human Behavior*, 21, 79–95.

Todeschin, A.S., Winkelmann-Duarte, E.C., Jacob, M.H.V., Aranda, B.C.C., Jacobs, S., Fernandes, M.C., et al. (2009). Effects of neonatal handling on social memory, social interaction, and number of oxytocin and vasopressin neurons in rats. *Hormones and Behavior*, 56, 93–100.

Ulrich-Lai, Y.M., & Herman, J.P. (2009). Neural regulation of endocrine and autonomic stress responses. *Nature Reviews Neuroscience*, 10, 397–409.

Ungar, P., Grine, F.E., Teaford, M.F., & El Zaatari, S. (2006). Dental microwear and diets in early African *Homo*. *Journal of Human Evolution*, 50, 78–95.

Uvnas-Moberg, K. (1998). Oxytocin may mediate the benefits of positive social interaction and emotions, *Psychoneuroendocrinology*, 23, 819–835.

van der Meij, L., Buunk, A.P., van de Sande, J.P., & Salvador, A. (2008). The presence of a woman increases testosterone in aggressive dominant men. *Hormones and Behavior*, 54, 640–644.

van der Vegt, E.J.M., van der Ende, J., Kirschbaum, C., Verhulst, F.C., & Tiemeier, H. (2009). Early neglect and abuse predict diurnal cortisol patterns in adults: A study of international adoptees. *Psychoneuroendocrinology*, 34, 660–669.

Voland, E., Chasiotis, A., & Schiefenhövel, W. (2005). *Grandmotherhood : The evolutionary significance of the second half of female life*. New Brunswick, NJ: Rutgers University Press.

Wagner, J.D., Flinn, M.V., & England, B.G. (2002). Hormonal response to competition among male coalitions. *Evolution and Human Behavior*, 23(6), 437–442.

Walker, R.S., Flinn, M.V., & Hill, K. (2010). The evolutionary history of promiscuous mating and partible paternity in lowland South America. *Proceedings of the National Academy of Sciences*, 107(45), 19195–19200.

Walvoord, E.C. (2010). The timing of puberty: Is it changing? Does it matter? *Journal of Adolescent Health* 47(5), 433–439.

Wiedenmayer, C.P. (2009). Plasticity of defensive behavior and fear in early development. *Neuroscience and Biobehavioral Reviews*, 33, 432–441.

Williams, R.W., & Herrup, K., 1988. The control of neuron number. *Annual Review of Neuroscience*, 11, 423–453.

Wrangham, R.W. (1999). Evolution of coalitionary killing. *Yearbook of Physical Anthropology*, 42, 1–30.

Wrangham, R.W., & Peterson, D. (1996). *Demonic males*. New York: Houghton Mifflin Company.

Wynne-Edwards, K.E. (2001). Hormonal changes in mammalian fathers. *Hormones and Behavior*, 40, 139–145.

Wynne-Edwards, K.E. (2003). From dwarf hamster to daddy: The intersection of ecology, evolution, and physiology that produces paternal behavior. In P. J.B. Slater, J.S. Rosenblatt, C.T. Snowden, & T.J. Roper (Eds.), *Advances in the study of behavior* (32, 207–261). San Diego: Academic Press.

Young, L.J. (2009). Love: Neuroscience reveals all. *Nature, 457*, 148.

Young, L., Wang, Z., & Insel, T.R. (2002). Neuroendocrine bases of monogamy. In J.T. Cacioppo, G.G. Berntson, R. Adolphs, C.S. Carter, R. J. Davidson, M.K. McClintock, et al. (Eds.), *Foundations in social neuroscience* (pp. 809–816). Cambridge, MA: MIT Press.

Ziegler, T.E., & Snowdon, C.T. (1997). Role of prolactin in paternal care in a monogamous New World primate, *Saguinus oedipus*. The integrative neurobiology of affiliation. *Annals of the New York Academy of Sciences, 807*, 599–601.

CHAPTER 3

The Evolutionary History of Pair-bonding and Parental Collaboration

Bernard Chapais

Abstract

Most evolutionarily oriented studies on the human pair-bond infer its origins from its present-day functional aspects and adaptive character and propose on this basis that the family was born as a parental partnership. They view monogamy and the sexual division of labor as having evolved together as part of the same adaptive suite. They also assume, explicitly or implicitly, that the human pair-bond was born from a background of sexual promiscuity. The primate evidence discussed here rather suggests that human monogamy originated from a prior stage of polygyny and therefore as a result of constraints on the profitability of polygyny. This implies that both monogamy and polygyny were part of our evolutionary heritage. The primate data suggest that monogamy originated as a male strategy of mate guarding favoring paternity confidence and father–offspring recognition, and that it operated as a preadaptation for the evolution of parental cooperation in the provisioning of progressively altricial (helpless) children.

Keywords: Monogamy, pair-bond, polygyny, human family, sexual division of labor, paternal investment, cooperative breeding

Marriage is what many anthropologists would call, often reluctantly, a "human universal." Reluctantly, because the word *universal* might suggest that the phenomenon has similar forms or meanings cross-culturally, which is obviously not the case. The ethnographic repertoire is particularly telling about the diversity of marriage practices. It includes the following forms, among several others: a man taking a wife in the name of a dead brother for whom he acts as a substitute (so-called *ghost marriage*); a sterile woman marrying another woman and having children with her through a male genitor, the sterile woman being considered a man and called father by her children; or a young man entering a lifelong relationship with a woman (his future mother-in-law) whom he must supply with game, in return for which he will marry her daughters to be born (Evans-Pritchard, 1951; Goodale, 1962). Not only are marital unions extremely diverse across cultures, but marriage is a multidimensional phenomenon combining sexual, reproductive, parental, cooperative, economic, religious, institutional, jural, and political aspects. Notwithstanding that complexity, all conjugal bonds have one fundamental aspect in common, namely, reciprocal sexual access between spouses. On this basis, the anthropologist Ward Goodenough concluded his quest for "a generally applicable definition of marriage" by defining the latter as "a transaction and resulting contract in which a person (male or female, corporate or individual, in person or by proxy) establishes a continuing claim to the right of sexual access to a woman . . . and in which the woman involved is eligible to bear children" (1970, pp. 12–13). This definition is particularly significant because it fits precisely with what one would expect from an evolutionary perspective.

As will be amply discussed in this chapter, the enduring reproductive bond between a man and a woman—the pair-bond—is the defining aspect of the human mating system in a comparative (interspecific) perspective, and in all likelihood, the evolutionary precursor of marriage.

Remarkably, most studies on the evolution of the human pair-bond are about its adaptive character, or Darwinian function, not about its evolutionary history, or phylogeny. Darwinian function and phylogeny are the two sides of the evolutionary coin. Whereas functional studies test hypotheses about the adaptive character of traits based on contemporary, synchronic data, phylogenetic studies seek to establish the evolutionary sequence of events that led to the trait's present state. The vast majority of evolutionarily oriented studies on the human family test hypotheses about the adaptive character of the enduring bond between the mother and the father. They attempt, in particular, to characterize the exact contribution of the father to family life as a way to establish why, at some point in the course of human evolution, the father joined the mother on a long-term basis (Bird, 1999; Gurven & Hill, 2009; Gurven, Winking, Kaplan, von Rueden, & McAllister, 2009; Hawkes, 1993; Hawkes, O'Connell, & Blurton Jones, 2001; Kaplan, Hill, Lancaster, & Hurtado, 2000; Marlowe, 2003a; Quinlan, 2008). The preponderance of functional over phylogenetic studies on the human family certainly reflects to a large extent the abundance of ethnographical data relevant to functional analyses of the human family and the relative scarcity of data available for evolutionary reconstructions of human behavior. Social behavior leaves few traces in the fossil record. But the fossil record is only one of two sources of data available for reconstructing the phylogeny of behavior. Another is behavioral primatology, and considering its significance in phylogenetic reconstructions, that source appears to have been significantly underexploited.

Information about the evolutionary history of the human pair-bond is important because a strict focus on the adaptive character of complex traits such as the human family may easily lead to misleading inferences about these traits' evolutionary *origins* and, by way of consequence, about the exact nature of their biological foundation. This shortcoming seems to apply particularly clearly to analyses of human pair-bonding. I refer to the predominant evolutionary model on the subject as the *parental cooperation hypothesis*, a label that describes, in effect, a family of models that view human pair-bonds as cooperative partnerships serving parental functions, including the extensive care, food provisioning, and transfer of information required by highly dependent (altricial) children (Fisher, 1992, 2006; Flinn, Quinlan, Coe, & Ward, 2007; Gurven & Hill, 2009; Kaplan et al., 2000; Kaplan, Hooper, & Gurven, 2009; Lovejoy, 1981, 2009; for earlier versions see Alexander & Noonan, 1979; Hill, 1982; Isaac, 1978; Washburn & Lancaster, 1968).

The parental function of human pair-bonds is not at issue here. The importance of parental cooperation in the evolution of the human family has received much empirical support. The human brain is three times bigger than the brain of a primate of comparable size, and as a result, the human baby is born at a relatively earlier stage in its development and humans have slower life histories. Humans are born with brains that represent 25% of adult brain size, whereas the corresponding figure for newborn apes is 40%. At 1 year of age, the human brain is only 50% of its adult size, whereas the ape brain is 80% (Coqueugniot, Hublin, Veillon, Houët, & Jacob, 2004). While the chimpanzee brain stops growing at 3–4 years of age, the human brain continues to grow until a little past 10 years. The protracted period of juvenile dependency in humans entails that the biological costs of raising human children are disproportionately high compared to the situation in other primates. Human mothers provision slow-maturing offspring well into adolescence, so that they commonly take care of several dependent children simultaneously (Kaplan et al., 2000; Lancaster & Lancaster, 1987). The provisioning of juvenile offspring never occurs in nonhuman primates. Thus, while maternal care is a sequential activity in other primates, it is a cumulative one in humans. Importantly, ethnographical evidence from hunter-gatherer societies indicates that the father, along with other categories of helpers, does alleviate the costs of maternity by provisioning his family (Gurven, 2004; Gurven & Hill, 2009; Kaplan et al., 2000, 2009; Marlowe, 2003a; Quinlan, 2008). Successful hunters often give a large proportion of the carcass to individuals other than their family, as if they hunted for reasons other than feeding their own family. Although it is likely that the functions of hunting are not limited to feeding one's close kin (Hawkes 1991, 1993, 2004; Hawkes et al., 2001), hunting is part of a system of reciprocity, direct or indirect, among hunters and their families, so that mothers and their offspring receive meat both from their husband/father and from other hunters (Hill, Barton, & Hurtado, 2009; Kaplan et al., 2009).

Moreover, in most societies, the hunter's family receives considerably more than other families (Gurven, 2004).

What is at issue here is the reasoning that, because human pair-bonds serve important parental functions, they came into existence as such. The parental cooperation model indeed states that pair-bonding *originated* in selective pressures for paternal investment. More specifically, it sees the evolution of protracted juvenile dependency and the concomitant increase in the costs of raising children as creating the conjugal family through the evolution of paternal investment in the form of male provisioning. Accordingly, all aspects of the human family—sexual, parental, and economic—are seen as having evolved in interrelations with each other as part of the same adaptive suite. For example, Kaplan et al. (2009) described the functional relations between pair-bonding and the sexual division of labor in hunter-gatherer societies in the following terms: "The human foraging niche, and particularly hunting, promotes cooperation between men and women and high levels of male parental investment because it favours sex-specific economic specialization . . . This sex-specialization . . . yields a complementarity between male and female roles . . . encouraging the formation of long-term pair-bonds" (p. 3291). Using the functional links between hunting, sexual specialization, and pair-bonding in contemporary societies to reason about the very origin of pair-bonding illustrates the potential pitfall of using the present-day state of complex traits to infer their evolutionary history (Chapais, 2008). The sexual, parental, and economic aspects of contemporary human families form a highly coherent and functional system in any particular society. From this plain ethnographic fact, it is easy to make two inferences likely to be erroneous. First, it is tempting to reason that, since all aspects of the system are necessary for the whole system to work, they are coevolved traits that were part of the same adaptive suite; that is, it is easy to form a somewhat contracted conception of the human family's evolutionary history. Second, it is tempting to explain the very origin of the whole entity in terms of its present-day Darwinian function, that is, to confuse the trait's contemporary function with its initial function. Accordingly, the parental cooperation model views the human family as emerging right from the outset with all its major components in place (Fisher 1992, 2006; Flinn, Quinlan, Coe & Ward, 2007; Kaplan et al., 2000, 2009; Lovejoy 1981, 2009) rather than as the last stage in a long evolutionary series of intermediary forms that followed one another over a large portion of human evolution. For example, it implicitly excludes the possibility that pair-bonded families might have thrived in the absence of male provisioning, a possibility that cannot be discarded, as we shall see. Both problematic inferences appear to reflect the focus on the adaptive aspects of pair-bonding and the relative neglect of its phylogeny.

The circumstances in which a trait originated can hardly be known without a consideration of the prior phylogenetic stage out of which that trait evolved. Understanding the origin of the modern family requires inferences about the nature of the social organization and mating system that *preceded* the human family. For example, whether pair-bonding originated from a background of sexual promiscuity (a mating arrangement in which both sexes have short-term mating relations with several partners), or from a background of polygyny (an arrangement in which each male forms enduring breeding bonds with a number of females simultaneously) has distinct implications regarding both the evolutionary processes involved in the corresponding transition and the nature of the biological underpinnings of pair-bonding. Fossil evidence is certainly the most direct source of information about phylogeny. Paleontological data provide essential markers for the timing of a number of aspects in the evolutionary history of the human family. For example, sexual dimorphism is a potential marker of the intensity of sexual competition, hence of the mating system (Clutton-Brock, Harvey, & Rudder, 1977; McHenry, 1996; Plavcan, 2001), while dental maturation is a marker of growth patterns (Dean, Leakey, Reid, Schrenk, Schwartz, & Stringer, 2001; Smith, Toussaint, Reid, Olejniczak, & Hublin, 2007), hence of the biological costs of raising children. But, however crucial that information may be, paleoanthropology is largely silent about the evolutionary history of the social systems that followed each other in the course of human evolution. Behavioral primatology is not, however. As will be argued here, the primate data, in combination with ethnographical data on hunter-gatherer societies, make it possible to infer stages in the evolution of the human mating system and of the particular form taken by parental cooperation in our species, the sexual division of labor.

Breaking Down the Human Pair-Bond into Phylogenetic Components

If a number of primatologists were asked to define the human pair-bond from a primatological perspective, this would probably produce a variety of answers depending on the angle from which they look at the problem. Some might remark that pair-bonding is an integral part of the specific composition of human groups, others might emphasize that it is the central feature of the human mating system, while still others might say that the parental bond is one of the most basic loci of cooperation in subsistence activities. All three perspectives are relevant for characterizing human pair-bonding within the framework of primate social systems and for assessing its originality, and I examine each of them separately.

An Integral Part of the Modal Composition of Human Groups

Defined in primatological terms, the overwhelming majority of human societies are multifamily communities—or communities of conjugal families (Rodseth, Wrangham, Harrigan & Smuts, 1991). A multifamily group is composed of a number of families interacting with each other on a regular basis and forming a cohesive entity. The primate social structure closest to the human multifamily structure is the multiharem group, a rare type exemplified by a small number of species such as the hamadryas baboon (*Papio hamadryas*), the gelada baboon (*Theropithecus gelada*), and Asian colobines, such as snub-nosed monkeys (*Rhinopithecus* spp.) (Grueter & van Schaik, 2010; Stammbach, 1987). In these species, several polygynous units form a cohesive group. If such groups are rare in nonhuman primates, this is not because monogamous units or polygynous units are rare, but because in most species each unit is an independent group. For example, gibbons (*Hylobates lar*) form independent monogamous units, and gorillas (*Gorilla gorilla berengei*) form independent polygynous units. In both species, reproductive units do not aggregate to form cohesive groups composed of several reproductive units interacting together (hereafter, multiunit groups).

In species where several breeding males and females do live together in large mixed-sex groups, long-term breeding bonds between particular males and females are most often absent; mating is promiscuous, with both sexes having short-term mating relations with several partners, as in chimpanzees. Thus, the modal composition of human groups combines two primate features that are usually found in distinct species: (a) the multimale–multifemale composition (or mixed-sex group), and (b) the stable reproductive unit, monogamous or polygynous (Chapais, 2008, 2010). How these two features got together in our species is a central issue in the evolutionary history of the human family.

The Defining Characteristic of the Human Mating System

The human mating system features two types of sexual bonds, enduring and short-term. Both types of bonds are consistently present in all human societies. Enduring bonds are marital, or marital-like, unions that are either monogamous or polygynous (polygyny's mirror arrangement, polyandry, is extremely rare in humans). Short-term sexual bonds take place premaritally, in which case they are most often accepted, or postmaritally, in which case they are universally disapproved of, an observation that underlines the importance of marital bonds in the human mating system. The co-occurrence of sexual promiscuity and stable breeding bonds in all human societies may be seen as a correlate of the modal composition of human groups, with the consistent proximity of families certainly facilitating extramarital sexual activity.

A particularly original feature of the human mating system from a primatological perspective—one that is so basic as to be missed—is the systematic coexistence of distinct types of enduring sexual bonds, both at the level of the species and that of particular societies. Monogamy is legally enforced in about 17% of human societies, whereas about 80% exhibit both monogamous and polygynous unions, in which case the majority of unions are monogamous in any society (Low, 2003; Marlowe, 2003b). This is a unique primate pattern in two respects. First, in no primate species other than humans do we find cohesive groups composed exclusively of several interacting monogamous families. In the few primate species that form multiunit groups the units are polygynous. The community of monogamous pairs is thus specifically human. Another uniquely human trait is the coexistence in the same society of monogamous and polygynous unions. The coexistence of both types of unions is in fact the modal configuration of marital unions in humans; I refer to it as the *monogamy–polygyny set*. In other primate species that practice polygyny—whether the reproductive units are independent, as in gorillas, or aggregated, as in hamadryas baboons—polygyny is the exclusive type of sexual bond: adult males are either polygynously mated, or they have no females. Monogamous bonds may be observed in these species, but they are temporary arrangements characterizing young males in the initial phase of harem building. Human monogamy is thus pervasive, and this is why pair-bonding may be considered the central feature of the human mating system, despite the fact that polygyny is practiced in the vast majority of human societies, and sexual promiscuity in all.

A Locus of Cooperative Subsistence Activities

The human parental bond is no less original from a primatological perspective. Humans lived in hunter-gatherer societies for over 99% of the evolutionary history of the genus *Homo*. In hunter-gatherer societies, three dimensions of the parental bond consistently co-occur: sexual access (in theory exclusive), the cooperative care of children, and cooperative subsistence (mutual provisioning) between spouses. If the first two dimensions are observed in other primates, the third is not. Mutual provisioning is uniquely human in the primate order, and so is the particular form it takes: the sexual division of labor, with men specializing in hunting and women in gathering (Kaplan et al., 2000).

Traditionally, the sexual division of labor has been treated as if it constituted an irreducible entity, probably because this is how it works in human societies. But a phylogenetic perspective indicates that it is doubtful that it evolved as such (Chapais, 2008). From an evolutionary perspective, the most primitive aspect of the sexual division of labor concerns food acquisition, as opposed to other more recent activities such as cooking, cultivating, herding, building, or crafting. The food acquisition dimension of the sexual division of labor breaks down into three components: (a) the capacity to transport food, (b) sexual differences in subsistence activities, and (c) food sharing between mates. Although the three components are always present in any society, from the viewpoint of phylogeny, they are logically independent of each other in the sense that each may exist in the absence of the other two. Food transport is dependent neither on food sharing nor on sex differences in subsistence: Males and females could carry the same food types and eat solitarily—as when chimpanzees carry bananas bipedally. Similarly, sex differences in subsistence are independent of food sharing and food transport: Males and females could eat certain food types at different rates without systematically transporting or sharing them; this is what chimpanzees actually do (discussion below). Last, food sharing between mates does not require that food be transported, nor that males and females differ in their subsistence activities; it might simply have to do with sex differences in the control of food resources. A male and a female could eat the same types of food and share them on the spot—as when primates practice cofeeding at a monopolizable food source, or pair-bonded mates engage in food transfers (Fox, 1984; van Noordwijk & van Schaik, 2009; Wolovich et al., 2007). Based on this reasoning, I shall argue that the three components of the sexual division of labor are separate building blocks that evolved at different times and for different reasons, rather than aspects of an irreducible entity that evolved as a block, as is commonly assumed.

Any evolutionary model of the human pair-bond must account for the three major notions just discussed: the multifamily composition, the polygyny–monogamy set, and the cooperative dimension of the parental bond. These are the object of the next three sections.

The Origin of the Multifamily Composition

As noted earlier the multiunit composition of human groups combines two traits: the multimale-multifemale composition and the stable reproductive unit (monogamous or polygynous). In theory, two distinct categories of processes could have produced that combination, which I refer to as the *fractionation hypothesis* and the *expansion hypothesis*.

The Fractionation Hypothesis

The human–chimpanzee split is the point in time, some 7 MYA, when the lineage leading to humans began to diverge from the lineage including our two closest living relatives, the chimpanzee and the bonobo (Fig. 3.1) (Brunet et al., 2002; Enard & Pääbo, 2004; Goodman et al., 1998; Goodman, Grossman, & Wildman, 2005). According to the fractionation hypothesis, the earliest hominins, immediately after the human–chimpanzee split, had a social system featuring the multimale–multifemale composition and sexual promiscuity. This assumption is supported by the observation that the human species and its two closest relatives, the chimpanzee and the bonobo, form large mixed-sex groups. Accordingly, it has been suggested that the multimale–multifemale composition was *homologous* in the three species (Ghiglieri, 1987; Wrangham, 1987). Homologous traits are similarities between closely related species, inherited through descent from their last common ancestor. By identifying likely homologous traits among humans, chimpanzees, and bonobos, it is possible to form a virtual

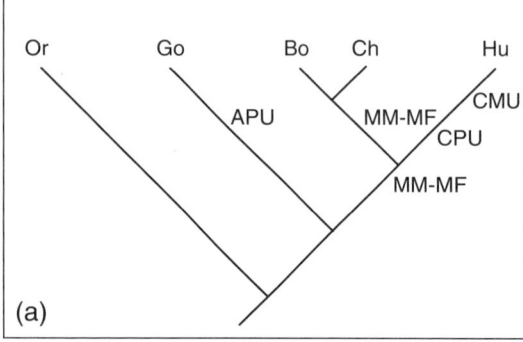

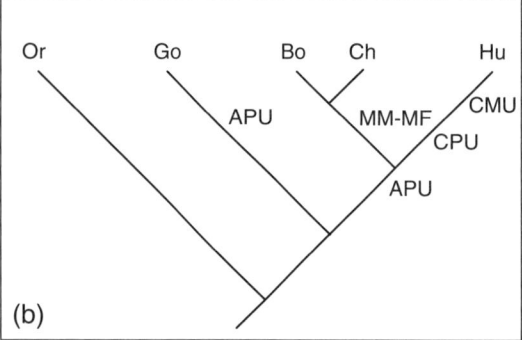

Fig. 3.1 Two hypotheses about the evolution of human society mapped upon the phylogeny of humans and the great apes. (**A**) fractionation hypothesis, (**B**) expansion hypothesis. Or: orangutan; Go: gorillas; Bo: bonobos; Ch: chimpanzees; Hu: humans; MM-MF: multimale–multifemale group; APU: autonomous polygynous units; CPU: community of polygynous units; CMU: community of monogamous units

model of their last common ancestor's social structure. Importantly, such a model is not a representation of the chimpanzee or bonobo; it is not a so-called *referential* model. Rather, it is a representation of the last common ancestor of all three species abstracted solely from, and limited to, the traits that they have *in common*.

Assuming that the earliest hominins formed large mixed-sex groups and practiced sexual promiscuity, it follows that enduring breeding bonds between particular males and females evolved later in the history of the human lineage. When this happened, the multiunit composition was born de facto. The next question, then, is whether enduring breeding bonds were initially polygynous or monogamous. A number of authors have assumed that they were monogamous right from the outset. They proposed that monogamy evolved from sexual promiscuity in response to an increase in the dependency of children and to selective pressures for the evolution of paternal investment in the form of provisioning (Fisher, 2006; Kaplan et al., 2000, 2009;

Lovejoy, 1981, 2009). For example, Kaplan et al. (2000) and Hill et al. (2009) reasoned that, upon the adoption of big game hunting in the course of human evolution, children could not acquire food by themselves and had to be provisioned by adult males—as this is the case in present-day hunter gatherer societies. However, our current knowledge on the evolution of mammalian mating systems does not support the view that the benefits of paternal investment drive the evolution of monogamy. In a phylogenetic analysis of mammalian mating and parental care systems, Brotherton and Komers (2003) found that in most monogamous species paternal care had evolved *after* monogamy was already established, and therefore that monogamy had evolved for reasons other than parental collaboration, namely as an adaptive mating arrangement. This explains why paternal care is absent in several monogamous primate species (van Schaik & Kappeler, 2003). The implication is that monogamy, which entails high levels of paternity confidence and allows systematic father-offspring recognition, is a prerequisite for, rather than the consequence of paternal investment (Dunbar, 1995; Ross & MacLarnon, 2000; van Schaik & Kappeler, 2003).

If monogamy did not evolve from sexual promiscuity as a parental strategy, what about the possibility that it evolved as a *mating* strategy? This is also unlikely. The community of monogamous families is not documented in nonhuman primates; polygyny is the rule in all multiunit primate species. Presumably, this is because the mere spatial cohesion of females in large mixed-sex groups always makes it possible for a male to monopolize more than one female at a time; in other words, monogamy does not appear to be an adaptive mating arrangement in multimale-multifemale groups.

One is left, therefore, with the possibility that the fractionation of the initial multimale-multifemale group in the course of human evolution produced polygynous units, not monogamous ones. (Fig. 3.2). Current models on the behavioral ecology of nonhuman primates (e.g., Clutton-Brock, 1989; van Hooff, 1999; van Schaik, 1996) are compatible with that view. Multiunit group structures, such as those of hamadryas and gelada baboons, are seen as adaptations to food resources too widely dispersed to support large foraging groups and, at the same time, dense enough so as not to impose solitary foraging patterns. In such a situation, ecological pressures favoring the spatial dispersion of females to minimize feeding competition are expected to interact with the males' centripetal mate guarding tactics to produce small foraging units that move relatively independently of each other and reunite on a regular basis. The type of group that best satisfies the interests of both sexes— which minimizes feeding competition and satisfies the polygyny pressure—is the polygynous unit; it is not the unisexual unit (all-male or all-female), nor the polyandrous unit (one female with several males). This ecological model finds preliminary empirical support in the observation that chacma baboons, which typically form large mixed-sex groups, may sometimes subdivide into semiautonomous polygynous units in harsher ecological conditions (Barton, 1999). That said, we know little about the exact ecological conditions underlying the multiunit composition in nonhuman primates.

The Expansion Hypothesis

The alternative to the fractionation hypothesis—the expansion hypothesis— posits that the social system of the earliest hominins was the autonomous polygynous unit and therefore that the multiunit group evolved afterward (Fig. 3.2). One possibility is that several independent polygynous units aggregated to form a multiunit group. Another possibility is that a single polygynous unit gave rise to a multiunit group as males remained in their natal group instead of emigrating at puberty, forming as many distinct polygynous units that stayed together. Regardless of the exact process involved, the expansion hypothesis finds support in the observation that the modal social system of our third closest relative, the gorilla, is the autonomous polygynous unit. That system might have characterized the last common ancestor of gorillas, chimpanzees, bonobos, and humans, in which case enduring sexual bonds would predate the evolution of the large mixed-sex group (Fig. 3.1B).

Based on available data, the fractionation hypothesis appears more likely than the expansion hypothesis (Chapais, 2008). If one takes the human-chimpanzee split as a starting point, the expansion hypothesis is less parsimonious in terms of the number of evolutionary changes needed to produce the social structures of chimpanzees and humans. The fractionation hypothesis implies a single evolutionary change, namely, the transition from the multimale–multifemale group to the community of polygynous units along the human lineage (Fig. 3.1A). In contrast, the expansion hypothesis involves two evolutionary changes from the initial autonomous polygynous unit (Fig. 3.1B). Moreover, it implies that the same initial structure gave rise to two very different social structures, namely, the sexually promiscuous multimale–multifemale group along the chimpanzee lineage, and the community of polygynous units along the human lineage. Another argument in favor of the fractionation hypothesis is the fossil record indicating that early hominins were anatomically more similar to chimpanzees and bonobos than to gorillas (McHenry, 1992). The fact that early hominins had a chimpanzee-like body mass suggests that their diet had more in common with the chimpanzee diet than with the low-quality diet of gorillas, which in turn suggests that the behavioral ecology of early hominins resembled more that of chimpanzees in terms of group size, group composition, ranging pattern, and so forth.

That said, the fractionation hypothesis and the expansion hypotheses appear equally likely when assessed in relation to our present knowledge about the phylogeny of multiunit groups in nonhuman primates. Cercopithecine species exhibiting a multiunit composition (e.g., hamadryas baboons and gelada baboons) appear to be derived from an ancestral species that had a multimale–multifemale group composition (Barton, 1999), a result supporting the fractionation hypothesis. On the other hand, colobine species that form multiunit groups (e.g., snub-nosed monkeys) appear to be derived from an ancestral species that formed autonomous polygynous units (Grueter & van Schaik, 2010), a result that supports the expansion hypothesis.

Polygyny As an Obligate Evolutionary Step

In any case, it is noteworthy that both the fractionation and expansion hypotheses concur on a basic point that has far-reaching implications, namely, the existence of the community of polygynous units as a necessary stage in the evolutionary history of the human mating system, a stage that would have given rise to the human mating system as we know it, as illustrated in Fig. 3.2.

A further argument in support of an intermediary polygyny stage is that it provides a phylogenetic explanation for the modal configuration of marital unions in human societies – the monogamy-polygyny set. Indeed, the view that monogamy was derived from polygyny accounts both for the fact that polygyny is present in the majority of human societies and for the preponderance of monogamous unions in almost all human societies. By contrast, the hypothesis that polygyny was absent in the evolutionary history of the human species and that monogamy evolved directly from sexual promiscuity

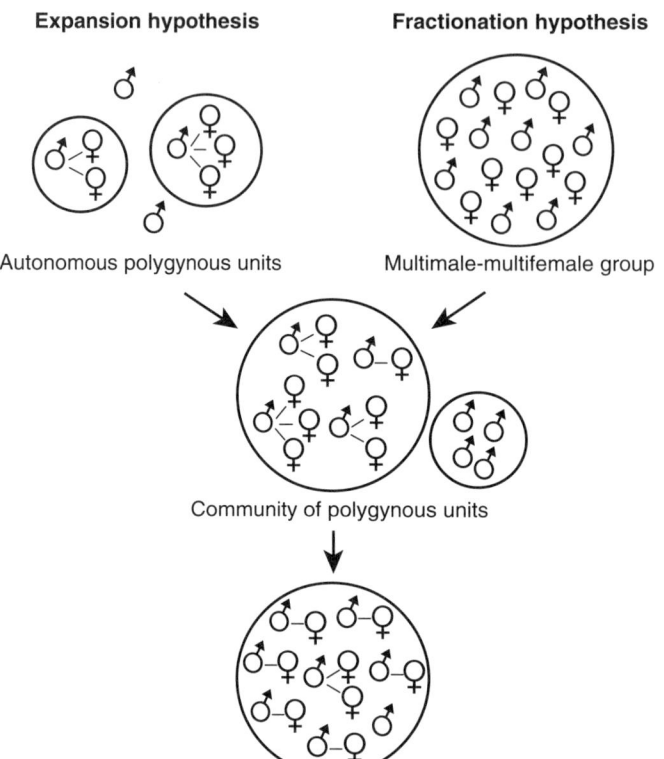

Fig. 3.2 The evolutionary sequence that led to the modal human mating system (community of mostly monogamous families). The expansion and fractionation hypotheses posit distinct initial group compositions immediately after the human-chimpanzee split, but agree on the existence of a polygyny stage prior to the evolution of monogamy

hardly accounts for the importance of polygyny in the human mating system.

The Evolution of Monogamy

The concordance of the fractionation and expansion hypotheses about an intermediary polygyny stage implies that human monogamy evolved through a reduction in the number of females monopolized by the average male; in other words, as a result of the evolution of *constraints on polygyny*. I consider two hypotheses that may account for the transition. Both see polygyny as becoming prohibitive, but for distinct reasons. The *provisioning hypothesis* states that it became progressively more advantageous for a female to be the single beneficiary of a male's provisioning effort; the *leveling hypothesis*, that it became progressively more costly for males to try to monopolize more than one female.

The Provisioning Hypothesis

The provisioning hypothesis explains the transition from polygyny to monogamy in terms of the benefits of male provisioning for mothers and their offspring. To my knowledge, this hypothesis has never been applied to a phylogenetic background of polygyny, it was applied to a background of sexual promiscuity (Kaplan et al., 2000, 2009; Lovejoy 2009), which makes a big difference. For example, consider the idea that hunting in modern hunter-gatherer societies is a skill-intensive activity requiring several years of practice before it becomes truly efficient, and therefore that juvenile hominins, upon the evolution of big-game hunting, could not acquire meat by themselves and were dependent on provisioning by adult males (Hill et al., 2009; Kaplan et al., 2000, 2009). Positing a prior state of polygyny (as opposed to sexual promiscuity) upon the evolution of big-game hunting entails that the two major conditions for the evolution of paternal investment—paternity confidence and father–offspring recognition—were met and therefore that males were in a position to provision their offspring selectively. As juvenile dependency and the costs of maternity kept increasing, the provisioning of several females by a single male would necessarily become proportionately less satisfactory in terms of the mother's needs. As a result, females belonging to smaller polygynous units, or females monogamously mated, would enjoy a larger share of the father's parental contribution. This would produce selective pressures for the evolution of smaller polygynous units, up to the unit size that maximizes the amount of paternal investment per mother: the pair-bond. Put differently, monogamy would have replaced polygyny when the provisioning capacity of the father went below the *polygyny threshold* (sensu Orians, 1969).

Crucially, for males to reduce the size of their harems and forego mating opportunities for paternal investment, one must necessarily assume a substantial reduction in levels of sexual competition between males; that is, the provisioning hypothesis implies a drastic reduction in the motivation of males for fighting over females: It implies a shift from mating effort to parental effort.

The Leveling Hypothesis

The leveling hypothesis implies no shift from mating to parental effort. It conceives of the evolution of monogamy as a response to an increase in the costs of aggressive competition between males. The following thought experiment (Chapais, 2008) illustrates the reasoning. Hamadryas baboons and gelada baboons form cohesive groups comprised of several polygynous units. The mean size of units in hamadryas baboons is 1.9 females, with some males having up to nine females; in geladas, mean harem size is 3.5 females, with males having up to ten females (Stammbach, 1987). Male competition for females is thus intense in these species; at any point in time, a substantial fraction of adult males have no females. Now, let us suppose that all males were given similar fighting abilities. In such a situation, aggressive conflicts between males would be extremely costly because both the risks of injuries and the duration of fights would rise dramatically. For any male attempting to monopolize more than one female, there would be a number of males deprived of females and ready to challenge the hopeful possessor with equally powerful means to do so. Polygyny would become prohibitive, and the evolutionarily most stable strategy would be the equal distribution of females among all males, or generalized monogamy. Defending a single female is indeed the arrangement that maximizes the net fitness gain of the average male—the difference between a male's benefits in terms of reproductive success and the costs of defending females. At this point, one may wonder why hamadryas and gelada baboons should end up forming enduring sexual bonds. The answer lies in males being harem builders in both species; if polygyny were to be severely constrained, males would be expected to keep forming stable breeding bonds, but they would end up with a single female. The same thought experiment carried out with the sexually promiscuous chimpanzee produces a different outcome: Extremely high levels of sexual promiscuity and sperm competition (Chapais, 2008).

This reasoning provides a hypothesis for the transition from the community of polygynous units to the community of mostly monogamous pairs in the course of human evolution. The development of weaponry is a factor likely to have equalized substantially the competitive abilities of hominin males. The reasoning rests on the assumption that weapons markedly reduce discrepancies in the competitive ability of males based on their sheer physical power. Of all the weapons likely to compensate for a deficit in physical force, projectile weapons such as hand-thrown spears, spearthrower-delivered darts, and bows and arrows, would stand as the most efficient ones because their capability to wound or kill is largely independent of the user's physical strength; see Shea (2006) and Churchill & Rhodes (2009) for the evolution of projectile weaponry in the context of subsistence activities. That said, any kind of weapons, from simple uncarved stones to wooden digging tools, could inflict serious injuries or kill others, provided the targeted individual was inattentive or sleeping. Chimpanzees may use stones as hammers to crack open nuts (Boesch & Boesch, 1984, 1990; McGrew, 1992, 2004), but they rarely use them as weapons against conspecifics. Thus, an important difference between chimpanzees and humans lies in the use of tools with the *intention* to wound or kill others. As soon as that capacity had evolved, any hominin was in a position to seriously hurt physically stronger males. In such a context, it should have become much more risky for a male to monopolize several females on a permanent basis. To use a blunt analogy, polygyny (and, for that matter, the monopolization of all types of resources) is feasible among males that differ clearly in their physical power and form a stable dominance order, but it is hardly feasible if every male has a gun. Generalized polygyny, with its consistent exclusion of a large fraction of males from the pool of reproductive individuals, would have become prohibitive. It would likely have given way to some sort of polygyny–monogamy mix, with most males being monogamously mated and just a few males forming polygynous units.

According to the leveling hypothesis, monogamy is the form taken by polygyny when the latter is maximally constrained. From that perspective, monogamous bonds, like polygynous bonds, are mate guarding tactics, and their origin lies in male mating effort, not parental effort as in the provisioning hypothesis (see also Hawkes, 2004; Hawkes, Rogers & Charnov, 1995). Importantly, the leveling hypothesis sees monogamy and male provisioning as evolving sequentially, whereas the provisioning hypothesis sees them as evolving concomitantly. Monogamy would have evolved in a first step and later operated as a preadaptation for the evolution of male provisioning once the costs of maternity had begun to increase.

Differentiating Between the Provisioning and Leveling Hypotheses

How are we to differentiate between the two hypotheses? Both agree on the importance of paternal investment in the form of provisioning, except that the first sees it as driving the evolution of monogamy, the second as evolving after monogamy was already in place. The two hypotheses also differ in their treatment of polygyny. The provisioning hypothesis accounts for the transition from polygyny to monogamy without invoking any change in the costs of defending females. It rather invokes the selection of males having a lower motivation for polygyny and, concomitantly, a higher drive for paternal investment. It sees the drive for polygyny as being selected against, not merely refrained, and it thus conceives of men as basically monogamous. In short, the provisioning hypothesis predicts generalized monogamy across human societies.

In contrast, the leveling hypothesis propounds that the drive for polygyny was repressed, or inhibited, owing to the costs of aggression; it does not imply that the motivation for polygyny was selected against. The leveling hypothesis thus predicts that polygyny should reemerge whenever some males succeed in securing more competitive power, or in attracting several females based on attributes other than physical prowess, notably their ability to control resources valued by females. Ethnographical evidence provide support for the leveling hypothesis. In socially stratified societies, males ranking higher in the socioeconomic scale have higher reproductive success (Cronk, 2006; Marlowe, 2003b). One may thus surmise that, prior to the advent of socioeconomic stratification brought about by the adoption of agriculture and cattle herding, monogamy was the predominant type of union—as it is in the vast majority of hunter-gatherer societies—and that the monogamy–polygyny set, as we know it, was subsequent to the advent of food production. In short, the human mating system is readily compatible with the leveling hypothesis, less so with the provisioning hypothesis.

The Evolutionary History of the Sexual Division of Labor

Earlier, I identified three major perspectives from which the human family is best characterized: as an integral part of the modal composition of human groups (multifamily group), as the central feature of the human mating system (monogamy–polygyny set), and as the basic locus of cooperative subsistence (sexual division of labor). I have hitherto been mainly concerned with the first two aspects. From the outset, it is important to note that cooperative subsistence is not limited to the father's contribution. Other categories of helpers, such as older siblings and grandmothers, contribute importantly to raising children (Hawkes et al., 1998; Hawkes, 2003; Hrdy, 1999, 2007). Notwithstanding this important fact, I am specifically concerned here with the evolution of cooperation between spouses. I argued earlier that the sexual division of labor breaks down into three components—food transport, food-sharing between pair-bonded mates, and sexual specialization in subsistence activities—and that because the three components are independent of each other it is likely that they evolved for distinct reasons. In what follows, I discuss the evolution of the three components separately. The general argument may be summarized in three propositions: (a) it is extremely likely that some levels of food transport and some degree of sex differences in subsistence activities predated by far the evolution of monogamy; (b) upon the evolution of monogamy, the merging of stable breeding bonds with food transport produced a primitive form of mutual provisioning among family members; and (c) the four traits taken together—monogamy, food transport, sex differences in subsistence activities, and food-sharing—amounted to a primitive version of the sexual division of labor, a version that operated as a preadaptation for the evolution of higher levels of sexual specialization when the costs of maternity began to increase substantially. The whole reasoning is summarized in Fig. 3.3.

Food Transport As a Correlate of Bipedalism

Food transport is in all likelihood the most primitive building block of the sexual division of labor, and it probably antedated it by millions of years; that is to say, hominins carried food around whether they formed multimale–multifemale groups, polygynous

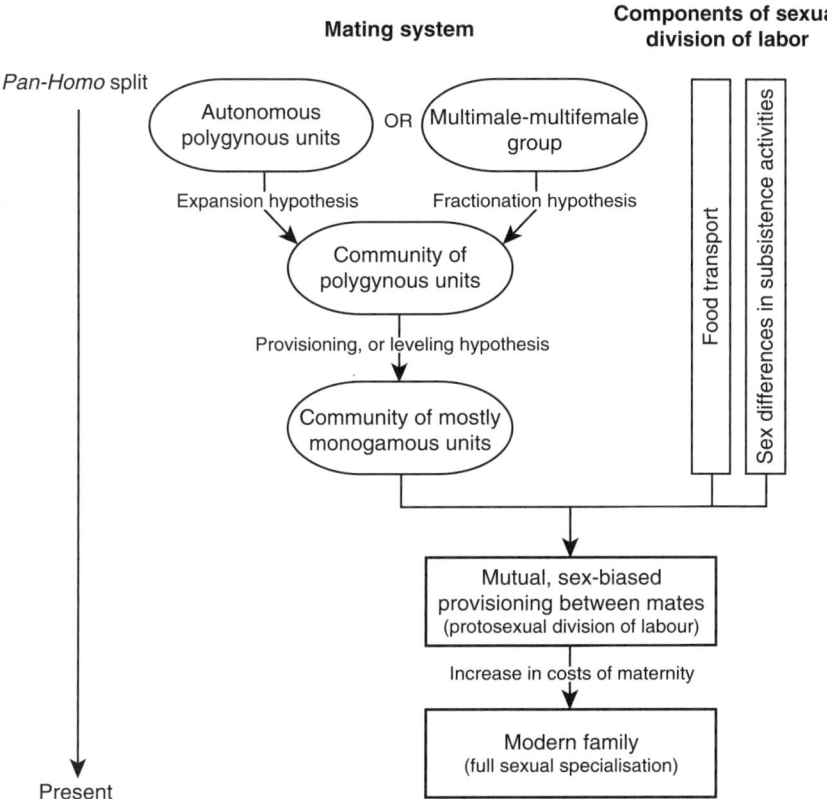

Fig. 3.3 The timing of the components of the sexual division of labor in relation to the evolutionary history of the human mating system. A primitive form of mutual provisioning and the sexual division of labor are seen as originating in the fortuitous combination of monogamy with food transport and sex differences in subsistence activities

units, or pair-bonds, and whether they provisioned other individuals or not. The basic argument here is that the ability to transport things around was a correlate of bipedalism, whether the latter was atypical and temporary, or humanlike and habitual. As soon as bipedalism had evolved and the hands were freed, hominins had the ability to transport food. Fossil evidence indicates that hominins were bipeds more than 4 MYA (Leakey, Feibel, McDougall, & Walker, 1995; White et al., 2009) and possibly up to 7 MYA (Brunet et al., 2002). It is possible that the advantages of transporting food played a role in the evolution of bipedalism, but it is equally possible that bipedalism evolved for reasons unrelated to transport (for a review, see Stanford, 2003), in which case the ability to carry food and tools around was an ancillary consequence of bipedalism. Thus, whatever the exact causal relation between bipedalism and food transport, the two aspects evolved concomitantly.

One of the most basic advantages of transporting food is perhaps that it provided a means for eating in safer locations, for example on higher ground with a view, or in trees. Early bipeds, such as *Ardipithecus ramidus*, present a mosaic of anatomical traits suggesting that they were still climbing trees (White et al., 2009). The importance of shelters against predators for hominins is illustrated by the observation that chimpanzees inhabiting mosaic savanna environments concentrate their activities in forest patches, moving rapidly and alertly in the more open parts of their environment (Hunt & McGrew, 2002). Predator avoidance is a self-centered benefit of transporting food, and it involves no cognitively sophisticated process. To explain the evolution of transportation on that basis, one needs invoke no particular selective pressures; food transport is some sort of by-product trait, an ancillary consequence of bipedalism combining with predation pressure. For a biped, the act of walking while holding something in its hand, or dragging it, is a behavior that is easily learned individually. It is also easily acquired through social learning because it involves no complex motor sequence, hence it is easily culturally transmissible and stabilized. From this perspective, it is extremely unlikely that the evolution of food transport awaited cognitively demanding food-sharing objectives, such as those involved in the sexual division of labor. For that matter, chimpanzees may carry tools for self-centered activities such as cracking nuts (Boesch & Boesch, 1984). In sum, upon the evolution of pair-bonds, it is likely that hominins had been transporting food and tools for ages.

The Origins of Sex Differences in Subsistence Activities

It is also likely that some levels of sex differences in subsistence activities characterized early hominins and predated the evolution of monogamy. Sex differences in subsistence activities are well documented in our closest relative, the chimpanzee. Females spend more time than males fishing for termites and ants, and cracking nuts with hammers and anvils (Boesch & Boesch, 1984, 1990; McGrew, 1979, 1992). As noted by McGrew (1992), these activities are readily compatible with maternal caretaking and infant monitoring; they are offspring-friendly. On the other hand, hunting is essentially a male activity. Males are responsible for 70% to more than 90% of kills, depending on the population (Boesch, 1994; Boesch & Boesch, 1989; Goodall, 1986; Mitani & Watts, 1999, 2001; Stanford, 1996, 1999; Stanford et al., 1994; Teleki, 1973; Watts & Mitani, 2002).

The reasons why males hunt more than females are particularly significant for the present discussion because they provide hypotheses about the origin of sex differences in subsistence activities in hominins. Male chimpanzees hunt prey that are more difficult to catch, such as colobus monkeys, more often than do females, whereas females hunt smaller and less dangerous prey (small ungulates) more often than males (McGrew, 1992). A recent study by Pruetz and Bertolani (2007) confirms that principle: Female chimpanzees use tools to extract lesser bush babies (prosimians weighing 200 g) from cavities in hollow branches or tree trunks. The male hunting bias in chimpanzees is attributable to a number of differences between males and females. First, males are larger, stronger, and have bigger canines. As a result, they can more easily overpower large prey and run smaller risks of being injured by them (McGrew, 1992). Second, adult females are most of the time pregnant or lactating and carrying their offspring (lactation lasts over 5 years in chimpanzees), and hence less mobile than males (McGrew, 1992).

Third, males cover longer distances daily than do females, 5 kilometers versus 3 kilometers at Gombe (Stanford, 1996) and stand a higher chance of encountering prey. Fourth, males display higher levels of social coordination than females, and social coordination is an asset in hunting because males often hunt in groups, and their success rates are higher than when they hunt solitarily (Boesch, 1994; Boesch & Boesch, 1989; Goodall, 1986; Stanford, 1996; Stanford et al., 1994). Fifth, males that possess meat have been observed to share it preferentially with their male allies, and on this basis, it has been suggested that hunting serves to reinforce male alliances (Mitani & Watts, 2001). It has also been proposed that males share meat preferentially with estrous females (McGrew, 1992; Stanford, 1996, 2001; Teleki, 1973) and with sexual partners on a long-term basis (Gomes & Boesch, 2009). However, a detailed analysis of long-term data in two populations of chimpanzees does not support the hypothesis that male chimpanzees share meat with females in exchange for short-term sexual benefits (Gilby, Emery Thomson, Ruane, & Wrangham, 2010).

The chimpanzee data suggest that the origin of the male hunting bias in humans had nothing to do with provisioning others and with paternal investment, and that it did not evolve as part of a system of cooperative provisioning. They also suggest that, when hominins began to hunt large and/or highly mobile prey, this activity was from the outset male biased for the reasons listed above. The earliest recorded zooarchaeological evidence that hominins butchered mammals is dated 2.5 MYA and concerns *Australopithecus garhi* from Ethiopia (Asfaw et al., 1999; de Heinzelin et al., 1999). Sexual specialization at that stage was probably fragmentary, with both sexes essentially gathering the same types of food. Nonetheless, males were bringing back large and/or difficult-to-catch game more often than were females. In all likelihood, therefore, sexual differences in subsistence activities predated by far the evolution of monogamy and might have operated as a preadaptation for the evolution of full sexual specialization (males and females bringing back different food types).

Mutual Provisioning As a Correlate of Pair-Bonding

Provisioning—bringing food to others—is the key dimension of the sexual division of labor. How did it evolve? Explanations based on the present-day function of provisioning would hold that the initial function of that behavior was helping one's mate and children (Kaplan et al., 2000, 2009; Lovejoy, 1981, 2009). This type of explanation implies the invention of a complex behavior pattern requiring some level of planning and coordination. This is certainly not impossible, but a cognitively less demanding view is that provisioning came into existence as a by-product trait, without hominins anticipating its consequences. I argue here that, upon the evolution of monogamy, the enduring bond between the father and the mother combined fortuitously with two older traits, food transport and sex differences in subsistence activities, and that this novel set of behavior patterns produced a de facto form of mutual provisioning.

The main assumption underlying the present reasoning is that pair-bonded hominins enjoyed high levels of mutual tolerance, for example that they commonly practiced cofeeding as they traveled around, and that they did so solely by virtue of being pair-bonded; that is, well before the evolution of parental collaboration. Before pursuing the reasoning, I justify this assumption using empirical evidence from nonhuman primates. Pair-bonded siamangs are closer to each other when feeding than when traveling, and closest in food trees (Chivers, 1974). As noted by Gittins and Raemaekers (1980, p. 71), in pair-bonded gibbons "the adult pair are extremely tolerant of each other . . . often feed close together and very rarely does one supplant the other." In a captive study of siamangs, Fox (1984) reported active food transfers between pair-bonded adults, in which the female confiscated food from the male's hand without resistance from him, and concluded that "the male's exceptional tolerance . . . was undoubtedly influenced by the strong pair-bond between these two individuals" (Fox, 1984, p. 327). Similarly, Wolovich et al. (2007) reported food transfers between pair-bonded mates in wild owl monkeys (*Aotus azarai*) and suggested that food sharing strengthened pair-bonds. Another source of evidence comes from primate species that do not normally form enduring pair-bonds, but in which sexually receptive females form temporary pair-bonds with males (called *consortships*). Interestingly, levels of mutual tolerance, food sharing, and food transfer rise dramatically in such relationships. Van Noordwijk and van Schaik (2009) reported a consistent pattern of food transfers between adult males and sexually receptive females in wild orangutans (*Pongo pygmaeus*), in which the female took food from the male's hand, mouth, or foot. They noted that sexual associations could end if males refused to share food. As another example, in an experimental study carried out in a free-ranging population of rhesus macaques (*Macaca mulatta*), Dubuc, Hughes, and Santos (n.d.) found that sexually receptive females in consort with a male enjoyed significantly higher levels of tolerance from their partner near a monopolizable food source, compared to females that were near an adult male with whom they were not in consort.

On may thus conclude that pair-bonding in nonhuman primates, whether temporary or prolonged, translates into disproportionate levels of mutual tolerance, including passive forms of food sharing. On this basis, it is likely that pair-bonded hominins too enjoyed high levels of tolerance and cofeeding, which might also have involved food transfers of the sort observed in orangutans, siamangs, and owl monkeys. Importantly, hominins had another ability, this one lacking in nonhuman primates: They were bipeds who could carry food around. This is a major difference, with far-reaching implications. Let us suppose, as argued previously, that pair-bonded mates transported food, either sporadically or on a regular basis, in order to eat it at some places, shifting or fixed. While eating in proximity, the father and the mother were cofeeding, as other primates do; they were engaged in a passive form of food sharing. Crucially, however, they were cofeeding out of food that had been gathered and transported by either one or both of them; they were thus engaged in a de facto form of mutual provisioning because individual A had contributed (transported) some portion of individual B's share, and vice-versa. Such de facto coprovisioning required no food sharing objective. Ego was not carrying food *in order to* feed its mate. Provisioning was a by-product of the correlates of pair-bonding—mutual tolerance, cofeeding, and spatial coordination—after these had merged with the tendency to eat food away from the place where it was collected. In short, the common practice of cofeeding had operated as a preadaptation for the passive sharing of gathered food; cofeeding had been co-opted in a novel context.

It is easy to see that such de facto provisioning, coupled with incipient sexual specialization, would set the stage for further levels of coordination between pair-bonded individuals. Paleontological data indicate that a prolonged childhood and its correlate, juvenile dependency and higher costs of maternity, were a late acquisition in human evolution, perhaps as late as the evolution of *Homo sapiens* (Smith et al., 2007). One may thus surmise that hominins practiced various forms and degrees of mutual provisioning, parental cooperation and sexual specialization well before the costs of raising children increased significantly as a result of brain expansion and delayed maturation. When this happened, males and females would have undergone selective pressures for more goal-oriented collaboration involving higher degrees of anticipation and sexual specialization.

Full sexual specialization in subsistence activities and, correlatively, maximal economic interdependence between spouses, is the rule in modern hunter-gatherer societies. Borrowing from economic models of marriage markets and resource allocation, Gurven and Hill (2009) argued that sexual specialization is more productive than the summed production of individuals doing the same type of work. Their reasoning may be summarized as follows: (a) the human omnivorous diet comprises several categories of food; (b) essential macronutrients—lipid, proteins, and carbohydrates—are found in different types of food (for example, meat is rich in protein and lipids, whereas plant products are rich in carbohydrates and sugars); (c) different food types involve different acquisition techniques, some of which requiring learning periods that are so extensive that maximal competence is reached only during adult life (Kaplan et al., 2000); and (d) in such a situation, it is more productive for males and females to learn different subsistence techniques and concentrate their subsistence activities in different spheres, that is, sexual specialization is adaptive (see also Gurven & Hill, 2009; Kaplan et al., 2009).

To these factors one must add biological differences between males and females, as discussed previously in relation to the subsistence activities of chimpanzees. Because men and women differ in their physical potentialities, this creates initial biases that are culturally amplified until they produce separate sets of activities. The fact that the content of such activities varies considerably across cultures—that the type of work performed by men and women differs cross-culturally—is in no way incompatible with the two basic principles stated here: Biological differences between the sexes produce initial biases in subsistence activities, and specialization is more efficient than nonspecialization.

Conclusion

The argument presented in this chapter may be summarized in the following propositions.

Using the current state and adaptive character of a complex behavioral phenomenon to infer its evolutionary history may be misleading because this naturally leads to the view that all aspects of the phenomenon were part of the same adaptive suite and that its initial and actual functions were the same. Functional studies of the human family exemplify this problem, and for this reason, they are likely to benefit from the integration of information on phylogeny. The comparative analysis of human and nonhuman social systems makes it possible to break down the human pair-bond and its cooperative dimension into a number of phylogenetically distinct building blocks and to reconstruct part of its evolutionary history.

The modal composition of human societies is the multifamily community. The modal configuration of marital unions is the monogamy–polygyny set, with the majority of unions being monogamous in any society. The cohesive community of predominantly monogamous pairs is a uniquely human trait in the primate order. The parental bond features other uniquely human traits, notably the provisioning of highly dependent children long after weaning, mutual provisioning between spouses, and the sexual division of labor.

The primate data suggest a three-stage evolutionary sequence for the evolution of the human pair-bond since the human-chimpanzee split: (a) the sexually promiscuous multimale–multifemale community, (b) the community of polygynous units, and (c) the community of mostly monogamous families. The main arguments for that sequence are that polygyny is practiced in the majority of human societies, that two competing hypotheses about the initial composition of human groups nonetheless agree on the existence of an intermediary polygyny stage, and that the alternative sequence (the evolution of monogamy directly from sexual promiscuity) is unlikely for a number of reasons.

The idea that human monogamy originated from a prior stage of polygyny—as opposed to sexual promiscuity, as is often assumed—significantly reduces the number of possibilities concerning the origin of monogamy. It indicates that monogamy evolved as a result of constraints on the profitability of polygyny. One possibility, labeled the provisioning hypothesis, explains the transition in terms of the benefits of male provisioning for mothers and their offspring, by positing that it became progressively more advantageous for mothers to be the single beneficiaries of a male's provisioning effort. This hypothesis predicts generalized monogamy in human societies. Another, the leveling hypothesis, propounds that, with the evolution of weaponry, it became progressively more costly for males to try to monopolize more than one female. The leveling hypothesis predicts a variable mixture of polygyny and monogamy depending on the possibility for males to control resources valued by females. The importance of polygyny in human societies is more compatible with the leveling hypothesis.

The primate evidence indicates that monogamy initially evolved as a mating arrangement, not as an adaptation for parental cooperation. Mate guarding by males is a particularly efficient means for ensuring paternity confidence and father–offspring recognition, two major prerequisites for the evolution of paternal care. In other words, it is possible that monogamous bonds predated the evolution of protracted juvenile dependency and high costs of maternity, and that monogamy later operated as a preadaptation for the evolution of paternal investment in the form of male provisioning. The human family would thus harbor two sets of Darwinian adaptations relating, respectively, to mate guarding and parental cooperation, a phylogenetic argument that finds support in functional and comparative analyses of human societies (Marlowe, 2003b; Quinlan, 2008).

In that vein, it is commonly assumed that the human mating system and parental cooperation (the sexual division of labor) evolved together as part of the same adaptive suite and over a continuous evolutionary period. But it is plausible that they did not. It is highly likely that some important aspects of the sexual division of labor (food transport and sex differences in subsistence activities) were already present upon the evolution of pair-bonding and that the combination of all three features produced de facto a sex-biased structure of mutual provisioning between family members, which later operated as a preadaptation for the evolution of the sexual division of labor.

Future Directions

Whether the multifamily composition characterizing human groups evolved through the fractionation of a large mixed-sex group into a number of polygynous units that stayed together, or through the expansion of an initial autonomous polygynous unit is still unclear. Detailed phylogenetic (cladistic) analyses of the evolution of multiunit groups in nonhuman primates and other species are needed.

Humans share the multi unit group composition with a small number of primate species such as hamadryas baboons, gelada baboons and snub-nosed monkeys. These species may represent the best available models for understanding the evolution of human social structure. We still know extremely little about them, especially about the ecological correlates of the multiunit composition. The existing socioecological models are badly in want of detailed empirical tests combining ecological and demographic parameters.

To obtain a timeline for the phylogenetic sequence that led to the modern human family, we need paleontological data on the anatomical markers of life-history traits, so that we can better assess the evolutionary history of the human growth pattern. This is crucial for assessing the extent of juvenile dependency and its phylogenetic timing, and the concomitant increase in the costs of raising children.

A particularly important question is the timing of the evolution of monogamy (e.g., as assessed by degree of sexual dimorphism) in relation to the evolution of juvenile dependency. Such information would make it possible, for example, to test the hypothesis that monogamy evolved prior to the increase in the costs of maternity and operated as a preadaptation for the evolution of parental collaboration.

In relation to the leveling hypothesis for the evolution of monogamy, we need to establish the timing of the evolution of weapons used against conspecifics, on the basis of anatomical markers of weapon-induced wounds. The leveling hypothesis predicts a concordance between such markers and monogamy.

Acknowledgments

I thank Carol Berman, Constance Dubuc, Kim Hill, Catherine Salmon, Todd Schakelford, Shona Teijeiro, and Richard Wrangham for several helpful comments on the manuscript, and Constance Dubuc for technical assistance with the figures.

References

Alexander, R.D., & Noonan, K.M. (1979). Concealment of ovulation, parental care, and human social evolution. In N.A. Chagnon & W. Irons (Eds.), *Evolutionary biology and human social behavior: An anthropological perspective* (pp. 436–453). North Scituate, MA.: Duxbury Press.

Asfaw, B., White, T., Lovejoy, O., Latimer, B., Simpson, S., & Suwa, G. (1999). *Australopithecus garhi*: A new species of early hominid from Ethiopia. *Science, 284*, 629–635.

Barton, R.A. (1999). Socioecology of baboons: The interaction of male and female strategies. In P. M. Kappeler (Ed.), *Primate males: Causes and consequences of variation and group composition* (pp. 97–107). Cambridge: Cambridge University Press.

Bird, R. (1999). Cooperation and conflict: The behavioral ecology of the sexual division of labor. *Evolutionary Anthropology, 8*, 65–75.

Boesch, C. (1994). Cooperative hunting in wild chimpanzees. *Animal Behaviour, 48*, 653–667.

Boesch, C., & Boesch, H. (1984). Possible causes of sex differences in the use of natural hammers by wild chimpanzees. *Journal of Human Evolution, 13*, 415–440.

Boesch, C., & Boesch, H. (1989). Hunting behavior of wild chimpanzees in the Taï National Park. *American Journal of Physical Anthropology, 78*, 547–573.

Boesch, C., & Boesch, H. (1990). Tool use and tool making in wild chimpanzees. *Folia Primatologica, 54*, 86–99.

Brotherton, P.M.N., & Komers, P.E. (2003). Mate guarding and the evolution of social monogamy in mammals. In U.H. Reichard & C. Boesch (Eds.), *Monogamy: Mating strategies and partnerships in birds, humans and other mammals* (pp. 42–58). Cambridge: Cambridge University Press.

Brunet, M., Guy, F., Pilbeam, D., Mackaye, H.T., Likius, A., Ahounta, D., et al. (2002). A new hominid from the Upper Miocene of Chad, Central Africa. *Nature, 418*, 145–152.

Chapais, B. (2008). *Primeval kinship: How pair-bonding gave birth to human society.* Cambridge, Mass.: Harvard University Press.

Chapais, B. (2010). The deep structure of human society: Primate origins and evolution. In P.M. Kappeler & J.B. Silk (Eds.), *Mind the gap: Tracing the origins of human universals* (pp. 19–51). Berlin: Springer.

Chivers D.J. (1974). The siamang in Malaya: A field study of a primate in tropical rain forest. *Contributions to primatology*, Vol. 4. Basel: Karger.

Churchill, S.E., & Rhodes, J.A. (2009). The evolution of the human capacity for "killing at a distance": The human fossil evidence for the evolution of projectile weaponry. In J.J. Hublin & M.P. Richards (Eds), *The evolution of hominin diets: Integrating approaches to the study of Paleolithic subsistence* (pp. 201–210). Berlin: Springer.

Clutton-Brock, T.H. (1989). Mammalian mating system. *Proceedings of the Royal Society of London, B, 236*, 339–372.

Clutton-Brock, T.H., Harvey, P., & Rudder, D. (1977). Sexual dimorphism, socioeconomic sex-ratio, and body weight in primates. *Nature, 269*, 797–800.

Coqueugniot, H., Hublin, J.J., Veillon, F. Houët, F., & Jacob, T. (2004). Early brain growth in *Homo erectus* and implications for cognitive ability. *Nature, 431*, 299–302.

Cronk, L. (2006). Behavioral ecology and the social sciences. In J. Barkow (Ed.), *Missing the revolution: Darwinism for social scientists* (pp. 166–185). Oxford: Oxford University Press.

de Heinzelin, J., Clark J.D., White T., Hart W., Renne, P., WoldeGabriel, et al. (1999). Environment and behavior of 2.5-million-year-old Bouri Hominids. *Science, 284*, 625–629.

Dean C., Leakey, M.G., Reid, D., Schrenk, F., Schwartz, G.T., & Stringer, C. (2001). Growth processes in teeth distinguish modern humans from *Homo erectus* and earlier hominins. *Nature, 414*, 628–663.

Dubuc, C., Hughes, K.D., & Santos, L. (n.d.). Food-sharing in a despotic primate: co-feeding between consortship partners in rhesus macaques.

Dunbar, R.I.M. (1995). The mating system of Callitrichid primates, I, conditions for the coevolution of pair-bonding and twining. *Animal Behaviour, 50*, 1057–1070.

Enard, W., & Pääbo, S. (2004). Comparative primate genomics. *Annual Review of Genomics and Human Genetics, 5*, 351–378.

Evans-Pritchard, E.E. (1951). *Kinship and marriage among the Nuer.* Oxford: Clarendon Press.

Fisher, H. (1992). *Anatomy of love: The natural history of monogamy, adultery, and divorce.* New York: W.W. Norton.

Fisher, H. (2006). *Why we love: The nature and chemistry of romantic love.* New York: Henry Holt.

Flinn, M.V., Quinlan, R.J., Coe, K., & Ward, C.V. (2007). Evolution of the human family: Cooperative males, long social childhoods, smart mothers, and extended kin networks. In C.A. Salmon & T.K. Schakelford, *Family relationships: An evolutionary perspective* (pp. 16–38). Oxford: Oxford University Press.

Fox, G.J. (1984). Food transfers in gibbons. In H. Preuschoft, D.J. Chivers, W.Y. Brockelman, & N. Creel (Eds.). *The lesser apes: Evolutionary and behavioral biology* (pp. 324–332). Edinburgh: Edinburgh University Press.

Ghiglieri, M.P. (1987). Sociobiology of the great apes and the hominid ancestor. *Journal of Human Evolution, 16*, 319–357.

Gilby, I., Emery Thompson, M., Ruane, J.D., & Wrangham, R. (2010). No evidence of short-term exchange of meat for sex among chimpanzees. Doi: 10.1016/j.jhevol.2010.02.006.

Gittins, S.P., & Raemaekers, J.J. (1980). Siamang, lar and agile gibbons. In D. J. Chivers (Ed.), *Malayan forest primates: Ten years' study in tropical rain forest* (pp. 63–105). New York: Plenum Press.

Gomes, C.M., & Boesch, C. (2009). Wild chimpanzees exchange meat for sex on a long-term basis. *PLoS ONE, 4*, 1–6.

Goodale, J.C. (1962). Marriage contracts among the Tiwi. *Ethnology, 1*, 452–466.

Goodall, J. (1986). *The chimpanzees of Gombe: Patterns of behavior.* Cambridge, MA: Harvard University Press.

Goodenough, W. (1970). *Description and comparison in cultural anthropology.* Chicago: Alidine.

Goodman, M., Grossman, L.I., & Wildman, D.E. (2005). Moving primate genomics beyond the chimpanzee genome. *Trends in Genetics, 21*, 511–517.

Grueter, C.C., & van Schaik, C.P. (2010). Evolutionary determinants of modular societies in colobines. *Behavioral Ecology, 21*, 63–71.

Gurven, M. (2004). To give and to give not: The behavioral ecology of human transfers. *Behavioral and Brain Sciences, 27*, 543–583.

Gurven, M., & Hill, K. (2009). Why do men hunt? A re-evaluation of "man the hunter" and the sexual division of labor. *Current Anthropology, 50*, 51–74.

Gurven, M., Winking, J., Kaplan, H., von Rueden, C., & McAllister, L. (2009). A bioeconomic approach to marriage and the sexual division of labor. *Human Nature, 20*, 151–183.

Hawkes, K. (2004). Mating, parenting, and the evolution of human pair bonds. In B. Chapais & C.M. Berman (Eds.), *Kinship and behavior in primates* (pp. 443–473). New York: Oxford University Press.

Hawkes, K. (1991). Showing off: Tests of an hypothesis about men's foraging goals. *Ethology and Sociobiology, 12*, 29–54.

Hawkes, K. (1993). Why hunter-gatherers work: An ancient version of the problem of public goods. *Current Anthropology, 34*, 341–361.

Hawkes, K. (2003). Grandmothers and the evolution of human longevity. *American Journal of Human Biology, 15*, 380–400.

Hawkes, K., O'Connell, J.F., & Blurton Jones, N.G. (2001). Hunting and nuclear families: Some lessons from the Hadza about men's work. *Current Anthropology, 42*(5), 681–709.

Hawkes, K., O'Connell, J.F., Blurton-Jones, N.G., Alvarez, H., & Charnov, E.L. (1998). Grandmothering, menopause, and the evolution of human life histories. *Proceedings of the National Academy of Sciences, 95*, 1336–1339.

Hawkes, K., Rogers, A.R., & Charnov, E.L. (1995). The male's dilemma: Increased offspring production is more paternity to steal. *Evolutionary Ecology, 9*, 662–677.

Hill, K. (1982). Hunting and human evolution. *Journal of Human Evolution, 11*, 521–544.

Hill, K. Barton, K., & Hurtado, M. (2009). The emergence of human uniqueness: Characters underlying behavioral modernity. *Evolutionary Anthropology, 18*, 187–200.

Hrdy, S.B. (1999). *Mother nature: A history of mothers, infants and natural selection.* New York: Random House.

Hrdy, S.B. (2007). Evolutionary context of human development: The cooperative breeding model. In C.A. Salmon & T.K. Schakleford (Eds.), *Family relationships: An evolutionary perspective* (pp. 39–67). New York: Oxford University Press.

Hunt, K.D., & McGrew, W.C. (2002). Chimpanzees in the dry habitats of Assirik, Senegal and Semliki Wildlife Reserve, Uganda. In C. Boesch, G. Hohmann & Marchant, L.F. (Eds.), *Behavioural diversity in chimpanzees and bonobos* (pp. 35–51). New York: Cambridge University Press.

Isaac, G. L. (1978). The food-sharing behaviour of proto-human hominids. *Scientific American, 238*, 90–108.

Kaplan, H.S., Hill, K.R., Lancaster, J.B., & Hurtado, A.M. (2000). A theory of human life history evolution: Diet, intelligence, and longevity. *Evolutionary Anthropology, 9*, 156–185.

Kaplan, H.S., Hooper, P.L., & Gurven, M. (2009). The evolutionary and ecological roots of human social organization. *Philosophical Transactions of the Royal Society, B, 364*, 3289–3299.

Lancaster, J.B., & Lancaster, C. (1987). The watershed: Change in parental-investment and family-formation strategies in the course of human evolution. In J. B. Lancaster, J. Altmann, A.S. Rossi, & L.R. Sherrod (Eds.), *Parenting across the life span: Biosocial dimensions* (pp. 187–205). New York: Aldine de Gruyter.

Leakey, M.G., Feibel, C.S., McDougall I., & Walker, A. (1995). New four-million-year-old hominid species from Kanapoi and Allia Bay, Kenya. *Nature 376*, 565–571.

Lovejoy, O. (1981). The origin of man. *Science, 211*, 341–350.

Lovejoy, C.O. (2009). Reexamining human origins in light of *Ardipithecus ramidus. Science, 326* (5949), 108–115.

Low, B.S. (2003). Ecological and social complexities in human monogamy. In U.H. Reichard & C. Boesch (Eds.), *Monogamy: Mating strategies and partnerships in birds, humans and other mammals.* Cambridge: Cambridge University Press.

Marlowe, F.W. (2003a). A critical period for provisioning by Hadza men: Implications for pair-bonding. *Evolution and Human Behavior, 24*, 217–229.

Marlowe, F.W. (2003b). Paternal investment and the human mating system. *Behavioural Processes, 51*, 45–61.

McGrew, W.C. (1979). Evolutionary implications of sex differences in chimpanzee predation and tool use. In D. A. Hamburg & E.R. McCown (Eds.), *Perspectives on human evolution, Vol. 5: The great apes* (pp. 440–463). Menlo Park, NJ: Benjamin/Cummings.

McGrew, W.C. (1992). *Chimpanzee material culture: Implications for human evolution.* Cambridge: Cambridge University Press.

McGrew, W.C. (2004). *The cultured chimpanzee: Reflections on cultural primatology.* Cambridge: Cambridge University Press.

McHenry, H.M. (1992). Body size and proportions in early hominids. *American Journal of Physical Anthropology, 87*, 407–431.

McHenry, H.M. (1996). Sexual dimorphism in fossil hominids and its socioecological implications. In J. Steele & S. Shennan (Eds.), *The archaeology of human ancestry: Power, sex and tradition* (pp. 91–109). New York: Routledge.

Mitani, J.C., & Watts, D.P. (1999). Demographic influences on the hunting behaviour of chimpanzees. *American Journal of Physical Anthropology, 109*, 439–454.

Mitani, J.C., & Watts, D.P. (2001). Why do chimpanzees hunt and share meat? *Animal Behaviour, 61*, 915–924.

Orians, G.H. (1969). On the evolution of mating systems in birds and mammals. *American Naturalist, 103*, 589–603.

Plavcan, J.M. (2001). Sexual dimorphism and primate evolution. *Yearbook of Physical Anthropology, 44*, 25–53.

Pruetz, J.D., & Bertolani, P. (2007). Savanna chimpanzees, *Pan troglodytes verus*, hunt with tools. *Current Biology, 17*, 1–6.

Quinlan, R.J. (2008). Human pair-ponds: Evolutionary functions, ecological variation, and adaptive development. *Evolutionary Anthropology, 17*, 227–238.

Rodseth, L., Wrangham, R.W., Harrigan, A.M., & Smuts, B.B. (1991). The human community as a primate society. *Current Anthropology, 32*, 221–254.

Ross, C., & MacLarnon, A. (2000). Evolution of non-maternal care in anthropoid primates: A test of the hypotheses. *Folia Primatologica, 71*, 93–113.

Shea, J.J. (2006). The origins of lithic projectile point technology: Evidence from Africa, the Levant, and Europe. *Journal of Archaeological Science, 33*, 823–846.

Smith, T.M., Toussaint, M., Reid, D.J., Olejniczak, A.J., & Hublin, J.J. (2007). Rapid dental development in a Middle Paleolithic Belgian Neanderthal. *Proceedings of the National Academy of Sciences, 104*, 20220–20225.

Stammbach, E. (1987). Desert, forest and montane baboons: Multi-level societies. In B.B. Smuts, D.L. Cheney, R.M. Seyfarth, R.W. Wrangham, & T.T. Struhsaker (Eds.), *Primate societies* (pp. 112–120). Chicago: University of Chicago Press.

Stanford, C.B. (2003). *Upright: The evolutionary key to becoming human.* New York: Houghton Mifflin.

Stanford, C.B. (1996). The hunting ecology of wild chimpanzees: Implications for the evolutionary ecology of Pliocene hominids. *American Anthropologist, 98*, 96–113.

Stanford, C.B. (1999). *The hunting apes: Meat eating and the origins of human behavior.* Princeton, NJ: Princeton University Press.

Stanford, C.B. (2001). The ape's gift: Meat-eating, meat-sharing, and human evolution. In F.B.M. de Waal (Ed.), *Tree of origin: What primate behavior can tell us about human social evolution* (pp. 95–117). Cambridge, MA: Harvard University Press.

Stanford, C.B., Wallis, J., Matama, H., & Goodall, J. (1994). Patterns of predation by chimpanzees on red colobus monkeys in Gombe National Park, 1982–1991. *American Journal of Physical Anthropology, 94*, 213–228.

Teleki, G. (1973). *The predatory behavior of chimpanzees.* Lewisburg, PA: Bucknell University Press.

van Hooff, J.A.R.A.M. (1999). Relationships among non-human primate males: A deductive framework. In P.M. Kappeler (Ed.), *Primate males: Causes and consequences of variation in group composition* (pp. 183–191). Cambridge: Cambridge University Press.

van Noordwijk, M.A., & van Schaik, C.P. (2009). Intersexual food transfer among orangutans: Do females test males for coercive tendency? *Behavioral Ecology and Sociobiology, 63,* 883–890.

van Schaik, C.P. (1996). Social evolution in primates: The role of ecological factors and male behavior. *Proceedings of the British Academy, 88,* 9–31.

van Schaik, C., & Kappeler, P.M. (2003). The evolution of social monogamy in primates. In U.H. Reichard & C. Boesch (Eds). *Monogamy: Mating strategies and partnerships in birds, humans and other mammals* (pp. 59–80). Cambridge: Cambridge University Press.

Washburn, S.L., & Lancaster, C. (1968). The evolution of hunting. In R.B. Lee & I. deVore (Eds.), *Man the hunter* (pp. 293–303). Chicago: Aldine.

Watts, D.P., & Mitani, J.C. (2002). Hunting behavior of chimpanzees at Ngogo, Kibale National Park, Uganda. *International Journal of Primatology, 23,* 1–28.

White, T.D., Asfaw B., Beyene, Y, Haile-Selassie, Y., Lovejoy, C.O., Suwa, G., & WoldeGabriel, G. (2009). *Ardipithecus ramidus* and the paleobiology of early hominids. *Science 326* (5949), 75–86.

Wolovich, C.K., Perea-Rodriguez, J.P., & Fernandez-Duque, E. (2007). Food transfers to young and mates in wild Owl monkeys (*Aotus azarai*). *American Journal of Primatology, 69,* 1–16.

Wrangham, R. (1987). The significance of African apes for reconstructing human social evolution. In W.G. Kinzey (Ed.), *The evolution of human behavior: Primate models* (pp. 51–71). Albany: State University of New York Press.

CHAPTER 4

The Evolution of Relationships in Nonhuman Families

Douglas W. Mock

Abstract

Sexual reproduction generates genetic novelties, such that the individual members of a simple nuclear family have both shared and unshared evolutionary interests in the others. Hamilton's rule is widely recognized as specifying how such relatedness can promote altruism and cooperation among close kin, but it simultaneously shows the evolutionary limits of selfishness. In addition, the pervasive tendency for parents to overproduce (to create more offspring than can normally be supported) exacerbates competition within the nursery, generating a rich array of behavioral dynamics that span the social range from nepotistic suicide to filial infanticide and siblicide. Full understanding of the three social dimensions of family life (parent–parent, parent–offspring, sibling–sibling) thus requires attention to the ecological limits on resource supply, the developmental requirements affecting demand, and the evolutionary genetics of kinship.

Keywords: Hamilton's rule, relatedness, parent-offspring conflict, sibling rivalry, sexual conflict, overproduction, nepotism, selfishness

For purposes of this chapter, a family will consist of one or two parents plus offspring, coexisting for a variable period in a limited-space "nursery" while parental investment flows from adult to progeny. As defined by Trivers (1972), parental investment consists of any goods or services that enhance one offspring's fitness at the cost of parents being able to provide for its siblings. The explicit zero-sum game is easiest to envision with two or more contemporary sibling nursery-mates, but the principle applies equally well to siblings that are produced sequentially and may never even know of each other's existence. For simplicity, I also restrict attention to species that reproduce sexually and, for most discussions, are diploid (having two sets of homologous chromosomes). Even so, there is much to consider.

This chapter's goal is first to summarize some theoretical themes that apply to all such families and then to illustrate how that framework has been useful in understanding basic but complex family tensions in taxa ranging from fruit trees to leeches to insects to birds to mammals. The implication for our understanding of human families is simply that one ignores broad evolutionary currents at one's peril: Theory sufficiently robust and general to offer testable predictions across myriad forms of life has much to say about the forces that shaped our own behavioral and other reproductive features. Furthermore, different scientific tools—especially a wider range of experimental manipulations—are available for studies of other life forms than can be applied logistically and ethically to humans.

Background Theory

The evolutionary study of social behavior came of age in the 1960s and 1970s with the development and appreciation of inclusive fitness theory (Hamilton, 1964a, 1964b) and evolutionary game theory (reviewed in Maynard Smith, 1982; Parker & Maynard Smith, 1990), plus the rediscovery of

Darwinian sexual selection (Campbell, 1972). At the same time, vague assumptions about selection operating effectively at the level of demes and whole species (the classical "group selection" of Wynne-Edwards [1962]) were being replaced by the realization that selection acts most potently at the level of alleles (thus expressing its phenotype-shaping power mainly on individuals) (Lewontin, 1970; Williams, 1966a). This shift also made previously unitary-looking social units (pair-bond, family, parent–offspring bond) seem less so. All these ideas were applied explicitly to family social relationships by the mid 1970s (Alexander, 1974; Dawkins 1976; O'Connor 1978; Trivers 1974; Wilson 1975), especially against the backdrop of early life-history theory (Cole, 1954) and its seminal notion of a quantity versus quality trade-off for offspring (Lack, 1947; Lloyd, 1987; Smith & Fretwell, 1974; Williams, 1966b).

It now seems clear that each member of a family is pulled in two diametrically opposite directions by fitness incentives for acting selfishly and others for acting nepotistically (altruistically toward close kin). The genetic reasons for such inner conflict are rooted in sexual reproduction itself, which involves a shuffling and mixing of parental genomes across generations. Recall that sex cells (gametes) are produced by meiosis, cell-division that requires a diploid cell first to halve its chromosome number by sending only one member of each homologous chromosome pair into the stockpile of future ova (if female) or sperm (if male). This reduction-division step means that copies of a given gene (e.g., a rare mutant that differs from its partner allele on the chromosomal homologue) will be present in only half of the gametes. Accordingly, when one gamete is involved later in a sexual union with a complementary gamete from the mating partner, there is the same 0.5 chance that the successful gamete is one of the mutation's carriers. This probability is known formally as the *coefficient-of-relatedness* (Hamilton, 1964a), symbolized as r between parent and offspring. One way of looking at this is that a diploid offspring, having half of its alleles from each parent, is the vehicle that conveys their genes into future generations and thus into their representation of gene pool composition. But note that each zygote is a glass half-full and half-empty from each parent's perspective, not a full copy (as would be the case in an asexual lineage). Sexual reproduction thus brings together novel sets of genes (via recombination of the two parents' haplotypes), and the very diversity it creates also means that each individual is unique (with the exception of identical twins, which start life as a single diploid zygote and then separate into two embryos). The genetic individuality produced by sex, in turn, means that family members have only partial overlap of genetic constitutions (expressed by r). The overlap can favor nepotism under certain circumstances specified in *Hamilton's rule* (explained more fully in Box 4.1), even as the non-overlapping proportion offers fitness incentives for selfishness. It follows that organisms that reproduce asexually tend to be highly cooperative and interdependent relative to those that always reproduce via sex. And some species that use sex part of the time and asexual reproduction part of the time show a parallel fluctuation between cooperation and selfishness. Still other species segregate certain members for sexual reproductive duties (these tend to be highly selfish), whereas others lack such options (and are altruistic). The most familiar cluster of these is probably the honeybees, where female workers labor on behalf of the single reproductive queen but cannot breed themselves.

Supply, Demand, and Parental Overproduction

Parallels abound within even the simplest of nursery-based families because genetically unique individuals share only partial interests with other family members. When resources are insufficient for all to flourish, competition kicks in and selfishness pays, but that social stress is automatically reversed, favoring cooperation and aid-giving, whenever competition relaxes. It follows that factors likely to produce an excess of demand over supply should indicate points at which self-promotion overrides the genial bonds of kinship.

One such factor is parental overproduction—parents creating more offspring than they can afford to raise well. At face value, this seems logically unlikely, because it should be generally to the breeders' advantage to match family size precisely to their local carrying capacity, especially the food budget they will be able to generate. There are, however, several reasons why parents can seldom muster such precision (reviewed in Mock & Forbes, 1995), mainly having to do with unpredictable future events, and why they should respond by overproducing instead of underproducing. Taking the second matter first, it is easy to see that natural selection is a reproductive race: At the conservative extreme, genes favoring the habit of creating only one offspring over a lifetime would be quickly swamped by alternative alleles favoring a greater

> **BOX 4.1 Hamilton's Rule**
>
> Altruistic behavior, wherein the net fitness cost of a social act to its performer (symbolized as c) delivers a fitness benefit (b) to some fellow conspecific, was problematic for classical Darwinism. Alleles typically spread via the personal reproductive success achieved by the bodies they inhabit. Accordingly, Darwin famously characterized the existence of sterile castes in social insects as "one special difficulty, which at first appeared to be insuperable, and actually fatal to the whole theory" (Darwin, 1859, p. 236). If natural selection is a reproductive race, then refusing to run is not an obvious way to win. Not knowing about particulate inheritance (genes), Darwin guessed that selection must somehow be able to operate at the "family level," because he could see that sterile workers did enhance the reproductive success of their mother, the queen. There the matter remained for another century, despite attracting the attention of many important thinkers like Sir Ronald Fisher, J.B.S. Haldane, and Sewall Wright.
>
> Parental care is the unpuzzling form of altruism. Reproductive adults commonly make prodigious personal sacrifices that enhance the survival prospects of their own progeny. Here, it is obvious how such largess is favored by natural selection because the offspring are clearly the vehicles for propagation of parental genes. More formally, alleles predisposing parents to make such sacrifices benefit because they exist as identical copies in the recipients. Much research has shown that adults are generally careful to direct investment toward their own offspring.
>
> W.D. Hamilton (1964a,b) pointed out that parent–offspring relatedness is merely the direct or lineal version of the broader genetic relationships linking all kin. Specifically, he noted that lateral kin also carry identical copies of a sexual individual's alleles. Accordingly, social behavior that confers fitness gains (enhanced lifetime reproductive success) to siblings, nieces, nephews, cousins, and so forth, can be selected because of their net positive contributions to the performer's overall or "inclusive" fitness. Furthermore, he identified the boundary conditions that must exist for nepotism to be favored in this way, expressing it in an elegant inequality containing just three variables. The simplest version of "Hamilton's rule" is $rb > c$, which can be rendered easily in words: alleles favoring altruism can spread via natural selection if the actor's net fitness cost is repaid by the recipient's fitness gain after it has been corrected for their degree of genetic relatedness. If they are full siblings, with $r = 0.50$, then the benefit must at least double the cost; if they are half-siblings, it must quadruple the cost, etc.
>
> Among the many demonstrations of this insight's power, perhaps the most dramatic was Hamilton's own observation that haplodiploid sex determination systems can boost r and thereby preadapt the resulting families for heightened degrees of cooperation and altruism. Darwin's "one special difficulty" (as well as his proposed family-level solution) became much more tractable because the social hymenoptera (including ants, bees, and wasps) have this type of genetic structure. Males are haploid, carrying DNA from their mothers only, so that when they make sperm, there can be no reduction-division: As a result, the millions of sperm produced by each male are genetically identical to each other (and to every cell in his body). Females are diploid, producing endlessly variable ova. But if a female mates with only one male, her daughters have an inflated relatedness ($r = 0.75$), midway between the value one expects in regular diploid siblings and that found in identical twins. Such sisters are thus particularly suited to evolve altruistic behavior toward each other (including the special sisters that will be sexually functional and active). This appears largely responsible for the taxonomic distribution of sister-run eusocial societies, where one finds extreme degrees of cooperation (including food-gathering and colony maintenance) and overt self-sacrifice (suicidal defense of the colony and sterility). These social features, in turn, have led to phenomenal ecological success for the insect order Hymenoptera (Hölldobbler & Wilson, 1990). Across the much broader taxonomic sweep of diploid organisms, Hamilton's rule also defines the boundary conditions for cooperative versus selfish tendencies of individuals within nuclear families (Mock & Parker, 1997), the chief focus of this chapter.

measure of profligacy. Because natural selection is most potent at the allele level (its effects most visible at the individual level), parents are best viewed as engaged in a scramble competition to reproduce in such a way as to maximize their lifetime totals of strong, breeding progeny (and grand-progeny, etc.). Thus, they are rewarded for aiming high as a first step toward maximizing their output of truly viable offspring across their whole breeding lifespan. The costs that incur as a result of such overproduction must be evaluated relative to the potential fitness gains.

At least three types of advantages may accrue for parents choosing to create an oversized family within a given breeding cycle (Mock & Forbes, 1995). Most famously, it has been pointed out that parents seldom possess perfect information about the availability of future key resources at the moment when they must commit to an integer number of offspring. In nursery species, the passage of time between fertilization and the peak of offspring food consumption, for example, may range from days (in, say, leeches: Burd et al., 2006) to many weeks (e.g., in large birds and mammals), as development proceeds.

Obviously, ecological conditions can sour or soar during that interval, dragging the amount of support parents can provide with them. If the family's future budget cannot be predicted accurately, the best parental strategy is often to start with a surplus of expendable offspring, which will be affordable and fitness-generating vehicles if conditions prove beneficent, but to trim family size secondarily through some process if resources prove scant. In formulating this argument, Lack (1947) was thinking about small insectivorous swifts (*Apus apus*) that lay either three eggs or only two, and whose offsprings' peak food demand is reached 3 weeks or more afterward. He reasoned that a good food year enables parents to capitalize on the existence of the third egg, but a short breeding season does not allow them the option of adding such later. On the other hand, when conditions are unfavorable, all three nestlings cannot be supported and one must be culled (via starvation). If that misfortune can be focused on just one chick, the other two may come through in good condition. Noting that the parents commence incubation prior to the completion of laying, thereby giving the earlier-laid embryos a 1- to 2-day developmental head start, he interpreted the resulting hatching asynchrony and nestling size hierarchy as a parental strategy for facilitating that subsequent downward adjustment in chick numbers. Both hatching asynchrony and its resulting partial-brood mortality ("brood reduction," Ricklefs, 1965) have since been found to be extremely widespread across avian species that depend critically on parental food deliveries, with various analogous systems for producing hierarchical sibships occurring in other nursery taxa (Mock & Parker, 1997). Thus, parental overproduction is seen as a means by which parents can gamble for the benefits of resource-tracking (Mock & Forbes, 1995). The components of this logic have been demonstrated empirically with songbirds (Forbes et al., 1997; Magrath, 1989; Mock et al., 2009) and falcons (Wiebe & Bortoloti, 1994).

A second incentive for overproduction recognizes that a somewhat larger family gives parents a bit of useful flexibility, because marginal/extra offspring may be able to serve as replacements for those otherwise viewed as members of the core brood. In particular, even if the parents' true carrying capacity for provisioning were known exactly, there are uncertainties about offspring numbers and/or qualities that might be repaired by having one or more backups. For example, even if the British swifts mentioned above never encountered benign weather that made it possible to raise all three chicks well, such that two was the maximum possible, the laying of a third egg could help insure parents against falling short of even that modest mark. Because eggs sometimes fail to hatch, the presence of a third egg cuts the parents' risk of having only one chick to raise. More to the point, various developmental failures can occur at any stage prior to fledging (delayed expressions of deleterious genes, accidents befalling individual nestlings, diseases or parasites infesting only part of the brood, etc.), at which point a marginal offspring that has not already been culled may suddenly rise in rank and prospects.

This insurance value of marginal chicks has been demonstrated vividly with field experiments. First, in American white pelicans (*Pelecanus occidentalis*) the parents typically lay two eggs but raise only one chick to fledging, because this species practices obligate siblicide. That is, in most nests the senior (A) chick attacks and kills its 2- to 3-day younger sibling shortly after B hatches. To test the insurance hypothesis for the value of the B egg as a backup, Cash and Evans (1986) removed the second egg from a sample of nests and showed that parents without a backup were less successful. In another sample of their nests, the simple expedient of marking which chicks came from A versus B eggs showed that about 20% of all fledglings actually started life in the backup position, indicating once again that the early investment (the insurance "premium") paid off (with a "claim"). In a more extensive series of experiments using more abundant red-winged blackbirds (*Agelaius phoeniceus*) as a model system, Forbes et al. (1997) quantified the impact that senior chicks have on their junior siblings and vice versa. As predicted by insurance logic, the parentally conferred competitive asymmetries meant that loss of one core sibling boosted the survival rate of marginal nest-mates by an impressive 31%, but the converse (removal of a junior sib) had no demonstrable effect on seniors.

The other way that producing a replacement offspring might compensate parents for its startup costs is by providing parents with a choice of whom to raise. Replacement value here is not tied to brood size, but to average brood quality. By creating extra young and then *selectively* investing in a subset from the total array, parents might terminate investment on the basis of various criteria (gender, genetic defects, parasite load, etc.) that give higher fitness returns. This process is likely to be very common in plants (Buccholz, 1922), which may overproduce on a truly massive scale, but seems less suited for small animal families and quite ill-suited for species in which parents impose handicaps like hatching asynchrony because competitive asymmetries that are uncorrelated with the qualities supposedly being favored are likely to impair the hypothetical screening process (Forbes & Mock, 1998).

The third general incentive for parental overproduction concerns ways that marginal offspring might boost the personal fitness of core siblings, even if they are unlikely to breed successfully themselves. Such services might be as simple as providing temporary insulation (huddling with nursery-mates and thereby reducing their surface exposure to chill) or as extreme as storing nutrients in body tissues that are then used as a meal subsequently by senior siblings. Sibling cannibalism is quite common in many nursery insects and larval amphibians, and some evidence exists to show that valuable nutrients enhance the fitness of survivors (reviewed in Elgar & Crespi, 1992). Finally, it should be mentioned that these three classes of overproduction incentives may sometimes be additive—that is, mutually compatible and reinforcing—if, for example, an individual offspring holds value as a potential replacement but then turns out to be affordable when local food levels rise unexpectedly.

Whether a particular marginal offspring makes a net benefit to parental fitness hinges partly on the combination of contributions it makes and partly on how much it costs to build, maintain, and, in some cases, terminate. Sketching roughly, one can note the materials for the gametes (especially the ovum), for its upkeep while attached to the mother, for its provisions after detachment (lactation, food deliveries, etc.), and so on. Furthermore, if the marginal offspring eventually has to be shut off from the family budget, it may not go quietly but resist that fate in any number of ways. In siblicidal birds, for example, the victim may succumb only after being assaulted repeatedly and perhaps after fighting back strenuously. There are no physiological measurements of the expenses required, but the killing process can last days and involve many vigorous struggles. Even in an obligately siblicidal bird like the African black eagle (*Aquila verreauxi*), where the A chick hatches several days ahead of its nestmate, one such execution was observed to include 38 separate assaults and a total of 1,569 pecks before the B chick was dead (Gargett, 1978). Demonstrations of the earlier (parental) costs are also emerging. Simple field experiments show that forcing a female black-headed gull (*Larus ridibundus*) to lay one egg more than her usual three (a "determinate" layer, she responds to a single-egg removal by adding to guarantee three) results in the loss of maternal body condition and other problems for the brood after they hatch (Monaghan et al., 1998). Similarly, giving common tern (*Sterna hirundo*) pairs one extra egg to incubate (but removing it upon hatching to restrict the extra parental costs to the incubation period) produces similar effects of wearing down the incubating parents and reducing the welfare of the chicks they raise (Heaney & Monaghan, 1996).

The Three-dimensional Family

With a simple two-parents-and-two-kids model family, we can identify three integrated social dimensions, one vertical (between generations) and two horizontal, that impinge heavily on each other by virtue of each individual's genetic uniqueness (the legacy of sex) in tandem with a tight resource budget. Substantial bodies of theory exist for each of these, summarized here only fleetingly.

The Sibling Dimension

Two (or more) nursery-mates can produce possibilities ranging from extreme sibling rivalry to similar extremes of altruism and cooperation, depending largely on the nature of the resource base. For example, if food is severely limiting (or even if it is likely to become so during the period of dependency on parental support), such that the closest of genetic relatives is also a dangerous ecological competitor, selection can even favor obligate siblicide to be performed well in advance of the actual shortage (Stinson, 1979), the proverbial pre-emptive strike. Alternatively, brood reduction may involve milder levels of overt aggression, such that a fatal result is less likely overall and/or is decided by whether the subordinate nursery-mate manages to inherit enough food (usually after the dominant has been satiated) to overcome any physical abuse it suffers. Moving on to less exaggerated forms of sibling rivalry, most brood reduction includes no aggression at all, but results from "scramble" forms of competition, wherein weaker nursery-mates consume too little to thrive (e.g., in many songbirds).

If nursery resources are sufficient for all, siblings generally tolerate and may even assist one another, presumably because each represents indirect fitness to the other(s). A dramatic example of toleration hinging on food levels is found in larval amphibians (toads and salamanders) that inhabit ephemeral pools during the nursery period. In the arid and semi-arid American West, shallow puddles and other small bodies of water may evaporate and vanish if not replenished by (unpredictable) rains. One solution to that ecological catastrophe, which has evolved repeatedly, is for offspring to switch from a generalized detritivore diet (consuming organic materials off the bottom) to a carnivorous diet that permits faster metamorphosis and thus an earlier option of leaving the water. Not all larvae take this option, apparently because there are future breeding penalties associated with maturing fast (smaller adult body size cuts reproductive potential), but many do and these transform physically with hypertrophied jaws that support their cannibalism (Pfennig, 1992; Pfennig & Collins, 1993). Of special interest to us in this context is that some species demonstrate dietary preference for nonkin victims. Specifically, if a cannibal-morph larva seizes a potential victim, it can taste (from the epithelial mucus) whether it has a sibling or a nonrelative, preferentially releasing the former (unless it has not eaten in a long time) and ingesting the latter (Pfennig et al., 1993, 1994).

In yet other systems where resources are sufficient for kin but cannot accommodate additional (unrelated) consumers, siblings may contribute to the parents' defense of nursery (e.g., nestling birds in colony-dwelling species), effectively helping protect their favored access to food provisions. In certain insects, such protectionism can take extraordinary forms, with huge colonies of ants and bees serving to illustrate. Here, the self-sacrifice can be total, as with the suicidal stings of worker honeybees in protecting the hive (including queen and brood of siblings). This is not a "simple family" of course, but the principles remain the same. Another unorthodox case involves a parasitoid wasp (*Copidosoma floridanum*), in which the mother typically lays two eggs, one male and one female, inside the body of its paralyzed caterpillar host. Several remarkable events ensue. First, there is a cloning extravaganza called *polyembryony*, during which the one female egg becomes approximately 1,200 identical twins (so r among these sisters is 1.0), and the one male egg becomes approximately 200 identical male twins. Next, a small fraction of the females then develop rapidly as a "precocial" morph with oversized jaws and no gonads. It is this transformation that represents altruism because these sisters, although genetic copies of the others, can never achieve any direct fitness and so rely entirely on their siblings for the indirect component of inclusive fitness. They are specialized as killing machines, but the big question is: Whom do they kill? The answer turns out to be that they have two classes of targets. Most obviously, they defend the family caterpillar against other broods that may have been inserted, so their personal sacrifice is easily interpreted through the traditional application of Hamilton's rule (Giron et al., 2004). But they also devote themselves to finding and killing many of their own brothers (Grbíc et al., 1992). To understand this second aspect, one has to know that this insect (and many others) have brother–sister mating, which typically occurs before anyone leaves the nursery. Because a few males can fertilize many more females, the optimal brood sex ratio is heavily female-biased. From the perspective of the females, though, the optimal ratio seems to be even more biased than the 6:1 skew achieved by polyembryony alone. (The details are not essential here, but ants, bees, and wasps are not diploid but haplodiploid, which means that females are often more closely related to their sisters than to their brothers, a factor that compounds the facts that these are clones and have incestuous mating.) In any case, the nonreproductive warrior females reduce the amount of caterpillar flesh devoted to brothers by pursuing sex-based siblicide that eliminates most of the males (sparing only a few that manage to hide in the moth's fat bodies). These remaining few males fertilize the reproductive sisters and the precocial warriors die.

In summary, sibling relationships can range from positive and supportive (for a useful review of these possibilities, see Forbes, 2007) to fatally negative, with all intermediate combinations, according to the nature of the resources available. This varies widely across animal and plant taxa, but also within even a single family unit as the supply–demand balance fluctuates. Applying Hamilton's rule to the family budget, it is easy to show that each dependent offspring should consume the next unit of parental investment, so long as those resources boost its own personal fitness at least half as much as they would boost the prospects of a full sibling (or four times as much as they would boost those of a half-sib). That is, each individual is "related to itself" by $r = 1.0$ and to its full sibling by 0.5, so the impact on its inclusive fitness balances when $b = 2c$ (Hamilton, 1964a; Mock & Parker, 1997; Parker et al., 1989; Trivers, 1974).

The Parent–Offspring Dimension

Extending that Hamiltonian logic to the fitness interests of separate generations, Trivers (1974, p. 249) challenged the harmonious view of parents as being consistently solicitous and of offspring as "passive vessels into which parents pour the appropriate care."

Instead, he argued that the two generations are likely to have divergent interests, hence "parent–offspring conflict" in a deeply evolutionary sense. Although it is certainly true that producing offspring and promoting their success is the chief business of mating and parental care, it does not necessarily follow that everyone is on the same page throughout the process. Hamilton's inclusive fitness concept exposed an unexamined facet of the full relationship, essentially viewing parent–offspring relations through the prism of sibling rivalry. This caught many by surprise, as theoretical biologist Geoff Parker (2010, p. 446) wrote recently, it was "something I simply hadn't realised, and the proposition came as a shock."

The heart of Trivers's theory is couched in terms of how the two generations view the optimal division of parental investment. From the parent's vantage, each offspring is equally related to it (by the meiosis-conferred r of 0.50), but from an individual offspring's position, self is worth two siblings. On the basis of these relatedness asymmetries alone, Trivers reasoned that parents should favor equal investment in all offspring, whereas offspring should favor a pronounced skew toward self (at the expense of sib fitness, as explained above).

There are, of course, other differences between adults and neonates, most conspicuously having to do with the superior size, strength, and experience of the former. Trivers (1974, p. 257) conceded this point in a delicious phrase ("an offspring cannot fling its mother to the ground at will and nurse"), before pressing on to suggest that it might use psychological manipulation in obtaining more investment than is in the parent's best interests to provide. Specifically, the offspring might exaggerate its level of true need, exploiting the parent's imperfect knowledge of same. Through such deceit and other coercive ploys (e.g., tantrums), Trivers made a seductive case for the empowerment of offspring and inspired serious consideration of whether offspring can indeed usurp control over the system to the degree that they lower parental fitness (this criterion is important because it defines why this is an evolutionary conflict). A brief dispute arose on this last point (Alexander, 1974; Dawkins, 1976), the so-called "battleground controversy," which led soon to positive mathematical confirmation (e.g., Blick, 1977; Parker & Macnair, 1978; Stamps et al., 1978) that true evolutionary conflict between the generations is quite possible.

This does not address a second side of the problem, viz. how such genetic conflicts are resolved (Godfray, 1995a), specifically whether offspring ever "win" in nature. This is important because the parent-wins solution does not require any theoretical framework beyond orthodox Darwinism: Parents routinely exercise their physical prerogatives, imposing their own wishes on offspring by fiat (e.g., building eggs too small to maximize each offspring's fitness but that promote parental interests in the long run). The exciting and inspiring part of Trivers' theory was that it simultaneously offered genetic incentives for offspring turning the tables, while suggesting plausible tricks they might use.

Even accepting the battleground logic of parent–offspring conflict, one can remain skeptical over whether the concept has provided compelling explanations for many social dynamics within families (reviewed in Mock & Forbes, 1992; Mock & Parker, 1997). Beleaguered human parents may find an argument that makes sense out of tantrums highly attractive, but alternative explanations abound for that and many other traits (e.g., mammalian "weaning conflict") that have been causally—and perhaps casually—ascribed to it. A small handful of exceptions (see Curley et al., 2004; Le Masurier, 1987; Mueller, 1991) give hope that the matter can be explored more critically in the future, but for now it remains to be seen whether many offspring can pull off the predicted psychological manipulations.

One obvious cloud over the topic concerns the starting assumption that relatedness is paramount in determining the parents' optimal distribution of investment. In a historical context, it is interesting that Trivers's original emphasis on r arose during the first flush of excitement over Hamilton's rule, when lateral relatedness was the conceptual novelty. This is not the place to elaborate fully on the complications that return when one scrutinizes the rule's other two variables (b & c), except to note that parents most assuredly do not always value their offspring equally (as explained above re: initial overproduction and the parental engineering of handicaps for marginal progeny). In short, parents often provide strikingly *un*equal postzygotic investment, boosting the prospects of some offspring at the expense of others. This means that we seldom know the optimal degree of skew for parents, which automatically means that we can hardly infer that any particular observed investment skew runs counter to adult interests! For example, if parent egrets perceive that they cannot afford to raise all three of their chicks to independence, they might regard siblicidal aggression by the senior siblings as a solution (Mock, 1987) and not as a challenge to their hegemony (O'Connor, 1978). This, in turn, offers a parsimonious explanation for the puzzling fact that egret parents, like many other siblicidal birds, do little or nothing to disrupt overt sib-killing (Mock, et al. 1990; Mock & Parker, 1997), even though their relatedness to seniors and juniors is equal.

Adaptive parental favoritism can be far more extreme than passively tolerating siblicide, as when parents themselves perform the execution of certain offspring on behalf of others. In some penguins, the lesser of two chicks is given no food (Boersma & Stokes, 1995); in others, the smaller egg is physically evicted by its own mother (St. Clair et al., 1995). Numerous plant species feature multiple waves of spontaneous abortion whereby the maternal sporophyte abscises fruits or seeds (offspring) that are in some obvious jeopardy, such as developing in too much shade (where the supportive metabolism of local leaves is inadequate), receiving too little water from unproductive roots, or under attack from herbivorous insects (Lloyd, 1980; Stephenson, 1981). Furthermore, large numbers of undamaged and apparently viable offspring are also dropped unilaterally, despite being as related to the parent as those retained for full investment. In the case of navel orange trees, more than 99% of all zygotes are discarded eventually (Kozlowski, 1973)! Thus, matters of parental favoritism, overt and otherwise, are likely to be both common and complex.

Because precise measurement of fitness—and hence of investment optima for both generations—is usually beyond our empirical grasp, rigorous evaluation of parent–offspring conflict theory is likely to require experimentation. This may be quite straightforward, at least in principle. Let us take a candidate behavioral trait that is commonly interpreted as stemming from parent–offspring conflict: the solicitation behavior of dependent offspring (i.e., "begging"), which has been offered as likely to contain deceit (Trivers, 1974) or, conversely, to be honest signals of true offspring need (Godfray, 1991; Godfray, 1995b; Kilner & Johnstone, 1997; Wright & Leonard, 2002). If true evolutionary conflict lies at its foundation, then it remains for experimenters to manipulate that trait and assess the fitness effects on both parties. It is an offspring phenotype, so increasing its expression should enhance the fitness of the performer and depress that of the parents; conversely, reducing its expression should have the reverse effects. On the other hand, if this seesaw relationship is not demonstrable, then we should be open to the possibility that there is no real evolutionary conflict (Mock & Forbes, 1992; Mock & Parker, 1997).

To date, few clear demonstrations of parent–offspring conflict exist (but see Curley et al., 2004; Mueller, 1991). Overall, it seems clear that parents and their offspring frequently do have disparate optima for how parental investment should be distributed, but it is considerably less clear that offspring have traits enabling them to extract more investment than is in the parents' interests to provide.

The Parent–Parent Dimension

In parallel with the preceding sections' historical shift of emphasis from assumed cooperation to assumed self-interest, the term "pair-bond" from classical descriptive ethology has been largely eclipsed in the modern behavioral ecology literature by "sexual conflict," recognizing that even fundamentally cooperative members of a two-member team also are likely to have somewhat different agendas. Male and female partners obviously need each other to create zygotes, but their degree of cooperation beyond that point can range from zero (in most sexual forms, males provide only gametes before departing) to effectively lifelong (e.g., certain swans and geese virtually never change mates while the first partner remains alive; Black, 1996). A key feature of this, and all other forms of cooperation, is iteration (Axelrod & Hamilton, 1981; Trivers, 1971): Partners engaged in a one-off shared venture need not concern themselves with the possibility that poor performance will invite future retaliation, as those anticipating repeat business may. It follows that taxa whose offspring require such expensive postzygotic investment that both parents opt to stay (Maynard Smith, 1977) and provide biparental care may also be in position to remain together for a shared future. At the theoretical extreme of "true monogamy" (Parker, 1985), where neither partner can take a second mate (even if the first one dies), the two have perfectly congruent fitness interests and thus no incentives for exploiting the other: Cooperation is imperative. But as one moves increasingly from that ideal, selfishness is expected to rise, and the puzzle of how biparental care can be evolutionarily stable rises with it.

The taxonomic distribution of biparental care is spotty and revealing. The larger the postzygotic investment needed, the more likely that two parents derive personal benefits from extending their individual contributions. Offspring requirements jumped sharply with the evolution of endothermy (Clutton-Brock, 1991), as the costs of neonatal growth and development steepened additionally from the physiological surcharge for maintaining warm-bloodedness. Accordingly, avian and mammalian parents must provide copious nutrients to fuel all these functions. Endothermic young also tend to have narrower temperature limits, thus often need exogenous warmth from insulated nests and/or parental heat-transfer (brooding). But these two vertebrate classes diverged sharply in evolving solutions to this problem, with mammals following the pattern of one parent becoming increasingly specialized for managing the job alone (internal gestation, lactation, etc.) and birds producing the greatest array of truly biparental care. Among other things, oviparity (the shedding of each zygote and its attached nutrient supply into a nursery/nest within 24 hours of its fertilization and prior to the fertilization of the next ovum in the clutch) cuts male incentives for departing immediately after copulation. And, once the proto-offspring has been thus deposited, the opportunity for both parties to share in its protection (from predators and the elements) materializes, even while the more burdened female must forage to metabolize additional eggs.

Although birds are the primary practitioners of biparental care (with >90% of all known avian species showing it to varying degrees; Lack, 1968), it is patchily distributed across the animal kingdom as exceptions to various taxonomic clades' usual pattern. For example, males provide direct care in fewer than 5% of all mammalian species (Kleimann, 1977; Kleimann & Malcolm, 1981), but in 30%–40% of both primates and carnivores (Clutton-Brock, 1991). Perhaps the most detailed studies of male care in a mammal centers on voles, where some *Microtus* species mate monogamously, whereas most are highly polygynous (e.g., Lim et al., 2004). Similarly, biparental contributions are found here and there in taxonomically disparate invertebrates, including burying beetles, in which parents prepare and defend a small vertebrate corpse as the brood's food source (e.g., Bartlett, 1988), and wood cockroaches, in which parents supply hindgut microfauna critical to the digestion of cellulose for months and even years (Nalepa, 1990; Nalepa & Bell, 1996).

Theoretical models of biparental care (Chase, 1980; Houston & Davies, 1985; McNamara et al., 1999; Parker, 1985; Winkler 1987) fall generally into two categories, according to whether partners play out preset effort levels (paralleling, for example, how "sealed bids" are submitted once for a construction contract) or engage in some kind of back-and-forth "negotiations" (with each adjusting effort in response to what the other offers, then readjusting, etc.). In fact, both modeling approaches allow adjustment between mates, but the former operates over evolutionary time, whereas the latter can operate in real-time (e.g., hour to hour). The basic appeal of negotiation is complicated somewhat by each player's ability to assess the other's contribution often being incomplete, hence potentially inadequate for retaliatory sanctions to discourage unilateral reductions. Negotiation's basic prediction for biparental care is that such a reduction should be met only with "partial compensation." That is, a self-interested parent is expected to weigh the personal fitness costs associated with escalating its own effort against the benefits accruing to offspring. It is expected to compromise by providing an intermediate increase, making up only part of the shortfall. To do less might jeopardize the offspring unnecessarily (e.g., if the partner will soon resume its full share), but providing full compensation may invite further slacking by the partner.

This conceptual framework has led to several empirical field tests of biparental negotiation, which take the general form of experimentally handicapping one parent so as to slow its deliveries of food and then assessing the subsequent actions of the unencumbered mate. In the first of these, small lead fishing weights were crimped onto the tail feathers of European starlings (*Sturnus vulgaris*) and not to their mates (Wright & Cuthill, 1989). Over the years, the procedural details of the handicap have varied (removals of a few flight feathers, implantation of time-release testosterone, continued use of tail weights, etc.), and all manner of results have been obtained, ranging from the predicted partial compensation (e.g., Markman et al., 1995) to no change in provisioning by the unencumbered partner (Saether et al., 1993; Slagsvold & Lifjeld, 1988, 1990), and even to "complete compensation" (Wright & Cuthill, 1990a, 1990b). Some parents show remarkable steadiness, regardless of manipulations, lending support to the "sealed bid" alternative to negotiation (Schwagmeyer et al., 2002). In short, the behavioral rules by which parents may coordinate shared provisioning remain rather unclear at this point (Sanz et al., 2000), and whether parents even have adequate information on partner effort to make corrective adjustments merits closer scrutiny.

Taken all together, these three social dimensions within the nuclear family (sib–sib, parent–offspring, and parent–parent) are inextricably related to one another. If parents abridge total investment because of their dealings with each other, then sibling rivalry intensifies automatically, quite possibly pulling parent–offspring conflict to a higher level as a result. Conversely, if parents function well as a team, thereby delivering more resources, those other conflicts may relax.

Conclusion
Future Directions

What are parents really trying to accomplish in a given reproductive cycle? The glib answer ("whatever is most likely to maximize lifetime reproductive success") is not simple, and researchers tend to forget that less is often more. Because parents routinely produce more offspring initially as a first step toward a smaller optimal brood by the end of parental investment, we seldom know whether their interim objectives differ from those of their surviving offspring. The potential for parent–offspring conflict may be virtually ubiquitous, but its impact remains unknown.

What do offspring solicitation signals really mean? Despite considerable work on the functional significance of "begging" over the past two decades, rather little is clear. Specifically, the quantitative issue of whether signal costs are sufficiently high to force honesty and the qualitative issue of what the messages express are, or should be seen as, wide open.

How is biparental care stabilized? Do parents have a fixed range of effort they are willing to provide, or are they sensitive to partner contributions along the way, perhaps readjusting in response? Are offspring necessarily better off with two caregiving parents, or does sexual conflict lead to a net reduction in total investment?

What proximate cues do siblings use to determine when a nursery-mate is a liability and when it is a fitness asset?

More generally, in all three of the family's social dimensions, how is the balance between competition and cooperation regulated? And, how well can the players recognize it when the tipping points have been reached?

References

Alexander, R.D. (1974). The evolution of social behavior. *Annual Review of Ecology and Systematics*, 5:325–383.

Axelrod, R. & Hamilton, W.D. (1981). The evolution of cooperation. *Science*, 211(4489): 1390–1396.

Bartlett, J. (1988). Male mating success and parental care in *Nicrophorus vespilloides* (Coleoptera: Silphidae). *Behavioral Ecology & Sociobiology*, 23(5), 297–303.

Black, J.M. (Ed.) (1996). *Partnerships in birds: The study of monogamy*. Oxford, UK: Oxford University Press.

Blick, J.E. (1977). Selection for traits which lower individual reproduction. *Journal of Theoretical Biology*, 67(3), 597–601.

Boersma, P.D. & Stokes, P.D. (1995). Mortality patterns, hatching asynchrony, and size asymmetry in Magellanic penguin (*Spheniscus magellanicus*) chicks. In P. Dann and P. Reilly (Eds.), *Penguin biology, Volume 2* (pp. 15–43). Chipping Norton NSW, Australia: Surrey Beatty & Sons.

Buchholz, J.T. (1922). Developmental selection in vascular plants. *Botanical Gazette*, 73(4), 249–286.

Burd, M., Govedich, F.R., & Bateson, L. (2006). Sibling competition in a brood-tending leech. *Proceedings of the Royal Society of London, Series B*, 273(1600), 2461–2466.

Campbell, B. (Ed.) (1972). *Sexual selection and the descent of man, 1871–1971* (pp.136–179). Chicago, IL: Aldine Atherton.

Cash, K., & Evans, R.M. (1986). Brood reduction in the American white pelican (*Pelecanus erythrorhynchos*). *Behavioral Ecology & Sociobiology*, 18(6), 413–418.

Chase, I.D. (1980). Cooperative and noncooperative behavior in animals. *American Naturalist*,115(6), 827–857.

Clutton-Brock, T. (1991). *The evolution of parental care*. Princeton, NJ: Princeton University Press.

Cole, L.C. (1954). The population consequences of life history phenomena. *Quarterly Review of Biology*, 29(2), 103–137.

Curley, J.P., Barton, S., Surani, A., & Keverne, E.B. (2004). Coadaptation in mother and infant regulated by a paternally expressed imprinted gene. *Proceedings of the Royal Society of London, Series B*, 271(1545), 1303–1309.

Dawkins, R. (1976). *The selfish gene*. Oxford, UK: Oxford University Press.

Elgar, M.A., & Crespi, B.J. (1992). *Cannibalism. Ecology and evolution among diverse taxa*. Oxford, UK: Oxford University Press.

Forbes, L.S. (2007). Perspectives in ornithology: Sibling symbiosis in nestling birds. *The Auk*, 124(1), 1–10.

Forbes, L.S., & Mock, D.W. (1998). Parental optimism and progeny choice: When is screening for offspring quality affordable? *Journal of Theoretical Biology*, 192(1), 3–14.

Forbes, L.S., Thornton, S., Glassey, B., Forbes, M., & Buckley, N.J. (1997). Why parent birds play favourites. *Nature*, 390(6658), 351–352.

Gargett, V. (1978). Sibling aggression in the black eagle in the Matapos, Rhodesia. *Ostrich*, 49(1), 57–63.

Giron, D., Dunn, D.W., Hardy, I.C.W., & Strand M.R. (2004). Aggression by polyembryonic wasp soldiers correlates with kinship but not resource competition. *Nature*, 430(7000), 676–679.

Godfray, H.C.J. (1991). The signalling of need by offspring to their parents. *Nature*, 353(6342), 328–330.

Godfray, H.C.J. (1995a). Evolutionary theory of parent-offspring conflict. *Nature*, 376(6536), 133–138.

Godfray, H.C.J. (1995b). Signalling of need between parents and young: Parent-offspring conflict and sibling rivalry. *American Naturalist*, 146(1), 1–24.

Grbíc, M., Ode, P.J., & Strand, M.R. (1992). Sibling rivalry and brood sex ratios in polyembryonic wasps. *Nature*, 360(6401), 254–256.

Hamilton, W.D. (1964a). The genetical evolution of social behaviour. *Journal of Theoretical Biology*, 7(1), 1–16.

Hamilton, W.D. (1964b). The genetical evolution of social behaviour. *Journal of Theoretical Biology*, 7(1), 17–52.

Heaney, V., & Monaghan, P. (1996). Optimal allocation of effort between reproductive phases: The trade-off between incubation costs and subsequent brood rearing capacity. *Proceedings of the Royal Society of London, Series B*, 263(1389), 1719–1724.

Hölldobler, B., & Wilson, E.O. (1990). *The ants*. Cambridge, MA: Harvard University Press.

Houston, A.I., & Davies, N.B. (1985). The evolution of co-operation and life history in the dunnock *Prunella modularis*. In R. Sibly, and R. Smith (Eds.), *Behavioural ecology: The ecological consequences of adaptive behaviour* (pp. 471–487). Oxford, UK: Blackwell Scientific Publishers.

Kilner, R., & Johnstone, R.A. (1997). Begging the question: Are offspring solicitation behaviours signals of need? *Trends in Ecology & Evolution, 12*(1), 11–15.

Kleimann, D.G. (1977). Monogamy in mammals. *Quarterly Review of Biology, 52*(1), 39–69.

Kleimann, D.G., & Malcolm, J.R. (1981). The evolution of male parental investment in mammals. In D.J. Gubernick, & P.H. Klopfer (Eds.), *Parental care in mammals* (pp. 347–387). New York: Plenum Press.

Kozlowski, T.T. (1973). Extent and significance of shedding plant parts. In T.T. Kozlowski (Ed.), *Shedding of plant parts* (pp. 1–44). New York: Academic Press.

Lack, D. (1947). The significance of clutch size. *Ibis, 89*(2), 302–352.

Lack, D. (1968). *Ecological adaptations for breeding in birds*. London: Methuen & Co.

LeMasurier, A.D. (1987). A comparative study of the relationship between host size and brood size in *Apateles* spp. (Hymenoptera: Braconidae). *Ecological Entomology, 12*(4), 383–393.

Lewontin, R.C. (1970). The units of selection. *Annual Review of Ecology & Systematics, 1*, 1–19.

Lim, M.M., Wang, Z., Olazábal, D.E., Ren, X., Terwilliger, E.F., & Young, L.J. (2004). Enhanced partner preference in a promiscuous species by manipulating the expression of a single gene. *Nature, 429*(6993), 754–758.

Lloyd, D. (1980). Sexual strategies in plants. I. An hypothesis of serial adjustment of maternal investment during one reproductive session. *New Phytologist, 86*(1), 69–79.

Lloyd, D. (1987). Selection of offspring size at independence and other size-versus-number strategies. *American Naturalist, 129*(6), 800–817.

Magrath, R.D. (1989). Hatch asynchrony and reproductive success in the blackbird. *Nature, 339*(6225), 536–538.

Markman, S., Yom-Tov, Y., & Wright, J. (1995). Male parental care in the orange-tufted sunbird: Behavioural adjustments in provisioning and nest guarding effort. *Animal Behaviour, 50*(3), 655–669.

Maynard Smith, J. (1977). Parental investment: A prospective analysis. *Animal Behaviour, 25*(1), 1–9.

Maynard Smith, J. (1982). *Evolution and the theory of games*. Cambridge, UK: Cambridge University Press.

McNamara, J.M., Gasson, C.E., and Houston, A.I. (1999). Incorporating rules for responding into evolutionary games. *Nature, 401*(6751), 368–371.

Mock, D.W. (1987). Siblicide, parent-offspring conflict, and unequal parental investment by egrets and herons. *Behavioral Ecology Sociobiology, 20*(4), 247–256.

Mock, D.W., Drummond, H., & Stinson, C.H. (1990). Avian siblicide. *American Scientist, 78*(5), 438–449.

Mock, D.W., Schwagmeyer, P.L., & Dugas, M.B. (2009). Parental provisioning and nestling mortality in house sparrows. *Animal Behaviour, 78*(3), 677–684.

Mock, D.W., & Forbes, L.S. (1992). Parent-offspring conflict: A case of arrested development? *Trends in Ecology & Evolution, 7*(12), 409–413.

Mock, D.W., & Forbes, L.S. (1995). The evolution of parental optimism. *Trends in Ecology & Evolution, 10*(3), 130–134.

Mock, D.W., & Parker, G.A. (1997). *The evolution of sibling rivalry*. Oxford, U.K. : Oxford University Press.

Monaghan, P., Nager, R.G., & Houston, D.G. (1998). The price of eggs: Increased investment in egg production reduces the offspring rearing capacity of parents. *Proceedings of the Royal Society of London Series B, 265*(1), 1–5.

Mueller, U. (1991). Haplodiploidy and the evolution of facultative sex ratios in a primitively eusocial bee. *Science, 269*(5222), 442–444.

Nalepa, C.A. (1990). Early development of nymphs and establishment of the hindgut symbiosis in *Cryptocercus punctulatus* Scudder (Dictyoptera: Cryptocercidae). *Annals of the Entomological Society of America, 83*(4), 786–789.

Nalepa, C.A., & Bell, W.J. (1996). Post-ovulation parental investment and parental care in cockroaches. In J.C. Choe, & B.J. Crespi (Eds.), *Social competition in insects and arachnids: Vol. 2. Evolution of sociality*. Princeton, NJ: Princeton University Press.

O'Connor, R.J. (1978). Brood reduction in birds: Selection for infanticide, fratricide, and suicide? *Animal Behaviour, 26*(1), 79–96.

Parker, G.A. (1985). Models of parent-offspring conflict. V. Effects of the behaviour of the two parents. *Animal Behaviour, 33*(2), 519–533.

Parker, G.A. (2010). Reflections before dusk. In L.C. Drickamer, & D. Dewsbury (Eds.), *Leaders in animal behavior: The second generation* (pp. 429–464). Cambridge, UK: Cambridge University Press.

Parker, G.A., & Macnair, M.R. (1978). Models of parent-offspring conflict. I. Monogamy. *Animal Behaviour, 26*(1), 97–111.

Parker, G.A., & Maynard Smith, J. (1990). Optimality theory in evolutionary biology. *Nature, 348*(6296), 27–33.

Parker, G.A., Mock, D.W., & Lamey, T.C. (1989). How selfish should stronger sibs be? *American Naturalist, 143*(6), 846–868.

Pfennig, D.F. (1992). Polyphenism in spadefoot toad tadpoles as a locally adjusted evolutionarily stable strategy. *Evolution, 46*(5), 1408–1420.

Pfennig, D.W., & Collins, J.P. (1993). Kinship affects morphogenesis in cannibalistic salamanders. *Nature, 362*(6423), 836–838.

Pfennig, D.W., Reeve, H.K., & Sherman, P.W. (1993). Kin recognition and cannibalism in spadefoot toad tadpoles. *Animal Behaviour, 46*(1), 87–94.

Pfennig, D.W., Sherman, P.W., & Collins, J.P. (1994). Kin recognition and cannibalism in polyphenic salamanders. *Behavioral Ecology, 5*(2), 225–232.

Ricklefs, R.E. (1965). Brood reduction in the curve-billed thrasher. *Condor, 67*(6), 505–510.

Saether, B., Anderson, R., & Pedersen, H.C. (1993). Regulation of parental effort in a long-lived seabird: An experimental manipulation of the cost of reproduction in the Antarctic petrel, *Thalassoica antarctica*. *Behavioral Ecology & Sociobiology, 33*(3), 147–150.

Sanz, J.J., Kranenbarg, S., & Tinbergen, J.M. (2000). Differential response by males and females to manipulation of partner contribution in the great tit (*Parus major*). *Journal of Animal Ecology, 69*(1), 74–84.

Schwagmeyer, P.L., Mock, D.W., & Parker, G.A. (2002). Biparental care in house sparrows: Negotiation or sealed bid? *Behavioral Ecology, 13*(5), 713–721.

Slagsvold, T., & Lifjeld, J.T. (1988). Ultimate adjustment of clutch size to parental feeding capacity in a passerine bird. *Ecology, 69*(6), 1918–1922.

Slagsvold, T., & Lifjeld, J.T. (1990). Influence of male and female quality on clutch size in tits (*Parus* spp.). *Ecology, 71*(4), 1258–1266.

Smith, C.C., & Fretwell, S.D. (1974). The optimal balance between size and number of offspring. *American Naturalist, 108*(962), 499–506.

Stamps, J., Metcalf, R.A., & Krishnan, V.V. (1978). A genetic analysis of parent-offspring conflict. *Behavioral Ecology & Sociobiology, 3*(4), 369–392.

St. Clair, C.C., Waas, J.R., St. Clair, R.C., & Boag, P.T. (1995). Unfit mothers? Maternal infanticide in royal penguins. *Animal Behaviour, 50*(5), 1177–1185.

Stephenson, A.G. (1981). Flower and fruit abortion: Proximate causes and ultimate functions. *Annual Review of Ecology & Systematics, 12*, 253–280.

Stinson, C.H. (1979). On the selective advantage of fratricide in raptors. *Evolution, 33*(4), 1219–1225.

Trivers, R.L. (1971). The evolution of reciprocal altruism. *Quarterly Review of Biology* 46 (1):35–57.

Trivers, R.L. (1972). Parental investment and sexual selection. In B. Campbell (Ed.), *Sexual selection and the descent of man, 1871–1971* (pp.136–179). Chicago, IL: Aldine Atherton.

Trivers, R.L. (1974). Parent-offspring conflict. *American Zoologist, 14*(1), 249–264.

Wiebe, K.L., & Bortolotti, G.D. (1994). Food supply and hatching spans of birds: Energy constraints or facultative manipulations? *Ecology, 75*(3), 813–823.

Williams, G.C. (1966a). *Natural selection and adaptation*. Princeton, NJ: Princeton University Press.

Williams, G.C. (1966b). Natural selection, the costs of reproduction, and a refinement of Lack's principle. *American Naturalist, 100*(916), 687–690.

Wilson, E.O. (1975). *Sociobiology, the new synthesis*. Cambridge, MA: Belknap Press.

Winkler. D.W. (1987). A general model for parental care. *American Naturalist, 130*(4), 526–543.

Wright, J., & Cuthill, I. (1989). Manipulation of sex differences in parental care. *Behavioral Ecology & Sociobiology, 25*(3), 171–181.

Wright, J., & Cuthill, I. (1990a). Biparental care: Short-term manipulations of partner contribution and brood size in the starling, *Sturnus vulgaris*. *Behavioral Ecology, 1*(1), 116–124.

Wright, J., & Cuthill, I. (1990b). Manipulation of sex differences in parental care: The effect of brood size. *Animal Behaviour, 40*(3), 462–471.

Wright, J., & Leonard, M.L. (Eds.). (2002). *Begging in birds*. Dordrecht: Kluwer Academic Publishers.

Wynne-Edwards, V.C. (1962). *Animal dispersion in relation to social behaviour*. Edinburgh, UK: Oliver & Boyd.

PART 2

Human Families

CHAPTER 5

Parent–Child Relationships

Marco Del Giudice *and* Jay Belsky

Abstract

The chapter provides an integrative framework for the evolutionary analysis of parent–child relationships. Starting from basic concepts in life history theory, the chapter examines the effect of ecological factors on parent–child relations and discusses how parents modulate their levels of investment depending on children's characteristics such as sex, age, and physical similarity to the father. Next, the chapter explores children's provision of care and resources, the possibility of exploitation by parents, and cross-cultural variation in children's role in the family. The final section introduces genomic imprinting and discusses how conflict between maternal and paternal genes can affect child development and parent–child relations.

Keywords: Attachment, caregiving, differential susceptibility, father-child resemblance, genomic imprinting, helping, life history strategy, parental investment, plasticity, sex-biased investment

Introduction

Few topics in psychology can rival the emotional appeal of parent–child relationships. At the same time—and perhaps for the same reasons—few areas of psychology cling so strongly to a romanticized view of human nature. Most of current developmental psychology is based, implicitly if not explicitly, on the idea that parent–child relationships are designed to be invariably fulfilling, maximally cooperative, and virtually free of conflict. Deviations from this ideal are usually treated as manifestations of individual or social pathology.

And this is exactly why the evolutionary approach to the family is so revolutionary: Biology shatters this romantic worldview at its foundations, by making conflict an essential and unavoidable feature of family relations (Trivers, 1974; see Chapter 6 by Salmon and Malcolm). This is possibly the single most important contribution of evolutionary biology to the study of families, as it illuminates and enriches our understanding of virtually all the processes involved in parent–child, spousal, and sibling relations. However, despite the 35 years since Trivers' (1974) landmark paper and a number of key evolutionary-oriented publications in leading developmental journals (e.g., Belsky, Steinberg, & Draper, 1991; Bjorklund & Pellegrini, 2000), developmentalists remain perhaps the most recalcitrant psychologists when it comes to embracing an evolutionary mindset. This is unfortunate, because what emerges from the evolutionary approach to the family is not a gloomy mirror image of the romantic worldview; rather, parent–child relations are revealed to reflect a fascinating and complex game, the central rules of which involve cooperation *and* conflict, positive *and* negative emotions, and a continuum of adaptive strategies instead of pervasive dysfunction. It is the rules of this game that are the focus of this chapter.

Affective Dynamics and Investment Dynamics

There are two basic ways to look at parent–child relations. One is to focus on what could be labeled "affective dynamics"—the emotional, communicative, and affiliative processes that take place between parents and children. This is the traditional focus of developmental research, and is currently best represented by work informed by attachment theory (Cassidy & Shaver, 2008). Attachment theory was originally developed with a strong biological and ethological basis (Bowlby, 1969/1982, 1973, 1980), although it drifted away from biology as it entered the mainstream (but see Belsky, 1997a; Chisholm, 1999; Del Giudice, 2009; Ein-Dor, Mikulincer, Doron, & Shaver, 2010; Simpson & Belsky, 2008). On another level, parent–child relationships may be understood from the perspective of "investment dynamics": In the ultimate sense, the biological function of parental care is to provide food, protection, shelter, and information (e.g., teaching of social and practical skills) to children. Parental investment results in a net fitness cost to the parent and a net fitness benefit to the child (for a more technical treatment of parental investment in human families, see Sear, in press).

These two levels of analysis are fully complementary: Investment dynamics underlie and motivate affective dynamics, and are the ultimate reason for their evolution. A child's motivation to maintain closeness to his or her mother, the fear, protest, and despair if the mother is not there, and the sense of comfort that arises when in the arms of a loving parent are all crafted by natural selection to ensure parental investment—both in the here and now (e.g., protection from a possible danger) and in the future (by fostering mutual affection and love). Evolutionary biologists and psychologists use the analysis of investment dynamics as a tool to explain, understand, and predict the working of affective and behavioral dynamics. This approach has yielded a number of crucial insights into the psychology of parent–child relationships, some of which overlap with traditional theories, although others are novel and, in some cases, highly counterintuitive.

Overview of the Chapter

The aim of this chapter is not to provide a comprehensive treatment of the psychological processes involved in parent–child relationships. Rather, we offer the reader an integrative conceptual framework for thinking about parents and children from a modern evolutionary perspective. The unifying theme of the chapter is that of investment dynamics; we will examine the evolutionary logic of parental investment in a hierarchical fashion, starting from broad individual differences in life history strategies and ending up with the regulation of genetic expression. We begin by presenting the basics of life history theory and by reviewing its main implications for individual and social differences in parent–child relationships. We then examine how parents modulate investment depending on children's characteristics, such as sex, age, and physical similarity to their father. Next, we look at the family as a cooperation network in which children reciprocate by providing help to parents, but where there are also opportunities for exploitation, and we discuss cross-cultural variation in the role of children within the family. Finally, we introduce one of the most fascinating topics in the biology of parent–child relations, genomic imprinting and the conflict between paternal and maternal genes *within* the child's genome.

A Life History Perspective on Parent–Child Relationships
Life History Theory

Life history theory is a branch of evolutionary biology dealing with the strategies that organisms use to allocate their limited time and energy to the various activities that comprise their lifecycle (see Hill, 1993; Kaplan & Gangestad, 2005; McNamara & Houston, 1996; Penke, 2010). All organisms live in a world of limited resources; the energy that can be extracted from the environment in a given amount of time, for example, is intrinsically limited. Time itself is also a limited good; the time spent by an organism looking for mates cannot be used to search for food or care for already-born offspring. Since all these activities contribute to an organism's evolutionary fitness, devoting time and energy to one will typically involve both benefits and costs; and natural selection strongly favors organisms that are able to adopt an optimal scheduling of activities—with optimal being defined as that which maximizes the individual's inclusive fitness.

Life history theory employs formal modeling to solve the complex optimization problem of how—and when—to allocate limited resources to gain the maximum reproductive success. Life history strategies (LHS) are, in a nutshell, adaptive solutions to a number of simultaneous fitness trade-offs. Use of the term "strategy" does not, however, imply conscious planning or deliberation or even awareness. The most basic trade-offs are between *somatic effort* (i.e., growth, body maintenance, and learning) and *reproductive effort*; and, within reproductive effort, between *mating* (i.e., finding and attracting mates, conceiving offspring) and *parenting* (i.e., investing resources in already conceived offspring). From another perspective, the crucial decisions involved in an LHS can be summarized by the trade-offs between *current* and *future reproduction*, and between *quality* and *quantity of offspring* (see Belsky, Steinberg, & Draper, 1991; Ellis, Figueredo, Brumbach, & Schlomer, 2009). Is the organism going to reproduce as soon as it can, or to wait longer, in order to accumulate resources that can then increase offspring "quality" and reproductive success—and thereby the parent's own inclusive fitness? The more time spent waiting, the more resources (e.g., energy reserves, but also ability and social status) could become available, but the risk of dying before reproducing will increase as well. And, is the organism going to put all of its reproductive effort into increasing the number of offspring, or will it channel resources and parenting effort into increasing the quality and long-term prospects of a few, selected descendants?

One of the most important implications of life history theory is that no strategy can be optimal in every situation; more specifically, the optimal (i.e., fitness-maximizing) strategy for a given organism depends on its ecology and on a series of factors such as resource availability, mortality, and environmental uncertainty. Indeed, organisms usually embody mechanisms that allow them to fine-tune their life histories according to the environmental cues they encounter during development. Within the same species, different individuals can find themselves in dramatically different environmental conditions, which may call for adjustment in the way that strategic trade-offs are resolved. Some individuals, for example, may face higher mortality, perhaps because of predation or diseases; others may live in a place or time in which food is scarce; others still may face unpredictable and rapidly changing conditions in which anticipating the future is extremely difficult. Due to such environmental variability, life history traits and strategies tend not to be genetically fixed, but rather evolve to show adaptive *developmental plasticity* (for an example, see Belsky et al., 1991; Ellis, Jackson, & Boyce, 2006; for a comprehensive account, see West-Eberhard, 2003). Organisms assess their local environments and adjust their strategic allocation choices, following evolved rules that maximize expected fitness in different ecological conditions.

A crucial factor affecting LHS is the pattern of extrinsic mortality; that is, mortality that cannot be prevented by altering the organism's behavior. More generally, all (totally or partially) uncontrollable factors that negatively affect reproductive success can be considered sources of *extrinsic mortality-morbidity* (Ellis et al., 2009). When mortality-morbidity is high (e.g., because of virulent diseases, risk of predation, or high levels of aggressive competition), it is adaptive to favor current reproduction by starting mating early, even at a cost for one's future reproductive potential. Moreover, high extrinsic mortality means that investing in parental care has quickly diminishing returns: As (by definition) parental effort cannot decrease extrinsic mortality-morbidity, offspring's fitness will not respond to parental care beyond a certain amount. Thus, environmental hazard favors quantity versus quality of offspring and current versus future reproduction, and selects for life histories that invest in mating at the expense of parenting. The same is expected from increases in environmental *unpredictability* (see Belsky et al., 1991; Ellis et al., 2009; Pennington & Harpending, 1988). Resource scarcity, in contrast, *in absence of elevated harshness/unpredictability* has the opposite effect, favoring "slow" life histories and high parental investment in a smaller number of offspring. This happens because in resource-scarce but safe and predictable environments, investment by parents can reliably enhance the fitness prospects of progeny and, thereby, parents' own inclusive fitness.

Although organisms can gather information about their local environment through direct experience, useful cues can also be provided by conspecifics; especially during the early phases of development, one's parents can be an excellent source of indirect information (Belsky et al., 1991). Parental behavior and parental investment vary according to the local ecology, to the parent's own LHS, and to offspring characteristics (see below); thus, offspring can use parents as a source of useful cues about the micro- and macroecological conditions they will (probabilistically) face in the future.

LIFE HISTORIES AND THE SEXES

In sexual species, the two sexes predictably differ on life history–related dimensions; they thus can be expected to employ somewhat different strategies in response to the same cues in the environment. In most species, males tend to engage in higher mating effort and lower parental effort than do females (Geary, 2002; Kokko & Jennions, 2008; Trivers, 1972). In addition, males usually undergo stronger sexual selection (i.e., their reproductive success is more variable) and tend to mature more slowly in order to gain the competitive abilities and qualities needed for successful competition for mates. Sexual asymmetries in life history strategies can be attenuated in species with monogamous mating systems, and when both parents contribute to offspring care. Compared with other mammals, humans show an unusual degree of paternal investment, and are clearly adapted for the *possibility* of monogamous, long-term relationships (see Chapter 2, by Flinn). However, human paternal care is highly variable and facultative (e.g., Geary, 2005; Quinlan, 2008), and strict monogamy is rarely found, if ever (Marlowe, 2000, 2003).

As a result of basic biological differences, the various components of LHS do not carry the same weight for men and women. The current versus future reproduction trade-off is somewhat more pressing for women: Women's reproductive rate is limited by the long duration of gestation and the conspicuous energetic investment of pregnancy and lactation, and their window for successful reproduction necessarily ends with menopause. In contrast, men can potentially sire many offspring in a very short time, as well as for a more extensive period of their lives. Men's crucial trade-off is the *mating versus parenting* one: The payoffs of high mating effort are potentially much larger for males, who can benefit directly from having access to a large number of partners; women can have only one child at a time (twin pregnancies aside), and thus benefit relatively less from multiple matings.

Life History Strategies and Parent–Child Relationship

Life history theory is a useful tool for understanding individual and societal differences in parent–child relations. Parents' strategies define their levels of investment in children, whereas children may use parental behavior as a cue to ecological conditions and thus adjust their developing life history strategies accordingly. The behavioral calibration of LHS is expected to work alongside genetic and epigenetic transmission, and genetic differences in plasticity can result in developmental patterns of gene-by-environment (G×E) interactions (Belsky et al., 2009; Belsky & Pluess, 2009).

PARENTS' STRATEGIES

Parental investment is one of the key dimensions of LHS. Harsh and unpredictable environmental conditions should reduce parental investment, and men should switch to a reduced investment strategy more readily than women when faced with equivalently harsh and unpredictable conditions. Based on cross-cultural evidence, Quinlan (2007) showed that levels of paternal care decline steadily with increasing risk of disease (pathogen stress), whereas maternal care decreases at high levels of pathogen stress but *increases* at moderate levels (possibly to compensate for reduced contribution by fathers). In contrast, severity of famine and warfare is associated with reduced maternal care, but only weakly related to paternal care. Another cross-cultural study by Schmitt and colleagues (2003) found that dismissiveness in romantic attachment (associated with low couple stability and low parental investment) increases with increasing mortality rates, fertility rates, and disease risk. Interestingly, the association was stronger in women; men are more dismissing than women at low and moderate levels of environmental stress, but sex differences shrink as environments become harsher.

As indicated above, the crucial LH trade-off for men is that between mating and parenting effort. Indeed, mating opportunity affect men's LHS more strongly than women's. A survey of four hunter-gatherer societies by Blurton Jones and colleagues (2000) showed that the availability of potential new partners for men (indexed by a low sex ratio, i.e., a low proportion of men relative to fertile women) was the strongest negative predictor of marital stability. Marital stability, in turn, is a major determinant of continued paternal investment across cultures. When sex ratios are low, young men tend not to marry, although they are able to marry more easily when they become older (Kruger & Schlemmer, 2009a, 2009b); at the same time, low sex ratios predict higher sexual promiscuity in both sexes (Schmitt, 2005). The local mating system is another key variable. Polygyny often correlates with reduced paternal investment (Marlowe, 2000, 2003), and the relationship between disease risk and reduced paternal investment reported by Quinlan (2007) appears to be mediated—at least in part—by increased polygyny. Another ecological determinant of couple stability is the degree of complementarity between men's and women's contribution to subsistence. In societies in which the sexes contribute resources in approximately equal parts, couple relationships are more stable than in societies in which one of the sexes provides most or all resources (Quinlan, 2008). At the individual level, the allocation of resources to mating versus parenting also depends on age: In men, there is a widely observed tendency to invest preferentially in mating during the first phase of reproductive life, then switch to increased paternal investment (e.g., Kruger & Schlemmer,

2009a, 2009b; Winking, Kaplan, Gurven, & Rucas, 2007).

In summary, life history theory explains how a number of ecological and social factors modulate parental investment and, in turn, affect the quality of parent–child relationships. Romantic attachment is likely a major component of parents' life history strategies (Belsky, 1997a; Chisholm, 1996; Del Giudice, 2009), as romantic attachment styles influence couple stability, fidelity, and long-term commitment, all conductive to parental investment and affectionate parent–child relations. In harsh and unpredictable environmental conditions, parenting becomes harsh, too; parents tend to be less involved, less affectionate, and more prone to neglect their children. Compared with paternal care, however, maternal care is somewhat more resistant to the undermining effects of harsh environments. Fathers' investment in their children is much more variable and heavily influenced by the availability of potential partners, especially when men are relatively young. Low sex ratios are a risk factor for familial instability and father absence (Messner & Sampson, 1990); social factors that lower the sex ratio (e.g., male incarceration, war) or otherwise reduce the number of men who have the resources to be potentially attractive husbands (e.g., unemployment) tend to switch LHS away from parenting and toward short-term mating.

Note that, as a rule, a given population or society will show internal variation in life history–relevant factors; for example local sex ratios may differ widely between cities (or, in large cities, between different neighborhoods), and different subgroups may experience different levels of violence and disease. The possession of adequate resources (e.g., at the family level) may also buffer adverse macroenvironmental effects to some degree—by, for example, reducing the unpredictability of the future (both actual and perceived). In general, it should be kept in mind that an individual's "environment" is a nested hierarchy of ecologies (Bronfenbrenner, 1979), from the macroecological level (e.g., population mortality rates, disease epidemics) to the microecological level (e.g., one's family conditions, but also one's specific place in that family). Individual differences in LHS also depend on genetic differences. All the life history–related traits investigated so far, from sexual maturation timing to romantic attachment, show at least moderate heritability (e.g., Brussoni, Lang, Livesley, & Macbeth, 2000; Figueredo et al., 2004; Mendle et al., 2006, 2009; Rowe, 2000). Moreover, an individual's genetic make-up influences his or her responsivity to environmental factors (Belsky et al., 2009; Belsky & Pluess, 2009), so that not all people are equally sensitive to the factors we have examined here (see below).

CHILDREN'S STRATEGIES

In the preceding section, we discuss how parental investment and caregiving behavior are affected by ecological factors. In turn, children can use their parents' behavior as sources of information about their own present and future environment. Belsky and colleagues (1991) proposed that attachment security in the first 5–7 years of life acts as a summary of the safety and quality of the child's environment, channeling the child's developmental trajectory along alternative developmental pathways. Attachment is closely linked to the stress response system and regulates the child's feelings of distress, pain, fear, and loneliness; and although attachment security can change during the individual's lifetime, it shows a prototype-like dynamics in which early security/insecurity (established in the first years of life) can continue to affect behavior and development later in life, including adulthood (Fraley, 2002). Secure attachment would lead to later sexual maturation, later reproduction, high parental investment, and a trusting, cooperative interpersonal style; in contrast, insecure attachment would lead to earlier maturation and reproduction, higher mating effort, and an opportunistic, selfish interpersonal orientation. Again, both macro- and microecological factors influence the quality of parent–child relations and children's attachment styles; indeed, the latter instantiate the former, thereby providing guidance to the child.

Even within the same family, parents may invest little in a given child because of a number of reasons, including parents' mental illness, low phenotypic quality of the child (e.g., disabilities, chronic health problems), or the presence of stepparents (Chapter 7, by Anderson). Here, we discuss how the child's sex, age, and birth order can be powerful determinants of parental investment. Parental behaviors are informative because they correlate with macroecological factors (Belsky, 1984; McLoyd, 1990), but also because investment received in the present is an indicator of the investment that the child can expect to receive in the future (Ellis, 2004).

The original evolutionary model of socialization advanced by Belsky and colleagues has been integrated and revised over the years (e.g., Belsky, 1997a; Chisholm, 1993, 1996, 1999; Del Giudice, 2009;

Simpson & Belsky, 2008) and has received extensive empirical support. For example, recent genetically informed studies have confirmed the predicted relationship between stressful, negative parent–child relationships and earlier puberty timing in girls (Belsky et al., 2007; Ellis & Essex, 2007; Tither & Ellis, 2008). More recently, data show that attachment security in infancy, known to be causally influenced by quality of parental care, itself predicts pubertal maturation; just as predicted, early insecurity forecasts earlier onset and completion of pubertal development, as well as earlier age of menarche (Belsky, Houts, & Fearon, 2010).

Subsequent elaborations of the model have emphasized that early strategic calibration may be revised at later developmental stages; LHS are not set in stone during early childhood and thus can respond to changes in the environment and to the new information provided by social interaction with peers (see Del Giudice & Belsky, 2010). Evolutionary theory and cross-cultural evidence also indicate that maternal and paternal investment respond in different ways to the same ecological factors (see above); thus, attachment relationships with the two parents may carry distinct types of information, conceivably influencing child development in different ways. Although some evidence suggests that insecure attachment to the mother and to the father predict different developmental outcomes (reviewed in Del Giudice, 2009), the data are still too sketchy to draw reliable conclusions. Unfortunately, the very research that now shows that early insecurity in the infant–mother relationship forecasts earlier pubertal maturation lacks measurement of infant–father attachment security.

Because of parent–offspring conflict about investment, children do not simply accept whatever parents do with them; rather, they actively try to maximize parental investment and commitment. In this vein, Chisholm (1996) proposed that children's insecure attachment styles are adaptive strategies designed to respond to different "safety threats." In the case of parents who are willing, but *unable* to consistently invest in offspring—for example because of scarce resources or competing demands on parents' time—the insecure-ambivalent strategy maximizes the available investment by increasing signaling of need, immature behavior, and emotional dependence. When parents are *unwilling* to invest, however, the insecure-avoidant strategy is favored; emotional distancing and self-reliance reduce the demands on parents, thus protecting the child from being abandoned or abused while still vulnerable. From this perspective, attachment styles are not the passive result of the child's experience with parents, but rather the outcome of an active negotiation process based on investment dynamics.

INDIVIDUAL DIFFERENCES IN PLASTICITY

A central premise of much developmental psychology focused on the family is that early experiences influence the child's future psychological and behavioral development. As a result, not only is there extensive research on how mothers, fathers, siblings, peers, child care, schooling, and even neighborhoods shape children's functioning over the short and long term, but also on the psychological, physiological, and neurological mechanisms that mediate such effects of experience on development. What is rarely considered, however, and yet is central to an evolutionary analysis of development, is why natural selection should even craft an organism whose future development is shaped by childhood experiences.

The minute one appreciates that the future always has been uncertain and will always, presumably, remain that way, there are grounds for questioning the assumption that experience shapes development. Would not this only make biological sense if contexts of development, broadly conceived, proved tolerably stable within a generation and perhaps across adjacent ones? Otherwise, how could setting one's developmental sail on the basis of the winds encountered early in life achieve a destination later in life? Unstable environments would blow the ship of development off course.

Such reasoning led Belsky (1997b,c, 2005) to hypothesize that children should vary in their susceptibility to rearing, with some being more susceptible to parenting and other experiential influences in and outside of the family and some being less susceptible. By bearing such diverse children, parents would end up hedging their bets on an uncertain future. If things turned out as consciously or unconsciously expected—both within and across generations—then a child whose development was guided by parentally shaped earlier experience should flourish; but if it did not, then it could be the child who proved less responsive to such developmental experiences who would realize a fitness advantage. Variation in susceptibility would benefit both parents and siblings, whose inclusive fitness would be increased through their relatedness to the "successful" offspring (the relatedness coefficient between siblings and between parent and offspring is 0.5, where 1.0 indicates a complete overlap of genetic interests).[1]

Boyce and Ellis (2005) have come to a similar conclusion, that children should vary in their susceptibility to rearing influences, but for different evolutionary reasons. On the basis of conditional adaptation logic, they hypothesize that those growing up in especially good conditions should be especially responsive to the environment, as this would enable them to take advantage, indeed embody, many of these resources, making them more competitive in the world in which they would eventually function. At the same time, those growing up under harsh conditions should prove highly susceptible, too, as this would promote antagonism and vigilance, making them more likely to survive and cope in the hostile world that they have been prepared to encounter. All others, according to this analysis, should prove to be more "fixed" than "plastic" strategists, to borrow Belsky's (2000, 2005) terminology.

As it turns out, evidence increasingly indicates that some individuals appear more susceptible than others to environmental influences—"for better *and* for worse," meaning that they are more likely than others to both benefit from supportive conditions *and* be adversely affected by negative conditions (Belsky, Bakermans-Kranenburg, & van IJzendoorn, 2007). Indeed, evidence indicates that this may be true of highly negatively emotional infants and toddlers, highly physiological reactive individuals, and those carrying certain genes (Belsky & Pluess, 2009; Orbadovic & Boyce, 2009). In fact, after carefully scrutinizing recent research on G×E interactions in predicting behavioral development, Belsky and associates (2009; Belsky & Pluess, 2009) have concluded that multiple alleles regarded by many psychiatric geneticists as "vulnerability genes" because they apparently increase the likelihood of psychiatric disorder in the face of stress may actually be better referred to as "plasticity genes" (Belsky et al., 2009; Belsky & Pluess, 2009). And this is because those carrying these genes not only function more poorly than all others under adverse circumstances, but function better than all others under benign and supportive conditions. The existence of plasticity genes and the resulting G×E interactions help to explain why, in behavior genetic studies, "shared" environmental effects (those which make siblings in the same family more alike) are consistently found to be small compared to "nonshared" ones. Individual differences in susceptibility also contextualize the claim, based on the findings of behavior genetics, that parental behavior has no lasting effects on children's development (e.g., Harris, 1998; Pinker, 2002). Whether parents' behavior affect a child's development seems to depend, in large part, on the child itself and his or her genetic make-up.

Children's Characteristics and the Modulation of Parental Investment

Morally upsetting as it may appear, evolution does not favor indiscriminate parental investment—or unconditional love—regardless of offspring's characteristics (Daly & Wilson, 1988). Limited resources must be allocated wisely, and parents embody evolved decision mechanisms designed to channel investment toward those offspring who offer the best chances of high fitness returns. In humans, parental discrimination may become manifest in the parent's feelings; for example, some children may elicit more affection and caring than others, even if the actual decision mechanisms work partially or completely outside the parent's awareness. Parental discrimination inevitably becomes more intense when resources are especially scarce; an extreme, dramatic example of parental discrimination is infanticide, which is especially frequent in harsh ecologies (see Hrdy, 1999). Even in more benign environments, not all children are necessarily equal in the eyes of their parents, and the consequences for children may be very real—for better or for worse. In this section, we explore three characteristics of children—sex, age, and physical resemblance to the father—that have been shown to affect parental investment across cultures.

Sex-biased Investment

Preferences for sons or daughters are extremely common in human families, yet very complex to predict and analyze. Parents can benefit from investing preferentially in children of one sex for a number of different reasons, and patterns of sex-biased investment depend in subtle ways on personal and ecological variables (Sieff, 1990). The underlying

---

[1] By a simplified account, the relatedness coefficient *r* can be defined as the probability that two individuals share the same allele at any given locus by (recent) common descent. As a probability, *r* ranges between 0 and 1. For example, in diploid species the parent–offspring relatedness is *r* = 0.5, since (with Mendelian transmission) an allele present in one of the parents has a 50% probability of ending up in any given offspring. Relatedness can be defined more generally (and rigorously) as the genetic similarity between two individuals, A and B, relative to the average genetic difference between A and a randomly chosen member of the population. Thus, *r* can be treated as a regression coefficient and can take negative values (see Grafen, 1985).

logic is that parents should prefer to invest in the sex with the best expected fitness returns. In turn, the fitness returns of a child depend on many ecological and cultural factors. For example, if daughters provide more help to their parents by caring for younger siblings, they may "repay" their investment costs more than sons; securing bridewealth is another way daughters in which may contribute to the welfare of parents and siblings. On the other hand, in some contexts, it is sons who provide more help than daughters—by, for example, providing food or economic resources and staying with the family for a longer time (e.g., because daughters marry young and then live with the husband's family). This kind of effect (known in the literature as *local resource enhancement*) has been used to explain the patterns of daughter favoritism in breastfeeding observed in Dominica (Quinlan, Quinlan, & Flinn, 2005) and in North American Hutterites (Margulis, Altmann, & Ober 1993).

Another important perspective on sex-biased parental investment is provided by the Trivers-Willard hypothesis (TWH; Trivers & Willard, 1973). The TWH stipulates that, when one sex benefits from high investment more than the other, parents in good conditions (i.e., with lots of resources to invest) should invest preferentially in that sex, whereas parents in poor conditions should invest in the other. Because males usually have higher reproductive variance than females, they benefit relatively more than females from good conditions; this is due to the fact that males in good conditions can outcompete other males. Moreover, in stratified societies, women can marry into higher classes more easily than men, and generally face less competition for mates than do low-status men; thus, parents of low social status may improve their inclusive fitness by investing in daughters, whereas high-status parents do so by investing preferentially in sons. Parents can fulfill the TWH in three independent ways: (1) by biasing the sex ratio at birth, so that mothers in poorer conditions give birth to more daughters; this can be accomplished by physiological mechanisms that respond to stress, nutritional level, and so on; (2) by selective infanticide or abandonment of neonates of one sex; and (3) by differential investment in nutrition, health, education, and in general by sex-biased distribution of family wealth.

The effect of maternal conditions (i.e., nutrition, education, socioeconomic status) on the sex ratio at birth has received some support from demographic studies in modern societies (Almond & Edlund, 2007; Chacon Puignau & Jaffe, 1996; Gibson & Mace, 2003; Mathews, Johnson, & Neil, 2008; see also Cameron & Dalerum, 2009). In some of this work, maternal conditions also predict sex biases in infant mortality (Almond & Edlund, 2007; Chacon et al., 1996; Voland, Dunbar, Engel, & Stephan, 1997), suggesting differential investment in already-born infants. However, effects tend to be rather small, and other investigations have failed to find evidence in favor of the TWH (e.g., Guggenheim, Davis, & Figueredo, 2007; Stein, Zybert, & Lumey, 2004). The TWH also provides an explanation of the fact that female infanticide has been historically more frequent in upper social strata, such as Indian high castes (Dickemann, 1979). However, it has been considerably more difficult to find consistent support for Trivers-Willard effects when measuring parental investment indicators like breastfeeding, investment in children's education and health, and so on. The strongest evidence in favor of the TWH comes from research on small-scale societies such as the Kipsigi and Mukogodo in Kenya, the Arsi Oromo in Ethiopia, the Yomut in Iran, and Hungarian Gypsies (Bereczkei & Dunbar, 1997; Borgerhoff Mulder, 1998; Cronk, 1989, 1991a,b; Irons, 2000). Cronk (2007) discusses the many theoretical and methodological difficulties involved in properly testing the TWH in large-scale industrialized societies.

An important insight emerging from evolutionary research on sex-biased investment is that parents are often unaware of their actual favoritism patterns. Marked patterns of daughter-biased investment, for example, have been found in populations in which parents express strong and culturally shared preferences for sons (Cronk, 1991a; Gibson, 2008; Pennington & Harpending, 1993). This, of course, adds to the difficulty of studying parental investment through self-report data. Finally, parents do not always agree in their preferences for sons versus daughters. Studies in various societies have found that fathers tend to invest more in sons, and mothers tend to invest more in daughters, although there are exceptions (reviewed in Gibson, 2008; Godoy et al., 2006). Godoy and colleagues (2006) proposed to explain this effect with an extension of the TWH, whereby the parent facing less resource constraints (usually the father) maximizes his (or her) fitness returns by investing in sons.

Age-related Preferences and Birth Order

In humans, mortality is highest around birth and decreases through childhood, with an all-time minimum in middle and late childhood, whereas fertility peaks in late adolescence and early adulthood. A child's *reproductive value* at a given age is his or her expected number of future offspring, and is a function of expected survival and expected reproduction; reproductive value is lowest at birth and rises steadily until early adulthood, then declines (see Sear, in press). When faced with difficult allocation decisions, parents should choose—all else being equal—to invest more in older children, whose reproductive value is highest. Preferences for older children are widespread and may have dramatic implications. Research on infanticide shows that younger children are consistently at higher risk of being killed by parents (e.g., Daly & Wilson, 1984; Hill & Hurtado, 1996). When Meryl Streep was required to give up one of her children for extermination in the film *Sophie's Choice*, about the legacy of the world War II, chances are that she would have chosen to save her older child and surrender her younger one to the Nazi murderers, had she been the real mother of a real child confronting this horrendous situation.

Firstborns are also favored when resource transfer from parents is concerned; cross-culturally, primogeniture is by far the most common pattern of inheritance. The advantages of firstborns can be counterbalanced by the fact that, as parents age, they face fewer competing demands for investment allocation (mating effort and investment in future offspring). Thus, laterborns can also end up getting a relatively large share of investment from parents, with middleborns receiving the least (see Salmon & Daly, 1998). Finally, the effects of age often interact with those of sex; for example, in societies in which sons are favored, children with many older brothers may be at special disadvantage (for extended discussion see Sear, in press).

Father–Child Resemblance

Genetic relatedness between a man and his putative children, including uncertainty about that relatedness (i.e., paternity uncertainty), is one of the crucial factors determining how much the man is expected to invest (see Chapter 11, by Goetz and Romero). Investing one's resources in a genetically unrelated child entails large fitness costs; thus, natural selection can be expected to favor discrimination and selective investment by fathers. Because females can gain material, social, and genetic benefits from extra-pair mating, cuckoldry is a real risk in most paternally investing species. To mitigate this risk, natural selection has favored psychological and behavioral mechanisms in males that function to increase paternity certainty and limit investment in unrelated offspring (e.g., Møller & Birkhead, 1993; Whittingham, Taylor, & Robertson, 1992).

One way for fathers to assess the likelihood that a child is their biological offspring is to rely on phenotypic similarity. Given the heritability of most physical traits, the more a child resembles his or her putative father, the greater the father's paternity confidence is likely to be. Greater perceived similarity, therefore, should translate into greater investment. Based on this logic, several empirical studies have tested—and confirmed—the impact of father–child similarity on paternal investment. Perceived facial resemblance in children positively predicts fathers' emotional closeness and investment (time spent with the child, involvement in the child's education; Alvergne, Faurie, & Raymond, 2010; Apicella & Marlowe, 2004, 2007; Li & Chang, 2007). There seems to be a good match between actual similarity (as rated by external judges) and fathers' perceived similarity (Alvergne et al., 2010).

The impact of similarity on paternal investment is even stronger when the father and the mother are separated; that is, when the father has no extra reasons to engage in parental care—for example, maintaining a good relationship with the mother or displaying one's good qualities as a partner (Apicella & Marlowe, 2004, 2007). Burch and Gallup (2000) found an association between perceived resemblance and the self-reported quality of father–child relationships in a sample of men who had committed domestic violence. Interestingly, phenotypic similarity seemed to affect the quality of paternal care only with respect to (possibly) biologically related children; when the child was *known* to be biologically unrelated, father–child resemblance had no significant effect.

Facial resemblance is not the only cue of phenotypic similarity available to fathers. Olfactory similarity also predicts paternal investment (Alvergne, Faurie, & Raymond, 2009), and fathers are more affectionate and attentive toward the children they can recognize by their smell (Dubas, Heijkoop, & van Aken, 2009). Some effects of olfactory recognition have been reported in mothers, too; mothers punish less frequently those children whose smell they can recognize (Dubas et al., 2009).

While discussing parent–child resemblance, it should be noted that infants and children do not, on average, resemble their parents very closely. Correct recognition rates are above chance but still far from perfect. Taken together, the empirical data suggest that children resemble both the mother and the father, with an overall tendency for newborns and infants to resemble their *mother* more than their father (see Alvergne, Faurie, & Raymond, 2007; Bressan & Grassi, 2004). In the study by Alvergne and colleagues (2007), male (but not female) children started to resemble their father more than their mother at about 2–3 years of age, an intriguing finding still in need of replication and (if confirmed) explanation.

Despite the weak resemblance between fathers and infants at birth, mothers and other maternal relatives are especially prone to attribute paternal resemblance to their newborns. This can be interpreted as a way to manipulate fathers' perception of similarity, thus increasing paternal commitment and investment (Alvergne et al., 2007; Bressan, 2002; Daly & Wilson, 1982). So far, there have been no investigations of how children who do not resemble their father react psychologically. An evolutionary-informed perspective suggests that the lack of similarity may be a specific source of distress, and that children (like their mothers) should actively manipulate their father's perception of similarity so as to maximize their commitment and parental investment.

Given that fathers are so sensitive to phenotypic similarity, should it not be the case that children evolve to resemble their biological fathers as closely as possible? The answer to this question turns out to be far from obvious. On the one hand, children benefit from advertising their identity to their putative father when he actually is the biological father; on the other, however, they also benefit from concealing their identity when the putative father is *not* the biological one. The mathematical models developed so far give contrasting results, with some models predicting increased selection for resemblance with increased paternity uncertainty (Johnstone, 1997) and others predicting the opposite effect (Bressan, 2002; Pagel, 1997). In any event, these models converge on the prediction that enhanced father–child resemblance should not evolve easily (if it can evolve at all). The benefits of concealing one's identity may account for the relatively low degree of resemblance between human infants and their fathers. Note in this regard that it might not just be nonbiological offspring who benefit from relative infant anonymity, but the cuckolding female partner as well.

Children As Providers: Caring, Helping and Exploitation

As in other animal families, the primary role of children is that of receiving investment from parents. At the same time, however, human children actively contribute to the family system as resource providers and caregivers. The anthropological literature clearly shows that daughters play a crucial role as helpers and alloparents (i.e., individuals who provide care without being the young's parents; see Hrdy, 2005). In traditional societies, women who can count on the help of daughters have higher reproductive success than do women who only have sons or young children (e.g., Flinn, 1989; Turke, 1988). Several studies show that the presence of older siblings improves child survival (Sear & Mace, 2008).

Whereas daughters often provide care to younger siblings, they can also contribute to the household economy by helping in domestic work. In traditional societies, children of both sexes spend considerable time foraging; in safe, resource-rich ecologies they may contribute substantially to their own caloric intake (see Kramer, 2005). For example, Maya children produce about 50% of what they consume by the age of 6 or 7 years (Kramer, 2002). Even though children are less efficient foragers than adults, they can devote more time to foraging because they have fewer competing activities to carry out, and the costs of helping can be relatively low compared to their fitness benefits.

The onset of juvenility, or *juvenile transition* (Del Giudice, Angeleri, & Manera, 2009), seems to be a crucial turning point in children's helping behavior. Juvenility is the biological label for middle childhood (from about 6–7 to 10–11 years of age in modern societies); it is a period of intense social learning and dramatic cognitive development, marked by specific hormonal and neurobiological changes and by the intensification of behavioral sex differences (Campbell, 2006; Del Giudice et al., 2009). For example, in the Maya population studied by Kramer (2005), juveniles play a substantial role as resource providers during the second phase of marriages (from about 10 to 20 years of marriage), when parents must support many children still living at home.

More generally, Lancy and Grove (in press) argued, based on cross-cultural evidence, that juvenility is the time when children start "getting noticed" by adults. For the first time, juveniles are assigned tasks involving expectations of responsibility. Indeed, in many societies young children are more or less ignored by adults, but as juveniles, they start to become involved in duties and chores and to assume a recognized social identity. Children help in a wide range of tasks, including gardening, herding, hunting, weaving, ceramics, and canoe-making; girls seem to undergo this transition from play to work earlier than boys (see Lancy and Grove, in press).

The importance of children's help should not lead us to ignore the fact that, because the relatedness between parents and children is only partial, the interests of parents and children do not fully coincide; in fact, at times they may clash with one another. Children's helping can take any shape from harmonious cooperation to parasitic exploitation by parents. The line is especially fine in impoverished Third World societies, in which child labor is a common and growing phenomenon. As extensively documented by Lancy (2008, ch. 10), in many countries, children are forced to begin earning their keep at younger and younger ages; the dismantling of traditional institutions and extended kin networks takes children out of the village and into the city, where the traditional, slow transition to adult work is dramatically accelerated. Moreover, the loss of social control on parents by kin members and neighbors means that child abuse can go unchecked.

Parents in harsh and unpredictable ecological conditions react by lowering their investment in children, leading to typical high mortality/high fertility patterns and unconcerned, neglectful, or abusive parenting. Parents may come to see children as a resource to exploit, in a paradoxical game in which children provide for their parents (sometimes they may be the family's primary income earners), and the border between cooperation and exploitation becomes blurred. It has been argued that, in some cases, street children may be better off by themselves (or with their siblings as caretakers) than at home with their abusive parents (e.g., Aptekar, 1992). These social and economic processes depend on a number of psychological mechanisms that are products of our evolutionary history: facultative parental investment, the modulation of LHS in response to environmental stress, and the willingness of children (especially juveniles) to help their parents and to actively engage in chores that contribute to their family's welfare.

Modern Childhood: Overprotection or Adaptive Strategy?

Anthropologists who study childhood in traditional societies are struck by the contrast between the traditional view of childhood and the modern ideal that is prevalent in the West and in East Asia. The modern ideal sees childhood as taking place in the context of a nuclear, egalitarian family in which parents share their caretaking responsibilities and unconditionally love and invest in their offspring. Every child is inherently worthy and has a right to life and happiness; the well-being of children is the primary concern of their parents, who instruct them and care for them well into adolescence. This ideal pattern is complemented by high investment in intellectual stimulation right from birth (or even before), supervised learning, formal schooling, an extended period of play and immaturity, and a protracted adolescence.

The traditional view of children is strikingly different from the modern one: children are regarded as the lowest-ranking members of the society, grow up in extended families, and are cared for by a network of individuals which includes older siblings and grandmothers (but with fathers rarely involved in direct caretaking). Selective infanticide and abandonment are relatively common, especially for children of the wrong sex or with developmental defects, making it clear that offspring are expendable. Children are largely ignored by adults and considered somewhat uninteresting as individuals, at least until they reach juvenility; they are then expected to return some of their parents' investment in the form of helping (Lancy, 2008). Of course, this does not mean that parent–child relations in traditional societies are unloving or careless, although they may appear as such to the eye of a modern Western parent (or developmental psychologist).

In the tension between these views (and between the corresponding cultural practices), modern childhood stands out as absurdly overprotected, excessively long, and even "out of touch" with our evolved dispositions. Lancy (2008) notes that "our society is a neontocracy where kids rule" (p. 373), in contrast with the gerontocratic organization of traditional cultures. This, however, may be a premature conclusion: In fact, the Western pattern of hyperinvestment in children could reflect an adaptive strategy responding to recent dramatic changes in social and ecological conditions. Modern industrialized societies have extremely low mortality rates (especially in the first years of life), and the most common sources of extrinsic mortality/morbidity (diseases, warfare, predation) are greatly reduced compared with their premodern levels. This alone should push LHS toward high levels of parental investment.

In parallel, social competition increases and technology becomes more sophisticated. Both high-level jobs and daily living require unprecedented amounts of cognitive flexibility and information manipulation (Gottfredson, 2007). As a result, children become more costly, and the main currency of parental investment becomes education. Because of reduced environmental harshness and increased need for high-quality cognitive skills, the threshold of diminishing returns for parental investment is shifted upward. The predicted outcome is a reduction in fertility and a corresponding increase in the amount of parental investment expended on each child (e.g., Kaplan, 1996; Kaplan & Lancaster, 2000; Shenk, 2009). This facultative plastic response of life history–related psychological mechanisms may capitalize on recent genetic selection for increased biparental care and higher cognitive flexibility, driven by the social and environmental changes brought about by agriculture (Cochran & Harpending, 2009).

In summary, modern childhood may turn out to be—at least in part—an adaptive response to modern environments. From an evolutionary standpoint, idealizing traditional childrearing could be just as myopic as taking for granted the romantic worldview criticized earlier. Children in traditional societies learn casually and mostly by observation rather than through formal schooling; but then, they only need to master a fraction of the knowledge required for successful living in a stratified and technologically advanced society. Likewise, intellectual stimulation from infancy and an extended phase of play and exploration may be advantageous in a competitive and fast-changing society where creativity, flexibility, and innovation are highly rewarded.

The Family Within: Imprinted Genes and Parent–Child Conflict

So far, we have discussed how investment dynamics are played out by individuals whose genetic interests are partly conflicting. Evolutionary genetics, however, shows that conflicts of interest run much deeper than that: In fact, conflicts about parental investment can arise not only between parents and children, but also between different genes *within the child*—specifically, between genes inherited from the mother and genes inherited from the father. This form of intragenomic conflict derives from the special characteristics of imprinted genes, and its evolutionary implications are spelled out in the *kinship theory* of genomic imprinting (Haig, 1997, 2004; Wilkins & Haig, 2003).

The Kinship Theory of Imprinting

A gene is said to be *imprinted* if its expression depends on its parent of origin (i.e., on whether it was contained in an ovum or a sperm). For example, *IGF2* (a gene coding for an important growth factor) is paternally expressed in humans, and its homologues are paternally expressed in various mammals including rats, mice, and sheep. This means that although every individual inherits two copies of the gene (one from each parent), only the paternally derived copy is actually expressed, whereas the maternally derived one is silenced and has no effect on the organism's development. Gene silencing is accomplished through reversible epigenetic mechanisms; complex imprinting patterns can be observed as, for example, some genes show parent-specific expression only in specific cell types or only during certain phases of development. To date, imprinted genes have only been found in mammals and angiosperm plants; according to current estimates, less than 1% of the mammalian genome is imprinted (Wilkins, 2008).

Let us consider parent–offspring conflict from the perspective of imprinted genes. A maternally derived allele in the offspring has a 50% probability of ending up in a future sibling. But if there is any degree of multiple paternity, this probability will be lower than 50% (possibly much lower). In other words, the relatedness between siblings is *asymmetric* when one looks at the maternal and paternal halves of the genome. For imprinted genes, this phenomenon has remarkable implications: Because a paternally expressed gene is always less strongly related to future siblings than its maternally expressed counterparts, it can be expected to function in a way that discounts the well-being of future siblings to the benefit of the individual offspring in which it resides. Thus, paternally expressed genes are expected to "side" with the offspring in the (up) regulation of maternal investment, and to evolve so as to increase the transfer of maternal resources to the offspring—for example, by increasing the rate of fetal growth. Maternally expressed genes are expected to evolve in the opposite direction, thus inhibiting the transfer of maternal resources to the offspring (so as to conserve resources for future offspring or those already born). The intensity of conflict between maternally and paternally expressed genes is expected to increase with increasing likelihood of multiple paternity, and can be completely avoided only in truly monogamous mating systems (that is, in exceedingly rare conditions).

In summary, the kinship theory of imprinting predicts that paternally expressed genes will evolve as "resource enhancers," increasing maternal investment toward the individual offspring; they are also expected to increase the demand behavior of offspring in direct sibling competition. In contrast, maternally expressed genes should become "resource inhibitors" and reduce the individual offspring's demands in order to favor siblings as a group (Haig & Wilkins, 2000). In species like humans, in which both mothers and fathers provide parental investment, the *generalized kinship theory* developed by Úbeda (2008) predicts that the effects of imprinted genes should *reverse* later in development (typically after weaning), with paternally expressed genes reducing offspring demands and maternally expressed genes increasing them. In other words, paternal genes should increase the offspring's cost when the mother is investing the most (i.e., during pregnancy and lactation), but reduce the offspring's cost as soon as the father's own contribution increases. Crucially, such reversal is expected even if the father always contributes less than the mother—all it takes is a *relative* increase in paternal investment over the course of development.

The Role of Imprinted Genes in Human Development

Many imprinted genes are involved in the regulation of fetal growth and affect the level of maternal investment before birth. Examples include the insulin-like growth factor II gene (*IGF2*; paternally expressed); *H19* (maternally expressed), which acts as a suppressor of the action of *IGF2*; and the placental gene *IPL* (also maternally expressed), which prevents placental overgrowth (see Haig, 2004). Many imprinted genes, however, are active after birth, and a substantial proportion are expressed in the brain (Isles, Davies, & Wilkinson, 2006). Thus, imprinted genes may continue to participate in the regulation of investment dynamics by affecting infant and child behavior. Likely targets of genetic action are hunger and food preferences, but several other behaviors can potentially act as resource enhancers/inhibitors—including crying, attention-seeking, emotional dysregulation, dependency, and so on (Brown & Consedine, 2004; Isles et al., 2006). Indirect evidence suggests that imprinted genes are probably involved in the regulation of critical neurotransmitter systems such as dopamine, serotonin, and γ-aminobutyric acid (GABA). Even more intriguingly, there are cues that imprinted genes may exert an impact on the oxytocin and vasopressin systems, which are crucially involved in the neurobiology of parent–child attachment (Davies, Lynn, Relkovic, & Wilkinson, 2008).

At present, most of the empirical evidence for behavioral effects of imprinted genes in human children comes from the study of two imprinting-related syndromes caused by mutations or deletions on the long arm of chromosome 15, Angelman syndrome (AS) and Prader-Willi syndrome (PWS). These disorders result from opposite patterns of genetic disruption and, as predicted by the kinship theory, show broadly opposite effects on infant investment demands (see Brown & Consedine, 2004; Crespi & Badcock, 2008; Úbeda, 2008). Angelman syndrome, resulting from paternal overexpression and/or maternal underexpression, is associated with increased demands on the mother (e.g., enhanced activity, prolonged suckling, bouts of laughter, and sleeping problems), whereas PWS, resulting from maternal overexpression and/or paternal underexpression, is associated with reduced demands on the mother (e.g., decreased activity, poor suckling, undergrowth, weak crying, and sleepiness). In PWS, hunger regulation changes dramatically after infancy, with PWS-affected children developing insatiable appetites and often becoming obese. An early explanation for this inversion is that the child's growing appetite for other kinds of food reduces consumption of breast milk, thus lowering the metabolic burden on the mother (Haig & Wharton, 2003). However, the generalized kinship theory (Úbeda, 2008) provides a more elegant explanation, as the reversal of genetic effects observed between infancy and childhood is fully consistent with the pattern predicted by the theory. Overexpression of maternal genes is expected to reduce offspring's demands during infancy, when the mother's relative contribution is highest (e.g., poor suckling and undergrowth reduce the cost of lactation), but increase them when the father's relative contribution becomes more substantial (e.g., weaned children can feed on paternally provided food).

We have just begun to understand the implications of genomic imprinting for the development of children's behavior and parent–child relations—and so far there has been virtually no application of these ideas to mainstream developmental psychology. Imprinted genes participate in the key neurobiological processes underlying emotional regulation, attachment, and social behavior. Human family life is complex, and parental investment in our species can extend for very long periods of time and even through multiple generations. It is thus reasonable to anticipate that imprinted genes will be found to affect a wide range of processes, including parent–child attachment, adolescent conflict, and the development of psychopathology.

Crespi and Badcock (2008) reviewed a large body of evidence linking imprinted genes to the etiology of autism and psychosis, and proposed that autistic spectrum conditions are associated with a "paternally biased" pattern of brain development (i.e., overexpression of paternal genes and/or underexpression of maternal genes), whereas psychotic spectrum syndromes would be associated with a "maternally biased" development (see Del Giudice et al., 2010, for a sexual selection perspective on the evolution of autism- and psychosis-related personality traits and the associated imprinted patterns). Haig (2010) proposed that imprinted genes could have been conspicuously involved in the evolution of several key features of the human life history, such as early weaning and slow childhood growth (see Chapter 2, by Flinn); finally, a recent model by Úbeda and Gardner (2010) linked imprinted genes to the development of altruism versus selfishness in children.

Conclusion

Long, emotionally intense parent–child relationships are a defining feature of our species and a crucial aspect of our psychology. Adopting the perspective of investment dynamics makes it possible to build a sophisticated general theory of these relationships. The evolutionary framework presented here gives meaning and organization to many psychological phenomena at different levels of analysis—from the impact of macroecological factors on parents' behavior to the subtleties of genomic imprinting and G×E interactions. As we anticipated, evolutionary-informed predictions are often in good agreement with mainstream developmental psychology—for example, both emphasize the role of harsh environments in determining negative parenting and insecure parent–child relations. The evolutionary approach puts these findings in a broader perspective and adds specificity to the theory, for example by singling out *extrinsic mortality-morbidity* and *unpredictability* as crucial features of the environment—among many possible others—that parents and children use to calibrate their life history strategies. In other instances (e.g., father–child resemblance), evolutionary predictions have some correspondence in folk knowledge, but took an explicitly biological focus to be precisely articulated and tested. Finally, several of the most intriguing phenomena described here simply could not be discovered (or understood) without the benefit of an evolutionary approach. They include the effect of early parent–child relations on puberty timing, the conflict between maternal and paternal genes in determining infant behavior, and the existence of differential susceptibility to the rearing environment.

Concentrating on individual phenomena, however, is not the best way to appreciate the contribution of evolutionary theory to the understanding of family relations. The real promise of evolutionary psychology lies in its integrative nature: What could be a collection of weakly related phenomena, hypotheses, and mini-theories turns into a well connected and hierarchically structured theoretical edifice. Most importantly for developmental psychologists, inhabiting that edifice does not require one to throw away the empirical yield of decades of research; rather, old insights find new explanations, previous knowledge is transformed and connected in unexpected ways, and new opportunities for discovery are revealed. Careful biological reasoning is also a powerful antidote to idealistic distortions of childhood and parenthood, to which—as experience shows—it is very easy to succumb. The psychology of parent–child relationships can no longer afford to remain disconnected from its biological roots.

Future Directions

One of the most important tasks for the next future will be to explore and clarify the relations between what we have called "investment dynamics" and "affective dynamics." Attachment theory can be thoroughly redescribed in an evolutionary perspective (e.g., Simpson & Belsky, 2008), thus raising a number of interesting and still unasked questions: What is the relationship between parents' life history strategies and children's attachment styles? How do factors such as children's sex and parent–child resemblance affect the formation and development of emotional bonds? What behaviors on children's part may be interpreted as attempts to gather reliable information about the local ecology? Which emotional systems are involved in these processes? How do macro- and microecological factors interact to shape attachment security? And so on. Evolutionary psychology may provide excellent theoretical foundations to the study of development, but it will not be embraced until it can be readily connected to the emotional life of parents and children.

Another crucial and under-researched topic is that of the decision-making mechanisms mediating parental investment. Evolutionary models make predictions about parental behavior, but they do not specify the proximate mechanisms that enable adaptive decision-making. In part, decision processes can be expected to work automatically and outside consciousness; in many cases, however, they may also depend on conscious thought and deliberate reasoning. These two levels may act synergistically, but disconnections are also possible (see, for example, the section on sex-biased investment). In addition to understanding how these mechanisms work, it would be extremely interesting to understand when a given decision-making process should be carried out automatically—and when it should be *designed* so as to remain out of the parent's awareness. The same questions can be asked of decision-making in children; for example, is deliberate reasoning involved in the behavioral manifestations of LHS? Do children possess conscious representations of environmental unpredictability and other life history–relevant parameters, and will changes in these representations feed back on children's behavioral strategies?

Finally, future progress in this area will depend on tighter integration with neurobiology and genetics. Parent–child relations are mediated by intricate neural and hormonal systems, which in turn depend on genetic expression and regulation. Modern genetics is sophisticated enough to deal with individual differences in plasticity, experience-dependent epigenetic regulation, and conflict between maternal and paternal genes. Evolutionary endocrinology (Ellison & Grey, 2009) and evolutionary neuroscience (Platek & Shackelford, 2009) are rapidly advancing fields that can bring invaluable contributions to the study of family relations.

References

Almond, D., & Edlund, L. (2007). Trivers–Willard at birth and one year: Evidence from US natality data 1983–2001. *Proceedings of the Royal Society of London B, 274*, 2491–2496.

Alvergne, A., Faurie, C., & Raymond, M. (2007). Differential facial resemblance of young children to their parents: Who do children look like more? *Evolution and Human Behavior, 28*, 135–144.

Alvergne, A., Faurie, C., & Raymond, M. (2009). Father–offspring resemblance predicts paternal investment in humans. *Animal Behaviour, 78*, 61–69.

Alvergne, A., Faurie, C., & Raymond, M. (2010). Are parents' perceptions of offspring facial resemblance consistent with actual resemblance? Effects on parental investment. *Evolution and Human Behavior, 31*, 7–15.

Apicella, C. L., & Marlowe, F.W. (2004). Perceived mate fidelity and paterna resemblance predict men's investment in children. *Evolution and Human Behavior, 25*, 371–378.

Apicella, C.L., & Marlowe, F.W. (2007). Men's reproductive investment decisions. Mating, parenting and self-perceived mate value. *Human Nature, 18*, 22–34.

Aptekar, L. (1992). Are Colombian street children neglected? The contributions of ethnographic and ethnohistorical approaches to the study of children. *Anthropology and Education Quarterly, 22*, 326–349.

Belsky, J. (1984). The determinants of parenting: A process model. *Child Development, 55*, 83–96.

Belsky, J. (1997a). Attachment, mating, and parenting: An evolutionary interpretation. *Human Nature, 8*, 361–381.

Belsky, J. (1997b). Theory testing, effect-size evaluation, and differential susceptibility to rearing influence: The case of mothering and attachment. *Child Development, 68*, 598–600.

Belsky, J. (1997c). Variation in susceptibility to rearing influences: An evolutionary argument. *Psychological Inquiry, 8*, 182–186.

Belsky, J. (2000). Conditional and Alternative Reproductive Strategies: Individual Differences in Susceptibility to Rearing Experience. In J. Rodgers, D. Rowe, & W. Miller (Eds.), *Genetic influences on human fertility and sexuality: Theoretical and empirical contributions from the biological and behavioral sciences* (pp. 127–146). Boston, MA: Kluwer.

Belsky, J. (2005). Differential susceptibility to rearing influences: An evolutionary hypothesis and some evidence. In B. Ellis, & D. Bjorklund (Eds.), *Origins of the social mind: Evolutionary psychology and child development* (pp. 139–163). New York: Guildford.

Belsky, J., Bakermans-Kranenburg, M.J., & van IJzendoorn, M.H. (2007). For better and for worse: Differential susceptibility to environmental influences. *Current Directions in Psychological Science, 16*, 300–304.

Belsky, J., Houts, R., & Fearon, R.M.P. (2010). Infant attachment security and timing of puberty: Testing an evolutionary hypothesis. *Psychological Science, 21*, 1195–1201.

Belsky, J., Jonassaint, C., Pluess, M., Stanton, M., Brummett, B., & Williams, R. (2009). Vulnerability genes or plasticity genes? *Molecular Psychiatry, 14*, 746–754.

Belsky, J., & Pluess, M. (2009). Beyond diathesis-stress: Differential susceptibility to environmental influences. *Psychological Bulletin, 135*, 885–908.

Belsky, J., Steinberg, L., & Draper, P. (1991). Childhood experience, interpersonal development, and reproductive strategy: An evolutionary theory of socialization. *Child Development, 62*, 647–670.

Belsky, J., Steinberg, L.D., Houts, R.M., Friedman, S.L., DeHart, G., Cauffman, E., et al. (2007). Family rearing antecedents of pubertal timing. *Child Development, 78*, 1302–1321.

Bereczkei, T., & Dunbar, R.I.M. (1997). Female-biased reproductive strategies in a Hungarian Gypsy population. *Proceedings of the Royal Society of London B, 264*, 26417–26422.

Bjorklund, D.F., & Pellegrini, A.D. (2000). Child development and evolutionary psychology. *Child Development, 71*, 1687–1708.

Blurton Jones, N.G., Marlowe, F.W., Hawkes, K., & O'Connell, J.F. (2000). Paternal investment and hunter-gatherer divorce rates. In L. Cronk, N. Chagnon, & W. Irons (Eds.), *Adaptation and human behavior: An anthropological perspective* (pp. 69–90). New York: Aldine De Gruyter.

Borgerhoff Mulder, M. (1998). Brothers and sisters: How sibling interactions affect optimal parental allocations. *Human Nature, 9*, 119–161.

Bowlby, J. (1969/1982). *Attachment and loss. Vol. 1. Attachment.* New York: Basic Books.

Bowlby, J. (1973). *Attachment and loss. Vol. 2. Separation.* New York: Basic Books.

Bowlby, J. (1980). *Attachment and loss. Vol. 3. Loss*. New York: Basic Books.

Boyce, W.T., & Ellis, B.J. (2005). Biological sensitivity to context: I. An evolutionary-developmental theory of the origins and functions of stress reactivity. *Development and Psychopathology, 17*(2), 271–301.

Bressan, P. (2002). Why babies look like their daddies: Paternity uncertainty and the evolution of self-deception in evaluating family resemblance. *Acta Ethologica, 4*, 113–118.

Bressan, P., & Grassi, M. (2004). Parental resemblance in 1-year-olds and the Gaussian curve. *Evolution and Human Behavior, 25*, 133–141.

Bronfenbrenner, U. (1979). *The ecology of human development*. Cambridge, MA: Harvard University Press.

Brown, W.M., & Consedine, N.S. (2004). Just how happy is the happy puppet? An emotion signalling and kinship theory perspective on the behavioural phenotype of children with Angelman syndrome. *Medical Hypotheses, 63*, 377–385.

Brussoni, M.J., Lang, K., Livesley, W.J., & Macbeth, T.M. (2000). Genetic and environmental influences on adult attachment styles. *Personal Relationships, 7*, 283–289.

Burch, R.L., & Gallup, G.G., Jr. (2000). Perceptions of paternal resemblance predict family violence. *Evolution and Human Behavior, 21*, 429–435.

Cameron, E.Z., & Dalerum, F. (2009). A Trivers-Willard effect in contemporary humans: Male-biased sex ratios among billionaires. *Public Library of Science ONE, 4*, e4195.

Campbell, B. (2006). Adrenarche and the evolution of human life history. *American Journal of Human Biology, 18*, 569–589.

Cassidy, J., & Shaver, P.R. (Eds.) (2008), *Handbook of attachment: Theory, research and clinical applications* (2nd ed.). New York: Guilford.

Chacon Puignau, G.C., & Jaffe, K. (1996). Sex ratio at birth deviations in modern Venezuela: The Trivers-Willard effect. *Social Biology, 43*, 257–270.

Chisholm, J.S. (1993). Death, hope, and sex: Life-history theory and the development of reproductive strategies. *Current Anthropology, 34*, 1–24.

Chisholm, J.S. (1996). The evolutionary ecology of attachment organization. *Human Nature, 7*, 1–38.

Chisholm, J.S. (1999). *Death, hope and sex: Steps to an evolutionary ecology of mind and morality*. New York: Cambridge University Press.

Cochran, G., & Harpending, H. (2009). *The 10,000 year explosion. How civilization accelerated human evolution*. New York: Basic Books.

Crespi, B., & Badcock, C. (2008). Psychosis and autism as diametrical disorders of the social brain. *Behavioral and Brain Sciences, 31*, 241–320.

Cronk, L. (1989). Low socioeconomic status and female-biased parental investment: The Mukogodo example. *American Anthropologist, 91*, 414–429.

Cronk, L. (1991a). Intention vs. behaviour in parental sex preferences among the Mukogodo of Kenya. *Journal of Biosocial Science, 23*, 229–240.

Cronk, L. (1991b). Preferential parental investment in daughters over sons. *Human Nature, 2*, 387–417.

Cronk, L. (2007). Boy or girl: Gender preferences from a Darwinian point of view. *Reproductive Biomedicine Online, 15*, 23–32.

Daly, M., & Wilson, M.I. (1982). Whom are newborn babies said to resemble? *Ethology and Sociobiology, 3*, 69–78.

Daly, M., & Wilson, M. (1984). A sociobiological analysis of human infanticide. In G. Hausfater, & S.B. Hrdy (Eds.), *Infanticide: Comparative and evolutionary perspectives* (pp. 487–502). New York: Aldine de Gruyter.

Daly, M., & Wilson, M. (1988). The Darwinian psychology of discriminative parental solicitude. *Nebraska Symposium on Motivation, 35*, 91–144.

Davies, W., Lynn, P.M.Y., Relkovic, D., & Wilkinson, L.S. (2008). Imprinted genes and neuroendocrine function. *Frontiers in Neuroendocrinology, 29*, 413–427.

Del Giudice, M. (2009). Sex, attachment, and the development of reproductive strategies. *Behavioral and Brain Sciences, 32*, 1–67.

Del Giudice, M., Angeleri, R., & Manera, V. (2009). The juvenile transition: A developmental switch point in human life history. *Developmental Review, 29*, 1–31.

Del Giudice, M., Angeleri, R., Brizio, A., & Elena, M.R. (2010). The evolution of autistic-like and schizotypal traits: A sexual selection hypothesis. *Frontiers in Psychology, 1*, 41.

Del Giudice, M., & Belsky, J. (2010). The development of life history strategies: Toward a multi-stage theory. In D.M. Buss, & P.H. Hawley (Eds.), *The evolution of personality and individual differences* (pp. 154–176). Oxford, UK: Oxford University Press.

Dickemann, M. (1979). Female infanticide, reproductive strategies and social stratification: A preliminary model. In N.A. Chagnon, & W. Irons (Eds.), *Evolutionary biology and human social behaviour* (pp. 321–367). North Scituate, RI: Duxbury Press.

Dubas, J.S., Heijkoop, M., & van Aken, M.A.G. (2009). A preliminary investigation of parent–progeny olfactory recognition and parental investment. *Human Nature, 20*, 80–92.

Ein-Dor, T., Mikulincer, M., Doron, G., & Shaver, P.R. (2010). The attachment paradox: How can so many of us (the insecure ones) have no adaptive advantages? *Perspectives on Psychological Science, 5*, 126–141.

Ellis, B.J. (2004). Timing of pubertal maturation in girls: An integrated life history approach. *Psychological Bulletin, 130*, 920–958.

Ellis, B.J., & Essex, M.J. (2007). Family environments, adrenarche and sexual maturation: A longitudinal test of a life history model. *Child Development, 78*, 1799–1817.

Ellis, B.J., Jackson, J.J., & Boyce, W.T. (2006). The stress response system: Universality and adaptive individual differences. *Developmental Review, 26*, 175–212.

Ellis, B.J., Figueredo, A.J., Brumbach, B.H., & Schlomer, G.L. (2009). The impact of harsh versus unpredictable environments on the evolution and development of life history strategies. *Human Nature, 20*, 204–268.

Ellison, P.T., & Grey, P.B. (2009). *Endocrinology of social relationships*. Cambridge, MA: Harvard University Press.

Figueredo, A.J., Vásquez, G., Brumbach, B.H., & Schneider, S.M.R. (2004). The heritability of life history strategy: The K-factor, covitality, and personality. *Social Biology, 51*, 121–143.

Flinn, M.V. (1989). Household composition and female reproductive strategies. In A. Rasa, C. Vogel, & E. Voland (Eds.), *Sexual and reproductive strategies*, pp. 206–233. London: Chapman and Hall.

Fraley, R.C. (2002). Attachment stability from infancy to adulthood: Meta-analysis and dynamic modeling of developmental mechanisms. *Personality and Social Psychology Review, 6*, 123–151.

Geary, D.C. (2002). Sexual selection and human life history. *Advances in Child Development and Behavior, 30,* 41–101.

Geary, D.C. (2005). Evolution of paternal investment. In D.M. Buss (Ed.), *The evolutionary psychology handbook* (pp. 483–505). Hoboken, NJ: John Wiley & Sons.

Gibson, M.A. (2008). Does investment in the sexes differ when fathers are absent? *Human Nature, 19,* 263–276.

Gibson, M.A., & Mace, R. (2003). Strong mothers bear more sons in rural Ethiopia. *Proceedings of the Royal Society of London B, 270,* S108–S109.

Godoy, R., Rejer-García, V., McDade, T., Tanner, S., Leonard, W.R., Huanca, T., Vadez, V., & Patel, K. (2006). *Human Nature, 17,* 169–189.

Gottfredson, L.S. (2007). Innovation, fatal accidents, and the evolution of general intelligence. In M.J. Roberts (Ed.), *Integrating the mind: Domain general versus domain specific processes in higher cognition* (pp. 387–425). Hove, UK: Psychology Press.

Grafen, A. (1985). A geometric view of relatedness. *Oxford Surveys in evolutionary Biology, 2,* 28–90.

Guggenheim, C.B., Davis, M.F., & Figueredo, A.J. (2007). Sons or daughters: A cross-cultural study of sex ratio biasing and differential parental investment. *Journal of the Arizona-Nevada Academy of Science, 39,* 73–90.

Haig, D. (1997). Parental antagonism, relatedness asymmetries, and genomic imprinting. *Proceedings of the Royal Society of London B, 264,* 1657–1662.

Haig, D. (2004). Genomic imprinting and kinship: How good is the evidence? *Annual Review of Genetics, 38,* 553–585.

Haig, D. (2010). Transfers and transitions: Parent–offspring conflict, genomic imprinting, and the evolution of human life history. *Proceedings of the National Academy of Sciences, 107,* 1731–1735.

Haig, D., & Wharton, R. (2003). Prader-Willi syndrome and the evolution of human childhood. *American Journal of Human Biology, 15,* 320–329.

Haig, D., & Wilkins, J.F. (2000) Genomic imprinting, sibling solidarity, and the logic of collective action. *Philosophical Transactions of the Royal Society of London B, 355,* 1593–1597.

Harris, J. R. (1998). *The Nurture Assumption: Why Children Turn Out the Way They Do.* New York: The Free Press.

Hill, K. (1993). Life history theory and evolutionary anthropology. *Evolutionary Anthropology, 2,* 78–88.

Hill, K., & Hurtado, A.M. (1996). *Ache life history: The ecology and demography of a foraging people.* New York: Aldine de Gruyter.

Hrdy, S.B. (1999). *Mother nature.* New York: Pantheon.

Hrdy, S.B. (2005. Evolutionary context of human development: The cooperative breeding model. In C.S. Carter, L. Ahnert, K.E. Grossmann, S.B. Hrdy, M.E. Lamb, S.W. Porges, & N. Sachser (Eds.), *Attachment and bonding: A new synthesis* (pp. 9–32). Cambridge, MA: MIT Press.

Irons, W. (2000). Why do the Yomut raise more sons than daughters? In L. Cronk, N. Chagnon, & W. Irons (Eds.), *Adaptation and human behavior: An anthropological perspective* (pp. 223–236). New York: Aldine De Gruyter.

Isles, A.R., Davies, W., & Wilkinson, L.S. (2006). Genomic imprinting and the social brain. *Philosophical Transactions of the Royal Society B, 361,* 2229–2237.

Johnstone, R.A. (1997). Recognition and the evolution of distinctive signatures: When does it pay to reveal identity? *Proceedings of the Royal Society of London B, 264,* 1547–1553.

Kaplan, H. (1996). A theory of fertility and parental investment in traditional and modern human societies. *Yearbook of Physical Anthropology, 39,* 91–135.

Kaplan, H.S., & Gangestad, S.W. (2005). Life history theory and evolutionary psychology. In D.M. Buss (Ed.) *Handbook of evolutionary psychology* (pp. 68–95). Hoboken, NJ: Wiley.

Kaplan, H., & Lancaster, J. (2000). The evolutionary economics and psychology of the demographic transition to low fertility. In L. Cronk, N. Chagnon, & W. Irons (Eds.), *Adaptation and human behavior: An anthropological perspective* (pp. 283–322). New York: Aldine De Gruyter.

Kokko, H., & Jennions, M. (2008). Parental investment, sexual selection and sex ratios. *Journal of Evolutionary Biology, 21,* 919–948.

Kramer, K.L. (2002). Variation in juvenile dependence: Helping behavior among Maya children. *Human Nature, 13,* 299–325.

Kramer, K.L. (2005). Children's help and the pace of reproduction: Cooperative breeding in humans. *Evolutionary Anthropology, 14,* 224–237.

Kruger, D., & Schlemmer, E. (2009a). When men are scarce, good men are even harder to find: Life history, the sex ratio, and the proportion of men married. *Journal of Social, Evolutionary, and Cultural Psychology, 3,* 93–104.

Kruger, D., & Schlemmer, E. (2009b). Male scarcity is differentially related to male marital likelihood across the life course. *Evolutionary Psychology, 7,* 280–287.

Lancy, D.F. (2008). *The anthropology of childhood. Cherubs, chattel, changelings.* New York: Oxford University Press.

Lancy, D.F., & Grove, M.A. (in press). Getting noticed: Middle childhood in cross-cultural perspective. *Human Nature.*

Li, H., & Chang, L. (2007). Paternal harsh parenting in relation to paternal versus child characteristics: The moderating effect of paternal resemblance belief. *Acta Psychologica Sinica, 39,* 495–501.

Margulis, S.W., Altmann, J., & Ober, C. (1993). Sex-biased lactational duration in a human population and its reproductive costs. *Behavioural Ecology and Sociobiology, 32,* 41–45.

Marlowe, F. (2000). Paternal investment and the human mating system. *Behavioural Processes, 51,* 45–61.

Marlowe, F. (2003). The mating system of foragers in the standard cross-cultural sample. *Cross-Cultural Research, 37,* 282–306.

Mathews, F., Johnson, P.J., & Neil, A. (2008). You are what your mother eats: Evidence for maternal preconception diet influencing foetal sex in humans. *Proceedings of the Royal Society of London B, 275,* 1661–1668.

McLoyd, V.C. (1990). The impact of economic hardship on black families and children. *Child Development, 61,* 311–346.

McNamara, J.M., & Houston, A.I. (1996). State-dependent life histories. *Nature, 380,* 215–221.

Mendle, J., Turkheimer, E., D'Onofrio, B.M., Lynch, S.K., Emery, R.E., Slutske. W.S., & Martin, N.G. (2006). Family structure and age at menarche: A children-of-twins approach. *Developmental Psychology, 42,* 533–542.

Mendle, J., Harden, K.P., Turkheimer, E., Van Hulle, C.A., D'Onofrio, B.M., Brooks-Gunn, J., et al. (2009). Associations between father absence and age of first sexual intercourse. *Child Development, 80,* 1463–1480.

Messner, S.F., & Sampson, R.J. (1990). The sex ratio, family disruption, and rates of violent crime: The paradox of demographic structure. *Social Forces, 69,* 693–713.

Møller, A.P., & Birkhead, T.R. (1993). Certainty of paternity covaries with paternal care in birds. *Behavioral Ecology and Sociobiology, 33*, 261–268.

Obradovic, J., & Boyce, W.T. (2009). Individual differences in behavioral, physiological, and genetic sensitivities to contexts: Implications for development and adaptation. *Developmental Neuroscience, 31*, 300–308.

Pagel, M. (1997). Desperately concealing father: A theory of parent–infant resemblance. *Animal Behaviour, 53*, 973–981.

Penke (2010). Bridging the gap between modern evolutionary psychology and the study of individual differences. In D.M. Buss, & P.H. Hawley (Eds.), *The evolution of personality and individual differences*. New York: Oxford University Press.

Pennington, R., & Harpending, H. (1988). Fitness and fertility among Kalahari! Kung. *American Journal of Physical Anthropology, 77*, 303–319.

Pennington, R., & Harpending, H. (1993). *The structure of an African pastoralist community: Demography, history and ecology of the Ngamiland Herero*. Oxford, UK: Clarendon Press.

Pinker, S. (2002). *The blank slate: The modern denial of human nature*. London: Penguin.

Platek, S.M., & Shackelford, T.K. (2009). *Foundations in evolutionary cognitive neuroscience*. New York: Cambridge University Press.

Quinlan, R.J. (2007). Human parental effort and environmental risk. *Proceedings of the Royal Society of London B, 274*, 121–125.

Quinlan, R.J. (2008). Human pair-bonds: Evolutionary functions, ecological variation, and adaptive development. *Evolutionary Anthropology, 17*, 227–238.

Quinlan, R.J., Quinlan, M.B., & Flinn, M.V. (2005). Local resource enhancement and sex-biased breastfeeding in a Caribbean community. *Current Anthropology, 46*, 471–480.

Rowe, D.C. (2000). Environmental and genetic influences on pubertal development: Evolutionary life history traits? In J.L. Rodgers, D.C Rowe, & W.B. Miller (Eds.), *Genetic influences on human fertility and sexuality: Recent empirical and theoretical findings* (pp. 147–168). Boston, MA: Kluwer.

Salmon, C.A., & Daly, M. (1998). Birth order and familial sentiment: Middleborns are different. *Evolution and Human Behavior, 19*, 299–312.

Schmitt, D.P. (2005). Sociosexuality from Argentina to Zimbabwe: A 48-nation study of sex, culture, and strategies of human mating. *Behavioral and Brain Sciences, 28*, 247–311.

Schmitt, D.P., Alcalay, L., Allensworth, M., Allik, J., Ault, L., Austers, I., et al. (2003). Are men universally more dismissing than women? Gender differences in romantic attachment across 62 cultural regions. *Personal Relationships, 10*, 307–331.

Sear, R. (in press. Parenting and families. In V. Swami (Ed.), *Evolutionary psychology: A critical introduction*. Oxford, UK: Wiley-Blackwell.

Sear. R., & Mace, R. (2008). Who keeps children alive? A review of the effects of kin on child survival. *Evolution and Human Behavior, 29*, 1–18.

Shenk, M.K. (2009). Testing three evolutionary models of the demographic transition: Patterns of fertility and age at marriage in urban South India. *American Journal of Human Biology, 21*, 501–511.

Sieff, D.F. (1990). Explaining biased sex ratios in human populations: A critique of recent studies. *Current Anthropology, 31*, 25–48.

Simpson, J.A., & Belsky, J. (2008). Attachment theory within a modern evolutionary framework. In P.R. Shaver, & J. Cassidy (Eds.), *Handbook of attachment: Theory, research, and clinical applications* (2nd ed.). New York: Guilford.

Stein, A.D., Zybert, P.A., & Lumey, L.H. (2004). Acute undernutrition is not associated with excess of females at birth in humans: The Dutch Hunger Winter. *Proceedings of the Royal Society of London B, 271*, S138–S141.

Tither, J.M., & Ellis, B.J. (2008). Impact of fathers on daughters' age at menarche: A genetically- and environmentally-controlled sibling study. *Developmental Psychology, 44*, 1409–1420.

Trivers, R.L. (1972). Parental investment and sexual selection. In B. Campbell (Ed.), *Sexual selection and the descent of man 1871–1971* (pp. 136–179). Chicago, IL: Aldine.

Trivers, R.L. (1974). Parent-offspring conflict. *American Zoologist, 14*, 249–264.

Trivers, R.L., & Willard, D.E. (1973). Natural selection of parental ability to vary the sex ratio of offspring. *Science, 17*, 990–992.

Turke, P. (1988). Helpers at the nest: Childcare networks on Ifaluk. In L. Betzig, M. Borgerhoff Mulder, & P. Turke (Eds.), *Human reproductive behavior* (pp. 173–188). Cambridge, MA: Cambridge University Press.

Úbeda, F. (2008). Evolution of genomic imprinting with biparental care: Implications for Prader-Willi and Angelman syndromes. *Public Library of Science Biology, 6*, 1678–1692.

Úbeda, F., & Gardner, A. (2010). A model for genomic imprinting in the social brain: Juveniles. *Evolution, 64*, 2587–2600.

Voland, E., Dunbar, R.I.M., Engel, C., & Stephan, P. (1997). Population increase and sex-biased parental investment in humans: Evidence from 18th and 19th century Germany. *Current Anthropology, 38*, 129–135.

West-Eberhard, M.J. (2003). *Developmental plasticity and evolution*. New York: Oxford University Press.

Whittingham, L.A., Taylor, P.D., & Robertson, R.J. (1992). Confidence of paternity and male parental care. *American Naturalist, 139*, 1115–1125.

Wilkins, J.F. (2008) (Ed). *Genomic imprinting. Advances in experimental medicine and biology, 626*.

Wilkins, J.F., & Haig, D. (2003). What good is genomic imprinting: The function of parent-specific gene expression. *Nature Reviews Genetics, 4*, 359–368.

Winking, J., Kaplan, H., Gurven, M., & Rucas, S. (2007). Why do men marry and why do they stray? *Proceedings of the Royal Society B, 274*, 1643–1649.

CHAPTER 6

Parent–Offspring Conflict

Catherine A. Salmon *and* James Malcolm

Abstract

At first glance, the relationship between parent and offspring seems to begin in perfect harmony. In particular, the image of human parents' devotion to their infant is one that has been depicted in art for thousands of years. It often seems to stand in sharp contrast to the modern image of the typical adolescent–parent relationship, usually portrayed as full of strife. It's also in contrast to the abrupt end of parent–child relations seen in many animal species. But are either really accurate? Should we expect total harmony or total conflict? What factors affect the degree of conflict between parent and child? Are there particular stages in the life of a child or parent that attenuate or exaggerate the degree of conflict? An evolutionary perspective on human and animal families provides useful insights to these and other questions.

Keywords: Parental investment, parent–offspring conflict, fitness, maternal–fetal conflict, kin selection

Introduction

Although most people think of parental investment in offspring as something that occurs post-birth, and although a significant portion of investment in humans does occur during childhood and adolescence (and sometimes goes on for much longer!), mothers begin to invest in their offspring long before they are born. For 9 months, the mother's body provides all the nutrients for her baby's development, as well as a safe haven in which to grow. At this stage, it would appear that the fetus and mother have identical interests: the continuing safety and development of the fetus. But their genetic interests are not identical. The fetus is more closely related to itself than to either its mother or any future siblings and, as a result, pregnancy becomes a balancing act between the fetus's attempts to secure a larger a share of the mother's resources than she is willing to give, and the mother's attempts to retain resources for herself and her future offspring. Thus, selection will favor fetal genes that serve to increase the transfer of nutrients to the fetus and maternal genes that limit any transfers in excess of the ideal from the maternal perspective. The results of this balancing act can include a variety of unpleasant maternal symptoms and can occasionally create serious pregnancy complications. Haig (1993, 1998) has suggested that such maternal–fetal conflict is responsible for some previously puzzling aspects of pregnancy.

Gestational diabetes affects up to 10% of women in the United States. The regulation of blood glucose levels is altered during pregnancy, with fasting blood sugar levels falling initially and then stabilizing at a new lower level by the end of the first trimester (Lind & Aspillaga, 1988). However, fasting insulin levels are unchanged for the first two trimesters, only rising in the third, along with the growth of the fetus. When women are not pregnant, blood glucose levels rise after a meal, but rapidly return to fasting levels in response to the release of insulin. During the later stages of pregnancy, maternal blood glucose and insulin both reach higher levels and remain elevated for a longer duration. This occurs because the placental hormone human placental lactogen (hPL) acts on maternal prolactin receptors to increase maternal resistance to insulin. If there is no opposition, hPL will maintain higher blood glucose levels for longer periods after eating. However, this usually is opposed by increased maternal production of insulin. As a result, in the third trimester, the same meal will produce an exaggerated insulin response, which is less effective at reducing blood glucose levels (Buchanan et al., 1990; Catalano et al., 1991).

This occurs because the mother is attempting to restrict fetal access to blood glucose. Why do mothers enact this restriction, and why do mothers increase insulin production while also becoming resistant to it? One approach to answering these questions is that, if fetal demands for glucose are unopposed, the fetus may remove more glucose from maternal blood than is in the mother's interests to give. For much of human history, food was not an unlimited resource, and so, from both a maternal and fetal perspective, nutritional resources are in high demand. Each maternal meal entails conflict over the share of blood glucose that mother and fetus will receive, and the longer the mother takes to reduce blood sugar levels, the greater the share obtained by the fetus. The insulin resistance of late pregnancy is caused by placental hormones producing increased blood glucose levels and a corresponding increased production of insulin by the mother (Haig, 1993). For pregnant women without preexisting diabetes, maternal glucose levels 2 hours after a meal have been positively correlated with infant birth weight (Tallarigo et al., 1986). However, this benefit of increased maternal glucose levels for the fetus can come at a cost to the mother's health. If blood glucose levels remain elevated, gestational diabetes can develop when the mother becomes unable to increase her insulin production sufficiently to match the insulin resistance that developed during the pregnancy.

Five percent of all pregnancies in the United States include the condition called preeclampsia, which is a form of gestational hypertension. Less than 0.02% progress from preeclampsia to the more severe eclampsia (Guy & Silverberg, 2009). However, worldwide, over 63,000 women and their fetuses die from eclampsia annually, mainly in places with poor health care (Langer et al., 2008). Blood pressure has two components, the cardiac output (or flow rate) and resistance (influenced by the size of the structures it flows through). During pregnancy, the fetus depends on the mother's circulatory system for all its needs. Conflict can arise over the relative flow of blood to the uteroplacental circulation (from which the fetus obtains its nutrients) and the nonplacental remainder. Theoretically, the fetus can increase its share of the cardiac output by decreasing resistance in the uteroplacental circulatory subsystem or by increasing resistance in the nonplacental subsystem. The mother can reduce the fetal share of the output by doing the opposite, increasing uteroplacental resistance or decreasing nonplacental resistance (Haig, 1993). As a result, we expect placental factors to increase maternal blood pressure and maternal factors to decrease maternal blood pressure.

A fetus benefits from increases in maternal blood pressure. More resources mean more, and faster, development. And we know that gestational hypertension typically results in a positive outcome from the fetal perspective. Hypertensive pregnancies have lower perinatal mortality than do normotensive pregnancies (Symonds, 1980). For Anglo American women, birthweight is correlated positively with maternal blood pressure for mothers with low prepregnancy weight and low weight gain during pregnancy (Naeye, 1981). Studies also suggest that chronic hypertension is associated with higher birth weights, and chronic hypotension is associated with lower birth weights (Ng & Walters, 1992; Salafia et al., 1990). However, there are risks associated with pregnancy-induced hypertension when it is extreme and occurs along with proteinuria (excessive protein in maternal urine).

These examples of parent–offspring conflict are striking in their intensity but represent a widespread phenomenon. Traditionally, such conflicts were interpreted from a Freudian perspective or by suggesting that the child was innately selfish. In 1974, Robert Trivers provided an evolutionary analysis for understanding these conflicts. His argument was, in turn, framed in the theory of kin selection published by W.D. Hamilton (1964). Trivers' paper has been influential, and there is continuing interest in the topic from both biologists and psychologists. In the remainder of this chapter, we review current theory about parent–offspring conflict, discuss variables that have been shown to be important in conflicts, and discuss the fitness consequences of this conflict and whether parents or their offspring win. Evidence for parent–offspring conflict is widespread, from plants (Shaanker, 1988) and insects (e.g., Rauter & Moore, 1999) to birds and mammals.

Parent–Offspring Conflict Theory

Parent–offspring conflict follows from Hamilton's fundamental inequality for social behavior, $br_0 - c > 1$, where b is the benefit in terms of reproductive success that an individual receives from an interaction, c is the cost that the actor incurs, and r_0, termed the *degree of relatedness*, is the chance that actor and recipient share a gene by common descent. This simple model can be applied to parents and offspring.

Parent–offspring conflict can be seen most simply as a corollary of sibling conflict. Imagine two nestlings. They are equally related to their parents, but each values contribution from their parents more highly than contributions to its sibling. The result will be sibling rivalry over parental resources. From the parent's perspective, it values each offspring equally, while each offspring wants more from the parent than the parent is selected to provide.

Parent–offspring conflict applies equally with one child and one parent. In the one-child case, conflict occurs because the reproductive success of the parent derives from his or her offspring. The offspring's reproductive success is from its own children, to which the parent is only related by .25. Parents and offspring do not have the same reproductive interests. The extent of the conflict is dictated, in part, by the degree of relatedness. In strict monogamy, the offspring is expected to accept food from the parent whenever its benefit is greater than twice the cost to the parent. The parent views it differently and only provides care when the benefit is greater than the cost. With more than one offspring in the nest, the parent values each offspring equally but each offspring values itself over its siblings. This produces conflict over the allocation of food. The outcome of any interaction should lie between the parent's and offspring's desired results. There is, therefore, a zone of conflict. The outcome, in terms of natural selection, is expected to lie in this zone of conflict, and winning or losing on the part of parent or offspring depends on whose desired cost–benefit ratio is attained.

As Trivers (1974) noted, at all times and for all interactions in which benefits are distributed to offspring, there will be a divergence of interests such that the offspring wants more than the parent is selected to provide. However, these inequalities are constrained by the fact that the actors are related, and this sets limits on the selfishness of each party. When the benefits to the offspring are greater than twice the cost to the parent, the offspring suffers a net cost from the reduced fitness it is inflicting on its parent. In the other direction, a parent who provisions such that the benefits to the offspring are less than the cost to itself, is reducing its own reproductive success by its harm to the offspring.

These constraints differentiate conflicts over reproductive resources that involve genetic kin from those that do not. Trivers' (1974) article presented primarily a verbal and graphical argument. After its publication, several authors produced mathematical models. In 1979, Parker et al. demonstrated mathematically that a gene with the properties proposed by Trivers would spread. In 1994, Godfray reviewed all published models addressing parent–offspring conflict to that time. These models and much of the empirical work on parent–offspring conflict have used altricial birds begging at a nest. This system is relatively straightforward to study empirically and has allowed for the implementation of interesting experimental procedures.

In 1991, Godfray published an influential article in which he used an evolutionarily stable strategy (ESS) framework arguing that if the offspring solicitation was costly, there would come a point at which extra energy from solicitation would not be compensated by extra parental investment. In this situation, begging becomes self-limiting and a stable evolutionary strategy. Regardless of which point in the zone of conflict the self-limitation occurs, the offspring loses the ability to manipulate the level of investment and the parental contribution is expected to gravitate to the parental optimum.

This model assumes that parents can assess their offspring's need accurately. Begging or solicitation becomes an honest signal—that is, the offspring's solicitation reflects its true need, and parents can make the appropriate allocations. Under these conditions, much of the conflict is removed. Numerous studies (reviewed in Johnstone & Godfray, 2002) have shown that parents do indeed respond to increased level of solicitation. However, without the provision that solicitation is costly and self-limiting, there is no reason to believe that the offspring's signal is honest. A graded signal can carry misinformation. At the same time, where it has been possible to measure the costs of begging, most studies have shown any cost to be extremely small (Chappell & Bachman, 2002). Chappell and Bachman (2002) concluded that there was no convincing evidence from the five studies reviewed that the costs of begging in birds was large enough to influence parent–offspring conflict. However, Kilner (2002) measured a decline in growth rate in canaries *Serinus canaria* induced to beg for long periods in the lab. (Human infants may be another example: Up to 5% of metabolic costs in infants may be spent in crying [Furlow, 1997].)

Costly signals also seem unlikely for some elements of begging displays, such as brightly colored gapes, which appear to have limited cost beyond their initial production. Bell (2008) studied banded mongooses (*Mungos mungo*) and found that a juvenile begged with different intensities to different members of the pack. This is not expected if a begging honestly indicates need. In response to concerns about the cost of signals, Johnstone and Godfray (2002) proposed several new models that are limited by the zone of conflict but incorporate variable degrees of begging. These models remain largely untested.

Another model that has been influential was generated by Parker and colleagues (e.g., Parker et al., 2002; Royle et al., 2002). However, the model is based on the same assumptions as the models presented by Godfray (1994)—that is, costly and hence honest signals. In this model, the distribution of resources to nestlings is analyzed and parents use the sum of the begging calls from the young to allocate resources.

Proximate Factors Influencing Parental Investment

Numerous factors can influence the amount of investment delivered to an offspring. If all investment is contested, as the fundamental model of parent–offspring conflict indicates, then all variations in investment will be the basis for conflict. We discuss some of the factors that influence investment and the outcome of parent–offspring conflict.

Parental Age

Life history theory suggests that the age of the parent should affect the degree of conflict with offspring (Salmon & Daly, 1998). In species in which the probability of death increases systematically with age, a parent is selected to give an increasing proportion of parental investment to offspring, which tends to benefit laterborn offspring more than the earlier born ones that have already matured. Relative to older parents, younger parents should be harboring resources to maximize lifetime reproductive success. Increasing investment by older parents, however, may be constrained by senescent decline.

Only a small fraction of the animal kingdom shows an increasing rate of mortality with age but they include many large mammals such as humans. The final extension of this perspective is that a parent should invest all available energy into a last child. Although for most animals it must be rare for the last child to be a predictable event, menopause allows a woman (and perhaps pilot whales) to recognize a child as her last (Austad, 1997).

Some data show that older parents invest more than do younger parents (Salmon & Daly, 1998; Voland & Gabler, 1994). Clutton Brock et al. (1984) showed that older red deer females had calves in better physical condition, and this was unlikely to be an effect of superior foraging skills acquired with age. In many seabirds (Ryder, 1980), older pairs fledge more offspring than do younger birds and, at least in some species (e.g., California gull *Larus californicus*; Pugusek, 1987), parents may die as a consequence of increased reproductive effort.

Studies of infanticide in humans indicate that the age of the mother is a significant factor in the likelihood of maternal infanticide. Young women, those likely to have many future opportunities to reproduce, might be expected to be more willing to sacrifice a current child when conditions for successfully raising the child are poor. Older women, close to the end of their reproductive years, who pass up the opportunity to invest, may not have the opportunity again. As the likelihood of future reproduction decreases, delaying childbirth becomes more costly. Selection should favor older women who invest immediately and to a significant extent in children rather than delaying investment. The dramatic cross-culturally observed decrease in the rate of maternally perpetrated infanticide with increasing maternal age reflects the change over time of the weight the maternal psyche places on a current offspring versus possible future offspring (Daly & Wilson, 1995; Lee & George, 1999; Overpeck, Brenner, Trumble, Trifiletti, & Berendes, 1998).

Number of Offspring

The number of children parents have at any one time also is expected to have an impact on parental investment (and levels of conflict between parent and child). Parental investment is a limited resource (whether measured in food, time, money, etc.) that must be allocated among offspring, and most parental resources will be in shorter supply when there are multiple children in the home. More children translates into fewer resources for any individual child. This is one reason existing children are often so resistant to adding another child to the household, not being keen on sharing their parents with a sibling, and sometimes reverting to more juvenile behavior themselves to try and retain as much parental attention and investment as possible (Michalski & Euler, 2008; Sulloway, 2007).

Gender of Parent

It would seem that the two parents in a monogamous species would agree on the distribution of parental resources to their offspring. Both are invested equally in the success of the brood. However, there are numerous examples of males contributing less than females (e.g., Briskie et al., 1994). Several studies in captivity have quantified the effect: for example, budgerigars (*Melopsittacus undulates*; Stamps, 1985), parrotlets (*Forpus passerinus*; Budden & Beissinger, 2009), canaries (*Serinus canaria*; Kilner, 2002), and great tits (*Parus major*; Kollicker et al., 1998). In the first three species, females take time to distribute food to all nestlings, compensating for size differences. In contrast, males give to the most ostentatious and larger chicks. In great tits, males did not respond to more begging with more food, unlike the females. There appears to be no simple explanation for these sex differences in providing care. In several cases, it appears that males allocate efforts to find more mates at the expense of feeding their young (Briskie, 1994). In other cases, males provide more food to strongly begging offspring (e.g., superb fairy wrens; MacGregor, 2000 in Kilner, 2002).

Age of Offspring

When it comes to the age of the offspring, there is often a greater fitness payoff to parents for investing in older children. Any specific offspring's expected contribution to parental fitness is found mainly in his or her reproductive value (expected future reproduction). This value increases with age until reproductive maturity, making an older, immature offspring more valuable from the parental perspective than a younger one (Montgomerie & Weatherhead, 1988). In humans, this increase is mainly due to significant childhood mortality rates in developing societies and over most of our evolutionary history. The average teenager has a higher reproductive value than the average infant because some infants do not survive to become teenagers. But it is also important to remember that, on average, the older a particular offspring gets, the less valuable is a unit of parental investment, especially certain kinds of investment (such as breast milk), compared to its value to younger offspring. The survival and reproductive future of young children is highly dependent on significant parental investment. Parents must weigh these costs and benefits when they have more than one offspring to care for.

Parents clearly respond to the changing needs of their offspring. Human infants require more time and attention, which they typically get, sometimes to the consternation of their slightly older siblings. But when times are very tough, and parents may not be able to invest in all their children, it is a cross-cultural universal that the youngest is the likeliest casualty (Daly & Wilson, 1984). Studies of familial homicides also support the hypothesis that older children are more highly valued. Daly and Wilson (1988) have studied homicide for over 20 years. Their examination of the risk of homicide of a child by a genetic parent in relation to offspring age revealed that infants are at a much higher risk of being killed than any other group of children. The rates drop dramatically after 1 year of age, until they approach zero at 17 years of age. One might suggest that this is because it is easier to kill a baby than a teenager. However, the risk of a child being killed by a nonrelative shows a different pattern: 1-year-olds are more likely to be killed than infants, and teenagers are the most likely to be killed.

Child's Expected Future Prospects

An offspring's future prospects are also relevant to parental returns on investment. The survival and reproductive success of a child define the benefit to parents. Natural selection would be unlikely to favor mechanisms that direct investment toward a child who is unlikely to survive and reproduce in turn. A child's expected future prospects are related to the ability to best utilize parental investment and, as a result, parental solicitude should be sensitive to cues of offspring "quality" or the ability to convert parental care into future reproductive success.

Poor infant quality does have an impact on parental investment. Human infants born with severe physical deformities are more likely than healthy infants to be the victims of infanticide, particularly in societies in which there is no institutional care for the disabled (Daly & Wilson, 1984, 1988). Hill and Ball (1996) examined the reasons given for infanticide cross-culturally in the ethnographic literature. The majority involved abnormal birth circumstances, but they noted that many factors were associated with conditions that increase the likelihood of death during infancy or childhood. Such children require a higher level of investment for a lower evolutionary payoff (as they are less likely to reproduce even if they do survive). This means that parents are better off, from a fitness perspective, if they terminate investment early (Haig, 2009) and start investing in a new offspring (one of several reasons why so many pregnancies end in spontaneous abortions—the mother's body rejects a less than optimal child, a situation in which the parent "wins" the conflict). And, even in North America, children with physically disabilities are at greater risk of abuse and more likely to suffer injuries at the hands of their parents requiring a visit to hospital than are healthy children (Daly & Wilson, 1984).

Another factor that reveals the importance of a child's future prospects as a predictor of parental investment is the offspring's sex. Trivers and Willard (1973) pointed out that when one sex has a greater variance in lifetime reproductive success than the other, and parents (particularly mothers) vary in their physical condition or access to resources in a way that influences offspring success, differences in preferences for sex of offspring are likely to evolve. If male reproductive success depends on the individual's condition, mothers who are able to invest heavily will be able to influence the reproductive success of their sons more successfully than will mothers with poor access to resources (nutritional or otherwise). They should prefer to have sons, or to invest more in their sons than in their daughters (Trivers & Willard, 1973; Bercovitch et al., 2000). Mothers in poor condition should prefer daughters because daughters are less of a reproductive risk (females generally have lower variance in reproductive success than males). This is known as the *Trivers-Willard effect*.

In humans, the evidence for Trivers-Willard effects has been mixed. Several studies have shown such sex-biased investment (Gaulin & Robbins, 1991; Hopcroft, 2005; Kanazawa, 2004), whereas others have found no such effects (Beaulieu & Bugental, 2008; Freese & Powell, 1999; Keller et al., 2001; Sieff, 1990). Dickemann's (1979) review of infanticide in the Indian caste system indicates that, before the 20th century, infanticide was common in higher-caste families, with the victims overwhelmingly female. Under these circumstances, there were very few marriage options for higher-caste daughters, who could only marry within their own caste, not into a lower one. In higher-caste families, investment in sons (who could marry females from their own or lower castes) resulted in more grandchildren. As a result, parental investment was heavily male biased (Gupta, 1987). For lower-caste families, the tendency for males to marry down in social status meant daughters out-reproduced sons, and lower-caste parents biased their investment toward daughters. One result was a much lower rate of female infanticide among the lower castes. Studies in the United States (Gaulin & Robbins, 1991) and Kenya (Cronk, 1989) have suggested that female infants from low-income families are nursed more than males. Pollet, Fawcett, Buunk, and Nettle (2009) reported that lower-ranking polygynous wives in Rwanda have significantly more daughters than do higher-ranking polygynous wives or monogamously married women in a population in which male reproductive success is extremely variable and strongly dependent on adult status and access to resources.

Bereczkei and Dunbar's (1997, 2002) studies of Hungarian Gypsy populations also reveal Trivers-Willard effects. Compared to native Hungarians, Gypsies have substantially more daughters than sons, and Gypsies are lower in social status. Gypsy women are also much more likely to marry up the social scale than are men, and they typically out-reproduce their Gypsy brothers. They also, on average, have healthier babies than those Gypsy women who marry within their own group. Like the lower-caste Indians, Gypsy parents invest more heavily in their daughters than in their sons. Bereczkei and Dunbar (1997) also found that Gypsy women spent more time nursing their firstborn daughters than their sons, when compared to native Hungarians, and provided more education for their daughters (their education was not free and came at a significant cost to the parents). Almond and Edlund's (2007) study of natality data for white females in the United States between 1983 and 2001, found that younger, more highly educated, and married women gave birth to more sons. When they looked at infant deaths, there were more male deaths when the mothers were younger and unmarried.

As was the case for Almond and Edlund's (2007) highly educated married mothers, there are times when investment favors sons over daughters. In societies in which the possession of resources significantly improves male reproductive success (such as India's caste system), a preference for sons, or for investing heavily in them, will be seen among the wealthy (as it has been in India). This was also the case in 18th-century northern German villages (Voland, 1998) and has been noted in the records of probated wills in British Columbia (Smith, Kish, & Crawford, 1987). Cameron and Dalerum's (2009) study of Trivers-Willard effects in the Forbes list of billionaires indicated that people in the top economic bracket have more grandchildren via their sons than their daughters and that mothers at this highest socioeconomic status have more sons.

Degree of Relatedness

In the opening paragraphs of this chapter, we noted that the inequality that lies at the heart of parent–offspring conflict is that the offspring will benefit so long as its benefit was less than twice the cost to the parent. This factor of two was in turn derived from the degrees of relatedness between siblings in a faithful monogamous situation. However, if offspring share only one parent, the degree of relatedness drops to one-quarter. Now, the inequality changes, and the offspring benefits as long as the benefit is greater than the cost to the parent divided by four. Parent–offspring conflict is expected to more intense with the lower the degree of relatedness between siblings.

An extreme example is provided by brood parasites, in which the chick is unrelated to the parent. Nestling cuckoos beg loudly (Payne, 2005) and at a volume that is considerably louder than a host chick. However, the loud noises of cuckoo chicks may not always represent unconstrained solicitation. Davies (2000) and Kilner, Noble and Davies (1999) have argued that the common cuckoo (*Cuculus canorum*), which throws out the host eggs, has to beg loudly to produce a begging signal that the full brood would produce.

In cowbirds, in which the parasitic nestling is raised with the host nestlings, Boncoraglio et al. (2009) showed that the brood parasite affected begging by the host chicks. Across 31 species, begging intensity was positively correlated with the degree of brood parasitism. However, the more subtle results come from situations in which the host young in the nest may not be full siblings. This happens when the female of a pair seeks mating opportunities with extra-pair mates. These extra-pair copulations are not an uncommon feature of bird biology. Briskie et al. (1994) documented a positive correlation between nestling loudness and the frequency of extra-pair copulations that reduce degrees of relatedness within broods. In cross-fostering experiments in the barn swallow (*Hirundo rustica*), nestlings of different parentage in the same nest begged more loudly than natural nestmates. However, the parents did not discriminate in their feeding (Boncoraglio et al., 2009).

In humans, the degree of relatedness also influences the costs and benefits of parental investment. Relatedness in a parent–offspring context is influenced by paternity uncertainty, stepparenting, and adoption. Paternity uncertainty is one reason why women typically invest more in parenting than do men. From a genetic perspective, men should invest preferentially in children that they are sure are theirs. For women, with internal fertilization and gestation, maternity has never been in doubt. Men do not have that degree of certainty and, therefore, should be alert to cues of paternity, investing only when such cues are present (although men may also invest in children that are not theirs as part of mating effort when their desired mate already has children). There are numerous studies that suggest that paternity uncertainty has a significant impact on human paternal investment. Daly and Wilson's (1982) study of spontaneous comments made by Canadian parents and grandparents after the birth of a child suggests that mothers and maternal grandparents make many more references to paternal resemblance than to maternal resemblance ("Oh look, he has his father's chin."). A Mexican replication founds similar results (Regalski & Gaulin, 1993). Maternal kin make an effort to reinforce the image of the baby as the father's child—especially if the "father" is around to hear.

The impact of stepparenting is that the stepparent is not genetically related to any of their stepchildren. In this case, lack of paternity (or maternity) is clear, and we would expect that mechanisms for parental allocation of resources will direct such resources away from stepchildren and toward any existing (or future) genetic children. This can cause conflict between parents, as well as between parents and offspring. For example, a woman with children from her previous as well as current relationship is equally related to all her children and might desire to allocate her investment equally. Her current partner, however, would likely desire to allocate resources preferentially toward the children that are the product of their union, as opposed to her previous one (Hofferth & Anderson, 2003). The stepsiblings, who are related through just one parent, will be expected to value themselves even higher in relation to their stepsiblings than they do to their genetic siblings, increasing the degree of conflict they experience over parental resources.

Daly and Wilson's (1984, 1988, 2001) numerous studies of discriminative parental solicitude have often focused on stepparenting. If parental care can be viewed on a continuum, self-sacrifice would be found at one end (parents who not only sacrifice their own desires, but their health and their lives for their children), whereas at the other end we find child neglect, abuse, and homicide. Inclusive fitness theory suggests that genetic relatedness to a child is one predictor of the willingness to invest, so that the less genetically related an adult is to a child, the lower the likelihood of investment (and the higher the risk of abuse or homicide). Daly and Wilson tested this in a study (Daly & Wilson, 1988) of child abuse in Hamilton, Ontario. They found that children living with a genetic parent and a stepparent were about 40 times more likely to be physically abused than were children living with both genetic parents. This occurred even when controlling for poverty and socioeconomic status (which also influence rates of child abuse).

Cases of parental infanticide provide similar evidence. Rates of infanticide are far higher for stepparents than for genetic parents, with the risk highest for the very young, those under 2 years of age. In fact, the risk of a preschool-aged child being killed ranges from 40 to 100 times higher for stepchildren than for children living with two genetic parents (Daly & Wilson, 1988). It is not so much that the stepparent actively desires the child's demise, but that they are not as cautious or caring as a genetic parent might be. As a result, the child often dies from a lack of care or intolerance rather than from targeted hostility. It's also important to remember that not all stepparents are uncaring; many are very good parents. But even some of those caring stepparents report that their affection for their stepchildren is not as great as that for their own biological children (Ganong & Coleman, 1986; Hobart, 1988, 1989).

One does not need to only focus on extreme examples to see discriminative parental solicitude. One can look at the degree of investment, rather than the decision to maintain or terminate investment. Stepfathers invest less financial resources in their stepchildren than in their biological children. A study of Albuquerque, New Mexico, men reported that genetic children were 5.5 times more likely to receive money for college than were stepchildren. In fact, genetic children received, on average, $15,500 more for college and had 65% more of their college expenses paid for than did stepchildren (Anderson, Kaplan, & Lancaster, 1999). It has also been suggested that when stepparental investment is seen, it may often reflect mating effort on the part of males (intended to make themselves more attractive to their new mate) rather than parental effort as such (Hofferth & Anderson, 2003; Anderson et al., 1999; Rohwer et al., 1999).

Adoption also changes the degree of relatedness, and it can do so to varying degrees. The adoption of related children (such as nieces or nephews) results in lesser parent–offspring genetic relatedness than for biological parent and child, but the parent and adopted child are nevertheless partly related. When unrelated children are adopted, there is no genetic relatedness. As a result, we would expect a lesser degree of parental investment in adopted related children than in one's own genetic children (Silk, 1980).

But from this perspective, we expect little to no parental investment in an unrelated adopted child as there is no genetic link. And yet (as Chapter 7 discusses in detail), adoptive parents do invest, most often very highly, in their genetically unrelated offspring.

The majority of historical accounts of adoption practices in traditional societies have documented the prevalence of the adoption of genetically related individuals. There is no theoretical reason to expect a mechanism designed specifically to deal with the adoption of genetically unrelated individuals, as the historical evidence suggests it was infrequent. It seems likely that in the relatively benign environment of the developed world, strong parental and cultural desires lead some individuals to adopt unrelated offspring. Many personal accounts of the relationship between adopted children and parents in the modern Western world suggest that it typically is much the same as that between genetic parent and child, particularly when the adopted child is an infant.

Other Factors
Many other factors have been shown to influence offspring begging and parental food-giving behavior, including immunocompetence (Saino & Moller, 2002), rate of digestion (Budden & Wright, 2008), and testosterone levels (Goodship & Buchanan, 2006). These variables could affect the outcome of parent–offspring conflict, but there are no data to date.

Signals of Solicitation
Signals of solicitation are often complex, with multiple components, many of them of graded intensity. Most signals are expressed without prior experience, but some can be modified by elements of the environment. In the house sparrow (*Passer domesticus*), nestlings adjust their begging to the schedule on which they are fed (Kedar et al., 2000). However, all solicitation signals must (a) act on the parent to elicit investment, (b) have the potential to extract more than the parent is selected to give, and (c) be adapted to the environment both in terms of the physics of the surroundings and the sensory capacities of predators.

Physical Environment
Begging usually occurs over short distances and is unlikely to have features that mitigate environmental degradation. A possible exception has been studied in the meerkat (*Suricata suricata*; Kunc et al., 2007) and the related banded mongoose. In these species,

individual young follow a caregiving adult around. The young produce an almost continuous stream of high-pitched squeaks that would appear to be easily locatable in an open environment and act to elicit provisioning behavior. In birds, Horn and Leonard (2002) discuss how the calls of hole-nesting birds are likely to be constrained. It appears that vocalizations are adapted to the dimensions of the hole to avoid reverberations. The begging noises of hole nesters end up with a broader frequency range and shorter duration than comparable calls from open-nesting species.

Some studies have reported a relationship between the brightness of the begging gapes in birds and the ambient light in the nest (Kilner & Davies, 1999). However, a more detailed method for quantifying reflected light may be necessary to bolster these findings (Kilner, 1999).

Predation

It would seem that a nest full of noisy chicks would attract predators. However, data on this point are not as convincing as might be expected The begging calls of the parasitic cowbird (*Molothrus ater*) are louder than the chicks of the host indigo buntings (*Passerina cyanea*). However, nests with parasites show no more predation than those without (Dearborn, 1999). In blackbellied magpies (*Pica pica*), Redondo and Castro (1992) found no correlations between the number of nestlings and the noise level and predation. On the other side, Haskell (1994) set up empty nests with quail (*Coturnix coturnix*) eggs and broadcast begging calls from the nests. Vocalizations of tree-nesting birds broadcast on the ground attracted predators, but not vice versa. With respect to physical forces and predation acting on signals of solicitation, it seems wise to understand what features of the signals may have been shaped by these factors of the environment before generating hypotheses based on social dynamics.

Eliciting Care

Are signals of solicitation designed specifically to elicit care? The work of Lorenz published in 1943 (cited in Eibl Eibesfeldt, 1974) suggested that the facial features of babies with large foreheads acted as a releaser of caregiving behavior. The "baby schema" has received support from a magnetic resonance imaging (MRI) study of nulliparous women, which showed that baby faces activates the nucleus accumbens (important in the brain reward system; Glocker et al., 2009). It has also been shown that babies in the first weeks of life adjust the cadence of their crying to match their mothers (e.g., Germans babies cry with a German inflection; Mampe et al., 2009). The young of brood parasites mimic the solicitation behavior of their hosts, most notably in the viduine finches (e.g., Davies, 2000). Races within several species of cuckoo also have begging calls adjusted to their hosts (Payne, 2005).

Exaggerated Solicitation

Do signals of solicitation support the prediction that offspring are trying to elicit more than the parents are adapted to give? From an intuitive view, the seemingly unnecessarily loud and annoying noise is reasonable evidence for parent–offspring conflict. However, it is difficult to assess to what extent a signal is more than is needed. Krebs and Dawkins (1984) suggested that, in situations in which both sender and receiver gained from an interaction, all that would be needed are "cost minimizing conspiratorial whispers" (p. 391). However, what is a whisper and what is a manipulative shout is not clear. Sibling rivalry produces another force, as vocalization must be heard in a social situation. It should be possible to compare solicitations to calls that are not potentially deceptive. However, in most cases, the other calls have themselves been selected for other contexts (e.g., alarm calls and contact calls are often selected to be inconspicuous, and mobbing calls to be loud; Harper, 1991; Horn & Leonard, 2002). For all the caveats, some qualitative results are clear. African wild dogs (*Lycaon pictus*), use high-pitched low-intensity noises in cooperative greetings. However, when a dependent adolescent begs, it uses an intense whining noise, which is grating to the human ear (accompanied by nudges to the belly of the intended donor; Malcolm, personal observation).

The spectrographic structure of human crying is aperiodic (Wolgemoth, personal communication), a sound element known to be annoying to the listener. Humans and chimps seem to act so as to quiet a crying infant as soon as possible. Loud crying certainly acts to interfere with any other communication by the parent or others around. Horn and Leonard (2002) mention data showing that some birds have auditory filters reducing input in the dominant frequencies of the cries of their begging offspring.

Zahavi & Zahavi (1997) suggested that loud calls act to attract predators, giving the parents a strong incentive to quiet them. However, the risk to the offspring seems greater than that to the parent;

it seems unlikely to work, and we currently lack the empirical evidence to judge. Such blackmail may work in other contexts. Andrews (2006) showed that adolescent threats of suicide in humans acted to increase investment by parents. Trivers provides a strikingly similar analysis of begging tantrums in pink-backed pelicans (*Pelecanus rufuescens*): "By going into convulsions it may convince the parent that withholding food will have dire consequences for the health of the chick" (Trivers, 1985, p. 157).

Complex Signals

Most displays of solicitation contain multiple elements, usually including sound and movement. It is often possible to distinguish between different intensities for elements of the signal (e.g., Kilner, 2002; Villasenor & Drummond, 2007). Kilner (2002) has analyzed the extent to which different components of displays represent different messages that can be interpreted as graded signals. Her conclusion is that, although elements of the display, such as gape color, may have some restricted meaning, it is part of a whole display that acts to elicit resources from the parents.

It seems possible that the multiplicity of graded signals could arise from a form of redundancy. An original signal by the offspring may be co-opted by the parent, so that this signal no longer has the power to induce the extra investment that the offspring desires. At that point, a new signal could arise, with a more immediate connection to need, but one which is still capable of eliciting more than the parents want to give. The old signal may be retained if it acts to enhance the total display.

Ultimate Considerations

Can we asses who wins in parent–offspring conflict? Is it possible to measure the costs and benefits of the interactions between parents and young? The problem has proved largely intractable except for certain eusocial haplodiploid species discussed below.

In assessing costs and benefits, it is perhaps convenient to distinguish "skirmishes" involving a single interaction from "battles"—a reiterated set of interactions, such as begging, during the period of offspring dependence—and finally, from "war" or the sum of all interactions over the period of raising an offspring.

As we can almost never assign, we can only make reasonable guesses about winners and losers. Would the conflict we see be expected if the interests of the two parties were the same? This may be more easily estimated for skirmishes than for battles or for the war. Goodall (1986) describes tantrums in weaning chimps. She states that the mother chimp "almost always does give in" and lets the infant nurse. (The mother's behavior, if translated, might read "Anything for Peace," p. 576.). It seems clear who wins this skirmish. However, the outcome of this one event may not reflect the degree to which the offspring was able to acquire more milk than the mother would want to give on other occasions.

Graves, Whiten, and Henzi (1991, p. 28), studying fledging in gulls, listed four criteria that should be satisfied to show parent–offspring conflict: "(a) the parents decrease their investment, and the reduction in food given to the chicks is not simply because there is less food available to the parents, (b) the offspring show behavior geared to increasing the level of parental investment, (c) investment has a cost to the parents and (d) failure to decrease investment has a cost to the parents." In this study, they made strong plausibility arguments for criteria the first three points but could bring little evidence to bear on the last point.

In some extreme cases, winners and losers are evident. The young of nest parasites (cuckoos and others) win in the competition for food and often impose direct costs on the host by eliminating their eggs. Two other extreme examples are human eclampsia and gestational diabetes, discussed earlier in this chapter. Not infrequently, both mother and fetus die, indicating tragically high costs of a competition in which neither party wins.

At least one group of organisms provides both behavioral evidence and quantifiable measures of parent–offspring conflict (Trivers & Hare, 1976). The extraordinary social systems of the eusocial haplodiploids is a result of offspring conflict. Sisters in haplodiploids are related to one another by .75 and are related to their brothers by .25. The altruistic raising of reproductives by females is the hallmark of eusociality. Females therefore help to raise sisters to whom they are unusually closely related, but they also raise brothers to whom they are unusually distantly related. The reproductive advantage that a female can gain by raising sisters is directly offset by the costs of raising brothers. Haplodiploidy by itself does not lead to eusociality.

However, there is a way that females can bias reproduction in their favor. They can invest differentially in sisters over brothers. The queen is equally related to her sons as her daughters and would prefer to invest equally in the two sexes. Her daughters would like to invest in a ratio of three females to one male (assuming reproductives of the two sexes are equally costly to produce). There is a conflict between the queen and her daughters, and it is the daughter's ability to bias investment in their direction that provides a primary selective advantage for daughters to stay in the nest. Numerous behavioral manifestations of this conflict have been reported. Workers kill males in many species (e.g., *Iridomyrmex*; Aron, 1994), and workers appear to imprison males and prevent access to food in some wasps, with preferential rearing of females (Starks & Poe, 1997). Workers can also insert their own haploid, male eggs into the brood. Queen bees (*Apis mellifera*) devote time to patrolling the brood, probably to detect these worker-produced eggs. Queen control of sex allocation can be complex. In some bumblebees, females produce only male eggs at the start of the season, giving the workers no reproductive option other than to raise males (Bourke & Ratnieks, 1997).

In species in which it is possible to catch the entire year's production of reproductives, it is also possible to calculate the investment in males versus females and to determine whether it is closer to the equal sex ratio optimum of the queen or the workers. The original dataset collect by Trivers and Hare (1976) showed an average sex ratio from monogynous ant species to be above 1:2.2, with some species at the predicted 1:3 or above. These results have been corroborated by later work (Bourke & Franks, 1995). There is consensus that workers usually control the ratio of investment (Mehdiabadi et al., 2003). Given their vast numerical superiority, this may not be surprising. These numbers represent the best that are so far available on the outcome of parent–offspring conflict.

Conclusion

Conflict is an inevitable component of relationships between parents and their offspring in sexually reproducing species. Conflicts range from those in ant colonies to those between a mother and her fetus. Parent–offspring conflict is governed by Hamiltonian degrees of genetic relatedness, and evidence, at least from birds, indicates that nestlings respond to quite subtle differences in the degree of relatedness among nest mates.

A subtle balance exists in the solicitation behavior of offspring. They must elicit caregiving, attempt to gain more resources than the parent is selected to provide, and at the same time not induce so much investment that the parents' reproductive success is jeopardized. Signals used for solicitation are expected to be complex and multilayered.

Active debate persists over whether the parent's or the offspring's optimal level of investment is achieved. If young provide honest signals, it is often not difficult for parents to adjust their investment. However, it is not clear how often signaling is honest. In one system, the outcome of parent–offspring conflict is clear. Reproductive sex ratios in monogynous ants suggest that offspring win this conflict over the number of males-to-females raised, but the vast numerical superiority of the workers versus the queen must bias this case.

Many aspects of the relationship between parent and offspring show remarkable consistency throughout history and between not only human cultures but also between species. Psychological mechanisms have evolved to manage these relationships. And, these mechanisms are sensitive to the many social and ecological variables that influence such relationships, including the various costs and benefits of investment from both parent and offspring perspectives. A better understanding of the conflicts that can arise (from before birth to adolescence) across species and cultures will enable us to not only understand our own behavior but that of our children (and our own parents).

Future Directions

1. One of the most important issues to resolve is whether signals of solicitation are honest or not. If such signals are consistently honest, much of the conflict is taken out of parent-offspring relationships. Presumably, no simple answer exists, as signals at different times in the period of parental investment may change in costliness, and some signals may be costly—allowing honest investment—whereas others are not costly.

2. Unraveling the complex signaling behavior to understand how behaviors sum to produce their effects and the extent to which filtering occurs on the part of the parents would be useful and interesting.

3. A difficult challenge is to quantify the effects on parent–offspring conflict on the fitness of the participants. Are the costs of exaggerated solicitation repaid with increased investment?

4. From an applied perspective, it would be helpful to have a better understanding of how parent–offspring conflict over investment plays out (and the factors that influence it) in mixed-composition families, in which the mother might have a number of children, each with different fathers.

5. In a similar vein, a better understanding of the cues of relatedness and how they affect paternal investment (and how they may function for maternal investment) may help us better ease the conflicts that arise in the adoption of unrelated children, as well as the introduction of children born through the use of reproductive technology.

References

Almond, D., & Edlund, L. (2007). Trivers-Willard at birth and one year: Evidence from US natality data 1983–2001. *Proceedings of the Royal Society B, 274*, 2491–2496.

Anderson, J.G., Kaplan, H.S., & Lancaster, J.B. (1999). Paternal care by genetic fathers and step-fathers: 1. Reports from Albuquerque men. *Evolution and Human Behaviour, 20*, 405–431.

Andrews, P.W. (2006). Parent-offspring conflict and cost-benefit analysis in adolescent suicidal behavior. *Human Nature, 17*, 190–211.

Aron, S., Passera, L., & Keller, L. (1994). Queen-worker conflict over sex ratio: A comparison of primary and secondary sex ratios in the Argentine ant *Iridomyrmex humilis*. *Journal of Evolutionary Biology, 7*, 403–418.

Austad, S.N. (1997). *Why We Age*. New York: John Wiley.

Beaulieu, D.A., & Bugental, D. (2008). Contingent parental investment: An evolutionary framework for understanding early interaction between mothers and children. *Evolution and Human Behavior, 29*, 249–255.

Bell, M.B.V. (2008) Receiver identify modifies begging intensity independent of need in banded mongoose (*Mungos mungo*) pups. *Behavioral Ecology, 19*, 1087–1094.

Bercovitch, F.B., Widdig, A., & Nurnberg, P. (2000). Maternal investment in rhesus macaques (*Macaca mulatta*): Reproductive costs and consequences on raising sons. *Behavioral Ecology and Sociobiology, 48*, 1–11.

Bereczkei, T., & Dunbar, R.I.M. (1997). Female-biased reproductive strategies in a Hungarian Gypsy population. *Proceedings of the Royal Society, London, B, 264*, 17–22.

Bereczkei, T., & Dunbar, R.I.M. (2002). Helping-at-the-nest and sex-biased parental investment in a Hungarian Gypsy population. *Current Anthropology, 43*, 804–809.

Boncoraglio, G., Caprioli, M., & Saino, N. (2009). Fine-tuned modulation of competitive behavior according to kinship in barn swallow nestlings. *Proceedings of the Royal Society, B, 276*, 2117–2123.

Bourke, A.F.G., & Franks, N.R. (1995). *Social evolution in ants*. Princeton, NJ: Princeton University Press.

Bourke, A.F.G., & Ratnieks, F.L.W. (1997). Kin selected conflict in the bumble bee *Bombus terrestris* (Hymenoptera: Apidae). *Proceedings of the Royal Society, B, 268*, 347–355.

Briskie, J.V., Naugler, C.T., & Leech, S.M. (1994). Begging intensity of nestling birds varies with sibling relatedness. *Proceedings of the Royal Society, London, B, 258*, 73–78.

Buchanan, T.A., Metzger, B.E., Freinkel, N., & Bergman, R.N. (1990). Insulin sensitivity and B-cell responsiveness to glucose during late pregnancy in lean and moderately obese women with normal glucose tolerance or mild gestational diabetes. *American Journal of Obstetrics and Gynecology, 162*, 1008–1014.

Budden, A.E., and Beissinger, S.R. (2009) Resource allocation varies with parental sex and brood size in the asynchronously hatcing green-rumped parrotlet *(Forpus passerinus)*. *Behavioural Ecology and Sociobiology, 63*, 637–647.

Budden, A.E., & Wright, J. (2008). Effects of feeding frequency on nestling begging and digestion. *Ibis, 150*, 234–241.

Cameron, E.Z., & Dalerum, F. (2009). A Trivers-Willard effect in contemporary humans: Male-biased sex ratios among billionaires. *Public Library of Science ONE, 4*, e4195.

Catalano, P.M., Tyzbir, E.D., Roman, N.M., Amini, S.B., & Sims, A.H. (1991). Longitudinal changes in insulin release and insulin resistance in nonobese pregnant women. *American Journal of Obstetrics and Gynecology, 165*, 1667–1672.

Chappell, M.A., & Bachman, G.C. (2002). Energetic costs of begging behavior. In J. Wright, & M.L. Leonard (Eds.), *The evolution of begging: Competition, cooperation and communication* (pp. 143–162). London: Kluwer.

Clutton Brock, T.H. (1984). Reproductive effort and terminal investment in iteroparous mammals. *American Naturalist, 123*, 212–229.

Cronk, L. (1989). Low socioeconomic status and female-based parental investment: The Mokogodo example. *American Anthropologist, 91*, 414–429.

Daly, M., & Wilson, M. (1982). Whom are newborn babies said to resemble? *Ethology and Sociobiology, 3*, 69–210.

Daly, M., & Wilson, M. (1984). A sociobiological analysis of human infanticide. In G. Hausfater, & S.B. Hrdy (Eds.), *Infanticide: Comparative and evolutionary perspectives* (pp. 487–502). New York: Aldine.

Daly, M., & Wilson, M. (1988). *Homicide*. Hawthorne, NY: Aldine.

Daly, M., & Wilson, M. (1995). Discriminative parental solicitude and the relevance of evolutionary models to the analysis of motivational systems. In M. Gazzaniga (Ed.), *The Cognitive Neurosciences* (pp. 1269–1286). Cambridge, MA: MIT Press.

Daly, M., & Wilson, M. (2001). An assessment of some proposed exceptions to the phenomenon of nepotistic discrimination against stepchildren. *Annales Zoologici Fennici, 38*, 287–296.

Davies, N.B. (2000). *Cuckoos, cowbirds and other cheats*. Oxford: Princeton University Press.

Dearborn, D. C. (1999). Brown headed cowbird nestling vocalizations and risk of nest predation. *The Auk, 116*, 448–457.

Dickemann, M. (1979). Female infanticide, reproductive strategies, and social stratification: A preliminary model. In N.A. Chagnon, & W. Irons (Eds.), *Evolutionary biology and human social behavior* (pp. 321–367). North Scituate, MA: Duxbury Press.

Eibl-Eiblesfeldt, I. (1974) *Love and Hate*. Berlin: Springer.

Freese, J., & Powell, B. (1999). Sociobiology, status, and parental investment in sons and daughters: Testing the Trivers-Willard hypothesis. *American Journal of Sociology, 106*, 1704–1743.

Furlow, H.B. (1997). Human neonatal cry quality as an honest signal of fitness. *Evolution and Human Behavior, 18*, 175–193.

Ganong, L.H., & Coleman, M. (1986). Stepchildren's perceptions of their parents. *Journal of Genetic Psychology, 148*, 5–17.

Gaulin, S.J.C., & Robbins, C.J. (1991). Trivers-Willard effect in contemporary North American society. *American Journal of Physical Anthropology, 85*, 61–69.

Glocker, M.L., Langleben, D.D., Ruparle, K., Loughead, J.W., Valdez, J.N., Griffin, M.D., et al. (2009). Baby schema modulates the brain of nulliparous women. *Proceedings of the National Academy of Sciences, 106*, 9115–9119.

Godfray, H.C.J. (1991). Signaling of need by offspring to their parents. *Nature, 352*, 328–330.

Godfray, H.C.J. (1995). Evolutionary theory of parent-offspring conflict. *Nature, 376,* 133–138.

Goodall, J. (1986). *The chimpanzees of Gombe: Patterns of behavior.* Cambridge, MA: Harvard University Press.

Goodship, N.M., & Buchanan, K.L. (2006). Nestling testosterone is associated with begging behaviour and fledging success in the pied flycatcher *Fidecula hypoleuca. Proceedings of the Royal Society, London, B, 272,* 71–76.

Graves, J., Whitten, A., & Henzi, S.P. (1991). Parent-offspring over independence in the herring gull *Larus argentatus. Ethology, 88,* 20–34.

Gupta, D. (1987). Selective discrimination against female children in rural Punjab. *Population and Development Review, 13,* 77–100.

Guy, A.M. & Silverburg, M.A. (2009). Pregnancy, Eclampsia. Retrieved from http://emedicine.medscape.com/article/797603-overview

Haig, D. (1993) Genetic conflicts in human pregnancy. *The Quarterly Review of Biology, 68,* 495–532.

Haig, D. (1998). Genetic conflicts of pregnancy and childhood. In S.C. Stearns (Ed.), *Evolution in Health and Disease,* pp. 77–90. Oxford, UK: Oxford University Press.

Haig, D. (2009). Transfers and transitions: Parent-offspring conflict, genomic imprinting, and the evolution of human life history. *Proceedings of the National Academy of Sciences, 107*(1), 1731–1735. Retrieved from www.pnas.org_cgi_doi_10.1073_pnas.0904111106

Hamilton, W.D. (1964). The genetical evolution of social behavior. *Journal of Theoretical Biology, 7,* 1–52.

Harper, D.G.C. (1991). Communication. In J.R. Krebs, & N.R. Davies (Eds.), *Behavioural Ecology* (3rd ed., pp. 374–398). Oxford, UK: Blackwells.

Haskell, D. (1994) Experimental evidence that nestling begging behavior incurs a cost due to nest predation. *Proceedings of the Royal Society, London, B, 257,* 161–164.

Hill, C.M. & Ball, H.L. (1996). *Abnormal births and other "ill omens": The adaptive case of infanticide.* Human Nature, 7, 381–401.

Hobart, C. (1988). Perceptions of parent-child relationships in nuclear and remarried Families. *Family Relations, 37,* 175–182.

Hobart, C. (1989). Experiences of remarried families. *Journal of Divorce, 13,* 121–144.

Hofferth, S. & Anderson, K.G. (2003). Are all dads equal? Biology versus marriage as basis for paternal investment. *Journal of Marriage and Family, 65,* 213–232.

Hopcroft, R.L. (2005). Parental status and differential investment in sons and daughters: Trivers-Willard revisited. *Social Forces, 83,* 1111–1136.

Horn, A.G., & Leonard, M.L. (2002). Efficacy and the design of begging signals. In J. Wright, & M.L. Leonard (Eds.), *The evolution of begging: Competition, cooperation and communication* (pp. 127–142). London: Kluwer.

Johnstone, R.A., & Godfray, H.C.J. (2002). Models of begging as signals of need. In J. Wright, & M.L. Leonard (Eds.), *The evolution of begging: Competition, cooperation and communication* (pp. 1–20). London: Kluwer.

Kanazawa, S. (2004). Big and tall parents have more sons: Further generalizations from the Trivers-Willard hypothesis. *Journal of Theoretical Biology, 235,* 583–590.

Kedar, H., Rodriguez-Girones, M.A., Yedvab, S., Winkler, D.W., & Lotem, A. (2000). Experimental evidence for offspring learning in parent-offspring communication. *Proceedings of the Royal Society, London, B, 267,* 1723–1727.

Keller, M.C., Nesse, R.M., & Hofferth, S. (2001). The Trivers-Willard hypothesis of parental investment: No effect in the contemporary United States. *Evolution and Human Behavior, 22,* 343–366.

Kilner, R.M. (1999). Family conflicts and the evolution of nestling mouth colour. *Behaviour, 136,* 779–804.

Kilner, R.M., & Davies, N.B. (1999). Nestling mouth colour: Ecological correlates of a begging signal. *Animal Behaviour, 56,* 705–712.

Kilner, R.M. (2002). The evolution of complex begging displays. In J. Wright, & M.L. Leonard (Eds.), *The evolution of begging: Competition, cooperation and communication* (pp. 87–106). London: Kluwer.

Kilner, R. M., Noble, D.G., & Davies, N.B. (1999). Signals of need in parent-offspring communication and their exploitation by the common cuckoo. *Nature, 397,* 667–672.

Kollicker, M., Richner, H., Werner, I., & Heeb, P. (1998). Begging signals and biparental care: Nestling choice between feeding locations. *Animal Behaviour, 55,* 215–222.

Krebs, J.R., & Dawkins, R. (1984). Animal signals: Mind reading and manipulation. In J.R. Krebs, & N.B. Davies (Eds.), *Behavioural ecology: An evolutionary approach* (2nd ed.) (pp. 380–402). Sunderland, MA: Sinauer Associates.

Kunc, H.P., Maden, J.R., & Manser, M.B. (2007). Begging signals in a mobile feeding system: The evolution of different call types. *American Naturalist, 107,* 617–624.

Langer, A., Villar, J., Tell, K., Kim, T., & Kennedy, S. (2008). Reducing eclampsia-related deaths: A call to action. *The Lancet, 43,* 705–706.

Lee, B.J., & George, R.M. (1999). Poverty, early childbearing and child maltreatment: A multinomial analysis. *Children and Youth Services Review, 21,* 755–780.

Lind, T., & Aspillaga, M. (1988). Metabolic changes during normal and diabetic pregnancy. In E.A. Reece, & D.R. Coustan (Eds.), *Diabetes mellitus in pregnancy: Principles and practice* (pp. 75–102). New York: Churchill Livingstone.

MacGregor, N.A. (2000). Nestling begging and parental response in the superb fairy wren *Malurus cyaneus.* Honours Thesis, Australian National University.

Mampe, B., Friederich, A., Christophe, A., & Wremke, K. (1994–1997). Cry melody is shaped by the native language. *Current Biology, 19.*

Mehdiabadi, N.J., Reeve, H.K., & Mueller, U.G. (2003). Queens versus workers: Sex ratio conflict in eusocial hymenoptera. *Trends in Ecology and Evolution, 18,* 88–93.

Michalski, R.L., & Euler, H.A. (2008). Evolutionary perspectives on sibling relationships. In C.A. Salmon, & T.K. Shackelford (Eds.), *Family relationships: An evolutionary perspective* (pp. 185–204). New York: Oxford University Press.

Montgomerie, R.D., & Weatherhead, P.J. (1988). Risks and rewards of nest defense by parent birds. *Quarterly Review of Biology, 63,* 167–187.

Naeye, R.L. (1981). Maternal blood pressure and fetal growth. *American Journal of Obstetrics and Gynecology, 141,* 780–787.

Ng, P.H., & Walters, W.A.W. (1992). The effects of chronic maternal hypertension during pregnancy. *Australian and New Zealand Journal of Obstetrics and Gynecology, 32,* 14–16.

Overpeck, M.D., Brenner, R.A., Trumble, A.C., Trifiletti, L.B., & Berendes, H.W. (1998) Risk factors for infant homicide in the United States. *New England Journal of Medicine, 339,* 1211–1216.

Parker, G.A. (2002). Begging scrambles with unequal chicks: Interactions between need and competitive ability. *Ecology Letters, 5*, 206–215.

Payne, R.B. (2005). *The Cuckoos.* Oxford, UK: Oxford University Press.

Pollet, T.V., Fawcett, T.W., Buunk, A.P., & Nettle, D. (2009). Sex-ratio biasing toward daughters among lower-ranking co-wives in Rwanda. *Biology Letters, 5*, 765–768.

Rauter, C.M., & Moore, A.J. (1999). Do honest signaling models of offspring solicitation apply in insects. *Proceedings of the Royal Society, London, B, 266*, 1691–1696.

Redondo, T. & Castro F. (1992). The increase in the risk of predation with begging activity in magpies *Pica pica. Ibis, 134*, 180–187.

Regalski, J.M., & Gaulin, S.J.C. (1993). Whom are Mexican infants said to resemble? Monitoring and fostering paternal confidence in the Yucatan. *Ethology and Sociobiology, 14*, 97–113.

Rohwer, S., Herron, J. C., & Daly, M. (1999). Stepparental behavior as mating effort in birds and other animals. *Evolution and Human Behavior, 20*, 367–390.

Royle, N.J., Hartley, I.R., & Parker, G.A. (2002). Begging for control: When are offspring solicitation behaviours honest? *Trends in Ecology and Evolution, 17*, 434–440.

Ryder J.P. (1980). The influence of age on the breeding biology of colonial nesting seabirds. In J. Burger, B.L. Offa, & H.E. Winn (Eds.), *The behavior of marine animals, Vol. 4 Marine birds.* New York: Plenum Press.

Saino, N., & Moller, A.P. (2002). Immunity and begging. In J. Wright, & M.L. Leonard (Eds.), *The evolution of begging: Competition, cooperation and communication* (pp. 245–268). London: Kluwer.

Salafia, C.M., Xenophon, J., Vintzileos, A.M., Lerer, T., & Silberman, L. (1990). Fetal growth and placental pathology in maternal hypertensive diseases. *Clinical and Experimental Hypertension, B 9*, 27–41.

Salmon, C.A., & Daly, M. (1998). Birth order and familial sentiment: Middleborns are different. *Evolution and Human Behavior, 19*, 299–312.

Shaankar, R.U., Ganeshaiah, K.N., & Bawa, K.S. (1988). Parent-offspring conflict, sibling rivalry, and brood size patterns in plants. *Annual Review of Ecology, Evolution, and Systematics, 19*, 177–205.

Sieff, D.F. (1990). Explaining biased gender ratios in human populations. *Current Anthropology, 31*, 25–48.

Silk, J.B. (1980). Adoption and kinship in Oceania. *American Anthropologist, 82*, 799–820.

Smith, M.S., Kish, B.J., & Crawford, C.B. (1987). Inheritance of wealth and human kin investment. *Ethology and Sociobiology, 8*, 171–182.

Sulloway, F.J. (2007). Birth order and sibling competition. In R. Dunbar & L. Barrett (Eds.), *The Oxford handbook of evolutionary psychology* (pp. 297–311). Oxford: Oxford University Press.

Stamps, J.A., Clark A., Arrowood P., & Kus, B. (1985) Parent-offspring conflict in budgerigars. *Behaviour, 94*, 1–40.

Starks, P., & Poe, E. (1997). Male stuffing in wasp societies. *Nature, 389*, 450.

Symonds, E.M. (1980). Aetiology of pre-eclampsia: A review. *Journal of the Royal Society of Medicine, 73*, 871–875.

Tallarigo, L., Giampietro, O., Penno, G., Miccoli, R., Gregori, G., & Navalesi, R. (1986). Relation of glucose tolerance to complications of pregnancy in nondiabetic women. *New England Journal of Medicine, 316*, 1343–1346.

Trivers, R.L. (1974). Parent-offspring conflict. *American Zoologist, 14*, 249–264.

Trivers, R. L. (1985) *Social Evolution.* Menlo Park, CA.: Benjamin/Cummings.

Trivers, R.L., & Hare, H. (1976). Haplodiploidy and the evolution of the social insects: The unusual traits of the social insects are uniquely explained by Hamilton's kinship theory. *Science, 191*, 249–263.

Trivers, R.L., & Willard, D. (1973). Natural selection of parental ability to vary the sex-ratio of offspring. *Science, 179*, 90–92.

Villasenor, E., & Drummond, H. (2007). Honest begging in the blue-footed bobby: Signaling, food deprivation and body condition. *Behavioral Ecology and Sociobiology, 61*, 1133–1142.

Voland, E. (1998). Evolutionary ecology of human reproduction. *Annual Review of Anthropology, 27*, 347–374.

Voland, E., & Gabler, S. (1994). Differential twin mortality indicates a correlation between age and parental effort in humans. *Naturwissenschaften, 81*, 224–225.

Zahavi, A., & Zahavi, A. (1997). *The Handicap Principle, a missing piece of Darwin's puzzle.* Oxford: Oxford University Press.

CHAPTER 7

Stepparenting, Divorce, and Investment in Children

Kermyt G. Anderson

Abstract

Human males routinely invest in offspring, but union dissolution and subsequent union formation result in complex family relationships, with men expected to provide care for children from current and previous unions. Many men face the challenge of how much to invest in genetic offspring following divorce, and whether to invest (and if so, how much) in stepchildren following remarriage. Men bias parental care toward their genetic offspring from current mates, with genetic offspring from former relationships and stepchildren from current relationships both receiving lower levels of investment. This chapter reviews the empirical evidence regarding investments in children following divorce, as well as investments in stepchildren, and presents a biosocial model that attempts to explain men's investment patterns in genetic children and stepchildren from current and previous relationships, a synthetic approach lacking in most models of male parental care.

Keywords: Child support, cohabitation, divorce, stepfather, union dissolution

Introduction

Biparental care, in which two parents cooperate to raise offspring, is found in every human culture. The emergence of the human nuclear family plays a central role in many theories of human evolution (see Gray & Anderson, 2010, for a recent summary). These models typically emphasize the establishment of male–female bonds, in which resources (such as hunted meat and gathered vegetable products) are shared in exchange for sexual fidelity; the resulting high paternity confidence led to males investing highly in the offspring of their mates, and the human family was born.

Although human parenting arrangements are typically biparental, tremendous variation exists, both within and across cultures, in the extent to which men are involved in raising children. Furthermore, marriages in many cultures are not permanent, and divorce raises additional questions about male parental care. To what extent do men invest in children following the end of a relationship with the children's mothers? And, if a man remarries a woman who already has children from a previous relationship—that is, he becomes a stepparent—to what extent does he invest in her offspring? This chapter examines these two related questions and reviews the implications that divorce and the formation of stepfamilies have for investment in children.

Divorce

Although some people think of divorce as a modern phenomenon that has arisen in recent decades primarily in urban settings in industrialized nation-states, it has an ancient pedigree. Divorce is common among hunter-gatherers; for example, 25%–40% of marriages among Aka, Hadza, and !Kung hunter-gatherers end in divorce (Blurton Jones, Marlowe, Hawkes, & O'Connell, 2000; Hewlett, 1991b). Not every culture allows marriages to dissolve; in a cross-cultural sample of 94 nonindustrialized societies, divorce was found in about 70% of cultures sampled, and was common or universal in 46% of them (Broude & Green, 1983). Even in industrialized nations, the frequency and acceptability of divorce varies; in Ireland, for example, divorce was legalized only in 1995, under the 15th amendment to the Irish constitution (which allows divorce only after couples have been separated for at least 4 of the past 5 years). In the United States today, about half of legal marriages end in divorce, typically within 8 years (Kreider, 2005).

This cross-cultural variance in the acceptability of divorce reflects underlying variation in marriage itself. Although marriage is essentially a human universal—in virtually every known culture, men and women form medium- to long-term unions in which they pool resources and raise children—the details vary tremendously. Marriage may involve a formal ceremony and celebratory feast, thus gaining social approval by the community. But in some cultures marriage is much more casual. Among Ache hunter-gatherers of Paraguay, for example, marriage occurs when a man and a woman begin sleeping together at the same fire at night (Hill & Hurtado 1996). Although not marked by formal ceremonies, these unions are socially sanctioned, and any offspring that result are socially legitimate; thus, for the purposes of this chapter, these unions will be considered marriages.

In industrialized nations-states, cohabitation (in which two unmarried people live together and have a sexual relationship) is emerging as an alternative form of union formation. Cohabitation is legally and culturally distinct from marriage, but it has marriage-like properties. Cohabitational relationships are often characterized as "trial marriages," giving the couple an opportunity to assess their relationship without the expense and commitment of formal marriage. In the United States, in 2002, 54% of women aged 19–44 had ever cohabited, and 19% of currently unmarried women were cohabiting at the time of survey (Kennedy & Bumpass, 2008). Most cohabitational relationships are fairly short-term, ending within about 2 years; they either transition to legal wedlock, or the couple moves apart (Bumpass, Sweet, & Cherlin, 1991; Wu & Balakrishnan, 1995). In the United States, the majority of marriages are preceded by cohabitation; for example, 62% of women whose first marriage occurred between 1997 and 2001 lived with their partners before marriage (Kennedy & Bumpass, 2008). In northern Europe, over 80% of marriages are preceded by cohabitation, whereas in southern Europe the rate is much lower at 18% (Kalmijn, 2007). Ending a cohabitational relationship differs from divorce, because there are usually fewer legal and social hurdles to simply moving out if a couple is not married. For the purposes of this chapter, I will examine studies of both formally married as well as informally cohabiting couples, and I will use the term "union dissolution" to encompass both legal divorce as well as the cessation of cohabitational unions.

Divorce impacts parental investment in children because most reproduction takes place in the context of unions (marriages or cohabitational relationships) in which two parents cooperate to raise offspring (Gray & Anderson, 2010). For example, a recent study of first births to men in the United States found that 66% were to married couples, 18% were to cohabiting couples, and 16% were to unmarried individuals who were living apart (Martinez, Chandra, Abma, Jones, & Mosher, 2006). Even that last category, however, is likely to mostly comprise individuals in medium-term relationships, rather than casual sex partners or one-night stands. Smock (2000) notes that a large proportion of what surveys identify as births to "single mothers" actually occur within unmarried two-parent households, and Bumpass and Lu (2000) argue that the recent increase in nonmarital births in the United States is due to increased cohabitation rates and not to increases in births to women without partners.

Following divorce (or union dissolution), a child typically no longer resides with both parents. In one study of which parent has custody of children following divorce in 45 cultures, children stayed with their mothers following divorce in 17.8% of societies, and with their fathers in 20.0%; divorce was not allowed in 8.9% of the sample; whereas in the remaining 53.3%, who gets custody following divorce depends on factors such as the children's ages or the circumstances of the divorce (Frayser, 1985). Children in industrialized nation-states are overwhelmingly likely to remain with their mothers upon divorce. In 2005, 13.6 million single parents were living with children under 21 in the United States, 84% of whom were mothers (Grall, 2007). Heuveline, Timberlake, and Furstenberg (2003) examined American family arrangements from birth through age 15 and estimated that 51% of children will spend part of their lives with a single parent. They calculated that over the first 15 years of life, American children can expect to spend 2.70 years living with a single mother, versus 9.88 years living with both biological parents and 2.42 years in other living arrangements. Heuveline et al. also report that children spend a significant amount of time living with single mothers in some European countries as well; for example, children in Germany will spend about 2.69 years living with a single mother, and for Swedish children the figure is 2.08 year. (In contrast, they report that children in Italy, Belgium, Spain, and Switzerland, can expect to spend a year or less living with a single mother.)

In the nonindustrial societies that characterized most of human evolution, father absence is frequently caused by paternal death, as well as by union dissolution. For example, among Ache hunter-gatherers in Paraguay, 25% of 15-year-old children have experienced parental divorce, and 20% have experienced paternal death (Hurtado & Hill, 1992). Paternal mortality is typically more common than maternal mortality, so children who live with single mothers may do so by default if their father is dead.

Causes of Divorce

Many factors contribute to divorce, including personality differences, age differences, conflicts over how to spend money, education level, and so forth (e.g., White, 1990). In recent decades, women with a college education have become less accepting of divorce, whereas the acceptability of divorce has increased among women with less education (Martin & Parashar, 2006). Sex ratio may also play a role; divorce is more likely when new potential partners are abundant. Trent and South (1989) used data from 66 countries and found that high sex ratios (more men than women) predicted lower divorce rates; men are less likely to leave their partners when fewer single women are available.

Although individual personalities play a role in which marriages succeed and which fail, cross-culturally some factors appear to contribute to union dissolution more than others. Betzig (1989) surveyed causes of divorce given for 160 societies. She found that infidelity was the most common grounds for divorce, followed by infertility, cruelty or mistreatment, and "displeasingness."

Divorce for any reason may decrease male involvement with children, but infidelity, as the leading cross-cultural cause of divorce (reported by 55% of the societies in Betzig's [1989] sample), has additional implications for paternal care. Men may respond strongly to sexual infidelity by their partners (either real or imagined) because it has a direct bearing on their paternity confidence; that is, the probability that their putative genetic children are actually theirs. Simply put, a man who unknowingly raises a child who does not carry his genes has expended effort that will not produce any evolutionary benefit for him (Alexander, 1974; Trivers, 1972).

Men are thus vigilant about their partner's sexual behavior, and may react to infidelity—or the perception of infidelity—by ending the relationship, rather than risk being cuckolded.

Because female infidelity may decrease male paternity confidence, whereas male infidelity will not decrease a woman's relatedness to her own offspring, there is a sex bias in the relationship between infidelity and divorce, with men more than women much more likely to divorce an unfaithful spouse. Men are much more likely than women to name adultery as grounds for divorce in England and Wales (Buckle, Gallup, & Rodd, 1996). Among the 88 societies reported by Betzig (1989) in which adultery is given as a valid reason for divorce, divorce followed adultery by either partner in 25 of these societies (28%), by only the wife's infidelity in 54 societies (61%), and by only the husband's infidelity in just two (2%). Using a sample of men living in Albuquerque, New Mexico, Anderson, Kaplan, and Lancaster (2007) found that when men had low paternity confidence in a pregnancy (that is, they had doubts about whether they were the father), they were almost five times more likely to divorce their wives (or leave their girlfriends if they were not married) than when they were convinced the child was theirs.

The third most common cross-cultural justification for divorce, cruelty or mistreatment (found in 34% of Betzig's [1989] cultures), also has implications for male parental investment. Men often use violence to control women's behavior, in particular their sexual behavior (e.g., Daly & Wilson, 1988); suspicions of infidelity may result in the man using violence to punish his spouse, and to discourage future extra-pair copulations. Yet, men's use of violence may eventually lead to women ending the union. In England and Wales, for example, cruelty is the most common grounds for divorce among women, who are far more likely than men to mention this as a reason for ending the marriage (Buckle, Gallup, & Rodd, 1996). In her cross-cultural data, Betzig (1989) noted that cruelty as grounds for divorce is ascribed exclusively to men in 45 out of 51 cultures, and to both spouses in five cultures, whereas in no culture is cruelty ascribed exclusively to women. Betzig also notes that ethnographic material supports the suggestion that male cruelty often results from actual or perceived female infidelity.

Thus, infidelity (by women) and violence (by men), which may often be caused by male concerns about female infidelity) both increase the odds of union dissolution. They may also decrease the man's confidence of paternity in his putative offspring. Reliable data on the frequency of nonpaternity (i.e., the proportion of men raising putative children who were actually sired by other men) are scarce, as most available datasets are biased either toward men with high paternity confidence (such as family genetic studies sampling married couples) or men with low paternity confidence (such as data from paternity-testing laboratories) (Anderson, 2006). A review of published data by Anderson (2006) found that median nonpaternity rates for 36 samples likely to be biased toward men with high paternity confidence was 1.7%–3.3%. Only one study has published data on men's assessment of paternity; using a sample of men living in Albuquerque, New Mexico; Anderson, Kaplan, and Lancaster (2006) found that men expressed doubts that they might be the real father in only 1.46% of pregnancies attributed to them. Low paternity confidence is associated with increased probability that a pregnancy will be aborted (Anderson, Kaplan, & Lancaster, 2006) and with reduced involvement by men with children (Anderson, Kaplan, & Lancaster, 2007). Thus, female infidelity (actual or perceived) may impact investment in children through two pathways: by increasing the probability of divorce, and by lowering the father's paternity confidence in his putative offspring.

Divorce and Paternal Investment

How does divorce itself influence men's investment in offspring? First, it is worth noting that the decisions men face upon divorce—whether or not to continue investing in their children, and if so how much—are a uniquely human conundrum. Only in humans do absent fathers frequently maintain contact with and continue to invest in nonresident dependent offspring (Gray & Anderson, 2010).

When children remain with their mother following union dissolution, forms of male investment that are constrained by proximity, such as spending time with children, must be altered. Most resident fathers see their children every day; in contrast, approximately half of American and Canadian nonresident fathers see their children several times a month or more, versus half who see them several times per year or less (Juby, Billette, Laplante, & Bourdais, 2007; Manning & Smock, 1999). Studies in Albuquerque, New Mexico, and Cape Town, South Africa have also found that men who do not live with their children see them less frequently than men who do (Anderson, Kaplan, Lam, & Lancaster, 1999; Anderson, Kaplan, & Lancaster, 1999). Paternal involvement is associated with distance: Men spend less time with children the further away from them they live (Manning, Stewart, & Smock, 2003). Other forms of contact, such as phone calls and e-mails, can be substituted for face-to-face contact, helping to maintain close emotional bonds between men and their nonresidential children—although evidence suggests that such forms of contact tend to decrease over time following divorce (e.g., Juby et al., 2007).

Men's financial expenditures on children also typically decrease following divorce. Parents who live with a child automatically share their income with that child, but parents who live apart from the child may not (e.g., Lin & McLanahan, 2007). Men typically have lower voluntary financial expenditures—pocket money, purchases such as clothing and food, school or college tuition, etc.—for nonresident genetic offspring than for resident ones (e.g., Anderson, Kaplan, & Lancaster, 1999). Perhaps the most salient form of postdivorce paternal investment in industrialized societies is child support (or maintenance). To give an idea of the scale of child support payments, in the United States, custodial mothers received $22.4 billion in child support in 2005 (Grall, 2007), clearly a substantial investment in children.

Many men pay child support willingly, and feel it is morally the right thing to do. Nonresident fathers who do not pay child support are judged negatively and often labeled "deadbeat dads." Despite this, many men who have child support obligations either pay no support or only part of what they are supposed to pay. In the United States, in 2005, 23% of custodial mothers who were supposed to receive child support did not receive any payments, while 30% received only partial payments; only 47% received the full amount awarded (U.S. Census Bureau, 2009). Because approximately 92% of women who receive child support from noncustodial fathers do so through formal legal arrangements (Grall, 2007), this implies that a large fraction of nonresident fathers are not contributing financially to their offspring, despite the moral opprobrium associated with this course of action.

Divorce and Children's Outcomes

Another way to examine how divorce impacts paternal investment in children is to compare the outcomes of children living with genetic fathers versus those who do not. Children's outcomes (such as survival, health, educational attainment, socioeconomic status, etc.) presumably reflect cumulative investment received from a variety of sources, so if children from father-absent households fare worse than children from father-present homes, the inference is that the difference is due (at least in part) to less investment by absent fathers (although other paternal factors, such as genes shared by fathers and children, may also contribute to these outcomes).

The impact of fathers on children's outcomes may begin even before the child is born. One study of birth certificates in the American state of Georgia found that babies with no father listed on the birth certificate (a proxy for father absence) were more likely to be underweight and to be born prematurely, factors that put them at a disadvantage right from the start (Gaudino, Jenkins, & Rochat, 1999). Children with no father listed on the birth certificate were also about twice as likely to die in their first year of life, even controlling for differences across children in background factors such as maternal socioeconomic status, maternal smoking, pregnancy duration, and birthweight.

In industrialized societies, infant mortality is a fairly rare occurrence; for example, in the United States about 7 out of 1,000 children born will die before their first birthday (U.S. Census Bureau, 2009). In nonindustrialized cultures lacking access to modern medical interventions, infant mortality rates are much higher. For example, among extant hunter-gathers, about 20.3 out of every 1,000 babies born will not reach their first birthday, whereas for horticulturalists and pastoralists the rate is 21.0 out of 1,000 (Hewlett, 1991a). Clearly, child mortality has a strong impact on evolutionary fitness, because only children who survive to adulthood and reproduce count toward one's reproductive success. Does divorce increase the odds of child mortality in traditional societies?

In one of the few studies to specifically examine the effect of divorce on children in a traditional population, Hill and Hurtado (1996) examined child mortality among Ache hunter-gatherers of Paraguay. Children whose parents had divorced were 1.09 times more likely to die than were children whose parents were married. This effect is almost identical to that observed for paternal death: Children whose fathers have died were 1.1 times more likely to die than were children whose fathers were alive. Because the leading cause of child mortality among the Ache is homicide, Hill and Hurtado attribute the protective effect of fathers to their role in maintaining male coalitions that resulted in decreased violence against their children, rather than increased direct investment (such as food provisioning) from fathers.

In industrialized societies, father absence due to divorce has been associated with a host of negative children's outcomes, including increased risk of dropping out of school and lower educational attainment, poorer physical and mental health, and behavioral problems (Amato, 2000; Anderson, Kaplan, & Lancaster, 1999; Biblarz & Gottainer, 2000; Hofferth, 2006; Mott, Kowaleski-Jones, & Menaghan, 1997). These effects can extend into the children's adulthood, influencing marital status and marital quality as well (Amato & Cheadle, 2005; Amato & Keith, 1991).

Negative effects of father absence on children's social outcomes have been found in non-Western societies as well. Scelza (2010) examined the timing of male initiation among the Martu of Australia. Initiation is a rite of passage that signals that a boy has become a man, and is necessary for social status as an adult (including being able to marry). It is an expensive as well as arduous ritual, but has important fitness consequences, as men who underwent initiation at earlier ages have higher fertility by age 30. Scelza found that boys who have fathers present in their lives undergo initiation at earlier ages than do boys with no fathers present.

Father involvement following divorce is not necessarily an all-or-nothing phenomenon, and there is tremendous variation in the extent to which divorced fathers maintain contact with their nonresidential children (Leite & McKenry, 2002; Mott, 1990). Higher levels of involvement by nonresident fathers may assuage the negative effects of father absence on children's outcomes (Amato & Gilbreth, 1999; King & Sobolewski, 2006). Quality of the parents' relationship before divorce, or of the predivorce father–child relationship, can also be an important factor: Children fare worse following divorce when predivorce relationships were good and fare better when predivorce relationships were poor (Booth & Amato, 2001; Strohschein, 2005), suggesting that children are sometimes better off without a father if the father's relationship to the child or the mother was not good.

Stepfathers

A man becomes a stepfather when he enters a relationship with a woman who already has biological children (Gray & Anderson, 2010). This is distinct from adoption or fostering (in which a couple jointly parents a child who is the offspring of neither of them), as well as nonpaternity (in which a man raises a child who is supposedly his but actually is not). The stepchildren are present from the start of the relationship, and the man faces the question of whether to invest in them and, if so, how much, from the moment the union begins.

Stepparenting necessarily follows from union dissolution, for at least one partner. Stewart (2007) notes that "traditional" stepfamilies form when a pair of divorced individuals, at least one of whom had kids, marry each other. However, the increase in cohabitation and in nonmarital births has changed the nature of stepfamily formation, and the adults in stepfamilies need neither to be currently nor previously married: Couples may live together without being married, or marriage may involve at least one partner who has never have been married before (Stewart, 2007). The vast majority of research on stepfamilies has focused on married couples (Stewart, 2007), and most target families in which the stepparent is male.

Stepfamilies are not a uniquely human arrangement, nor do they occur solely in modern industrialized societies as a result of high divorce rates. Many animal studies, mostly on birds, have reported cases in which incoming males tolerate or provide care for existing offspring of female mates (Rohwer, 1986; Rohwer, Herron, & Daly, 1999). Stepparenting has been observed in several primate species as well (Smuts & Gubernick, 1992). For example, primatologist Barbara Smuts (1985), observing olive baboons in Kenya, found that females often associate with males that Smuts labeled "friends." These friends spend significantly more time near females' infants than nonfriend males, and are significantly more likely to interact with them and to protect the infants when other, potentially aggressive males approach. Some of these male friends are possible fathers of the infants, but a good many were not. Smuts avoids describing these nonfather males as stepfathers, yet they apparently fulfill a similar role.

Stepfamilies are not necessarily uncommon among preindustrial populations, where mortality and divorce both lead to remarriage. Among Aka hunter-gatherers of central Africa, 18% of children aged 11–15 live with a mother and stepfather, and another 6% live with a father and stepmother (Hewlett, 1991b). Among the Yora of Peru, 15% of children with at least one living biological parent, and 12.5% of children with two living parents, live with a stepfather (Sugiyama & Chacon, 2005). Among both !Kung hunter-gatherers in southern Africa and Hadza hunter-gatherers in Tanzania, children often identify their stepfathers as "father" after remarriage, but they can identify their biological fathers if they are asked (Howell, 2000; Marlowe, 1999).

In modern nation-states, the increase in divorce and nonmarital births in recent decades has led to more children living with stepparents, usually stepfathers. Recent cross-sectional estimates suggest that 7% of American children aged birth through 17 live with a biological parent and a stepparent—approximately 6% with a stepfather and 1% with a stepmother (Federal Interagency Forum on Child and Family Statistics, 2007).

Cross-sectional measures of family structure will underestimate the proportion of children living with stepfathers, because many children now living with both biological parents or with a single mother will eventually live with a stepfather. Precise estimates of the cumulative proportion of children who will live with a stepparent are difficult to obtain, in part because many demographic surveys do not distinguish between biological fathers and stepfathers, or do not identify stepfamilies arising from unmarried couples, and the like (Stewart, 2007). Bumpass, Raley, and Sweet (1995) estimated that 30% of American children will spend time living in a stepfamily, whereas Heuveline, Timberlake, and Furstenberg (2003) calculate that American children aged birth to 15 will spend 1.9 years (or 13% of their childhood) living with a mother and a stepfather. In European countries, there is great variation in the cumulative percentage of their youth that children will spend living with a stepfather, ranging from 1.1% in Italy and 2.3% in Spain, to 10.5% in Latvia and 11.4% in the Czech Republic (Heuveline et al., 2003).

Stepfathers and Parental Care

Numerous studies have shown that stepfathers invest less in stepchildren than genetic fathers do in genetic offspring. In the United States, men spend less time with stepchildren, and they spend less money on them (Anderson, Kaplan, & Lancaster, 1999; Evenhouse & Reilly, 2004; Hofferth & Anderson, 2003; Hofferth, 2006; Thomson, Hanson, & McLanahan, 1994; Zvoch, 1999). Stepchildren have poorer grades and complete less education than do children without stepparents (Case, Lin, & McLanahan, 2001; Downey, 1995; Hofferth, 2006); those stepchildren who go to college receive less financial support from stepfathers (Anderson, Kaplan, & Lancaster, 1999). Stepfathers also evince less emotional warmth for stepchildren (Hofferth & Anderson, 2003), and stepchildren are more likely to have emotional and behavioral problems (Hofferth, 2006; Mott, Kowaleski-Jones, & Menaghan, 1997).

Outside of the United States, stepfathers invest less in stepchildren as well. Hadza hunter-gatherers spend less time near, in communication with, or nurturing stepchildren than biological children, and they never play with stepchildren (Marlowe, 1999). Men in Trinidad spend less time interacting with their stepchildren than their genetic children (Flinn, 1988), and high school students in South Africa report spending less time with and receiving less money from stepfathers than from coresident genetic fathers (Anderson, Kaplan, Lam, & Lancaster, 1999).

Incoming stepfathers do not necessarily have to invest in their stepchildren at all. Rohwer, Herron, and Daly (1999), discussing mating patterns among nonhuman species, note that a stepparent has three options when entering a mating relationship that brings with it preexisting offspring: kill them, tolerate them, or actively invest in them. Males in many species exercise the first option; infanticide by an incoming male may bring the mother back into a fertile state, allowing him to have a new offspring with her, thereby increasing his reproductive success (Hrdy, 1979; Rohwer et al., 1999). Humans are much more likely to invest in or at least tolerate offspring than murder them. Marsiglio (1991) found that, although many stepfathers have negative perceptions of stepparenting, many also feel positively toward the experience. For example, 52% of men felt the statement "It is harder to love stepchildren than it is to love your own children" was somewhat false or definitely false, whereas 55% felt the statement "Having stepchildren is just as satisfying as having your own children" was somewhat or definitely true. Some men are as close to their stepchildren as they could possibly be to their own genetic offspring.

At one point, sociologists felt that the increase in stepfathers due to rising levels of divorce and remarriage would benefit children, as stepfathers stepped in to replace absent fathers (Cherlin & Furstenberg, 1994). This optimistic view turned out to be inaccurate; stepfathers are generally not replacement fathers, and in terms of many outcomes, stepchildren are much more like children living with single mothers than children living in households with two biological parents (Case, Lin, & McLanahan, 2001; McLanahan & Sandefur, 1994), although there is evidence that children who have close relationships with their stepfathers have better outcomes (Amato & Rivera, 1999; White & Gilbreth, 2001). Indeed, there is a great deal of ambiguity regarding whether stepfathers are expected to act as replacement fathers.

Cherlin (1978) argued that remarriage is an incomplete institution, subject to a certain degree of social and cultural ambiguity. Unlike first marriages, in which the roles of spouses are fairly clearly defined, the roles of stepparents are not standardized, and thus stepparents do not have clear-cut expectations regarding how they should behave. Additionally, in industrialized societies, the stepchildren's biological father is usually still alive, reducing even further the need for the stepfather to step into the role of father. The general consensus is that stepfathers are not expected to do exactly what "real" fathers do (Coleman, Ganong, & Cable, 1996).

Although stepfathers may not be openly hostile to their stepchildren, the stepparent–stepchild relationship is acknowledged to often be difficult, characterized by conflicts of interest between the parties involved. Two biological parents share a similar perspective on their joint children—they both benefit from investments in the children—but in a stepfamily, investments that benefit the children may be favored by the biological parent but not the stepparent, resulting in a conflict of interest (Daly & Wilson, 1998). Stepfathers and stepsiblings do not share genes, do not share a personal history, and may resent the other due to the demands each makes on the person who is their intersection point, the mother of the child.

Although most human stepfathers either invest in or at least tolerate their stepchildren, a subset have more aggressive relationships. Stepfathers are perceived as having great potential for physical and sexual abuse. In one study of college students, 34% felt that stepfathers were more likely to physically abuse male children than genetic fathers, 56% felt that stepfathers and genetic fathers were about equally likely to abuse children, and only about 10% felt that stepfathers were less likely to abuse children than genetic fathers (Claxton-Oldfield & Whitt, 2003). Among respondents who felt that stepfathers represented a greater risk, the most common reason given for this perception was lack of a biological relationship between the man and the child (Claxton-Oldfield & Whitt, 2003).

Stepfathers are also more likely to actually abuse stepchildren, as well as kill them, compared to biological fathers. Martin Daly and Margo Wilson began documenting stepfathers' increased potential for violence in 1981 (Daly & Wilson, 1981), and have substantiated this line of research with numerous other publications using multiple datasets (e.g., Daly & Wilson, 1988, 1994, 1998, 2001). Controlling for background factors (such as the fact that stepchildren tend to be older than genetic offspring, and differences in parental income and education), they find that children were between 40 and 100 times more likely to be abused or murdered if they lived in a stepfather household than if they lived in a household with two biological parents. These results are rather startling, and have received some criticism (e.g., Malkin & Lamb, 1994), yet have stood up under repeated analyses (Daly & Wilson, 2001). These results have also been subject to misinterpretation; some people feel Daly and Wilson's research implies that stepfathers in general are extremely violent, and some of the negative reactions to their findings are based on this misinterpretation. Daly and Wilson themselves are quick to point out that, although the relative risk of abuse or homicide is much greater for stepfathers than for genetic fathers, the absolute levels of violence directed toward children by stepfathers are extremely low (1998). Assuming that increased rates of violence found among stepfathers imply that most stepfathers are violent is a logical fallacy, but unfortunately a common one based on a misunderstanding of relative risks.

As noted above, some men form extremely close bonds with their stepchildren. Daly and Wilson have focused on abuse and homicide in their analyses not because these outcomes are commonplace but because they are less likely to go unreported (particularly homicide). The greater risks experienced by stepchildren are probably not the result of a conscious "homicidal agenda" on the part of stepfathers, but more likely due to numerous factors, such as men having fewer "brakes" on aggressive or violent behavior toward unrelated children than toward their own offspring; stepfathers preferentially directing care and resources (and protection) toward genetic offspring and away from stepchildren; and perhaps the very presence of stepchildren, and the conflicts of interest they induce between parents, resulting in more arguments and fights that end in lethal outcomes (Daly & Wilson, 1998). None of this behavior need be conscious. For example, men could follow a simple rule of thumb, such as "act more nicely toward children you knew as infants"; because men typically do not meet stepchildren until the children are somewhat older, this simple rule could account, at a proximate level, for men's reduced investment in stepchildren. Relatively little empirical analysis has examined whether men's investment in stepchildren is correlated with the children's age when the relationship began, although studies show no general trend toward men investing more in stepchildren they began to parent at younger ages (Gray & Anderson, 2010).

The so-called Cinderella Effect—greater levels of abuse and aggression experienced by stepchildren relative to genetic offspring—has been observed in cross-cultural settings as well. Flinn (1988) observed that men in Trinidad were more likely to behave agonistically toward stepchildren than genetic children, a behavior category that includes any form of physical or verbal conflict, as well as screaming or crying that is likely to have been the result of conflict. Flinn also found that stepchildren go out of their way to avoid contact with stepfathers: Children under 20 with stepfathers were much more likely to live with their grandparents instead of their mothers than were children without a stepfather, whereas young adults over 20 were much more likely to have emigrated from their village if their mother coresided with a stepfather. Flinn and England (1997) documented greater levels of stress hormones in stepchildren than in genetic offspring, as well as poorer health outcomes for stepchildren, among children living in the Caribbean nation of Dominica. Although he did not document conflict with stepfathers, Marlowe (2005) found that Hadza children were much more likely to be held by a mother or maternal grandmother when a stepfather was present than when a genetic father was present. These kin may have been compensating for the stepfather's reduced level of care, relative to the genetic father—and they may have been safeguarding the child as well.

At least 27 distinct theories have been proposed to explain how stepfamilies work (Stewart, 2007). Cherlin's (1978) description of remarriage as an incomplete institution, discussed above, has proved highly influential, although it has received little direct empirical testing (Stewart, 2007). From an evolutionary perspective, individuals who direct resources toward their own offspring are expected to leave more descendents than are those who invest in unrelated offspring (Alexander, 1974). Viewed in this light, the reduced investment of men in stepchildren relative to genetic offspring makes evolutionary sense (Daly & Wilson, 1998). A counter-strategy of "invest more in stepchildren than in genetic children" would be less likely to leave descendents.

And yet, as reviewed above, a substantial fraction of children live with stepfathers. If investing in stepchildren is evolutionary disadvantageous, why is it not rare? Can evolutionary theory shed some light on why so many men are willing to invest in stepchildren—many quite willingly?

A Biosocial Model of Paternal Investment in Children

In an earlier set of papers (Anderson, Kaplan, Lam, & Lancaster 1999; Anderson, Kaplan, and Lancaster 1999; Hofferth & Anderson, 2003; see also Gray & Anderson, 2010), I developed a biosocial model of parental investment in offspring. Most theories of parental investment—from both evolutionary and nonevolutionary perspectives—focus on the benefit to offspring as the goal of the investment. A parent provides care for an offspring because the care increases the well-being (or fitness) of the recipient child. This model has strong intuitive appeal, and clearly applies to many cases. And yet, it does not explain the decrease in parental care observed following divorce, nor does it explain (from an evolutionary perspective at least) investment in stepchildren.

Evolutionary models have posited that fundamental trade-offs exist between mating effort (expenditures of time and resources that lead to the acquisition of a sexual partner, and the maintenance of such relationships) and parental effort (the production of and investment in offspring) (e.g., Low, 1978; Trivers, 1972). Under this heuristic model, effort allocated to one end (such as acquiring a mate) cannot be used for the other (such as improving the fitness of offspring). And yet, this trade-off may be relaxed under certain circumstances (Anderson, Kaplan, & Lancaster, 1999; Rohwer, Herron, & Daly, 1999; Smuts, 1985). Consider a species in which parental care exists. If providing care to offspring enhances one's appeal to the opposite sex, then parental care can function as both mating effort and parental effort—it can simultaneously increase one's appeal as a reproductive partner while increasing the fitness of existing offspring. Mating and parental effort can thus overlap.

Table 7.1 demonstrates how the model applies to different types of father–child relationships. Paternal care for men's genetic offspring through their current partners (upper left cell) is a combination of parental effort and mating effort: The care both benefits the child and improves the man's relationship with the child's mother. This is predicted to be the highest level of investment. Following divorce, the man is no longer in a sexual relationship with the child's mother, and thus care provided for that child is only parental effort, with no mating effort component (upper right cell of the table). Men will reallocate resources away from children following divorce, so that they can invest in new mating relationships (and possibly in new offspring); thus, investment in genetic offspring decreases following union dissolution.

The model also explains investment in stepchildren. From an evolutionary perspective, investment in stepchildren cannot be parental effort, since stepchildren do not carry the stepparent's genes. But if the biological parent of the stepchild is selecting a mate in part based on the mate's willingness and ability to invest in that child, then care provided to a stepchild is in fact mating effort. By investing in stepchildren, men are investing in their relationships with the stepchildren's mothers. This is shown in the lower left corner of the table.

The final cell of the table, at the lower right, represents stepchildren of former relationships, that is, following union dissolution. Because the stepparent has no genetic relatedness to the child, and is no longer in a relationship with the child's biological parent, postdivorce stepparental care can be classified as neither parental effort nor mating effort. As such, we expect to see minimal investment in stepchildren following union dissolution.

Support for the Biosocial Model

The biosocial model posits that parental care can also be a form of mating effort. Thus, men who willingly invest more in children may be more appealing as spouses, increasing their likelihood of initiating and maintaining long-term relationships. Several lines of evidence support this. Kalmijn (1999) found that Dutch families in which men were more involved in parental care had more stable marriages, because "the wife is happier if the husband is strongly involved with the children" (p. 409). One American study found that divorce is less likely following the birth of a boy than a girl, an effect which may result from men being more involved with sons than daughters (Morgan, Lye, & Condran, 1988); greater investment of men in their sons thus raises their attractiveness as partners, reducing the probability of divorce.

The biosocial model's premise that men's investments in stepchildren may be a form of mating effort is consistent with several lines of evidence. Smuts (1985), discussing baboons, suggests that males provide care and protection for infants because they receive reciprocal benefits from the infants' mothers. Several studies have found that men's potential willingness to invest in children influences women's perception of men as potential dates, sexual partners, or marital partners (Brase, 2006; La Cerra, 1994; Roney, Hanson, Durante, & Maestripieri, 2006). Other research has found that males appear to adjust their behavior toward children according to whether women are observing them. In Trinidad,

Table 7.1 Father–child relationships, by the man's relatedness to child and relationship with child's mother

Relatedness to Child	Relationship with Child's Mother	
	Current partner	*Previous partner*
Genetic child	Parental and mating investment (Highest level of investment)	Parental investment (Intermediate level of investment)
Stepchild	Mating investment (Intermediate level of investment)	Minimal investment

Mark Flinn (1988) found that men were more likely to have agonistic interactions with stepchildren when the mothers were not in view than when they were; in contrast, men's agonistic interactions with genetic offspring were not influenced by the presence or absence of the mother. This finding echoes the results of an experimental study with vervet monkeys, which found that subordinate males behaved more nicely toward infants who were separated from their mothers when the males could see the mother than when the mothers were not visible (Keddy Hector, Seyfarth, & Raleigh, 1989).

In reproductive terms, many stepfathers benefit from marrying (or partnering with) women who already have children. Some couples with stepchildren will have a child together to strengthen and validate their marital bond (Stewart, 2005). Stewart (2002) finds that, although American men desire fewer additional biological children as the number of stepchildren increases, in reality actual fertility patterns are not suppressed by the presence of stepchildren, a finding echoed by Li (2006). Many, perhaps most men, would prefer to marry women who do not already have children, and the evidence suggests that they would have greater fertility from doing so. But in terms of fertility, marrying a woman who already has children—and thus becoming a stepfather—produces greater fitness returns than never marrying at all. Anderson (2000) found that American men with one stepchild were more likely to have a child in a new marriage than were men with no stepchildren. Men with two stepchildren and with no stepchildren were equally likely to have a child within a new marriage, whereas men with three stepchildren were less likely than men with no stepchildren to have a child. Looking at lifetime fertility for American men aged 45 and older, Anderson (2000) found that among ever married men, lifetime fertility decreased with each additional stepchild parented, so that the highest overall fertility is observed among men who never raised stepchildren. The lowest levels of fertility, by a wide margin, are observed in men who never married. Men who parented one or two stepchildren over their lives averaged about two births more than men who never married, whereas even men who had raised three stepchildren had about 1.1 more births over their lifetimes than never married men.

In cultures in which divorce is rare and adult mortality is low, most men can obtain a wife who has never married. But when union dissolution is commonplace, the laws of supply and demand dictate that there will be fewer childless women looking for husbands than there are men looking for wives. Many men will be willing to accept a spouse with children than remain single. Investing in (or at least tolerating) stepchildren is the price many men are willing to pay to acquire a partner (Anderson, 2000).

The biosocial model presented in Table 7.1 makes implicit claims about the relative levels of care received by both genetic offspring and stepchildren, both before and after divorce. We have already seen that men invest less in genetic offspring following divorce, and invest less in stepchildren through their current mates than genetic children through their current mates. How do the other offspring categories of the table compare with one another in terms of men's investment patterns?

Very few studies have compared men's investments in genetic children by former mates with stepchildren by current mates. The model predicts that both will receive reduced levels of care relative to resident biological offspring. In a study of children parented by men living in Albuquerque, New Mexico, Anderson, Kaplan, and Lancaster (1999) found that both genetic offspring of previous mates and stepchildren of current mates were equally likely to attend college; among those attending college, both kinds of offspring were equally likely to receive financial support for education from the focal man. No differences were found between the two groups in terms of non–school-related financial expenditures, for either younger (aged birth through 17) or older (aged 18 through 24) offspring. Only for time involvement with children aged 5 through 12 was there a statistically significant difference: Due to proximity, men spend more time with stepchildren who live with them than with genetic offspring who do not. Similar results were found for self-reported involvement with parental figures by black township high school students living in Cape Town, South Africa, who reported minimal differences in financial expenditures for stepfathers and non-resident genetic fathers, but greater differences in time involvement (Anderson, Kaplan, Lam, & Lancaster, 1999).

Virtually nothing is known about stepchildren from previous relationships. Stewart (2007) notes that most demographic datasets do not even identify such children, and thus undercount the number of children who have ever been stepchildren. Ganong, Coleman, and Mistina (1995, p. 313) conducted a study of American beliefs about men's obligations to children following divorce, finding that "[f]ormer stepfathers were almost universally seen as no longer obligated towards stepchildren. In fact, this is the clearest consensus found in this study." Actual data on men's parental care for children following divorce has been gathered exclusively on genetic offspring, with one exception. Anderson, Kaplan, and Lancaster (1999), using a sample of men living in Albuquerque, New Mexico, examined investments and outcomes in stepchildren from men's former relationships. Compared not only with stepchildren of current mates but with both genetic offspring of current and former mates as well, stepchildren of former mates are the least likely to attend college and the least likely to receive money for college; they also received the lowest financial expenditures for non–school-related activities.

There are numerous explanations for why men invest less in biological offspring following divorce. Some of these focus more on proximate explanations of the phenomenon. Nonresident fathers may have less money to spend on children because of the fixed costs of maintaining a household; it is more expensive for two adults to maintain independent households than to have one joint household, leaving less income to spend on children (Weiss & Willis, 1993). Men may also reduce investments that are channeled through the child's mother because they cannot monitor or control whether she is using the money in ways consistent with his desires (Arendell, 1995; Weiss & Willis, 1993). This may explain why positive and friendly relationships between ex-spouses are associated with greater child support compliance (Kurdek, 1986)—perhaps the father trusts, or can better monitor, that the mother is spending the money appropriately if they are on better terms. Both child support and involvement with children have been found to increase when the physical distance between men's and children's residences is less (Manning, Stewart, & Smock, 2003; Seltzer, 1991), and some studies (although not all) have found that men who visit their children more frequently are more likely to pay child support (e.g., Juby, Billette, Laplante, & Bourdais, 2007; Sonenstein & Calhoun, 1990). Shackelford, Weekes-Shackelford, and Schmitt (2005) note that the causality of the relationship between distance and child support compliance is unclear—perhaps men who plan to invest more in their children choose to live closer to them—and they posit that men who pay more child support may visit their nonresidential children more frequently in order to monitor how the mother is spending the money. The idea that men decrease investments in children following divorce because women may redirect the money elsewhere does not explain, however, the decrease in forms of parental care that are channeled directly to children, such as pocket money and financial support for college (Anderson, Kaplan, Lam, & Lancaster 1999; Anderson, Kaplan, & Lancaster, 1999).

Male income is, not surprisingly, an important factor in child support compliance; men who earn more money are more likely to pay child support (Lin, 2000; Manning, Stewart, & Smock, 2003). Perceived fairness is also an issue with meeting child support obligations. Men who think their child support award is fair will pay it; further governmental involvement (such as garnishing wages) does not increase their compliance. In contrast, men who view their awards as unfair are less willing to pay the amount they owe; in these men, compliance is increased by methods such as withholding child support payments from their wages (Lin, 2000).

No studies measure investments by the same men both before and after divorce, and track their subsequent marital, cohabitational, or reproductive patterns following union dissolution. The biosocial model predicts that a trade-off will occur between high postdivorce investment in genetic offspring and subsequent mating or reproductive success (Anderson, Kaplan, & Lancaster, 1999). Consistent with this, Flinn (1992) found that men in Trinidad who were single were more likely to interact with their nonresident children than were men who had a new mate. Additionally, several studies have examined whether men who pay child support are less likely to remarry or father additional children than men who do not. The results are inconclusive, with several studies finding that men who pay child support are less likely to remarry, to form new sexual partnerships, or to have children (Anderson, 2010; Bloom, Conrad, & Miller, 1998; Huang & Han, 2007), whereas other studies have shown that men who have children within new relationships are subsequently less likely to pay child support (Manning & Smock, 2000; Manning, Stewart, & Smock, 2003). However, some studies have found no effect of child support payments on subsequent union formation (Stewart, Manning, & Smock, 2003). Still, the model may explain why many men are often resistant to paying child support, at least in full. Although men recognize their moral responsibility to paying child support, even if they subsequently remarry or have a new baby (Lin & McLanahan, 2007), men often complain that child support awards are unfair and too high (Arendell, 1995), and 53% of men with child support obligations either do not pay any money or pay only partially (U.S. Census Bureau, 2009). It is possible that the perceived unfairness of child support obligations results in part from the trade-offs between mating and parental effort men experience following union dissolution, when they are keen to reallocate resources away from the old relationship (in the form of parental care for biological offspring) into new avenues of mating effort.

Future Directions

Many unanswered questions remain and merit closer attention. A common theme is that data collection must change in order to address these unresolved questions. In particular, longitudinal data—in which detailed data are collected from the same individuals over time—can answer many questions that cross-sectional data cannot, for example by providing measures of parental involvement both before and after divorce. Unfortunately, longitudinal data collection has the disadvantage of being very labor-intensive, as it involves tracking and reinterviewing people several times (a difficult task as people are increasingly mobile, especially after union dissolution). Measurements of household composition and family dynamics must be more nuanced as well, to capture the increased complexity observed in contemporary culture, including short-term relationships and nonmarital unions. Improved data collection is essential if we are to advance our knowledge in the following areas:

1. How important is self-selection in influencing men's investments in children? Cross-sectional data generally compare groups of men—for example, investments in genetic offspring by men who are currently married versus men who are divorced. And yet, men who choose to leave a relationship may differ in important ways from men who choose to remain. Similarly, men who choose to become a stepparent may differ from men who only raise genetic offspring. To what extent are the differences observed in investment patterns due to differences in the types of men in different relationships, as opposed to the relationships themselves? Some studies have examined blended households—men who have both stepchildren and genetic children by the same woman—and have found reduced, but still significant, differences in investments between the two types of offspring being compared (e.g., Case, Lin, & McLanahan, 2001; Evenhouse & Reilly, 2004; Hofferth & Anderson, 2003; Hofferth, 2006). Yet, there are still selection issues in blended families, as men who have a biological child within a stepfamily may differ from men who do not. No study has yet examined investments by the same men both before and after divorce, to examine whether poor investors after divorce were less involved with children before divorce as well.

2. How does parental care vary across cohabiting versus married families? An increasing percentage of births occur in the context of unmarried cohabiting couples, and many stepfamilies are composed of unmarried couples as well. These are often undetected by recent surveys, who consider women single if they are unmarried, even if they are living with a long-term partner. Some studies have suggested that unmarried genetic fathers and stepfathers invest less in children than do married ones, and are associated with poorer outcomes (Hofferth & Anderson, 2003; Hofferth, 2006). Nonmarital births may also be associated with weaker social bonds between parents, as well as weaker legal protection for mothers once the relationship ends (including reduced likelihood of obtaining a child support award) (Case, Lin, & McLanahan, 2003). Do married stepfathers behave more like unmarried resident biological fathers rather than unmarried stepfathers?

3. To what extent do single women with children use cues of men's quality as a potential investor in their children as a mate choice guideline? What specific indicators do women use, and how important are they? Although some studies suggest women do pay attention to potential parental investment cues in men (La Cerra, 1994; Roney, Hanson, Durante, & Maestripieri, 2006), no research has specifically examined single mothers. One potential study that could be done is to have single women with children keep longitudinal "dating diaries," enumerating the qualities (including perceived potential level of parental care) associated with prospective partners, to examine whether how important potential care is to women selecting a mate who will be a stepfather to her children.

4. How do trade-offs in mating and parental effort influence investments in children across the life course? As reviewed above, men decrease investments in children following union dissolution as they reallocate resources to new relationships (including, possibly, investments in new genetic offspring and stepchildren). Yet, for many men, this subsequent relationship will come to an end as well. As multipartnered fertility becomes increasingly common (e.g., Guzzo & Furstenberg, 2007; Harknett & Knab, 2007), some men will experience successive cycles of unions (with or without children) followed by periods without a partner. How do these patterns influence men's investments in children from previous unions? Do men's investments wax and wane as new partners come and go? Most research on men's investments following divorce assumes men have had children through only one previous partner, but for some men, family dynamics are more complex, and we simply do not know how union dissolution, repartnering, and subsequent union dissolution influences men's involvement with children from earlier unions.

Conclusion

In conclusion, a great deal is known about men's patterns of care for both genetic children and stepchildren, before and after divorce. Yet, much remains to be learned. Many different theories (far more than can be reviewed here) have been proposed to explain the decrease in men's investments in children following divorce, and men's lower investments in resident stepchildren compared to resident genetic offspring. Only one theory—the biosocial model of parental and mating effort reviewed in this chapter—offers a theoretical basis that explains all of these investment patterns simultaneously. The biosocial model also explains why investment occurs at all in these offspring, which is as important an issue (especially for stepchildren) as why investment levels are reduced. Other theories may be developed that encompass men's overall investments in all kinds of offspring—biological and step, from current and former relationships—although so far only evolutionarily minded researchers have attempted to address the "big picture" of men's investments in children. The increasing complexity of family patterns makes disentangling men's investments in children fathered across partners both a challenge and a necessity if we are to fully understand how men provide care for the children they have parented.

References

Alexander, R.D. (1974). The evolution of social behavior. *Annual Review of Ecology and Systematics, 5*, 325–383.

Amato, P.R. (2000). The consequences of divorce for adults and children. *Journal of Marriage and the Family, 62*, 1269–1287.

Amato, P.R., & Keith, B. (1991). Parental divorce and the well-being of children: A meta-analysis. *Psychological Bulletin, 110*, 26–46.

Amato, P.R., & Gilbreth, J.G. (1999). Nonresident fathers and children's well-being: A meta-analysis. *Journal of Marriage and the Family, 61*, 557–573.

Amato, P.R., & Rivera, F. (1999). Paternal involvement and children's behavior problems. *Journal of Marriage & the Family, 61*, 375–384.

Amato, P.R., & Cheadle, J. (2005). The long reach of divorce: Tracking marital dissolution and child well-being across three generations. *Journal of Marriage and Family, 67*, 191–206.

Anderson, K.G. (2000). The life histories of American stepfathers in evolutionary perspective. *Human Nature, 11*, 307–333.

Anderson, K.G. (2005). Relatedness and investment in children in South Africa. *Human Nature, 16*, 1–31.

Anderson, K.G. (2010). Does paying child support reduce men's subsequent remarriage and fertility? Unpublished manuscript, Department of Anthropology, University of Oklahoma.

Anderson, K.G., Kaplan, H., Lam, D., & Lancaster, J.B. (1999). Paternal care by genetic fathers and stepfathers II: Reports by Xhosa high school students. *Evolution and Human Behavior, 20*, 433–451.

Anderson, K.G., Kaplan, H., & Lancaster, J.B. (1999). Paternal care by genetic fathers and stepfathers I: Reports from Albuquerque men. *Evolution and Human Behavior, 20*, 405–431.

Anderson, K.G., Kaplan, H., & Lancaster, J.B. (2006). Demographic correlates of paternity confidence and pregnancy outcomes among Albuquerque men. *American Journal of Physical Anthropology, 131*, 560–571.

Anderson, K.G., Kaplan, H., & Lancaster, J.B. (2007). Confidence of paternity, divorce, and investment in children by Albuquerque men. *Evolution and Human Behavior, 28*, 1–10.

Arendell, T. (1995). *Fathers and Divorce*. Thousand Oaks, CA: Sage Publications.

Betzig, L. (1989). Causes of conjugal dissolution: A cross cultural study. *Current Anthropology*, 30, 654–676.

Biblarz, T.J., & Gottainer, G. (2000). Family structure and children's success: A comparison of widowed and divorced single-mother families. *Journal of Marriage and the Family*, 62, 533–548.

Bloom, D.E., Conrad, C., & Miller, C. (1998). Child support and fathers' remarriage and fertility. In I. Garfinkel, S.S. McLanahan, D.R. Meyer, & J.A. Seltzer (Eds.), *Fathers under fire: The revolution in child support enforcement* (pp. 128–156). New York: Russell Sage Foundation.

Blurton Jones, N.G., Marlowe, F., Hawkes, K., & O'Connell, J.F. (2000). Paternal investment and hunter-gatherer divorce rates. In L. Cronk, N. Chagnon, & W. Irons (Eds.), *Adaptation and human behavior: An anthropological perspective* (pp. 69–90). New York: Aldine.

Booth, A., & Amato, P.R. (2001). Parental predivorce relations and offspring postdivorce well-being. *Journal of Marriage and the Family*, 63, 197–212.

Brase, G.L. (2006). Cues of parental investment as a factor in attractiveness. *Evolution and Human Behavior*, 27, 145–157.

Broude, G.J., & Greene, S.J. (1983). Cross-cultural codes on husband-wife relationships. *Ethnology*, 22, 263–280.

Buckle, L., Gallup, Jr., G.G., & Rodd, Z.A. (1996). Marriage as a reproductive contract: Patterns of marriage, divorce, and remarriage. *Ethology and Sociobiology*, 17, 363–377.

Bumpass, L.L., Raley, R.K., & Sweet, J.A. (1995). The changing nature of stepfamilies: Implications of cohabitation and nonmarital childbearing. *Demography*, 32, 425–436.

Bumpass, L., & Lu, H. (2000). Trends in cohabitation and implications for children's family contexts in the United States. *Population Studies*, 54, 29–41.

Bumpass, L., Sweet, J., & Cherlin, A. (1991). The role of cohabitation in declining rates of marriage. *Demography*, 53, 913–927.

Case, A., Lin, I., & McLanahan, S. (2001). Educational attainment of siblings in stepfamilies. *Evolution and Human Behavior*, 22, 269–289.

Cherlin, A. (1978). Remarriage as an incomplete institution. *American Journal of Sociology*, 84, 634–650.

Cherlin, A.J., & Furstenberg, Jr., F.F. (1994). Stepfamilies in the United States: A reconsideration. *Annual Review of Sociology*, 20, 359–381.

Claxton-Oldfield, S., & Whitt, L. (2003). Child abuse in stepfather families: Do people think it occurs more often than it does in biological father families? *Journal of Divorce and Remarriage*, 40, 17–33.

Coleman, M., Ganong, L.H., & Cable, S.M. (1996). Perceptions of stepparents: An examination of the incomplete institutionalization and social stigma hypotheses. *Journal of Divorce and Remarriage*, 26, 25–48.

Daly, M., & Wilson, M. (1981). Abuse and neglect of children in evolutionary perspective. In R. Alexander and D.W. Tinkle (Eds.), *Natural Selection and Social Behavior* (pp. 405–416). New York: Chiron.

Daly, M., & Wilson, M. (1988). *Homicide*. New York: Aldine.

Daly, M., & Wilson, M. (1994). Some differential attributes of lethal assaults on small children by stepfathers versus genetic fathers. *Ethology and Sociobiology*, 15, 207–217.

Daly, M., & Wilson, M. (1998). *The truth about Cinderella: A Darwinian view of parental love*. New Haven, CT: Yale University Press.

Daly, M., & Wilson, M. (2001). An assessment of some proposed exceptions to the phenomenon of nepotistic discrimination against stepchildren. *Annales Zoologici Fennici*, 38, 287–296.

Downey, D.B. (1995). Understanding academic achievement among children in stephouseholds: The role of parental resources, sex of stepparent, and sex of child. *Social Forces*, 73, 875–894.

Evenhouse, E., & Reilly, S. (2004). A sibling study of stepchild well-being. *Journal of Human Resources*, 39, 248–276.

Federal Interagency Forum on Child and Family Statistics. (2007). *America's children: Key national indicators of well-being*. Federal Interagency Forum on Child and Family Statistics, Washington, DC: U.S. Government Printing Office.

Flinn, M.V. (1988). Step- and genetic parent/offspring relationships in a Caribbean village. *Ethology and Sociobiology*, 9, 335–369.

Flinn, M.V. (1992). Paternal care in a Caribbean village. In B.S. Hewlett (Ed.), *Father-child relations* (pp. 57–84). New York: Aldine.

Flinn, M.V., & England, B.G. (1997). Social economics of childhood glucocorticoid stress response and health. *American Journal of Physical Anthropology*, 102, 33–53.

Frayser, S.G. (1985). *Varieties of sexual experience: An anthropological perspective on human sexuality*. New Haven, CT: HRAF Press.

Ganong, L.H., Coleman, M., & Mistina, D. (1995). Normative beliefs about parents' and stepparents' financial obligations to children following divorce and remarriage. *Family Relations*, 44, 306–315.

Gaudino, J.A., Jenkins, B., & Rochat, R.W. (1999). No fathers' names: A risk factor for infant mortality in the state of Georgia, USA. *Social Science and Medicine*, 48, 253–265.

Grall, T.S. (2007). *Custodial mothers and fathers and their child support: 2005*. Washington, D.C.: United States Census Bureau.

Gray, P., & Anderson, K.G. (2010). *Fatherhood: Evolution and human paternal behavior*. Cambridge, MA: Harvard University Press.

Guzzo, K.B., & Furstenberg, Jr., F.F. (2007). Multipartnered fertility among American men. *Demography*, 44, 583–601.

Harknett, K., & Knab, J.T. (2007). More kin, less support: Multipartnered fertility and kin support among new mothers. *Journal of Marriage and the Family*, 69, 237–253.

Heuveline, P., Timberlake, J.M., & Furstenberg, Jr., F.F. (2003). Shifting childrearing to single mothers: Results from 17 western countries. *Population and Development Review*, 29, 47–71.

Hewlett, B.S. (1991a). Demography and childcare in preindustrial societies. *Journal of Anthropological Research*, 47, 1–37.

Hewlett, B.S. (1991b). *Intimate fathers: The nature and context of aka pygmy paternal infant care*. Ann Arbor, MI: University of Michigan Press.

Hill, K., & Hurtado, A.M. (1996). *Ache life history: The ecology and demography of a foraging people*. New York: Aldine de Gruyter.

Hofferth, S. (2006). Residential father family type and child well-being: Investment versus selection. *Demography*, 43, 53–77.

Hofferth, S., & Anderson, K.G. (2003). Are all dads equal? Biology vs. marriage as basis for paternal investment in children. *Journal of Marriage and Family*, 65, 213–232.

Howell, N. (2000). *Demography of the Dobe !Kung* (2nd ed.). New York: Aldine de Gruyter.

Hrdy, S. (1979). Infanticide among animals: A review, classification, and examination of the implications for the reproductive strategies of females. *Ethology and Sociobiology, 1*, 13–40.

Huang, C-C., & Han, W-J. (2007). Child support enforcement and sexual activity of male adolescents. *Journal of Marriage and Family, 69*, 763–777.

Hurtado, A.M., & Hill, K. (1992). Paternal effect on offspring survivorship among Ache and Hiwi hunter-gathers: Implications for modeling pair-bond stability. In B.S. Hewlett (Ed.), *Father-child relations: Cultural and biosocial contexts* (pp. 31–55). New York: Aldine de Gruyter.

Juby, H., Billette, J.M., Laplante, B., & Le Bourdais, C. (2007). Nonresident fathers and children: Parents' new unions and frequency of contact. *Journal of Family Issues, 28*, 1220–1245.

Kalmijn, M. (1999). Father involvement in childrearing and the perceived stability of marriage. *Journal of Marriage and the Family, 61*, 409–421.

Kalmijn, M. (2007). Explaining cross-national differences in marriage, cohabitation, and divorce in Europe, 1990–2000. *Population Studies, 61*, 243–263.

Keddy Hector, A.C., Seyfarth, R.M., & Raleigh, M.J. (1989). Male parental care, female choice and the effect of an audience in vervet monkeys. *Animal Behaviour, 38*, 262–271.

Kennedy, S., & Bumpass, L. (2008). Cohabitation and children's living arrangements: New estimates from the United States. *Demographic Research, 19*, 1663–1692.

King, V., & Sobolewski, J.M. (2006). Nonresident fathers' contributions to adolescent well-being. *Journal of Marriage and Family, 68*, 537–557.

Kreider, R.M. (2005). Number, timing, and duration of marriages and divorces: 2001. In *Current Population Reports* (pp. 70–97). Washington, DC: U.S. Census Bureau.

Kurdek, L.A. (1986). Custodial mothers' perceptions of visitation and support and payment of child support by noncustodial fathers in families with low and high levels of preseparation interparent conflict. *Journal of Applied Developmental Psychology, 7*, 307–323.

La Cerra, M.M. (1994). *Evolved mate preferences in women: Psychological adaptations for assessing a man's willingness to invest in offspring*. Doctoral dissertation. Department of Psychology, University of California, Santa Barbara.

Leite, R.W., & McKenry, P.C. (2002). Aspects of father status and post-divorce father involvement with children. *Journal of Family Issues, 23*, 601–623.

Li, J.-C.A. (2006). The institutionalization and pace of fertility in American stepfamilies. *Demographic Research, 14*, 237–266.

Lin, I.-F. (2000). Perceived fairness and compliance with child support obligations. *Journal of Marriage and the Family, 62*, 388–398.

Lin, I.-F., & McLanahan, S.S. (2007). Parental beliefs about nonresident fathers' obligations and rights. *Journal of Marriage and Family, 69*, 382–398.

Low, B.S. (1978). Environmental uncertainty and the parental strategies of marsupials and placentals. *American Naturalist, 112*, 197–213.

Malkin, C., & Lamb, M. (1994). Child maltreatment: A test of sociobiological theory. *Journal of Comparative Family Studies, 25*, 121–133.

Manning, W.D., & Smock, P.J. (1999). New families and nonresident father-child visitation. *Social Forces, 78*, 87–116.

Manning, W.D., & Smock, P.J. (2000). Swapping families: Serial parenting and economic support for children. *Journal of Marriage and the Family, 62*, 111–122.

Manning, W.D., Stewart, S.D., & Smock, P.J. (2003). The complexity of fathers' parenting responsibilities and involvement with nonresident children. *Journal of Family Issues, 24*, 645–667.

Marlowe, F. (1999). Male care and mating effort among Hadza foragers. *Behavioral Ecology and Sociobiology, 46*, 57–64.

Marlowe, F. (2005). Who tends Hadza children? In B. Hewlett, & M. Lamb (Eds.), *Hunter-gatherer childhoods: Evolutionary, developmental and cultural perspectives* (p. 177–190). New Brunswick, CT: Transaction.

Marsiglio, W. (1991). Paternal engagement activities with minor children. *Journal of Marriage and the Family, 53*, 973–986.

Martin, S., & Parashar, S. (2006). Women's changing attitudes towards divorce, 1974–2002, evidence for an educational crossover. *Journal of Marriage and the Family, 68*, 29–40.

Martinez, G.M., Chandra, A., Abma, J.C., Jones, J., & Mosher, W.D. (2006). *Fertility, contraception, and fatherhood: Data on men and women from Cycle 6 (2002) of the National Survey of Family Growth*. Vital and Health Statistics 23. Washington, D.C.: National Center for Health Statistics.

McLanahan, S., & Sandefur, G. (1994). *Growing up with a single parent: What hurts, what helps*. Cambridge, MA: Harvard University Press.

Morgan, S.P., Lye, D., & Condran, G. (1988). Sons, daughters, and the risk of marital disruption. *American Journal of Sociology, 94*, 110–129.

Mott, F.L. (1990). When is a father really gone? Paternal-child contact in father-absent homes. *Demography, 27*, 499–517.

Mott, F.L., Kowaleski-Jones, L., & Menaghan. E.G. (1997). Paternal absence and child behavior: Does a child's gender make a difference? *Journal of Marriage and Family, 59*, 103–118.

Rohwer, S. (1986). Selection for adoption versus infanticide by replacement mates in birds. *Current Ornithology, 3*, 353–395.

Rohwer, S., Herron, J.C., & Daly, M. (1999). Stepparental behavior as mating effort in birds and other animals. *Evolution and Human Behavior, 20*, 367–390.

Roney, J.R., Hanson, K.N., Durante, K.M., & Maestripieri, D. (2006). Reading men's faces: Women's mate attractiveness judgments track men's testosterone and interest in infants. *Proceedings of the Royal Society, Series B, 273*, 2169–2175.

Scelza, B.A. (2010). Fathers' presence speeds the social and reproductive careers of sons. *Current Anthropology, 51*, 295–303.

Seltzer, J.A. (1991). Relationships between fathers and children who live apart: The father's role after separation. *Journal of Marriage and the Family, 53*, 79–101.

Shackelford, T., Weekes-Shackelford, V.A., & Schmitt, D.P. (2005). An evolutionary perspective on why some men refuse or reduce their child support payments. *Basic and Applied Social Psychology, 27*, 297–306.

Smock, P.J. (2000). Cohabitation in the United States. *Annual Review of Sociology, 26*, 1–20.

Smuts, B. (1985). *Sex and friendship in baboons*. Hawthorne, NY: Aldine.

Smuts, B.B., & Gubernick, D.J. (1992). Male-infant relationships in nonhuman primates: Paternal investment or mating effort? In B.S. Hewlett (Ed.), *Father-child relations: Cultural and biosocial contexts* (p. 1–30). New York: Aldine de Gruyter.

Sonenstein, F.L., & Calhoun, C.A. (1990). Determinants of child support: A pilot survey of absent parents. *Contemporary Policy Issues, 8*, 75–94.

Stewart, S.D. (2002). The effect of stepchildren on childbearing intentions and births. *Demography, 39*, 181–197.

Stewart, S.D. (2005). How the birth of a child affects involvement with stepchildren. *Journal of Marriage and Family, 67,* 461–473.

Stewart, S.D. (2007). *Brave new stepfamilies: Diverse paths towards stepfamily living.* Thousand Oaks, CA: Sage Publications, Inc.

Stewart, S.D., Manning, W.D., & Smock, P.J. (2003). Union formation among men in the U.S.: Does having prior children matter? *Journal of Marriage and Family, 65,* 90–104.

Strohschein, L.A. (2005). Parental divorce and child mental health trajectories. *Journal of Marriage and Family, 67,* 1286–1300.

Sugiyama, L.S., & Chacon, R. (2005). Juvenile responses to household ecology among the Yora of Peruvian Amazonia. In B. Hewlett & M.E. Lamb (Eds.), *Hunter-gatherer childhoods: Evolutionary, developmental and cultural perspectives* (pp. 237–261). New Brunswick, CT: Aldine Transaction.

Thomson, E., Hanson, T.L., & McLanahan, S.S. (1994). Family structure and child-well being: Economic resources vs. parental behaviors. *Social* Forces, 73, 221–242.

Trent, K., & South, S.J. (1989). Structural determinants of the divorce rate: A cross-societal analysis. *Journal of Marriage and the Family, 51,* 391–404.

Trivers, R. (1972). Parental investment and sexual selection. In B.C. Campbell (Ed.), *Sexual selection and the descent of man* (pp. 136–179). Chicago: Aldine.

U.S. Census Bureau. (2009. *Statistical Abstract of the United States: 2010 (129th ed..* Washington, DC. Retrieved December 28, 2009 from http://www.census.gov/compendia/statab/.

Weiss, Y., & Willis, R.J. (1993). Transfers among divorced couples: Evidence and interpretation. *Journal of Labor Economics, 11,* 629–679.

White, L. (1990). Determinants of divorce: A review of research in the eighties. *Journal of Marriage and the Family, 52,* 904–912.

White, L., & Gilbreth, J.G. (2001). When children have two fathers: Effects of relationships with stepfathers and noncustodial fathers on adolescent outcomes. *Journal of Marriage and Family, 63,* 155–167.

Wu, Z., & Balakrishnan, T.R. (1995). Dissolution of premarital cohabitation in Canada. *Demography, 32,* 521–532.

Zvoch, K. (1999). Family type and investment in education: A comparison of genetic and stepparent families. *Evolution and Human Behavior, 20,* 453–464.

CHAPTER 8

Adoption: Forms, Functions, and Preferences

Anthony A. Volk

Abstract

A significant body of literature has examined human families from an evolutionary perspective. Another significant body of literature has examined adoptive families. Unfortunately, these two bodies of literature have generally been kept separate from each other. To address this gap, I examine adoption from an evolutionary perspective. My goal is to both better understand adoption via evolutionary theory, as well as to better understand the evolution of families via adoption. I examine several forms and functions of adoption, including adoption as a substitute for biological children, adoption as a means of kin support, and adoption as a means of social exchange and manipulation. From an evolutionary perspective, what stands out about adoption is its ubiquity and its diversity, its emphasis on biological kinship, and its potential utility as a social tool. I recommend further studies on the ecology of adoption, as well as unifying adoption with other modern approaches to families, including cognitive psychology and neuroscience.

Keywords: Adoption, evolution, cross-cultural, facial cues

Adoption, the Family, and Evolution

Family is most often discussed and conceptualized as a grouping of kin (Salmon & Shackelford, 2007). Indeed, one definition of family is "all persons descended from the same ancestors, such as parents, children, aunts, uncles, cousins" (Weber, 1984, p. 378). Anderson (1991) comments that the dominant North American definition of a "real" family is the "nuclear unit of a father-head, mother, and their children, all held together as a... natural or biological arrangement (p. 235)." Most of the chapters in this volume emphasize relatedness as the central evolutionary context for understanding the conceptualization and functioning of families. From a general biological/evolutionary viewpoint, one could argue that the sole purpose of a family is to allow two adults to successfully form a pair-bond within which to produce and raise biological offspring to thereby pass on copies of their genes to future generations. This gene-centric view of the family explicitly highlights how important kinship is to families (Dawkins, 1989). In line with these theoretical statements, the majority of Americans believe that the crucial defining element of kinship is shared genes (Schneider, 1980).

Justifiably then, Hamilton's theory of kin selection (1963, 1964) has proven influential as an evolutionary approach to understanding families and family behaviors (e.g., Daly & Wilson, 1988; Hrdy, 1999). According to Hamilton (1963, 1964), a wide range of cooperative behaviors (including parenting) can be explained by the idea that an individual sacrifices personal resources to help another individual because the recipient shares genes with the helper. This help is therefore aimed ultimately at increasing the reproduction of copies of those genes that reside in the bodies of kin. With parents and siblings sharing 50% of their genes, and cousins 12.5% of their genes, the logic of kin selection is illustrated by a quote from the biologist

J. B. Haldane. When asked if he would sacrifice his life for his brother's, he replied "No, but I would lay down my life for two brothers or eight cousins"(McElreath & Boyd, 2007, p. 82), Since its appearance, the theory of kin selection has gained enormous evidential support from a wide range of disciplines, including the study of the human family from an evolutionary perspective (Bellow, 2003; Eberhard, 1975; Nowak, 2006). The idea that families consist of genetically related individuals motivated (unconsciously) to help each other pass on their genes allows us to explain a host of family traits and behaviors (Salmon & Shackelford, 2007). The importance of shared genes for understanding families makes it ironic that perhaps one of the most illuminating views of families may come from studying the *absence* of kinship bonds in adoptive families. I propose that, in the absence of standard kinship motives, studying adoption from an evolutionary viewpoint can shed light on adoption itself, as well as help us to better understand all human families. By its very nature, adoption stretches the definition and functions of families. It is through adoption's testing of the limits of human families that we can gain insights into the evolution of all human families.

Adoption is a highly varied affair, both in form and in function (Terrell & Modell, 1994). Adoption may be defined as permanently caring for offspring who are recognized as not your own biological children. An estimated 2%–4% of American children are adopted (Stolley, 1993). The form of adoption most familiar to Westerners is parents adopting unrelated children as substitutes for biological children (Wegar, 2000). However, cross-culturally, this form of adoption is relatively rare. Adoption can occur between related or unrelated individuals, it can be permanent or temporary in duration, it can be formal or informal, and it can serve a wide range of (sometimes competing) goals. A common source of confusion regarding adoption is the difference between fosterage and adoption. To a large extent, the two phenomena are similar in that they are based on providing care to a child who is not biologically one's own. Fosterage tends to be temporary in nature, with the child retaining his or her original biological/name, but these distinctions are not absolute, as some adoptions are temporary, and some adoptions allow a child to retain his or her biological name/identity. Thus, while we generally refer to adoption as permanent care associated with changes of family name and affiliation, not all cultures draw the same, or even a firm, distinction between adoption and fosterage.

What is interesting is that only rarely have the various forms and functions of adoption been examined from an evolutionary perspective (Betzig, 1988; Hamilton, Cheng, & Powell, 2007; Silk, 1990). Instead, most of the accounts of adoption, even those that explicitly discuss kinship, fail to take an evolutionary perspective on adoption (e.g., Bowie, 2004; Brodzinksy & Pinderhughes, 2002; Wegar, 2000). Because evolutionary perspectives on families have generally not considered adoption, and traditional accounts of adoption have not considered evolutionary theory, the study of adoption from an evolutionary perspective appears to be a worthwhile and timely endeavor. I therefore propose examining three forms of adoption that each reveal different aspects of adoptive families: adoption as an altruistic parental substitution, adoption as a form of kin support, and adoption as a form of social networking. Even these three general forms of adoption are not internally homogeneous. I discuss some of the possible variations of these three forms of adoption, describe their sociocultural contexts, and explore how evolutionary thinking can inform our understanding of them. Finally, I propose some general evolutionary lessons about the family that are revealed through the evolutionary study of adoption, and potential future directions for researching adoption using an evolutionary perspective.

Adoption as an Altruistic Parental Substitution

The form of adoption most familiar to, and most common in, Western cultures is adoption as an altruistic substitution for biological children (Terrell & Modell, 1994; Wegar, 2000). The adoption is altruistic in the sense that it can benefit the child (Brodzinsky & Pinderhughes, 2002), but does not directly benefit the genetic fitness of the adopting parent (Silk, 1980). The typical Western adoptive parent is relatively wealthy, educated, white, and in their late 30s to early 40s (Hamilton et al., 2007). The typical adopted child is an unrelated younger child (often an infant), white, and generally healthy (Hamilton et al., 2007; Stolley, 1993). The typical motivation for these kinds of adoptions is to meet the psychological needs of adoptive parents to raise a child and the developmental needs of children who lack a capable biological parent. Thus, this adoption may be equal for parents and child at a social level, but from a biological perspective, it is an altruistic investment by the parents in an unrelated individual (Silk, 1990). The disparities are greater between the biological parents and adoptive parents, as the former are poorer, less educated, younger, and (particularly in the recent past) motivated by religious and social conventions against infants born to unwed mothers (Sokoloff, 1993). From an evolutionary point of view, the biological parents receive free care for their offspring while the adoptive parents receive nothing in return (and indeed, may even offer significant financial compensation to the biological parents; Miller, 2005). Thus, this form of adoption is, by most definitions, significantly altruistic. The "only" biological rewards for the adoptive parents are the feelings of love and joy that can accompany raising a child.

What's interesting is that even though these adoptions are explicitly between unrelated individuals, adoptive parents nevertheless (or perhaps because of this) feel a crucial concern toward building strong emotional ties with the adopted child and incorporating that child into their new kinship circle (Howell, 2006; Modell, 1996). This process, termed "kinning," is an explicit attempt by adoptive parents to expose their adopted child to behaviors and circumstances that confirm their status as the child of the adoptive parents (Howell, 2003). Typically, this means spending more time with the child, engaging in more family-oriented behaviors, in more stereotypical family behaviors, and deliberately exposing the child to other members of their new kinship network, above and beyond what is normally seen in biological families (Howell, 2003, 2004). This idea of using intense exposure to simulate or even generate feelings of kinship may not be purely cultural, as it greatly resembles (in principle) the phenomenon of long-term exposure triggering kin-related feelings of incest avoidance (Lieberman, Tooby, & Cosmides, 2007). In the latter case, children who spend long periods of time together during their early childhood tend to feel less sexual attraction toward each other as adults, presumably due to evolved incest-avoidance mental modules that use proximity as a proxy for genetic relatedness (Lieberman et al., 2007). In the case of adoption, the intense exposure of the infant or child to their adoptive family may be meant to stimulate/simulate feelings of genetic relatedness. Indeed, a recent study demonstrated that, compared to a control group, an experimental group of fathers who were taught infant massage (and thus spent considerably more time with their infants) perceived greater physical resemblance of themselves to their infant (Volk, Darrell, & Marini, 2010). Frequent, intense family interactions as a means of generating perceptions or cognitions of resemblance may be a viable strategy for adoptive parents.

A significant concern of many adoptive parents who adopt unrelated children is that the child will someday abandon them (and their significant emotional and physical investments) in favor of returning to their birth parents (Borgman, 1982; Howell, 2004). Indeed, even when the biological parents are from another continent and completely absent during childhood, adopted children still sometimes feel that their biological kin are "incredibly important to [them], and will always be so" (Yngvesson, 2004, p. 222). This quote is hardly unique, and it supports to some degree the concern of adoptive parents that their investment may not be reciprocated to the same degree as are biological parents' investments. In most cases, this fear appears to be unfounded. For example, open adoptions do not lead to a decrease in adoptive family functioning or closeness (Brodzinksy & Pinderhughes, 2002). That this fear nevertheless persists in the absence of compelling evidence suggests some deeper psychological anxiety. Whether it is cultural or biological in origin, it highlights that, even when Western adoption is explicitly about adopting unrelated children, kinship (and perceptions of kinship) can still play a primary role in defining the family.

The importance of kinship to the adoption of strangers is not unique to Western culture. People from many cultures adopt as a means of coping with infertility, adopting unrelated infants (if necessary) as a substitution for biological children (Bowie, 2004; Silk, 1990). Amongst the Maasai pastoralists of Kenya, it is considered ill-luck, or even immoral, for a woman to be infertile (Talle, 2004). There is therefore a strong demand for infertile women to adopt a child, for it is the presence of a child, rather than the biological relationship, that removes the negative stigma of infertility (Talle, 2004). Yet, biological relatedness still matters, with parents showing a preference for adopting kin over strangers. The adopted child most often comes from the husband's side of the family. This patrilineal pattern of investment ensures that men are still able to invest in their side of the family, whether it be passing a child from a fertile wife to an infertile wife, or demanding a sister to provide a child to his wife/her sister-in-law. These adoptions are formalized from birth by the initial shared care of the infant between biological and adoptive mother, until the adoptive mother begins to produce milk herself (Talle, 2004). The biological mother is typically given a cow as compensation. Interestingly, the adoption is sometimes protested, but only by biological mothers. Unfortunately for these mothers, within Maasai society, men generally have the final say. Nevertheless, this highlights again the important of relatedness because it shows how difficult it is for some mothers to give up their biological offspring (presumably, paternity uncertainty and mating effort mitigate men's concerns), and how (when possible) men attempt to direct any adoptive investment toward their own kin rather than toward the adoptive mother's kin. This leads us to a consideration of another form of adoption: adoption as kin support.

Adoption as a Form of Kin Support

This form of adoption was perhaps the most common within ancestral human populations. Due to the high mortality associated with premodern adult lives (Cunningham, 2005; Howell, 2000), children frequently faced the possibility of losing one or both parents (Briggs, 1970; Rawson, 2003). In these cases, children who lost their parents required substitute parental care to have any chance of surviving to maturity (Hrdy, 1999). In many ways, this form of adoptive parenting resembles a kind of alloparenting (Hrdy, 2009), only taken to a more extreme form. Alloparenting is the provision of (typically modest, partial) parental care by someone other than the biological parents (Hrdy, 1999). In the case of adoption, alloparenting occurs not via assisting another parent, but by replacing the biological parent. Generally speaking, the loss of a young child's mother is associated with a much greater probability of mortality than is the loss of a father (Hrdy, 1999). However, infants can be—and are—successfully raised in Western and traditional societies by adoptive mothers who are capable of initiating lactation postadoption (Auerbach & Avery, 1981; Talle, 2004). In the past, wet nurses could also be employed to tide over an adopted infant until it was able to eat solids (Cunningham, 2005). So, although people in most cultures still prefer to adopt after a child has weaned (Silk, 1980), weaning is not an absolute barrier to adoption.

Adoption of kin due to deceased, impoverished, absent, or incompetent parents is found in virtually all cultures, including Western cultures (Stolley, 1993), Brazil (Fonseca, 2004), Peru (Leinaweaver, 2008), Inuit (Briggs, 1970), Oceanic cultures (Silk, 1980), West Africa (Silk, 1987), the !Kung (Howell, 2000), ancient Rome (Rawson, 2003), Late Imperial China (Hsiung, 2005), and medieval Europe (Cunningham, 2005). The common theme for these types of adoptions is a scarcity (or lack) of parental resources that is made up for by kin who possess the requisite resources. The logic of this decision is sometimes explicit. For example, among the Inuit, adoption of kin is an explicit alternative to infanticide when the biological parents' resources are scarce (Silk, 1990). The desire to have kin adopt the child is believed to be related to an increased probability that kin will better care for the child than will nonkin (Bowie, 2004), and is also sometimes an explicit factor. For example, among the Kiribati of the Gilbert Islands, awarding a child to nonkin for adoption is regarded as an insult to kin if there are kin willing and able to adopt the child (Silk, 1980). In nonhuman animals, environmental constraints such as scarce breeding resources or food sources requiring cooperative foraging strategies influence the occurrence of alloparenting and adoption (Riedman, 1982). In recent history, human kin adoption often was a temporary response to scare resources, resembling foster care more than adoption, in that the biological parents could reclaim their child when conditions improved. This was widely practice in 17th-century Europe: Parents would drop off children to wealthier family members (or orphanages) for adoption during difficult economic times with the intention of reclaiming them once the economic climate improved (Cunningham, 2005). A similar system was used until recently in Brazil, in which mothers preferred to leave their infants with kin, but would use government agencies as temporary care providers if suitable kin support was unavailable (Fonseca, 2004). Sadly, Brazilian children who are now placed into government care are removed permanently from their parents, much to the tragic surprise of many mothers who still hold traditional beliefs about adoption and offer up their infants under the incorrect assumption that they will later be able to reclaim them (Fonseca, 2004).

In North America, it is estimated that just under half of all adoptions are adoptions by kin as a means of supporting the children of a relative who is unable to properly care for those children (Stolley, 1993). The importance and suitability of kin as adoptive parents has been acknowledged in the United States, resulting in a recent surge in kin-adoption rates from 15% in 1998 to 21% in 2000, and kin fosterage rates from 18% in 1986 to 31% in 1990 (Testa, 2004). In many cases, the adoption is not formalized, and thus the care is labeled as foster-care or guardianship instead of adoption (Testa, 2004). Although this changes the legal responsibilities, it rarely changes the actual responsibilities of the adoptive parent (Berrick, 1998; Testa, 2004). In contrast to what is seen in nonkin adoptions, demographic evidence suggests that kin adoptive caregivers are more likely to be African American, older, single, unemployed, and of a lower socioeconomic status compared to nonadoptive parents/caregivers (Cuddeback, 2004). The single most common adoptive parent is the maternal grandmother (Cuddeback, 2004), which is just what evolutionary theories of grandparenting that emphasize kin selection and paternity uncertainty predict (Euler & Weitzel, 1996). The most common reason for adoption in these families is substance abuse and/or child neglect by the birth mother (Cuddeback, 2004).

An alternative form of kin substitution occurs in East Cameroon, where children are adopted frequently by kin in a polygynandrous society (Noterman, 2004). The two primary motivations for adopting kin appear to be the economic benefits associated with a large family (e.g., extra workers and future providers) and preventing one's spouse from investing too much in his or her side of the family at the same time as one tries to invest as much as possible in one's own family (Noterman, 2004). The latter motivation results from the tension between unrelated husbands and wives who each seek to direct their combined resources toward adopted kin from their family rather than the family of their spouse.

Thus, there is a highly kin-related investment strategy whereby mothers' brothers, fathers' sisters, and mothers' mothers all compete for adoptive children in order to enhance the relative fitness of their kin at the expense of their in-law(s). By adopting a related child when one has a surplus of resources, this frees the related birth parents to have another child sooner while their kin provide care to the existing child, thus optimizing resource allocation across a related network of kin. This competition for kin-related fitness can be so intense that at times maternal grandmothers (who exert significant control over their daughters) are known to attempt blackmail young fathers into relinquishing their official fatherhood of their children in exchange for the opportunity to remain married and eventually gain fatherhood over future children (Noterman, 2004). This is possible because birth certificates are often not completed and filed until well after a child's birth, allowing for false paternity claims to be made by the mother's family (Noterman, 2004).

Silk (1980, 1988) tested kin biases among Inuit, West African, and Oceanic adoptions. In these cultures, adoption is widely practiced, with a substantial fraction of children being adopted (10%+). Silk (1980, 1988) found a strong bias toward kin being chosen as the adoptive parents, particularly aunts, uncles, and grandparents. Intriguingly, however, there was a bias among parents with both biological and adopted children to invest more heavily in their biological children (Silk, 1980). Investment by kin and parental biases toward biological children both fit well with the theory of kin selection and inclusive fitness. The exceptions to this general pattern typically occurred when a biological child neglected his duties toward his parents, usually in their old age, allowing a more devoted adopted child to receive greater investment (particularly through wills; Silk, 1980). This suggests that kin adoption may sometimes contain an element of economic motivation (that will be discussed shortly) in addition to the evolutionary motivation of inclusive fitness.

The Yukpa of South America also practice adoption as a form of kin support. Upon the death of a parent, an older brother, or more often an older sister, will adopt a younger sibling to provide parental care for them (Halbmayer, 2004). Grandparents, aunts, and uncles may also adopt orphaned relatives, but in these cases, the Yupka assume a more economic motive than when the adoption is by more immediate relatives (Halbmayer, 2004). Thus, the form of the kin support depends on the closeness of the blood relation and the age of the adoptive parents. The more distant the genetic relationship and/or the older the adoptive parent, the greater the economic motive for children to be adopted, both for cheap labor and to function as future providers for the family when they are adults. Economics may therefore act as a supplemental motivation when kinship motives are insufficient (or absent).

Perhaps the most extreme version of adoption as a form of kin support is found among the Baatombu in Northern Benin. Although kin adoption is common in much of West Africa (up to 50% in some societies; Alber, 2004; Silk, 1987), it is particularly prevalent among the Baatombu. Traditionally, virtually all Baatombu children were raised by adults other than their biological parents. Boys are raised by male relatives, girls by female relatives, with the father's side of the family getting the firstborn, the mother's the secondborn, and so on (Alber, 2003; Alber, 2004). So, for example, if a family has a girl, then a boy, a female relative on the father's side would adopt the girl, while a male relative on the mother's side would adopt the boy. In both cases, the biological parents were expected to, and virtually always (>98% of documented cases) did, comply with requests from one of the child's aunts, uncles, or grandparents to adopt the child (Alber, 2003). Although the rates of adoption are lower today (dropping from roughly 98%, to 67%, to 35% over the last three generations), the practice still continues among the Baatombu (Alber, 2003). Biological parents are still openly discouraged from actively supporting their biological children (e.g., cannot call them publicly by their first name), although some may surreptitiously do so (particularly mothers; Alber, 2004). Highlighting the pervasive power of relatedness and kin selection, even when publicly sanctioned from providing any form of care, biological parents (i.e., mothers) strive to secretly invest in their biological offspring.

The Baatombu people offer three reasons for their high levels of adoption and fosterage (Alber, 2003). First, having a network of potential parents can alleviate resource-related stresses on parents, ensuring that children are adopted only by those who have the resources to raise them. This may help alleviate resource-related child mortality and/or impoverished child development (Brodzinksy & Pinderhughes, 2002; Hrdy, 1999; Silk, 1990). Second, this process reinforces kin networks by offering the most precious resource, children, to members of that kin network. This dramatic level of reciprocity (trading children) may create such strong feelings of solidarity that conflict is reduced and cooperation is increased both by sharing a common goal (the fitness of the offspring) and by feelings of reciprocity (Nowak, 2006). Finally, adults believe that parents are too lenient with their biological children, and are unable to teach them the strict rules and respect necessary within Baatombu society. This last explanation makes the least sense from a Darwinian perspective. Instead, it may represent an implicit conflict between a desire to care for and nurture one's offspring (thus "spoiling" them) and a desire to follow strict social rules aimed at creating group cohesion and elder respect. Thus, the Baatombu's extreme form of adoptive parenting appears to be geared largely to assisting the survival of related children and preserving the cultural fabric of Baatombu society.

Adoption As a Form of Social Networking

Perhaps the least familiar form of adoption is adults' use of children as a form of social networking. Although unfamiliar to many Westerners, a wide range of cultures employ children as means of forming and strengthening both kin and nonkin bonds. Among many Oceanic cultures, children are used as a form of economic support (Silk, 1980).

Among the Papua New Guinea Suau (a Southern Massim society), adoption is used as a substitute for biological children by infertile parents, but it is also used a form of social networking (Demian, 2004). In the island of Wogeo, it is fairly common for adults without children, or with few children, to adopt a child to gain economic assistance from that child later in life (Demian, 2004). In this case, the child lives with, and is raised by, the adoptive parent. In return, the child works for the adoptive parents, and in particular, provides for them when they get older. That these adoptions do not always proceed smoothly is revealed by the fact that children are allowed to leave their adoptive parents to return to their birth parents, presumably because they were not treated satisfactorily (Demian, 2004). In most cases, the birth parents must pay a fine to cover the expenses of raising the child to that date (typically paid with one or more pigs). The lack of either altruistic or inclusive fitness motivations may be an important factor in why these adoptions sometimes fail.

A similar economic motive for adoption is found among the Yap of Micronesia (South Pacific; Kirkpatrick & Broder, 1976). Only a small percentage of Yap adoptions were motivated by infertility, with the majority related to either elder care or transactions involving trading children for land or access to land among both kin and nonkin (Kirkpatrick & Broder, 1976). As in other cultures (Silk, 1980), children who were poorly cared for (e.g., in families that abused alcohol) had the option of returning to their birth parents, resulting in the revoking of land privileges for the adoptive parents (Treide, 2004). Adopted Yap children enjoyed a higher status among their adoptive and adoptee families for playing the role of bridge-maker between different families (Treide, 2004). In common with other cultures (e.g., Talle, 2004), Yap women are also less enthusiastic about adopting away their own children than are Yap men, and must sometimes be coerced to give up their child for adoption (Treide, 2004). Finally, Yapese who do not own land are usually barred from adopting Yapese children whose parents own land. Among the nearby Ifaluk of the Western Caroline Islands, there is a positive correlation between wealth or high status and adopting out infants (Betzig, 1988). This is believed to offer a reproductive advantage to high-status men who are able to get other, lower-status men, to invest in their offspring while they avoid reciprocal investments in the offspring of the lower-status men (Betzig, 1988). Thus, among the Yap, as well as many other Oceanic groups, adoption can be an economic tool used to provide retirement insurance for the elderly, a way to balance a wealth of children with a wealth of land, or a way to convert economic power into greater reproductive success. But these forms of adoption appear to be more fragile due to the absence of strong altruistic or kin-related motives.

The Yupka of South America also practice grandparental adoption as a form of elder support. In their view, it is preferable for parents to allow grandparents to adopt a child, rather than have the parents take in the grandparents, because this situation preserves the autonomy and power of grandparents (Halbmayer, 2004). In addition being adopted to provide economic and material help, grandchildren are sometimes adopted to keep a grandparent company. In these cases, the child typically retains greater contact with her birth parents (Halbmayer, 2004). This retention of the biological parents may reflect the weakness of socially motivated, rather than attachment-motivated, parent–adopted child bonds (Smith & Howard, 1999).

In other areas of New Guinea (e.g., Wogeo island), adoption is used directly to manipulate social networks (Anderson, 2004). First, adoption can be used as a form of reconciliation. The Wogeo have a saying, "I can't hurt him when he has my blood." This refers to the situation in which a man adopts his child to a potential rival or enemy, and is thereafter unwilling to harm that rival or enemy because of the risk of harming his own (now adopted) biological child. Thus, adoption can be used to repair damaged social relationships or as a buffer to avoid damaging conflict (Anderson, 2004). Furthermore, across Papua New Guinea there is a widely held traditional belief in both a place identity (where you grow up) and a matrilineal identity. Matrilineal filiations can be powerful socially, as long and large matrilineal lines are able to generate considerable social support (sometimes in the perceived form of sorcery; Demian, 2004). Yet, these lengthy matrilineal lines are also rendered vulnerable by their size to perceived social threats in the form of sorcery (Demian, 2004). So, adoption is used to confuse and disguise matrilineal lines by bringing in individuals from external groups. In this way, social tensions regarding power and vulnerability are diffused (Demian, 2004).

Adoption was also used by many North and South American groups as a way of dealing with captive children from enemy groups (Halbmayer, 2004; Trigger, 1969). These children were raised to be members of their captors' families. In this way, losses associated with group warfare were potentially offset by gains from adopting members of the losing or victimized tribe (e.g., the Iroquois; Richter, 1983). Furthermore, as in New Guinea, adoption was used by these groups as a way to end conflicts between groups. A similar practice was used by the ancient Romans with many of their neighbors. Typically, the Romans would adopt a prince from a neighboring country both as a means of securing peace as well as a means of acculturating a powerful potential ally (Mackay, 2007).

Adoption amongst the Yupka is also used as a way of obtaining brides. Older men are known to adopt younger girls, whom they raise as future brides (Halbmayer, 2004). In these cases, sexual contact between the adoptive "father" and his bride are forbidden until the girl reaches puberty. Violation of this no-contact rule can result in the return of the girl to her birth family (Halbmayer, 2004). A more frequent form of adoption-related marriage occurs between a stepfather and his stepdaughter in a form of mother–daughter polygyny. Thus, by marrying a woman with a daughter from another man, the husband gains, in effect, two wives. This practice is found not only in the Yupka (Halbmayer, 2004), but also in a number of other cultures (Rivière, 1984).

A final form of adoption as a means of social networking is the adoption of heirs to a dynasty. This practice is common in cultures with stratified social levels and/or nobility (Davis, 2006; Sokoloff, 1993). The preference was, in the absence of direct biological heirs, to adopt related biological heirs. For example, (Gaius) Julius Caesar adopted his great-nephew Augustus. Born Gaius Octavius Thurinus, he was renamed Gaius Julius Caesar Augustus and not only brought fame and wealth to the family, but also transformed the very name Caesar to represent all future Roman emperors! Thus, even distant kin could serve as important adoptive candidates for powerful families. In the absence of adoptable kin, the children of powerful friends or potential allies could be nominated as adoptive heirs (Hsiung, 2005). When used in this fashion, adoption resembles the more common practice of using marriages to create political ties between powerful families, and it represents a powerful social tool for creating or maintaining political power (Davis, 2006; Mackay, 2007). Adoption, therefore, has an diverse set of forms and functions. But what are some of the factors that affect the likelihood of individual adoptions?

General Adoption Preferences

In any form of adoption, central to any decision to adopt, are the adoptive parents' resources and social situation. As has been demonstrated, adults are sensitive to environmental cues of family support, cultural rules, and social contexts. Yet, adoptions are not solely influenced by the traits and context of the adoptive parents. The traits and attributes of the adopted child are also of great importance. This raises an important question: Assuming adults have a choice in the matter, what are the relevant cues that adults look for in adoptive children? Although there are a host of potential characteristics for adults to examine, three of the more important appear to be age, health, and resemblance.

Adults prefer to adopt healthy, younger children, presumably because they are more malleable, easier to form an attachment bond with, and less likely to have accumulated a negative developmental history or medical problems (Brooks, James, & Barth, 2002). Older children are more likely to be adopted by kin than by nonkin (Testa, 2004). A child's gender is generally not a concern, unless there is an imbalance of gender within the adoptive family (Bowie, 2004). In traditional societies, children are most often adopted after they are weaned from their mothers (Bowie, 2004), although this is not always the case (Talle, 2004). Research has shown that not only do adults prefer to adopt younger children, but adults perceive younger children's faces as more attractive and more desirable for adoption even when they are not interested in adopting a child (Volk, Lukjanczuk, & Quinsey, 2007). This data comes from the use of the Hypothetical Adoption Paradigm (HAP), which presents adults with a series of faces in a slide show and asks them to rate the faces on one or more scales, including hypothetical adoption preference (Chin, Wade, & French, 2006; Volk & Quinsey, 2002).

Health is another critical factor in adoption. Caring for a sick child represents a significant increase in both the risks assumed as well as the total costs involved (Miller, 2005). One of the strongest preferences of Western adoptive parents is for healthy children, which in part explains the drive away from less healthy, but simpler domestic adoptions to potentially healthier, but much more costly and complex transnational adoptions (Dorow, 2006; Sokoloff, 1993; Stolley, 1993). Among international adoptions, a common feature is the review of the medical health records of the child, sometimes including a photograph that is professionally analyzed by a pediatrician (Miller, 2005). The relationship between facial cues and health is well established, and can be traced as far back as ancient Chinese texts from the 11th century that refer to the importance of facial cues as an indicator of infant health (Hsiung, 2005). Studies using the HAP have shown that a wide range of facial cues influence adults' adoption preferences. Adults show a preference for healthy faces (Volk & Quinsey, 2002), as well as faces indicating normal body weight (Volk, Lukjanczuk, & Quinsey, 2005; Volk & Quinsey, 2006), and faces without cues of fetal alcohol syndrome (Waller, Volk, & Quinsey, 2004). There is a sex difference, as women tend to emphasize cues of health (and cuteness) more than men do, perhaps due to their greater typical share of the parental burden (Volk & Quinsey, 2002).

Resemblance has also received significant attention with regard to adoption preferences. HAP studies of resemblance have confirmed a male bias in terms of the importance of resemblance cues (Platek, Burch, Panyavin, Wasserman, & Gallup, 2002; Platek et al., 2003; Volk, 2009; Volk & Quinsey, 2002, 2007). The primary difference between men's and women's preferences is that, for reasons of paternity uncertainty, men value cues of resemblance most strongly whereas women value cues of infant quality (health, happiness) most strongly (Volk & Quinsey, 2002). This male emphasis on cues of resemblance appears to be cross-cultural (Volk, 2009), and it fits with what is seen in actual adoptions. Anecdotally, it was long suspected that the Chinese government used pictures submitted by international adoptive fathers to match for resemblance with prospective children. In North America, social workers (who are not consciously aware of, or advocating, inclusive fitness) often focus on resemblance. According to one social worker, "I think it helps with the bonding process when people look at your baby and say, 'Oh, he has your eyes' and that kind of thing, that helps solidify the bonding"(Wegar, 2000, p. 367). A majority of social workers viewed the matching of physical and mental characteristics as an important mechanism in ensuring "successful" adoptions (Wegar, 2000). However, it is worth nothing that resemblance may not only be important to men. As Volk and Quinsey (2002; 2007) note, and others have found (e.g., Bressan, Bertamini, Nalli, & Zanutto, 2009; DeBruine, 2004), women also significantly value cues of resemblance in the HAP. This cannot be explained by issues surrounding maternity certainty (which is functionally 100%), and instead it likely reflects the preference of both sexes to adopt related children over unrelated children. In this light, kin selection (Hamilton, 1964) predicts that adoptive parents may look for signs of physical or behavioral resemblance in their adopted child (Howell, 2004). Again, we can turn to quotes from North American adoption social workers (Wegar, 2000, p. 367): "We also try to match physical appearance. I had one family that I was able to match a child, a little girl, with a family that the mother looked remarkably like a biological parent. I mean, if you look at the pictures you would think that they were related…It was a fantastic match…because the child looks like she belongs to that family…" and "we make an effort to match people in terms of physical appearance, in terms of values…religious beliefs, those sorts of things."

Thus, cues of age, health, and resemblance all appear to be important in adults' adoption decisions. Certainly child cues, and in particular child facial cues, are not the sole determinants of adoption. The host of environmental, social, and cultural factors previously discussed can exert strong influences on adults' adoption decisions. Nevertheless, it would be incorrect to assume that the traits of the adopted child, including his or her physical traits, do not matter. So, although infant and child faces are certainly not the only determinants of adults' adoption decisions, they can influence those decisions— particularly in modern-type adoptions between unrelated (and unknown) individuals, where the simulation of a genetic family is often desired.

Common Themes

Evolutionary theory is a powerful tool for understanding human behavior. It has proven highly successful in studying a wide range of different aspects of families and family life (Salmon & Shackelford, 2007). In this chapter, I have applied evolutionary theory toward understanding adoption, and I have explored what the study of adoptive families can tell us about all families. I propose three main themes that have been revealed from this evolutionary analysis of adoption. First, adoption appears to be a universal human behavior that is both highly variable and (generally) adaptive. Second, issues of kinship are ironically central to most forms and functions of adoptions. Adoption therefore is not only influenced by kinship, but the study of adoption expands our understanding of kinship, in general. Finally, adoption highlights the flexibility of human parenting. Almost any competent adult, regardless of age, gender, or kinship, can be an effective parent to a child.

Adoption Is Universal, Varied, and (Generally) Adaptive

Adoption appears to be a universal human phenomenon. This ubiquity suggests that adoption may have had significant evolutionary advantages, both to those who were adopted as well as to those who adopted children. Although it is easy to imagine how adoption could be beneficial to orphaned children or to children from suboptimal birth families, it is more puzzling to consider how adoption could be of benefit to those who expend their finite resources on either distant kin or unrelated children. Indeed, on the face of it, this is just the sort of behavior that stereotypical neo-Darwinian thinking generally argues against. A potential parallel to the ubiquity of adoption may be the ubiquity of stepparenting. Stepparenting has received much more attention from an evolutionary perspective, and a large body of literature exists suggesting that stepparents are less interested in investing in unrelated stepchildren (e.g., Daly & Wilson, 1998, 1999; Marlowe, 1999; Zvoch, 1999). Presumably, stepparents choose to do so because that investment is a trade-off for access to a new sexual partner. In some cases, the same appears to be true for adoption (Halbmayer, 2004). Adults (almost always men) gain sexual partners either by exchanging a child for sexual access to an adult woman or by adopting a child who will become a future sexual partner (Halbmayer, 2004). There have not been any formal tests of the success of these strategies, although the former does appear to be similar to what is observed in stepfamilies, in which fathers sacrifice investing their resources in their own, related children to gain or to maintain access to a sexual partner (Marlowe, 1999). In the latter case, it would be interesting to investigate whether incest-avoidance mechanisms triggered by long periods of cohabitation (Lieberman et al., 2007) make the adoption of young children as future brides a poor reproductive strategy. A broadly similar strategy is seen in some animals that delay reproduction and invest in unrelated offspring, apparently as a trade-off for expected future mating opportunities (e.g., African wild dogs [*Lycaon pictus*]; McNutt, 1996). But overall, direct mating effort may explain only a small proportion of adoption in a few societies. What other evolutionary advantages can explain the ubiquity of adoption? Among animals, adoption appears to offer at least the following evolutionary advantages: exploitation of fostered young, reciprocal altruism, and increased inclusive fitness (Riedman, 1982). Are any of these advantages also present in humans who adopt?

First, adoption appears to offer economic benefits to many adoptive or foster parents. Particularly in agriculturalist societies, in which child labor is valuable, the adoption of a child may increase a families' overall wealth (Kirkpatrick & Broder, 1976). For elderly couples, adoption may be a means of replacing the economic value of dead (or never conceived) biological children (Demain, 2004; Silk, 1980). Although there has not been a formal test of this hypothesis, it is reasonable to assume that in some cases, investing in nonrelated offspring may generate opportunities for reciprocal altruism by the adopted child directed toward the biological relatives of the adoptive parents. For parents who adopt children into an existing biological family, the same logic may apply (Rawson, 2003). The adopted child can help the relatives of the person who adopts them (e.g., carrying on a family name or dynasty; Hsiung, 2005). Thus, exploitation of adopted/fostered young appears to offer evolutionary advantages in humans.

A second form of reciprocation is social in nature instead of economic. Offering one's child for adoption is perhaps the greatest single offering an individual can make. It has the potential to forge new relationships, strengthen existing relationships, and end hostile relationships (Anderson, 2004; Halbmayer, 2004; Rawson, 2003; Richter, 1983). Adopted children are thus powerful social tools that can be wielded to create social effects that are of great importance. Adoption can also be used to maintain social order (Demian, 2004) and social conventions regarding balances of power and definitions of family, respectively. Adoption can also be used to boost populations after costly violent conflict, or to increase the military/economic strength of a group (Richter, 1983). Thus, social benefits (including reciprocal altruism) appear to offer evolutionary advantages for adoption in humans.

Third, adoption can represent a means for a group of kin to optimize their collective resources. There is a strong preference toward adopting kin in virtually all adoptive societies. A young couple who are fertile, but limited in their resources (physical, emotional, and/or social) may adopt out their children to relatives who have sufficient resources to care for those children (Silk, 1980; Noterman, 2004). This is sometimes a temporary solution more reminiscent of fosterage, but it can become permanent if the situation so dictates (Cunningham, 2005). Adoption can also be a means of invigorating a family line or dynasty (Bellow, 2003; Rawson, 2003). Although this involves bringing in unrelated individuals, it is possible that the long-term benefit to kin is significant. Regardless of its duration, this form of adoption is consistent with theories of kin selection (Hamilton, 1963, 1964; Nowak, 2006). Thus, human adoption can serve an economic function, a social function, or offer kin selection advantages. These functions match very closely with the three functions of animal adoptions mentioned above (Riedman, 1982): exploitation of fostered young, reciprocal altruism, and increased inclusive fitness also offers evolutionary advantages of adoption in humans. So, there appears to be a strong degree of convergent evolution between the evolutionary functions of human adoption and the evolutionary functions of adoption in other animal species.

Finally, in some cases, adoption may not offer evolutionary advantages, but instead may be the by-product of other powerful adaptations—the motivations to procreate and to parent (Papoušek & Papoušek, 2002). For infertile adults who want children, adoption may offer an outlet for powerful evolved desires, emotions, and cognitions (e.g., attachment, Bowlby, 1982). This emphasizes not only the existence and importance of the human drive to parent, it also emphasizes its strength. That adults willingly go to exceptional lengths to forgo investing in themselves or kin, and instead direct their resources toward children who are obviously unrelated to them speaks strongly about both the external (Terrell & Modell, 1994) and internal (Bowlby, 1982; Brodzinksy & Pinderhughes, 2002; Sprengelmeyer et al., 2009; Strathearn, Li, Fonagy, & Montague, 2008) motivations toward caring for children. Other animals also appear to occasionally engage in behaviors believed to be caused by a mismatch of proximate factors incorporating "reproductive errors" that lead to an adult adopting altruistically an unrelated infant or juvenile (Riedman, 1982). Thus, even when it is possibly the result of an evolutionary by-product, human adoption resembles animal adoption.

Kinship Is Central to Adoption

No matter what the form or function of adoption, kinship is an important consideration. All else being equal, biological parents tend to show a bias toward selecting kin as the adoptive parents. Even in the United States, roughly half of all adoptions involve kin (Stolley, 1993). In some cultures, this preference for kin adoptions is so intense that it can lead to competition between the two adoptive parents to adopt a child from their side of the family (Noterman, 2004).

Kinship is also an issue with regard to maintaining an adoption. When the biological parents are available, there is a tendency for them to try to supplement their biological child's development through indirect investments (Alber, 2004). There is also an equivalent tendency for the adopted child to seek out his biological parents, even when there has been no contact between them. There seems to be a strong human desire to connect with people who are identified as biological kin (Yngvesson, 2004). The strength of this attraction on both sides can be seen in cultures that prohibit contact, or even knowledge of, biological parents and their adopted children (Alber, 2004; Borgman, 1982). The importance of replicating biological relatedness can also be seen in adoptive parents' efforts to "create" kinship through "kinning" activities that involve intense, frequent family activities aimed at creating perceptions of resemblance and intensifying the family bond (Howell, 2003, 2004).

The value of kinship is also visible in adults' preferences for infant facial cues (Platek et al., 2002; Volk & Quinsey, 2007). Cross-culturally, resemblance appears to be an important factor in adults' hypothetical adoption decisions (Volk, 2009). The numerous quotes given earlier in this chapter (Wegar, 2000) illustrate how explicitly conscious adoption workers are about the importance of resemblance and how they attempt to create feelings of biological kinship in adoptive parents through parent–child resemblance. The same social workers also emphasize how important a sense of (biological-like) kinship is for the success of adoptions (Wegar, 2000). In agreement with some studies of paternal care (e.g., Alvergne, Faurie, & Raymond, 2009, 2010; Heijkoop, Semon-Dubas, & van Aken, 2009), resemblance appears to be particularly important for men's adoption decisions (Volk & Quinsey, 2007). Certainly, open adoptions can succeed, with both parents and adopted children being capable of a mutually loving relationship in the explicit absence of biological kinship. This does not mean that kinship isn't important. Rather, it means that, as in stepfamilies (Daly & Wilson, 1998, 1999), biological kinship is one of many important factors in adoptive families.

Age and health are two other important factors that influence adoption. In many cases, the two factors are at odds with each other, for infants are desired (Stolley, 1993), but are more likely to have health issues and/or die (Miller, 2005; Volk & Atkinson, 2009). This is perhaps why in many (but not all) cases, infants are adopted only after they have been weaned (Silk, 1990). The preference for health (Volk et al., 2005) can also be at odds with the preference for youth (Volk et al., 2007) in Western culture when adoptive parents must decide between adopting a healthy older child, or a younger child with special needs (Miller, 2005). Thus, although adults prefer to adopt younger and healthy children, these preferences are not absolute.

Ecological factors such as wealth, family support, and cultural values influence adults' adoption decisions (Brodzinsky & Pinderhughes, 2002; Bowie, 2004). They combine with information about health and age to inform adoptive parents' decisions. Although these other factors are universally important, the one factor that appears to be most powerful, enduring, and universal is kinship.

Anyone Can Be a Parent

The final common theme is the flexibility of human parenting. Virtually any adult can potentially, and successfully, adopt a child. To be sure, not all adoptive parents are good parents, but in general, adoptive families are well-functioning (Brodzinsky, 1993). This reinforces arguments that humans are an inherently alloparental species (Hrdy, 1999, 2009). Human adoption may be an example of convergent evolution, as humans share many characteristics with other alloparental animals that display adoptive behaviors: production of single offspring, prolonged or energetically intensive parental investment, limited lifetime reproductive output, small groups with tight kinship bonds, and highly social or cooperative group structure (Riedman, 1982). When seen together, this combination of features greatly strengthens the evolutionary argument for adoption being an adaptive response present in humans. The possibility of anyone being a suitable adoptive parent may not only have been strengthened by these factors—adoption may have also reinforced them in return. Hrdy suggests that alloparenting generated a strong evolutionary pressure to develop the flexible, prosocial, reciprocal social groups that characterize humans (Hrdy, 2009). By logical extension, adoption could have played a similar role in the evolution of the human species and the human mind. The evolutionary advantages of adoption may have driven humans to behave, more nepotistically, more economically, and more altruistically. Human parenting has certainly evolved to be flexible enough that it does not require birth or kinship as a trigger for parenting (as in many species; e.g., Rosenblatt, 2002), and it is possible for men or women, relatives or nonkin, young or old adults to be interested in, and successful at, raising a child. This suggests two things: First, a basic capacity to raise a child is present in most (if not all) adults. Second, human social and cultural systems have evolved to support, if not encourage, this diversity of parenting.

Future Directions

The use of evolutionary theories to examine adoption has revealed numerous theoretical and practical aspects of family life. However, this field is relatively new and unexplored. Although adoption is intimately connected with themes of genes, kinship, intergenerational transfer, and adaptation, there has been relatively little contact between adoption researchers and evolutionary theory. I therefore propose four directions for future research: exploring the range of human adoption, cross-species studies of adoption, multidisciplinary perspectives on adoption, and the study of adoption to better understand nonadoptive families.

1. What is the range of human adoption? As has been described, adoption is a diverse subject to study. Both within and between groups, there are a range of different forms and functions for adoptions. Yet, these have only been described for a handful of the range of human societies (and histories). The absence of any direct reference to adoption in the *Ethnographic Atlas* is a significant limitation for those interested in studying the forms and functions of adoption (Terrell & Modell, 1994). If we are to understand adoption from an evolutionary perspective, we require an understanding of adoption in all of its forms. The exclusion of but a single culture could significantly impact our understanding of adoption (e.g., the extreme ubiquity and flexibility of Baatombu adoptions; Alber, 2004). Therefore, a crucial future direction is expanding the range of anthropological data on adoption in different cultures.

2. How does human adoption compare to animal adoption? This chapter presents several similarities between the forms, functions, and ecologies of human and animal adoption. These tantalizing similarities have not been explicitly investigated in great depth. This is an open invitation for future researchers to focus on testing cross-species hypotheses on adoption. The functions of animal (Riedman, 1982) and human (this chapter) adoption have been laid out; they simply require researchers to gather the appropriate data to test them using cross-species models and hypotheses. For example, how do within-species variations in the production of single offspring, prolonged or energetically intensive parental investment, limited lifetime reproductive output, small groups with tight kinship bonds, and highly social or cooperative group structure influence adoption in humans as compared to animals?

3. What do multidisciplinary perspectives bring to the understanding of adoption? One of the intriguing aspects of adoption is how closely it resembles "regular" parenting. Although there has been much stereotyping of adoption as being "inferior" to regular parenting (Popenoe, 1999; Wegar, 2000), adoptive parents appear to function and cope as well as do nonadoptive parents (Brodzinsky, 1993). The majority of psychological research on adoption has focused on the developmental adjustment of parents and children. As has been mentioned, little research has considered evolutionary theory, and even less has examined neurological or cognitive perspectives of adoption. Does adoptive parenting activate the same neural structures as "regular" parenting? What role does cognitive dissonance play in the creation of perceptions of resemblance in adoptive families?

4. What does the study of adoption reveal about nonadoptive families? As has been stressed in this chapter, adoption often pushes the boundaries of what is considered a family. Economic and social forces are often laid bare for observers to see and measure, as is the strong drive to raise a child. These factors are often hidden, complicated, or unmeasured in nonadoptive family research, so the study of adoption offers much promise for those interested in studying the evolution of human families. By making kinship an explicit and variable issue, adoption allows us to view family systems functioning in a broad range of ecological and social contexts. Ironically, adoption with its absence of direct kinship reinforces the importance of kinship for human families. It allows for the clear measurement of various family factors without the confounding influence of genetic similarity. This basic principle has been exploited for decades by behavioral geneticists at the same time as it has been ignored by some traditional and evolutionary psychologists. Adoptive families are not a rare exception; they appear to be a regular feature of human families. Adoption stretches the definition of "family," and by doing so, it forces any theory of families to accommodate a broader context. By developing

more inclusive and predictive theories, we can improve our understanding of all human families. Finally, from an evolutionary perspective, the ubiquity and importance of adoption suggest that a strong element of flexibility is inherent to the form, function, and preferences of human families. As clear as it is that evolution has shaped human adoption, it is equally clear that adoption has shaped human evolution.

References

Alber, E. (2003). Denying biological parenthood: Fosterage in Northern Benin. *Ethnos, 68*, 487–506.

Alber, E. (2004). The real parents are the foster parents: Social parenthood among the Baatombu in Northern Benin. In F. Bowie (Ed.), *Cross-cultural approaches to adoption* (pp. 33–46). New York: Routledge.

Alvergne, A., Faurie, C., & Raymond, M. (2009). Father-offspring resemblance predicts paternal investment in humans. *Animal Behavior, 78*, 61–69.

Alvergne, A., Faurie, C., & Raymond, M. (2010). Are parents' perceptions of offspring facial resemblance consistent with actual resemblance? Effect on parental resemblance. *Evolution and Human Behavior, 31*, 7–15.

Anderson, A. (2004). Adoption and belonging in Wogeo, Papua New Guinea. In F. Bowie (Ed.), *Cross-cultural approaches to adoption* (pp. 111–126). New York: Routledge.

Anderson, M.L. (1991). Feminism and the American family ideal. *Journal of Comparative Family Studies, 27*, 235–246.

Auerbach, K.G., & Avery, J.L. (1981). Induced lactation. *American Journal of Diseases of Children, 135*, 340–343.

Bellow, A. (2003). *In praise of nepotism: A natural history.* Toronto: Doubleday.

Berrick, J.D. (1998). When children cannot remain home: Foster family care and kinship care. *Future of Children, 8*, 72–87.

Betzig, L.L. (1988). Adoption by rank on Ifaluk. *American Anthropologist, 90*, 111–119.

Bressan, P., Bertamini, M., Nalli, A., & Zanutto, A. (2009). Men do not have a stronger preference than women for self-resemblant child faces. *Archives of Sexual Behavior, 38*, 657–664.

Borgman, R. (1982). The consequences of open and closed adoption for older children. *Child Welfare, 61*, 217–226.

Bowie, F. (2004). *Cross-cultural approaches to adoption.* New York: Routledge.

Bowlby, J. (1982). *Attachment.* New York: Basic Book Publishers.

Briggs, J.L. (1970). *Never in anger.* Cambridge, MA: Harvard University Press.

Brooks, D., James, S., & Barth, R.P. (2002). Preferred characteristics of children in need of adoption: Is there a demand for available foster children. *Social Service Review, 76*, 575–602.

Brodzinsky, D.M. (1993). Long-term outcomes in adoption. *The Future of Children, 11*, 153–166.

Brodzinksy, D.M., & Pinderhughes, E. (2002). Parenting and child development in adoptive families. In Marc H. Bornstein (Ed.), *Handbook of parenting, Vol. 1* (pp. 279–311). Mahwah, NJ: Lawrence Erlbaum.

Chin, S.F., Wade, T.J., & French, K. (2006). Race and facial attractiveness: Individual differences in perceived adoptability of children. *Journal of Cultural and Evolutionary Psychology, 4*, 215–229.

Cunningham, H. (2005). *Children and childhood in Western society since 1500* (2nd ed.). Toronto: Pearson-Longman Press.

Daly, M., & Wilson, M. (1988). *Homicide.* New Brunswick, NJ: Aldine Transaction.

Daly, M., & Wilson, M. (1998). *The truth about Cinderella: A Darwinian view of parental love.* Newhaven, CT: Yale University Press.

Daly, M., & Wilson, M. (1999). Stepparental investment. *Evolution and Human Behavior, 20*, 365–366.

Davis, R.H. (2006). *A history of medieval Europe.* Toronto: Pearson Press.

Dawkins, R. (1989). *The selfish gene.* Toronto: Oxford University Press.

DeBruine, L.M. (2004). Resemblance to self increases the appeal of child faces to both men and women. *Evolution and Human Behavior, 25*, 142–154.

Demian, M. (2004). Transaction in rights, transactions in children: A view of adoption from Papua New Guinea. In F. Bowie (Ed.), *Cross-cultural approaches to adoption* (pp. 97–110). New York: Routledge.

Dorow, S.K. (2006). *Transnational adoption: A cultural economy of race, gender, and kinship.* New York: New York University Press.

Eberhard, M.J. (1975). The evolution of social behavior by kin selection. *Quarterly Review of Biology, 50*, 1–33.

Euler, H.,A., & Weitzel, B. (1996). Discriminative grandparental solicitude as reproductive strategy. *Human Nature, 7*, 39–60.

Fonseca, E. (2004). The circulation of children in a Brazilian working-class neighborhood: a local practice in a globalized world. In F. Bowie (Ed.), *Cross- cultural approaches to adoption* (pp. 165–181). New York: Routledge.

Halbmayer, E. (2004). The one who feeds has the rights: Adoption and fostering of kin, affines, and enemies among the Yukpa and other Carib-speaking Indians of Lowland South America. In F. Bowie (Ed.), *Cross-cultural approaches to adoption* (pp. 145–164). New York: Routledge.

Hamilton, W.D. (1963). The evolution of altruistic behavior. *American Naturalist, 97*, 354–356.

Hamilton, W.D. (1964). The genetic evolution of social behavior. II. *Journal of Theoretical Biology, 7*, 17–52.

Hamilton, L., Cheng, S., & Powell, B. (2007). Adoptive parents, adaptive parents: Evaluating the importance of biological ties for parental investment. *American Sociological Review, 72*, 95–116.

Heijkoop, M., Semon-Dubas, J., & van Aken, M. (2009). Parent-child resemblance and kin investment: Physical resemblance or personality similarity? *European Journal of Developmental Psychology, 6*, 64–69.

Howell, N. (2000). *Demography of the Dobe! Kung* (2nd Ed.). New York: Aldine de Gruyter.

Howell, S. (2003). Kinning: The creation of life trajectories in transnational adoptive families. *Journal of the Royal Anthropological Institute, 9*, 465–484.

Howell, S. (2004). The backpackers that come to stay: New challenges to Norwegian transnational adoptive families. In F. Bowie (Ed.), *Cross-cultural approaches to adoption* (pp. 227–241). New York: Routledge.

Howell, S. (2006). *The kinning of foreigners: Transnational adoption in a global perspective.* New York: Berghahn Books.

Hrdy, S.B. (1999). *Mother Nature.* New York: Pantheon.

Hrdy, S.B. (2009). *Mothers and others.* Cambridge, MA: Harvard University Press.

Hsiung, P.-C. (2005). *A tender voyage: Children and childhood in Late Imperial China*. Stanford, CA: Stanford University Press.

Kirkpatrick, J.T., & Broder, C.R. (1976). Adoption and parenthood on Yap. In I. Brady (Ed.), *Transactions in kinship, adoption, and fosterage in Oceania* (pp. 200–227). Honolulu, HI: University of Hawaii Press.

Leinaweaver, J.B. (2008). *The circulation of children: Kinship, adoption, and morality in Andean Peru*. Durham, NC: Duke University Press.

Lieberman, D., Tooby, J., & Cosmides, L. (2007). The architecture of human kin detection. *Nature, 445*, 727–731.

Mackay, C.S. (2007). *Ancient Rome: A military and political history*. New York: Cambridge University Press.

Marlowe, F. (1999). Male care and mating effort among Hadza foragers. *Evolution and Human Behavior, 20*, 57–64.

McElreath, R., & Boyd, R. (2007). *Mathematical models of social evolution: A guide for the perplexed*. Chicago: University of Chicago Press.

McNutt, J.W. (1996). Adoption in African wild dogs, Lycaon pictus. *Journal of Zoology of London, 240*, 163–173.

Miller, L.C. (2005). *The handbook of international adoption medicine*. Toronto: Oxford.

Modell, J.S. (1994). *Kinship with strangers*. Berkley, CA: University of California Press.

Notermans, C. (2004). Fosterage and the politics of marriage and kinship in East Cameroon. In F. Bowie (Ed.), *Cross-cultural approaches to adoption* (pp. 48–63). New York: Routledge.

Nowaks, M.A. (2006). Five rules for the evolution of cooperation. *Science, 314*, 1560–1563.

Papoušek, H., & Papoušek, M. (2002). Intuitive parenting. In Marc H. Bornstein (Ed.), *Handbook of parenting, Vol. 1* (pp. 183–203). Mahwah, NJ: Lawrence Erlbaum.

Platek S.M., Burch R.L., Panyavin I.S., Wasserman B.H., & Gallup G.G. Jr. (2002). Reactions towards children's faces: resemblance matters more for males than females. *Evolution and Human Behavior, 23*, 159–166.

Platek, S.M., Critton, S.R., Burch, R.L., Frederick, D.A., Myers, T.E., & Gallup Jr., G.G. (2003). How much paternal resemblance is enough? Sex differences in hypothetical investment decisions, but not in the detection of resemblance. *Evolution and Human Behavior, 24*, 81–87.

Platek S.M., Raines D.M., Gallup G.G. Jr., Mohamed F.B., Thomson J.W., Myers T.E., et al. (2004). Reactions to children's faces: Males are more affected by resemblance than females are, and so are their brains. *Evolution and Human Behavior, 25*, 394–405.

Popenoe, D. (1993). American family decline, 1960–1990: A review and appraisal. *Journal of Marriage and the Family, 55*, 527–542.

Rawson, B. (2003). *Children and childhood in Roman Italy*. Toronto: Oxford University Press.

Richter, D.K. (1983). War and culture: The Iroquois experience. *The William and Mary Quarterly, 40*, 528–559.

Riedman, M.L. (1982). The evolution of alloparental care and adoption in mammals and birds. *Quarterly Review of Biology, 57*, 404–435.

Rivière, P. (1984). *Individual and society in Guiana*. New York: Cambridge University Press.

Rosenblatt, J.S. (2002). Hormonal bases of parenting in mammals. In M.H. Bornstein (Ed.), *Handbook of parenting, Vol. 1* (pp. 31–60). Mahwah, NJ: Lawrence Erlbaum.

Salmon, C.A., & Shackelford, T.K. (Eds.). (2007). *Family relationships: An evolutionary perspective*. Toronto: Oxford University Press.

Schneider, D.M. (1980). *American kinship: A cultural account*. Chicago, IL: University of Chicago Press.

Silk, J.B. (1980). Adoption and kinship in Oceania. *American Anthropologist, 82*, 799–820.

Silk, J.B. (1987). Adoption and fosterage in human societies: Adaptations or enigmas? *Cultural Anthropology, 2*, 39–49.

Silk, J.B. (1990). Human adoption in evolutionary perspective. *Human Nature, 1*, 25–52.

Smith, S.L., & Howard, J.A. (1999). *Promoting successful adoptions: Practice with troubled families*. New York: Sage.

Sokoloff, B.Z. (1993). Antecedents of American adoption. *The Future of Children, 3*, 17–25.

Sprengelmeyer, R., Perrett, D.I., Cornwell, R.E., Lobmaier, J.S., Sprengelmeyer, A., Aesheim, H., et al. (2009). The cutest little baby face: Differences in adults' sensitivity to cuteness in infant faces. *Psychological Science, 20*, 149–154.

Stolley, K. (1993). Statistics on adoption in the United States. *The Future of Children, 3*, 26–42.

Strathearn, L., Li., J., Fonagy, P., & Montague, P.R. (2008). What's in a smile? Maternal brain responses to infant facial cues. *Pediatrics, 122*, 40–51.

Talle, A. (2004). Adoption practices among the pastoral Maasai of East Africa: Enacting fertility. In F. Bowie (Ed.), *Cross-cultural approaches to adoption* (pp. 64–78). New York: Routledge.

Terrell, J., & Modell, J. (1994). Anthropology and adoption. *American Anthropologist, 96*, 155–161.

Testa, M.F. (2004). When children cannot return home: Adoption and guardianship. *The Future of Children, 14*, 115–129.

Tried, D. (2004). Adoptions in Micronesia: past and present. In F. Bowie (Ed.), *Cross- cultural approaches to adoption* (pp. 127–141). New York: Routledge.

Trigger, B.G. (1969). *The Huron: Farmers of the North*. Toronto: Holt, Rinehart, & Winston.

Volk, A.A. (2009). Chinese infant facial cues. *Journal of Evolutionary Psychology, 7*, 225–240.

Volk, A.A., & Atkinson, J. (2008): Is child death the crucible of human evolution? *Journal of Social and Cultural Evolutionary Psychology, 2*, 247–260.

Volk, A.A., Darrell-Chang, C., Marini, Z.A. (2010). Paternal care may influence perceptions of paternal resemblance. *Evolutionary Psychology, 8*, 516–529.

Volk, A.A., Lukjanczuk, J.M., & Quinsey, V.L. (2005). Influence of infant and child facial cues of low body weight on adults' ratings of adoption preference, cuteness, and health. *Infant Mental Health Journal, 26*, 459–469.

Volk, A.A., Lukjanczuk, J.M., & Quinsey, V.L. (2007). Perceptions of child faces as a function of child age. *Evolutionary Psychology, 5*, 801–814.

Volk, A., & Quinsey, V.L. (2002). The influence of infant facial cues on adoption preferences. *Human Nature, 13*, 437–455.

Volk, A.A., & Quinsey, V.L. (2006). The influence of cues of high and low body weight on adults' ratings in the Hypothetical Adoption Paradigm. *The Scientific World Journal, 6*, 1574–1582.

Volk, A.A., & Quinsey, V.L. (2007). Parental investment and resemblance: Replications, revisions, and refinements. *Evolutionary Psychology, 5*, 1–14.

Waller, K.L., Volk, A., & Quinsey, V.L. (2004). The effect of infant fetal alcohol syndrome facial features on adoption preferences. *Human Nature, 15*, 101–117.

Weber, K. (1984). *The globe modern dictionary.* Toronto: Globe Curriculum Press.

Wegar, K. (2000). Adoption, family, ideology, and social stigma: Bias in community attitudes, adoption research, and practice. *Family Relations, 49*, 363–370.

Yngvesson, B. (2004). National bodies and the body of the child: "completing" families through international adoption. In F. Bowie (Ed.), *Cross-cultural approaches to adoption* (pp. 211–226). New York: Routledge.

Zvoch, K. (1999). Family type and investment in education: A comparison of genetic and stepparent families. *Evolution and Human Behavior, 20*, 453–464.

CHAPTER 9

An Evolutionary Perspective on Siblings: Rivals and Resources

Thomas V. Pollet *and* Ashley D. Hoben

Abstract

In this chapter, we examine two important questions in evolutionary psychology pertaining to the study of sibling relationships. These questions are: Which mechanisms assist in the detection of kin generally, and siblings, in particular? And, which selection pressures played a key role in determining whether an individual helps or competes with a sibling? One area of biological literature views siblings as rivals, whereas another views them as important resources. Using the tools of kin selection theory, parent–offspring conflict theory, and parental investment theory, we review the evidence for the view that human sibling relationships can be typified in terms of rivalry or mutualism. We discuss important factors, such as birth spacing and gender, for example, which determine when siblings are rivals and when they are resources. Our conclusion is that, although sibling competition is widespread and can be fierce both during development and in adulthood, siblings are also an important resource throughout one's life. Yet, the degree to which siblings are rivals or resources is dependent on many contextual factors, such as gender, birth order, and reproductive value. Finally, we conclude by discussing future directions for research on sibling relationships from an evolutionary point of view.

Keywords: Sibling ties, sibling rivalry, kin selection theory, helpers-at-the-nest, genetic relatedness

What is so special about the sibling tie? Sibling solidarity appears to have a unique status across societies. Fraternity, for example, has been core a value in many societies and some societies, such as postrevolutionary France, have even attempted to model society and social order in the spirit of sibling solidarity. Why does the sibling tie evoke such pervasive imagery, that one would model a society after it? Perhaps this is because the sibling tie is the most enduring human relationship throughout one's life (Ainsworth, 1993; Cicirelli, 1995). In striking contrast to the importance of the sibling tie in the sociocultural domain, relatively little attention has been paid to research on siblings throughout the history of family psychology (Irish, 1964; Lee, Mancini, & Maxwell, 1990). Here, we provide an overview of research on sibling relationships following an evolutionary approach. The key question that we address is: From an evolutionary perspective, under which conditions are siblings rivals and under which conditions are siblings resources?

Before discussing the main evolutionary theories, it is important to note that there are different types of questions that aid our understanding of the importance of sibling relationships. In evolutionary biology, the distinction is made between the four why's for explaining a trait or behavior: Proximate, Ontogenetical, Phylogenetical, and Ultimate (Tinbergen, 1963). This chapter will focus on the proximate question (*Which mechanisms allow detecting kin/siblings?*) and the functional question (*What is the selection pressure behind helping or competing with a sibling?*), as the impact of the evolutionary psychological approach is the most profound on these questions. For those who want to read more about the ontogeny of the sibling relationship (*How do sibling relationships develop?*) and the phylogeny (*What is the evolutionary history of the sibling relationship? How different or how similar is it to sibling relationships in other primates?*), we refer to other works dealing with these topics in more detail, respectively, for ontogeny, Cicirelli (1995: 42-ff) and Teti (1992), and for phylogeny, Lee (1987).

Before addressing these questions, we give an overview of the key evolutionary theories necessary for understanding sibling relationships. Subsequently, we review research that documents that siblings are respectively rivals and resources. Finally, we review several factors that can explain under which circumstances a sibling is either a rival or a resource. We conclude by making some recommendations for future research.

Understanding Sibling Relationships in an Evolutionary Framework: Kin Selection Theory, Parent–Offspring Conflict

In line with Michalski and Euler (2008), we argue that three theories are of particular importance to understanding family relationships, and more specifically sibling relationships: Kin selection theory, parent–offspring conflict theory, and parental investment theory. We briefly discuss these theories here.

Kin Selection Theory

Dobzhnansky (1958) argued that nothing in biology makes sense except in the light of evolution. By analogy, for an evolutionary family psychologist, little in family relationships makes sense without kin selection theory. Hamilton (1964a,b) formulated his, now famous, equation, $r * b > c$, in order to better understand the evolution of altruism. In his equation, r corresponds to the degree of relatedness, b to the (fitness) benefit, and c is the (fitness) cost. So, if the benefit times the relatedness is larger than the cost, a gene underpinning this altruistic behavior can evolve and is likely to be maintained throughout the population. This is also known as *Hamilton's rule* and elegantly explains the behavior of many eusocial insects, for example (Bourke, 1997). It is important to bear in mind that Hamilton's rule is formulated taking into consideration that all other factors are constant (or can be converted into some cost or benefit).

Hamilton's rule leads to basic predictions concerning behavior toward kin and nonkin, which are generally supported in humans. For example, Hamilton's rule leads to predict that, all else being constant, individuals are more likely to engage in costly behavior that yields some benefit for kin than for nonkin (e.g., Madsen et al., 2007). Moreover, it leads to predict that, all else being constant, people will be more willing to perform a costly behavior if it yields a benefit for a more closely related individual than for a distantly related individual. For example, individuals should be much more willing to donate an organ to a sibling than to a cousin. This is typically consistent with data on human behavior (e.g., Neyer & Lang, 2003). Hamilton's rule also leads to predictions on the evolution of harmful or aggressive behavior. All else being equal, harmful or aggressive behavior should be less frequent among close relatives, siblings for example, than among distant relatives, such as cousins. We also refer to Flinn (Chapter 2) in which the evidence for kin selection theory and its role in understanding human behavior is reviewed in more detail.

Parent–Offspring Conflict Theory

Apart from kin selection theory, parent–offspring conflict theory as formulated by Trivers (1974) is important for understanding sibling dynamics. Because parents are expected to invest whatever is necessary to ensure the survival of their offspring, it is generally thought that parents will allocate the maximum amount of resources available, possibly to their own detriment and that of other potential offspring (Trivers, 1974). While parents are investing as much as possible to their offspring, an offspring may at the same time attempt to obtain more resources than the parents are able to give to maximize its own reproductive success (Trivers, 1974). Therefore, there is a conflict between the wants of the individual offspring and what the parent is able or willing to give. This leads to the prediction that offspring will continue to extract resources even to the detriment of its parents.

The clearest example of parent–offspring conflict is over weaning (e.g., in pigs, Drake, Fraser, & Weary, 2008). Initially, the fitness benefits of nursing an infant typically outweigh the fitness costs to the parent. If an infant is expected to survive, then the benefits of nursing are high, the cost to the mother (which is measured by the ability to produce additional offspring) are low. As the infant grows and becomes capable of feeding itself, the benefits of nursing may decrease and the costs to the mother increases. At a certain point, the costs of nursing to the mother may exceed the benefits to the offspring, and the net reproductive success of the mother decreases as well. However, for the infant, this is not important because it is 100% related to itself and will be at the most 50% related to future siblings. Conflict is expected to be greater in species in which unrelated males tend to father a female's successive offspring than in those species in which succeeding offspring are fathered by the same male (Trivers, 1974). That is, in monogamous species, there should be less conflict than in species that use other strategies. For further information on parent–offspring conflict theory, we refer to Salmon and Malcolm (Chapter 6) and Salmon (2005).

Parental Investment Theory

Parental investment is defined as the total energy and resources that parents must utilize in order to produce offspring and ensure that it survives, but this is done at the cost of investing in other offspring (Trivers, 1972). Among mammals, a substantial difference exists between the parental investment of males and females. This difference occurs even prior to conception. Male gametes are much smaller than those of the female and are less costly to produce (Halliday, 1994). Furthermore, given the process of internal fertilization among human females, there is an initial prenatal investment of a 9-month gestation and then postnatal investment of lactation for another 2 or more years. On the other hand, human males have a minimum investment of sperm at the time of copulation, and they may choose to abandon the female at any point post conception, knowing that their offspring will be taken care of (Trivers, 1972). This differential investment influences a whole host of behaviors, such as mate preferences, sexual strategies, risk taking, and child care and rearing (e.g., Buss & Schmitt, 1993; Buss, 1989; Gangestad & Simpson, 2000; Low, 1989; Wilson & Daly, 1985).

Kin Recognition

To be able to invest in one's brother or sister, it is necessary to recognize kin and be able to discriminate. In this section, we briefly review research on kin recognition and pay special attention to its role in sibling ties.

Recognition of kin is a necessary prerequisite for investment in kin and is especially important for group-living species such as humans. Hamilton (1987) proposed that the ability to distinguish kin members from nonkin members will become most highly developed in those species that live in large groups and where there are opportunities for costly fitness-reducing behaviors and simple cues are not enough to determine kin members. As such, kin recognition is often thought to function as a key mechanism in facilitating parental care, inbreeding avoidance, and altruism toward kin (Weisfeld, Czilli, Phillips, Gall, & Lichtman, 2003). Because investing in offspring, mating with relatives, and behaving altruistically are all extremely costly acts, it is important to know who is kin and who is not (Silk, 2002).

Cues used in kin recognition mechanisms are thought to be highly automated heuristics (Park, Schaller, & Van Vugt, 2008). These cues are proximate mechanisms that serve ultimate functions in terms of Tinbergen's four why's. Kinship cues have been classified into two broad categories: familiarity and phenotypic matching. Each of these categories has its own set of mechanisms that help assist kin recognition (Park et al., 2008). Which cues are used will vary as a function of the local ecology, innate biases, and temporal conditions (e.g., visibility). For example, in certain environments, auditory signals will more beneficial to the sender and receiver than visual cues. The first category of kin recognition cues includes those which connote familiarity, such as spatial location (Park et al., 2008). The most common mechanisms used to identify relatives during development are through patterns of association and interaction (Holmes & Sherman, 1983). For example, among primate groups, close association early in life is thought to be the foundation of kin recognition for maternal kin (Bernstein, 1991; Walters, 1987). Monkeys are thought to use age similarity as a proxy to distinguish kin from nonkin (Silk, 2008; also see Chapter 15, by Berman). Use of spatial location is a simple heuristic that does not require a lot of cognition. Cross-fostering experiments among warblers demonstrate that they are unable to distinguish between their own and foster eggs, or between their own or foster nestlings. This indicates that these birds rely heavily upon special location cues to be able to detect their own offspring (Komdeur, Richardson, & Burke, 2004). Familiarity and spatial cues to relatedness are also important for humans (Park et al., 2008). The importance of these cues can be traced back to Westermarck (1889), who argued that early cohabitation was an indication of sibling relationships and thus a mechanism to prevent incest. Westermarck (1889) observed that siblings rarely find each other sexually attractive. He proposed that cohabitation early in life, which is typical of siblings, leads to sexual aversion in adulthood. Natural experiments testing the Westermarck effect among unrelated individuals have occurred in Israel and Taiwan. In Israeli kibbutz, both male and female children are taken away from their parents at a young age and are raised together in a commune. Shepher (1971, 1983) examined a sample of 2,769 Israeli couples and found that marriages between individuals raised together during the first 6 years of their lives rarely occurred. In Taiwan, there are two types of arranged marriages, the major and the minor. In the major form of marriage, the parents arranged the marriages and the bride and groom typically do not meet until the day of their marriage (Lieberman, 2009). In the minor form of marriage, a girl between the ages of a few days to 4 years old is adopted into the family. The bride and groom are raised together until puberty, at which time their marriage was to occur (Lieberman, 2009). Wolf (1966, 1970) found that in the minor form of marriage, there was a higher frequency of sexual problems, divorce, and extramarital affairs. Both these natural experiments provide support for the idea that early coresidence serves as a cue for relatedness. After reanalysis of the Taiwanese data, Wolf (1995, 2005) found that age of first association only predicted martial fertility rates among the younger partner, but not the older. This suggests that multiple kin recognition cues are being used. For younger siblings, childhood coresidence duration is the primary cue used for sibling recognition, whereas for older siblings, observing their mother caring for an infant is a very reliable cue despite duration of coresidence or age of first association. Therefore, this is the primary cue used by older siblings. Consequently, Lieberman (2009) speculates that one explanation for the fact that age of first association only predicts fertility among the younger partners is because older partners rely on other cues that are not dependent upon coresidence duration or age of first association.

Apart from studying natural experiments, researchers have examined the Westermarck effect among siblings in Western societies, typically using university student populations. Bevc and Silverman (1993, 2000) found that there is a positive relationship between early separation and sexual behavior, and those siblings who were separated were more likely to engage in sexual intercourse. Furthermore, it was concluded that prolonged cohabitation reduces genital intercourse, but does not necessarily reduce sexual interest. A different field of studies examined individuals' moral reactions toward incest. This research found that respondents raised with siblings reported more disgust (Fessler & Navarrete, 2004; Lieberman, Tooby, & Cosmides, 2003), and those females with male siblings reported more disgust than those without (Fessler & Navarrete, 2004). This was also the same for males with female siblings. It was also found that, overall, females reported higher aversion to the sibling incest than did males (Fessler & Navarrete, 2004).

Other researchers have hypothesized that maternal perinatal association (MPA) is another important cue to kinship within a nuclear family (Lieberman, Tooby, & Cosmides, 2007). The ability of a mother to recognize her own offspring begins at the time of birth and is reinforced through postnatal care. Consequently, this cue may also be important for siblings, as they observe their mothers caring for siblings and consequently through this association know that the infant is related. The results of Lieberman and colleagues' study found that, when MPA was absent, duration of coresidence predicted altruistic behavior and opposition to first- and third-party incest. This would be consistent with the case for younger siblings, as this cue would be unavailable to them. When MPA is present, levels of altruism and sexual aversion are high; this would be in the case of older siblings. It was also found that MPA was the only variable predicting altruistic behavior towards younger siblings.

The second category of kin detection cues is matching of phenotypic features or similarity of the individual in question to a kin prototype (Hauber & Sherman, 2001; Park et al., 2008). This is also referred to as *self-referent phenotype matching*, "which is the ability of animals to learn and use their own phenotype as referents for recognition of relatives" (Mateo & Johnston, 2000, p. 695). Dawkins (1982) labeled this the "arm-pit effect." This is extremely important for those animals living in larger groups, where spatial cues are not sufficient and there is an increased possibility of being exploited by nonkin (Silk, 2002). This type of kin recognition has been documented in a large variety of species, ranging from bacteria to primates (Dal Martello & Maloney, 2006). Self-referent phenotypic matching may mediate nepotistic behavior and also prevent inbreeding. Among golden hamsters in captivity, for example, individuals are able to distinguish between the flank odors of kin and nonkin. Those individuals who are recognized as siblings are treated differently than those who are recognized as nonsiblings (Mateo & Johnston, 2000). Cross-fostered females behaved differently toward odors of kin (unfamiliar related) versus those of nonkin (unfamiliar unrelated), showing more interest in the odors of kin than of nonkin. Even "simple" organisms such as sea squirts are able to distinguish those sea squirts who are related and those who are not by use of chemical cues (Pfennig & Sherman, 1995). Apart from odor and chemical signals, visual and auditory cues are commonly used to discriminate between kin and nonkin members (Holmes & Sherman, 1983). These mechanisms are also found in our closest primate relatives. A study of chimpanzees demonstrated that they have the ability to match the faces of mothers and sons, but not mothers and daughters (Parr & De Waal, 1999). Furthermore, a study on rhesus monkeys found that when individuals were presented with calls from both kin and nonkin members, they responded each time to a playback of a kin call. This demonstrates that they are indeed able to distinguish a call from kin and nonkin (Rendall, Rodman, & Emond, 1996)

Studies have also documented evidence for phenotypic matching in humans. Research shows, for example, that infants who are being breastfed are able to distinguish between the breastfeeding pad of their mothers and the breastfeeding pad of an unfamiliar mother (Macfarlane, 1975). In a study by Porter and Moore (1981) on the ability of individuals to identify the t-shirt worn by family members by scent alone, they found that 19 out of the 24 children were able to correctly identify the t-shirt worn by their sibling. They also examined the ability of the mothers to identify the t-shirt worn by their children; 17 out the 18 mothers were able to correctly identify the t-shirt. In a second study, they examined the ability of both parents to identify the t-shirt worn by their children and distinguish between the t-shirts worn by their children. 16 out of 18 parents (10 mothers, 8 fathers) were able to correctly identify the t-shirt worn by their children and were able to distinguish between their children.

Studies on facial recognition of siblings demonstrated that participants were able to correctly match pairs of siblings when the bottoms of the faces were masked (Dal Martello & Maloney, 2006). But, participants' performance decreased significantly when the upper part of the face was masked. This shows that certain areas of the face are important in kin recognition. It has also been demonstrated that fathers tend to favor children who resemble them more (Apicella & Marlowe, 2004; Burch & Gallup, 2000). Adults also report higher willingness to help unrelated children who happen to have common facial features (DeBruine, 2004; Platek, Burch, Panyavin, Wasserman, & Gallup, 2002; Platek et al., 2003). In addition, facial similarity has also been shown to increase trustworthiness, but not sexual attraction (DeBruine, 2002).

It has also been speculated that kinship may also be indicated through similarity in attitudes (Park & Schaller, 2005). Using an implicit association task (IAT), Park and Schaller (2005) found that participant's perception of individuals with similar attitudes activates kinship cognition.

In sum, kin recognition cues play an important role in the development of bonding between mother and infant, preventing mating between close relatives, and facilitating nepotism between kin members. However, apart from kin recognitions cues that connate familiarity and similarity, it has been speculated that there may be a third category of cue (Pollet, 2007). This category includes third-party knowledge of kinship. That is, because an individual is told that a person is his or her sibling, then he or she will be treated accordingly. Culture then perpetuates this norm through, for example, classification of kin members. Among the Slavey Dene of northern Canada, the same word is used for both siblings and cousins and consequently they are treated similarly (Asch & Smith, 1999).

In this section, we briefly reviewed kin recognition and its importance for sibling relationships. For further information on kin recognition we refer the reader to Krupp, DeBruine, and Jones (Chapter 20). Kinship recognition is important as it delineates the potential mechanisms for sibling ties. In the following sections, we move from the proximate level (mechanism) to the ultimate level (What are the selection pressures for conflict between siblings or for helping of siblings?).

Siblings As Rivals
Sibling Rivalry and Resource Dilution

As outlined above, Trivers (1974) formulated parent–offspring conflict theory to understand parental decision making. An extension of Trivers' parental-investment theory leads to predict that it will pay siblings to compete intensely with one another. It can pay to be selfish even to the detriment of not only one's parents but also to one's siblings, as long as the total fitness benefits of doing so outweigh the total costs. In fact, mathematical models and empirical studies among many species (e.g., Lack, 1947; Mock & Parker, 1997, for review; also Mock, Chapter 4), suggest that it can be a good adaptive strategy for an individual to extract as much parental resources as possible, even to the detriment of one's siblings. As in many other species, such as birds, human offspring are in direct competition with one another to gain parental resources. Therefore, one can expect that rivalry and competition will likely be a fundamental aspect of human sibling relationships, especially during development.

What is the empirical evidence for sibling rivalry in humans? Research from developmental psychology suggests that, throughout development, sibling rivalry is common and can be intense (Cicirelli, 1995). For example, factor analyses of sibling relationships typically find conflict and rivalry as a dimension of children's sibling types of relations (e.g., Furman and Buhrmester, 1985; Stocker, Lanthier, & Furman, 1997). Yet, it is hard to draw solid conclusions from this area of research as there is much dispute on what constitutes conflict, or aggression, between siblings. Moreover, there is a widespread lay belief that conflicts between siblings, even when frequent and fierce, is a normal part of development (Cicirelli, 1995). This can lead to under- or over-reporting of conflict, which is problematic as most studies rely (solely) on parental reports, rather than on direct observation (for example, Cicirelli, 1995). The consensus from the literature appears to be that sibling conflict and rivalry is omnipresent and can be fierce at times, with, in the extreme cases having negative effects on development. On the other hand, sibling conflict and rivalry are part of a normal developmental process and have been suggested to have positive outcomes on children's development (e.g., Bedford et al., 2002; Leung & Robson, 1991; Raffaeli, 1992).

The degree of sibling rivalry and conflict is not constant, however. Relatively few longitudinal studies look at the degree of sibling rivalry throughout childhood (e.g., White, 2001). The scarce existing studies from Western societies suggest that, over time, sibling relationships become more egalitarian and thus suggest less conflict (Buhrmester & Furman, 1987, 1990). Yet, this effect is moderated by birth order: Throughout childhood, older siblings report more or less the same level of conflict and rivalry throughout their childhood. In contrast, young siblings report a peak in conflict and rivalry around young adolescence and a drop in late adolescence. The decline in late adolescence makes sense from an evolutionary perspective: Once competition for parental resources ceases and/or individuals have started their own reproductive career, it makes little sense for siblings to continue fierce competition over resources that do not affect their reproductive success anymore (Pollet & Nettle, 2007, 2009b). Therefore, one would predict, for example, that there would be relatively little conflict between siblings once they have dispersed from the household and/or have started their own reproductive careers.

In this section, we focused on sibling rivalry but so far have not discussed the developmental consequences of sibling rivalry. Sulloway (1996, 2001) extended parent–offspring conflict theory and argued that different birth positions occupy and exploit different developmental niches, leading to different personalities. For example, this would lead firstborns to be relatively more conservative and authoritarian than laterborns. There is mixed evidence for Sulloway's arguments, with some authors finding evidence for some of his predictions (e.g., Healey & Ellis, 2007; Rohde et al., 2003; Salmon, 2003), whereas others find no effects supporting his predictions (e.g., Freese et al., 2003; Hardman et al., 2007). We will not review Sulloway's theory in detail (or the evidence for his claims), but at the end of this chapter we briefly review the evidence for birth order effects on family relationships and sibling ties. Apart from Sulloway"s (1996) influential contribution on birth order, there is an ongoing and longstanding debate regarding the role of birth order on intellectual outcomes. Zajonc and Markus (1975) formulated the confluence model. In their model, the educational attainment of a child is thought to be a function of the intellectual environment he or she is raised in. This intellectual environment is thought to be roughly the average of the total family's intellect. As a consequence, the arrival of every new sibling dilutes the intellectual environment. This is, however, contingent upon birth spacing; if widely spaced, then younger siblings should not negatively impact on the intellectual attainment of older ones. Overall, firstborns should do relatively better as they have the advantage of the full undiluted intellectual environment, at least during a period. This is similar to what would one would predict from models on sibling rivalry in other animals (see Mock & Parker, 1997)—firstborns are at an advantage because, for a period, they are not competing with other dependent offspring. The confluence model leads to predict that firstborns with siblings should have worse outcomes in terms of educational attainment than would single children (Zajonc & Markus, 1975; Steelman et al., 2002). This was, however, not supported by data; in fact, firstborns seemed to do better in terms of achievement than singletons. In order to explain this effect, Zajonc and Markus (1975) argued that firstborns benefited from teaching their younger siblings. However, there are numerous theoretical and methodological problems with the confluence model (reviewed in Steelman et al., 2002), and some studies have failed to find empirical support for the confluence model (e.g., Hauser & Sewell, 1985; Rodgers et al., 2000). The role of birth order for intellectual development, as proposed by Zajonc and Markus (1975), is thus called into question. The full debate on birth order and educational attainment falls outside the scope of this chapter, and we refer here to Steelman and colleagues (2002), who reviewed the literature in detail. In the sections on birth order, birth spacing, sibship size, and SES, we will briefly discuss whether these factors affect siblings social relationships; whether they affect educational attainment is a different question, however, that we will not address.

Sibling Rivalry to the Extreme: When Does It Pay to Kill Your Sibling?

Intuitively, one might think it makes little adaptive sense to kill a close relative, such as your sibling, given that you are likely to carry shared genes. Yet, kin selection theory is not at odds with the finding that siblicide does occur in humans. Under certain circumstances, it can literally pay to kill your sibling. Although, on average, the likelihood that you share a gene with your sibling is 50%, you still share 100% with yourself. Therefore, evolutionary theory leads to the prediction that, if the fitness benefits (strongly) outweigh the fitness costs, it might pay to kill your close relative. There is ample evidence that siblicide is in fact common among many animal species (Mock & Parker, 1997). For example, among many bird species, extreme sibling rivalry occurs among hatchlings, often leading to death (Mock & Parker, 1998). While intuitively such extreme competition might seem maladaptive (O'Connor, 1978), research over the past decades shows that lethal sibling competition is not at odds with an adaptive explanation. In birds, and other species, for example, it has been demonstrated that it can be in the parents' genetic interest to induce strong, even fatal, sibling competition (Mock & Parker, 1997, 1998). Moreover, evolutionary theory can help us understand which conditions are likely to lead to extreme sibling competition. Among humans, siblicide does occur but, as in most mammals (Hudson & Trillmich, 2007), it definitely occurs to a far lesser extent than among many bird species. Throughout human history, famous cases of siblicide have been described and are often the subject for literature and art (in China, Davis, 2000; in Judo-Christian literature, Quinones, 1991; in Roman history, Bannon, 1997; in historical England, McCullen, 1952 on Shakespeare); however, these events appear to be rare in reality. For example, only 1.4% of 508 homicides in Daly and Wilson's (1988) Detroit sample were siblicides, and a more recent sample from Canada showed an estimate of 2% (Bourget & Gagne, 2006). Research by Gebo (2002) and Underwood and Patch (1999) shows that the vast majority of siblicides are fratricides (respectively: 73% of 4,668 siblicides and 76% of 514 siblicides; both from United States samples.). Also, if we limit the comparison to murders within the nuclear family, siblicides, the majority of which are fratricides, remain very rare events (Daly & Wilson, 1988; Mouzos & Rushforth, 2003). Data from Australia suggest that, within the family homicides, siblicide is the least frequent type, 12 times less frequent than homicide between intimate partners (Mouzos & Rushforth, 2003). Estimates across different Western samples suggest that less than 5% of homicides occur between siblings. The published estimates for siblicide are somewhat higher for non-Western samples, but still siblicide can be considered as relatively rare (Daly & Wilson, 1988; Daly et al., 2001).

A good example of "adaptive siblicide," in this case fratricide, can be found in the analyses by Dunbar and colleagues (1995). Dunbar and colleagues analyzed two Viking sagas and showed that fratricide did occur when the payoffs were very high. Similar findings are found for analyses of homicides within the English monarchy (1039–1945 AD): If one can rise to the throne, then it can pay to kill your brother (Johnson & Johnson, 1991). It is important also that in these historical samples, in absolute terms, siblicides are very uncommon (e.g., Johnson & Johnson, 1991). Interestingly, the majority of the fratricides in the Daly and Wilson's Detroit sample (1988) also appeared to revolve around competition for resources. The results thus concur with the analyses of Dunbar (1995) and the data on the English monarchy (Johnson & Johnson, 1991). At a broader scale, it is also generally in line with what one would expect from the mathematical models applied to sibling competition and siblicide in birds (Mock & Parker, 1997): If scarce resources matter for achieving reproductive success, sibling competition will be more intense.

Hamilton's rule can be used to predict that, all else equal, siblicides—most of which are fratricides—will be far less common than brothers forming an alliance and committing homicide against an unrelated individual (e.g., Daly & Wilson, 1988; Johnson & Johnson, 1991). If fratricides do occur, and are not caused by some pathology or substance abuse (see Bourget & Gagne, 2004), they typically appear to revolve around the access to (limited) resources (Daly & Wilson, 1988). Although siblicide is an extremely rare form of homicide in most Western societies, in certain societies it is an important cause of death for many women. For example, in many Islamic societies, such as Palestine (Ruggi, 1998) and Jordan (Faqir, 2001), women are expected to be sexually pure and chaste. The family's honor is dependent on the perceived sexual reputation of its women. Consequently, any female family member who severely taints the family honor is typically killed by her brother or father. Statistics from Jordan (although drastically under-reported) show that honor killings are mostly committed by brothers (61.9%), followed by fathers (14.3%), and finally nephews (10%) (Faqir, 2001). The extent to which this behavior is in line with predictions from kin selection theory, and is more broadly adaptive, is unclear.

Sulloway (1996) argued that there would be an asymmetry in siblicides: Elder siblings would be more inclined to murder their younger sibling than vice versa. The reasoning behind this argument is the presumed asymmetry in reproductive value. However, empirical research covering Western and non-Western samples fails to find any support for this prediction (Daly et al., 2001; Marleau & Saucier, 1998). If anything, it appears that, among young children, older siblings are only slightly more likely to commit homicide than the younger siblings (Daly et al., 2001), but this effect disappears after taking into account the age-specific likelihood of aggression. For adults, there appears to be no evidence for Sulloway's prediction at all. It is also likely that if birth order is to play a role in the occurrence of siblicide, it will be contingent on the inheritance patterns within a culture (primogeniture/ultimogeniture). It is unlikely that there would be a universal human pattern, indifferent to culture or ecology, whereby one birth order is significantly more likely to kill the other one, rather than vice versa.

Conclusion

Sibling rivalry is common and a normal aspect of human development. The intensity of sibling rivalry typically declines in adulthood. In rare cases, extreme sibling conflict can occur, and siblings even murder each other. It is, however, more likely that siblings form alliances against nonkin than that they murder each other. Analyses indicate that the majority of siblicide that cannot be attributed to pathology is triggered by a conflict revolving around access to resources, at least in Western societies.

Siblings As Resources

Although sibling relationships are by nature marked by conflict and, in extreme circumstances, can even end with siblicide, research also shows that siblings are an important asset throughout one's life. The evidence, mostly from family psychology and developmental psychology, appears clear: siblings, especially older siblings, are a resource to the individual, financially and emotionally.

Helper-at-the-Nest and the Evolution of Sibling Caretaking

From an evolutionary perspective, sibling caretaking in humans, especially during development, has been framed within a helpers-at-the nest paradigm. Helping-at-the nest is also sometimes referred to as *local resource enhancement* (see Barrett et al., 2002). In many other species, individuals who are not currently breeding or reproducing, such as siblings, provide care that helps a breeding pair to maximize their reproductive output (Clutton-Brock, 2002). In several species (e.g., scrub jays, Woolfenden & Fitzpatrick, 1984), but not all (e.g., among the fairy wren: Dunn, Cockburn, & Mulder, 1995), the helpers are closely related to the breeding pair.

For humans, there is evidence that helping-at-the-nest is common. Some authors, for example Hrdy (2005), have argued that cooperative breeding and helping-at-the nest are key characteristics of our human ancestral past. There is, however, considerable debate on whether siblings, especially older female siblings, function as helpers-at-the-nest. Cross-cultural evidence suggests that older siblings, in particular older female siblings, commonly take care of younger siblings (Cicirelli, 1994; Weisner & Gallimore, 1977). Consequently, several researchers following an evolutionary perspective have argued that sibling caretaking can be interpreted within a helper-at-the-nest framework. However, evidence that sibling caretaking forms a clear-cut case of helpers-at-the-nest is mixed at best. Several studies do provide evidence in line with a helpers-at-the-nest perspective on sibling caretaking. For example, a now classic study by Turke (1988) among the Ifaluk of Micronesia demonstrated that the presence of a firstborn daughter was positively related to parental reproductive success. Turke (1988) reasoned that a daughter would provide assistance to the mother, thereby reducing her workload and increasing maternal reproductive success. In contrast to this study, however, Flinn (1989) found no effect of sex of the firstborn on parental reproductive success in rural Trinidadian families. Flinn (1989) did, however, find evidence in line with a different aspect of helping-at-the nest: reproductive suppression. He showed that, among other things, daughters' reproduction was delayed when dependent siblings were present in the household. Perhaps the clearest support for a helpers-at-the-nest view of human sibling caretaking can be found in a study among Hungarian Gypsies by Bereczkei and Dunbar (2002). The presence of a firstborn daughter was shown to shorten interbirth intervals, and would thus help maximize parental reproductive success. Moreover, this study clearly showed that daughters were indeed more likely to provide childcare than sons were. Thus, in this study, a mechanism was clearly demonstrated. In contrast, a study among Berber women in Morocco found no evidence for childcare as a mechanism helper-at-the nest (Crognier et al., 2001). A different study among the Aymara of Bolivia also failed to find any strong evidence for child caretaking as a mechanism for helpers-at-the-nest (Crognier et al., 2002). Bove and colleagues (2002) found some evidence that siblings acted as helpers-the-nest in the Toba of Argentina. More specifically, daughters, especially elder daughters, reduced the maternal workload drastically (by over 15%), which could lead to increased maternal reproductive success. However, the data were not longitudinal and the help provided was not tied to maternal reproductive success in this study. In an extension of their earlier work (Draper & Hames, 2000), Hames and Draper (2004) found little support for helpers-at-the-nest among the Ju/Hoansi (!Kung) of Botswana. There was no evidence that the sex of the firstborn child had an influence on female fertility. Children do not provide any substantial domestic or material labor in this society, and older siblings are not involved in childcare.

Recently, Quinlan and Flinn (2005) found some evidence in line with siblings as helpers-at- the-nest in a Dominican sample. In this sample, the presence of younger sisters, who provide childcare, increased female reproductive success as measured by number of grandchildren. Their data, did, however, also show a negative effect of brothers on male reproductive success. The negative relationship between number of brothers and male reproductive success can be explained by competition over access to resources and land. All in all, there is mixed evidence for siblings as helpers-at-the nest. The evidence for siblings, and especially older female siblings, as helpers-at-the-nest is definitely much weaker than for many animals (also see Crognier et al., 2002). Although some studies (e.g., Bereczkei & Dunbar, 2002) find good evidence, other studies fail to find any evidence at all for siblings as helpers-at-the-nest (e.g., Hames & Draper, 2004). Further cross-cultural research, documenting sibling caretaking as a mechanism, is necessary to show that siblings are in fact helpers and have measurable effects on their parents' reproductive success, as they do in many other social species.

It is important that from a helpers-at-the nest perspective, rather than acting in their own genetic interest, offspring are to a certain extent being manipulated by the breeding pair. While in some cases, the genetic interest of the breeding pair might considerably overlap with the (related) helpers, this certainly is not always the case. Apart from cases in which ecological constraints play a powerful part in the decision to stay and help, what would be the benefit of sticking around and helping? Why not simply be selfish or leave? In animals, it turns out that there might be many good adaptive reasons for helpers to stick around (Cockburn, 1998). For example, the inheritance of a good territory might outweigh the costs of not helping, as has been suggested for *Callitrichids* (Dunbar, 1995). It appears, however, that one key reason, which has also been argued to explain helping behavior in animals (e.g., Cockburn, 1998), might be especially relevant for why caretaking among human siblings is so prevalent, even when it might appear against their genetic interest to do so. This reason is benefits in terms of *acquiring social skills*. In the following section, we briefly review the developmental benefits of sibling caretaking.

Developmental Benefits

Rather than coercion, it is possible that caretaking of younger siblings yields some developmental benefit for older siblings. Here, we review the evidence that siblings are important socializing agents and caregivers, and that both giver and receiver benefit from this behavior.

Several studies document developmental benefits from sibling interactions. Studies show that older siblings tend to be the leader in sibling interactions, demonstrating prosocial behavior, along with some aggressive behaviors, whereas younger siblings tend to imitate their older siblings (Cicirelli, 1995; Lamb, 1978). Older siblings also teach their younger siblings certain physical skills, such as how to play games and use toys (Azmitia & Hesser, 1993; Cicirelli, 1995: 42-ff). This interaction develops social skills in older siblings, while at the same time younger siblings are gaining cognitive abilities through imitation (Teti, 1992). There are sex differences in terms of interaction of older siblings with younger siblings: Older girls are more likely to interact with their younger siblings than are older boys. Consequently, it may be argued that older sisters will have a stronger developmental influence than older brothers (e.g., Lamb, 1978). Older siblings also have a substantial impact on the development of the communication skills of younger siblings (Cicirelli, 1995: 42-ff). Studies have shown that older siblings initiate communication with younger siblings (Dunn & Kenrick, 1982). When the younger sibling is learning to talk, older siblings are capable of inferring what the younger sibling is attempting to say. Older siblings have also been shown to be a source of comfort and support for younger children, as demonstrated by experiments by Stewart (1983) and, Stewart and Marvin (1984). In these studies, with older siblings ranging in age from 30 to 58 months, around half of them displayed nurturing behavior toward their younger siblings when they became upset in the absence of their mother. In a different experimental study, Samuels (1980) found that in an unfamiliar environment, younger siblings left their mothers' sooner, explored more, were less distressed, and were more independent when their older sibling was present. Studies have also demonstrated that individuals who are taught by their siblings obtain higher marks than those who are taught by their peers (Azmintia & Hesser, 1993; Cicirelli, 1972). Siblings may also act as a safeguard during periods of transition and potential turmoil in an individual's life. For example, it been found that siblings help lessen the distress of parental divorce (e.g., Kempton, Armistead, Wierson, & Forehand, 1991). As siblings grow up, the influence and amount of power those older siblings have over younger siblings' changes. Also, the amount of instruction that older siblings provide decreases as the younger sibling ages (Buhrmester & Furman, 1990). Using 3rd-, 6th-, 9th-, and 12th-graders, Buhrmester and Furman (1990) examined changes in sibling relationships. They found that sibling relationships become more egalitarian and less asymmetrical with age. There is a decrease in nurturing and dominating behavior of the older sibling toward the younger. It was also found that sibling relationships become less intense as children grow older. This can be partially attributed to the decrease in time that siblings spend together as they grow up. In sum, sibling relationships seem to have positive impacts for both the elder and younger individual. The younger one is able to learn through observing and imitating the older sibling, while the elder sibling develops her or his social skills. The general consensus is that siblings play an important role as socializing agents in development, and thus they are resources.

Siblings As Resources in Adult Life

In the previous section, we discussed the potential developmental benefits of siblings, and we concluded that they are typically resources with positive outcomes on development. But, are siblings also important resources in adulthood? Although siblings in adulthood typically do not live in the same household and are thus not part of each other's routine, research shows that, even if siblings are far apart, they remain important sources, primarily of emotional and financial support. For example, studies on biological kinship and altruism generally find that, next to parents, siblings are the only kin for which one is willing to make very costly sacrifices, such as donating a kidney (e.g., Neyer & Lang, 2003). As individuals age, relationships between siblings tend to change; rivalry between the siblings typically is quite low after adolescence, and adult siblings are primarily seen as a support system (Connidis, 1992; White, 2001). Studies have found that most elderly individuals sustain contact with siblings until very late in life (Cicirelli, 1980, 1981). Yet, studies have shown that life events have significant effects on the sibling relationship. Siblings are more likely to report a decrease in emotional closeness after a marriage than the birth of a child, for example. On the other hand, death and poor health of family members was shown to have significant positive effect on sibling relationships (Connidis, 1992; Cicirelli, 1995). Siblings also serve as an important source of support for individuals who are unmarried or childless (e.g., Connidis, 1992).

Relatively few studies have documented the importance of sibling ties over the lifespan. A longitudinal study by White (2001) using a large sample of 20- to 60-year-olds from the United States found that exchanges of help between siblings typically decline over time. Contact and proximity between siblings also declines over time but stabilizes around middle adulthood.

Furthermore, research indicates that having a sibling may have a positive impact on one's health in old age, although this appears to depend on gender.

For both men and women, having a positive relationship with a sister had a positive impact on well-being, whereas a negative relationship had negative effect on well-being. The presence of a brother had no impact on well-being for both men and women. Studies on happiness in old age have found that the presence of a sister and frequent contact with a sister is a strong predictor of overall happiness among elderly women (O'Byrant, 1988; Scott, 1990). In addition, a study by Cicirelli (1989) found that for both older men and women closeness to their sisters had a significant negative correlation to depression. That is, the closer these individuals felt to their sisters, the less likely they were to feel depressed. Also for women, conflict with sisters and indifference toward sisters had a significant positive relationship with depression. For both men and women with brothers, there were no significant findings. However, a later study by Ryan and Willits (2007) found no support for the role of sisters for happiness in old age. This study found that contact with siblings had no effect on overall health and psychological well-being for either elderly men or women.

Cross-cultural data suggest that siblings are also important for marriage arrangements. Cicirelli (1994) noted that in many traditional societies, siblings, predominantly older male siblings negotiate the bride wealth or dowry, dependent on the local custom. In certain instances, the older sibling does this for his selfish interest, although there are cases in which the negotiation benefits the younger sibling as well.

Conclusion

From an evolutionary point of view, the existence of helping (nonreproductive) siblings can be understood from a helpers-at-the-nest perspective in many species. The evidence that in humans, siblings function as helpers-at-the-nest increasing parental fitness is mixed at best. What is evident, however, is that across a wide range studies, siblings play a pivotal role in development and are typically an asset. Not only younger siblings benefit from having a sibling around, older siblings appear to benefit as well. Although siblings typically disperse from the household in adulthood and are often not part of one's day-to-day routine, they remain an important source of financial and emotional support.

When a Resource and When a Rival?: Factors Affecting Sibling Relationships

In the preceding sections, we reviewed the evidence for the arguments that siblings are rivals or resources. However, whether they are a rival or a resource is a function of a whole host of other factors, some of which we have already hinted at (e.g., gender). The factors that we discuss in this section are not an exhaustive list, but we have attempted to summarize the key issues that influence when siblings are more likely to be competitive with another and when they are more likely to help each other. We will not discuss age or life stages in great detail, as we have already outlined how age and life stages influence the dynamics of conflict and cooperation between siblings.

Relatedness

Several studies have found evidence for the role of biological kinship in altruism between individuals (e.g., Korchmaros & Kenny, 2001; Madsen et al., 2007; Neyer & Lang, 2003) that is in line with kin selection theory. However, the role of relatedness for sibling relationships has been relatively understudied. Emlen (1997) suggested that individuals will invest more in full siblings than in half-siblings or stepsiblings. Sibling ties are predicted to be weaker and display more conflict when siblings are not fully related. There has been relatively little research testing this prediction, but the research that has been done generally supports these predictions: With increasing relatedness sibling ties become stronger, all else being equal. This is demonstrated, for example in a study among Mormons by Jankowiak and Diderich (2000). Although there is a strong ideological pressure to treat half-siblings as equal to full-siblings, individuals showed a clear preference for their full sibling over their half-sibling. While understudied, research on relatedness is especially relevant for modern Western societies as *patchwork families*, families in which children from the previous and current marriage are raised together, are on the rise (see Beck-Gernsheim, 1998). Despite the fact that there has been considerable research on parent–offspring relations in these patchwork families (Cherlin & Furstenberg, 1994; Stewart, 2005; Zvoch, 1999), the study of sibling relationships within these families has been largely neglected. Pollet (2007) found that relatedness predicted interaction patterns between siblings in a large sample of Dutch adults (see White & Riedmann (1992b) for similar findings in a U.S. sample). In addition, relatedness appears positively related with the possession of some very basic knowledge about one another (Pollet & Nettle, 2009a). Full siblings virtually always knew whether or not their sibling was still alive. In stark contrast, step and half-siblings were far more likely to not have any notion of whether or not their sibling was alive. This is an important finding, as some basic knowledge about a sibling's want state is a necessary prerequisite for investing in that sibling. Relatedness between siblings also appears to influence the occurrence of siblicide. Michalski and colleagues (2002) found a negative relationship between the likelihood of homicide between siblings and genetic relatedness in an historical sample of Chicago 1870–1930, but while the pattern is clear, it did not reach statistical significance.

Earlier research within family psychology also supports Emlen's prediction (1997) that relatedness will influence sibling relationships. For example, parents and children report more conflict when siblings are not fully related than when they are fully related (Hetherington, 1988; Aquilino, 1991 for a review). There also is more contact between fully related siblings than between step-/half-siblings (White & Riedmann, 1992b). Yet, factors affecting contact between siblings, such as geographical distance or gender, appear to influence sibling relationships in a similar way, regardless of the degree of relatedness.

Gender

We have already discussed how gender influences sibling-oriented behavior when discussing helpers-at-the nest. During development, older sisters appear differentially more likely to function as helpers-at-the nest (e.g., Bove et al., 2002) and also appear more likely to take care of their sibling. This asymmetry between the sexes in sibling ties remains the case in adult life. For example, research demonstrates that sister–sister relationships are typically much stronger than brother–sister relationships (e.g., Pollet, 2007; White & Riedman, 1992a). This is in line with a more general finding that women are typically more oriented toward kin than men are (Rosenthal, 1985). It is also consistent with the view that, in our ancestral past, alloparenting was widespread and women relied on their kin networks for childcare (Hrdy, 2005; Sear & Mace, 2008). As, argued earlier, such sibling caretaking, especially by older female siblings, during development might serve to develop the parenting skills of the elder sibling. From an ultimate point view, this asymmetry between elder daughters and elder sons in sibling caretaking can be traced back to parental investment theory. In general, women typically have a lot more to lose when not having access to helping kin (e.g., Sear & Mace, 2008), than men do.

Birth Order and Reproductive Value

An abundance of literature exists on birth order effects on personality and intellectual development (e.g., Sulloway, 1996; Zajonc & Markus, 1975). Here, we focus on birth order effects and their influence on family relations, especially sibling relationships. Studies document consistently that middleborns differ from other birth positions in their kin relations: Middleborns perceive their close kin more negatively than do firstborns or lastborns (Kidwell, 1981, 1982; Kennedy, 1989; Rohde et al., 2003; Salmon & Daly, 1998; Salmon, 2003). Salmon and colleagues have shown in a series of studies that middleborns tend to perceive their parents as more punitive and less generous, and feel less close to their parents and family, than do firstborns or lastborns (Salmon & Daly, 1998; Salmon, 1999; Salmon, 2003 but see Hardman, Villiers & Roby, 2007). Middleborns also tend to prefer a (close) friend over family members and have less contact with family members than other birth orders. Perceived parental favoritism also appears to follow a curvilinear function according to birth order, with middleborns reporting lowest favoritism (Kidwell, 1981, 1982; Rohde et al., 2003). However, most of these studies have used an (undergraduate) student, rather than adult population. Little is known about whether middleborns continue to report worse family relations in later life. One recent study by Hardman and colleagues (2007) failed to find any evidence for a "neglected middleborn effect," not only in an adult sample but also in a sample of children. In a large-scale study of Dutch adults by Pollet and Nettle (2007), middleborns did not consistently differ from other birth orders in face-to-face contact with their sibling. The study did, however, find that firstborns were significantly more likely than laterborns to have frequent face-to-face contact with their sibling. In a subsequent study, Pollet and Nettle (2009b) demonstrated that adult firstborns reported better sibling relationships than laterborns. The only evidence for a neglected middleborn in adulthood in this study was found when using a within-family design and was limited to relationships with siblings and the comparison to a firstborn. The finding that firstborns invest more in laterborns and rate their relationship as better, rather than vice versa, is in line with Sulloway's (1996, 2001) prediction that firstborns are more likely to act as surrogate parents than are laterborns. It also fits with the helpers-at-the nest paradigm. All else being equal, adult firstborns can increase their inclusive fitness to a greater extent by investing in an adult laterborn than vice versa, due to age differentials in reproductive value (Hughes, 1988; Pollet & Nettle, 2007, 2009b). This leads to the prediction that, among adults, generally, adult firstborns will invest more in laterborns than vice versa. More research is necessary into birth order effects on sibling relationships at various life stages, preferably from cohort studies. As we will point out in the next section, many confounds might be at play and what appears to be a birth order effect could be explained by a conjunction of other factors.

Birth Spacing and Sibship Size

Although some authors (e.g., Teti, 1992, 2002; Zajonc & Markus, 1975) typically discuss birth order, birth spacing, and sibship size as one factor, it is necessary to consider age differentials and sibship size not solely as important moderators for birth order but in their own right. While birth spacing and overall sibship size are important moderators for birth order effects (Sulloway, 1996, 2001), conversely, some effects framed as birth order might in fact be effects due to age differentials between siblings, rather than true birth order effects (Steelman, 1985; Steelman & Powell, 1985; see Steelman et al., 2002). For example, the effect reported earlier—that firstborns are more likely to maintain contact than vice versa—is likely attributable to age difference effects rather than a true birth order effect. Here, we discuss the importance of sibship size and birth spacing for competition dynamics as factors in their own right.

With regards to sibship size, sometimes also referred to as *family size* instead of sibship size, it is important to stress the quality–quantity trade-off (e.g., Gillespie, Russell, & Lummaa, 2008; Walker, Gurven, Burger, & Hamilton, 2008; Borgerhoff Mulder, 2000). As in many other animals, the intensity of competition between human siblings is a function of how many dependent offspring parents have to divide their finite resources among. As such, one can predict that sibling rivalry is more intense if parents have multiple dependent offspring. There is evidence that in humans sibship, size has a profoundly negative effect on (intellectual) development (e.g., Powell & Steelman, 1993), which would also affect reproductive success. Resource dilution might be a key explanation at play here (e.g., Downey, 1995, 2001) and fits nicely with evolutionary reasoning on the quality–quantity trade-off. Some parents have a larger number of dependent offspring, and resource allocation per child can thus be lower than in the case of parents who have fewer offspring. This lower allocation per capita can then lead to adverse outcomes on intellectual development in family. The resource dilution explanation in sociology and economics is typically supported (see Steelman et al., 2002). It is flexible and can incorporate other factors such as family SES. Yet, as previously argued, it is important to bear in mind that severe methodological challenges remain. For example SES and sibship size can be confounded. Low-SES parents might have more children, and more closely spaced children, than high-SES parents, as proposed by the quality–quantity trade-off. Family size, in turn, has consequences on the children's intellectual development. So, the negative relationship between sibship size and educational attainment might be spurious, at least to a certain extent, and attributable to parental SES. Parental SES in conjunction with parental age and birth spacing, might thus explain what at first appears to be a sibship size effect. Still, one can easily understand that even if sibship size is less important than SES, this argument is still compatible with a resource dilution explanation. Carefully designed longitudinal studies are necessary to examine sibship size effects and their interactions with other variables such as parental SES. Thus, much work remains to be done, and the current evidence from some recent longitudinal studies is mixed. Even though some studies found little or no effect of sibship size on educational attainment and/or development (e.g., Guo & van Wey, 1999), others have found profound effects (e.g., Baydar et al., 1997; Downey, 1995, 2001; Lawson & Mace, 2008). Yet, the balance appears to be in favor of the resource dilution hypothesis, and it can incorporate potential moderators/mediators and is thus a suitable theoretical paradigm (Steelman et al., 2002)

It should be noted, however, that whichever birth order gets the upper hand in this competition for parental resources can be a function of cultural rules such as primogeniture (e.g., on Gabbra, Mace, 1996) or ultimogeniture (e.g., in the historical Krummhörn population; Voland & Dunbar, 1995). These rules can be seen as solutions to prevent resource dilution. As such, perhaps future research on birth order effects should pay more attention to understanding locally adapted resource allocation strategies by parents and less looking for (universal) birth order effects in favoritism and intellectual attainment.

It is also important to note here that sibship size potentially accounts for documented "middleborn effects" (also see Steelman, 1985; Steelman &

Powell, 1985; see Steelman, Freese, & Powell, 2002). Simply controlling for sibship size is not sufficient, as the likelihood of being coded as firstborn/middleborn/lastborn is intrinsically confounded with sibship size. Consider a family with five children: The chance of being coded as a middleborn is 3/5. For this family, the chance of being coded as either a firstborn or a lastborn is 1/5. For a family with two children, the chance of being coded as a middleborn is 0, whereas the chance of being coded as either a firstborn or lastborn is 1/2 each. One can therefore see that middleborns are especially likely to be part of larger families. Statistically controlling for sibship size does not solve this coding issue, as both variables are intrinsically confounded. As such, it is desirable to also test birth order effects in samples with just three children, as in this case the likelihood of being coded either as firstborn, middleborn, or lastborn is always equal, 1/3 (e.g., Pollet & Nettle, 2007). Restricting samples to individuals with three siblings, while at a cost of sample size, effectively rules out that any birth order effects are due to effects of sibship size in the sample.

Apart from sibship size, it is necessary to consider the role of sibling density as a factor for sibling competition. During development, having a closely spaced sibling typically increases competition and has been predicted and found to have sizeable negative effects on development, survival, and educational attainment (e.g., Cleland & Sathar, 1984; Minnett et al., 1983; Miller et al., 1992; Powell & Steelman, 1993). An abundance of evidence corroborates that close birth spacing negatively impacts health and development, both in Western and non-Western societies (e.g., Powell & Steelman, 1990; Rutstein, 2005; Zenger, 1993). Work by sociologists and economists showed that family size is among the key determinants of an individual's educational attainment (e.g., Downey et al., 1996, 2001; Hanushek, 1992; See Steelman et al., 2002 for a review). But, as argued above, as with birth order effects, more research is necessary on educational attainment, and many confounding factors might be at play (overall family size, maternal age, SES, birth order).

Even though during childhood and development large age differences with siblings appear to be generally positive, in adulthood, larger age differences are typically not beneficial for sibling ties. Larger age differences between siblings appear to decrease contact frequency between siblings (e.g., Lee, Mancini, & Maxwell, 1990; Pollet, 2007), and would hence negatively impact on investments between siblings. So, while during development it would be generally beneficial to be widely spaced with a sibling, in adulthood this is not necessary the case, as one might miss out on a resource in terms of financial and emotional support.

Socioeconomic Background and Inheritance of Wealth

As already indicated in the preceding sections, SES plays an important role in sibling rivalry. If a finite number of resources exist to divide among a large number of siblings, it is likely that this will influence sibling dynamics. This is the same as in many non-human species, especially birds (Mock & Parker, 1997). If only a limited amount of resources is available, and these directly tie into parental fitness, fierce competition is to be expected. So, in several instances, socioeconomic background serves as an important moderator for birth order, birth spacing, and/or sibship size effects. Some effects ascribed to birth order, sibship size, and/or birth spacing could ultimately boil down to socioeconomic variables (Steelman et al., 2002). From an evolutionary perspective, this ultimately boils down to a parental allocation problem and points to the quality–quantity tradeoff (e.g., Stearns, 1992; Voland, 1998), which is also known to economists and demographers (e.g., Becker, 1991; Hanushek, 1992; Van Bavel, 2005). This is an important explanation for changes in demographic behavior: For parents, it is important to divide their scarce resources so as to generate a maximum possible return in terms of long-term reproductive success. In addition, the resource allocation problem can lead to an unequal allocation, investing more to one birth order (e.g., firstborn/lastborn) than another (e.g., Mace, 1996; Voland & Dunbar, 1995). As discussed, resource dilution is a plausible explanation for the negative relationship between sibship size and educational attainment.

Apart, from the finding that socioeconomic background can be a factor in its own right for sibling rivalry and parental resource allocation, it also influences exchanges of support between adult siblings. Research from family studies shows, for example, that individuals who are less educated typically are less likely to give and receive support from their sibling than are those who are highly educated (e.g., Miner & Uhlenberg, 1997; Pollet, 2007; White & Riedman, 1992a; White, 2001).

Childlessness

There is some evidence that childlessness influences investment patterns between siblings. For example,

Essock-Vitale and McGuire (1985) showed that childless aunts were more likely to invest in their nieces. Pollet and colleagues (2006) showed that Belgian women who currently had no children had relatively more contact with their nieces and nephews than did women with their own children. Childless women also reported feeling closer to their nieces/nephews than women with children. Moreover, childless women appeared to take into account reproductive value, as no effect of childlessness was found for investment in relationships with uncle/aunts. While an uncle/aunt has on average the same likelihood of carrying a gene as a nephew/niece ($r = 0.25$), the reproductive value of a niece/nephew is generally much higher than that of an uncle/aunt. The importance of reproductive value for allocating investment is reinforced by another study (Pollet & Dunbar, 2008), which found that childless couples were also more likely to take care of a niece/nephew than were couples with children in a large sample covering the United States in 1910. In this study, childless couples were also more likely to have more and younger nieces/nephews in their home than were couples with children. In line with the findings of the Belgian sample, childless individuals apparently took into account reproductive value, as no differences were found in caretaking of a parent between couples with children and childless couples. Even though the coefficient of relatedness to a parent ($r = 0.5$) is double that of a niece/nephew ($r = 0.25$), the reproductive potential of the latter is much higher, and this is apparently what matters more for deciding to whom to allocate care.

The data on childlessness are generally in accordance with kin selection theory and the helpers-at-the-nest idea: If an individual currently has no offspring and is unlikely to produce offspring, then the optimal strategy should be to channel investment toward closely related kin. In fact, for childless individuals, the only way to increase their fitness is indirectly via investing in kin. Moreover, these studies highlight the importance of taking into account reproductive value, rather than just relatedness. For example, from a genetic point of view, it makes little sense for childless individuals to invest heavily in postreproductive kin. In contrast, it makes good adaptive sense to direct all investment toward kin that have a high potential of propagating their genes. Childless individuals appear to behave in line with this prediction.

Geographical Distance

Several studies have shown that geographical distance plays an important role in sibling relationships (e.g., Lee, Mancini & Maxwell, 1990; Pollet, 2007; White & Riedmann, 1992a). The old adage, "out of sight, out of mind" definitely holds true with regards to the sibling tie. Geographical distance appears to break down sibling ties, regardless of whether siblings were fully related (White & Riedmann, 1992a). However, more work is necessary, and it might be plausible that relatedness does interact with distance, leading to lower-quality sibling relationships. An analysis of the impact of distance on sibling relationship strength by use of survival analysis in a large Dutch sample indicates that distance accelerates decay of the sibling tie as a function of relatedness between siblings (Pollet, unpublished data). Distance broke down sibling ties faster for unrelated siblings than for full siblings. Thus, there might be a kernel of truth in the saying "birds of a feather flock together."

Cross-cultural Differences and Norms

In traditional societies, sibling relationships typically have a stronger normative component than in modern societies: One is expected to help one's sibling, even if the cost is high (Cicirelli, 1994, 1995). This is also the case for caretaking of siblings during development: Across traditional societies, sibling caregiving is the norm, with older siblings, especially female older siblings, taking care of younger siblings (Weisner & Gallimore, 1977; Weisner, 1987). By contrast, in modern Western societies, sibling relationships can be seen as more voluntary. Nonetheless, the predominant pattern across societies is that it is common for siblings to take care of one another, especially during development (Cicirelli, 1994). However, this is not to say that in every society children function as helpers, as in, for example (as previously discussed), the case of the Ju/Hoansi (!Kung), in which sibling caretaking is virtually absent (Hames & Draper, 2004). Cross-cultural comparative evidence that measures sibling caretaking at fixed age brackets in a consistent way is thus lacking. Therefore, it is hard to determine exactly how prevalent sibling caretaking is, even in Western societies. While the cross-cultural data are scattered, it appears that in traditional, communally oriented societies, sibling ties are generally stronger than in Western, individualistic societies (Cicirelli, 1994, 1995).

Norms and expectations about sibling relationships also play a pivotal important role in explaining sibling tie strength within a society. Within Western societies, expectations about what a sibling is supposed to do were strong predictors of the strength of sibling tie (Lee et al., 1990). Similarly, symmetrical relationships, —for example, in which the siblings take turns in initiating contact—are on average also rated as higher-quality relationships (see Pollet, 2007).

Conclusion

In this chapter, we reviewed two aspects of what might be a human's most enduring social bond, the sibling relationship. From an evolutionary perspective, we can expect that siblings are important as a great asset in terms of resources, while at the same time acting as a rival and competitor. In many other species, as in humans, whether or not kin are a rival or resource is contingent upon many factors. In our chapter, we have discussed the role of life stages in sibling relationships and a series of factors that can cause either intensified competition (e.g., close birth spacing) or increased help to and from siblings (e.g., geographical proximity). However, it is important to stress that sibling relationships remain understudied, and in order to get a better understand of the relationship between siblings it necessary to explore this topic further. Here, we have outlined some possibilities for future research.

Future Directions

1. With regards to proximate cues for sibling ties, research has successfully uncovered important cues such as proximity and physical resemblance. Yet, it is unknown what the relative importance of these cues is: Are some cues more important than others? Also, what happens if conflicting cues exist?

2. A lot of work remains to be done on the role of biological relatedness for sibling ties throughout the lifespan. Most studies conducted so far have been cross-sectional rather than longitudinal. In addition, although there is some knowledge about differences between full sibling, half-sibling, and stepsibling relationships, little is known about to whether relationships with adopted siblings differ from full sibling relationships.

3. Assessing the role of birth order effects remains a challenge for the future. The evidence for birth order effects on sibling relationships remains mixed. Carefully designed longitudinal studies incorporating potential confounds, such as maternal age, parental SES, sibship size, and birth spacing are necessary to assess its importance for sibling relationships throughout the lifespan.

4. Currently, there is a paucity of cross-cultural studies on sibling relationships. A challenge for the future is to run comparable longitudinal studies across cultures. Ideally, these would combine different methodologies (parental report, individual report, observation).

References

Aquilino, W.S. (1991). Family structure and home-leaving: A further specification of the relationship. *Journal of Marriage and the Family, 53,* 999–1010.

Ainsworth, M.D.S. (1991). Attachments and other affectional bonds across the life cycle. In C.M. Parkes, J. Stevenson-Hinde, & P. Marris (Eds.), *Attachment across the life cycle* (pp. 33–51). London: Routledge.

Apicella, C.L., & Marlowe, F.W. (2004). Perceived mate fidelity and paternal resemblance predict men's investment in children. *Evolution and human behavior, 25,* 371–378.

Asch, M., & Smith, S. (1999). Slavey Dene. In R.B. Lee, & R. Daly (Eds.), *The Cambridge encyclopedia of hunter gatherers* (pp. 46–50). Cambridge, UK: Cambridge University Press.

Azmitia, M., & Hesser, J. (1993). Why siblings are important agents of cognitive development: A comparison of siblings and peers. *Child Development, 64,* 430–444.

Barrett, L., Dunbar, R.I.M., & Lycett, J. (2002). *Human evolutionary psychology.* Princeton, NJ: Princeton University Press.

Bannon, C.J. (1997). *The brothers of Romulus: Fraternal pietas in Roman law, literature, and society.* Princeton, NJ: Princeton University Press.

Baydar, N., Greek, A., & Brooks-Gunn, J. (1997). A longitudinal study of the effects of the birth of a sibling during preschool and early grade school years. *Journal of Marriage and Family, 59,* 957–965.

Beck-Gernsheim, E. (1998). On the way to a post-familial family: From a community of need to elective affinities. *Theory, Culture & Society, 15,* 53–70.

Becker, G.S. (1991). *A treatise on the family. Enlarged edition.* Cambridge, MA: Harvard University Press.

Bedford, V.H., Volling, B.L., & Smith, P.A. (2000). Positive consequences of sibling conflict in childhood and adulthood. *International Journal of Aging and Human Development, 51,* 53–70.

Bereczkei, T., & Dunbar, R.I.M. (2002). Helpers-at-the-nest among Hungarian Gypsies. *Current Anthropology, 43,* 804–809.

Bernstein, I.S. (1991). The correlation between kinship and behaviour in non-human primates. In P.G. Hepper (Ed.), *Kin recognition* (pp. 6–29). Cambridge, UK: Cambridge University Press.

Bevc, I., & Silverman, I. (1993). Early proximity and intimacy between siblings and incestuous behavior: A test of the Westermarck hypothesis. *Ethology and Sociobiology, 14,* 151–161.

Bevc, I., & Silverman, I. (2000). Early separation and sibling incest: A test of the revised Westermarck theory. *Evolution and Human Behavior, 21,* 151–161.

Borgerhoff Mulder, M. (2000). Optimizing offspring: The quantity-quality tradeoff in agropastoral Kipsigis. *Evolution and Human Behavior, 21,* 391–410.

Bourke, A.F.G. (1997). Sociality and kin selection in insects. In J.R. Krebs, & N.B. Davies (Eds.), *Behavioural Ecology,* 4th ed. (pp. 203–227). Oxford, UK: Blackwell.

Bourget, D., & Gagne, P. (2006). Fratricide: A forensic psychiatric perspective. *Journal of American Academy of Psychiatry Law, 34*, 529–533.

Bove, R.B., Valeggia, C.R., & Ellison, P.T. (2002). Girl helpers and time allocation of nursing women among the Toba of Argentina. *Human Nature, 13*, 457–472.

Buhrmester, D., & Furman, W. (1987). The development of companionship and intimacy. *Child Development, 58*, 1101–1113.

Buhrmester, D., & Furman, W. (1990). Perceptions of sibling relationships during middle childhood and adolescence. *Child Development, 61*, 1387–1398.

Burch, R.L., & Gallup, G.G., Jr. (2000). Perceptions of paternal resemblance predict family violence. *Evolution and Human Behavior, 21*, 429–435.

Buss, D.M. (1989). Sex differences in human mate preferences: Evolutionary hypotheses tested in 37 cultures. *Behavioral and Brain Science, 12*, 1–49.

Buss, D.M., & Schmitt, D.P. (1993). Sexual strategies theory: An evolutionary perspective on human mating. *Psychological Review, 100*, 204–232.

Cicirelli, V.G. (1972). The effect of sibling relationship on concept learning of young children taught by child-teachers. *Child Development, 43*, 282–287.

Cicirelli, V.G. (1980). Relationship of family background variables to locus of control in the elderly. *Journal of Gerontology, 35*, 108–114.

Cicirelli, V.G. (1981). *Helping elderly parents: The role of adult children*. Boston, MA: Auburn House.

Cicirelli, V.G. (1989). Feelings of attachment to siblings and well being in later life. *Psychology and Aging, 4*, 211–216.

Cicirelli, V.G. (1994). Sibling Relationships in Cross-Cultural Perspective. *Journal of Marriage and the Family, 56*, 7–20.

Cicirelli, V.G. (1995). *Sibling relationships across the life span*. New York: Plenum Press.

Cleland, J., & Sathar, Z.A. (1983). The effect of birth spacing on childhood mortality in Pakistan. *Population Studies, 38*, 401–418.

Clutton-Brock, T.H. (2002). Breeding together: Kin selection and mutualism in cooperative vertebrates. *Science, 5*, 69.

Cockburn, A. (1998). Evolution of helping behavior in cooperatively breeding birds. *Annual Review of Ecology, Evolution and Systematics, 29*, 141–177.

Connidis, I.A. (1992). Life transitions and the adult sibling ties: A qualitative study. *Journal of Marriage and the Family, 54*, 972–982.

Crognier, E., Baali, A. & Hilali, H.K. (2001) Do "helpers at the nest" increase their parents' reproductive success? *American Journal of Human Biology, 13*, 365–373.

Crognier, E., Villena, M., & Vargas, E. (2002). Helping patterns and reproductive success in Aymara communities. *American Journal of Human Biology, 14*, 372–379.

Dal Martello, M.F., & Maloney, L.T. (2006). Where are kin recognition signals in the human face. *Journal of Vision, 6*, 1356–1366.

Daly, M., & Wilson, M. (1982). Whom are new born babies said to resemble? *Ethology and Sociobiology, 3*, 69–78.

Daly, M., & Wilson, M. (1988). *Homicide*. Hawthorne, NY: de Gruyter.

Daly, M., Wilson, M., Salmon, C.A., Hiraiwa-Hasegawa, M., & Hasegawa, T. (2001). Siblicide and seniority. *Homicide Studies, 5*, 30–45.

Davis, A. (2000). Fraternity and fratricide in late imperial China. *The American Historical Review, 105*, 1630–1640.

Dawkins, R. (1982). *The extended phenotype: The gene as the unity of selection*. Oxford, UK: Oxford University Press.

DeBruine, L.M. (2002). Facial resemblance enhances trust. *Proceedings of the Royal Society of London B: Biological Sciences, 269*, 1307–1312.

DeBruine, L.M. (2004). Resemblance to self increases the appeal of child faces to both men and women. *Evolution and Human Behavior, 25*, 142–154.

DeBruine, L.M. (2005). Trustworthy but not lust-worthy: Context specific effect of facial resemblance. *Proceeding of the Royal Society B: Biological Sciences, 272*, 919–922.

Dobzhansky, T. (1973). Nothing in biology makes sense except in the light of evolution. *The American Biology Teacher, 35*, 125–129.

Downey, D.B. (1995). When bigger is not better: Family size, parental resources, and children's educational performance. *American Sociological Review, 60*, 746–761.

Downey, D.B. (2001). Number of siblings and intellectual development: The resource dilution explanation. *American Psychologist, 56*, 497–504.

Drake, A., Fraser, D., & Weary, D.M. (2008). Parent-offspring resource allocation in domestic pigs. *Behavioral Ecology and Sociobiology, 62*, 309–319.

Draper, P., & Hames, R. (2000). Birth order, sibling investment and fertility among the Ju/`Hoansi (!Kung). *Human Nature, 11*, 117–156.

Dunbar, R.I.M. (1995). The mating system of callitrichid primates: II. The impact of helpers. *Animal Behaviour, 50*, 1071–1089.

Dunbar, R.I.M., Clark, A., & Hurst, N.L. (1995). Conflict and cooperation amongst Vikings: Contingent behavioral decisions. *Ethology and Sociobiology, 16*, 233–246.

Dunn P.O., Cockburn, A., & Mulder, R.A. (1995). Fairy-wren helpers often care for young to which they are unrelated. *Proceedings of the Royal Society of London B: Biological Sciences, 259*, 339–343.

Dunn, J., & Kendrick, C. (1982). The speech of two and three year olds to infant siblings; "Baby talk" and the context of communication. *Journal of Child Language, 9*, 579–595.

Emlen, S.T. (1984) Cooperative breeding in birds and mammals. In J.B. Krebs, & N.B. Davies (Eds.), *Behavioral ecology: An evolutionary approach* (pp. 245–281). Sunderland, MA: Sinauer Associates.

Emlen, S.T. (1995). An evolutionary theory of the family. *Proceedings of the National Academy of Science (USA), 92*, 8092–8099.

Emlen, S.T. (1997). The evolutionary study of human family systems. *Social Science Information, 34*, 563–589.

Essock-Vitale, S.M., & McGuire, M.T. (1985). Women's lives viewed from an evolutionary perspective. II. Patterns of helping. *Ethology and Sociobiology, 6*, 155–173.

Faqir, F. (2001). Intrafamily femicide in defence of honour: The case of Jordan. *Third World Quarterly, 22*, 65–82.

Fessler, D.M.T., & Navarrete, C.D. (2004). Third-party attitudes toward sibling incest: Evidence for Westermarck's hypothesis. *Evolution and Human Behavior, 25*, 277–294.

Flinn, M.V. (1989). Household composition and female reproductive strategies in a Trinidadian village. In A.E. Rasa, C. Vogel, & E. Voland (Eds.), The sociobiology of sexual and reproductive strategies (pp. 206–233). New York: Chapman & Hall.

Freese, J., Powell, B., & Steelman, L.C. (1999). Rebel without a cause or effect: Birth order and social attitudes. *American Sociological Review, 64*, 207–231.

Furman, W., & Buhrmester, D. (1985). Children's perceptions of the qualities of sibling relationships. *Child Development, 56*, 448–461.

Gebo, E. (2002). A contextual exploration of siblicide. *Violence and Victims, 17*, 157–168.

Gillespie, D., Russell, A., & Lummaa, V. (2008). When fecundity does not equal fitness: Effects of an offspring quantity versus quality trade-off in pre-industrial humans. *Proceedings of the Royal Society B: Biological Sciences, 275*, 713–722.

Guo, G., & Van Wey, L. (1999). Sibship size and intellectual development: Is the relationship causal? *American Sociological Review, 64*, 169–187.

Halliday, T.R. (1994). Sex and evolution. In P.J.B. Slater, & T.R. Halliday (Eds.), *Behavior and evolution* (pp. 150–192). Cambridge, UK: Cambridge University Press.

Hames, R.D., & Draper, P. (2004). Women's work, childcare and helpers at the nest in a traditional hunter–gatherer society. *Human Nature, 15*, 319–341.

Hamilton, W.D. (1964a-b). The genetic evolution of social behavior, I and II. *Journal of Theoretical Biology, 7*, 1–52.

Hamilton, W.D. (1987). Discriminating nepotism: Expectable, common, overlooked. In D.J.C Fletcher, & C.D. Michener (Eds.), *Kin recognition in animals* (pp. 417–637). New York: Wiley.

Hanushek, E.A. (1992). The trade-off between child quantity and quality. *Journal of Political Economy, 100*, 84–117.

Hardman, D., Villiers, C., & Roby, S. (2007). Another look at birth order and familial sentiment: Are middleborns really different? *Journal of Evolutionary Psychology, 5*, 197–211.

Harris, J.R. (1998). *The nurture assumption: Why children turn out the way they do.* New York: Free Press.

Hauber, M.E., & Sherman, P.W. (2001). Self-referent phenotype matching: Theoretical considerations and empirical evidence. *Trends in Neuroscience, 24*, 609–616.

Hauser R.M., & Sewell, W.H. (1985). Birth order and educational attainment in full sibships. *American Educational Research Journal, 22*, 1–23.

Healey, M.D., & Ellis, B.J. (2007). Birth order, conscientiousness, and openness to experience: Tests of the family-niche model of personality using a within-family methodology. *Evolution and Human Behavior, 28*, 55–59.

Hetherington, E.M. (1988). Parents, children and siblings six years after divorce. In R.A. Hinde, & J.S. Hinde (Eds.), *Relationships within the family: Mutual influences* (pp. 311–331). Oxford, UK: Clarendon Press.

Holmes, W.G., & Sherman, P. (1983). Kin recognition in animals. *American Naturalist, 71*, 46–55.

Hrdy, S.B. (2005). Evolutionary context of human development: The cooperative breeding model. In S.C. Carter, L. Ahnert, K. Grossman, S.B. Hrdy, M.E. Lamb, S.W. Porges, & N. Sachser (Eds.), *Attachment and bonding: A new synthesis* (pp. 9–32). Cambridge, MA: MIT Press.

Hudson, R., & Trillmich, F. (2007). Sibling competition and cooperation in mammals: Challenges, developments and prospects. *Behavioral Ecology and Sociobiology, 62*, 299–307.

Hughes, A.L. (1988). *Evolution and Human Kinship.* Oxford, UK: Oxford University Press.

Irish, D.P. (1964). Sibling interaction: A neglected aspect in family life research. *Social Forces, 42*, 279–288.

Jankowiak, W., & Diderich, M. (2000). Sibling solidarity in a polygamous community in the USA: Unpacking inclusive fitness. *Evolution and Human Behavior, 21*, 125–139.

Kempton, T., Armistead, L., Weirson, M., & Forehand, R. (1991). Presence of a sibling as a potential buffer following parental divorce: An examination of young adolescents. *Journal of Clinical Child Psychology, 20*, 434–438.

Kennedy, G.E. (1989). Middleborns' perceptions of family relationships. *Psychological Reports, 64*, 755–760.

Kidwell, J.S. (1981). Number of siblings, sibling spacing, sex and birth order: Their effects on perceived parent–adolescent relationships. *Journal of Marriage and the Family, 43*, 315–332.

Kidwell, J.S. (1982). The neglected birth order: Middleborns. *Journal of Marriage and the Family, 44*, 225–235.

Komdeur, J., Richardson, D.S., & Burke, T. (2004). Experimental evidence that kin discrimination in the Seychelles warbler is based on association and not on genetic relatedness. *Proceedings of the Royal Society of London B: Biological Sciences, 271*, 963–969.

Korchmaros, J.D., & Kenny, D.A. (2001). Emotional closeness as a mediator for the effect of genetic relatedness on altruism. Psychological Science, 12, 262–265.

Lack, D. (1947). The significant of clutch size. *Ibis, 89*, 302–352.

Lamb, M.E. (1978). The development of sibling relationships in infancy: A short-term longitudinal study. *Child Development, 49*, 1189–1196.

Lawson, D.W., & Mace, R. (2008). Sibling configuration and childhood growth in contemporary British families. International Journal of Epidemiology, 37, 1408–1421.

Lee, P.C. (1987). Sibships: Cooperation and competition among immature vervet monkeys. *Primates, 28*, 47–59.

Lee, T.R., Mancini, J.A., & Maxwell, J.A. (1990). Sibling relationships in adulthood: Contact patterns and motivations. *Journal of Marriage and the Family, 52*, 431–440.

Leung, A.K.D., & Robson, W.L.M. (1991). Sibling rivalry. *Clinical Pediatrics, 30*, 314–317.

Lieberman, D., Tooby, J., & Cosmides, L. (2003). Does morality have a biological basis? An empirical test of the factors governing moral sentiments relating to incest. *Proceedings of the Royal Society of London B: Biological Sciences, 270*, 819–826.

Lieberman, D., Tooby, J., & Cosmides, L. (2007). The architecture of human kin detection. *Nature, 445*, 727–731.

Lieberman, D. (2009). Rethinking the Taiwanese minor marriage data: Evidence the mind uses multiple kinship cues to regulate inbreeding avoidance. *Evolution and Human Behavior, 30*, 153–160.

Low, B.S. (1989). Cross-cultural patterns in the training of children: An evolutionary perspective. *Journal of Comparative Psychology, 103*, 311–319.

Mace, R. (1996) Biased parental investment and reproductive success in Gabbra pastoralists. *Behavioral Ecology and Sociobiology, 38*, 75–81.

Macfarlane, A. (1975). Olfaction in the development of social preferences in human neonate. *Ciba Foundation Symposium, 33*, 103–117.

Madsen, E.A., Tunney, R.J., Fieldman, G., Plotkin, H.C., Dunbar, R.I.M., Richardson, J.M., et al. (2007). Kinship and altruism: A cross-cultural experimental study. *British Journal of Psychology, 98*, 339–359.

Mateo, J.M., & Johnston, R.E. (2000). Kin recognition and the "armpit effect": Evidence of self referent phenotype matching. *Proceedings of the Royal Society of London B: Biological Sciences, 267*, 695–700.

McCullen, Jr., J.T. (1952). Brother hate and fratricide in Shakespeare, *Shakespeare Quarterly, 3,* 335–340.

Marleau, J.D., & Saucier, J.F. (1998). Birth order and fratricidal behavior in Canada. *Psychological Reports, 82,* 817–818.

Michalski, R.L., Russell, D.P., Shackelford, T.K., & Weekes-Shackelford, V.A. (2006). Siblicide and genetic relatedness in Chicago, 1870–1930. *Homicide Studies, 11,* 231–237.

Michalski, R.L., & Euler, H.A. (2008). Sibling relationships. In C.A. Salmon, & T.K. Shackelford (Eds.), *Family relationships: An evolutionary perspective* (pp. 185–204). New York: Oxford University Press.

Miner, S., & Uhlenberg, P. (1997). Intragenerational proximity and the social role of sibling neighbors after midlife. *Family Relations, 46,* 145–153.

Minnett, A.M., Lowe Vandell, D., & Santrock, J.W. (1983). The effects of sibling status on sibling interaction: Influence of birth order, age spacing, sex of child, and sex of sibling. *Child Development, 54,* 1064–1072.

Miller, J.E., Trussel, J., Pebley, A.R., & Vaughan, B. (1992). Birth spacing and child mortality in Bangladesh and the Philippines. *Demography, 29,* 305–318.

Mock, D.W., & Parker, G.A. (1997). *The evolution of sibling rivalry.* New York: Oxford University Press.

Mock, D.W., & Parker, G.A. (1998). Siblicide, family conflict and the evolutionary limits of selfishness. *Animal Behavior, 56,* 1–10.

Mouzos, J., & Rushforth, C. (2003). Family homicide in Australia. *Australian Institute of Criminology: Trends and Issues, 255,* 1–6.

Neyer, F.J., & Lang, F.R. (2003). Blood is thicker than water. Kinship orientation across adulthood. *Journal of Personality and Social Psychology, 84,* 310–321.

O'Bryrant, S.L. (1988). Sibling support and older widow's well being. *Journal of Marriage and Family, 50,* 173–183.

O'Connor, R.J. (1978). Brood reduction in birds: Selection for fratricide, infanticide and suicide? *Animal Behavior, 33,* 519–533.

Park, J.H., & Schaller, M. (2005). Does attitude similarity serve as a heuristic cue for kinship? Evidence of an implicit cognitive association. *Evolution and Human Behavior, 26,* 158–170.

Park, J.H., Schaller, M., & Van Vugt, M. (2008). The psychology of human kin recognition: Heuristic cues, erroneous inferences, and their implications. *Review of General Psychology, 12,* 215–235.

Parr, L.M., & de Waal, F.B.M. (1999). Visual kin recognition in chimpanzees. *Nature, 399,* 647–648.

Pfennig, D.W., & Sherman, P.W. (1995). Kin recognition. *Scientific American, 272,* 98–103.

Platek, S.M., Burch, R.L., Panyavin, I.S., Wasserman, B.H., & Gallup, G.G., Jr. (2002). Reactions to children's faces: Resemblance affects males more than females. *Evolution and Human Behavior, 24,* 159–166.

Platek, S.M., Critton, S.R., Burch, R.L., Frederick, D.A., Myers, T.E., & Gallup, G.G., Jr. (2003). How much paternal resemblance is enough? Sex differences in hypothetical investment decisions but not in the detection of resemblance. *Evolution and Human Behavior, 24,* 81–87.

Pollet, T.V. (2007). Genetic relatedness and sibling relationship characteristics in a modern society. *Evolution and Human Behavior, 28,* 176–185.

Pollet, T.V., & Dunbar, R.I.M. (2008). Childlessness predicts helping of nieces and nephews in United States, 1910. *Journal of Biosocial Science, 40,* 761–770.

Pollet, T.V., Kuppens, T., & Dunbar, R.I.M. (2006). When nieces and nephews become important: Differences between childless women and mothers in relationships with nieces and nephews. *Journal of Cultural and Evolutionary Psychology, 4,* 83–93.

Pollet, T.V., & Nettle, D. (2007). Birth order and face-to-face contact with a sibling: Firstborns have more contact than laterborns. *Personality and Individual Differences, 43,* 1796–1806.

Pollet, T.V., & Nettle, D. (2009a). Dead or alive? Knowledge about a sibling's death varies by genetic relatedness in a Modern society. *Evolutionary Psychology, 7,* 57–65.

Pollet, T.V., & Nettle, D. (2009b). Birth order and family relationships in adult life: Firstborns report better sibling relationships than laterborns. *Journal of Social and Personal Relationships, 26,* 1029–1046.

Porter, R.H., & Moore, J.D. (1981). Human kin recognition by olfactory cues. *Physiological Behavior, 27,* 493–495.

Powell, B., & Steelman, L.C. (1990). Beyond sibship size: Sibling density, sex composition, and educational outcomes. *Social Forces, 69,* 181–206.

Powell, B., & Steelman, L.C. (1993). The educational benefits of being spaced out: Sibship density and educational progress. *American Sociological Review, 58,* 367–381.

Quinlan, R.J., & Flinn, M.V. (2005). Kinship, sex, and fitness in a Caribbean community. *Human Nature, 16,* 32–57.

Quinones, R.J. (1991). *The changes of Cain: Violence and the lost brother in Cain and Abel literature.* Princeton, NJ: Princeton University Press.

Raffaeli, M. (1992). Sibling conflict in early adolescence. *Journal of Marriage and Family, 54,* 652–663.

Rendall, D., Rodman, P.S., & Emond, R.E. (1996). Vocal recognition of individuals and kin in free-ranging rhesus monkeys. *Animal Behavior, 51,* 1007–1015.

Retherford, R.D., & Sewell, W.H. (1991). Birth order and intelligence: Further tests of the confluence model. *American Sociological Review, 56,* 141–158.

Rodgers J.L., Cleveland, H.H., van den Oord, E., & Rowe D.C. (2000). Resolving the debate over birth order, family size, and intelligence. *American Psychologist, 55,* 599–612.

Rohde, P.A., Atzwanger, K., Butovskaya, M., Lampert, A., Mysterud, I., Sanchez-Andres, A., & Sulloway, F. J. (2003). Perceived parental favoritism, closeness to kin, and the rebel of the family: The effects of birth order and sex. *Evolution and Human Behaviour, 24,* 261–276.

Rosenthal, C.J. (1985). Kinkeeping and the familial division of labor. *Journal of Marriage and the Family, 47,* 965–974.

Rossi, A.S., & Rossi, P.H. (1990). *Of human bonding: Parent-child relations across the life course.* New York: Aldine.

Ruggi, S. (1998). Commodifying honor in female sexuality: Honor killings in Palestine. *Middle East report, 206,* 12–15.

Rutstein, E. (2005). Effects of preceding birth intervals on neonatal, infant and under-five years mortality and nutritional status in developing countries: Evidence from the demographic and health surveys. *International Journal of Gynecology and Obstetrics, 89,* S7–S24.

Ryan, A.K., & Willits, F.K. (2007) Family ties, physical health and psychological well being. *Journal of Aging and Health, 19,* 907–920.

Salmon, C.A. (1999). On the impact of sex and birth order on contact with kin. *Human Nature, 10*, 183–197.

Salmon, C.A. (2003). Birth order and relationships: Family, friends, and sexual partners. *Human Nature, 14*, 73–88.

Salmon, C.A. (2005). Parental investment and parent-offspring conflict. In D.M. Buss (Ed.), *Handbook of evolutionary psychology* (pp. 506–527). Hoboken, NJ: John Wiley & Sons, Inc.

Salmon, C.A., & Daly, M. (1998). Birth order and familial sentiment: Middleborns are different. *Evolution and Human Behavior, 19*, 299–312.

Samuels, H.R. (1980). The effect of an older sibling on infant locomotor exploration of a new environment. *Child Development, 51*, 607–609.

Scott, J.P. (1990). Siblings' interactions later in life. In T. Brubaker (Ed.), *Family relationships later in life*. (2nd ed., pp. 86–99). Newbury Park, CA: Sage.

Sear, R., & Mace, R. (2008). Who keeps children alive? A review of the effects of kin on child survival. *Evolution and Human Behavior, 29*, 1–18.

Shepher, J. (1971). Mate selection among second generation kibbutz adolescents and adults: Incest avoidance and negative imprinting. *Archives of Sexual Behavior, 1*, 293–307.

Shepher, J. (1983). *Incest: A biosocial view*. New York: Academic Press.

Silk, J.B. (2002). Kin selection in primate groups. *International Journal of Primatology, 23*, 849–975.

Steams S.C. (1992). *The evolution of life histories*. Oxford, UK: Oxford University Press.

Steelman, L.C. (1985). A tale of two variables: A review of the intellectual consequences of sibship size and birth order. *Review of Educational Research, 55*, 353–386.

Steelman, L.C., & Powell, B. (1985). The social and academic consequences of birth order: Real, artifactual, or both? *Journal of Marriage and the Family, 47*, 117–124.

Steelman, L.C., Powell, B., Werum, R., & Carter, S. (2002). Reconsidering the effects of sibling configuration: Recent advances and challenges. *Annual Review of Sociology, 28*, 243–269.

Stewart, R.B. (1983). Sibling attachment relationships: Child-infant interactions in the strange situation. *Developmental Psychology, 19*, 192–199.

Stewart, R.B., & Marvin, R.S. (1984). Sibling relations: The role of conceptual perspective taking in the ontogeny of sibling caregiving. *Child Development, 55*, 1322–1332.

Stewart, S.D. (2005). How the birth of a child affects involvement with step-children. *Journal of Marriage and Family, 67*, 461–473.

Stocker, C.M., Lanthier, R.P., & Furman, W. (1997). Sibling relationships in early adulthood. *Journal of Family Psychology, 11*, 210–221.

Stockley, P., & Parker, G.A. (2002). Life history consequences for mammalian sibling rivalry. *Proceedings of the National Academy of Science (USA), 99*, 12932–12937.

Sulloway, F.J. (1996). *Born to rebel: Birth order, family dynamics, and creative lives*. London: Abacus.

Sulloway, F.J. (2001). Birth order, sibling competition, and human behavior. In P.S. Davies & H.R. Holcomb III (Eds.), *Conceptual challenges in evolutionary psychology* (pp. 39–83). Dordrecht, NL: Kluwer Academic Publishers.

Teti, D.M. (1992) Sibling interaction. In V.B. Van Hasslet, & M. Hersen (Eds.), *Handbook of social development: A lifespan perspective* (pp. 201–226). New York: Plenum Press.

Teti, D.M. (2002). Retrospect and prospect in the psychological study of sibling relationships. In J. McHale, & W. Grolnick. (Eds.), *Retrospect and prospect in the psychological study of families* (pp. 193–224). Hillsdale, NJ: Erlbaum.

Tinbergen, N. (1963). On aims and methods of ethology. *Zeitschrift für Tierpsychologie, 20*, 410–433.

Trivers, R.L. (1972). Parental investment and sexual selection. In B. Campbell (Ed.), *Sexual selection and the descent of man* (pp. 136–179). Chicago, IL: Aldine Publishing Company.

Trivers, R.L. (1974). Parent-offspring conflict. *American Zoologist, 14*, 249–264.

Turke, P.W. (1988). Helpers at the nest: Childcare networks on Ifaluk. In, L.L. Betzig, M. Borgerhoff Mulder, & P.W. Turke (Eds.), *Human reproductive behaviour* (pp. 178–188). Cambridge, UK: Cambridge University Press.

Turke, P.W. (1989). Evolution and the demand for children. *Population and Development Review, 15*, 61–90.

Underwood, R.C., & Patch, P.C. (1999). Siblicide: A descriptive analysis of sibling homicide. *Homicide Studies, 3*, 333–348.

Van Bavel, J. (2006). The effect of fertility limitation on intergenerational social mobility: The quality-quantity trade-off during demographic transition. *Journal of Biosocial Science, 38*, 553–569.

Voland, E. (1998). Evolutionary ecology of human reproduction. *Annual Review of Anthropology, 27*, 347–374.

Voland, E., & Dunbar, R.I.M. (1995). Resource competition and reproduction. *Human Nature, 6*, 33–49.

Walker, R.S., Gurven, M., Burger, O., & Hamilton, M.I. (2008). The tradeoff between number and size of offspring in humans and other primates. *Proceedings of the Royal Society B: Biological Sciences, 275*, 827–834.

Walters, J.R. (1987). Kin recognition in non-human primates. In D.J.C. Fletcher, & C.D. Michener (Eds.), *Kin recognition in animals* (pp. 359–393). New York: Wiley.

Weisfeld, G.E., Czilli, T., Phillips, K.A., Gall, J.A., & Lichtman, C.M. (2003). Possible olfaction based mechanisms in human kin recognition and inbreeding avoidance. *Journal of Experimental Child Psychology, 85*, 279–295.

Weisner, T.S., & Gallimore, R. (1977). My brother's keeper: Child and sibling caretaking. *Current Anthropology, 18*, 169–190.

Weisner, T.S. (1987). Socialization for parenthood in sibling caretaking societies. In J. Lancaster, A. Rossi, J. Altmann, & L. Sherrod (Eds.), *Parenting across the life span* (pp. 237–270). New York: Aldine.

Westermarck, E. (1889). *The history of human marriage*. New York: Allerston Press.

White, L. (2001). Sibling relationships over the life course: A panel analysis. *Journal of Marriage and the Family, 63*, 555–568.

White, L.K., & Riedmann, A. (1992a). Ties among adult siblings. *Social Forces, 71*, 85–102.

White, L.K., & Riedmann, A. (1992b). When the Brady bunch grows up: Step/half- and full sibling relationships in adulthood. *Journal of Marriage and the Family, 54*, 197–208.

Wolf, A.P. (1966). Childhood association, sexual attraction and the incest taboo: A Chinese case. *American Anthropologist, 68*, 883–889.

Wolf, A.P. (1970). Childhood association and sexual attraction: A further text of the Westermarck hypothesis. *American Anthropologist, 72*, 503–515.

Woolfenden, G.E., & Fitzpatrick, J.W. (1984). The Florida scrub jay: Demography of a cooperative-breeding bird. In R.M. May (Ed.), *Monographs in population biology*. Princeton, NJ: Princeton University Press.

Zajonc, R.B., & Markus, G.B. (1975). Birth order and intellectual development. *Psychological Review, 82*, 74–88.

Zenger, E. (1993). Siblings' neonatal mortality risks and birth spacing in Bangladesh. *Demography, 30*, 477–488.

Zvoch, K. (1999). Family type and investment in education: A comparison of genetic and stepparent families. *Evolution and Human Behavior, 20*, 453–464.

CHAPTER 10

Trials and Tribulations of Childhood: An Evolutionary Perspective

Virginia Periss *and* David F. Bjorklund

> **Abstract**
>
> All humans face a prolonged and arduous trek on their way to becoming adults. Humans, compared to other primates, are not only born relatively immature but also take a dangerously long time to reach adulthood. Here we review how our species was able to combat the many diverse challenges faced at different stages between conception and adulthood. We first examine the selection pressures that helped shaped humans' unique ontogeny. We then examine the many costs associated with each stage of development, focusing in particular on how offspring have evolved specific adaptations at certain times in ontogeny to contend with these trials, all while having to master the many necessary skills needed to become a successful adult. In addition, we discuss the role of social support systems on development, including the importance of caregivers to children, specifically the mother, early in life and the influence of peers later in life.
>
> **Keywords:** deferred adaptations, ontogenetic adaptations, benefits of immaturity, social-brain hypothesis, cooperative breeding, alloparents, parental investment theory, infanticide, risk-taking, young male-syndrome

Childhood is not for the faint of heart. The journey to become a successful adult capable of reproduction occurs for only a privileged few. Even when a sperm successfully fertilizes an egg, the offspring has only about a 40% chance of making it through the first 6 weeks of life (Wang, Chen, Wang, Chen, Guang, & French, 2003). After this point, the offspring's chances of surviving, at least until birth, are greatly improved. Once the offspring leaves the protective nurturing environment of the womb, however, it still faces an uphill battle. Although the likelihood of dying prior to adolescence in developed countries today is less than 1%, that rate is closer to 50% in traditional cultures, as it was for Western cultures in the not-too-distant past, and was surely even higher for our hunter-gatherer ancestors (Volk & Atkinson, 2008).

The potential difficulties of surviving until adulthood in humans is in part reflected by the disproportionate amount of time humans, compared to other primates, take to attain adulthood. Indeed, the closer a species' common ancestor is with *Homo sapiens*, the longer its period of immaturity: approximately 2 years in lemurs, 4 years in macaques, and 8 years in chimpanzees, compared to approximately 15 years in humans (Poirier & Smith, 1974). In fact, based on historical data and data from traditional cultures (e.g., Hill & Hurtado, 1996; Kaplan, Hill, Lancaster, & Hurtado, 2000), it is likely that our ancient ancestors were closer to 18 to 20 years of age before being fully reproductive. Primates that take longer to reach maturity, therefore, should be expected to have higher child mortality rates compared with primates that reach maturity faster. In accordance with this, wild lemurs (25% juvenile mortality rate; Karpanty, 2005) and Japanese macaques from Yaskushima (11% juvenile mortality rate; Hanya et al., 2004) are more likely to survive until maturity than chimpanzees (52% juvenile mortality rate; Robbins, 1995).

Although this extended period of immaturity must have provided great benefits for our ancestors (see discussion to follow), it also came with great costs. Waiting so long to reach sexual maturity has associated with it the likelihood of death before reproducing, and thus the termination of one's genetic line. Because of the costs of an extended childhood, natural selection surely operated at least as strongly on the early stages of the lifespan as the later stages. Although evolutionary psychology has understandably focused on the adult—the individuals who do the mating and childrearing—the prolonged journey to adulthood required that infants and children evolved adaptations to survive the long trek to maturity (Bjorklund & Pellegrini, 2002).

At least two general types of adaptations during the early stages of development can be identified: deferred adaptations and ontogenetic adaptations (Hernández Blasi & Bjorklund, 2003). *Deferred adaptations* refer to aspects of children's learning or social behavior that have been shaped by natural selection in preparation for adulthood. This can be most easily seen in some sex differences, such as play styles or interest in infants, in which the different types of experiences of boys and girls prepare them for the life they will lead (or would have led in the environment of evolutionary adaptedness) as adults. *Ontogenetic adaptations*, in contrast, refer to features of infancy and childhood that serve to adapt children to their immediate environments and not necessarily to prepare them for a future one (Bjorklund, 1997; Oppenheim, 1981). This can be most readily seen in some prenatal and early postnatal physiological adaptations, such as when fetuses obtain their oxygen and nutrition from the placenta via the umbilical cord, or neonatal reflexes that facilitate survival, such as the sucking reflex, that disappear when they are no longer needed (when the infant is born and moves from being surrounded by amniotic fluid to being surrounded by air, or when sucking can be intentionally controlled). There may also be many such *behavioral/cognitive adaptations* that assist the survival of a young animal but that disappear when they are no longer functional. For example, young infants' poor perceptual abilities might protect them from overstimulation and competition between developing senses (Turkewitz & Kenny, 1982), and neonates' reflex-like tendency to copy facial expressions may facilitate mother–infant attachment at a time when infants cannot control their own social behavior (Bjorklund, 1987; see discussion later in this chapter).

In addition, like adults, infants and children are highly sensitive to local environmental conditions and may adjust aspects of their developmental trajectory depending on such conditions. For instance, Belsky, Steinberg, and Draper (1991) proposed that children during their first 5 or so years of life are sensitive to the quality of the rearing environment and follow different life history patterns consistent with how life will likely be as adults. For instance, girls who experience father absence, economic stress, and insecure attachment relationships reach sexual maturity earlier, engage in sexual activity sooner, and invest less in resulting offspring than do girls whose early experiences include father presence, lack of economic stress, and secure attachment relationships. Although research since the publication of this influential paper has shown that many factors can influence the rate at which females attain menarche and their subsequent mating strategies, the basic idea that children's early rearing environments influence aspects of their development has received substantial support (see Belsky, 2007; Del Giudice, 2009; Ellis, 2004 for reviews).

The extended period of immaturity, however, characteristic of our species not only resulted in selection pressures on infants and children, but also on their parents. The special nature of humans' life history surely required adaptations to childcare practices. In this chapter, we examine some of the adaptations of infancy, childhood, and parenthood and the dangers they were evolved to combat. First, we examine the nature of human ontogeny, some of the reasons why *Homo sapiens* may have evolved this unique life history, and some of the consequences for childcare. We then examine the numerous perils humans face throughout the various stages of development, beginning shortly after conception and continuing through adolescence. In light of this, we discuss how humans have evolved to contend with these challenges, as well as learning the necessary skills needed to be successful in adulthood. Although we discuss the active role the offspring plays in survival throughout these stages of development, we also address the importance of social support systems, with a focus on the role of mothers early in life and the impact of peers later in development.

Evolution of Human Life History
The Invention of Childhood and Adolescence

Humans spend an inordinate amount of time as prereproductives. However, humans not only take longer to achieve adulthood than other mammals, they have evolved new stages of the lifespan. There are at least three life history stages, for example, that all mammals experience: *infancy*, when an infant nurses from its mother; the *juvenile period*, when the young animal is weaned and can reasonably fend for itself but is still not able to reproduce; and *adulthood*. According to anthropologist Barry Bogin (1999, 2001, 2003), humans invented two new stages, each having its own distinct physical and psychological features: *childhood*, the time between weaning and the juvenile period (about 3 to 7 years), and *adolescence*, a brief 2–3 years following menarche in girls.

Childhood is characterized by a continued dependence on adults, due mainly to limitations in physical and cognitive abilities. For example, although the majority 3- and 4-year-old children in most cultures are no longer nursing (or at least receive most of their calories from sources other than breast milk), they do not have the strength or manual dexterity to forage and care for themselves. A more competent individual, therefore, must do the procuring of food, usually the child's mother. Moreover, preschool-age children still have primary teeth, which, because of their small size, make it necessary that food be specially prepared for them. In addition to their physical shortcomings, 3- to 7-year-old children have cognitive limitations that prevent them from living independently. Piaget (1983) described children at this time of life as *preoperational* thinkers. Unlike infants, preoperational children think symbolically. However, their thinking is intuitive, not logical. According to Piaget, preschool-age children lack the logical cognitive operations characteristic of older children, so-called *concrete operations*. Although more contemporary research has questioned many aspects of Piaget's theory, his description of preoperational children as cognitively unsophisticated has generally been supported. Young children, for example, have limited problem-solving abilities, difficulties regulating their thought and behavior, and perform poorly in social situations requiring both cooperation and competition, relative to older children (see Bjorklund, 2005, 2011; Siegler & Alibali, 2004).

It is difficult to imagine children much before the age of 7 years surviving on their own, that is, without an adult to support them. Although we do not expect juveniles (i.e., children older than 7 years) to be able to function independently in human society either, they stand a much better chance than preschool-age children. Juveniles are developing secondary teeth, have increased strength and dexterity, and display enhanced cognitive and social skills that permit them to fend for themselves, at least marginally. Millions of juveniles living on the streets around the world today eke out an existence without the support of adults (Amnesty International, 1990; Brooks, 1991). Furthermore, although the likelihood of dying before adulthood is surely higher for such street children than for youngsters who continue to receive parental care, street children, nonetheless, possess the minimal physical, social, and cognitive abilities to at least have a chance of surviving without substantial adult assistance. (For a discussion of the significance of the juvenile period to human development see Del Giudice, Angeleri, & Manera, 2009.)

The second "new" life history stage is adolescence, characterized by a rapid growth spurt, a period of postmenarche infertility for girls, and substantial neural reorganization (Giedd et al., 1999; Spear, 2007). Although we often refer to subadult animals as "adolescents," no other species displays the rapid growth spurt typical to that of humans, although chimpanzees (*Pan troglodytes*) and bonobos (*Pan paniscus*) apparently do have a postmenarchal period of infertility (see Bogin, 1999).

According to Bogin (1999, 2003), based on fossil evidence such as bone size and dental development, our ancestors developed these different life stages gradually, over the course of hominin evolution. Figure 10.1 presents the proposed life stages for *H. sapiens*, early and late *H. erectus*, *H. habilis*, *Australopithecus afarensis*, and modern chimpanzees (*P. troglodytes*). As you can see, Bogin identified the first evidence of the childhood stage in *H. habilis*, which became extended in *H. erectus* and *H. sapiens*; he identified adolescence only in *H. sapiens* (see also Gibbons, 2008).

The Benefits of Extending Immaturity

There are great perils in extending immaturity well into the second decade of life. In evolutionary biology, when there are great costs to something, there must also be great benefits, else it would have been eliminated by natural selection. What can be the offsetting benefits of humans' unique extended life history? Arguably, the most important benefit of delayed maturation, and perhaps its "cause," is the expansion of the brain and the cognitive systems it supports. In adulthood, human brains are proportionally larger relative to body size and weight than those of any other species. The encephalization quotient (EQ) is a measure of the size of an animal's brain compared to its "expected" size, given its

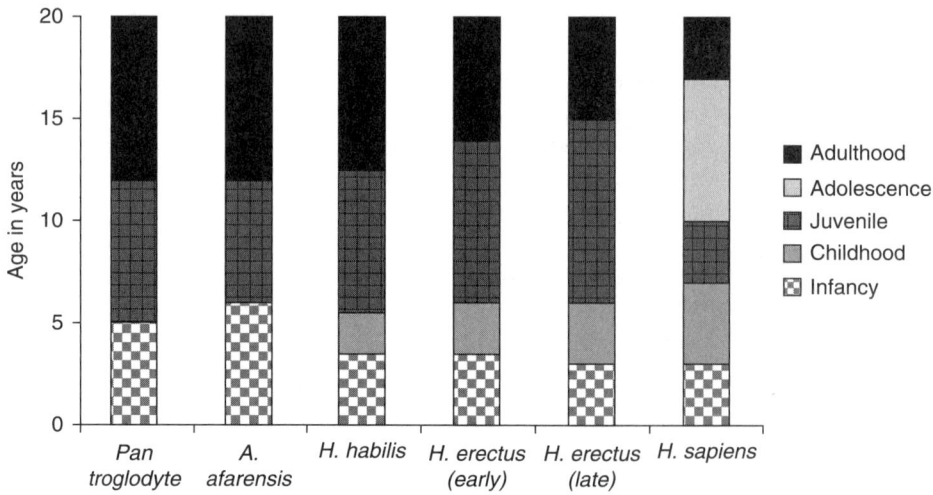

Fig. 10.1 Evolution of human life history stages (from Bogin, 2001). According to Bogin, humans evolved two new life stages: childhood and adolescence. Adapted from Bogin, B. (2001). *The growth of humanity*. New York: Wiley-Liss, with permission of the publisher

weight (Jerison, 1973). Animals with brains as large as expected given their body weight have an EQ of 1.0; animals with brains larger than expected for their body weight have an EQ greater than 1.0; and animals with an EQ less than expected for their body weight have an EQ of less than 1.0. Chimpanzees, humans' closest genetic relatives, have an impressive EQ of 2.3; humans, in contrast, have an EQ nearly three times as large, 7.6 (Jerison, 1973, 2000; Rilling & Insel, 1999). Figure 10.2 presents the estimated EQs of modern chimpanzees (*P. troglodytes*), modern humans (*H. sapiens*) and three presumed human ancestors. As you can see, there has been a steady increase in brain size over hominid evolution. As a result, humans have more cortical neurons than any other mammal (including much larger whales) and nearly twice as many as chimpanzees (see Roth & Dicke, 2005).

A large brain means a large skull, and this caused problems for our bipedal ancestors. (Bipedality preceded increased brain size, as can be seen in the recently described 4.4-million-year-old fossil *Ardipithecus ramidus*; White et al., 2009.) The brain of a human newborn could only get so large and still fit through the birth canal of a bipedal woman (Rosenberg & Trevathan, 1996). As a result, human infants are born "premature" relative to their primate cousins. If human neonates' brains were as well developed as

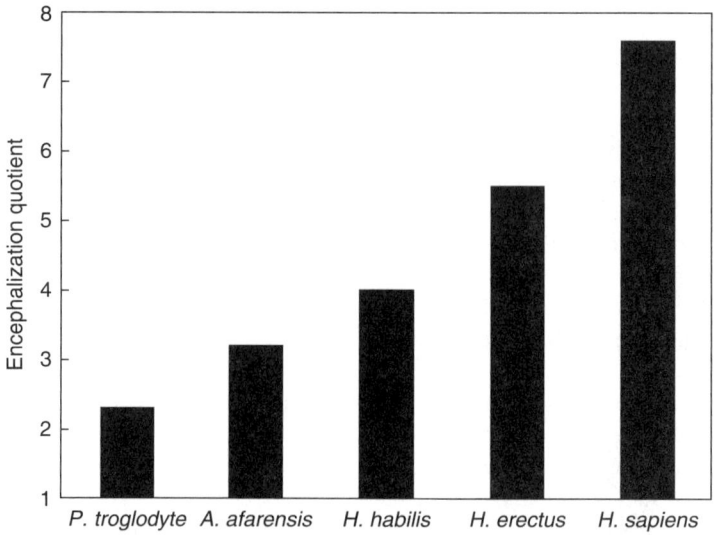

Fig. 10.2 Estimated encephalization quotients for chimpanzees (*Pan troglodytes*) and four hominid species

those of other primates, it has been estimated that gestation would need to continue for another 9 to 12 months (see Gould, 1977; Montagu, 1961), and the head would then be too large for a vaginal birth. As a result, human infants are born "prematurely," and they maintain their rapid rate of brain development characteristic of the prenatal period well into the second year of life (Gould, 1977).

Human bipedalism limited the maximum size of a human neonate brain to about 350 cc; anything larger would not pass thorough the birth canal (Dienske, 1986). In all other primates, there is a ratio of approximately 0.5 between prenatal and postnatal brain growth. So, for example, an infant born with a 350 cc cranial capacity could only possibly reach a brain of 700 cc by adulthood. Although *H. habilis* and *H. ergaster* had adult cranial capacities around 700 cc (McHenry & Coffing, 2000), *H. erectus* had a cranial capacity of 1,250 cc and modern humans between 1,350 and 1,500 cc. For *H. erectus* to have evolved such a large brain implies that, at some point during our evolutionary past, the ratio between pre- and postcranial growth changed from that of chimpanzees. Humans were able to accomplish this through retention of fetal growth rates caused in part by premature birthing.

Having a large brain affords greater learning abilities. Moreover, having a brain that develops slowly, with substantial changes occurring in adolescence and into young adulthood (e.g., Giedd et al., 1999; Sowell, Thompson, Holmes, Jernigan, & Toga 1999; Spear, 2007), provides the possessor of such a brain with greater plasticity—the ability to change and to adjust to novel environments—and memory capacity. Delayed brain maturation, for example, creates an extension of dendritic and synaptic growth, allowing humans the ability to produce more interconnections among neurons than any other primate (Gibson, 1991).

Many scholars have argued that larger brains evolved to meets the demands of living in highly social groups, known as the *social-brain hypothesis* (e.g., Alexander, 1989; Bjorklund & Harnishfeger, 1995; Whiten & Byrne, 1988; Dunbar, 2003; Geary & Flinn, 2001; Humphrey, 1976; Tomasello & Moll, 2010). Complex social groups created selection pressures for primates to meet the daily challenges of cooperation and competition among other intelligent group members. Some have argued that it was the confluence of a large brain, extended juvenile period, and social complexity that is responsible for humans' social intelligence (Bjorklund & Bering, 2003; Bjorklund, Cormier, & Rosenberg, 2005). Human cultures are incredibly complex and diverse, and it requires a large and pliable brain and a long time to master the ways of any particular social group.

An extended childhood also provides children more time to master the technologies that *H. sapiens* are so famous for (Kaplan et al., 2000). Although we are not the only tool users, no other species manufactures and uses tools to the extent that humans do (see Bjorklund & Gardiner, 2011). However, even if a big brain is necessary for acquiring and generalizing technological skills, the transmission of such skills is most readily accomplished via humans' exceptional social learning abilities (e.g., Horner, Whiten, Flynn, & de Waal, 2006), permitting the nongenetic transmission of acquired information from one generation to the next with high fidelity.

Humans' extended period of immaturity was an evolutionary gamble that seemed to have paid off. Despite the perils of dying before reproducing (and dying at birth due to complications of fitting a large head through a narrow birth canal), *H. sapiens* has survived, and its large, slow-developing brain has permitted it to establish ecological dominance over the globe. However, this could not have been achieved merely by inventing new life stages or by taking a few extra years to mature. The extraordinary physical changes in human life history had to be accompanied by changes in how infants and children were cared for, a topic we turn to now.

Evolution of Childcare
Having a long period of immaturity also required humans to evolve new patterns of childcare. As for nearly all mammals, human mothers are the primary caregivers to their offspring, and this relationship has been described as having "the greatest number of special-purpose anatomical, physiological, and psychological mechanisms" (Salmon & Shackelford, 2008, p. 8). However, humans are among about 5% of mammals in which the father also provides some care to offspring (Clutton-Brock, Hodge, Russell, Jordan, Bennett, Sharpe, & Manser, 2006), resulting most likely from increased demands generated by the extended period of dependency of human children. The presence of fathers lowers child mortality rates and creates an alternative mating strategy for men (see Geary, 2005). The goal of reproduction is to produce an offspring that will not only survive, but that will go on to successfully be a parent itself. It would not be enough for a man to employ a quantitative approach to increase his inclusive fitness if the offspring failed to survive

to reproductive age. Rather, a more successful method for getting genes passed to the next generation involves his active participation in child rearing. For example, Hrdy (1986) argued that father–child bonds may have been the foundation for mother–father–child bonds typical of human families. This change in mating strategies toward social monogamy equipped our ancestors with the necessary tools for successfully rearing offspring that take nearly two decades to reach sexually maturity.

Although human fathers provide some care for their children, in all cultures and throughout historical time, mothers still provide the vast majority of care, and this has required further modifications in how children are reared. One example of this is reflected in humans' tendencies to engage in *cooperative breeding* (Hrdy, 2007, 2009), in which mothers share the responsibility for childcare with others in the family and the larger social group. In addition to the father, most *alloparents*, individuals other than the genetic mother who provide childcare, are the mother's female kin, frequently the mother's mother, sisters, or older female offspring. According to Hrdy, this increased social support allowed women to space their slow-developing children more closely, permitting them to care for and nourish more children than they possibly could if they alone were responsible for them. Consistent with the cooperative breeding hypothesis, human mothers much more readily permit other individuals to hold and care for their infants, in contrast to other primates (Schön & Silven, 2007), a seeming requirement for cooperative breeding.

Alloparenting, however, is not unique to humans but has been observed in a number of other mammals, including elephants, lions, Cebus monkeys, and bats (see Hrdy, 1999). Alloparenting provides benefits not only for the offspring but also for the mother and the alloparent. For example, research looking at a variety of species has shown that there is a positive relationship between the number of alloparents and survivorship of the infant (e.g., Clutton-Brock, 2006), and these effects are heightened when surrogates are genetically related to the child (Griffin & West, 2003). For the mother, the presence of alloparents reduces her workload, allowing her to produce more offspring or have shorter interbirth intervals (e.g., Bales et al., 2001; Powell & Friend, 1992; Russel et al., 2003; Solomon, 1991). In line with this, Quinlan and Quinlan (2008) examined alloparenting and weaning ages in 58 traditional societies. They found that availability of helpers was significantly correlated with age of weaning, with higher numbers of alloparents being related to earlier ages of weaning.

Because most alloparents are related to the infants they help care for, they improve their inclusive fitness by increasing the chance that the infant will survive; they also gain valuable experiences in childcare. In communal species, juveniles assist in rearing offspring through activities such as feeding, carrying, babysitting, and pup thermal regulation (Russel, 2004; Solomon & French, 1997). Evidence of the benefits of parenting experience for juvenile alloparents in future parenting endeavors has been demonstrated in prairie voles (Stone, Mathieu, Griffin, & Bales, 2010). Similar to humans, prairie voles (*Microtus ochrogaster*) are cooperative breeders with monogamous mating systems in which the males assist in childrearing. Stone and colleagues (2010) showed that prairie voles that had no alloparenting experience spent more time in pup care, whereas experienced prairie voles tended to produce larger pups and engaged in more licking behaviors. In addition, the researchers found that, although the sex of the alloparent had an effect on time spent in nest alloparenting, with females spending more time on average than males, no sex differences in adulthood were found in total time spent or quality of contact with pups. The authors attributed these findings as reflecting the positive long-term benefits of alloparenting on later parental displays of care.

Other evidence for the importance of alloparents comes from research demonstrating that the chances of a child's survival increase substantially when mothers have help rearing their children, with maternal grandmothers having the greatest overall effects on children's survival (e.g., Beise & Voland, 2002; Gibson & Mace, 2005; Lahdenperä, Lummaa, Helle, Tremblay, & Russell, 2004; Sears & Mace, 2008). In accordance with this, a recent study by Parker and Short (2009) revealed that maternal grandmothers living in Lesotho play a critical role in grandchild care. Lesotho, like many other sub-Saharan African countries, has among the highest HIV/AIDS rates in the world, with over 26% of the people between the ages of 15 and 29 years having HIV/AIDS, and out of those only 14% receive treatment. As a result, there is a high mortality rate for mothers. This and other factors leave 46% of children between the ages of 6 and 16 years without biological mothers (UNAIDS, 2007). A review of Lesotho's Demographic and Health data revealed that of the children who have lost a mother, those with a maternal grandmother did equally as well later in life, as measured by school attendance, as did children raised by their biological mothers. Both groups did significantly better than children who lost their mothers and who did not have a maternal grandmother.

Childrearing practices vary widely among different groups of humans. The underlying foundation of these practices revolves around meeting the basic needs of the offspring while helping them to reach adulthood. This task may be easy for contemporary humans today, complete with hospitals and modern conveniences, but for our ancestors this presented a much more difficult challenge. It is believed that ancestral parents engaged in "natural" or "instinctual" parenting (Schön & Silvén, 2007), which involves mothers paying close attention to communicative signs from their children and quickly responding to their needs. Modern-day proponents of natural parenting note that for 99% of our species' history, infants over the first year of life, and perhaps longer, experienced constant contact and continuous care. For instance, an examination of modern hunter-gatherers reveals that infants sleep with their mothers, typically continue breastfeeding until after their second birthdays or beyond, and are held about 50% of the day before they begin to crawl (Lozoff & Brittenham, 1979). Similar patterns of infant care were found in 176 nonindustrialized societies that practice fishing, herding, or agriculture (Lozoff & Brittenham, 1979; see also Keller et al., 2004). Schön and Silven (2007) have argued that these "natural" practices are contingent on parents having "an innate sensitivity to their child's cues and an instinctive knowledge of their required responses" (p. 2). We will examine some of these "innate sensitivities," as well as children's adaptations to their parents, in the sections to follow.

Making It to Birth

Although the difficulty surviving after birth has been greatly reduced by modern technology, the probability of making it to birth is less optimistic. It is estimated, for example, that only one-fourth of fertilized eggs ever get implanted, and the ones that do have about a one-third chance of being spontaneously aborted before they become embryos.

According to Robert Trivers' (1972) parental investment theory, conflict exists between how much time and resources an individual puts into mating effort versus parenting effort. This can be seen even in the earliest stages of pregnancy. Shortly after conception is an optimal time for a female to "decide" whether to invest in the offspring, in that the costs of pregnancy (loss in mating opportunities) at this time are still relatively low. This may have been particularly important for our ancestors, when women would have suffered higher mortality rates while pregnant due to increased vulnerability to predation, as well as increased risk of death during childbirth.

Consistent with this, "maternal physiology may have evolved to select among early embryos on the basis of small differences that need only be weakly correlated with subsequent vigor" (Stearns, 1987, p. 25). With this strategy, the cost of a month delay in reproduction is insignificant compared to the cost of raising an offspring that is of low genetic fitness. In support of this, Clark and colleagues (1993) argued that menstruation functions as a means of removing defective embryos before pregnancy has gone too far. Similarly, menstruation has also been argued to eliminate normal embryos when social or ecological conditions are unsuitable for pregnancy (Haig, 1990).

During this time, the fetus is not without its own defenses against possible attempts at termination. Shortly after conception, a "game" begins between the mother and fetus. The fetus will attempt to deceive the mother into not aborting via hormones and communication between fetal and maternal cells. Evidence for this comes from research showing that, on average, 10%–20% of embryos that successfully block menstruations subsequently miscarry in the first trimester (Mackslon, Geraedts, & Fauser, 2002). These aborted embryos are often the result of chromosomal abnormalities, suggesting that some offspring may have been able to avoid termination up until this point by misleading the mother into thinking that it was of higher quality than was actually the case (Fritz et al., 2001).

Once the 12th week of pregnancy is reached, the chances of miscarriage are greatly reduced, partly because the mother has already endured costs associated with investment and is unlikely to reject the embryo at this point. In addition to the greater costs to reproductive fitness associated with longer investment, other benefits to the mother in keeping the offspring alive result from the increased rate of maternal infection should she miscarry at this time (Haig, 1993). For the mother, a decision to abort investment at this point would be costly, and as a result, miscarriages typically occur only in extreme situations. In both the second and third trimester, for instance, there is only about a 15% chance of miscarriage (Miscarriage: Causes of Miscarriage. HealthSquare. com, downloaded September 9, 2007), with most fetal deaths resulting from uterine malformations, in utero growth restrictions, and cervical and umbilical cord problems (Regine & Marot, 2007).

Related to Trivers' ideas about parental investment is his theory about parent–infant conflict. Trivers (1974) proposed that an offspring attempts to maximize its own fitness by extracting as much parental resources as possible. Parents, in contrast, do not want to provide all of their resources to a single offspring, which may jeopardize the welfare of current or future offspring, or of the parent him- or herself. Offspring, in turn, have developed adaptations to extract resources from parents beginning before birth (Haig, 1993). This conflict is two-sided, however, with mothers also evolving mechanisms to counter their offsprings' attempts.

Haig (1993) documented mechanisms involved in human mother–child conflict during pregnancy. For example, as we discussed briefly above, early in pregnancy, mothers may attempt to abort an unfit embryo. However, the embryo/fetus is not a passive player in this "tug of war" between itself and its mother. For example, the fetus produces human chorionic gonadotrophin (hCG), a hormone that prevents the mother from menstruating and thus shedding her uterine lining along with the newly implanted embryo. The fetus then projects trophoblasts into the mother's endometrial arteries (arteries that supply nutrients to the fetus), preventing the arteries from narrowing and reducing blood flow to the fetus. The fetus then releases human placental lactogen (hPL) that decreases the effects of insulin in the mother's blood. This results in higher amounts of glucose (fuel) being available for the developing fetus, even though these fetal manipulations may be harmful, in some cases, to the mother, causing *gestational diabetes*. In effect, the fetus strong-arms the mother into providing adequate resources to ensure its healthy development.

Once a fetus has survived 38 weeks of gestation, it must make the transition from the protective environment of the uterus to the outside world. As we mentioned previously, the birthing process in humans was complicated by the expansion of brain size coupled with bipedalism, requiring that human infants be born "prematurely." Even with a shortened gestation period, however, the birthing process is still risky for both the mother and infant. The neonatal mortality rate in developing countries today, likely similar to that of our ancestors, is estimated at around 1,250 per 100,000 successful births (World Health Organization, 2005). In addition, unlike other mammals, the birthing process in humans is typically socialized, because the mother is unable to assist herself or the infant during labor (Schön & Silven, 2007). There are numerous potential birth complications, including breeched birth, anoxia, failure of decent of the fetal head, and poor uterine contraction strength (World Health Organization, 2005). Additionally, there is always the risk of infection for both the mother and offspring, with it being the major cause of maternal mortality (World Health Organization, 2005).

Infancy

Following birth, the offspring once again faces an increased risk of death. No longer protected by the womb, the child is now left vulnerable and completely dependent on others for survival. Although infants have evolved mechanisms that promote maternal care, mothers and other caretakers have also evolved mechanisms that cause them to evaluate the benefit of further investing in an offspring, and we examine each briefly in the following sections. Note that although we discuss infant and parent adaptations in separate sections, they are actually interactive and surely coevolved.

Adaptations of Infants to Promote Survival

Humans are born prematurely relative to other primates, and as such, infants seem especially helpless and dependent on others for care. Shortly after birth, the mother looks for both physical and behavioral traits in her offspring as cues for genetic fitness. Infants, therefore, who were better able to display these features would have increased their likelihood of survival (Bjorklund & Pellegrini, 2002). Neonates, for instance, have been shown to match various facial expressions of others including tongue protrusions or mouth openings, termed *neonatal imitation* (e.g., Field, Woodson, Greenberg, & Cohen, 1982; Meltzoff & Moore, 1977). Such matching behavior disappears by 2 months, not to reappear until the latter part of the first year (Abravanel & Sigafoos, 1984; Jacobson, 1979). Even newborn chimpanzees (Bard, 2007; Myowa-Yamakoshi, Tomonaga, Tanaka, & Matsuzawa, 2004) and rhesus monkeys (Ferrari et al., 2006) have been shown to imitate facial expressions, and these behaviors also decline after 2 months. Although Meltzoff and Moore (1977) originally interpreted neonatal imitation as a form of social learning, others have interpreted it as an adaptive means of fostering parent–infant interaction at a time when infants have little intentional control over their actions (Bjorklund, 1987; Byrne, 2005; Legerstee, 1991; Nagy, 2006).

Consistent with this interpretation, neonatal imitation appears to be under the control of subcortical regions of the brain, unlike the "true" imitation observed in children and adults. For example, neonates who were later shown to be cortically blind, were nonetheless able to orient to objects visually in the first month of life before losing their ability (Dubowitz, Mushon, DeVries, & Arden, 1986), suggesting that early visual processing is done primarily by subcortical regions. Other research has shown that infants as young as 3 days have recognition memory for a 2-minute retention period, and this early recognition memory is largely controlled by subcortical structures (Pascalis & de Schonen, 1994). Not too long into development, however, these abilities move under the control of cortical circuits (Nagy, 2006). The relationship, therefore, between subcortical regions and early neonatal imitation may reflect adaptations possessed exclusively by the infant early in life that serve to elicit caretaking and resources from parents.

Nagy and Molnar (2004) argue that human neonates not only engage in imitation but also "provocation," in which they spontaneously produce previously imitated gestures. Psychophysiological analysis has revealed differences in neonatal heart rate responses between imitation and provocation, with neonates displaying an increase in heart rate during imitation and a decrease in heart rate during provocation. The authors interpreted these findings as suggesting that two different mechanisms are responsible for this pattern, one for modeling the movements of the actor (imitation) and a second for engaging the actor using a previously effective response (provocation).

Neonatal imitation can be argued, therefore, to be a highly complex social skill that seemingly disappears relatively soon in life. When the ability to imitate facial gestures emerges later in infancy, it is controlled by different brain regions and likely has a different function (as part of a suite of more general social-cognitive abilities). During our evolutionary past, infants who were better able to engage their mothers during the first few weeks of life, when chances of abandonment are high, may have increased their likelihood of surviving. Once attachment becomes more established and infants develop better intentional control of their own actions, they may "give up" this reflexive-like matching behavior. From this perspective, neonatal imitation reflects an important ontogenetic adaptation that is intended to serve the infant at a specific time in development and not as preparation for adulthood (Bjorklund & Pellegrini, 2002).

Consistent with this, Heimann (1989) reported a significant correlation between the level of neonatal imitation and subsequent quality of infant–mother interaction, with greater levels of neonatal imitation being associated with increased quality of interaction 3 months later.

As infants grow older and are better able to refine motor movements and convey intention, they are increasingly able to facilitate interactions with caretakers. For example, infants past the neonatal stage engage in behaviors (e.g., sustained eye contact, smiling) that have been described in other cultures as "flirting" (Eibl-Eibesfeldt, 1970). Through such behaviors, infants may not only display their genetic fitness but may also in doing so generate greater sustained and repeated social contact with their mothers, that in turn fosters infant–mother attachment, thus increasing their likelihood of surviving. For instance, infants labeled "socially competent" are able to effectively communicate their needs to their mothers and to respond to mothers' attempts at engagement (e.g., smiling in response to eye contact) better than less socially competent infants (Goldberg, 1977). Reinforcement of parental behavior in turn may affect a mother's feeling of competence and increase the quality of maternal care (see Goodman et al., 2005; Murray & Trevarken, 1986).

Other features that may serve to elicit care from adults are less under the direct control of the offspring but are important nonetheless, such as physical cues of immaturity. Lorenz (1943), for instance, argued that certain immature physical characteristics (e.g., large head and eyes, round checks) serve to evoke positive affect from parents and caregivers. Bowlby (1982) similarly argued that infantile facial features evolved through natural selection to facilitate the development of attachment. In support of this, a study by Alley (1981) revealed that that when adults were shown images depicting children with varying head shapes and asked to rate them in terms of "cuteness," their ratings decreased as the head shape became less infant-like and more adult-like (see also Alley, 1983; Fullard & Reiling, 1976; Zebrowitz, Kendall-Tackett, & Fafel, 1991). More recent research has found that young (19–26 years old) and middle-aged (45–51 years old) women were more sensitive to individual differences in the "cuteness" of infant faces than were men of any age and older (menopausal) women (53–60 years), suggesting that cuteness sensitivity is modulated by female reproductive hormones (Sprengelmeyer et al., 2009).

These positive perceptions of infantile features may be particularly important for infants and very young children, who are more costly to their parents in terms of fitness and thus may be more vulnerable to rejection or abandonment by a caretaker. Consistent with this are studies by Volk and his colleagues (Volk, Lukjanczuk, & Quinsey, 2007; Waller, Volk, & Quinsey, 2004), who found that cuteness and attractiveness are the single best predictors of the likelihood of people making hypothetical adoption decisions. In one study, Volk, Lukjanczuk, and Quinsey (2007) showed 200 adults 12 different images of children at eight different ages ranging from 6 months to 6 years. Adults were asked to rate the level of cuteness based on a photo of the child. The study revealed that adults were more likely to rate the more immature-looking child as cute, and these ratings were also correlated with their likelihood to make an adoption decision.

The preference for infantile features is actually an evolved adaptation in adults, of course, and has been confirmed in studies with nonhuman species (Maestripieri & Roney, 2006) and in studies examining differences in mother–infant interactions in mothers of infants with craniofacial deformities. These mothers were significantly less nurturing than mothers of "normal" infants (Barden et al., 1989). Other research by Frodi and her colleagues (1978) revealed that, when coupled with premature faces, infant cries were rated as more unpleasant compared to when the cry was paired to normal infant faces. Infant facial cues therefore may serve as a powerful influence on adults' perceptions, attributions, and parental care behaviors.

Parental Investment Decisions

Prior to birth, the mother has had only indirect knowledge of the genetic quality of her offspring. Once born, however, the mother has visual and auditory confirmation of genetic fitness. Since the reproductive value of a child is lowest at birth, increasing with age as a function of the likelihood of survival (Salmon, 2005), additional costs to the fitness of the infant (e.g., as reflected by deformities) may actually decrease the inclusive fitness of the mother.

In some of these cases, when the costs are too high (loss of reproductive opportunities) relative to the overall benefit to the parent (inclusive fitness), it may be in the best interest of the mother to stop investment via abandonment or infanticide, opting instead to focus resources on past and/or future offspring. Consistent with this, youthful mothers (under the age of 25) are not only more likely to kill their infants, but these effects increase when older offspring are present (Ramsey, 1982). The most likely reasons surrounding infanticide include lack of genetic relatedness (for a cuckolded father or stepparent), low genetic value of infant, and unpropitious circumstances for the mother (Haapasalo & Petäjä, 1999; Overpeck, Brenner, Trumble, Trifiletti, & Berendes, 1998; Pitt & Bale, 1995; Stone, Steinmeyer, Dreher, & Krischer, 2005). Looking at filicide (the killing of a child) rates in Canada between 1974 and 1983, Daly and Wilson (1988) reported that, prior to adolescence, a parent was more likely to kill a child than an unrelated person, and that the filicide rate was highest during the first year of life and dropped drastically thereafter. Whereas fathers are the most likely perpetrators of filicide for older children, genetic mothers are the most likely culprits during infancy (Harris, Hilton, Rice, & Eke, 2007). This is especially true for newborns. When a neonate is killed or abandoned to die, it is usually the mother who performs the act (Overpeck et al., 1998).

In support of these findings from developed societies, Hill and Ball (1995) reviewed ethnographical literature for reasons surrounding infanticide and found that the most common scenario for infant death at the hands of a parent occurred in cases of abnormal births (see also Schiefenhövel, 1988). In many cases, abnormal births transpire when the infant suffers injuries during decent down the birth canal, such as loss of oxygen.

It may be argued, therefore, that distal causation of infanticide results from parental investment strategies. Mechanisms for parental investment may in turn result in changes in the mother's physiological and emotional processing systems. Oxytocin levels, for example, have been shown to not only regulate birth and increase lactation rates but also to play an essential role in maternal care and attachment (Carter, 2002; Fleming, O'Day, & Kraemer, 1999). Consistent with this, if prereproductive female rats are injected with oxytocin, they will engage in increased maternal care compared with female rats that were not given the hormone. During pregnancy, however, if oxytocin is inhibited, it will result in an interference in the rat's ability to care for her pups (Carter, 2002). Production of oxytocin can also be affected by interactions between the mother and infant. Suckling, for example, elevates oxytocin levels in rodents, and as a result, milk production is increased (see Flinn, Ward, & Noone, 2005). In addition, increases in oxytocin have been shown to decrease activation in the hypothalamic-pituitary-adrenal (HPA) system, resulting in an increased feeling of contentedness (Uvnäs-Moberg, 1996). It may be of advantage for a female to feel calm during the time she is rearing her young as a means to reinforce maternal care. In addition, although hormonal activation inducing maternal care seems essential for new rat mothers to initiate nursing, once the bonding has begun hormones are no longer needed. Interestingly, however, if reinforcement from the olfactory or somatosensory systems is disabled, the mother will stop engaging in maternal care (Fleming et al., 1994) demonstrating the importance of the mother's ability to correctly interpret cues from her offspring in regulating her own caretaking behavior.

In humans, similar effects of oxytocin inhibition are seen in cases of postpartum depression. Postpartum depression is argued to result from changes in the mother's psychological basis of investment (Kurland & Gaulin, 2005), resulting in an increased likelihood of infanticide (Spinelle, 2003). Fluctuations in psychological states, such as in the case of postpartum depression, have been argued to constitute an internal reward system focused on the costs related to offspring fitness (Nesse, 1990; Tooby & Cosmides, 1990). Therefore, postpartum depression may not necessarily reflect psychopathology but a strategy to "neutralize any elation a new mother might feel and thus permit a more objective evaluation of offspring quality and environmental conditions" (Kurland & Gaulin, 2005, p. 467). In line with this, the psychological pains produced in sufferers of postpartum depression may have influenced our ancestors to cease investment in offspring. Daly and Wilson (1995), for example, argue that variations in severity of postpartum depression may reflect differences in life circumstances of the mother. Consistent with this, cases of postpartum depression are more typical in young single mothers or when the infant is suffering from poor health (Hagen, 1999).

In terms of inclusive fitness, a mother who lacks social support systems (e.g., mate, kin, alloparents) may be ill equipped to raise an infant to adulthood, even if the infant is of high genetic quality (Lancaster, 1971). In these cases, lack of social support plays a larger role than genetic fitness because of the large amount of time and resources needed to raise human offspring. In accordance with this, an examination of Canadian data for 1974–1983 showed that the rate of infanticide decreased with maternal age and was higher for single relative to married mothers (Daly & Wilson, 1988). Moreover, the occurrence of infanticide in single mothers was unrelated to the age of the mother, suggesting that lack of social support plays a critical role in child rearing (Tooby & Cosmides, 1990).

Childhood

The period of childhood, perhaps unique to humans, begins with the cessation of nursing, which, in traditional cultures, typically occurs around 3 years of age (Bogin, 2003). Most infants begin eating solid food sometime during their first year, so that the transition from mother's milk to solid food is usually not abrupt, although weaning is often a time of great conflict for the child and his or her mother.

Breast milk is tailored to an infant's physical needs, providing not only nutrition but also natural immunities that afford protection from infection through coating of the gastrointestinal tract and the neutralizing of viruses and toxins (Cripps et al., 1987, 1991). Consistent with this, breastfeeding has been shown to be an effective defense against infant morbidity, such as that caused by diarrhea (The World Health Organization, 1999). In fact, research with newborn infants in Ghana showed that infantile death rates could be reduced by 22% if all infants were breastfed within the first hour of life (Edmond et al., 2006). In addition to the nutritional and immunological benefits of breast milk, the act of nursing serves two other important functions for the infant. One is the suppression of maternal ovulation, which in turn increases birth spacing and prolongs the period of undivided investment from the mother (Vitzthum, 1994; Wood, 1994). The second is to provide the foundation for the formation of secure attachment that will have an effect on later emotional functioning. Infants, therefore, may be highly motivated to continue to nurse even when it may no longer be nutritionally beneficial to do so. Consistent with this, infants will maintain a desire to nurse even when increases in their biomass result in higher demands for caloric intake that are no longer able to be met by breast milk alone (Committee on Nutrition, 1980, 1992; Institute of Medicine, 1991; Pierse et al., 1991). In addition, shortly after the neonatal period, various immunological factors (e.g., SigA) produced in mother's milk begin to gradually decline, with little left by the onset of weaning (Goldman et al., 1982; Ogra & Ogra, 1978). An infant's motivation for continued nursing, therefore, might reflect less of a nutritional need and more of a desire to sustain parental investment. For the mother, however, prolonged nursing can have detrimental consequences not only on future reproductive opportunities but also on maternal health. Maternal depletion syndrome, for instance, results when maternal energy expenditure, biomass, and micronutrients (e.g., calcium) are lost through sustained nursing (Hayslip et al., 1989; Prentice, 1994; Sowers, 1993).

Mothers, then, are typically motivated to begin the weaning process before infants are, and, as a result, the weaning period typically results in great stress and anxiety for the infant, resulting from the infant's desire to combat the mother's efforts to stop nursing. Consistent with this, Nash (1978) found that, in baboons, maternal aggression, rejection, and tantrums toward their infants peaked at the same time as cessation of nursing. Furthermore, conflicts between mother and infant were most intense during mother's attempts at mating.

With the cessation of nursing, women may begin ovulating once again and therefore can become pregnant. For many young children, this means the presence of a sibling and the corresponding loss of parental attention. With the birth of a sibling, it is quite common for children to "regress"—exaggerating their own needs by acting younger (wanting to nurse/engaging in behaviors they had previously abandoned) or pretending to be distressed in order to receive more parental care (Salmon & Shackelford, 2008, p. 10). Quality of attachment may also decrease between a mother and her young child with the birth of a baby, and this is especially apparent for children 2 years of age and older (Teti, Sakin, Kucera, Corns, & Eiden, 1996). This effect has also been demonstrated in nonhuman primates. For example, Devore (1963) found that, in chimpanzees, infants have been shown to alter their behavior during resumption of their mother's estrus, including crescendoing cries, greater amount of time spent trying to cling to mother, and futile attempts at nursing.

Most children, nevertheless, survive weaning and the birth of a sibling and begin to fend for themselves, at least somewhat. Although worldwide (and surely for our ancestors), children die from infectious diseases at higher rates than juveniles, adolescents, and adults, their mortality rates are substantially lower than in infancy. For instance, for the period of 1999–2006 in the United States, the death rate per 100,000 for infants between birth and 2 years of age was approximately 750; in comparison, the death rate for children under 4 years of age plunged to 28.5 per 100,000 (CDC/National Health Statistics, downloaded February 5, 2010). These rates are considerably higher in developing countries, and were higher in Western countries in earlier centuries, but the pattern of increased likelihood of survival for children relative to infants appears to be universal.

Children are also less likely to be victims of filicide than infants (Daly & Wilson, 1988). However, much as infants, children are potential victims of abuse and murder, particularly at the hands of a stepparent (Daly & Wilson, 1988; Harris et al., 2007; Wilson, Daly, & Daniele, 1995). Stepparents, which are becoming increasingly common in modern societies given the high rates of divorce and remarriage, were also likely a common feature of ancient environments, when mortality rates for adults were higher than today. From an inclusive fitness perspective, stepparents should invest relatively little in their stepchildren, compared to their biological children. Consistent with this, stepparents find it more difficult to develop warm parental feelings for their stepchildren (Pitt & Bale, 1995) and may not be as easily able to inhibit aggressive behavior when an infant or young child misbehaves, resulting in abuse and, in rare cases, filicide. The increase risk of death in stepfamilies has even been reported for unintentional deaths, for instance, drowning (Tooley, Karakis, Stokes, & Ozanne-Smith, 2006), resulting from overall less parental care and protection.

Children, of course, are not defenseless against potential abuse. Most children maintain secure attachments to their biological parents, established in infancy, that decrease the risk of abuse (Schön & Silvén, 2007). Preschool-age children also still possess many of the infantile facial features that adults find endearing, thus likely fostering nurturing from adults (Volk et al., 2007). As we mentioned earlier, the thinking of children of this age has been labeled preoperational by Piaget and in turn results in many intellectual errors, some of which adults find amusing that in turn may bias adults to view them more positively. For example, in one set of studies, adults read short scripts from hypothetical children, some expressing mature cognition and others expressing immature cognition typical of preschool-age children (Bjorklund, Hernández Blasi & Periss, 2010). When children's immature thought involved supernatural causation (e.g., "The sun's not out because it's mad," "The mountain has a big peak for long walks and a small peak for short walks"), adults rated children expressing such reasoning higher on statements reflecting positive affect (e.g., cute, endearing, friendly) and lower on statements reflecting negative affect (e.g., sneaky, likely to lie, feel more aggravated with) than children expressing mature cognition. There was no such positive bias when immature thought did *not* involve some supernatural causation (e.g., failing to inhibit a response, overestimating one's abilities). Preschool-age children's cognition is strongly biased toward supernatural thinking, reasoning about events and objects in terms of *purpose*, what Kelemen (2004) has referred to as *promiscuous teleology*. Although this research demonstrates that not all aspects of cognitive immaturity of young children is viewed positively by adults, some forms of their thinking are, and this may serve to evoke caring in (or restrain aggression from) adults.

The Juvenile Period

The transition from childhood to the juvenile period is typically a gradual one, as children gain size and strength. Depending on the community in which a child lives, juveniles may be given substantial freedom to explore the surrounding environment, usually in the company of other juveniles. They may also be expected to perform certain chores, for example caring for younger siblings (especially girls), or to partake in some adult activities, such as foraging or hunting.

The physical changes associated with the transition from childhood to the juvenile period are accompanied by underlying hormonal changes. Typically beginning around 6 to 8 years of age, the adrenal glands in both sexes begin to produce a form of androgen called dehydroepiandrosterone (DHEA), a precursor of both testosterone and estrogen. This onset of androgen production is known as *adrenarche* and has been referred to as the "the awakening of the adrenal glands" and the beginning of *adrenal puberty* (Del Giudice et al., 2009; Ellis & Essex, 2007). To date, adrenal puberty has been observed only in humans, chimpanzees, and gorillas, three species with extended juvenile periods. Adrenal androgens appear to have minimal effects on the physical body, although they are related to a slight acceleration of skeletal growth, the initial growth of underarm and pubic hair, and oily skin. However, adrenal androgens appear to be related to aggression during this time, with high levels being associated with conduct disorder in boys, and there is some speculation that adrenal androgens are responsible for the first romantic/sexual feelings occurring between 7 and 10 years of age (see Del Giudice et al., 2009). In addition, the onset of adrenal puberty is also associated with the appearance and development of emotional, psychological, and behavioral problems (McGee et al., 1992). Increased psychological and psychosocial risk factors for major depressive disorder have been linked to disturbances in the basal levels of adrenal steroids (Goodyer et al., 1998, 2000, 2001).

Del Giudice and his colleagues (2009) proposed that the juvenile period, triggered by adrenarche, is a major life history transition, establishing reproductive strategies in both boys and girls, based on their genetic and environmental characteristics. This is achieved, in part, through interactions with the peer group and assessment of the likelihood of mating opportunities and support in the future based on current conditions.

The peer group becomes especially important during the juvenile period. The presence of peers has been shown to be critical for children (i.e., juveniles) to learn a variety of social skills, with the absence of peers during development having distressing effects in humans and other primates (e.g., Harlow, Harlow, Dodsworth, & Arling, 1966). In fact, according to group socialization theory, children's peer groups, rather than families, are the primary socializing agent (Harris, 1995, 1998).

Friendship becomes especially important during the juvenile period, being central to children's psychological development. For example, children without friends or who are unpopular/rejected, attest to feeling lonely, are more apt to be aggressive (especially boys), disruptive, and hyperactive. Rejected girls are often socially withdrawn (see Asher & McDonald, 2009; Dodge et al., 2003; Rubin, Bukowski, & Parker, 2006). There are long-term consequences to being socially rejected during the juvenile period. For example, in one study, researchers assessed the social status of children in the 5th grade and followed these children until the completion of high school (Kupersmidt & Coie, 1990). They reported that children who had been rejected in the 5th grade displayed more behavior problems in high school than other children and were more likely to drop out of school, get in trouble with the police, and experience other behavior problems (see also Ladd, 2006).

Although juveniles are susceptible to the effects of social isolation/rejection and the long-term consequences this can bring, this is generally the time in life when people are, on average, the healthiest they will ever be, with the lowest mortality rates (CDC/National Health Statistics, downloaded February 5, 2010). The most common cause of deaths for juveniles in most parts of the world is accidents, frequently during play or exploration with peers. In support of this, data from 2001 reveal that American children aged 4 years of age or younger were more than twice as likely to be hospitalized with respiratory system diseases or other immunological disorders than were children aged 5 to 14 years. Conversely, in 2001, children aged 5 to 14 years were 65% more likely to die as a result of injury than were children 4 years of age or younger (U.S. Department of Health and Human Services, 2001). In many cases, injuries for older children result from increased competitive social interactions with peers. As children begin to form more complex social groups, boys especially may be more prone to engage in riskier behaviors in an attempt increase social status within the group.

Across the globe, and presumably across time, peer social interaction has been the emphasis of the juvenile period, and it remains so today. This focus may conflict, however, with modern environments and their emphasis on formal schooling. For example, Geary (2007, p. 8) states, "schools are not a central interface between evolution and culture… [rather, schools are] contexts in which children must learn about novel abilities and knowledge needed to function as an adult in modern society." Geary argues that the driving forces behind human evolution revolved around abilities to learn about climatic fluctuations, hunting and other ecological domains, and social complexity. Although attaining these skills remains important today, contemporary children must acquire evolutionarily novel skills, such as reading, writing, and arithmetic, for which they have no endogenous motivation to learn and that must be acquired via practice that is usually "out of context" (i.e., not in environments in which they will be applied "in real life"). As such, although *H. sapiens* juveniles obviously have the cognitive wherewithal to acquire these skills, their attainment is at odds with their more "natural" motivation for social interaction. This can result in a failure to master these important technological skills and subsequent problems functioning in the economies of the contemporary world. Children, for example, value achievements in sports and organized competitions between groups over academic achievement (Geary-Byrd, Caven, Hoard, Vigil, & Numtee, 2003). Consistent with this, a study by Csikszentmihalyi and Hunter (2003) demonstrated that the lowest levels of happiness were experienced by children and adolescents engaged in school activities such as doing homework or listening to lectures. The highest levels of happiness were found when children engaged in social activities such as talking on the phone or engaging in social interactions with peers during the weekend. None of this should be surprising, but it points out a perhaps unanticipated peril of this period—failing to acquire the important, but evolutionarily novel, skills needed to function well in modern societies.

Adolescence

The beginning of puberty, with its growth spurt and onset of secondary sexual characteristics, appears much more abrupt than the earlier transitions. Adolescents have more independence of action in most cultures, and they extend the trend begun during the juvenile period of spending increasing amounts of time with peers. Whereas most interactions during the juvenile period were with same-sex peers, interactions with opposite-sex peers increases in adolescence, beginning a process of mate selection/intimate relationships that will characterize much of their adult lives.

Because adolescents are at the threshold of adulthood, aspects of their social behavior can become exacerbated at this time, sometimes putting them in danger. Children have always formed social hierarchies, with some children being of higher status than others, but social dominance and the benefits that high social status can afford become greater during adolescence. Young people are establishing their adult identities and competing with one another (especially intrasexual competition) for access to the opportunities that high status provides, particularly mating opportunities. Although there is status striving within both sexes, competition tends to be greater among males than females, as predicted by parental investment theory (Trivers, 1972). According to Trivers, the sex that invests the least in parenting (in humans and most mammals, males) should compete more vigorously for access to members of the more investing sex, which in humans and most mammals are females. Although females compete (often vigorously) among themselves for access to high-quality mates, most females will find a mate, even if he is less than desirable. Males, however, have greater reproductive variability, with some having mating opportunities with multiple females, whereas others may be entirely shut out from the mating game. From an evolutionary perspective, this makes risk-taking and the use of highly aggressive (and potentially dangerous to oneself as well as one's opponent) actions at this time in life worth the costs.

Risk-taking

Research has consistently documented that boys of all ages take more risks than girls (Benenson, 2005), with risk-taking and risky decision-making increasing at adolescence and then decreasing into early adulthood (Boyer, 2006; Gardner & Steinberg, 2005). The benefits of risk-taking can be increased status, gaining of valuable skills (if attaining those skills doesn't kill you), and the attention of members of the opposite sex. However, the consequences of risk-taking in adolescence can be dire, resulting in injuries or death. These include unsafe sex practices, automobile accidents caused by reckless or drunken driving, and the use of addictive drugs (for modern adolescents, anyway). For example, the rate of deaths due to automobile accidents increases sharply for males during the late teens and continues to rise into the mid-20s before decreasing. Females show a similar pattern, but despite the comparable number of male and female drivers, the death rate is two to three times higher for males at the same age (Center for Health Statistics, 1999).

Researchers have also documented increases in sensation- and novelty-seeking behaviors during adolescence (Spear, 2000; Steinberg, 2008; Steinberg Albert, Cauffman, Banich, Graham, & Woolard, 2008). Such behaviors may be adaptive, as they serve to increase independence from parents, promote the exploration of new environments, and perhaps help to avoid inbreeding by getting exposure to potential mates outside of one's immediate group (Casey, Getz, & Galvan, 2008). Yet, such adaptive behaviors have obvious risks associated with them.

Adolescents seem especially sensitive to peer pressure to engage in risky behaviors (Berndt, 1979; Cohen & Prinstein, 2006; Lewis & Lewis, 1984). For example, Cohen and Prinstein (2006) asked 16- and 17-year-old male high school students to participate in a "chat room" with other real adolescents. In reality, the "other adolescents" were confederates of the experimenter. The adolescents were likely to approve of aggressive and health-risk behaviors, including substance abuse, vandalism, verbal teasing, and physical aggression, that were suggested by their chat room partners. Conformity was especially strong when such behaviors were endorsed by adolescents presumed to be of high-status peers.

Peer pressure can be implicit as well, with merely the presence of peers resulting in increased risk-taking behavior. This is illustrated in a study in which adolescents (13–16 years old), young adults (average age = 19 years), and adults (average age = 37 years) participated in a video driving game (Gardner & Steinberg, 2005). The number of "crashes" made by the three age groups was comparable when they played the game alone. However, risk-taking (and "crashes") increased substantially for the adolescents (and moderately for young adults) when they played the game in the presence of friends. The presence of friends had no effect on risk-taking for adults. These experimental results are consistent with actual driving statistics for vehicular deaths. Adolescents are not only involved in proportionally more vehicle deaths per miles driven than older adults, but the death rate increases in proportion to the number of people (usually other teens) in the vehicle (Chen, Baker, Braver, & Li, 2000); there is no relationship between vehicular deaths and the number of passengers for older drivers.

The Young-male Syndrome

Although displays of physical aggression generally decrease over childhood and into adolescence, what aggression occurs during adolescence and young adulthood is more serious than that occurring earlier in development, sometimes resulting in death. At the extreme, the rates of being both a perpetrator and victim of homicide are greatest during adolescence and young adulthood, in all cultures studied, than at any other time in life, with rates being greater for males than for females (Daly & Wilson, 1988).

Consistent with parental investment theory, homicide rates are highest during the ages when males are most likely to be in the "mating market." Deaths among teenage boys and young men often occur over insults to one's reputations, fights for resources, or arguments over females. Although such violent behavior can result in injury, incarceration, or one's own death, human males have inherited a psychology that was adapted to different conditions, in which risky competition, on average, resulted in increased inclusive fitness, and it likely still does today, at least in some contexts. For example, taking risks and using aggression to attain resources to enhance one's status or to impress females is likely to be greatest when resources are limited, life expectancy is low, and competition is thus heightened. This pattern can be seen when we compare homicide rates for white versus African American males in the United States. Although both groups display the same pattern of elevated levels of death by homicide during the late teen and early adulthood years, levels are exaggerated for African Americans, who, on average, have less access to educational and economic opportunities than do whites (National Center for Health Statistics, United States, 1999).

Conclusion

For any species, surviving until reproductive age is no small feat, and this is especially the case for slow-developing, highly altricial animals such as humans. The battle for survival begins shortly after conception and continues throughout all stages of development. The first challenge an offspring faces is its ability to successfully interact with its mother via hormonal exchanges with the placenta. After birth, humans must continue to maintain a strong relationship with a caretaker while fighting for access to resources and care. This is done in part by adaptations focused on attending to and engaging in sustained social interactions. It is critical for infants, starting shortly after birth, to actively engage with caretakers as a means to promote care. In contrast, for the mother, cues of infant sociability early in life provide insight into the offspring's fitness and in turn may influence her level of investment. Once old enough to begin fending for themselves, children must learn to navigate in the most complex and taxing of worlds, the human social group.

Despite all of the inherent dangers surrounding development, humans have nonetheless not only survived but have flourished, in large part because their extended life course afforded them a large brain with exceptional learning abilities. But to survive, natural selection has "prepared" children for the many trials and tribulations they would face, equipping them with behavioral and cognitive processes tailored to facilitate social interaction and the acquisition of a suite of skills necessary for a slow-developing, "thinking" species. Natural selection also prepared children's parents and their kin to deal with a big-headed, dependent offspring for an extended period of time. In retrospect, given the dangers a prolonged period of dependency brought with it, *H. sapiens* is lucky to be alive. Delayed development was an evolutionary gamble, but one that, up to now, has paid off handsomely for our kind.

References

Alexander, R.D. (1989). Evolution of the human psyche. In P. Mellers, & C. Stringer (Eds.), *The human revolution: Behavioural and biological perspectives on the origins of modern humans* (pp. 455–513). Princeton, NJ: Princeton University Press.

Alley, T.R. (1981). Head shape and the perception of cuteness. *Developmental Psychology, 17,* 650–654.

Alley, T.R. (1983). Growth-produced changes in body shape and size as determinants of perceived age and adult caregiving. *Child Development, 54,* 241–248.

Asher, S.R., & McDonald, K.L. (2009). The behavioral basis of acceptance, rejection, and perceived popularity. In K.H. Rubin, W.M. Bukowski, & B. Laursen (Eds.) *Handbook of peer interactions, relationships, and groups* (pp. 232–248). New York: Guilford.

Bales, K.L., O'Herron, M., Baker, A.J., & Dietz. J. (2001). Sources of variability in numbers of live births in wild golden lion tamarins (*Leontopithecus rosalia*). *American Journal of Primatology, 54,* 211–221.

Bard, K. (2007) Neonatal imitation in chimpanzees (*Pan troglodytes*). *Animal Cognition, 10,* 233–242.

Barden, R.C., Ford, M.E., Jensen, A.G., Rogers-Salyer, M., & Salyer, K.E. (1989). Effects of craniofacial deformity in infancy on the quality of mother-infant interactions. *Child Development, 60,* 819–824.

Beise, J., & Voland, E. (2002). A multilevel event history analysis of the effects of grandmothers on child mortality in a historical German population (Krummhorn, Ostfriesland, 1720–1987). *Demographic Research, 7,* 469–498.

Belsky, J. (2007). Experience in childhood and the development of reproductive strategies, *Acta Psychologica Sinica, 39,* 454–468.

Belsky, J., Steinberg, L., & Draper, P. (1991). Childhood experience, interpersonal development, and reproductive strategy: An evolutionary theory of socialization. *Child Development, 62,* 647–670.

Benenson, J.F. (2005). Sex differences. In B. Hopkins (Ed.), *The Cambridge encyclopedia of child development* (pp. 366–373). New York: Cambridge University Press.

Berndt, T.J. (1979). Developmental changes in conformity to peers and parents. *Developmental Psychology, 15,* 608–616.

Bjorklund, D.F. (1987). A note on neonatal imitation. *Developmental Review, 7,* 86–92.

Bjorklund, D.F. (1997). The role of immaturity in human development. *Psychological Bulletin, 122,* 153–169.

Bjorklund, D.F. (2005). *Children's thinking: Cognitive development and individual differences* (4th ed.). Belmont, CA: Wadsworth.

Bjorklund, D.F. (2011). Cognitive development: An overview. In P.D. Zelazo (Ed.), *Oxford handbook of developmental psychology.* Oxford, UK: Oxford University Press.

Bjorklund, D.F., & Bering, J.M. (2003). Big brains, slow development, and social complexity: The developmental and evolutionary origins of social cognition. In M. Brüne, H. Ribbert, & W. Schiefenhövel (Eds.). *The social brain: Evolutionary aspects of development and pathology* (pp. 133–151). New York: Wiley.

Bjorklund, D.F., Cormier, C., & Rosenberg, J.S. (2005). The evolution of theory of mind: Big brains, social complexity, and inhibition. In W. Schneider, R. Schumann-Hengsteler, & B. Sodian (Eds.), *Young children's cognitive development: Interrelationships among executive functioning, working memory, verbal ability and theory of mind* (pp. 147–174). Mahwah, NJ: Erlbaum.

Bjorklund, D.F., & Gardiner, A.K. (2011). Object play and tool use: Developmental and evolutionary perspectives. In A.D. Pellegrini (Ed.), *Oxford handbook of play* (pp. 153–171). Oxford, UK: Oxford University Press.

Bjorklund, D.F., & Harnishfeger, K.K. (1995). The role of inhibition mechanisms in the evolution of human cognition and behavior. In F.N. Dempster, & C.J. Brainerd (Eds.), *New perspectives on interference and inhibition in cognition* (pp. 141–173). New York: Academic Press.

Bjorklund, D.F., Hernández Blasi, C., & Periss, V. (2010). Lorenz revisited: The adaptive nature of children's supernatural thinking, *Human Nature, 21,* 371–392.

Bjorklund, D.F., & Pellegrini, A.D. (2002). *The origins of human nature: Evolutionary developmental psychology.* Washington, DC: American Psychological Association.

Bogin, B. (1999). *Patterns of human growth* (2nd ed.). Cambridge, UK: Cambridge University Press.

Bogin, B. (2001). *The growth of humanity*. New York: Wiley-Liss.

Bogin, B. (2003). The human pattern of growth and development in paleontological perspective. In J.L. Thompson, G.E. Krovitz, & A.J. Nelson (Eds.), *Patterns of growth and development in the genus* Homo (pp. 15–44). Cambridge, UK: Cambridge University Press.

Bowlby, J. (1982). Attachment and loss: Retrospect and prospect. *American Journal of Orthopsychiatry, 52*, 664–678.

Boyer, T.W. (2006). The development of risk-taking: A multi-perspective review. *Developmental Review, 26*, 291–345.

Byrne, R.W. (2005). Social cognition: Imitation, imitation, imitation. *Current Biology, 15*, R489–R500.

Casey, B.J., Getz, S., & Galvan, A. (2008). The adolescent brain. *Developmental Review, 28*, 62–77.

Chen, L.-H., Baker, S.P., Braver, E.R., & Li, G. (2000). Carrying passengers as a risk factor for crashes fatal to 16- and 17-year-old drivers. *Journal of the American Medical Association, 283*, 1578–1582.

Clark, D.A., Banwatt, D., & Chaouat, G. (1993). Stress-triggered abortion in mice prevented by alloimmunization. *American Journal of Reproductive Immunology, 29*, 141–147.

Clutton-Brock, T.H. (2006). Cooperative breeding in mammals. In P.M. Kappeler, & C.P. van Schaik (Eds.), *Cooperation in primates and humans: Mechanisms and evolution* (pp. 173–190). Berlin: Springer-Verlag.

Clutton-Brock, T.H., Hodge, S.J., Russell, A.F., Jordan, N.R., Bennett, N.C., Sharpe, L.L., & Manser, M.B. (2006). Intrasexual competition and sexual selection in cooperative mammals. *Nature, 444*, 1065–1068.

Cohen, G.L., & Prinstein, M.J. (2006). Peer contagion of aggression and health risk behaviors among adolescent males: An experimental investigation of effects on public conduct and private attitudes. *Child Development, 77*, 967–983.

Committee on Nutrition, American Academy of Pediatrics. (1980). On the feeding of supplemental foods to infants. *Pediatrics, 65*,1178–1181.

Committee on Nutrition, American Academy of Pediatrics. (1992). The use of whole cow's milk in infancy. *Pediatrics, 89*, 1105–1109.

Cripps, A.W., Clancy, R.L., Gleeson, M., Hensley, M.J., Dobson, A.J., Firman, D.W., et al. (1987). Mucosal immunocompetence in man: The first five years. *Advances in Experimental Medicine and Biology, 216B*, 1369–1376.

Cripps, A.W., Gleeson, M., & Clancy, R.L. (1991). Ontogeny of the mucosal immune response in children. *Advances in Experimental Medicine and Biology, 310*, 87–92.

Csikszentmihalyi, M., & Hunter, J. (2003). Happiness in everyday life: The uses of experience sampling. *Journal of Happiness Studies, 4*, 1–15.

Daly, M., & Wilson, M. (1988). *Homicide*. New York: Aldine.

Daly, M., & Wilson, M. (1995). Discriminative parental solicitude and the relevance of evolutionary models to the analysis of motivational systems. In M Gazzaniga (Ed.), *The cognitive neurosciences* (pp. 1269–1286). Cambridge MA: MIT Press.

Del Giudice, M. (2009). Sex, attachment, and the development of reproductive strategies. *Behavioral and Brain Sciences, 32*, 1–21.

Del Giudice, M., Angeleri, R., & Manera, V. (2009). The juvenile transition: A developmental switch point in human life history. *Developmental Review, 29*, 1–31.

Devore, I. (1963). Mother-infant relations in free-ranging baboons. In H. Rheingold (Ed.), *Maternal behavior in mammals* (pp. 305–355). New York: Wiley.

Dienske, H. (1986). A comparative approach to the question of why human infants develop so slowly. In J.G. Else, & P.C. Lee (Eds.), *Primate ontogeny, cognition and social behavior* (pp. 145–154). Cambridge, UK: Cambridge University Press.

Dodge, K.A., Lansford, J.E., Burks, V.S., Bates, J.E., Pettit, G.S., Fontaine, R., et al. (2003). Peer rejection and social information-processing factors in the development of aggressive behavior problems in children. *Child Development, 74*, 374–393.

Dubowitz, L.M., Mushin, J., De-Vries, L., & Arden, G.B. (1986). Visual function in the newborn infant: Is it cortically mediated. *Lancet, 8490*, 1139–1141.

Dunbar, R.I.M. (2003). The social brain: Mind, language, and society in evolutionary perspective. *Annual Review of Anthropology, 32*, 163–181.

Eibl-Eibesfeldt, I. (1970). *Ethology: The biology of behavior*. New York: Holt, Rhinehart & Winston.

Ellis, B.J. (2004). Timing of pubertal maturation in girls: An integrated life history approach. *Psychological Bulletin, 130*, 920–958.

Ellis, B.J., & Essex, M.J. (2007). Family environments, adrenarche, and sexual maturation: A longitudinal test of a life history model. *Child Development, 78*, 1799–1817.

Ferrari, P.F,. Visalberghi, E., Paukner, A, Fogassi, L., Ruggiero, A., et al. (2006). Neonatal imitation in rhesus macaques. *Public Library of Science Biology, 4*, 302.

Field, T.M., Woodson, R., Greenberg, R., & Cohen, D. (1982). Discrimination and imitation of facial expression by neonates. *Science, 218*, 179–181.

Fleming, A.S., Kuchera, C., Lee, A., & Winocur, G. (1994). Olfactory-based social learning varies as a function of parity in female rats. *Psychobiology, 22*, 37–43.

Fleming, A.S., O'Day, D., & Kraemer, G.W. (1999). Neurobiology of mother-infant interactions: Experience and central nervous system plasticity across development and generations. *Neuroscience and Biobehavioral Reviews, 23*, 673–685.

Flinn, M.V., Ward, C.V., & Noone, R. (2005). Hormones and the human family. In D. Buss (Ed.), *Handbook of evolutionary psychology* (pp. 552–580). New York: Wiley.

Fritz, B., Aslan, M., Kalscheuer, V., Ramsing, M., Saar, K., Fuchs, B., & Rehder, H. (2001). Low incidence of UPD in spontaneous abortions beyond the 5th gestational week. *European Journal of Human Genetics, 9*, 910–916.

Frodi, A.M., & Lamb, M.E. (1978). Sex differences in responsiveness to infants: A developmental study of psychophysiological and behavioral responses. *Child Development, 49*, 1182–1188.

Fullard, W., & Reiling, A.M. (1976). An investigation of Lorenz's "babyness." *Child Development, 47*, 1191–1193.

Gardner, M., & Steinberg, L. (2005). Peer influence on risk taking, risk preference, and risky decision making in adolescence and adulthood: An experimental study. *Developmental Psychology, 41*, 625–635.

Geary, D.C. (2005). Evolution of paternal investment. In D.M. Buss (Ed.), *The handbook of evolutionary psychology* (pp. 483–505). New York: Wiley.

Geary, D.C. (2007). Educating the evolved mind: Conceptual foundations for an evolutionary educational psychology. In J.S. Carlson, & J.R. Levin (Eds.), *Educating the evolved mind: Conceptual foundations for an evolutionary educational psychology* (pp. 1–99). Charlotte, NC: Information Age Publishing.

Geary, D.C., & Flinn, M.V. (2001). Evolution of human parental behavior and the human family. *Parenting: Science and Practice, 1*, 5–61.

Geary, D.C., Byrd-Craven, J., Hoard, M.K., Vigil, J., & Numtee, C. (2003). Evolution and development of boys' social behavior. *Developmental Review, 23*, 444–470.

Gibbons, A. (2008). The birth of childhood. *Science, 322* (14 November), 1040–1043.

Gibson, K.R. (1991). Myelination and behavioral development: A comparative perspective on questions of neoteny, altriciality and intelligence. In K.R. Gibson, & A.C. Petersen (Eds.), *Brain maturation and cognitive development: Comparative and cross-cultural perspectives.* New York: Aldine de Gruyter.

Gibson, M.A., & Mace, R. (2005). Helpful grandmothers in rural Ethiopia: A study of the effect of kin on child survival and growth. *Evolution and Human Behavior, 26*, 469–482.

Giedd, J.N., Bluenthal, J., Jeffries, N.O., Castellanos, F.X., Liu, H., Zijdenbos, A., et al. (1999). Brain development during childhood and adolescence: A longitudinal MRI study. *Nature Neuroscience, 2*, 861–863.

Goldberg, S. (1977), Social competence in infancy: A model of parent–infant interaction. *Merrill-Palmer Quarterly, 23*, 163–177.

Goldman, A.S., Garza, C., Nichols, B.L., & Goldblum, R.M. (1982). Immunologic factors in human milk during the first year of lactation. *Pediatrics, 100*, 563–567.

Goodman, E., McEwen, B.S., Dolan, L.M., Schafer-Kalkhoff, T., & Adler, N.E. (2005). Social disadvantage and adolescent stress. *Journal of Adolescent Health, 37*, 484–492.

Goodyer, I.M., Herbert, J., Altham, & P.M.E. (1998). Adrenal steroid secretion and major depression in 8 to 16 year olds, III. Influence of cortisol/DHEA ratio at presentation on subsequent rates of disappointing life events and persistent major depression. *Psychological Medicine, 28*, 265–273.

Goodyer, I.M., Herbert, J., Tamplin, A., & Altham, P.M.E. (2000). Recent life events, cortisol and DHEA in the onset of major depression in high-risk adolescents. *British Journal of Psychiatry, 177*, 499–504.

Goodyer, I.M., Park, R.J., & Herbert, J. (2001). Psychosocial and endocrine features of chronic first-episode major depression in 8–16 year olds. *Biological Psychiatry, 50*, 351–357.

Gould, S.J. (1977). *Ontogeny and phylogeny.* Cambridge, MA: Harvard University Press.

Griffin, A.S., & West, S.A. (2003). Kin discrimination and the benefit of helping in cooperatively breeding vertebrates. *Science, 302*, 634–636.

Haapasalo, J., & Petäjä, S. (1999). Mothers who killed or attempted to kill their child: Life circumstances, childhood abuse and types of killing. *Violence & Victims, 14*, 219–239.

Haig, D. (1990) New perspectives on the angiosperm female gametophyte. *The Botanical Review, 56*, 236–274.

Haig, D. (1993). Genetic conflicts in human pregnancy. *Quarterly Review of Biology, 68*, 495–532.

Harlow, H.F., Harlow, M.K., Dodsworth, R.O., & Arling, G.L. (1966). Maternal behavior of rhesus monkeys deprived of mothering and peer associations as infants. *Proceedings of the American Philosophical Society, 110*, 88–98.

Harris, G.T., Hilton, N.Z., Rice, M.E., & Eke, A.W. (2007). Children killed by genetic parents versus stepparents. *Evolution and Human Behavior, 28*, 85–95.

Harris, J.R. (1995). Where is the child's environment? A group socialization theory of development. *Psychological Review, 102*, 458–489.

Harris, J.R. (1998). *The nurture assumption: Why children turn out the way they do.* New York: Free Press.

Hayslip, C.C., Klein, T.A., Wray, H.L., & Duncan, W.E. (1989). The effects of lactation on bone mineral content in healthy postpartum women. *Obstetrics & Gynecology, 73*, 588–592.

Heimann, M. (1989). Neonatal imitation gaze aversion and mother-infant interaction. *Infant Behavior & Development, 12*, 495–505.

Hernández Blasi, C., & Bjorklund, D.F. (2003). Evolutionary developmental psychology: A new tool for better understanding human ontogeny. *Human Development, 46*, 259–281.

Hill, C.M., & Ball, H.L. (1995). Abnormal births and other "ill omens." *Human Nature, 7*, 381–401.

Hill, K., & Hurtado, A.M. (1996). *Ache life history: The ecology and demography of a foraging people.* New York: Aldine de Gruyter.

Horner, V., Whiten, A., Flynn, E., & de Waal, F.B.M. (2006). Faithful replication of foraging techniques along cultural transmission chains by chimpanzees and children. *Proceedings of the National Academy of Sciences, 103*, 13878–13883.

Hrdy, S.B. (1986). Sources of variation in the reproductive success of female primates. In *Proceedings of the International Meeting on Variability and Behavioral Evolution* (pp. 191–203). Problemi Attuali di Scienza e di Cultura, N. 259. Rome, IT: Accademia a Nazionale dei Linceli.

Hrdy, S.B. (1999). *Mother nature: A history of mothers, infants, and natural selection.* New York: Pantheon Books.

Hrdy, S.B. (2007). Evolutionary context of human development: The cooperative breeding model. In C. Solomon, & T.K. Shackelford (Eds.), *Family relationships: Evolutionary perspectives.* New York: Oxford University Press.

Hrdy, S.B. (2009). *Mothers and others: The evolutionary origins of mutual understanding.* Cambridge, MA: Belknap Press.

Humphrey, N.K. (1976). The social function of intellect. In P.P.G. Bateson, & R.A. Hinde (Eds.), *Growing points in ethology* (pp. 303–317). Cambridge, UK: Cambridge University Press.

Institute of Medicine, National Academy of Sciences. (1991). *Nutrition during lactation.* Washington, DC: National Academy Press.

Jacobson, S.W. (1979). Matching behavior in the young infant. *Child Development, 50*, 425–430.

Jerison, H.J. (1973). *Evolution of the brain and intelligence.* New York: Academic Press.

Jerison, H.J. (2000). Evolution of intelligence. In R.J. Sternberg (Ed). *Handbook of human intelligence* (2nd ed.). Cambridge, UK: University Press.

Kaplan, H., Hill, K., Lancaster, J., & Hurtado, A.M. (2000). A theory of human life history evolution: Diet intelligence, and longevity. *Evolutionary Anthropology, 9*, 156–185.

Kelemen, D. (2004). Are children "intuitive theists"? Reasoning about purpose and design in nature. *Psychological Science, 15*, 295–301.

Keller, H., Lohaus, A., Kuensemueller, P., Abels, M., Yovsi, R., Voelker, S., et al. (2004). The bio-culture of parenting: Evidence from five cultural communities. *Parenting: Science and Practice, 4*, 25–50.

Kupersmidt, J.B., & Coie, J.D. (1990). Preadolescent peer status and aggression as predictors of externalizing problems in adolescence. *Child Development, 61*, 1350–1362.

Kurland, J.A., & Gaulin, S.J.C. (2005). Cooperation and competition among kin. In D. Buss (ed.), *Handbook of evolutionary psychology* (pp. 447–482). New York: Academic Press.

Ladd, G.W. (2006). Peer rejection, aggressive or withdrawn behavior, and psychological maladjustment from ages 5 to

12: An examination of four predictive models. *Child Development, 77,* 922–846.

Lahdenperä, M., Lummaa, V., Helle, S., Tremblay, M., & Russell, A.F. (2004). Fitness benefits of prolonged post-reproductive lifespan in women. *Nature, 428,* 178–181.

Lancaster, J.B. (1971). Play-mothering: Relations between juvenile females and young infants among free-ranging vervet monkeys (*Cercopithecus aethiops*). *Folia Primatology, 15,* 161–182.

Legerstee, M. (1991). The role of person and object in eliciting early imitation. *Journal of Experimental Child Psychology, 51,* 423–433.

Lewis, C.E., & Lewis, M.A. (1984). Peer pressure and risk-taking behaviors in children. *American Journal of Public Health, 74,* 580–584.

Lorenz, K.Z. (1943). Die angeboren Formen moglicher Erfahrung [The innate forms of possible experience]. *Zeitschrift fur Tierpsychologie, 5,* 233–409.

Lozoff, B., & Brittenham, G. (1979). Infant care: Cache or carry. *The Journal of Pediatrics, 95,* 478–483.

Mackslon, N.S., Geraedts, J.P.M., & Fauser, B.C.J.M. (2002). Conception to ongoing pregnancy: The "black box" of early pregnancy loss. *Human Reproductive Update, 8,* 333–343.

Maestripieri, D., & Roney, J.R. (2006). Evolutionary developmental psychology: Contributions from comparative research with nonhuman primates. *Developmental Review, 26,* 120–137.

McHenry, H.M., & Coffing, K.E. (2000). Australopithecus to Homo: Transformations of body and mind. *Annual Review of Anthropology, 29,* 125–166.

Meltzoff, A.N., & Moore, M.K. (1977). Imitation of facial and manual gestures by human neonates. *Science, 198,* 75–78.

Miscarriage: Causes of miscarriage. Online at HealthSquare.com (accessed September 18, 2007).

Montagu, A. (1961). Neonatal and infant immaturity in man. *Journal of the American Medical Association, 178,* 56–68.

Murray, L., & Trevarthen, C. (1986). The infant's role in mother-infant communication. *Journal of Child Language, 13,* 15–29.

Myowa-Yamakoshi, M., Tomonaga, M., Tanaka, M., & Matsuzawa, T. (2004). Imitation in neonatal chimpanzees (*Pan troglodytes*). *Developmental Science, 7,* 437–442.

Nagy, E. (2006). From imitation to conversation: The first dialogues with human neonates, *Infant and Child Development, 15,* 223–232.

Nagy, E., & Molnar, P. (2004). Homo imitans or homo provocans? Human imprinting model of neonatal imitation. *Infant Behavior and Development, 27,* 54–63.

Nash, L.T. (1978). Development of mother-infant relationship in wild baboons (*Papio anubis*). *Animal Behavior, 26,* 746–759.

National Center for Health Statistics. *Health, United States.* (1999). Hyattsville, MD.

Nesse, R. (1990). The evolutionary functions of repression and ego defenses. *Journal of the American Academy of Psychoanalysis, 18,* 260–285.

Ogra, S.S., & Ogra, P.L. (1978). Immunologic aspects of human colostrum and milk, II. Characteristics of lymphocyte reactivity and distribution of E-Rosette forming cells at different times after the onset of lactation. *Journal of Pediatrics, 92,* 550–555.

Oppenheim, R.W. (1981). Ontogenetic adaptations and retrogressive processes in the development of the nervous system and behavior. In K.J. Connolly, & H.F.R. Prechtl (Eds.), *Maturation and development: Biological and psychological perspectives* (pp. 73–108). Philadelphia, PA: International Medical Publications.

Overpeck, M.D., Brenner, R.A., Trumble, A.C., Trifiletti, L.B., & Berendes, H.W. (1998). Risk factors for infant homicide in the United States. *New England Journal of Medicine, 339,* 1211–1216.

Pascalis, O., & de Schonen, S. (1994). Recognition memory in 3- to 4-day-old human neonates. *NeuroReport: Learning and Memory, 5,* 14.

Piaget, J. (1983). Piaget's theory. In J.H. Flavell & E.M. Markman (Eds.), *Cognitive development,* Vol. 3 of P.H. Mussen (Gen. Ed.), *Handbook of child psychology* (4th ed.). New York: Wiley.

Pierse, P., VanAerde, J., & Clandinin, M. (1991). Nutritional value of human milk. *Progress in Food and Nutrition Science, 12,* 21–47.

Pitt, S.E., & Bale, E.M. (1995). Neonaticide, infanticide and filicide: A review of the literature. *Bulletin of the American Academy of Psychiatry and Law, 23,* 375–386.

Poirier, F.E., & Smith, E.O. (1974). Socializing functions of primate play. *American Zoologist, 14,* 275–287.

Powell, R.A. & Friend, J.J. (1992). Helping by juvenile pine voles (*Microtus pinetorum*), growth and survival of younger siblings, and the evolution of pine vole sociality. *International Society for Behavioral Ecology, 3,* 325–333.

Prentice, A. (1994). Maternal calcium requirements during pregnancy and lactation. *The American Journal of Clinical Nutrition, 59,* 477–482.

Quinlan, M.B., & Quinlan, R.J. (2008). Cross-cultural analysis in evolution and human behavior studies. *Cross-Cultural Research, 42,* 199–2000.

Ramsey, P. (1982). Introduction. In D. Horan & M. Delahoyde (Eds.), *Infanticide and the handicapped newborn* (pp. 1–8). Provo, UT: Brigham Young University Press.

Regine, L.M., & Marot, C.P. (2007). What to do when miscarriage strikes. In R.A. Munoz (Ed.), *The PDR family guide to women's health and prescription drugs* (pp. 345–350). Montvale, NJ: Medical Economics.

Rilling, J.K., & Insel, T.R. (1999). The primate neocortex in comparative perspective using magnetic resonance imaging. *Journal of Human Evolution, 37,* 191–223.

Rosenberg, K., & Trevathan, W.R. (1996). Bipedalism and human birth: The obstetrical dilemma revisited. *Evolutionary Anthropology, 4,* 161–168.

Roth, G., & Dicke, U. (2005). Evolution of the brain and intelligence. *Trends in Cognitive Sciences, 9,* 249–257.

Rubin, K.H., Bukowski, W.M., & Parker, J.G. (2006). Peer interactions, relationships, and groups. In W. Damon & R.M. Lerner (Gen. Eds.), *Handbook of child psychology* (6th ed.), N. Eisenberg (Vol. Ed.), Vol. 3, *Social, emotional, and personality development* (pp. 571–645). New York: Wiley.

Russell, A.F. (2004) Mammals: Comparisons and contrasts. In W.D. Koenig & J.L. Dickinson (Eds.), *Ecology and evolution of cooperative breeding in birds* (pp. 210–228). Cambridge, UK: Cambridge University Press.

Salmon, C.A. (2005). Parental investment and parent-offspring conflict. In D.M. Buss (Ed.), *The handbook of evolutionary psychology* (pp. 506–527). New York: Wiley.

Salmon, C.A. & Shackelford, T.K. (2008). Toward an evolutionary psychology of the family. In C.A. Salmon, & T.K. Shackelford (Eds.), *Family relationships an evolutionary perspective* (pp. 3–16). New York: Oxford University Press.

Schiefenhövel, W. (1988). *Geburtsverhalten und reproduktive Strategien der Eipo - Ergebnisse humanethologischer und ethnomedizinischer Untersuchungen im zentralen Bergland von Irian Jaya (West-Neuguinea), Indonesien.* Berlin: Reimer.

Schön, R.A., & Silvén, M. (2007). Natural parenting: Back to basics in infant care. *Evolutionary Psychology, 5*, 102–183.

Sears, R., & Mace, R. (2008). Who keeps children alive? A review of the effects of kin on child survival. *Evolution and Human Behavior, 29*, 1–18.

Siegler, R.S., & Alibali, M.W. (2004). *Children's thinking* (4th ed.). Upper Saddle River, NJ: Prentice Hall.

Solomon, N.G. (1991). Current indirect fitness benefits associated with philopatry in juvenile prairie voles. *Behavioral Ecology and Sociobiology, 29*, 277–282.

Solomon, N.G., & French, J.A. (1997). The study of mammalian cooperative breeding. In N.G. Solomon, & J.A. French (Eds.), *Cooperative breeding in mammals* (pp. 1–11). Cambridge, UK: Cambridge University Press.

Sowell, E.R., Thompson, P.M., Holmes, C.J., Jernigan, T.L., & Toga, A.W. (1999). In vivo evidence for post-adolescent brain maturation in frontal and striatal regions. *Nature Neuroscience, 1*, 859–861.

Sowers, M. (1993). Epidemiology of calcium and vitamin D in bone loss. *Journal of Nutrition, 123*, 413–417.

Spear, L.P. (2000). Neurobehavioral changes in adolescence. *Current Directions in Psychological Science, 9*, 111–114.

Spear, L.P. (2007). Brain development and adolescent behavior. In D. Coch, K.W. Fischer, & G. Dawson (Eds.), *Human behavior, learning, and the developing brain: Typical development* (pp. 362–396). New York: Guilford.

Sprengelmeyer, R., Perrett, D.I., Fagan, E.C., Cornwell, R.E., Lobmaier, J.S., Sprengelmeyer, A., et al. (2009). The cutest little baby face: A hormonal link to sensitivity to cuteness in infant faces. *Psychological Science, 20*, 149–154.

Stearns, S.C. (1987). The selection arena hypothesis. In S.C. Stearns (Ed.), *The evolution of sex and its consequences* (pp. 299–311). Birkhaeuser Verlag, AG.

Steinberg, L. (2008). A social neuroscience perspective on adolescent risk-taking. *Developmental Review, 28*, 78–106.

Steinberg, L., Albert, D., Cauffman, E., Banich, M., Graham, S., & Woolard, J. (2008). Age differences in sensation seeking and impulsivity as indexed by behavior and self-report: Evidence for a dual systems model. *Developmental Psychology, 44*, 1764–1778.

Stone, M.H., Steinmeyer, E., Dreher, J., & Krischer, M. (2005). Infanticide in female forensic patients: The view from the evolutionary standpoint. *Journal of Psychiatric Practice, 11*, 35–45.

Stone, A.I., Mathieu, D., Griffin, L., & Bales, K.L. (2010). Alloparenting experience affects future parental behavior and reproductive success in prairie voles (*Microtus ochrogaster*). *Behavioral Processes, 83*, 8–15.

Teti, D.M., Sakin, J.W., Kucera, E., Corns, K.M., & Eiden, R.D. (1996). And baby makes four: Predictors of attachment security among preschool-age firstborns during the transition to siblinghood. *Child Development, 67*, 579–596.

The World Health Organization. (1999). *Essential newborn care. Report of a technical work group.* Geneva: The World Health Organization, 2010.

The World Health Organization. (2005). *Perinatal morality: A listing of available information.* Geneva: The World Health Organization; 2010.

Tomasello, M., & Moll, H. (2010). The gap is social: Human shared intentionality and culture. In P.M. Kappeler, & J.B. Silk (Eds.), *Mind the gap: Tracing the origins of human universals* (pp. 331–350). New York: Springer.

Tooby, J., & Cosmides, L. (1990). The past explains the present: Emotional adaptations and the structure of ancestral environments. *Ethology and Sociobiology, 11*, 375–424.

Tooley, G.A., Karakis, M., Stokes, M., & Ozanne-Smith, J. (2006). Generalising the Cinderella effect to unintentional childhood fatalities. *Evolution and Human Behavior, 27*, 224–230.

Trivers, R.L. (1972). Parental investment and sexual selection. In B. Campbell (Ed.), *Sexual selection and the descent of man, 1871–1971* (pp. 136–179). Chicago, IL: Aldine.

Trivers, R.L. (1974). Parent-offspring conflict. *American Zoologist, 14*, 249–264.

Turkewitz, G., & Kenny, P. (1982). Limitations on input as a basis for neural organization and perceptual development: A preliminary theoretical statement. *Developmental Psychobiology, 15*, 357–368.

Uvnäs-Moberg, K. (1996). Neuroendocrinology of the mother–child interaction. *Trends in Endocrinology and Metabolism, 7*, 126–131.

Vitzthum, V. (1994). Comparative study of breast-feeding structure and its relation to human reproductive ecology. *Yearbook of Physical Anthropology, 37*, 307–349.

Volk, A.A., Lukjanczuk, J.L., & Quinsey, V.L. (2007). Perceptions of child facial cues as a function of child age. *Evolutionary Psychology, 5*, 801–814.

Volk, T., & Atkinson, J. (2008). Is child death the crucible of human evolution? *Journal of Social, Cultural, and Evolutionary Psychology, 2*, 247–260.

Waller, K., Volk, A., & Quinsey V.L. (2004). The effect of infant fetal alcohol syndrome facial features on adoption preference. *Human Nature, 15*, 101–117.

Wang, X., Chen, C., Wang, L., Chen, D., Guang, W., & French, J. (2003). Conception, early pregnancy loss, and time to clinical pregnancy: A population-based prospective study. *Fertility and Sterility, 79*, 577–584.

White, T.D., Asfaw, B., Beyene, Y., Haile-Selassie, Y., Lovejoy, C.O., Suwa, G., WoldeGabriel, G. (2009). *Ardipithecus ramidus* and the paleobiology of early hominids. *Science, 326*, 75–86.

Whiten A., & Byrne, R. (1988) Tactical deception in primates. *Behavioral Brain Science, 12*, 233–273.

Wilson, M., Daly, M., & Daniele, A. (1995) Familicide: The killing of spouse and children. *Aggressive Behavior, 21*, 275–291.

Wood, B.A. (1994). The oldest hominid yet. *Nature, 317*, 280–281.

Zebrowitz, L.A., Kendall-Tackett, K., & Fafel, J. (1991). The influence of children's facial maturity on parental expectations and punishments. *Journal of Experimental Child Psychology, 52*, 221–238.

CHAPTER 11

Family Violence: How Paternity Uncertainty Raises the Stakes

Aaron T. Goetz *and* Gorge A. Romero

Abstract

The male-specific problem of paternity uncertainty underlies several psychological mechanisms designed to prevent the unwitting investment of resources into genetically unrelated offspring. In this chapter, we establish how the costs of paternity uncertainty have come to shape male psychology in such a way that family dynamics are often disrupted by men's violence against women. Specifically, we take an evolutionary approach to elucidate why violence erupts between intimate partners as a consequence of paternity uncertainty. In doing so, we review the emotion of sexual jealousy, which produces mate guarding. We also argue that, from an evolutionary perspective, intimate partner violence (IPV) may be best understood as a form of punishment. We discuss the occurrence of partner killing in light of adaptive and nonadaptive explanations for the behavior and conclude with a review of theoretical and empirical work on sexual coercion in intimate relationships.

Keywords: Intimate partner violence, sexual conflict, paternity uncertainty, infidelity, sexual jealousy

In a Texas hospital in 1999, Morgan Wise was informed that the results of his genetic tests indicated that he was not a carrier for any strain of cystic fibrosis. Although a relief, the circumstances could not explain why his 6-year-old son manifested a disease that requires both biological parents to carry the gene. Wise, a divorced father of four, was urged by his physician to seek out paternity testing to elucidate the perplexing situation. Results from this and subsequent paternity tests revealed not only that Wise was not the genetic father of the 6-year-old, but also that two other children born to his wife during their marriage were not his genetic offspring either. Although not the biological father of the three children he was supporting, Wise was required to continue paying $1,100 a month in child support even after contesting the imposed financial costs. This is the life of Morgan Wise (Lewin, 2001) and is now well known in the small town where he resides. The justification for demanding child support from Wise is still debated and with the amount of attention attributed to his story, a growing number of cases from men in similar situations are now becoming publicized. Consider the case of Frank Hatley, a man once labeled a deadbeat by the media for not having the ability to pay child support for a genetically unrelated child. Hatley lost his job and eventually became homeless before being jailed for not paying child support (Castillo, 2009). Both Wise and Hatley are examples of men who share the modern-day consequences of an evolutionarily recurrent problem—the unwitting investment of resources into genetically unrelated children, what biologists call *cuckoldry*.

With current estimates of nonpaternity ranging from 2%–10% (Anderson, 2006; Bellis, Hughes, Hughes, & Ashton, 2005), we can appreciate that the problem of paternity uncertainty for men may have been sufficiently common throughout human evolutionary history to the extent that male psychology has been shaped to be sensitive to cues that potentially indicate an increased risk of cuckoldry.

In this chapter, we lay out the evolutionary foundations for the problem of paternity uncertainty and its consequences in family dynamics. We begin our discussion by elaborating on the costs of cuckoldry, followed by a review of literature that has unraveled some of the psychological mechanisms involved in detecting and preventing cuckoldry. We discuss how intimate partner violence (IPV), motivated by paternity uncertainty, sometimes leads to uxoricide (wife killing) by exploring two contrasting evolutionary ideas: the slip-up hypothesis (Daly & Wilson, 1988) and homicide adaptation theory (Buss & Duntley, 1998), and we apply evolutionary game theory in an attempt to better understand whether partner killing is a by-product or the result of an evaluative process from evolved psychological mechanisms. We end our discussion of how paternity uncertainty causes conflict in intimate relationships by discussing sexual violence and forced in-pair copulation. Throughout this chapter, we argue that male sexual jealousy—one of the leading contributors to violence in intimate partner relationships—can be understood as a form of punishment. Although there are potentially numerous causes of conflict within intimate relationships, the research reviewed in this chapter compiles an abundance of evidence that allows for a concise understanding of conflict within human pair-bonds.

Paternity Uncertainty and the Costs of Cuckoldry

Due to internal fertilization and gestation, ancestral males could not have been certain that their children were, in fact, genetically their own. Ancestral women, having given birth to the child, had maternity certainty. Internal fertilization and gestation imply that ancestral men could have faced paternity uncertainty, but did they? Even without direct observation of the ancestral environment, the answer is a resounding yes. When considering (a) cross-cultural infidelity and paternal discrepancy rates; (b) the cross-cultural ubiquity and power of male sexual jealousy (e.g., Buss, 2000; Daly et al., 1982); (c) women's fertile-phase sexuality, which functions primarily in the context of extra-pair mating (e.g., Gangestad & Thornhill, 1998; Gangestad & Thornhill, 2008; Penton-Voak et al., 1999); (d) men's overperception of female infidelity (Andrews, Gangestad, Miller, Haselton, & Neale, 2008; Goetz & Causey, 2009); (e) adaptations associated with sperm competition in humans (e.g., Goetz & Shackelford, 2006; Shackelford & Goetz, 2007); (f) the matrilateral bias associated with grandparental and avuncular investment (e.g., Euler & Weitzel, 1996; Gaulin, et al., 1997; Jeon & Buss, 2007); and (g) paternity inferences and willingness to invest associated with paternal resemblance (Platek et al., 2002, 2003, 2004, 2005), it is clear that female infidelity and cuckoldry were recurrent features of our evolutionary history. Indeed, the threat of cuckoldry is so devastating that its consequences are perhaps only rivaled by parasites (Goetz, Shackelford, Romero, Kaighobadi, & Miner, 2008).

As we saw with the stories of Morgan Wise and Frank Hatley, the costs of cuckoldry can involve loss of time, effort, resources spent on attracting a partner, resources directed at raising a rival's offspring, and reputational damage if the incident becomes public. Given these costs, we can see why natural selection might have favored male strategies that can prevent the occurrence of cuckoldry. Research performed by social scientists has begun to uncover that the execution of these strategies are the responses of psychological mechanisms—that is, neural-based features of human psychology that have been designed by natural selection to solve specific adaptive problems. We illustrate the functional design of these mechanisms by examining the purpose of an emotion that functioned to monitor threats to relationships: the emotion of sexual jealousy.

Psychological Mechanisms Equipped to Detect and Prevent Cuckoldry
Male Sexual Jealousy

Jealousy is an emotion that is experienced when a valued relationship is threatened by a real or imagined rival, and it generates contextually contingent responses aimed at reducing or eliminating the threat. Jealousy can be viewed as an emotion that functions to produce behavior aimed to prevent the derailment of a relationship. When jealousy is triggered, the resulting changes in behavior attempt to deter mates from infidelity or departure from the relationship (Buss, Larsen, Westen, & Semmelroth, 1992; Daly, Wilson, & Weghorst, 1982; Symons, 1979). Although both men and women experience jealousy, paternity uncertainty has arguably shaped the elicitation of jealousy in men differently than that of women. Men and women express jealousy similarly in regards to frequency and intensity (Shackelford, LeBlanc, & Drass, 2000; White, 1981); however, research has repeatedly demonstrated that sex differences emerge in light of sexual and emotional jealousy (e.g., Buss, 2000; Symons, 1979). These differences are rooted in the divergent adaptive problems faced by men—ensuring that offspring produced in the relationship are genetically the man's own—and women—keeping her mate continuously investing exclusively in her and her offspring. The evidence for these sex differences has been established on several research fronts, including experimental data (e.g., Schützwohl & Koch, 2004), physiological data (Buss et al., 1992), patterns of relationship termination (Betzig, 1989; Shackelford, Buss, & Bennett, 2002), and the behavioral output of jealousy (e.g., Buss & Shackelford, 1997). Male sexual jealousy alone cannot prevent cuckoldry. Emotions elicit mechanisms that in turn guide specific behavior (Cosmides & Tooby, 2000). Thus, we can perceive jealousy as a warning signal that, if triggered, could lead to preemptive monitoring or preventative behavior to prohibit relationship defection (temporary or permanent).

Maintaining Relationships

Mate retention is an example of the behavioral output that results from jealousy. Buss (1988) noted several mate guarding tactics, such as enhanced vigilance of partner whereabouts, concealment of a mate from potential rivals in social settings, and efforts to monopolize a partner's time. These tactics, as we will see, are a first line of defense that serve to help reduce the probability of paternity uncertainty. Buss and Shackelford (1997) demonstrated that men tend to monitor their partners more closely when they are of greater reproductive value (an indicator that may reflect a higher likelihood to be poached) and when the perceived probability of extra-pair copulation is higher. Additionally, men who are mated to women who possess characteristics that make them more likely to commit sexual infidelity guard their partners more intensely (Goetz et al., 2005). Men also guard their partners more intensely after spending a greater proportion of time apart from them—a situation that increases the likelihood of female sexual infidelity (Starratt, Shackelford, Goetz, & McKibbin, 2007)—and when she is near ovulation, a time when an extra-pair copulation or sexual infidelity would be most detrimental (Gangestad, Thornhill, & Garver, 2002). Research also suggests that when mate guarding fails, men turn to violent tactics. Kaighobadi, Starratt, Shackelford, and Popp (2008) documented that the relationship between accusations of female infidelity and female-directed violence is mediated by nonviolent guarding behaviors, suggesting that there exists a temporal hierarchy of mate retention behaviors that begin nonviolently and escalate to violence.

Intimate Partner Violence
Violence as Punishment

Given that humans are a biparental species marked by extraordinarily high paternal investment, it may seem paradoxical that female-directed IPV is so common among humans. Research addressing proximate explanations of violence has emphasized risk factors such as alcoholism (Stith, Smith, Penn, Ward, & Tritt, 2004), feelings of patriarchy (Watts & Zimmerman, 2002), and lack of communication skills (Babcock, Waltz, Jacobson, & Gottman, 1993), for example. However, recent research has been finding that the salience of these risk factors are not as compelling when taking into account the ultimate explanations for this violence. For example, Foran and O'Leary (2008) found that the relationship between alcohol use and IPV is moderated by feelings of jealousy, such that nonsevere forms of physical aggression are attributed to feelings of jealousy alone. Alcohol use increases the frequency of severe forms of physical aggression only when men reported (or were reported by their partner to have) stronger feelings of jealousy. We emphasize here that appreciating "ultimate" causes in investigating IPV can help elucidate research as an alternative, but compatible, approach to understanding proximate causes. Rather than viewing IPV as a short-lived, state-dependent behavior, evolutionary perspectives have explicated violence between intimate partners as a form of punishment that is designed to negotiate fitness costs presented by past infidelity and facilitate the deterrence of suspected future female infidelity (Goetz et al., 2008). Clutton-Brock and Parker (1995) argued that punishment is a functional behavior aimed at reducing conflicts of interest, with individuals expressing fitness threatening behaviors to the aggressor. This framework suggests that the severity of violence used against intimate partners is contingent on men's perceptions of how detrimental a partner's behavior is to their fitness. In line with this, research has found that men's violence against their intimate partners varies according to how serious a threat was perceived (e.g., Fitness, 2001; Fitness & Peterson, 2008). Fitness (2001) documented that punishment in a relationship varied with the perceived seriousness of the offense, such that retaliation for sexual infidelity received the most severe punishment, followed by less critical offenses such as trivial lying. Although the propensity to engage in physical violence was influenced by whether a partner had been forgiven for the offense, it was the severity of betrayal that largely determined whether a partner could be forgiven. Upon these foundations, researchers are now beginning to appreciate that the risk that cuckoldry poses to men's fitness allows one to predict that the occurrence of IPV should be directly related to perceptions of threats to fitness, such as sexual infidelity and relationship termination (Goetz et al., 2008).

Punishment can be costly to those who institute it and, thus, we can expect to see it explicitly used under specific contexts in which the behavior of others is non-cooperative. Intimate partner violence could have posed costs to ancestral males in the form of reputational damage and retaliation from a female's nearby male kin, for example. Figueredo et al. (2001) presented evidence for this latter prediction by demonstrating that women who lived in an area near to several of their male kin were physically abused less often by their partners. Nevertheless, punishment is still utilized, and although there are costs associated with its use, punishment may prove to be an effective behavior at reducing the occurrence of cuckoldry. In order to make predictions about the effectiveness of punishment, we look to research performed in game theory to assess its potential functionality.

Game theory acknowledges that an individual's social behavior does not occur in a vacuum, but rather must be considered in conjunction with the behavior of others. Evolutionary game theory (Fisher, 1930; Maynard-Smith, 1982) magnifies this logic by generations to show that the evolution of a trait depends on how it interacts with other extant and evolving traits. Because game theory considers the cost and benefits of interactions between competing strategies (e.g., people), it has notable relevance for the understanding of punishment as a male tactic against intimate partners. Given competing interests of the individuals involved in an interaction, game theory can evaluate competing strategies to determine the most effective approach to a particular interaction.

As reviewed above, much evidence suggests that female infidelity and cuckoldry were recurrent features of our evolutionary history. Women's sexual infidelity is in direct conflict with men's evolutionary interests, setting the stage for a game theoretical analysis. If a woman's sexual infidelity goes without retaliation, it is probable that future defection will occur (Axelrod & Hamilton, 1981) and the man will continue to incur costs. With this in mind, punishment (i.e., IPV) can begin to be viewed as retaliation against a defecting partner. Game theoretical studies examining the practicality of punishment as retaliatory strategy suggest that, even with the accrued costs from punishing over time, defection is effectively reduced (Gächter, Renner, & Sefton, 2008; Fehr & Gächter, 1999). Using game theory, we can argue that IPV might have directly or indirectly served as an effective form of punishment by limiting the benefits gained from defecting from a relationship, deterring the occurrence of future defecting behavior, and preventing defection from occurring in the first place by establishing and promoting severe punishment as a consequence for defection (Hauert, Traulsen, Brandt, Nowak, & Sigmund, 2007; Fehr & Gächter, 1999; Rauhut & Junker, 2009).

Male Proprietariness and Violence

Male sexual jealousy or male sexual proprietariness (Daly, Wilson, & Weghorst, 1982) is frequently found to be one of the causes of IPV, both physical and sexual (e.g., Buss, 2000; Daly & Wilson, 1988; Dobash & Dobash, 1979; Dutton, 1998; Frieze, 1983; Gage & Hutchinson, 2006). Moreover, suspicion or knowledge of infidelity reliably provokes violent behavior (Goetz & Shackelford, 2006, 2009; Kaighobadi et al., 2008; Starratt, Shackelford, Goetz, & McKibbin, 2009). Recognizing that male mate retention behaviors are manifestations of elicited sexual jealousy, Shackelford, Goetz, Buss, Euler, and Hoier (2005) investigated associations between male mate retention behaviors and IPV. Shackelford and his colleagues found across three studies that male use of specific mate retention behaviors was related to partner violence in a predictable fashion. For example, men who dropped by unexpectedly to see what their partner was doing or who told their partner that they would "die" if she ever left him were most likely to use serious violence against their partners, whereas men who attempted to retain their partners by expressing affection and displaying resources were least likely to use violence against their partners. These findings corroborated those by Wilson, Johnson, and Daly (1995), who found that women who affirmed that their partner insisted on knowing their whereabouts or limited their social contacts, were twice as likely to have experienced serious violence at the hands of their partners.

Physical violence has been identified as a tactic used by men to restrict an intimate partner's behavior, especially her sexual behavior outside the intimate relationship (Daly & Wilson, 1988; Goetz & Steele, 2009; Wilson & Daly, 1996) and is best understood in the context of female infidelity. Goetz (2007) hypothesized that men possess evolved psychological mechanisms dedicated to generating risk assessments of a partner's sexual infidelity, and that these mechanisms selectively process information associated with assessments of time spent apart from the partner, the presence of potential mate poachers, the partner's reproductive value and fertility, and the partner's personality characteristics. Moreover, mechanisms designed to detect the likelihood of sexual infidelity in males seem to overestimate the probability of its occurrence (Goetz & Causey, 2009). Together with risk assessment of a partner's sexual infidelity, contextual factors—such as social and reputational costs, proximity of the partner's kin capable of retaliation, and economic dependency (Figueredo & McCloskey, 1993; Wilson & Daly, 1993)—are processed during decisions to inflict violence on a partner.

Evolutionary perspectives appreciate that IPV is not sex-specific and is not isolated to human relationships (e.g., Goetz et al., 2008). The role of male sexual jealousy in IPV within humans is significant and is sometimes ignored or is undervalued by alternative approaches to studying partner violence (e.g., Graham-Kevan & Archer, 2009; Felson & Outlaw, 2007). Multiple factors contribute to the occurrence of IPV; however, we argue that paternity uncertainty is an important facet to understanding and predicting female-directed violence. As we will discuss in the following section, conceptualizing IPV from the evolutionary framework of male proprietariness allows us to explain several cases of partner violence and to predict the severity of violence based on detection of a threat to fitness.

Variances in the Severity of Violence
When unrelated offspring, such as stepchildren, coreside in the same home, male jealousy progressively elevates. Men may become more unwilling to allocate resources towards nongenetic offspring, as compared to the biological mother, and the resulting inequality of investment can transcend from minor conflict to violence (Brewer & Paulsen, 1999; Daly, Wiseman, & Wilson, 1997). Documented cases of domestic violence feature an overwhelming amount of women who reside with offspring from former intimate partners (Brownridge, 2004; Daly, Singh, & Wilson, 1993; Figueredo & McCloskey, 1993). Uninhibited by the presence of offspring genetically related to her current partner, these women consistently become the victims of violence (Daly et al., 1993). Furthermore, preliminary data demonstrates that women residing in stepfamilies have an increased probability of experiencing severe expressions of physical violence (Brownridge, 2004). Even in the most extreme case of uxoricide, women residing with offspring unrelated to their current partner are at a higher risk of being killed as compared with women who have offspring sired from their current partner (Brewer & Paulsen, 1999; Daly et al., 1997).

Relationships that potentially lack commitment, such as those seen among cohabitating partners as compared to married couples, also agitate male sexual jealousy. Unwed women residing with their partners have been found to be at an elevated risk for female-directed violence when compared to married women (Brownridge, 2008; Shackelford, 2001; Shackelford & Mouzos, 2005; Wilson, Daly, & Wright, 1993; Wilson et al., 1995). Notwithstanding, cohabitation as a risk factor for female-directed violence may be receding in impact as unwed intimate relationships become more prevalent (Brownridge, 2008). Although we see that the escalation and severity of violence can be influenced by a number of factors, we next turn to focus on the most serious form of female-directed violence—uxoricide—and attempt to understand its role in male psychology.

Male Proprietariness and Uxoricide
Of the 3,078 reported female homicides that occurred in the United States alone, 35% of them were perpetrated by a husband or boyfriend (Crime in the United States, 2008), and as research has established, the killing of an intimate partner is often found with the elicitation of male sexual jealousy (Daly & Wilson, 1988; Serran & Firestone, 2004). As mentioned earlier, inflicting punishment on a partner can be costly; consequently, we can assume that the killing of an intimate partner will be met with severe repercussions. With this in mind, we ponder whether uxoricide could have been substantially beneficial for men, so that selection pressures operated to favor those who carried out intimate femicide. Wilson and Daly (Daly & Wilson, 1988; Wilson & Daly, 1998; Wilson, Daly, & Daniele, 1995) address this question by proposing that partner killing is likely to be the consequence of a mishap from evolved mechanisms designed to influence and restrict a partner's behavior. This by-product hypothesis, otherwise known as the *slip-up hypothesis*, does not view partner killing as adaptive behavior and hence, suggests that selection would not favor the development of this behavior as a part of evolved male psychology. Altercations between intimate couples that result in men killing

their partner are therefore misapplied control tactics. Recognizing that many partner homicides are premeditated and not accidental, Buss and Duntley (1998, 2003; see also Buss, 2005) have suggested that many instances of lethal IPV result from evolved psychological mechanisms specifically designed to motivate killing a partner under certain conditions. Discovering a partner's sexual infidelity, Buss and Duntley argue, may be a special circumstance that might trigger specialized psychology in men. Homicide adaptation theory does not argue that discovering a partner's infidelity invariantly leads to partner killing, but that this situation activates evolved mechanisms associated with weighing the costs and benefits of homicide, and that under certain circumstances, partner killing by men might be the designed outcome (Buss, 2005).

Wilson and Daly's (1998; Wilson, Johnson, & Daly, 1995) and Buss and Duntley's (1998, 2003) contrasting hypotheses have not yet been tested concurrently, so that a single hypothesis remains to be found that best accounts for the data. Recent research has critiqued the proposition that the killing of an intimate partner is the result of an evaluation from adaptive mechanisms. Durrant (2009) argued that ancestral societies upheld sanctions against killing that would have made uxoricide too costly to be adaptive. Durrant also highlights many shortcomings in using comparative research as support for the homicide adaptation theory and ultimately suggests that understanding partner killing from a by-product standpoint would prove more parsimonious until further evidence is provided to support the existence of evolved mechanisms associated with committing uxoricide. Although we appreciate, as do Buss and Duntley, that assuming a priori that a trait may be an adaptation is a heuristic that guides research questions and methods, an adaptationist's hypothesis is merely a starting point. Nevertheless, we turn once again to evolutionary game theory and consider the costs associated with lethal IPV, in an effort to further inform the ongoing debate.

As game theory is the study of multiple competing strategies, we consider a simplified model of lethal IPV to see how it performs against similar strategies. Consider, first, the consequences of an ancestral male killing an intimate partner after discovering her infidelity. Given an ancestral group size of 150 individuals (Dunbar, 1993), a roughly equal sex ratio, and given that approximately 50% of the population would be of reproductive age, this reduces the pool of reproductive aged men and women to 38 each. Just one case of lethal IPV results in nearly a 3% reduction in the available mating pool (from 38 potential mates to 37). Thus, the male's action to eliminate his partner is more costly to him than if he would have not eliminated her and simply terminated the relationship. By eliminating his partner, other males' options have become limited also, as the 38 men are now competing for 37 women. If, however, the male terminates the relationship instead, there remain 38 men competing for 38 women. Thus, the actions of just one male killing his partner decreases the pool of available mates and, more importantly, intensifies mating competition for himself. This simplified model did not assume other parameters (e.g., polygyny) that would have exacerbated these results. Also, the calculations were based on Dunbar's (1993) research arguing that our ancestors evolved in groups of roughly 150 individuals, but note that the results change by only 1% for every change in 50 members. Moreover, the mating competition intensification is exponentially greater when applied to an entire community of men who eliminate cheating partners. Other costs associated with killing an intimate partner include incurring the wrath of her kin and the local community, experiencing a significant decrease in mate value (e.g., Burkett & Kirkpatrick, 2006), and if they had children together, depriving the children of maternal investment.

Thus, given the simplified game theoretical analysis, the many costs associated with killing an intimate partner, the absence of research identifying the computational mechanisms of an intimate partner homicide, and other criticisms emphasized by Durrant (2009), the most parsimonious explanation for intimate femicide remains Wilson and Daly's (1998; Wilson, Daly, & Daniele, 1995) by-product hypothesis. Future research, of course, is needed to concurrently test the adaptation and by-product hypotheses.

Sexual Coercion

Between 10% and 26% of women experience rape in marriage (Abrahams, Jewkes, Hoffman, & Laubscher, 2004; Dunkle et al., 2004; Finkelhor & Yllo, 1985; Hadi, 2000; Painter & Farrington, 1999; Russell, 1982; Watts, Keogh, Ndlovu, & Kwaramba, 1998). Rape also occurs in nonmarital intimate relationships. Goetz and Shackelford (2006) secured prevalence estimates of rape in intimate relationships from a sample of young men and from an independent sample of young women in a committed relationship for at least 1 year, but not necessarily married. Goetz and Shackelford documented that 7.3% of men admitted to raping their current partner at least once, and 9.1% of women reported that they had experienced at least one rape by their current partner. Although these percentages are astonishingly high, they likely do not reflect the true incidence of partner rape. Questions concerning sexual coercion and rape in relationships are emotionally loaded and can be subject to social desirability, and therefore such percentages may be underestimates of the prevalence of rape in intimate relationships among young men and women. Several hypotheses have been proposed to explain why, across cultures, reliable percentages of women are sexually coerced by their partners. Here we highlight two approaches: (a) viewing sexual coercion as a result of male desire for domination and control, and (b) understanding sexual coercion as a result of paternity uncertainty.

Some researchers have hypothesized that sexual coercion in intimate relationships is motivated by men's attempts to dominate and control their partners (e.g., Basile, 2002; Bergen, 1996; Frieze, 1983; Gage & Hutchinson, 2006; Gelles, 1977; Meyer, Vivian, & O'Leary, 1998; Watts et al., 1998) and that this expression of power is the product of men's social roles (e.g., Brownmiller, 1975; Johnson, 1995; Yllo & Straus, 1990). Results relevant to this hypothesis are mixed. Several studies have found that physically abusive men are more likely than nonabusive men to sexually coerce their female partners (Apt & Hurlbert, 1993; DeMaris, 1997; Donnelly, 1993; Finkelhor & Yllo, 1985; Koziol-McLain, Coates, & Lowenstein, 2001; Shackelford & Goetz, 2004), supporting the domination and control hypothesis. Gage and Hutchinson (2006), however, found that women's risk of sexual coercion by their partners is not related to measures assessing the relative dimensions of power in a relationship, such as who maintains control over decision making. That is, women mated to men who hold the dominant position in the relationship are not more likely to experience sexual coercion than do women mated to men who do not hold the dominant position in the relationship, thus contradicting the domination and control hypothesis. Although many researchers agree that individual men may sexually coerce their partners to maintain dominance and control, proponents of the domination and control hypothesis often argue that men are motivated as a group to exercise "patriarchal power" or "patriarchal terrorism" over women (e.g., Brownmiller, 1975; Johnson, 1995; Yllo & Straus, 1990).

An alternative hypothesis has been advanced by researchers studying sexual coercion from an evolutionary perspective: Sexual coercion in intimate relationships may be related to paternity uncertainty, with its occurrence related to a man's suspicions of his partner's sexual infidelity (Camilleri, 2004; Goetz & Shackelford, 2006; Goetz, Shackelford, & Camilleri, 2008; Lalumière, Harris, Quinsey, & Rice, 2005; Thornhill & Thornhill, 1992; Wilson & Daly, 1992). Sexual coercion in response to cues of his partner's sexual infidelity might function to introduce a man's sperm into his partner's reproductive tract at a time when there is a high risk of cuckoldry (i.e., when his partner has recently been inseminated by a rival male). This sperm competition hypothesis was proposed following recognition that forced in-pair copulation (i.e., partner rape) in nonhuman species followed female extra-pair copulations (e.g., Barash, 1977; Cheng, Burns, & McKinney, 1983; Lalumière et al., 2005; McKinney, Cheng, & Bruggers, 1984) and that sexual coercion and rape in human intimate relationships often followed accusations of female infidelity (e.g., Finkelhor & Yllo, 1985; Russell, 1982). We turn our discussion to research that has focused on establishing evidence for the occurrence of forced in-pair copulation (FIPC) in humans.

Partner Rape

Wilson and Daly (1992) suggested in a footnote that "sexual insistence" in the context of a relationship might act as a sperm competition tactic in humans as well. Thornhill and Thornhill (1992) also hypothesized that FIPC may be an anticuckoldry tactic designed over human evolutionary history by selective pressures associated with sperm competition. Thornhill and Thornhill argued that a woman who resists or avoids copulating with her partner might thereby be signaling to him that she has been sexually unfaithful and that the FIPC functions to decrease his paternity uncertainty. Thornhill and Thornhill argued that the fact that the rape of a woman by her partner is more likely to occur during or after a breakup—times in which men express great concern about female sexual infidelity—provides preliminary support for the hypothesis. Thornhill and Thornhill, for example, cited research by Frieze (1983) indicating that women who were physically abused and raped by their husbands rated them to be more sexually jealous than did women who were abused but not raped.

Similar arguments presented by Thornhill and Palmer (2000), and Lalumière et al. (2005) suggest that men who suspect that their female partner has been sexually unfaithful may be motivated to engage in FIPC. Both indirect and direct empirical evidence supporting this hypothesis has been documented. Frieze (1983) and Gage and Hutchinson (2006), for example, found that husbands who raped their wives were more sexually jealous than husbands who did not rape their wives. Shields and Hanneke (1983) documented that victims of FIPC were more likely to have reported engaging in extramarital sex than women who were not raped by their in-pair partner. Studying men's partner-directed insults, Starratt, Goetz, Shackelford, McKibbin, and Stewart-Williams (2008) found in two studies that a reliable predictor of a man's sexual coercion is his accusations of his partner's sexual infidelity. Specifically, men who accuse their partners of being unfaithful (nominating items such as "I accused my partner of having sex with many other men" and "I called my partner a 'whore' or a 'slut'") were more likely to be sexually coercive. Direct empirical evidence supporting this hypothesis is accumulating. Camilleri (2004), for example, found that risk of a partner's infidelity predicted sexual coercion among male participants but not female participants. Goetz and Shackelford (2006) documented in two studies that a man's sexual coercion in the context of an intimate relationship is related positively to his partner's infidelities. According to men's self-reports and women's partner-reports, men who used more sexual coercion in their relationship were mated to women who had been or were likely to be unfaithful, and these men also were likely to use more mate retention behaviors. In a forensic sample, Camilleri and Quinsey (2008) found that convicted partner rapists, compared to nonsexual partner abusers, experienced more cuckoldry risk events prior to committing their offense; and in a second study involving a community sample, direct and recent cues to female infidelity predicted men's self-reported propensity for sexual coercion. Most recently, Goetz and Shackelford (2009) collected data on the proximate and ultimate causes of men's sexual coercion in intimate relationships to explore how these variables interact. In two studies involving men's self-reports and women's partner-reports, men's sexual coercion of their partners was consistently predicted by female infidelity even after controlling for men's dominate personalities and men's controlling behavior. Because cuckoldry poses a substantial reproductive cost for males of paternally investing species, men are expected to have evolved a host of adaptations to confront the adaptive problem of paternity uncertainty. One such adaptation may be a sperm competition tactic whereby sexual coercion and FIPC function to increase likelihood that the in-pair male, and not a rival male, sires the offspring that his partner might produce. It may be that a proportion of sexually coercive behaviors (in the context of an intimate relationship) are performed by antisocial men who aim to punish, humiliate, or control their partners, independent of their perception of cuckoldry risk. We are not arguing that all sexual coercion and FIPCs are the output of evolved psychological mechanisms designed to reduce the risk of being cuckolded. Instead, we are suggesting that sexual coercion might sometimes be the result of male evolved psychology associated with male sexual jealousy.

Conclusion

Paternity uncertainty posed a significant threat to ancestral males. As we saw in the introduction of this chapter with the stories of Morgan Wise and Frank Hatley, men are still faced with threat of cuckoldry and suffer the many of the consequences that ancestral males may have faced. Our efforts in this chapter have been to demonstrate that the consequences of paternity uncertainty can be a notable contributor to the conflict that occurs within intimate relationships and in particular, in female-directed violence. Evolutionary psychologists have revealed several mechanisms in men that are used to detect threats to established relationships and to prevent the defection of a partner. This approach focuses on the ultimate causes in behavior and has allowed researchers to pose a concise and parsimonious explanation for several cases of IPV. As researchers venture forward, they will need to continue identifying and establishing evidence for the existence of psychological mechanisms that govern conflict in close relationships. Moreover, more effort is needed to make the distinction between adaptive behaviors and byproducts. The progression of research in this area will allow for a more comprehensive understanding of human behavior in intimate relationships and will improve our ability to explain IPV when considered alongside with proximate causes of behavior.

Directions for Future Research

1. *Intimate partner violence during pregnancy.* Considering the implications of understanding IPV as a form of punishment, future research should reexamine men's violence against their intimate partners in the context of pregnancy. Some research has shown that women are more

likely to be the recipients of IPV during pregnancy by their jealous partners (e.g., Burch & Gallup, 2004). Intimate partner violence during pregnancy may seem counterintuitive but should be predicted by men's suspicion of their paternity. For example, Campbell, Pugh, Campbell, and Visscher (1995) performed a qualitative study on women's likelihood to experience IPV during pregnancy. A recurring theme was that severe IPV during pregnancy was motivated by paternity uncertainty. An evolutionary approach to IPV during pregnancy would not only predict that men's violence directed at their pregnant partners would vary according to their suspicion of paternity, but might also hypothesize that physical aggression would be aimed at the abdomen in order to terminate the pregnancy.

2. *Neuroimaging the sexually proprietary brain.* Future research might benefit from employing neuroimaging techniques. Because men have a proprietary view of the intimate partners (i.e., men view their partners as property that they privately own and control), perhaps neuroimaging would reveal that the same neurological structures associated with thinking about actual personal property (e.g., a car or a house) are also involved when men think about their partners. It is not unreasonable to consider that the frugal engineering process of natural selection might have used the same neurological structures to govern cognition about personal property and sexual property.

3. *Understanding the proximate correlates of IPV.* Additionally, research should also aim to understand many of the correlations found with IPV and individual differences. For example, research has shown that socioeconomic status is a risk factor for IPV (Cunradi, Cactano, Clark, & Schafer, 2000); however, this may be a proximate cause to explain why some men might become more vigilant and potentially jealous when they are at higher risk of becoming cuckolded. Through these avenues of research, we can obtain a richer understanding of IPV in the hopes of reducing its occurrence.

References

Abrahams, N., Jewkes, R., Hoffman, M., & Laubscher, R. (2004). Sexual violence against intimate partners in Cape Town: Prevalence and risk factors reported by men. *Bulletin of the World Health Organisation, 82,* 330–337.

Anderson, K.G. (2006). How well does paternity confidence match actual paternity? Results from worldwide nonpaternity rates. *Current Anthropology, 48,* 511–518.

Andrews, P.W., Gangestad, S.W., Miller, G.F., Haselton, M.G., & Neale, M.C. (2008). Sex differences in detecting sexual infidelity: Results of a maximum likelihood method for analyzing the sensitivity of sex differences to underreporting. *Human Nature, 19,* 347–373.

Apt, C., & Hurlbert, D.F. (1993). The sexuality of women in physically abusive marriages: Comparative study. *Journal of Family Violence, 8,* 57–69.

Axelord, R., & Hamilton, W.D. (1981). The evolution of cooperation. *Science, 211,* 1390–1396.

Babcock, J.C., Waltz, J., Jacobson, N.S., & Gottman, J.M. (1993). Power and violence: The relation between communication patterns, power discrepancies, and domestic violence. *Journal of Consulting and Clinical Psychology, 61,* 40–50.

Barash, D.P. (1977). Sociobiology of rape in mallards (*Anas platyrhynchos*): Response of the mated male. *Science, 197,* 788–789.

Basile, K.C. (2002). Prevalence of wife rape and other intimate partner sexual coercion in a nationally representative sample of women. *Violence and Victims, 17,* 511–524.

Bellis, M.A., Hughes, K., Hughes, S., & Ashton, J.R. (2005). Measuring paternal discrepancy and its public health consequences. *Journal of Epidemiology and Community Health, 59,* 749–754.

Bergen, R.K. (1996). *Wife rape: Understanding the response of survivors and service providers.* Thousand Oaks, CA: Sage.

Betzig, L. (1989). Causes of conjugal dissolution: A cross-cultural study. *Current Anthropology, 30,* 654–676.

Brewer, V.E., & Paulsen, D.J. (1999). A comparison of U.S. and Canadian findings on uxoricide risk for women with children sired by previous partners. *Homicide Studies, 3,* 317–332.

Brownmiller, S. (1975). *Against our will: Men, women, and rape.* New York: Simon & Schuster.

Brownridge, D.A. (2004). Male partner violence against women in stepfamilies: An analysis of risk and explanations in the Canadian milieu. *Violence and Victims, 19,* 17–36.

Brownridge, D.A. (2008). The elevated risk for violence against cohabitating women: A comparison of three nationally representative surveys of Canada. *Violence Against Women, 14,* 809–832.

Burch, R., & Gallup, G.G., Jr. (2004). Pregnancy as a stimulus for domestic violence. *Journal of Family Violence, 19,* 243–247.

Burkett, B.N., & Kirkpatrick, L.A. (2006). *What are deal breakers in a mate: Characteristics that are intolerable in a potential mate.* Paper presented at the Annual Meeting of the Human Behavior and Evolution Society, Philadelphia, PA, June 10, 2006.

Buss, D.M. (1988). From vigilance to violence: Tactics of mate retention in American undergraduates. *Ethology and Sociobiology, 9,* 291–317.

Buss, D.M. (2000). *The dangerous passion.* New York: The Free Press.

Buss, D.M., Larsen, R J., Westen, D., & Semmelroth, J. (1992). Sex differences in jealousy: Evolution, physiology and psychology. *Psychological Science, 3,* 251–255.

Buss, D.M., & Shackelford, T.K. (1997). From vigilance to violence: Mate retention tactics in married couples. *Journal of Personality and Social Psychology, 72,* 346–361.

Buss, D.M., & Duntley, J.D. (1998). *Evolved homicide modules.* Paper presented at the Annual Meeting of the Human Behavior and Evolution Society, Davis, CA, July 10, 1998.

Buss, D.M., & Duntley, J.D. (2003). Homicide: An evolutionary perspective and implications for public policy. In N. Dress

(Ed.), *Violence and public policy* (pp. 115–128). Westport, CT: Greenwood Publishing Group, Inc.

Buss, D.M. (2005). *The murderer next door*. New York: The Penguin Press.

Camilleri, J. (2004). *Investigating sexual coercion in romantic relationships: A test of the cuckoldry risk hypothesis*. Unpublished master's thesis, University of Saskatchewan, Saskatoon, Saskatchewan, Canada.

Camilleri, J.A., & Quinsey, V.L. (2008). *Testing the cuckoldry risk hypothesis of partner sexual coercion in forensic and community samples*. Manuscript submitted for publication.

Campbell, J.C., Pugh, L.C., Campbell, D., & Visscher, M. (1995). The influence of abuse on pregnancy intention. *Women's Health Issues, 5*, 214–223.

Castillo, M. (2009). *Childless man freed after serving time for child support violations. CNN*.com. Retrieved January 2, 2010 from http://www.cnn.com/2009/CRIME/07/15/georgia.child.support/

Cheng, K.M., Burns, J.T., & McKinney, F. (1983). Forced copulation in captive mallards III. Sperm competition. *The Auk, 100*, 302–310.

Clutton-Brock, T.H., & Parker, G.A. (1995). Punishment in animal societies. *Nature, 373*, 209–216.

Cosmides, L., & Tooby, J. (2000). Evolutionary psychology and the emotions. In M. Lewis & J.M. Haviland-Jones (Eds.), *Handbook of emotions* (2nd ed., pp. 91–115). New York: Guilford Press.

Cunradi, C.B., Caetano, R., Clark, C., & Schafer, J. (2000). Neighborhood poverty as a predictor of intimate partner violence among White, Black, and Hispanic couples in the United States: A multilevel analysis. *Association of Educational Psychologists, 10*, 297–308.

Daly, M., Singh, L.S., & Wilson, M. (1993). Children fathered by previous partners: A risk factor for violence against women. *Canadian Journal of Public Health, 84*, 209–210.

Daly, M., Wilson, M., & Weghorst, J. (1982). Male sexual jealousy. *Ethology and Sociobiology, 3*, 11–27.

Daly, M., & Wilson, M. (1988). *Homicide*. Hawthorne, NY: Aldine de Gruyter.

Daly, M., Wiseman, K.A., & Wilson, M.I. (1997). Women with children sired by previous partners incur excess risk of uxoricide. *Homicide Studies, 1*, 61–71.

DeMaris, A. (1997). Elevated sexual activity in violent marriages: Hypersexuality or sexual extortion? *Journal of Sex Research, 34*, 361–373.

Dobash, R.E., & Dobash, R.P. (1979). *Violence against wives*. New York: The Free Press.

Donnelly, D.A. (1993). Sexually inactive marriages. *The Journal of Sex Research, 30*, 171–179.

Dunbar, R.I.M. (1993). Coevolution of neocortical size, group size and language in humans. *Behavioral and Brain Sciences, 16*, 681–735.

Dunkle, K.L., Jewkes, R.K., Brown, H.C., Gray, G.E., McIntyre, J.A., & Harlow, S.D. (2004). Gender-based violence, relationship power and risk of prevalent HIV infection among women attending antenatal clinics in Soweto, South Africa. *Lancet, 363*, 1415–1421.

Durrant, R. (2009). Born to kill? A critical evaluation of homicide adaptation theory. *Aggression and violent Behavior, 14*, 374–381.

Dutton, D.G. (1998). *The abusive personality*. New York: Guilford Press.

Euler, H.A. & Weitzel, B. (1996). Discriminative grandparental solicitude as reproductive strategy. *Human Nature: An Interdisciplinary Biosocial Perspective, 7*, 39–59.

Fehr, E., & Gächter, S. (1999). Cooperation and punishment in public goods experiments. *American Economic Review, 90*, 980–994.

Felson, R., & Outlaw, M.C. (2007). The control motive and marital violence. *Violence and Victims, 22*, 387–407.

Figueredo, A.J., & McCloskey, L.A. (1993). Sex, money, and paternity: The evolution of domestic violence. *Ethology and Sociobiology, 14*, 353–379.

Figueredo, A.J., Corral-Verdugo, V., Frías-Armenta, M., Bachar, K.J., White, J., McNeill, P.L., et al. (2001). Blood, solidarity, status, and honor: The sexual balance of power and spousal abuse in Sonora, Mexico. *Evolution and Human Behavior, 22*, 295–328.

Finkelhor, D., & Yllo, K. (1985). *License to rape: Sexual abuse of wives*. New York: Holt, Rinehart, & Winston.

Fisher, R.A. (1930). *The genetical theory of natural selection*. Oxford, UK: Clarendon Press.

Fitness, J. (2001). Betrayal, rejection, revenge and forgiveness: An interpersonal script. In M. Leary (Ed.), *Interpersonal Rejection* (pp. 73–103). New York, NY; Oxford University Press.

Fitness, J. & Peterson, J. (2008). Punishment and forgiveness in close relationships: An evolutionary, social-psychological perspective. In J.P. Forgas, & J. Fitness (Eds.), *Social relationships: Cognitive, affective, and motivational processes* (pp. 255–270). New York: Psychology Press.

Foran, H.M., & O'Leary, K.D. (2008). Problem drinking, jealousy, and anger control: Variables predicting physical aggression against a partner. *Journal of Family Violence, 23*, 141–148.

Frieze, I.H. (1983). Investigating the causes and consequences of marital rape. *Signs: Journal of women in culture and society, 8*, 532–553.

Gage, A.J., & Hutchinson, P.L. (2006). Power, control, and intimate partner sexual violence in Haiti. *Archives of Sexual Behavior, 35*, 11–24.

Gächter, S., Renner, E., & Sefton, M. (2008). The long-run benefits of punishment. *Science, 322*, 1510.

Gangestad, S.W. & Thornhill, R. (1998). Menstrual cycle variation in women's preferences for the scent of symmetrical men. *Proceedings of the Royal Society B, 265*, 927–933.

Gangestad, S.W., Thornhill, R., & Garver, C.E. (2002). Changes in women's sexual interests and their partner's mate-retention tactics across the menstrual cycle: Evidence for shifting conflicts of interest. *Proceedings of the Royal Society of London, 269*, 975–982.

Gangestad, S.W. & Thornhill, R. (2008). Human oestrus. *Proceedings of the Royal Society B, 275*, 991–1000.

Gaulin, S.J.C., McBurney, D.H., & Brakeman-Wartell, S.L. (1997). Matrilateral biases in the investment of aunts and uncles: A consequence of measure of paternity uncertainty. *Human Nature: An Interdisciplinary Biosocial Perspective, 8*, 139–151.

Gelles, R. (1977). Power, sex and violence: The case of marital rape. *Family Coordinator, 26*, 339–347.

Goetz, A.T. (2007). Violence and abuse in families: The consequences of paternal uncertainty. In C. Salmon, & T.K. Shackelford (Eds.), *Family relationships: An evolutionary perspective* (pp. 259–274). New York: Oxford University Press.

Goetz, A.T., & Causey, K. (2009). Sex differences in perceptions of infidelity: Men often assume the worst. *Evolutionary Psychology, 7*, 253–263.

Goetz, A.T., & Shackelford, T.K. (2006). Sexual coercion and forced in-pair copulation as sperm competition tactics in humans. *Human Nature, 17*, 265–282.

Goetz, A.T., & Shackelford, T.K. (2009). Sexual coercion in intimate relationships: A comparative analysis of the effects of women's infidelity and men's dominance and control. *Archives of Sexual Behavior, 38*, 226–234.

Goetz, A.T., Shackelford, T.K., & Camilleri, J.A. (2008). Proximate and ultimate explanations are required for a comprehensive understanding of partner rape. *Aggression and Violent Behavior, 13*, 119–123.

Goetz, A.T., Shackelford, T.K., Romero, G.A., Kaighobadi, F., & Miner, E.J. (2008). Punishment, proprietariness, and paternity: Men's violence against women from an evolutionary perspective. *Aggression and Violent Behavior, 13*, 481–489.

Goetz, A.T., & Steele, K. (2009). *Men's proprietary view of their romantic partners is specific to sexuality: An experimental study.* Paper presented at the 3rd International Conference on The Evolution of Human Aggression: Lessons for Today's Conflicts. Salt Lake City, UT, February 27, 2009.

Goetz, A.T., Shackelford, T.K., Weekes-Shackelford, V.A., Euler, H.A., Hoier, S., Schmitt, D.P., & LaMunyon, C.W. (2005). Mate retention, semen displacement, and human sperm competition: A preliminary investigation of tactics to prevent and correct female infidelity. *Personality and Individual Differences, 38*, 749–763.

Graham-Kevan, N., & Archer, J. (2009). Control tactics and partner violence in heterosexual relationships. *Evolution and Human Behavior, 30*, 445–452.

Hauert, C., Traulsen, A., Brandt, H., Nowak, M.A., & Sigmund, K. (2007). Via freedom to coercion: The emergence of costly punishment. *Science, 316*(5833), 1905–1907.

Hadi, A. (2000). Prevalence and correlates of the risk of martial sexual violence in Bangladesh. *Journal of Interpersonal Violence, 15*, 787–805.

Jeon, J., & Buss, D.M. (2007). Altruism towards cousins. *Proceedings of the Royal Society B, 274*, 1181–1187.

Johnson, M.P. (1995). Patriarchal terrorism and common couple violence: Two forms of violence against women. *Journal of Marriage and the Family, 57*, 283–294.

Kaighobadi, F., Starratt, V.G., Shackelford, T.K., & Popp, D. (2008). Male mate retention mediates the relationship between female sexual infidelity and female-directed violence. *Personality and Individual Differences, 44*, 1422–1431.

Koziol-McLain, J. Coates, C.J., & Lowenstein, S.R. (2001). Predictive validity of a screen for partner violence against women. *American Journal of Preventative Medicine, 21*, 93–100.

Lalumière, M.L., Harris, G.T., Quinsey, V.L., & Rice, M.E. (2005). *The causes of rape: Understanding individual differences in male propensity for sexual aggression.* Washington, DC: APA Press.

Lewin, T. (2001). In genetic testing for paternity, law often lags behind science. *The New York Times*, pp. 1, 28.

Maynard Smith, J. (1982). *Evolution and the theory of games.* Cambridge, UK: Cambridge University Press.

McKinney, F., Cheng, K.M., & Bruggers, D.J. (1984). Sperm competition in apparently monogamous birds. In R.L. Smith (Ed.), *Sperm competition and evolution of animal mating systems* (pp. 523–545). New York: Academic Press.

Meyer, S., Vivian, D., & O'Leary, K.D. (1998). Men's sexual aggression in marriage: Couple's reports. *Violence Against Women, 4*, 415–435.

Painter, K., & Farrington, D.P. (1999). Wife rape in Great Britain. In R. Muraskin (Ed.), *Women and justice: Development of international policy* (pp. 135–164). New York: Gordon and Breach.

Penton-Voak, I.S., Perrett, D.I., Castles, D.L., Kobayashi, T., Burt, D.M., Murray, L.K., & Minamisawa, R. (1999). Female preference for male faces changes cyclically. *Nature, 399*, 741–742.

Platek, S.M., Burch, R.L., Panyavin, I.S., Wasserman, B.H., & Gallup, G.G. (2002). Reactions to children's faces: Resemblance matters more for males than females. *Evolution and Human Behavior, 23*, 159–166.

Platek, S.M., Critton, S.R., Burch, R.L., Frederick, D.A., Myers, T.E., & Gallup, G.G. (2003). How much resemblance is enough? Sex difference in reactions to resemblance, but not the ability to detect resemblance. *Evolution and Human Behavior, 24*, 81–87.

Platek, S.M., Raines, D.M., Gallup, G.G., Mohamed, F.B., Thomson, J.W., Myers, T.E., et al. (2004). Reactions to children's faces: Males are still more affected by resemblance than females are, and so are their brains. *Evolution and Human Behavior, 25*, 394–405.

Platek, S.M., Keenan, J.P., & Mohamed, F.B. (2005). Sex differences in neural correlates of child facial resemblance: An event-related fMRI study. *NeuroImage, 25*, 1336–1344.

Rauhut, H., & Junker, M. (2009). Punishment deters crime because humans are bounded in their strategic decision-making. *Journal of Artificial Societies and Social Simulation, 12(3)*, 1. Online at <http://jasss.soc.surrey.ac.uk/12/3/1.html>.

Russell, D.E.H. (1982). *Rape in marriage.* New York: Macmillan Press.

Serran, G., & Firestone, P. (2004). Intimate partner homicide: A review of the male proprietariness and the self-defense theories. *Aggression and Violent Behavior, 9*, 1–15.

Schützwohl, A., & Koch, S. (2004). Sex differences in jealousy: The recall of cues to sexual and emotional infidelity in personally more and less threatening context conditions. *Evolution and Human Behavior, 25*, 249–257.

Shackelford, T.K. (2001). Cohabitation, marriage, and murder: Woman-killing by male romantic partners. *Aggressive Behavior, 27*, 284–291.

Shackelford, T.K., & Goetz, A.T. (2004). Men's sexual coercion in intimate relationships: Development and initial validation of the Sexual Coercion in Intimate Relationships Scale. *Violence and Victims, 19*, 21–36.

Shackelford, T.K., & Goetz, A.T. (2006). Comparative psychology of sperm competition. *Journal of Comparative Psychology, 120*, 139–146.

Shackelford, T.K., & Goetz, A.T. (2007) Adaptation to sperm competition in humans. *Current Directions in Psychological Science, 16*, 47–50.

Shackelford, T.K., & Mouzos, J. (2005). Partner killing by men in cohabitating and marital relationships: A comparative, cross-national analysis of data from Australia and the United States. *Journal of Interpersonal Violence, 20*, 1310–1324.

Shackelford, T.K., LeBlanc, G.J., & Drass, E. (2000). Emotional reactions to infidelity. *Cognition and Emotion, 14*, 643–659.

Shackelford, T.K., Buss, D.M., & Bennett, K. (2002). Forgiveness or breakup: Sex differences in responses to a partner's infidelity. *Cognition and Emotion, 16*, 299–307.

Shackelford, T.K., Goetz, A.T., Buss, D.M., Euler, H.A., & Hoier, S. (2005). When we hurt the ones we love: Predicting violence against women from men's mate retention tactics. *Personal Relationships, 12*, 447–463.

Shields, N.M., & Hanneke, C.R. (1983). Battered wives' reactions to marital rape. In R. Gelles, G. Hotaling, M. Straus, & D. Finkelhor (Eds.), *The dark side of families* (pp. 131–148). Beverly Hills, CA: Sage.

Starratt, V.J., Shackelford, T.K., Goetz, A.T., & McKibbin, W.F. (2007). Male mate retention behaviors vary with risk of female infidelity and sperm competition. *Acta Psychologica Sinica, 39*, 523–527.

Starratt, V.G., Goetz, A.T., Shackelford, T.K., McKibbin, W.F., & Stewart-Williams, S. (2008). Men's partner-directed insults and sexual coercion in intimate relationships. *Journal of Family Violence, 23*, 315–323.

Starratt, V.G., Shackelford, T.K., Goetz, A.T., & McKibbin, W.F. (2009). Only if he thinks she's cheating: Perceived risk of female infidelity moderates the relationship between objective risk of female infidelity and sexual coercion. Manuscript under editorial review.

Stith, S.M., Smith, D.B., Penn, C.E., Ward, D.B., & Tritt, D. (2004). Intimate partner physical abuse perpetration and victimization risk factors: A meta-analytic review. *Aggression and Violent Behavior, 10*, 65–98.

Symons, D. (1979). *The evolution of human sexuality*. New York: Oxford Univ. Press.

Thornhill, R., & Thornhill, N.W. (1992). The evolutionary psychology of men's coercive sexuality. *Behavioral and Brain Sciences, 15*, 363–421.

Thornhill, R., & Palmer, C.T. (2000). *A natural history of rape*. Cambridge, MA: MIT Press.

United States Department of Justice, Federal Bureau of Investigation. (2009). *Crime in the United States, 2008*. Retrieved from http://www.fbi.gov/ucr/cius2008/offenses/expanded_information/homicide.html

Watts, C., Keogh, E., Ndlovu, M., & Kwaramba, R. (1998). Withholding of sex and forced sex: Dimensions of violence against Zimbabwean women. *Reproductive Health Matters, 6*, 57–65.

Watts, C., & Zimmerman, C. (2002). Violence against women: Global scope and magnitude. *The Lancet, 359*, 1232–1237.

White, G.L. (1981). Some correlates of romantic jealousy. *Journal of Personality, 49*, 129–147.

Wilson, M., & Daly, M. (1992). The man who mistook his wife for a chattel. In J.H. Barkow, L. Cosmides, & J. Tooby (Eds.), *The adapted mind* (pp. 289–322). New York: Oxford University Press.

Wilson, M., & Daly, M. (1993). An evolutionary psychological perspective on male sexual proprietariness and violence against wives. *Violence and Victims, 8*, 271–294.

Wilson, M., & Daly, M. (1996). Male sexual proprietariness and violence against women. *Current Directions in Psychological Science, 5*, 2–7.

Wilson, M., & Daly, M. (1998). Lethal and nonlethal violence against wives and the evolutionary psychology of male sexual proprietariness. In R.E. Dobash, & R.P. Dobash (Eds.), *Rethinking violence against women* (pp. 199–230). Sage: Thousand Oaks, CA.

Wilson, M., Daly, M., & Daniele, A. (1995). Familicide: The killing of spouse and children. *Aggressive Behavior, 21*, 275–291.

Wilson, M., Johnson, H., & Daly M. (1995). Lethal and nonlethal violence against wives. *Canadian Journal of Criminology, 37*, 331–361.

Wilson, M., Daly, M., & Wright, C. (1993). Uxoricide in Canada: Demographic risk patterns. *Canadian Journal of Criminology, 37*, 331–361.

Yllo, K., & Straus, M.A. (1990). Patriarchy and violence against wives: The impact of structural and normative factors. In M.A. Straus & R.J. Gelles (Eds.), *Physical violence in American families: Risk factors and adaptations to violence in 8145 families* (pp. 383–399). New Brunswick, NJ: Transaction.

CHAPTER 12

Grandparents and Extended Kin

Harald A. Euler

Abstract

The four categories of grandparents differ in their investment in grandchildren, with the maternal grandmother investing the most and taking an outstanding position, followed usually by the maternal grandfather, the paternal grandmother, and the paternal grandfather. This discriminative grandparenting is manifest in many investment proxies, like contact and care, expressions of affection, grandchild survival, and others. The recurrent rank order of the four grandparent categories is best explained by two basic reproductively relevant variables: relationship uncertainty and sex-specific reproductive strategy. The expression of these variables is moderated by several conditions, among others residential proximity, marital status of grandparent, family size, type of joint activity, age of child, and grandparent–grandchild similarity. In natural fertility populations, the availability of the maternal grandmother increases chances for child survival. In industrialized countries, the positive impact of grandparental support is still evident in high-risk family conditions under circumstances of duress.

Keywords: Grandparental care, grandparental investment, grandparental solicitude, relationship uncertainty, reproductive strategy, grandmother hypothesis, sex-chromosome relatedness, animal grandparenting, matrilineal bias, sex-biased investment

Introduction

Grandparenting is a rare phenomenon in the animal kingdom but a ubiquitous and universal feature of human societies. In forager or hard-scrabble subsistence societies, the availability of a grandmother promotes infant survival and may be a matter of life or death for the child. The disappearance of traditional vertical family structures in industrialized societies and their replacement by horizontal friendship structures has been proclaimed by social scientists in the recent past. If the three-generation family were a thing of the past, grandparents and grandparenting would matter no longer. But the empirical evidence contradicts this. Despite media-promoted youth ideals, middle-aged people generally do not mind becoming grandparents. Rather, the first grandchild is welcomed with pride and joy (Fischer, 1983). Even modern grandparents dote on their grandchildren, prefer to have at least a few of them, and eagerly reveal the number if there are many. On the other side, the relationships with one's own grandparents are in general not considered irrelevant, boring, or wearing. At least some grandparents, most often the maternal grandmother, are considered an enrichment for oneself and the family and remain life-long in one's heart with cherished memories.

Modern demographic changes have the potential to impact family relationships pervasively. Birth rates and conjugal stability have decreased, while life expectancy and residential mobility have increased. In most Western countries, siblings, aunts, uncles, and cousins dwindle in number ("bean-pole" families). Due to past increases in life expectancy, the shared lifespan of grandparents and grandchildren is currently greater than ever (Coall & Hertwig, 2010a; Uhlenberg, 2004) but on the decline because of increasing age at first childbirth. Whereas in the past, the few surviving grandparents had many grandchildren, in the top-heavy families of today many surviving grandparents have only few grandchildren or grandchild sets[1] (Hagestad, 2006). Conjugal instability makes patch-work and single-parent families more the rule than an exception, and adoptions between unrelated individuals blur biological ties. State welfare provisions have largely crowded out dependence on kin support in raising children, whereas increased female participation in the labor force increases the at least occasional demand for kin support. Rising divorce rates and child custodies typically given to mothers marginalizes men from their families and opens the back door for a reentrance of matrilineal or at least matrifocal family structures (Bridges, Roe, Dunn, & O'Connor, 2007; Dench & Ogg, 2003). Compared to earlier times, many grandparents in industrialized countries are relatively affluent. Do all these changes make for completely new family dynamics? In this chapter, I argue that a biological core of human family relationships exists, including transgenerational and extended family relationships, which remains largely unaffected by these demographic changes but finds its expression in various societal circumstances. At the same time, it is clearly acknowledged that biological factors do not express themselves purely but always in interaction with environmental contexts.

Next to evolutionary theories, the topic of grandparenting is primarily addressed in sociological theories, occasionally also in economic (e.g., Cox, 2003) or rational, exchange-theoretic accounts (e.g., Friedman, Hechter, & Kreager, 2008). Sociologists have conducted research on grandparenting earlier than evolutionary biologists and produced more publications, which deliver valuable empirical information but are mostly atheoretical, with no or little attention paid to biological aspects. Therefore, reference is made to sociological studies only when they provide evidence for or against evolutionary hypotheses. Disregarded are, for example, U.S.-ethnocentric studies on racial or ethnic differences in grandparenting (see Hunter & Taylor, 1998; Kamo, 1998; Williams & Torrez, 1998), or studies that categorize grandparents into nonevolutionary phenomenological typologies[2] (e.g., homemaker, young-and-connected, remote, frail grandmothers, Baydar & Brooks-Gunn, 1998; apportioned, symbolic, individualized, remote grandparenting styles, Wood & Robertson, 1976). With exceptions (e.g., Cherlin & Furstenberg, 1986; Dench & Ogg, 2003; Fingerman, 2004; Kennedy, 1990; King, 2003; Kivett, 1991; Rossi & Rossi, 1990; Troll, 1983), sociological studies about grandparent–grandchild relationships do not consider sex differences inherent in human nature, but are generally unisex and gender-blind. These studies use generic children, generic parents, and generic grandparents, rather than, for example, maternal grandmothers, fathers, and granddaughters. All four categories[2] of grandparents are frequently lumped into one category. If grandmothers and grandfathers are differentiated, lineage may be not discerned, a variable of undeniable importance. Sometimes, a distinction is not even made between consanguineal and affinal relatives, or aunts/uncles and grandparents are lumped together (e.g., Robins & Tomanec, 1962). In an evolutionary approach, Socrates' wise advice to cut nature at its joints (like the butcher does) must be heeded.

For a comprehensive understanding of grandparenting, it is advisable to look beyond one's own disciplinary borders. Sociological and economic theories take a social macroperspective or elaborate the influence of norms and values (Coall & Hertwig, 2010a), which is typically underexposed in Darwinian accounts. Unfortunately, a disciplinary divide exists with respect to the topic of grandparenting. Publications from the "other side" are referred to only in a minority of works (Coall & Hertwig, in press). It appears wise to be open to nonevolutionary findings, but a restriction to works with some relevance for Darwinian explanations of grandparent–grandchild relationships is necessary here.

In this chapter, I argue that, to understand grandparent–grandchild relationships, their Darwinian fitness consequences need to be understood. Grandparenthood is characterized by relationship-specific features of an evolutionary heritage, and the same applies to relationships with aunts and uncles, nieces and nephews, and cousins. An evolutionary analysis can also shed light on grandparent–parent relationships, including in-law conflicts, because

---

[1] A grandchild set is constituted by the children of one adult child.

[2] Grandparent "categories" in this chapter denote the four different kinds of grandparents given by grandparent sex (grandfather, grandmother) and lineage (maternal, paternal).

parents are mediators of grandparent and grandchild relationships. Intergenerational relationships, with their mutual investments and emotional distances, are characterized by a robust structural core that can be parsimoniously accounted for by a few basic reproductively relevant variables, most notably genetic relatedness and reproductive strategy (Euler, Hoier, & Rohde, 2009; Euler & Michalski, 2007). Both variables—sex of grandparent and sex of parent (Uhlenberg & Hamill, 1998)—lead to pervasive asymmetries in family relationships and result in gender biases with a natural core.

The Biology of Grandparenting

Universal species-specific features are candidates for adaptations caused by particular evolutionary selection pressures. It is hypothesized that grandparenthood triggers psychological adaptations with relationship-specific features shaped by ancestral Darwinian fitness consequences, and the accumulated evidence relevant to this hypothesis is presented. Two basic human reproductive conditions are clearly sex-specific: (1) Because of their higher obligatory investment into each single reproduction (Trivers, 1972), females could, in the ancestral past, best maximize their genetic replication by maximizing maternal care, whereas for human males, with their high reproductive potential, the opportunity costs for parental investment were higher than for females. (2) Maternity is certain, whereas paternity may be uncertain. These two sex-specific conditions led to asymmetries that still pervade various aspects of family relationships, including grandparental investment into their adult children and their grandchildren.

Relationship Uncertainty

The Romans knew that *pater semper incertus est*, the Code Napoléon recognized the legal importance of paternity uncertainty, and the often-unspoken relevance of paternity assurance is rather ubiquitous (e.g., Daly & Wilson, 1982). The role of paternity certainty in grandparenting, which should be called *relationship certainty*, was first mentioned by Dawkins (1976). Throughout human history up to the present, grandparents had varying degrees of biological relatedness to their grandchildren and corresponding relationship certainties. Because maternity always has been certain (except for occasional modern maternity ward mix-ups), the relationship of the maternal grandmother is certain. The maternal grandfather and the paternal grandmother, however, each have one link of paternity uncertainty, and the paternal grandfather has two links.

The prevalence of misattributed paternity is often indicated to be around 10% (e.g., Buss, 2003, p. 236), but this estimate may be too high. A more conservative and arguably more accurate estimate of the prevalence in modern Western populations is around 3%, and there is some evidence that the prevalence of misattributed paternity has been on a slight decline for decades (Voracek, Haubner, & Fisher, 2008)—which supports the assumption that, in ancestral times, it might have been higher. Estimates from the magnitude of differences of investments into relatives of the next generation (nephews, nieces, and grandchildren) between matrilines and patrilines suggest that the average paternity discrepancy during our evolutionary past has been over 10% (Gaulin, McBurney, & Brakeman-Wartell, 1997; Hoier, Euler, & Hänze, 2001). Under the assumption that, with respect to paternity uncertainty, we execute adaptations to our ancestral environments, even if this entails a current mismatch (perceived cuckoldry is higher than actual cuckoldry), relationship certainty is a feature to be considered when evaluating preferential grandparental investment. In their own fitness interests, that is, in their unconscious effort to maximize their genetic replications in future generations, maternal grandmothers can be expected to invest, relatively, the most into their grandchildren, paternal grandfathers the least, with the maternal grandfather and the paternal grandmother in between.

Sex-chromosome Relatedness

The coefficient of relatedness between grandparent and grandchild, with mislabeled paternity and marriages between relatives ignored, is usually quantified as $r = 0.25$. The parent and his or her biological child share half of the genes ($r = 0.50$) by common descent (allele configurations), which makes half of half for the grandparent–grandchild relatedness, irrespective of grandparent or grandchild sex. This calculation, however, applies only for autosomal genes. The sex chromosomes complicate the matter because males are heterozygous (XY) for the sex chromosome. The Y chromosome passes directly down from the grandfather to his grandsons, whereas the X chromosome undergoes recombination. The heterosomal relatedness between grandparent and grandchild is thus asymmetrical with respect to sex of grandparent and grandchild (Table 12.1). With respect to Y-chromosome relatedness, the paternal grandfather is 100% related to

Table 12.1 Heterosomal Relatedness Between Grandparents and Grandchildren

	Grandfathers (Y-chromosome relatedness)		Grandmothers (X-chromosome relatedness)	
	Maternal	Paternal	Maternal	Paternal
Grandsons	**0** (4.41)	**100** (3.61)	**25** (4.97)	**0** (4.10)
Granddaughters	**0** (4.58)	**0** (3.75)	**25** (5.31)	**50** (4.35)

Bold numbers: Average % of shared sex-chromosome genes; numbers in parentheses: mean ratings of grandparental solicitude by adult grandchildren; data from author (N = 2,965; 1,050 males, 1,915 females).

his grandsons and 0% related to granddaughters, whereas the maternal grandfather is 0% related to both grandsons and granddaughters. With respect to X-chromosome relatedness, the paternal grandmother is 50% related to her granddaughters and 0% to her grandsons. The maternal grandmother is 25% related to both her granddaughters and grandsons (for a graphical illustration, see Fox, Sear, Beise, Ragsdale, Voland, & Knapp, 2010, p. 3). The X-chromosome contains approximately 8% of all human genes (National Center for Biotechnology Information, 2009), many of them affecting reproductive success and linked with autosomes that are associated with fertility and intelligence.

Two studies have investigated whether sex-chromosomal relatedness affects grandparental preferences for the sex of the grandchild. Chrastil, Getz, Euler, and Starks (2006) analyzed two sizeable samples of questionnaire data from adolescent and adult recipients of grandparental care. Various predictions based on sex-chromosome similarities were not supported. For example, paternal grandfathers did not show a preference for grandsons over granddaughters, as seen in the second data column in Table 12.1, such that paternal grandfathers did not receive higher solicitude ratings by grandsons than by granddaughters. Fox et al. (2010) investigated in mostly historical data from seven traditional populations how the presence of the grandmother (coresiding in the same home or village vs. living somewhere else) affected grandchild survival, differentiated according to grandmaternal and grandchild sex. Obvious associations between the extent of X-chromosome relatedness, as shown in the right part of Table 12.1 (bold numbers), and child survival were evident. In all seven populations, boys survived better with the maternal grandmother around than with the paternal grandmother around, whereas in four of the seven populations girls survived better with the paternal grandmother than with the maternal grandmother around. In all but one population, the presence of the paternal grandmother added more to granddaughter survival than to grandson survival.

A reanalysis of the solicitude data of the Chrastil et al. (2006) study with respect to the X-chromosome relatedness between grandmothers and grandchildren also failed to find evidence of impact on grandparental solicitude. As can be seen in the values in parentheses on the right part of Table 12.1, paternal grandmothers received higher solicitude ratings by granddaughters than by grandsons, but so did maternal grandmothers, even with a larger effect size (d = 0.19) than for the paternal grandmothers (d = 0.08). With respect to grandparental solicitude, heterosomal relatedness had no detectable effect.

Fox et al. (2009) conjecture that the differences between the studies could be due to mechanism differences between survivorship and "conscious behaviour" (p. 5). Although it may be contested that grandparental solicitude is a prototypic or even adequate example of conscious behavior, it is agreed that there are differences, possibly categorical ones, between grandparentally influenced infant survival in traditional societies and grandparental solicitude as rated by adult grandoffspring in modern societies. Otherwise, speculations about the reason for the differences between the two study results seem premature.

Reproductive Strategy

If relationship uncertainty was the only factor influencing the magnitude of grandparental investment, the maternal grandfather and the paternal grandmother should, all else being equal, show an equal amount of grandparenting. Two confounding factors must be taken into account. First, grandparents tend to come in pairs, so that by in-pair mutual influence, the maternal grandmother elevates the engagement of her husband with the grandchildren, whereas the paternal grandmother has a mate with the lowest relationship certainty. Second, in heterosomal relatedness, the paternal grandmother has a slight edge over the maternal grandfather (Table 12.1). These factors would have opposing effects. The first factor is not so strong and so robust that it alone can satisfactorily explain the larger involvement of the maternal grandfather as compared to the paternal grandmother. Therefore, along with other researchers, the sex-specific reproductive strategy is incorporated into the model to explain preferential grandparental investment (e.g., Euler & Michalski, 2007; Euler & Weitzel, 1996; Huber & Breedlove, 2007).

For a female mammal, the obligatory minimal amount of investment in each single reproduction is incomparably larger than the corresponding investment of the male (Trivers, 1972), with the consequence that the male reproductive potential is orders of magnitude larger than the female potential and the opportunity costs for the sexes are different. To maximize the number of grandoffspring, a female must maximize maternal investment, whereas a male may, but must not necessarily, maximize paternal investment to the same extent. Thus, maternal investment is more obligatory, paternal investment more facultative. This asymmetry between the sexes has consequences for intergenerational solidarity, as does the asymmetry of relational certainty.

Compared with other mammals, humans have a very long period of dependence. In hunter-gatherer societies, the capabilities for food acquisition surpass own caloric needs only in late adolescence (Kaplan, Hill, Lancaster, & Hurtado, 2000). To be able to fulfill these demands, ancestral human mothers needed help to raise offspring, as mothers still do today. According to current Western ideology, the child's father or the current mate of the mother is considered the most important helper. He is expected to deliver meat (hunter-gatherers) or provide financial support (modern societies), to give protection, to help socialize the child, and so on. Indeed, all over the world, women prefer as husbands men who are able to deliver resources (Buss, 1989).

However, apart from indirect care (e.g., providing shelter) the actual contribution of fathers to the chores of raising children is, on average, smaller than thought or wished. It depends with whom human fathers are compared. If human fathers are compared with other primate or mammal fathers, men do well because in other species paternal investment occurs rarely. If men are compared with women, their contribution to direct child care is rather small, for both forager fathers and modern fathers. Two kinds of fathers might be considered models of good fathering: Aka pygmy fathers and progressive U.S.-American academic faculty members. As for pygmy fathers, their time investment for direct care pales in comparison to the investment by mothers (Hewlett, 1991). For young U.S.-American professors who tried to obtain tenure and had a child under 2 years old, 75% agreed with the statement that husband and wife ought to share equally in child care, household work, and paid work (Rhoads & Rhoads, 2004). The actual performance, however, did not match the professors' attitudes. Whereas 67% of eligible female professors took the available paid leave, only 12% of the males did so. Questioned on 25 child care tasks that covered the gamut of daily care that can be split between both parents, the female academics did all 25 tasks significantly more often than did the male academics. Whether one looks at hunting returns in preagricultural societies or child care in industrialized societies (e.g., Presser, 1989), men are not as dependable as once thought (Hawkes, O'Connell, & Blurton Jones, 1997; but see Peccei, 2001). They roam and rage, fight and philander, are busy outdoors, or prefer to work at the office. But the baby needs constant and dependable attention.

Like many other species, human females have resorted to cooperative breeding and the engagement of so-called *allomothers* to manage child care (Hrdy, 1999, 2009), rather than to rely only on the father. Preferred allomothers are female kin—own mother, sisters, and preadolescent daughters or nieces. The largest contributions seem to come from the maternal grandmother and maybe the infant's older siblings (Sear & Mace, 2008). The allomothers contribute to the survival of the infant and to the mother's rate of reproduction. The average interbirth interval in ancestral populations was probably about 3 years. This appears long compared to birth rates of the recent past, before the onset of the modern demographic transition, but in the Pleistocene there was no stored baby food, no baby carriages, nor other conveniences that enabled mothers to become pregnant again soon after delivery. Compared to other great apes, a birth interval of 3 years is rather short (Galdikas & Wood, 1990).

The various kin allomothers have different qualifications. Sisters typically have own infants to care for, but to watch two babies is not much more work than to watch one. Daughters or nieces are well equipped by their life history; that is, their long duration of late childhood. But the mother's own mother is the best possible candidate. She is experienced both in child care and food gathering, her mental and somatic capabilities are still considerable, she is willing to help as she has a fitness interest in the grandchildren's well-being (Hawkes, O'Connell, & Blurton Jones, 1989), and due to early menopause and the long postmenopausal period, she is not burdened with provisioning her own infants. Her husband, the maternal grandfather, may be of additional help, but his opportunity costs are higher, which means that he is generally less inclined to help his daughter than is his spouse.

Grandparental resources are limited, and their allocation between sons and daughters[3] must be maximized. How much should be invested in the adult son and his offspring, compared to the daughter and her offspring? The son is not as burdened with child care as is the daughter, but he can be supported in his reproductive effort, not by time for child care, but by the transfer of status and wealth if socioecological conditions permit transformation of status and wealth into sexual access. Such conditions lead to a comparably high reproductive variance of males, as seen in traditional pastoral societies with a mating system of optional polygyny. Ancestral Pleistocene environments, however, were presumably not characterized by extreme sex differences in reproductive variance. Under conditions of relative pervasive monogamy, be it ecologically imposed, as in the Pleistocene, or culturally imposed, as in modern societies, time investment into the adult daughter and her children rather than in the adult son and his children should be the more desirable option for postmenopausal women. Whether these investments are offered by the grandparent or asked for by the daughter is a moot question; in general a mutual understanding can be assumed. Whether daughter-biased investment is subsumed under matrilateral bias, allomothering, or cooperative breeding, the ultimate cause derives from the sex-specific reproductive strategy of humans.

---

[3] For consistency of relationship terms, the three involved generations are generally referred to as grandparent (grandmother, grandfather), child (son, daughter) or parent, and grandchild (grandson, granddaughter). The "child/son/daughter" is thus an adult and parent to the grandchild.

The Grandmother Hypothesis

A postreproductive lifespan is rare and short among animals (Cohen, 2004), because reproductive and other physiological systems tend to fail in tandem. The early, nonfacultative, and irreversible cessation of fertility in humans followed by potentially many healthy postmenopausal life years is, on first sight, biologically anomalous and in need of explanation. For the first half of the past century, until it was refuted by Medawar (1957), the prevailing view of the biological value of the elderly was expressed in the Lotka model (Lotka, 1907), which assumed that elderly individuals did not contribute substantially to the fitness of populations. Williams (1957) was the first to consider human menopause to be an adaptation by arguing that " . . . it may have become advantageous for a woman of forty-five or fifty to stop dividing her declining faculties between the care of extant offspring and the production of new ones" (pp. 407–408). This idea was later labeled the "grandmother hypothesis," not quite correctly so because Williams was considering the role of the woman as a mother. It was Hamilton (1966) who first described the "special value of the old woman as mother *or grandmother*" (p. 37, italics added), but was uncertain whether it was an adaptation in its own right. The hypothesis presented by Williams has also been called the "stopping early hypothesis" (Hawkes, O'Connell, Blurton Jones, Alvarez, & Charnov, 1998, p. 1336), the "prudent mother hypothesis" (Hrdy, 1999, p. 275), the "altriciality lifespan hypothesis" (Peccei, 1995), or simply the "mother hypothesis" (Peccei, 2001), depending on which aspects of the hypothesis are highlighted. Also the grandmother hypothesis (or hypothes*es*) comes in different versions, depending on whether the focus is on the timing of menopause, the postmenopausal lifespan ("grandmother's clock hypothesis," Hrdy, 1999), or the investment in grandchildren (Hrdy, 1999; Peccei, 2001). When the question is about investment in children or grandchildren, however, the "or" might make for the wrong question. Both parts often cannot be disentangled because much support from grandparents to grandchildren is indirect via parents (Hagestad, 2006).

As can be gathered from the many different labels for the intuitively appealing grandmother hypothesis, the debate continues in biological anthropology about whether menopause is indeed an adaptation, a by-product, or modern artifact (for a summary see Voland, Chasiotis, & Schiefenhövel, 2005). However, there is convincing evidence that grandmaternal help can contribute to the fitness of the mother and to the survival of the grandoffspring (Hawkes et al., 1989; Hawkes, O'Connell, Blurton-Jones, Alvarez, & Charnov, 2000; Lahdenperä, Lummaa, Helle, Tremblay, & Russell, 2004; Sear & Mace, 2008), and thus to the fitness of the grandmother herself.

A Grandfather Hypothesis?

Women throughout the world live longer than men, but a long life also characterizes the latter. Also, men, although they do not experience menopause, do experience a postreproductive lifespan that might not be solely an artifact of modern longevity. Even among many contemporary foragers, many men are older than 50 years. Can men also boost their fitness by helping their offspring and by grandfathering? Although there is some supportive evidence, it seems restricted to particular life history traits and particular living conditions. Men do not generally gain more fitness (i.e., have more grandchildren) by grandfathering, at least not in monogamous societies (Lahdenperä, Russell, & Lumma, 2007). Compared to grandmothers, the investment of grandfathers is small (even when, as investment, all transfers of material, embodied, and relational resources are considered), as is also attested in modern societies by the amount of grandpaternal solicitude that is not prompted by the grandfathers' spouses (see below).

Greve and Bjorklund (2009) suggested a kind of sex-fair grandparent hypothesis called the *Nestor effect*, named after the respected oldest member of the Greek troop that beleaguered Troy. In addition to grandmotherly help in terms of child care, the experience and wisdom of elder group members, including men, as well as the bequests of their possessions, could have benefitted kin as well as other group members and—according to the authors—thus been a target of natural selection (kin and/or group selection). The emergence of old age in both sexes could thus be claimed to have contributed to the evolution of advanced culture. At present, the Nestor effect, the "fitness-enhancing effect of cumulative and integrative knowledge of some group members" (p. 163), is not yet supported by evidence, but is testable by investigating intergroup correlations between the number of Nestors in a group and the thriving of the group. Currently, there is no evidence regarding the adaptive significance of grandfathering.

Animal Grandparenting

Grandparenting refers to specific beneficial behaviors directed selectively toward the grandoffspring or its mother, not to the beneficial effects of the mere presence of the grandparent or the contribution of the elderly to the population in general. Occasional grandmothering has been observed in the context of general allomothering in various primates (Paul, 2005), including wild chimpanzees (Wroblewski, 2008), captive gorillas (Nakamichi, Silldorff, Bringham, & Sexton, 2004), wild baboons (Collins, Busse, & Goodall, 1984), captive vervet monkeys (Fairbanks, 2000), and in dolphins (Norris & Pryor, 1991). Grandfathering has not been observed, with the possible exception of bottle-nosed dolphins (Wells, 1991). However, ape and monkey mothers do not seem to routinely share infant care preferentially with their mothers. Rather, they let other trusted females, including their mother among others, hold and protect their infants. If monkey mothers live in the same group, they might preferentially assist their daughters in various ways (see Hrdy, 2009; Paul, 2005), for example, rush to help defend the grandoffspring against attacks from infanticidal males, provide safety, and secure the young monkey's group rank. In addition, essential care of grandoffspring, including suckling, has been observed recently (Nakamichi, Onishi, & Yamada, 2009). All these forms of support might add in the long run to the daughter's birth rate and to the survival of the grandoffspring, as does the support by other related females in the group. However, regular infant care handed over from the daughter preferentially to her mother seems to be absent. Hrdy (2009) suggests the possibility of adaptive neurological or hormonal differences between human and other primate mothers, particularly postpartum oxytocin, but comparative evidence is lacking. The adaptation is hypothesized by Hrdy (2009) to have appeared with *Homo erectus* due to climate-induced dietary requirements for more nutritious plant foods, particularly provided by tubers, which are difficult to locate, access, and process. Aged group members, particularly postmenopausal women, were well equipped with botanical knowledge and sufficient endurance to take the role of provisioners for their daughters and their daughters' children (O'Connell, Hawkes, & Blurton Jones, 1999). The helping grandmothers had entered at this stage of human evolution. Her job qualifications, in the words of Hrdy (2009, p. 267), included that she was "experienced in child care, sensitive to infant cues, adept at local subsistence tasks, undistracted by babies of their own or even the possibilities of having them, . . . repositories of useful knowledge, [and] . . . unusually altruistic."

As to animals other than primates, potentially fitness-promoting grandparenting is reported to have been observed occasionally. For example, postreproductive bottlenose dolphin and pilot whale grandmothers are said to babysit, guard, and even suckle their grandoffspring (Carey & Gruenfelder, 1997). In the Seychelles warbler, a fraction of breeding females are deposed each year from their dominant position, and thereafter most of them help in feeding their grandoffspring nestlings rather than breed themselves (Richardson, Burke, & Comdeur, 2007).

Notwithstanding these animal examples of grandmothering, human grandparenting has a variety of features that, as an ensemble, make it unique (Broadfield, 2010). Three outstanding features are the regularity of grandparenting, the existence of grandfathering, and the extremely long female postreproductive lifespan. Contrary to earlier views, menopause is not restricted to humans (Paul, 2005) but occurs in several long-lived nonprimate species, such as some whales and dolphins (Perrin, Brownell, & DeMaster, 1984), and maybe elephants. However, the long human female postreproductive lifespan, which for many years or even decades can be productive and which enables a potentially long shared lifespan between grandparent and grandchild, sometimes even between great-grandparent and great-grandchild, is unrivalled in the animal kingdom.

Grandparents, Parents, and Grandchildren

In this section, methods to assess grandparental investment are detailed and the large body of empirical evidence for preferential grandparenting is reported. The predictions by evolutionary theory are generally straightforward, but a host of moderating variables complicates the matter. What are called *moderating variables* here may be considered primary variables from a nonbiological perspective, but the position is taken and defended that human nature is basic rather than negligible or secondary, also in grandparent–grandchild relationships. The question of parent–grandparent relationships in their connectedness to grandparent–grandchild relationships is also discussed, not in all necessary detail but only as offshoots of the evolutionary structure of grandparent–grandchild relationships. At the end of the chapter, I consider the practical consequences for modern societies by addressing two questions: What is the relevance of the findings for public policies? Do modern-day grandparents, apart from being a reserve babysitter, benefit measurably the grandchild's cognitive, emotional, and social development, and their health and well-being?

Assessment of Grandparental Investment

Investment in offspring is generally defined as any behavior that increases the offspring's fitness at some fitness opportunity costs to the investor (e.g., Clutton-Brock, 1991). In evolutionary theories of animal behavior, investments are grouped into three types (e.g., Daly & Wilson, 1983): calories, time, and risk acceptance. Getting food for children is still of prime importance in premodern societies, but rarely in industrialized states. Risk acceptance is likewise of less importance for human behavior, for whom to eat or avoid being eaten is not the primary survival task. But time is as limited as it has ever been. The time devoted to a grandchild, in terms of contact frequency and duration, is thus one of the main grandparental investment measures, not the least because contact is a pre-requisite for the formation of attachments. Additionally, transfer of possessions, in the form of inter vivos transfers or bequests, have become important grandparental investments since humans settled.

The time typically devoted to a grandchild is mostly measured by paper-and-pencil ratings (e.g., Euler & Weitzel, 1996). Who is asked to do the rating? For three reasons, adult grandchildren are often preferred over grandparents as study participants: (1) Everybody has had grandparents, but not everybody is a grandparent; (2) older study participants are more difficult to recruit than younger ones, and more often unsatisfied by a quick assessment procedure; and (3) if the rating questions imply preferential grandparenting, norms of impartiality may prevent grandparents from expressing favoritisms in self-descriptive statements. For example, Norwegian grandparents who were asked whether there was one grandchild with whom they felt a particularly strong connection did not reveal any preferences (Hagestad, 2006). Preferences of grandparents ought to be measured indirectly when grandparents are questioned. For example, instead of asking which grandchild is the dearest or the emotionally closest grandchild, one can ask: "Tell me an interesting story about any of your grandchildren that comes to your mind." (More often children of daughters than of sons came to mind in an unpublished study.[4])

---

[4] I thank Sabine Hoier for this observation.

Questioning grandparents about contact frequencies ("How often during the last 12 months have you seen grandchild X?") or contact latencies ("When did you last see grandchild X?") do not seem to carry a reporting bias. Such self-descriptive statements reveal the same or similar differences between grandparent categories as do retrospective statements about received grandparental investment (Pollet, Nelissen, & Nettle, 2008; Pollet, Nettle, & Nelissen, 2007; Uhlenberg & Hamill, 1998). Michalski and Shackelford (2005) have argued that contact frequencies could be an inadequate measure of grandparental investment as they do not indicate who initiated the contact. However, in light of the general correspondence between contact data and received investment data, this potential bias appears negligible. Pollet et al. (2007) controlled for contact initiative by restricting the sample to grandparents with children less than 16 years of age and by questioning grandparents about who usually initiates the contact (Pollet et al., 2007). Their results are comparable to the usual findings.

Adult or adolescent grandchildren do not have any qualms about stating which grandparent is the favorite, or even to respectively rank all four grandparents, and their statements about received grandparental care, even during childhood, show sufficient construct validity, as do ratings of emotional closeness. However, grandparental survival biases must be controlled for when adult grandchildren are asked about received grandparental care. The typical ranking of grandparent categories, with maternal grandmother on top and paternal grandfather at bottom (see below), may be confounded by the fact that, during childhood, more maternal grandmothers are alive than paternal grandfathers, due to later parenthood and earlier death of men as compared to women. Tran, Fisher, and Voracek (2009) argue that the methods used so far to remove the confounders of exposure time to the various grandparents were insufficient. An analysis of covariance with repeated measures, with exposure time as covariate, is deemed by these authors to be too general and, therefore, does not result in a targeted removal of only the specific covariate for each grandparent category. If, on the other hand, the analysis of retrospective solicitude ratings is restricted to the complete set of four grandparents alive during the participant's childhood, the different exposure time to the grandparents *after* childhood may, according to Tran et al. (2009), nevertheless bias the ratings.

Parents may be questioned about grandparental involvement. Among studies with an evolutionary approach, this was done first by Littlefield and Rushton (1986), who asked parents whose child had died about the amount of mourning of each grandparent.

The three generations of information sources (grandparents, parents, grandchildren) yield mostly comparable results, but grandparents themselves tend to ascribe the greatest importance to and express the highest satisfaction with the grandparental role, feel most closeness to kin, and claim the highest rate of contact (Dench & Ogg, 2003). This finding is not unexpected in the light of life history theory. During the last part of life, extra-parental nepotistic efforts often become the most salient life effort (Alexander, 1987). But comparable results cannot always be expected because families are not only asymmetrical due to sex asymmetries, but also asymmetrical depending on where the focal kin is anchored (Hagestad, 2006), and whether one looks up from there to the older or down to the younger generation.

As to samples reported in the empirical literature about grandparenting, they range from large, nationally representative samples (e.g., Hank & Buber, 2009; Pollet, Nettle, & Nelissen, 2006; Pollet et al., 2007, 2008; Uhlenberg & Hammill 1998) to student or community convenience samples (Bishop, Meyer, Schmidt, & Gray, 2009; Euler & Weitzel, 1996; Tran et al., 2009).

The Rank Order of Grandparent Categories

One of the most robust findings, across a wide range of grandparent–grandchild relationship variables and investment proxies, is the rank order of grandparent categories, as predicted by evolutionary theory: The top position, often by a considerable margin, is taken by the maternal grandmother, followed usually (exceptions in Pollet et al., 2008; Tran et al., 2009) by the maternal grandfather, the paternal grandmother, and the paternal grandfather (Bishop et al., 2009; Bridges et al., 2007; Daly & Wilson, 1980; DeKay, 1995; Dubas, 2001; Eisenberg, 1988; Euler & Weitzel, 1996; Fischer, 1983; Hartshorne & Manaster, 1982; Hodgson, 1992; Hoffman, 1978/1979; Kahana & Kahana, 1970; Kennedy, 1990; Laham, Gonsalkorale, & von Hippel, 2005; Littlefield & Rushton, 1986; Matthews & Sprey, 1985; McBurney, Pashos, & Gaulin, 2006; Mills, Wakeman, & Fea, 2001; Monserud, 2008; Pashos, 2000; Robins & Tomanec,

1962; Pollet et al., 2006, 2007, 2008; Rossi & Rossi, 1990; Russell & Wells, 1987; Salmon, 1999; Schiefenhövel & Grabolle, 2005; Scholl Perry, 1996; Smith, 1988, 1991; Steinbach & Henke, 1998; Uhlenberg & Hamill, 1998; van Ranst, Verschueren, & Marcoen, 1995). This rank order has also been obtained by many social science researchers who did not consider evolutionary predictions, were not (yet) aware of them, or can be assumed to have been theoretically disinclined to consider them. Most of the studies are from North America or Europe. Depending on the type of grandparental activity, marital status, cultural or other factors (see below), and method to control for exposure time to grandparents (Tran et al., 2009), the maternal grandfather and the paternal grandmother may change positions.

Tran et al. (2009) maintain that the insufficient control of residential distance and exposure time to the various grandparents may account for the laterality effect, at least partially and with respect to retrospective ratings of adult grandchildren. Unlike the effect of grandparent sex, which is agreed to be caused by biological causes, the laterality effect is assumed to be socially engendered. Whether this assumption is justified and generalizable, and is not sample- or measurement-specific, appears debatable. The laterality effect has been reported in many studies in which grandparents have been questioned about various proxies for investment, with different methods of data analysis (e.g., Cox, 2003; Michalski & Shackelford, 2005; Pollet et al., 2006, 2007, 2008).

CONTACT AND CARE
Preferential grandparental investment from an evolutionary perspective was first investigated by Smith (1988, 1991) with respect to jointly spent time. Differential investment among grandparents was derived only on the basis of relationship uncertainty, which would predict (1) most investment for the maternal grandmother, (2) less and equal investment for the paternal grandmother and the maternal grandfather, and (3) least investment for the paternal grandfather. Although predictions 1 and 3 were confirmed, prediction 2 was not confirmed; maternal grandfathers spent more time with the grandchildren than did paternal grandmothers. This pattern was seen in unilineal grandparents (those with grandchildren only through daughters or through sons) as well as in bilineal grandparents (grandchildren through daughters and sons). Moreover, the difference between the investment of grandmothers and grandfathers should have been the same as the difference between maternal and paternal grandparents, because in both comparisons there is a difference of two uncertainty links. The difference in the second comparison, however, was larger than in the first comparison. These two deviations from the predictions in the form of a matrilineal bias were explained post hoc by resorting to other factors.

Because a matrilineal bias of grandparental–grandchildren relationships had been evident from prior nonevolutionary studies (e.g., Fischer, 1986; Kahana & Kahana, 1970; Rossi & Rossi, 1990), Euler and Weitzel (1996) deduced an ordered prediction about grandparental solicitude from the combined effects of both sex-specific reproductive strategy (matrilineal bias) and paternity uncertainty. A convenience sample of both student and community participants (16–80 years old) were asked how much each grandparent had cared for them (*gekümmert*) up to the age of 7 years. The German verb *kümmern* has both a behavioral and a cognitive-emotional meaning, namely to care for, to look after, and to be emotionally and/or cognitively concerned about. From the total sample of 1,857 respondents, a subset of 603 cases were selected for analysis whose four grandparents were all still alive when the participant was 7 years old. The usual rank order of grandparent categories was obtained, and the maternal grandfather was rated significantly higher than the paternal grandmother. The effect sizes (partial η^2, that is, the variance attributable to the effect of interest divided by this variance plus error variance) were 0.11 for the lineage effect (maternal vs. paternal) and 0.17 for the effect of sex of grandparent. Also, Pollet et al. (2008) report the effect of grandparent sex to be larger than the lineage effect. Both effects account for a sizable proportion of the variance.

Of special interest, apart from the insufficiency of paternity uncertainty as the only basic determinant, is the finding that the maternal grandfather cared more than the paternal grandmother. If grandparental care giving were solely determined by a traditional gender role that ascribes child care predominantly to women, then both categories of grandmothers should provide more care than both grandfathers. Accordingly, this argument should apply particularly to the older grandchildren in the sample, whose grandparents presumably subscribe more to traditional gender roles than do grandparents of younger participants. However, the difference was statistically significant in the opposite direction.

For the older participants of the sample (40 years or more), the difference in favor of the maternal grandfather over the paternal grandmother was larger than for the younger participants.

The noted rank order of grandparent categories with respect to various contact measures (e.g., frequencies, durations, time since last contact; face-to-face or telephone contact) has been obtained in many studies (e.g., Hartshorne & Manaster, 1982; Laham et al., 2005; Pollet et al., 2006, 2007, 2008; Salmon, 1999; Scholl Perry, 1996; Uhlenberg & Hammill, 1998). As to care or solicitude measures (given care vs. received care), the same can be said (e.g., Bishop et al., 2009; Pashos, 2000; Steinbach & Henke, 1998). All these studies, however, have been done in modern states and not in traditional pastoral, expressedly patrilocal, or otherwise patrifocal societies or societal milieus. There are indications that, in the latter kind of samples, paternal grandparent–grandchild relationships play a more important role (Huber & Breedlove, 2007; King & Elder, 1995; Pashos, 2000) than maternal grandparent–grandchild relationships (see the section "Cultural Context"). Even within the contemporary United States, rural youths, particularly those adolescents living on farms, have more frequent contact with paternal grandparents than do urban youths (King, Silverstein, Elder, Bengtson, & Conger, 2003).

So far, occasional and facultative contact and care has been considered, but foster care means permanent and obligatory contact and care. When we think of foster parents or adoptive parents, we tend to think of strangers from outside the family who were identified by a social agency. In traditional societies, however, kinship care is the rule, and kinship foster care placements are increasingly favored in Western countries as well (Hegar & Scannapieco, 1995, 1999). Which kin is preferred as foster parent?

In several traditional societies from which data are available (Inuit, East Pacific Rotuman, Trobiand), the favored adopter is the maternal grandmother (Daly & Wilson, 1980; Schiefenhövel & Grabolle, 2005). Among the Trobriand people, firstborn children are given away for adoption more often than laterborn children (Schiefenhövel & Grabolle, 2005). Of these firstborn children ($n = 50$), 19 (38%) were given to the maternal grandmother. Of the 69 laterborn children, 14 (20%) were given to the maternal grandmother. If maternal grandparents are compared with paternal grandparents, the former were adopters in 60 cases, the latter in only five cases.

In several U.S. states, the majority of foster care placements are kinship care (Scannapieco & Hegar, 2002). Over 50% of these placements go to the maternal grandmother, followed by an aunt in 33% of the placements.

EXPRESSIONS OF AFFECTION

One of the most frequently used measures for assessing the closeness between grandparent and grandchild is a rating of the emotional closeness or relationship closeness (e.g., Bishop et al., 2009; Bridges et al., 2007; Cox, 2003; Dench & Ogg, 2003; Eisenberg, 1988; Fischer, 1983; Hoffman, 1978/1979; Kennedy, 1990; Laham et al., 2005; Matthews & Sprey, 1985; McBurney et al., 2006; Mills et al., 2001; Robins & Tomanec, 1962; Rossi & Rossi, 1990; Russell & Wells, 1987; Scholl Perry, 1996; Silverstein & Ruiz, 2006). Such a rating is generally swiftly, willingly, and discriminatively provided by adolescent and adult grandchildren. It appears that the rating of emotional closeness is one of the best, if not the best, single indicator of grandparental investment. Out of available alternative indicators, it seems to be the least influenced by situational factors, such as residential proximity, and personal factors, such as age of the grandchild. Time investments in infants and young children, if done sensitively and responsively, lead to lifelong emotional bonds between the caregiver and the recipient of care (Bowlby, 1969). Because the amount of grief upon the loss (separation or death) of one of the bond members is correlated with the strength of the bond, it is no surprise that Littlefield and Rushton (1986) found the grandparental parent-rated mourning upon the death of a (grand)child was differentiated along the recurrent hierarchy of grandparent categories, with the maternal grandmother rated to mourn the most.

Affection can also be expressed in terms of verbal address. A loved person is often addressed with a diminutive and endearing name, which is often self-invented. Euler, Hoier, and Pölitz (1998) asked study participants how in childhood they addressed their four grandparents. The maternal grandmother stood out. She was significantly more often than the other three grandparents addressed with a love-expressing name. For example, the maternal grandmother might be addressed with the English equivalent of something like "dear granny" (German: *liebes Omilein*), whereas the paternal grandmother was referred to by a generic name (e.g., "the other grandmother," or "the grandmother from Hanover").

TANGIBLE TRANSFERS

The empirical analysis of tangible transfers from grandparents to grandchildren has received little attention from evolutionarily informed scientists (but see Pollet et al., 2008), with a few exceptions from outside psychology or anthropology (e.g., Cox, 2003). Therefore, not much more than a few hypotheses derived from evolutionary considerations can be presented.

Various types of tangible transfers to the next or next-but-one generation must be distinguished, particularly inter vivos transfers and bequests. Tied transfers, like housing down payments or tuition fees, may be yet another category. Especially, the many, small, and clandestine inter vivos transfers are not comparable to bequests or intended bequests. The former are more responsive to economic and demographic circumstances than the latter (McGarry, 1999), are given more often by donors who are themselves under liquidity constraints, and go more often to less well-off children, whereas the latter are more often divided equally, as they are more responsive to equity norms. Therefore, inter vivos transfers, especially small ones, can be expected to go more often to children of daughters than of sons (Pollet et al., 2008), not the least because of more contact with children of daughters. A hypothesis that specifies more differences between the four grandparents will not be ventured here. The paternal grandparents, as well as the maternal grandfather, might want to make up for the lesser time investment in the grandchild, compared to the maternal grandmother. Thus, Pollet et al. (2008) found maternal grandparents to provide a wider range of benefits, more essentials, gifts, and extras for the infant than paternal grandparents, but with respect to money for household costs and childcare, as well as loaning money, there were no lineage differences. Finally, larger material or financial bequests might be better translated into reproductive success by a son than by a daughter. All these considerations are additionally under the proviso of legal constraints and cultural norms of the particular population.

In hunter-gatherer and traditional societies, the net flow of the resources is from the old to the young. In postmodern societies, however, like the United States, Europe, and Japan, the net flow is to the old because of public pensions, government-financed care, and the like (Lee, 2010). Despite this massive resource consumption by the old, they still assist the younger generations with their time and also with money.

CHILD SURVIVAL

Child survival is a preferred fitness indicator for a woman in behavioral ecology and biological anthropology. The contributions of various kin to child survival have, therefore, been studied repeatedly, and the results are summarized by Sear and Mace (2008). The authors reviewed 45 studies, from a variety of historical and contemporary (typically natural fertility) populations, as to whether the presence of various kin persons had a positive, negative, or neutral effect on child survival. Next to the mother, who had a positive effect on child survival in all 28 populations with relevant information, the availability of a maternal grandmother was the best survival insurance for the child. Her presence increased child survival in nine out of 13 studies. Possibly as beneficial were older siblings, but only six studies included relevant data. Men (fathers, maternal and paternal grandfathers) all had in the overall balance score detrimental effects on child survival, perhaps because men eat a share of the food (with possibly priority servings), leaving less to dish out to the children. If a sum survival benefit score for each category of kin is calculated, with +1 for a positive, –1 for a negative, and 0 for a neutral effect, and the sum divided by the number of studies, the following scores (+1.00: always beneficial; –1.00: always detrimental) are obtained: mother 1.00, father –.36, maternal grandmother 0.46, paternal grandmother 0.18, maternal grandfather –.67, paternal grandfather –.27, older sibling 0.67. It needs to be mentioned that the summary of Sear and Mace (2008), as well as its conclusions, recently have been disputed by Strassman and Kurapati (2010), who concluded on the basis of the same data that overall nonsignificant findings predominate, even in the case of the maternal grandmother.

Compared to the generally supportive maternal grandmother, the presence of the paternal grandmother (the mother-in-law of the child's mother) increased child mortality in six out of 17 studies (e.g., Voland & Beise, 2002). How can this be explained, when the paternal grandmother cannot be characterized by mischievous personality traits because she is (usually) also a maternal grandmother to her daughter's children? Because women are the reproductively limiting sex, the control of female reproduction is in the inclusive fitness interest of family members in natural fertility populations, with a conflict of interest between the maternal and paternal family members. The maternal grandmother has already invested extensively in her daughter, whereas the paternal grandmother has hardly invested in the same woman, her daughter-in-law. The fitness interests of mother and daughter thus overlap considerably, but those of mother and daughter-in-law are restricted to the time of marriage (Voland, 2007; Voland & Beise, 2005). A daughter-in-law is in principle replaceable, a daughter is not. The fitness interest of the maternal grandmother is thus the conservation of her daughter's maternal resources, whereas the fitness interest of the paternal grandmother is exploitation of her daughter-in-law's maternal resources. Available maternal grandparents, especially maternal grandmothers, thus add to grandchildren's survival and well-being, whereas the presence of paternal grandparents, especially the paternal grandmother, tends to push maternal fecundity, earlier reproduction, and shorter interbirth intervals (Mace & Sear, 2005). The conflict of interest between the matriline and the patriline can even be traced down to the genetic level, in which maternally imprinted genes may inhibit fetal growth and paternally imprinted genes may stimulate fetal growth (Burt & Trivers, 2006).

Moderating Variables

Human evolutionary behavioral approaches tend to strip the subject matter of various kinds of particular distal (past developmental) and proximate (current situational) influences to make the gestalt of human nature more salient. The basic biological variables, like grandparental and parent sex, do indeed explain a sizeable share of the variance in the grandparent–grandchild relationship, but variance is left unaccounted for or is not even tapped by the samples. It comes, therefore, as no surprise that the matter gets complicated when other variables are taken into account. What are called moderating variables here may sound belittling because, for social scientists, these variables may be those of foremost interest, whereas grandparent or parent gender are at best mere confounding variables. But because the intention is to provide an evolutionarily informed account, which is still a minority position among family researchers, this position is defended while at the same time remaining open to an interdisciplinary approach, which is needed here (Coall & Hertwig, in press) as elsewhere. A listing of variables influencing grandparenting is found also in Pollet et al. (2006, 2007) and Uhlenberg and Hamill (1998).

RESIDENTIAL PROXIMITY

The effect of residential distance between grandparent and grandchild, which can vary between coresidence to halfway around the globe, has an understandable effect on grandparental investment. The effect is strongest with respect to frequency of visits and shows up dependably in almost every study that includes residential distance as a variable (e.g., Cherlin & Furstenberg, 1986; Hodgson, 1992; Lawton, Silverstein, & Bengtson, 1994; Pollet et al., 2006, 2007, 2008; Rossi & Rossi, 1990; Uhlenberg & Hamill, 1998; for an exception, see Salmon, 1999). Other measures also are responsive to distance, like gift giving (Bishop et al., 2009), solicitude ratings (Euler & Weitzel, 1996), amount of grandchild care (Hank & Buber, 2009), time spent together (Smith, 1991), and closeness of relationship (Robins & Tomanec, 1962). Obviously, modern communication means, such as telephone or e-mail, reduce the influence of geographical distance (Salmon, 1999).

Residential distance is thus a factor to be controlled for, especially when comparing populations that vary in residence patterns (matri-, patri-, neolocality). In the studies from industrialized countries, which generally have neolocal residence patters, the residential distances generally do not differ between the categories of grandparent (e.g., Euler & Weitzel, 1996; Pashos, 2000; Smith, 1991; Thomas, 1989), but there are exceptions of closer proximity to paternal (e.g., King & Elder, 1995; Salmon, 1999) or to maternal grandparents (Michalski & Shackelford, 2005).

The general lack of a shorter distance to maternal grandparents than to paternal grandparents in neolocal societies is at odds with the strong version of the grandmother hypothesis (Hawkes et al., 2000). The problem may be explained by other and overriding sex-biased dispersal determinants in non-natural fertility populations (Koenig, 1989), or by romantic expectations of dependable male support with child care when a new couple initiates joint residence. Moreover, the grandmother is really needed when the mother suffers from hardship or duress, as when the father has deserted, when financial support is insufficient, or when the mother is suffering for other reasons. In these situations, either the grandmother or the mother might reduce their geographical distance, which remains undetected when looking at general dispersal patterns in industrialized states. The pattern of moving closer during hardship is reported from natural fertility populations, in which the contribution of the father to child care is mixed (Mace & Sear, 2005; Sear & Mace, 2008) because the father may desert or die. The woman's mother may move nearby to help if the child's father is absent or if the mother remarries (Marlow, 2005).

For an evolutionary analysis, the interaction between residential proximity and the categories of grandparents is of interest. Euler and Weitzel (1996) reported that the negative correlations between residential distance and solicitude ratings varied with the number of the grandparent's uncertainty links. The negative correlation was lowest for the maternal grandmother and highest for the paternal grandfather, with the other two categories of grandparents in between. This observation points to the fact that the caregiving of the maternal grandmother is the least facultative of all four grandparents—that is, the least dependent on conducive opportunities and circumstances—a suggestion also supported by the effect of separation from the partner (see the next section). The maternal grandmother is the grandparent to count on, particularly during times of hardship.

MARITAL STATUS OF GRANDPARENT, PARENT, AND GRANDOFFSPRING

Married grandparents care more for the grandchild than do unmarried grandparents (Baydar & Brooks-Gunn, 1998; King, 2003; Pollet et al., 2007; Reitzes & Mutran, 2004; Silverstein & Marenco, 2001). Unmarried grandparents may be differentiated into widowed, divorced, and separated grandparents, and married grandparents into those married once and those remarried after widowhood or divorce. Widowhood has less negative effect on grandparenting than does divorce (King, 2003; Pollet et al., 2007), separation, and remarriage (Uhlenberg & Hamill, 1998).

Grandparental marital status can be associated with other factors relevant for grandparental involvement. For example, divorced persons have fewer children than married persons and thus fewer grandchildren, and the more grandchildren, the less care for each focal grandchild. Because most studies are cross-sectional, care must be taken to eliminate confounds. However, the decline in contact with grandchildren also showed up in the longitudinal study by Cherlin and Furstenberg (1986).

Of interest for an evolutionary approach is the interaction of marital status of grandparent with grandparent sex and lineage; that is, the effect of marital status of each grandparent on involvement with grandchildren. Because grandparents typically come in pairs, their care is similar due to shared obligations that act as a confound when assessing the independent involvement of each grandparent category. Partnership can end because of death of a partner, separation, or divorce. Widowhood and separation/divorce have different implications with respect to trade-offs in life efforts (i.e., mating effort vs. nepotistic effort), which is manifest in the comparison of grandparental solicitude between widowed grandparents, on the one hand, and separated or divorced grandparents, on the other. Whereas widowed grandparents did not differ from nonwidowed grandparents, there are obvious differences between the grandparent categories as to the effect of living separated from the spouse (Euler & Weitzel, 1996). For maternal grandmothers, the permanent presence of a mate had no effect on her solicitude; for the paternal grandmother it had some negative effect. For the grandfathers, however, there was a large difference attributable to whether they were living with a spouse (see also Dench & Ogg, 2003; Uhlenberg & Hamill, 1998). Paternal grandfathers living separately from their spouses (or ex-spouses) got a mean solicitude rating of 1.77, which is on a 6-point rating scale (1 = no solicitude) next to nothing. What is true for fathers is equally and still true for grandfathers: Putative paternal effort is actually to a large portion mating effort (Anderson, Kaplan, & Lancaster, 1999).

If parents divorce, the grandparent–grandchild relationship often suffers, particularly or only on the patrilineal side (Hagestad, 2006; Silverstein, Giarrusso, & Bengtson, 2003). The divorce of a daughter may even increase the contact between the maternal grandparents and the grandchildren, due to increased parental support solicited by the daughter and offered by her parents (see Denham & Smith, 1989). During and after divorce, mothers turn to their mothers, often as confidants, whereas fathers reduce contact and communication with their parents (Hagestad, Smyer, & Stierman, 1984) and pick up dating again (Johnson, 1988). The negative impact of parental divorce on grandparent–grandchild relations is found primarily in contact frequency, less so or not at all in emotional closeness (Bridges et al., 2007).

One study (Pollet et al., 2007) included the marital status of the adult grandchild as a variable, and it was not associated with grandparental contact frequencies.

FAMILY COMPOSITION
Number of Grandchildren
When investigating the effect of number of grandchildren in the family on grandparenting, it may be important to differentiate between grandchildren

and grandchild sets (Uhlenberg, 2004; Uhlenberg & Hamill, 1998), a distinction which is rarely made. The children of one adult child comprise a grandchild set. To babysit two children together (one set) is less than double the effort of babysitting two children in different sets. A grandmother with four children in four sets of one grandchild each is more in demand than with four children in one set. From the grandchild's view, the number of grandchild sets determines with how many cousin sets the child has to compete for the grandparent's attention.

Basic investment economics and demand considerations let us predict that the more grandchildren or grandchild sets a grandparent has, the higher is the total investment into grandchildren but the greater the dilution of investment; that is, the smaller the share for each particular grandchild. This is indeed a repeated finding (e.g., Coall, Meier, Hertwig, Wänke, & Höpflinger, 2009; Uhlenberg & Hamill, 1998; Smith, 1991). The more cousins (Laham et al., 2005) or the more aunts or uncles (Euler et al., 2009) an adult grandchild reports, the lower is the solicitude rating for the grandparent.

Relational uncertainty alone does not explain why maternal grandfathers invest more than the paternal grandmothers, as is commonly found. This finding also can be explained, in part, by coresidence of grandparents (Gaulin et al., 1997; McBurney et al., 2002) and/or by preferential investment in daughters over sons due to sex-specific reproductive strategy (Euler & Weitzel, 1996). Laham et al. (2005) suggest an alternative explanation (*preferential investment hypothesis*), which may be called *outlet theory*. The maternal grandfather and the paternal grandmother differ, on average, in the number of paternity-certain grandchildren ("outlets"). The maternal grandfather has the more certain outlets in the children of his daughter rather than in the children of his son for whom he would be the paternal grandfather. The paternal grandmother, however, who might also be a maternal grandmother, prefers to invest as the maternal grandmother in the children of her daughter rather than as a paternal grandmother in the children of her son. This outlet bias adds to the investment of the maternal grandfather and detracts from the investment of the paternal grandmother. Laham et al. (2005) present empirical support for their preferential investment hypothesis. If the maternal grandfather has other grandchildren through daughters, but the paternal grandmother does not, the preference for the maternal grandfather over the paternal grandmother should be most evident.

If, in contrast, the paternal grandmother has other grandchildren through daughters, but the maternal grandfather does not, the hypothesis would predict a preference for the paternal grandmother over the maternal grandfather. Laham et al. did find a preference for the maternal grandfather only in the first case, but not in the second one. However, a preference reversal in the second case was not observed.

As Laham et al. (2005) concede, their outlet considerations amount to small effect sizes. The outlets may constitute a bias and might need to be controlled, but they alone cannot account for the generally found higher solicitude of the maternal grandfather over the paternal grandmother. My database does not contain information about the existence of other grandchildren, but rather about the number of parents' siblings. If the father has as siblings only a sister, and the mother only a brother, the solicitude of the paternal grandmother is not rated higher by the adult grandchild than that of the maternal grandfather, and neither is it rated higher if the father has as siblings only sisters and the mother only brothers. Bishop et al. (2009) tested the outlet hypothesis and did not find support for it. Contrary to the prediction, various investment behaviors of the maternal grandfather were not rated higher by the grandchildren than were investment behaviors of the paternal grandmother when there were more certain outlets (cousins through the father's sister) available for the paternal grandmother.

Whether the maternal grandfather invests more than the paternal grandmother depends mainly on the gender-specificity of the investment behavior in question (Euler & Michalski, 2007). In most behaviors, the maternal grandfather is on average more engaged than the paternal grandmother, except for strongly gendered behaviors, such as cooking or making clothes for the grandchild.

Sibling Constellation of Parent
Euler et al. (2009) found a particular deviation from the pattern of lower grandparental solicitude ratings by adult grandchildren the more siblings the linking parent had. If the parent was a singleton, the solicitude ratings were higher, compared with a parent having a sibling, only for singleton mothers, not for singleton fathers. That is, grandparents who had as the only child a son received slightly lower solicitude ratings than grandparents who had a son plus another sibling, irrespective of the sex of the sibling. Various hypotheses were examined (e.g., sibling competition, conflict between mother-in-law and

daughter-in-law) and discarded. The best explanation for this phenomenon was a cohort sampling artifact. Many German parents of the recent past (maybe at present as well) preferred to have a name heir. If the first child was a boy, a second child was not desired. If the first child, however, was a girl, the parents gave it another try in hope for a boy. Such parents thus do not get children solely out of longing and love for a child irrespective of its sex, but partially for genealogical reasons (status display). Among the population of parents with a singleton son are, therefore, assumedly more parents with such genealogical interests than among parents with a singleton daughter. If such parents do not love children as much as other parents, they also care less for grandchildren.

Birth Order of Parent
Because children, except for twins, are born successively into the family, they get different amounts of parental attention even if parents try to invest equally in their children (Hertwig, Davis, & Sulloway, 2002). This and the order-induced differential niche-picking of siblings lead to a variety of personality differences between siblings (Sulloway, 1996, 2007), typically of small magnitude. Particularly, middleborns show less family solidarity and identity than do firstborns or lastborns (Salmon, 2003; Salmon & Daly, 1998).

Because parents are the mediators between grandparents and grandchildren, the parent's births order could also influence the investment of the grandparent. Indeed, Salmon (1999) found that, according to adult grandchildrens' reports, grandparents had significantly less contact with grandchildren of their middleborn daughters or sons than with grandchildren of firstborn and lastborn offspring. In contrast, Euler and Michalski (2007) found only minimal and largely statistically nonsignificant effects of parental birth order on grandparental solicitude ratings provided by adult grandchildren. Although the topic of birth order was not brought up first by evolutionary theorists, but is of psychoanalytic origin (Adler, 1927) and has been investigated intensively in developmental psychology and related disciplines (e.g., Ernst & Angst, 1983), the author is not aware of any works outside of evolutionary psychology on grandparenting and parent's birth order.

Number of Living Grandparents
If grandparental engagement is partially determined by grandchild demand, one could expect that this engagement also depends on the number of still living grandparents. If there are three other grandparents potentially available, the grandchild demand could be split among these grandparents, whereas it would concentrate on one grandparent if he or she were the only one still around. However, neither Euler and Weitzel (1996) nor Pashos (2000) found support for this possibility. The participants' ratings of a grandparent's past solicitude were not influenced by the number of other grandparents still alive during the participants' childhood.

The author is not aware of any other study that addressed this question. Uhlenberg and Hammill (1998) do not list the number of still-living grandparents of a child as one of the factors that make a difference with respect to mutual contact.

Genetic Relatedness
Apart from paternity uncertainty and differences in sex-chromosomal relatedness, stepparenting introduces another obvious relatedness factor with clear impact on grandparenting. Grandparental investment is reduced if there are one or more stepchildren in the family (Eggebreen, 1992). The relationship with stepparents is less close than with biological parents (Aldous, 1995; Patterson, Hurt, & Mason, 1998).

AGE OF GRANDPARENT, MOTHER, AND GRANDCHILD

Evolutionary theory predicts grandparental investment to depend on its age-dependent fitness effect. For an infant grandchild, a caloric investment might mean child survival, whereas the same amount of food may have little fitness effect for an adolescent grandchild. The reproductive value of the grandchild—its age-specific reproductive potential—is highest at the beginning of the reproductive career. The first prediction is clearly supported by data. The frequency of contact is highest after the birth of the grandchild and gradually declines with age (Bridges et al., 2007; Dench & Ogg, 2003; Dench, Ogg, & Thomson, 1999; Kivett, 1985). Because grandchild age is correlated with grandparent age, and grandparent–grandchild contact frequencies may decline with increasing grandparent age (see below), care must be taken to disentangle both effects. The decrease of contact, however, is not correlated with closeness between grandparent and grandchild (Bridges et al., 2007), presumably because emotional closeness is an expression of a lasting attachment. As to the second prediction, the evidence is less clear, with the possible exception of high-risk conditions, like teenage pregnancies (Coall & Hertwig, 2010a).

Where maternal age has been investigated, it has been found to correlate negatively with grandparental investment (Fergusson, Maughan, & Golding, 2008; Smith, 1991; Uhlenberg & Hamill, 1998).

How grandparental investment varies with the age of the grandparent is less clear, for several reasons. Because the four categories of grandparents are on average of different ages, the effect of grandparent age must be separated from grandparent category, which sometimes has been neglected. With advanced age, somatic resources decrease but nepotistic interest in the well-being of descendants can be assumed to increase (Alexander, 1987), and it is unclear what the net effect could be. Furthermore, with increasing age, the physiological differences between older persons increase and with them the somatic and mental resources to invest in grandchildren, possibly clouding within-subject age effects in error variance. Finally, age effects can be assumed to differ between investment measures. Understandably, contact frequencies have been reported to decrease with advanced grandparent age (Baydar & Brooks-Gunn, 1998), whereas solicitude ratings by adult grandchildren showed only small and nonsignificant negative correlations with grandparents' age (Euler & Weitzel, 1996; Pashos, 2000). With respect to monetary transfers, the matter might be different again.

SEX OF GRANDCHILD

We have repeatedly seen that the sex of the grandparent and the sex of the parent (lineage) are important determinants of grandparental investment. How about the sex of the grandchild? Just as the parent–offspring conflict concerns both sexes equally and not primarily boys (Daly & Wilson, 1990), as assumed in the Freudian Oedipus complex, there is no theoretical reason to assume a main effect for a sex-biased grandparental investment. In interaction with other variables, however, such as cultural factors, parental resource capacity (Trivers & Willard, 1973), and type of joint activity, the matter is different.

It thus comes to no surprise that most studies find no or only small main effects (Euler & Weitzel, 1996; Pashos, 2000; Pollet et al., 2007; Spitze & Ward, 1998; van Ranst et al., 1995). If grandparents are asked about their overall investment or their emotional closeness to a grandchild, the sex of the grandchild does not matter (Robins & Tomanec, 1962; Thomas, 1989), but here a reluctance to express favoritism cannot be excluded. If adult grandchildren are questioned, females gave slightly higher ratings in some studies (e.g., Euler & Weitzel, 1996; Salmon, 1999), but not in others (e.g., Laham et al., 2005; Pashos, 2000; Robins & Tomanec, 1962; Spitze & Ward, 1998). A sex difference could here be due to a grandparental preference for females, or to the higher family sentiment of female compared to male respondents (Salmon & Daly, 1996), which would result in a positive rating bias in female grandoffspring. Such a bias, however, would assumedly have to affect all four grandparents equally. But Euler and Michalski (2007) reported that females rated only the care of the maternal grandparents and of the paternal grandmother higher than did male participants, whereas there was no difference for paternal grandfathers. But then, paternal grandfathers show the least devotion to grandchildren anyway, so that, for female respondents, they are only at the fringe of family.

A sex-biased preference appears if different types of joint activities are considered (Euler & Michalski, 2007). Because girls are in general emotionally and socially more responsive and ask more for help than boys do (Bischof-Köhler, 2006), assumedly grandchild-driven sex biases appear with certain activities, like cuddling. Across generations, same-sex dyads are slightly closer than cross-sex dyads (Thomas, 1994; Godoy et al., 2006). The principle "Like father, like son; like mother, like daughter" applies to grandparent–parent dyads (Euler et al., 2009), but also to grandparent–grandchild dyads (Euler & Michalski, 2007; Salmon, 1999).

The Trivers-Willard hypothesis (Trivers & Willard, 1973) states that parents "in better condition" (p. 91) can be expected to bias their investment toward male offspring and thus boost their fitness. In human behavior, this effect is sometimes supported, sometimes not supported, but rarely contradicted, where "better condition" is often defined as socioeconomic status (SES). Does the Trivers-Willard hypothesis apply to grandparental investment as well? Do grandparents bias their investment toward male grandchildren, if the parents are of high SES, and toward female grandchildren, if the parents are low in SES? The evidence is scanty at best. Serendipitous findings in favor of the hypothesis may be found (Duflo, 2003), but two studies that systematically addressed the question (Euler & Weitzel, 1996; Leek & Smith, 1991) found no clear support.

GRANDPARENT–GRANDCHILD RESEMBLANCE

If the four categories of grandparent invest in grandchildren according to their relationship certainty, genetic relationship certainty is referred to, not individual relationship certainty. For the latter, resemblance to the grandchild is a grandparent's cue for his or her individual relationship certainty. Because fathers are more willing to invest in their children according to their resemblance to their putative children than are mothers (e.g., Platek, Burch, Panyavin, Wasserman, & Gallup, 2002), the hypothesis is justified that phenotypical similarity between grandparent and grandchild influences grandparental investment depending on the number of paternal uncertainty links. Concretely, paternal grandfathers can be expected to make their investment the most dependent on similarity to the grandchild, maternal grandmothers the least. There is some, although not strong, evidence for this prediction. Leek and Smith (1991) found positive correlations between help given and personality similarity to adult offspring as well as to grandchildren. However, without differentiation as to grandparent and parent sex, this finding is too vague to bear on the hypothesis. Euler (1994) reported that the correlation between resemblance in behavior and/or appearance and the past solicitude rated by adult grandchildren were—over the four grandparent categories—inversely related to solicitude ($r = 0.37$ for the maternal grandmother, 0.39 for the maternal grandfather, 0.42 for the paternal grandmother, and 0.47 for the paternal grandfather). The differences between these coefficients, however, were not statistically significant.

TYPE OF JOINT ACTIVITIES

Men and women differ in their interests and thus also in their activities (e. g., Baron-Cohen, 2003; Mealey, 2000), and the same applies as a matter of course to grandparents. Social science studies have described the differences in role content between grandmothers and grandfathers, assumed to reflect traditional gender roles (summarized in Spitze & Ward, 1998). Grandfathers tend to engage more in instrumental, outside, and nonfamily activities in their relations with grandchildren (e.g., make repairs or teach swimming), whereas grandmothers do the "warmer," emotional supportive, family-related, or interpersonal activities with their grandchildren, especially the time-consuming activities. In the author's research (partially reported in Euler & Michalski, 2007), 230 students rated over 55 different activities (e.g., "picked me up from school"; "played games with me"; "was proud of me") how much each grandparent had done with them when they were a child. For 49 items, the standard pattern applied: Grandmothers did more than grandfathers, and matrilineal grandparents more than patrilineal grandparents (see also Bishop et al., 2009, for comparable results). There were two exceptions where grandfathers had been more engaged than grandmothers: "taught me skills" and "made repairs for me," but again, maternal grandfathers got higher ratings than did paternal grandfathers. Significant differences between grandmothers and grandfathers and/or between matrilineal and patrilineal grandparents were lacking only for four of the 44 activities that occurred rarely (e.g., "gave me a pet," "bought financial investments for me"), assumedly due to a psychometric floor effect.

Two questions, apart from the rarely occurring transfer of financial investments like bonds, stocks, or trust funds, asked for money received from grandparents ("gave me money," "gave money regularly outside of pocket money, like helped pay for my education or for a car"). For both questions, the pattern was standard as well; grandmothers more than grandfathers, and matrilineal grandparents more than patrilineal grandparents. However, other studies (e.g. Cox, 2003) report or claim that paternal grandparents tend to make more money transfers than maternal grandparents.

To determine which activities were the best predictors of grandparental solicitude, the overall solicitude rating for each grandparent was correlated with the 55 activity ratings (Euler & Michalski, 2007). The highest correlations (mostly $r > 0.60$) were obtained for time-consuming activities (e.g., "Spent time with me," "Played games with me") and for activities indicating empathy and emotional closeness (e.g., "Was proud of me," "Complimented me," "Encouraged me"). Devoted time and emotional closeness seem to be the best behavioral and subjective proxies of kin investment.

GRANDPARENT–PARENT RELATIONSHIP

In social science research, the quality of the relationship between parents and grandparents is considered as an important factor in determining the relationship between grandparent and grandchild (e.g., Chan & Elder, 2000; Hagestad, 2006; Uhlenberg & Hammill, 1998). This finding is a truism, because parents as legal guardians determine the amount of contact with the grandparents. More remarkable, however, is that the grandparent–parent relationship is typically considered as a sufficient explanation for the amount of grandparental involvement. From an evolutionary perspective, however, the question arises whether the grandparent–parent relationship itself might be explained by ultimate causes. Heeding Occam's razor, might the same basic evolutionary principles that explain differential grandparental investment also explain differences in grandparent–parent relationships?

The correlation between the quality of the grandparent–parent relationship and the grandparent's solicitude was found to be higher for mothers than for fathers, with the correlation differences decreasing in the well-known order of the four grandparent categories, from maternal grandmother to paternal grandfather (Euler & Michalski, 2007). This finding supports the assumption that the grandparent–parent relationships, rather than being an exclusively independent causal factor, can be seen as an integral part of the evolutionarily programmed basic intergenerational relationship structure and are themselves shaped by reproductive determinants and their adaptive consequences.

Euler et al. (2001, 2009) predicted the relationship quality of each of the eight possible grandparent–parent dyads by three fitness-relevant factors:

- *Consanguinity*: The ties to own adult offspring are closer than to their in-law spouses.
- *Sex-specific reproductive strategy*: The relationship to the adult daughter, and to her husband as her reproductive assistant, is better than the relationship to the adult son, because the daughter is more restricted to a strategy of maximizing parental care, whereas the son may have alternative options of maximizing mates. The loss of the daughter-in-law, who would care for her kids with her mother's help after an eventual separation, is—from the grandparental reproductive viewpoint—less detrimental than the loss of the son-in-law.
- *Paternity uncertainty*: A better relationship is expected between grandmothers and adult offspring than between grandfathers and offspring. Paternity uncertainty diminishes the value of the spouse; that is, it makes the relationship with the welcomed spouse, the son-in-law, less positive and the relationship with the "rejected" spouse, the daughter-in-law, less negative. As to in-law offspring, the relationship between mother-in-law and son-in-law would be predicted to be comparatively good, the one between mother-in-law and daughter-in-law relatively poor.

In agreement with these predictions, the grandparent–parent relationships were in the following order, from best to worst: mother–daughter, father–daughter, mother–son, father–son, mother-in-law–son-in-law, father-in-law–son-in-law, father-in-law–daughter-in-law, and mother-in-law–daughter-in-law. Comparable results for several of these dyads or combinations thereof are found in Fingerman (2004), Rossi and Rossi (1990), Szydlik (1995), and Young and Willmott (1957).

The core, or pivot, of intergenerational family relations is the mother–daughter relationship. The mother-in-law–son-in-law relationship is comparatively good, contrary to deprecative male jokes about the mother-in-law. The mother-in-law–daughter-in-law relationship, however, in agreement with cross-cultural stereotypes about the mother-in-law irritating the daughter-in-law, is the most contentious of all grandparent–parent relationships.

CULTURAL CONTEXT

Even if all the variables mentioned so far are taken into account, there still remains a considerable variance in grandparental investment between countries, cultures, and subcultures (Huber & Breedlove, 2007). For example, the common investment order of the four grandparents (matrilateral > patrilateral, grandmothers > grandfathers) may not hold for patrifocal societies. Pashos (2000) found among urban Greeks the standard pattern, but rural Greeks, particularly male respondents, rated the care by paternal grandparents higher than that by maternal grandparents. A comparable within-country difference has been observed in the United States. Grandchildren in farm families, as compared to rural nonfarm families or urban families, lived closer to their paternal than to their maternal grandparents, visited them more frequently, and rated the quality of their relationship higher (King & Elder, 1995; King et al., 2003). Urbanization alone, however, does not seem to make a difference, at least not in European countries (Pashos, 2000; Pollet et al., 2007; Tran et al., 2009).

Within Europe, a particular North–South gradient can be seen with respect to grandparental investment (Hank & Buber, 2009). Across ten European countries, the prevalence of *any* care (over the last 12 months) was negatively correlated with the prevalence of *regular* care (almost weekly or more often over the last 12 months). The probability for any care was highest in Denmark, Netherlands,

France, and Sweden, and lowest in Italy and Spain. Regular care, however, was provided more in Greece, Italy, and Spain, and less in Denmark, Sweden, and France. Coall and Hertwig (2010a) correlated over the ten countries the prevalence of regular grandparental care with fertility rate and found an amazingly high negative rank correlation ($\rho = -.88$). The reason for this correlation appears to be what economists call *crowding out*, the replacement of private investment (here grandparental care) by public investment (state-financed institutional child care). Northern European countries value gender equality and female participation in the work force and thus provide relatively generously state-financed institutional child care, as well as institutional and financial support for working women. In Southern European countries, in contrast, fewer women work in paid labor. If a Mediterranean mother decides to combine a job with having children, she has to rely on her parents' (particularly her mother's) regular and dependable support with child care more than a Nordic mother. Thus, the hurdle for combining job and child is higher for a Southern than for a Northern European mother.

The variables relevant for grandparental care are not covered exhaustively up to this point, because many variables are of minor relevance for an evolutionary analysis. Mentioned, without discussing the methodological problem of possible confounds, might be maternal education (divergent findings; Fergusson et al., 2008; Vandell, McCartney, Owen, Booth, & Clarke-Stewart, 2003), the mother's perception of her childhood attachment to her mother (if good, more grandparenting; Fergusson et al., 2008), grandparental education (divergent findings; Pollet et al., 2007; Uhlenberg & Hammill, 1998), grandparental health status (no effect; Cherlin & Furstenberg, 1986; Uhlenberg & Hammill, 1998), and grandparental religiosity (more investment from religious grandparents; King & Elder, 1999).

Grandparenting in Modern Societies
EFFECTS OF GRANDPARENTING
Effects in Grandchildren
If passages of this chapter might have sounded like an encomium on grandparental solicitude, we may ask the crucial question in science: How about the evidence? Does grandparental investment have a measurable impact on the development of the grandchild in developed countries? Or, is grandparenting a child survival insurance only in hard-scrabble traditional fertility populations, just a handy convenience for busy modern mothers, and otherwise a harmless mismatch between ancestral demands for survival and modern amenities? Coall and Hertwig (2010a) collected and evaluated the available publications and arrived at the following conclusions. Despite the considerable investment of time and money by grandparents, only a few studies have investigated the impact on dimensions softer than infant survival, like the grandchild's cognitive, verbal, and social abilities, and mental health and happiness. However, for risk families or situations of duress (e.g., teenage pregnancy, maternal depression, drug misuse), where paternal support is often absent, the available evidence suggests that emotionally close grandparents can be an invaluable asset, fostering the grandchild's development and buffering stressors. Help follows the economic principle of diminishing marginal utility: the worse the predicament, the more help matters (Cox, 2010).

Effects for Grandparents
Psychology textbooks on human motivation do not treat grandparenting as a pleasurable activity, but neither is parenting considered a motive in its own right (Daly & Wilson, 1995), an omission criticized a century ago by McDougall (1908). Life history theory, however, lists extra-parental nepotistic effort as one of the life efforts that people strive to undertake (Alexander, 1987). It thus comes to no surprise that grandparents generally find satisfaction in grandchild care (e.g., Giarrusso, Silverstein, & Feng, 2000) and bemoan the loss of a grandchild or when denied contact. Grandparenting has been shown to benefit the grandparents' physical and mental health (McClellan, Stanwyck, & Anson, 1993) and reduce the risk of morbidity and mortality (Brown, Consedine, & Magai, 2005; Brown, Nesse, Vinokur, & Smith, 2003). However, there is the proviso of moderation. If grandparents are forced into the role of primary caregivers, the impact on health and well-being may be negative (see Coall & Hertwig, 2010a). Grandparents like to provide a helping hand if needed, but they reject to overtake the permanent primary or exclusive responsibility for the grandchild.

CONSEQUENCES FOR PUBLIC POLICIES
Findings from evolutionary approaches may inform public policy makers, but an in-depth analysis is beyond the scope of this chapter, not the least because of differences between countries as to legal and social systems and availability of state-financed institutional child care. The implications for kinship foster care are obvious and have already begun

to be taken into account (Herring, 2008). Here, I restrict myself to a telling example of disregard for grandparental gender differences and to a recent suggestion that appears noteworthy.

To achieve racial parity, the South African government drastically increased public pensions to the country's poor elderly, who by 1993 received relatively high amounts, namely twice the median per capita income in rural areas. Many of these recipients were grandparents living with their grandchildren in "skip-generation" extended households, in which parents work and live elsewhere. Duflo (2003) investigated the impact of these allowances on the grandchildren's weight and was surprised to find that only the pensions given to grandmothers, and not to grandfathers, redounded to the benefit of grandchildren, and then only to granddaughters. In the last sentence of the paper, the authors asked why grandmothers prefer girls. This chapter gives the explanation: Maternal grandmothers are the most reliable investors, and *poor* grandmothers prefer granddaughters, in agreement with the Trivers-Willard hypothesis.

A noteworthy policy suggestion derived from the cooperative breeding hypothesis has recently been made by Sear and Dickins (2010). In Western countries, most pronouncedly in Europe, the decreasing birth rate jeopardizes the stability of social security systems, and the timing of reproduction, with teenage pregnancies on the one hand and delayed first birth on the other, is of great concern. Sear and Dickins suggest that the availability of a supportive kin network may explain why many women reproduce too early or too late. In low socioeconomic milieus, males tend to be undependable, but the kin network, particularly the mother, is frequently intact, coupled with pro-natal attitudes. This situation may trigger an ancestral mechanism to welcome a baby. In higher socioeconomic milieus, women prefer to invest in their human capital (education and professional career), and because of employment opportunities, disperse from their kin network. These women, consequently, opt for a shift away from a kin-based cooperative breeding strategy and lose the signal that reproduction is feasible and desirable. Instead, they hope to meet the right male partner whose probability of appearance drops with the woman's advanced career while her fertility decreases, too.

Aunts, Uncles, and Cousins

The analysis of investment by aunts and uncles has the advantage of avoiding coresidence as a confound. Brothers and sisters of a parent, unlike grandmothers and grandfathers, typically do not live together and thus invest into nieces and nephews independently of each other. Several studies have investigated the investment of consanguineal aunts and uncles by letting college students rate whether maternal or paternal aunts or uncles showed more concern or care (Gaulin, McBurney, & Brakeman-Wartell, 1997; Hoier, Euler, & Hänze, 2000; McBurney, Simon, Gaulin, & Geliebter, 2001; Tran et al., 2009; see also Rossi & Rossi, 1990). More care for the offspring of sisters than of brothers was reported, and more by aunts than by uncles, supporting the predictions from evolutionary theory. In addition, Tran et al. (2009) found that matrilateral aunts or uncles care more for nieces, whereas patrilateral aunts or uncles cared more for nephews.

If the familial investment by aunts and uncles is compared with that of grandparents, we may predict more investment, on average, by grandparents than by consanguineal aunts and uncles, although both kinds of relatives have the same degree of relatedness. However, both kinds of relatives, especially the females, typically differ in their reproductive value due to their age differences. In most cases, the grandmother is past her reproductive age, whereas the aunt is not. The reproductive opportunity costs for aunts, and to a lesser extend for uncles as well, is higher than that for grandmothers and grandfathers.

The role of genetic relatedness for feelings of closeness to nieces and nephews has been demonstrated by Segal, Seghers, Mechanic, and Castillo (2007). Monozygotic twins expressed greater closeness toward the children of their cotwin than did dizygotic twins. In accordance with previous studies, female twins from same-sex pairs expressed greater closeness toward their nieces/nephews than male twins from same-sex pairs. Correlations between perceived similarity to niece/nephew and closeness ratings were slightly higher for twins with male cotwins than for twins with female cotwins.

The relationship with cousins differs due to paternity certainty. The relationship is genetically more certain with the children of a mother's sister and less certain with children of a father's brother. Closeness of relationship, as measured by willingness to help, emphatic concern, and contact frequency covaried accordingly (Jeon & Buss, 2007).

Conclusion

The approach to intergenerational relations informed by evolutionary theory and adaptationist hypotheses has furthered our understanding of kin structures and is still relevant in modern societies because our motivational architecture has been shaped by ancestral reproductive effects. Such an approach can help to integrate contributions from separate disciplines, to ask meaningful questions, to guide research, to inform public policies, and to provide personal insights into one's own family life.

The basic reproductive asymmetry between the sexes is evident in various asymmetries of intergenerational family relationships. The matrilineal bias bestows the maternal grandmother with a unique and prominent role in grandparental relationships, as evident in many different forms of investment in grandchildren and particularly in feelings of emotional closeness, which can be considered the proximate process mediating the various forms of investment.

Mothers in ancestral environments often lived long enough to become grandmothers and make relationship-specific contributions to their inclusive fitness, and could thus become equipped with grandparent-specific adaptations (Daly, Salmon, & Wilson, 1997). For example, whereas parental investment is relatively insensitive to sex of offspring (Daly & Wilson, 1990) except in combination with parental status, grandparental investment is clearly sensitive to the parental sex and at the same time insensitive to the sex of the grandchild. Likewise, we ought not be surprised if studies were to reveal that fondness of grandoffspring does not match parental fondness of offspring. Grandparents frequently seem to take a particular grandparental pride in the sheer number of their grandchildren, which appears not to be equalled by parental pride in number of own offspring.

Family relationships is a topic addressed by various disciplines, which often take insufficient notice of each other (Coall & Hertwig, in press) but frequently can complement each other with their relative contributions. Evolutionary biology is our most esteemed model, but social science researchers have the longest research tradition here and have accumulated the largest body of data. Anthropologists remind us of the danger of ethnocentrisms. Evolutionary psychology appears to be the best candidate to advance an interdisciplinary approach to the study of intergenerational relationships and contribute to a theoretical integration by highlighting ultimate causations in modern environments and proximate causations mediated by social, institutional, economic, and legal contexts.

Future Directions

1. The increased availability of databases with large and even representative samples call for multivariate analyses that enable researchers to control for many variables and to identify configurations of relevant variables. Such analyses could—among other things—provide information as to the existence of the Trivers-Willard effect with respect to grandparental investment or the possible differences between inter vivos transfers and bequests. Multivariate designs may also shed light on the relation between residential distance and the grandmother hypothesis, when the latter predicts smaller distances to the maternal than the paternal grandparents.

2. A systematic comparison of matrifocal versus patrifocal societies and their impact on the investment hierarchy of the four grandparent categories is needed to put into perspective the typical investment hierarchy found in industrialized countries. Is there evidence for the lineage-specific conservation versus exploitation hypothesis in modern countries? For example, is grandparental pride in the number of grandchildren more pronounced for paternal than maternal grandparents?

3. The contributions of grandparents to the development of grandchildren is another area in which resilient evidence from divergent fields would be welcome.

4. Little is known on the impact of grandchildlessness on grandparents' happiness and well-being. If grandparents miss grandchildren dearly, is there a difference between voluntary and involuntary childlessness of the grandparents' adult offspring?

5. How is the contemporary information transfer accomplished between grandparents and grandchildren, in both directions?

6. What is the relation between fertility behavior in modern countries and grandparental investment, taking social and economic factors, as well as gender norms and attitudes, into account?

References

Adler, A. (1927/2008). *Menschenkenntnis* [Knowledge of human nature]. Köln, Germany: Anaconda Verlag.

Aldous, J. (1995). New views of grandparents in intergenerational context. *Journal of Family Issues, 16*, 104–22.

Alexander, R.D. (1987). *The biology of moral systems*. New York: Aldine de Gruyter.

Anderson, K.G., Kaplan, H., & Lancaster, J.B. (1999). Paternal care by genetic fathers and stepfathers I: Reports from

Albuquerque men. *Evolution and Human Behavior, 20,* 405–431.

Baron-Cohen, S. (2003). *The essential difference. Men, women and the extreme male brain.* London: Allen Lane/Penguin Books.

Baydar, N., & Brooks-Gunn, J. (1998). Profiles of grandmothers who help care for their grandchildren in the United States. *Family Relations, 47,* 385–393.

Bischof-Köhler, D. (2006). *Von Natur aus anders. Die Psychologie der Geschlechtsunterschiede* (3rd ed.) [Different by nature. The psychology of sex differences]. Stuttgart, Germany: Kohlhammer.

Bishop, D.I., Meyer, B.C., Schmidt, T.M., & Gray, B.R. (2009). Differential investment behavior between grandparents and grandchildren. The role of paternity uncertainty. *Evolutionary Psychology, 7,* 66–77.

Bowlby, J. (1969). *Attachment.* London: The Hogarth Press.

Bridges, L.J., Roe, A.E.C., Dunn, J., & O'Connor, T.G. (2007) Children's perspectives on their relationships with grandparents following parental separation: A longitudinal study. *Social Development, 16,* 539–54.

Broadfield, D.C. (2010). The epiphenomenon of menopause in recent human history. *Behavioral and Brain Sciences, 33,* 19–20, in press.

Brown, S.L., Nesse, R.M., Vinokur, A.D., & Smith, D.M. (2003). Providing social support may be more beneficial than receiving it: Results from a prospective study of mortality. *Psychological Science, 14,* 320–27.

Brown, W.M., Consedine, N.S., & Magai, C. (2005). Altruism relates to health in an ethnically diverse sample of older adults. *The Journals of Gerontology. Series B: Psychological Sciences and Social Sciences, 60B,* P143–P152.

Burt, A., & Trivers, R. (2006). *Genes in conflict. The biology of selfish genetic elements.* Cambridge, MA: The Belknap Press of Harvard University Press.

Buss, D.M. (1989). Sex differences in human mate preferences: Evolutionary hypotheses tested in 37 cultures. *Behavioral and Brain Sciences, 12,* 1–49.

Buss, D.M. (2003). *The evolution of desire: Strategies of human mating* (2nd ed.). New York: Basic Books.

Carey, J.R., & Gruenfelder, C. (1997). Population biology of the elderly. In K.W. Wachter, & C.E. Finch (Eds.), *Between Zeus and the salmon: The biodemography of longevity* (pp. 127–160). Washington, DC: National Academy Press.

Chan, C.G., & Elder, G.H., Jr. (2000). Matrilineal advantage in grandparent–grandchild relations. *The Gerontologist, 40,* 179–190.

Cherlin, A.J., & Furstenberg, F.F., Jr. (1986). *The new American grandparent: A place in the family, a life apart.* New York: Basic Books.

Chrastil, E.R., Getz, W.M., Euler, H.A., & Starks, P.T. (2006). Paternity uncertainty overrides sex chromosome selection for preferential grandparenting. *Evolution and Human Behavior, 27,* 206–223.

Clutton-Brock, T.H. (1991). *The evolution of parental care.* Princeton, NJ: Princeton University Press.

Coall, D.A., & Hertwig, R. (2010a). Grandparental investment: Past, present, and future. *Behavioral and Brain Sciences, 33,* 1–19, in press.

Coall, D.A., & Hertwig, R. (in press). Grandparental investment: A relic of the past or a resource for the future? Paper submitted to *Current Directions in Psychological Science.*

Coall, D.A., Meier, M., Hertwig, R., Wänke, M., & Höpflinger, F. (2009). Grandparental investment: The influence of reproductive timing and family size. *American Journal of Human Biology, 21,* 455–63.

Cohen, A.A. (2004). Female post-reproductive lifespan: A general mammalian trait. *Biological Reviews, 79,* 733–750.

Collins, D.A., Busse, C.D., & Goodall, J. (1984). Infanticide in two populations of savanna baboons. In G. Hausfater, & S.B. Hrdy (Eds.), *Infanticide: Comparative and evolutionary perspectives* (pp. 193–215). Hawthorne, NY: Aldine.

Cox, D. (2003). Private transfers within the family: Mothers, fathers, sons, and daughters. In A.H. Munnell & A. Sundén (Eds.), *Death and dollars: The role of gifts and bequests in America* (pp. 168–209). Washington, DC: Brookings Institution Press.

Cox, D. (2010). Integrating evolutionary and social science approaches to the family. *Behavioral and Brain Sciences, 33*(1), in press.

Daly, M., & Wilson, M. (1980). Discriminative parental solicitude: A biological perspective. *Journal of Marriage and the Family, 42,* 277–288.

Daly, M., & Wilson, M. (1982). Whom are newborn babies said to resemble? *Ethology and Sociobiology, 3,* 69–78.

Daly, M., & Wilson, M. (1983). *Sex, evolution, and behavior* (2nd ed.). Belmont, CA: Wadsworth.

Daly, M., & Wilson, M. (1990). Is parent-offspring conflict sex-linked? Freudian and Darwinian models. *Journal of Personality, 58,* 163–189.

Daly, M., & Wilson, M. (1995). Discriminative parental solicitude and the relevance of evolutionary models to the analysis of motivational systems. In M.S. Gazzaniga (Ed.), *The cognitive neurosciences* (pp. 1269–1286). Cambridge, MA: MIT Press.

Daly, M., Salmon, C., & Wilson, M. (1997). Kinship: The conceptual hole in psychological studies of social cognition and close relationships. In J.A. Simpson, & D.T. Kenrick (Eds.), *Evolutionary social psychology* (pp. 265–296). Mahwah, NJ: Lawrence Erlbaum.

Dawkins, R. (1976). *The selfish gene.* Oxford, UK: Oxford University Press.

DeKay, W.T. (1995, July). *Grandparent investment and the uncertainty of kinship.* Paper presented at the Seventh Annual Meeting of the Human Behavior and Evolution Society, Santa Barbara, CA.

Dench, G., & Ogg, J. (2003). *Grandparenting in Britain: A baseline study* (2nd ed.). Eastbourne, UK: Antony Rowe Ltd.

Dench, G., Ogg, J., & Thomson, K. (1999). The role of grandparents. In R. Jowell, J. Curtice, A. Park, & K. Thomson (Eds.), *British Social Attitudes, the 16th report* (pp. 127–135). Aldershot, UK: Ashgate Publishing.

Denham, T.E., & Smith, C.W. (1989). The influence of grandparents on grandchildren: A review of the literature and resources. *Family Relations, 38,* 345–350.

Dubas, J.S. (2001). How gender moderates the grandparent–grandchild relationship: A comparison of kin-keeper and kin-selector theories. *Journal of Family Issues, 22,* 478–492.

Duflo, E.C. (2003). Grandmothers and granddaughters: Old age pensions and intrahousehold allocation in South Africa. *World Bank Economic Review, 17,* 1–25.

Eggebeen, D.J. (1992). Family structure and intergenerational exchanges. *Research on Aging, 14,* 427–47.

Eisenberg, A.R. (1988). Grandchildren's perspectives on relationships with grandparents: The influence of gender across generations. *Sex Roles, 19,* 205–217.

Ernst, C., & Angst, J. (1983). *Birth order: Its influence on personality*. Berlin, Germany: Springer.

Euler, H.A. (1994, October). *Diskriminative großelterliche Fürsorge* [Discriminative grandparental solicitude]. Paper at the Congress "Anthropologie Heute" of the Gesellschaft für Anthropologie, Humboldt-University of Berlin and University Potsdam, Potsdam, Germany.

Euler, H.A., Hoier, S., & Pölitz, E. (1998, May/June). *Kin investment of aunts and uncles: Why is the matrilateral bias stronger in women?* Paper at the 21st Annual Meeting of the European Sociobiological Society (ESS), Russian State University for the Humanities, Moscow, Russia.

Euler, H.A., Hoier, S., & Rohde, P.A. (2001). Relationship-specific closeness of intergenerational family ties: Findings from evolutionary psychology and implications for models of cultural transmission. *Journal of Cross-Cultural Psychology*, 32, 163–174.

Euler, H.A., Hoier, S., & Rohde, P. (2009). Relationship–specific intergenerational family ties: An evolutionary approach to the structure of cultural transmission. In U. Schönpflug (Ed.), *Cultural transmission: Psychological, developmental, social, and methodological aspects* (pp. 70–91). New York: Cambridge University Press.

Euler, H.A., & Michalski, R. (2007). Grandparental and extended kin relationships. In C.A. Salmon, & T.K. Shackelford (Eds.), *Family relationships: An evolutionary perspective* (pp. 230–255). New York: Oxford University Press.

Euler, H.A., & Weitzel, B. (1996). Discriminative grandparental solicitude as reproductive strategy. *Human Nature*, 7, 39–59.

Fairbanks, L.A. (2000). Maternal investment throughout the life span in Old World monkeys. In P.F. Whitehead, & C.J. Jolly (Eds.), *Old World monkeys* (pp. 341–367). Cambridge, UK: Cambridge University Press.

Fergusson, E., Maughan, B., & Golding, J. (2008). Which children receive grandparental care and what effect does it have? *Journal of Child Psychology and Psychiatry*, 49, 161–169.

Fingerman, K.L. (2004). The role of offspring and in-laws in grandparents' ties to their grandchildren. *Journal of Family Issues*, 25, 1026–1049.

Fischer, L.R. (1983). Transition to grandmotherhood. *International Journal of Aging and Human Development*, 16, 67–78.

Fischer, L.R. (1986). *Linked lives: Adult daughters and their mothers*. New York: Harper & Row.

Fox, M., Sear, R., Beise, J., Ragsdale, G., Voland, E., & Knapp, L.A. (2010). Grandma plays favourites: X-chromosome relatedness and sex-specific childhood mortality. *Proceedings of the Royal Society B*, 277, 567–573.

Friedman, D., Hechter, M., & Kreager, D. (2008). A theory of the value of grandchildren. *Rationality and Society*, 20, 31–63.

Galdikas, B.M.F., & Wood, J.W. (1990). Birth spacing patterns in humans and apes. *American Journal of Physical Anthropology*, 83, 185–191.

Gaulin, S.J.C., McBurney, D.H., & Brakeman-Wartell, S.L. (1997). Matrilaterial biases in the investment of aunts and uncles. *Human Nature*, 8, 139–151.

Giarrusso, R., Silverstein, M., & Feng, D. (2000). Psychological costs and benefits of raising grandchildren: Evidence from a national survey of grandparents. In C. Cox (Ed.), *To grandmother's house we go and stay: Perspectives on custodial grandparents* (pp. 71–90). New York: Springer.

Godoy, R., Reyes-García, V., McDade, T., Tanner, S., Leonard, W.R., Huanca, T., et al. (2006). Why do mothers favor girls and fathers, boys? A hypothesis and a test of investment disparity. *Human Nature*, 17, 169–189.

Greve, W., & Bjorklund, D.F. (2009). The Nestor effect: Extending evolutionary developmental psychology to a lifespan perspective. *Developmental Review*, 29, 163–179.

Hagestad, G.O. (2006). Transfers between grandparents and grandchildren: The importance of taking a three-generation perspective. *Zeitschrift für Familienforschung*, 18, 315–332.

Hagestad, G., Smyer, M., & Stierman, K. (1984). Parent-child relations in adulthood: The impact of divorcing in middle age. In R. Cohen, S. Weissman, & B. Cohler (Eds.), *Parenthood: Psychodynamic perspectives* (pp. 246–262). New York; NY: Guilford Press.

Hamilton, W.D. (1966). The moulding of senescence by natural selection. *Journal of Theoretical Biology*, 12, 12–45.

Hank, K., & Buber, I. (2009). Grandparents caring for their grandchildren: Findings from the 2004 Survey of Health, Ageing and Retirement in Europe. *Journal of Family Issues*, 30, 53–73.

Hartshorne, T.S., & Manaster, G.L. (1982). The relationship with grandparents: Contact, importance, role conceptions. *International Journal of Aging and Human Development*, 15, 233–245.

Hawkes, K., O'Connell, J.F., & Blurton Jones, N.G. (1989). Hardworking Hadza grandmothers. In V. Standen, & R.A. Foley (Eds.), *Comparative socioecology: The behavioural ecology of humans and other mammals* (pp. 341–366). London: Basil Blackwell.

Hawkes, K., O'Connell, J.F., & Blurton Jones, N.G. (1997). Hadza women's time allocation, offspring provisioning, and the evolution of long postmenopausal time spans. *Current Anthropology*, 38, 551–578.

Hawkes, K., O'Connell, J.F., Blurton Jones, N.G., Alvarez, H., & Charnov, E.L. (1998). Grandmothering, menopause, and the evolution of human life histories. *Proceedings of the National Academy of Sciences of the United States of America*, 95, 1336–1339.

Hawkes, K., O'Connell, K.J.F., Blurton-Jones, N.G., Alvarez, H., & Charnov, E. (2000). The grandmother hypothesis and human evolution. In L. Cronk, N. Chagnon, & W. Irons (Eds.), *Adaptation and human behavior: An anthropological perspective* (pp. 237–258). Hawthorne, NY: Aldine de Gruyter.

Hegar, R.L., & Scannapieco, M. (1995). From family duty to family policy: The evolution of kinship care. *Child Welfare*, 74, 200–216.

Hegar, R.L., & Scannapieco, M. (1999) (Eds.), *Kinship foster care: Policy, practice, and research*. New York: Oxford University Press.

Herring, D.J. (2008). Kinship foster care: Implications of behavioral biology research. *Buffalow Law Review*, 56, 495–556.

Hertwig, R., Davis, J.N., & Sulloway, F.J. (2002). Parental investment: How and equity motive can produce inequality. *Psychological Bulletin*, 128, 728–745.

Hewlett, B.S. (1991). *Intimate fathers: The nature and context of Aka pygmy paternal care*. Ann Arbor, MI: University of Michigan Press.

Hodgson, L.G. (1992). Adult grandchildren and their grandparents: The enduring bond. *International Journal of Aging and Human Development*, 34, 209–225.

Hoffman, E. (1978/79). Young adults' relations with their grandparents: An exploratory study. *International Journal of Aging and Human Development, 10*, 299–310.

Hoier, S., Euler, H.A., & Hänze, M. (2001). Diskriminative verwandtschaftliche Fürsorge von Onkeln und Tanten. Eine evolutionspsychologische Analyse [Discriminative solicitude of aunts and uncles. An evolutionary analysis]. *Zeitschrift für Differentielle und Diagnostische Psychologie, 22*, 206–215.

Hrdy, S.B. (1999). *Mother nature. Natural selection and the female of the species.* London: Chatto & Windus.

Hrdy, S.B. (2009). *Mothers and others. The evolutionary origins of mutual understanding.* Cambridge, MS: The Belknap Press of Harvard University Press.

Huber, B.R., & Breedlove, W.L. (2007). Evolutionary theory, kinship, and childbirth in cross-cultural perspective. *Cross-Cultural Research, 41*, 196–219.

Hunter, A.G., & Taylor, R.J. (1998). Grandparenthood in African American families. In M.E. Szinovacz (Ed.), *Handbook on grandparenthood* (pp. 70–86). Westport, CT: Greenwood Press.

Jeon, J., & Buss, D.M. (2007). Altruism towards cousins. *Proceedings of the Royal Society B: Biological Sciences, 274*, 1181–1187.

Johnson, C.L. (1988). Postdivorce reorganization of relationships between divorcing children and their parents. *Journal of Marriage and Family, 50*, 221–231.

Kahana, B., & Kahana, E. (1970). Grandparenthood from the perspective of the developing grandchild. *Developmental Psychology, 3*, 98–105.

Kamo, Y. (1998). Asian grandparents. In M.E. Szinovacz (Ed.), *Handbook on grandparenthood* (pp. 97–112). Westport, CT: Greenwood Press.

Kaplan, H., Hill, K., Lancaster, J., & Hurtado, A.M. (2000). A theory of human life history evolution: Diet, intelligence, and longevity. *Evolutionary Anthropology, 9*, 156–185.

Kennedy, G.E. (1990). College students' expectations of grandparent and grandchild role behavior. *The Gerontologist, 30*, 43–48.

King, V. (2003). The legacy of a grandparent's divorce: Consequences for ties between grandparents and grandchildren. *Journal of Marriage and the Family, 65*, 170–183.

King, V., & Elder, G.H., Jr. (1995). American children view their grandparents: Linked lives across three rural generations. *Journal of Marriage and the Family, 57*, 165–178.

King, V., & Elder, G.H., Jr. (1999). Are religious grandparents more involved grandparents? *Journal of Gerontology: Social Sciences, 54B*, S317–S328.

King, V., Silverstein, M., Elder, G.H., Jr., Bengtson, V.L., & Conger, R.D. (2003). Relations with grandparents. Rural Midwest versus urban southern California. *Journal of Family Issues, 24*, 1044–1069.

Kivett, V.R. (1985). Grandfathers and grandchildren: Patterns of association, helping and psychological closeness. *Family Relations, 34*, 565–571.

Kivett, V.R. (1991). The grandparent–grandchild connection. *Marriage and Family Review, 16*, 267–290.

Koenig, W.D. (1989). Sex-biased dispersal in the contemporary United States. *Ethology and Sociobiology, 10*, 263–278.

Laham, S.M., Gonsalkorale, K., & von Hippel, W. (2005). Darwinian grandparenting: Preferential investment in more certain kin. *Personality and Social Psychology Bulletin, 31*, 63–72.

Lahdenperä, M., Lummaa, V., Helle, S., Tremblay, M., & Russell, A.F. (2004). Fitness benefits of prolonged post-reproductive lifespan in women. *Nature, 428*, 178–181.

Lahdenperä, M., Russell, A.F., & Lummaa, V. (2007). Selection for long lifespan in men: Benefits of grandfathering? *Proceedings of the Royal Society B, 274*, 2437–2444.

Lawton, L., Silverstein, M., & Bengtson, V. (1994). Affect, social contact, and geographic distance between parents and their adult children. *Journal of Marriage and the Family, 56*, 57–68.

Lee, R.D. (2010). Population aging and the role of the elderly: Bonanza or burden? *Behavioral and Brain Sciences, 33*(1), in press.

Leek, M., & Smith, P.K. (1991). Cooperation and conflict in three-generation families. In P.K. Smith (Ed.), *The psychology of grandparenthood. An international perspective* (pp. 177–194). London: Routledge.

Littlefield, C.H., & Rushton, J.P. (1986). When a child dies: The sociobiology of bereavement. *Journal of Personality and Social Psychology, 51*, 797–802.

Lotka, A.J. (1907). Relation between birth rates and death rates. *Science, 26*, 12–22.

Mace, R., & Sear, R. (2005). Are humans cooperative breeders? In Voland, E., Chasiotis, A., & Schiefenhövel, W. (Eds.), *Grandmotherhood. The evolutionary significance of the second half of female life* (pp. 143–159). New Brunswick, NJ: Rutgers University Press.

Marlowe, F.W. (2005). Who tends Hadza children? In B.S. Hewlett, & M.E. Lamb (Eds.), *Hunter-gatherer childhoods* (pp. 177–190). Piscataway, NJ: Aldine Transaction.

Matthews, S.H., & Sprey, J. (1985). Adolescents' relationships with grandparents: An empirical contribution to conceptual clarification. *Journal of Gerontology, 40*, 621–626.

McBurney, D.H., Pashos, A., & Gaulin, S.J.C. (2006, June). *Family relationships and kin investment biases: A two generational questionnaire study.* Paper presented at the 18th Annual Meeting of the Human Behavior Evolution Society, Philadelphia, PA.

McBurney, D., Simon, J., Gaulin, S.J.C., & Geliebter, A. (2001). Matrilateral biases in the investment of aunts and uncles: Replication in a population presumed to have high paternity uncertainty. *Human Nature, 13*, 391–402.

McClellan, W.M., Stanwyck, D.J., & Anson, C.A. (1993). Social support and subsequent mortality among patients with end-stage renal disease. *Journal of the American Society of Nephrology, 4*, 1028–34.

McDougall, W. (1908). *An introduction to social psychology.* London: Methuen.

McGarry, K. (1999). Inter vivos transfers and intended bequests. *Journal of Public Economics, 73*, 321–351.

Mealey, L. (2000). *Sex differences: Development and evolutionary strategies.* San Diego, CA: Academic Press.

Medawar, P.B. (1957). *The uniqueness of the individual* (2nd ed.). New York: Dover Publications.

Michalski, R.L., & Shackelford, T.K. (2005): Grandparental investment as a function of relational uncertainty and emotional closeness with parent. *Human Nature, 16*, 293–305.

Mills, T.L., Wakeman, M.A., & Fea, C.B. (2001). Adult grandchildren's perceptions of emotional closeness and consensus with their maternal and paternal grandparents. *Journal of Family Issues, 22*, 427–55.

Monserud, M.A. (2008). Intergenerational relationships and affectual solidarity between grandparents and young adults. *Journal of Marriage and Family, 70*, 182–95.

Nakamichi, M., Onishi, K., & Yamada, K. (2009). Old grandmothers provide essential care to their young granddaughters in a free-ranging group of Japanese monkeys (*Macaca fuscata*). *Primates*, 51, 171–174. DOI 10.1007/s10329-009-0177-7.

Nakamichi, M., Silldorff, A., Bringham, C., & Sexton, P. (2004). Baby-transfer and other interactions between its mother and grandmother in a captive social group of lowland gorillas. *Primates*, 45, 73–77.

National Center for Biotechnology Information (2009). *Homo sapiens Chromosome: X. Map Viewer.* Bethesda, MD: US National Library of Medicine.

Norris, K.S., & Pryor, K. (1991). Some thoughts on grandmothers. In K. Pryor, & K.S. Norris (Eds.), *Dolphin societies: Discoveries and puzzles* (pp. 287–292). Berkeley, CA: University of California Press.

O'Connell, J.F., Hawkes, K., & Blurton Jones, N.G. (1999). Grandmothering and the evolution of *Homo erectus*. *Journal of Human Evolution*, 36, 461–485.

Pashos, A. (2000). Does paternal uncertainty explain discriminative grandparental solicitude? A cross-cultural study in Greece and Germany. *Evolution and Human Behavior*, 21, 97–109.

Patterson, C.J., Hurt, S. & Mason, C.D. (1998) Families of the lesbian baby boom: Children's contact with grandparents and other adults. *American Journal of Orthopsychiatry*, 68, 390–99.

Paul, A. (2005). Primate dispositions for human grandmaternal behavior. In E. Voland, A. Chasiotis, & W. Schiefenhövel (Eds.), *Grandmotherhood. The evolutionary significance of the second half of female life* (pp. 21–37). New Brunswick, NJ: Rutgers University Press.

Peccei, J.S. (1995). The origin and evolution of menopause: The altriciality–lifespan hypothesis. *Ethology and Sociobiology*, 16, 425–449.

Peccei, J.S. (2001). A critique of the grandmother hypotheses: Old and new. *American Journal of Human Biology*, 13, 434–452.

Perrin, W.F., Brownell, R.L. Jr., & DeMaster, D.P. (Eds.). (1984). *Reproduction in whales, dolphins, and porpoises*. Cambridge, MA: Report of the International Whaling Commission.

Platek, S.M., Burch, R.L., Panyavin, I.S., Wasserman, B.H., & Gallup, G.G., Jr. (2002). Reactions to children's faces. Resemblance affects males more than females. *Evolution and Human Behavior*, 23, 159–166.

Pollet, T.V., Nelissen, M., & Nettle, D. (2008). Lineage based differences in grandparental investment: Evidence from a large British cohort study. *Journal of Biosocial Science*, 41, 355–379.

Pollet, T.V., Nettle, D., & Nelissen, M. (2006). Contact frequencies between grandparents and grandchildren in a modern society: Estimates of the impact of paternity uncertainty. *Journal of Cultural and Evolutionary Psychology*, 4, 203–214.

Pollet, T.V., Nettle, D., & Nelissen, M. (2007). Maternal grandmothers do go the extra mile: Factoring distance and lineage into differential contact with grandchildren. *Evolutionary Psychology*, 5, 832–843.

Presser, H.B. (1989). Some economic complexities of child care provided by grandmothers. *Journal of Marriage and the Family*, 51, 581–591.

Reitzes, D.C., & Mutran, E.J. (2004). Grandparenthood: Factors influencing frequency of grandparent-grandchildren contact and grandparent role satisfaction. *Journal of Gerontology: Social Sciences*, 59B, S9–S16.

Rhoads, S.E., & Rhoads, C.H. (2004). *Gender roles and infant/toddler care: The special case of tenure track faculty*. Paper presented at the Annual Meeting of the MidWest Political Science Association, April 16, 2004. Retrieved July 23, 2009 from http://faculty.virginia.edu/sexdifferences/NewFiles/paper1.pdf

Richardson, D.S., Burke, T., & Komdeur, J. (2007). Grandparent helpers: The adaptive significance of older, postdominant helpers in the Seychelles warbler. *Evolution*, 61, 2790–2800.

Robins, L.N., & Tomanec, M. (1962). Closeness to blood relatives outside the immediate family. *Marriage and Family Living*, 24, 340–346.

Rossi, A.S., & Rossi, P.H. (1990). *Of human bonding: Parent–child relations across the life course*. New York: Aldine de Gruyter.

Russell, R.J.H., & Wells, P.A. (1987). Estimating paternity confidence. *Ethology and Sociobiology*, 8, 215–220.

Salmon, C. (2003). Birth order and relationships: Family, friends, and sexual partners. *Human Nature*, 14, 73–88.

Salmon, C.A. (1999). On the impact of sex and birth order on contact with kin. *Human Nature*, 10, 183–197.

Salmon, C.A., & Daly, M. (1996). On the importance of kin relations to Canadian women and men. *Ethology and Sociobiology*, 17, 289–297.

Salmon, C.A., & Daly, M. (1998). Birth order and familial sentiment: Middleborns are different. *Evolution and Human Behavior*, 19, 299–312.

Scannapieco, M., & Hegar, R.L. (2002). Kinship care providers: Designing an array of supportive services. *Child and Adolescent Social Work Journal*, 19, 315–327.

Schiefenhövel, W., & Grabolle, A. (2005). The role of maternal grandmothers in Tobriand adoptions. In E. Voland, A. Chasiotis, & W. Schiefenhövel (Eds.), *Grandmotherhood. The evolutionary significance of the second half of female life* (pp. 177–193). New Brunswick, NJ: Rutgers University Press.

Scholl Perry, K. (1996). Relationships among adolescents' ego development, their academic achievement, and the amount of their contact with and social distance from grandparents. Doctoral dissertation, Pace University, New York. *Dissertation Abstracts International*, DAI-B 57/08, p. 5391.

Sear, F., & Dickins, T.E. (2010). The generation game is the cooperation game. *Behavioral and Brain Sciences*, 33, 34–35.

Sear, R., & Mace, R. (2008). Who keeps children alive? A review of the effects of kin on child survival. *Evolution and Human Behavior*, 29, 1–18.

Segal, N.L., Seghers, J.P., Marelich, W.D., Mechanic, M.B., & Castillo, R.R. (2007). Social closeness of MZ and DZ twin parents toward nieces and nephews. *European Journal of Personality*, 21, 487–506.

Silverstein, M., & Marenco, A. (2001). How Americans enact the grandparent role across the family life course. *Journal of Family Issues*, 22, 493–522.

Silverstein, M., & Ruiz, S. (2006). Breaking the chain: How grandparents moderate the transmission of maternal depression to their grandchildren. *Family Relations*, 55, 601–612.

Silverstein, M., Giarrusso, R., & Bengtson, V. (2003). Grandparents and grandchildren in family systems. A sociodevelopmental perspective. In V. Bengtson, & A. Lowenstein (Eds.), *Global aging and challenges to families* (pp. 75–102). New York: Aldine de Gruyter.

Smith, M.S. (1988). Research in developmental sociobiology: Parenting and family behavior. In K.B. MacDonald (Ed.), *Sociobiological perspectives on human development* (pp. 271–292). New York: Springer.

Smith, M.S. (1991). An evolutionary perspective on grandparent–grandchild relationships. In P.K. Smith (Ed.), *The psychology of grandparenthood. An international perspective* (pp. 157–176). London: Routledge.

Spitze, G., & Ward, R.A. (1998). Gender variations. In M.E. Szinovacz (Ed.), *Handbook on grandparenthood* (pp. 113–127). Westport, CT: Greenwood Press.

Steinbach, I., & Henke, W. (1998). Grosselterninvestment—eine empirische interkulturelle Vergleichsstudie [Grandparental investment–An empirical cross-cultural comparative study]. *Anthropologie, 36,* 293–301.

Strassman, B.I., & Kurapati, N. (2010). Most studies of natural fertility populations do not support the grandmother hypothesis. *Behavioral and Brain Sciences, 33,* 35–39.

Sulloway, F.J. (1996). Born to rebel: Birth order, family dynamics, and creative lives. New York: Pantheon.

Sulloway, F.J. (2007). Birth order and sibling competition. In R.I.M. Dunbar, & L. Barrett (Eds.), *The Oxford handbook of evolutionary psychology* (pp. 297–311). Oxford, UK: Oxford University Press.

Szydlik, M. (1995). Die Enge der Beziehung zwischen erwachsenen Kindern und ihren Eltern - und umgekehrt [The closeness of relationship between adult children and their parents—and vice versa]. *Zeitschrift für Soziologie, 24,* 75–94.

Thomas, D. (1994). Like father, like son; like mother, like daughter: Parental resources and child height. *The Journal of Human Resources, 29,* 950–988.

Thomas, J.L. (1989). Gender and perceptions of grandparenthood. *International Journal of Aging and Human Development, 24,* 269–282.

Tran, U.S., Fisher, M.L., & Voracek, M. (2009). Spousal age differences and sex differences in life expectancy are confounders of matrilateral biases in kin investment. *Basic and Applied Social Psychology, 31,* 295–303.

Trivers, R.L. (1972). Parental investment and sexual selection. In B. Campbell (Ed.), *Sexual selection and the descent of man 1871–1971* (pp. 136–179). Chicago, IL: Aldine.

Trivers, R.L., & Willard, D.E. (1973). Natural selection of parental ability to vary the sex ratio of offspring. *Science, 179,* 90–91.

Troll, L.E. (1983). Grandparents: The family watchdogs. In T.H. Brubaker (Ed.), *Family relationships in later life* (pp. 63–74). Beverly Hills, CA: Sage Publications.

Uhlenberg, P. (2004). Historical forces shaping grandparent-grandchild relationships: Demography and beyond. In M. Silverstein (Ed.), *Intergenerational relations across time and place. Annual Review of Gerontology and Geriatrics, 24,* 77–97.

Uhlenberg, P., & Hammill, B.G. (1998). Frequency of grandparental contact with grandchild sets: Six factors that make a difference. *The Gerontologist, 38,* 276–285.

van Ranst, N., Verschueren, K., & Marcoen, A. (1995). The meaning of grandparents as viewed by adolescent grandchildren: An empirical study in Belgium. *International Journal of Aging and Human Development, 41,* 311–324.

Vandell, D.L., McCartney, K., Owen, M.T., Booth, C., & Clarke-Stewart, A. (2003). Variations in child care by grandparents during the first three years. *Journal of Marriage and Family, 65,* 375–381.

Voland, E. (2007). Evolutionary psychology meets history: Insights into human nature through family reconstitution studies. In R.I.M. Dunbar, & L. Barrett (Eds.), *The Oxford handbook of evolutionary psychology* (pp. 415–432). Oxford, UK: Oxford University Press.

Voland, E., & Beise, J. (2002). Opposite effects of maternal and paternal grandmothers on infant survival in historical Krummhörn. *Behavioral Ecology and Sociobiology, 52,* 435–443.

Voland, E., & Beise, J. (2005). "The husband's mother is the devil in the house." Data on the impact of the mother-in-law on stillbirth mortality in historical Krummhörn (1750–1874) and some thoughts on the evolution of the postgenerative female life. In E. Voland, A. Chasiotis, & W. Schiefenhövel (Eds.), *Grandmotherhood. The evolutionary significance of the second half of female life* (pp. 239–255). New Brunswick, NJ: Rutgers University Press.

Voland, E., Chasiotis, A., & Schiefenhövel, W. (Eds.). (2005). *Grandmotherhood. The evolutionary significance of the second half of female life.* New Brunswick, NJ: Rutgers University Press.

Voracek, M., Haubner, T., & Fisher, M.L. (2008). Recent decline in nonpaternity rates: A cross-temporal meta-analysis. *Psychological Reports, 103,* 799–811.

Wells, R.S. (1991). The role of long-term study in understanding the social structure of bottlenose dolphin community. In K. Pryor, & K.S. Norris (Eds.), *Dolphin societies: Discoveries and puzzles* (pp. 199–226). Berkeley, CA: University of California Press.

Williams, G.C. (1957). Pleiotropy, natural selection, and the evolution of senescence. *Evolution, 11,* 398–411.

Williams, N., & Torres, D.J. (1998). Grandparenthood among Hispanics. In M.E. Szinovacz (Ed.), *Handbook on grandparenthood* (pp. 87–96). Westport, CT: Greenwood Press.

Wood, V., & Robertson, J.F. (1976). The significance of grandparenthood. In J. Gubrium (Ed.), *Time, roles, and self in old age* (pp. 278–304). New York: Human Sciences Press.

Wroblewski, E.E. (2008). An unusual incident of adoption in a wild chimpanzee (*Pan troglodytes*) population at Gombe National Park. *American Journal of Primatology, 70,* 1–4.

Young, M., & Willmott, P. (1957). *Family and kinship in East London.* Harmondsworth, UK: Penguin.

PART 3

Animal Families

CHAPTER 13

Kin Recognition

Peter Hepper

Abstract

Kinship appears to be a major influence on the lives of animals. This chapter examines three key questions. First, do animals respond differentially to kin and nonkin? Examples are presented to illustrate that in all animal classes, in a wide variety of situations, kinship is a determinant of social behavior. Second, why do animals respond differentially to kin and nonkin? The answer lies in the benefits in fitness an animal receives through differential responding to kin and nonkin, as described by inclusive fitness and kin selection theory. Cooperative behavior, parental care, mate choice, and social cohesion, also benefit from this differential responding. The third question addresses how individuals recognize their kin. The three central components of kin recognition: the cues used, the classification of kin, and the development of kin recognition, are discussed with a view to describing how these elements must be constructed to ensure that individuals recognize their kin and discriminate degrees of relatedness. Some future directions for a greater understanding of kin recognition are presented at the end of the review.

Keywords: Kin recognition, kin discrimination, inclusive fitness, cues of kinship, development of kin recognition, animals

Introduction

Kinship is embedded in human society (chapter 1 and 2, this volume). Our activities with, and in response to, others are often influenced by kinship and how closely related we are. We give very little consideration to our ability to recognize our kin: parents, siblings, grandparents, cousins, nephews, etc. It is part of our lives. However, what about other animals? Adopting a decidedly anthropomorphic outlook, it seems obvious that kinship should also be important to animals as well. Animals display parental care, live in social groups, and appear to form bonds. It is perhaps somewhat surprising then to note that the scientific study of kin recognition in animals is a relatively recent phenomenon (Hepper, 1991a). Indeed, today, it is difficult to envisage the time when kinship was not a central consideration when discussing the social behavior of animals and its evolution. However, it was not until 1963, when W.D. Hamilton proposed his kinship theory (Hamilton, 1963), that the issue of kinship was first raised as having the potential to influence evolution. It was even later, in 1975, with E.O. Wilson's publication of *Sociobiology* (Wilson 1975), that the importance of kinship in social behavior was fully made apparent. The realization that relatedness was a major driving force behind social behavior stimulated researchers to examine the phenomenon of kinship in animals. It is the aim of this chapter to discuss kin recognition in animals.

This chapter is organized into three main sections. Each will address a key question for kin recognition: Do animals respond differentially to kin and nonkin? Why should animals respond differentially to kin and nonkin? And, finally, how do animals recognize their kin? These discussions will focus on central issues pertinent to these questions. In addressing these, I use selective examples of evidence to illustrate the issue under scrutiny rather than provide a comprehensive review of all studies (readers are referred to Blaustein, Porter, & Breed, 1988; Fletcher & Michener, 1987; Hepper, 1991b; Starks, 2004; Tang-Martinez, 2001 for additional information). I conclude the chapter with a brief discussion of some of the issues that remain unresolved and that future research must address. I begin, however, by considering the question "What is kin recognition?"

What Is Kin Recognition?

Kin recognition may be defined as the ability of individuals to distinguish kin from nonkin, or to differentiate between different classes of kin (e.g., siblings and cousins). Researchers have used two different terms, "kin discrimination" and "kin recognition", to refer to different aspects of the general process of responding differentially to kin and nonkin.

Kin discrimination refers to the exhibition of a differential response to kin and nonkin or to individuals of different degrees of relatedness. For example, when an Emperor penguin (*Aptenodytes forsteri*) parent seeks out its own chick from the crèche containing many similarly aged, unrelated chicks and selectively feeds it and not other chicks (Prévost, 1961), this is termed kin discrimination. The individual, in the same situation, responds to kin in one way but to nonkin in another; that is, it discriminates. The observation of a differential response to kin and nonkin implies nothing about the intentions of the animal in undertaking this response. Nor does it imply conscious intent. The animal is simply responding as if it has determined the degree of relatedness of the other animal. There is much evidence of kin discrimination in animals, and selective examples will be discussed later.

Kin recognition has been used to refer to the underlying mechanism(s) that individuals are presumed to use in identifying others as kin or nonkin, or in determining their degree of relatedness. Kin recognition, as used here, is the process that enables an individual, on encountering a conspecific, to determine if the conspecific is kin or nonkin, or how closely related the conspecific is. A number of different mechanisms have been proposed to explain how individuals recognize their kin, and these will be reviewed later.

I use these definitions throughout the remainder of this review. It is important to distinguish between kin recognition and kin discrimination. If there are evolutionary advantages to being able to respond to kin and nonkin differentially, then it is kin discrimination that is vital to obtain these benefits. Kin recognition is a means to achieve this. It must be noted that behavior in one area, for example, kin discrimination, may have no implications for the other, kin recognition. The fact that individuals show no evidence of kin discrimination does not necessarily mean that they are unable to recognize kin. For example, rat (*Rattus norvegicus*) mothers are able to recognize their offspring (Beach & Jaynes, 1956) and my early studies of kin recognition found that the young rat pups, and their mothers, have very good abilities to recognize each other (Hepper, 1986a). A staple methodology of laboratory research examining the mechanisms of kin recognition is cross-fostering (Mateo & Holmes, 2004). This involves the creation of new litters, often comprising varying percentages of kin and nonkin, to examine the recognition abilities of kin reared apart and nonkin reared together. However, despite excellent recognition abilities, rat mothers will still rear unrelated pups (Hepper, 1983), showing a lack of kin discrimination. Thus, inferences about recognition abilities must be drawn cautiously from observations of kin discrimination and vice versa.

Do Animals Respond Differentially to Kin and Nonkin?

This section reviews the evidence that animals respond differentially to kin and nonkin. Kin discrimination is a ubiquitous phenomenon. In virtually all animal classes there is evidence that individuals behave differently to kin and nonkin. I will draw examples from invertebrates and across all the major animal classes to illustrate the widespread occurrence of kin discrimination. It is not intended to review all studies demonstrating kin discrimination; rather this will be a highly selective review to demonstrate the range of animals exhibiting kin discrimination and the different situations in which kin discrimination occurs.

It needs to be borne in mind when reviewing this evidence that, although individuals may exhibit kin discrimination in one circumstance, this does necessarily mean they will exhibit this discrimination in all situations. I will pick up this point again when considering the challenges facing future research in the area.

Invertebrates

Perhaps the best known examples of kin discrimination in invertebrates are those presented by the eusocial insects, for example, ants, termites, bees (Wilson, 1971). Colonies constructed of relatives exhibit clearly defined divisions of labor, queens, guards, workers, and some individuals even forego their reproductive ability to maintain the colony to ensure the success of their kin and colony mates. However, kin discrimination is present throughout invertebrates.

The lace bug (*Gargaphia solani*) may abandon its eggs, leaving them to be reared by other individuals. These bugs lay egg masses that are then guarded by the parent of the eggs. However, some individuals will lay their eggs within the egg masses of others and then leave them to be cared for by the parents of the original egg mass. Observation of this egg dumping behavior indicates that the bugs deposit and leave their eggs with egg masses of siblings over nonkin (Loeb, Diener, & Pfennig, 2000), thus entreating the care of their young to their relatives.

Subsocial spiders may hunt large prey cooperatively, and once the prey is captured, they digest the food as a group. Spiders must "dissolve" their food externally before being able to ingest it. To do this they produce enzymes that are injected into their prey, breaking down the body, and enabling it to be consumed by the spider. However, enzyme production is costly and when feeding as a group, an opportunity exists for cheating if some individuals do not produce any digestive enzyme and just extract the food when digested. Observations of the subsocial spider genus, *Stegodyphus tentoriicola* (Ruch, Heinrich, Bilde, & Schneider, 2009) and *S. lineatus* (Schneider & Bilde, 2008) indicate that when siblings feed together, they gain more weight and exhibit greater feeding efficiency (as assessed by the amount of food extracted from their prey) than do groups of nonsiblings feeding together. It is suggested that siblings compete less with one another and are less likely to cheat each other, and through this cooperation they gain more food overall from their prey.

Earwig nymphs of the European earwig (*Forficula auricularia*) remain with nest mates during the first 10 days after emergence before dispersing. During this time, juveniles may cannibalize one another. Dobler and Kölliker (2010) observed that earwig nymphs will kill unrelated nest mates earlier than their siblings and more often cannibalize unrelated nymphs. The young earwigs adjust their behavior to preferentially cannibalize unrelated nest mates.

Fish

Many animal species live in groups. One manifestation of this is shoaling, or schooling, in fish. Shoaling may confer advantages to individuals in the shoal due to an enhanced ability to avoid predatory attack. This may arise from risk dilution, better vigilance, and greater predator confusion. Moreover, the greater the social cohesion in the shoal, the greater the defence against predatory attack. Kin groups of juvenile bluegill (*Lepomis macrochirus*) display greater cohesion when exposed to predator odor than do nonkin groups (Hain & Neff, 2009). Close association with kin may enhance their own, and their kin's, ability to avoid predators over shoals of nonkin. Shoals of related individuals exhibit less aggression to other shoal members than do shoals of unrelated individuals (Brown & Brown, 1993) in both Atlantic salmon (*Salmo salar*) and Rainbow trout (*Oncorhynchus mykiss*). Furthermore, higher survival rates have been reported in pike (*Esox lucius*) when groups are composed of related individuals compared with groups of unrelated individuals (Bry & Gillet, 1980). Thus, associating with kin during shoaling may reduce predation, decrease aggression, and improve survival.

Amphibians

Shoaling is also a feature of tadpole behavior, and tadpoles of the American toad (*Bufo americanus*) preferentially form shoals with siblings (Waldman, 1982). This may provide benefits arising from reduced predation, aposematic advertisement, and enhanced growth and survival.

Spadefoot toad tadpoles (*Scaphiopus bombifrons*) may become either cannibals or omnivores depending on their early feeding habits. If tadpoles feed on fairy shrimp, they develop cannibalistic feeding habits, whereas those feeding on vegetation and detritus maintain their omnivorous diet. These feeding habits affect their association behavior; "omnivores" associate preferentially with siblings, whereas "cannibals" associate preferentially with nonsiblings. Furthermore' cannibals will nip at all tadpoles they encounter; however, if they nip a sibling they let them go, whereas if they nip a nonsibling they do not let them go but eat them (Pfennig, Reeve, & Sherman, 1993). Tadpoles avoid cannibalizing their siblings.

Agonistic behavior is influenced by kinship in the fire salamander (*Salamandra infraimmaculata*) and marbled salamander (*Ambystoma opacum*). The larvae of both species exhibit less aggression to sibs and more closely related individuals than to nonkin, leading to a reduction in injuries experienced by kin (Markman, Hill, Todrank, Heth, & Blaustein, 2009; Walls & Roudebush, 2001).

Reptiles

Reptiles are not normally considered social and perhaps due to this there has been little investigation of the role of kinship in the social behavior of reptiles compared to other animal classes. However there is some evidence that kinship may influence behavior(s) in certain reptilian species.

Of all the snakes the crotalids (a subfamily of the family Viperidae) including rattlesnakes and pit vipers, are the most social. Females may aggregate together and exhibit parental care of young, although whether this is specifically directed at their own young is unknown. Observations of timber rattlesnakes (*Crotalus horridus*) indicate that female siblings aggregate together more closely and are more often in contact with one another than nonsiblings (Clark, 2004). The reasons for this are unknown at present.

A number of studies have suggested that skinks can recognize their kin (gidgee skinks, [*Egernia stokesii*], Main & Bull, 1996; tree skinks [*E. striolata*], Bull, Griffin, Bonnett, Gardner, & Cooper, 2001; black rock skinks [*E. saxatilis*], O'Connor & Shine, 2006), although exactly how this influences behavior remains to be fully elucidated. The shingleback lizard (*Tiliqua rugosa*) forms monogamous pairs and gives birth to large offspring in clutches of one to five. Mothers pay more attention to their own young than to unrelated young (Bull, Doherty, Schulze, & Pamula, 1994). Recognition may thus play a role in parental behavior.

Birds

Peacocks (*Pavo cristatus*) display a lek mating system, in which males congregate to display with the aim of attracting females and subsequently mating with them. Displaying in a group increases the number of females that are attracted to the lek. However, the number of matings each male achieves in the lek is not equal. Some males achieve many more matings than other members of the group. Petrie, Krupa, and Burke (1999) found that the males within the leks were more closely related than were individuals in different leks. Peacock males appear to preferentially congregate in leks together with their siblings to increase their attractiveness to females.

Ostriches (*Struthio camelus*) lay their eggs in a communal nest guarded by the major hen. However, there is a limit to the number of eggs (approximately 20) that can be successfully incubated, and there are often many more in the nest than this (30–40). To overcome this, the major hen pushes out eggs to maintain a manageable number to incubate. Bertram (1979) reports that the major hen pushes out the other females' eggs, leaving hers behind to be incubated.

Learning by observation from other individuals may be an effective way of acquiring knowledge about the environment and its resources and dangers. Common ravens (*Corvus corax*) were given the opportunity to watch another bird (the modeler) interact with novel objects. They observed this interaction but could not interact with the object themselves at this stage. When given the opportunity to interact with the object, the degree of relatedness between the observer and modeler influenced the subsequent interaction. When the observer bird watched a sibling interact with the object, the observer spent significantly longer manipulating the object than when the modeler was a nonsibling (Schwab, Bugnyar, Schloegl, & Kotrschal, 2008). Relatedness influences social, observational learning.

Mammals

A detailed study of the breeding habits of wild male African elephants (*Loxodonta africana*) indicates that kinship exerts a major influence on their reproductive behavior. Elephants live in matrilineal groups, with males living separately from these groups once they reach reproductive maturity. When females enter estrous, they are sought out by males who then follow them, prevent access to them by other males, and copulate with them. Males avoid mating with females of their family (matrilineal kin) and exhibit typical male reproductive behaviors (following, defending, and copulation) less when the estrous female is related compared with when the estrous female is unrelated (Archie, Hollister-Smith, Poole, Lee, Moss, Maldonado, Fleischer, & Alberts, 2007).

Many animals live in social groups (Wilson, 1975). One interesting example is presented by the spotted hyena (*Crocuta crocuta*), in which individuals live in complex social groups (clans) that cooperate to hunt, defend their territory, and care for their young. In these groups, kin associate together more than nonkin, and there is much less aggression and conflict between kin than between unrelated individuals. Mothers respond preferentially to the calls of their own cubs over unrelated young. Cubs direct less aggression to their fathers than to unrelated males. Clans may be large, and there is competition between clan members for resources, for example, prey. Kin cooperate more in hunting prey than do nonkin, and then associate together to defend successful kills (Holekamp, Sakai, & Lundrigan, 2007).

Kinship permeates all aspects of the social behavior of the clan.

The formation of alliances between males may have benefits for holding territories, hunting, and providing access to females. In dolphins, stable male associations cooperate in aggressive encounters and are more successful in securing reproductively receptive females. In male bottlenose dolphins (*Tursiops truncatus*), established alliances were more likely composed of closely related males than expected by chance (Parsons, Durban, Claridge, Balcomb, Noble, & Thompson, 2003). Similar male associations based on kinship are reported in African lions (*Panthera leo*; Packer, Gilbert, Pusey, & O'Brien, 1991). Forming an alliance with male kin benefits reproductive success.

Primates

Living in social groups is a complex process. Individuals need to conform to the conventions of the group, respect relationships (e.g., dominance), and respond to social interactions appropriately. No matter how skilled, disputes will arise and their resolution forms a major backdrop to social living. Observations of some primate societies indicate that kinship is one important factor in determining the outcomes of disputes. Individuals will intervene in disputes on behalf of their kin more than they do for nonkin, as for example, in pigtailed macaques (*Macaca nemestrina*; Massey, 1977) and rhesus macaques (*M. mulatta*; Kaplan, 1977, 1978).

Play behavior is considered essential for the behavioral development of the individual. It allows the practice of behaviors required for later life (e.g., fighting, hunting) in a nonthreatening and safe environment, as well as developing physical abilities among many other functions (Burghardt, 2005; Fagen, 1981). Adults engage in play behavior with young and often "handicap" themselves such that the play behavior may proceed on an equal footing (Hayaki, 1985; Spinka, Newberry, & Bekoff 2001). Adult male chimps (*Pan trogdolytes*) play more with their own offspring than with unrelated offspring (Lehman, Fickenscher, & Boesch, 2006). However, when it comes to their own brothers, it appears males will preferentially affiliate with their maternal siblings over paternal siblings (Langergraber, Mitani, & Vigilant, 2007). Chimps prefer kin as play partners.

The recognition of kinship may not be limited to the recognition of own kin. Humans are well aware, as third parties, of the kin relationships of others, for example, the mother/father of a child. Although not part of this kin group, we are able to recognize relationships within it. The same may be true of some primates. Vervet monkeys (*Cercopithecus aethiops*) exhibit alarm calls, and mothers respond to the calls of their own offspring (Cheney & Seyfarth, 1980). However, others may also recognize the relationship. When the distress calls of young are played, unrelated vervet monkeys direct their gaze to the mother of the young who has called (Cheney & Seyfarth, 1980, 1982).

Summary

Kin discrimination appears universal across the animal kingdom. It must also be noted that kin discrimination is not restricted to animals. Plants also have to compete for resources. Root systems provide the lifeline for many plants to acquire resources; the larger the root mass of a plant the better able to obtain resources. The Great Lakes sea rocket (*Cakile edentula lacustris*), an annual plant, develops a larger fine root mass when growing next to nonkin than when growing next to their kin (Dudley & File, 2007). The results suggest that plants compete less with kin than nonkin.

The above review has been, by necessity, selective but it has served to illustrate the fact that kinship occurs in a wide range of animals with very different life ecologies, in variety of contexts, and influences a wide range of behaviors. This raises the question, to be addressed in the next section, why?

Why Do Animals Recognize Their Kin?

This section reviews some of the theories that have suggested differentially responding to kin and nonkin affords benefits to those individuals able to do so.

Inclusive Fitness

A key concept for explaining why individuals may benefit from responding differentially to kin and nonkin is that of inclusive fitness. In Darwin's natural selection, fitness is considered a measure of the individual's reproductive success and is measured ultimately in terms of the number of genes that the individual successfully passes to the next generation. This is termed an individual's *personal fitness*. Related individuals have a number of genes in common. Siblings, on average in diploid species, share 50% of their genes that are identical by descent. Thus, an individual may achieve genetic representation in the next generation through the success of his or her kin. Hamilton (1963, 1964a,b) argued that an individual's fitness should be considered as the total of the individual's own personal reproductive success, plus the reproductive success of relatives that arises from the actions of the individual. This is termed an individual's *inclusive fitness*. This forms a cornerstone of Hamilton's kinship theory and underpins explanations of why discriminating between kin and nonkin provides advantages for individuals able to do so.

Altruism and Kinship Theory

It is perhaps worth noting, especially having recently celebrated the 150th anniversary of the publication of Darwin's *The Origin of Species by Means of Natural Selection* (1859), that one particular behavioral phenomenon posed a problem for Darwin, one he thought "actually fatal" to his theory (1859, p. 257). This was the existence of sterile castes in insects. Darwin postulated, in his theory of natural selection, that as individuals compete for resources, differences between individuals will mean that some are more successful than others and thus will have an increased opportunity to reproduce. This differential reproduction will enable species to evolve and change. It was difficult to see how sterile insects could have evolved as, even if they did possess some advantage, how could they reproduce? More recently, researchers faced a similar problem with the observations of altruistic behavior, for example, alarm calling (Caro, 2005; Sherman, 1977). Individuals, upon detecting a predator, emit an alarm call to draw the attention of other conspecifics to its presence. In doing so, the caller may draw the attention of the predator to itself and increase its risk of predation. How could a behavior in which one individual suffers a loss in fitness, possibly death, evolve?

The solution to these problems was provided by the kinship theory of Hamilton (1963, 1964a,b) and was termed *kin selection* (Maynard Smith, 1964). Using the concept of inclusive fitness, kinship theory demonstrated how behaviors that appeared to result in a loss in an individual's personal fitness could evolve if the gain in their relatives' fitness through their actions was greater than any loss in personal fitness; that is, their inclusive fitness was increased.

This was encapsulated in the formula

$$b * r > c$$

Where, b is the benefit in fitness gained by the recipient of an individual's behavior, c is the cost incurred by the individual in undertaking the behavior, and r is the coefficient of relatedness between the recipient and individual.

This provided a means to explain how behaviors that appeared to result in only a cost to the individual could evolve. If the gain in fitness of relatives is greater than the loss in personal fitness, there is an overall gain in fitness and thus the behavior could evolve. So, the behavior of rhesus macaques (*Macaca mulatta*) who intervene on behalf of their kin in agonistic encounters where they may suffer injury (Kaplan 1977, 1978, Massey 1977); peacocks (*Pavo cristatus*) who sacrifice mating opportunities for siblings to lek with them and attract more females (Petrie et al. 1993); and, vervet moneys (*Cercopithecus aethiops*) who give alarm calls that may attract the attention of the predator to them while allowing others to escape (Seyfarth, Cheney, & Marler, 1980), may all evolve if the benefits in fitness to the conspecifics who benefit from these acts is greater than the loss in fitness to individual undertaking the behavior.

Kin selection explains how differentially responding to kin and nonkin, and to different classes of kin, may confer benefits on individuals who do so, allowing them to maximize their fitness over individuals unable to do so.

Cooperation

Although initially proposed to explain altruistic behavior, kinship theory and inclusive fitness also have implications for cooperative behavior, where by acting together both individuals gain advantages in their fitness. This may explain, for example, the feeding behavior of subsocial spiders (*Stegodyphus tentoriicola, S. lineatus*), where cooperation results in more food (Ruch et al., 2009; and Schneider & Bilde, 2008); male associations in dolphins (*Tursiops truncatus*) and lions (*Panthera leo*), which lead to increased resources and access to females (Packer et al., 1983; Parsons et al., 2003). Individuals engaging in cooperative acts with kin may gain a greater increase in their fitness than if they cooperate with nonkin. Moreover cooperating with more closely related kin will provide greater benefits in fitness.

Parental Care

Although the publication of Hamilton's kinship theory raised the profile of kinship in social behavior and generated, although some years later, research in kin recognition, interest in one area where "kinship" plays a central role had been recognized and researched for many years. This is the area of parental care. Although the first studies of kin recognition may be traced to the 1970s, recognition of the importance and study of parent–offspring recognition may be found in late 19th century (Hepper, 1991b). For example, Romanes (1883a,b), in plotting his scale of intelligence, placed the ability to recognize offspring at level 20, something to be possessed by insects and higher-order taxonomic groups. This early interest is reflected by studies of parent–offspring behavior reported throughout the 20th Century. For example, MacGinitie (1939) reports that blind goby parents (*Typhlogobius californiensis*) do not eat their own young but will eat young from other parents' broods. Parent-offspring recognition has now been demonstrated in insects and all higher orders (Hepper, 1991b). The importance of parental care for the development and survival of young has long been recognized.

From the perspective of parents, producing and rearing offspring represents a significant investment and subsequent cost if things fail. The greater the amount of parental care required, the greater the investment. Thus, it would be expected that parents would be selective in their provision of care and recognize their offspring to ensure they provide care to genetically related individuals.

If parents recognize their offspring, this potentially places a requirement on the offspring to recognize their parents. Immediately after birth, the newly born or hatched young have little investment in their parents. Indeed, at this stage, their prime goal would be to obtain parental care, from anyone, to ensure they survive to reproductive maturity. Parents, however, if they recognize their young may attack unrelated young, for example, the sea elephant (*Mirounga leonina*; Laws 1956). The ability to recognize their parents and respond to them may be particularly important at the stage when young may be mobile but still requiring parental care, and where they could encounter unrelated adults. Young animals, to avoid attack and receive care, would thus be expected to respond differentially to their parents and other adults.

Recognition of parents and of offspring is particularly pertinent for seasonal breeders, in which young are born and reared in large communal crèches, for example, penguins. Many penguin species have been shown to demonstrate parent–offspring recognition that enables parents to find and feed their own young among many others in the crèche, and young seek out their parents (e.g., the Snares crested penguin [*Eudyptes robustus*], Proffitt & McLean, 1991; the Jackass penguin [*Spheniscus demersus*], Seddon & van Heezik, 1993; and, the Fiordland crested penguin [*Eudyptes pachyrhynchus*], Studholme, 1994).

Kinship theory may also account for the occurrence of alloparenting, in which individuals other than the biological parents care for the young, as for example, when the lace bug (*Gargaphia solani*) leaves its eggs with kin to rear (Loeb et al., 2000). Given that "parental" care is vital for the survival of the young, it might be expected that other related individuals may also provide care for the young, and in doing so, increase their own inclusive fitness through enhancing the survival of related young.

Mating

If "reproductive success" is key to promoting both individual and/or inclusive fitness, then the choice of a mate is vital to ensure fitness is maximized. Many factors are important in choosing the best possible mate (Bateson, 1983a). One factor is that of kinship. Breeding between related individuals, inbreeding, reduces fitness (Charlesworth & Charlesworth, 1987 1999; Keller & Waller, 2002). One means to avoid inbreeding is to recognize kin and thus avoid mating with relatives, as for example, in the African elephant (*Loxodonta africana*; Archie et al., 2007).

However, complete avoidance of inbreeding may also be detrimental in terms of fitness (Bateson, 1980; Mitton 1993; Peer & Taborski, 2005) leading to the view that individuals should strike a balance between inbreeding and outbreeding, termed *optimal outbreeding* by Bateson (1978, 1983b). Indeed, Bateson (1982) showed that Japanese quail (*Coturnix coturnix*) preferred their first cousins over siblings, third cousins, or unrelated individuals.

Social Cohesion

One further area where kinship may be important is a more general theme of social cohesion. For animals that live in social groups a certain level of order and regulation is required for the group to function as a whole and be effective. Continual disputes over resources, food, access to females, and the like would lead to disruption and eventually the group would disintegrate. Social order undoubtedly provides greater advantages to the individuals living in groups than does social disorder. Kinship may be one factor within a group that enables it to maintain its structure. Related individuals may support others in the group, provide protection from attack, and generally cooperate—as in the hyena (*Crocuta crocuta*) clan (Holekamp et al., 2007)—and this may promote social order. The ability to recognize kinship relationships within the group—for example, vervet monkeys (*Cercopithecus aethiops*), Cheney & Seyfarth, 1982—would also promote social group stability.

Thus, there are a number of reasons why individuals could benefit from responding differentially to kin and nonkin, and to different classes of kin. At the crux of each is that kin discrimination brings greater gains in fitness than nondiscriminative responding. Given the benefits of responding differentially to kin and nonkin, the question is raised of how might individuals achieve this?

How Do Individuals Recognize Their Kin?

In proposing his kinship theory, Hamilton argued that one means to avail of the benefits in inclusive fitness arising from differentially responding to kin and nonkin would be through a mechanism that enabled individuals to recognize their kin (Hamilton, 1964b). In the following section, I review how individuals might recognize their kin.

Early research identified four basic mechanisms that individuals could use to recognize their kin (Barnard, 1990; Hepper, 1986b; Holmes & Sherman, 1983).

Spatial Location

The individual achieves recognition through cues presented by the environment and not any cues presented by their conspecifics. An individual may respond to all conspecifics it encounters in its nest as kin; for example, the parent black-legged kittiwake (*Rissa tridactyla*) accepts and feeds any young placed into its nest (Cullen, 1957). The parent uses the physical cues of its nest to determine who its young are. Individuals within the nest are treated as own offspring, individuals outside of the nest are treated as not own offspring, irrespective of actual relatedness. Similarly, if individuals have a home range, conspecifics encountered in the home range would be treated as kin, whereas conspecifics encountered outside the range are treated as nonkin. To operate successfully, this requires a good correlation between spatial location and genetic relatedness.

Association or Familiarity

Individuals learn about their kin from encounters with conspecifics. Individuals respond to familiar individuals as kin and unfamiliar individuals as nonkin. This requires a good correlation between familiarity and relatedness. The degree of familiarity may enable the degree of relatedness to be determined. Evidence for this mechanism arises from studies in which litters of unrelated individuals are reared together. In subsequent two-choice tests, individuals are given a choice between familiar unrelated conspecifics and unfamiliar unrelated conspecifics individuals (e.g., Hepper, 1983; Holmes & Sherman, 1982; Kareem & Barnard, 1982). The preference for familiar but unrelated individuals is taken as evidence for recognition by association or familiarity.

Phenotype Matching

As with association/familiarity, recognition of kin by phenotype matching is achieved through use of cues presented by conspecifics. Here, however, the learning of cues is assimilated into a single template and conspecifics are compared to this. Based on the assumption that genetically related individuals possess similar cues, it allows for recognition of individuals not previously encountered. Evidence for this mechanism has focussed on examining an individual's preference between an unrelated and unfamiliar conspecific and a related but unfamiliar individual. This may have been achieved by cross-fostering (Hepper, 1983), or giving a choice of paternal half-siblings (Kareem & Barnard, 1982; Waldman, 1981) or individuals from successive litters (Grau, 1982). When individuals exhibit a discriminative response between the unfamiliar but related, and unfamiliar and unrelated conspecific, this is taken as evidence for recognition by phenotype matching. This mechanism also allows for the identification of the degree of relatedness by the closeness of match to the template.

Recognition Genes

The ability to recognize kin could be directly encoded by the individual's genes. There have been two suggestions for recognition genes. First, as proposed by Hamilton (1964b), individuals have a supergene that determines "(a) some perceptible feature of the organism, (b) the perception of that feature, and c) the social response consequent upon what was perceived" (p. 25), termed the "greenbeard" effect (Dawkins, 1982). Alternatively, a recognition gene could determine only the cue and recognition of this, and any response consequent on this recognition is determined by a separate gene (Hepper, 1986c). Although there has been some evidence for "recognition" genes (e.g., Grosberg & Quinn, 1986; Keller & Ross, 1998), there are many methodological problems to overcome to demonstrate the existence of a recognition gene (Hepper, 1986b). Furthermore, there has been much debate surrounding whether a recognition gene could exist (e.g., Crozier, 1986; Gardner & West, 2010; Grafen, 1990; Rousset & Rowe, 2007).

Mechanisms of Kin Recognition

These mechanisms, or variants thereof, have been considered to be the mechanisms of kin recognition. However, their general nature poses problems for an understanding of exactly how individuals recognize kin. Each has points of strength but also points of weakness. For example, although "spatial distribution" provides information on the cues used in recognition it does not elucidate how these are acquired. "Association/familiarity" describes how individuals may learn cues, but not how they use this information. "Phenotype matching" provides an answer to how individuals use cues via a comparison against a template, but exactly how this is acquired is less clearly identified. "Recognition genes" may be extremely difficult to demonstrate, even if they could exist.

Recognizing these problems, individuals attempted to refine and revise descriptions of possible mechanisms. For example, Waldman (1988) proposed mechanisms could be categorized by the cues that are used. If individuals use cues presented by their conspecifics, this he termed *direct recognition*, whereas if individuals used cues not presented by their conspecifics, for example the environment, he termed this *indirect recognition*. Porter (1988) proposed another dichotomy based on whether the individuals recognize kin by associating with them, *direct familiarity* or they recognize kin with whom they are unfamiliar by the fact they have associated with other kin who bear similar cues to these unfamiliar kin, *indirect familiarity*. Although clarifying particular aspects of recognition, for example, the cues used, or how recognition may be acquired, they do not account for all aspects of the recognition process.

One important issue to clarify is that individuals are not restricted to recognizing kin by a single mechanism. Often, when discussing mechanisms of kin recognition, it is explicitly, or implicitly, implied that individuals use one mechanism or another. Mechanisms of kin recognition are not mutually exclusive. Given the importance of recognizing kin, and the potential consequences of making errors in recognition, the overriding concern must be to make an accurate decision on relatedness. Thus, individuals could be expected to use a number of mechanisms.

For example, the bank vole (*Clethrionomys glareolus*) has been demonstrated to use mechanisms of "association/familiarity" and "phenotype matching" (Kruczek, 2007). Prepubertal females, when given a two-choice test between males differing in relatedness and familiarity, were found to prefer the familiar males (whether siblings or foster brothers) over unfamiliar males (whether siblings or unrelated males). Actual experience of the conspecific seems important here. However, mature females, when given a choice, preferred the novel odor of a genetically unrelated male to siblings regardless of whether this conspecific was familiar or unfamiliar. Here, the odor of relatedness, whether experienced or not, determined the preference. Thus, different mechanisms of recognition may coexist in the same individual (see also Villavicencio, Marquez, Quispe, & Vasquez, 2009).

A final issue to consider is the importance of differentiating between experimental manipulations and the natural ecology of the animal. Individuals will acquire their ability to recognize kin in their natural setting. Experimentally, it is very easy to undertake manipulations (e.g., cross-fostering animals), however, this situation may not occur naturally. For example, I cross-fostered rat pups to elucidate the role of familiarity in the development of sibling recognition (Hepper, 1983). Pups did learn about the nonkin they were reared with. However, rat pups are born into a nest that is protected and defended by their mother (Barnett, 1975). Thus, there will be little opportunity for pups to learn about unrelated individuals. Cross-fostering only has relevance for confirming that learning is required in the acquisition of kin recognition. Care must be taken in extrapolating further that individuals may learn about nonkin.

One of the main problems with the mechanisms as described is that they cover a number of different aspects of the kin recognition process at a very general level and provide little detail of the fundamental processes involved. Deconstructing kin recognition, defined as the underlying process enabling an individual to determine the degree of relatedness of other individuals, reveals three broad components (Hepper, 1991c; Mateo, 2004). These are: cues used to indicate kinship, a mechanism to enable the individual to compare cues of conspecifics to assess kinship, and a process enabling the individual to acquire information about its kin.

The remainder of the chapter will discuss each of these elements in turn. I concentrate upon theoretical aspects of each to illustrate what each component must deliver to enable an individual to be able to recognize kin.

The Cues of Recognition

In order to recognize conspecifics as kin or nonkin, individuals must use some cue that is associated with kinship. Any cue that is used in the recognition of kin must satisfy a number of conditions.

First, the cue must reliably delimit kin from nonkin in the situations in which it is used. Cues may be used in specific situations or at particular times in the individual's life. Individuals may use different cues at different times or multiple cues at any specific time. However, whatever cue is used it must correlate highly with kinship. Ideally, the cue used should be able to provide information on the degree of relatedness.

Second, there must be stability and continuity of the cue between the individual undertaking the recognition and the conspecific "presenting" the cue for inspection. If the cue used is highly labile and influenced by external factors, it could be different each time encountered and hence valueless in enabling the discrimination of kinship. Both animals must use the same cue; that is, there is continuity of cue between individuals.

Cues may be divided into two broad categories: cues presented by nonconspecifics and cues presented by conspecifics.

NONCONSPECIFIC CUES

The vital element for individuals to accrue the benefits in fitness as espoused by kinship theory is the ability to respond differentially to kin and nonkin. This could be achieved in the absence of using any specific cue that delineates kin from nonkin. Individuals, if by fact of their lifestyle only encounter kin, then this may give the impression of kin recognition. There are a number of situations where this may occur. For example, guards of the sweat bee (*Lassioglossum zephyrum*) prevent nonkin from entering the hive (Greenberg, 1979). Thus, the workers in the colony may not encounter nonkin. Similarly, newly hatched chicks in the nest may only experience kin if their parents have prevented unrelated individuals from laying eggs in the nest, and only they, the parents, care for them. In both cases, individuals may respond to all individuals encountered as kin, as others have ensured that these individuals will not encounter nonkin. Thus, a combination of a restricted environment with little opportunity to encounter nonkin, perhaps due to the guarding behavior of parents or other colony members, would enable individuals to respond to all conspecifics as kin. Such a mechanism, however, does not allow for the recognition of degrees of relatedness.

Environmental/Spatial Cues

Individuals may rely on their environment to provide cues that enable them to assess kinship. One example is presented by the Strawberry poison frog (*Oophaga pumilio*). Mothers leave a single egg in the water-filled axil of a bromeliad or other water-holding plant. The tadpole develops in this location, and the mother returns to the plant to feed the tadpole by laying unfertilized eggs into the water pool. This continues for about 6 weeks, with the mother returning to the same location. If the tadpole is moved and substituted for another unrelated tadpole, which may differ in age by up to 10 days, the mother still continues to provision the original "nest site" (Stynoski, 2009). It appears that the mother has no recognition of her tadpole, but has an accurate recognition of where she deposited her egg. Here, recognition is achieved by spatial location cues. Given the lack of mobility of tadpoles, there is little chance of moving location by themselves and so a recognition system based on spatial location will accurately determine kinship in this case.

More generally, any environmental cue—home range, nest site, food source, etc.—could be used as a cue of kinship if the cue correlates with relatedness. Individuals encountered within a specific physical location are kin, and those encountered outside are nonkin. It is more difficult to see how the degree of relatedness could be determined from these cues (e.g., the nest site).

Internal State

Individuals may use their internal state to influence their behavior (Hepper, 1986b). Many adult male mammals will kill young but appear to inhibit killing their own young and may prevent other adult males from killing them (Elwood, 1991). Males appear to inhibit their infanticidal tendencies around the time when their young are born and, cohabitation with females and copulation appear important in the inhibition of infanticide (Elwood, 1991). Given the potential costs of killing offspring, such an internal cue is advantageous. The selectivity of any "recognition" achieved here must be questioned. A change in an individual's state that influences behavior would apply globally across all the individual's behavioral encounters. Thus, a change in state from infanticidal to noninfanticidal would not only inhibit killing of own offspring but also any similarly aged offspring encountered. However, such an error may be acceptable given the huge costs (in terms of fitness) of killing one's own offspring.

It is difficult to see how, if this cue were to operate, the degree of relatedness could be determined.

CONSPECIFIC CUES

Cues presented by conspecifics may provide greater opportunities for accurate determination of kinship, and there are two general types of cues. Animals could use individual cues, in which all conspecifics are represented by an individually distinct cue. Alternatively, individuals may use a group cue, in which all members of the kin group are represented by, and share, the same "group" cue.

Individual Cues

Recognition could be achieved through the use of cues of individuality. Many species produce individual cues that are stable over time and are able to be reliably discriminated by other conspecifics (Halpin, 1986; Johnston, 2008; Thom & Hurst, 2004). Although accurately denoting individuality, they would not immediately depict kinship and the degree of relatedness, unless associated with some other factor (see the development of kin recognition). True cues of individuality are considered at the level of the population, and with the exception of identical twins, reliably depict each individual distinctively. However, individuals often live in groups and not the whole population, at least for part of their lives, and here other factors may mark conspecifics as individuals within this group, for example, dominance. In groups in which there is a single dominant male, most likely the father of the group's offspring (e.g., the silverback in gorillas), dominance would represent a cue of individuality (Hepper & Wells, 2010). Thus, there may be cues that single out conspecifics as individuals that may not be true signals of individuality, but in a specific context serve reliably as an indicator of individuality.

Group Cues

Recognition could be achieved through the use of "group" cues. These are cues that all individuals in a particular kin group possess. With regard to the recognition of kin, the best example would be a genetic cue—that is, a cue that is shared by all members of the family and varies with relatedness. The more closely related two individuals are, the more similar are their cues. There is much evidence for the existence of a genetically based cue. Studies that have examined individual preferences for unfamiliar but related individuals imply that conspecifics share a genetically determined cue (e.g., Breed, 1983; Brown, Brown, & Crosbie, 1993; Hepper, 1983; Kareem & Barnard, 1982; Waldman, 1981). Furthermore, some studies have found evidence that the cue varies with genetic relatedness (Bateson, 1982; Greenberg, 1979; Hepper, 1987).

It should be noted that although talking about a "genetic" cue, an individual's underlying genes are represented through their phenotypic expression and this is what is actually perceived by conspecifics. To accurately predict relatedness there must be a good correlation between genotype and phenotype.

Evidence for a more direct genetic contribution to an identifying cue arises from studies examining the discrimination of individuals differing in major histocompatibility complex (MHC) type or in major urinary proteins (MUP). Tadpoles of the African clawed toad (*Xenopus laevis*) prefer siblings who are identical in MHC type compared to siblings who are nonidentical (Villinger & Waldman, 2008). Male outbred derived mice (*Mus musculus*) treat siblings with the same MUP type as themselves differently from siblings with a different MUP type (Hurst et al., 2001). These studies indicate that a link exists between the individual's genotype and the expression of the phenotype, and that a genetically determined cue can influence discrimination.

Individuals could possess a "group" cue shared by all those living together that arises through common environmental factors. For example, diet may influence odor production (Albone, 1984). If related individuals feed on similar foods, they may come to produce a similar odor that enables recognition. For example, juvenile Atlantic salmon (*Salmo salar*) and Brook trout (*Salvelinus fontinalis*) are unable to discriminate kin from nonkin when kin are fed different diets but can when fed the same diet (Rajakaruna & Brown, 2006). To operate successfully, this would require all kin eat the same diet and have a diet sufficiently different from other kin groups to enable discrimination.

A common group cue could be acquired through labelling (Porter, 1988). Individuals living in a group become labelled with a common cue, specific to the group, and recognition is achieved through this cue. This is possible in mammals during the suckling process. Siblings sucking from the mother could become labelled with her odor, and siblings recognize each other through the presentation of a common odor, that of the mother. Such a cue could operate in circumstances in which individuals are continually being labelled, but once labelling stops, for example after weaning, such a cue would no longer be operational.

Summary
Thus, there are a number of different possibilities for cues that could be used to signal kinship. All cues require a good correlation between relatedness and the particular cue used. Different cues could be used in different circumstances, and the use of cues could develop over time. For example, for those species that are born into a confined, protected nest, early in development an absence of recognition or, spatial cues provided by the nest site, may provide sufficient information that correlates highly with kinship, and these cues are able to be used accurately. However, as the individual develops and leaves the nest, other cues will need to be involved to enable kin recognition.

Cues may also operate in combination to influence the salience of any one cue. For example, an individual presenting an unfamiliar conspecific cue of kinship in a familiar spatial location may arouse more concern than the same conspecific cue encountered in an unfamiliar location. Members of paper wasp (*Polistes fuscatus*) colonies are more tolerant of non-nestmates when encountered off the nest than the same non-nestmates encountered on the nest (Gamboa, 1991). Whether this is due to a more salient cue or a differential response determined by an individual's location is unknown. However, a number of different cues may operate in conjunction to enhance the salience of the conspecific's identity.

DETERMINING KINSHIP
Underlying the ability to recognize kin is the neural process that assesses the cue and produces an "answer" regarding the kinship status of the conspecific presenting the cue. Irrespective of what cues are used, an individual will encounter a conspecific and at that point a decision about relatedness is required to determine the appropriate behavioral response. At its most basic level, this process must involve a comparison of the cue perceived by the individual against some "standard" of kinship possessed by that individual. Two processes are involved: first, a comparison of cues, and second a decision regarding kinship and the degree of relatedness.

Comparison of Cue(s)
With regard to the comparison, individuals may possess no "standard" but simply respond to all conspecifics as kin. As long as individuals do not encounter nonkin, this will assess kinship correctly. This may function for individuals in the nest. This may be the individual's original state at the time of emergence, be it hatching or birth.

If individuals do undertake a comparison against a standard, there are two possibilities. Individuals have a stored internal standard within their neural system that provides the necessary information. Alternatively, individuals may have no stored representation but rather generate a comparator when needed. I shall first discuss how kinship may be determined without any stored representation of kin. There are two possibilities, and both require the use of conspecific cues to operate.

First, individuals may use the cues of self to determine relatedness. Any cue presented by self is 100% related to the individual and thus provides an accurate comparator against which to compare conspecifics. In the case of odours, individuals could simply compare their own odor with that presented by their conspecific, and how closely the odours match determines the degree of relatedness. It would be more difficult for auditory cues and somewhat impossible for animals to use visual cues, although the recognition of the relationships within other kin groups could be undertaken by auditory and visual cues (e.g., Parr & De Waal, 1999). Such self-matching has been termed the "armpit effect" by Dawkins (1982). Possible evidence for self-matching has been found in diverse animal groups, for example, the cichlid fish (*Pelvicachromis taeniatus*; Thünken, Waltschyk, Bakker, & Kullman, 2009), brown-headed cowbirds (*Molothrus ater*; Hauber, Sherman, & Paprika, 2000), and golden hamsters (*Mesocricetus auratus*; Mateo & Johnstone, 2000a). However, there are methodological issues in attempting to demonstrate this conclusively, and whether true self-matching has been demonstrated has been debated (Hare, Sealy, Underwood, Ellison, & Stewart, 2003; Hauber & Sherman, 2003; Mateo, 2004).

Second, recognition could be achieved through the process of dishabituation. Individuals habituate to their own cue, and when presented with a different cue, dishabituate, with the degree of dishabituation having the potential to determine the degree of relatedness (Hepper, 1991b).

Alternatively individuals may form a "permanent" representation of their kin. Through their experience individuals form a template(s) that denotes kinship, and individuals are compared against this. This template may take one of two forms. First, an animal may store individual representations of all cues used, for example, individual signatures of all conspecifics encountered. Individuals do not amalgamate cues but rather "store" each individual (or their cues) as separate entities.

Second, individuals may form a single template made up of the conspecific cues it has encountered. The composition of the template needs to be carefully considered. Acquiring the template from a number of individuals has both advantages and disadvantages. The more cues of kin used, the wider the applicability of the template. This could be beneficial if the decision to be made is simply whether a conspecific is kin or nonkin. The broader the representation, the more likely kin will be included. However, if the decision is to assess the degree of relatedness, then the broader the representation, with more kin included in its generation, the more difficult this becomes. To determine relatedness, a template constructed of a single cue would be advantageous; in this case, self provides the best cue.

Decision of Kinship

Upon encountering a conspecific, the individual has to make a determination of kinship. At its simplest level, this is a bimodal decision about whether the individual is kin or nonkin. This raises the issue about where the cutoff for kinship is placed. For diploid species individuals will be related to their kin by 100% (identical siblings), 50% (parents) and on average 50% (siblings), 25% (half siblings), 12.5% (cousins), to 0% (unrelated conspecifics). Individuals could thus place the point at which they determine an individual is kin anywhere along this range (100–0). This is an area requiring further study, but evidence has indicated animals are able to make very fine discriminations of kinship. Male Oldfield mice (*Peromyscus polionotus rhoadsi*) show a preference for more distantly related females over less distantly related females who differ by an average of 1.3% in their kinship (Ryan & Lacy, 2003). Thus, if individuals do make a bimodal decision of kin or nonkin, individuals would be able to make fine discriminations around any cutoff.

Kin selection provides additional benefits if the degree of kinship can be determined, not just a determination of kin or nonkin. Thus, individuals could be expected to evaluate the degree of relatedness.

Many studies of kin recognition only give individuals a choice of kin and nonkin in a two-choice test; therefore, the opportunity to display discriminations of degrees of relatedness is not present. When presented with conspecifics of different degrees of relatedness, however, individuals do appear to discriminate between them (Bateson, 1982; Greenberg, 1979; Hepper, 1987).

The natural behavior of animals also provides evidence of recognition of degrees of relatedness. For example, the aoudad (Barbary sheep, *Ammotragus lervia*) is adapted to the rugged desert mountains of North Africa, an environment that requires conservation of energy. As a consequence, behaviors of lying and resting predominate. Observations of the animals resting demonstrates that kin rest more closely together than nonkin and, more closely related kin rest closer than less closely related kin (Cassinello & Calabuig, 2008). This implies the ability to discriminate different degrees of relatedness rather than the operation of a bimodal decision of kin and nonkin.

Summary

None of the above proposals are mutually exclusive and those that are used may be determined by the developmental stage of the individual. Moreover, different species will undoubtedly use different means. The ability to store individual representations of conspecifics may be beyond species lacking the required underlying neural structures, and this may limit the mechanisms that can be used to assess kinship in those species. Similarly, what neural structures are required to make discriminations of different degrees of relatedness are unknown and some species, or animals at particular developmental stages, may be limited to decisions of kin and nonkin due to the absence of sufficient neural structure to enable fine-grain discriminations. Presently, there is little understanding of the underlying neural processes that enable a determination of kinship and relatedness.

THE DEVELOPMENT OF KIN RECOGNITION

If individuals must acquire knowledge about their kin before being able to recognize them, then the issue of how they acquire this information must be considered. Given the unlikelihood that this information is hardwired through an individual's genes (Hepper, 1986b), it would be expected that an individual has to learn about its kin before being able to recognize them. The most vital consideration for the individual is that the information acquired does reflect kinship. Two assumptions can be made. First, the individual begins as a tabula rasa regarding its kin. Second, individuals will learn nonselectively from the most salient individuals (cues) in their environment. That is, individuals do not know who, for example, their mother is and acquire information from her. Rather, individuals will simply acquire information from the conspecific who provides care for them. Thus, it is vital that learning contingencies are established that ensure the individual learns information from its kin. This section concentrates on how such selectivity can be achieved, rather than the actual mechanisms of learning (e.g., classical conditioning, exposure learning, etc.).

The most reliable option would be to acquire information from self, as this ensures that any information learned is from a genetically related individual, in this case 100% related. There are a number of studies indicating individuals may learn from self (Hauber & Sherman, 2001).

If, however, information is acquired from others, then the individual must ensure it learns about kin. There are a number of possibilities to ensure this.

Individuals could commence learning before birth or hatching, an ability that appears universal across all vertebrate groups: fish (Brannon, 1972), amphibians (Hepper & Waldman, 1992), reptiles (Sneddon, Hepper, & Manolis, 2001), birds (Sneddon, Hepper, & Hadden, 1998), and mammals (Wells & Hepper, 2006); and has been found in invertebrates as well (Isingrini, Lenoir, & Jaisson, 1985). Given the likelihood that "prenatal" experiences will be restricted to either self or siblings, or from parents, learning about conspecific cues at this stage may ensure any information acquired is from related individuals.

If individuals learn about kin after birth, then learning from their caretaker(s) or "nestmates" presents opportunities to ensure the individual learns from kin. Parents or caretakers recognize their own young and thus ensure the primary experience of young is with kin. Similarly, if there is more than one offspring born, parents may keep their offspring together, thus providing individuals with the opportunity to learn from nestmates (kin).

To ensure that individuals learn about their kin, environmental contingencies must be arranged to ensure any learning is from kin. The timing of learning becomes crucial in ensuring that the individual does in fact learn about genetically related individuals. Individuals should acquire their knowledge about kin when kin are naturally present. Thus, rat (*Rattus norvegicus*) pups who live in the nest with their mother until weaning at 3 weeks are provided an opportunity to learn about kin, and only kin, during this 3-week period. Indeed, during this period, they develop the ability to recognize their siblings and parents (Hepper, 1983). Exactly when during this period rat pups first "know" their siblings is unknown. In other species, there is a well-defined period for the acquisition of information about kin. For example, the zebra fish (*Danio rerio*) must experience its siblings on day 6 post fertilization to be able to recognize them subsequently. Exposure either up to day 5 or beginning day 7 does not result in recognition (Gerlach, Hodgins-Davis, Avolio, & Schunter, 2008).

A second factor that influences the timing of any learning is that individuals should be able to recognize kin by the time nonkin are first encountered. Learning need not necessarily be complete by then, but individuals should be able to discriminate kin from nonkin, allowing any further learning (if required) to be from related individuals. A number of studies demonstrate that recognition appears just prior to the time of encountering nonkin (e.g., starlings [*Sturnus vulgaris*]; van Elsacker, Pinxten, & Verheyen, 1988; Belding's ground squirrels [*Spermophilus beldingi*]; Holmes, 1988).

It appears that individuals may also be monitoring their ability to recognize and be recognized by kin, and this influences their behavior. For example, the Fur seal (*Arctocephalus tropicalis*) gives birth to its young in large colonies, containing many other mothers and their young, and thus posing problems for recognition. There is an additional pressure as mothers have to leave their offspring to return to the sea to hunt and provide food for themselves and support their nursing pups. Mothers may be foraging for periods of 2–3 weeks and return to the pups for 3–4 days before departing again. Mothers and offspring recognize each other using vocal cues, and this is established within 2–5 days of birth. Most interestingly, it is only when mother–offspring recognition has been established that the mother will depart on her first hunting trip to sea after birth (Charrier, Mathevon, & Jouventin, 2001). Not only is the process of learning timed to ensure mother and young learn about each other, but mothers do not leave their young until such recognition has been established.

Once knowledge about kin is acquired, it may require continued experience of kin to maintain this information. It appears that some species need constant exposure to maintain recognition. The Spiny mouse (*Acomys cahirinus*) loses its ability to recognize kin following some 8 days of isolation (Porter & Wyrick, 1979). However, Belding's ground squirrels (*Spermophilus beldingi*) retain knowledge of their kin after hibernation (Mateo & Johnston, 2000b). The necessity for exposure may depend on the recognition being undertaken. The domestic dog (*Canis familiaris*) demonstrates mother–offspring recognition even after separation for

2 years after weaning, whereas the ability to recognize siblings is lost unless siblings remain in contact during this period (Hepper, 1994).

One final consideration is how individuals acquire information on the degree of relatedness. In situations in which an individual uses a single template to make decisions about kinship, the degree of matching enables the degree of relatedness to be assessed. The closer the match to the template, the more closely related the individual can be assumed to be. However, if recognition is achieved through matching of conspecific cues to many individual templates, then these need to be associated with some other factor that will enable the determination of the degree of relatedness. Familiarity provides one such cue, as long as familiarity correlates with kinship. The more familiar an individual is, then the more closely related that individual is assumed to be. How the association between familiarity and relatedness takes place is unknown. Presumably, some factor, exposure, or perhaps positive reinforcement, contribute to the association of familiarity with individual cues. Individuals thus assess the degree of familiarity, and as long as this correlates highly with relatedness, individuals can successfully discriminate how closely related conspecifics are.

SUMMARY: RECOGNIZING KIN

The preceding review has attempted to identify the components that may exist to enable an individual to recognize its kin. None are mutually exclusive within or between the three components, and they may combine in a variety of ways to enable the recognition of kin. Although the experimental evidence indicates that animals do recognize kin, exactly how they achieve this is requiring of further study.

Conclusion

Throughout the animal kingdom, kinship is a major factor in influencing the behavioral responses of animals. Who animals aid, cooperate with, care for, and avoid mating with, are all influenced by kinship. It is clear that individuals who differentially respond to kin and nonkin can gain significant advantages in their fitness over individuals unable to do so. Thus, it is not surprising that individuals will possess mechanisms that enable them to recognize kin, although exactly how this is achieved is unknown.

Future Directions

The ubiquity of kin recognition across all animal species indicates that this is a major influence on the individual's behavior. Although it is only since the mid-1970s that studies of kin recognition began, significant advances have been made in our understanding of kin recognition and kin discrimination. However, some key issues remain to be addressed.

Evidence is accumulating that animals discriminate kin from nonkin—but not in all situations. Kin selection theory should provide the answers to why individuals differentiate kin from nonkin in some situations but not others. Very simply, they should discriminate when there are gains in fitness and not discriminate where there are no gains. Evidence to prove a negative is difficult both methodologically and statistically (and in terms of publication), thus reports of a lack of kin discrimination are far fewer than reports of kin discrimination. More naturalistic studies are needed to fully describe the kin-directed behaviors—and nonkin-directed behaviors—of animals. This is an onerous task requiring the careful documentation of kin relationships either through longitudinal observations, or with the advent of new technologies, DNA sampling. Of particular interest is whether behaviors are directed to others in proportion to their degree of relatedness. For example, if a primate is intervening in an agonistic encounter, do they contribute more effort the more closely related the other individual is? Information on the distribution of behaviors to differently related kin will provide information on both the ultimate cause of kin discrimination (kin selection) and the proximate causes of kin recognition (how finely attuned an individual's recognition system is).

If, as is most likely, individuals have to learn who their kin are, there is much to be understood about this process. How does the individual's environment or ecology ensure kin are learned about? The development of kin recognition has attracted some interest, but how kin recognition develops has not. By the development of kin recognition, I refer to the newborn, newly hatched, or newly emerged individual's acquisition of information about kin. As this chapter shows, this has been well documented. What is less clear is how this develops as the individual ages. For example, a female rat pup may have a sequence of kin to learn about: first its mother; then its siblings. At reproductive maturity, it needs to avoid related adult males, and after successfully mating, it has to recognize its own offspring. Little attention has been paid to this development and what mechanisms underlie it. It appears to have been assumed that this is a single mechanism and developmental process, but this is not necessarily the case.

Given the fact that the acquisition of kinship is nondirectional, and the individual acquires this information from whoever is available, the contingencies that have been evolved to ensure that the individual acquires information about kin are worthy of more detailed investigation. How do individuals ensure they learn about kin? The easiest solution to the problem is to use information acquired from self. As the individual is 100% related to self, this information provides the most secure information of genetic relatedness. Although easy to see this operating when cues are olfactory, it becomes more problematic for species whose primary senses are auditory and, particularly, visual. How could learning about self contribute here?

The underlying neural processes of kin recognition are enshrouded in mystery. Some neural processing must occur, but where and what are unknown. Not only should attention be paid to what neural processes occur, but also to how the animal's neural structures and abilities limit or enable certain mechanisms of kin recognition. We might expect fine discriminations of kinship to be made in primates due to their neural and cognitive capacity, but how might we explain similar discriminations in insects, who have a markedly different neural capacity? Indeed, the similarity of function across different species may elucidate some of the mysteries of how the neural system and brain operate.

Kin discrimination and kin recognition are fascinating phenomena that appear to determine many aspects of an individual's social behavior across all animal species. Further investigation is needed to fully comprehend how this ability influences so many aspects of animal's lives.

References

Albone, E.S. (1980). *Mammalian semiochemistry: The investigation of chemical signals between mammals.* Chichester, UK: Wiley.
Archie, E.A., Hollister-Smith, J.A., Poole, J.H., Lee, P.C., Moss, C.J., Maldonado, J.E., et al. (2007). Behavioural inbreeding avoidance in wild African elephants. *Molecular Ecology, 16,* 4138–4148.
Barnard, C.J. (1990). Kin recognition. Problems, prospect and the evolution of discrimination systems. *Advances in the Study of Behaviour, 19,* 29–82.
Barnett, S.A. (1975). *The rat: A study in behaviour.* Chicago: University of Chicago Press.
Bateson, P. (1978). Sexual imprinting and optimal outbreeding. *Nature, 273,* 659–660.
Bateson, P. (1980). Optimal outbreeding and the development of sexual preferences in Japanese quail. *Zeitschrift für Tierpsychologie, 53,* 231–244.
Bateson, P.P.G. (1982). Preferences for cousins in Japanese quail. *Nature, 295,* 236–237.
Bateson, P.P.G. (Ed.). (1983a). *Mate choice.* Cambridge: Cambridge University Press.
Bateson, P.P.G. (1983b). Optimal outbreeding. In P.P.G. Bateson (Ed.), *Mate choice* (pp. 257–277). Cambridge: Cambridge University Press.
Beach, F.A., & Jaynes, J. (1956). Studies of maternal retrieving in rats. 1: Recognition of young. *Journal of Mammalogy, 37,* 177–180.
Betram, B.C.R. (1979). Ostriches recognise their eggs and discard others. *Nature, 279,* 233–234.
Blaustein, A.R., Porter, R.H., & Breed, M.D. (1988). Kin recognition in animals–empirical evidence and conceptual issues. *Behavior Genetics, 18,* 405–407.
Brannon, E.L. (1972). Mechanisms controlling migration of sockeye salmon fry. *International Pacific Salmon Fish Commission Bulletin, 21,* 1–86.
Breed, M.D. (1983). Nestmate recognition in honey bees. *Animal Behaviour, 31,* 86–91.
Brown, G.E., & Brown J.A. (1993). Social dynamics in salmonid fishes: Do kin make better neighbours? *Animal Behaviour, 45,* 863–871.
Brown, G.E., Brown, J.A., & Crosbie, A.M. (1993). Phenotype matching in juvenile rainbow trout. *Animal Behaviour, 46,* 1223–1225.
Bry, C., & Gillet, C. (1980). Reduction of cannibalism in Pike (*Esox lucius*) fry by isolation of full-sib families. *Reproduction Nutrition and Development, 20,* 173–182.
Bull, C.M., Doherty, M., Schulze, L.R., & Pamula, Y. (1994). Recognition of offspring by females of the Australian skink, *Tiliqua rugosa. Journal of Herpetology, 28,* 117–120.
Bull, C.M., Griffin, C.L., Bonnett, M., Gardner, M.G., & Cooper, S.J.B. (2001). Discrimination between related and unrelated individuals in the Australian lizard, *Egernia striolata. Behavioral Ecology and Sociobiology, 50,* 173–179.
Burghardt, G.M. (2005). *The genesis of animal play.* Cambridge, Mass; MIT Press.
Caro, T. (2005). *Antipredator defenses in birds and mammals.* London: University of Chicago Press.
Cassinello, J., & Calabuig, G. (2008). Spatial association in a highly inbred ungulate population: Evidence of fine-scale kin recognition. *Ethology, 114,* 124–132.
Charlesworth, B., & Charlesworth, D. (1999). The genetic basis of inbreeding depression. *Genetical Research, 74,* 329–340.
Charlesworth, D., & Charlesworth, B. (1987). Inbreeding depression and its evolutionary consequences. *Annual Review of Ecology and Systematics, 18,* 237–268.
Charrier, I., Mathevon, N., & Jouventin, P. (2001). Mother's voice recognition by seal pups. *Nature, 412,* 873.
Cheney, D.L., & Seyfarth, R.M. (1980). Vocal recognition in free ranging vervet monkeys. *Animal Behaviour, 28,* 362–367.
Cheney, D.L., & Seyfarth, R.M. (1982). Recognition of individuals within and between groups of free-ranging Vervet monkeys. *American Zoologist, 22,* 519–529.
Clark, R.W. (2004). Kin recognition in rattle snakes. *Proceedings of the Royal Society of London B (Suppl), 271,* S243–S245.

Crozier, R.H. (1986). Genetic clonal recognition abilities in marine invertebrates must be maintained by selection for something else. *Evolution, 40*, 1100–1101.

Cullen, E. (1957). Adaptations in the kittiwake to cliff nesting. *Ibis, 99*, 275–305.

Dawkins, R. (1982). *The extended phenotype.* Oxford: Oxford University Press.

Darwin, C. (1859). *The origin of species by natural selection.* London: J Murray.

Dobler, R., & Kölliker, M. (2010). Kin-selected siblicide and cannibalism in the European earwig. *Behavioral Ecology, 21*, 257–263.

Dudley, S.A., & File, A.L. (2007). Kin recognition in an annual plant. *Biological Letters.* Doi: 10.1098/rsbl.2007.0232

Elwood, R.W. (1991). Parental states as mechanisms for kinship recognition and deception about relatedness. In P.G. Hepper (Ed.), *Kin recognition* (pp. 289–307). Cambridge: Cambridge University Press.

Fagen, R. (1981). *Animal play behavior.* New York: Oxford University Press.

Fletcher, D.J.C., & Michener, C.D. (1987). *Kin recognition in animals.* Chichester: J Wiley & Sons.

Gamboa, G.J., Foster, R.L., & Scope, J.A. (1991). Effects of stage of colony cycle, context, and intercolony distance on conspecific tolerance by paper wasps (*Polistes fuscatus*). *Behavioural Ecology & Sociobiology, 29*, 87–94.

Gardner, A., & West, S.A. (2010). Greenbeards. *Evolution, 64*, 25–38.

Gerlach, G., Hodgins-Davis, A., Avolio, C., & Schunter, C. (2008). Kin recognition in zebrafish: A 24 hour window for olfactory imprinting. *Proceedings of the Royal Society of London B, 275*, 2165–2170.

Grafen, A. (1990). Do animals really recognise kin? *Animal Behaviour, 39*, 42–54.

Greenberg, L. (1979). Genetic component of bee odor in kin recognition. *Science, 206*, 1095–1097.

Grosberg, R.K., & Quinn, J.F. (1986). The genetic control and consequences of kin recognition by the larvae of a colonial marine invertebrate. *Nature, 322*, 456–459.

Grau, H.J. (1982). Kin recognition in white-footed deermice (*Peromyscus leucopus*). *Animal Behaviour, 30*, 497–505.

Hain, T.J.A., & Neff, B.D. (2009). Kinship affects innate responses to a predator in bluegill *Lepomis macrochirus* larvae. *Journal of Fish Biology, 75*, 728–737.

Halpin, Z.T. (1986). Individual odors among mammals: Origins and functions. *Advances in the Study of Behaviour, 16*, 39–70.

Hamilton, W.D. (1963). The evolution of altruistic behaviour. *American Naturalist, 97*, 354–356.

Hamilton, W.D. (1964a). The genetical evolution of social behaviour, I. *Journal of Theoretical Biology, 7*, 1–16.

Hamilton, W.D. (1964b). The genetical evolution of social behaviour, II. *Journal of Theoretical Biology, 7*, 17–52.

Hare, J.F., Sealy, S.G., Underwood, T.J., Ellison, K.S., & Stewart, R.L.M. (2003). Evidence of self-referent phenotype matching revisited: Airing out the armpit effect. *Animal Cognition, 6*, 65–68.

Hauber, M.E., & Sherman, P.W. (2003). Designing and interpreting experimental tests of self-referent phenotype matching. *Animal Cognition, 6*, 69–71.

Hauber, M.E., Sherman, P.W., & Paprika, D. (2000). Self-referent phenotype matching in a brood parasite: The armpit effect in brownheaded cowbirds (*Molothrus ater*). *Animal Cognition, 3*, 113–117.

Hayaki, H. (1985). Social play of juvenile and adolescent chimps in the Mahale Mountains National Park, Tanzania. *Primates, 26*, 343–360.

Hepper, P.G. (1983). Sibling recognition in the rat. *Animal Behaviour, 31*, 1177–1191.

Hepper, P.G. (1986a). Parental recognition in the rat. *Quarterly Journal of Experimental Psychology, 38B*, 151–160.

Hepper, P.G. (1986b). Kin recognition: Functions and mechanisms. A review. *Biological Reviews of the Cambridge Philosophical Society, 61*, 63–93.

Hepper, P.G. (1986c). Can recognition genes for kin recognition exist? In L. Passera, & J.-P. Lachaud (Eds.), *The individual and society* (pp. 31–35). Toulouse, FR: Editions Privat.

Hepper, P.G. (1987). The discrimination of different degrees of relatedness in the rat: Evidence for a genetic identifier? *Animal Behaviour, 35*, 549–554.

Hepper, P.G. (1991a). Introduction. In P.G. Hepper (Ed.), *Kin recognition* (pp. 1–5). Cambridge, UK: Cambridge University Press.

Hepper, P.G. (Ed.). (1991b). *Kin recognition.* Cambridge, UK: Cambridge University Press.

Hepper, P.G. (1991c). Recognizing kin: Ontogeny and classification. In P.G. Hepper (Ed.), *Kin recognition* (pp. 259–288). Cambridge, UK: Cambridge University Press.

Hepper, P.G. (1994). Long-term retention of kinship recognition established during infancy in the domestic dog. *Behavioural Processes, 33*, 3–14.

Hepper, P.G., & Waldman, B. (1992). Embryonic olfactory learning in frogs. *Quarterly Journal of Experimental Psychology, 44B*, 179–197.

Hepper, P.G., & Wells, D.L. (2010). Individually identifiable body odors are produced by the Gorilla and discriminated by humans. *Chemical Senses,* This is now print published with details Vol-35, pp. 263–268.

Holekamp, K.E., Sakai, S.T., & Lundrigan, B.L. (2007). Social intelligence in the spotted hyena (*Crocuta crocuta*). *Philosophical Transactions of the Royal Society B, 362*, 523–538.

Holmes, W.G. (1988). Kinship and the development of social preferences. In E.M. Blass (Ed.), *Handbook of behavioral neurobiology, 9. Developmental psychobiology and behavioral ecology* (pp. 389–413). New York: Plenum.

Holmes, W.G., & Sherman, P.W. (1982). The ontogeny of kin recognition in two species of ground squirrels. *American Zoologist, 22*, 491–517.

Holmes, W.G., & Sherman, P.W. (1983). Kin recognition in animals. *American Scientist, 71*, 46–55.

Hurst, J.L., Payne, C.E., Nevison, C.M., Marie, A.D., Humphries, R.E., Robertson, D.H.L., et al. (2001). Individual recognition in mice mediated by major urinary proteins. *Nature, 414*, 631–634.

Isingrini, M., Lenoir, A., & Jaisson, P. (1985). Pre-imaginal learning as a basis of colony-brood recognition in the ant, *Cataglyphis cursor. Proceedings of the National Academy of Sciences, USA, 82*, 8545–8547.

Johnston, R.E. (2008). Individual odors and social communication: Individual recognition, kin recognition, and scent overmarking. *Advances in the Study of Behaviour, 38*, 439–505.

Kareem, A.M., & Barnard, C.J. (1982). The importance of kinship and familiarity in social interactions between mice. *Animal Behaviour, 30*, 594–601.

Kaplan, J. (1977). Patterns of fight interference in free-ranging rhesus monkeys. *American Journal of Physical Anthropology*, *47*, 279–288.

Kaplan, J. (1978). Fight interference and altruism in rhesus monkeys. *American Journal of Physical Anthropology*, *49*, 241–250.

Keller, L., & Ross, K.G. (1998). Selfish genes: A green beard in the red fire ant. *Nature*, *394*, 573–575.

Keller, L.F., & D.M. Waller. (2002). Inbreeding effects in wild populations. *Trends in Ecology and Evolution*, *17*, 230–241.

Kruczek, M. (2007). Recognition of kin in bank voles (*Clethrionomys glareolus*). *Physiology and Behaviour*, *90*, 483–489.

Langergraber, K.E., Mitani, J.C., & Vigilant, L. (2007). Wild male chimpanzees preferentially affiliate and cooperate with maternal but not paternal siblings. *American Journal of Physical Anthropology*, S44, 150.

Laws, R.M. (1956). The elephant seal (Mirounga leonina LINA). 2. General, social and reproductive behaviour. *Falklands 1st Dependency Survey, Scientific Report*, *13*, 18.

Lehrman, J., Fickenscher, G., & Boesch, C. (2006). Kin biased investment in wild chimpanzees. *Behaviour*, *143*, 931–955.

Loeb, M.L.G., Diener, L.M., & Pfennig, D.W. (2000). Egg-dumping lace bugs preferentially oviposit with kin. *Animal Behaviour*, *59*, 379–383.

MacGinitie, G.E. (1939). The natural history of the blind goby, *Typhlogobius californiensis* (Steindachner). *American Midl. Naturalist*, *21*, 489–505.

Main, A.R., & Bull, C.M. (1996). Mother-offspring recognition in two Australian lizards, *Tiliqua rugosa* and *Egernia stokesii*. *Animal Behaviour*, *52*, 193–200.

Markman, S., Hill, N., Todrank, J., Heth, G., & Blaustein L. (2009). Differential aggressiveness between fire salamander (*Salamandra infraimmaculata*) larvae covaries with their genetic similarity. *Behavioral Ecology and Sociobiology*, *63*, 1149–1155.

Massey, A. (1977). Agonistic aids and kinship in a group of pig-tailed macaques. *Behavioural Ecology and Sociobiology*, *2*, 31–40.

Mateo, J.M. (2004). Recognition systems and biological organization: The perception component of social recognition. *Annales Zoologici Fennici*, *41*, 729–745.

Mateo, J.M., & Holmes, W.G. (2004). Cross-fostering as a means to study kin recognition. *Animal Behaviour*, *68*, 1451–1459.

Mateo, J.M., & Johnston, R.E. (2000a). Kin recognition and the "armpit effect": Evidence of self-referent phenotype matching. *Proceedings of the Royal Society of London B.*, *267*, 695–700.

Mateo, J.M., & Johnston, R.E. (2000b). Retention of social recognition after hibernation in Belding's ground squirrels. *Animal Behaviour*, *59*, 491–499.

Maynard Smith, J. (1964). Group selection and kin selection. *Nature*, *201*, 1145–1147.

Mitton, J.B. (1993). Theory and data pertinent to the relationship between heterozygosity and fitness. In N.W. Thornhill (Ed.), *The natural history of inbreeding and outbreeding* (pp. 17–41). Chicago: University of Chicago Press.

O'Connor, D.E., & Shine, R. (2006). Kin discrimination in the social lizard *Egernia saxatilis* (Scincidae). *Behaviour and Ecology*, *17*, 206–211.

Packer, C., Gilbert, D.A., Pusey, A.E., & O'Brien, S.J. (1991). A molecular genetic analysis of kinship and cooperation in African lions. *Nature*, *351*, 562–565.

Parr, L.A., & de Waal, F.B.M. (1999). Visual kin recognition in chimpanzees. *Nature*, *399*, 647–648.

Parsons, K.M., Durban, J.W., Claridge, D.E., Balcomb, K.C., Noble, L.R., & Thompson, P.M. (2003). Kinship as a basis for alliance formation between male bottlenose dolphins, *Tursiops truncatus*, in the Bahamas. *Animal Behaviour*, *66*, 185–194.

Peer, K., & Taborsky, M. (2005). Outbreeding depression, but no inbreeding depression in haplodiploid ambrosia beetles with regular sibling mating. *Evolution*, *59*, 317–323.

Petrie, M., Krupa, A., & Burke, T. (1999). Peacocks lek with relatives even in the absence of social and environmental cues. *Nature*, *401*, 155–157.

Pfennig, D.W., Reeve, H.K., & Sherman, P.W. (1993). Kin recognition and cannibalism in spadefoot toad tadpoles. *Animal Behaviour*, *46*, 87–94.

Porter, R.H. (1988). The ontogeny of sibling recognition in rodents–superfamily Muroidea. *Behavior Genetics*, *18*, 483–494.

Porter, R.H., & Wyrick, M. (1979). Sibling recognition in spiny mice (*Acomys cahirinus*): Influence of age and isolation. *Behavioural Ecology and Sociobiology*, *3*, 61–68.

Prévost, J. (1961). *Ecologic du Manchot Empereur*. Paris: Hermann.

Proffitt, F.M., & McLean, I.G. (1991). Recognition of parents' calls by chicks of the Snares Crested penguin. *Bird Behaviour*, *9*, 103–113.

Rajakaruna, R.S., & Brown, J.A. (2006). Effect of dietary cues on kin discrimination of juvenile Atlantic salmon (*Salmo salar*) and brook trout (*Salvelinus fontinalis*). *Canadian Journal of Zoology*, *84*, 839–845.

Romanes, G.J. (1883a). *Animal intelligence*. London: Kegan, Paul and Trench.

Romanes, G.J. (1883b). *Mental evolution in animals*. London: Kegan, Paul and Trench.

Rousset, F., & D. Roze. (2007). Constraints on the origin and maintenance of genetic kin recognition. *Evolution*, *61*, 2320–2330.

Ruch, J., Heinrich, L., Bilde, T., & Schneider, J.M. (2009). Relatedness facilitates cooperation in the subsocial spider, *Stegodyphus tentoriicola*. *BMC Evolutionary Biology*, *9*, 257.

Ryan, K.K., & Lacy, R.C. (2003). Monogamous male bias behaviour towards females according to very small differences in kinship. *Animal Behaviour*, *65*, 379–384.

Schneider, J.M., & Bilde, T. (2008). Benefits of cooperation with genetic kin in a subsocial spider. *Proceedings of the National Academy of Sciences, USA*, *105*, 10843–10846.

Schwab, C, Bugnyar, T. Schloegl, C., & Kotrschal, K. (2008). Enhanced social learning between siblings in common ravens, *Corvus corax*. *Animal Behaviour*, *75*, 501–508.

Seddon, P.J., & van Heezik, Y. (1993). Parent-offspring recognition in the jackass penguin. *Journal of Field Ornithology*, *64*, 27–31.

Seyfarth, R.M., Cheney, D.L., & Marler, P. (1980). Monkey responses to 3 different alarm calls–evidence of predator classification and semantic communication. *Science*, *210*, 801–803.

Sherman, P.W. (1977). Nepotism and the evolution of alarm calls. *Science*, *197*, 1246–1253.

Sneddon, H., Hadden, R., & Hepper, P.G. (1998). Chemosensory learning in the chick embryo. *Physiology & Behavior, 64,* 133–139.

Sneddon, H., Hepper, P.G., & Manolis, C. (2001). Embryonic chemosensory learning in the Saltwater crocodile *Crocodylus porosus*. In G.C. Grigg, F. Seebacher, & C.E. Franklin (Eds.), *Crocodilian biology and evolution* (pp. 378–383). Chipping Norton, Australia : Surrey Beatty.

Studholme, B.J.S. (1994). Parent-offspring recognition in the Fiordland crested penguin (*Eudyptes pachyrhynchus*). *New Zealand Natural Sciences, 21,* 27–36.

Spinka, M., Newberry, R.C., & Bekoff, M. (2001). Mammalian play: Training for the unexpected. *Quarterly Review of Biology, 76,* 141–168.

Starks, P.E. (2004). Recognition systems. *Annals Zoologica Fennici, 41,* 689–892.

Stynoski, J.L. (2009). Discrimination of offspring by indirect recognition in an egg-feeding dendrobatid frog, *Oophaga pumilio*. *Animal Behaviour, 78,* 1351–1356.

Tang-Martinez, Z. (2001). The mechanisms of kin discrimination and the evolution of kin recognition in vertebrates: A critical re-evaluation. *Behavioural Processes, 53,* 21–40.

Thom, M.D., & Hurst, J.L. (2004). Individual recognition by scent. *Annals Zoologica Fennici, 41,* 765–787.

Thünken, T., Waltschyk. N., Bakker, T.C.M., & Kullman, H. (2009). Olfactory self-recognition in a cichlid fish. *Animal Cognition, 12,* 717–724.

Van Elsacker, L., Pinxten, R., & Verheyen, R.F. (1988). Timing of offspring recognition in adult starlings. *Behaviour, 107,* 122–130.

Villavicencio, C.P., Marquez, I.N., Quispe, R., & Vasquez, R.A. (2009). Familiarity and phenotypic similarity influence kin discrimination in the social rodent *Octodon degus*. *Animal Behaviour, 78,* 377–384.

Villinger, J., & Waldman, B. (2008). Self-referent MHC type matching in frog tadpoles. *Proceedings of the Royal Society B, 275,* 1225–1230.

Waldman, B. (1981). Sibling recognition in toad tadpoles– the role of experience. *Zeitschrift für Tierpsychologie, 56,* 341–358.

Waldman, B. (1982). Sibling association among schooling toad tadpoles: Field evidence and implications. *Animal Behaviour, 30,* 700–713.

Waldman, B. (1988). The ecology of kin recognition. *Annual Review of Ecology and Systematics, 19,* 543–571.

Walls, S.C., & Roudebush, R.E. (1991). Reduced aggression toward siblings as evidence of kin recognition in cannibalistic salamanders. *American Naturalist, 138,* 1027–1038.

Wells, D.L., & Hepper, P.G. (2006). Prenatal olfactory learning in the domestic dog. *Animal Behaviour 72,* 681–686.

Wilson, E.O. (1971). *Insect societies*. Cambridge, MA: Belknap Press.

Wilson, E.O. (1975). *Sociobiology: The new synthesis*. Cambridge, MA: Belknap Press.

CHAPTER 14

Kin Selection and Cooperative Courtship in Birds

Alan H. Krakauer *and* Emily H. DuVal

Abstract

The high level of genetic relatedness between parents and offspring is a key feature of family groups and is thought to be a major factor stabilizing social interactions within families. However, these families are only one type of persistent animal social group that strikes a balance between conflict and cooperation. In many species, males aggregate to court females; in a fascinating subset of species, these aggregations also include stable male alliances, and male partners perform elaborate and cooperative courtship displays. These complex social groups provide interesting systems for understanding the costs and benefits of group membership and how group formation occurs. Kinship, a central aspect of traditionally defined families, also exerts an influence in some male–male assemblages, yet the fitness consequences of nepotistic interactions are likely minor in most cases. In many other lekking birds, groupmates are not genetic relatives, and subordinates join male groups to obtain direct or delayed fitness benefits. The manner in which reproduction is shared, and the benefits accruing to subordinates in the group may help to determine how groups form. When kin-selected benefits drive reproductive coalitions, those coalitions can form early in animals' lives, when exposure to related potential partners is most frequent. However, when subordinate reproductive success is based on other benefits, males seem to choose among groups, sometimes delaying reproduction for years, apparently to find the best available display opportunity. Male display alliances offer an opportunity to investigate the factors stabilizing social interactions outside of a predetermined family structure, and the extent to which similar forces influence family and nonfamily groups. Clearly, leks in general and cooperative male alliances in particular have much to offer as laboratories for studying intrasexual behavior in addition to their well-established utility as model systems for understanding intersexual signaling and mate choice.

Keywords: Kin selection, lek, microsatellite, queuing, social network, manakin, nepotism, cooperation, cooperative breeding, *Meleagris gallopavo*

Introduction

Families are characterized by cooperative units that function to provision group members, protect young, share information, or defend territories. Families also inherently contain conflict, since we expect individuals to maximize their benefit from membership in any social group while minimizing the costs they pay for participation in the group. As we will see in this chapter, the push and pull of individual and group interests are not limited to parents and offspring, nor indeed, even to genetic relatives; they may be found in a variety of animal partnerships. Here, we focus on males that aggregate or even form partnerships for the sole purpose of attracting females and convincing them to mate.

Lek Mating Systems

Some of the most dazzling examples of sexual selection can be found in male display aggregations. Known as *leks*, from the Swedish word for "play," these consist of a group of males who hold small territories for the sole purpose of courtship. Females may assess many males before choosing their mate from among the prospective suitors. This choice is unimpeded by the social pairings that characterize 90% of bird species; in fact, females may even copy the mating decisions of other females visiting the lek (Gibson et al., 1991). This freedom of choice and inability of individuals to monopolize access to partners of the opposite sex often leads to highly skewed mating success in leks, with a few males garnering the majority of copulations, some males mating a few times, and the rest of the males failing to mate with any female at all. Because females have such unrestricted ability to choose, and because their choice is thought to be based primarily on the quality of the male rather than direct benefits of male provisioning skill or territory quality (Hamilton et al., 2006; Kirkpatrick & Ryan, 1991; Uy & Endler, 2004), leks are viewed as ideal situations in which to study sexual selection.

Much of the interest in lek mating systems has focused on the dynamics between males and females; for example, how male ornaments and behaviors might honestly convey genetic quality to females (Doucet & Montgomerie, 2003; Fiske et al., 1994; Petrie et al., 1991), and how genetic variability among males is maintained in the face of strong selection by females (i.e., the "lek paradox"; Cotton & Pomiankowski, 2007; Kirkpatrick & Ryan, 1991; Miller & Moore, 2007; Rowe & Houle, 1996). Although researchers have studied the correlates of male mating success in leks for decades, we are only now beginning to realize the answers to some of these important questions. Although mate choice behavior is often relatively easy to observe in leks, the genetic paternity studies required to more accurately measure evolutionary fitness or at least determine how reliably mating success describes male reproductive success have only been emerging over the past few years. This difficulty in obtaining parentage data is in part due to a common feature of lekking species—while the display grounds may be obvious and easily observed, the nest sites of females are often very difficult to find. Additionally, both mate quality and offspring quality can be tricky to define.

Males of lekking species usually exhibit delayed maturation, where males may take multiple years to achieve adult plumage and may require additional time to become a viable reproductive competitor in the population. These factors can make it very difficult for researchers to determine the consequences of mate choice for females, when understanding those consequences requires finding and then following the fate of offspring for such an extended period of time. Current research is finally beginning to reveal the full promise of leks as laboratories for studying sexual selection and mate choice; using modern molecular tools for assigning parentage to offspring and small, minimally invasive radio devices, careful long-term demographic analyses can overcome many of these obstacles.

Many of the features that make male display aggregations so important for studies of female mate choice (e.g., lack of social bond between parents, lack of paternal care by males) would seem to make them an odd choice for exploring family dynamics. What characteristics do leks and traditional animal families share? Four basic parameters determine family dynamics from an evolutionary perspective: (a) genetic coancestry, (b) dominance relationships, (c) the advantages of group living, and (d) the prospects for independent reproduction (Emlen, 1995). These four parameters are also critically important in determining patterns of reproductive success and group membership among lekking males. Like families, lek aggregations often persist beyond the lifespan of any one individual, sometimes lasting for several generations. Males are often faithful to leks both within and between seasons, thereby providing the opportunity for individuals to interact repeatedly over time. These aggregations accomplish specific, critical functions for participants (i.e., attracting females), and successful interactions required to accomplish those functions can be eroded by conflict among group members. Finally, paralleling Emlen's emphasis on genetic relatedness as a determinant of family dynamics, the topic of genctic relationships among males aggregating in leks will provide the backdrop for this chapter.

Cooperative Courtship in Leks

Although leks themselves are models for the study of sexual selection, cooperative behavior within these male aggregations presents a dilemma to evolutionary biologists. If ever there was a situation in which we would expect males to act alone and against the field of competitors, it would be during courtship, when the consequences of this competition leads directly to a key evolutionary currency: fathering a female's offspring. Why risk helping another male to mate if that help is at all costly? Yet, in a rare but evolutionarily diverse collection of birds, males either congregate in leks or otherwise form multimale teams to court or defend females. We find some obvious commonalities in the social organization of these species. These males do not participate in parental care. Similarly, we do not see extended pair-bonds between males and females. In these respects, species with cooperative courtship displays are much different from traditional "cooperative breeders," in which individuals other than the parents of a brood work together to provisions nestlings (Brown, 1987; Koenig & Dickinson, 2004; Mumme & Koenig, 1991). A wealth of empirical knowledge about cooperative breeding has developed since the behavior was first described. Only in recent years have molecular tools allowed us insight into the relationships among males in cooperative display groups, and to an understanding of which males truly are successful in the competition for females.

In this chapter, we will first ask the question of whether these groups of males are families in the traditional sense. Are the males close genetic relatives? And why might it be important for males to display with their relatives? We go on to expand our discussion to systems in which males may not be close relatives. What evolutionary forces bring individuals together in these systems? We then consider how these aggregations arise. Our focus will be on birds, although there is a rich literature on male–male associations in other animal taxa (Feh, 1999; Harcourt & De Waal, 1992; Packer et al., 1991; Sinervo et al., 2006).

Although cooperative courtship is an unusual occurrence in animal societies, it represents a complex coordination of competing interests among the participating males. The balance of costs and benefits that determine participation in these cooperative alliances takes place in a context separate from that of traditional cooperative breeding, allowing a novel examination of the generality of forces that have been shown to select for cooperation in caring for offspring. Our goal is to provide a detailed understanding of how kin selection influences cooperative display, but also to examine the other forces that create and maintain these unusual cooperative display partnerships. In doing so, we hope to assess the extent to which social dynamics in cooperative display partnerships are influenced by or reminiscent of family groups.

Kin Selection: Families in Action

The puzzle of how costly helping behavior evolves has been a challenge to evolutionary theory since Darwin's time. If helping other individuals requires that altruists give up their own reproductive opportunities, the genes for altruism should die out over time. For helping behavior to evolve in a competitive world, it is necessary for genes for altruistic behavior to spread even when the altruism itself carried some cost for the altruist. A major breakthrough in understanding how this could happen was W.D. Hamilton's concept of *inclusive fitness* (Hamilton, 1964a, b). Hamilton realized that close relatives are likely to share many identical copies of their genes through shared inheritance. Therefore, if an altruist can help its relatives produce more offspring, then it may be able to spread more copies of the altruism gene even while it produces fewer copies directly. This specific application of inclusive fitness theory is known as *kin selection* (Maynard Smith, 1964). Of course, we rarely know about the genetic basis for cooperative behavior itself—instead, Hamilton's model and related theory simply represent a way that selection could act on altruistic tendencies. Note that many theoreticians now support the mathematical equivalence between models of kin selection and modern models of multilevel (i.e., group) selection (McElreath & Boyd, 2007; Taylor & Nowak, 2007; Wilson & Wilson, 2007), although this equivalence is not universally accepted (Wild et al., 2009). We will focus on kin selection here.

Inclusive fitness benefits have been widely applied to explain how individuals benefit in traditional family systems, such as cooperative breeding. Kin selection is important for shaping many polyandrous mating systems in animals and even humans. It is therefore surprising how recently kin selection was first invoked as a possible explanation for male display aggregations such as leks (Höglund, 2003; Kokko & Lindstrom, 1996). Field studies often have found that larger aggregations attract more females, and yet females usually mate with just a small proportion of males in a lek (Höglund & Alatalo, 1995). Could low-ranking males benefit from aggregated display if they bring in additional mates for a related, higher-ranking male? In this section, we examine the evidence in support of the idea that male aggregations may in fact be families of related males, as well as evidence suggesting that male–male relationships may have their basis in other factors besides shared ancestry.

Evidence for Kin Selection

An important condition for kin selection to contribute to cooperative and aggregated display is the presence of kinship among males. What evidence do we have that family ties are shaping male display aggregations?

A survey of existing studies appears in Table 14.1. Most empirical tests of this idea have come only recently. Molecular tools such as microsatellite DNA genotyping now allow scientists to estimate the genetic similarity between individuals and infer whether they are related. In at least some species, males that gather together at leks tend to be (at least distantly) related. This is true for lesser prairie chickens (*Tympanuchus pallidicinctus*), in which patterns of genetic similarity within leks suggested that leks were composed of a mixture of relatives and nonrelatives (Bouzat & Johnson, 2004). This also appears to be true of the capercaillie (*Tetrao urogallus*), another species of grouse. Here, males in the same lek were on average significantly more related than expected by chance, a pattern possibly driven by the presence of a few close relatives (Regnaut et al., 2006). In another population of capercaillie, males belonged to one of two lineages, and membership of individual leks were often biased heavily toward one of these lineages (Segelbacher et al., 2007). In the blue manakin (*Chiroxiphia caudata*), some leks seemed to have mixed groups of close relatives and nonrelatives, whereas other leks contained mostly unrelated males (Francisco et al., 2009).

When leks are formed of individuals that vary in genetic relationships, it becomes important to ask how those clusters form: Are kin clusters a by-product of limited dispersal distances, which lead relatives to recruit into the same display group? Or, do males actively seek out and associate with male relatives? In at least some species, there is strong evidence for the latter. In the white-bearded manakin (*Manacus manacus*), males claim small display territories within a larger court in the understory of the Trinidadian forest. Like the blue manakin and capercaillie, males are related to some but not all males in a lek. Of the two leks investigated, males tended to cluster together spatially *within the lek* (Shorey et al., 2000). In other words, it appears that leks could be composed of multiple lineages of males, with those lineages tending to segregate from other such lineages on the scale of just a few meters.

One compelling explanation for how fine-scale kin structuring could occur is that males may learn to identify kin through brood associations as chicks, and then seek out familiar display associates later in life. An experimental study of feral peafowl (*Pavo cristatus*) found additional evidence for fine-scale

Table 14.1 Summary of evidence for kin clustering in lekking and cooperatively displaying birds

Species	Test of Kinship or Kin Aggregations	References
Wild turkey *Meleagris gallopavo*	Display coalitions of 2–4 same-aged males court and defend females. Males are close genetic relatives (mean pairwise R = 0.42); subordinates do not reproduce, but do gain sufficient inclusive fitness through helping the dominant display partner, so that helping is favored over solitary display.	Watts & Stokes, 1971; Krakauer, 2005a,b.
Peafowl *Pavo cristatus*	Unfamiliar full-sibs raised in separate nests, yet these genetically related males clustered together when displaying.	Petrie et al., 1999
Lesser prairie-chicken *Tympanuchus pallidicinctus*	Microsatellite analysis suggests leks are composed of a mixture of relatives and nonrelatives	Bouzat & Johnson, 2004
Capercaillie *Tetrao urogallus*	Relatedness of males in leks was higher than expected by chance. In a population with two major lineages, lek membership could be dominated by males from one or the other of the lineages.	Regnaut et al., 2006; Segelbacher et al., 2007
White-bearded manakin *Manacus manacus*	In at least two leks, there was nonrandom settlement of males, such that males formed clusters of relatives as determined from microsatellite genotypes.	Shorey et al., 2000
Blue manakin *Chiroxiphia caudata*	Microsatellite analysis revealed that some leks were formed of nonrelatives, some were composed of a mixture of relatives and nonrelatives.	Francisco et al., 2009
Satin bowerbird *Ptilonorhynchus violaceus*	Microsatellite analysis reveals some males settle near a close genetic relative; these dyads marauded each other's bower less frequently than the bowers of nonrelatives.	Reynolds et al., 2009

kin clustering, and also demonstrated that such learned associations are not necessary for kin structure to appear in leks (Petrie et al., 1999). As part of a separate study, peacock eggs were switched between nests of different mothers, meaning that males grew up with nestmates who were not actually related, and true genetic siblings were raised in different nests. These males were then released into a preserve and followed for several years, until they were adults and set up their own display territories. Unexpectedly, the researchers observed that true genetic brothers tended to cluster on the landscape. That they did so in the absence of any social cues for relatedness suggests that males might have based their choice of display associates on aspects of their own phenotype that were genetically based and therefore shared among siblings (a mechanism for identifying relatives known as *self-referent phenotype matching*) (Petrie et al., 1999; Sherman, 1999).

In addition to natal philopatry and actively choosing to display near certain males because they are close relatives, kin clusters could be the by-product of other processes. Saether (2002) listed several possible explanations for kin clusters that do not rely on cooperative interactions. For example, if males are successful over more than one season, young males could seek to be near attractive males that happen sometimes to be relatives (similar to the so-called "hotshot model" explaining why males may congregate in leks in the first place). Similarly, if the mate preferences of females vary spatially across the landscape, males who can best match their phenotype to the female audience could tend to end up near genetically similar males. This phenomenon could be particularly strong if reproduction is heavily skewed toward one or a few males, thereby creating lineages of half-brothers in subsequent cohorts.

It is important to note that associations among male relatives are not by themselves evidence for the action of kin selection. To fully understand why kin clusters occur, one must know about the fitness consequences for male clustering. For kin selection to explain an observed phenomenon, kin associations have to raise an individual's inclusive fitness above that which he would have enjoyed without interacting with relatives (Hamilton, 1964a,b). It is also possible that males have an antagonistic effect on each other rather than acting in a cooperative manner (Gardner & West, 2004; Platt & Bever, 2009).

What evidence besides associations of male relatives suggests a role for kin selection in cooperative and aggregated displays? The most compelling system yet demonstrating the role of kin selection in cooperative male display comes from studies of a common North American bird, the wild turkey (*Meleagris gallopavo*). An observational study conducted in the 1960s described coalitions of two to four males that competed with other males within the larger display aggregations. At most, only one male per coalition was seen mating; the authors believed that the teams were composed of brothers, and that kin selection could explain the apparent altruism by the males (Watts, 1969; Watts & Stokes, 1971). This hypothesis was finally tested several decades later. Microsatellite estimates of relatedness did reveal the males were close relatives (mean r = 0.42, between the expected values for half- and full siblings). Moreover, these same microsatellite genotypes allowed for paternity assignment in a sample of offspring. This facilitated the estimation of the reproductive success for dominant males in coalitions, subordinate males in coalitions, and solitary displaying males (that made up approximately half of the population). Combining these fitness data with the estimate of relatedness, it was found that subordinate males in coalitions achieve more fitness by helping their dominant display partner than they would as solitary breeders (see Box 14.1; Krakauer, 2005b). The exact nature of this help requires further study. Although females could prefer cooperative display (a hypothesis yet to be tested), subordinates also assisted in aggressively defending females. Subordinate males will chase competing males from the area while the dominant partner continues to display (Watts and Stokes, 1971).

Nepotistic interactions in male aggregations can also take the form of reduced aggression toward relatives. This has been found in the satin bowerbird (*Ptilonorhynchus violaceus*), a species in which males maintain individual display territories within a dispersed (or "exploded") lek. Males must construct sets of walls (the bower) within a cleared display court, and decorate the court with colorful objects. Females choose their mates based on a number of phenotypic and behavioral traits of the males, including the quality of the bower and its decorations. One way in which males compete for females is to raid the bowers of other males to abscond with valuable ornaments (Wojcieszek et al., 2007). When researchers generated microsatellite genotypes for the bower-holding males, they found that some males maintained a territory close to a genetic relative, and moreover, these males were less likely to disrupt the bowers of these relatives (Reynolds et al., 2009).

> **Box 14.1. Hamilton's rule in wild turkeys**
>
> Krakauer (2005a,b) provided the only quantification of kin-based benefits in a bird with male display aggregations. This analysis involved observations of display behavior and associations to define coalition membership, as well as construction of genotypes of hundreds of adults and offspring using ten microsatellite loci. These data were used to provide estimates for the variables in the simplified version of Hamilton's simple cost–benefit formula for the evolution of altruistic behavior among relatives ($r * b - c > 0$); if the benefits of aid, devalued by the coefficient of coancestry between the helper and the recipient of that help, outweigh the cost, then altruistic behavior should be favored.
>
> *Relatedness.* Relatedness between dominant and subordinate males in coalitions could be estimated using the microsatellite genotypes. Mean pairwise relatedness was 0.42 ± 0.07, a value expected for a mixture of half- and full siblings.
>
> *Benefit to the dominant male.* Male reproductive success was measured using a molecular parentage analysis, using a subset of approximately one-quarter of the sampled offspring that could be assigned unambiguously to a sampled male. The fitness benefit to having a helping subordinate was calculated as the difference between the mean fitness of dominant males and the mean fitness of solitary males. This required the assumption that dominant males breeding alone would expect the same fitness as the average solitary breeder.
>
> Dominant Fitness – Solitary Fitness = Benefit to Dominant
> 7.0 offspring/male – 0.9 offspring/male = 6.1 offspring/male
>
> *Cost of lost breeding opportunities for subordinate male.* This considers the fitness that subordinate males in coalitions would expect if they left their display team and attempted to breed alone (subordinates do not appear to sire any offspring when in coalitions). Similar to the assumption made to calculate the dominant's benefit, subordinates were assumed to have the same fitness as the average solitary breeder if they left.
>
> Solitary Fitness – Subordinate fitness = Cost to Subordinate
> 0.9 offspring/male – 0 offspring/male = 0.9 offspring/male
>
> *Putting it all together*
> With r, b, and c calculated, Hamilton's rule could now be evaluated:
> $r * b - c = 0.42 * (6.1) - 0.9 = +1.7$ offspring/male.
>
> Since this value is greater than zero, the costs of altruistic behavior are outweighed by indirect fitness gained by helping the dominant display partner, and kin selection can explain retention of subordinates in reproductive coalitions of wild turkeys.

The relationship between aggression and relatedness may differ quite dramatically in different species. In the white-bearded manakin, aggression was most intense with closest neighbors, but males didn't seem to reduce aggression when neighbors were close relatives: There was no relationship between pairwise relatedness and level of aggression (Shorey, 2002). In wild turkeys, there is dramatic seasonal variation in the patterns of aggressive behavior. One sees almost no aggression within display teams during the breeding season when males are courting females. At this time, all agonistic behaviors are directed toward other coalitions or solitary males. In contrast, some of the most violent and intense conflicts occur between display partners prior to the breeding season (Watts & Stokes, 1971), and other unique intrasexual behaviors such as prolonged bouts of circling or herding emerge within coalitions in the summer once females are no longer receptive (Krakauer, personal communication). These agonistic interactions are probably related to renegotiating dominance within a coalition. Although no dominance reversals were seen in a California population studied by Krakauer, other populations do exhibit changes in within-team dominance (A.B. Clark, unpublished data) across years. Although the indirect fitness benefits to helping more than make up for lost solitary opportunities, it is clearly better to be the dominant male receiving help from a related partner!

Evidence Against Kin Selection

Kin selection offers such a compelling explanation for cooperative behavior that it may be easy to forget that similarly complex behaviors can arise for completely different reasons. Just as some social groups of humans can function as "families" even when the individuals involved are not close relatives, the same cooperative display behaviors that are seen among familial relatives can also occur among unrelated individuals. Does cooperative or aggregated display also occur among *non*-relatives? If so, how do unrelated males maintain stable social alliances in the absence of kin-selected benefits?

The second major criterion for kin selection to influence cooperation—a positive fitness effect of helping—is a difficult one to test, especially in long-lived species. There are no rules about when in animals' lives the benefits of helping a relative have to be realized, and situations that seem to have no immediate fitness benefits may actually pay off much later, for example through increased survival of breeders or offspring (Crick, 1992; Khan & Walters, 2002; Kingma et al., 2010); but see (Pruett-Jones, et al. 2010). Although several studies have reported aggregations of relatives in leks (Höglund et al., 1999; Regnaut et al., 2006; Shorey et al., 2000), to our knowledge only the study of wild turkey alliances discussed above (Krakauer, 2005b) has been able to demonstrate that display aggregations allow subordinate males to more effectively pass on their genes than they would by displaying alone. Critical evidence that aggregating with kin in leks provides inclusive fitness payoffs is still lacking. Tests of this hypothesis are complicated by the potential for indirect fitness benefits to be relatively small, to be spread out over several years of lek attendance, or for only a subset of low-status males to follow a strategy based on associating with kin. Thus, although many studies have demonstrated males are on average unrelated to other males in the lek, it is more difficult to rule out less common or obvious strategies for accruing indirect fitness.

Although quantifying the fitness benefits of helping relatives is an ongoing challenge in the study of kin selection, studies that have rejected a role for kin selection in cooperatively displaying birds have generally put the brakes on this idea earlier in the logical progression of scientific proof: They have found that males in cooperative partnerships simply are not close relatives (Table 14.2). Researchers have tested for and failed to find patterns of genetic relatedness among cooperating or aggregating males in a variety of lekking birds. Even studies conducted on phylogenetically similar taxa have produced different answers to the question of whether leks are kin-structured. Spotted bowerbirds (*Chlamydera maculata*) neither avoid nor seek out kin in the placement of their courtship bowers. Unlike the satin bowerbirds discussed above, spotted bowerbirds don't avoid relatives' bowers when they invade the territories of other males to steal the courtship decorations (Madden et al., 2004). And greater sage grouse (*Centrocercus urophasianus*), unlike capercaillie and peafowl, show no fine-scale genetic structuring in their leks (Gibson et al., 2005). This result was seconded by a study testing genetic structure within and between leks in a different population of the greater sage grouse, with data spanning a 10-year time period (Bush et al., 2010). Although an early analysis of black grouse (*Tetrao tetrix*) leks provided evidence for greater-than-expected relatedness in leks (Höglund et al., 1999), a more comprehensive study in the same population found little support for the over-representation of relatives in leks (Lebigre et al., 2008). In another example, great bustards (*Otis tarda*) in Spain show no clear pattern of relatedness among males in leks (Martín et al., 2002). Critically, if aggregated males are not closely related, there is no possibility to pass on genes indirectly, no matter how much effort is invested in cooperation or lekking. The reason why some

Table 14.2 List of systems in which kin structure within or between leks has been tested but not found

Species of bird	References
Long-tailed manakin *Chiroxiphia linearis*	McDonald & Potts, 1994
Lance-tailed manakin *Chiroxiphia lanceolata*	DuVal, 2007a
Black grouse *Tetrao tetrix*	Lebigre et al., 2008
Great bustard *Otis tarda*	Martín et al., 2002
Spotted bowerbird *Chlamydera maculate*	Madden et al., 2004
Greater sage-grouse *Centrocercus urophasianus*	Gibson et al., 2005; Bush et al., 2010
Wire-tailed manakin *Pipra filicauda*	Loiselle et al., 2006
White-crowned manakin *Pipra pipra*	Loiselle et al., 2006
Blue-crowned manakin *Lepidothrix coronata*	Loiselle et al., 2006
Blue-backed manakin *Chiroxiphia pareola*	Loiselle et al., 2006

species show patterns of association based on relatedness and others do not remains an open question.

Manakins (family Pipridae) are a group of Neotropical birds including more than 40 species, almost all of which display for females in leks (Sick, 1967). Their elaborate and varied courtship displays and showy male plumages rival those of the birds of paradise (family Paradisaeidae) of New Guinea, and have attracted considerable attention as subjects for the study of sexual selection. Although results discussed above reported fine-scale genetic structure in two white-bearded manakin leks, none of the other species of manakins tested to date has shown kin-based associations (Francisco et al., 2009; Loiselle et al., 2007). If leks are kin-structured, there should be significant genetic differentiation among spatially discrete leks, but results from several manakin species directly contradict this prediction, and even the white-bearded manakin showed no genetic differentiation among nearby leks (Höglund & Shorey, 2003). It seems that leks may sometimes include relatives, but that relatedness is not the reason that manakins form leks.

The genus *Chiroxiphia* is one unusual branch of the manakin family tree in which males not only display in leks, but they do so cooperatively. *Chiroxiphia* males use complex multimale displays to attract females to their traditional display sites and convince them to mate. At each display site, only one alpha male ever has the chance to mate with females that the displaying males attract, and the alpha role is decided by male–male interactions, long before the female comes to watch the show (DuVal, 2007c; McDonald, 1989b). *Chiroxiphia* courtship displays are a remarkable mix of acrobatics and coordinated calls. In both the long-tailed manakin (*C. linearis*) and lance-tailed manakin (*C. lanceolata*), males perch side by side to sing duets. These duets are so tightly coordinated that it sounds as if the song comes from one bird. In all *Chiroxiphia*, males also perform dance displays when females come to visit their display areas. These dances include alternating up-and-down leaps, labored butterfly-like flights around the display perch, and a backward leapfrog display in which males leap and hover over one another in a pinwheel of color and sound, just centimeters from the female's beak. In most *Chiroxiphia*, displays are performed by pairs of males (DuVal, 2007b; Foster, 1981; Slud, 1957; Snow, 1963), but in the blue manakin (*C. caudata*), a similar behavior involves four to six males at once (Foster, 1981).

Cooperative courtship in *Chiroxiphia* manakins seems to be a situation much like that of the wild turkeys discussed above. In both situations, subordinates are an integral part of courtship, but help others copulate, rather than breeding themselves. Subordinate males in *Chiroxiphia* partnerships don't mate as long as they are subordinates, but may spend years in their supporting role (DuVal, 2007a; Foster, 1981; McDonald, 1989b). Paternity testing of lance-tailed manakin chicks has confirmed that, with vanishingly rare exceptions, only the alpha males are passing on their genes (DuVal, 2007a). Why then do subordinates cooperate?

It turns out that the reasons underlying manakin cooperation are vastly different from the forces promoting coalition formation in turkeys. The dominant alpha male and his subordinate beta partner are no more related than expected by random pairing from the population (DuVal, 2007a; McDonald & Potts, 1994). This means that beta male cooperation does not result from a drive to help close relatives reproduce. Instead of being the result of indirect fitness benefits, the cooperative displays of *Chiroxiphia* manakins seem to be the result of delayed direct benefits. This means that cooperation helps beta males pass on their genes by increasing their chances of copulating, but these chances come along well after their years of helpful dancing. *Chiroxiphia* manakins have been shown to reap delayed direct benefits in two distinct ways. In long-tailed manakins, males are quite literally waiting in line. In this simple queuing system, beta males become the next alpha when their display partners die (McDonald & Potts, 1994). When it's time to breed, female long-tailed manakins apparently return to places where they have copulated in the past, even if their previous mate no longer holds the alpha position. By helping attract a loyal clientele of females by cooperating as betas, males benefit by mating with the same females when they return to mate after those males ascend to alpha status. In contrast, lance-tailed manakins (which look remarkably similar to long-tailed manakins but which sport a much shorter tail) are not just waiting in line. Lance-tailed manakins have a complex queuing system in which some beta males inherit alpha status at the display areas where they helped as betas, but others establish new display perches or move to take over vacated areas elsewhere in the lek. When alpha males were experimentally removed from a lance-tailed manakin lek, their partners held on to alpha status for days or weeks, but the vast majority gave up their new alpha positions, and several moved to become beta to a different alpha partner, leaving their former display areas vacant and waiting to become an alpha later in life (DuVal, 2007a). It seems that by cooperating, beta male lance-tailed manakins are learning necessary skills or forming critical social alliances during their beta tenure. Delayed direct benefits in lance-tailed manakins are the result of complex queuing, in which males balance opportunities to take over vacant alpha positions with their own ability to be successful in that role. Differences in reproductive patterns between these sister species may reflect variation in ecological opportunities for breeding positions, male life histories (as long-tailed manakins mature 1 year later than lance-tailed manakins), or effects of population density on breeding behavior.

In some cases, the benefits of cooperative male display or male aggregations are much more immediate. In addition to indirect or delayed direct fitness increases, males can also benefit directly from coordinated displays by increasing their immediate chances of reproduction. Ruffs (*Philomachus pugnax*) are Old World sandpipers that display for females in leks and that have an unusual polymorphism in male plumage. Dominant "territorial" males sport a dark or rusty-colored ruff of feathers (which gives the species its name), subordinate "satellite" males have light-colored ruffs (vanRhijn, 1973), and female-like "faeders" have no ruff at all and apparently sire chicks by unobtrusively sneaking into other males' leks (Jukema & Piersma, 2006). These roles are genetically determined, and males keep the same role throughout their lives, although they may switch from lekking to following females throughout a breeding season (Lank & Smith, 1987). Territorial males may attack satellites when females are present, but at other times they allow their white-ruffed counterparts to share their territorial space without conflict, and satellites apparently do not try to steal display territories (vanRhijn, 1973). Interestingly, females prefer to visit territorial males that are displaying near a satellite partner (Hugie & Lank, 1997). Males of both morphs frequently mate with the females that they attract in mutual displays, and both sire chicks as a result of these matings (Lank et al., 2002). Similarly, female ruffs are attracted to leks that include more males in general, and the top male in a lek monopolizes a lower proportion of the copulations as the group gets larger (Widemo & Owens, 1995). Male ruffs benefit directly from aggregations by increasing their own chance of mating, whether via mutual display of satellite and territorial males, or simply by upping the numbers and attractiveness of a lekking group. Immediate increases in reproductive possibilities similarly underlie the key hypotheses (e.g., hotshot, hotspot, and female preference) that explain why males aggregate in lekking groups (Bradbury & Gibson, 1983; Höglund & Alatalo, 1995).

How Do Cooperative Alliances Form?

Understanding the processes by which males form cooperative partnerships is one approach to identifying critical periods that may be the targets of selection leading to complex social behavior. Unsurprisingly, cooperative alliances form in a variety of ways that vary in their similarity to the formation of family groups. Usually, when we think of a family, we think of intergenerational groups that persist on a territory or home range of sorts. Often we find that offspring postpone their independence, and either delay their dispersal to a new territory for some time or remain on the territory for their entire lives. But what happens in the case of male display aggregations? Many of the philopatry-based mechanisms that help create familial clusters (e.g., territoriality, parental nepotism) may not apply to males of polygynous species with non–resource-based mating systems. Additionally, cooperating males in courtship alliances appear to share little in common with males in monogamous partnerships: They typically lack any social bond with their mates, and do not participate in any way in raising their offspring. Thus, display territories are just that, and females leave these territories after mating. So, how do bonds between males arise, especially among young males making their first decisions on where and with whom to display? Although there is a rich literature on the evolution of leks that is beyond the scope of this chapter (Höglund & Alatalo, 1995), we focus here on individual decisions in a species where leks or aggregations have already evolved.

Development of Cooperative Alliances Among Kin

Probably the easiest way for male relatives to remain together is if they never go anywhere else. Birds in general have male-biased philopatry, meaning young females are more likely to disperse in search of a new, territory-holding male, while males stay closer to home as they learn the neighborhood and attempt to get a breeding territory (Greenwood, 1980). Lekking birds are no exception. For example, in the black grouse (*Tetrao tetrix*), any patterns of relatedness in leks are simply by-products of winter flock membership and do not reflect active choice for males of particular leks containing relatives (Lebigre et al., 2008).

Clearly, in some species, display aggregations containing related males can arise through processes other than simply lack of dispersal. The genetically similar clusters of males found on some leks of white-bearded manakins are separated by a few meters, not by kilometers, and spatial clustering of related lab-reared peacocks occurred even though related and unrelated males were released at the same location, so biased dispersal patterns are insufficient to explain observed grouping of kin. Instead, these males seem to be choosing to display in close spatial proximity to particular other males, either specifically because those males are relatives, or because related males tend to share a similar decision rule for display site selection (Höglund, 2003; Saether, 2002).

In wild turkeys, the relationships between members of a coalition seem to represent strong, lifelong partnerships among males. During the breeding season, males are quite mobile as they search for, court, and defend unpredictably dynamic groups of females. This behavior tends to mix the population of males, yet males in coalitions consistently are found together. Outside of the breeding season, males collect into same-sex flocks, and with the exception of birds that have disappeared (often through documented mortality events), coalitions emerge intact from these larger social flocks the next year (AHK, unpublished data). Adult males were never seen to "divorce" their display partner, nor were solitary males ever seen to join a coalition. All these observations point to the existence of unique and important partnerships in this species.

The actual process of partner choice in turkeys remains a mystery. Coalitions appear to be formed by the first winter, before adulthood, although the inconsistent display behavior of juvenile males (1-year-olds) makes it more difficult to identify these teams (AHK, personal communication). Does display partner choice occur in the large winter flocks when males have many choices, but also many chances to "incorrectly" partner with unrelated males? Or, do partnerships form earlier, perhaps as early as the first days after hatching, when only nestmates are around? Complicating matters, female turkeys frequently combine their precocial broods in a process known as "crèching," which creates groups of young turkeys of mixed parentage within several weeks of hatching. To be accurate, cues of relatedness based on learning the identity of nestmates would have to be incorporated into male–male interactions before crèching. The microsatellite genotypes of offspring in nests across the landscape suggest one should find low levels of relatedness among group members when these broods amalgamate into social groups of first-winter juveniles. If males initiate coalitions in large fall and winter yearling groups, or even in the smaller summer multifemale, multibrood crèches, they would require extremely adept kin recognition to reliably find relatives among the field of nonrelatives (Krakauer, 2005a).

In contrast, male turkeys would have a much greater expectation of encountering relatives if their partnerships were to form prior to brood amalgamation, in the first few days after hatching, but before mothers encountered each other and formed crèches. The complex mating patterns of turkeys can produce nests comprised of a mix of genetic full siblings, half-siblings through multiple mating by females or by quasi-parasitic multiple mating by males, and nonrelatives through brood parasitism (Krakauer, 2008). In spite of the variety of possible genetic relationships, males can expect, on average, that most nestmates will be sufficiently closely related to make cooperation advantageous. Males would be almost as effective at finding relatives using a contextual rule of thumb in which they assume male nestmates are related than they would in relying on a discrimination rule based on a mechanism such as phenotype matching, and could in fact be superior if the discrimination was error-prone (Krakauer, 2005a). Lab studies based on testing whether poults prefer to associate with unknown genetic relatives versus nonrelatives do show some potential role for a process like phenotype matching (Truong, 2003), although coalition formation remains poorly understood.

Nonkin Associations

Even when male coalitions or aggregations are formed of nonrelatives, the formation of alliances seems to be a nonrandom process. The choice of display partners or locations is often the result of years of social interaction, suggesting a mutual negotiation of partnership or lek occupation, whether cooperative or competitive. The processes by which males form nonkin alliances may also function in species that are more influenced by kin selection. One approach to assessing whether relatedness is truly important to the formation of male–male alliances or aggregations is to determine whether alliances among kin develop by a mechanism distinct from that governing the formation of groups of unrelated males. Consistent differences in routes of alliance formation among species with versus without kin associations would suggest meaningful differences in the nature of adaptive benefits gained by males in such alliances. To date, such comparative information is still unavailable, but future work may resolve this question.

In aggregations of lekking males, individual males usually return to and consistently display in the same location. Only rarely will territoriality break down, for example, in a display area lacking visual landmarks (Hovi et al., 1995) or following extreme weather events (Gibson & Bradbury, 1987). In several cases, researchers have shown that these consistent male locations are informative: Females tend to prefer males holding central territories, and males vie for these favored positions (Hovi et al., 1994; Wiley, 1991); but see (Saether et al., 2005). Both males and females may prefer central territories for reasons relating to sexual selection (males because centrality is preferred by females, and females because central males are successful competitors and presumably have "good genes"); or for reasons more directly linked to survival (e.g., protection from predators that may go undetected on peripheral display territories). Removing a male from a lek territory usually results in his rapid replacement. Interestingly, experimental manipulations of lekking great snipe (*Gallinago media*) suggest that peripheral males compete for display territories near the most successful central male: Removing a peripheral displayer resulted in his rapid replacement, whereas removing a successful central male resulted in the disbanding of the lekking group. Subordinate males were presumably gathered around the central male to intercept and mate with some of the many females that he attracted (Höglund & Robertson, 1990).

Territorial and satellite males in ruff leks provide an interesting comparison. Satellite males frequently follow female groups and can be highly mobile. Territorial males seem to actively solicit the approach of these satellite males, and the territorial males that attract the most satellites also attract the most females. Satellites seem to be using the same cues used by females in mate search. Alternately, females may be eavesdropping on male–male interactions to choose a mate. Although their mutual displays are particularly attractive to females, it is not clear whether some resident and satellite males form consistent long-term alliances, like *Chiroxiphia* manakins or wild turkeys. At least one study notes that the tolerance of resident males for the presence of satellites varied among residents, and according to which satellites were present (Hogan-Warburg, 1966).

Nevertheless, some nonkin alliances are long-lasting partnerships that may persist for years, with partners spending most of daylight hours together. Several life history traits predispose animals to complex formation of social alliances among nonrelatives. Animals that are long-lived, resident (nonmigratory), and have small clutch sizes find themselves interacting with the same individuals, month after month and year after year, but are unlikely to be in the company of relatives. Manakins typify these life history traits. All manakins have a maximum of only two eggs per clutch, and high rates of nest predation are counteracted by the relatively high survival of adults and impressive potential longevity. Long-tailed manakins may live to be more than 14 years old (McDonald, 1993b). Young males in many manakin species experience delayed plumage maturation: The time required for a young male to molt into his adult plumage is extended by a series of distinctive intermediate plumages, and varies by species (Doucet et al., 2007; DuVal, 2005; Foster, 1987; McDonald, 1993a). These distinctive subadult plumages seem to signal young males' subordinate social status, and may be instrumental in forming alliances with appropriate partners (McDonald, 1993a). Indeed, when the relative ages of display partners are known, the subordinate member is consistently younger than his alpha partner (DuVal, 2007c). *Chiroxiphia* manakins move through a complex age-graded dominance hierarchy to attain breeding alpha status, and a socially mediated progression of male interactions may occur in other species as well. Satin bowerbirds also show delayed plumage maturation. Young males are green or mottled until their seventh year after hatching, and older males tolerate their presence near display bowers as long as they don't have the glossy black plumage of a competitive adult male (Collis & Borgia, 1993).

To an extent that is unlikely in kin-based associations, males in alliances with nonkin may switch social partners several times during their reproductive lives. In some species, cooperative partnerships are obligate; for example, in the long-tailed manakin, only males with subordinate helpers ever hold breeding territories (McDonald, 1989a,b). In these cases, the ability to form a new alliance following the loss of a cooperative partner is an essential part of male reproductive success. In other species, like the lance-tailed manakin, males may display solitarily and successfully attract females as a solo male. Nevertheless, solo alpha males tend to form an alliance with a new male partner over time (DuVal, 2007c).

Signals of age may moderate behavioral interactions between individuals and facilitate the formation of alliances among potential partners, but cooperative display alliances are also influenced by interactive "practice" displays that occur months or years before true courtship dances. David McDonald reports that connectivity in a social network—a map of interacting individuals based on behavioral observations—predicts male's chances of rise to alpha status years later (McDonald, 2007). More closely connected young males were more likely to move into breeding alpha status later in life. Moreover, these early alliances were unaffected by relatedness (McDonald, 2009). Similarly, social connectivity was correlated with social rise to territory-holding status and the likelihood of siring offspring in the wire-tailed manakin (*Pipra filicauda*), a species that shows incipient cooperation in display (Ryder et al., 2008, 2009). Getting to be a territory-holding male—and keeping that social status—seems to be more than half the battle, at least in *Chiroxiphia* manakins. In lance-tailed manakins, most alpha males sire chicks but non-alphas almost never do so (DuVal & Kempenaers, 2008). Network results to date leave open the question of what it is about social connectivity that leads to later obtaining a breeding territory: male–male interactions may lead to improvement of display performance (e.g., through information exchange or simple physical exercise); males may form coalitions that actively help them attain breeding status; or healthy and vigorous males that survive to become alphas may simply interact with more individuals at a young age. Associations among nonkin seem to form deliberately and in ways that are important for later reproductive opportunities, but the behavioral rules governing the development of those alliances remain an active and exciting area of research.

Synthesis: Interindividual Dynamics

It is widely acknowledged that the diversity of lekking species represent independent evolutions of aggregated male display: Lek mating systems have arisen several times in birds, as well as in many other animal groups (Höglund & Alatalo, 1995). This rich historical backdrop has frustrated early attempts at explaining the evolution of male display aggregations, since the diverse natural history of lekking animals has led to different models being supported in different taxa (reviewed in Hogulund & Alatalo, 1995). Thus, it should not be surprising that we find such a diversity both in how males join cooperative alliances on leks, and how (particularly subordinate) males benefit from lek attendance and cooperation. This point is best made by examining the three groups possessing reproductive coalitions within larger display aggregations.

In each of these taxa (the ruff, the wild turkey, and the *Chiroxiphia* manakins), males have evolved a strategy to team up with a specific individual among the larger pool of competitors. Through some combination of intrasexual dominance and female mate choice, these associations confer an advantage to male–male coalitions over the other males. Ruff tandems of a territorial male and white-morphed satellite attract more females to the territory than do solitary territorial males. Both males have a good chance to mate, given that females frequently mate multiple times and the territorial male seems unable to monopolize all the matings in his territory (Lank et al., 2002). On the other hand, in both wild turkeys and *Chiroxiphia* manakins, the dominant male in the coalition rarely if ever cedes copulations to his subordinate helpers, but overt conflict over reproduction is rare. Presumably, females avoid coalitions in which males fight during courtship, enforcing stability in male alliances (McDonald, 1993a). Interestingly, turkeys and manakins benefit through completely different assurances from their dominant partner; in turkeys, the increased success of dominant males provides indirect fitness for the subordinate, whereas in *Chiroxiphia* manakins, subordinates increase their standing and likelihood of obtaining the coveted alpha position in the future, and may also increase their subsequent attractiveness through the practice of the complex song and dance.

How can we make sense of the variation in how male display aggregations are formed? Does the type of reproductive benefit promoting cooperation relate to the manner in which the aggregations form? The life histories of the species in question provide some help here. For example, wild turkeys have a large clutch size and a relatively short lifespan. These factors make the presence of related display partners early in life almost certain, and may also favor early coalition formation, since coalitions appear to be able to effectively "queue jump" via agonistic dominance of other males in the population. On the other hand, *Chiroxiphia* manakins have a much slower life history, with small clutch sizes and long time to maturation. Many male manakins lack a brother for a nestmate, which would hamper the early, life-long partnerships characterized by wild turkeys. Instead, they must jump into a connected social world in which their success in obtaining a breeding position relies on making many acquaintances or monitoring multiple queues. In the case of the ruff, leks are more ephemeral, as males migrate into an unpredictable arctic landscape. Territorial males have little assurance that a satellite partner will be alive or nearby in next breeding season, and the nonterritorial white-morph males have some ability to compare leks during the breeding season without risk of losing a display site for which they have fought.

Unfortunately, gross-level life history variation can only take us so far in this endeavor; many unanswered questions remain. Why do some lekking species with large broods show no evidence of any nepotistic behavior, while others, such as the peafowl, seem to possess sophisticated kin-recognition mechanisms with little obvious benefit? Why is nepotism apparently so rare in the long-lived species such as manakins, given that it would seem to be an effective strategy, especially for males who are cooperating subordinates for years, with no opportunity to breed? Given that there are clearly multiple routes that result in cooperative alliances among lekking males, why are species influenced by different types of adaptive benefits? We believe that answers to these questions will come down to (a) factors influencing male settlement decisions, (b) interaction characteristics among males, and (c) female mating patterns. In more detail, these are:

1. *What factors influence male settlement decisions within and between leks, and what are the consequences for these decisions?* With the exception of wild turkeys, kin selection likely does not provide the sole benefit for males to join (or remain in) a lek—most males do so because leks are the only place where they have a chance to breed. If the benefits to one lek over another are relatively small, they may be outweighed by costs of searching, and therefore may depend upon factors such as inter-lek distances, predation risk, and the spatial and temporal scale of the presettlement phase of a male's life cycle.

For some lekking species, shifting to a different lek involves many costs, with potentially few benefits. For example, male sage grouse tend to be faithful to the lek they settle in (Gibson & Bradbury, 1985, 1987). Switching to another lek would incur costs in terms of movement, vulnerability to predators, and having to establish a new territory elsewhere during a relatively short breeding season. On the other hand, perseverance on a lek could pay off, since even low-ranking males may have some slight opportunity to mate with females, either through disrupting the copulation attempts of higher-ranking males or if disturbance (e.g., from the presence of a predator) results in the absence of higher-ranking males. Ecological factors may also limit males' options: *Chiroxiphia* manakins spend several years visiting different dispersed display areas within a lek before they reach adult plumage. In DuVal's lance-tailed manakin population, beta and nonpair males have the opportunity to monitor many potential display territories to assess their activity and learn of vacancies (DuVal, 2007b). In McDonald's study of the long-tailed manakin, however, outside options appear to be less available to males once they have achieved beta status; beta males only rose to alpha status at their own territory (McDonald, 1989a, 1993a). In wild turkeys, density appears to play an important role in the presence of reproductive coalitions. Early reports of cooperative courtship were limited to a few high-density populations (Healy, 1992; Watts & Stokes, 1971); now, multimale teams are observed throughout the species' range as turkeys become common throughout much of North America.

2. *How do males interact in the lek? Do males in a lek take on different roles, and do partnerships remain together over extended periods of time?* One important question related to how males interact is whether males treat their neighbors differently. Males assort nonrandomly in some species, and as we have seen, such assortment may correlate with kinship among males. Although the recruitment process in these species has not been well described, one could imagine nepotism influencing settlement as in non-lekking, territorial red grouse, in which young males are permitted to squeeze into territories near older male relatives (Matthiopoulos et al., 1998; Piertney et al., 2008). Male settlement within leks is in general poorly understood, and it is likely that other factors related to males and their social environment may play a role (Greene et al., 2000; Sinervo et al., 2006).

Additionally, the stability and efficiency of inter- and intrasexual interactions may be overlooked in relation to the relationships males form in leks. A critical feature of both *Chiroxiphia* manakins and wild turkeys is that dominance within the display team is generally highly stable within a season. The reason this is so important is that minimal negotiation occurs among teammates regarding their roles when interacting with females or other males, which allows males to avoid costly conflict and confusion, and to direct most interactions outside of the group. Contrast this with species such as the greater sage grouse. Male sage grouse are relentlessly territorial, engaging in prolonged vocal and physical contests with familiar neighbors. This continued renegotiation would seem to make the formation of alliances difficult, since the benefits of joint action in competing with other males or attracting females could be eroded by the need to resolve within-group conflict during key interactions.

Leks are typically successful when aggregated males produce long-distance signals that attract receptive females. We now have some evidence that not all males in a lek work equally hard to produce these signals, and that patterns differ across species as to which males are shouldering most of the burden of courtship and advertising. In wild turkeys, the dominant male produces the majority of the strut displays (Krakauer, 2005b). This is also true of cooperatively displaying *Chiroxiphia* manakins; the dominant pair produce loud duets during much of the day, while lower-ranked males in the leks participate in duets much less frequently (DuVal, 2007c). In contrast, in some grouse species, the high-quality males (i.e., those who mated) actually displayed less when females were absent from the lek (Nooker & Sandercock, 2008; Patricelli & Krakauer, 2010). Further research is required to determine whether this pattern is evidence of a tactical decision on the part of high-quality males to save energy for close courtships. Alternately, lower-quality males may be forced to display more to maintain their territories in the lek.

3. *How does female mate choice structure male reproductive opportunities and the distribution of reproductive success among candidate males?* The obvious and showy displays of lekking male birds exist primarily because of females. Patterns of male reproductive success reflect the result of females' activities during mate search, which includes female preferences for certain behavioral types or morphological traits, and the effects of density (both of males and of other females), predator risk, and nest timing in relation to food abundance. Variation in mate preferences can also relate to intrinsic aspects of a female. For example, mate choice was predicted by different traits in older versus younger females in satin bowerbirds (Coleman et al., 2004), and an experimental study of captive wild turkeys in an artificial lek showed mate sampling behavior was affected by parasite load (Buchholz, 2004). The lion's share of research has therefore focused on why females select one male over another.

Increasingly, however, researchers are reporting evidence of multiple mating among females on the lek, drawing into question how females benefit from varied mating decisions. Multiple mating by females may make direct reproductive benefits more likely for a larger proportion of males in the lek—as lower-ranking males obtain a greater likelihood of mating, the relative pay-off for intensely altruistic behavior, such as seen in subordinate turkeys or beta-ranked *Chiroxiphia*, becomes less. Multiple mating does occur in these systems, but the strict dominance hierarchies within each coalition or display perch ensure that if females mate multiple times, they do so across rather than within these male groups. As noted above, female preferences for efficient courtship may be selecting for queue stability in these male aggregations.

Conclusion

These points show many similarities to the evolutionary factors structuring animal families. Family function hinges on the dynamics within social groups, the availability of outside options, the degree to which benefits are constrained or promoted by other members of the group, and by intersexual interactions (Emlen, 1995). However, these factors also have shaped the societies of lekking species to create types of associations rarely if ever found in more traditionally studied cooperatively breeding systems. For example, genetic families such as the wild turkey can form life-long coalitions of relatives that are not intergenerational families, and are not based upon defense of a shared nest site or territory. Similarly, competition has resulted in delayed reproduction in both lekking and cooperatively breeding species. Although many cooperative breeders delay dispersal as a plastic response due to lack of breeding vacancies, lek breeders may find reproduction as subadults exceedingly unlikely since they may take several years to achieve adult size or plumage. Note that this delayed maturation may actually facilitate dispersal, since it can allow prospecting for leks while incurring less aggression from older males. Finally, our review highlights the range of importance of genetic relatedness, from providing the incentive for male retention, to more subtle nepotistic effects, to the complete absence of kin groupings. Despite these similarities, studying group dynamics among lekking males obviously differs from the study of families in several informative ways. As the saying goes, "you can't choose your family," but males in leks apparently do make active choices to join particular groups. Furthermore, the role of helpers in traditional cooperative breeders is strongly constrained by inbreeding avoidance within the group, which is apparently not a factor in lekking alliances: lekking males are assessed by a large and unrestricted pool of females, suggesting that inbreeding avoidance has a relatively low influence on patterns of reproductive skew within the group. By investigating patterns of group formation in situations unrestricted by family structure (e.g., less likelihood of behaviors resulting from incest avoidance), we can hope to discover the extent to which family dynamics arise from direct selection on group dynamics, and to what extent they are by-products of the relatedness structure unique to family groups. We believe that this variability in structure makes display aggregations an exciting "new" venue for studying complex social systems.

In conclusion, by examining the evolutionarily diverse collection of avian taxa that form aggregated male displays, we have highlighted the different ways in which males may profit from displaying together. Cooperation in courtship and courtship aggregations may sometimes result from the indirect benefits of helping close relatives, but similar behaviors, including traditional lekking, can also result from selection through immediate and direct reproductive benefits or via delayed direct benefits. These represent three key pathways leading to male–male cooperation. The elaborate cooperative courtship behaviors of ruffs, wild turkeys, and *Chiroxiphia* manakins apparently represent a case of convergence, in which different selective environments result in similar patterns of cooperative male behavior. Although debate on the importance of kin and family structure in aggregated male display continues (Hatchwell, 2010), it's clear that even without the genetic incentive of helping related individuals there are multiple ways in which complex, cooperative behaviors can evolve.

Future Directions

1. Although DNA-based studies have revolutionized our understanding of male display aggregations, molecular tools have as yet been applied to only a small fraction of all lekking species, and rarely to multiple populations within a species. Greater taxonomic reach will be required to more fully explore how ecology and history relate to the types of partnerships and strategies available to males.

2. The juvenile and presettlement life stages of birds with non–resource-based mating systems are still poorly known. In some cases, careful long-term studies of sedentary species have illuminated the strategies males use to find a display site. For most species, however, technologies such as global positioning system (GPS) tracking or data-logging receivers will be required to uncover the behavior of males as they select leks and interact within leks.

3. Preliminary evidence for kin effects in display aggregations often takes the form of higher-than-expected level of mean relatedness in leks, or the over-representation of closely related dyads. Researchers also need to look carefully at patterns of male–male interactions within leks since these broader, molecular-based analyses may miss nepotistic interactions occurring among a relatively small subset of males. It is also unknown how males may acquire information about genetic relatedness.

4. We now understand that, in many species, kin selection does not explain male settlement behavior in leks nor coalition membership within display aggregations. In many of these cases, however, rigorous tests of alternative routes to fitness for low-ranking males are still needed. These alternatives may include low rates of direct reproduction, enhanced signaling through practice of courtship displays, or improved future status through linear or more complex queues.

5. Studies of female preferences in leks traditionally emphasize sexual selection for male traits and also why males aggregate. Female behavior may also be a critical determinant of male–male interactions (including display partnerships) in these aggregations. It is clear that an integrated understanding of both male and female mating behavior is required; the mechanisms underlying choice behavior offer a particularly promising area for future work.

References

Bouzat, J.L., & Johnson, K. (2004). Genetic structure among closely spaced leks in a peripheral population of lesser prairie-chickens. *Molecular Ecology, 13*, 499–505.

Bradbury, J.W., & Gibson, R.M. (1983). Leks and mate choice. In P.P.G. Bateson (Ed.), *Mate choice* (pp. 109–138). Cambridge, UK: Cambridge University Press.

Brown, J.L. (1987). *Helping and communal breeding in birds*. Princeton, NJ: Princeton University Press.

Buchholz, R. (2004). Effects of parasitic infection on mate sampling by female wild turkeys (*Meleagris gallopavo*): Should infected females be more or less choosy? *Behavioral Ecology, 15*, 687–694.

Bush, K.L., Aldridge, C.L., Carpenter, J.E., Paszkowski, C.A., Boyce, M.S., Coltman, D.W., & Scribner, K.T. (2010). Birds of a feather do not always lek together: Genetic diversity and kinship structure of greater sage-grouse (*Centrocercus urophasianus*) in Alberta. *The Auk, 127*, 343–353.

Coleman, S.W., Patricelli, G.L., & Borgia, G. (2004). Variable female preferences drive complex male displays. *Nature, 428*, 742–745.

Collis, K., & Borgia, G. (1993). The costs of male display and delayed plumage maturation in the satin bowerbird (*Ptilonorhynchus violaceus*). *Ethology, 94*, 59–71.

Cotton, S., & Pomiankowski, A. (2007). Sexual selection: Does condition dependence fail to resolve the "lek paradox"? *Current Biology, 17*, R335–R337.

Crick, H.Q.P. (1992). Load-lightening in cooperatively breeding birds and the cost of reproduction. *Ibis, 134*, 56–61.

Doucet, S.M., McDonald, D.B., Foster, M.S., & Clay, R.P. (2007). Plumage development and molt in long-tailed manakins (*Chiroxiphia linearis*): Variation according to sex and age. *The Auk, 124*, 29–43.

Doucet, S.M., & Montgomerie, R. (2003). Multiple sexual ornaments in satin bowerbirds: Ultraviolet plumage and bowers signal different aspects of male quality. *Behavioral Ecology, 14*, 503–509.

DuVal, E.H. (2005). Age-based plumage changes in the lance-tailed manakin: A two-year delay in plumage maturation. *Condor, 107*, 917–922.

DuVal, E.H. (2007a). Adaptive advantages of cooperative courtship for subordinate male lance-tailed manakins. *The American Naturalist, 169*, 423–432.

DuVal, E.H. (2007b). Cooperative display and lekking behavior of the Lance-tailed Manakin (Chiroxiphia lanceolata). *The Auk, 124*, 1168–1185.

DuVal, E.H. (2007c). Social organization and variation in cooperative alliances among male lance-tailed manakins. *Animal Behaviour, 73*, 391–401.

DuVal, E.H., & Kempenaers, B. (2008). Sexual selection in a lekking bird: The relative opportunity for selection by female choice and male competition. *Proceedings of the Royal Society of London, Series B, 275*, 1995–2003.

Emlen, S.T. (1995). An evolutionary theory of the family. *Proceedings of the National Academy of the Sciences USA, 92*(18), 8092–8099.

Feh, C. (1999). Alliances and reproductive success in Carmargue stallions. *Animal Behaviour, 57*, 705–713.

Fiske, P., Kalas, J.A., & Sæther, S.A. (1994). Correlates of male mating success in the lekking great snipe (*Gallinago media*): Results from a four-year study. *Behavioral Ecology, 5*, 210–218.

Foster, M.S. (1981). Cooperative behavior and social organization of the swallow-tailed manakin (*Chiroxiphia caudata*). *Behavioral Ecology and Sociobiology, 9*, 167–177.

Foster, M.S. (1987). Delayed maturation, neoteny, and social system differences in two manakins of the genus *Chiroxiphia*. *Evolution, 41*, 547–558.

Francisco, M.R., Gibbs, H.L., & Galetti, P.M. (2009). Patterns of individual relatedness at blue manakin (*Chiroxiphia caudata*) leks. *The Auk, 126*, 47–53.

Gardner, A., & West, S.A. (2004). Spite and the scale of competition. *Journal of Evolutionary Biology, 17*, 1195–1203.

Gibson, R., Pires, D., Delaney, K., & Wayne, R. (2005). Microsatellite DNA analysis shows that greater sage grouse leks are not kin groups. *Molecular Ecology, 14*, 4453–4459.

Gibson, R.M., & Bradbury, J.W. (1985). Sexual selection in lekking grouse: Phenotypic correlates of male strutting success. *Behavioral Ecology and Sociobiology, 18*, 117–123.

Gibson, R.M., & Bradbury, J.W. (1987). Lek organization in sage grouse variations on a territorial theme. *The Auk, 104*, 77–84.

Gibson, R.M., Bradbury, J.W., & Vehrencamp, S.L. (1991). Mate choice in lekking sage grouse revisited: The roles of vocal display, female site fidelity, and copying. *Behavioral Ecology, 2*, 165–180.

Greene, E., Lyon, B.E., Muehter, V.R., Ratcliffe, L., Oliver, S.J., & Boag, P.T. (2000). Disruptive sexual selection for plumage coloration in a passerine bird. *Nature (London), 407*, 1000–1003.

Greenwood, P.J. (1980). Mating systems, philopatry, and dispersal in birds and mammals. *Animal Behavior, 28*, 1140–1162.

Hamilton, I.M., Haesler, M.P., & Taborsky, M. (2006). Predators, reproductive parasites, and the persistence of poor males on leks. *Behavioral Ecology, 17*, 97–107.

Hamilton, W.D. (1964a). Genetical evolution of social behaviour I. *Journal of Theoretical Biology, 7*, 1–16.

Hamilton, W.D. (1964b). The genetical evolution of social behaviour II. *Journal of Theoretical Biology, 7*, 17–52.

Harcourt, A.H., & De Waal, F.B.M. (1992). *Coalitions and alliances in humans and other animals*. New York: Oxford University Press.

Hatchwell, B.J. (2010). Cryptic kin selection: Kin structure in vertebrate populations and opportunities for kin-directed cooperation. *Ethology, 116*, 203–216.

Healy, W.M. (1992). Behavior. In J.G. Dickson (Ed.), *The wild turkey: Biology and management* (pp. 46–65). Mechanicsburg, PA: Stackpole Books.

Hogan-Warburg, A.J. (1966). Social behavior of the ruff, *Philomachus pugnax* (L.). *Ardea, 54*, 109–229.

Höglund, J. (2003). Lek-kin in birds - provoking theory and surprising new results. *Annales zoologici Fennici, 40*, 249–253.

Höglund, J., & Alatalo, R.V. (1995). *Leks*. Princeton, NJ: Princeton University Press.

Höglund, J., Alatalo, R.V., Lundberg, A., Rintamaki, P.T., & Lindell, J. (1999). Microsatellite markers reveal the potential for kin selection on black grouse leks. *Proceedings of the Royal Society of London Series B-Biological Sciences, 266*, 813–816.

Höglund, J., & Robertson, J.G.M. (1990). Spacing of leks in relation to female home ranges habitat requirements and male attractiveness in the great snipe (*Gallinago media*). *Behavioral Ecology and Sociobiology, 26*, 173–180.

Höglund, J., & Shorey, L. (2003). Local genetic structure in a white-bearded manakin population. *Molecular Ecology, 12*, 2457–2463.

Hovi, M., Alatalo, R.V., Höglund, J., Lundberg, A., & Rintamaki, P.T. (1994). Lek center attracts black grouse females. *Proceedings of the Royal Society of London Series B-Biological Sciences, 258*, 303–305.

Hovi, M., Alatalo, R.V., & Siikamaki, P. (1995). Black grouse leks on ice: Female mate sampling by incitation of male competition? *Behavioral Ecology and Sociobiology, 37*, 283–288.

Hugie, D., & Lank, D. (1997). The resident's dilemma: A female choice model for the evolution of alternative mating strategies in lekking male ruffs (*Philomachus pugnax*). *Behavioral Ecology, 8*, 218–225.

Jukema, J., Piersma, T. (2006). Permanent female mimics in a lekking shorebird. *Biology Letters, 2*, 161–164.

Khan, M.Z., & Walters, J.R. (2002). Effects of helpers on breeder survival in the red-cockaded woodpecker (*Picoides borealis*). *Behavioral Ecology and Sociobiology, 51*, 336–344.

Kingma, S.A., Hall, M.L., Arriero, E., & Peters, A. (2010). Multiple benefits of cooperative breeding in purple-crowned fairy-wrens: A consequence of fidelity? *Journal of Animal Ecology, 79*, 757–768.

Kirkpatrick, M., Ryan, M.J. (1991). The evolution of mating preferences and the paradox of the lek. *Nature, 350*, 33–38.

Koenig, W.D., & Dickinson, J.L. (2004). *Ecology and evolution of cooperative breeding in birds*. New York: Cambridge University Press.

Kokko, H., Lindstrom, J. (1996). Kin selection and the evolution of leks: Whose success do young males maximize? *Proceedings of the Royal Society of London Series B-Biological Sciences, 263*, 919–923.

Krakauer, A.H. (2005a). The evolution of cooperative male courtship: Kin selection and the mating system of the wild turkey (*Meleagris gallopavo*). Doctoral dissertation, University of California, Berkeley, CA.

Krakauer, A.H. (2005b). Kin selection and cooperative courtship in wild turkeys. *Nature, 434*, 69–72.

Krakauer, A.H. (2008). Sexual selection and the genetic mating system of wild turkeys. *Condor, 110*, 1–12.

Lank, D.B., & Smith, C. (1987). Conditional lekking in the ruff. *Behavioral Ecology and Sociobiology, 20*, 137–145.

Lank, D.B., Smith, C.M., Hanotte, O., Ohtonen, A., Bailey, S., & Burke, T. (2002). High frequency of polyandry in a lek mating system. *Behavioral Ecology, 13*, 209–215.

Lebigre, C., Alatalo, R.V., Forss, H.E., & Siitari, H. (2008). Low levels of relatedness on black grouse leks despite male philopatry. *Molecular Ecology, 17*, 4512–4521.

Loiselle, B.A., Ryder, T.B., Duraes, R., Tori, W., Blake, J.G., & Parker, P.G. (2007). Kin selection does not explain male aggregation at leks of four manakin species. *Behavioral Ecology, 18*, 287–291.

Madden, J.R., Lowe, T.J., Fuller, H.V., Coe, R.L., Dasmahapatra, K.K., Amos, W., & Jury, F. (2004). Neighbouring male spotted bowerbirds are not related, but do maraud each other. *Animal Behaviour, 68*, 751–758.

Martín, C.A., Alonso, J.C., Alonso, J., Pitra, C., & Lieckfeldt, D. (2002). Great bustard population structure in central Spain: Concordant results from genetic analysis and dispersal study. *Proceedings: Biological Sciences, 269*, 119–125.

Matthiopoulos, J., Moss, R., & Lambin, X. (1998). Models of red grouse cycles. A family affair? *Oikos, 82*, 574–590.

Maynard Smith, J. (1964). Group selection and kin selection. *Nature, 201*, 1145–1147.

McDonald, D.B. (1989a). Cooperation under sexual selection: Age-graded changes in a lekking bird. *American Naturalist, 134*, 709–730.

McDonald, D.B. (1989b). Correlates of male mating success in a lekking bird with male-male cooperation. *Animal Behaviour, 37*, 1007–1022.

McDonald, D.B. (1993a). Delayed plumage maturation and orderly queues for status: A manakin mannequin experiment. *Ethology, 94*, 31–45.

McDonald, D.B. (1993b). Demographic consequences of sexual selection in the long-tailed manakin. *Behavioral Ecology, 4*, 297–309.

McDonald, D.B. (2007). Predicting fate from early connectivity in a social network. *Proceedings of the National Academy of Sciences USA, 104*, 10910–10914.

McDonald, D.B. (2009). Young-boy networks without kin clusters in a lek-mating manakin. *Behavioral Ecology and Sociobiology, 63*, 1029–1034.

McDonald, D.B., & Potts, W.K. (1994). Cooperative display and relatedness among males in a lek-mating bird. *Science, 266*, 1030–1032.

McElreath, R., & Boyd, R. (2007). *Mathematical models of social evolution: A guide for the perplexed*. Chicago, IL: University of Chicago Press.

Miller, C.W., & Moore, A.J. (2007). A potential resolution to the lek paradox through indirect genetic effects. *Proceedings of the Royal Society B-Biological Sciences, 274*, 1279–1286.

Mumme, R.L., & Koenig, W.D. (1991). Explanations for avian helping behavior. *Trends in Ecology & Evolution, 6*, 343–344.

Nooker, J., & Sandercock, B. (2008). Phenotypic correlates and survival consequences of male mating success in lek-mating greater prairie-chickens (*Tympanuchus cupido*). *Behavioral Ecology and Sociobiology, 62*, 1377–1388.

Packer, C., Gilbert, D.A., Pusey, A.E., & O'Brien, S.J. (1991). A molecular genetic analysis of kinship and cooperation in African lions. *Nature, 351*, 562–565.

Patricelli, G.L., & Krakauer, A.H. (2010). Tactical allocation of effort among multiple signals in sage grouse: An experiment with a robotic female. *Behavioral Ecology, 21*, 97–106.

Petrie, M., Halliday, T., & Sanders, C. (1991). Peahens prefer peacocks with elaborate trains. *Animal Behavior, 41*, 323–331.

Petrie, M., Krupa, A., & Burke T. (1999). Peacocks lek with relatives even in the absence of social and environmental cues. *Nature, 401*, 155–157.

Piertney, S.B., Lambin, X., Maccoll, A.D.C., Lock, K., Bacon, P.J., Dallas, J.F., et al. (2008). Temporal changes in kin structure through a population cycle in a territorial bird, the red grouse *Lagopus lagopus scoticus*. *Molecular Ecology, 17*, 2544–2551.

Platt, T.G., & Bever, J.D. (2009). Kin competition and the evolution of cooperation. *Trends in Ecology & Evolution, 24*, 370–377.

Pruett-Jones, S., Greig, E.I., Rowe, M., & Roche, E.A. (2010). The effects of sex, age, and social status on annual survival in the splendid fairy-wren. *Condor, 112*, 369–377.

Regnaut, S., Christe, P., Chapuisat, M., & Fumagalli, L. (2006). Genotyping faeces reveals facultative kin association on capercaillie's leks. *Conservation Genetics, 7*, 665–674.

Reynolds, S.M., Christman, M.C., Uy, J.A.C., Patricelli, G.L., Braun, M.J., & Borgia, G. (2009). Lekking satin bowerbird males aggregate with relatives to mitigate aggression. *Behavioral Ecology, 20*, 410–415.

Rowe, L., & Houle, D. (1996). The lek paradox and the capture of genetic variance by condition dependent traits. *Proceedings of the Royal Society of London Series B-Biological Sciences, 263*, 1415–1421.

Ryder, T.B., McDonald, D.B., Blake, J.G., Parker, P.G., & Loiselle, B.A. (2008). Social networks in the lek-mating wire-tailed manakin (*Pipra filicauda*). *Proceedings of the Royal Society B-Biological Sciences, 275*, 1367–1374.

Ryder, T.B., Parker, P.G., Blake, J.G., & Loiselle, B.A. (2009). It takes two to tango: Reproductive skew and social correlates of male mating success in a lek-breeding bird. *Proceedings of the Royal Society B-Biological Sciences, 276*, 2377–2384.

Saether, S.A. (2002). Kin selection, female preferences and the evolution of leks: Direct benefits may explain kin structuring. *Animal Behavior, 63*, 1017–1019.

Sæther, S.A., Baglo, R., Fiske, P., Ekblom, R., Höglund, J., & Kålås, J.A. (2005). Direct and indirect mate choice on leks. *The American Naturalist, 166*, 145–157.

Segelbacher, G., Wegge, P., Sivkov, A.V., & Höglund, J. (2007). Kin groups in closely spaced capercaillie leks. *Journal of Ornithology, 148*, 79–84.

Sherman, P.W. (1999). Birds of a feather lek together. *Nature, 401*, 119–120.

Shorey, L. (2002). Mating success on white-bearded manakin (*Manacus manacus*) leks: Male characteristics and relatedness. *Behavioral Ecology and Sociobiology, 52*, 451–457.

Shorey, L., Piertney, S., Stone, J., & Hoglund, J. (2000). Fine-scale genetic structuring on *Manacus manacus* leks. *Nature, 408*, 352–353.

Sick, H. (1967). Courtship behavior in manakins (Pipridae): A review. *The Living Bird, 6*, 5–22.

Sinervo, B., Chaine, A., Clobertt, J., Calsbeek, R., Hazard, L., Lancaster, L., et al. (2006). Self-recognition, color signals, and cycles of greenbeard mutualism and altruism. *Proceedings of the National Academy of Science USA, 103*, 7372–7377.

Slud, P. (1957). The song and dance of the long-tailed manakin, *Chiroxiphia linearis*. *The Auk, 74*, 333–339.

Snow, D.W. (1963). The display of the blue-backed manakin, *Chiroxiphia pareola*, in Tobago, W.I. *Zoologica, 48*, 167–176.

Taylor, C., Nowak, M.A. (2007). Transforming the dilemma. *Evolution, 61*, 2281–2292.

Truong, L.B. (2003). *Kin recognition in captive wild turkeys (Meleagris gallopavo)*. Masters thesis, University of Mississippi, Oxford, MS.

Uy, J.A.C, & Endler, J.A. (2004). Modification of the visual background increases the conspicuousness of golden-collared manakin displays. *Behavioral Ecology, 15*, 1003–1010.

vanRhijn, J.G. (1973). Behavioral dimorphism in male ruffs, *Philomachus pugnax* (L.). *Behaviour, 47*, 153–229.

Watts, C.R. (1969). *Social organization of wild turkeys on the Welder Wildlife Refuge, Texas*. Doctoral dissertation, Utah State University, Logan, UT.

Watts, C.R., & Stokes, A.W. (1971). The social order of turkeys. *Scientific American, 224*(6), 112–118.

Widemo, F., & Owens, I.P.F. (1995). Lek size, male mating skew and the evolution of lekking. *Nature, 373*, 148–151.

Wild, G., Gardner, A., & West, S.A. (2009). Adaptation and the evolution of parasite virulence in a connected world. *Nature, 459*, 983–986.

Wiley, R.H. (1991). Lekking in birds and mammals - Behavioral and evolutionary issues. *Advances in the Study Behavior, 20*, 201–291.

Wilson, D.S., & Wilson, E.O. (2007). Rethinking the theoretical foundation of sociobiology. *Quarterly Review of Biology, 82*, 327–348.

Wojcieszek, J.M., Nicholls, J.A., & Goldizen, A.W. (2007). Stealing behavior and the maintenance of a visual display in the satin bowerbird. *Behavioral Ecology, 18*, 689–695.

CHAPTER 15

Primate Kin Preferences: Explaining Diversity

Carol M. Berman

Abstract

Kinship has long been recognized as one of the major organizing principles of primate social organization. However, kin preferences are not ubiquitous, and vary widely between and within species. They are constrained by factors that determine the kinship structure of groups, mechanisms available for recognizing kin, and the availability and/or distribution of limiting resources. Within groups, kinship also interacts with sex, rank, and age. Enduring mother–offspring bonds serve as important building blocks of matrilineal kin relationships in many species, but they are not inevitable even when mothers and adult offspring coreside. Patrilineal kin preferences are just beginning to be examined in a variety of species, and mechanisms have yet to be identified. The question of kin selection as an explanation for kin preferences continues to pose challenges. Recent studies support the operation of kin selection, but suggest that its limits may be narrow, rarely going beyond parent–offspring and sibling relationships.

Keywords: Kinship, kin preferences, kin selection, matrilineal relationships, patrilineal relationships, socioecological theory, dominance style, attachment, parent–offspring bonds

Introduction

Kinship was one of the first principles of nonhuman primate social organization to be appreciated, and it remains an important focus for researchers today. The importance of kin relatedness in the social interactions of primates was first recognized by M. Kawai (1958), S. Kawamura (1958), and D.S. Sade (1965, 1967) in provisioned groups of Japanese (*Macaca fuscata*) and rhesus (*M. mulatta*) macaques. Their pioneering studies established kinship as a central organizing principle of primate social structure, along with age, sex, and dominance. However, over time, researchers have come to realize that kin preferences are not ubiquitous and that kin structures vary widely among species. Thus, efforts today focus on explaining interspecific and intraspecific diversity in kin-related behavior and on understanding the evolutionary processes involved in producing and maintaining it.

Early studies of kinship focused to a large extent on provisioned groups of macaques and other species with matrilineal social organizations. In these species enduring mother–daughter bonds form core building blocks of social organization. In fact, one can predict female affiliative relationships and dominance relationships with high accuracy by knowing matrilineal kin relationships (Kawai, 1958; Kawamura, 1958; Kurland, 1977; Sade, 1965, 1967). This stems from the fact that males typically disperse to other groups during adolescence, whereas females remain in their natal groups for life and continue to associate closely with their mothers. This brings females into close association with their maternal sisters, aunts, nieces and grandmothers etc., who are already close associates of the mother. In this way, matrilineages become subunits of social organization within the larger social group.

Close maternal kin not only affiliate preferentially, they also preferentially support one another in conflicts with others (e.g., Bernstein et al., 1993; Chapais, 1988a; Kaplan, 1978; Kurland, 1977). Within families, mothers tend to support younger daughters over older daughters (Datta, 1988). Largely as a result of these support patterns (Chapais, 1988a), dominance structures among females become closely linked with their kinship structures: adult daughters take on ranks immediately below their mothers, daughters rank in reverse order of age (termed youngest sister ascendancy), and lineages as a whole can be ranked in the same order as their matriarchs. These matrilineally based hierarchies are remarkably stable, maintained sometimes for many years (review in Kapsalis, 2004) by a combination of support from kin and other high-ranking females (Chapais, 1988a,b).

The early observation that enduring mother–daughters bonds form structural units in matrilineal societies dovetailed nicely with classic studies of mother–infant attachment that primarily used macaque models to test aspects of Bowlby's attachment theory of human attachment (Bowlby, 1969, 1973) and to provide an empirical basis for conceptualizing mother–offspring bonds within an integrated evolutionary framework (Hinde, 1974; Suomi, 1995). Attachment theory emphasizes the central and adaptive nature of mother–infant bonds during infancy and childhood, the persistence of emotional bonds with caregivers beyond the period of dependency, and the influence of parental bonds in shaping other close relationships throughout the lifetime. As such, early research on a small number of macaque species led to a view of matrilineal structure emerging from early mother–infant bonds that had roots in attachment processes (Suomi, 1999, 2005).

Over the years, studies on a wider range of primate species have revealed both more varied attachment patterns (Mason & Mendoza, 1998; Reite & Capitanio, 1985; Rosenblum & Kaufman, 1968) and more varied social/kinship structures (e.g., Chapais & Berman, 2004a), not all of which are based on enduring mother–daughter bonds. For example, females in some primate species disperse to other social groups around puberty (review in Strier, 2004), severing ties with mothers and other maternal kin and forming new and sometimes close relationships with unrelated individuals (bonobos [*Pan paniscus*]; White, 1996; chimpanzees [*P. troglodytes*]; Gilby & Wrangham, 2008; Langergraber et al., 2009; Lehmann & Boesch, 2008, 2009; Pepper et al., 1999). Thus, early mother–infant interaction may not invariably lead to long-term bonds, strong bonds may develop independently of mother–offspring relationships, and social structure may not be based on mother–offspring bonds. Given wide variation in social/kinship structure, explanatory models began to de-emphasize the role of early attachment processes in favor of ecological, life history, and demographic factors leading to particular group compositions, and selective pressures governing social interaction among group members at all stages of the life cycle. Kin selection, particularly in the case of matrilineally organized social groups, was viewed as the primary adaptive process driving strong affiliative and supportive relationships among maternal kin. Recently, however, the case for kin selection has been both boosted by evidence of paternal kin recognition and favoritism (Widdig, 2007) and challenged by demonstrations that some examples of kin-biased behavior in primates and other animals might be better explained in terms of mutualism, reciprocity, or nonadaptive processes (Chapais, 2001; Clutton-Brock, 2002). The latter has renewed interest in the possible importance of attachment processes by raising the possibility that matrilineal social structure may simply be a by-product of persistent filial bonds within the context of sex-biased dispersal patterns (Chapais, 2001; Warfield, 2005).

This chapter will survey the diversity of kin structures and preferences across nonhuman primate species, first exploring a number of factors that constrain the potential for the expression of kin preferences at a species level: sex-biased dispersal patterns, female reproductive and mortality rates, and cues for kin recognition. Next, it will examine evidence for and against kin selection as an explanation for the evolution and maintenance of kin preferences and kin structures among primates. Within this context, evidence for associations between classic attachment criteria, enduring parent–offspring bonds and social structure will also be explored. Finally, it will describe current ecological models concerned with the variability of kin preferences within species and between closely related species.

Theoretical Background: Attachment, Kin Selection, Reciprocity and Mutualism
Attachment Processes

John Bowlby's classic attachment theory (1969, 1973) concerns the processes underlying the formation of emotional bonds between human infants and their caregivers and the consequences of early experiences with caregivers for social/emotional development. It posits that infants are born with an innate behavioral and motivational system (the attachment system) that promotes the formation of an emotional bond with a primary caregiver. The behaviors function to maintain proximity and contact with the caregiver and to elicit interaction that will ultimately assure that the infant is nurtured and protected from the environment. As such, the attachment system is a set of physical, neurobiological, psychological, and behavioral adaptations shaped by natural selection that promote infant survival in the natural environments of nonhuman primates and in the "environment of evolutionary adaptedness" of humans (reviews in Cassidy & Shaver, 1999; Carter et al., 2005). Bowlby was primarily concerned with the processes underlying an infant's attachment to its mother, but he also conceptualized a complementary motivational system, derived from early infant attachment, that facilitates the attachment of mothers to their infants (Bowlby, 1988). He hypothesized that among humans, attachment to a primary caregiver leads to the construction and later dependence on internal cognitively based working models of the self and of the caregiver that reflect the quality of their attachment relationship. These working models not only govern the parent–offspring relationship beyond childhood and into adulthood, they are also hypothesized to come into play as sets of expectations and responses in the context of other close relationships later in life.

Our understanding of normative patterns of attachment in nonhuman primates relies heavily on research on a few macaque species. Dubbed by some as the "classic cercopithecine attachment model," primate attachment is conceptualized by some researchers as a special case of imprinting found in other mammals and birds (Immelmann & Suomi, 1981), and is characterized by (a) a repertoire of physical characteristics, signals, movements, and other behaviors adapted to and brought into play specifically to promote proximity and contact with the primary caregiver; (b) nearly continuous carrying of infants by caregivers in the early weeks; (c) discrimination of the caregiver from other individuals; (d) ongoing frequent and intimate contact between infants and caregivers; (e) physiological control characterized by decreased dependence on hormonal and olfactory stimulation in favor of increased executive brain involvement relative to other mammals; and (f) the persistence of bonds beyond the period of nutritional dependence

(Keverne, 2005; Suomi, 1999). These and other parallels with humans have been interpreted as support for a homologous relationship between human and at least some nonhuman primate attachment systems (Hinde, 1974; Maestripieri, 2003; Reite & Capitanio, 1985; Simpson, 1999; Suomi, 1995). Two parallels in particular are seen as diagnostic of filial attachment, particularly when they co-occur:

• *Secure base use*: Infants use their primary caregiver as a secure base for exploration of their physical and social environment, returning to the caregiver when distressed and using contact with her to reduce levels of behavioral and physiological arousal (Harlow & Zimmerman, 1959; Reite et al., 1981). In a similar manner, infants are less likely to respond with fear to environmental challenges in the presence of the primary caregiver than in her absence (Levine & Weiner, 1988; Mason & Capitanio, 1988; review in Mason & Mendoza, 1998).

• *Intense response to separation*: Infants display typical patterns of response to involuntary separation from their primary caregivers. Initial responses are of protest and apparent searching. Infants of some species go on to show a second stage of withdrawal and depression similar to that shown by many institutionalized children. Distress calling and searching appear to be mediated by endogenous opioid activity (Barr et al., 2008; Kalin et al., 1988), whereas other aspects of the response (freezing, threatening) are regulated by the limbic-hypothalamic-pituitary-adrenal (LHPA) system (reviewed in Gunnar, 2005). Unlike humans, nonhuman primate infants do not show a third stage of detachment from parents at reunion. Rather, mothers and infants typically display emotional reunions. A more prolonged period of clinginess by infants may follow (Hinde & McGinnis, 1977), but can be reduced by administering opioids (Kalin et al., 1995).

Although there are no standardized measures of caregiver attachment in nonhuman primates, researchers generally view the co-occurrence of selective (but not necessarily exclusive) care of one's own infant, highly protective and anxious monitoring of infant activity when it is out of contact, and responses of behavioral and physiological distress to separation from the infant as evidence of attachment (review in Maestripieri, 2003).

The two diagnostic criteria of infant attachment to their primary caregivers described above are widespread among Old World monkeys, apes, and humans, generally supporting Bowlby's hypothesis of an infant attachment system with deep phylogenetic roots and suggesting a homologous system at least in these taxa (Mason & Mendoza, 1998; Mineka & Soumi, 1978; Suomi, 1995, 1999). According to the criteria for caregiver attachment, it also appears to be widespread among Old World monkeys, apes, and humans (see review in Maestripieri, 2003). At the same time, variation among and within primate species, including some Old World monkeys and human societies, and lack of information about many species has led to uncertainty about the degree of homology versus homoplasy across the primate order (e.g., Reite & Capitanio, 1985) and even about the existence of cercopithecine-type attachment bonds versus other forms of mother–infant bonding found in nonprimate mammals and birds (Immelmann & Suomi, 1981; Keverne, 2005). Certainly, differences exist between humans and nonhumans (Maestripieri & Roney, 2006), for example, in responses to reunion and in the degree of cognitive involvement in attachment relationships. Thus, it is likely that some aspects of attachment in humans (e.g., internal working models, which are hypothesized to be predicated on fully developed abilities of intersubjectivity [Call & Tomasello, 2008]), may be derived, whereas others (e.g., those involving the regulation of fear via neuroendocrine and limbic activity), may be homologous over a wide range of species. As such, the long-term effects of mother–infant interaction are hypothesized to be less dependent on complicated cognitive mechanisms than on (a) neuroendocrine and limbic mechanisms affecting the offspring's ability to cope with social and environmental challenges (Fairbanks & McGuire, 1988, 1993; Gunnar, 2005; Hinde et al., 1978; Hinde & Spencer-Booth, 1971; Kraemer, 1992; Kraemer et al., 2005; Suomi, 1995, 1999; see also Maestripieri et al., 2009), and (b) on simpler social learning mechanisms mediated in part by the caregiver's regulation of the infant's social interaction with others (Berman, 1980, 2004; Roney & Maestripieri, 2003; Simpson, 1985; Simpson & Datta, 1990).

Other variations in infant attachment patterns undoubtedly represent environmentally contingent adaptations (Hrdy, 2009). For example, varied responses to separation are associated with differences in the availability of allocare among Old World monkey species and human societies, which are associated in turn with low levels of social risk within groups (Hrdy, 2009). When risk is low, mothers are less protective and allocare is extensive.

As a result, infants may form one or more secondary attachments within their social groups. In these cases, infants tend to spend less time in contact with the mother and are less likely to become withdrawn or depressed in her absence. Indeed, when separated from mothers, they may actively seek care from allocare givers, as in Hanuman langurs (*Presbytis entellus*; Dolhinow 1980), bonnet macaques (*Macaca radiata*; Kaufman & Rosenblum, 1969; Rosenblum & Kaufman, 1968; see reviews in Mineka & Suomi, 1978; Hrdy, 2009). However, when no allocare givers are available, their responses are more severe, resembling those of species that do not normally receive high levels of allocare. Examples include bonnet macaques (Kaufman & Stynes, 1978), ring-tailed lemurs (*Lemur catta*; Klopfer & Boskoff, 1979), and Hanuman langurs (Dolhinow, 1980).

Much variation in maternal attachment within human and nonhuman primate species is also seen in terms of environmentally contingent adaptation (Fairbanks, 2003; Hrdy, 1999; Mason & Mendoza, 1998) in a manner consistent with parental investment theory (Trivers, 1972). For example, mothers may abandon, neglect, or limit contact with infants when they lack necessary resources or support of conspecifics; when infants are weak, disabled, or highly vulnerable to predation; or when the mother's older immature offspring or future reproduction are threatened, as in vervet monkeys (*Chlorocebus aethiops*; Hauser & Fairbanks, 1988) and mountain baboons (*Papio cynocephalus ursinus*; Lycett et al., 1998; Barrett et al., 2006; Lycett et al., 1998; review in Lee, 1996).

Less is known about attachment in New World monkeys and prosimians, but a few studies suggest less uniform patterns. Suomi (1999) suggests that capuchin monkey infants (*Cebus apella*) are not strongly attached to their mothers based on observations that mother–infant interaction is both less frequent and less unique in content compared to rhesus. In particular, capuchin infants tend to seek comfort from a variety of group members when frightened (Bryne & Suomi, 1995). However, this behavior may simply be a consequence of having multiple allocare givers. Mother–infant interaction is even less frequent and less intimate in squirrel monkeys (*Saimiri sciureus*) (Fragaszy et al., 1991). Nevertheless, both mother and infant squirrel monkeys display typical patterns of distress and increased cortisol levels when separated, as well as alleviation of distress through interaction with the mother (Mendoza & Mason, 1997). Other New World monkey species, including cooperatively breeding marmosets and tamarins (*Callitrichines* spp.) and biparental titi monkeys (*Callicebus moloch*), show evidence of attachment to fathers rather than mothers (Kostan & Snowdon, 2002; Mason & Mendoza, 1998; see also Wolovich et al., 2008). For example, titi monkey infants show distress and elevated cortisol levels to the removal of their fathers even in the presence of their mothers, but do not show similar responses to removal of the mother unless their fathers are also absent (Hoffman et al., 1995; Mason & Mendoza, 1998). This is not inconsistent with attachment per se, since fathers are typically the primary caregivers in these species (Wolovich et al., 2008; Wright, 1984). On the other hand, there is little evidence that titi monkey parents form specific attachments to their infants. They neither appear to recognize, favor their own infants, nor respond with distress when separated from them (Mendoza & Mason, 1997).

Among prosimians, diurnal ring-tailed lemurs and brown lemurs (*Eulemur fulvus*) show similar patterns of contact and proximity as cercopithecine monkeys and appear to use their mothers as secure bases (Klopfer & Boskoff, 1979). They display typical protest and withdrawal following separation from mothers when left on their own. On reunion, infants seek additional contact with mothers, but mothers do not reciprocate (Klopfer & Boskoff, 1979). Nocturnal prosimians and tarsiers (*Tarsius* spp.) have radically different care patterns from most other primates that have not been studied from an explicit attachment perspective. Unlike other primates, mothers park their infants either for the entire night—for example, in pottos (*Arctocebus sp.*) and lorises (*Loris sp.*)—or cache and carry them from one spot to another at shorter intervals, for example in tarsiers and most galagoes (*Galaginae* spp.) (Gursky, 1997, 2007; Nekaris & Bearder, 2007). Mother–infant interaction appears to be less frequent than in monkeys or apes, with little maternal restraint, retrieval, or rejection of infants, and relatively equal responsibility for maintaining proximity. Intense responses to separation or typical secure base behavior have yet to be described (Doyle, 1979; Ehrlich, 1977; Ehrlich & MacBride, 1989, 1990; Erhlich & Musicant, 1977; Fitch-Synder & Erhlich, 2003; Gursky, 1997, 2007; Mascagni & Doyle, 1993; Nash, 2003; and citations within).

Clearly, definitive conclusions about the distribution of attachment criteria across species and about the question of homology must await information about a much larger range of species and formal phylogenetic analysis (e.g., Atz, 1970; Rendall & Di Fiore, 2007; Thierry et al., 2008). Nevertheless, based on current knowledge, it is possible to conclude tentatively that human, ape, and Old World monkey infants and their primary caregivers are typically attached to one another, and in some cases, infants are attached to secondary caregivers. Conversely, primary caregivers are typically attached to their infants. Among New World monkeys fewer species have been studied, and in some cases rates of mother–infant interaction may be lower. Nevertheless, similar attachment criteria have been observed in species in which care is provided primarily by mothers. In species in which fathers are primary caregivers, infants may be more strongly attached to their fathers than mothers. Titi monkeys represent a unique case in which parents do not appear to be attached to their infants. Diurnal prosimians that continuously carry their young also display attachment behavior not unlike that of classic cercopithecines. However, there is little evidence of cercopithecine-like attachment among nocturnal prosimians and tarsiers.

Kin Selection Theory

Since the 1970s, Hamilton's inclusive fitness or kin selection theory (Hamilton, 1964) has provided a powerful evolutionary explanation for the widespread occurrence of preferences among kin in addition to those between parents and offspring. According to Hamilton's theory, individuals that behave in ways that increase the reproductive success of their own offspring and/or the offspring of other genetic relatives, will be evolutionarily selected. This stems from the fact that individuals that are related through a common ancestor share a proportion of their genes in common. Thus, under some circumstances, one may increase the transmission of one's own genes in the next generation by promoting the reproduction of one's kin, even when helping them decreases one's own production of offspring (i.e., when the act is altruistic). The circumstances are described in a formal mathematical model, since called Hamilton's rule: $b * r > c$, where b represents the benefit of an act to the recipient (the amount that the act increases the recipient's reproductive success), c represents the cost of the act to the performer (the amount the act decreases the performers own reproductive success), and r represents the average degree of relatedness between the performer and the recipient due to common descent. Hamilton's rule posits that altruistic acts should be selected when the cost to the performer is smaller than the benefit to the recipient, discounted by their degree of relatedness. In reality, it has been difficult to test Hamilton's rule or to rule out alternative explanations (see "The Question of Selection" below).

Kin-biased Mutualism and Reciprocity

One alternative explanation for the evolution and maintenance of altruistic behavior is based on the idea of reciprocity (Trivers, 1971). Altruistic behavior should be selected when the cost of the act to the actor is relatively small compared with the benefit to the receiver, provided the receiver reciprocates in the future. In this way, both parties exchange relatively small costs for larger benefits. This process allows unrelated individuals to exchange net benefits, but reciprocity can be equally engaged in by kin. Indeed, when it occurs between close kin, individuals have the potential to reap both direct benefits from their interaction, as well as indirect benefits derived from augmenting the reproduction of genetic relatives (Wrangham, 1982). Since reciprocity involves a time lag between the initial altruistic act and it reciprocation, it is open to cheating (nonreciprocation) on the part of the initial receiver. Hence, Trivers (1971) speculated that the evolution of reciprocity would be accompanied by the evolution of mechanisms to detect and counteract cheating, and would involve both engaging in a series of contingent exchanges of benefits with the same individuals and keeping track of altruistic acts given and received from individual partners. Because of the cognitive demands of precise record keeping, many theorists have reasoned that reciprocal altruism should operate only on a very limited time scale for most nonhumans (e.g., Barrett et al., 2007; Barrett & Henzi, 2006; Stevens & Hauser, 2005). However, Schino and Aureli (2009) argue that record keeping can also operate on an emotional level, obviating the need for cognitive complexity. De Waal and Brosnan (2006) in particular describe two cognitively undemanding forms of reciprocity: (a) symmetry-based reciprocity that is based on tendencies for individuals to direct altruistic acts indiscriminately to whomever they associate with frequently, and (b) attitudinal reciprocity, in which individuals adopt positive attitudes toward individuals that behave positively toward them without keeping precise counts of benefits exchanged.

A final mechanism for explaining the evolution of behavior that benefits another individual is mutualism. Mutualism concerns the concurrent exchange of behavior that yields net benefits for both parties, or self-serving acts by one party that incidentally benefit another (by-product mutualism) (Dugatkin, 1997). Like reciprocal altruism, it can explain cooperative acts between nonkin, but it can potentially yield additional indirect benefits when kin interact. Since there is no time lag between the donation and receipt of benefits, mutualistic acts between two individuals should not be highly vulnerable to cheating. However, when multiple individuals are involved, free riders may step in to reap benefits without joining in the action to produce them (Nunn, 2000).

The Potential for Kin Bias

Although the adaptive processes discussed above suggest widespread opportunities for the evolution and maintenance of kin-biased behavior and social structure, a number of other phenomena pose constraints. Among them include sex-biased dispersal patterns, female reproductive and mortality rates, and male reproductive skew and limited mechanisms of kin recognition.

Dispersal Patterns

Primates have long lifespans, overlapping generations, and most species live in permanent social groups. Dispersal is usually sex-biased, a feature that has profound implications for kin-related behavior, because it largely determines the classes of kin that are present and absent within groups. When one sex tends to remain in its natal group for life, while the other sex disperses during puberty or early adulthood, the sex that remains (the philopatric sex) accumulates within groups. This allows extended networks of biological kin (matrilineal or patrilineal) to form and interact on a regular basis (Chapais & Berman, 2004b; Strier, 2008), but also generally limits the potential for kin bias to those that are present, because nonhuman primates rarely maintain close relationships with members outside their group (Rodseth et al., 1991).

In species in which females but not males remain for life (i.e., female philopatric/male dispersal groups), female matrilineal kin tend to accumulate within groups. As a result, female members often reside with a wide range of female maternal kin throughout their lives. However, they may also reside with fathers, paternal siblings (sisters and undispersed brothers), and other patrilineal kin (females and undispersed males). After dispersing, male contact with kin is usually limited to a small number of males (and their descendents) that disperse into the same social groups. Recent genetic studies generally reveal kin structures that are consistent with observed dispersal patterns. Examples include baboons (*Papio cynocephalus*; Altmann et al., 1996), long-tailed macaques (*M. fascicularis*; de Ruiter & Geffen, 1998); see reviews in DiFiore, 2009; Kappler, 2008; Morin & Goldberg, 2004. Adult females within these groups are more closely related to one another than are males, and females are more closely related to members of their own matrilines than to females in different matrilines.

In species in which males remain for life and females disperse (male philopatric/female dispersal groups), adult males are expected to reside with many categories of male paternal kin (fathers, sons, grandfathers, grandsons, brothers, nephews, uncles, cousins, etc.). Adults of both sexes should reside with only a few categories of matrilineal kin—males with mothers, brothers, and undispersed sisters, and females with sons and undispersed daughters, provided females disperse before reproducing. Both sexes may also live with the male and undispersed female descendants of male maternal kin and other matrilineal kin that may have dispersed into the same group (Chapais & Berman, 2004b). Genetic studies of relatedness have found relatively high levels of male relatedness in male philopatric woolly monkeys (*Lagothrix poeppigii*; DiFiore & Fleischer, 2005), but not in male philopatric bonobos (Gerloff et al., 1999). Nor are male philopatric chimpanzees more closely related to one another than are females (Lukas et al., 2005; Vigilant et al., 2001). Lukas et al. (2005) appear to resolve this discrepancy in a model of relatedness that takes not only dispersal patterns, but also reproductive skew and group size into consideration. The model predicts high male relatedness only in relatively small groups and is consistent with published data for a variety of primate and nonprimate taxa.

Kin structures can be variable when both sexes disperse. A common pattern is for one sex to be more likely to disperse or to disperse farther than the other (reviews in Kappler, 2008; DiFiore, 2009). Genetic studies provide several examples in which males appear to disperse farther than females, as in western lowland gorillas (*Gorilla gorilla gorilla*; Douadi et al., 2007), but see Bradley et al., 2004; orangutans (*Pongo pygmaeus*; Krutzen et al., 2008; Singleton & van Schaik, 2002; van Schaik & van Hooff, 1996); Coquerel's dwarf lemurs (*Mirza coquereli;* Kappler et al., 2002). When this occurs, a dispersed matrilineal population structure results.

Female Reproductive and Mortality Rates

Female reproductive patterns constitute another set of factors affecting the kin structure of groups and hence the potential for kin bias. Ages of first reproduction, intervals between infants and female lifespans, along with mortality patterns, influence the number of generations found within groups, the categories of kin residing at the same time, as well as the size and number of matrilines. Reproductive rates in particular can profoundly influence the availability of kin of various kinds (Dunbar, 1988). For example, when reproductive rates are slow, fathers and older siblings may disperse before younger ones are born. Similarly, if mortality rates are high, mothers and other close kin may die before they are able to provide youngsters with support necessary to attain high rank (Datta & Beauchamp, 1991). Availability may also influence the strength of kin relations when kin coreside (Berman et al., 2008; Perry et al., 2008). For example, the extent to which baboon females favor paternal sisters may depend on the scarcity of maternal kin (Silk et al., 2006; Smith et al., 2003; Widdig et al., 2001). Conversely, it has been hypothesized that the intensity of maternal kin preferences may be inversely related to availability of paternal kin (Schülke & Ostner, 2008). Availability is also hypothesized to affect the costs and benefits of favoring various categories of kin, particularly when time for social interaction is limited (S. Altmann, 1979). Chapais and Belisle (2004) argue, for example, that when individuals have few kin, they are likely to receive the greatest payoff in terms of indirect fitness by investing available time and energy into a range of kin categories. However, when they have many kin, they should benefit most by limiting their investment to a few of their closest kin.

Kin Recognition and Reproductive Skew

Individuals living in groups with extended kin networks, either paternal or maternal, are expected to associate preferentially with kin only if they can distinguish them from unrelated group members with similar characteristics. Thus, the potential for kin bias is constrained by the ability of individuals to recognize their relatives. Maternal kin recognize each other primarily through familiarity (review in Rendall, 2004). In strongly kin-structured societies, close association with mothers brings offspring into affiliative interaction with maternal siblings and other maternal kin in direct proportion to their degrees of relatedness through maternal lines, producing a linkage between familiarity, maternal kinship, and affiliation (Berman, 2004; Chapais, 2001; Rendall, 2004).

A combination of maternal transmission and independent learning mechanisms are likely to be involved in the development of kin bias via familiarity (review in Berman, 2004). From birth, primate infants show patterns of association that typically mirror those of the mother. This stems from the fact that mothers and infants remain in close proximity to one another and hence to the mother's close associates. The result is that infants in species with strong matrilineal bonds also show strong tendencies to associate with close matrilineal kin, whereas those in species with weaker matrilineal bonds display weaker or no kin preferences. In some species, this process is reinforced when mothers exert a large degree of control over infant's interactions with others, favoring their own close associates. Thus, initial forms of kin bias are largely the result of passive behavior on the part of the infant (Berman, 2004; de Waal, 1996). A more active form of kin bias appears when infants become progressively more independent from their mothers but continue to associate (often taking the initiative) with many of the same individuals with whom they interacted previously. In this sense, active kin bias develops through a process of social transmission through the mother. Several specific mechanisms of transmission are possible: differential exposure and interaction with kin and nonkin (MacKenzie et al., 1985; Martin, 1997; Welker et al., 1987), observational learning using the mother as a model (Altmann, 1980; Hakami et al., 1990), and/or active and selective intervention in the infant's interactions with others by the mother (Maestripieri, 1995). By late infancy and juvenescence, youngsters' networks no longer exactly duplicate those of their mothers (Berman & Kapsalis, 1999), suggesting that maternal transmission gradually gives way to other processes, particularly independent learning through direct interaction with kin and nonkin. In strongly kin-biased groups, older kin are more likely than nonkin to initiate friendly and supportive interaction and less likely to threaten or harass them (review in Berman, 2004). Youngsters' networks may also increasingly reflect attraction to similarly aged peers (possible paternal siblings, see below).

Until recently, researchers thought that the potential for patrilineal kin recognition was limited to a small number of monogamous and single male/multifemale species. In these species, most infants born into a group are sired by a single male, making familiarity well as paternity certainty high between fathers and offspring (Rendall, 2004). In species with more than one reproductive male, researchers were usually unable to assign paternity with certainty, so fathers were assumed to be unable to distinguish their own offspring from others. This inability would both make father–offspring favoritism impossible and preclude other kinds of patrilineal kin recognition (e.g., paternal siblings, cousins or uncles and nephews) through association with the father. However, with the recent application of genetic methods to determine paternity, researchers are beginning to find evidence of patrilineal kin recognition in some wild and free-ranging multimale primate groups (see review in "A Survey of Kin Preferences" below; Widdig, 2007).

Mechanisms of paternal kin recognition are not well understood. One major hypothesis is based on findings that male reproductive skew can be high even in groups that contain more than one adult male (e.g., Altmann et al., 1996; Cowlishaw & Dunbar, 1991; Pope, 1990). When one or a few high-ranking males sire most infants, rank can serve as a cue to paternity. Reproductive skew also leads to the production of similarly aged paternal siblings (J. Altmann, 1979), a finding that has been confirmed genetically in several species, such as in baboons (Altmann et al., 1996; Silk et al., 2006a), rhesus macaques (Widdig et al., 2002), Hanuman langurs (Launhardt et al., 2001), mandrills (*Mandrillus sphinx*; Charpentier et al., 2005), capuchin monkeys (*Cebus capucinus*; Muniz et al., 2006, Perry et al., 2008), great apes (Bradley et al., 2005; Gerloff et al., 1999; Robbins & Robbins, 2005; Vigilant et al., 2001; review in Widdig, 2007). Thus, offspring can potentially use age similarity as a cue for paternal relatedness with an accuracy approximating the degree of reproductive skew. However, this is more likely to be the case in female philopatric/male dispersal societies than in male philopatric/female dispersal societies (Chapais, 2006).

Peers often have preferential relationships (Janus, 1992; Nakamichi & Yamada, 2007; Pereira, 1988; Silk et al., 2006a; Watts & Pusey, 1993; Widdig et al., 2001, 2002; but see Charpentier et al., 2007; Schino et al., 2007), and researchers suggest that they may be mediated by a general attraction to similarly aged partners (de Waal & Luttrell, 1986). However, in some cases, individuals show small, but statistically significant preferences for paternal siblings over similarly aged unrelated group members (Silk et al., 2006; Widdig et al., 2001), suggesting that more specific mechanisms may be involved. Hypotheses based on familiarity, recognition of physical similarities such as odor or appearance (i.e., phenotypic matching) (Lacy & Sherman, 1983) or combinations of the two are under investigation, but few results for primates are available as yet (review in Widdig, 2007). Nevertheless, the fact that bonds are generally much weaker between paternal kin than maternal kin suggests that paternal kin recognition mechanisms may have relatively weak effects compared with those that mediate recognition with maternal kin (Chapais, 2008; Rendall, 2004).

A Survey of Kin Preferences
Female Philopatry/Male Dispersal Species
FEMALES

Many Old World monkeys display "classic matrilineal social structures" that feature high degrees of matrilineal kin bias, socially cohesive matrilines, and matrilineally based dominance hierarchies, similar to those described earlier for rhesus and Japanese macaques (see recent reviews in Berman, 2004; Chapais, 2001; Kapsalis, 2004; Silk, 2001, 2002, 2006; Strier, 2008). Generally, close maternal kin spend disproportionate amounts of time together and preferentially groom, feed, huddle, sleep, support, travel together, and reconcile with one another, as for example in vervets (Hunte & Horrocks, 1987), pig-tailed macaques (*Macaca nemestrina*; Judge, 1991), long-tailed macaques (Aureli et al., 1997), rhesus (Kapsalis & Berman, 1996a; Sueur & Petit, 2008), Japanese macaques (Aureli et al., 1997; Majolo et al., 2005; Nakamichi & Shazawa, 2003; Wada et al., 2007), and baboons (Silk et al., 2006a,b; Wittig et al., 2007). Matrilineal kin in these species appear to discriminate gradations of relatedness, favoring mothers and offspring over siblings and grandmothers over aunts, nieces, and others (reviewed in Kapsalis, 2004). Although maternal kin may show relatively high rates of aggression, it is generally relatively mild in intensity (Bernstein, 1991). Allocare is also highly kin-biased (Hrdy, 1976), and close maternal kin are among the most likely candidates to adopt infants if they are orphaned (e.g., Berman, 1982a; Hasegawa & Hiriwa, 1980; Nicolson, 1987; Nozaki, 2009; see also Waitt et al., 2004). In addition, maternal kin are preferred models for social learning (review in Chauvin & Berman, 2004). Finally, social groups typically fission by splitting along matrilineal lines, with different lineages settling in different daughter groups and close female kin remaining together (Chepko-Sade & Sade, 1979; Dittus, 1988; Koyama, 1970; Kuester & Paul, 1997; Li et al., 1996; Oi, 1988; Prud'homme, 1991; van Horn et al., 2007; Widdig et al., 2006a; review in Okamoto, 2004).

In some species, there is evidence that adult and/or juvenile paternal sisters also affiliate more with one another than with unrelated adult females, as in rhesus monkeys (Widdig et al., 2001, 2002), savanna baboons (Silk et al., 2006a; Smith et al., 2003), and mandrills (Charpentier et al., 2007). In agonistic encounters, rhesus females tend to refrain from supporting their paternal sisters' opponents, although they do not actively support them (Widdig et al., 2006b). In some cases, paternal kin remain together when groups fission, as in savanna baboons (Smith, 2000), but not in others, as in Barbary macaques (*Macaca sylvanus*; Kuester & Paul, 1997).

However, not all species with female philopatry/male dispersal conform to the classic matrilineal model. Their social structures are not as well known, but in general they display more moderate and less consistent tendencies to organize their behavior around kinship. For example, females of several Old World monkey species, including some macaques, guenons (*Cercopithecine* spp.), and langurs, show weaker tendencies to affiliate, co-feed, reconcile with, and/or support matrilineal kin and to split along matrilineal lines. These include Hanuman langurs (Borries, 1989; Hrdy & Hrdy, 1976), bonnet macaques (Defler, 1978), sooty mangabeys (*Cercocebus atys*; Ehardt, 1988), stumptail macaques (*M. arctoides*; Butovskaya, 1993; de Waal & Luttrell, 1989), Barbary macaques (Aureli et al., 1997; Menard et al., 2006; Patzelt et al., 2009), and moor macaques (*M. maura*; Matsumura & Okamoto, 1997; Okamoto & Matsumura, 2001; reviews in Thierry, 2000; Thierry & Aureli, 2006; Cords & Simpson, 2006; Thierry et al., 2008). Dominance hierarchies may also deviate from the "classic" matrilineal model to varying degrees. Specifically, individual competitive ability or support from unrelated individuals may determine ranks within and between families when support is rare or follows less strict matrilineal lines. Mother–daughter rank reversal has been described in Barbary macaques (Paul & Kuester, 1987), Tonkean macaques (*Macaca tonkeana*; Thierry, 2000), some savanna baboons (Combes & Altmann, 2001), bonnet macaques (Silk et al., 1981), and Hanuman langurs (Borries et al., 1991; Hrdy & Hrdy, 1976). When this occurs, mothers cannot help younger daughters gain rank over older daughters, and as a result, sisters may not rank in any consistent order (Chapais, 2004; Paul, 2006; Prud'homme & Chapais, 1993; Thierry & Aureli, 2006).

The best-known New World monkeys with female philopatry/male dispersal are white-faced capuchin monkeys (*Cebus capucinus*). Females preferentially groom, support, and reconcile with matrilineal kin, but unlike the classic matrilineal species, mothers and daughters do not affiliate any more than do sisters. Maternal sisters do not rank in reverse order of age, and paternal sisters show no evidence of kin bias (Perry & Manson, 2008; Perry et al., 2008). The best known diurnal prosimians, ring-tailed lemurs, preferentially groom mothers, daughters, and sisters (Nakamichi & Koyama, 1997; see also, Oda, 1996), and groups tend to split along matrilineal lines (review in Gould & Sauther, 2007). However, mothers rarely support daughters, and perhaps as a result, daughters' ranks are not similar to those of their mothers (Nakamichi & Koyama, 1997).

Males

Juvenile males in female philopatric/male dispersal species preferentially affiliate with and/or support maternal brothers and other close kin before they disperse, as in rhesus (Colvin, 1983a), bonnets (Silk, 1992), and Barbarys (Widdig et al., 2000; see also Barbaranelli, 1994, cited in Paul, 2006) and may preferentially handle related infants (Kümmerli & Martin, 2008). Conversely, females tend to favor related natal adult and juvenile males, affiliating, supporting, reconciling, and co-feeding preferentially with them (Fairbanks, 2000; Pereira & Fairbanks, 1993; Schino et al., 2007). In some species, matrilineal kin also facilitate rank acquisition in natal males (e.g., Berard, 1989; Colvin, 1983; Koford, 1963; Kuester & Paul, 1988; Paul, 2006).

Although a male's focus on female kin tends to weaken as he matures, many males maintain an orientation toward related males. In some species, groups of similarly aged males may disperse together and cooperate with one another in aggressive encounters with other males, such as Peruvian squirrel monkeys (*Saimiri boliviensis*; Mitchell, 1994), ring-tailed lemurs (Sauther et al., 1999; Sussman, 1992), vervet monkeys (Cheney & Seyfarth, 1983), and long-tailed macaques (van Noordwijk & van Schaik, 1985). In species with high reproductive skew, dispersal partners are likely to be paternal brothers, but it is not yet clear whether they preferentially choose paternal kin in these cases, or whether alliances with more closely related males are more successful or more enduring than those with fewer close kin. In other species, males may join groups in which maternal or paternal male kin already reside (Cheney & Seyfarth, 1983; but see Alberts & Altmann, 1995), easing their entry into new groups and increasing their chances of achieving high rank or at least of receiving support (Meikle & Vessey, 1981; Pusey & Packer, 1987; van Noordwijk & van Schaik, 1985; but see Melnick et al., 1984; Colvin, 1986).

Adult males in many female philopatric/male dispersal species form special relationships with particular infants or juveniles. However, the infants are frequently not their genetic offspring, and male care can be better explained as mating effort (Fernandez-Duque et al., 2008; Smuts, 1985; van Schaik & Paul, 1996) or agonistic buffering (Stein, 1984; Strum, 1984; review in MacKinnon, 2007). Nevertheless, recent studies suggest that males may favor their own offspring in some cases. For example, male savanna baboons preferentially intervene on behalf of their own juvenile offspring when they get into fights with other youngsters (Buchan et al., 2003). In addition, juvenile mandrills appear to recognize their own fathers and affiliate with them more than with unrelated males (Charpentier et al., 2007). Putative fathers may also attempt to protect their own offspring from infanticide by other males, as in Hanuman langurs (Borries et al., 1999), long-tailed macaques (de Ruiter et al., 1994), Japanese macaques (Soltis et al., 2000), chacma baboons (*Papio cynocephalus ursinus*; Weingrill, 2000; review in Widdig, 2007).

Male Philopatry/Female Dispersal Species
Males

Males in some, but not all male philopatric/female dispersal species maintain long-term ties to their mothers. Among bonobos, mother–adult son relationships are among the strongest in the group (Furuichi, 1989; White, 1996; but see Hohmann et al., 1999), and maternal support increases a son's chances of attaining a high rank (Furuichi, 1989; Ihobe, 1992). Chimpanzee mothers may also influence their son's dominance ranks (Boesch & Boesch-Achermann, 2000; Goodall, 1986; but see Williams et al., 2002). In contrast, muriquis males (*Brachyteles hypoxanthus*) do not maintain long-term preferential bonds with their mothers, even though they typically coreside for long periods of time (Tolentino et al., 2008).

There is evidence that male chimpanzees recognize their own offspring, although they generally show only low levels of care. For example, Lehmann et al. (2006) found that genetic fathers played longer with their offspring and directed less aggression toward them than toward unrelated juveniles. Recent genetic analyses confirm earlier reports that chimpanzee males also preferentially affiliate and cooperate with their maternal brothers (Langergraber et al., 2007; see also Goodall, 1986; Nishida, 1989). However, most cooperation and affiliation takes place between unrelated or distantly related males (Boesch et al., 2006, Langergraber et al., 2007). In contrast, paternal brothers show no preferences for one another (Langergraber et al., 2007, but see Lehmann et al., 2006). Male–male bonds are generally weak among bonobos (White, 1996; but see Furuichi & Ihobe, 1994), and at this point, there is no firm evidence that they are any stronger with either maternal or paternal siblings than with unrelated males (Furuichi & Ihobe, 1994; but see Hohmann et al., 1999). Male muriquis associate closely, cooperate in group defense and show high levels of mating tolerance, but there is no evidence that they favor maternal brothers (Strier et al., 2002). Similarly, male spider monkeys (*Ateles* spp.) have strong affiliative and cooperative relationships, but it is not known whether they favor close kin over others (review in Di Fiore & Campbell, 2007).

FEMALES

Most chimpanzee females disperse when they reach sexual maturity. Nevertheless, some remain in their natal groups or return after a period of time away (Goodall, 1986; Nishida, 1989; Stumpf, 2007). When mothers reside in the same community with adolescent or adult daughters, they tend to spend much more time together than do unrelated females (Williams et al., 2002; see also Langergraber et al., 2009). However, this is less likely to be the case when maternal sisters coreside as adults (Nishida, 1989). As juveniles, females enthusiastically care for and play with younger maternal siblings, and are likely to adopt younger ones if their mother dies (Goodall, 1986).

Unlike chimpanzees, when mother–adult daughter muriqui pairs occasionally find themselves together in the same social group, they tend to spend more time with one another than expected by chance, but they seldom form strong affiliative bonds with each other or with any other female (Strier, 1993, 1994). Among bonobos, female–female relationships are extremely prominent (Furuichi, 1989; White, 1996; but see Hohmann et al., 1999), and female–female support, affiliation, and sociosexual behavior are common (White, 1996). However, these relationships are not based on kinship (Gerloff et al., 1999; Hashimoto et al., 1996).

Species in Which Both Sexes Disperse
SOLITARY OR DISPERSED SOCIAL STRUCTURES

In orangutans and many small nocturnal prosimians, both sexes disperse, but males generally disperse farther than females. Although they generally forage alone, matrilineally related females typically occupy adjacent or overlapping home ranges, forming a matrilineal population structure. Among these are orangutans (Galdikas, 1988; Krutzen et al., 2008; Setia et al., 2009; Singleton et al., 2009; Singleton & van Schaik, 2002; van Schaik & van Hooff, 1996) and several galagoes (Bearder, 1987; Clark, 1978; reviews in Kappeler, 2008; Morin & Goldberg, 2004; Nash, 2004). Behavioral and genetic evidence has begun accumulating that in some species, maternal kinship also structures social relationships within these larger dispersed communities (Nash, 2004). For example, grey mouse lemurs (*Microcebus murinus*) forage solitarily during the night and sleep in hollow trees by day, sharing nests with two to five other matrilineally related females. Females raise their young cooperatively in the nests, favoring their own, but grooming and nursing all infants, particularly when the infants' mothers are out foraging. Interestingly, mothers carry only their own young, suggesting that they do not provide care to others merely because they fail to recognize their own (e.g., Eberle & Kappeler, 2006; Radespiel, 2006). In one galago (*G. senegalensis braccatus*), allonursing by older sisters and grandmothers has also been observed (Kessler & Nash, 2008). In contrast, Coquerel's dwarf lemurs display similar matrilineal ranging patterns and social structure, but do not share nests or interact cooperatively with maternal kin (e.g., Kappeler et al., 2002; Wimmer et al., 2002).

NONDISPERSED SOCIAL STRUCTURES

When both sexes disperse to other groups, access to kin may vary considerably. Nevertheless, both males and females commonly favor matrilineal kin when available. In mountain gorillas (*Gorilla beringei beringei*), silverback males sire most of the infants born into their breeding groups; thus, offspring are generally paternal siblings or full siblings. Most sons emigrate as young blackbacks, but some continue to reside with their fathers into adulthood, cooperating with them in intergroup conflicts. As a result, males in multimale groups are often father–son pairs or brothers (paternal and/or maternal) (Bradley et al., 2005; Robbins, 1995). Maternal brothers may also join the same all male groups (Robbins, 2007).

Within groups, adult males generally coexist by tolerating or avoiding one another rather than by forming highly affiliative or hostile relationships (review in Robbins, 2007). Nevertheless, relationships between related males have been described as more affiliative relationships than those between unrelated males (Harcourt, 1979; Harcourt & Stewart, 1981). Although most mountain gorilla females disperse from their natal groups, a minority remains in them or join groups containing female kin. As a result, about 80% spend part of their adult lives with other maternally or paternally related adult females (Watts, 1996, 2001). When that occurs, related adult females prefer to affiliate and support one another, particularly when they are related maternally rather than paternally (Stewart & Harcourt, 1987; Watts, 1994). See Douadi et al. (2007), Bradley et al. (2007), Levrero et al. (2006), and Breuer et al. (2009) for recent comparable information about Western lowland gorillas.

Hamadryas baboons (*Papio cynocephalus hamadryas*) live in one-male/multifemale groups within multilevel societies composed of associated one-male units (clans), associated clans (bands), and associated bands (troops). Related males appear to reside in the same clans more than expected by chance. They cooperate in decisions over clan movement and readily reconcile with one another after disputes. However, it is unclear whether they favor close kin over other clan males. Nevertheless, there is evidence that clans are more cohesive when they contain father–son pairs, full or maternal brothers, or other maternally related males (Colmenares, 1992). Females live in a series of units during their lives with other (generally unrelated) adult females and their young. They do not have strong bonds with other females, typically focusing their interaction on the unit male and on their own immature offspring (Abegglen, 1984; Kummer, 1968, 1990; Sigg et al., 1982). Nevertheless, mother–daughter pairs and paternal sisters, but not maternal sisters are not only found together more often than expected by chance, they also groom and support each other more than others (Colmenares, 1992, 2004).

Callitrichid (marmoset and tamarin) females are cooperative breeders in which single dominant females generally give birth to two sets of twins per year. Their rapid reproductive rate depends on receiving help with infant care and home range defense from adult males and nonbreeding group members (Bales et al., 2000; Garber, 1997). Nonbreeding helpers are frequently, but not exclusively close relatives of the breeding pair, often mature brothers and sisters of the infants (Huck et al., 2004) that are reproductively suppressed by the parents via physiological and/or behavioral mechanisms (review in Digby et al., 2007). In golden lion tamarins (*Leontopithecus rosalia*), a minority of dominant females allow subordinate females to reproduce, and are more likely to do so with daughters than sisters, and least likely to do so with unrelated females (Dietz, 2004).

Reproductive Benefits of Kin Bias

As illustrated above, examples of kin favoritism and cooperation among primates are abundant. Nevertheless, researchers are only beginning to document clear links between kin favoritism and components of fitness. Past efforts have been hampered by difficulties in quantifying short- and long-term costs and benefits of particular behaviors, as well as lifetime reproductive success of long-lived individuals. However, evidence that strong affiliative and supportive relationships with kin yield reproductive benefits is beginning to accumulate. Some of the best evidence comes from red howler monkeys (*Alouatta seniculus*) and wild chacma baboons.

When adolescent male red howler monkeys disperse from their natal groups, they do so with a small band of peers, preferring kin when available. The band remains together for years, cooperating to invade or defend another bisexual group. Once established in a group, the dominant male monopolizes reproduction. However, he depends on the male coalition to defend the group from takeovers by other (often infanticidal) males. Coalitions that are composed of related males tend to last much longer than those made up of unrelated males (8.2 vs. 2.3 years). Thus, kin coalitions provide greater direct benefits for the dominant male and appear to provide indirect benefits to his male kin (Pope, 1990, 2000b).

Red howler females attempt to stay within their natal groups and reproduce, but often face eviction as juveniles or adolescents when the number of adult females reaches a limit (Pope, 2000a). In an apparent effort to avoid eviction, young females vigorously pursue supportive relationships with their mothers and older sisters, but those without support from a high-ranking mother must invariably disperse. Dispersed females often travel over long distances to find unrelated females with whom they can jointly establish a territory. Even if they succeed, their reproduction is delayed for about 2 years, and their infants suffer higher mortality than those born into well-established groups.

As a result, there is an overall correlation between female reproductive success and relatedness within groups (Crockett & Pope, 1993; Pope, 2000a).

Offspring survival is also associated with strong kinship relationships in wild chacma baboons (Silk et al., 2009). Specifically, mothers who form stronger and more enduring bonds with their own mothers and daughters have longer-lived offspring than those that form weaker bonds with them. When females have no mothers or daughters in the group, offspring survival is enhanced for those that have relatively strong relationships with maternal sisters. The relationship between affiliative relationships and offspring survival carries well into the offspring's adulthood and can not be attributed to mothers' dominance, relationships with male protectors, or numbers of kin within the group. Rather it seems to be related specifically to the strength and persistence of affiliative relationships with a few close kin. Although the precise mechanisms are still unclear, Silk et al. (2009) suggest that females with strong relationships (and their young) may enjoy increased protection from predators, support in conflict, and/or lower levels of social stress (Crockford et al., 2008; Engh et al., 2006; Wittig et al., 2008).

Other researchers have found lower infant mortality for mothers that raise infants in the presence of grandmothers, such as vervets (Fairbanks, 1988) and Japanese macaques (Pavelka et al., 2002); earlier sexual maturity in females that grow up in the presence of mothers and maternal sisters, as in baboons (Charpentier et al., 2008); and shorter intervals between births when more maternal kin are present, as in white-faced capuchins (Fedigan et al., 2008). However, it is not always clear whether these advantages are due to the presence of kin, or whether the presence of kin is the result of higher fitness that runs in families for other reasons. High rank has also been tied to higher reproductive success in many groups, particularly for males (reviews in Cowlishaw & Dunbar, 1991; Widdig, 2007), but also for some females (Altmann & Alberts, 2003, 2005; Harcourt, 1987; Setchell et al., 2002; Silk, 1987; van Noordwijk, 1999). Thus, it has been argued that when support from kin is important in attaining high rank, kin relationships lead to increased fitness (e.g., Silk, 2006).

The Question of Selection
Nonadaptive Explanations
Artifact of Rank Relationships
The discovery of widespread kin preferences among primates in the 1970s and 1980s led many researchers to uncritically accept evidence of kin bias alone as evidence of kin selection. However, as critics pointed out, kin-biased behavior can be the result of a number of processes, some adaptive and others nonadaptive (Chapais, 2001; Clutton-Brock, 2002). The simplest explanation is that kin bias may be an artifact of processes that tend to bring individuals of similar rank into close association and cooperation. This is a plausible explanation for many species in which close kin occupy similar ranks. Individuals may simply be attracted to others that are similar to themselves in rank, age, and kinship (de Waal & Luttrell, 1986), or individuals may end up interacting with others of similar rank because they are both attracted to individuals of high rank, but constrained by competition from gaining access to them (Seyfarth, 1983). A number of studies indicate, however, that rank and age effects are not sufficient to explain kin bias. Strong kinship effects have been found even when rank or age differences are controlled in female rhesus, bonnet, and Tibetan macaques (*Macaca thibetana*) (Berman et al., 2004; de Waal, 1991; Kapsalis & Berman, 1996a,b; Silk, 1982). Indeed, the effects of rank and age are often weaker than those of kinship, for example in bonnet macaques (Silk, 1982), rhesus macaques (Kapsalis & Berman, 1996a,b), and baboons (Silk et al., 1999); or absent altogether, for example in capuchins (Schino et al., 2009). Similarly, kin-biased behavior is found in species in which dominance ranks are not correlated with kinship, such as Hanuman langurs (Borries et al., 1994) and gorillas (Watts & Pusey, 1993).

Persistent Mother–Offspring Bonds
Researchers have also raised the possibility that kin bias and matrilineal social organization may be nonadaptive by-products of enduring mother–offspring association patterns (Warfield, 2005). If relationships between infants and other maternal kin develop out of their common association with the mother, it is reasonable to ask to what extent an exchange of benefits is necessary to explain kin preferences and other key features of matrilineal social structure. In one version of the argument, it has been suggested that after infancy, offspring no longer receive substantial benefits from their mothers, but continue to associate closely with them as a nonadaptive consequence of early attachment processes (Warfield, 2004, 2005, personal communication). Warfield thus suggests that key features of matrilineal structure can be explained largely as a by-product of two factors: nonadaptive persistent

filial bonds and sex biased dispersal. If so, one might expect species that display strong infant attachment bonds to mothers (e.g., apes, Old World Monkeys, some New World monkeys, and diurnal lemurs) to also display strong bonds between adult offspring and mothers, provided mothers and offspring coreside within the same groups. This should be the case for both sons and daughters, since there is little evidence of sex differences in attachment strength during infancy (Mineka & Suomi, 1978). It should also occur regardless of whether adult sons and daughters appear to benefit from relationships with their mothers. Further, where mothers and more than one offspring coreside, one would expect strong relationships among maternal siblings and possibly other maternal kin. Where early classic attachment patterns are less certain or atypical (callictrichids, titi monkeys, and nocturnal prosimians), one would not necessarily expect enduring bonds between mothers and adult offspring nor close interaction between maternal kin.

As described earlier, in many female philopatric/male dispersal species, the following characteristics co-occur: strong infant attachment, mother–daughter bonds in adulthood, and matrilineal social structure marked by intense kin preferences for matrilineal kin and matrilineally based dominance hierarchies. Where infants form secondary attachments to allocare givers (i.e., where attachment to the mother is less exclusive, as indicated by less severe responses to maternal separation), preferential mother–daughter bonds are usually discernible in adulthood, but kin preferences for other maternal kin are less intense, and dominance hierarchies may deviate from the classic matrilineal model, as in bonnet macaques (Kaufman & Rosenblum, 1969; Rosenblum & Kaufman, 1968) and Hanuman langurs(Borries et al., 1991, 1993; reviews in Maestripieri, 1994; Thierry, 2000). Conversely, in some female philopatric/male dispersal species, individual males that delay dispersing until adulthood maintain close, supportive relationships with their mothers, such as in rhesus (Berard, 1989; Colvin, 1983b; Koford, 1963) and Barbary macaques (Kuester & Paul, 1988; Paul, 2006). In addition, in some male philopatric/female species, strong infant attachment to mothers and later supportive mother–son relationships also co-occur, as in chimpanzees (Boesch & Boesch-Achermann, 2000; Goodall, 1986; but see Williams et al., 2002) and bonobos (Furuichi, 1989; Ihobe, 1992). Finally, when individual chimpanzee and hamadryas baboon mother–adult daughter pairs are found in the same group, they also display preferential and supportive relationships with each other (Colmenares, 1992, 2004; Williams et al., 2002).

While these examples appear to support the co-occurrence of infant attachment and persistent mother–offspring relationships, a few exceptions argue that the persistence of filial bonds into adulthood may depend on potential benefits provided by mothers. For example, muriqui mothers typically do not maintain preferential relationships with either their sons or daughters mothers when they coreside in the same group (Strier, 1993,1994; Tolentino et al., 2008). Nor do Tibetan macaque mothers display affiliative or supportive relationships with individual upwardly mobile adult male sons that delay dispersing from their natal groups (Berman, unpublished data). In both species, maternal support is either unnecessary, given the egalitarian nature of relationships within the group, as in muriquis (Tolentino et al., 2008), or ineffective given differences in competitive ability between the sexes, as in Tibetan macaques (Berman, personal observation). Thus, the persistence of early attachment bonds into adulthood is not inevitable and may itself be a product of adaptive processes. Nor does the presence of persistent filial bonds necessarily lead to strong social relationships between maternal siblings: When chimpanzee and hamadryas mothers and daughters find themselves in the same group, daughters maintain preferential relationships with mothers but not necessarily with sisters (Colmenares, 1992, 2004; Nishida, 1989).

In species in which strong infant attachment is less clear or atypical, both sexes typically disperse, and frequent interaction with adult offspring is less common. Nevertheless, several species display dispersed matrilineal social structures, opening the door to cooperative or supportive interaction between mothers, female offspring, and other female matrilineal kin. The extent to which this actually occurs is still largely unknown and appears to be variable. Cooperative interaction is extensive some (e.g., grey mouse lemurs [Eberle & Kappeler, 2006; Radespiel, 2006]), but absent or minimal in others (e.g., Coquerel's dwarf lemur [Kappeler et al., 2002; Wimmer et al., 2002]). Nevertheless, this suggests that close relationships and matrilineal social structures can emerge even when infant attachment deviates from the typical "classic" pattern.

It is also necessary to consider the null hypothesis that associations between maternal kin other than the mother may merely be outcomes of common proximity with the mother. If so, they may not represent independent relationships. However, several studies suggest that this is not the case. For example, females have been found to display strong kin bias even when amount of time in proximity is controlled (e.g., Berman et al., 2004; Bernstein et al., 1993). Indeed, infant rhesus macaques have been shown to pursue relationships with others without regard to maternal proximity after a few months of age (Berman, 1982b). In addition, in many cases maternal sisters maintain strong relationships even in the absence of mothers. In baboons, bonds between maternal sisters actually become stronger following a mother's death (Silk et al., 2006a). Finally, the existence of preferential relationships among paternal kin suggests that kin bias can not be explained entirely as a byproduct of extended maternal ties.

Kin Selection Versus Mutualism/Reciprocity

Another possibility is that bonds between kin are "real," but are outcomes of mutualism or reciprocity rather than kin selection (Chapais, 2001, 2006; Chapais & Belisle, 2004). In mutualism and reciprocity, cooperating individuals receive direct immediate or delayed benefits from their interaction. In kin selection, individuals derive indirect benefits by augmenting the reproduction of genetic relatives. In reality, kin interaction often yields both direct and indirect benefits, and it is difficult to determine which are primary. For example, young tamarins that help their parents rear younger siblings may receive indirect benefits from helping kin, as well as direct benefits from being able to remain on their parent's territory. The direct benefits may be particularly important when their own chances of establishing a territory and reproducing are small. Two sets of findings suggest that direct benefits may be sufficient to explain helping behavior in some cases: Some helpers are unrelated to the parents and offspring, and help is often distributed without regard to kinship. However, other findings also suggest a role for indirect benefits: in other cases, both the amount of help given (Baker, 1991; cited in Dietz, 2004) and the probability that a dominant female shares reproduction with a subordinate (Baker et al., 2002) are correlated with degree of relatedness (reviewed in Dietz, 2004).

Although direct benefits may be sufficient to explain some forms of cooperation, individuals that form mutualistic or reciprocal relationships preferentially with kin should theoretically be at an advantage over those who cooperate with nonkin, because they are able to reap both direct and indirect benefits (Wrangham, 1982). Support for kin-biased reciprocity or mutualism comes from recent studies of female grooming patterns that have found independent effects of kinship and reciprocity across several primate species (Schino & Aureli, 2010), more equitable grooming relationships among close kin than distant or unrelated female baboons (Silk et al., 2006b), and kin-biased alliance patterns used against low-ranking targets (e.g., Chapais, 2001). When both partners rank above the target, the costs of aggression are low, and each alliance partner is likely to benefit directly by reinforcing its rank over the target and by obtaining resources it holds.

On the other hand, other factors, including competition, may offset some or all of the benefits of cooperating with kin. Chapais et al. (1994) describe a situation involving Japanese macaque females that are involved in fights with higher-ranking unrelated females. Normally, they could expect support from their younger sisters, but they may not receive it when their younger sisters are attempting to rise in rank over them and require support from higher-ranking individuals to succeed. Chapais (2006) also suggests that kin may not be optimal choices for interaction that requires partners with specific abilities. For example, it may be more beneficial to form an alliance with an unrelated high-ranking individual than with a low-ranking relative, because an alliance with a powerful ally is more likely to be effective. Similarly, it may be beneficial for juveniles to choose play partners that are well matched by size and sex over poorly matched related partners (Walters, 1986, 1987).

Clearly, comparing indirect benefits received from kin versus those received directly from cooperation versus costs of competing with kin is difficult in most cases. As a result, it is often difficult to come to firm conclusions about the role of kin selection versus mutualism or reciprocity in particular cases. Nevertheless, one class of behavior, unilateral altruism, is less problematic because it involves behavior that increases the fitness of another individual at a cost to the actor and is directed in only one direction—from the altruist to the recipient (Chapais & Belisle 2004). Here, the actor receives no immediate benefit from the act and incurs a clear cost for which it is not reciprocated. An example of unilateral altruism concerns agonistic support on behalf of a youngster involved in a fight with an individual that ranks above the supporter. Not only is such support risky for the supporter, the youngster is also incapable of reciprocating effectively. Several observational studies indicate that support against dominant opponents is highly kin-biased; examples include Japanese macaques (Chapais et al., 1997; Kurland, 1977; Watanabe, 1979), bonnet macaques (Silk, 1982), rhesus macaques (Chapais, 1983; Kaplan, 1978), baboons (Pereira, 1989; Walters, 1980), vervet monkeys (Hunte & Horrocks, 1987), long-tailed macaques (Netto & van Hooff, 1986), and gorillas (Harcourt & Stewart, 1989). Supporters are not only likely to support kin over nonkin, they also support close kin over distant kin (Chapais et al., 1997; Datta, 1983). However, these findings do not definitively demonstrate kin selection because they do not control for a number of possibly confounding factors: the availability of kin that require help, the availability of alternative helpers, and the helper's ability to gain access to needy kin (Chapais & Belisle, 2004). Nevertheless, a series of experiments that provided these controls produced similar results (Chapais, 1988a; Chapais et al., 1997, 2001): When three unrelated Japanese macaque juveniles were housed with a single adult female relative of the lowest-ranking juvenile, the low-ranking juveniles were capable of reversing ranks with higher-ranking peers only with the support of the adult. They received support regularly from mothers, sisters, grandmothers, and great-grandmothers, only rarely from aunts, and never from cousins or great-aunts.

Another form of unilateral altruism involves allowing a subordinate individual access to monopolizable food. Observational studies support the idea that both passive co-feeding (Berman et al., 2004; de Waal, 1986; Furuichi, 1983; Ihobe, 1989; Yamada, 1963; but see Pastor-Nieto, 2001) and active food sharing (Feistner & Price, 1990; Perry & Rose, 1994; McGrew, 1975; Silk, 1979) are highly kin-biased. In addition, Belisle and Chapais (2001) found similar results in an experimental study of Japanese macaques that controlled for variations in motivation (e.g., hunger) and costs of defending food (e.g., injury, loss of efficiency). Mothers and daughters co-fed more than grandmother–granddaughter or sister–sister pairs, who in turn co-fed more than aunt–niece pairs and unrelated females. However, when the costs of defending food were further reduced, females no longer favored their sisters or grandmothers, extending feeding tolerance only to daughters (Belisle, 2000). Thus, although these results support the notion of kin selection in unilateral altruism, they also suggest that when the costs of defending food are minimal, favoritism may extend only to one's closest kin (Chapais & Belisle, 2004).

A final approach to testing predictions for kin selection comes out of studies of rank reversals between baboon mothers and their mature daughters that often occur before mothers reach an advanced age (Combes & Altmann, 2001). Ordinarily females that are targeted for rank reversal resist vigorously, but Combes and Altmann (2001) suggest that reversals between mothers and mature daughters are "consensual," providing a way for mothers to reap indirect benefits that accrue when daughters attain high rank. This hypothesis stems from the fact that a mother's reproductive value may drop below that of their daughters as she ages, loses fertility, and has progressively shorter spans of time to continue reproducing. Combes and Altmann (2001) tested this idea using demographic records and Hamilton's rule to predict the ages at which such altruistic rank reversals should take place. They concluded that mothers should first begin to lose rank at about 15 years of age, be more likely to experience reversals as they age, and that the age at which they lose rank should depend on the age difference between the mother and daughter. In general, the actual ages of rank reversal were consistent with the predictions. However, further research is needed to ascertain whether or not mothers resisted the rank reversals or had the potential to counteract them (Chapais, 2004).

Ecological Models of Kin Bias

As described above, demographic and life history processes provide basic constraints on the potential for kin bias, and kin selection, reciprocity, and mutualism help explain its broad adaptive nature. However, these processes leave much remaining to explain about why kin-related behavior varies across and within primate species. To fill these gaps, several ecologically based models have been offered beginning in the 1960s. The earliest models relied on correlations between a few ecological variables (e.g., diet, habitat) and several global features of social groups, such as group size, dispersal patterns, diurnality, territoriality, or numbers of males per group (Crook & Gartlan, 1966; Crook, 1970) to categorize primate species. Although pioneering, they were unable to explain variation in social composition and dynamics within categories (e.g., Rubenstein & Wrangham, 1986). Current models focus on social relationships, conceptualizing social structure as the overall patterning of social relationships within groups. Relationships themselves are seen as emergent properties based on the nature, quality, and patterning of social interactions among individuals that have only partly overlapping interests (Hinde, 1976). In such systems, the divergent reproductive interests of males and females are considered particularly salient: Female reproductive success is limited by access to nutrition and protection, whereas male reproductive success is limited by access to fertile females. Since females represent a limiting factor for males, most models begin by considering female needs to distribute themselves with regard to protection and food resources, and then subsequently consider male needs to distribute themselves around fertile females (Van Schaik, 1989; Wrangham, 1979, 1980).

Socioecological Explanations

The most prominent current socioecological model of primate sociality begins with the premise that diurnal females form groups with one another when doing so effectively reduces risks of predation and infanticide (Sterck et al., 1997). Once in a group, however, they must contend with competition for limited food resources both within their group and with other groups. In this context, affiliative and supportive kin bias are viewed as adaptations to direct forms of competition. Females that experience high within-group contest competition (WGC) and low between-group competition (BGC) for monopolizable food resources (i.e., resident-nepotistic groups) should benefit by forming within-group coalitions with kin and with high-ranking individuals to increase their access to food. Kin are expected to be favored allies based on their long-term familiarity and potential indirect fitness gains. Females are also expected to favor kin as partners for affiliation, because alliances are widely believed to be maintained by grooming (Schino, 2007; but see Berman et al., 2008; Henzi & Barrett, 1999; Silk et al., 1999). The value of alliances should lead to female philopatry.

When females experience low WGC and high BGC (resident-egalitarian groups), they should benefit from group level coalitions but not from within-group alliances. As such, they should display much weaker tendencies to favor kin. Similarly, females that experience both high WGC and BGC (resident-nepotistic-tolerant) should show less intense kin bias and more tolerance toward nonkin than resident-nepotistic females in order to maintain cooperation in group level alliances. Finally, when females experience low WGC and low BGC (dispersal-egalitarian groups), they would not benefit from either within-group or group level alliances. Thus, they should not be expected to display either high degrees of kin bias or philopatry. Unfortunately, studies that have investigated links between WGC and tendencies for females to affiliate and form coalitions with one another have produced inconsistent results (e.g., Barton et al., 1996; Boinski, 1999; Hill, 1999, 2004; Mitchell et al., 1991; reviews in Koenig, 2002; Menard, 2004; Thierry, 2008), and none has found direct links between levels of WGC and intensities of affiliative and supportive kin bias (Berman et al., 2008; but see Majolo et al., 2009).

Dominance Style

Researchers have experienced somewhat more success explaining variations in kin bias in terms of species-typical, sex-specific dominance styles (e.g., Thierry, 2000). The dominance style concept hypothesizes that species can be arranged along a continuum based on the intensity and unidirectionality of aggression and on conciliatory tendencies following aggression. Despotic species form one end of the continuum, displaying intense and highly asymmetric aggression and low rates of reconciliation following conflicts. Relaxed or egalitarian species form the other end of the continuum, displaying mild, more symmetrical aggression and high rates of reconciliation. Additional aspects of social structure appear to covary with dominance style, most notably, kin bias, maternal protectiveness, and low rates of allocare.

A great deal of overlap occurs between dominance style designations and Sterck et al.'s (1997) socioecological categories. For example, resident-nepotistic species are generally classified as despotic and display intense kin bias, whereas resident-nepotistic-tolerant or resident-egalitarian species are generally classified as relaxed or egalitarian and display weak kin bias (e.g., Thierry, 2000). Some explanations for the covariation of dominance style and kin bias also focus on tendencies for kin to form within-group agonistic alliances (Thierry, 1990a,b). For example, Chapais (2004) hypothesizes direct links between affiliative kin bias, the profitability of alliances and the strength of WGC. However, others view dominance styles as emergent properties of self-organizing social systems driven by species-specific variations in kin bias (Thierry, 1990a,b) and/or intensities of aggression (Hemelrijk, 1999; Wendland et al., 2006). In this view, dominance styles reflect past rather than current ecological conditions and competitive regimes, and are somewhat independent of current ecological conditions because they represent evolutionary stable strategies

(Matsumura & Kobayashi, 1998). Specifically, current dominance styles are hypothesized to be outcomes of past biogeographical factors (Thierry, 2004) and phylogenetic inertia (Matsumura & Kobayashi, 1998, Matsumura, 1999, Thierry et al., 2000). However, current studies of kin bias show only weak evidence for a phylogenetic signal (Thierry et al., 2008).

A recent novel hypothesis suggests that relaxed dominance styles in macaques result from high levels of male reproductive skew. Citing a correlation between skew and position on Thierry's (2000) dominance style continuum, Schülke and Ostner (2008) argue that when skew is high, females have many paternal kin, and that this may dilute interaction rates with maternal kin and encourage widespread tolerance within the group.

Time Constraints
Dunbar's (1988, 1992) time constraints model represents an extension of Sterck et al.'s (1997) socioecological theory that attempts to explain variation in kin bias in terms of indirect links between WGC and affiliative networks. WGC is hypothesized to increase as groups increase in size, increasing the need for strong affiliative relationships and large within-group alliances. However, social time is likely to be limited, and at some point, females may not have enough time to maintain strong relationships with all other females in the group (Dunbar, 1984). Under these circumstances, the model suggests that females should benefit by focusing their affiliative interaction on a small proportion of group members, most likely one's closest kin (S. Altmann, 1979; Chapais, 2001). So far, studies of rhesus macaques (Berman et al., 1997; Berman & Kapsalis, 2009), Tibetan macaques (Berman et al., 2008), Tonkean macaques (Berman & Thierry, 2010a, b), and capuchin monkeys (Perry et al., 2008) are consistent with this prediction; bias among close kin is more intense when groups are large than when they are small.

Dispersal Costs/Foraging Efficiency
A final model by Isbell and her colleagues (review in Isbell, 2004) views female kin bias as a secondary outcome of group living rather than a driving force for group formation and female philopatry. Briefly, it hypothesizes that groups of female kin form by default when there is an advantage to group living. Adult daughters may attempt to remain on their mothers' home ranges when dispersal costs are high enough to make reproduction unlikely in a new area. Mothers are likely to allow them to stay when their own reproduction is not compromised by sharing their range with another female. Since mothers of different species vary in the extent to which they are energetically constrained both physiologically and ecologically, they also vary in the extent to which they can expand their ranges to accommodate daughters. In cases in which daughters are actually able to contribute to home range defense or expansion, matrilineal kin groups are likely to form, opening the door to inclusive fitness benefits through kin bias.

Conclusion
Studies of primate kinship began about 50 years ago with descriptions of maternal attachment and matrilineally based social organizations. Although theoretical work still relies heavily on matrilineally organized species, our view of kinship has expanded since then thanks to studies of a wide variety of species and to the application of noninvasive molecular genetic methods. Indeed, the use of genetic techniques has been perhaps the most far-reaching recent development, providing means to confirm and extend our knowledge of matrilineal relationships and to determine patrilineal relationships for the first time (Di Fiore & Gagneux, 2007; Morin & Goldberg, 2004; Woodruff, 2004). This has led to exciting discoveries of patrilineal kin favoritism, which have led to investigations paternal kin recognition mechanisms, the role of male reproductive skew in structuring kin relationships, and the possible interplay of matrilineal and patrilineal kin effects. All of these developments have contributed in turn to a greatly expanded appreciation for the diversity of kin effects among and within species, and particularly for the complex interaction of kinship with a host of other factors related to sex, dominance, life history characteristics, demography, and ecology.

Although researchers have a long way to go to explain diversity, they have begun to flesh out some common themes that shape kin relationship across species. Dispersal patterns, reproductive rates, mortality patterns, and reproductive skew shape the composition and kinship structure of groups, constraining preferential relationships to members that coreside. Within groups, kin relationships are further constrained by recognition mechanisms. The extent to which patrilineal kin recognize and favor one another is just beginning to be examined in a variety of species, and recognition mechanisms have yet to be identified in specific cases.

Currently, available data suggest that patrilineal kinship is generally weaker in shaping relationships than matrilineal kinship, even in cases in which patrilineal kin are available and recognizable. Recognition and preferences for maternal kin begin with common associations with the mother, although alternative mechanisms have not been ruled out. Persistent mother–offspring bonds serve as important building blocks of kin structure in many species, but the display of "classic" infant attachment does not appear to lead inevitably to enduring bonds in adulthood between coresident mothers and offspring. Preliminary evidence raises the possibility that variation in the persistence of filial bonds may depend on an exchange of benefits and may itself be the product of selection. Similarly, long-term bonds between close kin in matrilineal societies appear to be grounded in reproductive benefits related to increased infant survival and higher reproductive rates (Hrdy, 2009; Pope, 2000a,b; Silk et al., 2009). The potential benefits of interacting with kin appear to interact in complex ways with sex, age, dominance, and the availability of kin, as well as with the abundance and distribution of current and/or past limiting resources (food, time, mates, etc.). Several explanatory models based on these factors are under investigation.

Kin selection continues to pose intriguing questions and challenges. Primate researchers no longer accept evidence of kin bias alone as evidence for kin selection (Chapais, 2001; Clutton-Brock, 2002), but rather attempt to also examine alternative hypotheses for kin bias. As a result, they have uncovered examples of kin-biased behavior that can be better explained as kin-based mutualism or reciprocity. Current approaches that are being developed to probe more precise predictions of Hamilton's rule and to rule out alternative explanations are promising, and include experimental studies in captivity (Chapais & Belisle, 2004) and long-term field-based studies of demography and behavior (Combes & Altmann, 2001; Silk et al., 2006). Studies using these approaches have strengthened support for the operation of kin selection, while simultaneously indicating that the limits of kin selection may be narrow, rarely going beyond parent–offspring and sibling relationships.

Questions and Future Directions

1. Information about attachment, kinship, and kin-related behavior is still lacking or fragmentary for many taxa. Studies are needed to broaden our basic knowledge, particularly studies that generate both behavioral and genetic data and that follow populations over multiple generations.

2. Studies of the behavioral, physiological, and reproductive consequences of kin relationships are providing means to test predictions of kin selection theory and other adaptive and nonadaptive explanations for kin bias. Topics of particular interest include proximate mechanisms by which strong kin relationships lead to benefits, the extent to which relationships with nonkin can compensate for the absence of kin relationships, and whether specific constraints and opportunities are associated with particular kinds of kin relationships (e.g., with fathers, grandmothers, siblings, etc.).

3. Studies of paternal kin recognition and its mechanisms are in their infancy. Another intriguing question concerns the reasons why patrilineal kinship appears to be less important than maternal kinship in shaping relationships, even when paternal kin are available and recognizable.

4. Currently, there is no consensus over the relative importance of current versus past selection in shaping kin-related behavior, or about the role of complex adaptive systems versus self-organizing systems driven by a few initial conditions (Thierry, 2008). Future studies should profit from the application of both ecological and phylogenetic analysis, and should ultimately aim to encompass a wide range of species in order to correct an historically narrow concentration on matrilineal social structures.

5. Several recent efforts to apply primate research to specific questions about the evolution of the human family represent exciting areas of growth, but were beyond the scope of this chapter. They include anthropological questions about the evolution of human pair-bonds, menopause, cooperative breeding, and exogamy (e.g., Boehm, 1999; Chapais, 2008; Fox, 2004; Hawkes, 2004; Hrdy, 2009; Rodseth et al., 1991), and psychological questions about incest avoidance (Paul & Kuester, 2004) and links between early attachment quality and later reproductive strategies, romantic relationships, parenting style, and general sensitivity to environmental stimuli (e.g., Belsky, 1999; Belsky & Pluess, 2009; Del Guidice, 2009; Ellis, 2004; Maestripieri, 2005).

References

Abegglen, J.J. (1984). *On socialization in hamadryas baboons*. Cranbury, NJ: Associated University Presses.

Alberts, S.C., & Altmann, J. (1985). Balancing costs and opportunities: Dispersal in male baboons. *American Naturalist*, 145, 279–306.

Altmann, J. (1979). Age cohorts as paternal sibships. *Behavioral Ecology and Sociobiology*, 6, 161–164.

Altmann, J. (1980). *Baboon mothers and infants*. Cambridge, MA: Harvard University.

Altmann, J., & Alberts, S. (2003). Variability in reproductive success viewed from a life-history perspective in baboons. *American Journal of Human Biology*, 15, 401–409.

Altmann, J., & Alberts, S. (2005). Growth rates in a wild primate population: Ecological influences and maternal effects. *Behavioral Ecology and Sociobiology*, 57, 490–501.

Altmann, J., Alberts, S.C., Haines, S.A., Dubach, J., Muruthi, P., Coote, T., et al. (1996). Behavior predicts genetic structure in a wild primate group. *Proceedings of the National Academy of Science*, 93, 5797–5801.

Altmann, S. (1979). Altruistic behaviour: The fallacy of kin deployment. *Animal Behavior*, 27, 958–962.

Atz, J.W. (1970). The application of the idea of homology to behavior. In L.R. Aronson, E. Tobach, D.S. Lehrman, & J.S. Rosenblatt (Eds.), *Development and evolution of behavior* (pp. 53–74). San Francisco: W.H. Freeman.

Aureli, F., Das, M., & Veenema, H.C. (1997). Differential kinship effect on reconciliation in three species of macaques (*Macaca fascicularis, M. fuscata,* and *M. sylvanus*). *Journal of Comparative Psychology*, 111, 91–99.

Baker, A.J. (1991). *Evolution of the social system of the golden lion tamarin*. (Ph.D. thesis), University of Maryland, College Park, MD.

Baker, A.J., Bales, K., & Dietz, J.M. (2002). Mating system and group dynamics in golden lion tamarins (*Leontopithecus rosalia*). In D.G. Kleiman & A.B. Rylands (Eds.), *The lion tamarins of Brazil*. Washington, D.C: Smithsonian Institution Press.

Bales, K., Dietz, J., Baker, A., Miller, K., & Tardif, S.D. (2000). Effects of allocare-givers on fitness of infants and parents in callitrichid primates. *Folia Primatologica*, 7, 27–38.

Barbaranelli, G. (1994). *Sozialbeziehungen Zwishen Adulten Berberaffenmannchen (Macaca sylvanus L. 1758)*. (Unpublished Diploma thesis), University of Gottengen, Gottingen.

Barr, C.S., Schwandt, M.L., Lindell, S.G., Higley, J.D., Maestripieri, D., Goldman, D., Suomi, S.J., & Heilig, M. (2008). Variation at the mu-opioid receptor gene (OPRM1) influences attachment behavior in infant primates. *PNAS*, 105, 5277–5281.

Barrett, L., & Henzi, S.P. (2006). Monkeys, markets and minds: Biological markets and primate sociality. In P.M. Kappeler & C.P. van Schaik (Eds.), *Cooperation in primates and humans* (pp. 209–232). New York: Springer.

Barrett, L., Henzi, S.P., & Lycett, J.E. (2006). Whose life is it anyway? Maternal investment, developmental trajectories and life history strategies in baboons. In L. Swedell & S.R. Leigh (Eds.), *Reproduction and fitness in baboons: Behavioral, ecological and life history perspectives* (pp. 199–234). New York: Springer.

Barrett, L., Henzi, P., & Rendall, D. (2007). Social brains, simple minds: Does social complexity really require cognitive complexity? *Philosophical Transaction of the Royal Society of London, B*, 362(1480), 561–575.

Barton, R.A., Byrne, R.W., & Whitten, A. (1996). Ecology, feeding competition and social structure in baboons. *Behavioral Ecology and Sociobiology*, 38, 321–329.

Bearder, S.K. (1987). Lorises, bushbabies, and tarsiers: Diverse societies in solitary foragers. In B.B. Smuts, D.L. Cheney, R.M. Seyfarth, R.W. Wrangham, & T.T. Struhsaker (Eds.), *Primate societies* (pp. 11–24). Chicago: University of Chicago Press.

Bélisle, P. (2002). *Apparentement et co-alimentation chez le macaque Japonais (Macaca fuscata)*. (Ph.D. thesis). Université de Montréal, Montreal.

Bélisle, P., & Chapais, B. (2001). Tolerated co-feeding in relation to degree of kinship in Japanese macaques. *Behaviour*, 138, 487–509.

Belsky, J. (1999). Modern evolutionary theory and patterns of attachment. In J. Cassidy & P.R. Shaver (Eds.), *Handbook of attachment* (pp. 141–161). New York: Guilford Press.

Belsky, J., & Pluess, M. 2009. Beyond diathesis stress: Differential susceptibility to environmental influences. *Psychology Bulletin.*, 135, 185–908.

Berard, J.D. (1989). Life histories of male Cayo Santiago macaques. *Puerto Rican Health Sciences Journal*, 8, 61–64.

Berman, C.M. (1982a). The social development of an orphaned rhesus infant on Cayo Santiago: Male care, foster mother-orphan interaction and peer interaction. *American Journal of Primatology*, 3, 31–141.

Berman, C.M. (1982b). The ontogeny of social relationships with group companions among free–ranging infant rhesus monkeys II. Differentiation and attractiveness. *Animal Behavior*, 30, 63–170.

Berman, C.M. (2004). Developmental aspects of kin bias in behavior. In B. Chapais & C.M. Berman (Eds.), *Kinship and behavior in primates* (pp. 317–346). New York: Oxford University Press.

Berman, C.M., Ionica, C.S., & Li, J-H. (2004). Dominance style among *Macaca thibetana* on Mt. Huangshan, China. *International Journal of Primatology*, 25, 1283–1312.

Berman, C.M., & Kapsalis, E. (1999). Development of kin bias among rhesus monkeys: Maternal transmission or individual learning? *Animal Behavior*, 58, 883–894.

Berman, C.M., & Kapsalis, E. (2009). Variation over time in grooming kin bias among female rhesus macaques on Cayo Santiago supports the time constraints hypothesis. *American Journal of Physical Anthropology*, 48(Suppl), 89–90.

Berman, C.M., Ogawa, H., Ionica, C.S., Yin, H., & Li, J. (2008). Variation in kin bias over time in a group of Tibetan macaques at Huangshan, China: Contest competition, time constraints or stress response? *Behaviour*, 145, 863–896.

Berman, C.M., Rasmussen, K.L.R., & Suomi, S.J. (1997). Group size, infant development and social networks in free-ranging rhesus monkeys. *Animal Behavior*, 53, 405–421.

Berman, C.M., & Thierry, B. (2010a). Grooming kin bias varies with both group size and social style: A comparison of Cayo Santiago rhesus (*M. mulatta*), corral-living Tonkean (*M. tonkeana*) and wild Tibetan (*M. thibetana*) macaques at Huangshan, China. *American Journal of Primatology*, 72(Suppl. 1), 67.

Berman, C.M., & Thierry, B. (2010b). Variation in kin bias: Species differences and time constraints in macaques, *Behaviour*, 147, 1863–1887.

Bernstein, I.S. (1991). The correlation between kinship and behaviour in non-human primates. In P.G. Hepper (Ed.),

Kin recognition (pp. 7–29). Cambridge: Cambridge University Press.
Bernstein, I. S., Judge, P. G., & Ruehlmann, T. E. (1993). Kinship, association, and social relationships in rhesus monkeys (*Macaca mulatta*). *American Journal of Primatology, 31,* 41–53.
Boehm, C. (1999). *Hierarchy in the forest: The evolution of egalitarian behavior.* Cambridge, MA: Harvard University.
Boesch, C., & Boesch-Achermann, H. (2000). *The chimpanzees of the Taï Forest.* New York: Oxford University.
Boesch, C., Boesch, H., & Vigilant, L. (2006). Cooperative hunting in chimpanzees: Kinship or mutualism? In P.M. Kappeler & C.P. van Schaik (Eds.), *Cooperation in primates and humans: Mechanisms and evolutions* (pp. 139–150). New York: Springer.
Boinski, S. (1999). The social organizations of squirrel monkeys: Implications for ecological models of social evolution. *Evolutionary Anthropology, 8,* 101–112.
Borries, C. (1989). Mothers and adult daughters—on kinship in free-ranging Hanuman langurs (*Presbytis entellus*). *Primate Report, 25,* 10.
Borries, C. (1993). Ecology of female social relationships: Hanuman langurs (Presbytis entellus) and the van Schaik model. *Folia Primatology, 61,* 21–30.
Borries C., Sommer V., & Srivastava A. (1991). Dominance, age, and reproductive success in free-ranging female Hanuman langurs (*Presbytis entellus*). *International Journal of Primatology, 12,* 231–257.
Borries, C., Launhardt, K., Epplen, C., Epplen, J. T., & Winkler, P. (1999). Males as infant protectors in Hanuman langurs (*Presbytis entellus*) living in multi-male groups—defence pattern, paternity, and sexual behaviour. *Behavioral Ecology and Sociobiology, 46,* 350–356.
Borries, C., Sommer, V., & Srivastava, A. (1994). Weaving a tight social net: Allogrooming in free-ranging female langurs (Presbytis entellus). *International Journal of Primatology, 15,* 421–443.
Bowlby, J. (1969). *Attachment and loss. Vol. 1 Attachment.* New York: Basic Books.
Bowlby, J. (1973). *Attachment and loss. Vol. 2 Separation.* New York: Basic Books.
Bowlby, J. (1988). *A secure base.* New York: Basic Books.
Bradley, B.J., Doran, D.M., & Vigilante, L. (2007). Potential for female kin associations in wild western gorillas despite female dispersal. *Proceedings of the Royal Society, B, 274,* 2179–2185.
Bradley, B.J., Doran-Sheehy, D.M., Lukas, D., Boesch, C., & Vigilant, L. (2004). Dispersed male networks in western gorillas. *Current Biology, 14,* 510–513.
Bradley, B.J., Robbins, M.M., Williamson, E.A., Steklis, H. D., Steklis, N.G., Eckhardt, N., Boesche, C., & Vigilant, L. (2005). Mountain gorilla tug-of-war: Silverbacks have limited control over reproduction in multimale groups. *PNAS, 102,* 9418–9423.
Breuer, T., Hockemba, M., Olejniczak, Parnell, R.J., & Stokes, E.J. (2009). Physical maturation, life- history classes and age estimates of free-ranging western gorillas—Insights from Mbeli Bai, Republic of Congo. *American Journal of Primatology, 71,* 106–119.
Buchan, J., Alberts, S. C., Silk, J. B., & Altmann, J. (2003). True paternal care in a multi-male primate society. *Nature, 425,* 179–181.
Butovskaya, M. (1993). Kinship and different dominance styles in groups of three species of the genus Macaca (*M. arctoides, M. mulatta, M. fascicularis*). *Folia Primatology, 60,* 210–224.
Byrne, G.D., & Suomi, S.J. (1995). Activity patterns, social interaction and exploratory behavior in *Cebus apella* infants from birth to 1 year of age. *American Journal of Primatology, 35,* 255–270.
Call, J., & Tomasello, M. (2008). Does the chimpanzee have a theory of mind? *Trends in Cognitive Science, 12,* 187–192.
Carter, C.S, Ahnert, L., Grossman, K.E., Hrdy, S.B., Lamb, M.E., Porges, S.W., & Sachser, N. (2005). *Attachment and bonding.* Cambridge: MIT press.
Cassidy, J., & Shaver, P.R. (1999). *Handbook of attachment.* New York: Guilford Press.
Chapais, B. (1983). Dominance, relatedness and the structure of female relationships in rhesus monkeys. In R.A. Hinde (Ed.), *Primate social relationships: An integrated approach* (pp. 208–217). Oxford: Blackwell.
Chapais, B. (1988a). Experimental matrilineal inheritance of rank in female Japanese macaques. *Animal Behavior, 36,* 1025–1037.
Chapais, B. (1988b). Rank maintenance in female Japanese macaques: Experimental evidence for social dependency. *Behaviour, 104,* 41–59.
Chapais, B. (2001). Primate nepotism: What is the explanatory value of kin selection? *International Journal of Primatology 22,* 203–229.
Chapais, B. (2004). How kinship generates dominance structures: A comparative perspective. In B. Thierry, M. Singh, & W. Kaumanns (Eds.), *Macaque societies: A model for the study of social organization* (pp. 186–204). Cambridge: Cambridge University Press.
Chapais, B. (2006). Kinship, competence and cooperation in primates. In P.M. Kappeler & C.P. van Schaik (Eds.), *Cooperation in primates and humans* (pp. 47–64). New York: Springer.
Chapais, B. (2008). *Primeval Kinship: How pair-bonding gave birth to human society.* Cambridge: Harvard University.
Chapais, B., & Belisle, P. (2004). Constraints on kin selection in primate groups. In B. Chapais & C.M. Berman (Eds.), *Kinship and behavior in primates* (pp. 365–386). New York: Oxford University.
Chapais, B., & Berman, C.M. (2004). *Kinship and behavior in primates.* New York: Oxford University Press.
Chapais, B., & Berman, C.M. (2004b). Variation in Nepotistic Regimes and Kin Recognition: A Major Area for Future Research. In B. Chapais & C.M. Berman (Eds.), *Kinship and behavior in primates* (pp. 477–489). New York: Oxford University Press.
Chapais, B., Gauthier, C., Prud'homme, J., & Vasey, P. (1997). Relatedness threshold for nepotism in Japanese macaques. *Animal Behavior, 53,* 1089–1101.
Chapais, B., Prud'homme, J., & Teijeiro, S. (1994). Dominance competition among siblings in Japanese macaques: Constraints on nepotism. *Animal Behavior, 48,* 1335–1347.
Chapais B., Savard, L., & Gauthier, C. (2001). Kin selection and the distribution of altruism in relation to degree of kinship in Japanese macaques. *Behavioral Ecology and Sociobiology, 49,* 493–502.
Charpentier, M., Peignot, P., Hossaert-McKey. M., Gimenez, O., Setchell, J.M., & Wickings, E.J. (2005). Constraints on control: Factors influencing reproductive success in male mandrills (*Mandrillus sphinx*). *Behavioral Ecology, 16,* 614–623.

Charpentier, M., Peignott, P., Hossaert-McKey, M., & Wickings, E.J. (2007). Kin discrimination in juvenile mandrills, *Mandrillus sphinx*. *Animal Behavior, 73*, 37–45.

Charpentier, M., Tung, J., Altmann, J., & Alberts, S.C. (2008). Age at maturity in wild baboons: Genetic, environmental and demographic influences. *Molecular Ecology, 17*, 2026–2040.

Chauvin, C., & Berman, C.M. (2004). Intergenerational transmission of behavior. In B. Thierry, M. Singh, & W. Kaumanns (Eds.), *Macaque societies: A model for the study of social organization* (pp. 209–230). Cambridge: Cambridge University Press.

Cheney, D. L., & Seyfarth, R. M. (1983). Nonrandom dispersal in free-ranging vervet monkeys: Social and genetic consequences. *American Naturalist, 122*, 392–412.

Chepko-Sade, B.D., & Sade, D.S. (1979). Patterns of group spitting within matrilineal kinship groups: A study of social group structure in *Macaca mulatta* (Cercopithecidae: Primates). *Behavioral Ecology and Sociobiology, 5*, 67–87.

Clark, A.B. (1978). Sex ratio and local resource competition in a prosimian primate. *Science, 201*, 163–165.

Clutton-Brock, T.H. (2002). Breeding together: Kin selection and mutualism in cooperative vertebrates. *Science, 296*, 69–72.

Colmenares, F. (1992). Clans and harems in a colony of hamadryas and hybrid baboons: Male kinship, familiarity and the formation of brother-teams. *Behaviour, 121*, 61–94.

Colmenares, F. (2004). Kinship structure and its impact on behavior in multilevel societies. In B. Chapais & C.M. Berman (Eds.), *Kinship and behavior in primates* (pp. 242–270). New York: Oxford University.

Colvin, J.D. (1983a). Familiarity, rank and the structure of rhesus male peer networks. In R.A. Hinde (Ed.), *Primate social relationships: An integrated approach* (pp. 190–200). Oxford: Blackwell.

Colvin, J.D. (1983b). Influences of the social situation on male emigration. In R. A. Hinde (Ed.), *Primate social relationships: An integrated approach* (pp. 160–171). Sunderland, MA: Sinauer.

Colvin, J.D. (1986). Proximate causes of male emigration at puberty in rhesus monkeys. In R.G. Rawlins & M.J. Kessler (Eds.), *The Cayo Santiago macaques: History, behavior and biology* (pp. 131–157). Albany: SUNY Press.

Combes, S.L., & Altmann, J. (2001). Status change during adulthood: Life-history by-product or kin selection based on reproductive value? *Proceedings of the Royal Society of London, 268*, 1367–1373.

Cords, M., & Simpson, S. (2006). Limits to kin bias in wild blue monkey society. *International Journal of Primatology, 27*(Suppl 1), 266.

Cowlishaw, G., & Dunbar, R.I.M. (1991). Dominance rank and mating success in male primates. *Animal Behavior, 41*, 1045–1056.

Crockett, C.M., & Pope, T.R. (1993). Consequences of sex differences in dispersal for juvenile red howler monkeys. In M.E. Pereira & L.A. Fairbanks (Eds.), *Juvenile primates: Life history, development, and behavior* (pp. 104–118). New York: Oxford University Press.

Crockford, C., Wittig, R., Whitten, P.L., Seyfarth, R.A., & Cheney, D.L. (2008). Social stressors and coping mechanisms in wild female baboons (*Papio hamadryas ursinus*). *Hormones and Behavior, 53*, 254–265.

Crook, J.H. (1970). The socio-ecology of primates. In J.H. Crook (Ed.), *Social behaviour of birds and mammals* (pp. 103–166). London: Academic Press.

Crook, J.H., & Gartlan, J.S. (1966). On the evolution of primate societies. *Nature, 210*, 1200–1203.

Datta, S.B. (1983). Relative power and the acquisition of rank. In R.A. Hinde (Ed.), *Primate social relationships: An integrated approach* (pp. 93–103). Oxford: Blackwell.

Datta, S.B.(1988). The acquisition of dominance among free-ranging rhesus monkey siblings. *Animal Behavior, 36*, 754–772.

Datta, S.B., & Beauchamp, G. (1991). Effects of group demography on dominance relationships among female primates. I. Mother-daughter and sister-sister relations. *American Naturalist, 138*, 201–226.

Defler, T.R. (1978). Allogrooming in two species of macaque (*Macaca nemestrina* and *Macaca radiata*). *Primates, 19*, 153–167.

Del Guidice, M. (2009). Sex, attachment and the development of reproductive strategies. *Behavior and Brain Science, 32*, 1–67.

de Ruiter, J.R., & Geffen, E. (1998). Relatedness of matrilines, dispersing males and social groups in long-tailed macaques (*Macaca fascicularis*). *Proceedings of the Royal Society of London, B., 265*, 79–87.

de Ruiter, J.R., van Hooff, J.A.R.A.M., & Scheffrahn, W. (1994). Social and genetic aspects of paternity in wild long-tailed macaques. *Behaviour, 129*, 203–224.

de Waal, F.B.M. (1986). Class structure in a rhesus monkey group: The interplay between dominance and tolerance. *Animal Behavior, 34*, 1033–1040.

de Waal, F.B.M. (1991). Rank distance as a central feature of rhesus monkey social organisation: A sociometric analysis. *Animal Behavior, 41*, 383–395.

de Waal, F.B.M. (1996). Macaque social culture: Development and perpetuation of affiliative networks. *Journal of Comparative Psychology, 110*, 147–154.

de Waal, F.B.M., & Brosnan, S.F. (2006). Simple and complex reciprocity in primates. In P.M. Kappeler & C.P. van Schaik (Eds.), *Cooperation in primates and humans: Mechanisms and evolutions* (pp. 85–105). New York: Springer.

de Waal, F.B.M., & Luttrell, L.M. (1986). The similarity principle underlying social bonding among female rhesus monkeys. *Folia Primatology, 46*, 215–234.

de Waal, F.B.M., & Luttrell, L.M. (1989). Toward a comparative socioecology of the genus Macaca: Different dominance styles in rhesus and stumptail monkeys. *American Journal of Primatology, 19*, 83–109.

Dietz, J.M. (2004). Kinship Structure and reproductive skew in cooperatively breeding primates. In B. Chapais & C.M. Berman (Eds.), *Kinship and behavior in primates* (pp. 223–241). New York: Oxford University Press.

Di Fiore, A. (2009). Genetic approaches to the study of dispersal and kinship in New World primates. In P.A. Garber, A. Estrada, J.C. Bicca-Marquis, E.W. Heymann, & K.B. Strier (Eds.), *South American primates: Comparative perspectives in the study of behavior, ecology and conservation* (pp. 211–250). New York: Springer Press.

Di Fiore, A., & Campbell, C.J. (2007). The Atelines: Variations in ecology, behavior, and social organization. In C.J. Campbell, A. Fuentes, K.C. MacKinnon, M. Panger, & S.K. Bearder (Eds.), *Primates in perspective* (1st ed., pp. 155–185). New York: Oxford University Press.

Di Fiore, A., & Fleischer, R.C. (2005). Social behavior, reproductive strategies and population genetic structure of *Lagothrix poeppigii*). *International Journal of Primatology, 26*, 1137–1173.

Di Fiore, A., & Gagneux, P. (2007). Molecular primatology. In C.J. Campbell, A. Fuentes, K.C. MacKinnon, M. Panger, & S.K. Bearder (Eds.), *Primates in perspective* (1st ed. pp. 369–393). New York: Oxford University.

Digby, L.J., Ferrari, S.F., & Saltzman, W. (2007). Callitrichines: The role of competition in cooperatively breeding species. In C.J. Campbell, A. Fuentes, K.C. MacKinnon, M. Panger, & S.K. Bearder (Eds.), *Primates in perspective* (1st ed., pp. 85–106). New York: Oxford University Press.

Dittus, W.P.J. (1988). Group fission among wild toque macaques as a consequence of female resource competition and environmental stress. *Animal Behavior, 36*, 1626–1645.

Dolhinow, P. (1980). An experimental study of mother loss in the Indian langur monkey (*Presbytis entellus*). *Folia Primatology, 33*, 77–128.

Douadi, M.I., Gatti, S., Leverero, F., Duhamel, G., Bermejo, M., Vallet, D., Menard, N., & Petit, E. (2007). Sex-biased dispersal in western lowland gorillas (*Gorilla gorilla gorilla*). *Molecular Ecology, 16*, 2247–2259.

Doyle, G.A. (1979). Development of behavior in prosimians with special reference to the lesser bushbaby, *Galao senegalensis moholi*. In G.A. Doyle & R. D. Martin (Eds.), *The study of prosimian behavior* (pp. 157–206). New York: Academic Press.

Dugatkin, L.A. (1997). *Cooperation among animals.* New York: Oxford University Press.

Dunbar, R.I.M. (1984). *Reproductive decisions. An economic analysis of gelada baboon social strategies.* New Jersey: Princeton University Press.

Dunbar, R.I.M. (1988). *Primate social systems.* London: Croom Helm.

Dunbar, R.I.M. (1992). Time: A hidden constraint on the behavioural ecology of baboons. *Behavioral Ecology and Sociobiology, 31*, 35–49.

Eberle, M., & Kappeler, P.M. (2006). Family insurance: Kin selection and cooperative breeding in a solitary primate (*Microcebus murinus*). *Behavioral Ecology and Sociobiology, 57*, 60:582–588.

Ehardt, C.L. (1988). Absence of strongly kin-preferential behavior by adult female sooty mangabeys (*Cercocebus atys*). *American Journal of Physical Anthropology, 76*, 233–243.

Ehrlich, A. (1977). Social and individual behaviors in captive greater galagos. *Behaviour, 63*, 192–214.

Ehrlich, A., & MacBride, L. (1989). Mother-infant interactions in captive slow lorises (*Nycticebus coucang*). *American Journal of Primatology, 19*, 217–228.

Ehrlich, A., & MacBride, L. (1990). Mother-infant interactions in captive thick-tailed galagos (*Galago garnettii*). *Journal of the Mammal, 71*, 198–204.

Erhlich, A., & Musicant, A. (1977). Social and individual behaviors in captive slow lorises. *Behaviour, 60*, 196–220.

Eibl-Eibesfeldt, I. (1989). *Human ethology.* New York: Aldine.

Ellis, B.J. (2004). Timing of pubertal maturation in girls: An integrated life history approach. *Psychology Bulletin,130*, 920–958.

Engh, A.L., Beehner, J.C., Bergmann, T.J., Whitten, P.L., Hoffmeier, R.R., Seyfarth, R.M., & Cheney, D.L. (2006). Behavioural and hormonal responses to predation in female chacma baboons (*Papio hamadryas ursinus*). *Proceedings of the Royal Society of London B., 273*, 707–712.

Fairbanks, L. A. (1988). Vervet monkey grandmothers: Effects on mother-infant relationships. *Behaviour, 104*, 176–188.

Fairbanks, L.A. (2000). Maternal investment throughout the life span in Old World monkeys. In P.F. Whitehead & C.F. Jolly (Eds.), *Old world monkeys.* (pp. 341–367). Cambridge: Cambridge University.

Fairbanks, L.A. (2003). Parenting. In D. Maestripieri (Ed.), *Primate psychology* (pp. 144–170). Cambridge, MA : Harvard University Press.

Fairbanks, L.A., & McGuire, M.T. (1988). Long term effects of early mothering behavior on responsiveness to the environment in vervet monkeys. *Developmental Psychobiology, 21*, 711–724.

Fairbanks, L.A., & McGuire, M.T. (1993). Maternal protectiveness and response to the unfamiliar in vervet monkeys. *American Journal of Primatology, 30*, 119–129.

Fedigan, L.M., Carnegie, S.D., & Jack, K.M. (2008). Predictors of reproductive success in female white-faced capuchins (*Cebus capucinus*). *American Journal of Physical Anthropology, 137*, 82–90.

Feistner, A., & Price, E.C. (1990). Food-sharing in cotton-top tamarins (*Saguinus oedipu*s). *Folia Primatology, 54*, 34–45.

Fernandez-Duque, E., Juarez, C.P., & Di Fiore, A. (2008). Adult male replacement and subsequent infant care by male and siblings in socially monogamous owl monkeys (*Aotus azarai*). *Primates, 49*, 81–84.

Fitch-Synder, H., & Ehrlich, A. (2003). Mother-infant interactions in slow lorises (*Nycticebus bengalensis*) and pygmy lorises (*Nycticebus pygmaeus*). *Folia Primatology 74*, 259–271.

Fox, R. (2004). Primate kin and human kinship. In R. Parkin & L. Stone (Eds.), *Kinship and family: An anthropological reader* (pp. 424–437). Malden, MA: Blackwell Publ.

Fragaszy, D. M., Baer, J., & Adams-Curtis, L. (1991). Behavioral development and maternal care in tufted capuchins (*Cebus apella*) and squirrel monkeys (*Saimiri sciureus*) from birth through seven moths. *Developmental Psychobiology, 24*, 375–393.

Furuichi, T. (1983). Interindividual distance and influence of dominance on feeding in a natural Japanese macaque troop. *Primates, 24*, 445–455.

Furuichi, T. 1989. Social interactions and the life history of female *Pan paniscus* in Wamba, Zaire. *International Journal of Primatology, 10*, 173–197.

Furuichi, T., & Ihobe, H. (1994). Variation in male relationships in bonobos and chimpanzees. *Behaviour, 130*, 212–228.

Galdikas, B. (1988). Orangutan diet, range, and activity at Tanjung Puting, Central Borneo. *International Journal of Primatology, 9*, 1–35.

Garber, P.A. (1997). One for all and breeding for one: Cooperation and competition as a tamarin reproductive strategy. *Evolutionary Anthropology, 5*, 187–199.

Gartlan, J.S. (1968). Structure and Function in Primate Society. *Folia Primatology, 8*, 89–120.

Gerloff, U., Hartung, B., Fruth, B., Hohmann, G., & Tautz, D. (1999). Intracommunity relationships, dispersal pattern and paternity success in a wild living community of bonobos (*Pan paniscus*) determined from DNA analysis of faecal samples. *Proceedings of the Royal Society of London B., 266*, 1189–1195.

Gilby, I.C., & Wrangham, R. A. (2008). Association patterns among wild chimpanzees (*Pan troglodytes schweinfurthii*) reflect sex differences in cooperation. *Behavioral Ecology and Sociobiology, 62*, 1831–1842.

Goodall, J. (1986). *The chimpanzees of Gombe: Patterns of behavior.* Cambridge, MA: Harvard University.

Gould, L., & Sauther, M. (2007). Lemuriformes. In C.J. Campbell, A. Fuentes, K.C. MacKinnon, M. Panger, & S.K. Bearder (Eds.), *Primates in perspective* (1st ed., pp. 46–72). New York: Oxford University.

Gunnar, M.R. (2005). Attachment and stress in early development: Does attachment add to the potency of social regulators of infant stress? In C.S. Carter, L. Ahnert, K.E. Grossman, S.B. Hrdy, M.E. Lamb, S.W. Porges, & N. Sachser (Eds.), *Attachment and bonding* (pp. 245–255). Cambridge: MIT Press.

Gursky, S. (1997). Modeling maternal time budgets: The impact of lactation and gestation on the behavior of the spectral tarsier, *Tarsius spectrum*. Ph.D. dissertation. State University of NY: Stony Brook.

Gursky, S. (2007). Tarsiformes. In C.J. Campbell, A. Fuentes, K.C. MacKinnon, M. Panger, & S.K. Bearder (Eds.), *Primates in perspective* (1st ed., pp. 73–85). New York: Oxford University Press.

Hamilton, W.D. (1964). The genetical evolution of social behavior, I and II. *Journal of Theoretical Biology, 7*, 1–52.

Harcourt, A.H. (1987). Dominance and fertility among female primates. *Journal of Zoology, 213*, 471–487.

Harcourt, A.H. (1979). Social relationships between adult male and female mountain gorillas in the wild. *Animal Behavior, 27*, 325–342.

Harcourt, A.H., & Stewart, K.J. (1981). Gorilla male relationships: Can differences during immaturity lead to contrasting reproductive tactics in adulthood? *Animal Behavior, 29*, 206–210.

Harcourt, A.H., & Stewart K.J. (1989). Functions of alliances in contests within wild gorilla groups. *Behaviour, 109*, 176–190.

Harlow, H.F., & Zimmermann, R.R. (1959). Affectional responses in the infant monkey. *Science, 130*, 421–432.

Hasegawa, T., & Hiraiwa, M. (1980). Social interactions of orphans observed in a free-ranging troop of Japanese monkeys. *Folia Primatology, 33*, 129–158.

Hashimoto, C., Furuichi, T., & Takenaka, O. (1996). Matrilineral kin relationships and social behavior of wild bonobos (*Pan paniscus*): Sequencing the D-loop region of mitochondrial DNA. *Primates, 37*, 305–318.

Hauser, M.D., & Fairbanks, L.A. (1988). Mother-offspring conflict in vervet monkeys: Variation in response to ecological conditions. *Animal Behavior, 36*, 802–813.

Hawkes, K. (2004). Mating, parenting and the evolution of human pair bonds. In B. Chapais & C.M. Berman (Eds.), *Kinship and behavior in primates* (pp. 443–473). New York: Oxford University Press.

Hemelrijk, C.K. (1999). An individual-orientated model of the emergence of despotic and egalitarian societies. *Proceedings of the Royal Society of London B, 266* (1417), 361–369.

Henzi, S.P., & Barrett, L. (1999). The value of grooming to female primates. *Primates, 40*, 47–59.

Hikami, K., Hasegawa, Y., & Matsuzawa, T. (1990). Social transmission of food preferences in Japanese monkeys (*Macaca fuscata*) after mere exposure or aversion training. *Journal of Comparative Psychology, 104*, 233–237.

Hill, D.A. (1999). Effects of provisioning on the social behavior of Japanese and rhesus macaques: Implications for socioecology. *Primates, 40*, 187–198.

Hill, D.A. (2004). Intraspecific variation: Implications for interspecific comparisons. In B. Thierry, M. Singh, & W. Kaumanns (Eds.), *Macaque societies: A model for the study of social organization* (pp. 262–266). Cambridge: Cambridge University Press.

Hinde, R.A. (1974). *Biological bases of human social behaviour.* New York: McGraw-Hill Book Company.

Hinde, R.A. (1976). Interactions, relationships and social structure. *Man, 11*, 1–17.

Hinde, R.A., Leighton-Shapiro, M.E., & McGinnis, L. (1978). Effects of various types of separation experience on rhesus monkeys 5 months later. *Journal of Child Psychology, & Psychiatry & Allied Disciplines, 19*, 199–211.

Hoffman, K.A., Mendoza, S.P., Hennessy, M.B., & Mason, W.A. (1995). Responses of infant titi monkeys, *Callicebus moloch*, to removal of one or both parents: Evidence for paternal attachment. *Developmental Psychobiology, 28*, 399–407.

Hohmann, G., Gerloff, U., Tautz, D., & Fruth, B. (1999). Social bonds and genetic ties: Kinship, association and affiliation in a community of bonobos (*Pan paniscus*). *Behaviour, 136*, 1219–1235.

Hrdy, S.B. (1976). Care and exploitation of nonhuman primate infants by conspecifics other than the mother. *Advances in the Study of Behavior, 6*, 101–158.

Hrdy, S.B. (1999). *Mother nature: A history of mothers, infants and natural selection.* New York: Pantheon.

Hrdy, S.B. (2009). *Mothers and others: The evolutionary origins of mutual understanding.* Cambridge: Harvard University.

Hrdy, S.B., & Hrdy, D.B. (1976). Hierarchical relations among female Hanuman langurs (Primates: Colobinae, *Presbytis entellus*). *Science, 193*, 913–915.

Huck, M., Löttker, P., & Heymann, E.W. (2004). The many faces of helping: Possible costs and benefits of infant carrying and food transfer in wild moustached tamarins (*Saguinus mystax*). *Behaviour, 141*, 915–934.

Hunte, W., & Horrocks, J. A. (1987). Kin and non-kin interventions in the aggressive disputes of vervet monkeys. *Behavioral Ecology and Sociobiology, 20*, 257–263.

Ihobe, H. (1989). How social relationships influence a monkey's choice of feeding sites in the troop of Japanese macaques (*Macaca fuscata fuscata*) on Koshima Islet. *Primates, 30*, 17–25.

Ihobe, H. (1992). Male-male relationships among wild bonobos (*Pan paniscus*) at Wamba, Republic of Zaire. *Primates, 33*, 163–179.

Immelmann, K., & Suomi, S.J. (1981). Sensitive phases in development. In K. Immelmann, G.W. Barlow, L. Petrinovitch, & M. Main (Eds.), *Behavioral development: The Bielefeld project* (pp. 395–431). New York: Cambridge University.

Isbell, L.A. (2004). Is there no place like home? Ecological bases of female dispersal and philopatry and their consequences for the formation of kin groups. In B. Chapais & C.M. Berman (Eds.), *Kinship and behavior in primates* (pp. 71–108). New York: Oxford University Press.

Janus, M. (1992). Interplay between various aspects in social relationships of young rhesus monkeys: Dominance, agonistic help, and affiliation. *American Journal of Primatology, 26*, 291–308.

Judge, P.G. (1991). Dynamic and triadic reconciliation in pigtail macaques (*Macaca nemestrina*). *American Journal of Primatology, 23*, 225–237.

Kalin, N.H. Shelton, S.E., & Barksdale, C.M. (1988). Opiate modulation of separation-induced distress in non-human primates. *Brain Research, 440*, 285–292.

Kalin, N.H., Shelton, S.E., & Lynn, D.E. (1995). Opiate systems in mother and infant primate coordinate intimate contact during reunion. *Psychoneuroendocrinology, 20*, 735–742.

Kaplan, J.R. (1978). Fight interference and altruism in rhesus monkeys. *American Journal of Physical Anthropology, 49,* 241–249.

Kappeler, P.M. (2008). Genetic and ecological determinants of primate social systems. In J. Korb & J. Heinze (Eds.), *Ecology of social evolution* (pp. 225–243). London: Springer.

Kappeler, P. M., Wimmer, B., Zinner, D., & Tautz, D. (2002). Hidden matrilineal structure of a solitary lemur: Implications for primate evolution. *Proceedings of the Royal Society of London, B., 269,* 1755–1763.

Kapsalis. E. (2004). Matrilineal kinship and primate behavior. In B. Chapais & C.M. Berman (Eds.), *Kinship and behavior in primates* (pp. 153–176). New York: Oxford University Press.

Kapsalis, E., & Berman, C.M. (1996a). Models of affiliative relationships among free-ranging rhesus monkeys, *Macaca mulatta.* I. Criteria for kinship. *Behaviour, 133,* 1209–1234.

Kapsalis, E., & Berman, C.M. (1996b). Models of affiliative relationships among free-ranging rhesus monkeys, *Macaca mulatta.* II. Testing predictions for three hypothesized organizing principles. *Behaviour, 133,* 1235–1263.

Kaufman, I.C., & Rosenblum, L.A. (1969). Effects of separation from mother on the emotional behavior of infant monkeys. *Annals of the New York Academy of Science, 159,* 681–695.

Kaufman, I.C., & Stynes, A.J. (1978). Depression can be induced in a bonnet macaque infant. *Psychosomatic Medicine, 40,* 71–75.

Kawai, M. (1958). On the system of social ranks in a natural troop of Japanese monkey (I)—Basic rank and dependent rank. *Primates, 1,* 111–130.

Kawamura, S. (1958). Matriarchal social ranks in the Minoo-B Troop: A study of the rank System of Japanese monkeys. *Primates, 1–2,* 149–156.

Kessler, S.E., & Nash, L.T. (2008). Grandmothering in captive *Galao senegalensis braccata. Primate Eye, 96* (Suppl) 525.

Keverne, E.B. (2005). Neurobiological and molecular approaches to attachment and bonding. In C.S. Carter, L. Ahnert, K.E. Grossman, S.B. Hrdy, M.E. Lamb, S.W. Porges, & N. Sachser (Eds.), *Attachment and bonding* (pp. 101–117). Cambridge: MIT Press.

Klopfer, P.H., & Boskoff, K.J. (1979). Maternal behavior in prosimians. In G.A. Doyle & R.D. Martin (Eds.), *The study of prosimian behavior* (pp. 123–156). New York: Academic Press.

Koenig, A. (2002). Competition for resources and its behavioural consequences among female primates. *International Journal of Primatology, 23,* 759–783.

Koford, C.B. (1963). Rank of mothers and sons in bands of rhesus monkeys. *Science, 141,* 356–357.

Kostan, K.M., & Snowdon, C.T. (2002). Attachment and social preferences in cooperatively-reared cotton-top tamarins. *American Journal of Primatology, 57,* 131–139.

Koyama, N. (1970). Changes in dominance rank and division of a wild Japanese monkey troop in Arashiyama. *Primates, 11,* 335–390.

Kraemer, G.W. (1992). A psychobiological theory of attachment. *Behavioral and Brain Sciences, 15,* 493–541.

Kraemer, G.W., Lamb, M.E., Liotti, G.A., Lyons-Ruth, K., Meinlschmidt, G., Schölmerich, A., et al. (2005). Group report: Adaptive and maladaptive outcomes. In C.S. Carter, L. Ahnert, K.E. Grossman, S.B. Hrdy, M.E. Lamb, S.W. Porges, & N. Sachser (Eds.), *Attachment and bonding* (pp. 429–474). Cambridge: MIT press.

Krutzen, M., Arora, N., Nater, A., & van Schaik, C.P. (2008). Genetic estimates of male and female dispersal in multiple populations of Bornean and Sumatran orangutans (*Pongo spp.*). *Primate Eye, 96.*

Kuester, J., & Paul, A. (1988). Rank relations of juvenile and subadult natal males of Barbary macaques (*Macaca sylvanus*) at Affenberg Salem. *Folia Primatology, 51,* 33–44.

Kuester, J., & Paul, A. (1997). Group fission in Barbary macaques (Macaca sylvanus) at Affenberg Salem. *International Journal of Primatology, 18,* 941–966.

Krutzen, M., Arora, N., Nater, A., & van Schaik, C.P. (2008). Genetic estimates of male and female dispersal in multiple populations of Bornean and Sumatran orangutans (*Pongo spp.*) *Primate Eye, 96,* Abst 371.

Kummer, H. (1968a). *Social organization of hamadryas baboons.* Basel: Karger.

Kummer, H. (1990). The social system of hamadryas baboons and its presumable evolution. In T. de Mello, A. Whiten, & R.W. Byrne, R.W. (Eds.), *Baboons: Behaviour and ecology, use and care* (pp. 43–60). Selected Proceedings of the XIIth Congress of the International Primatological Society, Brasilia.

Kümmerli, R., & Martin, R.D. (2008). Patterns of infant handling and relatedness in Barbary macaques (*Macaca sylvanus*) on Gibraltar. *Primates, 49,* 271–282.

Kurland, J.A. (1977). *Kin Selection in the Japanese monkey.* Basel: Karger.

Lacy, R.C., & Sherman, P.W. (1983). Kin recognition by phenotypic matching. *American Naturalist, 121,* 489–512.

Langergraber, K.E., Mitani, J.C., & Vigilant, L. (2007). The limited impact of kinship on cooperation in wild chimpanzees. *PNAS, 104,* 7786–7790.

Langergraber, K., Mitani, J., & Vigilant, L. (2009). Kinship and social bonds in female chimpanzees (*Pan troglodytes*). *American Journal of Primatology, 71,* 840–851.

Launhardt, K., Borries, C., Hardt, C., Epplen, J.T., & Winkler, P. (2001). Paternity analysis of alternative male reproductive routes among the langurs (*Semnopithecus entellus*) of Ramnagar. *Animal Behavior, 61,* 53–64.

Lee, P.C. (1996). The meanings of weaning: Growth, lactation and life history. *Evolutionary Anthropology, 5,* 87–96.

Lehmann, J., & Boesch, C. (2009). Sociality of the dispersing sex: The nature of social bonds in West African female chimpanzees, *Pan troglodytes. Animal Behavior, 77,* 377–387.

Lehmann, J., Fickenscher, G., & Boesch, C. (2006). Kin biased investment in wild chimpanzees. *Behaviour, 143,* 931–955.

Levine, S., & Weiner, S.G. (1988). Psychoendocrine aspects of mother-infant relationships in nonhuman primates. *Psychoneuroendocrinology, 13,* 143–154.

Levrero, F., Gatti, S., Menard, N., Petit, E., Caillaud, D., & Gautier-Hion, A. (2006). Living in nonbreeding groups: An alternative strategy for maturing gorillas. *American Journal of Primatology, 68,* 275–291.

Li, J.H., Wang, Q.S., & Han, D.M. (1996). Fission in a free-ranging Tibetan macaque troop at Huangshan Mountain, China. *Kexue Tongbao/Chinese Science Bulletin, 41,* 1377–1381.

Lukas, D., Reynolds, V., Boesch, C., & Vigilant, L. (2005). To what extent does living in a group mean living with kin? *Molecular Ecology, 14,* 2181–2196.

Lycett, J.E, Henzi, S.P., & Barrett, L. (1998). Maternal investment in mountain baboons and the hypothesis of reduced care. *Behavioral Ecology and Sociobiology, 42,* 49–56.

MacKenzie, M.M., McGrew, W.C., & Chamove, A.S. (1985). Social preferences in Stumptailed macaques (*Macaca actoides*): Effects of companionship, kinship and rearing. *Developmental Psychobiology, 18*, 115–123.

MacKinnon, K.C. (2007). Social beginnings: The tapestry of infant and adult interactions. In C.J. Campbell, A. Fuentes, K.C. MacKinnon, M. Panger, & S.K. Bearder (Eds.), *Primates in perspective* (1st ed., pp. 571–591). New York: Oxford University Press.

Maestripieri, D. (1994). Social structure, infant handling, and mothering styles in group-living Old World monkeys. *International Journal of Primatology, 15*, 531–553.

Maestripieri, D. (1995). Assessment of danger to themselves and their infants by rhesus macaque (*Macaca mulatta*) mothers. *Journal of Comparative Psychology, 109*, 416–420.

Maestripieri, D. (2003). Attachment. In D. Maestripieri (Ed.), *Primate psychology* (pp. 108–143). Cambridge, MA: Harvard University.

Maestripieri, D. (2005). Effects of early experience on female behavioural and reproductive development in rhesus macaques. *Proceedings of the Royal Society of London B, 272*, 1243–1248.

Maestripieri, D., & Roney, J.R. (2006). Evolutionary developmental psychology: Contributions from comparative research with nonhuman primates. *Developmental Reviews, 26*, 120–137.

Maestripieri, D., Hoffman, C.L., Anderson, G.M., Carter, C.S., & Higley, J.D. (2009). Mother-infant interactions in free-ranging rhesus macaques: Relationships between physiological and behavioral variables. *Physiology & Behavior, 96*, 613–619.

Majolo, B., Schino, G., & Troisi, A. (2005). Towards thirty years of ethological research on the Japanese macaque (*Macaca fuscata*) colony of the Rome Zoo: A review. *Journal of Anthropological Science, 83*, 43–60.

Majolo, B., Ventura, R., Koyama, N.F., Hardie, S.M., Jones, B.M., Knapp, L.A., & Schino, G. (2009). Analysing the effects of group size and food competition on Japanese macaque social relationships. *Behaviour, 146*, 113–137.

Martin, D. A. (1997). *Kinship bias: A function of familiarity in pigtailed macaques (Macaca nemestrina)*. Ph.D. dissertation, University of Georgia.

Mascagni, O., & Doyle, G.A. (1993). Infant distress vocalizations in the southern African lesser bushbaby (*Galago moholi*). *International Journal of Primatology, 14*, 41–60.

Mason, W.A., & Capitanio, J.P. (1988). Formation and expression of filial attachment in rhesus monkeys raised with living and with inanimate mother substitutes. *Developmental Psychobiology, 21*, 401–430.

Mason, W.A., & Mendoza, S. P. (1998). Generic aspects of primate attachments: Parent, offspring and mates. *Psychoneuroendocrinology, 223*, 765–778.

Matsumura, S. (1999). The evolution of "egalitarian" and "despotic" social systems among macaques. *Primates, 40*, 23–31.

Matsumura, S., & Kobayashi, T. (1998). A game model for dominance relations among group-living animals. *Behavioral Ecology and Sociobiology, 42*, 77–84.

Matsumura, S., & Okamoto, K. (1997). Factors affecting proximity among member of a wild group of moor macaques during feeding, moving, and resting. *International Journal of Primatology, 18*, 929–940.

McGrew, W.C. (1975). Patterns of plant food sharing by wild chimpanzees. In S. Kondo, M. Kawai, & A. Ehara (Eds.), *Contemporary Primatology, Proceedings of the Fifth International Congress of Primatology* (pp. 304–309). Basel: Karger.

Meikle, D.B., & Vessey, S.H. (1981). Nepotism among rhesus monkey brothers. *Nature, 294*, 160–161.

Melnick, D.J., Pearl, M.C., & Richard, A.F. (1984). Male migration and inbreeding avoidance in wild rhesus monkeys. *American Journal of Primatology, 7*, 229–243.

Menard, N. (2004). Do ecological factors explain variation in social organization? In B. Thierry, M. Singh, & W. Kaumanns (Eds.), *Macaque societies: A model for the study of social organization* (pp. 237–262). Cambridge: Cambridge University Press.

Menard, N., Lathuilliere, M., Petit, E., Vallet, D., & Crouau-Roy, B. (2006). Philopatry of female macaques in relation to group dynamics and the distribution of genes - the case of the Barbary macaque (*Macaca sylvanus*). In J.K. Hodges & J. Cortes (Eds.), *The Barbary macaque: Biology, management and conservation* (pp. 129–147). Nottingham: Nottingham University Press.

Mendoza, S.P., & Mason, W.A. (1997). Attachment relationships in new world primates. *Annals of the New York Academy of Science, 807*, 203–209.

Mineka, S., & Suomi, S.J. (1978). Social separation in monkeys. *Psychology Bulletin, 85*, 1376–1400.

Mitchell, C.L. (1994). Migration alliances and coalitions among adult male South American squirrel monkeys (*Saimiri sciureus*). *Behaviour, 130*, 169–190.

Mitchell, C.L., Boinski, S., & van Schaik, C.P. (1991). Competitive regimes and female bonding in two species of squirrel monkeys (*Saimiri oerstedi* and *S. sciureus*). *Behavioral Ecology and Sociobiology, 28*, 5–60.

Morin, P.A., & Goldberg, T.L. (2004). Determination of genealogical relationships from genetic data: A review of methods and applications. In B. Chapais & C.M. Berman (Eds.), *Kinship and behavior in primates* (pp. 15–45). New York: Oxford University Press.

Muniz, L., Perry, S., Manson, J.H., Gilkenson, H., Gros-Louis, J., & Vigilant, L. (2006). Father-daughter inbreeding avoidance in a wild primate population. *Current Biology, 16*, R156–R157.

Nakamichi, M., & Koyama, N. (1997). Social relationships among ring-tailed lemurs (*Lemur catta*) in two free-ranging troops at Berenty Reserve, Madagascar. *International Journal of Primatology, 18*, 73–93.

Nakamichi, M., & Shazawa, Y. (2003). Distribution of grooming among adult females in a large, free-ranging group of Japanese macaques. *International Journal of Primatology, 24*, 607–625.

Nakamichi, M., & Yamada, K. (2007). Long-term grooming partnerships between unrelated adult females in a free-ranging group of Japanese monkeys (*Macaca fuscata*). *American Journal of Primatology, 69*, 652–663.

Nash, L.T. (2003). Sex differences in the behavior and social interactions of immature *Galago senegalensis braccatus*. *Folia Primatology, 74*, 285–300.

Nash, L.T. (2004). Kinship and behavior among nongregarious nocturnal prosimians. In B. Chapais & C.M. Berman (Eds.), *Kinship and behavior in primates* (pp. 200–222). New York: Oxford University.

Nekaris, A., & Bearder, S.K. (2007). The lorisiform primates of Asia and mainland Africa: Diversity shrouded in darkness. In C.J. Campbell, A. Fuentes, K.C. MacKinnon, M. Panger, & S.K. Bearder (Eds.), *Primates in perspective* (1st ed., pp. 24–45). New York: Oxford University Press.

Netto J.W., & van Hooff, J.A.R.A.M. (1986). Conflict interference and the development of dominance relationships in immature *Macaca fascicularis*. In J.G. Else & P.C. Lee (Eds.), *Primate ontogeny, cognition and social behaviour* (pp. 291–300). Cambridge: Cambridge University Press.

Nicolson, N.A. (1987). Infants, mothers, and other females. In B. B. Smuts, D.L. Cheney, R. M. Seyfarth, R.W. Wrangham, & T.T. Struhsaker (Eds.), *Primate societies* (pp. 330–342). Chicago: University of Chicago.

Nishida, T. (1989). Social interactions between resident and immigrant female chimpanzees. In P.G. Heltne & L.A. Marquardt (Eds.), *Understanding chimpanzees* (pp. 68–89). Cambridge, MA: Harvard University.

Nozaki, M. (2009). Grandmothers care for orphans in a provisioned troop of Japanese macaques (*Macaca fuscata*). *Primates*, 50, 85–88.

Nunn, C.L. (2000). Collective benefits, free-riders, and male extra-group conflict. In P.M. Kappeler (Ed.), *Primate males: Causes and consequences of variation in group composition* (pp. 192–204). Cambridge: Cambridge University.

Oda, R. (1996). Effects of contextual and social variables on contact call production in free-ranging ringtailed lemurs (*Lemur catta*). *International Journal of Primatology*, 17, 191–205.

Oi, T. (1988). Sociological study on the troop fission of wild Japanese monkeys (*Macaca fuscata yakui*) on Yakushima Island. *Primates*, 29, 1–19.

Okamoto, K. (2004). Patterns of group fission. In B. Thierry, M. Singh, & W. Kaumanns (Eds.), *Macaque societies: A model for the study of social organization* (pp. 112–116). Cambridge: Cambridge University.

Okamoto, K., & Matsumura, S. (2001). Group fission in moor macaques (*Macaca maurus*). *International Journal of Primatology*, 22, 481–493.

Pastor-Nieto, R. (2001). Grooming, kinship and co-feeding in captive spider monkeys (*Ateles geoffroyi*). *Zoo Biology*, 20, 293–303.

Patzelt, A., Pirow, R., & Fischer, J. (2009). Post-conflict affiliation in Barbary macaques is influenced by conflict characteristics and relationship quality, but does not diminish short-term renewed aggression. *Ethology*, 115, 658–670.

Paul, A. (2006). Kinship and behavior in Barbary macaques. In J.K. Hodges & J. Cortes (Eds.), *The Barbary macaque: Biology, management and conservation* (pp. 47–61). Nottingham: Nottingham University Press.

Paul, A., & Kuester, J. (1987). Dominance, kinship and reproductive value in female Barbary macaques (*Macaca sylvanus*) at Affenberg Salem. *Behavioral Ecology and Sociobiology*, 21, 323–331.

Paul, A., & Kuester, J. (2004). The impact of kinship on mating and reproduction. In B. Chapais & C.M. Berman (Eds.), *Kinship and behavior in primates* (pp. 271–291). New York: Oxford University.

Pavelka, M.S.M., Fedigan, L. M., & Zohar, S. (2002). Availability and adaptive value of reproductive and post-reproductive Japanese macaque mothers and grandmothers. *Animal Behavior*, 64, 407–414.

Pepper, J.W., Mitani, J.C., & Watts, D.P. (1999). General gregariousness and specific social preferences among wild chimpanzees. *International Journal of Primatology*, 20, 613–632.

Pereira, M.E. (1988). Effects of age and sex on intra-group spacing behaviour in juvenile savannah baboons, *Papio cynocephalus cynocephalus*. *Animal Behavior*, 36, 184–204.

Pereira, M.E. (1989). Agonistic interactions of juvenile savanna baboons. II. Agonistic support and rank acquisition. *Ethology*, 80, 152–171.

Pereira, M.E., & Fairbanks, L.A. (1993). *Juvenile primates: Life history, development and behavior*. New York: Oxford University Press.

Perry, S., & Rose, L. (1994). Begging and transfer of coati meat by white-faced capuchin monkeys, *Cebus capucinus*. *Primates*, 35, 409–415.

Perry, S., & Manson, J.H. (2008). *Manipulative monkeys: The capuchins of Lomas Barbudal*. Cambridge, MA: Harvard University Press.

Perry, S., Manson, J.H., Muniz, L., Gros-Louis, J., & Vigilant, L. (2008). Kin-biased social behaviour in wild adult female white-faced capuchins, *Cebus capuchins*. *Animal Behavior*, 76, 187–199.

Pope, T.R. (1990). The reproductive consequences of male cooperation in the red howler monkey: Paternity exclusion in multi-male and single-male troops using genetic markers. *Behavioral Ecology and Sociobiology*, 27, 439–446.

Pope, T.R. (2000a). Reproductive success increases with degree of kinship in cooperative coalitions of female red howler monkeys (Alouatta seniculus). *Behavioral Ecology and Sociobiology*, 48, 253–267.

Pope, T.R. (2000b). The evolution of male philopatry in Neotropical monkeys. In P.M. Kappeler (Ed.), *Primate males: Causes and consequences of variation in group composition* (pp. 219–235). Cambridge: Cambridge University Press.

Prud'homme, J. (1991). Group fission in a semifree-ranging population of Barbary macaques (*Macaca sylvanus*). *Primates*, 32, 9–22.

Prud'homme, J., & Chapais, B. (1993). Aggressive interventions and matrilineal dominance relations in semifree-ranging Barbary macaques (*Macaca sylvanus*). *Primates*, 34, 271–283.

Pusey, A.E., & Packer, C. (1987). Dispersal and philopatry. In B.B. Smuts, D.L. Cheney, R.M. Seyfarth, R.W. Wrangham, & T.T. Struhsaker (Eds.), *Primate societies* (pp. 250–266). Chicago: University of Chicago Press.

Radespiel, U. (2006). Ecological diversity and seasonal adaptations of mouse lemurs (*Microcebus spp.*). In L. Gould & M. L. Sauther (Eds.), *Ecology and Adaptation* (pp. 211–234). New York: Springer.

Range, F. (2006). Social behavior of free-ranging juvenile sooty mangabeys (*Cercopithecus torquatus atys*). *Behavioral Ecology and Sociobiology*, 59, 511–520.

Reite, M., & Capitanio, J.P. (1985). On the nature of social separation and social attachment. In M. Reite & T Field (Eds.), *The psychology of attachment and separation* (pp. 223–255). New York: Academic Press.

Reite, M., Short, R., Seiler, C., & Pauley, J.D. (1981). Attachment, loss and depression. *Journal of Child Psychology & Psychiatry*, 22, 141–169.

Rendall, D. (2004). "Recognizing kin": Mechanisms, media, minds, modules and muddles. In B. Chapais & C.M. Berman (Eds.), *Kinship and behavior in primates* (pp. 295–316). New York: Oxford University Press.

Rendall, D., & DiFiore, A. (2007). Homoplasy, homology, and the perceived special status of behavior in evolution. *Journal of Human Evolution*, 52, 504–521.

Robbins, M.M. (1995). A demographic analysis of male life history and social structure of mountain gorillas. *Behaviour, 132,* 21–47.

Robbins, A., & Robbins, M.M. (2005). Fitness consequences of dispersal decisions for male mountain gorillas (*Gorilla beringei beringei*). *Behavioral Ecology and Sociobiology, 5,* 295–309.

Robbins, M.M. (2007). Gorillas: Diversity in ecology and behavior. In C.J. Campbell, A. Fuentes, K.C. MacKinnon, M. Panger, & S.K. Bearder (Eds.), *Primates in perspective* (1st ed., pp. 305–321). New York: Oxford University Press.

Roney, J.R., & Maestripieri, D. (2003). Social development and affiliation. In D. Maestripieri (Ed.), *Primate psychology* (pp. 171–204). Cambridge, MA : Harvard University Press.

Rosenblum, L.A., & Kaufman, I.C. (1968). Variations in infant development and response to maternal loss in monkeys. *American Journal of Orthopsychiatry, 38,* 418–426.

Rubenstein, D.I., & Wrangham, R.W. (1986). Socioecology: Origins and trends. In D.I. Rubenstein & R.W. Wrangham (Eds.), *Ecological aspects of social evolution* (pp. 3–17). Princeton, NJ: Princeton University Press.

Sade, D.S. (1965). Some aspects of parent-offspring and sibling relations in a group of rhesus monkeys, with a discussion of grooming. *American Journal of Physical Anthropology, 23,* 1–17.

Sade, D.S. (1967). Determinants of dominance in a group of free-ranging rhesus monkeys. In S. Altmann (Ed.), *Social communication among primates* (pp. 99–114). Chicago: University of Chicago.

Sauther, M.L., Sussman, R.W., & Gould, L. (1999). The socioecology of ringtailed lemur: Thirty-five years of research. *Evolutionary Anthropology, 8,* 120–132.

Schino, G., & Aureli, F. (2009). Reciprocal altruism in primates: Partner choice, cognition and emotions. *Advances in the Study of Behavior, 39,* 45–69.

Schino, G., & Aureli, F. (2010). The relative roles of kinship and reciprocity in explaining primate altruism. *Ecology Letters, 13,* 45–50.

Schino, G., Tiddi, B., & Polizzi di Sorrentino. E. (2007). Agonistic support in juvenile Japanese macaques: Cognitive and functional implications. *Ethology, 113,* 1151–1157.

Schino, G., Di Giuseppe, F., & Visalberghi, E.A. (2009). Grooming, rank and agonistic support in tufted capuchin monkeys. *American Journal of Primatology, 71,* 101–105.

Schülke, O., & Ostner, J. (2008). Male reproductive skew, paternal relatedness, and female social relationships. *American Journal of Primatology, 70,* 695–698.

Setchell, J.M., Lee, P.C., Wickings, E.J., & Dixson, A.F. (2002). Reproductive parameters and maternal investment in mandrills (*Mandrillus sphinx*). *International Journal of Primatology, 23,* 51–68.

Setia, T.M., Delgado, R.A., Atmoko, S., Singleton, I., & van Schaik, C.P. (2009). Social organization and male-female relationships. In S.A. Wich, S. Atmoko, T.M. Setia & van Schaik, C.P. (Eds.), *Orangutans: Geographic variation in behavioral ecology and conservation* (pp. 245–253). New York: Oxford University Press.

Seyfarth, R.M. (1983). Grooming and social competition in primates. In R.A. Hinde (Ed.), *Primate social relationships: An integrated approach* (pp. 182–190). Oxford: Blackwell.

Sigg, H., Stolba, A., Abegglen, J.J., & Dasser, V. (1982). Life history of hamadryas baboons: Physical development, infant mortality, reproductive parameters and family relationships. *Primates, 23,* 473–487.

Silk, J.B. (1979). Feeding, foraging, and food sharing behavior of immature chimpanzees. *Folia Primatology, 31,* 123–142.

Silk, J.B. (1982). Altruism among adult female bonnet macaques: Explanation and analysis of patterns of grooming and coalition formation. *Animal Behavior, 79,* 162–187.

Silk, J.B. (1987). Social behavior in evolutionary perspective. In B.B. Smuts, D.L. Cheney, R.M. Seyfarth, R.W. Wrangham, & T.T. Struhsaker (Eds.), *Primate societies* (pp. 318–329). Chicago: University of Chicago Press.

Silk, J.B. (1992). Patterns of intervention in agonistic contests among male bonnet macaques. In A.H. Harcourt & F.B.M. de Waal (Eds.), *Coalitions and alliances in humans and other animals* (pp. 215–232). Oxford: Oxford University Press.

Silk, J.B. (2001). Ties that bond: The role of kinship in primate societies. In L. Stone (Ed.), *New directions in anthropological kinship* (pp. 71–92). New York: Rowman & Littlefield Publishers.

Silk, J.B. (2002). Kin selection in primate groups. *International Journal of Primatology, 23,* 849–875.

Silk, J.B. (2006). Practicing Hamilton's rule: Kin selection in primate groups. In P.M. Kappeler & C.P. van Schaik (Eds.), *Cooperation in primates and humans* (pp. 25–46). New York: Springer.

Silk, J.B., Alberts, S.C., & Altmann, J. (2003). Social bonds of female baboons enhance infant survival. *Science, 302,* 1231–1234.

Silk, J.B., Altmann, J., & Alberts, S.C. (2006a). Social relationships among adult female baboons (*Papio cynocephalus*) I. Variation in the strength of social bonds. *Behavioral Ecology and Sociobiology, 61,* 183–195.

Silk, J.B., Altmann, J., & Alberts, S.C. (2006b). Social relationships among adult female baboons (*Papio cynocephalus*) II. Variation in the quality and stability of social bonds. *Behavioral Ecology and Sociobiology, 61,* 197–204.

Silk, J.B., Samuels, A., & Rodman, P.S. (1981). The influence of kinship, rank, and sex on affiliation and aggression between adult female and immature bonnet *macaques* (*Macaca radiata*). *Behaviour, 78,* 111–137.

Silk, J.B., Seyfarth, R.M., & Cheney, D.L. (1999). The structure of social relationships among female savanna baboons in Moremi Reserve, Botswana. *Behaviour, 136,* 679–703.

Silk, J.B., Beehner, J.C., Bergman, T.J., Crockford, C., Engh, A., Moscovice, L.R., et al. (2009). The benefits of social capital: Close social bonds among female baboons enhance offspring survival. *Proceedings of the Royal Society of London B., 276,* 3099–3104.

Simpson, J.A. (1999). Attachment theory in modern evolutionary perspective. In J. Cassidy & P.R. shaver (Eds.), *Handbook of attachment* (pp. 115–140). New York: Guilford Press.

Simpson, M.J.A. (1985). Effects of early experience on the behavior of yearling rhesus monkeys (*Macaca mulatta*) in the presence of a strange object: Classification and correlation approaches. *Primates, 26,* 57–72.

Simpson, M.J.A., & Datta, S.B. (1990). Predicting infant enterprise from early relationships in rhesus monkeys. *Behaviour, 116,* 42–63.

Singleton, I., Knott, C.D., Morrogh-Bernard, H.C., Wich, S.A., & van Schaik, C.P. (2009). Ranging behavior of orangutan females and social organization. In S.A. Wich, S. Atmoko, T.M. Setia, & C.P. van Schaik (Eds.), *Orangutans: Geographic variation in behavioral ecology and conservation* (pp. 205–213). New York: Oxford University Press.

Singleton, I., & van Schaik, C.P. (2002). The social organization of a population of Sumatran orang-utans. *Folia Primatology, 73*, 1–20.

Smith, K. (2000). *Paternal kin matter: The distribution of social behavior among wild adult female baboons*. Ph.D. thesis, University of Chicago, Chicago.

Smith, K., Alberts, S.C., & Altmann, J. (2003). Wild female baboons bias their social behaviour towards paternal half-sisters. *Proceedings of the Royal Society of London, B., 270*, 503–510.

Smuts, B.B. (1985). *Sex and friendship in baboons*. New York: Aldine.

Soltis, J., Thomsen, R., Matsubayashi, K., & Takenaka, O. (2000). Infanticide by resident males and female counter-strategies in wild Japanese macaques (*Macaca fuscata*). *Behavioral Ecology and Sociobiology, 48*, 195–202.

Spencer-Booth, Y., & Hinde, R.A. (1971). Effects of brief separations from mothers during infancy on behaviour of rhesus monkeys 6–24 months later. *Journal of Child Psychology, Psychiatry & Allied Disciplines, 12*, 157–172.

Stein, D.M. (1984). *The sociobiology of infant and adult male baboons*. Norwood, NJ: Ablex Publishing Corporation.

Sterck, E.M.K., Watts, D.P., & van Schaik, C.P. (1997). The evolution of female social relationships in nonhuman primates. *Behavioral Ecology and Sociobiology, 41*, 291–309.

Stevens, J.R., & Hauser, M.D. (2005). Cooperative brains: Psychological constraints on the evolution of altruism. In S. Dehaene, J.R. Duhamel, M.D. Hauser, & G. Rissolati (Eds.), *From monkey brain to human brain* (pp. 159–187). Cambridge: MIT Press.

Stewart, K.J., & Harcourt, A.H. (1987). Gorillas: Variation in female relationships. In B.B. Smuts, D.L. Cheney, R.M. Seyfarth, R.W. Wrangham, & T.T. Struhsaker (Eds.), *Primate societies* (pp. 155–164). Chicago: University of Chicago Press.

Strier, K.B. (1993). Growing up in a patrifocal society: Sex differences in the spatial relations of immature muriquis. In M.E. Pereira & L.A. Fairbanks (Eds.), *Juvenile primates: Life history, development, and behavior* (pp. 138–147). New York: Oxford University Press.

Strier, K.B. (1994). Brotherhoods among atelines: Kinship, affiliation, and competition. *Behaviour, 130*, 151–167.

Strier, K.B. (2004). Patrilineal kinship and primate behavior. In B. Chapais & C.M. Berman (Eds.), *Kinship and behavior in primates* (pp. 177–199). New York: Oxford University Press.

Strier, K.B. (2008). The effects of kin on primate life histories. *Annual Review of Anthropology, 37*, 21–36.

Strier, K.B., Dib, L.T., & Figueira, J.E.C. (2002). Social dynamics of male muriquis (*Brachyteles arachnoides hypoxanthus*). *Behaviour, 139*, 315–342.

Strum, S.C. (1984). Why males use infants. In D.M. Taub (Ed.), *Primate paternalism* (pp. 146–185). New York: Van Nostrand Reinhold Company.

Stumpf, R. (2007). Chimpanzees and bonobos: Diversity within and between species. In C.J. Campbell, A. Fuentes, K.C. MacKinnon, M. Panger, & S.K. Bearder (Eds.), *Primates in perspective* (1st ed., pp. 321–344). New York: Oxford University Press.

Sueur, C., & Petit, O. (2008). Organization of group members at departure is driven by social structure in *Macaca*. *International Journal of Primatology, 29*, 1085–1098.

Suomi, S.J. (1995). Influence of attachment theory on ethological studies of biobehavioral development in nonhuman primates. In S. Goldberg, R. Muir, & J. Kerr (Eds.), *Attachment theory: Social developmental and clinical perspectives* (pp. 185–201). Hillsdale, NJ: Analytic Press.

Suomi, S.J. (1999). Attachment in rhesus monkeys. In J. Cassidy & P.R. Shaver (Eds.), *Handbook of attachment* (pp. 181–197). New York: Guilford Press.

Suomi, S.J. (2005). Mother-infant attachment, peer relationships, and the development of social networks in rhesus monkeys. *Human Development, 48*, 67–79.

Sussman, R.W. (1992). Male life history and intergroup mobility among ringtailed lemurs (*Lemur catta*). *International Journal of Primatology, 13*, 395–413.

Thierry, B. (1990a). Feedback loop between kinship and dominance: The macaque model. *Journal of Theoretical Biology, 145*, 511–522.

Thierry, B. (1990b). The state of equilibrium among agonistic behavior patterns in a group of Japanese macaques (*Macaca fuscata*). *CR Academy Science, Paris, 310*, 35–40.

Thierry, B. (2000). Covariation of conflict management patterns across macaque species. In F. Aureli & F.B.M. de Waal (Eds.), *Natural conflict resolution* (pp. 106–128). Berkeley: University California Press.

Thierry, B. (2004). Social epigenesis. In B. Thierry, M. Singh, & W. Kaumanns (Eds.), *Macaque societies: A model for the study of social organization* (pp. 267–290). Cambridge: Cambridge University Press.

Thierry, B. (2008). Primate socioecology, the lost dream of ecological determinism. *Evolutionary Anthropology, 17*, 93–96.

Thierry, B. and Aureli. F. (2006). Barbary but not barbarian: Social relations in a tolerant macaque. In J.K. Hodges & J. Cortes (Eds.), *The Barbary macaque: Biology, management and conservation* (pp. 29–45). Nottingham: Nottingham University Press.

Thierry, B., Aureli, F., Nunn, C.L., Petit, O., Abegg, C., & de Waal, F.B.M. (2008). A comparative study of conflict resolution in macaques: Insights into the nature of trait covariation. *Animal Behavior, 75*, 847–860.

Thierry, B., Iwaniuk, A.N., & Pellis, S.M. (2000). The influence of phylogeny on the social behavior of macaques (Primates: Cercopithecidae, genus *Macaca*). *Ethology, 106*, 713–728.

Tolentino, K., Roper, J.J., Passos, F.C., & Strier, K.B. (2008). Mother-offspring associations in northern muriquis, *Brachyteles hypoxanthus*. *American Journal of Primatology, 70*, 301–305.

Trivers, R.L. (1971). The evolution of reciprocal altruism. *Quarterly Review of Biology, 46*, 35–57.

Trivers, R.L. (1972). Parental investment and sexual selection. In B. Campbell (Ed.), *Sexual selection and the descent of man* (pp. 136–179). Chicago: Aldine.

van Horn, R.C., Buchan, J.C., Altmann, J., & Alberts, S.C. (2007). Divided destinies: Group choice by female savannah baboons during social group fission. *Behavioral Ecology and Sociobiology, 61*, 1823–1837.

van Noordwijk, M.A. (1999). The effects of dominance rank and group size on female lifetime reproductive success in wild long-tailed macaques, *Macaca fascicularis*. *Primates, 40*, 105–130.

van Noordwijk, M.A., & van Schaik, C.P. (1985). Male migration and rank acquisition in wild long-tailed macaques (*Macaca fascicularis*). *Animal Behavior, 33*, 849–861.

Van Schaik, C.P. (1989). The ecology of social relationships amongst female primates. In V. Standon & R.A. Foley (Eds.), *Comparative socioecology: The behavioural ecology of humans and other mammals* (pp. 195–218). Oxford: Blackwell Scientific Publications.

van Schaik, C.P., & Paul, A. (1996). Male care in primates: Does it ever reflect paternity? *Evolutionary Anthropology, 5*, 152–156.

van Schaik, C.P., & van Hooff, J.A.R.A.M. (1996). Toward an understanding of the orangutan's social system. In W.C. McGrew, L. Marchant, & T. Nishida (Eds.), *Great ape societies* (pp. 3–15). Cambridge: Cambridge University Press.

Vigilant, L., Hofreiter, M. Siedel, H., & Boesch, C. (2001). Paternity and relatedness in wild chimpanzee communities. *Proceedings of the National Academy of Science, 98*, 12890–12895.

Wada, K., Tokida, E., & Ogawa, H. (2007). The influence of snowfall, temperature and social relationships on sleeping clusters of Japanese monkeys during winter in Shiga Heights. *Primates, 48*, 130–139.

Waitt, C., Gerald, M.S., & Berard, J. (2004). Transfer from the natal group is related to presence of immature relatives in orphaned male rhesus macaques (*Macaca mulatta*). *Folia Primatology, 75*, 101–103.

Walters, J. (1980). Interventions and the development of dominance relationships in female baboons. *Folia Primatology, 34*, 61–89.

Walters, J.R. (1986). Transition to adulthood. In B. B. Smuts, D.L. Cheney, R.M. Seyfarth, R.W. Wrangham, & T.T. Struhsaker (Eds.), *Primate societies* (pp. 11–24). Chicago: University of Chicago.

Walters, J.R. (1987). Kin recognition in nonhuman primates. In D.F. Fletcher & C.D. Michener (Eds.), *Kin recognition in animals* (pp. 359–393). New York: John Wiley.

Warfield, J.J. (2004). The filial bond between offspring and mothers is the initial building block of cercopithecine social organization. *Folia Primatology, 75*(Suppl 1), 349–350.

Warfield, J.J. (2005). The filial bond offspring maintain with their mothers as the initial building block of cercopithecine social organization. *American Journal of Primatology, 66*(s1), 119.

Watanabe, K. (1979). Alliance formation in a free-ranging troop of Japanese macaques. *Primates, 20*, 459–474.

Watts, D.P. (1994). Social relationships of immigrant and resident female mountain gorillas: Relatedness, residence and relationships between females. *American Journal of Primatology, 32*, 13–30.

Watts, D.P. (1996). Comparative socio-ecology of gorillas. In W.C. McGrew, L. Marchant, & T. Nishida (Eds.), *Great ape societies* (pp. 16–28). Cambridge: Cambridge University Press.

Watts, D.P. (2001). Social relationships of female mountain gorillas. In M.M. Robbins, P. Sicotte, & K.J. Stewart (Eds.), *Mountain gorillas: Three decades of research at Karisoke* (pp: 215–240). New York: Cambridge University.

Watts, D.P. and Pusey, A.P. (1993). Behavior of juvenile and adolescent great apes. In M.E. Pereira & L.A. Fairbanks (Eds.), *Juvenile primates: Life history, development, and behavior* (pp. 148–167). New York: Oxford University.

Weingrill, T. (2000). Infanticide and the value of male-female relationships in mountain chacma baboons. *Behaviour, 137*, 337–359.

Welker, C., Schwibbe, M.H., Schaefer-Witt, C., & Visalberghi, E. (1987). Failure of kin recognition in *Macaca fascicularis*. *Folia Primatology, 49*, 216–221.

Wendland, J.R., Lesch, K.P., Newman, T.K., Timme, A., Gachot-Neveu, H., Thierry, B., & Suomi, S.J. (2006). Differential functional variability of serotonin transporter and monamine oxidase A genes in macaque species displaying contrasting levels of aggression-related behavior. *Behavior Genetics, 36*, 163–172.

White, F.J. (1996). *Pan paniscus* 1973 to 1996: Twenty-three years of field research. *Evolutionary Anthropology, 5*, 11–17.

Widdig, A. (2007). Paternal kin discrimination: The evidence and likely mechanisms. *Biology Reviews, 82*, 319–334.

Widdig, A., Nurnberg, P., Bercovitch, F.B., Trefilov, A., Berard, J.B., Kessler, M.J., et al. (2006b). Consequences of group fission for the patterns of relatedness among rhesus macaques. *Molecular Ecology, 15*, 3825–3832.

Widdig, A., Nurnberg, P., Krawczak, M., Streich, W.J., & Bercovitch, F.B. (2001). Paternal relatedness and age proximity regulate social relationships among adult females rhesus macaques. *Proceedings of the National Academy of Science, 98*, 13769–13773.

Widdig, A., Nurnberg, P., Krawczak, M., Streich, W.J., & Bercovitch, F.B. (2002). Affiliation and aggression among adult female rhesus macaques: A genetic analysis of paternal cohorts. *Behaviour, 139*, 371–391.

Widdig, A., Streich, W.J., Nurnberg, P., Croucher, P.J.P., Bercovitch, F.B., & Krawczak, M. (2006a). Paternal kin bias in agonistic interventions of adult female rhesus macaques (*Macaca mulatta*). *Behavioral Ecology and Sociobiology, 61*, 205–214.

Widdig, A., Streich, W.J., & Tembrock, G. (2000). Coalition formation among male Barbary macaques (*Macaca sylvanus*). *American Journal of Primatology, 50*, 37–51.

Williams, J.M., Lu, H., & Pusey, A.E. (2002). Costs and benefits of grouping for female chimpanzees at Gombe. In C. Boesch, G. Hohmann, & L.F. Marchant (Eds.), *Behavioral diversity in chimpanzees and bonobos.* (pp. 192–203). Cambridge: Cambridge University Press.

Wimmer, B., Tautz, D., & Kappeler, P. M. (2002). The genetic population structure of the gray mouse lemur (*Microcebus murinus*), a basal primate from Madagascar. *Behavioral Ecology and Sociobiology, 52*, 166–175.

Wittig, R.M., Crockford, C., Seyfarth, R.M., & Cheney, D.L. (2007). Vocal alliances in chacma baboons (*Papio hamadryas ursinus*). *Behavioral Ecology and Sociobiology, 61*, 899–909.

Wittig, R.A., Crockford, C., Lehmann, J., Whitten, P.L., Seyfarth, R.M., & Cheney, D.L. (2008). Focused grooming networks and stress alleviation in wild female baboons. *Hormones and Behavior, 54*, 170–177.

Wolovich, C.K., Perea-Rodriguez, J.P., & Fernandez-Duque, E. (2008). Food transfers to young and makes in wild owl monkeys (*Aotus azarai*). *American Journal of Primatology, 70*, 211–221.

Woodruff, D.S. (2004). Noninvasive genotyping and field studies of free-ranging nonhuman primates. In B. Chapais & C.M. Berman (Eds.), *Kinship and behavior in primates* (pp. 46–68). New York: Oxford University Press.

Wrangham, R.W. (1979). On the evolution of ape social systems. *Social Science Information, 18*, 335–368.

Wrangham, R.W. (1980). An ecological model of female-bonded primate groups. *Behaviour, 75*, 262–300.

Wrangham, R.W. (1982). Mutualism, kinship, and social evolution. In King's College Sociobiology Group (Ed.), *Current problems in sociobiology* (pp. 269–290). Cambridge: Cambridge University Press.

Wright, P.C. (1984). Biparental care in *Aotus trivirgatus* and *Callicebus moloch*. In M.F. Small (Ed.), *Female primates: Studies by women primatologists* (pp. 59–75). New York: Alan R. Liss.

Yamada, M. (1963). A study of blood-relationship in the natural society of the Japanese macaque—An analysis of co-feeding, grooming, and playmate relationships in Minoo-B-troop. *Primates, 4*, 43–65.

PART 4

Fictive Families

CHAPTER 16

Pet Keeping: A Case Study in Maladaptive Behavior

John Archer

Abstract

Natural selection leads to maladaptive behavior through several interrelated means. New adaptations may be constrained by designs resulting from past adaptations, there may be maladaptive by-products of adaptive responses, and environments may change faster than the capacity to respond to them. The behavior of hosts of avian brood parasites provides an example, and it is argued that human pet keeping is another, involving the manipulation of human responses that evolved for other purposes. This leads to strong attachments by humans to their pets, which are underpinned by the following: (a) infant schema, which may be maintained in adult pets; (b) anthropomorphism; (c) motherese or infant-directed speech, which further facilitates the development of the human–pet bond; and (d) the ability to regard attachments to pets more favorably than those to humans. Adaptations by pet species facilitate human attachments, and support the view that pets manipulate the human owners.

Keywords: Adaptation, maladaptive behavior, constraints, evolutionary arms race, social parasites, pets, attachment, infant schema, anthropomorphism, infant-directed speech

How Nonadaptive or Maladaptive Behavior Has Arisen by Natural Selection

Evolutionary psychology seeks to explain human behavior in terms of its adaptive significance—why certain ways of behaving, rather than alternatives, were maintained by natural selection. It also seeks to show how knowledge of the evolutionary function of behavior can inform present-day mechanisms. This approach has produced testable hypotheses in areas such as the social psychology of mate choice, sex differences in social behavior such as aggression and sexuality, and the social nature of human reasoning (Buss, 2008). Yet, there remain many aspects of human psychology that at first sight seem not to fit this framework because they appear be detrimental to an individual's survival and reproductive prospects. In this chapter, I first outline some of the ways in which such apparently non-adaptive behavior can be explained in evolutionary terms and then use as an example the phenomenon of humans forming a bond with another species, in the form of pets.

Before discussing the ways in which natural selection can produce maladaptive or nonadaptive behavior, it is necessary to clarify what is meant by these terms. Even when considering behavior that obviously serves an adaptive function, there are limits to the extent to which it is perfectly adapted in terms of providing the maximum possible fitness advantage. In most cases, animals have to settle for the best that is available in the circumstances, given the previous design of the species. Natural selection leads not to perfection but to ways of responding that enable the animal to operate and reproduce more efficiently than its competitors. In this context, maladaptive behavior is behavior that is detrimental to this process, and nonadaptive behavior is neutral to it.

The points that new adaptations are built upon (a) previous adaptations for past environments and

(b) longstanding designs that constrain the adaptive solutions that are possible, are important ones that have been emphasized in the works of biological critics of evolutionary psychology (Gould & Lewontin, 1979; Gould & Vrba, 1982; see Andrews, Gangestad, & Matthews, 2002; Buss, Haselton, Shackelford, Bleske, & Wakefield, 1998). From the perspective of Tinbergen's (1963) four explanations of behavior, evolutionary psychologists are concerned with one of these, function or survival value. A separate evolutionary explanation concerns phylogenetic history. Since this involves how one form (or behavioral disposition) becomes transformed into another over evolutionary time, it is therefore more concerned with the impact of existing design (and the constraints this involves), on the evolutionary process (e.g., Gould, 1980; Mithen, 1996; Shubin, 2007).

Eastwick (2009) adopted this phylogenetic approach to consider the evolution of human mating. He also cited a number of examples of historical constraints that have initially led to maladaptive behavior in a new environment, leading to what he termed an *adaptive workaround*. The extent to which the workaround becomes successful will depend on the time scale involved and the extent to which the old adaptation involves mechanisms that are easily changed. This analysis provides the first step in considering how natural selection can produce maladaptive behavior.

A consequence of current adaptations being limited by constraints is that adaptive responses must incorporate costs or trade-offs in coming to their adaptive workarounds. One example concerns the influence of testosterone and related hormones (androgens) on the behavior of male vertebrates. Steroid receptors and their associated hormones form part of the basic design plan of vertebrates (Baker, 1997). One consequence of this is that the males of most vertebrate species have their reproductive physiology and behavior controlled by testosterone or a related androgen. To evolve a new mechanism from scratch would not be feasible. Yet, high levels of androgens impose physiological and behavioral costs, such as higher energy turnover and increased risk of injury, leading to decreased survival and lower reproductive success (Vleck & Brown, 1999). In species where male–male competition is frequent and the opportunity to mate depends on its outcome, there is no alternative to incurring these costs, because high-risk intermale competition is an adaptive strategy. When competition is less pronounced, and paternal care is adaptive, a workaround is evident: Circulating testosterone levels are maintained at lower levels, so that their deleterious effects are less pronounced. Intermale competitive situations lead to short-term rises in testosterone levels that are not maintained over longer periods of time (Archer, 2006; Wingfield, Hegner, Dufty, & Ball, 1990). In this example, the mechanism that underlies the adaptive feature (testosterone increasing aggressiveness) has deleterious effects that cannot be removed by selection. Therefore, to increase aggressiveness through this particular route, the individual has either to incur certain costs, or to minimize these costs by restricting the times when testosterone levels are high.

Grief provides an example of a feature that is maladaptive when viewed in isolation, but can be viewed as a by-product of a wider set of characteristics that are adaptive. Grief involves a set of behavioral, emotional, and motivational processes that occur when a loved one dies. It is a universal human reaction, and parallels a similar response to separation and loss in social birds and mammals (Archer, 1999, 2001a,b, 2008). Yet, grief is associated with higher mortality rates, a greater number of illness symptoms, and lowered immune system function. Psychological health is typically poorer among bereaved people, as indicated by anxiety, depression, and a loss of interest in food, sex, and other activities. Viewed as a trait subject to natural selection, individuals who treat the loss of a significant other with emotional indifference and whose behavior is unaffected by the loss should be at a considerable adaptive advantage over those who grieve. Yet, such individuals are relatively rare (Archer, 2008; see Bonanno, 2004).

The answer to this puzzle lies in the evolutionarily ancient mechanisms that ensure the stability of important social relations despite separations of uncertain duration (Archer, 1999, 2001a,b; following Bowlby, 1980, and Parkes, 1972). These mechanisms involve the creation of internal models of a significant other, linked to strong emotional reactions. They ensure continued attachments when the significant other is absent, and they motivate the animal to seek reunification when separated. On those relatively few occasions when the separation is permanent through death, these separation reactions become ineffective, and hence maladaptive. In the case of nonhumans, and in most of human evolutionary history, separation and permanent loss would not be readily distinguishable (Archer, 1999, 2001a,b). Grief can therefore be viewed as a cost of human relationships being based on evolutionarily ancient adaptive attachment mechanisms: The inflexible nature of these constitute constraints on the evolution of a separate adaptive reaction in the case of separation involving death of a loved one.

In both of these examples, maladaptive behavior has arisen because natural selection acts on organisms that already exist, rather than being able to build a perfect design from scratch. Mechanisms adapted for one purpose have to be co-opted for another, and therefore often have side effects that would not—if design were perfect—occur.

In other cases, nonadaptive behavior occurs because the environment has changed at a faster rate than new adaptive solutions can evolve. The present human environments are in many aspects very different from the ancestral ones, so that there are numerous examples from humans in modern technological societies. For example, a phenotype that readily enables the storage of fat is likely to be adaptive in times of food scarcity, but is detrimental to health where cheap food rich in carbohydrate and fat is available (Wells, 2007). The stress response arises from a fight or flight response that acts as an emergency reaction to potentially life-threatening situations, activating sympathetic and neuroendocrine systems (Cannon, 1929; Selye, 1950; Mason, 1968a, b), to produce rapid energy mobilization, at the expense of growth, food storage, and reproduction (Mason, 1968a, b). These systems, designed to operate in the short-term when an active response is required, are in present-day human environments often mobilized for longer periods, when an active response is not possible. This leads to maladaptive changes in the form of stress-related diseases (Selye, 1950).

Such human examples are well known. Yet, they are a special case of the more general principle that environments may change faster than new adaptations can evolve to meet the changes. When this occurs in the context of the coevolution of adaptations in predators and prey, or parasites and hosts, it is referred to as an *evolutionary arms race* (Dawkins & Krebs, 1979). In such cases, one side may have evolved to manipulate or counter the other's adaptations, which are consequently rendered maladaptive at that particular time. Brood parasites such as cuckoos are, in evolutionary terms, ahead of their hosts, who are responding to the cuckoo eggs in a way that was adaptive in an ancestral environment without brood parasites. It would currently be adaptive to recognize such eggs and eject them from the nest. This does indeed occur where brood parasitism has occurred at a higher rate and over longer periods of time (Davies & Brooke, 1988).

New adaptive solutions may be slow to arise in new environments because the mechanisms underlying many behavioral reactions are relatively inflexible, which is another way of saying that they are constrained by past adaptations. The caregiving responses by the hosts of brood parasites are controlled by phylogenetically ancient mechanisms that work well under the environmental conditions their species and its ancestors will have typically encountered, where eggs and chicks in their nest are their own offspring. These mechanisms have led to adaptive behavior in the past and in most cases today. Yet, they are built on a simple principle and can readily lead the animal to respond inappropriately—maladaptively—when these adaptive assumptions are no longer fulfilled. The mechanism underlying the parenting response involves it being evoked by any eggs or chick the parent encounters in its nest.

Avian brood parasites exploit the generality of the mechanisms underlying the host bird's parental care, to the advantage of their own chicks and to the cost of the parents of the host species (e.g., Davies & Brooke, 1988). Had the ancestral parenting response evolved in an environment in which it was necessary to constantly discriminate one's own offspring from those of others, more discriminating responses would have evolved. Although we typically think of human behavior as being controlled by mechanisms that enable flexible behavior that tracks environmental conditions, there still remain a number of cases where important reactions are elicited by a relatively simple set of stimuli. Sexual interest and parental interest are two examples. Both rely on initial attraction based on a relatively simple set of stimuli. In the case of the parenting response, there are a common set of stimuli present in the infants of most birds and mammals. As indicated in later sections, this phylogenetically ancient response enables humans to become attached to individuals of other species that share these features, and this underlies the widespread tendency for humans to become attached to animals they keep as pets (Archer, 1997).

The Evolutionary Significance of Pet Keeping

So far, I have outlined some of the circumstances under which nonadaptive and maladaptive behavior can occur as a result of natural selection. The specific example I consider in detail is human pet keeping, mentioned at the end of the previous section. In evolutionary terms, pet keeping would seem to have few obvious fitness benefits. The affection, food, time, and energy devoted to a pet is not repaid in terms of related offspring or inclusive fitness, and it could have been more profitably spent caring for human offspring and relatives. As with other forms of maladaptive behavior, it has been suggested that pet keeping may, after all, be adaptive, because it has been shown to confer some benefits in terms of health, well-being, and social support (Serpell, 1986, 2003). Although this possibility cannot be ruled out, and there is evidence for such benefits (McNicholas, Gilby, Rennie, Ahmedzai, Dono, & Ormerod, 2005), balancing these benefits against the considerable costs involved renders it unlikely (Archer, 1997).

Alternatively, pet keeping can be considered as a by-product of adaptive mechanisms possessed by humans, mainly those that facilitate appropriate parental behavior and enable social interactions with other humans. These include nurturant responses to a simple set of facial and bodily stimuli associated with babies and young children, first identified by Lorenz (1943, 1950), and subsequently investigated in a number of studies (Archer, 1992, pp. 82–90). Since these "infant schema" are found in the young of most birds and mammals, people respond similarly to the young of these other species, including puppies and kittens, and to adults of other species possessing the features. A very important way in which humans are able to effectively interact with other humans is to treat them as intentional beings: This too is part of a generalized response, in this case the attribution of mental processes to any agents that behave with human-like characteristics (Epley, Waytz & Cacioppo, 2007; Mithen, 1996).

This view of pet keeping is that it is an accidental by-product of mechanisms that have an adaptive function when applied to humans. The features that set off these mechanisms are sufficiently general that they enable people to form strong attachments to appropriate members of another species. The question this raises is why the mechanisms have not become more specific to humans, so as to rule out such nonadaptive by-products. One answer might be that pet keeping is fairly new in evolutionary history. This does not seem to be the case, with evidence for the domestication of dogs in different parts of the world, dating back to 12,000 to 17,000 years ago (Clutton-Brock, 1977, 1981, 1995; Davis & Valla, 1978; Musil, 1970).

An alternative evolutionary view of pet keeping—one that also acknowledges that they are by-products of responses adaptive in other contexts—is one I suggested in an earlier article (Archer, 1997). Pets are viewed as equivalent to the social parasites found in nonhuman animals. They manipulate the host's responses by mimicking social releasers that control their behavior (Archer, 1997). For example, the beetle *Atemeles pubicollis* is a social parasite of ants that has "broken the code of the social insects" (Wilson, 1975) and is provisioned and cared for by its hosts as if it were their own offspring. In a similar way, pet dogs and cats appear to have evolved dispositions associated with human parenting. When such a process occurs over a long period of time, it leads to an evolutionary arms race, in which the manipulative species evolves further adaptations to facilitate its manipulation, and the manipulated species evolves responses to counter the other's adaptations. Since the selection pressures on the two species will be unequal, this is likely to lead to the manipulative species being ahead in the arms race. In the case of the avian brood parasites, failure of the eggs to be reared by the host species will lead to no offspring for the parasitic species. Failure to identify the host's eggs and chicks and to reject them will lower fitness for the host, but not to zero, if the risk of subsequent parasitism is low. As a result of these unequal selection pressures, the parasitic species is likely to be ahead in the arms race. As Dawkins and Krebs (1979) noted, this is a case of the "life-dinner" principle in arms races, apparent in predator–prey interactions, where one side (the prey) has to win to survive, but the other (the predator) does not, as there is always a further opportunity to chase other prey. Applied to brood parasitism, the parasite in the nest has to manipulate the host: If not, it will die, whereas the host can reproduce in other years if it is deceived.

Applying these principles to human pet keeping, if a pet is rejected by its human owner, its survival chances in the wild will be much reduced (but the existence of feral populations suggests that it will not be zero). The human pet keeper, by accepting a pet, reduces his or her fitness to a lesser extent, in terms of the diversion of resources to the pet from offspring and other relatives. Based on this reasoning, we would expect stronger selection pressure on pet species to modify their morphology and behavior so as to be more acceptable to their owners, than on the owner species to modify theirs so as to reject the pet species. Of course, many of these modifications in the pet species are the result of humans choosing animals that are more pleasing to them and hence with whom they can better bond. In a similar way, a brood-parasitized bird could be said to have gradually selected characteristics of the parasitic chicks, so that they exaggerate the typical calls and gaping responses of their own species, to produce what ethologists termed "supernormal stimuli" (McFarland, 1981; Tinbergen, 1951; Wickler, 1968). An analogy used by Dawkins and Krebs (1979), following earlier ethologists, was that the host species respond like "addicts" to these exaggerated stimuli. This is surely not too far away from the exaggerated parental responses shown by some pet owners to their beloved pets. In a later section, I consider possible adaptive changes in pet dogs and cats that can be considered in this light.

In the following sections, I first consider the evidence that people do form strong attachments to their pets, and follow this with discussions of some of the mechanisms through which this is achieved. These include the two mentioned so far: generalized infant features that act as social releasers, and anthropomorphism. I also consider the ability to communicate with pets (which forms an important basis of the attachment process), and the potential for valuing relationships with pets more than those with humans. Although these issues were considered in my previous article (Archer, 1997), there is now further evidence in all cases. I also consider how the pet species have changed their characteristics, so as to become more acceptable to humans, an issue not considered previously, but an essential component if we consider pets as coevolving for their relationship with humans.

Evidence for Human Attachment to Pets

There is a wide range of anecdotal evidence for the large amount of time, money, and affection devoted to pets in Western nations (Archer, 1997; Bonas, McNicholas, & Collis, 2000). A Gallup poll in the United States showed that 56% of pet owners stated that they would not sell their pet for a million dollars (El-Alayli, Lystad, Webb, Hollingsworth, & Ciolli, 2006), and numerous websites devoted to people's pets illustrate the affection and resources devoted to them. A review of historical and anthropological sources (Serpell, 1986, 1987) indicated that pet keeping is, and has been, widespread, so that it cannot be viewed as an aberration of modern Western life. Throughout all these accounts is evidence of love and affection shown toward pets.

A number of studies have sought to measure people's attachment to their pets. One of the earliest of these (Katcher, Friedmann, Goodman, & Goodman, 1983) found high levels on ten items regarded as indicative of attachment, such as carrying the pet's photograph around and regarding it as a family member, among a sample of veterinary clinic clients. Holcombe, Williams, and Richards (1985) used items from this scale, together with those derived from research on attachment styles in humans by Ainsworth (1969, 1979). Johnson, Garrity, and Stallones (1992) based their Lexington Attachment to Pets Scale (LAPS) on two earlier attitudinal scales combined with the companion animal bonding scale of Poresky, Hendrix, Mosier, and Samuelson (1987). Other scales measure concepts similar to attachment, such as commitment to the pet (Staats, Miller, Carnot, Rada, & Turnes, 1996). Stallones, Johnson, Garrity, and Marx (1990) designed the Companion Animal Attachment Scale and administered it to a national probability sample of 1,300: As expected, they found stronger attachment among those with sole responsibility for their pets.

With the partial exception of the scale by Holcombe et al. (1985), none of these measures was explicitly based on human studies of attachment, although they incorporate—to different extents—aspects of attachment in its original sense (Bowlby, 1969), such as an emotional or affective bond, and the use of the pet as a secure base (Crawford, Worsham, & Swinehart, 2006). The attachment-to-pets scale designed by Archer and Ireland (in press) was explicitly based on studies of human attachment (Bowlby, 1958, 1969). The questionnaire involved items measuring how important the pet is in the person's life, its contribution to self-worth, physical contact and interactions with it, its use as a secure base and to reassure the owner, the desire for the pet's presence, thinking about it when apart, and distress at thoughts of its loss. Among four samples of dog owners recruited in different ways, scores tended toward the strongly attached end of the scale, and reliability analysis revealed overall coherence in the measures, with factor analysis indicating three interrelated components, corresponding to degree of closeness with the pet, care and protection, and a source of security. A subsequent study (Archer & Monton, in press) found that the scale was applicable to cat owners as well as dog owners.

Most studies have implicitly or explicitly measured the *strength* of attachment people have toward their pets, following the original emphasis on attachment by infants to their parents, which was Bowlby's main concern. In contrast, Beck and Madrash (2008) transferred *styles* of attachment to people's relationship with their pets. Styles of attachment were initially an important focus for child-to-parent attachment (Ainsworth, 1969, 1979) and were later transferred to adult romantic relationships (Fraley, Waller, & Brennan, 2000; Griffin & Bartholomew, 1994a, 1994b; Hazan & Shaver, 1987).

Beck and Madrash used both a measure of the two dimensions found to underlie attachment style by Griffin and Bartholomew (1994a, 1994b), and descriptions of the four prototypes these orthogonal dimensions produced (secure, preoccupied, dismissing-avoidant, and fearful-avoidant attachment styles). These measures were adapted for pets, and together with the original version for partners, were administered to a web-based survey of 192 pet owners. The associations between the two versions of the scale were generally small. This may be because the attachment styles identified in children and in romantic partners do not generalize to attachments to pets. The items on the Pet Avoidance and Pet Anxiety scales do not appear to be appropriate for a nonhuman companion; for example, those involving concern over losing the pet's love or commitment, and avoiding showing one's feelings and emotions to the pet. It may be that attachment *styles* do not readily transfer to relationships that are largely caregiving, such as parenting and pet keeping, as opposed to security-seeking.

This speculation raises the issue of the type of attachment people have with their pets. Although this would generally seem to include caregiving, it may also involve some aspects of security-seeking, the type of relationship children have with their parents. The earlier evidence that both these aspects are involved, probably to different extents in different cases, was reviewed in my previous article (Archer, 1997, pp. 240–241). This is supported by the factor structure of the Dog Attachment Questionnaire (Archer & Ireland, in press), described above: Factors involving items related to care and protection, and to a source of security, were found. In a study investigating the types of relationship people have with their pets, Bonas et al. (2000) applied a measure initially designed for human relationships, which had a number of subscales measuring specific relationship provision, such as nurturance, companionship, conflict, antagonism, and instrumental aid. When applied to human–pet relationships, there were two main components, support and conflict. Support involved subscales for intimacy, nurturance, affection, admiration, and instrumental aid, indicating that security-seeking plays an important part in these human–pet relationships. This component was more pronounced in relationships with dogs than with cats. One suggestion for future research is to design questionnaires to measure either caregiving or care-seeking, and to assess the extent to which people with different types of pet show these features.

A further study indicates that attachment styles to other humans can influence how a person feels after interacting with a pet dog. Colby and Sherman (2002) measured human attachment styles, using the four categories described by Bartholomew and Horowitz (1991), among a sample of institutionalized older people. Human attachment styles were related to changes in mood following interactions with the dogs (as part of a pet visitation scheme). Securely attached people showed increases in positive mood, and decreases in depression after the interactions, whereas people characterized by a fearful avoidant style showed increased depression after the visit. These findings, albeit with a specialized population, raise the possibility that the styles of attachment people have with significant others may influence their feelings when interacting with their pets, and may come to influence the strength or type of attachment they have with them—although the study by Beck and Madrash (described above) suggests that it is more the strength rather than the style of attachment that is applicable to humans' relationships with their pets.

The Development of an Attachment Bond

In his writings on attachment, Bowlby (1958, 1969) concentrated on the child's developing bond to his or her parents, although he did subsequently refer to the development of attachment by parents to their infants (e.g., Bowlby, 1980, pp. 39–41). Bowlby (1969) emphasized the importance of exposure learning, and having satisfying interactions, as key processes leading to attachment formation. Daly and Wilson (1980, 1988) concentrated on attachment by parents to their offspring. They emphasized the importance of an initial assessment of the offspring's quality and of the mother's circumstances for starting a process that would lead to the development of attachment. In support of their view, they emphasized the negative consequences of absence of typical infant features, but there is also evidence that, within the normal range, mothers of more attractive infants show more affection and playfulness, and more positive attitudes toward them, than do mothers of less attractive infants (Langois, Ritter, Casey, & Sawin, 1995). The infant features that act as social releasers in the case of humans and generalize to the young of other species (see following section) would form an important part of this initial assessment of infant quality. Daly and Wilson (1988) described two further stages in the development of attachment, which occur after the initial stage. These were the development of attachment specific to the parent's own child, and the consolidation of the bond through mutually satisfying interactions over a period of months and years. As with all stage models, the three stages partially overlap.

A similar process of initial assessment is likely to occur with pets, the infant features mentioned above (see also the following section) providing an important source of attraction. Subsequently, exposure learning occurs when the animal becomes part of its owner's everyday life. As with the formation of a human relationship, mutually satisfying interactions are an important feature in the formation of a bond with a pet. Pet dogs and cats behave in ways that are appealing to their owners (Serpell, 1986, 1996). Dogs are more demonstrative in terms of their affection and attention to their owners (Smith, 1983), although cats seem to like being stroked and petted. Two studies identified the features that owners find most satisfying in their pets—dependence, play, fun, and relaxation (Berryman, Howells, & Lloyd-Evans, 1985)—and in the case of dogs, their expressiveness, loyalty, and affection (Serpell, 1983).

The hypothalamic peptide hormone oxytocin is involved in the process of attachment in mammals generally, and in several contexts in humans. For example, when it is administered to people, it increases their degree of trust in others (Kosfeld, Heinrichs, Zak, Fischbacher, & Fehr, 2005; Theodoridou, Rowe, Penton-Voak, & Rogers, 2009). Odendaal and Meintjex (2003) found that oxytocin and other physiological measures associated with bonding or affection increased following positive interactions with dogs in adult humans. Miller, Kennedy, DeVoe, Hickey, Nelson, and Kogan (2009) found that oxytocin levels increased in women but not men in a small sample of American dog owners interacting with their dogs after being separated from them all day. In a larger Japanese sample of dog owners, Nagasawa, Kikusui, Onaka, and Ohta (2009) found that oxytocin levels increased after they had interacted with their dogs for 30 minutes. There were no indications of moderation by the sex of participant in this study. Those owners who were recipients of longer periods of gaze from their dogs, and who reported closer relationships with them, showed a larger increase in oxytocin than did owners with shorter periods of gaze and less close relationships. Interactions that were initiated by the dogs' gaze led to greater increases in oxytocin.

These studies all provide evidence of physiological changes consistent with attachment formation with pet dogs. In the following sections, I examine some of the mechanisms that are important for being able to form a mutually satisfying relationship with a pet, beginning with their initial appeal (Daly and Wilson's assessment process) and going on to consider mechanisms that are crucial for being able to treat them as human-like entities, and becoming attached to them.

Mechanisms Promoting Attachment to a Pet
Social Releasers

Lorenz (1943, 1950/1971) suggested that a set of facial features, involving a high cranium, a small face, big eyes, pouch-like cheeks, and a small snout, were "social releasers" (Hinde, 1982) for parental behavior. Social releasers are a relatively simple set of stimuli that evoke a similar reaction from all members of a species (or from one sex or age group). They represent widespread mechanisms in the control of animal behavior. Because they are relatively automatic responses to simple stimuli, they may be set off outside their original adaptive context, and therefore they can be subject to manipulation by another species. In the case of the infant schema, these are shared with the young of most species of birds and mammals, so that humans readily respond to the young of other species with the same sort of response that they show to human infants. Experimental studies have demonstrated that the features described by Lorenz are viewed as "babyish" or "baby-faced" when viewed in black-and-white faces (Gardner & Wallach, 1965; Zebrowitz & Montepare, 1992), and that they are rated as attractive in drawings of infant faces (e.g., Sternglanz, Gray, & Murakami, 1977).

Some studies indicate a greater preference for infant schema among women than men (Archer, 1992, pp. 82–90). Using images of infant faces, computer-manipulated for differences in cuteness, Sprengelmeyer et al. (2009) found that women in their early 20s, and those aged 45 to 51 years were more sensitive to differences in cuteness than were women aged 53 to 60 years, and men of the same age or younger. This suggested that the greater sensitivity to these faces was maintained by female reproductive hormones, which are absent in men and in women of postreproductive age. This interpretation was supported by a further study showing that young women taking oral contraceptives were more sensitive to differences in cuteness in infant faces than were young women who were not taking oral contraceptives. The authors speculated that estrogen and progesterone may alter the emotional response to the cuter baby face, so that it is more rewarding, thus helping mothers to form attachments to such babies.

Further studies show that, in the context of adult faces, infant schema are associated with attributions of personality characteristics such as innocent, trustworthy, warm, compassionate, and having positive affect (Livingstone & Pearce, 2009; Zebrowitz, 1997; Zebrowitz & Montepare, 1992; Zebrowitz, Olson, & Hoffman, 1993). They also play a part in sexual attraction (e.g., Cunningham, Barbee, & Pike, 1990). The same features have also been incorporated into cultural artifacts such as teddy bears and cartoon characters. Increased conformity also has occurred over time to infant schema in teddy bears (Hinde & Barden, 1985), and in Mickey Mouse drawings (Gould, 1980).

Lorenz (1943, 1950/1971) suggested that a link exists between infant features and humans' attraction to those pets that are treated most like infants and children, such as Pekinese dogs and Cavalier King Charles spaniels, since they retain infant schema into adulthood. Archer and Monton (in press) obtained ratings of the attractiveness of facial photographs of the adults of common breeds of dogs and cats, some of which had infant features and some of which did not. These were compared with the ratings for photos of young dogs and cats, human infants, and teddy bears with and without infant schema. Faces with the infant features were generally rated as more attractive than those without. Human infant faces were found to be no more attractive than those of kittens or puppies. Women rated pets with infant features as more attractive than men did, although human infants or pets without infant features were rated similarly by both sexes. There were also preferences consistent with the owner's pet species. This is the first systematic study to demonstrate the attractiveness of baby features in the context of pet species. The heightened attractiveness of kittens and puppies, and of adult cats and dogs with infant features, provides a basis for humans wanting to continue to interact with them, and in some cases to their adoption as pets.

Infant features are not the only aspects of the pet involved in its initial attractiveness to potential owners. There is evidence from dog owners in the United States, Venezuela, and Japan that, in the case of pure breeds, owners pick dogs that resemble themselves (Nakajima, Yamamoto, & Yoshimoto, 2009; Payne & Jaffe, 2005; Roy & Christenfeld, 2004, 2005). Payne and Jaffe (2005) suggested that owners adopt a "like seeks like" rule when choosing a pet, and that this is a generalization of a process that people use when choosing a mate. If so, this would be another example of generalization to pets of mechanisms that were evolved for facilitating human social interactions.

Anthropomorphism

Humans readily attribute thoughts and feelings to anything that has human-like qualities, from non-human animals to computers or robots. Developmentally, this is first seen at around 3 to 4 years of age and is termed *theory of mind* by developmental psychologists. More generally, the process is known as *anthropomorphism* when it is applied to anything other than humans, be it an animal, inanimate object, or deity. This can be viewed as a by-product of the ability to view other humans as having mental states like our own. Possessing a theory of mind greatly facilitates interaction with them. People with autism, who lack this ability, dramatically illustrate the limitations of human interactions without it.

Mithen (1996) claimed that anthropomorphism is one of the defining features of modern *Homo sapiens*, and that it was absent in other hominids, including the Neanderthals. He argued that this way of thinking was highly adaptive in that it enabled more complex and successful hunting strategies based on an anthropomorphic understanding of the prey's behavior. One by-product of this was to enable animals to be introduced into human social life (Serpell, 2003), and this characteristic was essential for domestication and for pet keeping.

Epley et al. (2007) considered anthropomorphism as a particular type of inductive inference. It occurs when an external agent elicits existing knowledge relevant to humans, and it is influenced by the person's need and desire to form connections with other humans, and their need to interact effectively with the environment (effectance motivation). Egocentric bias is seen as the default position when dealing with another agent, to be corrected according to the person's capacity to do so and the specific information available. Perceived similarity to humans increases the likelihood of anthropomorphism, so that characteristics of pet species, such as their facial features (see previous section) and their similarity to humans in features such as motion, morphology, and emotions, will facilitate this process.

From this analysis, we would expect pet owners to use more mentalistic concepts than non–pet owners, when describing the behavior of pet species. To assess this, Fidler, Light, and Costell (1996) measured the degree to which people used phrases indicative of desires, feelings, and other mental states in response to a pet dog interacting with its owner. Consistent with the prediction, they found that a greater number of mentalistic descriptions by pet owners than by non-owners.

Epley et al.'s (2007) analysis explains a number of features of attachment to pets, and makes several further predictions. One of these was that people with a greater need for control would anthropomorphize more than those with a lower need for control, since this influences effectance motivation. Epley, Waytz, et al. (2008) found this to be the case in a study in which American undergraduates rated how human-like were two dogs they observed behaving in a video sequence. These dogs had been rated as differing in predictability in a pilot experiment. Those participants who were higher in the need for control rated the unpredictable dog in more anthropomorphic terms than did those who were low in the need for control, although both groups tended to rate the unpredictable dog in more anthropomorphic terms than they did the predictable dog.

Where people are in constant interaction with animals for utilitarian purposes, as in traditional cultures, they will, according to Epley et al. (2007), be less likely to anthropomorphize them. Where people have fewer social connections with other humans, they will be more prone to anthropomorphism. This will occur in individualist rather than collectivist cultures (Hofstede, 2001; Triandis, 1972, 1995) and within individualist cultures more in those with fewer social relationships. Epley, Waytz, Akalis, and Cacioppo (2008) found that American undergraduates who scored high on a standard loneliness scale tended to rate their pets higher on supportive anthropomorphic traits than did those who scored low on the loneliness measure. A further study showed that that inducing feelings of social isolation led to more anthropomorphic traits associated with social connection being attributed to the participants' pets than when participants did not have feelings of social isolation induced (Epley, Akalis, Waytz, & Cacioppo, 2008). The link between the tendency to anthropomorphism and lack of social connection was shown to extend to technological gadgets and to supernatural agents in two further studies (Epley, Akalis et al., 2008).

If lack of social connection is associated with a greater tendency to anthropomorphize, this may lead to greater attachment to pets among those with fewer social contacts. Consistent with this is evidence for an association between social connection and the degree of attachment to a pet. Studies of pet owners in the United States show that attachment to pets is stronger among: (a) those who had never married than those who had (Stallones et al., 1990); (b) divorced people than those who were married with children (Albert & Bulcroft, 1987, 1988); and (c) people from households with no children (Albert & Bulcroft, 1988; Holcomb et al., 1985; Johnson et al., 1992) than those from households with children. In an Australian sample, children from single-parent families were (according to their parents) more strongly attached to their pet dogs than were children from two-parent families (Bodsworth & Coleman, 2001). Following loss of a pet, people living alone show more distress than those living with others (Archer & Winchester, 1994; Carmack, 1985; Gerwolls & Labott, 1994).

Two rather different studies have investigated loneliness in relation to pet keeping. Among a sample of older women living in the community, Krause-Parello (2008) found a small tendency for those who were lonelier to be more attached to their pet dog or cat, and also to have slightly lower general health. There was also a small but significant mediating effect of attachment to a pet on the inverse relationship between loneliness and general health, so that this was lowered by attachment to a pet. Gilby, McNicholas, and Collis (2007) undertook a direct test of whether acquiring a pet reduced loneliness. They measured loneliness during a 6-month period among participants who reported that they were actively seeking to acquire a new pet. Over half had acquired one by the end of the study period, but the researchers found no evidence that their loneliness had decreased during this time.

The studies reviewed in this section indicate that anthropomorphism is a particular type of inductive inference that serves to facilitate human–human interactions, yet generalizes far beyond other humans, not only to nonhuman animals, but also to inanimate objects and hypothetical beings. It was shown that lack of human connections can lead to greater anthropomorphism of pets and technological objects, and this process could underlie the greater attachment to pets found in people with fewer social connections.

Communication with Pets

Humans' ability to communicate with their pets is based on the process of anthropomorphism, discussed in the previous section. This is facilitated further because dogs and cats share moods and emotions with humans, which people recognize in their communication with them. Pet owners compensate for the pets' lack of language by behaving as if the pet can understand them. Most pet owners talk to their pets as if they can understand them, and they believe that the animals are sensitive to their feelings (Katcher et al., 1983; Smith, 1983).

Of particular interest in relation to humans' communication with their pets is the use of motherese or infant-directed speech (IDS), which is the form of speech that is typically used by adults when interacting with young infants. It tends to involve a higher-pitch than adult-directed speech, the use of short utterances and sentences, repetitions, exaggerated vowels, imperatives and questions, particularly tag questions (such as "don't you" at the end), and a slower tempo (Falk, 2004). Distinct IDS exists in all languages, and Falk (2004) has argued that it has been important in the evolution of a protolanguage from primate communication systems. Infants usually prefer to listen to this form of speech and recognize and prefer it even in a foreign language (Bryant & Barrett, 2007). The first study of the use of IDS toward pets involved analyses of recordings of four female dog owners talking to their dogs (Hirsh-Pasek & Treiman, 1982). Most of the features of IDS were found in these interactions, although *deixis* or naming objects (such as "this is red"), a characteristic of speech by mothers to infants, was lacking.

In a more extensive study, both in terms of participants and speech analysis, Mitchell and Edmonson (1999) observed 23 people playing with two dogs, one of whom was their own pet and the other an unfamiliar dog (another participant's pet). They found many of the characteristics of IDS, such as short, highly repetitive utterances, but some differences. Seven words occurred in over half the utterances, notably "come," the dog's name, and "ball," and there were many questions directed to the dog. The authors suggested that underlying the communication by owners with their dogs is a desire to control them, which is less apparent in speech directed to infants. In a subsequent report on the same study, Mitchell (2001) compared the interactions with the dogs with the features of IDS to infants. Differences included shorter sentences when talking to dogs, more imperatives and exact definitions, and fewer questions, declarative statements, and deictic utterances (naming). This comparison is limited, since it did not involve the same

people talking to dogs and to infants. In addition, both this and the previous empirical study (Hirsh-Pasek & Treiman, 1982) involved dog owners. If instead, researchers studied people interacting with cats, or with breeds of dogs that have retained infant characteristics into adulthood, there may have been less control and more nurturance, and hence more similarities with speech directed to human infants.

Sims and Chin (2002) observed people interacting with a cat (which was not their own pet) and found various aspects of IDS in these interactions: People used short, repetitive utterances, imperatives ("look" and "come on"), questions ("what's this?"), encouragements ("there you go"), greetings ("hey"), attributions of thoughts to the cat, and expression of their own thoughts. The more the participant perceived the cat to be intelligent, the more they used questions when interacting with it, and the more they attributed thoughts to it. There was also evidence that speech was adjusted, so that it was more similar to IDS when the cat was regarded as more intelligent. This was particularly the case for the female participants.

A further study (Prato-Previde, Fallani, & Valsecchi, 2006) recorded dog owners' talking to their dogs in a series of episodes with owner, dog, and a stranger (Ainsworth's Strange Situation: see a later section), and again found considerable use of IDS. Women showed more utterances than men did, and more words, repetitions, diminutives, endearments, and pet names, although there were no sex differences in the frequency of commands and self-answers.

Burnham, Kitamura, and Vollmer-Conna (2002) compared the way in which 12 mothers talked to their infants, their pets (five cats and seven dogs), and other adults, in three domains relevant to IDS. They found that speech directed to infants and to pets was similar, and differed from speech directed to adults in terms of pitch and affect, although mothers only exaggerated vowels to their infants and not to their pets.

In spite of differences in the sort of IDS used with infants and with pet dogs found in some studies, the adoption of any form of IDS toward a nonlinguistic being is noteworthy. In the case of infants, IDS enables mothers to interact with their infants at a distance, and is likely to direct the infants' attention and to modulate their arousal and affect, calming them in the absence of direct physical contact (Falk, 2004). These aspects may also apply to the use of IDS with pets, although other aspects, such as a role in tutoring and as a basis for learning a specific language, are clearly lacking for pets. In the process of forming a bond with the pet, the use of IDS can be viewed as following from anthropomorphism and providing a way in which the bond can be facilitated and developed.

Unconditional Positive Regard

In a previous article (Archer, 1997), I suggested that, in some cases, people attribute positive features to their relationship with pets that compare them favorably with their close relations to other humans. Thus, the pet is seen as always available, always loving, and completely uncritical, features that other humans find it difficult to live up to. These features were apparent in a number of statements made by pet owners in various studies, but most of the evidence presented in the earlier article was anecdotal. A more recent finding consistent with the view that pets provide an unconditional source of security for their owners comes from the study by Beck and Madresh (2008), who applied human attachment styles to human–pet relationships. Participants rated their relationships with their pets as much more secure than those with their partners. There were fewer concerns about whether the pet loved them, about whether the pet wanted to stay with them, and whether it was difficult for them to become emotionally close.

El-Alayli, Lystad, Webb, Hollingsworth, and Ciolli (2006) assessed whether people had an inflated view of their own pets' personality compared to the personality of the typical pet or the typical pet owner's pet and found that this was indeed the case. This finding is consistent with research showing similar bias with regard to friends and to possessions. El-Alayli et al. also found that this bias was greater in those who were more strongly attached to their pets and in those people who rated themselves as similar to their pets in terms of personality. This is consistent with research showing that people prefer pets who are similar to them, described earlier (Nakajima et al., 2009; Payne & Jaffe, 2005; Roy & Christenfeld, 2004, 2005).

These limited studies extend the earlier anecdotal accounts that many pet owners attribute positive features to their relationships that are not possible in the more complex and nuanced relationships people form with one another. There is considerable scope for extending such investigations in the future.

Adaptations in Pet Species That Facilitate Pet Keeping

If human pet keeping is largely beneficial (in terms of fitness) to the pets, we would expect that the most common species will have been modified by selection so as to be more acceptable to their human owners. Overall, the various dog breeds in existence today are pedomorphic in morphology compared with the ancestral wolf (Clutton-Brock, 1995; Goodwin, Bradshaw, & Wickens, 1997). They therefore retain at maturity what in the ancestral wolf would be juvenile features. Among these are the infant facial schema described earlier. In many cases, the adult faces of pet dogs and cats retain these facial features into adulthood, although the extent to which this has occurred varies between breeds. Goodwin et al. (1997) examined displays of dominance and submission in ten breeds of dog selected for their physical dissimilarity to the ancestral wolf. The numbers of ancestral displays retained in the breed correlated with how closely it was judged to be physically similar to the wolf. Breeds with the smallest numbers of signals tended to use displays that appeared early in the development of the wolf. These behavioral differences from the wolf can be viewed as ways in which pet dogs have changed their repertoire to fit them for domestication, including the role of a pet.

In an earlier section, I outlined the evidence that owners form attachments to their pets. There is also evidence from observational studies that dogs form attachments to their owners. A standard observational method for assessing the extent to which infants and toddlers are attached to their caregivers is the Strange Situation Test (Ainsworth, 1969; Ainsworth & Bell, 1970), which involves a series of interactions between the infant, caregiver, and a stranger, in a strange situation. There are typically seven episodes involving the infant and caregiver, the introduction of a stranger, the caregiver leaving the room, the caregiver returning, the infant being left alone, the stranger reentering, and finally reunion with the caregiver.

Topál, Miklósi, Csányi, and Dóka (1998) modified the strange situation test for dog owners and their dogs to assess whether the dogs showed behavior indicating attachment. They did, in that they played more and showed more physical contact with their owners than with the strangers. The dogs also explored more and stood by the door less when the owner, rather than the stranger, was present. There was also evidence for individual differences consistent with Ainsworth's secure–insecure dimension.

A subsequent study (Prato-Previde, Sustance, Spiezio, & Sabatini, 2003) also used a modified Strange Situation, and analyzed changes from episode to episode, rather than aggregating the data as Topál et al. (1998) did. Prato-Previde et al. found clear evidence that the dogs were using their owners as a secure base (one of the criteria for attachment), in that the dogs played more with the strangers when their owners were present than when they were absent, and they explored more in the presence than in the absence of their owners. The dogs also showed a range of attachment behavior, such as searching and proximity-seeking when the owner was not there, spent time near to the owner's chair, and made contact with the owner's clothing in his or her absence.

Topál, Gácsi, Miklósi, Virányi, Kubinyi, and Csányi (2005) used the Strange Situation to compare the attachment of 16-week-old hand-reared dogs and wolves, and of puppies. They found the characteristic selective responses to owners in the hand-reared dogs and puppies, but not in the hand-reared wolves, who did not show a different response to the owner and a stranger. The authors concluded that attachment by dogs to their owners did not result from a socialization experience that operates similarly on the ancestral wolf (*Canis lupis*) species as well as on domesticated dogs (*Canis familiaris*). They concluded that "dogs have evolved a capacity for attachment to humans that is functionally analogous to that present in human infants" (Topál et al., 2005, p. 1373). If that is correct, the dog's capacity for forming an attachment to humans is the direct result of its evolution as a companion animal species. Consistent with this, there is evidence that adult dogs of placid temperament show physiological changes indicating bonding or affection following positive interactions with adult humans (Odendaal & Meintjes, 2002). The changes included higher levels of serum oxytocin, prolactin, and β-endorphin.

These studies show that pet dogs become attached to their owners. There are no comparable studies involving cats, although Turner (1991) observed interactions between cats and their female owners in 158 Swiss households. Particularly important was initiation—when either the owner or the pet showed the intent to interact—by vocalization to the other. Observations began when this was followed by a sequence of interaction. If the cat showed more initiations, there were more interactions between it and its owner. The cat's and the owner's willingness to comply with the other were positively correlated, so that if the owner complied with the cat at one time, the cat complied at another, and vice versa. This study demonstrates that cats, ancestrally an asocial species, show clear evidence of responding and reciprocally interacting with their human owners.

McComb, Taylor, Wilson, and Charlton (2009) explored the purrs of cats, recording these either when they were actively seeking food from their owners or in other contexts. Both cat owners and those with no cat owning experience found food purrs to be more urgent and less pleasant than other purrs. Embedded in the food purr was a high-pitched component, like a cry or meow, without which the purrs were viewed as less urgent and more pleasant. McComb et al. noted that the isolation cry of the cat is similar to the distress call of the human infant, and embedding this in the soliciting purr could be "a subtle means of exploitation, tapping into an inherent mammalian sensitivity to such cries" (p. R508). If correct, this would be another incidence of how the behavior of a pet species had been modified to evoke caregiving by their human owners.

Therefore, evidence suggests that both the morphology and the behavior of pet species have evolved to fit them for forming a close relationship with their human owners. This would fit the view that the human–pet bond represents coevolution between two species, either for mutual benefit or (as argued previously) because the pet species represent social parasites.

Alternatives to the Attachment View of Pet Keeping

The evolutionary social parasite view of pet ownership is based on the pet manipulating adaptive mechanisms that have evolved to facilitate bonds between humans, principally those between parents and dependent offspring. On this interpretation, the costs of pet keeping are borne by the human because the mechanisms of attachment formation are designed precisely to enable bonds to form to others who do not provide reciprocal benefits, notably children. In the case of pets, bearing these costs is maladaptive. An alternative view of pet ownership is based on exchange theory, which is a rational choice view of pet ownerships—the bond is maintained only when the benefits exceed the costs (e.g., Netting, Wilson, & New, 1987). Of course, it is not disputed that when the costs of pet ownership become too great, this will weaken the bond with the owner, but the difference between the two views is that the evolutionary-based attachment view of pet ownership would predict that the bond would be maintained beyond the point at which the costs exceed the benefits, and that it takes a considerable imbalance in favor of costs for the bond to be broken. This is relatively difficult to test at present since most studies of pet ownership concentrate on its benefits. One exception is that by Dwyer, Bennett, and Coleman (2006), who incorporated both positive and negative items into a questionnaire about people's relationships with their pet dogs. Although the positive aspects consisted of perceived emotional closeness (largely corresponding to attachment measures) the negative aspects, which were factorially distinct, involved aspects of time, money, and effort spent on the dog, and the restriction of other activities it causes. It would be interesting to study further the negative aspects of pet keeping, and in particular where these become particularly salient, leading to the pet being rejected.

Conclusion

The background to viewing human pet keeping as a form of maladaptive behavior is a consideration of the various ways in which behavior not currently adaptive could have arisen through the process of natural selection. Change in the environment from the ancestral one to the highly specialized human environments of the present day is the most obvious of these, but this represents a special case of the general principle that an animal's environment may change faster than its ability to evolve new adaptive traits. In some cases, this ability may be hindered or prevented by constraints that have arisen from the way in which past adaptive traits develop. In particular, the ability to produce new adaptive traits may be prevented if a trait is generally adaptive but maladaptive under specific circumstances.

These considerations apply to human pet keeping, in that the development of an attachment by humans to their pets depends on mechanisms that have their evolutionary functional origin in facilitating interactions with other humans. In the case of humans' reactions to infant schema, these involve a phylogenetically ancient mechanism. This illustrates the principle of constraints arising from previous adaptive features. Parental responses to infant schema are adaptive when viewed in their primary context, to facilitate the initial stages of attachment by a mother (and other adult relatives) to the infant. Their operation in other contexts can be viewed as costs that have to be borne, in view of the inflexibility of the mechanism involved. Similarly, the attribution of human-like mental processes to pet species can be viewed as arising from a trait that is of primary importance for dealing with other humans. Likewise, the use of IDS seems to be evoked by any dependent individual with whom an attachment bond has been formed: Again, it is a feature that is highly adaptive for facilitating bonds by mothers with their human infants (Falk, 2004), but not when extended to pet species.

The social parasite view of pet keeping goes beyond the view that these features are accidental by-products of features that are adaptive in the context of human relationships. It holds that they can also be considered as the result of a coevolutionary process, in which the pet species have become modified in ways that make them not only more likely to evoke caregiving responses from their human owners, but also more likely to form attachments with them. These modifications include morphological features that have been noted over 15,000 years ago from the fossil record (Musil, 1970), and behavioral ones that have been investigated in a number of recent studies.

Future directions

1. What is the relative extent to which different breeds of domestic dogs and cats have retained into adulthood the infant schema, described by Lorenz (1943, 1950/1971)?

2. To what extent are there individual differences in caregiving or care-seeking in relation to a pet, according to whether it is a cat or dog, or according to the breed of dog?

3. To what extent do the three stages proposed by Daly and Wilson (1988) for parents' attachment to their infants apply to people's developing attachment to pets?

4. If a set of facial photographs of pet species are manipulated to increase or decrease the extent to which they possess infant schema, do ratings of attractiveness vary accordingly?

5. Are there differences in the attraction of infant schema in the faces of pet animals between women of reproductive age and postmenopausal women (following the study by Sprengelmeyer et al., 2009)?

6. Can the tendency to show anthropomorphic thought toward a potential pet be increased by experimentally inducing feelings of social rejection?

7. To what extent does the use of motherese or IDS by pet owners follow the pet's possession of infant schema?

8. Can a precise cost–benefit assessment explain when owners reject their pets?

References

Ainsworth, M.D.S. (1969). Object relations, dependency and attachment: A theoretical review of the infant-mother relationship. *Child Development, 40*, 969–1025.

Ainsworth, M.D.S. (1979). Infant-mother attachment. *American Psychologist, 34*, 932–937.

Ainsworth, M.D.S. (1989). Attachments beyond infancy. *American Psychologist, 44*, 709–716.

Ainsworth, M.D.S., & Bell, S.M. (1970). Attachment, exploration, and separation: Illustrated by the behavior of one-year-olds in a strange situation. *Child Development, 41*, 49–67.

Albert, A., & Bulcroft, K. (1987). Pets and urban life. *Anthrozoös, 1*, 9–25.

Albert, A., & Bulcroft, K. (1988). Pets, families, and the life course. *Journal of Marriage and the Family, 50*, 543–552.

Andrews, P.W., Gangestad, S.W., & Matthews, D. (2002). Adaptationism–how to carry out an exaptationist program. *Behavioral and Brain Sciences, 25*, 489–553.

Archer, J. (1992). *Ethology and human development.* Savage, MD: Barnes & Noble.

Archer, J. (1997). Why do people love their pets? *Evolution and Human Behavior, 18*, 237–259.

Archer, J. (1999). *The nature of grief.* London & New York: Routledge.

Archer, J. (2001a). Grief from an evolutionary perspective. In M.S. Stroebe, W. Stroebe, R.O. Hansson, & H. Schut (Eds.), *Handbook of Bereavement Research: Consequences, Coping and Care* (pp. 263–283). Washington, DC: APA.

Archer, J. (2001b). Broad and narrow perspectives in grief theory: A comment on Bonanno and Kaltman (1999). *Psychological Bulletin, 127*, 554–560.

Archer, J. (2006). Testosterone and human aggression: An evaluation of the challenge hypothesis. *Neuroscience and Biobehavioral Reviews, 30*, 319–335.

Archer, J. (2008). Theories of grief: Past, present and future perspectives. In M. Stroebe, R.O. Hansson, & W. Stroebe (Eds.), *Handbook of Bereavement Research and Practice: 21st Century Perspectives* (pp. 45–65). Washington, DC: APA.

Archer, J., & Ireland, J.L. (in press). The development and factor structure of a questionnaire measure of the strength of attachment to pet dogs. *Anthrozoös.*

Archer, J., & Monton, S. (in press). Preferences for infant facial features in pet dogs and cats. *Ethology.*

Archer, J., & Winchester, J. (1993). Bereavement following death of a pet. *British Journal of Psychology, 85*, 259–271.

Baker, M.E. (1997). Steroid receptor phylogeny and vertebrate origins. *Molecular and Cellular Endocrinology, 135*, 101–107.

Bartholomew, K., & Horowitz, L.M. (1991). Attachment styles among young adults: A test of a four-category model. *Journal of Personality and Social Psychology, 61*, 226–244.

Beck, L., & Madresh, E.A. (2008). Romantic partners and four-legged friends: An extension of the attachment theory to relationships with pets. *Anthrozoös, 21*, 43–56.

Berryman, J.C., Howells, K., & Lloyd-Evans, M. (1985). Pet owner attitudes to pets and people: A psychological study. *The Veterinary Record, 117*, 659–661.

Bodsworth, W., & Coleman, G.J. (2001). Child-companion animal attachment bonds in single and two-parent families. *Anthrozoös, 14*, 216–223.

Bonas, S., McNicholas, J., & Collis, G.M. (2000). Pets in the network of family relationships: An empirical study. In A.L. Podberscek, E.S. Paul, & J.A. Serpell (Eds.), *Companion animals and us: Exploring the relationship between people and pets* (pp. 209–236). New York: Cambridge University Press.

Bonanno, G.A. (2004). Loss, trauma and human resilience: Have we underestimated the human capacity to thrive after extremely aversive events? *American Psychologist, 59*, 20–28.

Bowlby, J. (1958). The nature of the child's tie to his mother. *International Journal of Psychoanalysis, 39*, 350–373.

Bowlby, J. (1969). *Attachment and loss, volume 1. Attachment.* London: The Hogarth Press & Institute of Psychoanalysis. (Penguin edition, 1971).

Bowlby, J. (1980). *Attachment and loss, volume 3. Loss: Sadness and depression.* London: The Hogarth Press and Institute of Psychoanalysis. (Penguin edition, 1981).

Bryant, G.A., & Barrett, H.C. (2007). Recognizing intentions in infant-directed speech: Evidence for universals. *Psychological Science, 18*, 746–751.

Burnham, D., Kitamura, C., & Vollmer-Conna (2002). What's new, pussycat? On talking to babies and animals. *Science, 296*, 1435.

Buss, D.M. (2008). *Evolutionary psychology: The new science of the mind*, 3rd ed. Boston, MA: Pearson/Allyn and Bacon.

Buss, D. M., Haselton, M.G., Shackelford, T.K., Bleske, A.L., & Wakefield, J.C. (1998). Adaptations, exaptations, and spandrels. *American Psychologist, 53*, 533–548.

Cannon, W.B. (1929). *Bodily changes in pain, hunger, fear and rage*, 2nd ed. New York: Appleton.

Carmack, J. (1985). The effects on family members and functioning after death of a pet. *Marriage and Family Reviews, 8*, 149–161.

Clutton-Brock, J. (1977). Man-made dogs. *Science, 197*, 1340–1342.

Clutton-Brock, J. (1981). *Domesticated animals from early times.* London: British Museum (Natural history).

Clutton-Brock, J. (1995). Origins of the dog: Domestication and early history. In J. Serpell (Ed.), *The domestic dog: Its evolution, behaviour and interactions with people* (pp. 7–20). Cambridge, UK: Cambridge University Press.

Colby, P. M., & Sherman, A. (2002). Attachment styles impact on pet visitation effectiveness. *Anthrozoös, 15*, 150–165.

Crawford, E.K., Worsham, N.L., & Swinehart, E.R. (2006). Benefits derived from companion animals, and the use of the term "attachment." *Anthrozoös, 19*, 98–112.

Cunningham, M.R., Barbee, A.P., & Pike, C.L. (1990). What do women want? Facial metric assessment of multiple motives in the perception of male facial physical attractiveness. *Journal of Personality and Social Psychology, 59*, 61–72.

Daly, M., & Wilson, M.I. (1980). Discriminative parental solicitude: A biological perspective. *Journal of Marriage and the Family, 42*, 277–288.

Daly, M., & Wilson, M.I. (1988). The Darwinian psychology of discriminative parental solicitude. *Nebraska Symposium on Motivation, 35*, 91–144.

Dawkins, R., & Krebs, J.R. (1979). Arms races between and within species. *Proceedings of the Royal Society of London B 205*, 489–511.

Davies, N.B., & Brooke, M. (1988). Cuckoos versus reed warblers: Adaptations and counteradaptations. *Animal Behaviour, 36*, 262–284.

Davis, S.J.M., & Valla, F.R. (1978). Evidence for the domestication of the dog 12, 000 years ago in the Natufian of Israel. *Nature, 276*, 608–610.

Dwyer, F., Bennett, P.C., & Coleman, G.J. (2006). Development of the Monash Dog Owner Relationship Scale (MDORS). *Anthrozoös, 19*, 243–156.

Eastwick, P.W. (2009). Beyond the Pleistocene: Using phylogeny and constraint to inform the evolutionary psychology of human mating. *Psychological Bulletin, 135*, 794–821.

El-Alayli, A., Lystad, A.L., Webb, S.R., Hollingsworth, S.L., & Ciolli, J.L. (2006). Reigning cats and dogs: A pet-enhancement bias and its link to pet attachment, pet-self similarity, self-enhancement, and well-being. *Basic and Applied Social Psychology, 28*, 131–143.

Epley, N., Akalis, S., Waytz, A., & Cacioppo, J.T. (2008). Creating social connection through inferential reproduction: Loneliness and perceived agency in gadgets, gods, and greyhounds. *Psychological Science, 10*, 114–120.

Epley, N., Waytz, A., Akalis, S., & Cacioppo, J.T. (2008). When we need a human: Motivational determinants of anthropomorphism. *Social Cognition, 26*, 143–155.

Epley, N., Waytz, A., & Cacioppo, J.T. (2007). On seeing human: A three-factor theory of anthropomorphism. *Psychological Review, 114*, 864–886.

Falk, D. (2004). Prelinguistic evolution in early hominins: Whence motherese? *Behavioral and Brain Sciences, 27*, 491–541.

Fidler, M., Light, P., & Costell, A. (1996). Describing dog behavior psychologically: Pet owners versus non-owners. *Anthrozoös, 9*, 196–200.

Fraley, R.C., & Shaver, P.R. (2000). Adult romantic attachment: Theoretical developments, emerging controversies, and unanswered questions. *Review of General Psychology, 4*, 132–154.

Gardner, B.T., & Wallach, L. (1965). Shapes of figures identified as a baby's head. *Perceptual and Motor Skills, 20*, 135–142.

Gerwolls, M.K., & Labott, S.M. (1994). Adjustment to the death of a companion animal. *Anthrozoös, 9*, 172–187.

Gilby, A., McNicholas, J., & Collis, G.M. (2007). A longitudinal test of the belief that companion animal ownership can help reduce loneliness. *Anthrozoös, 20*, 345–353.

Goodwin, D., Bradshaw, J.W.S., & Wickens, S.M. (1997). Paedomorphosis affects agonistic visual signals of domestic dogs. *Animal Behaviour, 53*, 297–304.

Gould, S.J. (1980). *The panda's thumb*. New York: Norton.

Gould, S.J., & Lewontin, R.C. (1979). The spandrels of San Marco and the Panglossian paradigm: A critique of the adaptationist programme. *Proceedings of the Royal Society of London, Series B, 205*, 581–598.

Gould, S.J., & Vrba, E.S. (1982). Exaptation–a missing term in the science of form. *Paleobiology, 8*, 4–15.

Griffin, D., & Bartholomew, K. (1994a). The metaphysics of measurement: The case of adult attachment. In K. Bartholomew & D. Perlman (Eds.), *Advances in personal relationships, vol. 5: Attachment processes in adulthood* (pp. 17–52). London: Kingsley.

Griffin, D., & Bartholomew, K. (1994b). Models of the self and other: Fundamental dimensions underlying measures of adult attachment. *Journal of Personality and Social Psychology, 67*, 430–445.

Hazan C., & Shaver, P. (1987). Romantic love conceptualized as an attachment process. *Journal of Personality and Social Psychology, 52*, 511–524.

Hinde, R.A. (1982). *Ethology*. Oxford, UK: Oxford University Press.

Hinde, R.A., & Barden, L.A. (1985). The evolution of the teddy bear. *Animal Behaviour, 33*, 1371–1373.

Hirsh-Pasek, K., & Treiman, R. (1982). Doggerel: Motherese in a new context. *Journal of Child Language, 9*, 229–237.

Hofstede, G. (2001). *Culture's consequences: International differences in work-related values* (2nd ed.). Thousand Oaks, CA: Sage.

Holcomb, R., Williams, R.C., & Richards, P.S. (1985). The elements of attachment: Relationship maintenance and intimacy. *Journal of the Delta Society, 2*, 28–34.

Johnson, T.P., Garrity, T.F., & Stallones, L. (1992). Psychometric evaluation of the Lexington Attachment to Pets Scale (LAPS). *Anthrozoös, 5*, 160–175.

Krause-Parello, C.A. (2008). The mediating effect of pet attachment support between loneliness and general health in older females living in the community. *Journal of Community Health Nursing, 25*, 1–14.

Katcher, A.H., Friedmann, E., Goodman, M., & Goodman, L. (1983). Men, women, and dogs. *Californian Veterinarian, 2*, 14–16.

Kosfeld, M., Heinrichs, M., Zak, P.J., Fischbacher, U., & Fehr, E.H. (2005). Oxytocin increases trust in humans. *Nature, 435*, 673–676.

Langois, J.H., Ritter, J.M., Casey, R.J., & Sawin, D.B. (1995). Infant attractiveness predicts maternal behaviors and attitudes. *Developmental Psychology, 31*, 464–472.

Livingston, R.W., & Pearce, N.A. (2009). The teddy-bear effect: Does having a baby face benefit black Chief Executive Officers? *Psychological Science, 20*, 1229–1236.

Lorenz, K. (1943). Die angeborenen Formen möglicher Erfahrung. *Zeitschrift für Tierpsychologie, 5*, 235–409.

Lorenz, K. (1950/1971). Part and Parcel in Animal and Human Societies.' In K. Lorenz (R. Martin, Trans.), *Studies in animal and human behaviour, volume 2* (pp. 115–195). London: Methuen.

McComb, K., Taylor, A.M., Wilson, C., & Charlton, B.D. (2009). The cry embedded within the purr. *Current Biology, 19*, R507–508.

McFarland, D. (1981). *The Oxford companion to animal behaviour*. Oxford, UK: Oxford University Press.

McNicholas, J., Gilby, A., Rennie, A., Ahmedzai, S., Dono, J-A., & Ormerod, E. (2005). Pet ownership and human health: A brief review of evidence and issues. *British Medical Journal, 331*, 1252–1254.

Mason, J.W. (1968a). Organization of the multiple endocrine responses to avoidance in the monkey. *Psychosomatic Medicine, 30*, 774–790.

Mason, J.W. (1968b). "Over-all" hormonal balance as a key to endocrine organization. *Psychosomatic Medicine, 30*, 791–808.

Miller, S.C., Kennedy, C., DeVoe, D., Hickey, M., Nelson, T., & Kogan, L. (2009). An examination of changes in oxytocin levels in men and women before and after interaction with a bonded dog. *Anthrozoös, 22*, 31–42.

Mitchell, R.W. (2001). Americans' talk to dogs: Similarities and differences with talk to humans. *Research on Language and Social Interaction, 34*, 183–210.

Mitchell, R.W., & Edmonson, E. (1999). Functions of repetitive talk to dogs during play: Control, conversation or planning? *Society and Animals, 7*, 55–81.

Mithen, S. (1996). *The prehistory of the mind: A search for the origins of art, religion and science*. London: Thames & Hudson.

Musil, R. (1970). Domestication of the dog already in the Magdalenian. *Anthropologie, 8*, 87–88.

Nagasawa, M., Kikusui, T., Onaka, T., & Ohta, M. (2009). Dog's gaze at its owner increases owner's urinary oxytocin during social interaction. *Hormones and Behavior, 55*, 434–441.

Nakajima, S., Yamamoto, M., & Yoshimoto, N. (2009). Dogs look like their owners: Replications with racially homogeneous owner portraits. *Anthrozoös, 22*, 173–181.

Netting, F.E., Wilson, C.C., & New, J.C. (1987). The human-animal bond: Implications for practice. *Social Work, 32*, 60–64.

Odendaal, J.S.J., & Meintjes, R.A. (2002). Neurophysiological correlates of affiliative behavior between humans and dogs. *The Veterinary Journal, 165*, 296–301.

Parkes, C.M. (1972). *Bereavement: Studies of grief in adult life*. London and New York: Tavistock.

Payne, C., & Jaffe, K. (2005). Self seeks like: Many humans choose their dog pets following roles used for assortative mating. *Journal of Ethology, 23*, 15–18.

Poresky, R.H., Hendrix, C., Mosier, J., & Samuelson, M.L. (1987). The companion animal bonding scale: Internal reliability and construct validity. *Psychological Reports, 60*, 743–746.

Prato-Previde, E., Custance, D.M., Spiezio, C., & Sabatini, F. (2003). Is the dog-human relationship an attachment bond? An observational study using Ainsworth's Strange Situation. *Behaviour, 140*, 225–254.

Prato-Previde, E., Fallani, G., & Valsecchi, P. (2006). Gender differences in owners interacting with pet dogs: An observational study. *Ethology, 112*, 64–73.

Roy, M.M., & Christenfeld, N.J.S. (2004). Do dogs resemble their owners? *Psychological Science, 15*, 361–363.

Roy, M.M., & Christenfeld, N.J.S. (2005). Dogs still do resemble their owners. *Psychological Science, 16*, 743–744.

Selye, H. (1950). *The physiology and pathology of exposure to stress*. Montreal: Acta.

Scrpell, J. (1983). The personality of the dog and its influence on the pet-owner bond. In A.H. Katcher & A.M. Beck (Eds.), *New perspectives on our lives with companion animals* (pp. 57–65). Philadelphia: University of Pennsylvania Press.

Serpell, J. (1986). *In the company of animals*. Oxford: Blackwell.

Serpell, J. (1987). Pet-keeping in non-western societies. *Anthrozoös, 1*, 166–174.

Serpell, J.A. (1996) Evidence for an association between pet behavior and owner attachment levels. *Applied Animal Behaviour Science, 47*, 49–60.

Serpell, J. (2003). Anthropomorphism and anthropomorphic selection—beyond the "cute response." *Society and Animals, 11*, 83–100.

Shubin, N. (2007). *Your inner fish*. New York: Pantheon.

Sims, V.K., & Chin, M.G. (2002). Responsiveness and perceived intelligence as predictors of speech addressed to cats. *Anthrozoös, 15*, 166–177.

Smith, S.L. (1983). Interaction between pet dog and family members: An ethological study. In A.H. Katcher & A.M. Beck (Eds.), *New perspectives on our lives with companion animals* (pp. 29–36). Philadelphia: University of Pennsylvania Press.

Sprengelmeyer, R., Perrett, D.I., Fagan, E.C., Cornwell, R.E., Lobmaier, J.S., Sprengelmeyer, A., et al. (2009). The cutest little baby face: A hormonal link to sensitivity to cuteness in infant faces. *Psychological Science, 20*, 149–154.

Stallones, L., Johnson, T.P., Garrity, T.F., & Marx, M.B. (1990). Quality of attachment to companion animals among U.S. adults 21 to 64 years of age. *Anthrozoös, 3*, 171–175.

Staats, S., Miller, D., Carnot, M.J., Rada, K., & Turnes, J. (1996). The Miller-Rada Commitment to Pets Scale. *Anthrozoös, 9*, 88–94.

Sternglanz, S.H., Gray, J.L., & Murakami, M. (1977). Adult preferences for infantile facial features: An ethological approach. *Animal Behaviour, 25*, 108–115.

Theodoridou, A, Rowe, A.C., Penton-Voak, I.S., & Rogers, P.J. (2009). Oxytocin and social perception: Ocytocin increases perceived facial trustworthiness and attractiveness. *Hormones and Behavior, 56*, 128–132.

Tinbergen, N. (1951). *The study of instinct*. New York: Oxford University Press.

Tinbergen, N. (1963). On the aims and methods of ethology. *Zeitschrift für Tierpsychologie, 20*, 410–433.

Topál, J., Gácsi, M., Miklósi, A., Virányi, Z., Kubinyi, E., & Csányi, V. (2005). Attachment to humans: A comparative study on hand-reared wolves and differently socialized dog puppies. *Animal Behaviour, 70*, 1367–1375.

Topál, J., Miklósi, A., Csányi, V., & Dóka, A. (1998). Attachment behavior in dogs (*Canis familiaris*): A new application of Ainsworth's (1969) Strange Situation Test. *Journal of Comparative Psychology, 112*, 219–229.

Triandis, H.C. (1972). *The analysis of subjective culture*. New York: Wiley.

Triandis, H.C. (1995). *Individualism and collectivism*. Boulder, CO: Westview.

Turner, D.C. (1991). The ethology of the human-cat relationship. *Schweizer Archive für Tierheilkunde, 133*, 63–70.

Vleck, C.M., & Brown, J.L. (1999). Testosterone and social and reproductive behavior in *Aphelocoma* jays. *Animal Behaviour, 58*, 943–951.

Wells, J.C.K. (2007). The thrifty phenotype as an adaptive maternal effect. *Biological Reviews, 82*, 143–172.

Wickler, W. (1968). *Mimicry*. London: Weidenfeld & Nicholson.

Wilson, E.O. (1975). *Sociobiology: The new synthesis*. Cambridge, MA: Harvard University Press.

Wingfield, J.C., Hegner, R.E., Dufty Jr., A.M., & Ball, G.F. (1990). The "challenge hypothesis": Theoretical implications for patterns of testosterone secretion, mating systems, and breeding strategies. *American Naturalist, 136*, 829–846.

Zebrowitz, L.A. (1997). *Reading faces: Window to the soul?* Boulder, CO: Westview Press.

Zebrowitz, L.A., & Montepare, J.M. (1992). Impressions of babyfaced individuals across the life span. *Developmental Psychology, 28*, 1143–1152.

Zebrowitz, L.A., Olson, K., & Hoffman, K. (1993). Stability of babyfacedness and attractiveness across the life span. *Journal of Personality and Social Psychology, 64*, 453–466.

CHAPTER 17

Pets in the Family: An Evolutionary Perspective

James A. Serpell *and* Elizabeth S. Paul

Abstract

Pets have become such a common component of modern family life that we tend to take them for granted. Nevertheless, from an evolutionary standpoint, pets present us with a paradox comparable to—though even more puzzling than—that posed by the phenomenon of adoption. In the latter case, one can at least argue that adoptive parents may derive deferred fitness benefits from the future contribution of adopted children to the family economy (Kramer, 2005). But in the case of adopted pets, such contributions appear to be minimal at best, whereas the level of investment in their care and sustenance is sometimes considerable. The paradox further intensifies when one considers that pet keeping is not confined to modern, affluent societies, but is widespread among subsistence hunters and horticulturalists whose opportunities to engage in nonfitness enhancing behavior would appear to be much more constrained. This chapter critically examines theories that purport to explain how pet keeping evolved and why it continues to persist and flourish in a wide range of cultures. Given the current state of knowledge, few firm conclusions can be drawn at this time regarding the possible adaptive consequences of pet keeping. However, it is possible to highlight future areas of research that may help to illuminate the functional significance (if any) of this intriguing behavior.

Keywords: evolution; mutualism; pets; pet keeping; adoption; human-animal interaction

Introduction

Any discussion of the phenomenon of pet keeping, especially from an evolutionary perspective, needs to begin with a reasonable working definition of the word *pet*. The *Oxford English Dictionary* (OED) defines a pet as: "Any animal that is domesticated or tamed and kept as a favorite, or treated with indulgence and fondness." The OED thus tends to make a distinction between nonhuman animals (henceforth "animals") kept primarily for social, emotional, or sentimental reasons (i.e., pets) and those that are kept mainly for economic or practical purposes (i.e., working animals, livestock, research animals). Of course, the two categories frequently overlap in practice, as in the case of working guide dogs or sheepdogs, for example. However, the distinction remains critical to the present discussion because, although it is easy to account for the economic exploitation of animals using classical evolutionary theory, it is far less easy to explain the practice of keeping animals purely as "favorites," or of treating them with "indulgence and fondness."

In most modern, industrial societies, pets—in the OED sense of the word—have become a ubiquitous feature of family life. According to various opinion polls and surveys, between 86% and 97% of pet-owning Americans consider their pets to be members of the family (American Animal Hospital Association, 1996; Associated Press, 2009; Barker & Barker, 1988; Cain, 1985; Catanzaro, 1984; Harris Interactive, 2007; Pew Research Center, 2006), and up to 50% report that their pets are, "just as much a part of the family as any other person in the household" (Associated Press, 2009).

Further evidence suggests that pets fulfill primarily childlike roles within families. In one study, 75% of pet owners surveyed considered their pets akin to children, and nearly one-third of participants in another survey indicated that they felt closer to the family dog than to any other member of the family (American Animal Hospital Association, 1996; Barker & Barker, 1988). The familial status of pets is also confirmed by the kinds of things that people do with their animal companions. For example, 69% of American pet owners allow their pets to sleep in bed with them, and nearly two-thirds give them holiday and/or birthday gifts (Harris Interactive, 2007).

From an evolutionary perspective, the prevalence and status of pets within families presents an intriguing paradox. Expressed in simple terms, pet keeping entails a significant investment of time, energy, and resources on the part of pet owners, and yet appears to confer no obvious benefits in terms of their survival or genetic fitness. The goal of this chapter is to explore the extent and significance of the use of pets as family members in both Western and non-Western societies, while also examining different theories that have been proposed to explain the evolutionary origins and functional significance of this seemingly paradoxical behavior.

Extent of the Pet Keeping Phenomenon

Pet keeping is not a rare or unusual behavior. According to recent surveys, there are now about 75 million pet dogs in America living in roughly 44.8 million homes, 90.5 million cats in 38.4 million homes, 150 million pet fish in 15 million homes, and many millions more ferrets, rabbits, guinea pigs, hamsters, rats, mice, gerbils, and birds of various kinds, as well as a wide assortment of pet reptiles and amphibians (American Pet Products Manufacturers' Association [APPMA], 2008). The figures for the European Union (EU) are more modest but still impressive: 41 million dogs and 47 million cats distributed among 55 million households, and some striking differences in per capita numbers and proportions of pet animals within the different EU countries. Worldwide, the pet population has expanded recently and rapidly. The findings of market research suggest that the combined cat and dog population of the United States has increased by a factor of four since the mid-1960s; twice the rate of growth of the human population. Pet keeping is now a majority activity in the United States, with 63% of U.S. households owning at least one pet, and 45% owning more than one.

Although pet keeping seems to have achieved unprecedented levels of popularity in the last few decades, the practice of treating particular animals with "indulgence and fondness" appears to have ancient roots. Some of the oldest known archaeological remains of domestic wolf-dogs from the late Paleolithic of Europe and North America (8,000–14,000 years ago) were found buried together with humans in a manner indicative of strong mutual bonds of attachment (Benecke, 1987; Davis & Valla, 1978; Morey, 1992, 2006). Similarly, the discovery of nonindigenous cat remains buried in association with humans on the Mediterranean island of Cyprus about 9,500 years ago provides evidence that humans were taking tame wildcats with them on ocean voyages several thousand years before these animals became household pets or the objects of religious veneration in ancient Egypt (Malek, 1993; Serpell, 2000; Vigne et al., 2004).

The notion that Paleolithic humans may have been in the habit of capturing and taming wild animals and keeping them as pets is consistent with the observed behavior of more recent hunting and gathering peoples. According to numerous reports by explorers and anthropologists, pet keeping among subsistence hunting and horticultural peoples is the norm rather than the exception, and is typically characterized by intense emotional attachments to the animals involved, as well as strong moral taboos against killing or eating them. This is even the case when these animals belong to species that are hunted routinely for food (Erikson, 1987, 2000; Serpell, 1989). Furthermore, as with pets in industrialized countries, the owner–pet relationship among these hunting societies is typically understood as analogous to that between parent and child (Basso, 1973; Crocker, 1977; Fausto, 1999). In some cases, the connection is fairly explicit. Among the Bororo people of central Brazil, ownership of pet macaws (*Ara* sp.) is almost entirely limited to women, and the standard Bororo explanation for why some households keep more of these pets than others is that these are the homes of women who have previously lost many children (Crocker, 1977).

Pictorial and documentary evidence further suggests that pet keeping has been practiced continuously throughout human history, although its popularity has waxed and waned somewhat unpredictably over time and from place to place (Serpell, 1996). In Europe and colonial North America, pet keeping did not become widespread until the 18th century. Medieval and Renaissance moralists and theologians seem to have regarded most forms of intimacy between people and animals as morally suspect, and generally condemned the practice of keeping animals exclusively for companionship. Consequently, pet keeping remained chiefly the province of the upper classes and ruling élite until the end of the early modern period, when the emergence of both Enlightenment attitudes and an urban middle class saw the gradual spread of pets into all sectors of Western society (Grier, 2006; Harwood, 1928; Ritvo, 1988; Salisbury, 1994; Serpell & Paul, 1994; Thomas, 1983).

The Costs of Pet Keeping

In modern, industrialized societies, pets are not only tremendously popular and widespread, but also represent a significant cost to those who care for them. The average lifetime monetary costs of dog and cat ownership in the United States has recently been estimated at $13,330 and $8,506,[1] respectively, for an animal with a 13-year lifespan. By the end of 2010, Americans will be spending around $50 billion annually on their pets, chiefly on prepared foods and accessories (APPMA, 2008). Income also appears to be a limiting factor in the spread of pet keeping. According to some surveys, almost 70% of U.S. adults with annual incomes over $100,000 own pets compared with only 45% of those earning less than $30,000 (Pew Research Center, 2006). In addition to their economic impact, pets may also inflict emotional costs on both their owners and others. A significant number of pet owners experience severe and prolonged grief reactions following the deaths of their pets (Archer, 1997), and badly behaved pets can be a source of considerable stress and conflict within families, and among neighbors and friends (Voith, 2009).

Pet keeping also imposes costs on society. The U.S. Centers for Disease Control and Prevention estimates that 4.5 million Americans are bitten by pet dogs each year, of which nearly 900,000 require medical attention (Centers for Disease Control and Prevention, 2008). Pets are also sources of a variety of zoonotic diseases, as well as a common cause of allergies and asthma (Mandhane et al., 2009; Nafstad et al., 2001; Robertson & Thompson, 2002). The environmental impact of pet keeping on this scale may also be considerable. In their recent book, Vale and Vale (2009) calculate that a medium-size family dog eats around 360 pounds of meat and 210 pounds of cereal annually, roughly equivalent to the energy consumed by driving a 4×4 SUV 6,200 miles a year, including the energy required to build the vehicle. According to another estimate, America's 75 million pet dogs may consume as many calories as roughly 35 million people. Producing this much food would require the equivalent of approximately 20,000 square miles of productive farmland (Coppinger & Coppinger, 2001).

All of these statistics are derived from relatively affluent, developed countries where people can afford to invest substantial time and resources in a variety of superficially non–fitness enhancing activities, whether visiting casinos or shopping for fashionable clothes. Unfortunately, there appear to be no quantitative studies of pet-related investment among less affluent subsistence hunting or horticultural societies in which pet keeping is also common. It is apparent, however, that some individuals in such societies expend relatively large amounts of time and effort on their pets. For instance, Serpell (1996, pp. 61–66) cites numerous reports of women breastfeeding pets alongside their own infants, carefully premasticating fibrous plant foods to hand-feed pet birds and rodents, or spending several hours each day catching tiny fish to feed pet kingfishers.

Evolutionary Origins of Pet Keeping

Existing theories of pet keeping usually fail to distinguish between the evolutionary origins of this behavior and its possible functional consequences. The distinction is important because the two approaches involve different levels of analysis. Arguments about origins are concerned with a trait's initial appearance and spread within a population, whereas accounts based on function refer to the maintenance of a trait due to its current (or recent) effects on individual fitness (Emlen et al., 1991; Tinbergen, 1963). According to Williams (1966), a trait or a behavioral predisposition should only be considered an adaptation if it has been modified during its evolutionary history in ways that enhance its effectiveness as measured by fitness consequences to the performer.

The evolutionary origins of pet keeping are of particular interest because this behavior seems to be a manifestation of altruism in its purest form. That is, it enhances the survival and reproductive success of biologically unrelated animals while apparently contributing nothing to the fitness of their human owners. Pet keeping therefore appears to violate the assumptions of both natural and kin selection, according to which individuals should seek to maximize either their own survival and reproductive

---

[1] http://www.examiner.com/x-9729-Cats-Examiner~y2009m8d4-Cats-cost-less-to-own-than-dogs-research-firm-says

success and/or that of their genetic relatives, to an extent proportional to the latter's degree of relatedness and the relative fitness costs thereby incurred by the donor (Hamilton, 1964). In these respects, pet keeping shares much with both alloparenting and adoption—two behaviors that are widespread among birds and mammals, and which are sometimes also directed toward the infants and young of unrelated parents (Cäsar & Young, 2008; Riedman, 1982). Indeed, given the similarities, a reasonable alternative term for "pet keeping" within evolutionary psychology might be "cross-species adoption."

Although cross-species adoption is certainly unusually prevalent in *Homo s. sapiens*, it is not without precedent in the animal kingdom. Numerous examples of comparable behavior have been reported in both captive and free-ranging mammals,[2] and in some instances, these relationships are surprisingly strong and enduring. Izar et al. (2006), for example, describe a remarkable case of an infant marmoset (*Callithrix* sp.) adopted by a group of free-living capuchin monkeys (*Cebus* sp.) in Brazil who was physically carried and cared for by two different adoptive "mother" monkeys for a period of 14 months before eventually disappearing from the group.

The practice of adopting unrelated infants of either one's own or another species probably results from errors in the evolved mechanisms responsible for mother–infant bonding and care (Maestripieri, 2001). As Daly and Wilson (1987, p. 93) put it: "Some examples of misdirected 'parental' nurture surely represent nothing more than rare 'mistakes' generated by motivational mechanisms that are usually effective in promoting fitness." If this interpretation is correct, humans are evidently especially prone to these types of errors. Silk (1990, p. 39) explains this error-proneness in terms of "innate psychological predispositions" that promote an intense attraction to infants, as well as a lack of inborn kin recognition systems or stereotyped maternal bonding processes. In Silk's view, humans are unusually susceptible because, in the Pleistocene environments in which they evolved, there was little opportunity for human females to adopt nonkin and therefore few evolutionary pressures to develop mechanisms to discriminate between related and unrelated young. Hrdy (2009) has taken these ideas further by arguing that hypernurturing behavior, together with theory of mind and the capacity to empathize and cooperate with others are adaptations that facilitate cooperative breeding (see also Burkart et al., 2009). One could also apply signal detection theory (Green & Swets, 1966) to argue that overly discriminating systems of kin recognition might have been disadvantageous to our ancestors, if the costs of negative errors (not offering care to the offspring of kin) were significantly greater than the costs of positive errors (occasionally offering care to the infants of nonkin or other species). If this were the case, pet keeping could have evolved and spread as long as it involved relatively minimal costs to those who engaged in the behavior.

On a somewhat different tack, Serpell (1996, 2003) has suggested that both pet keeping and animal domestication are secondary by-products of the evolved human ability to use "reflexive consciousness" or theory of mind as a model for understanding the mental lives of others (Humphrey, 1983). This trait is believed to have evolved in the context of human social relationships, but due to obvious phylogenetic similarities it can also be applied to the task of understanding the minds of nonhumans. The archaeologist Steven Mithen (1996) refers to this specific application as *anthropomorphic thinking*, and he argues persuasively that it enabled our Paleolithic ancestors to become more successful hunters by conferring on them the ability to "think like" and therefore anticipate the behavior of their prey. It may also have had other far-reaching consequences: By enabling our ancestors to attribute humanlike thoughts, feelings, motivations, and beliefs to other animals, it opened the door to the incorporation of some animals into human families and social groups, first as pets and eventually as domestic dependents (Serpell, 2003). To some extent, this hypothesis and the previous one are complementary. The theory of hyperinclusive parental motivation helps to account for the initial human tendency to adopt, socialize, and care for young animals, while the concept of anthropomorphic thinking helps to explain why these same animals might have been tolerated and accepted as members of human families long after they passed the infantile stage of dependence.

Both of the above examples imply that pet keeping originated as an unavoidable side effect of other adaptive traits. Recently, Herzog (2010) has suggested that this behavior might have emerged and spread without any adaptive associations whatsoever. He argues that pet keeping may be a *meme* (Dawkins, 1976)—a unit of cultural selection—a relatively inconsequential but highly contagious

---

[2] http://daughterearth.blogspot.com/2008/12/cross-species-adoptions.html

mental virus that has spread itself through certain human populations by a process of social copying. In support of this idea, he cites evidence that pet keeping, and even the preference for particular types of pets, tends to run in families; that different nationalities, cultures, and ethnic groups vary widely in their liking for pets; and the fact that the practice once adopted can sometimes spread very rapidly within societies in which pet keeping was previously rare or unknown. Memes can also spread, at least in the short term, even when they are manifestly disadvantageous to the individuals who adopt them. Although it is hard to refute the meme theory of pet keeping, it is also difficult to explain why the cultural transmission of pet keeping would have persisted over thousands of years of human history in the absence of any obvious selective benefit to those who adopted this superficially costly behavior.

Functional Consequences of Pet Keeping

When framed in terms of its function, pet keeping can be explained using a variety of both adaptive and nonadaptive arguments (see Table 17.1). At the core of each of these is an attempt to explain the apparent paradox of humans choosing, at not inconsiderable cost to themselves, to care for and provide sustenance to individuals who are neither their own kin, nor even their own species. Central to this issue is the question of whether, at the level of the inclusive fitness of the humans concerned, the benefits of pet keeping outweigh the costs. Below, we consider various functional theories and hypotheses that have been proposed to explain this behavior. Our aim is to consider current evidence in favor of each proposal, and to suggest where further studies may be needed to distinguish between competing possibilities. Functional consideration of the phenomenon of pet ownership is particularly interesting because it highlights the interaction between ultimate and proximate causes of caregiving behavior. Humans, like other animals, do not always behave as optimally as some theorists might like to expect. Not only are we always likely to be at some stage within the process of adaptation, rather than at any notional endpoint of it, we are also inevitably constrained to some extent by the mechanisms (e.g., physiological, neural, behavioral) that natural selection has already provided us with (McNamara & Houston, 2009). When we care for, love, and trust animals as if they are kin, are we behaving against our better interests within a system that has evolved for other purposes Or, is our interest in pets in fact more fine-tuned, less paradoxical, and more advantageous to us than is at first apparent?

Table 17.1 Adaptive and Nonadaptive Hypotheses to Account for the Existence of Pet Keeping

Hypothesis	Benefits to Pet Owners	Fitness Effect (Adaptive) or Mechanism of Maintenance (Nonadaptive)
Adaptive		
Social Buffering	Enhanced survival	Keeping pets provides a social buffer against the negative health effects of psychosocial stress.
Parenting Experience	Increased reproductive success	Keeping pets provides experience of parenting/nurturing which translates into higher reproductive success when the pet owner breeds.
Honest Advertisement (of parenting ability)	Enhanced future probability of breeding	Keeping pets demonstrates an individual's parenting/nurturing skills, thereby increasing his/her probability of being chosen as a mate.
Nonadaptive		
Neutral trait	None	Pet keeping is a selectively neutral trait, maintained by genetic (and/or memetic) drift.
Social parasitism	None	Pet keeping is maintained as an unavoidable low-cost by-product of parental care motivations that are exploited by other species.

Modified from Emlen, S.T., Reeve, H.K., Sherman, P.W., Wrege, P.H., Ratnieks, F.L.W., & Shellman-Reeve, J. (1991). Adaptive versus nonadaptive explanations of behavior: The case of alloparental helping. *American Naturalist, 138*, 259–270, with permission.

Nonadaptive Consequences
PETS AS SOCIAL PARASITES

One solution to the evolutionary paradox posed by pet keeping is to argue that pets are essentially social parasites that manipulate the behavior of their owners (hosts) to obtain one-sided fitness benefits (Archer, 1997). Pets, according to this view, are comparable to avian brood parasites, such as cuckoos and cowbirds, which rely on their hosts' inability to distinguish reliably between its own and the imposter's eggs or nestlings. To the extent that this occurs frequently and is costly to the cuckolded species, an evolutionary "arms race" is likely to ensue (Dawkins & Krebs, 1979): Although the host becomes better at spotting and discriminating against the parasite's young, the young will become more similar to the young of the host to avoid detection. These kinds of changes have certainly taken place during the evolution of our most successful pet species—dogs and cats. And although neotenous morphological features, behavioral dependency, docility, sociality, playfulness, affection, and tactile responsiveness have all been enhanced and extended, often beyond infancy and into the adult animal (Coppinger et al., 1987; Dechambre, 1949; Fox, 1978; Lorenz, 1971; Sanefuji et al., 2007; Serpell, 2003), it is unclear who is being parasitized by whom in this context. For example, to improve their ability to serve as social companions, the vast majority of pet dogs and cats in the United States are surgically sterilized, while eugenicist breeding practices leave many of them crippled with genetic disease or anatomical deformities that are detrimental to their welfare and biological fitness (Arman, 2007; Serpell, 2003). It could therefore be argued that these animals are in fact the victims of *human* social parasitism rather than vice versa, and that the "cute" care-soliciting features of many pets are the products of selection for characteristics that enhance their ability to satisfy specific human needs.

The assumption that pet keeping confers no fitness advantages on humans may be false, or it may be that any parasitism by pets on humans is relatively weak, and that the costs incurred are far less severe than those inflicted on their hosts by brood parasites such as cuckoos or cowbirds. Alternatively, it may be more appropriate to characterize pet keeping as a case of *mutualism*, in which both human and pet derive benefits from the relationship comparable to those derived from interactions between, say, tropical cleaner-fish (*Labroides* sp.) and their clients/hosts (Herre et al., 1999; Johnstone & Bshary, 2002; Serpell, 2003). If this is the case, however, it is necessary to specify what the mutual benefits might be. Certainly, from the perspective of the pets, the advantages may seem obvious: By providing them with food, water, shelter, care, and protection from danger, humans have enabled these species to expand into a new ecological niche in which they have become hugely successful in evolutionary terms. But what kinds of benefits might people derive from the company of pets that could potentially offset the costs of caring for them?

Adaptive Consequences
PET KEEPING AS NONHUMAN SOCIAL SUPPORT

Social support is a theoretical construct that expresses the degree to which individuals are socially embedded and have a sense of belonging, obligation, and intimacy with others (Cobb, 1976; Eriksen, 1994; Schwarzer & Knoll, 2007). In practice, it tends to be broken down into different components, including (a) *emotional support*, or the sense of being able to turn to others for comfort in times of stress, the feeling of being cared for by others; (b) *social integration*, the feeling of being an accepted part of an established group or social network; (c) *esteem support*, the sense of receiving positive, self-affirming feedback from others regarding one's value, competence, abilities, or worth; (d) *practical, instrumental, or informational support*, the knowledge that others will provide financial, practical, or informational assistance when needed; and (e) *opportunities for nurturance and protection*, the sense of being needed or depended upon by others (Collis & McNicholas, 1998).

Social support (or a lack of it) is known to have a profound impact on human mental and physical health (House et al., 1988; Kiecolt-Glaser & Newton, 2001; Lim & Young, 2006; Monroe et al., 1986). A growing body of evidence has confirmed a strong positive link between social support and enhanced health and survival in humans. For example, social support factors have been shown to protect against cardiovascular disease and stroke, rheumatoid arthritis, diabetes, nephritis, pneumonia, and most forms of cancer, as well as depression, schizophrenia, and suicide (see e.g., Eriksen, 1994; Esterling et al., 1994; House, Landis, & Umberson, 1988; Kikusui et al., 2006; Sherbourne et al., 1992; Uchino, 2006; Vilhjalmson, 1993). The mechanisms underlying these effects of social support are still the subject of ongoing research, but at least some of the benefits appear to arise from the phenomenon of *social buffering*: That is, the capacity of supportive social relationships to buffer or ameliorate the deleterious health consequences of psychosocial stress. It is well established that prolonged psychosocial stress results in chronically elevated levels of circulating glucocorticoid (stress) hormones, and that these in turn can have a damaging impact on the immune system (Ader, Cohen, & Felten, 1995; Kikusui et al., 2006; Uchino, 2006). At least some of these effects of social support appear to be mediated by the neuropeptide hormones, oxytocin and vasopressin, which also play critical roles in the modulation of attachment behavior and social bonding in mammals (Donaldson & Young, 2008; Lim & Young, 2006). Furthermore, the elevation in oxytocin associated with pleasurable social interactions also has a down-regulating effect on the hypothalamic-pituitary-adrenal (HPA) axis that regulates the stress response (Heinrichs et al., 2003: Kikusui et al., 2006).

The findings of research on the role of pets in people's lives seem to fit this social support/social buffering paradigm. Pet owners, for example, have been shown to possess fewer physiological risk factors (high blood pressure; high serum triglycerides and cholesterol levels) for cardiovascular disease than nonowners, as well as exhibiting improved survival and longevity following heart attack (Anderson et al., 1992; Friedmann, Thomas, & Eddy, 2000; Garrity & Stallones, 1998). They also appear to be more resilient in the face of stressful life events, resulting in fewer health problems and fewer visits to doctors for medical care (Heady, 1998; Siegel, 1990). The acquisition of a new pet has been found to be associated with improvements in an owner's mental and physical health, and with sustained reductions in his or her tendency to overreact to stressful situations and stimuli (Allen et al., 1991, 2001; Serpell, 1991). Also, pet owners who report being very attached to their pets tend to report more benefits than those who are less attached, and dog owners tend to do better than cat owners, perhaps because the attachment to dogs, on average, is stronger (Freidmann & Thomas, 1995; Ory & Goldberg, 1983; Serpell, 1991).

These apparent links between pet keeping and human health are consistent with the view of pets serving as sources of social support (Collis & McNicholas, 1998; Garrity & Stallones, 1998; Serpell, 1996; Virués-Ortega & Buela-Casal, 2006). Additional recent findings suggest that the mechanisms underlying these effects of pet ownership may be similar to those thought to be responsible for the social buffering effect in human relationships. Two studies have demonstrated significant increases in plasma oxytocin levels in human subjects following interactions with their own (but not with unfamiliar) dogs (Odendaal & Meintjes, 2003; Miller et al., 2009), whereas another study detected significantly elevated levels of urinary oxytocin among dog owners who received greater amounts of visual attention (gaze) from their dogs in an experimental trial. When questioned, these owners also professed stronger attachments for their more attentive dogs (Nagasawa et al., 2009).

The social buffering idea may also go some way toward explaining the relatively recent and ongoing explosion in the popularity of pets among industrialized nations within the last 30–40 years. In the United States, for instance, the results of a variety of social and public health surveys have documented the gradual collapse or fragmentation of traditional social support systems, particularly since the 1960s. Such trends have been marked by a substantial rise in the number of people living alone, especially in urban areas; escalating divorce rates and an increase in the number of couples choosing to have fewer children or none at all (Morgan & Taylor, 2006); people spending less and less time socializing with their friends, or getting involved in their local communities; and families dispersing geographically, so that fewer close relatives now live within easy reach (Putnam, 2000). It seems plausible to argue in light of these trends that the recent growth of the pet population at least partly reflects people's attempts to augment their traditional support systems using pets (see also Archer, 1997).

Why humans should apparently be so dependent on the support of others to maintain their health and well-being in the face of psychosocial stress remains an important evolutionary question of its own. One can surmise that, ancestrally, the survival and reproductive advantages of being affiliated with closely knit social groups selected for individuals who experienced psychological distress when socially isolated and who were therefore highly motivated to seek out and maintain social attachments.

PETS AND THE ACQUISITION OF PARENTING SKILLS

Among *K*-selected animals, such as humans, in which females are only able to produce a limited number of offspring in a lifetime, and in which the young require a prolonged and intensive period of parental investment, parenting abilities are likely to have a disproportionate impact on the survival and reproductive success of each offspring. In such species, natural selection will therefore tend to favor the evolution of traits or behaviors that improve parenting skills (Hrdy, 2009; Silk, 1990). Among primates living in naturalistic social groups, for example, first-time mothers are more likely than multiparous mothers to neglect and abandon their infants or handle them clumsily. Conversely, the probability of infant abandonment is greatly reduced as females give birth to successive infants, and the quality of their maternal care typically improves as well. The experience of interacting with younger siblings or other females' infants during the juvenile period can also improve the quality of maternal care and the probability of infant survival of first-time mothers. In vervet monkeys (*Cercopithecus aethiops*), first-time mothers who had greater infant handling experience as juveniles were more likely to be competent mothers, and their infants had a higher probability of survival than did females with less juvenile experience with infants (Fairbanks, 1990; Maestripieri & Roney, 2006).

Based on evidence of this kind, several authors have proposed that the widespread and intense interest in infants shown by juvenile female primates (including humans), as well as phenomena such as alloparenting and the adoption of sometimes unrelated infants, represent adaptations for facilitating the acquisition of parenting skills (Hrdy, 2005, 2009; Maestripieri & Roney, 2006; Riedman, 1982). Identical arguments can also be applied to instances of cross-species adoption (pet keeping), if it is assumed that the experience gained from nurturing and caring for a young nonhuman animal can enhance an individual's subsequent efforts at child rearing (Hrdy, 2009). Regrettably, the possible relationship between pet keeping and reproductive success has never been investigated in any human population, although there is certainly abundant evidence of cross-species adoption of orphaned young animals among hunting and gathering peoples, and numerous reported instances of women in these societies caring for and even breastfeeding a wide variety of species (Erikson, 1987, 2000; Serpell, 1989). Evidence from a number of retrospective studies also suggests that people exposed to pet ownership in childhood may develop traits, such as enhanced empathy, that could contribute to improved parenting behavior (Bierer, 2001; Daly & Morton, 2009; Paul & Serpell, 1993; Poresky & Hendrix, 1990; Visek-Vidovic et al., 1999, 2001).

Two important predictions of the "parenting experience" hypothesis are that pet keeping should be more popular among women and girls than among men and boys, and that interest in pets should be strongest among preadolescent and adolescent females, since these groups stand to gain most from the acquisition of nurturing experience (Maestripieri & Pelka, 2002; Maestripieri & Roney, 2006). The evidence from research partially supports these predictions. Most studies suggest that enthusiasm for pets tends to be highest among girls in the 8- to 12-year age range, especially in those without access to younger siblings, and that overall interest in pet keeping tends to decline thereafter (Melson et al., 1997; Paul & Serpell, 1992). On the other hand, it is also clear that pet keeping is popular with both sexes throughout the human lifespan, even among postreproductive adults for whom additional parenting experience would, presumably, be nonfunctional.

PETS AS ADVERTISING

Although the possibility of pets acting as signals has not been extensively explored, evidence from a number of studies suggest that the presence of a pet can influence other people's perceptions of the owner or carer in ways that might influence fitness-relevant behaviors toward them. The most basic hypothesis that can be proposed in this respect is that pet keeping is (or was until relatively recently) a form of conspicuous consumption that advertises the owner's surplus wealth and ability to accrue resources. Although such effects may not be readily apparent in contemporary developed societies, where food (especially the protein rich foods required by pet dogs and cats) is relatively affordable, it may still apply to other species. In Britain, for example, where grazing land is particularly expensive, the keeping of some pet-like animals such as horses does frequently seem to carry with it connotations of wealth or elevated social rank. And, in the past, when food would have been scarcer, it was primarily the wealthy nobles and aristocracy who indulged passions for lap dogs and other intimates (Ritvo, 1988; Serpell, 1996; Thomas, 1983). Although the causes and fitness consequences of these kinds of displays may be hard to determine or quantify, it must at least be conceded that the keeping of certain types of pets, in certain societies or environments, may confer benefits to the owner by virtue of the high status thereby attributed to them by others.

Of course, being seen to be keeping and caring for a pet may transmit more information about a person than mere wealth. As a social activity, in particular, it might be expected to convey details of a person's overall temperament or willingness to display altruistic behavior. In the early years of human–animal research, a number of studies demonstrated that people tend to be perceived differently and more positively in the presence of pet animals than when unaccompanied (Lockwood, 1983; Serpell, 1996). A seminal study by Messent (1984) found that passers-by made more friendly social acknowledgments to a person walking with a dog through a public park than when they were alone. In a series of subsequent studies, similar results were obtained. Both adults and children using wheelchairs were acknowledged, spoken to, and smiled at more often by passers-by when in the presence of a dog (Eddy et al., 1988; Mader et al., 1989), although in more recent research, this apparent "social facilitation" of approachability or likeability was found to depend on the type of animal involved. Experimenters with puppies were acknowledged more than those with adult dogs, and a person was acknowledged less in the presence of a Rottweiler than a Labrador Retriever (Fridlund & MacDonald, 1998; Wells, 2004). Even more interesting from a fitness point of view was the finding of another recent study conducted in France in which an attractive male experimenter loitered in a pedestrian area and attempted to persuade young female passers-by to give him their phone numbers. He was three times as successful when he had a pet dog with him than when he did not (Guéguen & Ciccotti, 2008). Further studies are needed to dissect the precise processes by which the presence of a dog could have such effects, and additional research is needed to investigate the possible effect that more private types of pet keeping (e.g., cat ownership) might have. So far, however, the evidence is both intriguing and compelling: Being seen to be with, and perhaps caring for, a pet appears to have significant effects on the perception others have of us, and on the behavior they show toward us. Perhaps these effects are similar to those that accrue from being seen to engage in human-directed caregiving; indicating that, as a willing alloparent, an individual is honestly advertising his or her potential skills as a high-investing parent.

Conclusion

On the basis of relatively limited evidence, it appears most likely that pet keeping, or "cross-species adoption," originated among Paleolithic hunting peoples as a consequence of misdirected parental behavior. The human capacity for anthropomorphic thinking may have helped the process of assimilating these early pets into human families by enabling people to attribute human mental characteristics to these animals long after they were past the care-soliciting stage of infantile dependence. Various adaptive and nonadaptive theories have been proposed to explain the ongoing, although sporadic, popularity of pets among human cultures ever since. The least flattering of these "functional" hypotheses regards pet keeping as a nonadaptive or maladaptive consequence of hyperinclusive nurturing tendencies that render our species vulnerable to exploitation by nonhuman social parasites in the form of dogs, cats, rabbits, gerbils, hamsters, and so on. Most other theories take the view that human–pet relationships are essentially mutualistic, and that both participants gain fitness benefits by associating with the other. According to one such theory, pet keeping from the human perspective is the social equivalent of wearing warm clothes—i.e., adaptive behavior that can protect or buffer people from the "chill" of psychosocial stress. Another views pet keeping, at least ancestrally, as a means by which young humans acquire nurturing or empathic skills that enable them to become more successful at rearing their own offspring later in life. Still another sees this behavior as a potential way of signaling or advertising to other humans that one is capable of supporting and caring for a dependent, thereby enhancing one's social status—and perhaps increasing one's chances of being chosen as a mate. Based on current evidence, it is difficult to choose among these various competing hypotheses, and the task is further complicated by the fact that the functional value of pet keeping in modern Europe or North America (i.e., its current utility) may be quite different from its adaptive value in the past. It is also possible that pet keeping serves, or has served, all of these different functions at different times and in different cultural contexts during its long history. Additional research into the history and prehistory of pet keeping, as well as its current functions, is needed to explore these various alternatives. To this end, a number of potential research questions can be posed that may help to clarify our understanding of the significance of family pets, both in terms of current functions and possible evolutionary significance.

Future Directions

1. If pet keeping is genuinely adaptive, why isn't it universal? Conversely, if pet keeping confers no measurable adaptive benefits, why does its popularity continue to grow? What individual and cultural factors, apart from disposable income,

limit or encourage the spread of pet keeping within and between human societies?

2. What are the cumulative effects of pet keeping throughout the lifespan on human health and longevity? Most studies relating pet ownership to human health have focused on current pet ownership versus nonownership, and the results in some cases have been equivocal (Cutt et al., 2007; Wells, 2009). But perhaps the beneficial effects of pets are cumulative over the lifespan and depend on a person's lifetime exposure to these kinds of relationships. Investigating such effects might be possible with large, retrospective cohort studies of seniors in which pet ownership history is compared with long-term medical records. Such studies might also include a prospective followup component to explore the relationship between lifetime pet ownership and longevity.

3. Similarly, how, if at all, are the putative health benefits of pet ownership related to the quality (as opposed to the quantity) of these relationships? If pets are indeed serving as sources of nonhuman social support, then one would predict that their impact would depend on how effective these relationships are at satisfying each person's individual social support needs. Future studies could therefore consider the extent to which particular pets meet or conflict with their owner's expectations and perceived social requirements, and how this in turn affects the person's health. More focused studies could explore the possibility of an interaction between the health effects of pet keeping and the social support needs of the individuals concerned.

4. Does pet keeping in childhood/early adolescence produce measurable and significant changes in social and affective skills that are known to be important in mothering/parenting—such as empathy, social perspective taking, and nurturing? If the theory that pet keeping fosters nurturing/parenting skills is correct, it would predict enhanced skills in these areas among pet owning versus nonowning children/adolescents. Such research would need to be carefully designed to control for potentially confounding factors, such as the levels of empathy and nurturing that are shown by the parents and other caregivers of children and adolescents who do and do not keep pets.

5. Is pet keeping in childhood/adolescence related in any way to reproductive success? Again, if it is true that pet keeping fosters nurturing/parenting skills, one would predict a positive association between early exposure to pet care and subsequent parenting ability, and on the number, quality, and survival of a person's offspring. Again, it would be essential to control for other potentially confounding variables that might affect the results, such as parental nurturance, subcultural covariations in pet keeping and other cultural traditions, duration and intensity of childhood attachments to pets, and access to alternative nurturing objects (dolls, soft toys, infants, younger siblings, etc.). Such studies may also be more revealing in societies in which offspring mortality is higher and, consequently, the effects of parenting variation can be more readily observed.

6. How does pet ownership and/or the presence of a pet affect the way persons are perceived and evaluated by others, and how do these perceptions vary across different cultural groups?

Exploring the possible historical and adaptive significance of pet keeping will help us to further understand this apparently paradoxical and long-standing cultural phenomenon. It may also allow us to appreciate some of the more subtle, dynamic processes that go on in multispecies interactions, when ongoing relationships influence the life courses of all the partners involved. Investigation of the current functions of human–pet relationships, on the other hand, will have value in informing contemporary discussions about the future role for resource-expensive domestic animals in a world suffering from exponential human population growth and ever-increasing pressures to reduce carbon dioxide production. This is likely to prove an emotive academic and political discourse that may bring more attention to the fascinating and puzzling relationship between people and pets than ever before.

References

Ader, R.L., Cohen, N., & Felten, D. (1995). Psychoneuroimmunology: Interactions between the nervous system and the immune system. *The Lancet, 345,* 99–103.

Allen, K.M., Shykoff, B.E., & Izzo, J.L. (2001). Pet ownership, but not ACE inhibitor therapy, blunts home blood pressure responses to mental stress. *Hypertension, 38,* 815–820.

Allen, K.M., Blascovich, J., Tomaka, J., & Kelsey, R.M. (1991). Presence of human friends and pet dogs as moderators of autonomic responses to stress in women. *Journal of Personality and Social Psychology, 61,* 582–589.

Anderson, W.P., Reid, C.M., & Jennings, G.L. (1992). Pet ownership and risk factors for cardiovascular disease. *Medical Journal of Australia, 157,* 298–301.

American Animal Hospital Association (1996). *National Survey of People and Pet Relationships.* Denver, CO: AAHA.

American Pet Products Manufacturers' Association (APPMA). (2008). *APPMA National Pet Owners Survey: 2007–2008.* Greenwich, CT: American Pet Products Manufacturers Association Inc.

Archer, J. (1997). Why do people love their pets? *Evolution and Human Behavior, 18*, 237–259.

Arman, K. (2007). A new direction for kennel club regulations and breed standards. *Canadian Veterinary Journal, 48*, 953–965.

Associated Press (2009). The AP-Petside.com Poll. Retrieved March 2, 2010 from http://surveys.ap.org/.

Barker, S.B., & Barker, R.T. (1988). The human-canine bond: Closer than family ties? *Journal of Mental Health Counseling, 10*, 46–56.

Basso, C.B. (1973). *The Kalapalo Indians of Central Brazil*. New York: Holt, Rinehart & Winston.

Benecke, N. (1987). Studies on early dog remains from northern Europe. *Journal of Archaeological Science, 14*, 31–39.

Bierer, R.E. (2001). *The Relationship between pet bonding, self-esteem and empathy in pre-adolescents*. Unpublished PhD dissertation, University of New Mexico. Dissertation Abstracts International: Section B: The Sciences & Engineering. Vol. 61(11-B), June 2001.

Burkart, J.M., Hrdy, S.B. & van Schaik, C.P. (2009). Cooperative breeding and human cognitive evolution. *Evolutionary Anthropology, 18*, 175–186.

Cain, A.O. (1985). Pets as family members. *Marriage and Family Review, 8*, 5–11.

Cäsar, C., & Young, R.J. (2008). A case of adoption in a wild group of black-fronted titi monkeys (*Callicebus nigrifrons*). *Primates, 49*, 146–148.

Catanzaro, T.E. (1984). The human-animal bond in military communities. In R.K. Anderson, B.L. Hart, & L.A. Hart (Eds.), *The pet connection: Its influence on our health and quality of life* (pp. 341–347). Minneapolis: Center to Study Human-Animal Relationships and Environments, University of Minnesota.

Centers for Disease Control and Prevention (CDC). (2008). *Dog Bite Prevention*. Retrieved March 12, 2009 from http://www.cdc.gov/HomeandRecreationalSafety/Dog-Bites/biteprevention.html.

Cobb, S. (1976). Social support as a moderator of life stress. *Psychosomatic Medicine, 38*, 300–314.

Collis, G.M., & McNicholas, J. (1998). A theoretical basis for health benefits of pet ownership. In C.C. Wilson & D.C. Turner (Eds.), *Companion animals in human health* (pp. 105–222). Thousand Oaks, CA: Sage.

Coppinger, R., & Coppinger, L. (2001). *Dogs: A startling new understanding of canine origin, behavior & evolution*. New York: Scribner.

Coppinger, R.P., Glendinning, J., Torop, E., Matthay, C., Sutherland, M., & Smith, C. (1987). Degree of behavioral neoteny differentiates canid polymorphs. *Ethology, 75*, 89–108.

Crocker, J.C. (1977). My brother the parrot. In J.D. Sapir & J.C. Crocker (Eds.), *The social uses of metaphor: Essays on the anthropology of rhetoric* (pp. 164–192). Philadelphia: University of Pennsylvania Press.

Cutt, H., Giles-Corti, B., Knuiman, M., & Burke, V. (2007). Dog ownership, health and physical activity: A critical review of the literature. *Health and Place, 13*, 261–272.

Daly, B., & Morton, L.L. (2009). Empathic differences in adults as a function of childhood and adult pet ownership and pet type. *Anthrozoös, 22*, 371–382.

Daly, M., & Wilson, M. (1987). The Darwinian psychology of discriminative parental solicitude. In D.W. Leger (Ed.), *Comparative perspectives in modern psychology: Nebraska symposium on motivation, 1987* (Vol. 35, pp. 91–144). Lincoln: University of Nebraska Press.

Davis, S.J.M., & Valla, F. (1978). Evidence for domestication of the dog 12,000 years ago in the Natufian of Israel. *Nature, 276*, 608–610.

Dawkins, R. (1976). *The selfish gene*. Oxford: Oxford University Press.

Dawkins, R., & Krebs, J.R. (1979). Arms races between and within species. *Proceedings of the Royal Society of London, Series B, 205*, 489–511.

Dechambre, E. (1949). La Theorie de foetalization et la formationdes races chiens et de porc. *Mammalia, 13*, 129–137.

Donaldson, Z.R., & Young, L.J. (2008). Oxytocin, vasopressin, and the neurogenetics of sociality. *Science, 322*, 900–904.

Eddy, T.J., Hart, L.A., & Boltz, R.P. (1988). The effects of service dogs on social acknowledgements of people in wheelchairs. *Journal of Psychology, 122*, 39–45.

Emlen, S.T., Reeve, H.K., Sherman, P.W., Wrege, P.H., Ratnieks, F.L.W., & Shellman-Reeve, J. (1991). Adaptive versus nonadaptive explanations of behavior: The case of alloparental helping. *American Naturalist, 138*, 259–270.

Eriksen, W. (1994). The role of social support in the pathogenesis of coronary heart disease: A literature review. *Family Practice, 11*, 201–209.

Erikson, P. (1987). De L'apprivoisement à l'approvisionnement: Chasse, alliance et familiarisation en Amazonie Amérindienne. *Techniques et Cultures 9*, 105–140.

Erikson, P. (2000). The social significance of pet-keeping among Amazonian Indians. In A.L. Podberscek, E.S. Paul, & J.A. Serpell (Eds.), *Companion animals & us: Exploring the relationships between people & pets* (pp. 7–26). Cambridge: Cambridge University Press.

Esterling, B.A., Kiecolt-Glaser, J., Bodnar, J.C., & Glaser, R. (1994). Chronic stress, social support, and persistent alterations in the natural killer cell response to cytokines in older adults. *Health Psychology, 13*, 291–128.

Fairbanks, L. A. (1990). Reciprocal benefits of allomothering for female vervet monkeys. *Animal Behaviour, 40*, 553–562.

Fausto, C. (1999). Of enemies and pets: Warfare and shamanism in Amazonia. *American Ethnologist, 2*, 933–956.

Fox, M.W. (1978). *The dog: Its domestication and behaviour*. New York: Garland STPM Press.

Fridlund, A.J., & MacDonald, M. (1988). Approaches to Goldie: A field study of human response to canine juvenescence. *Anthrozoös, 11*, 95–100.

Freidmann, E., & Thomas, S.A. (1995). Pet ownership, social support, and one-year survival after acute myocardial infarction in the Cardiac Arrhythmia Suppression Trial (CAST). *American Journal of Cardiology, 76*, 1213–1217.

Friedmann, E., Thomas, S.A., & Eddy, T.J. (2000). Companion animals and human health: Physical and cardiovascular influences. In A.L. Podberscek, E. Paul, & J.A. Serpell (Eds.), *Companion animal and us* (pp. 125–142). Cambridge, Cambridge University Press.

Garrity, T.F., & Stallones, L. (1998). Effects of pet contact on human well-being: Review of recent research. In C.C. Wilson & D.C. Turner (Eds.), *Companion animals in human health* (pp. 3–22). Thousand Oaks, CA: Sage Publications.

Green, D.M., & Swets, J.W. (1966). *Signal detection theory and psychophysics*. New York: Wiley.

Grier, K.C. (2006). *Pets in America: A history*. Chapel Hill: University of North Carolina Press.

Guéguen, N., & Ciccotti, S. (2008). Domestic dogs as facilitators in social interaction: An evaluation of helping and courtship behaviors. *Anthrozoös, 21*, 339–349.

Hamilton, W.D. (1964). The genetical evolution of social behavior. *Journal of Theoretical Biology, 7*, 1–32.

Harris Interactive. (2007). *Pets are "members of the family" and two-thirds of pet owners buy their pets holiday presents.* Retrieved March 2, 2010 from http://www.harrisinteractive.com/harris_poll/index.asp?PID=840.

Harwood, D. (1928). *Love for animals and how it developed in Great Britain.* Lampeter: Edwin Mellen Press (republished 2002).

Headey, B. (1998). Health benefits and health cost savings due to pets: Preliminary estimates from an Australian national survey. *Social Indicators Research, 47*, 233–243.

Heinrichs, M., Baumgartner, T., Kirshbaum, C., & Ehlert, U. (2003). Social support and oxytocin interact to suppress cortisol and subjective responses to stress. *Biological Psychiatry, 54*, 1389–1398.

Herre, E.A., Knowlton, N. Mueller, U.G., & Rehner, S.A. (1999). The evolution of mutualisms: Exploring the paths between conflict and cooperation. *Trends in Ecology and Evolution, 14*, 49–53.

Herzog, H. (2010). *Some we love, some we hate, some we eat: Why it's so hard to think straight about animals.* New York: Harper Collins.

House, J.S., Landis, K.R., & Umberson, D. (1988). Social relationships and health. *Science, 241*(4865), 540–545.

Hrdy, S.B. (2005). *Mother Nature: A history of mothers, infants, and natural selection.* New York: Pantheon Books.

Hrdy, S.B. (2009). *Mothers and others: The evolutionary origins of mutual understanding.* Cambridge, MA: Harvard University Press.

Humphrey, N.J. (1983). *Consciousness regained.* Oxford: Oxford University Press.

Izar, P., Verderane, M.P., Visalberghi, E., Ottoni, E.B., Gomes de Oliveira, M., Shirley, J., & Fragaszy, D. (2006). Cross-genus adoption of a marmoset by wild capuchin monkeys (*Callithrix jacchus*). *American Journal of Primatology, 68*, 692–700.

Johnstone, R.A., & Bshary, R. (2002). From parasitism to mutualism: Partner control in asymmetric interactions. *Ecology Letters, 5*, 634–639.

Kikusui, T., Winslow, J.T., & Mori, Y. (2006). Social buffering: Relief from stress and anxiety. *Philosophical Transactions of the Royal Society, Series B. 361*, 2215–2228.

Kiecolt-Glaser, J.K., & Newton, T.L. (2001). Marriage and health: His and hers. *Psychological Bulletin, 127*(4), 472–503.

Kramer, K.L. (2005). Children's help and the pace of reproduction: Cooperative breeding in humans. *Evolutionary Anthropology, 14*, 224–237.

Lim, M.M., & Young, L.J. (2006). Neuropeptide regulation of affiliative behavior and social bonding in animals. *Hormones and Behavior, 50*, 506–517.

Lockwood, R. (1983). The influence of animals on social perception. In A. H. Katcher & A. M. Beck (Eds.), *New perspectives on our lives with companion animals* (pp. 64–71). Philadelphia: University of Pennsylvania Press.

Lorenz, K. (1971). *Studies in animal and human behaviour* (vol. 2). (Translation by R. Martin; First published 1950). Cambridge, MA: Harvard University Press.

Mader, B., Hart, L.A., & Bergin, B. (1989). Social acknowledgements for children with disabilities: Effects of service dogs. *Child Development, 60*, 1529–1534.

Maestripieri, D. (2001). Biological bases of maternal attachment. *Current Directions in Psychological Science, 10*, 79–83.

Maestripieri, D., & Pelka, S. (2002). Sex differences in interest in infants across the lifespan: A biological adaptation for parenting? *Human Nature, 13*, 327–344.

Maestripieri, D., & Roney, J.R. (2006). Evolutionary developmental psychology: Contributions from comparative research with nonhuman primates. *Developmental Review, 26*, 120–137.

Malek, J. (1993). *The Cat in Ancient Egypt.* London: British Museum Press.

Mandhane, P.J., Sears, M.R., Poulton, R., Green, J.M., Lou, W.Y.W., Taylor, D.R., & Hancox, R.J. (2009). Cats and dogs and the risk of atopy in childhood and adulthood. *Journal of Allergy and Clinical Immunology, 124*, 745–750.

McNamara, J.M., & Houston, A.I. (2009). Integrating function and mechanisms. *Trends in Ecology and Evolution, 24*, 670–675.

Melson, G.F., Schwarz, R.L., & Beck, A.M. (1997). Importance of companion animals in children's lives–Implications for Veterinary Practice. *Journal of the American Veterinary Medical Association, 211*, 1512–1518.

Messent, P.R. (1984). Correlates and effects of pet ownership. In R.K. Anderson, B.L. Hart, & L.A. Hart (Eds.), *The pet connection: Its influence of our health and quality of life* (pp. 331–340). Minneapolis: Centre to Study Human-Animal Relationships and Environments, University of Minnesota.

Miller, S.C., Kennedy, C., DeVoe, D., Hickey, M., Nelson, T., & Kogan, L. (2009). An examination of changes in oxytocin levels before and after interactions with a bonded dog. *Anthrozoös, 22*, 31–42.

Mithen, S. (1996). *The prehistory of the mind: A search for the origins of art, religion and science.* London: Thames & Hudson.

Monroe, S.M., Bromet, E.J., Connell, M.M., & Steiner, S.C. (1986). Social support, life events, and depressive symptoms: A 1-year prospective study. *Journal of Consulting & Clinical Psychology, 54*(4), 424–431.

Morey, D.F. (1992). Size, shape and development in the evolution of the domestic dog. *Journal of Archaeological Science, 19*, 181–204.

Morey, D.F. (2006). Burying key evidence: The social bond between dogs and people. *Journal of Archaeological Science, 33*, 158–175.

Morgan, S.P., & Taylor, M.G. (2006). Low fertility at the turn of the twenty first century. *Annual Review of Sociology, 32*, 375–399.

Nafstad P., Magnus P., Gaarder P.I., & Jaakkola J.J. (2001). Exposure to pets and atopy-related diseases in the first 4 years of life. *Allergy, 56*, 307–312.

Nagasawa, M., Kikusui, T., Onaka, T., & Ohta, M. (2009). Dog's gaze at its owner increases owner's urinary oxytocin during social interaction. *Hormones & Behavior, 55*, 434–441.

Odendaal, J., & Meintjes, R. (2003). Neurophysiological correlates of affiliative behavior between humans and dogs. *The Veterinary Journal, 165*, 296–301.

Ory, M.G., & Goldberg, E.L. (1983). Pet possession and life satisfaction in elderly women. In A.H. Katcher & A.M. Beck (Eds.), *New perspectives on our lives with companion animals* (pp. 303–317). Philadelphia: University of Pennsylvania Press.

Paul, E.S., & Serpell, J.A. (1992). Why children keep pets: The influence of child and family characteristics. *Anthrozoös, 5*, 231–244.

Paul, E.S., & Serpell, J.A. (1993). Childhood pet keeping and humane attitudes in young adulthood. *Animal Welfare, 2*, 321–337.

Pew Research Center. (2006). *Gauging family intimacy: Dogs edge cats (dads trail both)*. A Social Trends Report. Washington, DC: Pew Research Center.

Poresky, R.H., & Hendrix, C. (1990). Differential effects of pet presence and pet bonding on young children. *Psychological Reports, 67*, 51–54.

Putnam, R.D. (2000). *Bowling alone*. New York: Simon & Schuster.

Riedman, M.L. (1982). The evolution of alloparental care and adoption in mammals and birds. *Quarterly Review of Biology, 57*, 405–435.

Ritvo, H. (1988). The emergence of modern pet-keeping. In A.N. Rowan (Ed.), *Animals and people sharing the world* (pp. 13–31). Hanover, NH: University Press of New England.

Robertson, I.D., & Thompson, R.C. (2002). Enteric parasitic zoonoses of domesticated dogs and cats. *Microbes and Infection, 4*, 867–873.

Salisbury, J.E. (1994). *The beast within: Animals in the Middle Ages*. London & New York: Routledge.

Sanefuji, W., Ohgami, H., & Hashiya, K. (2007). Development of preference for baby faces across species in humans (Homo sapiens). *Journal of Ethology, 25*, 249–254.

Schwarzer, R., & Knoll, N. (2007). Functional roles of social support within the stress and coping process: A theoretical and empirical overview. *International Journal of Psychology, 42*, 243–252.

Serpell, J.A. (1989). Pet keeping and animal domestication: A reappraisal. In J. Clutton-Brock (Ed.), *The walking larder: Patterns of animal domestication, pastoralism & predation* (pp. 10–21). London: Unwin Hyman.

Serpell, J.A. (1991). Beneficial effects of pet ownership on some aspects of human health and behavior. *Journal of the Royal Society of Medicine, 84*, 717–720.

Serpell, J.A. (1996). *In the company of animals: A study of human-animal relationships*. Cambridge: Cambridge University Press.

Serpell, J.A. (2000). Domestication and history of the cat. In D.C. Turner & P.P.G. Bateson (Eds.), *The domestic cat: The biology of its behavior* (pp. 180–192). Cambridge: Cambridge University Press.

Serpell, J.A. (2003). Anthropomorphism and anthropomorphic selection–Beyond the "cute response." *Society and Animals, 11*, 83–99.

Serpell, J.A., & Paul, E.S. (1994). Pets and the development of positive attitudes to animals. In A. Manning & J.A. Serpell (Eds.), *Animals & human society: Changing perspectives* (pp. 127–144). London: Routledge.

Sherbourne, C.D., Meredith, L.S., Rogers, W., & Ware, J.E. (1992). Social support and stressful life events: Age differences in their effects on health-related quality of life among the chronically ill. *Quality of Life Research, 1*, 235–246.

Siegel, J.M. (1990). Stressful life events and use of physician services among the elderly: The moderating role of pet ownership. *Journal of Personality and Social Psychology, 58*, 1081–1086.

Silk, J.B. (1990). Human adoption in evolutionary perspective. *Human Nature, 1*, 25–52.

Thomas, K. (1983). *Man and the natural world: Changing attitudes in England, 1500–1800*. London: Allen Lane.

Tinbergen, N. (1963). On the aims and methods of ethology. *Zeitschrift fur Tierpsychologie, 20*, 410–433.

Uchino, B.N. (2006). Social support and health: A review of physiological processes potentially underlying links to disease outcome. *Journal of Behavioral Medicine, 29*, 377–387.

Vale, B., & Vale, R.J.D. (2009). *Time to eat the dog? The real guide to sustainable living*. London: Thames and Hudson.

Vilhjalmson, R. (1993). Life stress, social support and clinical depression: A reanalysis of the literature. *Social Science Medicine, 37*, 331–342.

Vigne, J.D., Guilaine, J., Debue, K., Haye, L., & Gérard, P. (2004). Early taming of the cat in Cyprus. *Science, 304*, 259.

Virués-Ortega, J., & Buela-Casal, G. (2006). Psychophysiological effects of human-animal interaction: Theoretical issues and long-term interaction effects. *The Journal of Nervous and Mental Disease, 194*, 52–57.

Visek-Vidovic, V., Stetic, V.V., & Bratko, D. (1999). Pet ownership, type of pet and socio-emotional development of school children. *Anthrozoös, 12*, 211–217.

Visek-Vidovic, V., Arambasic, L., Kerestes, G., Kuterovac-Jagodic, G., & Vlahovic-Stetic, V. (2001). Pet ownership in childhood and socio-emotional characteristics, work values and professional choices in early adulthood. *Anthrozoös, 14*, 224–231.

Voith, V.L. (2009). The impact of companion animal problems on society and the role of veterinarians. *Veterinary Clinics of North America–Small Animal Practice, 39*, 327.

Wells, D.L. (2004). The facilitation of social interactions by domestic dogs. *Anthrozoös, 17*, 340–352.

Wells, D.L. (2009). The effects of animals on human health and well-being. *Journal of Social Issues, 65*, 523–543.

Williams, G.C. (1966). *Adaptation and natural selection: A critique of current evolutionary thought*. Princeton, NJ: Princeton University Press.

CHAPTER 18

Fictive Kinship and Induced Altruism

Hector N. Qirko

Abstract

The concept of fictive kinship as used in the social sciences is ambiguous, but can be understood to reflect social understanding of the lack of biological relatedness between individuals or groups in contexts that are nevertheless deemed important enough for affinity to be designated. Because social and genetic kinship are generally congruent, kin labels and other cues to genetic kinship are likely related to evolved psychological mechanisms associated with kin recognition and altruistic dispositions. As these cues are subject to error and manipulation, altruistic behavior, including forms not subject to reciprocity and inclusive fitness calculations, may be induced through kin cue manipulation. This chapter reviews the arguments and literature associated with fictive kinship and induced altruism, and describes a test of the induced human altruism model. It is hypothesized that organizations and institutions requiring costly sacrifice by their members will tend to develop similar practices associated with kin cue manipulation. Support for this hypothesis is drawn from two examples of costly, unreciprocated altruism in nonkin settings: lifelong vows of celibacy and suicide bombing.

Keywords: Altruism, celibacy, fictive kinship, induced altruism, kin cue manipulation, suicide terrorism

Introduction

Fictive kinship (also variously described as artificial, social, quasi-, or pseudo-kinship) is a longstanding concept in anthropology and the social sciences. It refers to individuals unrelated by birth or marriage who label and treat one another as kin. In other words, fictive kinship involves the "extension of kinship obligations and relationships to individuals specifically not otherwise included in the kinship universe" (Wagner, 1995). There is general agreement in the literature that although modeled on locally accepted kinship roles and terminology, fictive kinship is recognized by participants to fall outside these roles and terminology. And although fictive kinship assignations are voluntary and achieved, they involve a set of reciprocal obligations in even the most informal contexts (e.g., Holy, 1996, p. 166; Parkin, 1997, pp. 124–125; Seltzer, 1993; Shipton, 1997; Wagner, 1995).

Examples of the use of the term(s) to describe relationships are numerous. A well-known one is godparenting, common worldwide but particularly associated with Catholicism in Latin America (*compadrazgo*). Beginning with a child's baptism, godfather and godmother agree to share responsibility for the child's spiritual and material welfare. This formalizes bonds between godparents and children, as well as between parents and godparents (*compadres*, literally coparents). Although it exhibits some historical and geographic variability, the *compadrazgo* is typically a highly institutionalized relationship marked by complex statuses and mutual obligations, as well as by ritualized behaviors and forms of address (Foster, 1953; Gudeman, 1975; Mintz & Wolfe, 1950). Other examples of fictive kinship related to parenting are various forms of adoption, fosterage, or other means through which adults assume parental or grandparental roles

(Howell, 2009; Silk, 1987; Terrell & Modell, 1994). Here again, reciprocal roles and obligations can be complex, especially in traditional societies in which offspring are responsible for the care of elderly parents once they are unable to provide for themselves (Ikels, 1998).

Fictive kin relationships are also often modeled on siblingship, created and cemented by common experience and the sharing of blood, food, or other substances. Examples include age-grade transitions to adulthood through rites of passage (van Gennep, 2004), gangs (Vigil, 1988), "brothers in arms" in military organizations (McCauley, 2002), and sororities and fraternities (Phillips, 2005). Fictive marriages are also common. Two examples are Chinese (Stockard, 1989) and Nuer (Evans-Pritchard, 1951) ghost marriages, in which one of the spouses is deceased. Among American Northwest native peoples such as the Kwakwaka'wakw (Kwakiutl), daughterless men could offer sons, body parts, even dogs in marriage to other men (Collins, 1994). In some cases, same-sex and immigration-related unions are also described as examples of fictive marriage (Freedman, 2004; Lau, 2006; Vanita, 2005, p. 172).

Fictive kinship ties may emulate more distant relationships, as in the case of cousins (e.g., Baumann, 1995; Bodenhorn, 2000), and the common American practice of individuals becoming "honorary" aunts or uncles to their friends' children (Slade, 1987). In addition, fictive kinship can parallel less specific and definable kin ties. Gubrium and Buckholdt (1982) describe a nursing home in which both friends and staff workers are assigned familial terminology by residents at the same time that some genealogical relatives are denied their status. Similar "family" ties have been noted in restaurants (Kim, 2009), businesses (Vlahos, 1985), prisons (Giallombardo, 1966), and many other settings.

Fictive kin labeling is therefore cross-culturally ubiquitous, but as an analytic concept fictive kinship presents several problems. This chapter attempts to inform these issues through an evolutionary psychological perspective. In many cases, the manipulation of kinship labels to create and strengthen bonds among unrelated individuals may be best understood as an aspect of induced altruism, in which cues associated with evolved cognitive mechanisms around kin recognition are manipulated to elicit altruistic behavior. Although induced altruism by means of such kinship deceit is well known in many species, the possibility of its relevance to understanding patterns of human altruistic behavior has not yet been rigorously explored. However, especially in religious, military, and other institutions that demand costly forms of altruism from their members, organizational practices consistently conform to predictions stemming from induced altruism theory. Thus, a reconceptualized theory of fictive kinship may illuminate some aspects of a common yet evolutionarily problematic behavior, human unreciprocated altruism in nonkin contexts.

Problems with the Fictive Kinship Concept

A major problem with the concept of fictive kinship is that it is applied so liberally that its usefulness for comparative purposes is open to question. Essentially, all that fictive kin relationships have in common is that, although they emulate procreative ties, they are defined "in their own terms" (Wagner, 1995) and used on an "as needed" basis (Seltzer, 1993, p. 158). Thus they can be as individualized as informal dyadic agreements and as extensive as interactions among clans (Collins, 2006, pp. 73–75) or between castes (Lambert, 2000). In what few typologies of fictive kinship have been attempted (e.g., Pitt-Rivers, 1968; Shipton, 1997), categories tend to overlap too much to be useful (Frishkopf, 2003). In addition, the bases for the concept's application by researchers are often tenuous: Kahn (2004) describes employees of an Israeli fertility clinic as fictive kin merely because they sometimes speak of "their" babies. And Maddy (2001) argues that medical practitioners constitute a fictive family largely because of their adherence to the Hippocratic Oath, in which they are described in kinship terms. Further, analytic and local interpretations of kinship assignations are often in conflict. Purportedly fictive kin terms are sometimes used not to label supplementary or replacement kin but simply to describe and validate familiarity (Ibsen & Klobus, 1972; Seltzer, 1993). The history of American adoptive and blended families (Modell, 1994) and of same-sex unions and families (Lewin, 1998) perhaps best illustrates this problem, given the many analytic and local reformulations of kinship assumptions these "families of choice" (Weston, 1991) entail. Thus, fictive kinship is, rather than a clearly operationalizable concept, a "catch-all" for describing, often misleadingly, relationships that do not follow a typical kinship pattern (Lambert, 2000, p. 74).

A more fundamental problem is the usefulness of the concept of kinship itself. Schneider (1984), Holy (1996), and others (e.g., Sahlins, 1977; Strathern, 1992) have argued that the view that kinship systems are universally based on biological relationships is shaped by Western notions of the natural and universal importance of "blood" ties. They point to a variety of cultures in which native conceptions of kinship challenge "natural fact" assumptions of immutability and procreative relatedness (Holy, 1996, p. 165). For example, Schneider reports that among the Yap of the West Caroline Islands, it is "doing" rather than "being" that defines bonds, and reproduction, although understood, is of little importance (1984, p. 132). Similarly, giving birth does not give one the status of parent among the Iñupiat of northern Alaska, and primary relations, "both in affect and moral weight, are formed with those who brought you up" (Bodenhorn (2000, p. 141; see also Langness, 1964; Schiefelin, 1976). And, North Indians value adoptive and residence-based kinship ties more highly than the "base" ones formed through reproduction (Lambert 2000, p. 79). Thus, to the extent that kinship can be based on factors in addition to or instead of reproduction, few distinguishing objective criteria are available for comparative purposes, and distinctions between "real" and "fictive" kin are rendered meaningless (Frischkopf, 2003, p. 4; Howell, 2009; Kemp, 1983, p. 95; Read, 2001).

In an attempt to revitalize kinship studies after these critiques, Carsten has argued for replacing "kinship" with "relatedness," which describes ties in terms of "indigenous statements and practices— some of which may seem to fall quite outside what anthropologists have conventionally understood as kinship" (2000, p. 3). She argues that, in this way, comparisons can be made without relying on an arbitrary biology/culture distinction. Biological relatedness can instead be held in "suspension" until its relevance to relationships in particular cases is ascertained (2000, p. 27). This advice, although perhaps meant to underscore the irrelevancy of biology to kinship studies, is also useful in attempting to more effectively explore biology's role in kinship labeling. If all kinship systems and terminologies are social, then "fictive" should refer only to cases reflecting social understanding of the lack of genetic relatedness between individuals or groups of individuals in contexts that are nevertheless deemed important enough for affinity to be designated.

With this in mind, two additional attributes of kinship become relevant. The first is that, notwithstanding that kinship assignations may often be based on nonprocreative factors, the assignations' underpinnings are generally reproductive, at least for close kin (Kronenfeld, 1996, p. 684). As van den Berghe (1979, p. 9) notes, "all cultural models of kinship and marriage bear a demonstrable relationship to [biological facts], although not all societies have equally accurate models of the biology of reproduction and heredity." Even where kinship conceptualizations drift from genetic underpinnings, or nonreproductive relationships are valued more highly than procreative ones, individuals are typically aware of the biological ties that connect them (Alexander, 1979; Bodenhorn, 2000; Lambert, 2000; van den Berghe, 1981). For example, the Zafimaniry of Madagascar differentiate cognitively and behaviorally among siblings, half-siblings, and more distant relatives, even though all are assigned the same kin label (Bloch, 1999). West African foster and adoptive parents similarly treat children in their care differently according to degrees of genetic relatedness (Silk, 1987). Yanomamo favor closer biological relatives in disputes and village fissioning irrespective of kinship labels that may obfuscate these relationships (Chagnon, 1979, 1981). Thus, "biology has not gone away," and genetic relatedness remains a "force behind the construction of kinship in the first place" (Stone, 2006, p. 21). As Bloch and Sperber argue, the fact that kinship is social does not mean that biological factors do not underlie its patterning, as a "predisposition to attend to reliable correlates of [genetic] relationships cognitively, emotionally, or behaviorally in one or several of a multiplicity of ways is likely to have evolved in many species, including the human species" (2004, p. 450).

A second relevant attribute of kinship is its manipulability. As Bloch explains, kinship terms "always do much more than label individuals, and most can be used by a skilful speaker of a language to refer to an almost unlimited number of people given the right situation and sufficient ability" (1971, p. 80; see also Read 2001). Kinship, whether fictive or not, entails obligations, and even at its most symbolic (e.g., Frishkopf, 2003), many of these obligations are directly related to individuals' somatic and reproductive success. Thus, kinship assignations have fitness consequences and are often manipulated strategically for material and reproductive gain. Yanomamo males manipulate kinship classifications for female kin to increase the number of potential mates (Chagnon, 1988). Iñupiat label themselves as cousins whether or not they are genealogically related in contexts that create "enormous tactical potential" (Bodenhorn, 2000, p. 136). Youth in a multiethnic London suburb do the same, irrespective of their varied kinship system rules and even when unable to describe the genealogical ties they might share (Baumann, 1995). Fictive kinship in American black communities has been used since slavery significantly more intensely than in parallel white communities to provide not only psychological but "essential" material support (Chatters, Joseph, & Jayakody, 1994, p. 305; see also Aschenbrenner, 1975; Gutman, 1977).

Another example of kinship's manipulability is *namesaking* (naming a child after oneself or a close relative), which can be an important means through which a child is accepted into kinship networks (Gutman, 1977). Naming a child after the father, particularly when there is some question as to paternity, may be a deliberate strategy on the part of a mother to strengthen child–father bonds (Furstenberg & Talvitie, 1980). Johnson, McAndrew, and Harris (1991) find that adopted children are significantly more likely than natural children to be named after parents or relatives. They suggest that naming a child in such a manner can reinforce parental behavior and generally enhance relatedness by making the child "instantly more similar, familiar, and hence, more likeable to potential caregivers" (1991, p. 368).

Therefore, kinship designations generally correlate with genetic relatedness; individuals are generally aware of genetic ties they share with others even where their social kinship systems value nonprocreative relationships as well or more; and individuals often manipulate kin designations for material and reproductive benefits. In sum, kin labels and roles can encourage behavior toward nonkin that is appropriate to genetic relatives. Carsten (2004, p. 137) has wondered about the emotional power such labeling possesses and the mechanisms that underlie it. A plausible theory is that kin labels are an aspect of evolved psychology in that they have served as reliable cues to genetic relatedness in human evolutionary history. If this is the case, because genetic relatedness is an important trigger in generating altruistic behavior, in some contexts fictive kin assignations may be a means through which individuals attempt to induce altruistic behavior from those to whom they are genetically unrelated (or only distantly related).

Induced Altruism

Altruism, in evolutionary terms, is simply behavior that benefits the reproductive success of its recipient at a cost to that of its provider (Badcock, 1991, p. 88). There are only three generally accepted contexts in which it could evolve and persist in populations. One is reciprocity: Tendencies to behave altruistically can be selected if they lead to behaviors that return benefits larger than their cost. Reciprocal altruism occurs when two individuals trade altruistic acts. As defined by Trivers (1971, 1985), it requires repeated interactions among specific individuals exchanging benefits of equal fitness values to minimize the risks and costs of being cheated. It appears to explain several categories of behavior among unrelated individuals within species (e.g., Wilkinson, 1984), particularly primates (e.g., Brosnan & de Waal, 2002; Schino, 2007; Seyfarth & Cheney, 1984), as well as some interspecies interactions, such as the relationship of "cleaner fish" to their hosts (Trivers, 1971). In humans, due to powerful cognitive abilities, lengthy lifespan, and cultural practices that can aid in tracking interactions, reciprocity is likely to require a smaller number of exchanges, and lengthier periods of time between them, than in many other species (Brosnan & de Waal, 2002, p. 101; Dawkins, 1989, p. 188). However, evidence that humans behave in accordance with predictions based on reciprocal altruism theory, as opposed to simply following cultural norms, remains difficult to obtain, although there is some support from models (e.g., de Vos & Zeggelink, 1997) and empirical research (Essock-Vitale and McGuire, 1985; Gurven, 2006; Schroeder et al., 1995). There is also some indirect evidence: Human ability to discriminate among many individuals, long memories with respect to actions, and emotional dispositions in areas such as friendships, gratitude, trust, and suspicion suggest reciprocal altruism to be an important evolved component of human behavior (Dawkins, 1989, p. 187).

Another context in which altruism can evolve is among genetic relatives, explained by kin selection theory (commonly, although they are not identical, inclusive fitness theory). First formally proposed by Hamilton (1964), kin selection theory predicts that any gene that lowers the fitness of an individual but confers an advantage to others sharing that gene can spread in a population. Inclusive fitness theory helps explain many apparent paradoxes in the natural world, including nonreproducing worker castes of social insects (Wilson, 1975, although see Wilson, 2005). Moreover, inclusive fitness predictions have received support in almost every species in which they have been tested (Emlen, 1995, 1997). It is becoming increasingly clear that humans often behave altruistically in accordance with inclusive fitness predictions as well (e.g., Badcock, 2000; Burnstein, Crandall, & Kitayama, 1994; Essock-Vitale & McGuire, 1980, 1985; Madsen et al., 2007). However, as in the case of reciprocal altruism, it remains difficult to evaluate the role of learned norms for aiding social kin relative to evolved altruistic dispositions.

A third evolutionarily plausible context for the evolution of altruism is its inducement. Induced altruism is therefore behavior that benefits the reproductive success of its recipient at a cost to that of its provider, but without a resulting benefit to the altruist (Badcock, 1991, p. 89). Although any act of predation would therefore qualify, there are specific adaptations in many fish, insect, and other species whereby altruism is induced (Trivers, 1985, p. 49). False cleaner fish mimic the behavior of genuine species in order to obtain a meal (Randall & Randall, 1960). An Amazonian parasitic nematode spreads by causing infected ants to resemble ripe fruits and so be eaten by birds (Yanoviak, Kaspari, & Poinar, 2008). There are many species parasitized in similar ways (see Badcock, 1991; Ridley, 1995; Trivers, 1985), and of particular relevance are those in which inducement involves kinship cues, or kinship deceit. The clearest examples are cuckoos, cowbirds, and other parasitic birds, in which host care is elicited by spatial location, shape, and color of eggs, hyperintense mimicry of host fledgling calls, and in some cases phenotypic similarity in host nestling plumage (Rothstein & Robinson, 1998; see also Davies, 2000). In these cases, the host–parasite relationship is typically coevolved, involving an "arms race" of increasingly sophisticated measures and countermeasures that can eventually result in evolutionary equilibrium. However, in some cases, parasitization may have emerged so recently that host defenses have not yet evolved (Rothstein & Robinson, 1998). This exploitation/defense coevolutionary process can take place within species as well (Dawkins, 1987, pp. 178–193; Ridley 1995, p. 257). Cosmides and Tooby (1992), for example, provide support for the possibility that aspects of evolved cognition facilitate "cheater-detection" in human social contracts. Sulloway (1996, p. xiv) describes how "an evolutionary arms race played out within the family" results in differing sibling strategies based on birth order (see also Michalski & Euler, 2007). Here too, in novel circumstances, manipulation may take place without counteradaptations being in place to combat it. As Pinker (1997, p. 42) points out, "[O]ur ancestral environment lacked the institutions that now entice us to nonadaptive choices, such as religious orders . . . so until very recently there was never a selection pressure to resist the enticements." Badcock suggests that as a consequence all moral systems are in fact a form of induced altruism (1991, p. 121). In sum, "[A]ll systems of altruism are vulnerable to parasitisms in which individuals pretend a degree of relatedness they do not possess or a degree of reciprocity they will not express . . . These considerations are by no means irrelevant to our own lives" (Trivers, 1985, pp. 51–52).

Human Kinship Recognition Cues

Critical to successful induced altruism through kinship deceit are the species-specific kinship cues that must be manipulated to produce desired behaviors. Since Hamilton's work on inclusive fitness, much research has been conducted on kin recognition abilities in animals (Alexander, 1990; Hamilton, 1964; Hepper, 1991a,b; Pfennig, 2002; Sherman & Holmes, 1985; Sherman, 2009; Wells, 1987; Wilson, 1987) and even in some plants (e.g., Dudley & File, 2007). This literature describes spatial distribution, association (especially during development), and phenotypic matching as the most common mechanisms, which can appear in combination (Hepper, 1991). Although direct genetic recognition, or the "green-beard" effect (Dawkins, 1989), is possible, it is rare (but see Keller & Ross, 1998; Queller, Ponte, Bozzaro, & Strassmann, 2003).

Primates clearly discriminate among relatives (e.g., Parr & De Waal, 1999; Silk, 2001), although the number of cues they use to do so remains unclear. In humans, association and phenotypic matching are the most likely to apply (Trivers, 1985; Wells, 1987). The clearest support for the importance of association as a cue of human relatedness recognition is found through the Westermarck effect, which predicts a lack of sexual interest among individuals raised together. It appears to operate even when the parties are unrelated genetically, as found in studies of Israeli kibbutzim, in which children reared together tend to avoid each other sexually (Talmon, 1964), and in Taiwanese arranged marriages, in which the practice of rearing children together who then marry results in disproportionately high levels of sexual dissatisfaction (Wolf, 1995). Less direct evidence is available for other societies (Brown, 1991, pp. 118–129; Wolf, 1995, pp. 423–438), as well as in some experimental work (e.g., Bressan, Colarelli, & Cavalieri, 2009). Although visual and auditory associative recognition is likely, olfaction has also been implicated: Mothers and infants can identify each other through scent (Hepper, 1991b; Porter, 1991), and there is evidence that adolescents and adults can discriminate among conspecifics on the basis of association through odor as well (Olsson, Barnard, & Turri, 2006; Lundström, Boyle, Zatorre, & Jones-Gotman, 2009; Weisfeld, Czilli, Phillips, Gall, & Lichtman, 2003). More recent reevaluations of kibbutzim and Taiwanese marriage data support the likelihood of an association cue in both cases (Lieberman, 2009a; Lieberman, Tooby, & Cosmides, 2003, Lieberman, Tooby, & Cosmides, 2007). Siblings of different birth orders appear to utilize different associative cues, suggesting that these cues are fine-tuned with respect to specific relationships (Lieberman, 2009a). Additionally, although incest rules clearly have a strong social component (e.g., Leavitt, 1989), negative emotional responses to the idea of incestuous acts involve dramatically increased activity in more extensive parts of the brain than responses to other behaviors viewed as immoral, suggesting the likelihood of a deep-seated, incest-related cue (Borg, Lieberman, & Kiehl, 2008).

The human brain appears particularly endowed to discriminate among human faces, which supports the importance of phenotypic similarity in kin recognition (Gauthier & Logothetis, 2000; Wilson, 1987; Zebrowitz, 1997, p. 23–26). Phenotypic similarity is regularly discussed cross-culturally as a marker of genetic affinity, especially as related to father–child ties (Daly & Wilson, 1982; Regalski & Gaulin, 1993), and third parties can successfully match siblings (DeBruine et al., 2009), and children to their parents (DeBruine, Jones, Little, & Perrett, 2008:71), on its basis. Further, a number of studies have established that humans react positively to facial resemblance (DeBruine et al., 2008). Self-resemblance increases trust (DeBruine, 2002) as well as monetary contributions (Krupp, DeBruine, & Barclay, 2008) in experimental games, and across-gender trust increases with resemblance as well (DeBruine, 2005). Here, as in association, the cue is context-specific, not simply a generalized preference for similarity, as similarity decreases interest in at least some forms of sexual relationships (DeBruine et al., 2008).

Lieberman (2009b) has suggested that the relatively recent development of language in human evolutionary history weakens the case for kin-labeling language serving as an evolved relatedness cue. However, children appear to seek, retain, and attend specifically to all markers of relatedness, however those markers are expressed (Bloch & Sperber, 2004). Daly, Salmon, and Wilson (1997, p. 289) suggest that children "acquire an understanding of kinship terminology in ways that cannot be accounted for by the hypothesis of domain-general inductive processes." Further, all societies exhibit ego-centered kinship terminology based on parent–offspring relationships, and distinguish between genders, generations, and degree of relatedness (Daly et al., 1997). Universal linguistic categories pertaining to kinship are therefore potentially an aspect of the innate structure of language (Pinker & Bloom, 1992) and emotions. Salmon (1998; see also Johnson, Ratwik, & Sawyer, 1987) has found that kin terms evoke more positive responses than other affiliative terms in political and patriotic speech. In an experiment involving e-mail solicitations, addressees were most likely to respond positively if they shared senders' names. Although the altruistic acts engendered were minor, "These results indicate that names elicit altruism because they function as salient cues of kinship" (Oates & Wilson, 2002:105).

Induced Altruism in Institutions

It is therefore reasonable to explore the possibility that association, phenotypic similarity, and linguistic kin referents are cues in evolved human psychological mechanisms related to kin recognition, and that these can evoke altruistic responses even among unrelated individuals. The manipulation of such cues would likely not have been relevant to the small, generally closely related groups that characterized living conditions throughout most of human history, although the cross-cultural examples of "tactical kinship" (Bloch, 1971) discussed earlier suggest tendencies, perhaps longstanding ones, in individuals to use it as a social strategy. However, when groups of biologically unrelated individuals are brought together in activities for which a willingness to behave altruistically is desirable, maintaining and reinforcing commitment to altruism through manipulation could be effective. This is particularly plausible because of a potential lag in the evolution of cognitive mechanisms to defend against manipulation. Precisely because we have lived in small kin groups for most of our history, mechanisms for recognition of genetic relatives presumably evolved in that context. Therefore, frequent interaction with nonkin is a novel development, a consequence of rapid population growth and increased mobility, and adaptations to defend against kin cue manipulation are unlikely to have evolved.

Institutions represent cases in which individual-level competitive and cooperative strategies have been systematized and reified to the point that original interests are often forgotten. For example, Wach (1962) outlines the stages through which institutional development of religious movements takes place. Charismatic individuals first attract followers who are integrated into the group primarily through personal contact and simple rules and practices. With the death of the founder and increasing membership, progressively more complex organizational structures emerge. Discipline becomes more important, and rites and rules are elaborated. Finally (if the movement continues to be successful) true institutions, involving ecclesiastical bodies, specialized clergy, and numerous, detailed rules for both are established. As the individual characteristics and motivations that sparked the movement are less and less relevant, methods to organize growing and increasingly unrelated membership become necessary. Personal devotion to specific charismatic leaders is transformed into behavior in the name of more abstract ideals and entities. It is at this point in the history of any institution demanding altruistic behavior from its members that organizational practices to maintain and reinforce commitment would be most needed, and when those most psychologically effective in doing so would be developed and maintained. This is not to say, however, that in some cases founders would not make use of such practices from the outset.

Several researchers have discussed the possible relevance of kin cue manipulation to the process of institutionalization. Balch (1985) describes how organizations (more properly, leaders of organizations) have historically attempted to minimize the disruptive effects of familial obligations by destroying or preventing family attachments and attempting to substitute themselves as kin. Although his emphasis is on the forcible manipulation of recruits, in which coercion maintains stability, Balch also discusses how kinship recognition cues such as association, familiarity, kinship-evoking language, and symbolism have been used to achieve this goal. van den Berghe (1981) has also emphasized the power of kinship-related manipulation in his cross-cultural discussion of ethnicity and unequal political systems. Kin terminology is commonly used to describe unrelated ethnics and nationals, and states are "are almost invariably bolstered by an ideology that disguises the parasitism of the ruling class as either kin selection or reciprocity" (1981, p. 60). van den Berghe also cites a predisposition to favor biological relatives that is manipulated in large groups through association and "filiation with known members" (1981, p. 28). Finally, Johnson (1986, 1989; Johnson et al., 1987), suggests that patriotic volunteerism, combat risk-taking, and combat suicide are elicited in military contexts through the manipulation of association, phenotypic similarity, and kin term cues.

In my own work, I've tried to further explore and test the possibility that kinship manipulation reinforces altruistic behavior (Qirko, 2002, 2004, 2009).

An initial problem in doing so is that altruism can entail behaviors of varying costs expressed in different contexts under which different theories may best apply. It is also too often conflated with related but dissimilar phenomena, such as cooperation (Rachlin, 2002). For example, in the military contexts Johnson describes, motivations to enlist may be financial (e.g., Carter & Flora, 2007), and so perhaps best understood via reciprocity theory, whereas combat suicide's cost precludes such an explanation. Attempts have been made to distinguish between classes of altruistic behavior. Altruism may be "hard-core," or irrational, as opposed to "soft-core" or calculated (E.O. Wilson, 1979), "strong" or "weak," in reference to absolute versus relative costs to the altruist (D.S. Wilson, 1990), and "pure," which affords no benefit to the altruist, as opposed to "generalized," in which the altruist receives some (presumably still unequal) benefits (Gaulin & Schlegel, 1980). Bressar et al. (2009) distinguish life-threatening behavior as the highest of four levels of altruism. But these categories are obviously too broad to provide much direction.

Therefore, in order to explore human kin cue manipulation, I have sought unambiguously costly examples of unreciprocated behavior in institutional (nonkin) contexts, acts that by definition limit the number and power of alternative Darwinian and other (e.g., cost–benefit assessments, risk strategies, etc.) explanations that might apply. These afford a good setting for testing the possibility that organizational practices related to kin cue manipulation are used to aid in maintaining and reinforcing commitment to sacrificial behavior. Five organizational practices can be predicted to be used by institutions for such purposes, the first three stemming directly from induced altruism and kin recognition theory. Institutions demanding costly sacrifice should encourage, particularly among new recruits (a) *close association* that replicates natural kin contexts (particularly parent–child and sibling relationships); (b) *the use of false phenotypic matches* (uniforms, emblems, hair styles, speech patterns, mannerisms, etc.); and (c) *the use of linguistic and other symbolic kin referents*.

There are, however, two additional relevant predictions not directly related to kin recognition cues themselves but to the process through which they are likely to engage an evolved kin-recognition psychology. The first is that institutions demanding costly sacrifice should (d) *prefer young recruits*. It is becoming increasingly clear that human learning, in addition to being biased toward domains related to selective pressures encountered over the course of evolution (Geary, 1995; Lumsden, 1984, p. 114), in many cases involves sensitive periods during which learning at a particular developmental stage is greatly facilitated. The most fully understood example is first language acquisition (Pinker, 1994), but sensitive periods appear to apply to a variety of domains. For example, Klaus et al. (1972) report that nonverbal cues picked up by newborns from their mothers have long-lasting effects on the developing mother–child relationship. Belsky, Steinberg, and Draper (1991; also Draper & Harpending, 1988) suggest that children raised in stressful familial environments develop insecure parental bonds, experience early puberty and, as adults, form unstable pair-bonds and limit their investment in childrearing. Recent studies support the likelihood of developmental stages related to social learning. Although the functional reasons remain unclear, adolescents experience dramatically different neural development around social cognition, basic emotions, and processing of emotional perspectives of others than do adults. "Adolescence is a period of social and psychological development during which social awareness and behavior undergo profound change" (Burnett, Bird, Moll, Frith, & Blakemore, 2009; Choudhury, Blakemore, & Charman, 2006), and adolescents are more likely to be more sensitive to social cognition–related information than later as adults (Blakemore & Choudhury, 2006). In general, areas of the adolescent social brain undergo "substantial structural and functional development" (Blakemore, 2008, p. 274). This suggests that individuals should be most susceptible to kinship manipulation during childhood.

A final prediction is that institutions should *(e) discourage association with actual kin*, as research suggests that severed familial attachments can be replaced. Although attachment theory is typically discussed in terms of the first 2 or 3 years of life, individuals may make several attachments during the course of development (Ainsworth, 1977, 1985; Cicchetti, Cummings, Greenberg, & Marvin, 1993; Cole & Cole, 1989). Further, children separated from their parents can successfully form substitute attachments with others who were once strangers (Bowlby, 1980; Cole & Cole, 1989, pp. 228–229; Dontas, Maratos, Fafoutis, & Karangelis, 1985; Sagi et al., 1985). Attachment theory is therefore relevant to humans' entire lifespans (Ainsworth, 1985; Goldberg, 1991, p. 396), and adolescence is a particularly fluid period with respect to attachment to peers (Nickerson & Nagle, 2005) and other authority figures (including religious ones; e.g., Kirkpatrick, 1998). Although the impact of severed primary attachments on this process is not discussed, surrogates are especially common when insecurity is associated with parents (Ainsworth, 1985), which suggests that institutions may better reinforce nonkin attachments if they sever or restrict actual kin relations.

The presence of institutional practices related to the predictions listed above in association with costly altruism would provide some support for the proposition that kin cues are manipulated to reinforce desired sacrificial behavior. This is particularly true if the practices are similarly present in very different cultural contexts. The predictions were therefore tested with historical and ethnographic data on two of the most costly examples of altruism in nonkin settings.

Celibacy

A good example of dramatically costly behavior in institutions is celibacy, or a vow of lifelong sexual and reproductive abstinence. It is altruistic in that organizations, rather than the celibate's offspring and close kin, benefit from his or her expenditures of time, labor, and energy. As the Apostle Paul wrote, "The unmarried man is busy with the Lord's affairs, concerned with pleasing the Lord; but the married man is busy with this world's demands and occupied with pleasing his wife" (Cholij, 1989, p. 201). In addition, through celibacy, institutions directly acquire and control members' preexisting wealth and future inheritances (Balch, 1985). From an evolutionary perspective, there is no benefit afforded celibates that can make up for the loss in fitness that the vow entails, and so evolved cognitive mechanisms associated with reciprocity would not appear to apply. Similarly, the taking of vows may benefit a celibate's family members in various ways, such as in heightened status or by resulting in one less mouth to feed. If the act benefits close genetic relatives, kin can receive gains that exceed the losses of the celibate, and this can explain why parents or other close relatives may wish, or even force, individuals into permanent abstinence (e.g., Betzig, 1995; Dickemann, 1979a,b; Hager, 1992). However, inclusive fitness does not fully explain the sacrifice from the point of view of the celibate. If he or she remains in close association with kin, then direct psychological reinforcement that maintains the individual's altruistic commitment can be generated. However, if the abstinent is denied close association with family members, as is typical in institutional cases, other means of reinforcement are likely to be necessary. Despite some suggestions to the contrary (e.g., Freyd & Johnson, 1992), many sources have noted that members of religious orders typically maintain their vows, if often with great difficulty (e.g., Ingersoll, 1966; Spiro, 1971; Wynne, 1988). Additionally, celibacy has historically elicited a great deal of controversy in the major religions due to its difficulty, and many branches and sects have been created specifically to escape its requirements (Wei-hsun Fu & Wawrytko, 1994; Wynne, 1988). Therefore, although inclusive fitness theory may be relevant, the maintenance of commitment to celibacy on the part of members would likely still be an institutional requirement.

Thus, institutionalized celibacy is a good setting in which to test kin cue manipulation predictions, and support for them can be found in a review of major religious institutions and well-known offshoots that require celibacy of their members (Qirko, 2004). Christianity, Hinduism, Buddhism, Jainism, Islamic dervish groups, and Protestant sects (such as the Shakers), notwithstanding their many dissimilarities, appear to share a similar pattern with respect to celibacy and its institutional reinforcement. Celibacy is, first, viewed in doctrine and statements by leaders, members, and researchers as altruistic. All of the major organizations discussed, including the most ascetic, are highly organized and successful with respect to the acquisition of resources from recruits and nonmembers. And in all cases, membership is associated with voluntary surrender of personal and family resources, efforts to gather additional resources, and sacrifice of time and labor for the benefit of the organization. There is therefore often a great deal to protect in organizations by means of the reinforcement of celibate vows. The organizational contexts are all also nonkin. Only some Protestant sects appear to exhibit some patterned instances of related recruits, but in these cases attempts are made to minimize the potentially disruptive impact of such relationships. Among the Shakers, for example, children who entered the sect with their parents were separated from them and cared for by others (Kitch, 1989). Further, all of these institutions rely on close association of members (even where wandering or missionary work are important); the severing or restricting of ties with nonmembers, particularly biological relatives; uniformity in dress and other accouterments and behaviors; and the institutional replication of family roles accompanied by extensive use of kin labels (including, in some cases, multigenerational fictive lineages tracing back to founders [Dazey, 1990]).

For example, as described by Roman sources, the Essenes were a Jewish religious order of approximately 4,000 members in present-day Syria and Palestine. Marriage was forbidden and celibacy the norm for many. New members, who relinquished all property, worked in various occupations but shared their earnings communally. All wore identical clothing. Although not confined to monasteries, Essenes lived in commonly occupied and supervised houses, shared communal meals, and are likely to have lived and traveled only in close association with each other. They referred to each other as kin, and their access to actual kin was restricted. Members could not aid their own relatives without special permission, and a Qumran scroll fragment suggests that "loving one's relatives" was considered an offense to the group. Finally, an important means of recruitment was the adoption of non-Essene children (Beall, 1988; Eshel, 1994; Vermes & Goodman, 1989). Similarly, recruits in European monasteries of the central Middle Ages, often infants whose parents "dedicated" them to lifelong service, were separated from kin upon entering the monastery. No property or wealth could be privately held. At all stages of their training, they wore identical clothing and, for males ("tonsure") hairstyles. They were "brothers" and "sisters" to each other, abbots were "fathers," and kin terms were similarly applied to their church and deities (Evans, 1968; Knowles, 1963). Buddhist monastic life also conforms to the predicted pattern, as illustrated in Burma and Thailand in the 1960s (e.g., Bunnag, 1973; Ingersoll, 1966; Nash, 1963; Pfanner, 1966; Spiro, 1971). Novices were typically 8 years old or younger. All members wore yellow robes, "disfigured" only by means of a small dot in order to make them individually identifiable (Horner, 1982, p. 407). Upon ordination, usually at age 20, candidates divested themselves of all possessions and rights to inheritable resources. Even later-acquired resources in the form of gifts belonged to the order upon the death or departure of the individual, and could not be transferred to laity. Monks were separated from kin by residence in a monastery, and strict rules restricting travel. They knew each other as "Sons of the Buddha," and their sponsors as "mother" and "fathers."

A cross-cultural review using Murdock and White's (1969) sample of 186 societies provides 26 examples of institutionalized celibacy, including several not related to the major religions and their offshoots (Qirko, 2002). Here too, the predicted pattern appears to apply. Priestesses of Vesta, goddess of the hearth ("Vestal Virgins"), served for 30 years as guardians of the sacred fire kept in the public temple in Rome. They were selected from among the populace between the ages of 6 and 10, separated until the end of their tenure, and obliged to wear special bridal dresses, at least on public occasions (Benko, 1971). Inca "Virgins of the Sun" were similarly set apart at age 8 or younger to live in permanent seclusion in the Temple of the Sun in Cuzco. They wore uniform clothing and identifying markers, and lived in close association with each other and overseeing *mama-cunas* (de la Vega, 1961). And the 19th-century "Amazons" of Dahomey, known to the general population as "our mothers" (Skertchly, 1974, p. 458), were typically celibate women chosen from the general populace while very young. Each of the several divisions of Amazons was identified with particular clothing, hairstyles, and names. Members' separation from the populace was complete: Even when outside the palace, they appeared only in heavily guarded processions.

A review of the historical development of religious movements and institutions also provides indirect support for the likely role of kin cue manipulative practices in reinforcing the altruistic commitment of their members. Incipient movements typically succeed only when they are able to successfully control self and kin interests, and celibacy is often an important means through which this is achieved (van den Berghe & Peter, 1988). It in turn, however, requires organizational reinforcement, and many movements fail as a consequence of their inability to encourage or maintain it (e.g., Andelson, 1983, Davis & Richardson, 1973). Organized monasticism and associated practices developed in the major religions only when societies grew sufficiently large that recruit pools were comprised of increasingly unrelated members (Horner, 1983; Olivelle, 1990; Timko, 1990). For example, the first Hindu monasteries arose in the company of demographic changes that resulting in centralized political authorities and increased contact across a relatively large area of North India (Olivelle, 1990). Their founder, Adi Sankaracharya (788–820 AD), developed administrative structures that remain in use to this day. Ascetics were organized in ten orders, each distinguished by kin terminology, uniform clothing, distinctive forms of address, and initiation rituals (Ghurye, 1964; Elder, 1990).

Suicide Terror

Although much is now known of the organizational and strategic rationales for suicide terrorism (e.g., Pape, 2005), the motivations of the human bombers themselves are not well understood, and poverty, educational deprivation, mental illness, familial instability, and other variables do not appear to be particularly relevant (Atran, 2003, 2004; Post, 2007; Sageman, 2004). Small-group dynamics, often cited as an explanation (e.g., Atran & Stern, 2005; Kruglanski & Golec, 2004; Schbley & McCauley, 2005), merely describe the influence that group ideologies and practices can have on individual commitment and behavior without specifying how these can reinforce individual decisions to commit such terminal acts of altruism. But as suicide bombing is another example of dramatically self-sacrificial behavior often exhibited in institutional contexts, the model of kin cue manipulation should apply to it as well. A review of the admittedly sketchy data on the inner workings of terrorist organizations suggests that it often does (Qirko, 2009).

Several researchers have noted a preference for young recruits, and parental and sibling kin term usage among recruits, trainers, and leaders in suicide terrorists organizations (Atran, 2003, 2004; Merari, 1990). Additionally, recruits tend to train in small, intense associations, both in camps, where the use of uniforms and other markers of phenotypic similarity is common, and in subsequent cells (Gunawardena, 2003). Recruits are also often separated from kin and community. They are typically unmarried, but sever marital ties if they have them (Sageman, 2004, pp. 79–80).

The Tamil Tigers of northern Sri Lanka are a good example. Recruits are typically very young, most often under the age of 15 (Becker, 2004). Upon recruitment, they sever ties with often strongly opposed families and communities to undergo secret, isolated training in close association only with each other and their trainers and leaders. Even the Black Tigers, the suicide arm of the organization, wear uniforms in training. The use of kinship terms for organization members is pronounced: Velupillai Pirapaharan, the leader, is known as "Elder Brother," and members refer to each other as siblings (Sornarajah 2004). Another example is the Party of Allah Iran under Ayatollah Khomeini in the 1980s. Here, too, young recruits were preferred. In one branch, the "Children of the Iman," children selected for martyrdom "no longer belong[ed] to their respective families" (Taheri, 1987, p. 191). In training camps and on missions, they wore distinctive red headbands, and referred to each other as brothers and sisters (Taheri, 1987; Reuter, 2004). To the Bassidj, also young martyrs, Khomemei was the "superlative father," and they "married" their organization, becoming brothers to their fellow members. These recruits were also cut off from family members to train and live in "unreal fraternisation behind closed doors" (Khosrokhavar, 2005, p. 88), where they wore identical uniforms. This pattern is also typical of al-Qaeda (Gunaratna, 2002), Muslim Brotherhood (Mishal & Sela, 2000), Iranian Fedayeen, and Lebanese Shi'ites (Taheri, 1987).

Some suicide contexts, however, do not appear to conform to the predicted pattern, and the recruitment and training of bombers seems much less formal than the model demands. This appears to be because indoctrination is less important when kin and community ties are strong (Argo, 2006; Sageman, 2004). In Chechnya, a relatively informal terrorist organizational structure is likely related to the fact that revenge for death or injury to relatives or spouses (hence the term "Black Widows" for female bombers) is the primary motivation for suicide bombers (Reuter, 2004). Here, and among some Palestinian terrorist groups (Oliver & Steinberg, 2005), the desire for revenge or protection that kinship ties engender may be sufficient to motivate individuals to commit altruistic suicide without the need for charismatic leadership, recruitment rhetoric, intensive training, or institutional manipulation.

In sum, it is likely no accident that suicide terrorists are often compared to monks and members of religious cults, or that the organizational structure of suicide terrorist camps mirrors that of military organizations. In all of these cases, costly sacrifice is required of members, and reinforcement of commitment to it would be an important contributor to organizational success.

Discussion

Clark McAuley has noted that terrorists, armies, monastic orders, religious cults, even drug treatment centers and residential schools separate recruits from families to create substitute families for which the recruits will be willing to sacrifice themselves (2002, p. 13). He refers to this process as "normal psychology" involving small-group dynamics. However, "normal" does not mean well understood, and the examples of institutional practices associated with celibacy and suicide bombing given above suggest that one explanation for the power of group dynamics in the context of altruistic behavior may be the effective manipulation of kinship cues. However, several additional points, as well as alternative possibilities, need to be briefly discussed.

First, *reinforced altruism* is likely a more apt term than induced altruism. Humans are rarely fooled into believing themselves related to nonkin. Instead, they commit to ideologies, including those that demand somatic and reproductive sacrifice from them, for a wide variety of reasons, such as the ideologies' logical and emotional appeal, adherence to group and community norms, and personal dispositions and circumstances. The altruism involved is rationally understood and, at least in many cases, voluntary. Institutional practices, whether consciously employed by leaders or historically inherited as organizational information, are therefore not designed to deceive but rather to reinforce, by whatever means prove effective, member behavior around a variety of issues related to organizational survival and the achievement of goals. Costly altruism may not even be a primary goal; in military organizations, for example, obedience is likely much more important than the occasional act of combat suicide (Henderson, 1985). For this reason, multiple reinforcers may be used. Terrorist organizations often offer substantial rewards to human bombers' kin, as well as make use of public pledges and titles, such as "living martyr," that render the suicidal act a foregone conclusion (Merari, 2005). In cases of costly altruism, many motivational practices should be expected to complement the various motivations and personalities of entering recruits (Moghadam, 2003).

However, it would be naïve to assume manipulation to be an unlikely aspect of organizational practice, given that deceit and its identification are fundamental components of human (and primate) relationships. Many aspects of human social interactions are predicated on it (Cronk, 1994), and mechanisms underlying "'Machiavellian intelligence'" (Byrne & Whiten, 1988) may even explain the explosive evolution of human cognitive abilities (Gavrilets & Vose, 2006). It is worth noting that leaders of organizations often benefit directly from the altruistic behavior of their followers—behaviors in which the leaders themselves do not engage. Rulers of Inca, Dahomey, and other societies requiring celibacy of their subjects were not enjoined to observe chastity, and in fact enjoyed increased reproductive opportunities. High-ranking medieval clergy and leaders of Protestant celibate sects alike often ignored sexual and familial restrictions (Betzig, 1995). Celibacy demanded of others has often been an avenue for increased reproductive success by leaders (Betzig, 1986). Similarly, an important distinction in suicide terror organizations is that between organizational leaders and trainers and the recruits committed to altruistic suicide. Organizers identify, train, and motivate human bombers in the interests of their causes, but they rarely become suicides themselves (Zartman, 2003).

The predicted, and to some extent supported, pattern of institutional kin cue manipulation discussed in this chapter, however, might be better explained by other theories. The presence of this pattern of practices may be due simply to diffusion, as both major religions and terrorist organizations have certainly influenced each other throughout their development. However, cultural traits diffuse only according to their perceived utility and fit with existing cultural patterns (Smith & Crano, 1977), and particular traits are not necessarily maintained in institutions as they are introduced into new settings (Lewis, 1986). An argument for diffusion would still have to explain why these particular practices are maintained in so many different contexts. Another possibility is that the predicted practices are found in institutions for reasons other than reinforcing altruistic behavior. For example, the need to organize large numbers of individuals might suffice to explain the use of uniforms. Kinship terms may be used as an organizing principle solely because of their linguistic universality. Young recruits may be preferred, as explained by some terrorist groups, because of their relative ease in moving among the enemy. Although this may certainly be the case, the five predictions were not chosen singly or at random, but are interrelated elements of an independently derived theory of kinship recognition. No alternative theory appears to better explain their associated traits' collective presence in organizations.

At least one alternative evolutionary hypothesis might apply as well. Kanter (1972) argued that sacrificial behavior in religious organizations, rather than requiring reinforcement, itself reinforces commitment. This is consistent with commitment theory (Frank, 1988; Nesse, 2001), wherein commitment to costly, apparently irrational behavior signals to others one's sincere willingness to act, resulting in net rewards to the signaler. Thus, the cost of many institutional practices may signal commitment to intragroup cooperation (Atran & Norenzayan, 2004; Sosis, 2000; Sosis & Alcorta, 2003). As Sosis put it, "celibacy is one of the costliest signals imaginable" (2000, p. 81). Atran (2003) similarly explores the potential relevance of this theory to suicide terror, suggesting that terrorist organizations may manipulate signaling dispositions in recruitment and training to engender and reinforce commitments to sacrifice. However, to the extent that signaling tendencies have evolved through natural selection, extremely costly altruism such as celibacy and suicide are not explained. "Handicap" signals arise because they promote individual fitness relative to survival and reproduction (Grafen, 1990; Zahavi & Zahavi, 1997); thus they cannot be so expensive as to preclude the goals they have been selected to achieve.

Conclusion

It is common knowledge that many human activities and groups are organized along the lines of what has traditionally been called fictive kinship, and that kinship assignations can imbue emotional power to the dispositions of participants (Carsten, 2004, p. 137). Ultimately, all that is argued in this chapter is that evolutionary psychology may illuminate the mechanisms underlying such assignations and their power, as organizations and institutions in a variety of cultural contexts appear to similarly develop practices associated with kin recognition and induced altruism. This simple observation has some important consequences. Human nonkin unreciprocated altruism remains problematic for evolutionists, as its relatively common presence is not easily explained through the use of traditional (i.e., neo-Darwinian) theories. Of course, evolutionary explanations may not be required for it. Enculturation, perhaps coupled with a human disposition to conform, may suffice (Boyd & Richerson, 1985; Logan & Qirko, 1996). However, given that human psychology seems to be biased in ways that conform to evolutionary expectations in so many other domains, it is premature to dismiss the possibility that evolutionary theory can inform this behavior as well.

Three current theories seek, at least in part, to explain human nonkin, unreciprocated altruism in evolutionary terms. All assume that this behavior is sufficiently widespread to require special explanation, and assume as well that humans are unique in expressing it. One is commitment theory, briefly discussed earlier. Herbert Gintis introduces Randolph Nesse's edited volume on the subject by reading from a newspaper: "[E]ach of these stories portrays individuals concerned with the well-being of other, unrelated people, and these individuals are willing to sacrifice in some material manner to help or hurt the objects of their attention" (Gintis, 2001, p. xiv). The problem commitment theory attempts to solve is that although "traditional sociobiology" has taught us that behavior is selfish, human behavior is often not: "[P]eople do not always act on calculated advantage, and many actions appear irreducibly costly to the actors themselves" (p. xv). Richard Dawkins similarly introduces memetic theory in *The Selfish Gene* (1989) by using institutionalized celibacy as an example of the need to "throw out the gene" to explain certain forms of human altruism. One of memetic theory's most well-known advocates, Susan Blackmore, devotes two chapters in *The Meme Machine* (2000) to human altruism, and argues that humans are unusual in that they "put enormous efforts into helping others who are not their relatives (i.e., do not share their genes) and who are unlikely or unable to reciprocate" (Blackmore 2001, p. 453). There is therefore an "extra something" in humans that allows for the existence of "true" altruism (2000, p. 154). Finally, In *Unto Others* (1999), Sober and Wilson defend their reformulation of group selection theory in large part because of the problem of human altruism: "The idea that human behavior is governed entirely by self-interest and that altruistic ultimate motives don't exist has never been supported by either a coherent theory or a crisp and decisive set of observations" (1999, p. 8). Group selection therefore has been a powerful force in human evolution because it can explain the special nature of human "groupishness."

Without arguing the merits of each of these theories (and there are more; the potential role of mirror neurons in the evolution of altruism is receiving some attention; e.g., Rizzolatti & Craighero, 2005), it seems reasonable to object that carefully examining contexts in which "special" altruism is expressed is a necessary first step to effective theory building. To the extent that much problematic altruism appears to take place in settings in which it is reinforced through practices that appeal to dispositions to aid genetic relatives, at least some of the problems it presents are mitigated.

As outlined here, at least, induced altruism by means of kinship deceit does not explain human unreciprocated, nonkin altruism, as the motivations to engage in such behavior must first be expressed in order to be reinforced. However, illuminating some of the contexts in which the behavior takes place can contribute to a fuller, evolutionarily based understanding of the phenomenon. Perhaps human unreciprocated, nonkin altruism is not really as big a problem for evolutionists as it appears to be.

Future Directions

1. Targeted ethnographies of monasteries, military training centers, and other nonkin settings in which costly altruism is exhibited could be undertaken to explore the use and effect of institutional practices potentially associated with kin cue manipulation.

2. Experimental and brain imaging studies would be helpful in exploring the effects of fictive kin labels on emotional states and altruistic dispositions.

3. Comparative historical analyses could be undertaken of institutions in which costly altruism is exhibited, to trace the specific development of institutional practices potentially associated with kin cue manipulation.

Acknowledgments

I am grateful to Bruce Tomaso and Emily Dahl for their contributions to earlier versions of this chapter.

References

Ainsworth, M.D.S. (1977). Attachment theory and its utility in cross-cultural research. In P.H. Leiderman, S.R. Tulkin, & A. Rosenfeld (Eds.), *Culture and infancy* (pp. 49–68). New York: Academic Press.

Ainsworth, M.D.S.(1985). Attachments across the life-span. *Bulletin of the New York Academy of Medicine, 61*, 792–812.

Alexander, R.D. (1979). *Darwinism and human affairs*. Seattle: University of Washington Press.

Alexander, R.D. (1990). Epigenetic rules and Darwinian algorithms. *Ethology and Sociobiology, 11*, 241–303.

Andelson, J.G. (1983). Communitarianism, familism, and individualism among the Inspirationists at Amana. *International Journal of Sociology of the Family, 13*, 45–62.

Argo, N. (2006, April). Human bombs: Rethinking religion and terror. *Audits of the Conventional Wisdom*, MIT Center for International Studies. Retrieved from http://web.mit.edu/cis/acw.html

Aschenbrenner, J. (1975). *Lifelines: Black families in Chicago*. New York: Holt Rinehart.

Atran, S. (2003). Genesis of suicide terrorism. *Science 299*, 1534–1539.

Atran, S. (2004). Mishandling suicide terrorism. *Washington Quarterly, 27*, 67–90.

Atran, S., & Norenzayan, A. (2004). Religion's evolutionary landscape: Counterintuition, commitment, compassion, communion. *Behavioral and Brain Sciences, 27*, 713–770.

Atran, S., & Stern, J. (2005). Small groups find fatal purpose through the web. *Nature, 437*, 620.

Badcock, C. (1991). Evolution and individual behavior: *An introduction to human sociobiology*. Oxford, UK: Basil Blackwell.

Badcock, C. (2000). *Evolutionary psychology: A critical introduction*. Cambridge, UK: Polity.

Balch, S.H. (1985). The neutered civil servant: Eunuchs, celibates, abductees and the maintenance of organizational loyalty. *Journal of Social and Biological Structures, 8*, 313–328.

Baumann, G. (1995). Managing a polyethnic milieu: Kinship and interaction in a London suburb. *Journal of the Royal Anthropological Institute, 1*, 725–741.

Beall, T.S. (1988). *Josephus' description of the Essenes illustrated by the Dead Sea Scrolls*. Cambridge, UK: Cambridge University Press.

Belsky, J., Steinberg, L, & Draper, P. (1991). Childhood experience, interpersonal development, and reproductive strategy: An evolutionary theory of socialization. *Child Development 62*, 647–670.

Benko, S. (1984). *Pagan Rome and the early Christians*. Bloomington: Indiana University.

Betzig, L. (1986). *Despotism and differential reproduction*. New York: Aldine.

Betzig, L. (1995). Medieval monogamy. *Journal of Family History, 20*, 181–216.

Blackmore, S. (2000). *The Meme machine*. Oxford, UK: Oxford University Press.

Blackmore, S. (2001). Meme. In C. Blakemore & S. Jennett (Eds.), *The Oxford companion to the body* (pp. 453–454). Oxford, UK: Oxford University Press.

Blakemore, S.J. (2008). The social brain in adolescence. *Nature Reviews Neuroscience, 9*, 267–277.

Blakemore, S.J., & Choudhury, S. (2006). Development of the adolescent brain: Implications for executive function and social cognition. *Journal of Child Psychology and Psychiatry, 47*, 296–312.

Bloch, M. (1971). The moral and tactical meaning of kinship terms. *Man, 6*, 79–87.

Bloch, M. (1999). Commensality and poisoning. *Social Research, 66*, 133–149.

Bloch, M., & Sperber, D. (2004). Kinship and evolved psychological dispositions: The mother's brother controversy reconsidered. In R. Parkin, & L. Stone (Eds.), *Kinship and family: An anthropological reader* (pp. 438–455). Boston, MA: Blackwell.

Bodenhorn, B. (2000). "He used to be my relative": Exploring the bases of relatedness among Iñupiat of northern Alaska. In J. Carsten (Ed.), *Cultures of relatedness: New approaches to the study of kinship* (pp. 128–148). Cambridge, UK: University Press.

Borg, J.S., Lieberman, D., & Kiehl, K.A. (2008). Infection, incest, and iniquity: Investigating the neural correlates of disgust and morality. *Journal of Cognitive Neuroscience, 20*, 1529–1546.

Boyd, R., & Richerson, P. J. (1985). *Culture and the evolutionary process*. Chicago, IL: University of Chicago Press.

Bressan, P.M. Colarelli, S.M., & Cavalieri, M.B. (2009). Biologically costly altruism depends on emotional closeness among step but not half or full siblings. *Evolutionary Psychology, 7*, 118–132.

Brosnan, S.F., & de Waal, F.B.M. (2002). A proximate perspective on reciprocal altruism. *Human Nature, 13*, 129–152.

Brown, D. (1991). *Human universals*. Philadelphia: Temple University Presso.

Bunnag, J. (1973). *Buddhist monk, Buddhist layman: A study of urban monastic organization in central Thailand*. Cambridge, UK: Cambridge University Press.

Burnett, S., Bird, G., Moll, J., Frith, C., & Blakemore, S.J. (2009). Development during adolescence of the neural processing of social emotion. *Journal of Cognitive Neuroscience, 21*, 1736–1750.

Burnstein, E., Crandall, C., & Kitayama, S. (1994). Some Neo-Darwinian decision rules for altruism: Weighing cues for inclusive fitness as a function of the biological importance of the decision. *Journal of Personality and Social Psychology, 67*, 773–789.

Byrne, R.W., & Whiten, A. (1988). *Machiavellian intelligence: Social expertise and the evolution of intellect in monkeys, apes, and humans*. Oxford, UK: Clarendon.

Carsten, J. (2000). Introduction: Cultures of relatedness. In J. Carsten (ed.), *Cultures of Relatedness: New Approaches to the Study of Kinship* (pp. 1–36). Cambridge, UK: University Press.

Carsten, J. (2004). *After kinship*. Cambridge, UK: Cambridge University Press.

Carter, P., & Flora, B. (2007). I want you . . . badly: A complete guide to Uncle Sam's recruiting incentives. *Slate*, November 7. Retrieved from http://www.slate.com/id/2177426?wpisrc=newsletter.

Chagnon, N.A. (1979). Mate competition, favoring close kin and village fissioning among the Yanomamö Indians. In N. A. Chagnon & W. Irons (Eds.), *Evolutionary biology and human social behavior: An anthropological perspective* (pp. 86–131). North Scituate, MA: Duxbury Press.

Chagnon, N.A. (1981). Terminological kinship, genealogical relatedness and village fissioning among the Yanomamö Indians. In R.D. Alexander & D.W. Tinkle (Eds.), *Natural selection and social behavior* (pp. 490–508). New York: Chiron.

Chagnon, N.A. (1988). Male Yanomamo manipulations of kinship classifications of female kin for reproductive advantage. In L. Betzig, M. Borgerhoff Mulder, & P. Turker (Eds.), *Human reproductive behavior: A Darwinian perspective* (pp. 23–48). Cambridge, UK: Cambridge University Press.

Chatters, L., Taylor, R.J., & Jayakody, R. (1994). Fictive kinship relations in black extended families. *Journal of Comparative Family Studies, 25*, 297–312.

Cholij, R. (1989). *Clerical celibacy in East and West*. Hereford, UK: Fowler Wright.

Choudhury, S., Blakemore, S.-J., Charman, T. (2006). Social cognitive development during adolescence. *Social Cognitive and Affective Neuroscience, 1*, 165–174.

Cicchetti, D., Cummings, E.M., & Marvin, R.S. (1993). An organizational perspective on attachment beyond infancy: Implications for theory, measurement, and research. In M.T. Greenberg, D. Cicchetti, & E.M. Cummings (Eds.), *Attachment in the preschool years: Theory, research, and intervention* (pp. 3–50). Chicago: University of Chicago Press.

Cole, M., & Cole, S.R. (1989). *The development of children*. New York: Scientific American Books.

Collins, J.M. (1994). Kinship, social class, and religion of northwest peoples. In R.J. DeMallie & A. Ortiz (Eds.). *North American Indian anthropology: Essays on society and culture* (pp. 82–107). Norman: University of Oklahoma Press.

Collins, K. (2006). *Clan politics and regime transition in Central Asia*. Cambridge, UK: Cambridge University Press.

Cosmides, L., & Tooby, J. (1992). Cognitive adaptations for social exchange." In J.H. Barkow, L. Cosmides, & J. Tooby (Eds.). *The adapted mind: Evolutionary psychology and the generation of culture* (pp. 163–228). New York: Oxford University Press.

Cronk, L. (1994). Evolutionary theories of morality and the manipulative use of signals. *Zygon, 29*, 81–101.

Daly, M., & Wilson, M.I. (1982). Whom are newborn babies said to resemble? *Ethology and Sociobiology, 3*, 69–78.

Daly, M., Salmon, C., & Wilson, M. (1997). Kinship: The conceptual hole in psychological studies of social cognition and close relationships. In J.A. Simpson & D.T. Kenrick (Eds.), *Evolutionary social psychology* (pp. 265–296). Mahwah, NJ: Erlbaum.

Davies, N.B. (2000). *Cuckoos, cowbirds and other cheats*. London UK: Academic Press.

Davis, R., & Richardson, J.T. (1993). The organization and functioning of the Children of God. In M.E. Mart (Ed.), *New and intense movements* (pp. 322–340). Munich, FRG: K.G. Saur.

Dawkins, R. (1987). *The blind watchmaker*. New York: W.W. Norton.

Dawkins, R. (1989). *The selfish gene* (2nd ed.). Oxford, UK: Oxford University Press.

Dazey, W.H. (1990). Tradition and modernization in the organization of the Dasanami Samyasins. In A.B. Creel & V. Narayanan (Eds.), *Monastic life in the Christian and Hindu traditions* (pp. 281–321). Lewiston, NY: Edwin Mellen.

DeBruine, L.M. (2002). Facial resemblance enhances trust. *Proceedings of the Royal Society of London B, 269*, 1307–1312.

DeBruine, L.M. (2005). Trustworthy but not lust-worthy: Context specific effects of facial resemblance. *Proceedings of the Royal Society of London B, 272*, 919–922.

DeBruine, L.M., Jones, B.C., Little, A.C., & Perrett, D.I. (2008). Social perception of facial resemblance in humans. *Archives of Sexual Behavior, 37*, 64–77.

DeBruine, L.M., Smith, F.G., Jones, B.C., Roberts, S.C., Petrie, M., & Spector, T.D. (2009). Kin recognition signals in adult faces. *Vision Research, 49*, 38–43.

De la Vega, G. (1961). *Commentarios reales*. New York: Orion.

de Vos, H., & Zeggelink, E. (1997). Reciprocal altruism in human social evolution: The viability of reciprocal altruism with a preference for "old-helping-partners." *Evolution and Human Behavior, 18*, 261–278.

Dickemann, M. (1979a). The ecology of mating systems in hypergynous dowry societies. *Social Science Information, 18*, 163–195.

Dickemann, M. (1979b). Female infanticide, reproductive strategies, and social stratification: A preliminary model. In N.A. Chagnon & W. Irons (Eds.), *Evolutionary biology and human social behavior: An anthropological perspective* (pp. 321–367). North Scituate, MA: Duxbury Press.

Dontas, C., Maratos, O., Fafoutis, M., & Karangelis, A. (1985). Early social development in institutionally reared Greek infants: Attachment and peer interaction. *Monographs of the Society for Research in Child Development, 50*, 136–146.

Draper, P., & Harpending, H. (1988). A sociobiological perspective on the development of human reproductive strategies. In K.B. MacDonald (Ed.), *Sociobiological perspectives on human development* (pp. 340–372). New York: Springer-Verlag.

Dudley, S.A., & File, A.L. (2007). Kin recognition in an annual plant. *Biology Letters, 3*, 435–438.

Elder, J.W.(1990). Some roots and branches of Hindu monasticism. A.B. Creel & V. Narayanan (Eds.), *Monastic life in the Christian and Hindu traditions* (pp. 1–36). Lewiston, NY: Edwin Mellen.

Emlen, S.T. (1995). An evolutionary theory of the family. *Proceedings of the National Academy of Sciences, 92*, 8092–8099.

Emlen, S.T. (1997). Predicting family dynamics in social vertebrates. In J.R. Krebs & N.B. Davies (Eds.), *Behavioural ecology: An evolutionary approach* (4th ed.) (pp. 228–253). Oxford, UK: Blackwell Science.

Eshel, E. (1994). 4Q477: The rebukes by the overseer. *Journal of Jewish Studies, 45*, 111–118.

Essock-Vitale, S.M., & McGuire, M.T. (1980). Predictions derived from the theories of kin selection and reciprocation assessed by anthropological data. *Ethology and Sociobiology, 1*, 233–243.

Essock-Vitale, S.M., & McGuire, M.T. (1985). Women's lives reviewed from an evolutionary perspective II: Patterns of helping. *Ethology and Sociobiology, 6*, 155–173.

Evans, J. (1968). *Monastic life at Cluny*. Hamden, CT: Archon.

Evans-Pritchard, E.E. (1951). *Kinship and marriage among the Nuer*. Oxford, UK: Clarendon.

Foster, G.M. (1953). Cofradia and compadrazgo in Spain and Spanish America. *Southwestern Journal of Anthropology, 9*, 1–28.

Frank, R.H. (1988). *Passions within reason: The strategic role of the emotions*. New York: Norton.

Freedman, E.B. (2004). Boston marriage, free love, and fictive kin: Historical alternatives to mainstream marriage. *Organization of American Historians Newsletter, 32, 1*, 16.

Freyd, J.J., & Johnson, J.Q. (1992). The evolutionary psychology of priesthood celibacy. *Behavioral and Brain Sciences, 15*, 385.

Frishkopf, M. (2003). Spiritual kinship and globalization. *Religious Studies and Theology, 22*, 1–26.

Furstenberg, F.F., & Talvitie, K.G. (1980). Children's names and paternal claims: Bonds between unmarried fathers and their children. *Journal of Family Issues, 1*, 31–57.

Gaulin, S.J.C., & Schlegel, A. (1980) Paternal confidence and paternal investment: A cross-cultural test of a sociobiological hypothesis. *Ethology and Sociobiology, 1*, 301–309.

Gauthier, I., & Logothetis, N.K. (2000). Is face recognition not so unique after all? *Cognitive Neuropsychology, 17*, 125–142.

Gavrilets, S., & Vose, A. (2006). The dynamics of Machiavellian intelligence. *Proceedings of the National Academy of Sciences, 103*, 16823–16828.

Geary, D.C. (1995). Reflections of evolution and culture in children's cognition. *American Psychologist, 50*, 24–37.

Ghurye, G.S. (1964). *Indian Sadhus* (2nd ed.). Bombay, India: Popular Prakashan.

Giallombardo, R. (1966). *Society of women: A study of a women's prison*. New York: John Wiley and Sons.

Gintis, H. (2001). Foreword: Beyond selfishness in modeling human behavior. In R.M. Nesse (Ed.), *Evolution and the capacity for commitment* (pp. xiii–xviii). New York: Russell Sage Foundation.

Goldberg, S. (1991). Recent developments in attachment theory and research. *Canadian Journal of Psychiatry, 36*, 393–400.

Grafen, A. (1990). Biological signals as handicaps. *Journal of Theoretical Biology, 144*, 517–546.

Gubrium, J.F., & Buckholdt, D.R. (1982). Fictive family: Everyday usage, analytic, and human service considerations. *American Anthropologist, 84*, 878–885.

Gudeman, S. (1975). Spiritual relationships and selecting a godparent. *Man, 10*, 221–237.

Gunaratna, R. (2002). *Inside Al Qaeda: Global network of terror*. New York: Columbia University Press.

Gunawardena, A. (2003). *Black Tigers: LTTE suicide terrorism - the Sri Lankan Experience*. MSc dissertation, University of Leicester, UK.

Gurven, M. (2006). The evolution of contingent cooperation. *Current Anthropology, 47*, 185–192.

Gutman, H.G. (1977). *The Black family in slavery and freedom, 1750–1925*. New York: Vintage.

Hager, B.J. (1992). Get thee to a nunnery: Female religious claustration in medieval Europe. *Ethology and Sociobiology, 13*, 385–407.

Hamilton, W.D. (1964). The genetical evolution of social behavior, I,II. *Journal of Theoretical Biology, 7*, 1–52.

Henderson, W.D. (1985). *Cohesion: The human element in combat*. Washington, DC: National Defense University Press.

Hepper, P.G. (Ed.) (1991a). *Kin recognition*. Cambridge, UK: Cambridge University Press.

Hepper, P.G. (1991b). Recognizing kin: Ontogeny and classification. In P.G. Hepper (Ed.), *Kin recognition* (pp. 259–288). Cambridge, UK: Cambridge University Press.

Holy, L. (1996). *Anthropological perspectives on kinship*. London: Pluto Press.

Horner, I.B. (Trans.). (1982). *The book of the discipline (Vinaya-Pitaka)*, Vol. II. London: Pali Text Society.

Horner, I.B. (Trans.). (1983). *The book of the discipline (Vinaya-Pitaka)*, Vol. IV. London: Pali Text Society.

Howell, S. (2009). Adoption of the unrelated child: Some challenges to the anthropological study of kinship. *Annual Review of Anthropology, 38*, 149–66.

Hurford, J.R. (1991). The evolution of the critical period for language acquisition. *Cognition, 40*, 159–201.

Ibsen, C.A., & Klobus, P. (1972). Fictive kin term use and social relationships: Alternative interpretations. *Journal of Marriage and Family, 34*, 615–662.

Ikels, C. (1998). Grandparenthood in cross-cultural perspective. In M. E. Szinovacz (Ed.), *Handbook on grandparenthood* (pp. 40–52). Westport, CT: Greenwood.

Ingersoll, J. (1966). The priest role in central village Thailand. In A. Suddard (Ed.), *Anthropological studies in Theravada Buddhism* (pp. 51–76). New Haven, CT: Yale University Southeast Asia Studies.

Johnson, G.R. (1986). Kin selection, socialization, and patriotism: An integrating theory. *Politics and the Life Sciences, 4*, 127–154.

Johnson, G.R. (1989). The role of kin recognition mechanisms in patriotic socialization: Further reflections. *Politics and the Life Sciences, 8*, 62–69.

Johnson, G.R., Ratwik, S.H., & Sawyer, T.J. (1987). The evocative significance of kin terms in patriotic speech. In V. Reynolds, V. Falger, & I. Vine (Eds.), *The sociobiology of ethnocentrism* (pp. 157–174). London: Croom Helm.

Johnson, J.L., McAndrew, F.T., & Harris, P.B. (1991). Sociobiology and the naming of adopted and natural children. *Ethology and Sociobiology, 12*, 365–375.

Kahn, S.M. (2004). Eggs and wombs: The origins of Jewishness. In R. Parkin, & L. Stone (Eds.), *Kinship and family: An anthropological reader* (pp. 362–377). Boston, MA: Blackwell.

Kanter, R.M. (1972). *Commitment and community: Communes and utopias in sociological perspective*. Cambridge, MA: Harvard University Press.

Keller, L. & Ross, K.G. (1998). Selfish genes: A green beard in the red fire ant. *Nature, 394*, 573–575.

Kemp, J. (1983). Kinship and the management of personal relations: Kin terminologies and the axiom of amity. *Bijdragen tot de Taal-, Land- en Volkenkunde, 139*, 81–98.

Kim, E.C. (2009). "Mama's family": Fictive kinship and undocumented immigrant restaurant workers. *Ethnography, 10*, 497–513.

Kirkpatrick, L.A. (1998). God as a substitute attachment figure: A longitudinal study of adult attachment style and religious change in college students. *Personality & Social Psychology Bulletin, 24*, 961–974.

Kitch, S.L. (1989). *Chaste liberation: Celibacy and female cultural status*. Urbana: University of Illinois Press.

Klaus, M.H., Jerauld, R., Kreger, N.C., McAlpine, W., Steffa, M., & Kenell, J.H. (1972). Maternal attachment: Importance of the first post-partum days. *New England Journal of Medicine, 286*, 460–463.

Knowles, D.D. (1963). *The monastic order in England* (2nd ed.). Cambridge, UK: Cambridge University Press.

Khosrokhavar, F. (2005). *Suicide bombers: Allah's new martyrs*. London: Pluto.

Kronenfeld, D.B. (1996). Kinship terminology. In D. Levinson & M. Ember (Eds.), *Encyclopedia of cultural anthropology* (Vol. 2, pp. 682–686). New York: Henry Holt.

Kruglanski, A.W., & Golec, A. (2004). Individual motivations, the group process and organizational strategies in suicide terrorism." In E. Meyersson Milgrom (Ed.), *Suicide missions and the market for martyrs, a multidisciplinary approach*. Princeton, N.J.: Princeton University Press. Retrieved from, http://www.wam.umd.edu/~hannahk/terror.html

Krupp, D.B., DeBruine, L.M., & Barclay, P. (2008). A cue of kinship promotes cooperation for the public good. *Evolution and Human Behavior, 29*, 49–55.

Lambert, H. (2000). Sentiment and substance in North Indian forms of relatedness. In J. Carsten (Ed.), *Cultures of relatedness: New approaches to the study of kinship* (pp. 73–103). Cambridge, UK: University Press.

Langness, L. (1964). Some problems in the conceptualization of High lands social structure. In J.B. Watson (Ed.), *New Guinea: The central highlands. American Anthropologist 66*, 162–182.

Lau, E.T. (2006). *Paper families: Identity, immigration administration and Chinese exclusion*. Durham, NC: Duke University Press.

Leavitt, G. (1989). Disappearance of the incest taboo. *American Anthropologist, 91*, 116–131.

Lewin, E. (1998). *Recognizing ourselves: Ceremonies of lesbian and gay commitment*. New York: Columbia University Press.

Lewis, I.M. (1986). *Religion in context*. Cambridge, UK: Cambridge University Press.

Lieberman, D. (2009a). Rethinking the Taiwanese minor marriage data: Evidence the mind uses multiple kinship cues to regulate inbreeding avoidance. *Evolution and Human Behavior, 30*, 153–160.

Lieberman, D. (2009b). It's all relative: The evolution of psychological mechanisms governing kin detection, incest avoidance, and altruism. Paper presented at the Evolution of Brain, Mind, and Culture Conference, Center for Mind, Brain, and Culture, Emory University, Atlanta GA, November 13.

Lieberman, D., Tooby, J., & Cosmides, L. (2003). Does morality have a biological basis? An empirical test of the factors governing moral sentiments relating to incest. *Proceedings of the Royal Society of London B, 270*, 819–826.

Lieberman, D., Tooby, J., & Cosmides, L. (2007). The architecture of human kin detection. *Nature, 445*, 727–731.

Logan, M.H., & H.N. Qirk. (1996). An evolutionary perspective on maladaptive traits. *American Journal of Human Biology, 8*, 615–629.

Lumsden, C.J. (1984). Parent-offspring conflict over the transmission of culture. *Ethology and Sociobiology, 5*, 111–129.

Lundström, J.N., Boyle, J.A., Zatorre, R.J., & Jones-Gotman, M. (2009). The neuronal substrates of human olfactory based kin recognition. *Human Brain Mapping, 30*, 2571–2580.

Maddy, R. (2000). Fictive kinship in American biomedicine. In L. Stone (Ed.), *New directions in anthropological kinship* (pp. 285–302). Lanham, MD: Rowman & Littlefield.

Madsen, E., Tunney, R., Fieldman, G., Plotkin, H., Dunbar, R. I., Richardson, J.-M., & McFarland, D. (2007). Kinship and altruism: A cross-cultural experimental study. *British Journal of Psychology, 98,* 339–359.

McCauley, C. (2002). Psychological issues in understanding terrorism and the response to terrorism. In C.E. Stout (Ed.), *The psychology of terrorism* (Vol. 3, pp. 3–29). Westport CT: Praeger.

Merari, A. (1990). The readiness to kill and die: Suicide terrorism in the Middle East. In W. Reich (Ed.), *Origins of terrorism: Psychological ideologies, theologies, states of mind* (pp. 192–207). Cambridge, UK: Cambridge University Press.

Merari, A. (2005). "Suicide terrorism." In R. I. Yufit & D. Lester (Ed.), *Assessment, treatment, and prevention of suicidal behavior* (pp. 431–453). New York: Wiley.

Michalski, R., & Euler, H. A. (2007). Sibling relationships. In C.A. Salmon & T.K. Shackelford (Eds.), *Family relationships: An evolutionary perspective* (pp. 185–204). New York: Oxford University Press.

Mintz, S.W., & Wolf, E.R. (1950). An analysis of ritual co-parenthood (compadrazgo). *Southwestern Journal of Anthropology, 6,* 341–368.

Modell, J.S. (1994). *Kinship with strangers: Adoption and interpretations of kinship in American culture.* Berkeley: University of California Press.

Moghadam, A. (2003). Palestinian suicide terrorism in the second intifada: Motivations and organizational aspects. *Studies in Conflict and Terrorism, 26,* 65–92.

Murdock, G.P., & White, D.R. (1969). Standard cross-cultural sample. *Ethnology, 8,* 329–369.

Nash, M. (1963). Burmese Buddhism in everyday life. *American Anthropologist, 65,* 285–295.

Nickerson, A.B., & Nagle, R.J. (2005). Parent and peer attachment in late childhood and early adolescence. *Journal of Early Adolescence, 23,* 223–249.

Oates, K., & Wilson, M. (2002). Nominal kinship cues facilitate altruism. *Proceedings of the Royal Society (Biological Sciences), 269,* 105–109.

Olivelle, J.P. (1990). Village vs. wilderness: Ascetic ideals and the Hindu world. In A.B. Creel & V. Narayanan (Eds.), *Monastic life in the Christian and Hindu traditions* (pp. 125– 160). Lewiston, NY: Edwin Mellen.

Oliver, A.M., & Steinberg, P.F. (2005). *The road to Martyr's Square: A journey into the world of the suicide bomber.* New York: Oxford University Press.

Olsson, S.B., Barnard, J., & Turri, L. (2006). Olfaction and identification of unrelated individuals: Examination of the mysteries of human odor recognition. *Journal of Chemical Ecology, 21,* 1635–1645.

Pape, R.A. (2005). *Dying to win: The strategic logic of suicide terrorism.* New York: Random House.

Parkin, R. (1997). *Kinship: An introduction to the basic concepts.* Oxford, UK: Blackwell.

Parr L.A., & de Waal, F.B.M. (1999). Visual kin recognition in chimpanzees. *Nature, 399,* 647–648.

Pfanner, D.E. (1966). The Buddhist monk in rural Burmese society. In A. Suddard (Ed.), *Anthropological studies in Theravada Buddhism* (pp. 77–96). New Haven, CT: Yale University Southeast Asia Studies.

Pfennig, D.W. (2002). Kin recognition. In M. Pagel (Ed.), *Encyclopedia of evolution* (pp. 592–595). Oxford, UK: Oxford University Press.

Phillips, C.M. (2005). Sisterly bonds: African American sororities rising to overcome obstacles. In T.L. Brown, G.S. Parks, & C.M. Phillips (Eds.), *African American fraternities and sororities: The legacy and the vision* (pp. 341–359). Lexington: University of Kentucky Press.

Pinker, S. (1994). *The language instinct: How the mind creates language.* New York: Harper Collins.

Pinker, S. (1997). *How the mind works.* New York: Norton.

Pinker, S., & Bloom, P. (1992). Natural language and natural selection. In J.H. Barkow, L. Cosmides, & J. Tooby (Eds.). *The adapted mind: Evolutionary psychology and the generation of culture* (pp. 451–493). New York: Oxford University Press.

Pitt-Rivers, J. (1968). Kinship: Pseudo kinship. In D.L. Sills & R.K. Merton (Eds.), *International encyclopedia of social sciences* (Vol. 8, pp. 408–413). New York: Macmillan.

Porter, R.H. (1991). Mutual mother-infant recognition in humans. In P.G. Hepper (Ed.), *Kin recognition* (pp. 125–160). Cambridge, UK: Cambridge University Press.

Post, J.M. (2007). *The mind of the terrorist: The psychology of terrorism from the IRA to al- Qaeda.* New York: Palgrave Macmillan.

Qirko, H.N. (2002). The institutional maintenance of celibacy. *Current Anthropology, 43,* 321–328.

Qirko, H.N. (2004). Altruistic celibacy, kin-cue manipulation, and the development of religious institutions. *Zygon, 39,* 681–706.

Qirko, H.N. (2009). Altruism in suicide terror organizations. *Zygon, 44,* 289–322.

Queller, D.C., Ponte, E., Bozzaro, S., & Strassmann, J.E. (2003). Single-gene green beard effects in the social amoeba *Dictyostelium discoideum. Science, 299,* 105–106.

Rachlin, H. (2002). Altruism and selfishness. *Behavioral and Brain Sciences, 25,* 239–296.

Randall, J.E., & Randall, H.A. (1960). Examples of mimicry and protective resemblance in tropical marine fishes. *Bulletin of Marine Science, 10,* 444–480.

Read, D.W. (2001). Formal analysis of kinship terminologies and its relationship to what constitutes kinship. *Anthropological Theory, 1,* 239–267.

Regalski, J.M., & Gaulin, S.J. (1993). Whom are Mexican infants said to resemble? Monitoring and fostering paternal confidence in the Yucatan. *Ethology and Sociobiology, 14,* 97–113.

Reuter, J. (2004). Chechnya's suicide bombers: Desperate, devout, or deceived? Washington DC: *The American Committee for Peace in Chechnya.* Retrieved from http://www.peaceinthecaucasus.org/reports/SuicideReport/SuicideReport.pdf

Ridley, M. (1995). *Animal behavior: An introduction to behavioral mechanisms, development, and ecology* (2nd ed.). Boston, MA: Blackwell.

Rizzolatti, G., & Craighero, L. (2005). Mirror neuron: A neurological approach to empathy. In J. P. Changeux, A.R. Damasio, W. Singer, & Y. Christen (Eds.), *Neurobiology of human values* (pp. 107–123). Berlin: Springer-Verlag.

Rothstein, S.I., & Robinson, S.K. (1998). The evolution and ecology of avian brood parasitism. In S.I. Rothstein & S.K. Robinson (Eds.), *Parasitic birds and their hosts: Studies in coevolution* (pp. 3–56). New York: Oxford University Press.

Sageman, M. (2004). *Understanding terror networks.* Philadelphia: University of Pennsylvania Press.

Sagi, A., Lamb, M.E., Lewkowicz, K.S., Shoham, R., Dvir, R., & Estes, D. (1985). Security of infant-mother, -father, and -metaplet attachments among kibbutz-reared Israeli children.

Monographs of the Society for Research in Child Development, 50, 257–275.

Sahlins, M.D. (1977). *The use and abuse of biology: An anthropological critique of sociobiology*. Ann Arbor: University of Michigan Press.

Salmon, C.A. (1998). The evocative nature of kin terminology in political rhetoric. *Politics and the Life Sciences, 17*, 51–57.

Schbley, A., & McCauley, C. (2005). Political, religious, and psychological characteristics of Muslim protest marchers in eight European cities: Jerusalem Day 2002. *Terrorism and Political Violence, 17*, 551–572.

Schieffelin, E. (1976). *The sorrow of the lonely and the burning of the dancers*. New York: St. Martin's Press.

Schino, G. (2007). Grooming and agonistic support: A meta-analysis of primate reciprocal altruism. *Behavioral Ecology, 18*, 115–120.

Schneider, D.M. (1984). *A critique of the study of kinship*. Ann Arbor: University of Michigan Press.

Schroeder, D.A., Penner, L.A., Dovidio, J.F., & Piliavin, J.A. (1995). *The psychology of helping and altruism: Problems and puzzles*. New York: McGraw-Hill.

Seltzer, M.M. (1993). Fictive kinship. In R. Kastembaum (Ed.), *Encyclopedia of adult development* (pp. 158–160). Phoenix AZ: Oryx.

Seyfarth, R.M., & Cheney, D.L. (1984). Grooming, alliances and reciprocal altruism in Vervet monkeys. *Nature, 308*, 541–543.

Sherman, P.W. (2009). The role of kinship. In D.W. Macdonald (Ed.), *The new encyclopedia of mammals* (pp. 162–163). Princeton, NJ: Princeton University Press.

Sherman, P.W., & Holmes, W.G. (1985). Kin recognition: Issues: evidence. In B. Holldobler & M. Lindauer (Eds.), *Experimental behavioral ecology and sociobiology* (pp. 437–460). New York: Gustav Fischer Verlag.

Shipton, P. (1997). Fictive kinship. In T. Barfield (Ed.), *Dictionary of anthropology* (pp. 186–187). Malden, MA: Blackwell.

Skertchly, J.A. (1974). *Dahomey as it is*. London: Chapman and Hall.

Silk, J.B. (1987). Adoption and fosterage in human societies: Adaptations or enigmas? *Cultural Anthropology, 2*, 39–49.

Silk, J.B. (2001). Ties that bind: The role of kinship in primate societies. In L. Stone (Ed.), *New directions in anthropological kinship* (pp. 71–92). Lanham, MD: Rowman & Littlefield.

Slade, M. (19August 87, 17). Relationships: Nurturing by adopted relatives. *The New York Times*. Retrieved from http://www.nytimes.com/1987/08/17/style/relationships-nurturing-by-adopted-relatives.html

Smith, F.J., & Crano, W.D. (1977). Patterns of cultural diffusion: Analyses of trait associations across societies by content and geographical proximity. *Cross-Cultural Research, 12*, 145–167.

Sober, E., & Wilson, D.S. (1999). *Unto others: The evolution and psychology of unselfish behavior*. Cambridge, MA: Harvard University Press.

Sornarajah, N. (2004). The experiences of Tamil women: Nationalism, construction of gender, and women's political agency. Part II. *Lines* 3(2). Retrieved from http://www.lines-magazine.org/index.html

Sosis, R. (2000). Religion and intra-group cooperation: Preliminary results of a comparative analysis of utopian communities. *Cross-Cultural Research, 34*, 70–87.

Sosis, R. (2004). The adaptive value of religious ritual. *American Scientist, 92*, 166–172.

Sosis, R., & Alcorta, C. (2003). Signaling, solidarity, and the sacred: The evolution of religious behavior. *Evolutionary Anthropology, 12*, 264–274.

Spiro, M.E. (1971). *Buddhism and society*. London: Allen and Unwin.

Stockard, J. (1989). *Daughters of the Canton delta: Marriage patterns and economic strategies in South China, 1860–1930*. Stanford, CA: Stanford University Press.

Stone, L. (2006). *Kinship and gender: An introduction* (3rd ed.). Boulder CO: Westview.

Strathern, M. (1992). *After nature: English kinship in the late twentieth century*. Cambridge, UK: Cambridge University Press.

Sulloway, F. J. (1996). *Born to rebel: Birth order, family dynamics, and creative lives*. New York: Pantheon.

Taheri, A. (1987). *Holy terror: Inside the world of Islamic terrorism*. Bethesda, MD: Adler & Adler.

Talmon, Y. (1964). Mate selection in collective settlements. *American Sociological Review, 29*, 491–508.

Terrell, J., & Modell, J. (1994). Anthropology and adoption. *American Anthropologist, 96*, 155–161.

Timko, P. (1990). Pray at fixed times, pray always: Patterns of monastic prayer. A.B. Creel & V. Narayanan (Eds.), *Monastic life in the Christian and Hindu traditions* (pp. 97–124). Lewiston, NY: Edwin Mellen.

Trivers, R.L. (1971). The evolution of reciprocal altruism. *Quarterly Review of Biology, 46*, 35–57.

Trivers, R.L. (1985). *Social evolution*. Menlo Park, CA: Benjamin/Cummings.

van den Berghe, P.L. (1979). *Human family systems: An evolutionary view*. New York: Elsevier.

van den Berghe, P.L. (1981). *The ethnic phenomenon*. New York: Elsevier.

van den Berghe, P.L., & Peter, K. (1988). Hutterites and kibbutzniks: A tale of nepotistic communism. *Man, 23*, 522–539.

van Gennep, A. (2004 [1909]). *The rites of passage*. London: Routledge.

Vanita, R. (2005). *Love's rite: Same-sex marriage in India and the West*. New York: Palgrave Macmillan.

Vermes, G., & Goodman, M.D. (1989). *The Essenes according to the classical sources*. Sheffield, UK: JSOT Press.

Vigil, J.D. (1988). Group processes and street identity: Adolescent Chicano gang members. *Ethos, 16*, 421–445.

Vlahos, O. (1985). *Doing business: The anthropology of striving, thriving, and beating out the competition*. New York: Franklin Watts.

Wach, J. (1962). *Sociology of religion*. Chicago, IL: University of Chicago Press.

Wagner, R.A. (1995). Fictive kinship. In *Marriage and family encyclopedia*. Retrieved from http://family.jrank.org/pages/630/Fictive-Kinship.html

Wei-hsun Fu, C., & Wawrytko, S.A. (1994). *Buddhist behavioral codes and the modern world*. Westport, CT: Greenwood.

Weisfeld, G.E., Czilli, T., Phillips, K.A., Gall, J.A., & Lichtman, C.M. (2003). Possible olfaction-based mechanisms in human kin recognition and inbreeding avoidance. *Journal of Experimental Child Psychology, 85*, 279–295.

Wells, P.A. (1987). Kin recognition in humans. In D.J.C. Fletcher & C.D. Michener (Eds.), *Kin recognition in animals* (pp. 395–415). New York: John Wiley.

Weston, K. (1991). *Families we choose: Lesbians, gays, kinship*. New York: Columbia University Press.

Wilkinson, G.S. (1984). Reciprocal food sharing in the vampire bat. *Nature, 308*, 181–184.

Wilson, D.S. (1990). Weak altruism, strong group selection. *Oikos, 59*, 135–48.

Wilson, E.O. (1975). *Sociobiology: The new synthesis*. Cambridge MA: Belknap Press.

Wilson, E.O. (1979). *On human nature*. Cambridge, MA: Harvard University Press.

Wilson, E.O. (1987). Kin recognition: An introductory synopsis. In D.J.C. Fletcher & C.D. Michener (Eds.), *Kin recognition in animals* (pp. 7–18). New York: John Wiley.

Wilson, E.O. (2005). Kin selection as the key to altruism: Its rise and fall. *Social Research, 72*, 159–166.

Wolf, A. (1995). *Sexual attraction and childhood association*. Stanford, CA: Stanford University Press.

Wynne, E.A. (1988). *Traditional Catholic religious orders: Living in community*. New Brunswick, NJ: Transaction Books.

Yanoviak, S.P., Kaspari, M., Dudley, R., & Poinar Jr., G. (2008). Parasite-induced fruit mimicry in a tropical canopy ant. *American Naturalist, 171*, 536–544.

Zahavi, A., & Zahavi, A. (1997). The handicap principle. Oxford, UK: Oxford University Press.

Zartman, W. (2003). Negotiating with terrorists. *International Negotiation, 8*, 43–450.

Zebrowitz, L.A. (1997). *Reading faces*. Boulder, CO: Westview.

CHAPTER 19

Passion and Compassion: Psychology of Kin Relations Within and Beyond the Family

Justin H. Park *and* Joshua M. Ackerman

Abstract

Family is special. People avoid sexual contact with close relatives, but at the same time are highly beneficent toward them. Such discriminatory behavior is guided by a set of psychological mechanisms, heuristics that facilitate evolutionarily adaptive behavior most of the time but may lead to overperception of kinship under specific circumstances. In this chapter, we describe psychological mechanisms of kin recognition in sexual and altruistic contexts, and we discuss the extent to which these mechanisms may influence close relationships between unrelated individuals, resulting in an experience of "psychological kinship." We suggest that friendship may provide a context within which overinclusive kin recognition is especially likely to occur, especially among women. We also identify questions for future research, including when men might be especially prone to overperceiving kinship.

Keywords: Altruism, family, friendship, incest avoidance, kin recognition, kinship

Introduction

In the American television series *Friends* (Crane et al., 1994–2004), the characters Joey and Rachel become infatuated with each other and attempt a romantic relationship after having been close friends for several years. Previously, two other characters—Chandler and Monica—had successfully gone from being friends to lovers. In the (anti)climactic episode (Buckner & Halvorson, 2003), Joey and Rachel reach the brink of sexual contact, only to hit a psychological wall: They find that the situation feels "weird" and "wrong." Eventually they give up, disappointed and bewildered. Rachel asks, "I wonder how Monica and Chandler could do it?" Joey answers, "I guess they weren't as good friends as we are." The reasoning is not articulated; presumably, viewers understand why being such good friends should pose a problem. An earlier episode (Reich, Cohen, & Weiss, 2002) provides a hint: The character Ross, having difficulty picturing Joey and Rachel as a couple, says to his sister Monica, "I mean it's . . . . It's like you and me going out, only weirder!" Perhaps what Joey and Rachel felt was a tinge (or more) of what a typical brother and sister would feel upon contemplating sex with each other.

To make interesting scientific discoveries, one must ask the right questions. A major benefit of adopting a functional–evolutionary perspective in psychology is that we are forced to go beyond the obvious, to pose what may at first seem like "dumb" questions. Why do we like the sight of beautiful faces? Why do we get upset when rejected by others? Why do we relish social acceptance? It is tempting to answer: We just do. Of course, when something just feels obvious, it is usually because the messy psychological details are enwrapped within human intuition and introspectively unavailable (James, 1890). As psychologists, these details are part of what we are trying to uncover; but being humans, our intuition often prevents us from recognizing the right questions in the first place (Cosmides & Tooby, 1994). A common consequence is that there exist conspicuously underexplored patches of psychological terrain, especially (and ironically) in intuition-rich areas requiring particular research attention.

Within social psychology—the field that deals with people's thoughts about and relations with other people—kinship represents one of those underexplored patches (Daly, Salmon, & Wilson, 1997). Despite the fact that thoughts about and relations with kin dominate social life, the social psychological literature has surprisingly little to say about kinship. A search of the database PsycINFO (in September, 2009) returned a total of 8,711 articles in the leading empirical journal, the *Journal of Personality and Social Psychology* (*JPSP*), going back to the year 1965. A search for articles containing the words "kin" or "kinship" in the title returned two articles (0.02% of the total). A search for titles containing the words "family" or "families" was more encouraging, turning up 38 additional articles (0.44% of the total), although only a handful of these were about family relations per se. These numbers don't tell the whole story, of course, but perhaps the low profile of kinship is not surprising, given how fundamental it is. People have deep intuitions regarding kinship (Jones, 2003; Lieberman, Oum, & Kurzban, 2008), and social psychologists—being people—may not have felt the need to probe those intuitions. Consider the following questions: Why do parents favor their own children over others? Why don't brothers and sisters have sex with each other? How do people know who their children, brothers, and sisters are? It is easy to dismiss such fundamental questions because they seem trivial: *Of course*, parents favor their own children; *of course*, siblings don't have sex; and we *just know* who our family members are.

In this chapter, we contemplate some of these questions and describe some of the psychological mechanisms underlying kin relations as revealed by empirical research. The emerging picture is not as clear-cut as one might think. For starters, the mind must rely on fairly simple—and fallible—heuristics to reckon genetic relatedness, and this may sometimes have some odd downstream repercussions, as Joey and Rachel discovered. And, although Joey and Rachel's feelings of unease appeared to be mutual, there are reasons to suspect that women may find the prospect of sex with close friends particularly aversive (in fact, it was Rachel who initiated the awkwardness by "unconsciously" slapping Joey's hand mid-courtship). As we describe below, women may be more likely to treat friends as though they were kin in a variety of nonsexual social contexts.

We also explore whether there may be circumstances under which men may be especially likely to share kinship sentiments with others.

As there already exist clear descriptions of how humans detect different classes of actual genetic kin (e.g., Lieberman, 2007; Tal & Lieberman, 2007), the bulk of this chapter focuses on the extent to which these and associated mechanisms may extend to close relationships between nonkin (e.g., Ackerman, Kenrick, & Schaller, 2007; Park, Schaller, & Van Vugt, 2008). In particular, we explore the extent to which our understanding of friendship (between nonkin) may be illuminated by considering the psychology of kin relations. Ultimately, whether—and how powerfully—kinship psychology influences nonkin relations is an empirical matter. The answer is not straightforward because, although humans likely possess domain-specific relationship schemas, these are unlikely to be encapsulated and mutually exclusive (Barrett & Kurzban, 2006). Joey and Rachel, despite knowledge that they are unrelated, may have run into trouble because of a spillover effect of their incest-avoidance mechanisms.

Evolution and the Psychology of Kin Relations

We first present a brief review of the psychological mechanisms underlying identification of kin within the contexts of sexual relations and helping behavior. Along the way, we attempt to clarify some issues, especially some common misunderstandings of the psychological implications of a biological perspective on kinship.

Incest Avoidance and the Role of Familiarity

People tend not to engage in sexual relations with biological relatives. This is not because individuals curb incestuous urges; most people find the mere thought of sex with close relatives emotionally disturbing (e.g., Park, 2008). This fact may seem self-evident, and it represents one of the many unexamined intuitions described above. Indeed, there are theoretical reasons to expect people to find family members especially desirable. Repeated in many social psychology textbooks is the notion that similarity and familiarity are among the key contributors to attraction (e.g., Aronson, Wilson, & Akert, 2005; Brehm, Kassin, & Fein, 2005)—and who is more similar and familiar to us than our genetically related family members? Families also tend to support each other, and we like people who are kind to us (Li, Bailey, Kenrick, & Linsenmeier, 2002).

So, why aren't we interested in jumping into bed with our parents and siblings?

Westermarck (1891) was one of the first scholars to recognize the significance of incest-avoidance tendencies. In fact, he proposed one of the earliest evolutionary psychological hypotheses: that humans are innately predisposed to find incest aversive and that early-life coresidence—which most often occurs among close kin—is what inspires the aversion. (Animals are expected to evolve incest-avoidance tendencies, due to the harmful consequences of inbreeding; see Lieberman, 2007.)

From the perspective of contemporary psychology, Westermarck's (1891) key insight was not that humans are innately incest-avoidant (although this idea was also significant, especially in the Freudian era), but that natural selection produces psychological information-processing mechanisms designed to take input from the developmental context and produce some functional output that drives adaptive behavior. Although he did not use this terminology, he essentially made a distinction between *ultimate* and *proximate* explanations: that sexual aversion emerges between family members is a proximate account of behavior; that this serves the function of inbreeding avoidance is the ultimate explanation of the proximate process. Hence, it is not the case that humans have evolved motivations to avoid inbreeding per se; rather, humans—and many other organisms—have evolved simple heuristics that appear to be directed toward the goal of inbreeding avoidance, under most circumstances. But not under all circumstances; in fact, the presence of sexual aversion between *unrelated* people has served as key evidence for Westermarck's hypothesis (e.g., Wolf, 1966).

One critical developmental variable that feeds into the incest-avoidance mechanism seems to be the number of years one has coresided with another person (e.g., Lieberman, Tooby, & Cosmides, 2003). Longer periods of coresidence produce stronger sexual aversions. A large-scale study of arranged marriages in China showed that those arrangements in which infants are adopted into families and reared with their future mates are marked by lower birth rates and higher rates of adultery and divorce than other forms of marriage (Wolf, 1995). Thus, it is not simply biological kin who can develop incest aversion, but unrelated people as well. Lieberman, Tooby, and Cosmides (2007) recently argued that duration of coresidence may be less important when more reliable information is available. Specifically, older siblings can observe the arrival of their younger siblings and can observe their mother caring for them. Lieberman et al. (2007) found that for such older siblings, aversion to incest is elevated regardless of coresidence duration; for younger siblings, who cannot observe their older siblings perinatally, coresidence duration is the best available cue and does reliably predict aversion to incest (see also Lieberman, 2009). Either way, it is a sense of familiarity that fuels sexual aversion (we should note that we use the term *familiarity* to refer to felt closeness such as that typically experienced among family members, not to refer to simple knowledge of another person).

The role of familiarity as a sexual barrier is also apparent when genetically related individuals sometimes do engage in incestuous behavior. The fictional world has no shortage of stories of incest, and in many of these there is a lack of normal familial association between the relevant individuals (Oedipus and Jocasta being the most famous). This is no coincidence. Even if two people are fully aware of their relatedness, without the appropriate level of familiarity they may not experience the normal aversion. Empirical research supports this conjecture. One set of studies found that (nonfictional) genetic siblings who engage in procreative incest (as opposed to nonprocreative incest) are more likely to have spent time apart during their childhood (Bevc & Silverman, 1993, 2000; according to these researchers, the incest-avoidance mechanism may have evolved to be highly domain-specific, deterring not just sexual feelings in general, but reproductive attempts more specifically). Even in the rare situations in which familiar genetic siblings end up committing incest, their familiarity is at the very least a nuisance. In Eugenides's (2002) novel *Middlesex*, Desdemona and Lefty (sister and brother who grew up with each other) develop romantic feelings and get married incognito: "Their honeymoon proceeded in reverse. Instead of getting to know each other, becoming familiar with likes and dislikes, ticklish spots, pet peeves, Desdemona and Lefty tried to *defamiliarize* themselves with each other" (pp. 71–72, emphasis added).

Westermarck's (1891) hypothesis also implied something that we normally take for granted—that people are capable of identifying and remembering specific *individuals* across extended periods. Familiarity with a specific person implies forming a representation of that person as an abstraction, which persists even as tangible features of the person (facial features, vocal qualities) change over time. This means that psychological processes underlying familiarity are likely to be distinct from processes typically studied by social cognition researchers, which mostly have to do with how individuals react to strangers under varying circumstances. Often within experimental settings, participants are presented with descriptions or photos of strangers, some key variables (e.g., gender, ethnicity, attractiveness) are manipulated, and some theoretically relevant responses are assessed. However, it is not feasible to experimentally manipulate long-term familiarity in order to assess its effects. Simply put, familiarity is not a "cue" in the same sense that those experimentally manipulable variables are cues. Rather, familiarity is what results when the relationship between two individuals—along with their mental representations—has been fundamentally altered as a result of experience. We stress this point because it has been common practice to employ the term "cue" to refer to familiarity as well as to other potential correlates of kinship, such as facial resemblance, that purportedly require no prior acquaintance. This practice may obscure psychologically distinct processes. In particular, confusion can arise when processes underlying identification of already-familiar individuals (e.g., identifying one's child via odor cues) are incorrectly described as examples of "kin recognition." (The ability to recognize an existing family member, based on some sensory cue, is not an instance of kin recognition because the underlying individual identification mechanism is a domain-general capacity that is useful across social contexts. The same mechanism might be employed, for instance, to identify a well-known enemy.)

As Harris (2006) put it, humans possess a "people-information acquisition device": Most of us know dozens or hundreds of people and have no difficulty telling them apart by the way they look and sound. Highly familiar individuals (such as family members) can indeed be identified by smell alone (e.g., Porter & Moore, 1981). The ability to individuate and to identify familiar persons by sight, sound, and smell are obviously useful components of an incest-avoidance mechanism. This ability is important for other reasons as well—namely, determining to whom we should direct our altruistic efforts.

Kin Selection and Altruism

Consider the set of people closest to you—those you can rely on when in trouble, and those you would help without hesitation. Often, such people are family members. When it comes to investing our valuable resources (e.g., time, money), we are extremely partial, directing much of it to close kin. Why is this? And what psychological mechanisms underlie this tendency? Here, the conventional biologically informed answer is that individuals are driven to enhance their inclusive fitness, which is achieved by "helping those who share your genes"; and Hamilton (1964) is cited as the author of that idea. But this is a misunderstanding (for discussions and clarifications, see Daly et al., 1997; Dawkins, 1979; Park, 2007). The intuition that "blood is thicker than water" is so deeply ingrained that it can seem like a fundamental law of nature; and we easily translate "blood" into "genes." However, genetic similarity per se is irrelevant to understanding what actually motivates altruistic behavior. What kin selection theory states is that genes underlying specific altruistic tendencies (e.g., being kind to one's coresidents) *can* evolve under specific circumstances, not that organisms are genetically omniscient and direct their altruistic efforts accordingly. Kin selection theory is thus a guide for identifying proximate psychological mechanisms (analogous to the proximate coresidence-based mechanism identified by Westermarck); it does not constitute a prescriptive rule for behavior.

A common error is to treat Hamilton's (1964) inequality ($c < b * r$) itself as the proximate psychological mechanism, a decision rule that should guide behavior (see Park, 2007). Consequently, animals are simply presumed to adjust their level of altruism according to degrees of relatedness. For instance, because the degree of relatedness is .5 between siblings and .125 between cousins, a simplistic prediction is that individuals should be exactly four times more helpful to a sibling than a cousin. This is what led to Haldane's famous response when asked whether he would give his life to save a drowning brother: "No, but I would to save two brothers or eight cousins" (McElreath & Boyd, 2007, p. 82). Hamilton's theory states only that such a tendency *can* evolve, not that it must or did. Because of this confusion, behavioral deviations from Hamilton's theory—which occur frequently—are sometimes incorrectly interpreted as evidence against kin selection theory.

Researchers who wish to apply kin selection theory to altruism must therefore tackle some important questions: What proximate psychological mechanisms actually evolved? Did evolution produce information-processing mechanisms that are finely attuned to degrees of relatedness, such as those between half-siblings, full siblings, and cousins? When we consider the empirical evidence, the picture is far from straightforward. Although humans and many nonhuman animals do tend to favor more closely related individuals (e.g., Chapais, Savard, & Gauthier, 2001; Judge & Hrdy, 1991; Stewart-Williams, 2007; Webster, 2003), evidence of sensitivity to precise degrees of relatedness is virtually nonexistent. But this should not be surprising, given that kin selection theory is not about the *psychology* of kin altruism (see Buss, 2008, p. 232). As with incest avoidance, what seem to have evolved are simple heuristics such as "if X grew up with me in the same nest/litter/home, then be responsive when X needs help." To expect organisms to behave strictly according to degrees of relatedness is to conflate the ultimate and proximate levels (just as humans do not possess motivations to avoid inbreeding per se, they do not possess motivations to be altruistic to genetic kin per se).

Empirical research indicates that the principal "kin recognition" process underlying incest avoidance—familiarity with specific individuals—underlies kin altruism as well. Lieberman et al. (2007) found that varying durations of coresidence with specific individuals calibrates altruistic tendencies toward those individuals (at least for altruistic tendencies toward older siblings; with respect to younger siblings, the experience of observing one's mother caring for them seems to suffice). The primacy of familiarity as a determinant of altruism is true in other primates as well (Goodall, 1986; Rendall, 2004). It would thus seem that mechanisms that allow individuals to recognize genetic relations without prior acquaintance are likely to play a relatively minor role, at least among primates. As Rendall (2004) noted, "mechanisms that actually identify and discriminate degrees of genetic relatedness (so-called true kin recognition mechanisms) appear rare" (p. 298). Rare, yes; but do they exist?

"True" Kin Recognition Mechanisms?

In the science fiction film *Back to the Future* (Canton et al., 1985), the protagonist Marty McFly travels 30 years into the past, just before his parents (were supposed to) meet each other. Marty is soon disturbed to discover that his mother, Lorraine, has become infatuated with him. In one memorable scene, Lorraine passionately kisses Marty. But she immediately appears confused, saying, "This is all wrong. I don't know what it is, but when I'm kissing you, it's like I'm kissing my brother." The audience (and Marty, although too stunned to think clearly) knows why she feels this way. But the mechanism is not made explicit. How did she know that something wasn't right? Did something about Marty's phenotype (his appearance, voice, smell) tip off Lorraine's kin recognition system?

If such a thing had really occurred (perhaps under a more realistic scenario of long-lost siblings unknowingly going on a date), it would indicate a different sort of kin recognition capacity, one that does not involve extended familiarity with a specific person. There are evolutionary reasons to expect such a capacity. Although familiarity is an eminently useful heuristic, it's less useful for close kin who do not share a home (e.g., half siblings). Familiarity is also a less-than-perfect indicator of relatedness for males with respect to offspring because of the problem of paternity uncertainty. If there is a chance that a man's partner has given birth to a child fathered by someone else (and this is common enough in people and other animals), the man cannot rely simply on the fact that he knows the child well. He needs more diagnostic information.

Indeed, there is evidence for what are known as *phenotype matching* mechanisms: Individuals attend to physical and behavioral characteristics that may connote genetic relatedness and react on the basis of those characteristics. Some of these mechanisms seem to be built upon the familiarity system, whereby newly encountered individuals are compared to already-familiar kin. For instance, because I am familiar with my brother and his characteristics, if I encounter someone—even a stranger—who resembles my brother, this may then trigger kin-relevant responses. Thus, comparisons may be made between unfamiliar others and a general *kin prototype* (i.e., an evolved heuristic may be "if someone resembles familiar kin, treat that person as kin"). Fostering studies with nonhuman animals have shown that genetically unrelated nestmates/littermates may indeed use each other's features (vocalizations, smells) to serve as the standard of comparison when assessing newly encountered individuals (Sharp, McGowan, Wood, & Hatchwell, 2005; Yamazaki et al., 1988). Of course, in such cases, the phenotype matching mechanisms are no more diagnostic than the familiarity mechanism on which they are based. Are there more foolproof phenotype matching mechanisms? Yes: There is evidence for mechanisms that allow individuals to assess genetic relatedness more directly by comparing a target's features to their own (known as *self-referent* phenotype matching; Hauber & Sherman, 2001).

Unlike familiarity, phenotypic resemblance is a cue that can be experimentally introduced in the absence of existing relationships, making it amenable to laboratory research. In recent years, several studies have investigated the effects of experimentally manipulated facial resemblance. The typical procedure is to take a photograph of a participant's face and to digitally combine it with faces of unfamiliar strangers (for a description, see DeBruine, Jones, Little, & Perrett, 2008). The result is a person who facially resembles the participant, but not so blatantly that the participant consciously notices it. This method has been used to test whether facial resemblance exerts effects that one would expect of a kinship cue—that is, dampening sexual attraction while heightening altruistic reactions; evidence supports these expectations (e.g., DeBruine, 2005). The method has also been used to test whether men are more sensitive than are women to self–child facial resemblance, as one might expect given paternity uncertainty; this hypothesis has received mixed support (e.g., DeBruine, 2004; Platek, Burch, Panyavin, Wasserman, & Gallup, 2002). What may be occurring in these self-morph studies is kin prototype-based phenotype matching (rather than self-referent phenotype matching). The reason is that ancestral humans would have had far greater exposure to the appearance of their family members than to their own (mirrors and cameras being in short supply). Thus, the observed effects of self-morphs may be a consequence of the fact that participants' faces actually resemble those of their family members and thus serve as a proxy for their kin-based prototype. Perhaps these experimental effects would be even stronger if participants viewed photos of strangers manipulated to resemble a close family member.

This burgeoning literature indicates that, although the picture is far from clear, people do respond in what appear to be functional ways to facial resemblance (see also DeBruine, Jones, & Perrett, 2005; Platek et al., 2003, 2004). Of course, these phenotype matching mechanisms can lead to errors as well, such as when the kin prototype is based on genetically unrelated individuals (e.g., one's adopted family). More generally, these experiments are set up precisely to stimulate kin-relevant responses in the absence of actual kinship. Thus, to the extent that the effects of manipulated facial resemblance actually recruit kin recognition mechanisms, these findings further demonstrate that it is not only possible but fairly easy to elicit kin-relevant responses in the absence of actual kinship, even when perceivers are consciously aware that no true kinship exists.

Assuming that the effects of manipulated resemblance do pertain to kinship, one must ask how ecologically relevant such cues are, considering that, as noted above, familiarity seems to do much of the "kin recognition" work. A handful of studies among actual family members have shown that resemblance cues do seem to matter. These studies focus on men's reactions to children, again highlighting the importance of paternity uncertainty. Burch and Gallup (2000) conducted a study among men convicted of spousal abuse, examining whether these men's beliefs about the resemblance between themselves and their children predicted various outcomes. The results showed that perceived resemblance was positively correlated with the quality of the men's relationships with their children, and negatively correlated with the frequency of spousal conflicts and the severity of the injuries suffered by their spouses. Another study found that men's perceived resemblance with their children was positively correlated with the level of investment in the children, operationalized as the amount of attention, time, and help devoted to the children (Apicella & Marlowe, 2004). Importantly, further research has found that actual resemblance (not just perceived resemblance) predicts emotional closeness between father and child, but not between mother and child (Alvergne, Faurie, & Raymond, 2010). A recent study tested men's and women's ability to identify their (purportedly biological) children by odor cues, and investigated their investment in the children (Dubas, Heijkoop, & van Aken, 2009). The results showed that 67.7% of the men and 79.4% of the women could identify their children by smell. More interestingly, men showed a tendency to invest more in children who were identifiable by smell; women showed no such bias. Thus, the experimental effects reviewed earlier appear indicative of real-life outcomes.

Furthermore, although the evidence is preliminary, it appears that other kinds of similarities, such as attitudinal similarity, may also serve as kinship cues, at least under some circumstances (e.g., Mobbs et al., 2009). Many of us have experienced meeting a person who "reminds" us of a family member and thus draws out charitable feelings (or perhaps mild aversions, in sexual situations). One study found that people who tend to trust their intuitions tend to make stronger implicit associations between an attitudinally similar stranger and "family" concepts, but not the broader category of "pleasant" concepts (Park & Schaller, 2005). Social psychological studies have shown that people possess rich mental representations of significant individuals (e.g., parent, sibling, spouse), and when presented with a novel target who resembles a significant individual, information processing of the target is influenced by those existing representations (Andersen, Glassman, Chen, & Cole, 1995). For example, after meeting a person who reminds me of my brother, I might mistakenly remember that the person likes to watch science fiction films because my brother does.

Finally, we mentioned earlier that according to conventional social psychological wisdom, people are attracted to "similar" (and "familiar") others. Does this contradict the view that familiarity and phenotypic resemblance should *reduce* attraction? Not at all. As it turns out, the social psychological literature on the impact of similarity/familiarity on "attraction" is not about sexual attraction, but about *liking* (see Park et al., 2008). That similarity promotes liking is fully consistent with the present perspective: Outside of sexual contexts, information connoting kinship is expected to increase affinity. This sort of divergent effect of similarity is consistent with other theoretical perspectives as well. Describing his Exotic Becomes Erotic theory, Bem (1996) noted that "similarity may promote friendship, compatibility, and companionate love, but it is dissimilarity that sparks erotic/romantic attraction and passionate love" (p. 323). Familiarity has similar consequences: Westermarck's (1891) theory implies that although familiarity may arouse compassion, it is novelty that fuels passion.

Psychology of Kin Relations Beyond the Family

In this section, we explain why the kin recognition processes described above inevitably lead to situations in which nonkin are perceived as kin, and vice versa. As we describe below, the tendency to treat nonkin as kin may underlie—at least to some extent—relationships between unrelated individuals; moreover, based on evolutionary cost–benefit analysis, it is possible to predict who should be especially prone to treating nonkin as kin, and when.

Overinclusive Kin Perception and Sex Differences

A key point concerning the kin recognition systems described above is that, although they are often effective (people who live with us and look like us are usually kin), they are not foolproof. Consider sibling relations. None of the kin recognition systems seems capable of reliably identifying true genetic siblings under all circumstances. Familiarity becomes unreliable the moment someone is switched at birth (or, more realistically, is adopted, is brought into a step family, or is a half-sibling who grows up in a different household). And, it is far from clear whether phenotype-matching mechanisms are sensitive enough to make fine distinctions such as those between a full sibling, half-sibling, and cousin. Even the self-referent phenotype matching process can be activated by a complete stranger who, by sheer coincidence, looks, sounds, smells, and acts like we do. Thus, kin recognition presents a signal-detection problem, inevitably producing false-positive and false-negative errors. Unrelated coresidents who refuse each other as sexual partners commit a false-positive error (they infer kinship in its absence). Genetic siblings who engage in incest commit a false-negative error (they fail to infer kinship in its presence). Assuming that it's impossible to eliminate these kinds of errors, is there any reason to expect bias toward one type of error?

When engaging in scientific hypothesis testing, we are deliberately biased against false-positive errors (i.e., inferring effects in their absence) because we find them to be more costly for science. Within biological organisms, natural selection can produce psychological mechanisms with biases against the type of error that is more costly in terms of reproductive fitness; thus, people tend to overperceive dangers, and men tend to overperceive sexual interest in women, as underperception in these particular contexts is more costly (Haselton & Nettle, 2006). Conversely, people tend to underperceive individuating characteristics of outgroup faces (Ostrom & Sedikides, 1992), and women tend to underperceive men's romantic commitment intentions, especially prior to the onset of sexual activity in relationships (Ackerman, Griskevicius, & Li, in press). Assuming a degree of ambiguity regarding genetic relatedness, is it more costly to over- or underperceive kinship?

Within the contexts of sexual relations and altruism, respectively, the consequences of false-negative errors are incest and failing to provide aid to real kin, whereas the consequences of false-positive errors are refusing a genetically suitable mate and providing aid to nonkin. Whether a bias toward one type of error is more adaptive will clearly depend on several factors, such as the sheer number of close kin in one's environment (Park et al., 2008). For instance, if most people you encounter happen to be kin (because you come from a big family in a small village), the odds of committing false-positive errors are low, so it may be more adaptive to be biased toward such errors.

One important variable that may modulate these kin recognition biases is one's sex (Ackerman et al., 2007). Inbreeding is costly, but it is more costly for females than males (as any unfit reproduction is more costly for mammalian females; Trivers, 1972). So, women are expected to harbor a stronger bias toward false-positive errors (i.e., a tendency to infer kinship in its absence) in the context of sexual relations than men. Indeed, women do seem to find the prospect of incest more aversive than do men under some circumstances (Fessler & Navarrete, 2004). More importantly, there should be a particularly large sex difference in aversion toward sex with close but unrelated individuals—instances in which women, but not men (unconsciously) perceive the target as kin. Likewise, providing gratuitous aid to nonkin is costly (although admirable), but it may be relatively less costly for females than for males. Female nonkin relationships tend to be more communal than men's, marked by tight connections and socioemotional bonds (Baumeister & Sommer, 1997; Geary & Flinn, 2002; Kashima et al., 1995), and the types of support provided in these relationships mirrors the altruism within families, given without strong expectation of reciprocity (Ackerman & Kenrick, 2008; Clark, Mills, & Powell, 1986). There is also historical evidence to suggest that humans were ancestrally patrilocal (i.e., at marriage, women moved into men's families and not the converse; Pasternak, Ember, & Ember, 1997), which may have created pressure for women to form supportive social alliances by overperceiving kinship. In contrast, men's nonkin relationships tend to be more hierarchical and task-oriented, with support following a reciprocal, exchange-based format. Within such situations, women's accidental altruism toward nonkin is likely to build social relationships, but men's altruism is less likely to do so. In fact, male altruism may even upset established or anticipated social hierarchies (e.g., consider two men fighting over who will pay the dinner bill). This is not to say that men never treat unrelated others like family, but simply that within the contexts of sexual or altruistic interaction, women are more likely to benefit from overperceiving kinship.

Psychological Kinship

As reviewed above, it is not genetic relatedness per se that underlies kinship-relevant behavior; what matters is the extent to which a particular person is perceived as "kin"—what Lieberman et al. (2007) referred to as the *kinship index*. The perception of kinship encompasses propositional knowledge that a particular person is a sibling, cousin, etc.; familiarity that one feels with respect to those persons; and implicit detection of other kinship cues. So, even if a person is genetically unrelated to us, we may consciously categorize that person as kin (e.g., as a "sibling," if there has been a history of coresidence) and/or we may experience cognitive and emotional reactions normally directed toward kin (such as dampened passion and heightened compassion) in interactions with this person. Wolf (1966) relates a girl's reply when asked why she refused to marry a boy whose family she had joined as a child: "I just couldn't do it. It was too embarrassing. Imagine marrying your brother!" (p. 893). Pinker (1997) referred to such erroneous perceptions as "kinship illusions." More generally, the perception and experience of kinship, erroneous or not, has been referred to as "psychological kinship" (Bailey, 1988).

A handful of social psychological studies have attempted to investigate psychological kinship—that is, the specific cognitive and emotional mediators of kin-directed behavior (Korchmaros & Kenny, 2001; Kruger, 2003; Maner & Gailliot, 2007; Neyer & Lang, 2003; Park & Schaller, 2005). These have all focused on mediators of altruism, and they have revealed that emotional closeness—and more specifically empathic concern—may be among the key mediators. Cognitive mediators such as perceived self–other overlap have been shown to predict helping behaviors as well (Maner et al., 2002). Park and Schaller (2005) found that, although an attitudinally similar stranger implicitly activates both "family" and "pleasant" concepts, only the former concept predicts desire to assist the target individual. Thus, one component of psychological kinship appears to be cognitive activation of family-related concepts, rather than activation of positive concepts more broadly. The cognitive processing of psychological kin may therefore recruit the same psychological mechanisms devoted to the processing of real kin (Ackerman et al., 2007; Park et al., 2008).

An important implication is that when a person experiences psychological kinship with someone else, even an unrelated person, this may trigger sexual aversion and/or altruistic behaviors. Of course, the experience of psychological kinship is not all-or-nothing, and people may sometimes actively ignore certain pieces of kin-connoting information; thus, reactions in the real world will likely comprise a mixture of thoughts and feelings at varying degrees of strength. For example, a woman who has a brother who looks uncannily like her, and with whom she has coresided, may experience a robustly high level of psychological kinship with him. On the other hand, a man who meets a woman who shares his attitudes and interests may experience a low level of psychological kinship, which may decrease to zero if he is romantically inclined toward her. Most instances of psychological kinship will fall within these extremes, thus emphasizing the importance of relationship context for modulating the perception of kinship. Below, we discuss some of these contexts, focusing our discussion explicitly on relationships and interactions between genetically unrelated individuals. Many of these have traditionally been studied as unique, independent relationship domains. Our perspective suggests instead that our understanding and treatment of people within a wide variety of relationships is influenced by mechanisms designed for the processing of kin, at least to a greater extent than we may recognize.

Friendship

We know that the key antecedents of psychological kinship are high levels of familiarity and perceived similarity, and that emotional closeness and empathy are key affective reactions. Are there nonkin relationships that are characterized by high familiarity, similarity, emotional closeness, and empathy? Yes: friendships.

Next to family members, friends seem to occupy an especially important place in most people's social networks. In some ways, friendship connotes a level of closeness that even exceeds what is typically experienced between siblings, as revealed by the intelligible statement "my sister and I are so close, we are practically best friends." (Of course, the blurring of relationship boundaries in the opposite direction occurs as well: "My friend and I are so close, we're like sisters.") As with kinship, the psychology of friendship seems to have received relatively little attention in social psychology (the same *JPSP* search returned 44 articles with "friend," "friends," or "friendship" in the title, representing 0.55% of the total; and only a subset of these articles appeared to be about friendship per se). What is friendship? How is it psychologically distinct from kinship? And, under what circumstances might psychological kinship underlie friendship?

Objectively, kinship and friendship (among unrelated individuals) are different. Kin are genetically related; friends are not. With many kin, a large chunk of childhood is spent living in the same household; this is rarely the case for friends. Friends do not suffer genetic fitness costs from engaging in sexual activity. Altruism toward friends also nominally falls outside the domain of kin selection. By default, then, helping between friends would seem to be best explained by reciprocal altruism (Trivers, 1971), the other major theory of the evolution of altruism, which explains the tendency to help as dependent on future opportunities to have that help repaid. On the surface this seems sensible, as friendship does involve give and take. However, theory and research in the social sciences—as well as our intuitions regarding friendship—tell a different story.

A common categorization of human relationships distinguishes between *communal* and *exchange* relationships (e.g., Clark & Mills, 1979; Fiske, 1992). Communal relationships are defined in part by a tendency for individuals to provide assistance to each other largely unconditionally; exchange relationships, on the other hand, are defined by the norms of reciprocal exchange. Interestingly, early theorists simply assumed that both friends and family fall within the communal category. More importantly, research has shown that friendship does indeed follow the communal pattern (Clark, Mills, & Corcoran, 1989), implying that people think of friendships as relationships that should not be governed explicitly by reciprocal exchange (see also Stewart-Williams, 2007). Indeed, a good way to nip a budding friendship is to return favors blatantly or to refuse them in the first place. Such considerations suggest a commonality between kinship and friendship. However, there are important differences as well. For example, people preferentially give help to kin or to friends under different circumstances. People provide more low-cost help to friends than to siblings, but more high-cost help to siblings than to friends (Stewart-Williams, 2007). Evidence also suggests that people prefer providing instrumental support to kin and emotional support to friends (Felton & Berry, 1992; Taylor & Chatters, 1986). Furthermore, despite similarities in the communal nature of the relationships, kinships may be more impervious to relationship threats. Even in those cases in which friends psychologically feel like kin, a long-term lack of reciprocity can lead to the dissolution of friendships (Ackerman & Kenrick, 2008; Argyle & Henderson, 1984). Kinship, on the other hand, is for life.

These considerations suggest that friendship is conceptually distinct from other relationships, that altruism toward friends is fully explained by neither kin selection nor reciprocal altruism. Indeed, evolutionary psychologists have proposed that friendship develops via alternative routes, such as positive feedback of mutual valuation (Tooby & Cosmides, 1996) and alliance formation (DeScioli & Kurzban, 2009). From the present perspective, one theoretical possibility is that friendships develop along a rather independent trajectory from that of kinships, but over time adopt many of the same psychological mechanisms. For instance, many newly formed alliances involve heightened sensitivity to reciprocal exchange and the overall equality that is maintained in the relationship (e.g., Clark & Mills, 1979). Over time, reciprocity becomes less important and communal (familial) feelings grow (Lydon, Jamieson, & Holmes, 1997). The costs of false-positive kinship-perception errors also drop as friendships develop (e.g., the risks of being cheated are lower within more established friendships). Thus, in many situations, and for many people, friends may become psychological kin.

Recent research reveals that the tendency to experience friendship as being akin to kinship may be more pronounced for some people than for others. We considered earlier why women might be more inclined to treat unrelated others as family members (i.e., because of the norms of female relationships, the higher costs of inbreeding, and ancestral patrilocality). Importantly, this does not mean women should treat *all* others as kin. The potential costs of responding to unfamiliar people as though they were family—from physical and economic harm to the loss of mating opportunities—can be quite high. Friends, however, represent an ideal combination of closeness and familiarity to encourage signal-detection errors among women.

Ackerman and colleagues tested this idea in several studies that examined emotional and behavioral reactions to three types of relationships: siblings, friends, and strangers. Two studies asked men and women to imagine either kissing (Study 1) or having sex with (Study 2) an opposite-sex person from one of the three relationship categories, and then to indicate the extent of various emotions they felt while imagining these scenarios (Study 2 is reported in Ackerman et al., 2007). Both studies revealed similar patterns (although kissing did not elicit as strongly negative or positive reactions as did sex). The thought of making out or having sex with a sibling was quite upsetting for most people: Men and women reported high levels of disgust and low levels of positive affect. The opposite was true for imagined strangers: Emotional responses were uniformly positive (presumably these were not undesirable imaginary strangers). However, reactions to friends were more complex: Men were as positive to romance with friends as they were to romance with strangers; women, on the other hand, were more negative to romantic thoughts about friends, and they felt especially strong disgust, an emotion tied to sexual aversion (e.g., Lieberman et al., 2007; Tybur, Lieberman, & Griskevicius, 2009). Consistent with this finding, in a study conducted by Park (2008), women reported greater disgust than did men when instructed to imagine having sex with a close friend, whereas men and women reported equally high levels of disgust when instructed to imagine having sex with close kin.

In another study, Ackerman et al. (2007) investigated the role of biological sex and relationship type on altruistic behavior. Here, people took part in an online quiz task in which they worked on logic questions in two-person team environments consisting of real kin (parents, children, and siblings), friends, and strangers. Each person attempted to complete as many questions as possible within a limited time. At the end, the total team score was calculated and provided to the participants (no individual performance feedback was given). Unbeknownst to participants, every team received the same score: 93% correct. Each person then judged which team member was most responsible for the outcome. As in the earlier studies, women and men responded identically within the kin and stranger pairings: Everyone gave credit to their family members and took credit from strangers. Thus, people were more altruistic with family than with unrelated others. However, with friends, judgments again diverged. Men treated their friends like strangers, taking credit for the successful outcome. Women treated their friends like kin, giving credit for success to their friends. These patterns indicate more than people simply being nicer to women than to men; the team partners were an equal mix of men and women in all conditions. Instead, a cogent explanation is that women treated their friends more like family members than did men, both in sexual and altruistic contexts.

These studies are consistent with the idea that women use psychological mechanisms associated with kinship to process friendship, at least more so than do men, but they also raise a number of intriguing questions. For instance, how might kin-relevant psychological mechanisms be activated? One possibility is that some implicit process is triggered during friendship formation, akin to a critical period in which friends are imprinted into women's kinship networks. Another possibility is that the cognitive and behavioral strategies women use when interacting with friends exploit kinship indicators such as familiarity and similarity. We have already mentioned female-biased interaction norms of cooperation and socioemotional connection. Other behaviors, such as mutual grooming and dressing alike, may also produce familial feelings. Finally, such norms and behaviors may facilitate cognitively taking the perspective of friends, an ability more indicative of biological than nonbiological relationships. If so, this might suggest that psychological kinship can be elicited through repeatedly simulating the mental perspective of others. These types of mechanisms are relevant to men as well, of course, but may be activated primarily under specific conditions. One of these specific conditions may be the presence of intergroup competition.

Intergroup Competition and Male Bonding

Why might intergroup competition lead men to treat their friends as though they were kin? Competition between individuals and groups, from families to teams to nations, is a central feature of humans' evolutionary history (Ackerman & Kenrick, 2008; Baumeister & Leary, 1995). The potential for social conflict may in fact be the primary motivator of nongenetic, nonromantic social bonding. However, across societies and primate species, one subset of individuals participates in and is responsive to intergroup conflict more than any other—males. In humans, men have historically been the soldiers in warfare and the players in team sports. This is not simply because men are more aggressive than are women. The mere suggestion of competition between groups triggers ingroup male bonding mechanisms. For example, telling people that researchers are studying the relative performance of groups leads male members of those groups, but not female members, to engage in costly ingroup cooperation (Van Vugt, De Cremer, & Janssen, 2007). In fact, this relatively minor intergroup threat also increases men's identification with their ingroup. Van Vugt and colleagues (2007; Van Vugt & Park, 2010) have proposed that such findings, and those from studies in many other cultures (e.g., Chagnon, 1988; Keegan, 1994), are evidence for a *male warrior hypothesis*. This hypothesis states that the behaviors and cognitions of men are more oriented toward between-group interactions than are those of women. The reason for this sex difference is that men stand to gain relatively more status and reproductive benefits through group-level competition.

The presence of intergroup threat thus motivates both ingroup solidarity and, potentially, improved ingroup performance. Sports teams may excel and gain fervent fan followings by emphasizing competition with close rivals, and the same is true for religious sects, nations, and even newly formed "minimal" groups (Ackerman, Shapiro, & Maner, 2009; Campbell, 1965; Hammond & Axelrod, 2006; Sherif, Harvey, White, Hood, & Sherif, 1961). Male bonding is especially likely to increase as a result of outgroup-threat signals. Under such conditions, men may begin to overperceive kinship among their friends and associates. If so, this suggests that intergroup competition will lead men not only to behave more altruistically toward their friends, but also to respond less positively toward suggestions of romantic relations with opposite-sex friends. Anecdotal and experimental evidence supports the former possibility (e.g., self-sacrificial behavior to save fellow soldiers during wartime; also see the above citations), although less is known about the latter possibility. Although designed to test somewhat different hypotheses, Ackerman and Kenrick (2009) conducted a series of studies on intragroup and intergroup romance that have implications both for altruistic behavior and for the prospect of decreased male attraction toward female friends.

"The Mating Game" refers to the social and competitive process of forming romantic relationships. People playing this game (i.e., attempting to attract a mate) must navigate murky romantic waters by convincing potential mates that they are desirable selections and by besting competitors for those mates. Therefore, for heterosexual individuals, romantic relationship formation involves a game of "intergroup competition" between men and women. Sometimes, though, this mating game is a team sport. That is, people may help each other to find, evaluate, and attract romantic partners. Historically, and at present in many cultures, these "teammates" consist of family members (see Kenrick & Keefe, 1992; Park, Dubbs, & Buunk, 2009). For example, parents or other kin may broker the selection of marriage partners (Apostolou, 2007), or people may simply try to influence the mating behavior of their relatives (Faulkner & Schaller, 2007). In relatively more mobile Western cultures, friends may act as psychological kin for similar purposes.

In a series of studies investigating cooperative courtship behaviors, Ackerman and Kenrick (2009) tested the possibility that friends would help each other to achieve romantic goals. The studies revealed that men and women in the United States did help their friends in ways akin to the help given by kin in other cultures. For instance, in many such societies (especially polygynous ones), it is the woman's family that attempts to negotiate a high threshold for a husband, whereas the man relies on his family to help pay an adequate bride-price (Anderson, 2007; Geary & Flinn, 2001). This pattern is indicative of differing romantic motivations that males and females hold as a result of evolved parental investment pressures. That is, the relatively higher potential costs borne by females from investing in offspring (e.g., pregnancy) lead women to be more romantically choosy than men. Thus, women are more likely to set up romantic thresholds for men to overcome by demonstrating their quality as a mate. Indeed, the studies showed that women were more likely to help each other build barriers to unwanted romance and even test the value of desirable males, whereas men were more likely to help each other break down those barriers (Ackerman & Kenrick, 2009). Interestingly, opposite-sex friends adjusted the type of help they gave in order to meet their friends' romantic goals. People even used counterfeit romantic partners to build and break down barriers. These behaviors carry high potential costs (e.g., helpers may "cheat" by attempting to attract a desirable target rather than aid a friend), and thus only people who share a high degree of trust and common fate make good teammates. We propose that the use of friends in these situations may signal that these friends feel a sense of psychological kinship. Further, the aid given by opposite-sex friends (e.g., women helping men attract other women, men helping women to block other men) may also suggest that these friends feel decreased romantic attraction toward each other. Regardless, the results of these studies indicate that both women *and* men can interact with friends much as they do kin. Women may generally be more likely to do so, but in the context of intergroup competition, men's friends may become more like family.

The Use and Misuse of Kinship Terms
The impact of psychological kinship may also be felt in our linguistic interactions. The wide array of terms used to identify kin highlights the importance of formally establishing rules of social relations and genetic heritage among family members. Kin can be distinguished by gender, lineage, degree of genetic overlap, and marriage, all to a fine degree. Contrast this with the far more imprecise identification of "friends." Here, if a qualification is made, it is usually limited to "friends" versus "best friends." An alternative way of identifying the closeness felt with such unrelated others is through the overapplication of kinship terminology.

People use kin terms to regulate social connections within a number of nonbiological relationships. Among friends, people might refer to "blood brothers" or "blood sisters," or label someone "a member of my family." Through marriage, people may become stepsiblings or cousins-in-law. Close friends of one's parents might become "aunts," "uncles," or even "godparents." Similar terminology is used within groups that share some common interest or distinguishing characteristic. Student coalitions such as sororities and fraternities allow "sisters" and "brothers" to bond through shared activities and communal living. Social groups bound by race or ethnicity may adopt these terms as well. Businesses may label themselves "happy families," even when their employees are unrelated. Organized criminal gangs, such as the Mafia or Yakuza, also profit from familial labels. Even nonhumans can benefit from the use of kinship terminology. Pets become "members of the family," and many religions construe deities as "father- and mother-figures" (and the members as "children"). In fact, there is evidence that political speech is especially evocative when it employs these sorts of kin terms (Johnson, Ratwik, & Sawyer, 1987; Salmon, 1998).

This broad application of kin terms can help to ensure that the same benefits provided to genetic relatives can spread to unrelated others. Simulated relatedness promotes the exchange of social support and encourages socialization within communities (Chatters, Taylor, & Jayakody, 1994). Fictive kinship can also kick start engagement in reciprocal relationships (e.g., Chatters et al., 1994). These relationships tend to involve more lenient reciprocation schedules than relationships with explicitly unrelated individuals, and thus overall cooperativeness is increased. Research suggests that those people who lack close kin and other sources of support may be most likely to form false familial relationships (MacRae, 1992). Interestingly, fictive kinship may sometimes be the result of donated social support, and not the elicitor of it (e.g., Karner, 1998).

Conclusion
In this chapter, we highlighted two major points about kin relations within and beyond the family. First, to understand kinship-relevant behavior, we must rigorously identify the underlying psychological

mechanisms. Behavior cannot be simply assumed to follow normative, biologically derived expectations, because organisms have not necessarily evolved to accurately calculate genetic relatedness between themselves and others and to behave accordingly. What seem to have evolved are psychological heuristics, which promote adaptive behavior but are not immune to "kinship illusions." The second important point is that the psychological processes underlying kin relations may exert influences within other social relationships; moreover, based on evolutionary cost–benefit analysis, we can predict when people's kinship psychology may be especially likely to be overapplied. We reviewed research showing that, across both sexual and altruistic contexts, women are especially likely to treat their friends as though they were kin. As we discussed above, however, men may treat their friends (or other close individuals) as though they were kin within the context of intergroup conflict.

Although our analysis of friendship does suggest that friendship is sometimes akin to kinship, we do not rule out the possibility that people possess distinct psychological mechanisms to process friendship. We are thus left with several important questions. To what extent do the observed effects (e.g., women reacting to friends as though they were kin) indicate activation of kin processing psychological mechanisms? How distinct are the psychological mechanisms underlying kinship and friendship? More broadly, to what extent are kin and other relationship-processing mechanism domain-specific?

These kinds of questions are not merely academic. Research on the psychology of kin relations is being closely followed by legal scholars, who in turn are publishing writings that could potentially influence policy in areas such as foster care and adoption (e.g., Herring, 2003, 2009). Thus, another area for future research concerns applying knowledge of kinship psychology toward maximizing high-quality care among children placed in foster or adoptive care. Is a child better off when placed with parents whom the child physically resembles? If so, is it especially important for the child to resemble male parents? More broadly, how might the psychology of kinship influence people's subjective definition of kinship? In custody battles involving biological and adoptive parents, might some people be more inclined toward perceiving that the adoptive parents (with their high level of familiarity) are the "real parents"? People's definitions of and reactions to incest might also be influenced by these psychological mechanisms. Such questions demonstrate the fundamental and practical importance of expanding our knowledge base on issues of kin relations, both within and beyond the family. We have barely scratched the surface on such matters.

References

Ackerman, J.M., Griskevicius, V., & Li, N. (in press) *Let's get serious: Communicating commitment in romantic relationships.* Journal of Personality and Social Psychology.

Ackerman, J.M., & Kenrick, D.T. (2008). The costs of benefits: Help-refusals highlight key trade-offs of social life. *Personality and Social Psychology Review, 12,* 118–140.

Ackerman, J.M., & Kenrick, D.T. (2009). Cooperative courtship: Helping friends raise and raze relationship barriers. *Personality and Social Psychology Bulletin, 35,* 1285–1300.

Ackerman, J.M., Kenrick, D.T., & Schaller, M. (2007). Is friendship akin to kinship? *Evolution and Human Behavior, 28,* 365–374.

Ackerman, J.M., Shapiro, J.R., & Maner, J.K. (2009). When is it good to believe bad things? *Behavioral and Brain Sciences, 32,* 510–511.

Alvergne, A., Faurie, C., & Raymond, M. (2010). Are parents' perceptions of offspring facial resemblance consistent with actual resemblance? Effects on parental investment. *Evolution and Human Behavior, 31,* 7–15.

Andersen, S.M., Glassman, N.S., Chen, S., & Cole, S.W. (1995). Transference in social perception: The role of chronic accessibility in significant-other representations. *Journal of Personality and Social Psychology, 69,* 41–57.

Anderson, S. (2007). The economics of dowry and bride price. *Journal of Economic Perspectives, 21,* 151–174.

Apicella, C.L., & Marlowe, F.W. (2004). Perceived mate fidelity and paternal resemblance predict men's investment in children. *Evolution and Human Behavior, 25,* 371–378.

Apostolou, M. (2007). Sexual selection under parental choice: The role of parents in the evolution of human mating. *Evolution and Human Behavior, 28,* 403–409.

Argyle, M., & Henderson, M. (1984). The rules of friendship. *Journal of Social and Personal Relationships, 1,* 211–237.

Aronson, E., Wilson, T.D., & Akert, R.M. (2005). *Social psychology* (5th ed.). Upper Saddle River, NJ: Pearson.

Bailey, K.G. (1988). Psychological kinship: Implications for the helping professions. *Psychotherapy, 25,* 132–141.

Barrett, H.C., & Kurzban, R. (2006). Modularity in cognition: Framing the debate. *Psychological Review, 113,* 628–647.

Baumeister, R.F., & Leary, M.R. (1995). The need to belong: Desire for interpersonal attachments as a fundamental human motivation. *Psychological Bulletin, 117,* 4970–529.

Baumeister, R.F., & Sommer, K.L. (1997). What do men want? Gender differences and two spheres of belongingness: Comment on Cross and Madson (1997). *Psychological Bulletin, 122,* 38–44.

Bem, D.J. (1996). Exotic becomes erotic: A developmental theory of sexual orientation. *Psychological Review, 103,* 320–335.

Bevc, I., & Silverman, I. (1993). Early proximity and intimacy between siblings and incestuous behavior: A test of the Westermarck hypothesis. *Ethology and Sociobiology, 14,* 171–181.

Bevc, I., & Silverman, I. (2000). Early separation and sibling incest: A test of the revised Westermarck theory. *Evolution and Human Behavior, 21,* 151–161.

Brehm, S.S., Kassin, S.M., & Fein, S. (2005). *Social psychology* (6th ed.). Boston: Houghton Mifflin.

Buckner, B., & Halvorson, G. (2002). The one with Ross's tan. [Television series episode]. In D. Crane, M. Kauffman, K. Bright, M. Borkow, A. Chase, M. Curtis, et al. (Producers), *Friends*. United States: Warner Bros. Television.

Burch, R.L., & Gallup, G. G., Jr. (2000). Perceptions of paternal resemblance predict family violence. *Evolution and Human Behavior, 21*, 429–435.

Buss, D.M. (2008). *Evolutionary psychology: The new science of the mind* (3rd ed.). Boston: Pearson.

Campbell, D.T. (1965). Ethnocentric and other altruistic motives. In D. Levine (Ed.), *Nebraska symposium on motivation* (pp. 283–311). Lincoln: University of Nebraska Press.

Canton, N., Gale, B., Kennedy, K., Marshall, F., Spielberg, S. (Producers), & Zemeckis, R. (Director). (1985). *Back to the future* [Motion picture]. United States: Universal Pictures.

Chagnon, N. A. (1988). Life histories, blood revenge, and warfare in a tribal population. *Science, 239*, 985–992.

Chapais, B., Savard, L., & Gauthier, C. (2001). Kin selection and the distribution of altruism in relation to degree of kinship in Japanese macaques (*Macaca fuscata*). *Behavioral Ecology and Sociobiology, 49*, 493–502.

Chatters, L.M., Taylor, R.J., & Jayakody, R. (1994). Fictive kinship relations in Black extended families. *Journal of Comparative Family Studies, 25*, 297–312.

Clark, M.S., & Mills, J. (1979). Interpersonal attraction in exchange and communal relationships. Journal of Personality and Social Psychology, 37, 12–24.

Clark, M.S., Mills, J., & Corcoran, D. (1989). Keeping track of needs and inputs of friends and strangers. *Personality and Social Psychology Bulletin, 15*, 533–542.

Clark, M.S., Mills, J., & Powell, M.C. (1986). Keeping track of needs in communal and exchange relationships. Journal of Personality and Social Psychology, 51, 333–338.

Cosmides, L., & Tooby, J. (1994). Beyond intuition and instinct blindness: Toward an evolutionarily rigorous cognitive science. *Cognition, 50*, 41–77.

Crane, D., Kauffman, M., Bright, K., Borkow, M., Chase, A., Curtis, M., et al. (Producers). (1994–2004). *Friends* [Television series]. United States: Warner Bros. Television.

Daly, M., Salmon, C., & Wilson, M. (1997). Kinship: The conceptual hole in psychological studies of social cognition and close relationships. In J. A. Simpson & D. T. Kenrick (Eds.), Evolutionary social psychology (pp. 265–296). Mahwah, NJ: Erlbaum.

Dawkins, R. (1979). Twelve misunderstandings of kin selection. *Zeitschrift für Tierpsychologie, 51*, 184–200.

DeBruine, L.M. (2004). Resemblance to self increases the appeal of child faces to both men and women. *Evolution and Human Behavior, 25*, 142–154.

DeBruine, L.M. (2005). Trustworthy but not lust-worthy: Context-specific effects of facial resemblance. *Proceedings of the Royal Society B, 272*, 919–922.

DeBruine, L.M., Jones, B.C., Little, A.C., & Perrett, D.I. (2008). Social perception of facial resemblance in humans. *Archives of Sexual Behavior, 37*, 64–77.

DeBruine, L.M., Jones, B.C., & Perrett, D.I. (2005). Women's attractiveness judgments of self-resembling faces change across the menstrual cycle. *Hormones and Behavior, 47*, 379–383.

DeScioli, P., & Kurzban, R. (2009). The alliance hypothesis for human friendship. *PLoS ONE, 4*, e5802.

Dubas, J.S., Heijkoop, M., & van Aken, M.A.G. (2009). A preliminary investigation of parent–progeny olfactory recognition and parental investment. *Human Nature, 20*, 80–92.

Eugenides, J. (2002). *Middlesex*. London: Bloomsbury.

Faulkner, J., & Schaller, M. (2007). Nepotistic nosiness: Inclusive fitness and vigilance of kin members' romantic relationships. *Evolution and Human Behavior, 28*, 430–438.

Felton, B.J., & Berry, C.A. (1992). Do the sources of the urban elderly's social support determine its psychological consequences? *Psychology and Aging, 7*, 89–97.

Fessler, D.M.T., & Navarrete, C.D. (2004). Third-party attitudes toward sibling incest: Evidence for Westermarck's hypothesis. *Evolution and Human Behavior, 25*, 277–294.

Fiske, A.P. (1992). The four elementary forms of sociality: Framework for a unified theory of social relations. *Psychological Review, 99*, 689–723.

Geary, D.C., & Flinn, M.V. (2001). Evolution of human parental behavior and the human family. *Parenting: Science and Practice, 1*, 5–61.

Geary, D.C., & Flinn, M.V. (2002). Sex differences in behavioral and hormonal response to social threat: Commentary on Taylor et al. (2000). *Psychological Review, 109*, 745–750.

Goodall, J. (1986). *The chimpanzees of Gombe: Patterns of behavior*. Cambridge, MA: Harvard University Press.

Hamilton, W.D. (1964). The genetical evolution of social behaviour. I, II. *Journal of Theoretical Biology, 7*, 1–52.

Hammond, R.A., & Axelrod, R. (2006). The evolution of ethnocentrism. *Journal of Conflict Resolution, 50*, 926–936.

Harris, J.R. (2006). *No two alike: Human nature and human individuality*. New York: Norton.

Haselton, M.G., & Nettle, D. (2006). The paranoid optimist: An integrative evolutionary model of cognitive biases. *Personality and Social Psychology Review, 10*, 47–66.

Hauber, M.E., & Sherman, P.W. (2001). Self-referent phenotype matching: Theoretical considerations and empirical evidence. *Trends in Neuroscience, 24*, 609–616.

Herring, D.J. (2003). Child placement decisions: The relevance of facial resemblance and biological relationships. *Jurimetrics, 43*, 387–414.

Herring, D.J. (2009). Fathers and child maltreatment: A research agenda based on evolutionary theory and behavioral biology research. *Children and Youth Services Review, 31*, 935–945.

James, W. (1890/1950). *The principles of psychology* (Vol. 2). New York: Dover.

Johnson, G.R., Ratwik, S.H., & Sawyer, T.J. (1987). The evocative significance of kin terms in patriotic speech. In V. Reynolds, V. Falger, & I. Vine (Eds.), *The sociobiology of ethnocentrism* (pp. 157–174). London: Croom Helm.

Jones, D. (2003). The generative psychology of kinship Part 1: Cognitive universals and evolutionary psychology. *Evolution and Human Behavior, 24*, 303–319.

Judge, D.S., & Hrdy, S.B. (1991). Allocation of accumulated resources among close kin: Inheritance in Sacramento, California, 1890–1984. *Ethology and Sociobiology, 13*, 495–522.

Karner, T.X. (1998). Professional caring: Homecare workers as fictive kin. *Journal of Aging Studies, 12*, 69–82.

Kashima, Y., Yamaguchi, S., Kim, U., Choi, S.-C., Gelfand, M.J., & Yuki, M. (1995). Culture, gender, and self: A perspective from individualism–collectivism research. *Journal of Personality and Social Psychology, 69*, 925–937.

Keegan, J. (1994). *A history of warfare*. New York: Random House.

Kenrick, D.T., & Keefe, R.C. (1992). Age preferences in mates reflect sex differences in human reproductive strategies. *Behavioral & Brain Sciences, 15*, 75–133.

Korchmaros, J.D., & Kenny, D.A. (2001). Emotional closeness as a mediator of the effect of genetic relatedness on altruism. *Psychological Science, 12*, 262–265.

Kruger, D.J. (2003). Evolution and altruism: Combining psychological mediators with naturally selected tendencies. *Evolution and Human Behavior, 24*, 118–125.

Li, N. P., Bailey, J.M., Kenrick, D.T., & Linsenmeier, J.A.W. (2002). The necessities and luxuries of mate preferences: Testing the tradeoffs. *Journal of Personality and Social Psychology, 82*, 947–955.

Lieberman, D. (2007). Aligning evolutionary psychology and social cognition: Inbreeding avoidance as an example of investigations into categorization, decision rules, and emotions. In J. P. Forgas, M. G. Haselton, & W. von Hippel (Eds.), *Evolution and the social mind: Evolutionary psychology and social cognition* (pp. 179–194). New York: Psychology Press.

Lieberman, D. (2009). Rethinking the Taiwanese minor marriage data: Evidence the mind uses multiple kinship cues to regulate inbreeding avoidance. *Evolution and Human Behavior, 30*, 153–160.

Lieberman, D., Oum, R., & Kurzban, R. (2008). The family of fundamental social categories includes kinship: Evidence from the memory confusion paradigm. *European Journal of Social Psychology, 38*, 998–1012.

Lieberman, D., Tooby, J., & Cosmides, L. (2003). Does morality have a biological basis? An empirical test of the factors governing moral sentiments regarding incest. *Proceedings of the Royal Society of London B, 270*, 819–826.

Lieberman, D., Tooby, J., & Cosmides, L. (2007). The architecture of human kin detection. *Nature, 445*, 727–731.

Lydon, J.E., Jamieson, D.W., & Holmes, J.G. (1997). The meaning of social interactions in the transition from acquaintance-ship to friendship. *Journal of Personality and Social Psychology, 73*, 536–548.

MacRae, H. (1992). Fictive kin as a component of the social networks of older people. *Research on Aging, 14*, 226–247.

Maner, J.K., & Gailliot, M.T. (2007). Altruism and egoism: Prosocial motivations for helping depend on relationship context. *European Journal of Social Psychology, 37*, 347–358.

Maner, J.K., Luce, C.L., Neuberg, S.L., Cialdini, R.B., Brown, S., & Sagarin, B.J. (2002). The effects of perspective taking on motivations for helping: Still no evidence for altruism. *Personality and Social Psychology Bulletin, 28*, 1601–1610.

McElreath, R., & Boyd, R. (2007). *Mathematical models of social evolution: A guide for the perplexed*. Chicago: University of Chicago Press.

Mobbs, D., Yu, R., Meyer, M., Passamonti, L., Seymour, B.J., Calder, A.J., Schweizer, S., Frith, C.D., & Dalgleish, T. (2009). A key role for similarity in vicarious reward. *Science, 324*, 900.

Neyer, F.J., & Lang, F.R. (2003). Blood is thicker than water: Kinship orientation across adulthood. *Journal of Personality and Social Psychology, 84*, 310–321.

Ostrom, T.M., & Sedikides, C. (1992). Out-group homogeneity effects in natural and minimal groups. *Psychological Bulletin, 112*, 536–552.

Park, J.H. (2007). Persistent misunderstandings of inclusive fitness and kin selection: Their ubiquitous appearance in social psychology textbooks. *Evolutionary Psychology, 5*, 860–873.

Park, J.H. (2008). Is aversion to incest psychologically privileged? When sex and sociosexuality do not predict sexual willingness. *Personality and Individual Differences, 45*, 661–665.

Park, J.H., Dubbs, S.L., & Buunk, A.P. (2009). Parents, offspring and mate-choice conflicts. In H. Høgh-Olesen, J. Tønnesvang, & P. Bertelsen (Eds.), *Human characteristics: Evolutionary perspectives on human mind and kind* (pp. 352–365). Newcastle, UK: Cambridge Scholars Publishing.

Park, J.H., & Schaller, M. (2005). Does attitude similarity serve as a heuristic cue for kinship? Evidence of an implicit cognitive association. *Evolution and Human Behavior, 26*, 158–170.

Park, J.H., Schaller, M., & Van Vugt, M. (2008). Psychology of human kin recognition: Heuristic cues, erroneous inferences, and their implications. *Review of General Psychology, 12*, 215–235.

Pasternak, B., Ember, C.R., & Ember, M. (1997). *Sex, gender, and kinship. A cross-cultural perspective*. Upper Saddle River, NJ: Prentice-Hall.

Pinker, S. (1997). *How the mind works*. New York: Norton.

Platek, S.M., Burch, R.L., Panyavin, I.S., Wasserman, B.H., & Gallup, G.G., Jr. (2002). Reactions to children's faces: Resemblance affects males more than females. *Evolution and Human Behavior, 23*, 159–166.

Platek, S.M., Critton, S.R., Burch, R.L., Frederick, D.A., Myers, T.E., & Gallup, G.G., Jr. (2003). How much paternal resemblance is enough? Sex differences in hypothetical investment decisions but not in the detection of resemblance. *Evolution and Human Behavior, 24*, 81–87.

Platek, S.M., Raines, D.M., Gallup, G.G., Jr., Mohamed, F.B., Thomson, J.W., Myers, T.E., et al. (2004). Reactions to children's faces: Males are more affected by resemblance than females are, and so are their brains. *Evolution and Human Behavior, 25*, 394–405.

Porter, R.H., & Moore, J.D. (1981). Human kin recognition by olfactory cues. *Physiology and Behavior, 27*, 493–495.

Reich, A., Cohen, T. (Writers), Weiss, B. (Director). (2002). The one where Joey tells Rachel [Television series episode]. In D. Crane, M. Kauffman, K. Bright, M. Borkow, A. Chase, M. Curtis, et al. (Producers), *Friends*. United States: Warner Bros. Television.

Rendall, D. (2004). "Recognizing" kin: Mechanisms, media, minds, modules, and muddles. In B. Chapais & C.M. Berman (Eds.), *Kinship and behavior in primates* (pp. 295–316). Oxford, UK: Oxford University Press.

Salmon, C.A. (1998). The evocative nature of kin terminology in political rhetoric. *Politics and the Life Sciences, 17*, 51–57.

Sharp, S.P., McGowan, A., Wood, M.J., & Hatchwell, B. J. (2005). Learned kin recognition cues in a social bird. *Nature, 434*, 1127–1130.

Sherif, M., Harvey, O.J., White, B.J., Hood, W.R., & Sherif, C.W. (1961). *Intergroup conflict and co-operation: The Robber's Cave experiment*. Hanover, NH: Wesleyan University Press, University Press of New England.

Stewart-Williams, S. (2007). Altruism among kin vs. nonkin: Effects of cost of help and reciprocal exchange. *Evolution and Human Behavior, 28*, 193–198.

Tal, I., & Lieberman, D. (2007). Kin detection and the development of sexual aversions: Toward an integration of theories on family sexual abuse. In C. A. Salmon & T.K. Shackelford (Eds.), *Family relationships: An evolutionary perspective* (pp. 205–229). Oxford, UK: Oxford University Press.

Taylor, R.J., & Chatters, L.M. (1986). Patterns of informal support to elderly Black adults: Family friends and church members. *Social Work, 31*, 432–438.

Tooby, J., & Cosmides, L. (1996). Friendship and the banker's paradox: Other pathways to the evolution of adaptation for altruism. In W.G. Runciman, J. Maynard Smith, & R.I.M. Dunbar (Eds.), *Evolution of social behaviour patterns in primates and man* (pp. 119–143). New York: Oxford University Press.

Trivers, R.L. (1971). The evolution of reciprocal altruism. *Quarterly Review of Biology, 46*, 35–57.

Trivers, R.L. (1972). Parental investment and sexual selection. In B. Campbell (Ed.) *Sexual selection and the descent of man, 1871–1971* (pp 136–179). Chicago, Aldine.

Tybur, J.M., Lieberman, D., & Griskevicius, V. (2009). Microbes, mating, and morality: Individual differences in three functional domains of disgust. *Journal of Personality and Social Psychology, 97*, 103–122.

Van Vugt, M., De Cremer, D., & Janssen, D.P. (2007). Gender differences in cooperation and competition: The male-warrior hypothesis. *Psychological Science, 18*, 19–23.

Van Vugt, M., & Park, J.H. (2010). The tribal instinct hypothesis: Evolution and the social psychology of intergroup relations. In S. Stürmer & M. Snyder (Eds.), *The psychology of prosocial behavior: Group processes, intergroup relations, and helping* (pp. 13–32). Chichester, UK: Wiley-Blackwell.

Webster, G.D. (2003). Prosocial behavior in families: Moderators of resource sharing. *Journal of Experimental Social Psychology, 39*, 644–652.

Westermarck, E. (1891). *The history of human marriage*. London: Macmillan.

Wolf, A.P. (1966). Childhood association, sexual attraction, and the incest taboo: A Chinese case. *American Anthropologist, 68*, 883–898.

Wolf, A.P. (1995). *Sexual attraction and childhood association: A Chinese brief for Edward Westermarck*. Stanford, CA: Stanford University Press.

Yamazaki, K., Beauchamp, G.K., Kupniewski, D., Bard, J., Thomas, L., & Boyse, E.A. (1988). Familial imprinting determines H-2 selective mating preferences. *Science, 240*, 1331–1332.

CHAPTER 20

Cooperation and Conflict in the Light of Kin Recognition Systems

Daniel Brian Krupp, Lisa M. DeBruine, *and* Benedict C. Jones

Abstract

Genetic relatedness is central to the problems of social evolution. Whenever individuals interact nonrandomly with respect to genotype, their actions may have indirect fitness consequences. Although population structure affects the frequency of interactions among relatives, kin recognition systems can help optimize behavior to the advantage of the actor's genetic posterity. Here, we review the functional and mechanistic foundations of kin recognition systems and demonstrate their effects on cooperation and conflict in a number of different species, devoting special attention to the case of *Homo sapiens*. We conclude by developing several testable hypotheses about the impact of kin recognition on social behavior.

Keywords: Kin recognition, social evolution, inclusive fitness theory, phenotype matching, green-beards

---

The Argentine ant, *Linepithema humile*, is a bit peculiar. Upon encountering a conspecific from an unfamiliar colony, individuals sometimes react violently. But, this behavior is contingent on the genetic diversity of the colony from which the ants are drawn, and can thus be asymmetrical: Individuals reared in genetically homogeneous colonies are typically aggressive toward foreign conspecifics, whereas those from heterogeneous colonies tend to be indifferent toward foreigners (Tsutsui, Suarez, & Grosberg, 2003). This dislike of "alien" phenotypes smacks of xenophobia (Starks, 2003). It also seems awfully human.

An appreciation for the evolved design of kin recognition systems sheds light on this phenomenon of formicine discrimination, among myriad other aspects of organismal sociality. Given the wide scope of the kin recognition literature, we cannot discuss the majority of the published works (including much of that which regards mate choice), but excellent reviews may be found in this volume (Chapter 13, by Hepper) and elsewhere (e.g., Fletcher & Michener, 1987; Hepper, 1991; Sherman, Reeve, & Pfennig, 1997; Waldman, 1988; volume 41, issue 6 of *Annales Zoologici Fennici*). Our aim in this review, rather, is to demonstrate the utility of kin recognition in solving the functional problems of cooperation and conflict, and the predictable consequences that result from its deployment in social contexts. Naturally, our analysis begins with social evolution theory.

Social Evolution Theory

W.D. Hamilton (1964, 1971b) provided the theoretical foundations for the study of kin recognition in his seminal work on social evolution. From the standpoint of evolutionary biology, an action performed by one or more individuals (the average actor) is said to be social when it has effects on the fitness of others (the average recipient).[1] We apply

---

[1] This definition is slightly at odds with the literature. Typically, social actions are defined as those having fitness effects on *both* the actor and recipient (e.g., Grafen, 1985; West, Griffin, & Gardner, 2007). The common definition, however, is overly restrictive: Actions that have consequences for others are surely "social" even when they do not affect the individuals performing them.

the term *cooperation* to the two kinds of action that increase the recipient's fitness: mutually beneficial behavior (actions that increase both the actor's and recipient's fitness) and altruism (actions that increase the recipient's fitness but decrease the actor's). Conversely, we apply the term *conflict* to the two kinds of action that reduce the recipient's fitness: selfishness (actions that decrease the recipient's fitness but increase the actor's) and spite (actions that decrease both the actor's and recipient's fitness). For reasons discussed at length elsewhere (West, Griffin, & Gardner, 2007), the fitness metric used here refers to the net consequences of the action on reproductive success—that is, summed over the lifetime of the organism—relative to the mean fitness of the population, rather than to other members of the same social group.

There are three general mathematical approaches to social evolution theory, each partitioning the fitness effects of a social action in different ways. Inclusive fitness treatments consider the effects of the action from the perspective of the actor (Hamilton, 1963, 1964, 1970; Taylor, Wild, & Gardner, 2007), whereas direct fitness/neighbor-modulated fitness/kin selection treatments consider the effects of the action from the perspective of the recipient (Frank, 1998; Taylor & Frank, 1996; Taylor, Wild, & Gardner, 2007). Finally, group or multilevel selection treatments decompose the effects of the action on fitness within and between groups (Grafen, 1984; Hamilton, 1975; Queller, 1992). All three methods are formally equivalent, but the inclusive fitness approach is perhaps the most intuitive, and so we make use of it here.

A social action will be favored when the sum of its direct (d) and indirect (i) fitness consequences are greater than the mean population fitness (set to 0 in a population of constant size), $d + i > 0$. Direct fitness is simply the increment or decrement in reproduction of the actor as a consequence of having performed the action. It is a proxy for the reproductive success of the focal allele via the actor's descendant line, and it is equivalent to the classical Darwinian notion of fitness. Conversely, indirect fitness is a proxy for the increment or decrement in reproduction of identical copies of the focal allele via individuals other than the actor or the actor's descendants; allele copies are typically housed in the bodies of collateral kin. As such, i can be partitioned into two components: the effect of the social action on the direct fitness of the recipient, x, weighted by the relatedness of the recipient to the actor, r, a measure of the probability that the actor and recipient share copies of the focal allele. Thus, the rule $d + rx > 0$, known as Hamilton's rule, specifies the ecological (d, x) and genetic (r) conditions under which natural selection favors any social action.[2]

Simple as it is, social evolution theory often engenders confusion, especially the concept of genetic relatedness. As relatedness is very much the focus of this chapter (and book), we clarify the concept below.

Genetic Relatedness

Genetic relatedness is usefully conceived of as a "genetic exchange rate" (Frank, 1998), as if the actor values the recipient's genetic currency against its own (Hamilton, 1964). The value of the recipient's reproduction to the actor lies in the former's likelihood of carrying identical copies of an allele influencing the actor's social behavior. From the actor's perspective, the more likely the two are to share copies of a focal allele, the greater the recipient's worth; conversely, the less likely the two share copies of the focal allele, the more expendable—undesirable, even—the recipient becomes. The issue at hand is how this likelihood is to be measured.

Since Hamilton's first works on social evolution (Hamilton, 1963, 1964), the concept of genetic relatedness has been appreciably modified (e.g., Frank, 1998; Grafen, 1985; Hamilton, 1970; Michod & Hamilton, 1980; Queller, 1994). Contemporary measures take into account the *chance* probability of bearing a copy of the focal allele, which is to say the likelihood of an individual, plucked at random from the population at large, bearing a copy. This is because a social action will cause no evolutionary change when the affected recipient bears the allele at chance levels. For instance, if the population mean frequency of the allele is $\bar{p}$ = 0.5, then adding or subtracting offspring from average recipient n with a frequency of bearing the allele of 0.5 (i.e., chance) will result in no subsequent change in the representation of the allele; it will remain $\bar{p}$ = 0.5. This result holds true at any allele frequency in the population, and so r = 0 for all pairs of individuals who hold copies of the focal allele at frequencies that do not deviate from chance.

---

[2] This rule is merely a restatement of the more familiar form $rb-c > 0$, where $x = b$ and $d = -c$. Unlike the standard form, the variant we present is not accompanied by any misleading connotations that c represents a cost to the actor (as any $c < 0$ represents a benefit) or that b represents a benefit to the recipient (as any $b < 0$ represents a cost).

Limited dispersal, or population "viscosity," characterizes many breeding systems, and it has the effect of increasing the genetic relatedness of neighbors. However, it also tends to increase the competition among neighbors for limited reproductive vacancies, such that the benefits of associating with kin are cancelled by their downstream competitive effects (Queller, 1994; Taylor, 1992a,b). This and other aspects of population structure lead us to formulate a general measure of the relatedness of actor m to recipient n as:

$$r = \frac{p_n - \bar{p}}{p_m - \bar{p}}$$

where p_m and p_n are the average frequencies of the focal allele of the actor and the recipient, respectively, and $\bar{p}$ is the average frequency of the focal allele in the actor's and recipient's competitive pool or "economic neighborhood" (Queller, 1994). We are most often interested in the direct and indirect effects of actions performed by individuals bearing the focal allele, so p_m will equal 1 in the typical analysis. Because recipients may be either more or less likely than chance to bear the focal allele, r can take on both positive and negative values. When $r > 0$, the recipient is more likely than chance to share the focal allele borne by the actor, and so the two are said to be positively related. Conversely, when $r < 0$, the actor and recipient are negatively related, because the recipient is less likely than chance to bear the focal allele borne by the actor. In other words, the actor and recipient will tend to bear *rival* alleles. Genetical evolution is the result of a change in the relative frequency of the allele in the population, so an action that decreases the reproduction of negative relatives is one that decreases the representation of rival genotypes, thereby increasing the relative representation of the focal allele. It has long been understood that positive relatedness is essential to the evolution of altruism (Foster, Wenseleers, & Ratnieks, 2006a; Hamilton 1963, 1964;). Likewise, negative relatedness is a requisite condition for the evolution of spite: As it entails costs to both actor and recipient ($d < 0$ and $x < 0$), r must also be < 0 to satisfy Hamilton's rule (Gardner & West, 2004; Hamilton, 1970).

The mathematics of relatedness may seem tangential to the problems of kin recognition, but they highlight an important aspect of its measurement: Relatedness is a relative concept. As gene frequencies in the relevant population change, so too does the relatedness of a particular pair of individuals (Gardner & West, 2004; West et al., 2007). Below, we will show how one particular mechanism of kin recognition—phenotype matching—is ably designed to make the relative judgments expected by the modern metrics of genetic relatedness.

Kin Recognition Systems

The ability to recognize kin is not required for an action to have indirect fitness consequences. Organisms may affect the reproduction of their relatives whenever population structure causes nonrandom assortment among kin, as in viscous populations (Hamilton, 1964), without any information about the relatedness of their neighbors. For instance, under certain competitive regimes, the pathogenic bacterium *Pseudomonas aeruginosa* evolves increasing degrees of cooperation when its neighbors are positively related (Diggle, Griffin, Campbell, & West, 2007; Griffin, West, & Buckling, 2004). Conversely, under different regimes, *P. aeruginosa* evolves to engage in conflict with negatively related neighbors (Inglis, Gardner, Cornelis, & Buckling, 2009). The effects of demography on social evolution are varied (see e.g., Frank, 1998; Queller, 1994; Taylor 1992a,b; Taylor, Day, & Wild, 2007; Wild, Gardner, & West, 2009); nonetheless, the point is that kin recognition is not strictly required to affect indirect fitness. Under certain conditions of population structure, a rule of "help thy neighbor" will suffice to benefit positive relatives.

And yet, kin recognition systems have been discovered many times over. Among species that interact in mixtures of more and less closely related individuals, discriminative responses toward relatives afford indirect fitness benefits, creating selection pressure on the design of kin recognition mechanisms. Design "options" abound for such systems—the informational inputs, computational algorithms, and consequent behavioral outputs may vary over time, place, and lineage—but all are selected to work to the same basic end: to optimize the expenditure of resources in nepotistic fashion, as if maximizing the genetic posterity of the focal allele through direct and indirect channels of reproduction.

Kin recognition has several connotations. It is often operationalized as the differential treatment of genetic relatives (*kin discrimination*), but is more appropriately defined as the collection of de facto sensory and perceptual mechanisms that function to assess the relatedness of a social partner, irrespective of the behavioral response. Of course, kin recognition systems must be in the service of action, or they would be irrelevant to selection, so confusion between these two meanings is not entirely problematic. The danger to be avoided, rather, is in drawing the conclusion that kin recognition is absent because of a lack of evidence of discrimination, even though discrimination is not always to be expected (Holmes, 2004; Liebert & Starks, 2004; Mateo, 2004; Waldman, 1988).

The ability to recognize kin can entail rather sophisticated mental "architecture," but in many cases it will be quite simple. Indeed, its implementation is at times positively brainless: There is recent evidence that the annual plant *Cakile edentula* recognizes kin, retarding root structure growth—and thereby reducing competition—when planted beside maternal siblings (Dudley & File, 2007). Likewise, sperm of the polyandrous deer mouse *Peromyscus maniculatus* help one another as a function of relatedness (Fisher & Hoekstra, 2010). Even malaria parasites seem capable of feats of kin discrimination (Reece, Drew, & Gardner, 2008). What mechanisms might underlie such nepotism?

Indirect Kin Recognition

The mechanisms of kin recognition may be *direct*, whereby individuals themselves are recognized as particular kin members (e.g., sibling 1 vs. sibling 2, etc.) or as belonging to a kin "class" (e.g., siblings vs. cousins), or they may be *indirect*, whereby individuals are not themselves recognized as kin, but are instead distinguished as a function of circumstance. Each has its virtues—indirect mechanisms are relatively inexpensive, direct mechanisms are more versatile—but each also entails a unique set of problems, and so their use is predicted to be favored by different ecologies (Waldman, 1988).

In many cases, context is intimately tied to genetic relatedness. Relatives are often reared together, tended to by the same individuals, and at least partly segregated from nonrelatives. As such, kinship can be assigned as a function of the context in which individuals may find themselves, and it is in these circumstances that we expect to find indirect kin recognition mechanisms at work. A simple indirect mechanism relies on location, treating individuals in one space, such as the nest, as kin and those located elsewhere as nonkin. Any organism that cares for juveniles (related and unrelated alike) placed in its nest, but not elsewhere, is effectively using location data to impute kinship. Such rules can be sensible: When recognition errors of acceptance (perceiving a nonrelative as kin) based on spatial information are rare—offspring are not ambulatory, for example, and so cannot accidentally wind up in the wrong nest—more complex mechanisms are a costly extravagance. Predictably, then, gulls with isolated nests, such as cliff-nesting kittiwakes (*Rissa tridactyla*), will accept unrelated conspecific young when artificially placed in their nests, whereas other, communally nesting gulls are less inclined to do so (Cullen, 1957). It is notable, however, that this difference between cliff-nesting and communally nesting gulls may lie not in the parents' offspring-recognition abilities per se, but in their adoption of decision rules to disregard this information in favor of indirect recognition (Storey, Anderson, Porter, & MacCharles, 1992).

Spatial cues ought often to be mitigated by developmental timing. As offspring of many species mature, they will tend to become more mobile, so age will correlate with the likelihood of committing a recognition error. Holmes and Sherman (1982) demonstrated a temporal sequence of acceptance and rejection of juveniles at the burrow by adult Belding's ground squirrels (*Spermophilus beldingi*) roughly corresponding to the age of offspring weaning. Adult females would accept juveniles, regardless of genetic relatedness, until about the age at which the juveniles emerge from the burrow on their own accord. Prior to this age, juveniles rarely mix with nonrelatives. After this age, however, when the risk of encountering nonrelatives in the burrow increases, adult females appear to make use of other mechanisms that reduce the likelihood of making an identification error.

Direct Kin Recognition

Context-based kin recognition systems may be inexpensive to develop and employ, but they entail increasing costs in terms of recognition errors as spatial aggregation becomes less predictive of relatedness. Once individuals begin to run a nontrivial risk of encountering nonrelatives (in previously reliable locations or elsewhere), it might pay to learn the phenotypes of various rearing associates—who, in many species, are typically parents, offspring, and siblings—instead of their locations. Early context can enable such direct kin recognition, as prior association with conspecifics in particular spatiotemporal contexts allows an individual to encode the phenotypes of its kin before it encounters nonrelatives (Mateo, 2004). Thus, individual or class recognition can be co-opted for the purpose of recognizing kin. Animals as diverse as rhesus macaques (*Macaca mulatta*; Rendall, Rodman, & Emond, 1996) and golden hamsters (*Mesocricetus auratus*; Todrank,

Heth, & Johnston, 1998) can recognize and distinguish kin on an individual basis, for instance, but *Homo sapiens* provides the most familiar example. Children who have been reared together and tended to by the same mother grow to individually recognize and treat each other as siblings, even when they have explicit knowledge that might be expected to obviate such familial sentiments (Lieberman, Tooby, & Cosmides, 2007).

Direct kin recognition mechanisms, however, are not limited to distinctions between familiar and unfamiliar individuals. Organisms may be reared among unequally related conspecifics (as in broods of mixed paternity), and they may frequently encounter genetically related strangers. Both circumstances can lead to the evolution of specialized mechanisms for the detection and evaluation of cues or *labels* associated with kinship that distinguish among familiar rearing associates and extend to interactions with unfamiliars. Rather than evaluating conspecifics on information regarding individual identity, organisms may search for labels indicative of genotype. In a process known as *phenotype matching*, individuals compare the labels expressed by conspecifics to internal, multidimensional representations (*templates*) of a variety of *referents*. A kin template is formed when the referents for the template are members of a particular kin class, and an average template is formed when its referents are members of the local population. An evaluator can compute the differences between these two templates to define the dimensions on which individuals are to be judged. When two unfamiliar individuals meet, for instance, they may effectively locate each other's phenotype along these dimensions: A phenotype that is more similar to the kin template than is the average template will be perceived as positively related, whereas a phenotype that is less similar to the kin template than is the average template will be perceived as negatively related (Fig. 20.1). The distance between the kin and average templates is expected to be a function of both the variance in and prevalence of label polymorphism to which the evaluator is exposed (Krupp, 2010).

Templates are generally the products of learning and may represent a weighted average of label values extracted from several individuals (other-referent phenotype matching), such as parents and siblings, values extracted from the evaluator itself (self-referent phenotype matching), or some combination of the two. As sex and age are typically uncorrelated with relatedness, kin templates are expected to overlook phenotypic differences

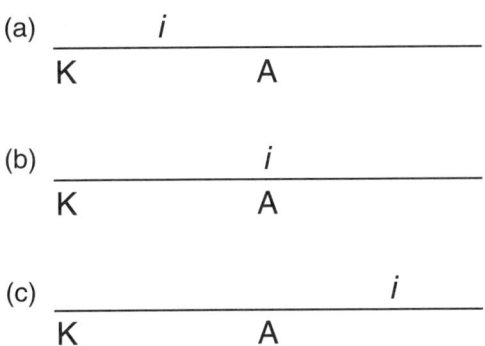

Fig. 20.1 Phenotype matching in one dimension. In a phenotype matching system, one or more dimensions are defined (*solid lines*); the phenotypic values of the prototypical kin (K) and average (A) templates are represented and located along these dimensions, as well as the phenotypic values of individuals i. When i is closer to the kin template than is the average template (a), i is perceived as a positive relative ($r > 0$). When i is no closer to the kin template than is the average template (b), i is perceived as a nonrelative ($r = 0$). Finally, when i is further from the kin template than is the average template (c), i is perceived as a negative relative ($r < 0$)

associated with these variables.[3] They may also be fixed at particular points in development, or they may be continuously updated, allowing for a more dynamic assessment of relatedness as the average population phenotype (and, presumably, genotype) changes with time and place.

When label polymorphism is directly attributable to genetic variability, recognition may not require learning (although it is often difficult to rule out). Rather, gene products may recognize copies in other bodies, although it has been difficult to demonstrate the existence of such "recognition alleles." In a sense, however, recognition alleles and individual recognition—any kind of direct kin recognition, really—represent special cases of phenotype matching, as the evaluator is in all cases matching the phenotypic labels expressed by an individual to an internal template. In the former case, the label is genetically determined and the template is (possibly) unlearned, whereas in the latter case the label and template are individual-specific. This is not to suggest that the differences among the various mechanisms of direct kin recognition ought to be overlooked in favor of their commonalities, but there is considerable overlap

---

[3] In point of fact, sex will correlate with kinship when it is genetically determined, and this can have behavioral consequences (e.g., Fox, Sear, Beise, Ragsdale, Voland, & Knapp, 2010). Whether kin templates are associated with relatedness at sex-determining alleles, however, is not known.

in the form and function of these various systems (see also Waldman, 1987).

At times, label polymorphism is caused by genetic differences among individuals. However, mere association between label and genetic diversity is often sufficient to support direct kin recognition. Common descent is the most frequent cause of genetic similarity, so the relatedness of two individuals at a given locus will tend to be correlated with relatedness across the whole genome. This makes genetic relatedness and kinship largely overlapping concepts (Grafen, 1985); thus, cues of kinship will reliably predict the relatedness of the interacting parties.[4] So, although genetic variation must be correlated with label polymorphism, it does not need to cause the polymorphism. For example, long-tailed tits (*Aegithalos caudatus*) produce nest-specific contact calls, known as a "churr" call; individuals distinguish the churr calls of their kin from those of nonkin (Sharp, McGowan, Wood, & Hatchwell, 2005). When young are cross-fostered into the nests of nonrelatives, they learn the churr call of their foster parents, so that the correlation in sound qualities of the call among unrelated foster siblings reared together is not significantly different from that of related siblings reared together, whereas both groups produce calls significantly more similar to their nestmates than do related siblings reared apart (Sharp et al., 2005). In principle, any feature of an organism (including culturally acquired accoutrements) could be used as a label of kinship, so long as it was reliably correlated with genetic relatedness and perceptible to conspecifics.

Kin Recognition in the Context of Cooperation and Conflict

A vast number of empirical demonstrations show that kinship is associated with cooperation and conflict. Yet, it is not always clear that recognition systems are the cause of any apparent nepotism, as population structure may produce similar patterns of association without appeal to discriminative abilities. Moreover, interactions among kin may not necessarily bring about indirect fitness benefits (Griffin & West, 2002), even though they are commonly expected. Nevertheless, careful studies of kin recognition, having flourished in the wake of social evolution theory, provide numerous examples of the effects of kin recognition on social behavior.

Kin recognition research typically investigates proximate and ultimate aspects of the three "components" of recognition systems (Reeve, 1989): (a) the *expression* component, corresponding to the mechanisms that produce the label (Tsutsui, 2004); (b) the *perception* component, corresponding to the mechanisms that interpret the label, generate the template, and test the match between the two (Mateo, 2004); and (c) the *action* component, corresponding to the mechanisms that produce the discriminatory behavioral outputs (Liebert & Starks, 2004). This work often involves divorcing genetic relatedness from any postulated kinship cue. If organisms discriminate conspecifics as a function of some cue that was associated with genetic relatedness in ancestral environments, then disturbing the relationship between genealogical kinship and cues thereof can result in recognition errors diagnostic of kin recognition systems. Effectively, the method by which researchers (or nature) can successfully create "fictive" kin reveals the design, if any, of the recognition system.

For example, indirect kin recognition mechanisms make the de facto "assumption" that individuals located in one particular place and time (juveniles in the nest, for instance) are close kin, and brood parasites have been quite successful at exploiting such mechanisms. Brood parasites impose significant costs on their hosts, so the regularity by which hosts accept and rear parasitic offspring remains an enduring puzzle (reviewed in Davies, 2000). Davies and Brooke (1989b) have nicely demonstrated that several host species of the common cuckoo (*Cuculus canorus*) fail to discriminate between parasitic chicks and their own progeny in the nest. Moreover, such ready acceptance of foreign chicks is not likely to be the result of a cuckoo trick, as host species also accept chicks of nonparasitic species. Current host species (as well as nonparasitized, but suitable, host species) do reject cuckoo *eggs* based on their appearance (Davies & Brooke, 1989a). As young, naïve hosts are more likely to accept cuckoo eggs than older, experienced hosts, host species likely learn to recognize their own eggs (Davies, 2000; Lotem, Nakamura, & Zahavi, 1992). So, host species use an indirect recognition mechanism at the chick stage, but reduce the initial risks of parasitism at the egg stage, using direct recognition when the risk of recognition errors by indirect means is elevated.

---

[4] Where relatedness at the focal locus and the remainder of the genome are orthogonal, "kinship" is not an entirely appropriate label. For lack of a more inclusive, well-recognized term, however, we continue to employ the term "kin recognition" in these rare instances.

Unlike the common cuckoo, the American coot (*Fulica americana*) parasitizes conspecific nests. Intraspecific brood parasitism such as this should make recognition of the host's eggs and hatchlings particularly difficult, as the objects being discriminated will undoubtedly be quite similar. Yet, American coots are able to distinguish their own eggs from those of conspecifics based on direct recognition mechanisms. They appear to evaluate egg color, rejecting those noticeably different from their own by burial or by relegating them to lesser incubation positions (Lyon, 2003). Furthermore, because the first eggs to hatch are almost always the host's own, they can recognize their young by phenotype matching, the first hatchlings being used as the referents (Shizuka & Lyon, 2010). As a result, juvenile parasites of this species have a significantly increased mortality risk, likely due to harm delivered by their host parents (Shizuka & Lyon).

At times, the very same recognition mechanisms can lead to both cooperative and competitive behaviors, as evidenced by the sea squirt *Botryllus schlosseri*. This marine invertebrate forms cooperative networks of colonies by fusion of blood vasculature with conspecifics. Individuals fuse strictly with clones or close relatives, and conflict is evident after contact between conspecific nonrelatives. Such interactions lead to a cytotoxic response that causes significant damage to the contacted tissues, followed by the formation of a necrotic barrier between individuals (Scofield & Nagashima, 1983). The recognition label controlling the acceptance/rejection response appears to be the product of a single, highly variable histocompatibility locus analogous to the vertebrate major histocompatibility complex (MHC) (Grosberg & Quinn, 1986). Thus, the very alleles used in immune defense also serve as labels of kinship.

It is not surprising that genes involved in immunity are sometimes involved in kin recognition. Selection will generally work against variation in traits whose primary function is to advertise kinship, because those recipients with common labels will find more opportunities to cooperate and fewer instances to compete with others (having a higher probability of encountering social partners with the same label), thus driving the most common label to fixation (Crozier, 1986, 1987; Grosberg & Quinn, 1989; Rousset & Roze, 2007). Selection will, however, tend to maintain label diversity when other, countervailing pressures favor allelic variation (Crozier, 1987; Gardner & West, 2007; Rousset & Roze, 2007). Loci coding for immune response are often highly variable because they are subject to antagonistic coevolution by parasites, so they tend to make good labels for kin recognition systems.

The same logic extends to kin recognition in parasites. The eusocial parasitic wasp *Copidosoma floridanum* is enveloped in an extraembryonic membrane during larval development inside the host. Giron and Strand (2004) propose that antagonistic coevolution between *C. floridanum* and its host has maintained polymorphism in the extraembryonic membrane, which has been subsequently exploited by the parasite as a kin recognition label. Having shown that the membrane conceals the parasite from the host's immune system, they also find that it serves as a kinship cue: Precocial soldier larvae discriminatively attack reproductive larvae enveloped in the membranes of nonrelatives, but spare larvae enveloped in the membranes of their genetically identical sisters. This is true even when the reproductive larvae have been experimentally excised from their own membranes and transferred to the membranes of other individuals—identical sisters enveloped in the membranes of nonrelatives, or unrelated females enveloped in the membranes of identical sisters, for instance.

When a kin label cannot be easily divorced from its bearer, unlike the situation of *C. floridanum*, researchers may instead rely on cross-fostering techniques, whereby responses of individuals reared with their genetic relatives are compared to those of individuals reared with unrelated "foster" families (for a review, see Mateo & Holmes, 2004). Such studies can be revealing, as a seminal kin recognition experiment by Buckle and Greenberg (1981) demonstrates. Sweat bees (*Lasioglossum zephyrum*) guard the entrances of their nests, generally allowing access only to resident conspecifics. Using cross-fostering, Buckle and Greenberg created colonies of six young bees, half from one colony (A) and the other half from a second colony (B), and demonstrated that guards of the original colonies admitted greater access to their unfamiliar relatives than to unfamiliar nonrelatives from the experimental colony (i.e., colony A guards accepted cross-fostered individuals derived from colony A at higher rates than cross-fostered individuals derived from colony B). The researchers also cross-fostered young bees singly into the nests of five nonrelatives—so that one bee from colony A was reared with five bees from colony B. In this experiment, the unique bee accepted the unfamiliar sisters of its unrelated nestmates but rejected its own, unfamiliar, related sisters, providing evidence for other-referent phenotype matching; in the case of *L. zephyrum*, as in many species, the referents for template composition are the individual's nestmates.

Other-referent phenotype matching appears to be a fairly common phenomenon, whereas self-referent phenotype matching has only rarely been confirmed. Peacocks (*Pavo cristatus*) are a lekking species, and males will often assemble in small groups to attract females. This sort of congregation behavior can be conceived of as a form of cooperative courtship, so it seems predictable that males sharing a lek tend to be positive relatives (Petrie, Krupa, & Burke, 1999; see also Krakauer, 2005; Shorey, Piertney, Stone, & Hoglund, 2000). What is surprising, however, is that the males are able to assort as a function of relatedness even when they have been cross-fostered and reared with nonrelatives (Petrie et al., 1999). Having few or no relatives upon which to base a kin template, this result suggests that male peacocks use self-referent phenotype matching to choose their lekking partners, although further research is needed to confirm this hypothesis. Self-referent phenotype matching is also strongly suspected in golden hamsters (*Mesocricetus auratus*; Heth, Todrank, & Johnston, 1998; Mateo and Johnston, 2000), brown-headed cowbirds (*Molothrus ater*; Hauber, Sherman, & Paprika, 2000), white-bearded manakins (*Manacus manacus*; Shorey et al., 2000), and chacma baboons (*Papio cynocephalus*; Alberts, 1999), among other species. Moreover, where paternity is relatively uncertain, self-referent phenotype matching may be involved in father–offspring recognition. In the future, we are likely to discover numerous other species that make use of self-referent mechanisms, as techniques to make a convincing demonstration have become further refined (see Hauber & Sherman, 2001; Mateo & Holmes, 2004).

Among the most spectacular mechanisms of kin recognition mediating social behavior concern those originally suggested by Hamilton (1964) and elaborated by Dawkins (1976, 1982): the *green-beards*. In order to convey the idea that altruistic behavior is in the furtherance of the focal allele (rather than the whole genome), Hamilton argued that an allele that expressed a label of its identity and acted altruistically toward those also bearing this label (in accordance with the rule $d + rx > 0$) would have a selective advantage over its rivals. Dawkins gave the example of individuals growing beards that are colored according to the identity of the allele they bear, whereby green-bearded individuals discriminatively cooperated with other green-beards (and likewise for any other color of beard); hence, "green-beard." Green-beard recognition is typically thought of as unlearned, but this is not a necessary condition, as the allele may simply encode a mechanism that learns its own label (Waldman, 1987). Moreover, green-beards are commonly envisioned as genetic enablers of altruistic behavior, but they can also lead to selfish, spiteful, or mutually beneficial behavior (Gardner & West, 2010; West & Gardner, 2010).

For various reasons, few thought that green-beards existed in nature, but several convincing examples have been found. One instance regards the violent "uprising" of red fire ant workers (*Solenopsis invicta*) against their queens (Keller & Ross, 1998). At the Gp-9 locus, individuals will tend to either bear two copies of the *B* allele or one of each of the *B* and *b* alleles, as workers and queens bearing two *b* alleles typically fall victim to a premature death. Homozygous (*BB*) queens rarely survive, however, as they are usually torn limb from limb by heterozygous (*Bb*) workers. When workers are rubbed against the cuticle of homozygous (*BB*) queens, other workers attack them, but workers rubbed against heterozygous (*Bb*) queens are spared, suggesting that the kin label is specified by an odor. All of this indicates that the *b* allele, or other, closely linked alleles encode a label, an algorithm that leads the labels of others to be compared to a template, and a violent reaction when there is a mismatch between the two.

Other examples are rosier by comparison. Haig (1996) has argued that green-beards may be ubiquitous but hidden in certain kinds of interactions, like those at the interface between mother and fetal placenta, which involve alleles coding for homophilic cell adhesion molecules; such molecules simultaneously express allele identity and show greater affinity to identical copies of themselves. Thus, the coordination of multiple cells—the very definition of multicellularity—may often be the consequence of a green-beard mechanism. In much the same way, individual cells of the slime mold *Dictyostelium discoideum* (a social amoeba) congregate and adhere preferentially to those bearing identical copies of a focal allele at the csA locus when they are starved, forming a mobile slug that differentiates into a stalk (~20% of the cells) and a fruiting body (Queller, Ponte, Bozzaro, & Strassmann, 2003; Strassman, Zhu, & Queller, 2000). Because cells in the stalk die in its formation, they do not reproduce and are thus sacrificed, altruistically, for the reproductive spores in the fruiting body. *D. discoideum* cells can discriminate as a function of kinship (Ostrowski et al., 2008), but readily form chimeras of multiple clonal lineages, some of which exploit others (Strassman et al., 2000). Cells of the related *D. purpureum*, however, do preferentially associate with close kin, avoiding chimeric assemblies (Mehdiabadi et al., 2006).

A strain of budding yeast, closely related to that which is commonly found in beer, also seems to make use of a green-beard to facilitate cooperative behavior, but in this case the consequences appear to be mutually beneficial (Smukalla et al., 2008). Expression of the gene *FLO1* in *Saccharomyces cerevisiae* leads to flocculation, wherein cells bind to one another, creating an agglomeration, or "floc," of cells. Flocculation appears to protect the cells interior to the floc from a variety of environmental stressors—a yeast's version of a "selfish herd" (Hamilton, 1971a). Those *S. cerevisiae* cells that do not express *FLO1* are excluded from joining flocs, so there is something like a green-beard mechanism at work here. It is unclear, however, whether cells recognize and show increased affinity to identical copies of the *FLO1* gene—that is, whether they discriminate potential floc partners as a function of beard "color"—or adhere to any *FLO1*-expressing cell, forming chimeras much like *D. discoideum*.

A final example of green-beard–influenced sociality regards cooperative mate guarding in the evocatively named side-blotched lizard (*Uta stansburiana*; Sinervo & Clobert, 2003). Male blue morphs of this lizard (*bb* genotype at the OBY locus) tend to aggregate with other blue males. This behavior appears to be to their reproductive advantage, as aggregated blue males have increased fitness relative to solitary blue males, presumably because cooperating blue morphs prevent yellow sneaker males (*by* and *yy* genotypes) from accessing their mates. Conversely, territory-usurping orange morphs (*oo*, *bo*, and *yo* genotypes) are significantly less likely to aggregate with one another, also to apparent reproductive advantage, arguably because this reduces competition among individuals bearing the *o* allele. The aggregation of blue males and disaggregation of orange males is independent of kinship (Sinervo & Clobert, 2003). There is, however, strong linkage disequilibrium between the genes at the OBY locus and much of the remainder of the *U. stansburiana* genome, so that a polygenic green-beard complex is the likely mechanism underlying certain key aspects of side-blotched lizard social organization.

We could go on, but we would rather devote the remaining pages to an especially tricky model species: *Homo sapiens*. We hope the reader shares our interest in this species.

Kin Recognition and the Human Condition

Homo sapiens has lived among genetic relatives throughout its entire evolutionary history. The family is the primary locus of human social organization and, until recently, humans could migrate only so far as their legs would carry them, so that the dispersion of genotypes over large distances has only happened slowly. Even today, considerable genetic structuring of human populations persists (e.g., Lao et al., 2008; Novembre et al., 2008). Nevertheless, interactions between individuals would have involved both close and distant relatives, and so kin recognition mechanisms may have been employed in human affairs. Indeed, the ubiquity of (often complex) terminological systems that delineate various categories of more proximal and distal kin points to the possibility that kin recognition is fundamental to human sociality. Studies of real-world behavior routinely uncover nepotistic discrimination in human action (e.g., Bowles & Posel, 2005; Chagnon, 1988; Daly & Wilson, 1980, 1988a,b; Hames, 1987), but, with rare exception, the recognition mechanisms involved have been given little attention. Below, we catalogue some of the findings concerning the influence of kin recognition on human sociality, much of which has been published only in the last decade.

Individual Recognition

In ancestral environments, children reared in the same household would almost certainly have been at least half, if not full, siblings. Selection may thus have favored an associative mechanism in childhood that attributes kinship to caretakers and other juvenile household members, particularly those who shared the residence for a lengthy period of time. Such a psychology might manifest itself as nepotism when competition includes nonrelatives, and it might also regulate sexual aversion toward close kin, because extreme inbreeding can have deleterious consequences. The latter notion underlies the Westermarck hypothesis, that incest aversion is the product of close association among individuals during childhood (Westermarck, 1894).

Three lines of inquiry implicate childhood coresidence in sexual aversion. First, unrelated children reared together in the same peer group on Israeli kibbutzim are extremely unlikely to marry or to have sexual relations with each other, seeking out mates from other peer groups, kibbutzim, or elsewhere

(Shepher, 1971; Talmon, 1964). Second, Taiwanese "minor" marriages—whereby a young girl was adopted into the household of, and raised alongside, her unrelated future husband—have yielded significantly higher divorce rates and fewer offspring than the "major" marriages of two adults who had little to no association prior to the wedding day (Wolf, 1993). Third, surveys of American undergraduates show that coresidence duration with opposite-sex individuals significantly predicts aversion to sexual behavior among opposite-sex siblings (Lieberman, Tooby, & Cosmides, 2007).

The Taiwanese marriage and American survey data also supply evidence that the kin recognition mechanisms involved in sexual aversion to siblings make use of parent–child association. Humans, like many other animals, are typically reared by at least one of their genetic parents, usually their mother. Witnessing one's mother rear subsequent individuals, then, informs the senior offspring that the junior is likely to be a sibling. Lieberman et al. (2007) argue that this cue is sufficient to infer kinship, reducing the utility of childhood coresidence duration as a predictor of sibling relatedness for senior offspring, and their results bear this out: Coresidence duration is only a significant predictor of sexual aversion among opposite-sex siblings for individuals who had no access to mother–neonate association cues (i.e., the younger sibling of a given pair), whereas siblings who could make use of mother–neonate association are generally averse to opposite-sex sibling incest, irrespective of coresidence duration. Similarly, sexual aversion varies as a function of coresidence duration in Taiwanese minor marriages for the younger of the two parties, but remains high for the elder spouse (Lieberman, 2009).

The effects of coresidence duration and mother–neonate association are not restricted to sexual aversion. Lieberman et al. (2007) find the same general pattern of results—mother–neonate association as a predictor in general, and coresidence duration as a predictor only in the absence of mother–neonate association cues—holds for sibling-directed cooperation. Thus, the very mechanisms that foment distaste for siblings in sexual contexts likely foster affection for these same individuals in nonsexual contexts. An experiment by DeBruine (2005), discussed below, nicely demonstrates the same context-dependent effect among strangers.

Phenotype Matching

Studying kin recognition systems in humans poses significant challenges. Data from the "field" are enlightening and important, but will too often be confounded by uncontrolled variables that obscure the details of the mechanisms involved. For obvious reasons, researchers do not cross-foster infants to expose the inner workings of human kin recognition, so a controlled method of investigation is not readily apparent. Certain labels of kinship, however, can be manipulated.

Recall that labels must be correlated with genotypes to make a useful kinship cue. As in many other organisms, there is a positive association between phenotypic and genetic similarity in humans. For instance, simple anthropometric measures and linguistic differences are correlated with genetic relatedness in the Yanomamö of Venezuela and Brazil (Spielman, 1973; Spielman, Migliazza, & Neel, 1974), and people typically perform above chance when judging the relatedness of unknown individuals to one another based on photographic (Kaminski, Dridi, Graff, & Gentaz, 2009; reviewed in DeBruine, Jones, Little, & Perrett, 2008) and olfactory stimuli (Porter, Cernoch, & Balogh, 1985)—an interesting quality in a highly social organism. Indeed, the method by which we judge relatedness is almost completely confounded with our assessment of the similarity between the individuals being judged, whereas age and sex seem to account for only a small fraction of the variance in relatedness judgments, as would be expected for a kin recognition mechanism (DeBruine, Smith, Jones, Roberts, Petrie, & Spector, 2009; Maloney & Dal Martello, 2006). With this in mind, technological innovations now make it possible to experimentally manipulate a postulated label of kinship—facial resemblance—to investigate phenotype matching mechanisms. In these studies, images of participants' own faces are used to digitally alter the appearance of a set of faces, unfamiliar to the participants, to generate realistic, self-resembling stimuli (Fig. 20.2). Participants' responses to self-resembling faces, relative to control faces, are then used as indices of cooperative and sexual inclinations toward kin (for a review of the methods and findings, see DeBruine et al., 2008).

In an experimental task assessing monetary transfers between pairs of individuals, DeBruine (2002) found that participants were more trusting of self-resembling partners than controls. Furthermore, in a test of theoretical predictions that cooperation in "tragedy of the commons" contexts—wherein there is a conflict between individual and collective interests—is enhanced by genetic relatedness, Krupp, DeBruine, and Barclay (2008) found group cooperation (as measured by monetary transfers to

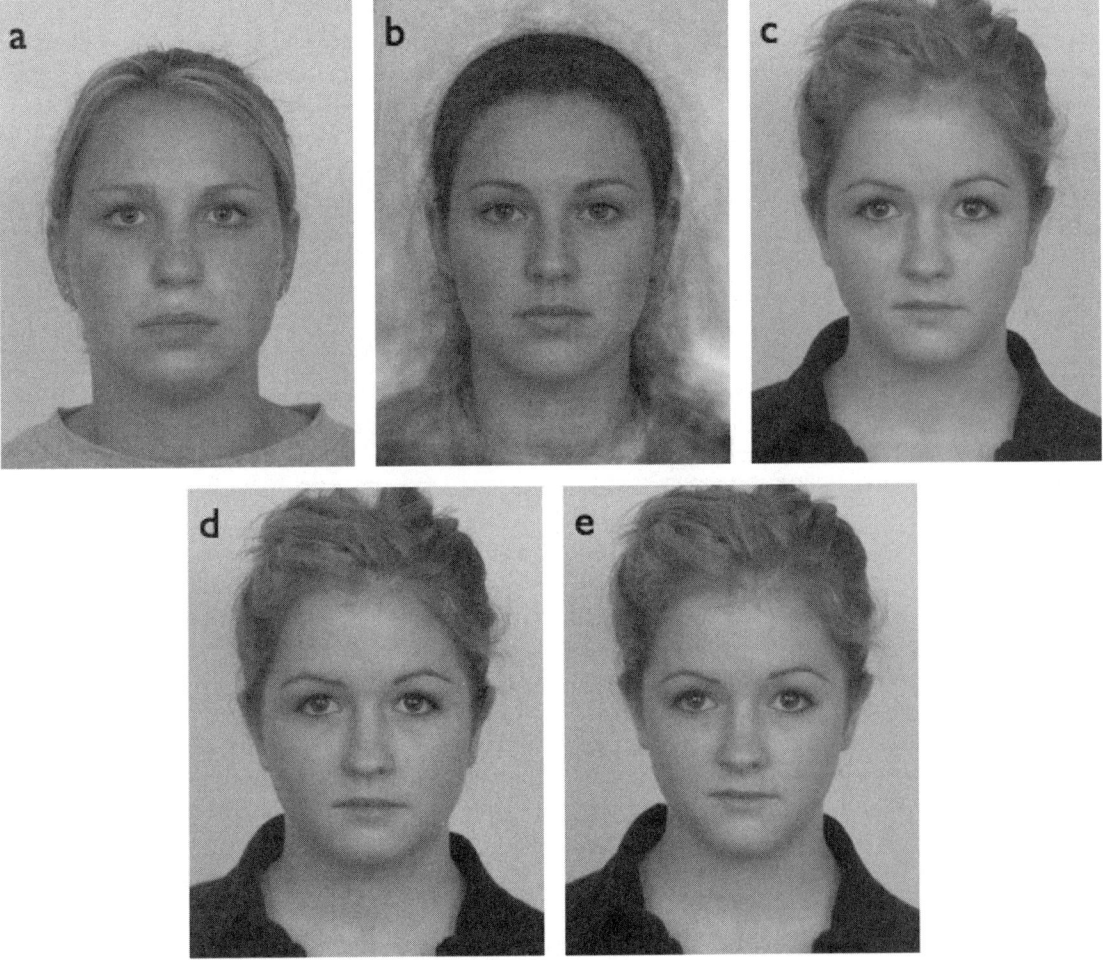

Fig. 20.2 Example of self- and antiself-resembling transformed images. In this example, 50% of the difference in shape between the participant's face (*a*) and an average face of the same sex and ethnicity (*b*) have been applied to a third, "base" face (*c*). When the differences are added to the base face, the result is a self-resembling transform (*d*) showing increased resemblance between the base face and the participant's face. When the differences are subtracted from the base face, the result is an antiself-resembling transform (*e*) showing decreased resemblance between the base face and the participant's face

the group) increased as a function of the number of self-resembling members of the group. Both studies restricted interactions to same-sex faces but, as above, there is an interesting prediction to be made with regard to opposite-sex faces.

All else being equal, individuals are expected to be more helpful toward kin. They are not, however, expected to find kin sexually attractive, especially in short-term contexts in which the genetic costs are not mitigated by the potential benefits of having a cooperative mate. For instance, several studies have shown associations between mate preferences and genetic similarity at the MHC, many of them demonstrating aversion toward MHC-similar individuals (reviewed in Havlicek & Roberts, 2009). To test the predictions that self-resemblance breeds trust but not sexual attractiveness, DeBruine (2005) assessed participants' preferences toward opposite-sex, self-resembling faces and found that, whereas self-resembling faces were perceived as more trustworthy than control faces, they were also perceived as less sexually attractive to participants in short-term contexts. This context-dependent effect provides strong support for the hypothesis that humans use facial resemblance as a label of kinship, and against the notion that the effects of self-resemblance are mere by-products of some general preference for familiarity. The hypothesis is further bolstered by differential responses to self-resemblance in male versus female faces (DeBruine, 2004a) and at different phases of the menstrual cycle (DeBruine, Jones, & Perrett, 2005).

Although the typical manipulation of facial resemblance makes the resulting stimuli more *self*-resembling, it is unlikely that humans had much experience with their own facial appearance before the advent of mirrors and photographs. Thus, effects of self-resemblance are likely due to the overlap between one's own phenotype and that of the kin template built on closely related referents, such as parents and siblings. It is remarkable, then, that a recent study of twins provides evidence of self-referent phenotype matching in humans. Bressan and Zucchi (2009) gauged participants' preferences for images of self-resembling faces over control faces that resembled their (monozygotic or dizygotic) same-sex twin, showing that participants favored the self-resembling faces in two different cooperative contexts.

Although fascinating, the results of Bressan and Zucchi (2009) should be interpreted with caution. It is debatable whether twins are an appropriate model for use in investigations of "typical" human kin recognition, since surviving twins were likely rare in ancestral environments. Moreover, the authors interpret their results as demonstrating that "human kin recognition is self- *rather than* family-referential" (emphasis ours), but their forced-choice design cannot test whether self-referent phenotype matching operates in exclusion of, or in conjunction with, other-referent phenotype matching. As the authors imply elsewhere in the article, it can only show that self-referent cues are used *over and above* other-referent cues and, in any case, the only other-referent comparison was one's twin, so that other family members (such as one's mother or father) cannot be excluded as making up a portion of the kin template. Indeed, numerous studies show considerable overlap between parental traits and offspring preferences; individuals' preferences for a mate's hair and eye color, for instance, are better explained by their opposite-sex parent's hair and eye color than by their own colors (Little, Penton-Voak, Burt, & Perrett, 2003; see also Bereczkei, Gyuris, Koves, & Bernath, 2002; Bereczkei, Gyuris, & Weisfeld, 2004; Wiszewska, Pawlowski, & Boothroyd, 2007). Nonetheless, theirs is a tantalizing result, and future research should investigate self-referent phenotype matching in humans further. A study of the kin templates of adopted individuals, although logistically difficult, seems to us a promising avenue.

Phenotype matching, whether self- or other-referent, may help to solve another important reproductive problem: whether a mate's child is also one's own. Because of internal fertilization, human females can be virtually certain of their relatedness to their offspring; males cannot be so sure. This poses a problem for men, since they often invest in their social mate's offspring. Theoretically, paternity uncertainty can be mitigated by the recognition of a reliable kinship label, but it is not entirely clear whether it is in the interests of offspring to signal or conceal their relatedness to putative fathers. Early work offered evidence that babies appeared more similar to their fathers than to their mothers, but methodologically superior studies have repeatedly failed to find this effect (reviewed in DeBruine et al., 2008). Despite this, men might still place more value on their putative offspring's appearance as a kinship label than women. Predictably, then, mothers seem more interested than fathers in noting resemblances between the father and his ostensible offspring (Daly & Wilson, 1982; McLain, Setters, Moulton, & Pratt, 2000; Regalski & Gaulin, 1993), and fathers invest in their ostensible offspring as a function of perceived resemblance (Alvergne, Faurie, & Raymond, 2009, 2010; Apicella & Marlowe, 2004). Again, experimental work initially showed that men were more influenced by facial self-resemblance than women (Platek, Burch, Panyavin, Wasserman, & Gallup, 2002; Platek et al., 2003, 2004), but this result has not proven robust to replication (Bressan, Bertamini, Nalli, & Zanutto, 2009; DeBruine, 2004b).

Facial resemblance is by no means the only kinship label available to humans. Some of the earliest work on human kin recognition, for instance, pertains to olfactory labels (reviewed in Porter, 1999). Human neonates can distinguish their own mother's scent from those of unfamiliar mothers, whether that scent occurred naturally or was artificially applied to the child's bassinet or its mother's breasts. Mothers are likewise able to discriminate their own child's odors from those of other children, and even to distinguish between the odors of their own children, suggesting individual recognition by odor. Third parties are also able to match the odors of unfamiliar children and mothers, implicating phenotype matching mechanisms in olfactory kin recognition. Olfactory labels associated with genetic variability, such as MHC alleles, whereas germane to mate choice (Havlicek & Roberts, 2009), are likely suspects for kin recognition labels in other contexts as well.

Culturally inherited labels, such as those based on naming practices, can present an altogether different sort of kinship cue. As implied by the term, family names are correlated with genetic relatedness (e.g., Sykes & Irven, 2000), and first names may also be so related (for instance, children are sometimes named after a same-sex parent or grandparent), so they may provide a culturally acquired cue of kinship. Oates and Wilson (2002) performed a "field" study to test the hypothesis that sharing of first and family names increases cooperative behavior, measured as the frequency of responses to a solicitation of help by the experimenters, masquerading as a stranger sharing none, one, or both names with the respondent. The researchers found that sharing names increased cooperation, the largest effect being the sharing of both names, followed by the family name alone, the first name alone, and least of all sharing neither name. Moreover, rare names had larger effects on cooperation than common names, as might be expected by the notion that rare names are more diagnostic of kinship than are common names (see also Krupp, 2010).

Conclusion

Kin recognition systems are widespread, and they play a pivotal role in social behavior. Despite volumes of research on their influence in the everyday affairs of other species, their impact is likely to have been underestimated in human social interaction (with, perhaps, the exception of mate choice decisions): Numerous models of human social evolution make much of interactions among non-relatives (e.g., Bowles, 2006; Boyd, Gintis, Bowles, & Richerson, 2003; Gintis, 2000; Nowak & Sigmund, 1998; Trivers, 1971), but by contemporary measures of relatedness, only a handful of individuals in the population are likely to be truly *unrelated* to their neighbors. Indeed, some models tend to characterize as nonrelatives individuals who are, in fact, related by virtue of limited dispersal (Foster et al., 2006b; West et al., 2008). Below, we outline directions for future research that address questions of considerable significance to organismal sociality.

Future Directions

We began this chapter with a discussion of *Linepithema humile*, the Argentine ant, arguing that its aggressive behavior toward alien conspecifics resembles xenophobia in humans (Starks, 2003). Recall that this antagonism is asymmetrical: Individuals drawn from genetically homogeneous colonies behaved more aggressively toward foreign conspecifics drawn from heterogeneous colonies than vice versa (Tsutsui et al., 2003). Does this asymmetrical response reflect a functional problem and, if so, how is it solved by the organism's proximate design?

Asymmetrical aggression can be understood in terms of genetic relatedness. If relatedness is measured as a function of deviation from the expected population frequency of the focal allele, then common and rare genotypes will be asymmetrically related (Krupp, 2010). All else being equal, actions will have proportionately larger consequences for rare genotypes than for common ones. Consider, for instance, two alleles in the population: A_1 at a frequency of 0.8, and A_2 at a frequency of 0.2. An action that has the consequence of bringing the frequency of A_1 down to 0.7 in the population—and thereby bringing A_2 up to 0.3—means that A_1 has lost 12.5% of its share of the gene pool. By contrast, the increase of A_2 to 0.3 represents a 50% increase in its share. Thus, an actor bearing the common allele is expected to value recipients bearing the rare allele—its rival—more negatively than the converse. As a corollary, actors bearing the rare allele are expected to value kin more positively than actors bearing the common allele.

Phenotype matching systems can readily generate asymmetrical perceptions of relatedness (Krupp, 2010). As perceptions of the kin and average templates are learned by the sampling of phenotypes in the population (the referents), the variance in label polymorphism and the frequency of particular label values will define the scale upon which the kin and average templates lie (Fig. 20.1). Individuals bearing common phenotypes will tend to develop kin and average templates that scale more closely to one another than will individuals bearing rare phenotypes, so the kinds of phenotypes that can be located between the two templates represent a narrower range of possible label values for bearers of common phenotypes than for bearers of rare phenotypes (Fig. 20.3). Thus, a greater range of phenotypes will be perceived as positively related to bearers of rare phenotypes than to bearers of common phenotypes and, correspondingly, a greater range of phenotypes will be perceived as negatively related to bearers of common phenotypes than to bearers of rare phenotypes.

In the case of *L. humile*, ants drawn from homogeneous colonies likely develop kin and average templates that are located much closer to one another than would those drawn from heterogeneous colonies, once placed on the same perceptual scale. Correspondingly, homogeneous colony-derived individuals likely "perceive" themselves to be of more

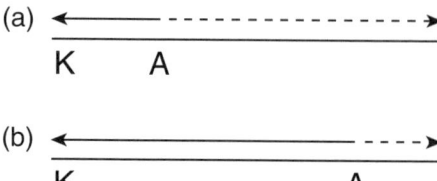

Fig. 20.3 The effect of label frequency on perceptions of relatedness. When individuals bear common label values (*a*), their kin (*K*) and average (*A*) templates are expected to be more similar, and thus scale more closely together than the templates of individuals bearing rare values (*b*). Consequently, a smaller range of possible phenotypes will be perceived as positively related (*solid arrows*) than negatively related (*dashed arrows*) among bearers of common label values than among bearers of rare values

common genetic stock than do heterogeneous colony-derived individuals. They should thus perceive ants from heterogeneous colonies as more negatively related to themselves than the converse, leading to the asymmetrical behavior reported in Tsutsui et al. (2003; see also Starks, 2003).

For similar reasons, we might expect much the same pattern among humans. Xenophobic and ethnocentric behaviors are commonplace (LeVine & Campbell, 1972; Van Den Berghe, 1981) and, like the asymmetric aggression of Argentine ants, might be an output of mental algorithms designed to assess and respond to ecological conditions (e.g., Olzak, 1992) and perceptions of relatedness (Van Den Berghe, 1981). This hypothesis can be difficult to test directly; nevertheless, laboratory analogues are possible. As discussed above, several studies have demonstrated that facial self-resemblance has effects predicted by the hypothesis that it is used as a cue of kinship. The same technology that generates self-resembling faces can be used to make "antiself-resembling" ones (e.g., Leopold, Rhodes, Müller, & Jeffery, 2005), faces that appear more dissimilar to the participant than does an average face (Fig. 20.2). It remains to be seen how participants treat such faces, but if they are perceived as negatively related, we would expect discriminatory responses that work in opposing directions to self-resembling faces.

The asymmetrical aggression seen in *L. humile* appears to change with repeated exposure to individuals drawn from neighboring colonies (Thomas, Tsutsui, & Holway, 2005; see also Sanada-Morimura, Minai, Yokoyama, Hirota, Satoh, & Obara, 2003). This kind of dynamic adjustment suggests that recognition systems can be updated with new information about the expected phenotypes of average individuals in the population. As genetic relatedness measures the likelihood that two individuals share the focal allele relative to chance, a shift in the population mean genotype ought to be accommodated by kin recognition systems. This can be done by updating the average template through exposure to new individuals. There is evidence that humans dynamically adjust their perceptions of sex and ethnicity (Webster, Kaping, Mizokami, & Duhamel, 2004), and so it is plausible that perceptions of relatedness shift as templates germane to kin recognition are updated.

Finally, at the proximate level of description, there remain numerous questions about the ontogeny and mechanistic design of kin recognition systems. Among the most pressing are those concerning the kinds of representations contained in an animal's brain, and the mental algorithms involved in building and integrating them, as it remains unclear how individuals integrate phenotypic information to produce kin and average templates, and whether these templates are maintained over time or rapidly constructed when called upon. Moreover, it is as yet unknown whether there are critical developmental periods that constrain the updating, if any, of recognition templates. Inroads have been made in the study of the cognitive and neural architecture underlying individual recognition (e.g., Calder & Young, 2005), but the appropriate psychophysical tools have only rarely been applied to kin recognition (e.g., Dal Martello & Maloney, 2006).

In short, much work remains to be done. If research continues to advance at the current pace, however, this review may soon find itself out of date. It is our hope that this will indeed be the case.

Acknowledgments

We dedicate this chapter to the memory of Margo Wilson, a pioneer in the evolution-minded study of human family dynamics, a mentor, and a dear friend. We thank Martin Daly, Warren Holmes, Adam Sparks, and Peter Taylor for many thoughtful comments, and acknowledge funding from the Social Sciences and Humanities Research Council of Canada in the form of a standard research grant to DBK.

References

Alberts, S.C. (1999). Paternal kin discrimination in wild baboons. *Proceedings of the Royal Society, Series B: Biological Sciences, 266*, 1501–1506.

Alvergne, A., Faurie, C., & Raymond, M. (2009). Father-offspring resemblance predicts paternal investment in humans. *Animal Behaviour, 78*, 61–69.

Alvergne, A., Faurie, C., & Raymond, M. (2010). Are parents' perceptions of offspring facial resemblance consistent with actual resemblance? Effects on parental investment. *Evolution and Human Behavior, 31*, 7–15.

Apicella, C.L., & Marlowe, F.W. (2004). Perceived mate fidelity and paternal resemblance predict men's investment in children. *Evolution and Human Behavior, 25*, 371–378.

Beecher, M.D. (1982). Signature systems and kin recognition. *American Zoologist, 22*, 477–490.

Bereczkei, T., Gyuris, P., Koves, P., & Bernath, L. (2002). Homogamy, genetic similarity, and imprinting: Parental influence on mate choice preferences. *Personality and Individual Differences, 33*, 677–690.

Bereczkei, T., Gyuris, P., & Weisfeld, G.E. (2004). Sexual imprinting in human mate choice. *Proceedings of the Royal Society, Series B: Biological Sciences, 271*, 1129–1134.

Bowles, S. (2006). Group competition, reproductive leveling, and the evolution of human altruism. *Science, 314*, 1569–1572.

Bowles, S., & Posel, D. (2005). Genetic relatedness predicts South African migrant workers' remittances to their families. *Nature, 434*, 380–383.

Boyd, R., Gintis, H., Bowles, S., & Richerson, P. J. (2003). The evolution of altruistic punishment. *Proceedings of the National Academy of Sciences, 100*, 3531–3535.

Bressan, P., Bertamini, M., Nalli, A., & Zanutto, A. (2009). Men do not have a stronger preference than women for self-resemblant child faces. *Archives of Sexual Behavior, 38*, 657–664.

Bressan, P., & Zucchi, G. (2009). Human kin recognition is self- rather than family-referential. *Biology Letters, 5*, 336–338.

Buckle, G.R., & Greenberg, L. (1981). Nestmate recognition in sweat bees (*Lasioglossum zephyrum*): Does an individual recognize its own odor or only odors of its nestmates? *Animal Behaviour, 29*, 802–809.

Calder, A.J., & Young, A. W. (2005). Understanding the recognition of facial identity and facial expression. *Nature Reviews Neuroscience, 6*, 641–651.

Chagnon, N.A. (1988). Life histories, blood revenge, and warfare in a tribal population. *Science, 239*, 985–992.

Crozier, R.H. (1986). Genetic clonal recognition abilities in marine-invertebrates must be maintained by selection for something else. *Evolution, 40*, 1100–1101.

Crozier, R.H. (1987). Genetic aspects of kin recognition: Concepts, models, and synthesis. In D.J.C. Fletcher & C.D. Michener (Eds.), *Kin recognition in animals* (pp. 55–73). New York: Wiley.

Cullen, E. (1957). Adaptations in the Kittiwake to cliff-nesting. *Ibis, 99*, 275–302.

Dal Martello, M.F., & Maloney, L.T. (2006). Where are kin recognition signals in the human face? *Journal of Vision, 6*, 1356–1366.

Daly, M., & Wilson, M. (1980). Discriminative parental solicitude: A biological perspective. *Journal of Marriage and the Family, 42*, 277–288.

Daly, M., & Wilson, M.I. (1982). Whom are newborn babies said to resemble? *Ethology and Sociobiology, 3*, 69–78.

Daly, M., & Wilson, M. (1988a). *Homicide*. Hawthorne, NY: Aldine de Gruyter.

Daly, M., & Wilson, M. (1988b). Evolutionary social psychology and family homicide. *Science, 242*, 519–524.

Davies, N.B. (2000). *Cuckoos, cowbirds and other cheats*. San Diego, CA: Academic Press.

Davies, N.B., & Brooke, M.D. (1989a). An experimental study of co-evolution between the cuckoo, *Cuculus canorus*, and its hosts, I: Host egg discrimination. *Journal of Animal Ecology, 58*, 207–224.

Davies, N.B., & Brooke, M.D. (1989b). An experimental study of co-evolution between the cuckoo, *Cuculus canorus*, and its hosts, II: Host egg markings, chick discrimination and general discussion. *Journal of Animal Ecology, 58*, 225–236.

Dawkins, R. (1976). *The selfish gene*. New York: Oxford University Press.

Dawkins, R. (1982). *The extended phenotype*. New York: Oxford University Press.

DeBruine, L.M. (2002). Facial resemblance enhances trust. *Proceedings of the Royal Society, Series B: Biological Sciences, 269*, 1307–1312.

DeBruine, L.M. (2004a). Facial resemblance increases the attractiveness of same-sex faces more than other-sex faces. *Proceedings of the Royal Society, Series B: Biological Sciences, 271*, 2085–8090.

DeBruine, L.M. (2004b). Resemblance to self increases the appeal of child faces to both men and women. *Evolution and Human Behavior, 25*, 142–154.

DeBruine, L.M. (2005). Trustworthy but not lust-worthy: Context-specific effects of facial resemblance. *Proceedings of the Royal Society, Series B: Biological Sciences, 272*, 919–922.

DeBruine, L.M., Jones, B.C., Little, A.C., & Perrett, D.I. (2008). Social perception of facial resemblance in humans. *Archives of Sexual Behavior, 37*, 64–77.

DeBruine, L.M., Jones, B.C., & Perrett, D.I. (2005). Women's attractiveness judgments of self-resembling faces change across the menstrual cycle. *Hormones and Behavior, 47*, 379–383.

DeBruine, L.M., Smith, F. G., Jones, B.C., Roberts, S.C., Petrie, M., & Spector, T. D. (2009). Kin recognition signals in adult faces. *Vision Research, 49*, 38–43.

Diggle, S.P., Griffin, A.S., Campbell, G.S., & West, S.A. (2007). Cooperation and conflict in quorum-sensing bacterial populations. *Nature, 450*, 411–4114.

Dudley, S.A., & File, A.L. (2007). Kin recognition in an annual plant. *Biology Letters, 3*, 435–438.

Fisher, H.S., & Hoekstra, H.E. (2010). Competition drives cooperation among closely related sperm of deer mice. *Nature, 463*, 801–803.

Fletcher, D.J.C., & Michener, C.D. (Eds.). (1987). *Kin recognition in animals*. Chichester, New York: Wiley.

Foster, K.R., Wenseleers, T., & Ratnieks, F.L.W. (2006a). Kin selection is the key to altruism. *Trends in Ecology & Evolution, 21*, 57–60.

Foster, K.R., Wenseleers, T., Ratnieks, F.L.W., & Queller, D.C. (2006b). There is nothing wrong with inclusive fitness. *Trends in Ecology & Evolution, 21*, 599–600.

Fox, M., Sear, R., Beise, J., Ragsdale, G., Voland, E., & Knapp, L.A. (2010). Grandma plays favourites: X-chromosome relatedness and sex-specific childhood mortality. *Proceedings of the Royal Society, Series B: Biological Sciences, 277*, 567–573.

Frank, S.A. (1998). *Foundations of social evolution*. Princeton, NJ: Princeton University Press.

Gardner, A., & West, S.A. (2004). Spite and the scale of competition. *Journal of Evolutionary Biology, 17*, 1195–1203.

Gardner, A., & West, S.A. (2007). The decline and fall of genetic kin recognition. *Current Biology, 17*, R810–R812.

Gardner, A., & West, S.A. (2010). Greenbeards. *Evolution, 64*, 25–38.

Gintis, H. (2000). Strong reciprocity and human sociality. *Journal of Theoretical Biology, 206,* 169–179.

Giron, D., & Strand, M. R. (2004). Host resistance and the evolution of kin recognition in polyembryonic wasps. *Proceedings of the Royal Society, Series B: Biological Sciences (Supplement), 271,* S395–S398.

Grafen, A. (1984). Natural selection, kin selection and group selection. In J.R. Krebs & N.B. Davies (Eds.), *Behavioural Ecology* (2nd ed., pp. 62–84). Oxford: Blackwell Scientific.

Grafen, A. (1985). A geometric view of relatedness. *Oxford Surveys in Evolutionary Biology, 2,* 28–89.

Griffin, A.S., & West, S.A. (2002). Kin selection: Fact and fiction. *Trends in Ecology & Evolution, 17,* 15–21.

Griffin, A.S., West, S.A., & Buckling, A. (2004). Cooperation and competition in pathogenic bacteria. *Nature, 430,* 1024–1027.

Grosberg, R.K., & Quinn, J.F. (1986). The genetic control and consequences of kin recognition by the larvae of a colonial marine invertebrate. *Nature, 322,* 456–459.

Grosberg, R.K., & Quinn, J.F. (1989). The evolution of selective aggression conditioned on allorecognition specificity. *Evolution, 43,* 504–515.

Haig, D. (1996). Gestational drive and the green-bearded placenta. *Proceedings of the National Academy of Sciences, 93,* 6547–6551.

Hames, R. (1987). Garden labor exchange among the Ye'kwana. *Ethology and Sociobiology, 8,* 259–284.

Hamilton, W.D. (1963). The evolution of altruistic behavior. *American Naturalist, 97,* 354–356.

Hamilton, W.D. (1964). The genetical evolution of social behaviour (I and II). *Journal of Theoretical Biology, 7,* 1–52.

Hamilton, W.D. (1970). Selfish and spiteful behaviour in an evolutionary model. *Nature, 228,* 1218–1220.

Hamilton, W.D. (1971a). Geometry for the selfish herd. *Journal of Theoretical Biology, 31,* 295–311.

Hamilton, W.D. (1971b). Selection of selfish and altruistic behaviour in some extreme models. In J. F. Eisenberg & W. S. Dillon (Eds.), *Man and beast: Comparative social behavior* (pp. 57–91). Washington, DC: Smithsonian Press.

Hamilton, W.D. (1975). Innate social aptitudes of Man: An approach from evolutionary genetics. In R. Fox (Ed.), *Biosocial Anthropology* (pp. 133–153). London: Malaby Press.

Hauber, M.E., & Sherman, P.W. (2001). Self-referent phenotype matching: Theoretical considerations and empirical evidence. *Trends in Neurosciences, 24,* 609–616.

Hauber, M.E., Sherman, P.W., & Paprika, D. (2000). Self-referent phenotype matching in a brood parasite: The armpit effect in brown-headed cowbirds (*Molothrus ater*). *Animal Cognition, 3,* 113–117.

Havlicek, J., & Roberts, S.C. (2009). MHC-correlated mate choice in humans: A review. *Psychoneuroendocrinology, 34,* 497–512.

Hepper, P.G. (Ed.). (1991). *Kin recognition.* New York: Cambridge University Press.

Heth, G., Todrank, J., & Johnston, R.E. (1998). Kin recognition in golden hamsters: Evidence for phenotype matching. *Animal Behaviour, 56,* 409–417.

Holmes, W.G. (2004). The early history of Hamiltonian-based research on kin recognition. *Annales Zoologici Fennici, 41,* 691–711.

Holmes, W.G., & Sherman, P.W. (1982). The ontogeny of kin recognition in two species of ground squirrels. *American Zoologist, 22,* 491–517.

Inglis, R.F., Gardner, A., Cornelis, P., & Buckling, A. (2009). Spite and virulence in the bacterium *Pseudomonas aeruginosa*. *Proceedings of the National Academy of Sciences, 106,* 5703–5707.

Kaminski, G., Dridi, S., Graff, C., & Gentaz, E. (2009). Human ability to detect kinship in strangers' faces: Effects of the degree of relatedness. *Proceedings of the Royal Society, Series B: Biological Sciences, 276,* 3193–3200.

Keller, L., & Ross, K.G. (1998). Selfish genes: A green beard in the red fire ant. *Nature, 394,* 573–575.

Krakauer, A.H. (2005). Kin selection and cooperative courtship in wild turkeys. *Nature, 434,* 69–72.

Krupp, D.B., DeBruine, L.M., & Barclay, P. (2008). A cue of kinship promotes cooperation for the public good. *Evolution and Human Behavior, 29,* 49–55.

Krupp, D.B. (2010). *Asymmetries of relatedness.* Manuscript in preparation.

Lao, O., Lu, T.T., Nothnagel, M., Junge, O., Freitag-Wolf, S., Caliebe, A., et al. (2008). Correlation between genetic and geographic structure in Europe. *Current Biology, 18,* 1241–1248.

Leopold, D.A., Rhodes, G., Müller, K.-M., & Jeffery, L. (2005). The dynamics of visual adaptation to faces. *Proceedings of the Royal Society, Series B: Biological Sciences, 272,* 897–904.

LeVine, R.A., & Campbell, D.T. (1972). *Ethnocentrism.* New York: Wiley.

Lieberman, D. (2009). Rethinking the Taiwanese minor marriage data: Evidence the mind uses multiple kinship cues to regulate inbreeding avoidance. *Evolution and Human Behavior, 30,* 153–160.

Lieberman, D., Tooby, J., & Cosmides, L. (2007). The architecture of human kin detection. *Nature, 445,* 727–731.

Liebert, A.E., & Starks, P.T. (2004). The action component of recognition systems: A focus on the response. *Annales Zoologici Fennici, 41,* 747–764.

Little, A.C., Penton-Voak, I.S., Burt, D.M., & Perrett, D.I. (2003). Investigating an imprinting-like phenomenon in humans: Partners and opposite-sex parents have similar hair and eye colour. *Evolution and Human Behavior, 24,* 43–51.

Lotem, A., Nakamura, H., & Zahavi, A. (1992). Rejection of cuckoo eggs in relation to host age: A possible evolutionary equilibrium. *Behavioral Ecology, 3,* 128–132.

Lyon, B.E. (2003). Egg recognition and counting reduce costs of avian conspecific brood parasitism. *Nature, 422,* 495–499.

Maloney, L.T., & Dal Martello, M.F. (2006). Kin recognition and the perceived facial similarity of children. *Journal of Vision, 6,* 1047–1056.

Mateo, J.M. (2004). Recognition systems and biological organization: The perception component of social recognition. *Annales Zoologici Fennici, 41,* 729–745.

Mateo, J.M., & Holmes, W.G. (2004). Cross-fostering as a means to study kin recognition. *Animal Behaviour, 68,* 1451–1459.

Mateo, J.M., & Johnston, R.E. (2000). Kin recognition and the "armpit effect": Evidence of self-referent phenotype matching. *Proceedings of the Royal Society, Series B: Biological Sciences, 267,* 695–700.

McLain, D.K., Setters, D., Moulton, M., & Pratt, A.E. (2000). Ascription of resemblance of newborns by parents and non-relatives. *Evolution and Human Behavior, 21,* 11–23.

Mehdiabadi, N.J., Jack, C.N., Farnham, T.T., Platt, T.G., Kalla, S.E., Shaulsky, G., et al. (2006). Kin preference in a social microbe. *Nature, 442,* 881–882.

Michod, R.E., & Hamilton, W.D. (1980). Coefficients of relatedness in sociobiology. *Nature, 288,* 694–697.

Novembre, J., Johnson, T., Bryc, K., Kutalik, Z., Boyko, A.R., Auton, A., et al. (2008). Genes mirror geography within Europe. *Nature, 456,* 98–101.

Nowak, M.A., & Sigmund, K. (1998). Evolution of indirect reciprocity by image scoring. *Nature, 393,* 573–577.

Oates, K., & Wilson, M. (2002). Nominal kinship cues facilitate altruism. *Proceedings of the Royal Society, Series B: Biological Sciences, 269,* 105–109.

Olzak, S. (1992). *The dynamics of ethnic competition and conflict.* Stanford, CA: Stanford University Press.

Ostrowski, E.A., Katoh, M., Shaulsky, G., Queller, D.C., & Strassmann, J.E. (2008). Kin discrimination increases with genetic distance in a social amoeba. PLoS Biology, 6, e287.

Petrie, M., Krupa, A., & Burke, T. (1999). Peacocks lek with relatives even in the absence of social and environmental cues. *Nature, 401,* 155–157.

Platek, S.M., Burch, R.L., Panyavin, I.S., Wasserman, B.H., & Gallup, G.G. (2002). Reactions to children's faces: Resemblance affects males more than females. *Evolution and Human Behavior, 23,* 159–166.

Platek, S.M., Critton, S.R., Burch, R.L., Frederick, D.A., Myers, T.E., & Gallup, G.G. (2003). How much paternal resemblance is enough? Sex differences in hypothetical investment decisions but not in the detection of resemblance. *Evolution and Human Behavior, 24,* 81–87.

Platek, S.M., Raines, D.M., Gallup, G.G., Mohamed, F.B., Thomson, J.W., Myers, T.E., et al. (2004). Reactions to children's faces: Males are more affected by resemblance than females are, and so are their brains. *Evolution and Human Behavior, 25,* 394–405.

Porter, R.H. (1999). Olfaction and human kin recognition. *Genetica, 104,* 259–263.

Porter, R.H., Cernoch, J.M., & Balogh, R.D. (1985). Odor signatures and kin recognition. *Physiology & Behavior, 34,* 445–448.

Queller, D.C. (1992). Quantitative genetics, inclusive fitness, and group selection. *American Naturalist, 139,* 540–558.

Queller, D.C. (1994). Genetic relatedness in viscous populations. *Evolutionary Ecology, 8,* 70–73.

Queller, D.C., Ponte, E., Bozzaro, S., & Strassmann, J.E. (2003). Single-gene greenbeard effects in the social amoeba *Dictyostelium discoideum. Science, 299,* 105–106.

Reece, S.E., Drew, D.R., & Gardner, A. (2008). Sex ratio adjustment and kin discrimination in malaria parasites. *Nature, 453,* 609–614.

Reeve, H.K. (1989). The evolution of conspecific acceptance thresholds. *American Naturalist, 133,* 407–435.

Regalski, J.M., & Gaulin, S.J.C. (1993). Whom are Mexican infants said to resemble? Monitoring and fostering paternal confidence in the Yucatan. *Ethology and Sociobiology, 14,* 97–113.

Rendall, D., Rodman, P.S., & Emond, R.E. (1996). Vocal recognition of individuals and kin in free-ranging rhesus monkeys. *Animal Behaviour, 51,* 1007–1015.

Rousset, F., & Roze, D. (2007). Constraints on the origin and maintenance of genetic kin recognition. *Evolution, 61,* 2320–2330.

Sanada-Morimura, S., Minai, M., Yokoyama, M., Hirota, T., Satoh, T., & Obara, Y. (2003). Encounter-induced hostility to neighbors in the ant *Pristomyrmex pungens. Behavioral Ecology, 14,* 713–718.

Scofield, V.L., & Nagashima, L.S. (1983). Morphology and genetics of rejection between oozooids from the tunicate *Botryllus schlosseri. Biological Bulletin, 165,* 733–744.

Sharp, S.P., McGowan, A., Wood, M.J., & Hatchwell, B.J. (2005). Learned kin recognition cues in a social bird. *Nature, 434,* 1127–1130.

Shepher, J. (1971). Mate selection among second generation kibbutz adolescents and adults: Incest avoidance and negative imprinting. *Archives of Sexual Behavior, 1,* 293–307.

Sherman, P.W., Reeve, H.K., & Pfennig, D.W. (1997). Recognition systems. In J. R. Krebs & N.B. Davies (Eds.), *Behavioural Ecology* (4th ed., pp. 69–96). Oxford: Blackwell.

Shizuka, D., & Lyon, B.E. (2010). Coots use hatch order to learn to recognize and reject conspecific brood parasitic chicks. *Nature, 463,* 223–226.

Shorey, L., Piertney, S., Stone, J., & Hoglund, J. (2000). Fine-scale genetic structuring on *Manacus manacus* leks. *Nature, 408,* 352–353.

Sinervo, B., & Clobert, J. (2003). Morphs, dispersal behavior, genetic similarity, and the evolution of cooperation. *Science, 300,* 1949–1951.

Smukalla, S., Caldara, M., Pochet, N., Beauvais, A., Guadagnini, S., Yan, C., et al. (2008). *FLO1* is a variable green beard gene that drives biofilm-like cooperation in budding yeast. *Cell, 135,* 726–737.

Spielman, R.S. (1973). Do the natives all look alike? Size and shape components of anthropometric differences among Yanomama Indian villages. *American Naturalist, 107,* 694–708.

Spielman, R.S., Migliazza, E.C., & Neel, J.V. (1974). Regional linguistic and genetic differences among Yanomama Indians. *Science, 184,* 637–644.

Starks, P.T. (2003). Selection for uniformity: Xenophobia and invasion success. *Trends in Ecology & Evolution, 18,* 159–162.

Storey, A.E., Anderson, R.E., Porter, J.M., & MacCharles, A.M. (1992). Absence of parent-young recognition in Kittiwakes—a reexamination. *Behaviour, 120,* 302–323.

Strassmann, J.E., Zhu, Y., & Queller, D.C. (2000). Altruism and social cheating in the social amoeba *Dictyostelium discoideum. Nature, 408,* 965–967.

Sykes, B., & Irven, C. (2000). Surnames and the Y chromosome. *American Journal of Human Genetics, 66,* 1417–1419.

Talmon, Y. (1964). Mate selection in collective settlements. *American Sociological Review, 29,* 491–508.

Taylor, P.D. (1992a). Altruism in viscous populations—an inclusive fitness model. *Evolutionary Ecology, 6,* 352–356.

Taylor, P.D. (1992b). Inclusive fitness in a homogeneous environment. *Proceedings of the Royal Society, Series B: Biological Sciences, 249,* 299–302.

Taylor, P.D., Day, T., & Wild, G. (2007). Evolution of cooperation in a finite homogeneous graph. *Nature, 447,* 469–472.

Taylor, P.D., & Frank, S.A. (1996). How to make a kin selection model. *Journal of Theoretical Biology, 180,* 27–37.

Taylor, P.D., Wild, G., & Gardner, A. (2007). Direct fitness or inclusive fitness: How shall we model kin selection? *Journal of Evolutionary Biology, 20,* 301–309.

Thomas, M.L., Tsutsui, N.D., & Holway, D.A. (2005). Intraspecific competition influences the symmetry and intensity of aggression in the Argentine ant. *Behavioral Ecology, 16,* 472–481.

Todrank, J., Heth, G., & Johnston, R.E. (1998). Kin recognition in golden hamsters: Evidence for kinship odours. *Animal Behaviour, 55,* 377–386.

Trivers, R.L. (1971). The evolution of reciprocal altruism. *Quarterly Review of Biology, 46*, 35–57.

Tsutsui, N.D. (2004). Scents of self: The expression component of self/non-self recognition systems. *Annales Zoologici Fennici, 41*, 713–727.

Tsutsui, N.D., Suarez, A.V., & Grosberg, R.K. (2003). Genetic diversity, asymmetrical aggression, and recognition in a widespread invasive species. *Proceedings of the National Academy of Sciences, 100*, 1078–1083.

Van Den Berghe, P.L. (1981). *The ethnic phenomenon*. Westport, CT: Praeger.

Waldman, B. (1987). Mechanisms of kin recognition. *Journal of Theoretical Biology, 128*, 159–185.

Waldman, B. (1988). The ecology of kin recognition. *Annual Review of Ecology and Systematics, 19*, 543–571.

Webster, M.A., Kaping, D., Mizokami, Y., & Duhamel, P. (2004). Adaptation to natural facial categories. *Nature, 428*, 557–561.

West, S.A., & Gardner, A. (2010). Altruism, spite, and greenbeards. *Science, 327*, 1341–1344.

West, S.A., Griffin, A.S., & Gardner, A. (2007). Social semantics: Altruism, cooperation, mutualism, strong reciprocity and group selection. *Journal of Evolutionary Biology, 20*, 415–432.

West, S.A., Griffin, A.S., & Gardner, A. (2008). Social semantics: How useful has group selection been? *Journal of Evolutionary Biology, 21*, 374–385.

Westermarck, E.A. (1894). *The history of human marriage*. London: Macmillan.

Wild, G., Gardner, A., & West, S.A. (2009). Adaptation and the evolution of parasite virulence in a connected world. *Nature, 459*, 983–986.

Wiszewska, A., Pawlowski, B., & Boothroyd, L.G. (2007). Father-daughter relationship as a moderator of sexual imprinting: A facial metric study. *Evolution and Human Behavior, 28*, 248–252.

Wolf, A.P. (1993). Westermarck redivivus. *Annual Review of Anthropology, 22*, 157–175.

PART 5

Conclusions and Future Directions

CHAPTER
21 Reflections on the Human Family

David C. Geary, Drew H. Bailey, *and* Jonathan Oxford

Abstract

Recreation of the socioecology in which the human family evolved can be guided by the paleontological record, comparisons of closely related species, and of course by the study of family formation across human cultures and the historical record. Following this approach, we propose that the socioecology of our australopithecine ancestors was similar to that found in modern gorillas (*Gorilla gorilla*); specifically, single-male harems with several females and their offspring. Such a social structure explains many features of the human family, including high levels of paternal investment, long-term male–female relationships, and concealed ovulation, that are not readily explained if our ancestors were more similar to modern chimpanzees (*Pan troglodytes*). Moreover, the evolutionary changes needed to move from a gorilla-like social structure to the current human pattern are much less complex than the changes needed to move from a chimpanzee-like social structure. After describing the gorilla-like start point for the human family and evolutionary changes in our socioecology, we reflect on how this model relates to the different patterns of family formation found across and within human cultures and to our understanding of sibling relationships and grandparental investment.

Keywords: Human family, evolution, gorilla, grandmother hypothesis, siblings, australopithecines, socioecology

---

To place the human family in an evolutionary perspective, and to more fully understand the proximate expression of maternal and parental investment, as well as relationships among other family members, it is critical to have the correct start point (Geary & Flinn, 2001; Lovejoy, 1981). In other words, to correctly interpret current patterns of family formation and dynamics, we have to know where we came from. These forms of evolutionary analysis are based on patterns in the fossil record (e.g., degree of sexual dimorphism or physical sex differences), knowledge about the traits of interest in living primates and other animals, and on the number of evolutionary steps needed to move from the proposed start point to the currently observed pattern (Foley & Lee, 1989; Ghiglieri, 1987). Such analyses cannot be considered definitive, but they nonetheless provide an empirical and logical means to narrow the range of evolutionary possibilities. A common approach is to combine core features of the fossil record with related traits in our closest living relatives—chimpanzees (*Pan troglodytes*), bonobos (*P. paniscus*), gorillas (*Gorilla gorilla*), and orangutans (*Pongo pygmaeus*)—to make inferences about the corresponding traits of the ancestor common to these species or subsets of them. These traits then provide the start point for reconstructing the evolutionary changes that led to the human traits of interest.

More general patterns among primates, mammals, or across a wider range of species provide further constraints on these reconstructions, as do correlations among traits (Harvey & Clutton-Brock, 1985). Mammals that live in large, complex social groups—those in which individuals have relationships with one another (i.e., it is not simply herding)—have lower juvenile and adult mortality risks, longer developmental periods and lifespans, and larger brains than do their cousins that live more solitary lives (Barton, 1996; Dunbar, 1993; Dunbar & Bever, 1998). For species in which males physically compete for social dominance or control of reproductively important resources (e.g., nesting sites), males are larger and more aggressive than females, and they tend to mature later and die younger (Alexander, Hoogland, Howard, Noonan, & Sherman, 1979; Allman, Rosin, Kumar, & Hasenstaub, 1998). The latter patterns are most pronounced for species in which males control large harems and are small or absent in monogamous species with paternal investment (Allman, Rosin, Kumar, & Hasenstaub, 1998; Clutton-Brock, Harvey, & Rudder, 1977). For a few species, males compete one-on-one for dominance, and they cooperate to form coalitions to compete against other male coalitions. In this context, large physical size becomes less important and strong social competencies more important for successful male–male competition. Accordingly, males of these species have larger brains than males of related species that only compete one-on-one, and the sex difference in physical size is smaller although still important (Plavcan & van Schaik, 1997).

We follow the same strategy in this chapter; specifically, we use the fossil record, studies of related primates and more general across-species patterns, as well as human cross-cultural research to guide our reflections on the evolution of the human family and to frame our understanding of the proximate dynamics of family relationships. We begin with the fossil record and related work on social dynamics in chimpanzees and gorillas to recreate the socioecology in which the human family evolved. In the second section, we use this socioecology as a means to enrich our understanding of currently observed family dynamics and variation therein.

Hominid Socioecology and Family Evolution

To build an evolutionary foundation for understanding the human family, we have to start with our ancestors and any associated paleontological information that provides insights into the social structure of these species and evolutionary change in this structure. We do so in the first section, but do not address the implications for the evolution of the human family until after we present brief reviews of the social structure of chimpanzees and gorillas. Chimpanzees are often used as a frame for trying to understand our australopithecine ancestors (e.g., Wrangham & Peterson, 1996), but Geary and Flinn (2001) argued the gorilla social structure might be even more useful. Once these foundations are laid, we provide a model for the socioecology in which the human family evolved.

Family Tree

There is of course debate about many aspects of our evolutionary past, but there is also consensus on the major hominid (i.e., bipedal) species and their most likely relations to one another (McHenry, 1994a, McHenry & Coffing, 2000; Wood & Collard, 1999). A pruned, so to speak, family tree is shown in the bottom section of Figure 21.1, and core changes that can be established with the fossil record are shown above this.

Dating the sediments found with the fossils shown in Figure 21.1 provides a means to estimate when these species existed. These methods suggest that *Australopithecus anamensis* existed about 4.0 million years ago (MYA) and *A. afarensis* from about 4.0 to 2.8 MYA (Leakey, Feibel, McDougall, Ward, & Walker, 1998; McHenry, 1994a). It has been proposed that *A. africanus* was the link between *A. afarensis* and the line that eventually led to humans, but this is debated due to the discovery of a contemporaneous species, *A. garhi* (Asfaw White, Lovejoy, Latimer, Simpson, & Suwa, 1999); *A. garhi* is dated at about 2.5 MYA, and *A. africanus* from about 3.0 to 2.3 MYA.

Homo habilis is a mosaic of traits, some of which are more similar to *Australopithecus* than to *Homo* (Dean, Leakey, Reid, Schrenk, Schwartz, Stringer, & Walker 2001; Wood & Collard, 1999), but in either case existed from about 2.5 to 1.5 MYA. *H. ergaster* and *H. erectus* appear to be earlier and later specimens of the same species, respectively (Asfaw et al., 2002), and is hereafter referred to as *H. erectus*. This species emerged in Africa about 1.8 MYA and began to move into Asia and possibly southern Europe (Gabunia et al., 2000), with separate populations evolving into *H. neanderthalensis* and *H. sapiens* (McHenry, 1994a). Genetic analyses suggest that modern humans evolved between 150,000 (Thomson, Pritchard, Shen, Oefner, & Feldman, 2000) and roughly 50,000 years ago (Horai, Hayasaka, Kondo, Tsugane, & Takahata, 1995).

EVOLUTIONARY CHANGE

The fossil record speaks to us in many ways. The physical size of our ancestors can be estimated based

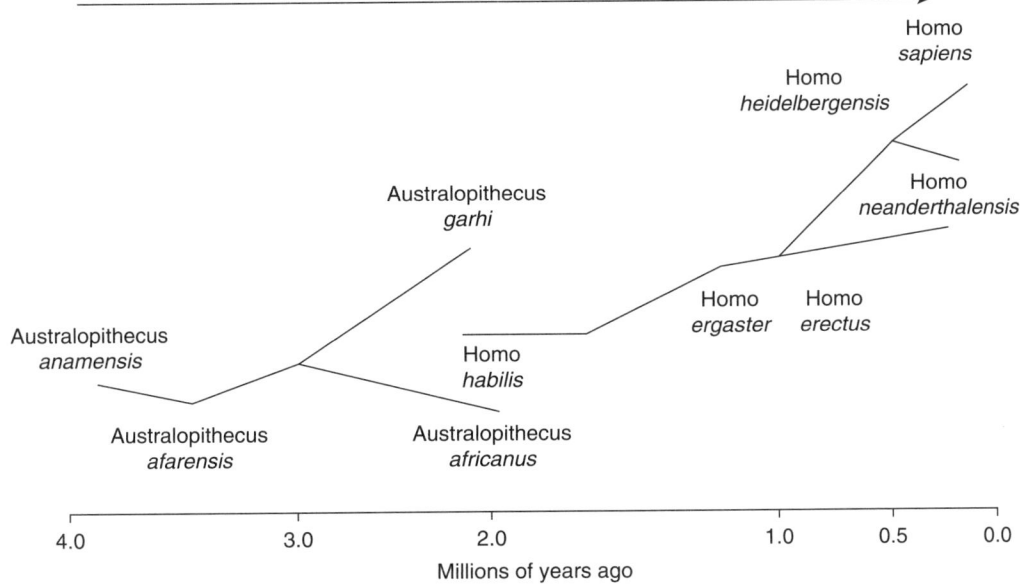

Fig. 21.1 Major changes

on the relation between the size of certain bones (e.g., the femur) and overall body size and weight in living humans and other primates. The equations used to predict human (or other primate) body weight are then applied to fossil bones to yield estimates of the weight and size of extinct species. The likely sex of the associated fossils can be determined in several ways, including shape of the pelvis and the structure of teeth. Teeth are also useful because they are abundant in the fossil record and because wear patterns allow for inferences about the diet of the species and any evolutionary change in diet. Here, we give an overview of evolutionary change in sexual dimorphism, brain volume, life history, and diet. When combined with our knowledge of living primates, especially our cousin species, these patterns allow us to bring into focus the socioecology in which the human family evolved.

Sexual Dimorphism

The fossil record indicates larger males than females in all *Australopithecus* and *Homo* species (McHenry, 1992, 1994b; McHenry & Coffing, 2000). The most striking difference is for *A. anamensis*, in which the sex difference may have been as large as that found in gorillas (Leakey et al., 1998). In other words, males of this species may have been twice the size (in terms of weight) of females. *A. afarensis* and *A. africanus* were also quite dimorphic, with males about 50% heavier than females (Richmond & Jungers, 1995). The sexual dimorphism in weight continued to decrease with the emergence of *Homo*, due to more dramatic increases in the size of our female than male ancestors. McHenry and Coffing (2000) estimated that males of *A. afarensis* were 151 cm tall and weighed 51 kg (i.e., about 4 feet, 11 inches and 100 pounds), whereas females were 105 cm tall and weighed 29 kg (i.e., about 3 feet, 5 inches and 64 pounds). Modern size for males and females emerged with *H. erectus*, possibly before this.

The sexual dimorphism for *A. anamensis* is in the range of that found with orangutans and gorillas, but this dimorphism and the corresponding social behaviors are more likely to have been similar to that of the gorilla than the orangutan; the latter species is arboreal and more solitary than most other primates (Rodman & Mitani, 1987). Specifically, the sexual dimorphism suggests intense one-on-one male–male physical competition, which is most likely to occur when males are competing for access to nondispersed multiple females or for control of territories that encompass the smaller territories of multiple, dispersed females (Clutton-Brock et al., 1997; Emlen & Oring, 1977). In either case, the large dimorphism suggests competition was between lone males, not coalitions of males.

A reduction in sexual dimorphism suggests the emergence of male coalitionary competition, less intense male–male competition, and thus a reduction in the degree of polygyny, or some combination. We note, however, that the sexual dimorphism in weight may potentially underestimate the degree of evolutionary change in mating system. This is because women have more body fat than men, more body fat than most other female primates in wild settings, and presumably more than our australopithecine ancestors. The result is a smaller sex difference in overall weight than we would obtain if men and women are compared on lean muscle mass. Here, the differences are quite large and for the upper body are as large as those found with gorillas (Tanner, 1990; Zihlman & McFarland, 2000).

Brain Size
There has been about a threefold increase in brain volume and substantial changes in brain organization since *A. anamensis* (Falk et al., 2000; Holloway, 1973; McHenry, 1994a; Tobias, 1987; Wood & Collard, 1999). Although the evolutionary change in brain volume is potentially confounded by species differences in body size, the encephalization quotient (EQ) can be used to control for this. The EQ value provides an index of brain size relative to that of a mammal of the same body weight (Jerison, 1973). The EQ of the typical mammal is set at 1.0 (about that of a domestic cat) and that of chimpanzees and gorillas is 2.3 and 1.6, respectively (Jerison, 1973). The EQ of australopithecines was about 3.0 and that of early *Homo* about 4.0. The EQ of modern humans, in comparison, is 6.0 to 7.5 (McHenry, 1994a; Ruff, Trinkaus, & Holliday, 1997).

The importance of these changes for understanding the human family depends on the pressures that drove them. Scientists have proposed three classes of such pressure; specifically, climatic, ecological, and social (Alexander, 1989; Ash & Gallup, 2007; Bailey & Geary, 2009; Kaplan, Hill, Lancaster, & Hurtado, 2000; Potts, 1998). Despite differences in the content of the proposed pressures, all of the models have a common core—the adaptive advantages of the ability to anticipate and mentally generate strategies to cope with anticipated future variation and change (for review, Geary, 2005). Climatic variation can result from long-term trends that affect populations that do not migrate (Potts, 1998), and from seasonal variation for hominid populations that migrated away from central Africa (Ash & Gallup, 2007; Kanazawa, 2008). Ecological models highlight the importance of hunting and other adaptations (e.g., tool use) that enable efficient extraction of biological resources from the many varied ecologies occupied by humans and our ancestors since *H. erectus*, and on the complex learning required to master these skills (Kaplan et al., 2000). The basic idea is supported by findings that species with complex foraging or predatory demands have larger brain volumes and higher EQ values than related species with less complex foraging or predatory demands (e.g., Barton, 1996). Changes in tooth morphology and tool sophistication with the emergence of australopithecines, and especially after *H. habilis*, are also consistent with coevolutionary change in hunting efficiency, diet, brain volume, and EQ (e.g., Aiello & Wheeler, 1995; Foley & Lahr, 1997).

Alexander's (1989) concept of ecological dominance merges ecological and social models of hominid brain evolution. The key idea is that hominids evolved adaptations that enabled increasingly efficient use of biological resources (e.g., hunting, cooking) and increasing control of physical ecologies (e.g., building shelters), resulting in a corresponding decrease in mortality risk and increase in population size. Expanding populations can result in rapidly decreasing ecological resources per capita, which, as originally argued by Malthus (1798), creates the potential for runaway within-species competition (Alexander, 1989; Flinn, Geary, & Ward, 2005; Geary, 2005). The result was a turning point in our evolutionary history, a shift from primarily ecologically-based selective pressures to primarily social ones. The shift in selection pressures is consistent with broad support for the social brain hypothesis; that is, that social competition and cooperation were core selective forces contributing to hominid brain and cognitive evolution (e.g., Brothers, 1990; Dunbar, 1998, 2003; Humphrey, 1976).

The result was almost certainly larger social communities and more frequent interactions between them, either in terms of cooperative trade, warfare, or some combination. The hominid family either emerged in the context of these sweeping social changes, or, as we propose below, already existed and became embedded within the expanding communities (Geary & Flinn, 2001). The expansion in brain size was associated with a lengthening of the developmental period and the resulting increasing demands on parents or other relatives for investment in children. The lengthening of the developmental period would, in theory, allow children to learn about the nuances of the pressures that drove this evolutionary change. In other words, if the fluidity and complexity of social relationships contributed strongly to the evolutionary change in brain volume and organization, then children's self-generated developmental activities should result in experiences that allow children to predict and cope with this social complexity.

Life History

Evolutionary change in the developmental period can be placed within a broader life history perspective; that is, the suite of traits that defines a species' maturational and reproductive pattern and the factors that govern the evolution of these traits and their expression during the lifespan. There are several ways to estimate the developmental trajectory of our ancestors, including the tight link between the timing of molar eruption and the timing of other life history milestones (Dean et al., 2001; Bogin, 1999; McHenry, 1994b). Across primate species, the age of first molar eruption is strongly correlated with age of weaning, age of sexual maturation, and adult brain size (Bogin, 1999; Kelley, 2004). On the basis of such relations, McHenry and Bogin estimated the age of maturation for *A. afarensis* and *A. africanus* to have been similar to that found in chimpanzees, 10–12 years. There is disagreement about the specific age of maturation for species of *Homo*, but the evolutionary pattern is more certain. Bogin estimated gradual increases in the length of the developmental period from *H. habilis* to *H. erectus* to modern humans, and proposed the emergence of two unique and qualitatively different developmental periods: childhood and adolescence (Bogin, 1999).

Chimpanzees and our early ancestors, to the best of our knowledge, had three relatively distinct developmental periods, as with other mammals. Infancy is the time of suckling, and juvenility is the time between weaning and reproductive maturation. For most primates, the juvenile period is initiated with the eruption of the first molar and independent feeding. Unlike most other primates, chimpanzees have a 12- to 18-month delay between the age of first molar eruption and weaning. During this time they learn, through observation and imitation, how to "fish" for termites, crack open nuts, and other survival-related skills (Goodall, 1986). Bogin (1999) proposed that human childhood emerged between infancy and juvenility, and extends from 2 to 3 years of age (weaning in traditional societies) to the age of eruption of the first molar at 6–7 years. Weaning is typically followed by a new pregnancy in traditional societies, leaving the 3-year-old dependent on a wider range of adults for food preparation, feeding, care, and protection.

The human juvenile period is the same as that found in other primates and lasts from age 7 to the onset of the hormonal changes that begin reproductive maturation. At this time, the earlier described sexual dimorphisms become exaggerated in preparation for the forms of reproductive competition experienced by our ancestors. These physical changes and the heightened focus on peer relationships in teenagers mark the evolutionarily novel human adolescence. Their highly social behavior is in keeping with intense social pressures as a core driver of hominid brain evolution (Joffe, 1997; Sawaguchi, 1997). The 15- to 20-year period between weaning and reproduction in traditional societies—compared with 5 to 7 years in chimpanzees and our early ancestors—is intriguing and indicates that activities during this developmental period are of critical evolutionary significance. Of course, many of these activities, even those that are peer oriented, would not be possible without an extended period of parental investment and potential investment from other kin.

Diet

Diet is important because it influences the cost–benefit trade-offs of competition and cooperation for food and appears to affect the social organization of females more than that of males (Sterck, Watts, & van Schaik, 1997; Wrangham, 1980); generally, females disperse or coalesce based on the ecological dispersal and value of their foods, and males follow females. Diets heavily dependent on access to limited patches of high-quality food, such as fruit trees, create conditions for the evolution of female kin-based coalitions that support social competition for access to these foods. A common pattern for these species is the formation of individual and kin-based dominance hierarchies that influence access to these foods and female philopatry: Females stay in their birth group and form life-long cooperative relationships with female kin, and males emigrate to other breeding groups at maturity. When food is readily available, as with species that largely feed on plants or high-quality foods in small, distributed patches, females do not benefit by forming coalitions and thus tend to be solitary or, if they do aggregate, show much lower levels of both cooperation and competition (i.e., they do not interact much) than found in species organized around female kin groups. Females of these species often show a pattern of dispersal from the birth group—males are either the philopatric sex, or both sexes leave the birth group—and egalitarian female–female relationships. The latter does not necessarily entail reciprocal altruism, but rather the absence of dominance hierarchies among females and tolerance of or indifference to the presence of other females.

This is where the australopithecine diet becomes potentially important for our analysis. The details remain to be sorted out, but it appears that the australopithecines had a more varied diet than that of extant great apes and likely fed on leaves, fruits, nuts or seeds, insects, and sedges (Sponheimer & Lee-Thorp, 1999, 2003; Strait et al., 2009; Teaford & Ungar, 2000); the latter are high-quality perennial plants that grow in moist soil. The variety of foods that appear to have been consumed by australopithecines and the likely abundance of many of them suggest relatively low levels of feeding competition. These are conditions that are more likely to support a dispersal-egalitarian social structure among females rather than, for instance, the formation of female kin-based coalitions and dominance hierarchies. In strong support of the dispersal aspect of this proposal is the finding that males are more likely to stay in their birth group and females emigrate to a new group in chimpanzees, bonobos, gorillas (although both sexes often leave the group), and humans living in traditional societies (Eriksson et al. 2006; Lawson Handley & Perrin, 2007; Manson & Wrangham, 1991; Pasternak, Ember, & Ember, 1997; Rodseth, Wrangham, Harrigan, & Smuts, 1991); when men leave their group, it is often to work for their in-laws for the right to marry their daughter (bride price) or because their wife's residence is in the same or a neighboring community as the men's kin (Marlowe, 2004).

In other words, the tendency for male philopatry and female emigration in humans and extant great apes is consistent with a similar pattern for the ancestor common to these species, which would include the australopithecines (Ghiglieri, 1987). The nature of female–female relationships is less certain of course, and could range from short-term cooperative relationships during feeding disputes or to counter male harassment, as with bonobos (Parish, 1996); more isolated females and their offspring, as with chimpanzees and orangutans (Goodall, 1986; Harcourt & Stewart, 2007); or female aggregation around a dominant male, with low levels of female–female conflict, as with gorillas (Harcourt & Stewart, 2007).

Great Apes

To help link the above discussion with our overview of the socioecology of chimpanzees and gorillas, we identified several core male, female, and life history traits in humans and compared these to similar traits in chimpanzees and gorillas (Bogin, 1999; Ghiglieri, 1987; Goodall, 1986; Harcourt & Stewart, 2007; Murdock, 1981; Pasternak, Ember, & Ember, 1997). For this exercise, we asked how much change would be required to move from a chimpanzee-like or a gorilla-like common ancestor to achieve the observed modal patterns for humans in traditional societies (Foley & Lee, 1989). The latter are the targets we are trying to explain. Traits coded 0 were determined to be similar enough across species—the differences between the chimpanzee or gorilla trait and the same target trait in humans—to require minimal evolutionary change, if a homologous trait existed in the common ancestor. Traits coded 1 were determined to require substantial change to evolve into the current human form. These are admittedly coarse codes, but nonetheless are useful anchors for placing constraints on the reconstruction of the socioecology in which the human family evolved. The core traits and our codes are shown in Table 21.1, and we will return to these in the section on "Hominid Socioecology."

CHIMPANZEES

Chimpanzee communities consist of up to 100 or so adult males and females, and their offspring, although the typical community consists of 35 to 40 individuals (Bygott, 1979; Goodall, 1986). Within these communities, groups of males define a territory that contains the smaller territories of adult females and their offspring (Goodall, 1986; Wrangham, 1979). In other words, families are female-centered and nested within larger territories that are maintained by the group's males. Females compete with one another for access to the best foraging areas within the group's territory, and successful females secure better resources for themselves and their offspring and thus achieve higher lifetime reproductive success than do less competitive females (Pusey, Williams, & Goodall, 1997). The result of this competition is the separation of females and their families into separate foraging areas. Females and their offspring often come together in communal areas within the larger territory and female-on-female threats or attacks are common in

Table 21.1 Estimates of Minimal (0) or Substantial (1) Change for the Human Trait to Evolve from a Chimpanzee-like or Gorilla-like Ancestor

Human Trait	Chimpanzee Model	Gorilla Model
Males		
Sexual dimorphism	0	1
One-on-one, nested in coalitional competition	0	1
Male philopatry	0	1
One-male families, with one or several wives	1	0
Paternal investment	1	0
High paternity certainty	1	0
Females		
Pair-bonded mating	1	0
Concealed ovulation	1	0
Continuous sexual receptivity	1	1
Female–female competition over resources	0	1
Life History		
Interbirth interval	1	1
Weaning age	1	0
Age at sexual maturity	1	1
Age of first birth	1	1
Menopause	1	1
Lifespan	1	1

Note. Traits coded 0 were determined to be similar enough across species to require minimal evolutionary change, if a homologous trait existed in the common ancestor. Traits coded 1 were determined to require substantial change to evolve into the current human form.

these areas, most typically over access to food or in the protection of their offspring (Goodall, 1986).

Males are the philopatric sex and compete one-on-one and in coalitions for status within their communities. With the latter, males cooperate when it allows them to move up the dominance hierarchy, and to mate guard, hunt, and patrol the groups' territorial boundaries (de Waal, 1982, 1993; Goodall, 1986; Mitani & Watts, 2005; Watts & Mitani, 2001; Williams, Oehlert, Carlis, & Pusey, 2004). Within communities, the behavior of coalition partners ranges from the mere physical presence of one male while the other threatens or attacks another male, to joint displays and, occasionally, joint attacks. Whether one-on-one or coalitional, moving up the dominance hierarchy has reproductive consequences. Dominant males aggressively achieve more matings with estrous females than do other males; even though chimpanzees mate promiscuously, DNA fingerprinting confirms that socially dominant males sire more offspring than do subordinates (Boesch, Kohou, Néné, & Vigilant, 2006; Constable, Ashley, Goodall, & Pusey, 2001).

Males also form larger coalitions for patrolling the border of their territory and for making incursions into neighboring communities (Mitani & Watts, 2005; Nishida, 1979; Watts, Muller, Amsler, Mbabazi, & Mitani, 2006; Watts & Mitani, 2001). "A patrol is typified by cautious, silent travel during which the members of the party tend to move in a compact group. There are many pauses as the chimpanzees gaze around and listen. Sometimes they climb tall trees and sit quietly for an hour or more, gazing out over the 'unsafe' area of a neighboring community" (Goodall, 1986, p. 490). When members of such patrols encounter one another, the typical response is pant-hooting (a vocal call) and physical displays on both sides, with the smaller group eventually withdrawing (Wilson, Hauser, & Wrangham, 2001). At other times, the meetings can be deadly. The primary benefit of winning these conflicts appears to be expansion of the groups' territory size, which allows females to expand their individual territories (Williams et al., 2004). The latter results in more food, shorter interbirth intervals, and thereby a higher reproductive success for the community's females and males. Territory expansion can also result in the recruitment of new females into the community but tends to occur only when all or nearly all of their community's males have been killed (Wilson & Wrangham, 2003).

Nonsuckling females go through a 36-day estrous cycle during which sexual organs swell conspicuously, with maximum swelling occurring at about the time of ovulation (Goodall, 1986). The swellings attract the sexual interest of male chimpanzees, and dominant ones tend to control mating activities during the days surrounding females' maximum swelling. On other days and, when they are able to, even on days of maximal swelling, females mate with multiple males. Once pregnant and nursing, females are generally not sexually receptive and do not typically affiliate with males. Given promiscuous mating, males are not aware of paternity and do not directly affiliate or protect offspring, although they do indirectly protect them by maintaining the integrity of the groups' territory—males from other communities will sometimes kill infants from other communities if they have not copulated with the infants' mother (Harcourt & Stewart, 2007).

GORILLAS

Gorilla communities are smaller than chimpanzee communities, and are often organized as single-male harems that typically include one reproductive male, two to four females, and their offspring (Fossey, 1984; Harcourt & Stewart, 2007; Stewart & Harcourt, 1987; Taylor, 1997). There is, however, considerable variation in this social structure, especially in groups of mountain gorillas (*Gorilla beringei*). Robbins (1999), for instance, found that 40% of these groups included several, typically related (e.g., uncle-nephew) males. Groups of lowland gorillas (*Gorilla gorilla*) maintain single-male harems, but several families will occupy the same geographical region, and encounters between them are often friendly, especially among the males (Bradley, Doran-Sheehy, Lukas, Boesch, & Vigilant, 2004; Douadi et al., 2007). DNA fingerprinting indicates that males in neighbouring groups tend to be related, which provides a ready explanation for the lower levels of male–male competition during group encounters in comparison to that found with mountain gorillas.

At maturation nearly all females will emigrate to the group of another male during between-group encounters. In mountain gorillas, these occur about once every 5 weeks and provide females their only opportunity to transfer. These encounters incite physical one-on-one male–male competition over females and male mate guarding of them, although joint defense by two males in multimale groups occurs as well (Harcourt & Stewart, 2007; Robbins & Sawyer, 2007). Most males also leave their birth group, but some will stay and eventually succeed the dominant silverback male (Harcourt & Stewart, 2007). When males leave the birth group, many of them stay in the same geographic area and will maintain a foraging range close to that of their father.

During their lifetime females may transfer from one male's group to another's a few times, but once they have chosen a long-term mate they will remain with him until he dies or is unable to protect her offspring from other males (Harcourt & Stewart, 2007). Unlike the unrestricted mating of female chimpanzees (during estrous) and a correspondingly low level of paternity certainty (Goodall, 1986), adult male and female gorillas often form long-term social relationships. DNA fingerprinting indicates that male lowland gorillas show high levels of paternity certainty (>95%; Bradley et al., 2004). For mountain gorillas in multimale groups, dominant males sire 70%–80% of the offspring, and other males in the group sire the remaining offspring (Nsubuga, Robbins, Boesch, & Vigilant, 2008). In the absence of intergroup encounters, behavioral observation reveals low levels of male mate guarding of females (e.g., compared to chimpanzees) and high levels of affiliation with their offspring. "Associated males hold, cuddle, nuzzle, examine, and groom infants, and infants turn to these males in times of distress" (Whitten, 1987, p. 346).

In contrast to female chimpanzees, female gorillas do not have conspicuous sexual swellings and primarily solicit copulations behaviorally (Stewart & Harcourt, 1987). Female gorillas experience comparatively low levels of feeding competition with one another, and as with the chimpanzee, can be classified as a dispersal-egalitarian species (Sterck et al., 1997); disputes do occur but tend to be minor and suppressed by the silverback male (Harcourt & Steward, 2007).

When threatened by another group or predator (e.g., humans), females may compete for proximity to the silverback.

Hominid Socioecology

Our hominid ancestor clearly differed from both chimpanzees and gorillas in many ways (e.g., being bipedal, larger EQ, and so forth), but at the same time there are likely to be common traits such that combing information from the fossil record with behavioral information on chimpanzees and gorillas, as well as on humans in traditional societies, narrows the range of our ancestral possibilities (e.g., Foley & Lee, 1989; Ghiglieri, 1987). Returning to Table 21.1, we see the core changes (0 = minimal, 1 = substantial) needed for common human reproductive relationships and life history traits to have evolved from a chimpanzee-like reproductive strategy or a gorilla-like strategy. Considering the bottom section of the table, we see that modern humans differ from both chimpanzees and gorillas and almost certainly our australopithecine ancestors on most core life history traits, suggesting the current human pattern is evolutionarily recent (Bogin, 1999; Dean et al., 2001). For this reason, we do not address these important changes in this section.

The top section of Table 21.1 indicates the broad-brush evolutionary changes that would be necessary to move from either the chimpanzee or gorilla model to the corresponding target traits in men. The first two rows concern the nature and intensity of male–male competition and the third row, male philopatry. On these dimensions, men are more similar to male chimpanzees than to male gorillas, and if we focused on these traits, a logical inference would be that the common ancestor was male philopatric and showed a moderate sexual dimorphism, with male–male competition having been both one-on-one and coalitional (Wrangham & Peterson, 1996). However, the degree of the sexual dimorphism in australopithecines is closer to that found in the gorilla than the chimpanzee. As noted in "Evolutionary Change," this degree of dimorphism suggests intense one-on-one male–male competition over harems or for control of territory that encompasses the smaller and independent territories of several females. Whether or not males stayed in the same geographic area as their male kin, the sexual dimorphism in male australopithecines suggests a different socioecology than that implied by the similarities between male chimpanzees and men.

The next three rows show a constellation of coevolving traits—family relationships, paternal investment, and paternity certainty—and, to confuse matters further, on these dimensions men are much more similar to male gorillas than to male chimpanzees. Across the male traits listed in Table 21.1, neither the chimpanzee nor the gorilla model is clearly better than the other. The same is true for the female traits listed in Table 21.1, with women's pair-bonded mating and concealed ovulation being closer to that of female gorillas than the promiscuous mating and conspicuous estrous swellings of female chimpanzees. Women are more competitive with one another than female gorillas, falling closer to the chimpanzee in this domain, but neither female chimpanzees nor female gorillas show continuous sexual receptivity across the ovulatory cycle. Given that a conclusion about the ancestral human family cannot be drawn from the comparative analysis and the fossil record, the focus turns to the evolutionary changes needed to move the trait or suite of coevolving traits from the chimpanzee- or gorilla-like start points to the human targets (Foley & Lee, 1989; Ghiglieri, 1987).

For males, the evolutionary changes needed to move from a gorilla-like model to the human pattern are less extensive than those needed to move from a chimpanzee-like model (Geary & Flinn, 2001). In fact, one key change could have set in motion selection pressures that would have moved many of the gorilla-like traits closer to the current human pattern. This change would have been the emergence of male coalitions and a corresponding strengthening of male-biased philopatry. Bradley et al.'s (2004) finding that male lowland gorillas stay in the same geographic area as kin and are generally friendly during intergroup encounters is a preadaptation for such a change. The evolutionary shift would only occur, however, if the benefits of cooperation become larger than the costs of shared mating with females of the group; we see some of these benefits with male cooperation and shared defense in mountain gorillas (Harcourt & Stewart, 2007). In other words, the human targets of male philopatry and coalitional competition could easily evolve from the socioecology of gorillas through males remaining in their birth group or lone males increasing their level of cooperation in threatening contexts (Chapais, 2008; Geary & Flinn, 2001).

Either change results in close-knit male kinships and the creation of the multimale, multifemale communities, as found in all human societies (Foley & Lee, 1989; Ghiglieri, 1987; Rodseth et al., 1991). If gorilla families were placed in closer proximity and if male kinship bonds were strengthened, the common structure of human families, including polygynous ones, in traditional societies would be formed. Moreover, the formation of male coalitions would lessen the importance of physical size and strength during male–male competition (Plavcan et al., 1995), and place a premium on the brain and cognitive systems that support the formation and functioning of these coalitions. The predicted result is the observed pattern of an evolutionary reduction in physical sexual dimorphisms and an increase in brain size. The unusually high levels of paternal investment in humans, in comparison to chimpanzees and most other mammals (Clutton-Brock, 1989), and the correspondingly high rate of paternity certainty (>90%; Anderson, 2006; Geary, 2000) also come into focus: These are not evolutionarily recent or unusual human traits, but rather have a deep evolutionary history, and follow logically for a species that evolved from a socioecology that was composed of single-male or only a few male family groups.

The formation of multimale, multifemale communities and the need for cooperation among males would not only result in larger populations, it would complicate social dynamics among males and females. One consequence is a reduction in polygyny, based on the assumption that males are more likely to cooperate in defense of their community if they have a mate and offspring. A reduction in polygyny results in an increase in the number of lower-quality males entering the reproductive pool. The combination of more available males and individual differences in male quality creates greater opportunity for and greater benefits of cuckoldry, especially when females are paired with a low-quality mate. In this situation, paternity rates are predicted to be lower than the 95% found in gorillas, but maintained at a high level by a variety of adaptations, including male mate guarding, sensitivity to potential affairs by their partners, and male–female pair-bonding (Andrews, Gangestad, Miller, Haselton, Thornhill, & Neale, 2008; McDonald, 1992). These adaptations, along with a high probability of paternity certainty, are consistent with the gorilla-like social and family structure.

An important trait that remains to be explained is women's continuous sexual receptivity across the ovulatory cycle. The emergence of this trait is almost certainly related to the maintenance of the male–female pair-bond and the continuation of paternal investment in the face of heightened female–female competition over male investment (Geary, 2010). As we described in "Evolutionary Trends," the australopithecine diet was varied and included many abundant, high-quality foods. Recall, that this is important because it was likely to have been associated with comparatively low levels of feeding competition among females. This situation allows multiple females to pair with the same high-quality male, with little cost to the females or their offspring, and allows for the formation of single-male harems if males provided a critical benefit to females, which they do in gorillas: Proximity to dominant silverbacks reduces risk of infanticide by extra-group males (Harcourt & Stewart, 2007). If the socioecology of australopithecines was organized around single-male harems, then a typical family group was relatively isolated and was composed of fewer than ten individuals (Harcourt & Stewart, 2007). During our evolutionary history, group sizes expanded to between 100 and 200 individuals (Dunbar, 1993), greatly complicating social life and providing a premium for social-cognitive competencies. If males in these larger communities differed in quality and provided social or other resources that were more limited than easily acquired foods (e.g., sedges), then female–female competition for pairing with these males would emerge. Continuous sexual receptivity in turn would provide females with a competitive edge over their more demure competitors.

In contrast to a gorilla-like socioecology, if our australopithecine ancestors were more chimpanzee-like, then many of the human target traits listed in Table 21.1 would have had to evolve de novo. In particular, there would need to be marked changes in female sexuality, male–female relationships, and male investment in their offspring. One could certainly construct a series of evolutionary changes that could potentially bring us from a chimpanzee-like model to the current human traits, but we will not do so here. Our point is that the number and complexity of changes needed to move from a chimpanzee-like socioecology to the human one make this start point much less likely than the gorilla-like socioecology we just described.

The Human Family Today

Even if our deep evolutionary history was centered on relatively isolated single-male family groups, the emergence of male coalitions and larger communities, as well as the evolved increases in brain size and cognitive sophistication make our current socioecology more fluid and flexible than those of our ancestors. We discuss the associated flexibility in family formation in the next section and then address two types of family relationships—grandparents and siblings—whose importance may be more evolutionarily novel than was the case for our australopithecine ancestors. Men's investment in families and children is of course an interesting evolutionary riddle, at least in comparison to chimpanzees and most other mammals (Clutton-Brock, 1989), but not much of a riddle if we evolved from a gorilla-like socioecology. For this reason, and because it has been addressed extensively elsewhere (Geary, 2000, 2005, 2010), we do not address it here.

Different Types of Families

Considerable variation exists in the composition of human families, including polygyny, polyandry, and monogamy, as summarized in Table 21.2. The social and ecological conditions that account for this variation are not fully understood, but general patterns have been identified (Flinn & Low, 1986). Ecological influences on family formation include the quantity, type, and distribution of food and other material resources, and whether these resources (e.g., cows) can be monopolized by male coalitions or not (e.g., sparse hunted game). Core social variables include rules for marriage, the extent of intragroup competition and warfare, and paternity certainty (White, 1988; White & Burton, 1988). A majority of traditional societies have marriage rules that allow polygynous or polyandrous unions, although the former is many times more common than the latter (Murdock, 1981), in keeping with

Table 21.2 Marriage Patterns and Family Formation

Marriage	System Variations of the System
Polygyny	1. Resource-based polygyny. In resource-rich environments and cultures in which polygyny is not legally prohibited, male kin-based coalitions compete for control of these resources (e.g., land, cows) and dominant men in successful coalitions marry polygynously. A common family structure is a husband who lives separately (e.g., in a different hut) from his wives and their children (e.g., Borgerhoff Mulder, 1990; Draper, 1989)
	2. Social power polygyny. In ecologies in which resources are abundant but not easily controlled by coalitions and in which polygyny is not prohibited, male kin-based coalitions compete for social dominance and power (e.g., through warfare). Dominant men in successful coalitions marry polygynously. A common family structure is a husband, two or three wives, and their children (e.g., Chagnon, 1988). Family units consisting of a husband, wife, and their children are common as well (Hames, 1996).
Polyandry	1. Fraternal polyandry. Although rare, in societies in which land is of low fertility and thus yields poor crops, families tend not to divide inherited land (Smith, 1998). In these societies, brothers share the land—which can only support a small number of children—and marry polyandrously. In these cases, the family consists of two husbands, one wife, and their children. If one brother acquires additional wealth, he will often marry another woman, who does not become the wife of his brother.
Monogamy	1. Ecologically imposed. In environments with sparse and widely distributed food sources, high levels of both maternal and paternal investment are needed to successfully raise offspring, and thus polygyny is rare. Monogamy and family units that consist of a husband, wife, and their children are common (Flinn & Low, 1986).
	2. Socially imposed. Legal prohibition of polygamy in Western culture suppresses the male tendency to form polygynous marriages in resource-rich ecologies. Monogamy and family units consisting of a husband, wife, and their children are thus more common than would otherwise be the case. Serial monogamy and single-parent (typically mother) families are also common in these societies.
	3. Serial. In resource-rich ecologies with socially imposed monogamy, men and women often have a series of legal marriages, although this pattern is sometimes found in other cultures as well (Hill & Hurtado, 1996). Men, but not women, who marry serially have, on average, more children than do men who stay monogamously married to one person (Buckle, Gallup, & Rodd, 1996; Johanna, Forsberg, & Tullberg, 1995).

Adapted from Geary, D. C., & Flinn, M. V. (2001). Evolution of human parental behavior and the human family. *Parenting: Science and Practice, 1,* p. 33, with permission of the publisher, Lawrence Erlbaum Associates.

our gorilla-like socioecology. In these societies, coalitions of related men cooperate to gain access to and maintain control of the resources women need to rear their children, or to control reproduction-related social dynamics; control of material resources results in resource-based polygyny (Borgerhoff Mulder, 1990), and control of social dynamics results in social power polygyny (Chagnon, 1988).

The material and social resources that are controlled by men's coalitions are not simply related to their mating efforts. They are often used to influence the social and reproductive interests of their children. With resource-based polygyny, younger men in the coalitions are often dependent on the wealth of their father, uncles, and other relatives to pay the bride price—such as cattle paid to the prospective bride's parents—needed to marry (e.g., Borgerhoff Mulder, 2000). At the same time, a young woman's parents and other relatives will often use their wealth and social power to facilitate her marriage to a wealthy or socially powerful man and kin group, and to influence her treatment by the man and his kin after she has married. A similar pattern is found with social power polygyny, whereby men's coalitions engage in negotiations to influence the reproductive prospects of their sons and daughters. In both forms of marriage system, women almost always marry, some monogamously and some into polygynous unions (Hartung, 1982). High-status men typically have several wives, other men marry monogamously, and some men never marry (Murdock, 1981). Polyandry is found in less than 1% of human societies and is also related to resource control (Smith, 1998); land tends to be inherited by sons but cannot be subdivided into smaller, functional plots (i.e., plots that can support a family). To keep this resource in the family and to provide sufficient resources to support children, brothers will marry the same woman and work the same land.

Monogamous marriages and families consisting of a husband, wife, and their children who reside in the same household are common in societies in which monogamy is ecologically or socially imposed. The result is a suppression of polygynous marriages in higher-status men, although serial monogamy is common in these societies, as are single-parent families (typically headed by mothers and aided by maternal kin). These societies are also unusual in that nuclear families are often physically isolated from the wider kin network, although kin are still a source of social and economic support; this isolation is more common in the professional classes, in which jobs often require moving away from kin (Argyle, 1994). In societies with socially imposed monogamy, kin-based negotiations for marriage partners are uncommon, but intergenerational transfer of wealth from parents to children, as related to children's later marriage prospects or the well-being of the donor's grandchildren, is common (Gaulin & Boster, 1990).

In short, both men and women are involved in family formation and parental investment, but the dynamics of these vary across differing physical and social ecologies. When it is not prohibited, men attempt to acquire the resources needed to marry polygynously but must do so through cooperation with their male kin, and often through the cooperation of prospective brides (e.g., Chagnon, 1997). The combination of male coalitions, their status within the coalition, and the distribution of resources in the wider ecology influences men's reproductive strategies and patterns of family formation, spousal warmth, paternal investment, and men's and women's mate choices. In some cultures, women influence these patterns, from attempting to bias men's negotiations for marriage of their daughters (e.g., Borgerhoff Mulder, 1990) to negotiating the nature of the spousal relationship. In other cultures, the mate choices of men but especially women are constrained because their spouses are often chosen by their parents or other kin (Apostolou, 2007). All of these dynamics are variations on the same theme—humans form complex kinship networks, including families that cooperate to control social dynamics and to gain access to resources in the wider community.

Nuclear and Extended Family Relationships

The gorilla model helps us to understand some features of the human family, such as paternal investment and long-term male–female bonds, but does not make specific predictions about other aspects. One of these is the seemingly at-odds shortening of the human interbirth interval and a corresponding lengthening of the developmental period. In traditional societies, the interbirth interval is about 3 years, as compared to 4–5 years for gorillas and about 6 years for chimpanzees (Bogin, 1999; Harcourt & Stewart, 2007). Moreover, human infants are born more altricial than infants of these other species and develop more slowly, suggesting an increase in selection for parental investment. Yet, somehow human families are producing more offspring. The key is that it is not simply direct investment from the parents, but an increase in alloparental care (i.e., care from other kin; Flinn & Leone, 2006; Sear & Mace, 2008). Grandmothers are one source of this care, as we describe in the second section, "Grandparents." In the first section, "Siblings," we reflect on how sibling relationships fit within our proposed gorilla-like family structure.

SIBLINGS

Siblings are a potential source of alloparental care during development and a frequent source of care of nieces and nephews in adulthood (Kurland & Gaulin, 2005). Siblings also provide emotional and financial support to one another as adults. We will review some of these patterns, but primarily want to provide an evolutionary scenario for conceptualizing empirical research on sibling relationships. We thus begin with a summary of sibling availability and relationships in chimpanzee and gorilla communities and follow with reflections on potential patterns of sibling relationships during human evolution. We close with potential links to empirical studies of sibling relationships today.

Chimpanzees and Gorillas

Sibling relationships are important for chimpanzees and gorillas both during the developmental period and oftentimes into adulthood (Bradley, Doran-Sheehy, & Vigilant, 2007; Goodall, 1986; Mitani, 2009; Watts, 1994). Chimpanzee siblings are often a source of support and alloparental care and may even adopt and raise siblings should their mother die (Goodall, 1986). Although female gorillas disperse from their birth group when they reach adulthood, sisters sometimes disperse together and lone females are more likely to join groups that include female kin (Bradley et al., 2007). For chimpanzees, maternal brothers often form long-term social relationships (Mitani, 2009) and, as noted, male lowland gorillas in neighboring families tend to be brothers or other kin and have friendly interactions during intergroup encounters (Harcourt & Stewart, 2007). This does not mean there is no conflict among siblings, but it does mean that siblings can be significant sources of social support in these species and almost certainly throughout much of our evolutionary history (Davis & Daly, 1997; Kurland & Gaulin, 2005).

Although there is little question that sib relationships were important during our evolutionary history, the nature of these relationships may have been different if the start point of family evolution was chimpanzee-like or gorilla-like. Chimpanzee families are organized around the mother, with no paternal investment, and with spacing between siblings of about 5 or 6 years (Goodall, 1986). Females will have, on average, three to five offspring survive infancy, and two or three survive to adulthood, meaning that most individuals will have one or two maternal sibs while growing up and an unknown number of paternal sibs (e.g., Sugiyama, 2004). The extent to which juvenile chimpanzees have contact with their peers, some of whom may be paternal sibs, depends on the sociability of their mother; some mothers have frequent contact with other females (and their offspring), whereas others are more solitary (Goodall, 1986). Because there are many males in chimpanzee communities and due to changes in dominance rank among males, chimpanzee sibs are more likely to be sired by different fathers than are gorilla sibs. Although this would result in more half sibs among chimpanzees, it is not clear if this affects their relationships. It appears that familiarity when growing up, as would happen with maternal sibs, and for males, similarities in age and mutual benefit from cooperation are the most important influences on long-term relationships (Goodall, 1986).

Gorilla families, as noted earlier, are organized around one or two dominant males, and thus female gorillas and their offspring are in closer physical proximity than female chimpanzees. Single-male family groups are, on average, composed of about ten individuals, about half of whom will be infants or juveniles (Harcourt & Stewart, 2007), all or most of whom will be paternal full sibs. Multi-male groups typically include two silverbacks, five females, and six or seven infants and juveniles. The dominant male sires about five out of six offspring, and the second-ranking male sires the remaining offspring; these males are sometimes brothers and sometimes not (Bradley et al., 2005). Due to changes in dominance positions, the offspring in the group may or may not be paternal sibs, but in any case are more frequently so than are juveniles in chimpanzee communities. Female gorillas will, on average, birth three or four offspring in their lifetime and two or three of these will survive to adulthood. Given the shorter interbirth interval, maternal sibs will be closer in age than chimpanzee maternal sibs. In all, gorillas will have one or two maternal siblings while growing up, and with four adult females in a typical one-male group, they may have four to eight paternal sibs.

The difference between these evolutionary start points includes more full and half paternal sibs and more frequent contact with juveniles of other mothers (many of whom will be paternal half sibs) in a gorilla-like community than in a chimpanzee-like community. The higher frequency of paternal sibs and the greater frequency of contact among juveniles of different mothers is a potentially important socioecology for the development of reproductively important relationships in adulthood. There are only hints of this in research on extant gorillas, but keep in mind that this is only our start point.

Human Evolution

If the human family emerged from a gorilla-like social ecology, then full and paternal half-siblings would have been common, and given group member's proximity to the dominant male, juveniles would have had frequent if not near continuous exposure to all other juveniles in the group. Paternal half sibs would have likely been closer in age than maternal full sibs. The importance of childhood familiarity for the development of long-term relationships into adulthood, the availability and familiarity with paternal full and half sibs, and similar ages of many paternal half sibs create conditions in which males or females could form relatively large kin-based coalitions. The pressure for females to do so would have been to facilitate competition over clumped, high-quality food sources, such as large fruit trees (Sterck et al., 1997). The pressure for males to do so would have been to facilitate competition over access to reproductive females (Geary, 2010; Wrangham, 1999). As described earlier, the australopithecine diet appears to have been varied and included plants that were likely abundant; thus, intense feeding competition among females seems less likely than intense male–male competition over groups of females. Recall, the latter is supported by the large sexual dimorphism in male australopithecines.

As the reader knows from the "Evolutionary History" section, the magnitude of this sexual dimorphism declined over the course of human evolution, in conjunction with increases in brain size and in the length of the developmental period. We argued this reflected the emergence of multimale kin-based coalitions and increased familiarity of juveniles in gorilla-like groups, their paternal relatedness, and male philopatry make the transition from single-male to multiple-male kin-based groups a straightforward evolutionary step. The corresponding increase in group size and likely reduction in degree of polygyny would have reduced the degree of paternal relatedness among juveniles in the group, but shortening of the interbirth interval from what was likely to have been 5–6 years to about 3 years would have resulted in full sibs closer in age (Bogin, 1999). The reduced age difference would allow for development of greater familiarity between sibs and a sharing of life histories, which would presumably increase rates and strength of cooperation (Chapais, 2008).

Again, this is not to say that sibling rivalry over paternal and social (e.g., peer relationships) resources were not important; they almost certainly were. Our points are that attempts to reconstruct the evolution of the human family need to consider sibling relationships and that the pattern of full and half paternal sibs that would result from a gorilla-like family structure fit well with our proposal regarding the evolutionary emergence of male kin-based coalitions.

Siblings Today

There are, of course, important anthropological and cross-cultural studies of children and their development (Whiting & Whiting, 1975), but most of these have been conducted in pastoral, farming, or economically developed communities and not in hunter-gatherer groups, and most of the research on the latter societies, with a few exceptions (e.g., Henry, Morelli, & Tronick, 2005), has not focused on children in general, much less sibling relationships in particular (Hewlett & Lamb, 2005). The research that has been conducted reveals that older children often have some responsibility for the care and monitoring of their younger siblings, and younger children will often imitate the behavior of their older sibs (Whiting & Edwards, 1988). There are also cross-cultural differences in sibling relationships. For instance, conflicts occur among siblings in all societies, but parents in some societies tend to allow sibs to work out their own relationship dynamics, whereas parents in others intervene and disrupt the conflict (Whiting & Edwards, 1988).

The majority of empirical studies on sibling relationships have been conducted in Western societies, in which norms about sibling roles are not well defined (McHale, Kim, & Whiteman, 2006). The study of sibling relationships in these cultures tends to focus on competition, privacy, and independence, as contrasted with the focus on caregiving in anthropological studies (Cicirelli, 1994; Hewlett & Lamb, 2005; Rabain-Jamin, Maynard, & Greenfield, 2003). Both research literatures touch on the importance of siblings for socialization. The focus in anthropological studies is often on, for instance, older children's disciplining of younger siblings, or on younger children imitating their older sibs (Whiting & Edwards, 1988). The emphasis of psychological studies in Western culture is more likely to be on topics such as emotional regulation and perspective taking, social problem solving, and conflict resolution (Azmitia & Hesser, 1995; Dunn, 1983; Dunn, Brown, Slomkowski, Tesla, & Youngblade, 1991; Maynard, 2002; Youngblade & Dunn, 1995).

The anthropological studies would benefit from the use of the methods used to assess these subtle social-psychological processes in sibling relationships, and the psychological studies would benefit from an evolutionary framing of these relationships and from a deeper appreciation of how growing up in modern societies may influence sibling and other relationships. The combination of nuclear families, socially imposed monogamy, and modern schooling, as just some examples, has almost certainly resulted in changes in sibling relationships, relative to those in traditional cultures and during our evolutionary history. As in other societies, siblings in modern ones are still a very common source of lifelong support (sometimes lifelong conflict; Kurland & Gaulin, 2005), but in comparison to traditional societies and a gorilla-like social structure during our evolutionary history, we have fewer siblings, less contact with them while growing up (due in part to age-segregated schooling, and in adulthood due to the job structure of modern economies; e.g., living farther apart), and we are more dependent on nonkin relationships for social support.

GRANDPARENTS

Older children can contribute to the well-being of their siblings and can relieve mothers from some parental investment and through this may have contributed to the evolutionary shortening of the interbirth interval, but this care is not a sufficient explanation for this dramatic evolutionary change. The evolving social structure of our ancestors must have included investment by others, presumably those with some genetic relatedness to the offspring. These adults may have included fathers (Geary, 2000), adult siblings (Hrdy, 2005), grandparents (Hawkes, O'Connell, Blurton Jones, Alvarez, & Charnov, 1998), or some combination; reciprocal care among unrelated females was also likely (Geary, 2002; Kurland & Gaulin, 2005). We focus on the investment provided by grandparents, and relevantly, the existence of a postreproductive lifespan in women; specifically, we review proposed ultimate-level explanations for these traits. The literature, and therefore our review, has focused primarily on grandmaternal investment, but we note that grandpaternal investment also presents an interesting human practice worthy of theoretical attention, just not in this chapter.

Menopause and the Grandmother Hypothesis

Among primates, humans are unique in that women have a long postreproductive lifespan (Alexander, 1990). Several ultimate-level explanations for women's long postreproductive lifespan have been proposed, but no consensus has been reached.

The *grandmother hypothesis* (Hawkes et al., 1998) proposes that women can increase their fitness by investing resources in their grandchildren to a higher extent than by continuing to produce children of their own, given the increasing age-related risks of maintaining a pregnancy and giving birth. The hypothesis focuses primarily on grandmothers' influence on grandchild survival via food production. In a comprehensive review, Sear and Mace (2008) found a positive relation between presence of maternal grandmother and child survival in 9 of 13 studies, whereas 9 of 17 studies found a positive relation between paternal grandmother presence and child survival.

However, several criticisms have been raised about the grandmother hypothesis. For example, Peccei (2001) argues that mathematical models indicate that grandmothering is not a more adaptive strategy than continued reproduction and that the assumption of female philopatry is flawed. We agree with the latter, but note that even with the male-biased philopatry assumed with our gorilla model, the increase in group size that would follow the formation of male kin-based coalitions result in more degrees of freedom in the characteristics of hominid groups. As size increased from a typical gorilla group of about ten individuals to human villages of 100 to 200 individuals (Dunbar, 1993), the potential number and variety of alloparents increased substantially. Although these traditional groups tend to be male biased in terms of philopatry, especially with high levels of local raiding and warfare (Pasternak et al., 1997), human groups and family organizations are highly flexible, as we described in the section "Different Types of Families," and the presence of the maternal grandmother is common. Moreover, as group size increased during our evolution, the need to emigrate to avoid inbreeding likely decreased, thus allowing for larger communities that could have included paternal and maternal kin. With respect to our gorilla model, these latter scenarios are more recent evolutionary changes.

Alternative Hypotheses

There are several alternative explanations of menopause (e.g., Cant & Johnston, 2008; Williams, 1957). Williams first proposed the *mother hypothesis*, specifically, that women's postreproductive lifespan evolved to enable the extended mothering needed for slowly developing offspring. The grandmother hypothesis, as initially proposed, focused on grandmothers' investments in terms of food and its subsequent impact on child survival. Kaplan and colleagues (2000) note that grandmothers in some populations do not produce enough food to share with grandchildren. However, as Peccei (2001) proposes, grandmothers may invest in children in other ways as well. For example, Scelza (2009) reported that, among the Martu Aborigines, grandmothers were responsible for a high proportion of difficult caretaking practices, such as soothing, disciplining, bathing, and grooming. These are important components of alloparenting that are not captured by studies of calories provided by grandmothers to their grandchildren. A full understanding of this form of alloparenting and of the evolved function of menopause will require inclusion of these potential influences on children's wellbeing.

Potential Moderators of Grandparental Investment

In humans, mothers invest more in their offspring than do fathers, in part because of nonpaternity risks (i.e., risk of cuckoldry; Geary, 2010). Therefore, paternal grandparents and maternal grandfathers face uncertainty about their genetic relatedness to their grandchildren, whereas maternal grandmothers do not. Paternal grandfathers encounter paternity uncertainty across two generations, paternal grandmothers and maternal grandfathers encounter paternity uncertainty in one generation, and maternal grandmothers never encounter paternity uncertainty. If a population's rates of maternal and paternal certainty were 100% and 95% respectively, then maternal grandmothers would be genetically related to their grandchildren 100% of the time, paternal grandmothers and maternal grandfathers would be genetically related to their grandchildren 95% of the time, and paternal grandfathers would be genetically related to their grandchildren 90.25% of the time.

Smith (1988) hypothesized that grandparental investment would track the pattern of paternity certainty across types of grandparents. Data collected across three decades and several cultures, generally consisting of grandchildren's reports of their grandparents' investment patterns, provide support for this hypothesis (Bishop, Meyer, Schmidt, & Gray, 2009; Chastril, Getz, Euler, & Starks, 2006; Euler & Weitzel, 1996; Hartshorne & Manaster, 1982; Hoffman, 1979-1980; Salmon, 1999; Pashos, 2000; Laham, Gonsalkorale, & von Hippel, 2005), as have parent reports of grandparental investment from a large British dataset (Pollet, Nelissen, & Nettle, 2009).

Sex chromosome relatedness has also been proposed as a potential moderator of grandparental investment patterns. The vast majority of human offspring inherit one sex chromosome from each parent. Females inherit an X chromosome from each parent, whereas males inherit an X chromosome from their mothers and a Y chromosome from their fathers. Because males have one Y chromosome and females have zero Y chromosomes, a male's Y chromosome must be inherited from his father, who must have inherited his Y chromosome from his father, who must have inherited his Y chromosome from his father, etc. Therefore, paternal grandfathers must share their Y chromosome with their male grandchildren. Because males inherit their X chromosome from their mothers, and because daughters inherit this same X chromosome from their fathers, paternal grandmothers must share an X chromosome with their granddaughters. Similarly, a grandson's X chromosome must come from a maternal grandparent.

Because genes on the sex chromosomes are clearly able to alter an individual's behavior, grandparents have been hypothesized to have undergone selection for differential investment in their grandchildren based on sex chromosome relatedness. Tests of this hypothesis have produced mixed results. A meta-analysis of seven studies of relations between grandmother presence and survival in historical and traditional modern populations concluded that the relationship between having a living paternal grandmother and survivorship was significantly more positive for granddaughters than for grandsons (Fox et al., 2009). However, the authors noted that the reasons for this finding are unclear, citing two null findings for correlations between preferential grandparental treatment and probability of shared sex chromosomes (Chastril et al., 2006; Pollet et al., 2009) and noting that X-linked traits may have been responsible for this finding.

Chastril et al. (2006) compared the consistency of grandparental investment patterns in German and

American samples with the paternity uncertainty and sex chromosome selection hypotheses. Based on grandchildren's reports of quality of grandparental care and amount of grandparental contact desired, the authors reported support for both the paternity uncertainty hypothesis (generally, these ratings tracked paternity certainty patterns) and the sex chromosome selection hypothesis (grandsons reported desiring more contact with paternal grandparents than did granddaughters). However, the authors note that the support for the paternity uncertainty hypothesis is stronger, is not compromised by the sex-specific investment patterns predicted by the sex chromosome selection hypothesis, and is consistent with the hypothesis that ancestral humans received moderate to high amounts of grandparental investment and had low to moderate amounts of paternity uncertainty.

As we described earlier, a gorilla-like family structure would have resulted in low paternity uncertainty, but that uncertainty would increase as community size increased and polygyny decreased. When combined with larger communities and increased opportunity to alloparenting, including that of grandparents, a bias in grandparental investment can be incorporated into our gorilla-model, but again, assuming that these biases emerged later in our evolutionary history.

Future Directions

The family is not only a human universal; it is arguably the core social organization of our species. Scientists and lay persons implicitly recognize the importance of the family for the development, socialization, and well-being of children; the very long human childhood would not be possible without intense investment by parents and other adults. Given this, it is not surprising that considerable research efforts are expended in attempts to better understand the human family and to develop ways to improve family functioning. Using PsychInfo, we identified 50,718 articles, chapters, books, commentaries, and so forth on the human family published between 1990 and 1999, inclusive. During the same time frame, there were 5,550 publications on human evolution, but the overlap between these two extensive research literatures was 459 publications, or 0.91% of the entire literature on the human family. From 2000 to 2009, inclusive, there are 79,811 publications on the human family and 12,218 on human evolution. The overlap was 786 publications or 0.98% of the entire literature on the human family. Despite the emergence of evolutionary psychology during the 1990s and beyond, the influence of evolutionary studies on human family research is surprisingly small.

To be sure, there have been many important evolutionary analyses of the human family and many empirical studies of family dynamics based on evolutionary hypotheses (e.g., Daly & Wilson, 1988; Salmon & Shackelford, 2007), but the core literature on the human family remains to be informed by evolutionary insights. The key goal for the future is to bring these insights to the wider group of researchers who study the human family, and to the practitioners who work with families to improve their well-being.

Conclusion

Following an earlier work by Geary and Flinn (2001), our core proposal is that the socioecology of our australopithecine ancestors was similar to that found in modern gorillas—that is, single-male harems with several females and their offspring. If correct, this form of social structure means that seemingly unusual features of the human family have a very deep evolutionary core, including high levels of paternal investment and long-term male–female relationships; Lovejoy (1981) also argued that male australopithecines invested in females but he did not propose a gorilla-like family structure as we have. Equally important, the evolutionary changes needed to move from a gorilla-like family structure to the current human pattern are much less complex than the changes needed to move from a chimpanzee-like structure. The key evolutionary change that would have set the stage for other changes would have been the strengthening of male–male bonds and the formation of male kin-based coalitions (Geary & Flinn, 2002). With this change, we would move gorilla-like families into larger communities. These communities would complicate social dynamics, but in ways consistent with the paleontological record and current human studies. Male cooperation, for instance, would likely reduce the degree of polygyny and the magnitude of the corresponding sexual dimorphism; increase the benefits of strong social competencies and presumably result in a corresponding increase in brain size; and increase cuckoldry risks.

Evolution did not end there, however. Community sizes continued to increase, as did the complexity of social dynamics, and our ancestors' ability to cope with novelty and change within the lifespan (Dunbar, 1993; Geary, 2005). Accompanying these were significant changes in human life history that differ from both gorilla and chimpanzee life histories, suggesting that the human pattern emerged more recently in our evolutionary past than did our very old gorilla-like base. Among the more important changes include a shortening of the interbirth interval, a lengthening of the developmental period, and menopause. We agree that these changes are consistent with an increase in either paternal investment or alloparental care, including investment by siblings, grandparents, or other kin. Our points here are that humans' ability to cope with very complex social dynamics has also resulted in an ability to form many different types of families, contingent on current social conditions. This variety, however, is not inconsistent with our gorilla-like start point, but rather reflects the expression of a more recently evolved ability to create evolutionarily novel solutions to cope with core human concerns (Geary, 2005), including investment in children.

References

Alexander, R.D. (1990). *How did humans evolve? Reflections on the uniquely unique species*. Museum of Zoology (Specialty Publication No. 1). Ann Arbor: The University of Michigan.

Alexander, R.D., Hoogland, J.L., Howard, R.D., Noonan, K.M., & Sherman, P.W. (1979). Sexual dimorphisms and breeding systems in pinnipeds, ungulates, primates, and humans. In N.A. Chagnon & W. Irons (Eds.), *Evolutionary biology and human social behavior: An anthropological perspective* (pp. 402–435). North Scituate, MA: Duxbury Press.

Allman, J., Rosin, A., Kumar, R., & Hasenstaub, A. (1998). Parenting and survival in anthropoid primates: Caretakers live longer. *Proceedings of the National Academy of Sciences USA, 95,* 6866–6869.

Anderson, K.G. (2006). How well does paternity confidence match actual paternity? Evidence from worldwide nonpaternity rates. *Current Anthropology, 47,* 513–520.

Andrews, P.W., Gangestad, S.W., Miller, G.F., Haselton, M.G., Thornhill, R., & Neale, M.C. (2008). Sex differences in detecting sexual infidelity: Results of a maximum likelihood method for analyzing the sensitivity of sex differences to underreporting. *Human Nature, 19,* 347–373.

Apostolou, M. (2007). Sexual selection under parental choice: The role of parents in the evolution of human mating. *Evolution and Human Behavior, 28,* 403–409.

Argyle, M. (1994). *The psychology of social class*. New York: Routledge.

Asfaw, B., Gilbert, W.H., Beyene, Y., Hart, W.K., Renne, P.R., WoldeGabriel, G., et al. (2002, March 21). Remains of *Homo erectus* from Bouri, Middle Awash, Ethiopia. *Nature, 416,* 317–320.

Asfaw, B., White, T., Lovejoy, O. Latimer, B., Simpson, S., & Suwa, G. (1999, April 23). Australopithecus garhi: A new species of early hominid from Ethiopia. *Science, 284,* 629–635.

Azmitia, M., & Hesser, J. (1993). Why siblings are important agents of cognitive development: A comparison of siblings and peers. *Child Development, 64,* 430–444.

Bailey, D.H., & Geary, D.C. (2009) Hominid brain evolution: Testing climactic, ecological, and social competition models. *Human Nature, 20,* 67–79.

Barton, R.A. (1996). Neocortex size and behavioural ecology in primates. *Proceedings of the Royal Society of London B, 263,* 173–177.

Bishop, D.I., Meyer, B.C., Schmidt, B.C., & Gray, B.R. (2009). Differential investment behavior between grandparents and grandchildren: The role of paternity uncertainty. *Evolutionary Psychology, 7,* 66–77.

Boesch, C., Kohou, G., Néné, H., & Vigilant, L. (2006). Male competition and paternity in wild chimpanzees of the Taï forest. *American Journal of Physical Anthropology, 130,* 103–115.

Bogin, B. (1999). *Patterns of human growth* (2nd ed.). Cambridge, UK: Cambridge University Press.

Borgerhoff Mulder, M. (1990). Kipsigis women's preferences for wealthy men: Evidence for female choice in mammals? *Behavioral Ecology and Sociobiology, 27,* 255–264.

Borgerhoff Mulder, M. (2000). Optimizing offspring: The quantity-quality tradeoff in agropastoral Kipsigis. *Evolution and Human Behavior, 21,* 391–410.

Bradley, B.J., Doran-Sheehy, D.M., Lukas, D., Boesch, C., & Vigilant, L. (2004). Dispersed male networks in Western gorillas. *Current Biology, 14,* 510–513.

Bradley, B.J., Doran-Sheehy, D. & Vigilant, L. (2007). Potential for female kin associations in wild western gorillas despite female dispersal. *Proceedings of the Royal Society B, 274,* 2179–2185.

Bradley, B.J., Robbins, M.M., Williamson, E.A., Steklis, H.D., Steklis, N.G., Eckhardt, N., et al. (2005). Mountain gorilla tug-of-war: Silverbacks have limited control over reproduction in multimale groups. *Proceedings of the National Academy of Sciences USA, 102,* 9418–9423.

Buckle, L., Gallup, G.G., Jr., & Rodd, Z.A. (1996). Marriage as a reproductive contract: Patterns of marriage, divorce, and remarriage. *Ethology and Sociobiology, 17,* 363–377.

Cant, M.A., & Johnstone, R.A. (2008). Reproductive conflict and the separation of reproductive generations in humans. *Proceedings of the National Academy of Sciences, 105,* 5332–5336.

Chagnon, N.A. (1997). *Yanomamö* (5th ed.). Fort Worth, TX: Harcourt.

Chagnon, N.A. (1988, February 26). Life histories, blood revenge, and warfare in a tribal population. *Science, 239,* 985–992.

Chapais, B. (2008). *Primeval kinship: How pair-bonding gave birth to human society*. Cambridge, MA: Harvard University Press.

Chastril, E.R., Getz, W.M., Euler, H.A., & Starks, P.T. (2006). Paternity uncertainty overrides sex chromosome selection for preferential grandparenting. *Evolution and Human Behavior, 27,* 206–223.

Cicirelli, V.G. (1994). Sibling relationships in cross-cultural perspective. *Journal of Marriage and the Family, 56,* 7–20.

Clutton-Brock, T.H. (1989). Mammalian mating systems. *Proceedings of the Royal Society of London B, 236,* 339–372.

Clutton-Brock, T.H., Harvey, P.H., & Rudder, B. (1977, October 27). Sexual dimorphism, socionomic sex ratio and body weight in primates. *Nature, 269,* 797–800.

Constable, J.L., Ashley, M.V., Goodall, J., & Pusey, A.E. (2001). Noninvasive paternity assignment in Gombe chimpanzees. *Molecular Ecology, 10,* 1279–1300.

Daly, M., & Wilson, M. (1988). Evolutionary social psychology and family homicide. *Science, 242,* 519–524.

Davis, J.N., & Daly, M. (1997). Evolutionary theory and the human family. *Quarterly Review of Biology, 72*, 407–435.

Dean, C., Leakey, M.G., Reid, D., Schrenk, F., Schwartz, G.T., Stringer, C., & Walker, A. (2001, December 6). Growth processes in teeth distinguish modern humans from Homo erectus and earlier hominins. *Nature, 414*, 628–631.

de Waal, F.B.M. (1982). *Chimpanzee politics: Power and sex among apes*. New York: Harper & Row.

de Waal, F.B.M. (1993). Sex differences in chimpanzee (and human) behavior: A matter of social values? In M. Hechter, L. Nadel, & R.E. Michod (Eds.), *The origin of values* (pp. 285–303). New York: Aldine de Gruyter.

Draper, P. (1989). African marriage systems: Perspectives from evolutionary ecology. *Ethology and Sociobiology, 10*, 145–169.

Douadi, M. I., Gatti, S., Levrero, F., Duhamel, G., Bermejo, M., Vallet, D., et al. (2007). Sex-biased dispersal in western lowland gorillas (*Gorilla gorilla gorilla*). *Molecular Ecology, 16*, 2247–2259.

Dunbar, R.I.M. (1993). Coevolution of neocortical size, group size and language in humans. *Behavioral and Brain Sciences, 16*, 681–735.

Dunbar, R.I.M., & Bever, J. (1998). Neocortex size predicts group size in carnivores and some insectivores. *Ethology, 104*, 695–708.

Dunn, J. (1983). Sibling relationships in early childhood. *Child Development, 54*, 787–811.

Dunn, J., Brown, J., Slomkowski, C., Tesla, C., & Youngblade, L. (1991). Young children's understanding of other people's feelings and beliefs: Individual differences and their antecedents. *Child Development, 62*, 1352–1366.

Emlen, S.T., & Oring, L.W. (1977, July 15). Ecology, sexual selection, and the evolution of mating systems. *Science, 197*, 215–223.

Eriksson, J., Siedel, H., Lukas, D., Kayser, M., Erler, A., Hashimoto, C., Hohmann, G., et al. (2006). Y-chromosome analysis confirms highly sex-biased dispersal and suggests a low male effective population size in bonobos (*Pan paniscus*). *Molecular Ecology, 15*, 939–949.

Euler, H.A., & Weitzel, B. (1996). Discriminative grandparental solicitude as a reproductive strategy. *Human Nature, 7*, 39–59.

Falk, D., Redmond, J.C. Jr., Guyer, J., Conroy, G.C., Recheis, W., Weber, G.W., & Seidler, H. (2000). Early hominid brain evolution: A new look at old endocasts. *Journal of Human Evolution, 38*, 695–717.

Flinn, M.V., & Leone, D.V. (2006). Early family trauma and the ontogeny of glucocorticoid stress response in the human child: Grandmother as a secure base. *Journal of Developmental Processes, 1*, 31–68.

Flinn, M.V., & Low, B.S. (1986). Resource distribution, social competition, and mating patterns in human societies. In D.I Rubenstein & R. W. Wrangham (Eds.), *Ecological aspects of social evolution: Birds and mammals* (pp. 217–243). Princeton, NJ: Princeton University Press.

Foley, R.A., & Lee, P.C. (1989, February 17). Finite social space, evolutionary pathways, and reconstructing hominid behavior. *Science, 243*, 901–906.

Fossey, D. (1984). *Gorillas in the mist*. Boston, MA: Houghton Mifflin Co.

Fox, M., Sear, R. Beise, J., Ragsdale, G., Voland, E., & Knapp, L.A. (2009). Grandma plays favourites: X-chromosome relatedness and sex-specific childhood mortality. *Proceedings of the Royal Society of London B, 277*, 567–573.

Gabunia, L., Vekua, A., Lordkipanidze, D., Swisher, C.C. III, Ferring, R., Justus, A., et al. (2000, May 12). Earliest Pleistocene hominid cranial remains from Dmanisi, Republic of Georgia: Taxonomy, geological setting, and age. *Science, 288*, 1019–1025.

Gaulin, S.J.C., & Boster, J.S. (1990). Dowry as female competition. *American Anthropologist, 92*, 994–1005.

Geary, D.C. (2000). Evolution and proximate expression of human paternal investment. *Psychological Bulletin, 126*, 55–77.

Geary, D.C. (2002). Sexual selection and sex differences in social cognition. In A.V. McGillicuddy-De Lisi & R. De Lisi (Eds.), *Biology, society, and behavior: The development of sex differences in cognition* (pp. 23–53). Greenwich, CT: Ablex/Greenwood.

Geary, D.C. (2005). *The origin of mind: Evolution of brain, cognition, and general intelligence*. Washington, DC: American Psychological Association.

Geary, D.C. (2010). *Male, female: The evolution of human sex differences* (2nd ed.). Washington, DC: American Psychological Association.

Geary, D.C., & Flinn, M.V. (2001). Evolution of human parental behavior and the human family. *Parenting: Science and Practice, 1*, 5–61.

Geary, D.C., & Flinn, M.V. (2002). Sex differences in behavioral and hormonal response to social threat: Commentary on Taylor et al. (2000). *Psychological Review, 109*, 745–750.

Ghiglieri, M.P. (1987). Sociobiology of the great apes and the hominid ancestor. *Journal of Human Evolution, 16*, 319–357.

Goodall, J. (1986). *The chimpanzees of Gombe: Patterns of behavior*. Cambridge, MA: The Belknap Press.

Hames, R. (1996). Costs and benefits of monogamy and polygyny for Yanomamö women. *Ethology and Sociobiology, 17*, 181–199.

Harcourt, A.H., & Stewart, K.J. (2007). *Gorilla society: Conflict, compromise, and cooperation between the sexes*. Chicago, IL: University of Chicago Press.

Hartung, J. (1982). Polygyny and inheritance of wealth. *Current Anthropology, 23*, 1–12.

Harvey, P.H., & Clutton-Brock, T.H. (1985). Life history variation in primates. *Evolution, 39*, 559–581.

Hawkes, K., O'Connell, J.F., Blurton Jones, N.G., Alvarez, H., & Charnov, E. (1998). Grandmothering, menopause and the evolution of human life histories. *Proceedings of the National Academy of Sciences of the United States of America, 95*, 1336–1339.

Henry, P.I., Morelli, G.A., & Tronick, E.Z. (2005). Child caretakers among Efe foragers of the Ituri forest. In B.S. Hewlett & M.E. Lamb (Eds.), *Hunter-gatherer childhoods: Evolutionary, developmental & cultural perspectives* (pp. 191–213). New Brunswick, NJ: Transaction Publishers.

Hewlett, B.S., & Lamb, M.E. (Eds.). (2005). *Hunter-gatherer childhoods: Evolutionary, developmental & cultural perspectives*. New Brunswick, NJ: Transaction Publishers.

Hill, K., & Hurtado, A.M. (1996). *Ache life history: The ecology and demography of a foraging people*. New York: Aldine de Gruyter.

Hartshorne, T.S., & Manaster, G.J. (1982). The relationship with grandparents: Contact, importance, role conception. *International Journal of Aging and Human Development, 15*, 233–245.

Hoffman, E. (1979-1980). Young adults' relations with their grandparents: An exploratory study. *International Journal of Aging and Human Development, 10*, 299–310.

Holloway, R.L. (1973). Endocranial volumes of early African hominids, and the role of the brain in human mosaic evolution. *Journal of Human Evolution, 2*, 449–459.

Horai, S., Hayasaka, K., Kondo, R., Tsugane, K., & Takahata, N. (1995). Recent African origin of modern humans revealed by complete sequences of hominoid mitochondrial DNAs. *Proceedings of the National Academy of Sciences USA, 92*, 532–536.

Hrdy, S.B. (2005). Comes the child before the man: How cooperative breeding and prolonged postweaning dependence shaped human potential. In B.S. Hewlett & M.E. Lamb (Eds.), *Hunter-gatherer childhoods: Evolutionary, developmental & cultural perspectives* (pp. 65–91). New Brunswick, NJ: Transaction Publishers.

Jerison, H.J. (1973). *Evolution of the brain and intelligence*. New York: Academic Press.

Joffe, T.H. (1997). Social pressures have selected for an extended juvenile period in primates. *Journal of Human Evolution, 32*, 593–605.

Johanna, A., Forsberg, L., & Tullberg, B.S. (1995). The relationship between cumulative number of cohabiting partners and number of children for men and women in modern Sweden. *Ethology and Sociobiology, 16*, 221–232.

Kaplan, H., Hill, K., Lancaster, J., & Hurtado, A.M. (2000). A theory of human life history evolution: Diet, intelligence, and longevity. *Evolutionary Anthropology, 9*, 156–185.

Kurland, J.A., & Gaulin, S.J.C. (2005). Cooperation and conflict among kin. In D.M. Buss (Ed.), *The evolutionary psychology handbook* (pp. 447–482). Hoboken, NJ: John Wiley & Sons.

Laham, S.M., Gonsalkorale, K., and von Hippel, W. (2005). Darwinian grandparenting: Preferential investment in more certain kin. *Personality and Social Psychology Bulletin, 31*, 63–72.

Lawson Handley, L.J., & Perrin, N. (2007). Advances in our understanding of mammalian sex-biased dispersal. *Molecular Ecology, 16*, 1559–1578.

Leakey, M.G., Feibel, C.S., McDougall, I., Ward, C., & Walker, A. (1998, May 7). New specimens and confirmation of an early age for Australopithecus anamensis. *Nature, 393*, 62–66.

Lovejoy, C.O. (1981, January 23). The origin of man. *Science, 211*, 341–350.

Manson, J.H., & Wrangham, R.W. (1991). Intergroup aggression in chimpanzees and humans. *Current Anthropology, 32*, 369–390.

Marlowe, F.W. (2004). Marital residence among foragers. *Current Anthropology, 45*, 277–284.

Maynard, A.E. (2002). The development of teaching skills in Maya sibling interactions. *Child Development, 73*, 969–982.

Mitani, J.C., & Watts, D.P. (2005). Correlates of territorial boundary patrol behavior in wild chimpanzees. *Animal Behaviour, 70*, 1079–1086.

MacDonald, K. (1992). Warmth as a developmental construct: An evolutionary analysis. *Child Development, 63*, 753–773.

McHale, S.M., Kin, J., & Whiteman, S.W. (2006). Sibling relationships in childhood and adolescence. In P. Noller & J. Feeney (Eds.), *Close Relationships: Functions, forms, & processes* (pp. 127–149). Hove, UK: Psychology Press.

McHenry, H.M. (1992). Body size and proportions in early hominids. *American Journal of Physical Anthropology, 87*, 407–431.

McHenry, H.M. (1994a). Tempo and mode in human evolution. *Proceedings of the National Academy of Sciences USA, 91*, 6780–6786.

McHenry, H.M. (1994b). Behavioral ecological implications of early hominid body size. *Journal of Human Evolution, 27*, 77–87.

McHenry, H.M., & Coffing, K. (2000). Australopithecus to Homo: Transformations in body and mind. *Annual Review of Anthropology, 29*, 125–146.

Mitani, J.C. (2009). Male chimpanzees form enduring and equitable bonds. *Animal Behaviour, 77*, 633–640.

Murdock, G.P. (1981). *Atlas of world cultures*. Pittsburgh, PA: University of Pittsburgh Press.

Nishida, T. (1979). The social structure of chimpanzees of the Mahale mountains. In D.A. Hamburg & E.R. McCown (Eds.), *The great apes* (pp. 73–121). Menlo Park, CA: The Benjamin/Cummings Publishing Company.

Nsubuga, A.M., Robbins, M.M., Boesch, C., & Vigilant, L. (2008). Patterns of paternity and group fission in wild multimale mountain gorilla groups. *American Journal of Physical Anthropology, 135*, 263–274.

Packer, C., Gilbert, D.A., Pusey, A.E., & O'Brien, S.J. (1991, June 13). A molecular genetic analysis of kinship and cooperation in African lions. *Nature, 351*, 562–565.

Parish, A.R. (1996). Female relationships in bonobos (*Pan paniscus*): Evidence for bonding, cooperation, and female dominance in a male-philopatric species. *Human Nature, 7*, 61–96.

Pashos, A. (2000). Does paternity uncertainty explain discriminative grandparental solicitude? A cross-cultural study in Greece and Germany. *Evolution and Human Behavior, 21*, 97–109.

Pasternak, B., Ember, C.R., & Ember, M. (1997). *Sex, gender, and kinship: A cross-cultural perspective*. Upper Saddle River, NJ: Prentice-Hall.

Peccei, J.S. (2001). A critique of the grandmother hypotheses: Old and new. *American Journal of Human Biology, 13*, 434–452.

Plavcan, J.M., & van Schaik, C.P. (1997). Intrasexual competition and body weight dimorphism in anthropoid primates. *American Journal of Physical Anthropology, 103*, 37–68.

Pollet, T.V., Nelissen, M., & Nettle, D. (2009). Lineage based differences in grandparental investment: Evidence from a large British cohort study. *Journal of Biosocial Science, 41*, 355–379.

Pusey, A., Williams, J., & Goodall, J. (1997, August 8). The influence of dominance rank on the reproductive success of female chimpanzees. *Science, 277*, 828–831.

Rabain-Jamin, J., Maynard, A.E., & Greenfield, P. (2003). Sibling teaching in two cultures. *Ethos, 31*, 204–231.

Richmond, B.G., & Jungers, W.L. (1995). Size variation and sexual dimorphism in *Australopithecus afarensis* and living hominoids. *Journal of Human Evolution, 29*, 229–245.

Riss, D., & Goodall, J. (1977). The recent rise to the alpha-rank in a population of free-living chimpanzees. *Folia Primatologica, 27*, 134–151.

Robbins, M.M. (1999). Male mating patterns in wild multimale mountain gorilla groups. *Animal Behaviour, 57*, 1013–1020.

Robbins, M.M., & Sawyer, S.C. (2007). Intergroup encounters in mountain gorillas of Bwindi Impenetrable National Park, Uganda. *Behaviour, 144*, 1497–1519.

Rodman, P.S., & Mitani, J.C. (1987). Orangutans: Sexual dimorphism in a solitary species. In B. B. Smuts, D.L. Cheney,

R.M. Seyfarth, R.W., Wrangham, & T.T. Struhsaker (Eds.), *Primate societies* (pp. 146–164). Chicago, IL: The University of Chicago Press.

Rodseth, L., Wrangham, R.W., Harrigan, A.M., & Smuts, B.B. (1991). The human community as a primate society. *Current Anthropology, 32*, 221–254.

Ruff, C.B., Trinkaus, E., & Holliday, T.W. (1997, May 8). Body mass and encephalization in *Pleistocene Homo*. *Nature, 387*, 173–176.

Salmon, C.A. (1999). On the impact of sex and birth order on contact with kin. *Human Nature, 10*, 183–197.

Sawaguchi, T. (1997). Possible involvement of sexual selection in neocortical evolution of monkeys and apes. *Folia Primatologica, 68*, 95–99.

Scelza, B.A. (2009). The grandmaternal niche: Critical caretaking among Martue Aborigines. *American Journal of Human Biology, 21*, 448–454.

Sear, R., & Mace, R. (2008). Who keeps children alive? A review of the effects of kin on child survival. *Evolution and Human Behavior, 29*, 1–18.

Smith, E.A. (1998). Is Tibetan polyandry adaptive? Methodological and metatheoretical analyses. *Human Nature, 9*, 225–261.

Smith, M.S. (1988). Research in developmental sociobiology: Parenting and family behavior. In K.B. MacDonald (Ed.), *Sociobiological perspectives on human development* (pp. 271–292). New York: Springer.

Salmon, C., & Shackelford, T. (Eds.). (2007). *Family relationships: An evolutionary perspective*. New York: Oxford University Press.

Sponheimer, M., & Lee-Thorp, J.A. (1999, January 15). Isotopic evidence for the diet of an early hominid, *Australopithecus africanus*. *Science, 238*, 368–370.

Sponheimer, M., & Lee-Thorp, J.A. (2003). Differential resource utilization by extant great apes and australopithecines: Towards solving the C4 conundrum. *Comparative Biochemistry and Physiology Part A, 136*, 27–34.

Sterck, E.H.M., Watts, D.P., & van Schaik, C.P. (1997). The evolution of female social relationships in nonhuman primates. *Behavioral Ecology and Sociobiology, 41*, 291–309.

Stewart, K.J., & Harcourt, A.H. (1987). Gorillas: Variation in female relationships. In B.B. Smuts, D.L. Cheney, R.M. Seyfarth, R.W. Wrangham, & T.T. Struhsaker (Eds.), *Primate societies* (pp. 155–164). Chicago, IL: The University of Chicago Press.

Strait, D.S., Weber, G.W., Neubauer, S., Chalk, J., Richmond, B.G., Lucas, P.W. et al. (2009). The feeding biomechanics and dietary ecology of *Australopithecus africanus*. *Proceedings of the National Academy of Sciences USA, 106*, 2124–2129.

Sugiyama, Y. (2004). Demographic parameters and life history of chimpanzees at Bossou, Guinea. *American Journal of Physical Anthropology, 124*, 154–165.

Taylor, A.B. (1997). Relative growth, ontogeny, and sexual dimorphism in gorilla (*Gorilla gorilla gorilla* and *G.G. beringei*): Evolutionary and ecological considerations. *American Journal of Primatology, 43*, 1–31.

Teaford, M.F., & Ungar, P.S. (2000). Diet and the evolution of the earliest human ancestors. *Proceedings of the National Academy of Sciences USA, 97*, 13506–13511.

Thomson, R., Pritchard, J.K., Shen, P., Oefner, P.J., & Feldman, M.W. (2000). Recent common ancestry of human Y chromosomes: Evidence from DNA sequence data. *Proceedings of the National Academy of Sciences USA, 97*, 7360–7365.

Tobias, P.V. (1987). The brain of *Homo habilis*: A new level of organization in cerebral evolution. *Journal of Human Evolution, 16*, 741–761.

Watts, D.P. (1994). Social relationships of immigrant and resident female mountain gorillas, II: Relatedness, residence, and relationships. *American Journal of Primatology, 32*, 13–30.

Watts, D.P., & Mitani, J.C. (2001). Boundary patrols and intergroup encounters in wild chimpanzees. *Behaviour, 138*, 299–327.

Watts, D.P., Muller, M., Amsler, S.J., Mbabazi, G., & Mitani, J.C. (2006). Lethal intergroup aggression by chimpanzees in Kibale National Park, Uganda. *American Journal of Primatology, 68*, 161–180.

Whiting, B.B., & Edwards, C.P. (1988). *Children of different worlds: The formation of social behavior*. Cambridge, MA: Harvard University Press.

Whiting, B.B., & Whiting, J.W.M. (1975). *Children of six cultures: A psycho-cultural analysis*. Cambridge, MA: Harvard University Press.

Williams, J.M., Oehlert, G.W., Carlis, J.V., & Pusey, A.E. (2004). Why do male chimpanzees defend a group range? *Animal Behaviour, 68*, 523–532.

Wilson, M.L., Hauser, M.D., & Wrangham, R.W. (2001). Does participation in intergroup conflict depend on numerical assessment, range location, or rank for wild chimpanzees? *Animal Behaviour, 61*, 1203–1216.

Wilson, M.L., & Wrangham, R.W. (2003). Intergroup relations in chimpanzees. *Annual Review of Anthropology, 32*, 363–392.

White, D.R. (1988). Rethinking polygyny: Co-wives, codes, and cultural systems. *Current Anthropology, 29*, 529–572.

White, D.R., & Burton, M.L. (1988). Causes of polygyny: Ecology, economy, kinship, and warfare. *American Anthropologist, 90*, 871–887.

Whitten, P.L. (1987). Infants and adult males. In B.B. Smuts, D.L. Cheney, R.M. Seyfarth, R.W. Wrangham, & T.T. Struhsaker (Eds.), *Primate societies* (pp. 343–357). Chicago, IL: The University of Chicago Press.

Williams, G.C. (1957). Pleiotropy, natural selection, and the evolution of senescence. *Evolution, 11*, 398–411.

Wood, B., & Collard, M. (1999, April 2). The human genus. *Science, 284*, 65–71.

Wrangham, R.W. (1980). An ecological model of female-bonded primate groups. *Behaviour, 75*, 262–300.

Wrangham, R.W. (1999). Evolution of coalitionary killing. *Yearbook of Physical Anthropology, 42*, 1–30.

Wrangham, R., & Peterson, D. (1996). *Demonic males*. New York: Houghton Mifflin Company.

Youngblade, L.M., & Dunn, D. (1995). Individual differences in young children's pretend play with mother and siblings: Links to relationship and understanding of other people's feelings and beliefs. *Child Development, 66*, 1472–1492.

Zihlman, A.L., & McFarland, R.K. (2000). Body mass in lowland gorillas: A quantitative analysis. *American Journal of Physical Anthropology, 113*, 61–78.

CHAPTER 22

Between Conflict and Cooperation: New Horizons in the Evolutionary Science of the Human Family

Gregory Gorelik, Todd K. Shackelford, *and* Catherine A. Salmon

Abstract

Familial relationships cannot be properly understood outside of an evolutionary framework. Pseudoscientific and traditional modes of thought have steered us away from an accurate account of ourselves and our kin. Recent theoretical and empirical advancements in the evolutionary sciences, such as the theories of inclusive fitness, parental investment, and parent–offspring conflict, have aided our understanding of familial conflict and cooperation. We suggest that a gene's-eye perspective of human families can likewise illuminate much of human psychology and behavior by contrasting individual interests with genetic interests. Furthermore, genetic imprinting and extended phenotypic action-at-a-distance have unveiled the extent to which coevolutionary arms races and manipulation may lie at the heart of familial interactions and psychological disorders. We posit that human cultural trends and morals can ultimately be grounded on an evolutionary foundation: Not only do human laws and institutions reflect group-level manifestations of gene-level cooperative adaptations, they may also reflect gene-level manipulative adaptations. An awareness of evolutionary dynamics can advance human well-being and unveil the hidden mechanisms beneath all human and nonhuman relationships.

Keywords: Family relationships, kin selection, inclusive fitness, evolutionary psychology, extended phenotype, cooperation, conflict, adaptation

Introduction

For all the time that we spend with and think about our kin, accurate information on the workings of the human family is hard to come by. Amid the current of popular talk shows like Dr. Phil or Dr. Laura, as well as a host of books and self-help phenomena, there is little honest, reality-based information to help us understand our familial relationships. There is, however, much proselytizing by religious figures and media ideologues on the breakdown of the modern family. Self-titled gurus and even some medically trained professionals are disseminating advice that is false and sometimes dangerous. Although this volume is not meant to offer therapeutic guidance for mending the wounds of familial conflict, it does provide an empirically tested account of the dynamics behind family relationships. By understanding our evolutionary past and the selection pressures that bombarded our ancestors, we can begin to form a stable foundation that will guide our academic, practical, and ethical decisions in dealing with the trials and tribulations of kinship.

The Unveiling of Familial Nature

Just as Rousseau's (1755) depiction of a wholly peaceful human nature was overturned by Darwin's (1859) theory of natural selection, current explorations in evolutionary biology and psychology cast doubt on the idea that a family is a coherent unit of cooperative individuals, with familial conflict only occurring when otherwise functional family relationships break down. With the modern evolutionary synthesis in biology, as well as the subsequent developments of kin selection and selfish gene theory, science has been unveiling the extent to which familial conflict is the product of selection. William Hamilton's (1964) theory of inclusive fitness provided a theoretical framework for predicting instances of familial discord as well as cooperation. According to this theory, the more genetically distant a relative is from another relative, the more likely it is that conflict between them will occur. In fact, when there is any genetic heterogeneity between interacting individuals, some form of conflict between them is inevitable, regardless of whether they are related. Distant relatives do not share as many genes for helping one another as do close relatives. For example, because monozygotic twins share 100% of their genes, they are likely to reproductively value each other as much as they value themselves. Meanwhile, parent–child and full sibling relationships, which are based on a genetic similarity of only 50%, are expected to exhibit conflict as well as cooperation. The same reasoning can be extended to more distant networks of interrelatedness, with individuals investing more in their grandchildren, for instance, than in their third cousins (see Chapter 12, by Euler). Of course, the proportion of shared genes is not the only factor determining how much investment is provisioned to family members. Ecological circumstances, such as the availability of food, as well as the health, age, and reproductive prospects of family members are also considerations that are taken into account when deciding whether to benefit one's kin (see Chapter 5, by Del Giudice and Belsky, for life history tradeoffs in parental care).

In general, organisms tend to behave indifferently toward one another. Outright cooperation and conflict are costly and are only engaged in if the reproductive benefits outweigh the expenditures in time and energy. In many species, even relatives tend to be ignorant of each other's existence. In some species, however, genes that code for altruism toward kin may spread within a gene pool by favoring relatives who are likely to carry copies of the same genes. Such is the case with humans. Our nepotistic tendency is a result of millions of years of selection for genes that selfishly benefited copies of themselves. Although our proximate thoughts and feelings enable us to feel love and affection for our family members, the ultimate evolutionary reason behind that love and affection is genetic self-interest—although, of course, this in no way invalidates the power and importance of such feelings. Furthermore, when genetic incongruity exists between kin that spend a great deal of evolutionary time interacting with one another (as parents and children do within our own species, which is characterized by a prolonged period of dependence on parental care; see Chapter 10, by Periss and Bjorklund), coevolutionary arms races are expected to occur. Far from being confined to predator–prey interactions, arms races characterize many of our most cherished familial relationships. The human family is rife with evolved weaponry for mutual exploitation.

All's Fair in Love and War
Following in Hamilton's footsteps, subsequent investigations in the biological sciences brought us face to face with the realization that familial conflict runs deeper than expected. In a series of groundbreaking papers, Robert Trivers examined a number of adaptations that organisms possess for manipulating and extracting resources from their kin. His theory of parental investment (1972), for instance, examined the diverging reproductive interests of males and females. According to parental investment theory, the sex with the greater minimum obligatory investment necessary to produce and rear offspring to reproductive age will be the more discriminating sex when it comes to choosing sexual partners. In most mammals, females incur greater minimum reproductive costs than males as a result of pregnancy and lactation. By choosing the wrong male, females risk jeopardizing their valuable reproductive resources by investing in genetically inferior offspring or risk copulating with a male who is unlikely to provide the resources needed to help her successfully raise an offspring to adulthood. As a result, females are expected to have evolved psychological adaptations for discriminating genetically superior and resource-rich suitors from genetically inferior and resource-deficient suitors. In contrast, males are likely to have evolved their own adaptations for attempting to copulate with as many females as they can (since males pay less in reproductive costs when copulating with genetically inferior females than vice versa) and for minimizing investment in offspring that they did not sire. This war of the sexes has been raging as a coevolutionary arms race between ancestral males and ancestral females. Although sexual reproduction can be a cooperative venture by which males and females replicate their genes, we must all come to terms with the possibility that human romantic relationships are rife with deceptive and manipulative strategies that were selected into each sex because they proved successful at manipulating members of the opposite sex.

In humans, women may manipulate men to extract resources (by promising them sexual favors, for example), prevent them from investing in rival women and their offspring through psychological manipulation and commitment jealousy, or cuckold them by surreptitiously producing offspring sired by genetically superior men (see Buss, 2003, for review). Men, on the other hand, are more likely to deceive women into thinking that they are of higher genetic quality or are better able and more likely to invest in long-term romantic commitment and childrearing than they actually are. Along with body language and verbal behaviors, members of both sexes may use clothing, makeup, and accessories to manipulate members of the opposite sex as part of their reproductive strategy. Manipulative reproductive strategies vary by sex (see Buss, 2003, for review): Women are more likely to engage in appearance-enhancing behaviors to communicate youth and fertility, and men are more likely to exaggerate their wealth, generosity, and social standing to communicate their willingness and ability to invest in a woman and her offspring. Men also possess a host of adaptations for manipulating the sexual behavior of their partners to minimize the risk of investing in offspring sired by a rival (see Chapter 11, by Goetz and Romero). These adaptations include abusive and intimidating tactics, as well as generous and affectionate behaviors aimed at preventing female infidelity (Miner & Shackelford, 2010). Male and female sexual strategies, however, do not all fit the same pattern and may vary across an individual's lifespan as a result of contextual and life history circumstances, although genetic differences can account for the influence of personality characteristics on sexual strategies (see Kaighobadi et al., 2009, for the effect of male personality traits on the risk of partner-directed violence). Sexual jealousy as an evolved response to ancestral selection pressures of paternity uncertainty and the risk of partner abandonment may thus shed light on such divergent behaviors as romantic affection and spousal abuse.

On average, men are more interested in sexual variety than are women. Some men, however, may eschew a polygynous strategy in favor of a long-term commitment to a single woman, provided that such a strategy was reproductively successful for their male ancestors. The evolution of long-term pair-bonding mechanisms within men and women may have brought about selection for the intensely felt and overpowering emotional reactions that characterize romantic love (see Buss, 1987, 2003). Such a seemingly irrational commitment to a member of the opposite sex may have been adaptive for our ancestors in motivating them to remain together to raise an altricial child. Future investigations into male–female interactions are needed to further map the structure and function of the adaptations employed by each sex against the opposite sex in the mating arena. The application of sexual selection theory (Miller, 2000) to human mating strategies may likewise illuminate our understanding of human culture as a tool that is used to attract mates by communicating one's genetic worth or resourcefulness. Evolutionary approaches to human psychology and behavior can thus provide valuable insights into the origins and functions of our most sublime passions and affections.

Parents and Children

Our conception of the parent–offspring relationship as the paragon of familial harmony is likewise being overturned by current investigations into parent–offspring conflict. The bond between a mother and her child is often regarded as the most pure and sacred of all family relationships. This sentiment is expressed in the iconic Christian image of Mary cradling her infant, a depiction of unbridled love and nurturance. Such idyllic cultural imagery, however, belies a more nuanced biological reality. Although the mother–child relationship is largely based on the evolutionary necessity for care and protection of altricial infants and children (see Chapter 10, by Periss and Bjorklund), and although there are countless examples of parents sacrificing their own lives on behalf of their children, Trivers's (1974) theory of parent–offspring conflict posits the existence of an arms race between the reproductive interests of parents and offspring that may even lead to instances of child abuse and filicide. The evolutionary reason for this conflict boils down to sibling rivalry. Disregarding factors such as offspring age and health, a diploid mother's genetic interests are usually best served by apportioning her resources equally among all her offspring because that mother shares the same proportion of her genes with each of them (50%). Each offspring, however, values its own genes over the genes of its mother and siblings, and although relatives are more likely to cooperate than nonrelatives, the genetic interests of the offspring are sometimes best served by extracting more resources from its mother than the mother is willing to allocate. This resource extraction comes at the cost of the reproductive success of the offspring's mother and its current or future siblings, leading to the evolution of adaptations for manipulation on the part of both parents and offspring. In certain contexts, therefore, the genetic interests of parents and offspring are at cross purposes (see Chapter 6, by Salmon and Malcolm). Even though we are one of a few mammalian species in which fathers also provide a certain amount of childcare, mothers are still the primary caregivers in almost every society. As a result of these selection pressures, parent–offspring conflict is mostly fought between mothers and offspring (but see Chapter 5, by Del Giudice and Belsky, for cases in which paternal and maternal genes compete within a single organism via genetic imprinting).

The tug-of-war between a mother and her offspring is evident at conception. Although the uterus is usually an ideal environment for a developing fetus, a fetus's adaptations for extracting nutrients from its mother may sometimes trigger the mother's physiological adaptations for limiting resource allocation to the fetus. In such instances, a fetus is considered to be parasitic on the mother and may even bring about a miscarriage. For an expectant mother, a miscarriage can be an earth-shattering experience. From an evolutionary perspective, however, it may reflect an adaptive response on the part of the mother's body that may ultimately save her life. This may have been a last line of defense for an ancestral mother whose Pleistocene environment lacked the amenities of modern medicine.

If the infant survives gestation, its struggle with its mother over nutrients and maternal affection takes on wider behavioral dimensions. Infant crying, for instance, may signal an infant's genuine need for protection or sustenance, or be used as an honest indicator of infant fitness, but it can also be manipulatively employed by the infant to prevent mothers from copulating and giving birth to sibling competitors (e.g., Lummaa et. al. 1997). For the same reason, a child may delay its time of weaning for the sake of limiting resource diversion to its current or future siblings. As children mature, sibling rivalry and parent–offspring conflict may be expressed in the contexts of playground privileges, priorities to the biggest portion of dessert, or demands for the best Christmas present. Once puberty arrives, adolescents and parents may engage in conflict over adolescent mating decisions (Apostolou, 2009). For example, parental genetic interests may be better served by their daughters engaging in long-term mating, but daughters may reproductively benefit their own genes by engaging in short-term mating and relying on parents to help them raise resultant offspring. Thus, parent–offspring conflict may be in motion whenever parents prevent adolescents from associating with members of the opposite sex of whom they disapprove. Likewise, adolescents can adaptively rebel against their parents' wishes by staying out late or keeping friends whose influence upon their sexual behavior may conflict with parental interests. The hidden biological dynamics of parent–offspring conflict over mating decisions may yet explain the timeless appeal of Shakespeare's *Romeo and Juliet*.

All evolutionary relationships fall along the continuum of conflict at one end and cooperation at the other. Relationships between different genes and organisms reflect the selection pressures that gave rise to them. Some of these relationships are characterized by mutual benefit, whereas others reflect generations of continuous conflict and arms races. Evolutionary relationships characterized by genetic kinship, however, fall somewhere in between the two extremes. Although an organism may reap genetic benefits by investing in kin with whom genes for benefitting kin are shared, exploitation of one's kin is also to be expected when there is genetic distance between the interacting kin. Furthermore, adaptations for dealing with kin may be extended or co-opted when genetically unrelated organisms benefit from or parasitize one another via the redirection of adaptations that are normally aimed at benefiting or manipulating relatives (see Chapter 16, by Archer; Chapter 17, by Serpell and Paul; Chapter 18, by Qirko; and Chapter 19, by Ackerman and Park).

The Long Reach of Our Genes

We are fractionated from within and without. No longer can we consider ourselves to be working solely for the evolutionary benefit of our individual selves. Hamilton's (1964) theory of inclusive fitness and Dawkins's (1976) popularization of selfish genes brought about the realization that genetic interests do not always coincide with the interests of the individual organism. It may be helpful to view the family as consisting of networks of genes that seek to propagate themselves by coding for programs that either benefit and form alliances with one another, or exploit one another, rather than as consisting of individual family members. The evolutionary success of these programs is ultimately judged by whether the genes coding for them are naturally selected over rival alleles within the gene pool. To the extent that a novel mutation contributes to the cooperative or manipulative effort of programs that function within the family environment, it will propagate itself within the gene pool and contribute to the coevolutionary processes that characterize kinship relations. Indeed, this perspective helps to illuminate the evolution of all biological systems.

The relationship between a gene and its phenotypic effect(s) is nonlinear. The developmental process is characterized by a complex bidirectionality, whereby a gene's expression is dependent upon the other genes within its environment, as well as upon the ecological cues that activate it (see, for review, Bjorklund & Pellegrini, 2002). This leaves much room for the influence of competing genes upon the development of a gene's phenotypic expression, whether anatomical, physiological, psychological, or behavioral. To the extent that we spend a substantial portion of our lives surrounded by kin, beginning with conception, there is much opportunity for our close kin to manipulate the developmental outcomes of our phenotypic programs. Our genes, however, are not idle pacifists and do not absorb without recourse the manipulation of their developmental expression; our ongoing evolution has likely brought about the selection for phenotypic defenses against the manipulative nature of certain genes possessed by our kin. This may have resulted in an arms race, whereby our kin's genes are selected for how well they can direct our ontogenetic course for their own benefit, and our own genes are selected based on the criteria of how well they can code for phenotypic expressions that resist being manipulated during our development (which may help to explain the paradoxical finding that parental rearing practices have little direct effect on subsequent offspring outcomes, although it remains to be seen whether parents may influence their offspring's development via more implicitly acting adaptations to parent–offspring conflict; see Harris, 2009). This genetic battle can even occur between the maternal and paternal genes within an individual organism, whereby one parent's genes can code for physiological processes or behaviors that inflict a cost upon the genes of the other parent (see Chapter 5, by Del Giudice and Belsky). In this sense, it is more accurate, biologically speaking, to view families as self-promoting networks of genes rather than as self-promoting individual organisms.

We likewise possess the same adaptations for manipulating, as well as benefitting, our own offspring, provided that we ourselves reproduce. Thus, when we are in the role of offspring, certain genetic programs and psychological mechanisms for extracting resources from our caregivers are turned on, while other contextually irrelevant programs and mechanisms are turned off. Once we become parents, latent genetic programs and psychological mechanisms for manipulating as well as benefitting our own offspring come online. In a spectacle of evolutionary irony, the inherited evolved programs and mechanisms used by our parents to manipulate us in our youth are used by us as tools to manipulate our own offspring. Such is the evolutionarily derived cycle that characterizes our developmental journey through life.

According to Del Giudice and Belsky (Chapter 5), parental investment strategies can influence offspring attachment styles, pubertal timing, and sexual behavior. Girls who form insecure attachments to their fathers, for instance, are more likely to experience an earlier onset of menarche and pregnancy than do girls who receive reliable paternal resources and care. This parallels Maestripieri et al.'s (2009) work showing how maternal styles can influence the subsequent developmental trajectories of rhesus macaques. These findings may be interpreted by positing that parents have evolved manipulative strategies to influence the physiological, psychological, and behavioral development of their children. On the opposite side of the arms race, children may have evolved defensive strategies to minimize the influence of parental strategies on their development. It may be that children's developmental outcomes are not only the results of parental manipulation but also reflect evolved solutions to the life history trade-offs that they experience throughout their development. Both scenarios should be investigated empirically.

Whenever one organism manipulates the behavior of a different organism (more specifically, whenever a gene manipulates the action of a different gene) for its own reproductive benefit, it is using the manipulated organism (or gene) as an extended phenotype of itself (Dawkins, 1982). This action-at-a-distance gives manipulator programs far-reaching power in manipulating their environments. The manipulated organisms can be viewed as phenotypic manifestations of manipulator organisms. This approach can help us to understand intersexual and intrasexual relationships, as well as parent–offspring relationships. Coevolutionary relationships between members of the same species may result in selection for mutually manipulative strategies that are either evolutionarily stable, in which each strategy is at its adaptive peak and can do no better, or evolutionarily unstable, in which a runaway arms race ensues and ever-more manipulative, counter-manipulative, and defensive strategies evolve. Both stable and unstable arms races are probably present in our own species, in which individuals have evolved strategies to use other individuals as extended phenotypic tools for their own benefit (see, for review, Dawkins, 1982).

Humans may manipulate each other in circumstances in which deception and manipulation helped our ancestors best their reproductive rivals by controlling the rivals' behaviors. Studies of language use within politics, economics, and everyday situations can aid our understanding of how our evolved predispositions for deceiving our rivals are verbally and culturally expressed, and how language and culture may in turn influence the evolutionary and developmental trajectories of our manipulative extended phenotypic adaptations. Likewise, the proximate manifestations of parent–offspring conflict can be examined from the perspective of the extended phenotype by measuring individuals' behaviors as a function of their kin's manipulative strategies. For example, young mothers with high future reproductive prospects may seek to limit their investment in reproductively unsuccessful offspring by manipulating their offspring's psychological state or behavior. In a study by Brown et al. (2009), university students' risk of suicide was predicted by their mother's age, how burdensome they felt they were to their families, and their degree of romantic satisfaction. Therefore, parents may possess adaptations for relieving their burden of a reproductively unsuccessful child by using that child as an extended phenotypic tool of their own reproductive interests. Thus, parental adaptations for manipulating offspring psychology and behavior may have been selected into our gene pool if these adaptations successfully brought about the death of a reproductively unpromising and resource-draining offspring. Parental manipulation of offspring depression and suicidal ideation may have had lower social costs than direct filicide and thus, along with filicide, may have been selected into our gene pool. Suicide may even prove adaptive to the offspring's own genetic interests, provided that the genes coding for kin-directed altruism are benefitted thereby. Likewise, parents may use their children as extended phenotypic tools to acquire sexual partners, similar to the way in which individuals may use their pets to show off their resources or empathetic qualities to potential mates (see Chapter 17, by Serpell and Paul). In the future, researchers might investigate the specific behavioral, neural, and hormonal pathways by which individuals influence the emotions, cognitions, and behaviors of other individuals. Of course, such a scientific investigation in no way excuses psychological abuse, filicide, or the manipulation of individuals; understanding the evolved strategies that humans employ against other humans does not morally sanction them.

The cultural correlates of parent–offspring conflict can be analyzed by examining the extent to which parents, offspring, and siblings use tools and technologies to influence each other's behavior. The telephone and internet may be useful tools for manipulating our families, friends, and neighbors. Parents may retain some extended phenotypic power over their children (regardless of whether their children are in the same household) if they continue to influence their children's behavior. For example, cellular phones and computers may provide parents with effective means of manipulating their physically distant children's reproductive behaviors by sending their offspring dating advice through e-mail or text messages. Likewise, children may acquire a larger extended phenotypic reach over their parents if they are technologically savvier than their parents and can use technology to extract resources from them. It is likely that the rapid increase in technological advancement that exemplifies our species has created novel selection pressures for unpredictable and innumerable runaway arms races between related and unrelated individuals. With the aid of modern technology, our manipulative and defensive psychological mechanisms have acquired unprecedented phenotypic powers.

Therapeutic Implications of the Extended Phenotype

In applying the extended phenotype model to therapeutic settings, we can automatically see the pitfalls of psychologically treating individuals in isolation from their families and social networks. Psychological conditions such as depression and bipolar disorder may in fact be indicative of genetic conflicts between patients and their kin, or internal conflicts between a patient's maternal and paternal genes. If individuals manipulate each other's psychological states and behaviors with evolved manipulative tactics, it is no longer enough to focus therapeutic treatments on individual patients—clinicians must be attentive to signs of the psychological manipulation of patients by their families, friends, social structures, and institutions, or by some of their own selfish genetic elements. Psychological symptoms such as paranoia may result from hyperactive adaptations that normally protect individuals from being manipulated by other individuals in their environments. Although the government may not be spying on a schizophrenic patient's every move, his or her paranoia may hint at a deeper conflict between the interests of state institutions and the patient's own reproductive interests.

Hearing voices or feeling conflicting emotions and cognitions may result from genetic imprinting of parental genes. Paternal genes may code for psychological systems that conflict with an individual's maternally coded psychological systems, and vice versa. The symptomatic results of this mismatch of psychological processes could be shame, guilt, or suicidal behavior. Patients may feel torn from within, and therapists may see no hope for recovery. Although medications can greatly reduce some of the worst symptoms of psychosis, and cognitive and behavioral treatments can give patients tools for managing their intrusive thoughts and behaviors, clinicians might devise novel methods for dealing with the reverberations of this internal genetic conflict. Medications for selectively suppressing the action of genes implicated in genetic imprinting may do well in conjunction with appropriate therapeutic techniques for lessening the burdens of patients.

Likewise, psychiatrists and psychologists might investigate the social and familial frameworks within which their patients operate. Interpersonal and family therapy, combined with evolutionary psychological approaches, can provide important insights for guiding future research into psychological treatments. More specifically, therapists may view the distressing symptoms of patients as effects of manipulative tactics of other individuals. By doing so, therapists can focus their treatments on lessening the burdens of such manipulative tactics, instead of treating symptoms as breakdowns in the normal functioning of individuals.

Many of our adaptations for manipulating and deceiving others have been naturally selected to target family members. The reason for this is that most of our ancestors' social interactions were limited to repeated encounters with kin. Thus, there may have been an implicit evolutionary rationale behind the psychoanalytic focus on maternal relationships within the therapeutic setting. Freud's folly, however, was in positing familial dynamics for which there was, and still is, little empirical support. The dynamics behind parent–offspring conflict, however, have been documented in a number of widely diverse species, including humans. Postpartum depression, for example, may represent an evolved response on the part of a young mother to a resource-draining infant (e.g., Hagen, 2002). By recognizing this evolutionary dynamic, therapists can devise effective treatments to inform their patients, improve their condition, and forestall the destructive effects that such evolutionary dynamics may have upon patients and their significant others.

In conclusion, future investigations into familial friction and therapeutic treatments may benefit from an examination of interpersonal and intrapersonal conflict from the perspective of extended phenotypic manipulation. Such an evolutionarily grounded investigation may improve upon earlier psychoanalytic discussions of familial conflict as expressed through unconscious processes. The examination of unconscious family dynamics from an evolutionary perspective may prove useful in isolating and examining the manipulative behaviors that family members employ against each other and against themselves as a result of genetic conflicts of interest.

Evolutionary Ethics of the Family

In the final section of this chapter, we focus on the roles that arms races and mutual manipulation play in human ethics and morality. This will not be a discussion of what is moral or ethical. We do not offer prescriptions for proper moral conduct, as this is beyond the scope of the present chapter. In any case, the foregoing treatment of human adaptations to the family environment has shown how difficult it is to decipher moral rectitude and responsibility in a species that is rife with manipulative and deceptive tactics. Can genes or gene networks be held accountable for the actions of their phenotypic effects? Who (or what) has moral responsibility if individual actions are coded for by gene networks that transcend individual bodies? We believe that moral responsibility should not be sought on the genetic level. Whatever the genetic (or cultural) correlates of behavior are, judicial systems of deterrence and punishment are probably right to focus on the individual when assigning personal responsibility. Although we should not excuse rape and murder by invoking biological motivations ("blame the genes!"), neither should we ignore the biological correlates of some of our most unsavory behaviors (for an excellent discussion of biology and moral responsibility, see Pinker, 2002).

Rather than devising methods for assigning genetic culpability, we discuss human morality from the perspective of evolved psychological mechanisms that maximize the replication of the genes coding for their development. We also examine the social and cultural correlates of adapted moral sentiments whose ancestral domains were limited to family and tribal interactions. Ours is a tentative approach and may be more useful for the questions posed than for the answers provided. It is incumbent upon investigators in the biological, psychological, and social sciences to take the reins in this endeavor and to empirically flesh out these issues.

For any social species, the benefits of interacting with other members of their species must exceed the costs of going solo. There are a number of evolutionary explanations as to why organisms engage in cooperative relationships (see Trivers, 1985, for a review). The first is genetic relatedness and the mutual possession of genes "for" helping kin. Eusocial insects are notorious cooperators for this very reason and even put our own "family values" to shame. A second explanation for cooperation between organisms is based on the mutual exchange of favors, or reciprocal altruism (Trivers, 1971). For reciprocal altruism to evolve, organisms must repeatedly interact with one another, and such interactions must persist for many generations. In these circumstances, the genetic interests of the interactants may be promoted through mutual cooperation. Provided that organisms gain a reproductive advantage over their entire cooperative period by cooperating with other reciprocators, immediate returns of favors are not necessary for the selection of general cooperative tendencies. What is necessary, however, is the ability to spot cooperators from non-cooperators, as cheaters may benefit by accepting favors without returning them. To guard against this threat, cooperators must evolve "cheater-detection" mechanisms to avoid and punish non-cooperators (see Cosmides & Tooby, 2005). This sets up an arms race in which cooperative strategies are pitted against non-cooperative or deceptive strategies across evolutionary time. As cooperators become better at detecting cheats, cheats should become better at deceiving and extracting resources from cooperators.

For humans, both kin favoritism and reciprocal altruism probably play a role in accounting for our sociality with respect to relatives as well as nonrelatives (for a different explanation of human generosity and altruism, see Miller's [2000] account of sexual selection in humans). Cooperation between kin may also involve reciprocity, and cooperation between nonkin may involve the redirection of modular processes for benefiting kin (see Chapter 18, by Qirko). For most of human evolutionary history, our ancestors lived in small tribal societies based mostly on kinship ties. If two individuals from the same society were unrelated, chances were high that both were related to a third individual. It is therefore likely that our moral and empathetic sentiments had their origins in adaptive acts of kindness directed toward individuals with whom genes "for" that kindness were shared. Likewise, the evolution of reciprocal altruism was enabled by the relatively small tribal societies within which individuals were forced into repeated interactions with their fellow tribesmen (the rudimentary forms of such cooperative structures can be witnessed in some of our great ape cousins—see Chapter 21, by Geary et. al.). With the increasing population density of early hominids, selection pressures came about that lead to the evolution of complex social dynamics. Our ancestors' cooperative and manipulative tendencies gained unprecedented reach as a result of these selection pressures, likely contributing to an increase in brain size and the evolution of language. With an increase in brain size came a prolonged developmental period and the need for parental and alloparental care. Children thus became increasingly dependent on their caregivers to acquire the knowledge needed to cooperate with and manipulate other individuals in their densely populated environments. Because humans are a cultural species (in that our evolved cognitive abilities are adapted to and express themselves within the contexts of rapidly changing informational and societal trends—i.e., language, technology, fashion, etc.), our evolved cooperative predispositions are dependent upon culturally acquired values and mores for their proper development. In this way, the development of human morality entails the adaptive attunement to certain familial and societal rules of conduct. Children's evolved learning mechanisms are specifically tuned to parental moral instruction early on in their development. This moral instruction was adaptive for children and parents alike, in that children could learn the effective means by which to negotiate their social surroundings to mate and successfully replicate their parents' genes. When reflecting upon the dynamics of parent–offspring conflict, however, we are forced to admit that mutual benefit and cooperation is not all there is to moral instruction. Some familial rules of conduct may ultimately reflect extended phenotypic means by which individuals selfishly manipulate the behavior of their kin.

Extending biological and psychological findings to wider cultural phenomena is a risky endeavor. Human culture may function under rules and mechanisms that are unique to its domain. Nevertheless, human culture is a product of biological evolution and possesses an indelible stamp of its "lowly origin." As such, we next examine the cultural expressions of our evolved moral sentiments to better understand how familial arms races and conflicts may play themselves out on our cultural stage. The tribal culture of our ancestors was different in many ways from our technologically interconnected global system. With advancements in transportation and communication technologies, the rate and extent of cultural change has been magnified to unprecedented levels. Taking into account this minefield of gene–culture coevolution, we limit our discussion and hypotheses to only a few societal trends. In doing so, we hope that researchers in diverse fields may apply some of these ideas to past and present societies across the globe.

If we are forced to define human culture, however tentatively, then we posit that culture entails the group-level expression of gene-level adaptations for transferring non-genetic information. Notwithstanding arguments for group-level selection, adaptation entails the selective retention of some alleles over others within a gene pool (Williams, 1966). The most salient vehicle of genetic expression is the individual organism, within which genes code for proteins in conjunction with other genes. On average, genes within an organism have been selected to cooperate with one another in building adaptations that are effective at propagating copies of those genes. Sometimes, however, genes can be selected at the expense of the other genes with which they share an organism, as in inclusive fitness or genetic imprinting, mentioned earlier. In humans, gene-level adaptations coding for individual-level psychological processes can be variously expressed as group-level cultural trends. In turn, group-level cultural trends may influence gene-level adaptations. Genes are still selected for how well they can replicate copies of themselves, but some of those selection pressures result from the incidental group-level effects of genetic programs. Therefore, there is no need to invoke any kind of higher-level selection to explain cultural or genetic evolution. Certain societies may, however, be more successful than other societies as a by-product of their culture, provided that certain cultural trends remain stable across generations and are more effective at promoting group survival than are other cultural trends. For example, whereas parents may violently discipline their children in one society, another society's cultural practice of patient instruction and compassion may ultimately have more longevity.

Humans, like most mammals, possess a variety of adaptations for enhancing our reproductive opportunities. We likely employ psychological process to maintain sexual access to desired mates, as well as to deceive and manipulate sexual rivals. Mate retention behaviors, for instance, may be used to prevent our sexual partners from abandoning us in favor of better reproductive opportunities. As mentioned earlier, such behaviors can be abusive as well as nurturing. To the extent that mate retention behaviors are employed to benefit one's genetic success, a certain amount of manipulation is inherent in such behaviors, even if they display generosity or compassion. Likewise, individuals can psychologically manipulate their sexual rivals via deception, as well as via intimidation and aggression. In both instances, strategies are employed to manipulate a sexual rival's behavior for one's own reproductive benefit. With the aid of language, humans may employ gossip and competitor derogation tactics to psychologically manipulate would-be mates away from sexual competitors—essentially manipulating the mate choices of their sexual targets in an extended phenotypic fashion, leading to the selection of genes that enable such manipulation (provided that the manipulation is evolutionarily successful). These tactics also vary by sex; because men more than women value physical attractiveness in a sexual partner, women are more likely than men to derogate their sexual competitors' appearance ("Look at her fat thighs!"). On the other hand, because women more than men value current or potential resource holdings in a sexual partner, men are more likely than women to derogate their sexual competitors' earning potential and lack of social standing ("He's not going anywhere in life!").

When applied to the moral systems of various cultures, manipulation of individuals for the sake of one's own reproductive interests is manifest on much larger scales. For example, men in polygynous societies whose wives reside in separate houses may lessen the threat of cuckoldry and sperm competition by requiring their wives or other men (their would-be sexual competitors) to undergo genital mutilation (Wilson, 2008). Whatever proximate explanations such cultural practices may have (i.e., religious, aesthetic, initiatory, etc.), they may ultimately serve the evolutionary function of reducing paternity uncertainty and preventing investment in genetically unrelated offspring. If correct, Wilson's analysis may have uncovered evidence for culture-wide manipulative practices that are still prevalent in many societies, including our own. Depending on society, failure to comply with such rituals may lead to social ostracism or even death. A similar phenomenon may be at the bottom of culturally sanctioned monogamy and its social repercussions. The moral values associated with monogamy may reflect manipulative strategies by which genetically inferior men maximize their reproductive prospects by limiting the sexual opportunities of genetically superior men (Pinker, 1997). Female dress codes within certain Muslim societies may likewise be strategies by which men manipulate the sexual opportunities of their wives and other female family members. Likewise, women whose reproductive prospects are at stake may be complicit and even supportive of such practices if they can thereby reduce their competitors' genetic success. As is reflected by studies into parent–offspring conflict over mating decisions, families in such societies may exert control over their daughters' or sisters' sexual choices via the institution of arranged marriage and the threat of an "honor" killing if they fail to comply. The fact that such practices are so prevalent in Arab cultures may reflect the long history of agropastoralism within these societies (Apostolou, 2010). The accumulation of wealth that comes with agropastoralism may put pressure upon male resource holders to maintain their wealth and to prevent the squandering of their resources on relatives who reduce their genetic prospects with their mate choices.

Our psychological processes are amenable to a wide variety of cultural contexts and can creatively synthesize cultural information in novel ways, which may explain why our culture changes so rapidly. Although our genetic processes and familial conflicts are more or less predictable, their cultural expression varies across time and space. For example, the universal experience of parent–offspring conflict emerges through widely different cultural manifestations. The counterculture movement of the 1960s, for instance, may have tapped into the psychological adaptations by which offspring counteract parental manipulation. Thus, the expression of "free love" may have been a culture-wide expression of evolved mechanisms used by offspring to rebel against the influence of parents on their mating decisions. Likewise, the recent embrace of rap music and urban dress by white, suburban youths may reflect adaptive niche-seeking behaviors by which individuals attract mates of their own choosing. In such instances, parental reproductive interests may be threatened by their offspring's free exercise of mate choice. Parents may in turn represent their genetic interests through their own cultural expressions.

Conservative ideals and "family values" may be extended phenotypic manifestations by which parents attempt to influence offspring behavior by influencing social norms and morals. Further research is needed to track the specific design features of various cultural trends and examine the extent to which they reflect the evolutionary products of familial conflict. For example, parallels may be drawn between various youth and revolutionary movements and the adaptive behaviors by which offspring manipulate caregivers. Likewise, personality and familial-context factors can be examined for correlations with individual membership in various groups, religions, and political movements.

Thus, many of our modern rules of conduct may reflect the overextension of normally functional adaptations for enforcing morals and values upon family members to densely populated environments for which they were not selected. Our ancestors did not evolve in environments containing millions of densely packed humans sharing a radius of a few square miles, as in Tokyo and Manhattan. Although selection may have sped up with the onset of agriculture (as population growth brought about a higher genetic diversity on which selection could act—see Cochran & Harpending, 2009), an interconnected world of close to 7 billion humans is historically unprecedented. The legal and judicial systems of modern states may reflect the co-optation of naturally or sexually selected moral sentiments to a much wider circle of interacting individuals. Thus, order and stability is achieved via the redirection of ancestral moral sentiments that were originally limited to intrafamilial and reciprocal interactions. Although governments (often aided by state religion) can bring about smooth and efficient systems of cooperation and nonviolent competition, they may also enforce rules and ordinances by which the reproductive interests of some individuals may be curbed for the benefit of others—usually those enforcing the particular rules and ordinances. This may be a result of the overextension of manipulative adaptations by which humans attempt to influence the behavior of family members and unwary reciprocators. This is only to be expected if family members and other interactants possess traits for manipulating the behavior of their reproductive rivals, effectively utilizing their fellow humans as extended phenotypes of their own selfish genes. Our lives may be saturated with interconnected webs of manipulation by which some individuals or groups influence the behavior of other individuals or groups. Nowadays, these webs have grown to unprecedented complexity and reach with the aid of modern communication and transportation technologies.

Even though all humans possess adaptations for benefitting kin and cooperating with reciprocators, the cross-cultural variation in morals, values, and taboos may reflect the wide variety of forms by which humans attempt to manipulate other humans in their environments. As touched on by Qirko (Chapter 18), religious and political systems may hijack our adaptations for benefitting kin into allocating investment to nonrelatives by loading sermons, rituals, and political speeches with kin-based terms such as "brothers and sisters." Likewise, our evolved tendencies to benefit those who may benefit us in the future may be taken advantage of by social systems that may never reciprocate (i.e., by promising heavenly rewards or utopian dreams). This is not to deny the potential reproductive benefits that individuals may enjoy by sacrificing on behalf of political or religious groups (Atran, 2002), but as with any cooperative relationship, there is always a risk of defection. Group-level systems of morality and ethics may reflect cooperative as well as manipulative adaptations, whether cognitive or emotional, by which individuals enforce rules of conduct upon their family members and acquaintances. Likewise, our adapted systems may be manipulatively subverted into pathways that are detrimental to our survival and reproductive prospects as easily as they can be co-opted for more benign purposes. For instance, evolved attachment systems that are usually directed toward caregivers may be activated by emotional pleas to "accept the love and guidance" of a "heavenly father" or a "holy mother" (see Kirkpatrick, 2004, for the application of attachment systems to supernatural agents). Similarly, manipulative adaptations used to maximize one's inclusive fitness may transform into nepotistic moral systems that support royal families and other dynasties. Provided that parents and offspring can adaptively manipulate each other's behavior through discipline, moral instructions, and emotional expressions (as is expected from the theory of parent–offspring conflict), then ethical systems may reflect manipulative as well as cooperative forms of behavioral control that are extended to the wider society. Finally, evolved defenses against manipulation may be culturally expressed as consumer protection services, government regulations, and media-generated information campaigns. Scholars should not shirk the opportunity to uncover the extent to which societal laws, norms, and morals reflect cooperative, manipulative, and defensive extensions of human biological traits. Such an investigation can be especially fruitful if conducted with a proper evolutionary perspective.

Conclusion
Toward an Evolutionarily Enlightened Humanity

Our discussion of the evolutionary processes that underlie many of our interactions with family, friends, coworkers, strangers, and social structures and institutions, should not be interpreted as value judgments on these relationships. Even if there are manipulative adaptations which humans and non-humans employ in their dealings with other organisms, we may ultimately accept the manipulative nature of such relationships and continue to engage in them. For example, if our pets are ultimately coevolved parasites that take advantage of our propensity to care for anything with infant-like features, should we then abandon our dogs and cats (see Chapter 16, by Archer; but also see Chapter 17, by Paul and Serpell, for possible health and reproductive benefits of pet-keeping)? Likewise, should we not adopt genetically unrelated offspring if adoption results from the misfiring of otherwise functional parental adaptations (see Chapter 8, by Volk)? Such questions are absurd precisely because our evolved nature enables us to circumvent our genetic interests. Natural selection has provided us with adaptations that were successful at propagating our ancestors' genes, but only on average, and only within ancestral environments. It does not guarantee that we will always pursue the best way to spread our genes in the here and now, or even spread our genes at all. Such a realization has even eluded some scholars. A similar phenomenon, often referred to as the *naturalistic fallacy*, is the mistaken assumption that explaining our biological nature is tantamount to an endorsement of it. If manipulating family members and friends for our own reproductive benefit is a result of evolved mechanisms and modules, should we then tacitly accept such manipulation as an unavoidable outcome of our evolutionary past? The selections within this volume are, in part, an attempt by researchers and scholars to tear down the veil of ignorance that enshrouds human nature. Only by understanding the evolutionary dynamics behind life's veneer can we hope to transcend our most sordid tendencies.

Of course we are not naïve. Overcoming our noxious predispositions may be a Sisyphean task. Our evolved capacities to deceive and manipulate one another may be unprecedented in their destructive potential. Nuclear, chemical, and biological weapons, nationalistic bigotries, religious fundamentalist threats, environmental degradation, and the power that communicative technologies provide for despots and demagogues intent on seducing the minds of millions, all speak to the dangers that our adapted mechanisms pose to our well-being. What gives us a sense of optimism, however, is the rapid advancement of human knowledge. By understanding evolutionary arms races and the nature of viruses and bacteria, we have been able to devise vaccines and cures for some of the deadliest diseases that have plagued humanity. With advancements in genetic engineering, we are able to feed millions of individuals with nutritious, calorie-rich foods. With market economies, we can bring about reciprocal relationships that transcend cultural, ethnic, racial, and national boundaries. With the aid of global communications systems, we can expand our circle of kinship and ingroup favoritism to include nonrelatives and even nonhuman endangered species. With an increasing awareness of our environmental impact, we have begun to take steps to alleviate our destructive footprints upon this planet. The future, however, is far from certain.

As evolutionary scientists, our aim is to uncover the ultimate explanations for the proximate workings of our biological world. We hope that this volume accomplishes this task by stripping away some of the self-deceptive layers with which humanity has been clothed for millions of years. We spend most of our lives interacting with kin. In understanding the evolutionary dynamics of the family, we believe that individuals can make more informed decisions regarding themselves, their kin, and their societies. Aside from such practical implications, we also hope that this volume instructs and enlightens those interested in the inner workings of human and nonhuman families. There is, however, much that remains undiscovered. It rests upon researches from diverse fields to correct many of our errors, oversights, and misconceptions. Empirical research is essential in corroborating or refuting the speculative nature of some of our inquiries. As with all of science, the study of human evolution is a work in progress.

References

Apostolou, M. (2009). Parent-offspring conflict over mating: The case of short-term mating strategies. *Personality and Individual Differences*, *47*, 895–899.

Apostolou, M. (2010). Sexual selection under parental choice in agropastoral societies. *Evolution and Human Behavior*, *31*, 39–47.

Atran, S. (2002). *In gods we trust: The evolutionary landscape of religion*. Oxford: Oxford University Press.

Bjorklund, D.F., & Pellegrini, A.D. (2002). *The origins of human nature: Evolutionary developmental psychology*. Washington, DC: American Psychological Association.

Brown, R.M., Brown, S.L., Johnson, A., Olsen, B., Melver, K., & Sullivan, M. (2009). Empirical support for an evolutionary model of self-destructive motivation. *Suicide and Life-Threatening Behavior*, *39*, 1–12.

Buss, D.M. (1987). Love acts: The evolutionary biology of love. In R.J. Sternberg & M.F. Barnes (Eds.), *The psychology of love* (pp. 100–118). New Haven: Yale University Press.

Buss, D.M. (2003). *The evolution of desire: Strategies of human mating (revised edition)*. New York: Basic Books.

Cochran, G., & Harpending, H. (2009). *The 10,000 year explosion: How civilization accelerated human evolution*. New York: Basic Books.

Cosmides, L. & Tooby, J. (2005). Neurocognitive adaptations designed for social exchange. In D.M. Buss (Ed.), *The handbook of evolutionary psychology* (pp. 584–627). Hoboken: Wiley.

Darwin, C.R. (1859/1964). *On the origin of species*. Cambridge, MA: Harvard University Press.

Dawkins, R. (1976). *The selfish gene*. Oxford: Oxford University Press.

Dawkins, R. (1982). *The extended phenotype*. Oxford: W. H. Freeman.

Hagen, E.H. (2002). Depression as bargaining: The case postpartum. *Evolution and Human Behavior*, *23*, 323–336.

Hamilton, W.D. (1964). The genetical evolution of social behaviour (I and II). *Journal of Theoretical Biology*, *7*, 1–52.

Harris, J.R. (2009). *The nurture assumption: Why children turn out the way they do* (rev. ed.). New York: Free Press.

Kaighobadi, F., Shackelford, T.K., Popp, D., Moyer, R.M., Bates, V.M., & Liddle, J.R. (2009). Perceived risk of female infidelity moderates the relationship between men's personality and partner-directed violence. *Journal of Research in Personality*, *43*, 1033–1039.

Kirkpatrick, L.A. (2004). *Attachment, evolution, and the psychology of religion*. New York: Guilford Press.

Lummaa, V., Vuorisalo, T., Barr, R.G., & Lehtonen, L. (1997). Why cry? Adaptive significance of intensive crying in human infants. *Evolution and Human Behavior*, *19*, 193–202.

Maestripieri, D., Hoffman, C.L., Anderson, G.M., Carter, C.S., & Higley, J.D. (2009). Mother-infant interactions in free-ranging rhesus macaques: Relationships between physiological and behavioral variables. *Physiology & Behavior*, *96*, 613–619.

Miller, G. (2000). *The mating mind: How sexual choice shaped the evolution of human nature*. London: Heineman.

Miner, E.J. & Shackelford, T.K. (2010). Mate attraction, retention, and expulsion. *Psicothema*, *22*, 9–14.

Pinker, S. (1997). *How the mind works*. New York: Norton.

Pinker, S. (2002). *The blank slate: The modern denial of human nature*. New York: Viking.

Rousseau, J.J. (1755/1994). *Discourse upon the origin and foundation of inequality among mankind*. New York: Oxford University Press.

Trivers, R.L. (1972). Parental investment and sexual selection. In B. Campbell (Ed.), *Sexual selection and the descent of man, 1871-1971* (pp. 136–179). Chicago: Aldine-Atherton.

Trivers, R. (1974). Parent-offspring conflict. *American Zoologist, 14*, 249–264.

Trivers, R. (1985). *Social evolution*. Menlo Park, CA: Benjamin-Cummings.

Williams, G.C. (1966). *Adaptation and natural selection: A critique of some current evolutionary thought*. Princeton, NJ: Princeton University Press.

Wilson, C.G. (2008). Male genital mutilation: An adaptation to sexual conflict. *Evolution and Human Behavior, 29*, 149–164.

INDEX

A

Ache hunter-gatherers of Paraguay, 98
Ackerman, J. M., 338–39
Adaptation, 6, 122, 170, 174, 387–96
    adaptive mating arrangement, 38
    adaptive parental favoritism, 58
    adaptive siblicide, 134
    adaptive workaround, 282
    as altruistic dispositions, 313–15
    behavioral/cognitive, 150
    deferred, 150
    environmentally contingent, 250–51
    of gorillas, 374
    grandmother hypothesis, 186–87
    hominids, 368
    of infants, 156–58
    information processing, role in, 12, 14
    of intercommunity alliances, 18
    monogamy as, 42, 47
    of multiunit group structures, 38–40
    and natural selection, 4–5, 250, 281–83
    ontogenetic, 150
    of pet keeping, 291–92, 300–1, 304
    relationship-specific, 7–9, 183
Adolescence, 162–63, 317
    brain development, 13
Adoption, 89, 158, 288, 318, 348
    among Papua New Guinea Suau, 118
    among Yap of Micronesia, 118
    as an altruistic parental substitution, 114–16
    ancient Romans, 119
    anyone can be a parent, 123–24
    within Baatombu society, 118
    in Brazil, 116
    cross-species, 300, 304
    definition, 114
    and degree of relatedness, 90
    difference with fosterage, 114
    factors influencing, 123
    as a form of kin support, 116–18
    as a form of social networking, 118–19
    general preferences, 120–21
    human *vs* animal, 124
    infant-directed speech (IDS), 290
    Inuit, West African, and Oceanic, 117
    and kinship, 116, 122–23
    motivation for, 114–15
    multidisciplinary perspectives, 124
    and nonadoptive families, 124–25
    in North America, 116
    open, 115
    range of human, 124
    of strangers, 115
    as a universal human phenomenon, 121–22
    use of, 122
    Western adoptive parent, 114, 120
    Yukpa of South America, 117, 119
Adrenal androgens, 161
Adrenal puberty, 161
Adrenarche, 161
Advertisement, and pets, 304–5
Aegithalos caudatus, 350
Affective dynamics, in parent–child relationships, 65–66
African black eagle (*Aquila verreauxi*), 55
African clawed toad (*Xenopus laevis*), 221
African elephants (*Loxodonta africana*), 214, 217
African lions (*Panthera leo*), 215
African wild dogs (*Lycaon pictus*), 121
Age-related preferences, 72–73
Ainsworth, M. D. S., 285
Akalis, S., 289
Alarm-calling, 9
Alexander, R. D., 368
Allele
    favoring altruism, 53
    and fitness notion, 346
    focal, 346–47, 352–53, 356
    grandparent–grandchild relatedness, 183
    identical, 5
    parent–off spring relatedness, 71, 76
    recognition, 349
    rival, 347, 389
    role in natural selection, 52–53
Alley, T. R., 157
Allomothers, 185
Alloparenting, 17, 116, 139
    benefits, 123, 154
    and grandmother hypothesis, 380–81
    kinship theory and, 217
    in pet keeping, 300
Allostatic load, 24
Almond, D., 88
Altruism, 78
    Hamilton's rule, 53, 129, 232, 234
    in haploid insects, 8
    induced, 313–14
    kin selection theory, 129, 313, 332–33
    kinship theory, 5, 137–38, 216, 253
    parental investment theory, 130
    reciprocal, 121–22, 253, 313, 337, 370, 393
    reinforced, 320
    sibling rivalry, 55–56
    unilateral, 262
Alvergne, A., 74
American coot (*Fulica americana*), 351
American Pet Products Manufacturers' Association (APPMA), 298
American toad (*Bufo americanus*), 213
American white pelicans (*Pelecanus occidentalis*), 54
Anderson, G. M., 390
Anderson, K., 8
Anderson, K.G., 99–100, 106–7
Anderson, M.L., 113
Andrews, P.W., 92
Androgens, 22–23, 161, 282
Angelman syndrome (AS), 77
Anglo American women, 84
Animal families, behavioral mechanisms of, 3–4. *See also* Animal kin recognition
    alarm-calling, 9
    in chimpanzee community, 15–16
    cues of nonpaternity, 16
    infanticide, 4, 16
    multiple-reproductive-male groups, 16
    parenting, 9
    polygamous mate competition, 16
    relationships between chimpanzee mother and her offspring, 3–4
    weaning conflict, 6
Animal grandparenting, 187–88
Animal kin recognition
    altruism and kinship theory, 216
    amphibians, 213
    birds, 214
    cooperative behaviors, 216
    development of, 223–25
    fish, 213
    implications for cooperative behavior, 216
    inclusive fitness theory, 215–16
    indirect/direct, 219
    invertebrates, 212–13
    kin selection, 215–16
    mammals, 214–15
    and mating behavior, 217
    mechanisms of, 218–25
    and parental care, 216–17

Animal kin recognition (cont'd)
  phenotyping matching, 218
  primates, 215
  reptiles, 214
  and social cohesion, 217–18
  timing of learning, 224
Anthropomorphic thinking, 300
Anthropomorphism, 288–89
  in *Homo sapiens*, 288
Aoudad (Barbary sheep, *Ammotragus lervia*), 223
APPMA. *See* American Pet Products Manufacturers' Association (APPMA)
Archer, J., 288
Ardipithecus ramidus, 43, 152
Arginine vasopressin (AVP), 16, 20–23
Arm-pit effect, 131
Arsi Oromo, 72
Asexual reproduction, 52
Asian colobines, 36
Asymmetrical aggression, 357–58
Atlantic salmon (*Salmo salar*), 213, 221
Atran, S., 321
Attachment behavior, 20–23, 69
  bonding, 120, 251, 261, 286, 293
Attachment to pet
  anthropomorphism, 288–89
  infant features and, 288
  infant schema, 287–88
  mechanisms promoting, 287–89
  social releasers, 287–88
Augustus, Gaius Julius Caesar, 119
Aureli, F., 253
Australopithecine diet, 370
Australopithecus species, 20
  A. anamensis, 366
  A. garhi, 44
Autonomic nervous system (ANS), 21
Autonomous polygynous unit, 39
Avian brood parasites, 283

B
Baboons (*Papio cynocephalus*), 253, 352
Baby schema, 91
Bachman, G.C., 85
Back to the Future, 333
Badcock, C., 78, 314
Balch, S. H., 316
Ball, H.L., 87, 158
Banded mongooses (*Mungos mungo*), 86
Bank vole (*Clethrionomys glareolus*), 219
Barbary macaques (*Macaca sylvanus*), 256
Barclay, P., 354
Barn swallow (*Hirundo rustica*), 89
Bartholomew, K., 286
Battleground controversy, 57
Beck, L., 285–86, 291
Beetles (*Atemeles pubicollis*), 59, 284
Begging call, 58, 85–87, 89–92
Behavioral primatology, 35
Belding's squirrels (*Spermophilus beldingi*), 224, 348

Belisle, P., 254
Bell, M.B.V., 86
Belsky, J., 69–71, 317, 390
Bem, D. J., 335
Bennett, P. C., 293
Bereczkei, T., 88
Betram, B.C.R., 214
Betzig, L., 99
Big-game hunting, evolution of, 40
Biological parents, 118
Biparental care, 22–23, 58–59, 97
Biparental negotiation, 59
Biparental titi monkeys (*Callicebus moloch*), 252
Bipedalism, evolution of, 42–44, 153, 156
Birds, survival rate of, 6. *See also* Lekking species (birds)
Birth order
  age-related preferences and, 72–73
  and degree of sibling rivalry and conflict, 133–35, 314–15
  as determinant of parental investment, 69
  of parent, 196
  and reproductive value, 139–41
Birthweight, 84, 101
Bjorklund, D.F., 187
Black grouse (*Tetrao tetrix*), 236, 238
Blackbellied magpies (*Pica pica*), 91
Blind goby parents (*Typhlogobius californiensis*), 217
Bloch, M., 312
Blood-brothers, 9, 340
Blood glucose and gestational diabetes, 83
Blood pressure and pregnancy, 84
Blood-sisters, 340
Blunt analogy, 41
Bogin, B., 151, 369
Bonas, S., 286
Boncoraglio, G., 89
Bonnet macaques (*Macaca radiata*), 251
Bonobos (*Pan paniscus*), 37, 151
Bororo people, and pet keeping, 298
Botryllus schlosseri, 351
Bowlby, J., 157, 249, 285–86
Boyce, W.T., 71
Bradley, B. J., 373
Bradshaw, J. W. S., 291
Brain. *See also* Autonomic nervous system (ANS)
  evolution of hominid, 368–69
  in human kinship recognition cues, 315
  size, 19, 152
Breast milk, 77, 87, 151, 159
Breastfeeding, 12, 21
  benefits, 159
  daughter favoritism in, 72
  kin recognition in, 132
  hunter-gatherer society, childrearing practices, 155
  of pets, 299, 304
Breeding bonds, 36

Breeding progeny, 53
Bressan, P., 356
Briskie, J.V., 89
Brood parasitism
  avian brood parasites, 283
  degree of, 89
Brood reduction, 55
Brook trout (*Salvelinus fontinalis*), 221
Brooke, M. D., 350
Brosnan, S.F., 253
Brotherton, P.M.N., 38
Brown-headed cowbirds (*Molothrus ater*), 222
Brown lemurs (*Eulemur fulvus*), 252
Buckholdt, D. R., 311
Buckle, G. R., 351
Budgerigars (*Melopsittacus undulates*), 87
Buhrmester, D., 137
Bumpass, L.L., 98
Burch, R. L., 334
Burke, T., 214
Burnham, D., 290
Buss, D.M., 171, 174
Bustards (*Otis tarda*), 236
Buunk, A.P., 88

C
Cacioppo, J. T., 288–89
Cakile edentula, 348
California gull (*Larus californicus*), 86
Callitrichids, 136
Cameron, E.Z., 88
Camilleri, J.A., 176
Canaries (*Serinus canaria*), 87
Canis lupis, 292
Cannibal-morph larva, 56
Cannibalism, 56
Capuchin monkey infants (*Cebus apella*), 251
Capuchin monkeys (*Cebus capucinus*), 255
Caregiving behavior, 91
Carsten, J., 312
Carter, C. S., 390
Cash, K., 54
Castillo, R.R., 201
Castro F., 91
Celibacy, induced altruism and, 317–19
Chacma baboons (*Papio cynocephalus ursinus*), 39, 257
Chapais, B., 254
Chappell, M.A., 85
Charlton, B. D., 292
Chastril, E. R., 380
Chat room partners, 163
Cheney, D.L., 218
Cherlin, A., 103–4
Childcare, evolution of, 153–55
Childhood, 150–51, 159–61
  preschool-age children, 160
  weaning process, 160
Childlessness, and investment patterns between siblings, 141–42
Childrearing practices, 155

Children, contribution in caring and helping, 74–76
Children's outcomes
  and divorce, 100–101
  impact of fathers on, 101
Child's reproductive value, 73
Chimpanzees (*Pan troglodytes*), 37, 151–52, 187, 215, 370–72
  human trait evolve from, 371
  life history, 369
  nonsuckling females, 372
  sex differences in subsistence activities in, 44
  siblings in, 377–78
Chin, M. G., 290
Chiroxiphia manakins, 237, 240–43
Chisholm, J.S., 70
Chrastil, E.R., 184
Chromosomal homologue, 52
Churchill, S.E., 41
Cichlid fish (*Pelvicachromis taeniatus*), 222
Cicirelli, V.G., 138
Cinderella Effect, 104
Ciolli, J. L., 291
Clark, D. A., 155
Clutton-Brock, T.H., 86
Coall, D. A., 200
Coefficient-of-relatedness, between parent and offspring, 52
Coevolutionary development, 18
Coffing, K., 367
Cognition, human, 13
Cohabitation, 98, 102, 107, 121, 130–31, 173, 220
Cohen, G.L., 163
Colby, P. M., 286
Coleman, G. J., 293
Coleman, M., 107
Collis, G. M., 286, 289
Colony-dwelling species, 56
Common cuckoo (*Cuculus canorum*), 89
Common ravens (*Corvus corax*), 214
Communication, with pets, 289–91. *See also* Vocalizations
  infant-directed speech, 290
  unconditional positive regard, 291
Compadrazgo, 310
Companion Animal Attachment Scale, 285
Concrete operations, 151
Consanguinity, 199
Consortships, 45
Cooperative and competitive behaviors, 113, 216
  in sea squirt, 351
Cooperative breeding hypothesis, 154
Cooperative grooming, 9
Cooperative subsistence, between spouses. *See* Mutual provisioning
Copidosoma floridanum, 351
Coquerel's dwarf lemurs (*Mirza coquereli*), 254
Cornwell, R. E., 287

Cortex, 12
Cortisol stress response, effect of family environment, 23, 26
  elevated levels, 25
  high-stress events, 25
  and maternal care, 26
  risk for associated health problems, 26
Cosmides, L., 331, 333, 336, 354
Costell, A., 289
Costs
  of cuckoldry and paternity uncertainty, 170
  dispersal of primates, 265
  of pet keeping, 299
Counseling psychology, 7
Crèching, 239
Crespi, B., 78
Cronk, L., 72
Cross cousin marriage, 19
Cross-cultural infidelity, 170
Cross-fostering experiments, 130
Cross-species adoption, 300
Crowding out, 200
Csányi, V., 291–92
Csikszentmihalyi, M., 162
Cuckoldry, 73
  and male sexual jealousy, 170–71
  paternity uncertainty and costs of, 170
  psychological mechanism to prevent, 170–71
Cuculus canorus, 350
Cue to paternity, 255
Cues of kinship, 9
  association and familiarity, 218
  comparison of cues, 222–23
  conspecific, 221–22
  decision-making about relatedness, 222–23
  environmental/spatial, 220
  group, 221
  individual, 221
  nonspecific, 220–21
  recognition genes, 218–19
  spatial location, 218
Cues of relatedness, 94, 239
Custance, D. M., 292
Cuteness, 157

D
Dalerum, F., 88
Daly, M., 8, 89, 103–4, 134, 158–59, 172, 286–87, 300
Darwin, C. R., 4, 216, 352, 386, 389
Darwinian sexual selection, 52
Darwin's "one special difficulty," 53
Dating diaries, 109
Daughter-biased investment, 72, 88
  caring and helping attitude, 74
Daughter favoritism, 72
Davies, N. B., 89, 350
Dawkins, R., 131, 284–85
De Cremer, D., 339
De Waal, F.B.M., 253

DeBruine, L. M., 354–55
Deer mouse (*Peromyscus maniculatus*), 348
Deferred adaptations, 150
Dehydroepiandrosterone (DHEA), 161
Deixis, 290
Del Giudice, M., 161, 390
Detritivore diet, 56
Developmental plasticity, 67
Developmental psychology, 7, 75
DeVoe, D., 287
Dickemann, M., 88
Dickins, T.E., 201
Dictyostelium discoideum, 352–53
Diet, hominid, 369–70
Dimorphism, 365
  in hominoids, 18
Diploid offspring, 52–53
Direct reproductive fitness, 5, 13, 243–44
Divorce
  among hunter-gatherers, 97–98
  causes of, 99–100
  and children's outcomes, 100–101
  cross-cultural justification for, 99
  impact on parental investment in children, 98
  in industrialized nations-states, 98
  in nonindustrial societies, 99
  and parental investment, 100
Dobler, R., 213
Dog Attachment Questionnaire, 286
Dóka, A., 291–92
Dolphins (*Tursiops truncatus*), 215–16
Domestic dog (*Canis familiaris*), 224, 292
Dopamine, 21–22, 77
Dopamine D2 receptors, 23
Draper, P., 136, 317
Dubuc, C., 45
Duflo, E. C., 201
Dunbar, R.I.M., 88, 134
Duntley, J.D., 174
Durrant, R., 174
DuVal, E.H., 242
Dwyer, F., 293

E
Eastwick, P. W., 282
Edlund, L., 88
Edmonson, E., 290
El-Alayli, A., 291
Ellis, B.J., 71
Emlen, S.T., 138–39
Emotional support, and pet keeping, 302
Emperor penguin (*Aptenodytes forsteri*), 212
Encephalization quotient (EQ), 151–52, 368
Endothermic young, 58
England, B.G., 104
Epley, N., 288–89
Esteem support, and pet keeping, 302
Estrogen, 21
Ethnographic Atlas, 18, 124
Eugenides, J., 331

Euler, H. A., 8, 184, 190–91, 195–96, 198, 380
European earwig (*Forficula auricularia*), 213
European starlings (*Sturnus vulgaris*), 59
Evans, R.M., 54
Evolutionary arms race, 283
Evolutionary ethics, of family, 392–96
Evolutionary game theory, 51
Evolutionary origins, of pet keeping, 299–301
Evolutionary perspective, on family
 adaptations as decision-makers, 6
 kinship theory, 5–6
 natural selection, 4–5
Evolutionary significance, of pet keeping, 283–85
Extended phenotype model, therapeutic implications of, 391–92

F

Facial resemblance, parent–child, 315, 332, 334
 and fathers' perceived similarity, 73–74
 role in kin recognition, 132, 354–56
Fagan, E. C., 287
Falk, D., 290
Familial homicides, 87
Familiarity
 as cues of kinship, 218
 defined, 331
 role in kin relation, 330–32
 as sexual barrier, 331
Family environment, cortisol stress response to, 26
Family evolution. *See also* Evolutionary perspective, on family
 evolutionary changes in hominid, 366–70
 family tree, 366–70
 great apes, 366–70
Father-absent households, 101
Father-present homes, 101
Father–child relationships, 106
 predivorce, 101
Father–child resemblance, 73–74, 78
Fatherhood, 7–8
Fawcett, T.W., 88
Female black-headed gull (*Larus ridibundus*), 55
Female body size, 19–20
Female–female competition, 374
Female infidelity, 99
Female sexual infidelity, 171–73
Fetal alcohol syndrome, 120
Fetal development, 7
Fictive kin labeling, 311
Fictive kin relationships, 311
Fictive kinship
 in American black, 312–13
 overview, 310–11
 problems with concept of, 311–14
 in Yanomamo, 312

Fictive kinship, 9, 311
Fidler, M., 289
Figueredo, A. J., 172
Filicide, 8–9, 160
Finches species, 6
Fiordland crested penguin (*Eudyptes pachyrhynchus*), 217
Fire salamander (*Salamandra infraimmaculata*), 213
Firstborns, favoritism for, 73
Fisher, M.L., 189
Fisher, Sir Ronald, 53
Fitness, J., 171
Flinn, M.V., 104, 106–7, 136
Flirting, 157
FLO1 gene, 353
Fluid intelligence, 13
Food sharing, between mates, 37
 passive forms of, 45
Food transport, in terms of sexual division of labor, 37, 42–44
 among bipeds, 43
 hominins, 42–44
 predator avoidance during, 43
Forbes, L.S., 54
Forced in-pair copulation (FIPC), in humans, 175–76
Fox, M., 184
Fractionation hypothesis, 37–39
Fragaszy, D., 300
Fratricides, 134
Friends, 329
Friendship, 9, 161, 181, 291, 299, 303, 311, 337–39
Frieze, I. H., 175–76
Fur seal (*Arctocephalus tropicalis*), 224
Furman, W., 137
Furstenberg, Jr., F.F., 98☒-aminobutyric acid (GABA), 77

G

Gácsi, M., 292
Gage, A.J., 175–76
Galagoes (*Galaginae* spp.), 252
Gallup, G. G., Jr., 334
Game theory, 172
Ganong, L.H., 107
Gardner, A., 78
Garrity, T. F., 285
Geary, D. C., 162
Gelada baboon (*Theropithecus gelada*), 36, 38, 41
Generalized kinship theory, 76
Genes
 and human family, 389–91
 manipulation, 390–91
 phenotypic effect of, 390
Genetic correlation, donor and recipient's offspring, 5
Genetic incongruity, in kin, 387
Genetic kinship, 5, 9, 389
Genetic relatedness, 9, 183, 218, 330, 393

closeness to nieces and nephews by aunts/uncles, 201
father–child resemblance, 73
grandparent investment, 379–80
Hamilton's rule for, 53, 346–48, 350
homicide between siblings and, 139
inclusive fitness theory, 89–90
infanticide and, 158
kinship and, 221, 312–13, 333, 335–36, 354, 357
for lekking males, 231, 236, 243
proxy for, 115
stepparenting and, 105, 196
Genomic imprinting, 76–78
Gestation (pregnancy), 13
Gestational diabetes, 6–7, 83, 156
Gestational hypertension, 84
Getz, W. M., 184, 380
Ghost marriage, 33
Gibbons (*Hylobates lar*), 36
 food transferring and sharing, 45
Gilby, A., 289
Giron, D., 351
Gittins, S.P., 45
Godfray, H.C.J., 85–86
Godoy, R., 72
Godparents, 9
Goetz, A.T., 9, 174, 176
Golden hamsters (*Mesocricetus auratus*), 131, 222
Gomes de Oliveira, M., 300
Goodall, J., 3–4, 92
Goodenough, W., 33
Goodwin, D., 291
Gorillas (*Gorilla gorilla berengei, Gorilla gorilla gorilla*), 36, 254, 372–73
 human trait evolve from, 371
 siblings in, 377–78
Grandfather hypothesis, 187
Grandmother hypothesis, 186–87, 379–80
Grandparental investment, allocation of, 8
 and genetic relatedness, 379–80
 sex-biased preference, 197
Grandparental investment, potential moderators of, 380–81
Grandparenting, 8, 16–17, 181, 376–81
 age factor, 196–97
 analysis of investment by aunts and uncles, 201
 animal, 187–88
 assessment of grandparental investment, 188–89
 child survival, 192–93
 and consequences for public policies, 200–201
 contact and care, 190–91
 cultural context, 199–200
 effect of residential distance between grandparent and grandchild, 193–94
 effects in grandchildren, 200
 emotional bonding, 17

empirical analysis of tangible transfers, 192
expressions of affection, 191
gender of grandchild, 197
and genetic relatedness, 201
grandfather hypothesis, 187
grandmother hypothesis, 186–87, 379–80
grandparent–grandchild resemblance, 198
grandparent–parent relationship, 198–99
and grandparents' physical and mental health, 200
heterosomal relatedness between grandparents and grandchildren, 184
impact of family composition, 194–96
marital status of grandparents, 194
matrilineal bias of grandparental–grandchildren relationships, 190
menopause and grandmother hypothesis, 379–80
potential moderators of grandparental investment, 380–81
rank order of grandparent categories, 189–93
and relationship uncertainty, 183
and reproductive strategy, 184–86
sex-chromosome relatedness, 183–84
and type of joint activities, 198
Graves, J., 92
Greenberg, L., 351
Greve, W., 187
Grief, natural selection and, 282
Griffin, D., 286
Group-against-group play, 14
Group selection, 52, 187, 232, 322
Gubrium, J. F., 311
Guenons (*Cercopithecine* spp.), 256
Gurven, M., 46

H

Hadza hunter-gatherers, 102–3
Haig, D., 6, 78, 83, 156
Haldane, J.B.S., 53, 114
Hamadryas baboon (*Papio hamadryas*), 36, 38, 41
Hames, R.D., 136
Hamilton, W.D., 5, 8, 53, 84, 130, 313, 332, 345, 352, 387, 389
Hamilton's kin selection theory, 113, 216, 252
Hamilton's rule, 52–53, 56–57, 84–85, 129, 134, 252
  altruism, 53, 129, 232, 234
  genetic relatedness, 53, 346–48, 350
  siblicide, 134–35
Hammill, B.G., 196
Hanneke, C.R., 176
Hanuman langurs (*Presbytis entellus*), 251
Haplodiploid sex determination systems, 53

Hardman, D., 139
Hare, H., 93
Harris, J. R., 332
Harris, P. B., 313
Hatching asynchrony, 54
Hatley, F., 169
Heimann, M., 157
Helpers-at-the nest paradigm, 135–36
Helping behavior, 74–75
Hendrix, C., 285
Henzi, S.P., 92
Herbivorous insects, 58
Hertig, R., 200
Herzog, H., 300
Heuveline, P., 98
Hickey, M., 287
Higley, J. D., 390
Hill, C.M., 87, 158
Hill, K., 38, 46, 101
Hindgut microfauna, 59
HIV/AIDS, 154
Hoben, A., 8
Hoffman, C. L., 390
Hoier, S., 191
Holcomb, R., 285
Hole-nesting birds, 91
Hollingsworth, S. L., 291
Holmes, W. G., 348
Holy, L, 311
Homicide, 163
  adaptation theory, 170, 174
  as a cause of child mortality among Ache hunter-gatherers, 101
  familial, 87
  siblicide, 134–35, 139
  impact of step-parenting, 8, 89, 104
Hominid socioecology, 373–74
  change in brain size, 368–69
  diet, 369–70
  evolutionary change, 366–70, 367
  family tree, 366–70
  great apes, 370–73
  life history, 369
  reduction in polygyny, 374
  sexual dimorphism, 367–68
  social behavior, 367, 369
Hominins, 20, 37, 39–46, 151
  cranial capacity, 13
  origin of sex differences in subsistence activities in, 42–44
Hominoids, 13
Homo erectus, 19, 153, 187
Homo ergaster, 153
Homo habilis, 153, 366
Homo neanderthalensis, 366
Homo sapiens, 19, 45, 149, 152, 162, 366
  anthropomorphism in, 288
  direct kin recognition in, 349
Homologous traits, 37
Hormonal mechanisms, in human–family relationships, 20–23
Horn, A.G., 91
Horowitz, L. M., 286

Hrdy, S. B., 154, 187, 300
Hughes, K.D., 45
Human brain, evolution of, 12–14, 34
  cognitive abilities, 13
  family environment and, 14
  hormonal basis for attachment and family love, 20–23
  information processing and communication, 13–14
  juvenile period, 13
  maternal attachment, 22
  problem solving skill, 14
  relations between family environment and cortisol stress response, 26
  social behavior, 14
  social environment, response to, 23–26
  structural changes, 13
Human crying, 91
Human family
  biological and psychological findings of culture, 393–96
  evolutionary ethics of, 392–96
  familial nature, 386–87
  genes and, 389–91
  grandparents, 379–81
  marriage patterns and family formation, 375
  modern, 374–81
  mother hypothesis, 380
  nuclear and extended family relationships, 376–81
  overview, 386
  parental investment, 387–88
  parents and children, 388–89
  potential moderators of grandparental investment, 380–81
  reproductive strategies, 387–88
  siblings, 377–79
  types of, 375–76
Human groups, modal composition of, 36
Human juvenile period, 369
Human kinship recognition cues, 314–15
  brain in, 315
  development of language, 315
Human kinship systems. *See also* Human brain, evolution of
  extended, and control of mating relationships, 17–18
  fathering, 14–16
  grandparenting, 16–17. *See also* Grandparenting
  human community and intergroup relations, 15
  mating relationships, 15
  paleontological evidence, 18–19
  parental cooperation, 34
  paternal care, 15
Human life, evolution of. *See also* Human family
  adolescence, 162–63
  childcare, 153–55
  childhood, 150–51, 159–61

INDEX | 403

Human life, evolution of (*cont'd*)
  early stages of pregnancy, 155–56
  extending immaturity, 151–53
  infancy, 156–59
  juvenile period, 161–62
Human mating system, 36–37
Human placental lactogen (hPL), 83–84
Human social relationships, 14
Human society, evolution mapped upon the phylogeny, 38
Hungarian Gypsies, 72
Hungarian Gypsy populations, 88
Hunter, J., 162
Hunter-gatherer societies, 149, 378
  Ache community of Paraguay, 98–99, 101
  Aka of central Africa, 102
  capabilities for food acquisition, 185
  childrearing practices, 155
  divorce, 97–98
  Hazda, 102–3
  modern, 46, 155
  net flow of resources, 192
  origin of sex differences in subsistence activities in, 42, 44
  pair-bonding, 37–38
  sexual division of labor in, 34–35
  stepfamilies, 102
Hurtado, A.M., 101
Hutchinson, P.L., 175–76
Hyena (*Crocuta crocuta*), 214
Hyperinvestment, in children, 75
Hypertensive pregnancies, 84
Hypothalamic-anterior pituitary-adrenal cortex system (HPA) activity, 21
Hypothalamic-pituitary-adrenal system, 16, 158
Hypothalamic-pituitary-gonadal system, 16
Hypothalamus, 21

I

Immaturity, period of, 150–53
Immunocompetence, 90
Implicit association task (IAT), 132
Imprinted genes, characteristics of, 76–78
Incest avoidance, 330–32
Inclusive fitness theory, 51, 57, 89
  animal kin recognition, 215–16
Inclusive reproductive fitness, 5
Indigo buntings (*Passerina cyanea*), 91
Indirect reproductive fitness, 5
Induced altruism, 313–14. *See also* Altruism
  attachment theory, 317
  celibacy, 317–19
  institutional practices and, 315–18
  suicide terror, 319–20
Infancy, 156–59
Infant altriciality, 20
Infant crying, 389
Infant mortality, 72, 154–58
  industrialized cultures, 101
  nonindustrialized cultures, 101

Infant quality, 87
Infant schema, 284
  attachment to pet, 287–88
Infanticide, 16, 116, 220, 257, 264, 374. *See also* Siblicide
  adoption of kin as an alternative, 116
  female, 72
  inclusive fitness theory, 158–59
  in Indian caste system, 88
  maternal, 4, 86–87
  parental, 71, 90
  at risk population, 73
  selective, 72, 75
  by stepfathers, 103
Infant–mother relationship, 70
Information processing (intelligence), 12–13
Initiation, 101
Insectivorous swifts (*Apus apus*), 54
Instinctual parenting, 155
Insulin-like growth factor II gene (*IGF2*), 76–77
Intensive parenting, 16
Intergenerational relationships, 183. *See also* Grandparenting
Intergroup competition, 339–40
Intimate partner violence (IPV), 170
  male sexual proprietariness and, 172–74
  partner rape, 175–76
  during pregnancy, 175–76
  proximate correlates of, 176
  as punishment, 171–72
  secual coercion, 174–75
  variance in severity, 173
Investment dynamics, in parent–child relationships, 65–66
Iridomyrmex, 93
Izar, P., 300

J

Jaffe, K., 288
Janssen, D. P., 339
Japanese macaques (*Macaca fuscata*), 9, 248, 257
Japanese quail (*Coturnix coturnix*), 217
Jerauld, R., 317
Johnson, H., 172
Johnson, J. L., 313
Johnson, T. P., 285
Johnstone, R.A., 86
Jones, B., 68
Journal of Personality and Social Psychology (*JPSP*), 330
Ju/Hoansi (!Kung) of Botswana, 136
Juvenile bluegill (*Lepomis macrochirus*), 213
Juvenile dependency, 40
Juvenile period, 13, 161–62
  immunological disorders, 162
  peer social interaction, 162
  psychological and psychosocial risk factors, 161
  social isolation/rejection, 161–62
Juvenile transition, 74–75

K

Kahn, S. M., 311
Kaighobadi, F., 171
Kanter, R. M., 321
Kaplan, H.S., 38, 99–100, 107, 380
Kelemen, D., 161
Kenell, J. H., 317
Kennedy, C., 287
Kenrick, D. T., 338–39
Kibbutz, 130
Kikusui, T., 287
Kilner, R. M., 85, 89, 92
Kin call, 132. *See also* Kin recognition
Kin cue manipulation, 315–19
Kin discrimination, 212, 215
Kinning, 115
Kin perception, overinclusive, 336
Kin prototype, 333
Kin recognition, 130–32, 347–50
  ability to, 348
  in animals. *See* Animal kin recognition
  components of, 350
  in context of cooperation and conflict, 350–53
  in cross-fostered females, 131
  culturally inherited labels and, 356–57
  definition, 212
  direct, 348–50
  in eusocial parasitic wasp, 351
  from facial resemblance, 132, 354–56
  green-beards effect, 352
  human condition and, 353–57
  indirect, 348
  individual recognition, 353–54
  label polymorphism, 350
  mechanism, 333–35
  peacocks, 352
  phenotype matching, 333, 354–57
  social evolution theory, 345–47
  spatial cues, 348
  sweat bees, 351–52
  third-party knowledge of kinship, 132
  underlying mechanism(s), 212
  weaning and, 224–25, 348
Kin relation
  evolution and psychology of, 330–35
  friendship and, 337–39
  incest avoidance and role of familiarity, 330–32
  overinclusive kin perception and sex differences, 335–36
  overview, 329–30
  psychology beyond family, 335–40
Kin selection, 215–16, 223
  altruism and, 313, 332–33
  lekking species, 232–38
  theory, 113, 129
Kinship
  biology's role in. *See* Fictive kinship
  critiques and, 312
  fictive. *See* Fictive kinship
  index, 336
  namesaking and, 313

psychological, 336–37
recognition cues, in human, 314–15
use and misuse of terms, 340
in Yanomamo, 312
Kinship theory, 5–6, 191
and animal psychology, 9
cues of kinship, 9
and friendship, 9
of genomic imprinting, 76–77
and human psychology, 7
Kipsigi, 72
Kitamura, C., 290
Kittiwakes (*Rissa tridactyla*), 218, 348
Klaus, M. H., 317
Kogan, L., 287
Kölliker, M., 213
Komers, P.E., 38
Krause-Parello, C. A., 289
Krebs, J. R., 284–85
Kreger, N. C., 317
Krupa, A., 214
Krupp, D. B., 354
Kubinyi, E., 292

L

Lace bug (*Gargaphia solani*), 213
Lack, D., 54
Laham, S.M., 195
Lalumière, M.L., 175
Lancaster, J.B., 99–100, 107
Lance-tailed manakins, 237
Lancy, D.F., 75
LAPS. *See* Lexington Attachment to Pets Scale (LAPS)
Larval amphibians, 55
Lasioglossum zephyrum, 351–52
Leek, M., 198
Lekking species (birds)
aggregations, 240
behavior of territorial and satellite males in ruff, 240
cooperative courtship in, 231–32
cooperative partnerships, 238–41
cues of relatedness, 239
factors influencing settlement decisions, 242
interindividual dynamics, 241–43
kin selection, 232–38
kin structure within or between, 236
mating systems, 230–31
nonkin associations, 239–41
reproductive patterns, 237–38
Leonard, M.L., 91
Leveling hypothesis, 41–42
Lexington Attachment to Pets Scale (LAPS), 285
Li, J.-C.A., 106
Lieberman, D., 131, 315, 331, 333, 336, 354
Life history, of hominid, 369
Life history theory, of parent–child relationships, 86. *See also* Parent–child relationships

and extrinsic mortality, 67
psychological mechanisms, 75–76
risk of disease (pathogen stress), 68
and sexual selection, 67–68
somatic effort–reproductive effort trade-offs, 66
Light, P., 289
Linepithema humile, 345, 357
Lions (*Panthera leo*), 216
Littlefield, C.H., 189
Lobmaier, J. S., 287
Local resource enhancement, 72, 135
Long-tailed macaques (*M. fascicularis*), 254
Lorenz, K. Z., 157, 284, 287–88
Lorises (*Loris sp.*), 252
Lu, H., 98
Lukjanczuk, J.L., 158
Lystad, A. L., 291

M

Maasai society, 116
Mace, R., 192, 379
MacGinitie, G.E., 217
Maddy, R., 311
Madrash, E. A., 285–86, 291
Maestripieri, D., 390
Maintaining relationships, 171
Maladaptive behavior
adaptive workaround, 282
arises by natural selection, 281–83
avian brood parasites and, 283
changing environment and, 283
grief, 282
Male bonding, 339–40
Male infidelity, 99
Male–male competition, 282, 373
in gorillas, 372
Male philopatry, 370
Male reproductive success, 88
Male sexual jealousy, 170–71
Male warrior hypothesis, 339
Mammalian mating systems, evolution of, 38
Manacus manacus, 352
Mandrills (*Mandrillus sphinx*), 255
Manipulative reproductive strategies, 388
Marbled salamander (*Ambystoma opacum*), 213
Marelich, W.D., 201
Marital stability, 68
Markus, G.B., 133–34
Marlowe, F., 104
Marriage, 97–98
dissolution of. *See* Divorce
Marsiglio, W., 103
Marvin, R.S., 137
Mate retention, 171
Maternal behavior and hormonal activation, 21–22
Maternal care, 34
and childhood stress, 26
Maternal genes, 6
Maternal infanticide, 86

Maternal investment decisions, 7
Maternal perinatal association (MPA), 131
Maternal resemblance, 89
Maternal resources
allocation of, 7
transfer to offspring, 76, 193
Maternal solicitude, 7
Maternal–fetal conflict, 83
Maternal–offspring bond, 23, 249
Mateship, 8–9
Mating game, 339
Matrilineal kin relationships, 248
Maturation, in gorillas, 372
McAlpine, W., 317
McAndrew, F. T., 313
McComb, K., 292
McDonald, D., 241
McHenry, H. M., 367
McKibbin, W.F., 176
McNicholas, J., 286, 289
Meadow vole (*Microtus pennsylvanicus*), 22
Mechanic, M.B., 201
Medium-term relationships, 98
Meerkat (*Suricata suricata*), 90
Meintjes, R. A., 287
Meltzoff, A.N., 157
Memes, 300–301
Menopause, 86
and grandmother hypothesis, 379–80
Mesocricetus auratus, 348, 352
Messent, P. R., 305
Mice (*Mus musculus*), 221
Michalski, R.L., 139, 189, 196
Microtus species, 58
Middlesex, 331
Miklósi, A., 291–92
Miller, S. C., 287
Misattributed paternity, 183
Miscarriage, 155
Mistina, D., 107
Mitchell, R. W., 290
Mithen, S., 288, 300
Mixed-sex groups, 36–39
Mobbing call, 91
Moderating variables, 188
Modern childhood, 75–76
Molnar, P., 157
Molothrus ater, 352
Monogamous primate species, 38
Monogamy,
differentiate between leveling and provisioning hypothesis, 42
evolution of, 40–42, 45–46
fractionation hypothesis, 36–38
in human families, 375–76, 379
leveling hypothesis, 41–42
mating strategies, 154, 186
moral values of, 395
provisioning hypothesis, 40–41
true/strict, 58, 68, 85
Monogamy–polygyny set, 36, 39, 46
Monozygotic twins, 201
Monton, S., 288

Moor macaques (*M. maura*), 256
Moore, M.K., 157
Mosier, J., 285
Mother–child relationship, 317, 388–89
Mother hypothesis, 380
Motherhood, 7
Mother–infant interaction, 251
Mother's reproductive fitness, 6
Mukogodo, 72
Multimale–multifemale group, 37–40, 42–43
Multipartnered fertility, 109
Multiple-reproductive-male groups, 16
Multiunit composition, of human groups
    expansion hypothesis, 39
    fractionation hypothesis, 37–39
    intermediary polygyny stage, 39–40
    multimale–multifemale group, 37–39
Murdock, G. P., 318
Mutual provisioning, 37, 44–46
Mutualism, 253, 302
Myelinated cortical neurons, 13

N

Nagasawa, M., 287
Nagy, E., 157
Namesaking, 313
Natural selection, 16, 66, 73, 301, 304, 321, 331, 386
    adaptation and, 4–5, 8, 170, 396
    and attachment behavior, 157, 250
    grief, 282
    Hamilton's rule, 53
    inclusive fitness theory, 215–16
    maladaptive behavior arises by, 281–83
    morphological changes, 19–20, 26
    parental investment and, 87
Naturalistic fallacy, 4, 396
Negotiation, biparental, 59
Nelson, T., 287
Neonatal imitation, 156–57
Nepotism, 52
Nested family social structure, 16
Nestling cuckoos, 89
Nestling size hierarchy, 54
Nestor effect, 187
Nettle, D., 88, 139
Neuroendocrine mechanisms, in human–family relationships, 20–23
Neurotransmitters, role in attachment behavior, 21
Noble, D.G., 89
Nonadaptive behavior. *See* Maladaptive behavior
Nonmarital births, 108
Nonpaternity, 8, 16, 100, 169, 380
Non-school-related financial expenditures, 106
North American Hutterites, 72
Nursery-based families, 52–60
    extremes of altruism and cooperation in, 55
    passage of time between fertilization and offspring food consumption, 53–54

O

Oates, K., 357
Occam's razor, 199
Odendaal, J. S. J., 287
Oedipus complex, 197
Offspring's reproductive fitness, 6
Ohta, M., 287
Oldfield mice (*Peromyscus polionotus rhoadsi*), 223
Onaka, T., 287
Ontogenetic adaptations, 150
Optimal outbreeding, 217
Orangutans (*Pongo pygmaeus*), 254
Origin of Species by Means of Natural Selection, The, 216
Ostriches (*Struthio camelus*), 214
Ottoni, E. B., 300
Outlet theory, 195
Overexpression of maternal genes, 77
Oxford English Dictionary (OED), 297
Oxytocin (OT), 16, 20–23, 159
    in attachment in mammals, 287

P

Pair-bonding, 16, 22–23, 52, 58, 113, 170. *See also* Mutual provisioning
    evolutionary history, 34–35
    food acquisition dimension of sexual division of labor, 37
    hunter-gatherer societies, 37
    in lekking species, 232
    mating, 371, 373
    parental cooperation model, 34–35
    phylogenetic perspective, 37
    primatological perspective, 35–37
Paleoanthropology, 35
Paleolithic human, pet keeping and, 298
Palmer, C.T., 175
Paper wasp (*Polistes fuscatus*), 222
Parasitic cowbird (*Molothrus ater*), 91
Parasitoid wasp (*Copidosoma floridanum*), 56
Parental care, 53, 216–17
    cohabitating *versus* married families, 108
Parental cooperation hypothesis, 34
Parental cost. *See also* Costs
    to incubation period, 55
    men's financial expenditures on children, 100
Parental discrimination, 71
Parental infanticide, 90
Parental investment, 51, 86
    in adopted related children, 90
    in children, biosocial model, 105–7
    decisions, 158–59
    divorce and, 100
    form, postdivorce, 100
    in lower-caste families, 88
    and offspring's future prospects, 87
    and self-selection, 108
    and sibling relationship, 130
Parental overproduction, 52–55
    advantages, 53–55
    insectivorous swifts (*Apus apus*), 54
    songbirds, 54
Parent–child relationships, 388–89
    affective dynamics, 65–66
    age-related preferences and birth order, 72–73
    characteristics of imprinted genes, 76–78
    children's contribution in caring and helping, 74–76
    children's strategies, 69–70
    in diploid species, 71
    father–child resemblance, 73–74
    impact of parents' behavior, 71
    individual differences in plasticity, 70–71
    investment dynamics, 65–66
    life history theory, 66–68
    macro- and microecological factors influencing, 69
    parental investment, 68–69
    puberty timing in girls, 70
    romantic attachment styles, 69
    sex-biased investment, 71–72
Parenting. *See also* Alloparenting; Parent–child relationships
    attachment bond, development of, 286–87
    experience hypothesis, 304
    skills, pets and acquisition of, 303–4
    stepparenting, 89–90
Parent–offspring bond, 52
Parent–offspring conflict, 6–7, 9, 56–58, 60, 76, 197, 388–89
    and age of offspring, 87
    battleground logic of, 57
    and begging noises, 91
    and child's expected future prospects, 87–88
    as a corollary of sibling conflict, 85
    cultural correlates of, 391
    and degree of relatedness, 88–90
    in evolutionarily stable strategy (ESS) framework, 85
    and gender of parent, 86–87
    and noise level and predation, 91
    and number of offspring, 86
    and parental age, 86
    and physical environment, 90–91
    and sibling relationship, 129–30
    and solicitation signals, 90–92
    theory, 84–86
Parent–offspring genetic relatedness, 90. *See also* Genetic relatedness
Parent–offspring recognition, 216–17
Park, J. H., 132, 336

Parker, G., 57, 86
Parrotlets (*Forpus passerinus*), 87
Pashos, A., 196
Paternal care
    as adaptive attachment mechanisms, 282
    benefits, 26
    divorce and, 99
    evolution of, 47
    hormonal basis for, 21–22
    in humans, 14–16, 68–69
    as mating effort and parental effort, 105
    in monogamous species, 38
    and phenotypic similarity, 73, 123
Paternal genes, code for psychological systems, 392
Paternal investment, 38, 40
Paternal resemblance, 8, 89. *See also* Resemblance
Paternal solicitude, 7
"Paternally biased" pattern, of brain development, 78
Paternity uncertainty, 89, 170–71, 199
Payne, C., 288
Peacocks (*Pavo cristatus*), 214, 216, 352
Peccei, J. S., 379–80
Peer pressure, 163
Perrett, D. I., 287
Personal fitness, 215
Pet keeping
    adaptations in pet species, 291–92
    adaptive and nonadaptive hypotheses, 301
    adaptive consequences, 302–5
    in America, 298
    attachment bond, development of, 286–87
    attachment view, alternatives to, 292–93
    as by-product of adaptive mechanisms, 284
    communication with pets, 289–91
    costs of, 299
    cross-species adoption, 300
    in European Union, 298
    evolutionary origins of, 299–301
    evolutionary significance of, 283–85
    functional consequences of, 301–5
    human attachment to pets, 285–86
    infant schema and, 284
    maladaptive behavior arises from natural selection, 281–83
    nonadaptive consequences of, 302
    as nonhuman social support, 302–3
    Paleolithic humans, 298
    pet rejection by humans, 284–85
    pictorial and documentary evidence for, 298–99
    supernormal stimuli, 285
Petrie, M., 214
Pets. *See also* Pet keeping
    and acquisition of parenting skills, 303–4
    adaptations in, 291–92
    adaptive and nonadaptive hypotheses, 297
    advertisement and, 304–5
    attachment bond, development of, 386–87
    communication with, 289–91
    definition of, 297
    human attachment to, 285–86
    mechanisms promoting attachment to, 287–89
    as social parasites, 302
Phenotype matching, 239,
    kin recognition and, 218–19, 347–49, 354–57
    paternal care and, 73, 123
    self-referent, 131, 234, 333–35, 349
Philopatric woolly monkeys (*Lagothrix poeppigii*), 254
Physical violence, 172
Physiological stress responses, 24
Piaget, J., 151
Pig-tailed macaques (*Macaca nemestrina*), 215, 256
Pike (*Esox lucius*), 213
Pink-backed pelicans (*Pelecanus rufuescens*), 92
Pinker, S., 314, 336
Placental gene *IPL*, 76
Plasticity genes, 71
Pleistocene, 13
Pölitz, E., 191
Pollet, T.V., 8, 88, 138–39, 142, 189
Polyembryony, 56
Polygamous mate competition, 16
Polygyny, 68, 174, 381
    as an obligate evolutionary step, 39–40, 378
    drive for, 42
    in human families, 375–76
    mother–daughter, 119
    multiunit group structures, 37–40
    primatological perspective, 35–36
    as reproductive-strategy, 186
    resource-based, 376
    sexual dimorphism and, 368, 374
    social power, 376
    threshold, 41
Polygyny–monogamy mix, 41
Popp, D., 171
Poresky, R. H., 285
Postmenopausal women, 8
Pottos (*Arctocebus sp.*), 252
Practiced sexual promiscuity, 38
Prader-Willi syndrome (PWS), 77
Prairie vole (*Microtus ochrogaster*), 22–23, 154
Prato-Previde, E., 292
Preeclampsia, 6, 84
Preferential investment hypothesis, 195
Pregnancy, early stages of, 155–56
Pregnancy conditions, in United States, 83–84
Preoperational thinkers, 151
Primate kin preferences
    attachment processes, 249–52
    dispersal costs/foraging efficiency, 265
    dominance style concept, 264–65
    ecological model of kin bias, 263–64
    female philopatry/male dispersal species, 256–57
    female reproductive patterns and mortality rate, 254
    filial attachment, 250
    kin-biased mutualism and reciprocity, 253
    kin recognition and reproductive skew, 254–56
    kin selection theory, 252–53
    kin selection *vs* mutualism/reciprocity, 262–63
    male philopatry/female dispersal species, 257–58
    matrilineal kin relationships, 248
    nondispersed social structures, 258–59
    persistent mother–offspring bonds, 260–62
    rank relationships, 260
    reproductive benefits of kin bias, 259–60
    sex-biased dispersal patterns, 253–54
    socioecological explanations, 264
    solitary or dispersed social structures, 258
    in terms of links between WGC and affiliative networks, 265
Prinstein, M.J., 163
Progesterone, 21
Projectile weaponry, 41
Prolactin (PRL), 16, 21
Promiscuous teleology, 161
Protectionism, 56
Provisioning hypothesis, 40–42
Pseudomonas aeruginosa, 347
Psychological kinship, 336–37
Psychosocial stress, 24, 303, 305
Punishment, violence as, 171–72
Putative fathers, 7
Pygmy fathers, 185

Q

Qirko, H. N., 9, 396
Quail (*Coturnix coturnix*), 91
Queen bees (*Apis mellifera*), 93
Quinlan, M.B., 154
Quinlan, R.J., 68, 136, 154
Quinsey, V.L., 158, 176

R

Raemaekers, J.J., 45
Rainbow trout (*Oncorhynchus mykiss*), 213
Rat (*Rattus norvegicus*), 212, 224
Reciprocal altruism, 253, 313, 337, 370
    evolutionary advantages, 121–22
    as cooperative relationships, 393
Reciprocity, 18, 253

Red fire ant workers (*Solenopsis invicta*), 352
Red-winged blackbirds (*Agelaius phoeniceus*), 54
Redondo, T., 91
Referential model, 38
Reinforced altruism, 320
Relational uncertainty, 195
Remarriage, 102–4, 194
Replacement offspring, 54
Reproductive fitness, 5–6, 155, 335
Reproductive strategists, 5
Reproductive success, 217
Resemblance, 7–8, 115
    and adoption, 120, 123
    facial, parent–child, 73–74, 315, 332–34, 354–56
    father–child, 73–74, 78
    grandparent–grandchild, 198
    paternal, 170
    phenotypic, 333, 335
    self, 315, 355–56–358
Resource inhibitors, 76
Rhesus macaques (*Macaca mulatta*), 45, 215–16, 248, 348
Rhodes, J.A., 41
Richards, P. S., 285
Ringtailed lemurs (*Lemur catta*), 251
Risk-taking behavior, 162–63
Romanes, G.J., 217
Romantic love, 21, 161
Romeo and Juliet, 389
Romero, G., 9
Rousseau, J. J., 386
Ruffs (*Philomachus pugnax*), 238
Rushton, J.P., 189
Ryan, A.K., 138

S

Sabatini, F., 292
Saccharomyces cerevisiae, 353
Sage grouse (*Centrocercus urophasianus*), 236
Saliva immunoassay techniques, 24
Salmon, C. A., 196
Samuels, H.R., 137
Samuelson, M. L., 285
Santos, L., 45
Scelza, B. A., 380
Schaller, M., 132, 336, 338
Schino, G., 253
Schmitt, D.P., 107
Schneider, D. M., 311–12
Schön, R.A., 155
Sea elephant (*Mirounga leonina*), 217
Sear, F., 201
Sear, R., 192, 379
Segal, N.L., 201
Seghers, J.P., 201
Self-referent phenotype matching, 131, 234, 333–35, 349
Self-resemblance, 315, 355–56–358
Self-sacrifice, 56

Semiautonomous polygynous units, 39
Serinus canaria, 85
Serotonin, 77
Serpell, J. A., 300
Sex-biased dispersal patterns, 253–54
Sex-biased investment, 71–72
    in Indian caste system, 88
Sex chromosome relatedness, 380
Sex differences, kin relation and, 335–36
Sex-specialization, 35
Sex-specific reproductive strategy, 199
Sexual coercion and violence, 174–76
Sexual dimorphism, 18
    in hominid, 367–68
Sexual division of labor, 16, 37
    cofeeding activity, 45
    food acquisition dimension, 37
    food transport perspective, 37, 42–44
    mutual provisioning, 37, 44–46
    phylogenetic perspective, 37
    sexual specialization in subsistence activities, 46
    in subsistence activities, 37, 44
Sexual jealousy, 170–73, 176, 388
Sexual reproduction, 52
Sexual swellings, in female gorillas, 372
Sexually proprietary brain, 176
Seyfarth, R.M., 218
Shackelford, T.K., 8, 107, 171, 174, 176, 189
Shared genes, 114
Shea, J.J., 41
Sherman, A., 286
Sherman, P. W., 348
Shields, N.M., 176
Shingleback lizard (*Tiliqua rugosa*), 214
Shirley, J., 300
Shoaling, 213
Siblicide, 9, 134–35
Sibling relationships, 8, 55–56
    in adult life, 137–38
    cannibalism, 55
    caretaking, 135–36
    competition, 5–6
    developmental benefits, 136–37
    factors affecting, 138–43
    in Israel, 130–31
    kin selection theory perspective, 129
    parental investment theory perspective, 130
    parent–offspring conflict theory perspective, 129–30
    as resources, 135–38
    rivalry and resource dilution, 132–34
    role in kin recognition, 130–32
    role of relatedness for, 138–39
    siblicide, 134–35
    in Taiwan, 131
Sibling tie, 128
Siblings, 377–79. *See also* Sibling relationships; Step-relationships
    anthropological studies, 379
    in chimpanzees and gorillas, 377–78

human evolution and, 378
todays, 378–79
Sibship, 8
    size, 140
Silk, J. B., 117, 300
Silvén, M., 155
Sims, V. K., 290
Skinks (*Egernia stokesii, Egernia striolata*), 214
Smith, M. S., 380
Smith, P.K., 198
Smock, P.J., 98
Snipe (*Gallinago media*), 240
Snub-nosed monkeys (*Rinopithecus* spp.), 36
Social behavior, 34, 238 369
    adolescent, 162
    as deferred adaptation, 150
    effects of kin recognition on, 211, 214–16, 350, 352
    genetic relatedness and, 346
    hominids, 367, 369
    human, 7, 14, 18, 20, 77, 136, 172
    inclusive fitness theory, 51, 53
    mammals, 215
    parent–offspring conflict theory, 84–85
    reptiles, 214
    role of OT and AVP, 22–23
    sex differences in, 281
Social-brain hypothesis, 153
Social buffering, pet keeping and, 302–3
Social communication (language), 12
Social competition, 17, 75, 368–69
Social evolution theory, 345–47
    conflict, 346
    cooperation, 346
    genetic relatedness, 346–47
    mathematical approaches to, 346
Social integration, and pet keeping, 302
Social learning, 13–14, 43, 74, 153, 317
    of infants, 251
    neonatal imitation as a form of, 156
    role of matrilineal kin, 256
Social parasites, pets as, 302
Social stress, 24–25, 52, 260
Social support, pet keeping as nonhuman, 302–3
Solicitation signals, 58, 85, 90–92, 315, 357
Somatic effort–reproductive effort trade-offs, 66
Sooty mangabeys (*Cercocebus atys*), 256
Sophie's Choice, 73
Spadefoot toad tadpoles (*Scaphiopus bombifrons*), 213
Sperber, D., 312
Spiders (*Stegodyphus tentoriicola, S. lineatus*), 213, 216
Spiezio, C., 292
Spiny mouse (*Acomys cahirinus*), 224
Spotted bowerbirds (*Chlamydera maculate*), 236

Sprengelmeyer, A., 287
Sprengelmeyer, R., 287
Squirrel monkeys (*Saimiri sciureus*), 251
Stallones, L., 285
Starks, P.T., 184, 380
Starlings (*Sturnus vulgaris*), 224
Starratt, V.G., 171, 176
Steelman, L.C., 134
Steffa, M., 317
Steinberg, L., 317
Step-relationships, 8
    among preindustrial populations, 102
    cross-sectional measures of family structure, 102
    father–child relationships, 106
    nature of stepfamily formation, 102
    stepchildren, 8
    stepfathers. *See* Stepfathers
    stepparenting, 89–90
    stepsiblings, 103
Stepfathers, 90
    benefits in reproductive terms, 106
    and parental care, 102–4
Sterile castes, in social insects, 53
Stewart, R.B., 137
Stewart, S.D., 106–7
Stewart-Williams, S., 176
Strand, M. R., 351
Strawberry poison frog (*Oophaga pumilio*), 220
Stress response systems, 21, 26
Suicide terror, induced altruism and, 319–20
Sulloway, F. J., 133, 135, 139, 314
Sweat bee (*Lassioglossum zephyrum*), 220

T

Taiwanese arranged marriages, and kinship, 314–15
Tamarins (*Callitrichines* spp.), 252
Tarsiers (*Tarsius* spp.), 252
Taylor, A. M., 292
Team sports, 14
Tern (*Sterna hirundo*), 55
Testosterone, 21
    and maladaptive behavior, 282
Theory of mind (ToM), 13, 288
Thornhill, N.W., 175
Thornhill, R., 175
Three-dimensional family
    parent–offspring dimension, 56–58

parent–parent dimension, 58–60
    sibling dimension, 55–56
Timber rattlesnakes (*Crotalus horridus*), 214
Timberlake, J.M., 98
Tinbergen, N., 282
Tits (*Parus major*), 87
Tonkean macaques (*Macaca tonkeana*), 256
Tooby, J., 331, 333, 336, 354
Topál, J., 291–92
Trade-offs, somatic effort–reproductive effort, 66, 68, 105
    birth spacing and sibship size, 140–41
    and investment in children, 109
Tran, U.S., 189–90, 201
Tree-nesting birds, 91
Trivers, R. L., 51, 56–57, 85, 88, 93, 132, 155–56, 162, 253, 313, 387–88
Trivers-Willard effect, 88
Trivers-Willard hypothesis (TWH), 72, 197
Trivers's theory, 57
Turner, D. C., 292
Two-parents-and-two-kids model family, 55

U

Úbeda, F., 78
Uhlenberg, P., 196
Uncarved stones, 41
Unsafe sex practices, 163
Uteroplacental circulatory subsystem, 84
Uxoricide, 173–74

V

Vale, B., 299
Vale, R. J. D., 299
Van den Berghe, P. L., 312, 316
Van Noordwijk, M.A., 45
Van Schaik, C.P., 45
Van Vugt, M., 339
Ventral palladium, 23
Verderane, M. P., 300
Vervet monkeys (*Cercopithecus aethiops*), 215–16, 218, 251, 304
Virányi, Z., 292
Visalberghi, E., 300
Vocalizations, 91
Volk, A.A., 158
Vollmer-Conna, 290
Voracek, M., 189
Vulnerability genes, 71

W

Wach, J., 315
Waytz, A., 288–89
Weaning, 159–60, 389
    and adoption, 116
    conflict, 6–7, 57, 129
    cues and, 221
    in human, 369, 371
    kin recognition and, 224–25, 348
    period, 129, 154
    in primates, 369
    solicitation and, 92
Webb, S. R., 291
Weekes-Shackelford, V.A., 8, 107
Weitzel, B., 8, 190
Westermarck, E., 130, 331, 335
Westermarck effect, 314
White, D. R., 318
White, L., 137
White-faced capuchin monkeys (*Cebus capucinus*), 256
Whitten, A., 92
Wickens, S. M., 291
Wild orangutans (*Pongo pygmaeus*), 45
Wild owl monkeys (*Aotus azarai*), 45
Willard, D., 88
Williams, G. C., 299
Williams, R. C., 285
Willits, F.K., 138
Wilson, C., 292
Wilson, M., 8, 89, 103–4, 134, 158–59, 172, 286–87, 300, 357
Wire-tailed manakin (*Pipra filicauda*), 241
Wise, M., 169
Wolf, A. P., 131, 336
Wood cockroaches, 59
Wooden digging tools, 41
Wright, Sewall, 53
Wynne-Edwards, V. C., 52

Y

Yanomamo, kinship in, 312
Yomut, 72
Young-male syndrome, 163

Z

Zahavi, A., 91
Zajonc, R.B., 133–34
Zebra fish (*Danio rerio*), 224
Zucchi, G., 356